The Broadview Anthology of
BRITISH LITERATURE

Volume 4
The Age of Romanticism

The Broadview Anthology of British Literature

The Medieval Period
The Renaissance and the Early Seventeenth Century
The Restoration and the Eighteenth Century
The Age of Romanticism
The Victorian Era
The Twentieth Century and Beyond

The Broadview Anthology of

BRITISH LITERATURE

Volume 4
The Age of Romanticism

GENERAL EDITORS

Joseph Black, University of Massachusetts
Leonard Conolly, Trent University
Kate Flint, Rutgers University
Isobel Grundy, University of Alberta
Don LePan, Broadview Press
Roy Liuzza, University of Tennessee
Jerome J. McGann, University of Virginia
Anne Lake Prescott, Barnard College
Barry V. Qualls, Rutgers University
Claire Waters, University of California, Davis

broadview press

LIBRARY AND ARCHIVES CANADA CATALOGUING IN PUBLICATION

The Broadview anthology of British literature / general editors, Joseph Black ... [et al].

Includes bibliographical references and index.
Contents: v.1. The Medieval period. —v.2. The Renaissance and the early seventeenth century. —v. 3. The Restoration and the eighteenth century.—v.4. The age of Romanticism.—v.5. The Victorian era.—v.6. The Twentieth century and beyond
ISBN 1-55111-609-x (v.1), —ISBN 1-55111-610-3 (v.2), —ISBN 1-55111-611-1 (v. 3), —ISBN 1-55111-612-x (v.4),—
ISBN 1-55111-613-8 (v.5),—ISBN 1-55111-614-6 (v.6)

1. English literature. I. Black, Joseph Laurence, 1962–

PR1109.B77 2006 820.8 C2006-900091-3

Broadview Press is an independent, international publishing house, incorporated in 1985. Broadview believes in shared ownership, both with its employees and with the general public; since the year 2000 Broadview shares have traded publicly on the Toronto Venture Exchange under the symbol BDP.

We welcome comments and suggestions regarding any aspect of our publications—please feel free to contact us at the addresses below or at broadview@broadviewpress.com.

North America
PO Box 1243,
Peterborough, Ontario
Canada K9J 7H5

3576 California Road,
Orchard Park, NY, USA 14127
Tel: (705) 743-8990;
Fax: (705) 743-8353
email: customerservice@broadviewpress.com

UK, Ireland, and continental Europe
NBN International
Estover Road
Plymouth
UK PL6 7PY
Tel: +44 (0) 1752 202301;
Fax: +44 (0) 1752 202331;
Fax Order Line: +44 (0) 1752 202333;
Cust Ser: enquiries@nbninternational.com
Orders: orders@nbninternational.com

Australia and New Zealand
UNIREPS,
University of New South Wales
Sydney, NSW, 2052
Australia
Tel: 61 2 9664 0999;
Fax: 61 2 9664 5420
email: info.press@unsw.edu.au

www. broadviewpress.com
Broadview Press gratefully acknowledges the financial support of the Government of Canada through the Book Publishing Industry Development Program for our publishing activities.

Cover design by Lisa Brawn

PRINTED IN CANADA

Contributing Editors and Writers

Managing Editor Don LePan
Editorial Coordinator Jennifer McCue
General Academic and Textual Editor Colleen Franklin
Design Coordinator Kathryn Brownsey

Contributing Editors

Sandra Bell
Emily Bernhard Jackson
Joseph Black
Robert Boenig
Laura Cardiff
Noel Chevalier
Mita Choudhury
Thomas J. Collins
Leonard Conolly
Dianne Dugaw
Stephen Glosecki
Amanda Goldrick-Jones
Michael Keefer
Don LePan
Roy Liuzza
Marie Loughlin
D.L. Macdonald
Anne McWhir
David Oakleaf
Jude Polsky
Anne Lake Prescott
Joyce Rappaport
Herbert Rosengarten
Peter Sabor
Janice Schroeder
Geoffrey Sill
Andrew Taylor
Peggy Thompson
Craig Walker
Claire Waters
James Winny

Contributing Writers

Laura Cardiff
Jude Polsky
Jane Beal
Rachel Beatty
Rachel Bennett
Emily Bernhard Jackson
Rebecca Blasco
Julie Brennan
Andrew Bretz
Emily Cargan
Wendy Eberle-Sinatra
Peter Enman
Jane Grove
Camille Isaacs
Erik Isford
Don LePan
John McIntyre
Kenna Olsen
Kendra O'Neal Smith
Laura Pellerine
Jason Rudy
Anne Salo
Janice Schroeder
Nicole Shukin
James Soderholm
Anne Sorbie
Jenna Stook
Candace Taylor
David van Belle
Shari Watling
bj Wray
Nicole Zylstra

Layout and Typesetting

Kathryn Brownsey
Susan Chamberlain

Illustration Formatting and Assistance

Cheryl Baldwin
Lisa Brawn
Susan Thomas

Production Coordinators

Barbara Conolly
Leonard Conolly
Judith Earnshaw

Permissions Coordinators

Emily Cargan
Jennifer Elsayed
Amy Nimegeer

Proofreaders

Jennifer Bingham
Martin Boyne
Lucy Conolly
Lynn Fraser
Anne Hodgetts
Amy Neufeld
Lynn Neufeld
Morgan Rooney
Kerry Taylor

Editorial Advisors

Rachel Ablow, University of Rochester
Rita Bode, Trent University
Susan Brown, University of Guelph
Catherine Burroughs, Wells College
Elizabeth Campbell, Oregon State University
Margaret Case, Ohio Northern University
Nancy Cirillo, University of Illinois, Chicago
Angelo Costanzo, Professor Emeritus, Shippensburg University
David Cowart, University of South Carolina
Alex Dick, University of British Columbia
Len Diepeveen, Dalhousie University
Daniel Fischlin, University of Guelph
Robert Forman, St. John's University
Barbara Gates, University of Delaware
Chris Gordon-Craig, University of Alberta
Stephen Guy-Bray, University of British Columbia
Elizabeth Hodgson, University of British Columbia
Michael Keefer, University of Guelph
Gordon Kipling, University of California, Los Angeles
William Liston, Ball State University
Peter Mallios, University of Maryland
Rod Michell, Thompson Rivers University
Byron Nelson, West Virginia University
Michael North, University of California, Los Angeles
Anna C. Patchias, formerly of the University of Virginia, Charlottesville
Alex Pettit, University of Northern Texas
John Pollock, San Jose State University
Carol Senf, Georgia Tech
Sharon Smulders, Mount Royal College
Goran Stanivukovic, St. Mary's University
Julian Yates, University of Delaware

Contents

APPENDICES

Preface

A Fresh Approach

To those with some awareness of the abundance of fresh material and lively debate in the field of English Studies in recent generations, it may seem surprising that this abundance has not been more fully reflected in the number of available anthologies. Thirty years ago there were two comprehensive anthologies designed for courses surveying British Literature: *The Norton Anthology of English Literature* and one alternative. In recent years there have been still two choices available—the *Norton* and one alternative. Over that time span *The Longman Anthology of British Literature* replaced *The Oxford Anthology of English Literature* in the role of "alternative," but there has been no expansion in range of available choices to match the expansion of content and of approach that has characterized the discipline itself. The number of available handbooks and guides to writing has multiplied steadily (to the point where there are literally hundreds of available choices), while the number of comprehensive anthologies of British literature has remained at two.

For those of us who have been working for the past three years on *The Broadview Anthology of British Literature*, it is not difficult to understand why. The very expansion of the discipline has made the task of assembling and editing an anthology that fully and vibrantly reflects the ways in which the British literary tradition is studied and taught an extraordinarily daunting one. The sheer amount of work involved is enormous, but so too is the amount of expertise that needs to be called on. With that background very much in mind, we have charted a new course in the preparation of *The Broadview Anthology of British Literature*. Rather than dividing up the work among a relatively small number of academics, and asking each of them to handle on their own the work of choosing, annotating, and preparing introductions to texts in their own areas of specialization, we have involved a large number of contributors in the process (as the pages following the title page to this volume attest), and encouraged a high degree of collaboration at every level. First and foremost have been the distinguished academics who have served as our General Editors for the project, but in all there have literally been hundreds of people involved at various stages in researching, drafting headnotes or annotations, reviewing material, editing material, and finally carrying out the work of designing and typesetting the texts and other materials. That approach has allowed us to draw on a diverse range of talent, and to prepare a large anthology with unusual speed. It has also facilitated the maintenance of a high degree of consistency. Material has been reviewed and revised in-house at Broadview, by outside editors (chief among them Colleen Franklin, an academic with a wide-ranging background and also a superb copy editor), by a variety of academics with an extraordinarily diverse range of backgrounds and academic specialities, and by our team of General Editors for the project as a whole. The aim has been not only to ensure accuracy but also to make sure that the same standards are applied throughout the anthology to matters such as extent and coverage in author introductions, level of annotation, tone of writing, and student accessibility.

Our General Editors have throughout taken the lead in the process of making selections for the anthology. Along the way we have been guided by several core principles. We have endeavored to provide a selection that is broadly representative, while also being mindful of the importance of choosing texts that have the capacity to engage readers' interest today. We have for the most part made it a policy to include long works in their entirety or not at all; readers will find complete in these pages works such as *Utopia*, *Confessions of an English Opium Eater*, *In Memoriam* and *A Room of One's Own* that are often excerpted in other anthologies. Where inexpensive editions of works are available in our series of paperback Broadview Editions, we have often decided to omit them here, on the grounds that those wishing to teach one or more such works may easily order them in a combination package with the anthology; on these grounds we have decided against including *Frankenstein*, *Pride and Prejudice*, or *Heart of Darkness*. (For both Mary Shelley and Jane Austen we have made exceptions to our general policy regarding excerpts, however, including selections from *The Last Man* to represent Shelley and the first four chapters of *Pride and Prejudice*, together with a complete shorter work, *Lady Susan*, to represent Austen.)

Any discussion of what is distinctive about *The Broadview Anthology of British Literature* must focus above all on the contents. In every volume of the anthology there is material that is distinctive and fresh–including not only selections by lesser-known writers but also less familiar selections from canonical writers. The anthology takes a fresh approach too to a great many canonical texts. The first volume of the anthology includes not only Roy Liuzza's translation of *Beowulf* (widely acclaimed as the most engaging and reliable translation available), but also new translations by Liuzza of many other works of Old English poetry and prose. Also included in the first volume of the anthology are a new verse translation of *Judith* by Stephen Glosecki, and new translations by Claire Waters of several of the *Lais* of Marie de France. The second volume includes *King Lear* not only in the full Folio version but also with three key scenes from the Quarto version; readers are thus invited to engage first-hand with the question of how textual issues may substantially affect larger issues of meaning. And so on through all six volumes.

In a number of these cases the distinctive form of the anthology facilitates the presentation of content in an engaging and practical fashion. Notably, the adoption of a two-column format allows for some translations (the Marie de France *Lais*, the James Winny translation of *Sir Gawain and the Green Knight*) to be presented in parallel column format alongside the original texts, allowing readers to experience something of the flavor of the original, while providing convenient access to an accessible translation. Similarly, scenes from the Quarto version of *King Lear* are presented alongside the comparable sections of the Folio text, and passages from four translations of the Bible are laid out parallel to each other for ready comparison.

The large trim-size, two-column format also allows for greater flexibility in the presentation of visual materials. Throughout we have aimed to make this an anthology that is fully alive to the connections between literary and visual culture, from the discussion of the CHI-RHO page of the Lindisfarne Gospels in the first volume of the anthology (and the accompanying color illustration) to the inclusion in Volume 6 of a number of selections (including Graham Greene's "The Basement Room," Hanif Kureishi's "My Son the Fanatic," Tom Stoppard's "Professional Foul," and several skits from "Monty Python's Flying Circus") that may be discussed in connection with film or television versions. Along the way appear several full-page illustrations from the Ellesmere manuscript of Chaucer's *Canterbury Tales* and illustrations to a wide variety of other works, from *Robinson Crusoe* and *Gulliver's Travels* to *A Christmas Carol* and *The Road to Wigan Pier*.

CONTEXTUAL MATERIALS

Visual materials are also an important component of the background materials that form an important part of the anthology. These materials are presented in two ways. Several "Contexts" sections on particular topics or themes appear in each volume of the anthology, presented independent of any particular text or author. These include broadly based groupings of material on such topics as "Religion and Spiritual Life," "Print Culture," "India and the Orient," "The Abolition of Slavery," "The New Art of Photography," and "The End of Empire." The groups of "In Context" materials each relate to a particular text or author. They range from the genealogical tables provided as a supplement to *Beowulf*; to materials on "The Eighteenth-Century Sexual Imagination" (presented in conjunction with Haywood's *Fantomina*); to a selection of materials relating to the Peterloo massacre (presented in conjunction with Percy Shelley's "The Mask of Anarchy"); to materials on "'The Vilest Scramble for Loot' in Central Africa" (presented in conjunction with Conrad's "An Outpost of Progress"). For the most part these contextual materials are, as the word suggests, included with a view to setting texts in their broader literary, historical, and cultural contexts; in some cases, however, the materials included in "Contexts" sections are themselves literary works of a high order. The autobiographical account by Eliza M. of nineteenth-century life in Cape Town, for example (included in the section in Volume 5 on "Race and Empire"), is as remarkable for its literary qualities as it is for the light it sheds on the realities of colonial life. In the inclusion of texts such as these, as well as in other ways, the anthology aims to encourage readers to explore the boundaries of the literary and the non-literary, and the issue of what constitutes a "literary text."

WOMEN'S PLACE

A central element of the broadening of the canon of British literature in recent generations has of course been a great increase in the attention paid to texts by women writers. As one might expect from a publisher that has played an important role in making neglected works by women writers widely available, this anthology reflects the broadening of the canon quantitatively, by including a substantially larger number of women writers than have earlier anthologies of British literature. But it also reflects this broadening in other ways. In many anthologies of literature (anthologies of British literature, to be sure, but also anthologies of literature of a variety of other sorts) women writers are set somewhat apart, referenced in introductions and headnotes only in relation to issues of gender, and treated as important only for the fact of their being women writers. *The Broadview Anthology* strenuously resists such segregation; while women writers are of course discussed in relation to gender issues, their texts are also presented and discussed alongside those by men in a wide variety of other contexts, including seventeenth-century religious and political controversies, the abolitionist movement and World War I pacifism. Texts by women writers are front and center in the discussion of the development of realism in nineteenth-century fiction. And when it comes to the twentieth century, both Virginia Woolf and Dorothy Richardson are included alongside James Joyce as practitioners of groundbreaking modernist narrative techniques.

"BRITISH," "ENGLISH," "IRISH," "SCOTTISH," "WELSH," "OTHER"

The broadening of English Studies, in conjunction with the expansion and subsequent contraction of British power and influence around the world, has considerably complicated the issue of exactly how inclusive anthologies should be. In several respects this anthology (like its two main competitors) is significantly more inclusive than its title suggests, including a number of non-British writers whose works connect in important ways with the traditions of British literature. We have endeavored first of all to portray the fluid and multilingual reality of the medieval period through the inclusion not only of works in Old and Middle English but also, where other cultures interacted with the nascent "English" language and "British" culture, works in Latin, in French, and in Welsh. In later periods the word "British" becomes deeply problematic in different respects, but on balance we have preferred it to the only obvious alternative, "English." There are several objections to the latter in this context. Perhaps most obviously, "English" excludes authors or texts not only from Ireland but also from Scotland and from Wales, both of which retain to this day cultures quite distinct from that of the English. "English literature," of course, may also be taken to mean "literature written in English," but since the anthology does not cover *all* literature written in English (most obviously in excluding American literature), the ambiguity would not in this case be helpful.

The inclusion of Irish writers presents a related but even more tangled set of issues. At the beginning of the period covered by the six volumes of this anthology we find works, such as the *Book of Kells*, that may have been created in what is now England, in what is now Scotland, in what is now Ireland—or in some combination of these. Through most of the seventeenth, eighteenth, and nineteenth centuries almost the whole of Ireland was under British control—but for the most part unwillingly. In the period covered in the last of the six volumes Ireland was partitioned, with Northern Ireland becoming a part of the United Kingdom and the

Republic of Ireland declared independent of Britain on 6 December 1921. Less than two months earlier, James Joyce had completed *Ulysses*, which was first published as a complete work the following year (in Paris, not in Britain). It would be obviously absurd to regard Joyce as a British writer up to just before the publication of *Ulysses*, and an Irish writer thereafter. And arguably he and other Irish writers should never be regarded as British, whatever the politics of the day. If on no other grounds than their overwhelming influence on and connection to the body of literature written in the British Isles, however, we have included Irish writers—among them Swift, Sheridan, Wilde, Shaw, Beckett, Bowen, Muldoon, and Heaney as well as Joyce—throughout this anthology. We have also endeavored to give a real sense in the introductions to the six volumes of the anthology, in the headnotes to individual authors, and in the annotations to the texts themselves, of the ways in which the histories and the cultures of England, Ireland, Scotland and Wales, much as they interact with one another, are also distinct.

Also included in this anthology are texts by writers from areas that are far removed geographically from the British Isles but that are or have been British possessions. Writers such as Mary Rowlandson, Olaudah Equiano, and Phillis Wheatley are included, as they spent all or most of their lives living in what were then British colonial possessions. Writers who came of age in an independent United States, on the other hand, are not included, unless (like T.S. Eliot) they subsequently put down roots in Britain and became important British literary figures. Substantial grey areas, of course, surround such issues. One might well argue, for example, that Henry James merits inclusion in an anthology of British literature, or that W.H. Auden and Thom Gunn are more American poets than British ones. But the chosen subject matter of James's work has traditionally been considered to mark him as having remained an American writer, despite having spent almost two-thirds of his life in England. And both Auden and Gunn so clearly made a mark in Britain before crossing the Atlantic that it would seem odd to exclude them from these pages on the grounds of their having lived the greater part of their adult lives in America. One of our competitors includes Sylvia Plath in their anthology of British literature; Plath lived in England for only five of her thirty years, though, and her poetry is generally agreed to have more in common with the traditions of Lowell, Merwin and Sexton than with the currents of British poetry in the 1950s and '60s.

As a broad principle, we have been open to the inclusion of twentieth and twenty-first century work in English not only by writers from the British Isles but also by writers from British possessions overseas, and by writers from countries that were once British possessions and have remained a part of the British Commonwealth. In such cases we have often chosen selections that relate in one way or another to the tradition of British literature and the British colonial legacy. Of the Judith Wright poems included here, several relate to her coming to terms with the British colonial legacy in Australia; similarly, both the Margaret Atwood and the Alice Munro selections include work in which these Canadian authors attempt to recreate imaginatively the experience of British emigrants to Canada in the nineteenth century; the Chinua Achebe story in the anthology concerns the divide between British colonial culture and traditional Nigerian culture; and so on. For convenience we have also grouped most of the post-World War II non-British authors together, following the "Contexts: The End of Empire" section. (Other than that, the table of contents for the anthology is arranged chronologically according to the birthdate of each author.)

The History of Language, and of Print Culture

Among the liveliest discussions we had at meetings of our General Editors were those concerning the issue of whether or not to bring spelling and punctuation into accord with present-day practice. We finally decided that, in the interests of making the anthology accessible to the introductory student, we should *in most cases* bring spelling and punctuation in line with present-day practice. An important exception has been made for works in which modernizing spelling and punctuation would alter the meaning or the aural and metrical qualities. In practice this means that works before the late sixteenth century tend to be presented either in their original form or in translation, whereas later texts tend to have spelling and punctuation modernized. But where spelling and punctuation choices in later texts are known (or believed on reliable authority) to represent conscious choice on the part of the author rather than simply the common practice of the time, we have in those cases, too, made an exception and retained the original spelling and punctuation. (Among these are texts by Edmund Spenser, by William Cowper, by William Blake, John Clare, and several other poets of the Romantic era, by George Bernard Shaw, and by contemporary figures such as Linton Kwesi Johnson.)

Beyond this, we all agreed that we should provide for readers a real sense of the development of the language and of print culture. To that end we have included in each volume examples of texts in their original form—in some cases through the use of pages shown in facsimile, in others by providing short passages in which spelling and punctuation have not been modernized. A list of these appears near the beginning of each volume of the anthology.

We have also included a section of the history of the language as part of the introduction to each volume. And throughout the anthology we include materials—visual as well as textual—relating to the history of print culture.

A DYNAMIC AND FLEXIBLE ANTHOLOGY

Almost all major book publishing projects nowadays are accompanied by an adjunct website, and most large-scale anthologies are accompanied by websites that provide additional background materials in electronic form. The website component of this anthology, on the other hand, is precisely that—a *component* of the anthology itself. The notion of a website of this sort grew organically out of the process of trying to winnow down the contents of the anthology to a manageable level—the point at which all the material to be included would fit within the covers of bound books that would not be overwhelmingly heavy. And we simply could not do it. After we had made a very substantial round of cuts we were still faced with a table of contents in which each volume was at least 200 or 300 pages longer than our agreed-upon maximum. Our solution was not to try to cut anything more, but rather to select a range of material to be made available in a website component of the anthology. This material is in every way produced according to the same high standards of the material in the bound books; the editorial standards, the procedures for annotation, the author introductions, and the page design and layout—all are the same. The texts on the web, in short, are not "extra" materials; they are an integral part of the full anthology. In accordance with that principle, we have been careful to include a wide range of texts by lesser-known writers within the bound books, and a number of texts by canonical writers within the web component of the anthology.

The latter may be used in a variety of ways. Most obviously, readings from the web component are available to any purchaser of the book. Instructors who adopt *The Broadview Anthology of British Literature* as a course text are also granted permission to reproduce any web material for which Broadview holds copyright in a supplementary coursepack. An alternative for instructors who want to "create their own" anthology is to provide the publisher with a list of desired table of contents; Broadview will then make available to students through their university bookstore a custom-made coursepack with precisely those materials included. Other options are available too. Volumes of the anthology itself may of course be shrink-wrapped together at special prices in any desired combination. They may also (for a modest additional charge) be combined in a shrink-wrapped package with one or more of the over 200 volumes in the Broadview Editions series.

We anticipate that over the years the web-based component of the anthology will continue to grow—every year there will be a greater choice of web-based texts in the anthology. And every year too we anticipate additional web "extras" (discussed below). But we never foresee a day when the web will be the only option; we expect physical books always to remain central to Broadview's approach to publishing.

THE BROADVIEW LIST

One of the reasons we have been able to bring a project of this sort to fruition in such a relatively short time is that we have been able to draw on the resources of the full Broadview list: the many titles in the Broadview Editions series, and also the considerable range of other Broadview anthologies. As the contributors' pages and the permissions acknowledgments pages indicate, a number of Broadview authors have acted as contributing editors to this volume, providing material from other volumes that has been adapted to suit the needs of the present anthology; we gratefully acknowledge their contribution.

As it has turned out, the number of cases where we have been able to draw on the resources of the Broadview list in the full sense, using in these pages texts and annotations in very much the same form in which they appear elsewhere, has been relatively small; whether because of an issue such as the level of textual modernization or one of style of annotation, we have more often than not ended up deciding that the requirements of this anthology were such that we could not use material from another Broadview source as-is. But even in these cases we often owe a debt of gratitude to the many academics who have edited outstanding editions and anthologies for Broadview. For even where we have not drawn directly from them, we have often been inspired by them— inspired to think of a wider range of texts as possibilities than we might otherwise have done, inspired to think of contextual materials in places where we might otherwise not have looked, inspired by the freshness of approach that so many of these titles exemplify.

EDITORIAL PROCEDURES AND CONVENTIONS, APPARATUS

The in-house set of editorial guidelines for *The Broadview Anthology of British Literature* now runs to over 40 pages, covering everything from conventions for the spacing of marginal notes, to the use of small caps for the abbreviations CE and BCE, to the approach we have adopted to references in author headnotes to name changes. Perhaps the most important core principle in the introductions to the various volumes, in the headnotes for each author, in the introductions in "Contexts" sections, and in annotations throughout the anthology, is to endeavor to provide a sufficient amount of information to enable students to read and interpret these texts, but without making evaluative judgements or imposing particular interpretations. In practice that is all a good deal more challenging than it sounds; it is often extremely difficult to describe why a particular author is considered to be important without using language that verges on the interpretive or the evaluative. But it is fine line that we have all agreed is worth trying to walk; we hope that readers will find that the anthology achieves an appropriate balance.

ANNOTATION: It is also often difficult to make judgments as to where it is appropriate to provide an explanatory annotation for a word or phrase. Our policy as been to annotate where we feel it likely that most first- or second-year students are likely to have difficulty understanding the denotative meaning. (We have made it a practice not to provide notes discussing connotative meanings.) But in practice the vocabularies and levels of verbal facility of first- and second-year students may vary enormously, both from institution to institution and within any given college or university class. On the whole, we provide somewhat more annotation than our competitors, and somewhat less interpretation. Again, we hope that readers will find that the anthology has struck a appropriate balance.

THE ETHICS AND POLITICS OF ANNOTATION: On one issue regarding annotation we have felt that principles are involved that go beyond the pedagogical. Most anthologies of British literature allow many words or phrases of a racist, sexist, anti-Semitic, or homophobic nature either to pass entirely without comment, or to be glossed with apologist comments that leave the impression that such comments were excusable in the past, and may even be unobjectionable in the present. Where derogatory comments about Jewish people and money-lending are concerned, for example, anthologies often leave the impression that money-lending was a pretty unsavory practice that Jewish people entered by choice; it has been all too rare to provide readers with any sense of the degree to which English society consistently discriminated against Jews, expelling them entirely for several centuries, requiring them to wear physical marks identifying their Jewish status, prohibiting them from entering most professions, and so on. *The Broadview*

Anthology endeavors in such cases, first of all, not to allow such words and phrases to pass without comment; and second, to gloss without glossing over.

DATES: We make it a practice to include the date when a work was first made public, whether publication in print or, in the case of dramatic works, made public through the first performance of the play. Where that date is known to differ substantially from the date of composition, a note to this effect is included in parentheses. With medieval works, where there is no equivalent to the "publication" of later eras, where texts often vary greatly from one manuscript copy to another, and where knowledge as to date of original composition is usually imprecise, the date that appears at the end of each work is an estimate of the date of the work's origin in the written form included in the anthology. Earlier oral or written versions are of course in some cases real possibilities.

TEXTS: Where translations appear in this anthology, a note at the bottom of the first page indicates what translation is being used. Similar notes also address overall textual issues where choice of copy text is particularly significant. Reliable editions of all works are listed in the bibliography for the anthology, which is included as part of the website component rather than in the bound books, to facilitate ready revision. (In addition to information as to reliable editions, the bibliography provides for each author and for each of the six periods a select lists of important or useful historical and critical works.) Copyright information for texts not in the public domain, however, is provided within the bound books in a section listing Permissions Acknowledgments.

INTRODUCTIONS: In addition to the introductory headnotes for each author included in the anthology, each "Contexts" section includes a substantial introduction, and each volume includes an introduction to the period as a whole. These introductions to the six volumes of the anthology endeavor to provide a sense not only of the broad picture of literary developments in the period, but also of the historical, social, and political background, and of the cultural climate. Readers should be cautioned that, while there is inevitably some overlap between information presented here and information presented in the author headnotes, an effort has been made to avoid such repetition as much as possible; the general introduction to each period should thus be read in conjunction with the author headnotes. The general introductions aim not only to provide an overview of ways in which texts and authors included in these pages may connect with one another, but also to give readers a sense of connection with a range of other writers and texts of the period.

READING POETRY: For much of the glossary and for the "Reading Poetry" section that appears as part of the appendices to each volume we have drawn on the superb material prepared by Herbert Rosengarten and Amanda Goldrick-Jones for *The Broadview Anthology of Poetry*; this section provides a concise but comprehensive introduction to the study of poetry. It includes discussions of diction, imagery, poetic figures, and various poetic forms, as well as offering an introduction to prosody.

MAPS: Also appearing within each of the bound books are maps especially prepared for this anthology, including, for each volume, a map of Britain showing towns and features of relevance during the pertinent period; a map showing the counties of Britain and of Ireland; maps both of the London area and of the inner city; and world maps indicating the locations of some of the significant places referenced in the anthology, and for later volumes showing the extent of Britain's overseas territories.

GLOSSARY: Some other anthologies of British literature include both glossaries of terms and essays introducing students to various political and religious categories in British history. Similar information is included in *The Broadview Anthology of British Literature*, but we have adopted a more integrated approach, including political and religious terms along with literary ones in a convenient general glossary. While we recognize that "googling" for information of this sort is often the student's first resort (and we recognize too the value of searching the web for the wealth of background reference information available there), we also recognize that information culled from the Internet is often far from reliable; it is our intent, through this glossary, through our introductions and headnotes, and through the wealth of accessible annotation in the anthology, to provide as part of the anthology a reliable core of information in the most convenient and accessible form possible.

OTHER MATERIALS: A chart of Monarchs and Prime Ministers is also provided within these pages. A range of other adjunct materials may be accessed through *The Broadview Anthology of British Literature* website. "Texts and Contexts" charts for each volume provide a convenient parallel reference guide to the dates of literary texts and historical developments. "Money in Britain" provides a thumbnail sketch of the world of pounds, shillings, and pence, together with a handy guide to estimating the current equivalents of monetary values from earlier eras. And the website offers, too, a variety of aids for the student and the instructor. An up-to-date list of these appears on the site.

Acknowledgments

The names of those on the Editorial Board that shaped this anthology appear on the title page, and those of the many who contributed directly to the writing, editing, and production of the project on the following two pages. Special acknowledgment should go to Jennifer McCue, who as Editorial Coordinator has been instrumental in tying together all the vast threads of this project and in making it a reality; to Laura Cardiff and Jude Polsky, who have carried larger loads than any others in drafting introductory materials and annotations, and who have done so with great skill and unfailing grace; to Kathryn Brownsey, who has been responsible for design and typesetting, and has continued to do a superb job and to maintain her good spirits even when faced with near-impossible demands; to Colleen Franklin, for the range of her scholarship as well as for her keen eye as our primary copy editor for the entire project; to Emily Cargan, Jennifer Elsayed and Amy Nimegeer who have together done superb work on the vast job of clearing permissions for the anthology; and to Michelle Lobkowicz and Anna Del Col, who have ably and enthusiastically taken the lead with marketing matters.

The academic members of the Advisory Editorial Board and all of us in-house at Broadview owe an enormous debt of gratitude to the hundreds of academics who have offered assistance at various stages of this project. In particular we would like to express our appreciation and our thanks to the following:

Rachel Ablow, University of Rochester
Bryan Alexander, Middlebury College
Sharon Alker, Whitman College
James Allard, Brock University
Laurel Amtower, San Diego State University
Rob Anderson, Oakland University
Christopher Armitage, University of North Carolina, Chapel Hill
Clinton Atchley, Henderson State University
John Baird, University of Toronto
William Baker, Northern Illinois University
Karen Bamford, Mount Allison University
John Batchelor, University of Newcastle
Lynn Batten, University of California, Los Angeles
Alexandra Bennett, Northern Illinois University
John Beynon, California State University, Fresno
Robert E. Bjork, Arizona State University
Rita Bode, Trent University
Robert Boenig, Texas A & M University
Rick Bowers, University of Alberta
David Brewer, Ohio State University
William Brewer, Appalachian State University
Susan Brown, University of Guelph
Sylvia Brown, University of Alberta
Sheila Burgar, University of Victoria
Catherine Burroughs, Wells College
Rebecca Bushnell, University of Pennsylvania
Elizabeth Campbell, Oregon State University
Cynthia Caywood, University of San Diego
Jane Chance, Rice University
Ranita Chatterjee, California State University, Northridge
Nancy Cirillo, University of Illinois, Chicago
Eric Clarke, University of Pittsburgh
Jeanne Clegg, University of Aquila, Italy
Thomas J. Collins, University of Western Ontario
Kevin Cope, Louisiana State University
David Cowart, University of South Carolina
Catherine Craft-Fairchild, University of St. Thomas
Carol Davison, University of Windsor
Alex Dick, University of British Columbia
Len Diepeveen, Dalhousie University

Mary Dockray-Miller, Lesley College
Frank Donoghue, Ohio State University
Chris Downs, Saint James School
Julie Early, University of Alabama, Huntsville
Siân Echard, University of British Columbia
Garrett Epp, University of Alberta
Daniel Fischlin, University of Guelph
Verlyn Flieger, University of Maryland
Robert Forman, St. John's University
Roberta Frank, Yale University
Jeff Franklin, University of Colorado, Denver
Maria Frawley, George Washington University
Mark Fulk, Buffalo State College
Andrew Galloway, Cornell University
Michael Gamer, University of Pennsylvania
Barbara Gates, University of Delaware
Daniel Gonzalez, University of New Orleans
Jan Gorak, University of Denver
Chris Gordon-Craig, University of Alberta
Ann-Barbara Graff, Georgia Tech University
Michael Griffin, formerly of Southern Illinois University
Elisabeth Gruner, University of Richmond
Stephen Guy-Bray, University of British Columbia
Ruth Haber, Worcester State College
Margaret Hadley, University of Calgary
Robert Hampson, Royal Holloway University of London
Michael Hanly, Washington State University
Lila Harper, Central Washington State University
Joseph Harris, Harvard University
Anthony Harrison, North Carolina State University
Douglas Hayes, Winona State University
Jennifer Hellwarth, Allegheny University
Peter Herman, San Diego State University
Kathy Hickock, Iowa State University
John Hill, US Naval Academy
Thomas Hill, Cornell University
Elizabeth Hodgson, University of British Columbia
Joseph Hornsby, University of Alabama
Scott Howard, University of Denver
Tara Hyland-Russell, St. Mary's College
Catherine Innes-Parker, University of Prince Edward Island
Jacqueline Jenkins, University of Calgary
John Johansen, University of Alberta
Richard Juang, Susquehanna University
Michael Keefer, University of Guelph
Sarah Keefer, Trent University
Jon Kertzer, University of Calgary
Helen Killoran, Ohio University
Gordon Kipling, University of California, Los Angeles
Anne Klinck, University of New Brunswick
Elizabeth Kraft, University of Georgia
Mary Kramer, University of Massachusetts, Lowell
Linda Leeds, Bellevue Community College
Mary Elizabeth Leighton, University of Victoria
William Liston, Ball State University
Sharon Locy, Loyola Marymount University
Peter Mallios, University of Maryland
Arnold Markley, Penn State University
Pamela McCallum, University of Calgary
Kristen McDermott, Central Michigan University
John McGowan, University of North Carolina
Thomas McLean, University of Otago, New Zealand
Rod Michell, Thompson Rivers University
Kitty Millett, San Francisco State University
Richard Moll, University of Western Ontario
Monique Morgan, McGill University
Lucy Morrison, Salisbury University
Byron Nelson, West Virginia University
Carolyn Nelson, West Virginia University
Claudia Nelson, Southwest Texas State University
Holly Faith Nelson, Trinity Western University
John Niles, University of Wisconsin, Madison
Michael North, University of California, Los Angeles
Mary Anne Nunn, Central Connecticut State University
David Oakleaf, University of Calgary
Tamara O'Callaghan, Northern Kentucky University
Karen Odden, Assistant Editor for *Victorian Literature and Culture* (formerly of University of Wisconsin, Milwaukee)
Erika Olbricht, Pepperdine University
Patrick O'Malley, Georgetown University
Patricia O'Neill, Hamilton College
Delilah Orr, Fort Lewis College
Cynthia Patton, Emporia State University
Russell Perkin, St. Mary's University
Marjorie G. Perloff, Stanford University
John Peters, University of North Texas

Alexander Pettit, University of North Texas
Jennifer Phegley, The University of Missouri, Kansas City
John Pollock, San Jose State University
Mary Poovey, New York University
Gautam Premnath, University of Massachusetts, Boston
Regina Psaki, University of Oregon
Katherine Quinsey, University of Windsor
Geoff Rector, University of Ottawa
Margaret Reeves, Atkinson College, York University
Cedric Reverand, University of Wyoming
Gerry Richman, Suffolk University
David Robinson, University of Arizona
Laura Rotunno, Pennsylvania State University, Altoona
Nicholas Ruddick, University of Regina
Jason Rudy, University of Maryland
Donelle Ruwe, Northern Arizona University
Michelle Sauer, Minot State University
SueAnn Schatz, Lock Haven University of Pennsylvania
Dan Schierenbeck, Central Missouri State University
Norbert Schürer, California State University, Long Beach
David Seed, University of Liverpool
Carol Senf, Georgia Tech University
Judith Slagle, East Tennessee State University
Sharon Smulders, Mount Royal College
Malinda Snow, Georgia State University
Goran Stanivukovic, St. Mary's University
Richard Stein, University of Oregon
Eric Sterling, Auburn University Montgomery
James Stokes, University of Wisconsin, Stevens Point
Mary-Ann Stouck, Simon Fraser University
Nathaniel Strout, Hamilton College
Lisa Surridge, University of Victoria
Beth Sutton-Ramspeck, Ohio State University
Nanora Sweet, University of Missouri, St. Louis
Dana Symons, Simon Fraser University
Andrew Taylor, University of Ottawa
Elizabeth Teare, University of Dayton
Doug Thorpe, University of Saskatchewan
Jane Toswell, University of Western Ontario
Herbert Tucker, University of Virginia
John Tucker, University of Victoria
Mark Turner, King's College, University of London
Eleanor Ty, Wilfrid Laurier University
Deborah Tyler-Bennett, Loughborough University
Kirsten Uszkalo, University of Alberta
Lisa Vargo, University of Saskatchewan
Gina Luria Walker, The New School, New York City
Kim Walker, Victoria University of Wellington
Miriam Wallace, New College of Florida
Hayden Ward, West Virginia State University
Ruth Wehlau, Queen's University
Lynn Wells, University of Regina
Chris Willis, Birkbeck University of London
Lisa Wilson, SUNY College at Potsdam
Anne Windholz, Augustana College
Susan Wolfson, Princeton University
Kenneth Womack, Pennsylvania State University
Carolyn Woodward, University of New Mexico
Julia Wright, Wilfrid Laurier University
Julian Yates, University of Delaware
Arlene Young, University of Manitoba
Lisa Zeitz, University of Western Ontario

The Age of Romanticism

Perhaps more than any other era in English history, the Romantic period expressed its ongoing evolution in its clothing. When the artistic, literary, and political changes that are usually associated with Romanticism began in the 1780s, the heavy and elaborate costumes of the eighteenth century still prevailed, constricting their wearers into a rigid formality mirrored in the contemporaneous social and aesthetic structures. In the years surrounding the French Revolution, heady with the possibility of greater freedom, these stiff garments gave way to loose, flowing dresses for women, cut from muslins and patterned cottons that had been rendered relatively inexpensive by increasing British Imperial control in the East and by technological advances in weaving in Britain itself. During the same period local militiamen, sporting gorgeous military uniforms, demonstrated both Britain's growing national pride and its persistent fear of French invasion. By the time the Romantic period drew to a close in the mid-1830s, these looser fashions and glittering uniforms had themselves been superseded by the tightly-laced corsets, salt-and-pepper trousers, and bell skirts heavily supported by hoops and petticoats that are now inextricably associated with English Victorianism.

Morning dress, c. 1800.

Ball Dress, c. 1800.

Richard Dighton, *George "Beau" Brummell*, 1805. Brummell, the leading "dandy" of the age, brought into fashion a new style of dress coat, pantaloons, and black evening dress for men. Brummell was fastidious about cleanliness as well as clothing, but denounced perfume for men and any form of showy display.

As the combination of freedom and militarism expressed in Romantic fashions suggests, the fifty years between the French Revolution and the reign of Queen Victoria were neither historically simple nor culturally straightforward. Despite its seeming cohesiveness and unity, the Romantic period was a complex nexus of revolution and conservatism, of bold iconoclasm and hidebound conventionality.

Revolutions played a central role in shaping the Romantic period—and continue to shape our perceptions of it. The form and structure of the British Romantic era, and of the concept "Romanticism" itself, have changed radically in recent decades. What in the mid-twentieth century was seen as a literary period centered on five or six major poets, all male, and a select number of prose writers, also all male, has gradually come to be seen as an era in which writers and thinkers of different genders, beliefs, and social backgrounds all contributed to shaping their era. Whereas students once covered British Romantic poetry by reading only William Blake, William Wordsworth, Samuel Taylor Coleridge, Lord Byron, Percy Shelley, and John Keats (collectively known as "The Big Six"), they now also hear the voices of Mary Robinson, Anna Letitia Barbauld, Felicia Hemans, and Letitia Landon—all respected and popular in their day but largely unstudied until recently. Whereas reading Romantic prose nonfiction once meant for the most part reading Coleridge, Charles Lamb, and William Hazlitt, students now explore the proto-feminist writing of Mary Wollstonecraft, the didactic prose of Hannah More and Maria Edgeworth, and myriad others. The prose fiction of the period (aside from a nod or two acknowledging Jane Austen and Sir Walter Scott) was once given short shrift, and the drama even less. Nowadays Mary Shelley's novels—particularly *Frankenstein* and *The Last Man*—receive at least as much critical attention as do the works of her spouse, with *Frankenstein* probably being read more widely than any other single work of the Romantic period; Austen's works are now seen to hold a central position in the history of the novel; and the work of other writers of fiction—from William Godwin to Mary Hays, Amelia Opie, Mary Robinson, and Charlotte Smith—has been much more fully and more favorably assessed. In the study of drama a similar if less marked shift has occurred, with the importance of the work of Hannah Cowley, Elizabeth Inchbald and Joanna Baillie, as well as that of Percy Shelley and of Byron, being newly recognized.

If recent decades have brought a substantial shift in the emphasis placed on various authors in the study of the Romantic period, they have also brought a shift in the way the period as a whole is perceived. Whereas Romantic literature in English was once discussed far more with reference to nature and to the imagination than it was with reference to politics or to ideology, a broader perspective is now almost universally acknowledged as essential to a comprehensive understanding of the period. At the same time, it is still almost universally accepted that the Romantic mind-set and the literary works it produced were shaped, above all, by the French Revolution and the Industrial Revolution.

For Romanticism, the French Revolution was epoch-making. When the Bastille fell on 14 July 1789 and the French National Assembly issued its democratic, anti-monarchical *Declaration of the Rights of Man and Citizen* on August 27 of the same year, it seemed to the people of Great Britain, a mere twelve miles across the Channel, that a new dawn was on the horizon. For liberals and for many authors, artists, and intellectuals, this dawn was a rosy one, promising not only greater equality and better government in France itself, but also the beginning of a thoroughgoing transformation of the world. Mary Robinson's "Ainsi Va Le Monde" (1791) provides a vivid sense of the degree to which a fervent faith in and enthusiasm for freedom knew no bounds in the breasts of many writers of the time:

> Hark! "Freedom" echoes thro' the vaulted skies.
> The goddess speaks! O mark the blest decree,—
> Tyrants Shall Fall—Triumphant Man Be Free!

Wordsworth, present in France during the early days of the Revolution, famously wrote of it later, "Bliss was it in that dawn to be alive!", while his friend and fellow poet Robert Southey recalled that "a visionary world seemed to open … [N]othing was dreamt of but regeneration of the human race." Mary Wollstonecraft, who had recently published *A Vindication of the Rights of Woman*, moved to Paris in 1792, also inspired by revolutionary idealism. The Revolution became a central metaphor in the works of William Blake, and a central psychological influence on all the first generation Romantic writers.

The younger generation too, particularly Byron and Shelley, were stirred by revolutionary fervor. What these poets hoped for, however was a continuation of the *spirit* of the French Revolution. For, in actuality, Wordsworth's new dawn soon darkened into a terrible thunderstorm and a rain of blood. In August of 1792, the leaders of the Revolution overthrew the French monarchy, and a month later a Paris mob massacred more than a thousand prisoners whom they believed to be royalist conspirators. Extremist Jacobins[1] now prevailed over more moderate Girondins, and the Revolution turned into the Reign of Terror (1793–94). In January 1793, King Louis XVI went to the guillotine; Marie Antoinette followed him in October. France declared war on Britain in 1793, and Britain reciprocated. As the terror progressed under the guidance of Maximilien Robespierre, thousands of aristocrats, clergy, and alleged opponents of the Revolution were guillotined including, eventually, Robespierre himself. In 1794 France offered to support any and all revolutions abroad, and then proceeded to invade its neighbors. In 1799, Napoleon had himself named First Consul for life, and in 1804 he crowned himself Emperor. When he invaded the Iberian Peninsula in 1807, Britain intervened to aid the Spanish and Portuguese: what became known as the Napoleonic Wars did not end until Napoleon was thoroughly routed at the Battle of Waterloo in 1815.

What had begun as a movement for democracy, then, had become a military dictatorship. Looking back from a distance of twenty-four years, Byron wrote that the French made themselves a fearful monument:

> The wreck of old opinions …
> … the veil they rent
> And what behind it lay all earth shall view.
> But good with ill they also overthrew,
> Leaving but ruins, wherewith to rebuild
> Upon the same foundation, and renew
> Dungeons and thrones … (*Childe Harold* 3.82)

The Revolution's promise of freedom died in a frenzy of oppression, destruction, violence, and imperialism, and many of Britain's intellectuals watched in horror, gradually turning from bold liberalism to a cautious conservatism they saw as both pragmatic and necessary. To use the political terminology that first developed out of the seating arrangements in the French National Constituent Assembly in 1789, they moved from the left of center to the right of center; Wordsworth, Coleridge, and Southey, all radical thinkers in their youth, were firm conservatives by the end of their

[1] Throughout the Romantic period the terms "Jacobin" and "anti-Jacobin" were employed to describe those in sympathy with and those opposed to revolutionary ideals of the sort that had been promulgated during the French Revolution.

William Heath, *The Battle of Waterloo* (detail), 1815. British infantrymen to the right are firing into the ranks of the French cavalry. The full battle involved approximately 75,000 French troops under Napoleon; the Duke of Wellington commanded an allied force of well over 100,000. The casualties totaled over 50,000—60 per cent of them French.

lives. Others—such as Barbauld—remained politically on the left, but became disillusioned both by the course that revolution had taken in France and by the failure of the British to embrace the principles of freedom. Barbauld surveyed what seemed to her a decadent and oppressive England in "Eighteen Hundred and Eleven"—"The worm is in thy core, thy glories pass away"—and Shelley despaired in "England in 1819" at "Rulers who neither see nor feel nor know, / But leech-like to their fainting country cling."

The British government's response to the developments in France had been swift and repressive. In 1794 they suspended the right of habeas corpus, which required the state to show legitimate cause for imprisonment and to carry out trials in a timely manner. As a result, those accused of crimes could be held for an indefinite period. In 1795, Parliament passed the Treasonable Practices Act, which made criticism of the government a crime; in the same year it passed an act that limited the size of public meetings and the places in which they could be held. The Combination Acts of 1799 and 1800 forbade workers to associate for the purposes of collective bargaining. To enforce all these restrictive measures, the government set loose a herd of spies, many of whom acted as *agents provocateurs*, infiltrating liberal and radical groups and prompting them to commit criminal acts they otherwise might not have committed. In at least one important case, that of the Cato Street Conspiracy of 1820 (a scheme to murder cabinet ministers and stage a government *coup*), these government agents first urged on and then exposed conspirators who were punished with hanging or with transportation to Australia. In Scotland and Ireland, authoritarianism could be even more severe, particularly since rebellion there required no instigating: in 1798, the United Irishmen, led by Theobald Wolfe Tone and Lord Edward Fitzgerald and assisted by French forces, attempted a country-wide uprising to achieve complete Irish independence. The rebellion ended in failure, and the oppression of the Irish under

British rule became more strongly entrenched than ever.

If the French Revolution and the 22 years of war with France that followed produced ruinous government authoritarianism, they also acted to create for the first time a widespread and shared sense among British citizens that England, Wales, Scotland and, to a lesser extent, Ireland, formed one cohesive nation: Great Britain. Scotland had been linked to England by the Union of 1707, while union with Ireland, which had been firmly under English control since the time of Cromwell, was made official with the Act of Union in 1800. The wars with France allowed the English people to see themselves as leading a larger body defending liberty and freedom (even if that liberty and freedom were now, ironically, defined by a conservative authoritarian mind-set). At the same time, the wars raised very real threats of invasion—there were scares in 1778, 1796–98, and 1803, and Wales was actually invaded in 1797. As so often happens, threats from without acted to foster cohesion within. Foreign travel was out of the question for all but the very rich or the very brave; Great Britain turned inward and discovered itself, instead. Sir Walter Scott's collection of folk-songs and ballads, *Minstrelsy of the Scottish Border* (1802–03), Thomas Moore's *Irish Melodies* (1807–34), and Felicia Hemans's *Welsh Melodies* (1822), all gave their readers a sense of the nation's rich past, while at the same time celebrating the blend of cultures that went into making up Great Britain. Regional poets such as Robert Burns and John Clare gave proud voice to those cultures, so that the individual nations which made up the one great nation were simultaneously celebrated in and recognized as within the British fold. Long poetical works such as John Thelwall's *The Hope of Albion; or Edwin of Northumbria* (1801) expanded the sense of an epic British mythology, while collections such as Hemans's *Tales and Historic Scenes* (1819), a celebration of military valor, fostered a sense of pride in present-day accomplishments.

T.W. Huffram, *Theobald Wolfe Tone*, date unknown.
Tone is shown in French uniform.

James Gillray, *United Irishmen in Training*, 1798. The famous English caricaturist here portrays the Irish as cruel buffoons; they are assaulting a British uniform stuffed with straw.

The sense of a larger Britain, though, did nothing to lessen the belief among the English that England was specifically and even divinely favored. Such notions were perhaps given their most memorable, if also most ambivalent, expression in the opening to William Blake's "Preface" to *Milton* (1804), in which ancient England is linked with Christ:

And did those feet in ancient time
Walk upon England's mountain's green?
And was the Holy Lamb of God
On England's pleasant pastures seen?
And did the countenance divine
Shine forth upon our clouded hills?[1]

Although Blake leaves it up to his reader to determine whether the answer to these rhetorical questions is yes or no, the stanza that follows explicitly figures England as a land worthy to be the new Jerusalem (if only sometime in the future):

I will not cease from mental fight,
Nor shall my sword sleep in my hand,
Till we have built Jerusalem
In England's green and pleasant land.

Between these invocations of the divine in Britain, however, Blake inserts an insidious question, and one that began to plague English writers and citizens more and more as the Romantic period progressed: "was Jerusalem builded here/Among these dark Satanic mills?" The phrase "dark Satanic mills" has become the most famous description of the force at the center of the industrial revolution. Even as the French Revolution changed the consciousness of the British people, this other revolution in their own country had as much impact on them as did any conflagration abroad.

Beginning in the sixteenth and seventeenth centuries the British Isles, and England in particular, had been undergoing wholesale changes in economic structure. The pace of change increased dramatically as the eighteenth century progressed. From being a largely rural

Thomas Girtin, *Westminster from Lambeth*, c. 1800.
Girtin's watercolor was one of a series of sketches for a panorama of London (now lost).

[1] *And did those feet … clouded hills* The opening two stanzas (a total of 16 lines) were set to music by Charles H.H. Parry in 1916; under the title "Jerusalem," these verses have become an unofficial national anthem for the English.

nation with a largely agricultural economy, Britain became an urban nation with an economy based in manufacturing. James Watt's refinement of the steam engine, and James Hargreaves's invention of the Spinning Jenny (a machine that allowed cotton to be woven on several spindles simultaneously) are only the most famous of a host of changes that produced a boom in industrialization. Factories sprang up in what had once been countryside: the populations of towns and cities, particularly those associated with manufacture, swelled. At the beginning of the 1770s, about a quarter of England's population lived in urban centers, but by 1801 that proportion had risen to one third, and by the 1840s half of the English population resided in cities. In 1750, the total English population was roughly 5.5 million; by the time of the first census in 1800, it had grown to 8 million, while the population of Scotland and Ireland totaled more than 6.5 million. By 1831, the total population of Great Britain was thus approximately 14 million. This increase fueled the Industrial Revolution from both ends, supplying more consumers eager to acquire goods and more able bodies to work in factories that produced those goods.

Illustration of an early locomotive engine, 1808.

Industrialization also contributed to an important shift in the country's social structure. The paradigm of classes and ranks that placed the nobility at the top with everyone else keeping to their places beneath had begun to change as early as the seventeenth century, as those involved in business and commerce grew wealthy enough to exert power of their own. The process was greatly accelerated in the late eighteenth and early nineteenth centuries as more and more factory owners and other men of business (they were exclusively male) amassed larger and larger fortunes. Still, the road that led from newly acquired wealth to social acceptance remained a long and circuitous one. An inherited fortune stemming from longstanding ownership of large amounts of land (and the rents thereby produced) remained the most respectable form of wealth. To possess a good deal of money as a result not of belonging to the "landed gentry" but rather of having amassed it through commercial activity was considered more than faintly disreputable. It might take two or three generations before the taint of anyone in the family having been "in trade" (a term applied to industrialists as much as to tradesmen) was removed, and the source of the family fortune forgotten. The social nuances involved in such transitions are vividly captured by Jane Austen, for example, when she describes the Bingley sisters in *Pride and Prejudice*:

> They were rather handsome, had been educated in one of the first private seminaries in town, had a fortune of twenty thousand pounds, were in the habit of spending more than they ought, and of associating with people of rank; and were therefore in every respect entitled to think well of themselves, and meanly of others. They were of a respectable family in the north of England; a circumstance more deeply impressed on their memories than that their brother's fortune and their own had been acquired by trade.

Fine gradations of respectability attached to every occupation, with social position often at odds with

George and I.R. Cruikshank, *Sporting a Toe at Almacks*, 1821. Many clubs were restricted to men; Almack's was an exclusive London club controlled by a group of society women. During "the season" a fashionable ball was held at Almack's every week.

financial circumstances. Members of the clergy and their families, for instance, though sometimes impecunious, were generally respected. Whether members of the gentry or born into the working class, they often moved in elevated social circles. Physicians, defined as those medical men who had a degree from a university, could sometimes move in the "best circles" in a community, although apothecaries and surgeons, who gained their knowledge through apprenticeship, could not.

Even the Romantic literary world reflects the increased social mobility possible in the period. John Keats, for example, was the son of a stable keeper who had increased his financial standing by marrying the daughter of the stable owner. Keats trained as a surgeon-apothecary (a job that combined the duties of present-day pharmacist, general practitioner, and surgeon), but at the age of 18 he came into an inheritance and devoted himself entirely to literature. He wrote to a friend that he thought he would "be among the English poets" after his death, and as it turned out, no social barriers could prevent that from occurring. Similarly, Samuel Taylor Coleridge, a parson's son who attended a London charity school as a child, ended his life lauded and respected as "The Sage of Highgate."

The Industrial Revolution may have increased social mobility, and certainly it allowed goods to be produced more efficiently. But it also devastated large portions of England's underclasses, the agricultural laborers and peasants who had benefited, however slightly, from the land-based economy that was passing away. Wordsworth's reference in "Tintern Abbey" to "vagrant dwellers in the houseless woods" describes a very real phenomenon. In the late eighteenth and early nineteenth centuries, a series of Enclosure Acts resulted in

Henry Fuseli, *The Nightmare*, 1790–91. The Swiss-born artist Fuseli (1741–1825) moved to England in 1779, and soon became one of the leading artistic figures of the day. Beginning in 1781, Fuseli painted several different versions of *The Nightmare* for which he became famous; it remains an iconic image of the Gothic sensibility, and of Romantic interest in what we now term "the unconscious."

Fuseli moved in London's artistic and intellectual circles through the 1790s, and was briefly involved romantically with Mary Wollstonecraft before her marriage to William Godwin.

William Blake, *The Sun Standing at his Eastern Gate*, illustration to John Milton's *L'Allegro*.

William Blake, *The Sick Rose*, from *Songs of Experience*, 1794.

Phillipe Jaques de Loutherbourgh, *Coalbrookdale By Night*, 1801. The small Shropshire town of Coalbrookdale has been sometimes described as the birthplace of the Industrial Revolution. Located in a gorge on the River Severn, it was the site of the first ironworks that used the modern method of smelting with coke rather than charcoal (an innovation of Joseph Darby in 1709). Together with the adjacent towns of Madeley, Ironbridge, Jackfield, and Coalport, Coalbrookdale was part of an early industrial powerhouse; at the end of the eighteenth century it had a greater concentration of furnaces and forges than anywhere else in the world. Darby's son Abraham also constructed the world's first iron bridge nearby in 1779; the bridge and much of the old ironworks remain today, and the Ironbridge Gorge has been declared a World Heritage Site.

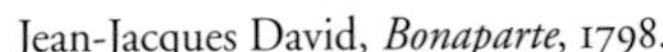

Jean-Jacques David, *Bonaparte*, 1798.

Artist unknown, *A Stoppage to a Stride over the Globe*, 1803.

Thomas Phillips, *George Gordon, Lord Byron*, 1814. Byron is wearing clothing of a sort native to the region of Epirus (then part of Albania, now part of northern Greece); he had bought this outfit while traveling through the area in 1809.

Elizabeth Levenson-Gower, *Mountain Landscape*, c. 1830. Levenson-Gower published two volumes based on her watercolor images of Scottish landscapes, the first collection of etchings, *Views of Orkney and the North-Eastern Coast of Scotland* (1807), and the second a volume of twenty aquatints, *Views on the Northern and Western Coasts of Sutherland* (1833). The artist intended that various of the wide Sutherland images be joined together to form 360 degree scenic panoramas.

J.M.W. Turner, *The Burning of the Houses of Parliament*, 1835. In the 1830s it became Turner's practice to send unfinished work (often with only rough underpainting completed) to the Royal Academy in advance of its annual exhibition. During the period devoted (in the case of other artists) to the varnishing of already-completed work, Turner would complete the painting itself, often watched by a sizeable crowd. An eyewitness, E.V. Rippingille, described Turner completing *The Burning of the Houses of Parliament* in 1835:

> For [the] three hours I was there ... he never ceased to work, or even once looked or turned from the wall in which his picture was hung. A small box of colors, a few very small brushes, and a vial or two, were at his feet ... In one part of the mysterious proceedings Turner, who worked almost entirely with his palette knife, was observed to be rolling and spreading a half-transparent stuff over his picture, the size of a figure in length and thickness. As Callcott was looking on I ventured to say ... "What is that he is plastering his picture with?" to which enquiry it was replied, "should be sorry to be the man to ask him" ... Presently the work was finished: Turner gathered his tools together, put them into and shut the box, and then with his face still turned to the wall, and at the same distance from it, went sidelong off, without speaking a word to anybody ... Maclise, who stood near, remarked, "There, that's masterly, he does not stop to look at his work; he knows it is done, and he is off!"

J.M.W. Turner, *Slavers Throwing Overboard the Dead and Dying—Typhoon coming on*, 1840. Turner's painting depicts a 1781 incident in which Captain Luke Collingwood of the slave ship "Zong," with his ship running short of water and other supplies when it had been blown off-course during a severe storm, ordered that all sick and dying slaves be thrown overboard; 133 were killed as a result. Insurance was a factor in Collingwood's decision; compensation could be claimed for property lost or jettisoned in storms, but not for slaves killed by disease or other natural causes. The incident became widely publicized and spurred support for the abolitionist movement. In the ensuing legal case the court upheld the insurance company's financial liability; no criminal charges were brought against the captain. In the twentieth century the incident became the basis for several literary works, including a long poem by David Dabydeen and a novel by Fred D'Aguiar.

the conversion of formerly common land into large, privately-held farms. The process of enclosure was not new; it had been occurring since the late Middle Ages, in response to population pressures and as Britain was transformed first into a largely mercantile economy and then into an industrial society. While enclosures did often result in something of an increase in agricultural production, they also often spelled ruin for thousands of small farmers. Large landholders benefitted from their enlarged acreage, but many of those who had heretofore been able to eke out a living from a tiny patch of land and sell their modest surpluses now lost all ability to support themselves. These smallholders and their families were forced either to labor for others for meager wages, to migrate to the city and enter the manufacturing workforce, or to turn to begging or thievery. Poor harvests in 1794–95, 1799–1800, and 1810–11 worsened the plight of the rural poor even further. The proliferation of vandals, vagrants, and beggars in the writing of this era reflected a growing social reality.

The leading literary figures of the day were for the most part sympathetic to the plight of the poor in a time of growing inequity, but beyond that held widely divergent attitudes concerning these developments, and concerning the commoners themselves. Barbauld was one who sought to ameliorate the inequities that had become so characteristic of English life; she cast a cold eye on the power relations involved and had harsh criticism for the privileged, but also took an un-idealized view of commoners, seeing them as prey to vice as much as virtue, in reaction to the circumstances in which they had been placed in through economic hardship, lack of education, and so on. As she wrote in *Thoughts on the Inequality of Conditions* (1800),

> Power enables the indolent and the useless not only to retain, but to add to their possessions, by taking from the industrious the natural reward of their labour, and applying it to their own use ... It is not sufficiently considered how many virtues depend upon comfort, and cleanliness, and decent apparel. Destroy dirt and misery, and you will destroy at once a great many vices.

It is the very different approach of William Wordsworth, however, that has come to be seen as characteristic of British Romanticism. Wordsworth's focus was much less on the struggle to ameliorate conditions than it was on the value of recognizing the worth inherent in the hearts and minds of rural common folk—and the poetic value that they represented. In the same year as Barbauld wrote *Thoughts on the Inequality of Conditions* Wordsworth expressed his ideals in this connection in the 1800 "Preface" to *Lyrical Ballads*:

> The principal object, then, proposed in these Poems was to choose incidents and situations from common life ... Humble and rustic life was generally chosen, because, in that condition, the essential passions of the heart find a better soil in which they can attain their maturity, are less under restraint, and speak a plainer and more emphatic language; because in that condition of life our elementary feelings coexist in a state of greater simplicity, and, consequently, may be more accurately contemplated, and more forcibly communicated; because the manners of rural life germinate from those elementary feelings, and, from the necessary character of rural occupations, are more easily comprehended, and are more durable; and, lastly, because in that condition the passions of men are incorporated with the beautiful and permanent forms of nature.

Poems such as "Michael," "The Ruined Cottage," "Idiot Boy" and "Resolution and Independence" represent Wordsworth's attempt to put those ideals into practice. In "Resolution and Independence," the poet encounters an old, poor, itinerant leech-gatherer, and ends by admiring "In that decrepit Man so firm a mind." Whereas Barbauld regarded theft as a justifiable response to the oppression of extreme poverty in an iniquitous social system, Wordsworth pays homage to the old leech-gatherer for earning an "honest maintenance" despite the "many hardships" he must endure.

If the rural poor fared badly during these years, life for the workers in the cities and the unemployed poor was just as bad. In 1815, at the instigation of large land holders who stood to benefit from high prices for grain, the government passed the Corn Laws to institute a substantial tariff on imports of grain from foreign countries, making such imports much more expensive. ("Corn" in Britain denotes grain, most commonly wheat; what North Americans call "corn" is referred to in Britain as "maize.") The effect of the tariff was to protect British grain producers, and to inflate the price of bread and other foodstuffs for the consumer. The poor in the cities suffered particularly, and from 1815 until the Corn Laws were finally repealed in 1845 they remained a lightning rod for political dissent.

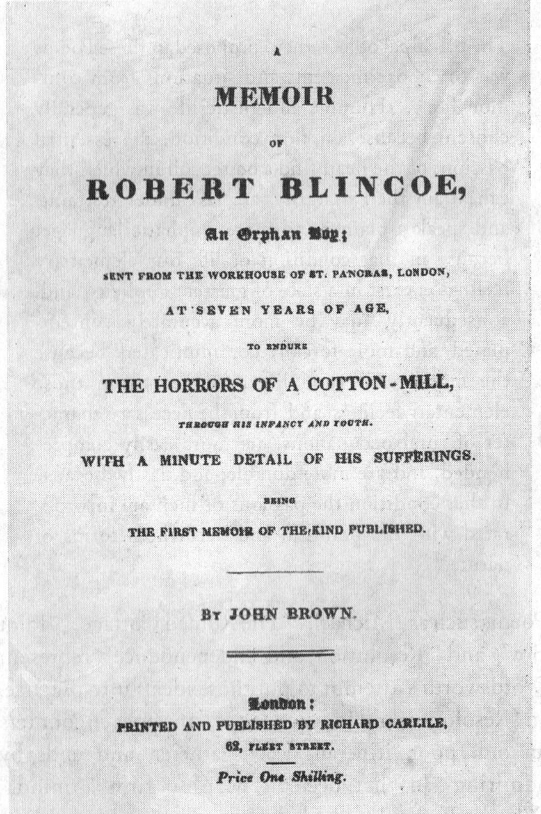

A

MEMOIR

OF

ROBERT BLINCOE,

An Orphan Boy;

SENT FROM THE WORKHOUSE OF ST. PANCRAS, LONDON,

AT SEVEN YEARS OF AGE,

TO ENDURE

THE HORRORS OF A COTTON-MILL,

THROUGH HIS INFANCY AND YOUTH.

WITH A MINUTE DETAIL OF HIS SUFFERINGS.

BEING

THE FIRST MEMOIR OF THE KIND PUBLISHED.

By JOHN BROWN.

London:

PRINTED AND PUBLISHED BY RICHARD CARLILE,

62, FLEET STREET.

Price One Shilling.

Title page, *A Memoir of Robert Blincoe*, first published in 1828, re-issued in 1832. Demonstrations in 1832 and 1833 for factory reform frequently cited the evidence of factory conditions that he had provided, and Blincoe testified before the Royal Commission that investigated the issue of child labor in 1833.

Had conditions for the urban poor been better in other respects, the Corn Laws might have had less impact. The British government, however, assured by Adam Smith's highly influential work of economic philosophy, *The Wealth of Nations* (1777), that the best way to encourage national economic success was to leave businesses free to grow without hindrance, for the most part adopted a *laissez-faire* approach to regulating treatment of employees and working conditions during this period. In practice, "laissez-faire" meant shifts of as much as 15 hours at a stretch, often for very young children. Wages were kept as low as manufacturers could manage, and injuries were common; children were the preferred workers for clearing jams in mechanized looms, for example, and the frequent result was the loss of the tiny fingers and hands that made them ideal for the job. Workers' health was often ruined by unsanitary working and living conditions (employers often owned not only the factories, but the slums in which their workers lived), and by unfettered pollution.

It is often assumed that the worst extremes of the Industrial Revolution in Britain occurred during the Victorian era, but by the time Victoria came to the throne, Parliament had already been pressed to take a succession of measures to restrict the abuse of children: the largely ineffectual Health and Morals of Apprentices Act (1802), the Regulation of Cotton Mills and Factories Act (1819), and the Act to Regulate the Labour of Children and Young Persons in the Mills and Factories of the United Kingdom (1833). Even after the passage of this last, children as young as nine could be forced to work nine hour days, and 13 year-olds to work 12 hour days, but that represented a degree of improvement from the late eighteenth and early nineteenth centuries. Robert Blincoe, for example, an orphan raised in a London workhouse and transported in 1799, at the age of seven, to work in the Lowdham Mill near Nottingham, described his life at the mill to John Brown in 1829:

> Blincoe heard the burring sound [of the machinery] before he reached the portals and smelt the fumes of the oil with which the axles of twenty-thousand wheels and spindles were bathed the moment he entered the doors. The noise appalled him, and the stench seemed intolerable. It was the custom at Lowdham Mills, as it is in most water mills, to make the apprentices work up lost time [i.e., time when the machines had been unable to run during regular working hours], by working over hours ... When

> children of seven years of age had to work fourteen hours every day in the week, Sundays excepted, any addition was severely felt ... Almost from the first hour [Blincoe] entered the Mill, till he arrived at a state of manhood, it was one continual round of cruel and arbitrary punishment.... I asked him if he could state the average number of times in which he might safely say he had suffered corporal punishment in a week. His answer invariably was, that his punishments were so various and so frequent, it was impossible to state with anything approaching to accuracy.... Supper consisted of milk-porridge, of a very blue complexion [together with] bread partly made of rye—very black, and so soft they could scarcely swallow it, as it stuck like bird-lime to their teeth.

If the Government addressed such outrages only with reluctance (sometimes Parliamentary committees looking into allegations would not hear any direct testimony of the workers), many citizens found them harder to ignore. Demonstrations of popular dissatisfaction were frequent and took various forms. Luddites, followers of the imaginary "General Ned Ludd," attacked and broke machinery during the years 1811–16, sometimes to force concessions from their employers but sometimes to express their dissatisfaction with creeping mechanization. After the bad harvests and the passage of the Corn Laws in 1815, food riots occurred across the country. Coercion Acts were passed in 1817 to try to stifle dissent, but they provoked strong antagonism, and both in London and in parts of Scotland some republican groups advocated revolution. Farm workers staged violent protests throughout the 1820s, that culminated in mass barn-burning in 1830. Perhaps the most famous popular uprising was the 1819 gathering of nearly a hundred thousand mill workers at St. Peter's Field, near Manchester. A peaceful demonstration that ended with an address to the crowd by the radical Henry "Orator" Hunt (1773–1835), this gathering so alarmed the local gentry that they sent drunken, armed militiamen to break it up and arrest Hunt. The militiamen attacked the crowd with their sabres when it jeered them, and the ensuing melee left eleven dead, including one trampled child, and more than four hundred injured, many from sabre wounds.

"Peterloo," as it came to be dubbed by the radical press, in reference to the British victory at Waterloo four years earlier, was a seminal event in nineteenth-century politics and economics. Parliament did nothing to relieve the sufferings of these poor or the hundreds of thousands like them, but rather strengthened its repressive powers by passing the Six Acts at the end of 1819. These Acts made it a crime to demonstrate; gave magistrates the power to enter private homes to search for weapons; outlawed meetings of more than 50 people unless all those attending a meeting were residents of the parish in which the meeting was held (thus effectively curtailing any kind of large gatherings); tightened the guidelines on what could be considered blasphemous or treasonous libel; and raised the newspaper tax, thus effectively cutting the circulation of formerly inexpensive radical newspapers. The Six Acts were so repugnant to certain members of the liberal Whig party who would later become powerful politicians that they led in the long run to the liberal Reform Act of 1832. Thus, the eventual result of the massacre was a measure of relief from the extraordinarily repressive measures it had spawned.

Political Parties and Royal Allegiances

For most of this period, the upheavals among the lower classes found little reflection in the English government, where the Tories held sway from 1783-1830, with only one short interruption. The Tories were the conservative party: they saw themselves as upholders of law and tradition, determined to preserve the prevailing political and social order. From 1793 to 1801, and again from 1804-1806, the Tories and the country were led by Prime Minister William Pitt, whose fiscal restraint and willingness to suppress political protest (sometimes with open brutality) made him a hero to some but a villain to many others. Pitt died in office in 1806, certainly of overwork and probably of alcoholism; his last words were either, "Oh, my country! how I leave my country!" or "I think I could eat one of Bellamy's veal pies," depending on the source. The Tories continued in power, on their own or in coalition, until 1830.

The Whigs, who remained the party of opposition during this time, ranged themselves against the Tories as advocates of greater civil and religious liberty. In reality, neither party would have been called "Liberals" or "Democrats" by today's standards, but the Whigs did advocate the abolition of the slave trade, Catholic emancipation (which would allow greater political participation to Catholics, heretofore barred from a role in government), and Parliamentary reform. From 1782–1806, the leader of the Whigs was the charismatic Charles James Fox, gambler, gourmand, and political colossus, whose political machinations made him as many enemies as friends. Not until 1806, a year after Fox's death, would the Whigs participate in government—and then for only a relatively short period, as part of a coalition. They would not gain power in their own right until 1830. They were then at last able to pass the Reform Act of 1832 (also known as the Great Reform Act), which extended voting rights to a broader spectrum of propertied males,[1] redistributed Parliamentary seats, and brought significantly fairer political representation.

While the politicians plotted and schemed, the British Royal Family suffered its own difficulties. George III, who had ascended the throne in 1760, embodied Toryism both politically and personally: traditionalist, ponderous, and domestic, he produced a large family, embraced conservative politics, and allegedly liked to wander the countryside incognito, chatting with farmers. In 1788, however, he suffered a bout of mental illness that lasted until early 1789. This illness, now believed to be the result of the hereditary blood disease porphyria, reappeared in 1810, leaving him permanently insane. In 1811, when it became apparent that the King would not recover, his eldest son was declared Regent.

Monarchs of the House of Hanover traditionally clashed with their eldest sons, and George III and the Prince who would become George IV were no different. Bred to wait for his father to die, growing ever fatter (at the end of his life he weighed more than 300 pounds), the Regent was a stark contrast to his thrifty father. In 1787, when he was 25, his debts totaled more than £160,000 (equivalent to about £8,000,000 today). He lived with a Roman Catholic mistress whom he later married, secretly and unconstitutionally, before abandoning her for a series of other mistresses. Later, to secure relief from debts, he married his cousin Caroline of Brunswick, a woman he found so totally and instantly loathsome that his first words upon seeing her were, "I am not well; pray get me a glass of brandy." Although they did manage to produce one daughter, Charlotte, who later died in childbirth, the Prince and his wife never lived together, and his attempt to divorce her after his accession in 1820 was one of the great scandals of the period.

Sir Thomas Lawrence, *The Prince Regent in Profile*, c. 1814. The Prince knighted Lawrence, the leading English portraitist of the day, in 1815, saying that he was "proud in conferring a mark of favor on one who had raised the character of British art in the estimation of all Europe."

George IV was not without redeeming virtues; notably, he was a keen patron of the arts, particularly architecture. In addition to a magnificent pavilion in Brighton, he and his architects built Trafalgar Square, modified and improved Buckingham House into

[1] The changes are estimated to have altered the composition of the electorate to approximately one in seven males from fewer than one in ten.

Buckingham Palace, and created parks, streets, and crescents throughout London. He was an enthusiastic reader and promoter of literature, as well as a generous patron of the sciences, establishing several fellowships and prizes. Nonetheless, the Prince became a figure of increasing public contempt. Leigh Hunt described him as "a libertine head over heels in debt and disgrace, a despiser of domestic ties," Percy Shelley called him, in prose, an "overgrown bantling [infant]," and, in poetry, "the dregs of [his] dull race." When he died in 1830, *The Times* wrote, "There never was an individual less regretted by his fellow creatures than this dead King."

Sir Thomas Lawrence, *Caroline Amelia Elizabeth of Brunswick*, 1804 (detail).

IMPERIAL EXPANSION

At the same time that Britain was experiencing its own internal power struggles and upheavals, the nation was expanding its presence around the globe. Throughout the first half of the nineteenth century, Britain was well on its way to forging the Empire that would reach full flower in the Victorian period. The East India Company, founded by a group of London merchants in 1600, controlled most of Eastern India by 1765, and thereafter continued to extend their administrative and governmental control over the sub-continent. British interest in China began in the late eighteenth century, when Britain began to import the tea that would soon become a staple of the British table, and rose throughout the 1800s. Increased contact with (and domination of) various parts of the Far East led to increased fascination with its cultures, a fascination widely reflected in literature. "Eastern" influence pervades the prose and poetry of this period, from William Beckford's novel *The History of the Caliph Vathek* (1786), to Byron's *Eastern Tales* (1813–14), to Percy Shelley's *Alastor* (1816), where the protagonist makes his way

> through Arabie
> And Persia, and the wild Carmanian waste,
> And o'er the aerial mountains which pour down
> Indus and Oxus from their icy caves,
> In joy and exultation [he] held his icy way,
> Till in the vale of Cashmire ...
> he stretched
> His languid limbs.

Wearing her India cotton frock, sipping her tea from Canton, coffee from Yemen, or chocolate from Mexico, the English consumer of the Romantic period felt the influence of imperial expansion not only in the commodities she purchased but in the pages she turned.

James Gillray, *Fashionable Contrasts, or the Duchess' Little Shoe Yielding to the Magnitude of the Duke's Foot*, 1792. At the time, the press had been fawning over Princess Frederica Charlotte Ulrica Catherina, who had just married Frederick Augustus, Duke of York; the daintiness of her feet had been particularly praised.

James Gillray, *The Plum Pudding in Danger*, 1805. Napoleon and British Prime Minister William Pitt are shown carving up the globe, with Napoleon skewering Europe and Pitt helping himself to the ocean. (1805 saw both the Battle of Trafalgar, at which the British under Lord Nelson established dominance at sea; and the Battle of Austerlitz, at which Napoleon defeated Russian and Austrian armies to cement his control of the Continent.)

Sir Charles D'Oyly, *The Emporium of Taylor & Co. in Calcutta*, c. 1825–28.

But if the British Empire brought rewards to the nation's citizens, it all too often entailed exploitation and horror in the colonies themselves. Chief amongst these was the slavery that fueled the economy of the British West Indies. The mass of sugar required to sweeten Britain's tea, coffee, and chocolate was cultivated, cut, and processed on these islands by slaves who worked under inhuman conditions until they literally wore out —at which point their white masters simply purchased fresh replacements. Over the course of the eighteenth century, British slavers transported some three million slaves to the West Indies and other agricultural colonies; the economic success of the port towns Bristol and Liverpool was based in large part on the important part they played in the English slave trade—and the trade in sugar from plantations that relied on slave labor. (At the start of the American Revolution, British imports from the largest sugar plantation center, Jamaica, were worth five times more than British imports from the 13 colonies.)

Arguably the strongest resistance to slavery in the West Indies came from the slaves themselves. The British invaded the formerly French island of Saint-Dominique in 1793 in order to aid in the suppression of a slave uprising led by Toussaint L'Ouverture, but withdrew five years later, having sent more troops to the West Indies over that period than they had sent to America during the War of Independence. When a subsequent effort by Napoleon also failed and the former slaves founded the Republic of Haiti in 1804, the message that emancipation was inevitable had registered widely in Britain.

Emancipation was also spurred by a widespread and effective protest movement within Britain. Between

1787, when protests first began, and 1791, abolitionists gathered 500 petitions against slavery from across Britain. In all some 400,00 signatures were collected; this was Britain's first large-scale petition campaign. The Abolitionist movement attracted support from Evangelicals, from Whig politicians, and from radicals, and has been described as the first British political movement in the modern sense. The leading figures in the movement were abolitionists Thomas Clarkson, Granville Sharp, and William Wilberforce, but it also drew considerable support from the poets of the day, among them William Cowper, Hannah More, William Blake, Mary Robinson, and Anne Cromarty Yearsley (whose *A Poem on the Inhumanity of the Slave Trade* [1788] inveighed against the very business that supported her home town of Bristol), and Letitia Barbauld.

Central to the literature of the abolitionist movement were books written by former slaves such as Olaudah Equiano and Mary Prince, which laid out plainly the horrors of a slave's life and openly sought sympathy and fellow-feeling from readers. In his autobiography, *The Interesting Narrative of the Life of Olaudah Equiano* (1786), Equiano described conditions both in West Indies and in America. As he observed with telling effect, the system bred degradation for "free negroes" as well as for slaves:

> I have often seen slaves, particularly those who were meagre, in different islands, put into scales and weighed; and then sold from three pence to six pence to nine pence a pound. My master, however, whose humanity was shocked at this mode, used to sell by the lump. And at or after a sale it was not uncommon to see negroes taken from their wives, wives taken from their husbands, and children from their parents, and sent off to other islands, and wherever else their merciless lords chose, and probably never more during life to see each other! ...
>
> [Free negroes] live in constant alarm for their liberty; and even this is but nominal, for they are universally insulted and plundered without the possibility of redress; for such is the equity of West Indian laws, that no free negro's evidence will be admitted in their courts of justice.

Accounts such as these, coupled with a determined and prolonged campaign and with the effects of the growth of the Asian sugar trade, led to the abolition of the slave trade in 1806–7, and (following another uprising, this time in Jamaica in 1831–32) to an Act in 1833 that provided for the full abolition of slavery. The persecution of blacks by whites, however, continued both in the West Indies and throughout the British Empire.

Noticeably absent from the list of abolitionist writers are several of the leading names of English Romantic poetry. Wordsworth,[1] Coleridge, Byron, Shelley and Keats were in general all sympathetic with the aims of the abolitionist movement, and Coleridge in particular spoke out strongly both against slavery itself and against the maintenance of the slave trade, memorably writing that "a slave is a person perverted into a thing," and slavery not so much "a deviation from justice as an absolute subversion of all morality." It has been plausibly suggested that some major works of Romantic poetry (notably Coleridge's "The Rime of the Ancient Mariner" and Keats's "Lamia") may usefully be read in relation to the slave trade. But directly pressing for the abolition of slavery through verse in the manner of Cowper, Robinson, and Yearsley was never a significant part of their poetic agenda.

The Romantic Mind and Its Literary Productions

It is not surprising that in a world overwhelmingly concerned with change, revolution, and freedom, the makers of literature should be similarly preoccupied; as discussed above, the French Revolution and its aftermath lent vital force to the Romantic impulse. That force, though, was not exerted on all the literary minds in the Romantic era with equal force, or in quite the same direction. For several of the leading figures of English Romanticism, the freedom that animated the poetic imagination was only tangentially related to the collectivist enterprise that the revolution in France had represented. Instead, it was very much an *individual*

[1] *The Prelude* Wordsworth admitted that in the 1790s "this particular strife had wanted power / To rivet my affections." He did write two sonnets (one to Clarkson, one to Toussaint L'Ouverture) in 1807, the year in which abolition of the slave trade was accomplished.

freedom; the freeing of the individual mind and the individual soul took pride of place. Subjective experience and the role that it played in the individual's response to and experience of reality are dominant themes in the works of the Romantics. Wordsworth's "Ode: Intimations of Immortality" surveys what becomes of the "heaven-born freedom" with which every individual who enters the world is born. Percy Shelley's *Mont Blanc is* an extended exploration of power and creativity, and Keats's Odes continually express their author's fascination with the connection between physical experience and the individual human imagination. In Byron, subjectivity, creativity, and epistemological questing all find expression in a series of heroes for whom the power of the Will is a central concern. The question of what it means to be an individual looms large in the works of all these authors.

Nature became a fulcrum in the balancing of subjective and objective in the Romantic construction of reality; most of the period's leading writers remained preoccupied with the relationship between the natural world and the individual mind. Percy Shelley appealed to the wind, "Make me thy lyre, even as the forest is," and in "Tintern Abbey" Wordsworth recognized nature as

> The anchor of my purest thoughts, the nurse
> The guide, the guardian of my heart, and soul
> Of all my moral being.

This commingling of self and nature was at least in part an expression of the late eighteenth- and early nineteenth-century tendency to see the natural world in opposition to the human world. In the same poem, for example, Wordsworth describes himself as coming to nature

> more like a man
> Flying from something that he dreads than one
> Who sought the thing he loved.

Less frequently did poets of the Romantic period comment on the relationship between humans and nature as an objective reality. The focus was much more often on what non-human nature had to offer to the individual human soul than on how humans in aggregate were reshaping the natural world. Barbauld was one who saw the latter clearly; in her grim survey of England in "Eighteen Hundred and Eleven" she described how

> Science and Art urge on the useful toil,
> New mould a climate and create the soil, ...
> On yielding Nature urge their new demands,
> And ask not gifts but tribute at her hands.

Such clear-eyed observations of human manipulation of nature were few and far between, however.

The importance of the subjective sense of reality to the Romantic imagination also comes out clearly in the widespread fascination in the period with the visions experienced in dreams, in nightmares, and other altered states. The question Keats poses at the end of "Ode to a Nightingale"—"Was it a vision, or a waking dream?" —is of a sort that occurs frequently in the literature of Romanticism. Among the many works of the period that touch on this theme are Coleridge's fragment "Kubla Khan" (which he claimed came to him during a drug-induced sleep); Keats's visionary *The Fall of Hyperion: A Dream*; Mary Shelley's *Frankenstein* (the story of which came to her in a dream, and in which Victor Frankenstein acquires the habit of taking "every night a small quantity of laudanum" in order to "gain the rest necessary for the preservation of life"); and De Quincey's *Confessions of an English Opium Eater*.

In the work of women writers of the period, interest in the individual and the mind often took different forms from those that engaged the interest of male writers. Many were concerned with education: Hannah More produced a series of Cheap Repository Tracts designed to enlighten the poor, while Maria Edgeworth gained fame as a children's writer and educationalist. Mary Wollestonecraft authored not only her famous *Vindication of the Rights of Woman*, but also *Thoughts on the Education of Daughters* (1787) and *The Female Reader* (1772). The Romantic period abounded in outspoken female writers who engaged with the issues of their day and sought to make a difference in their world. In their own time, however, such authors were often derided as "bluestockings," unnatural women who revealed their prudishness through their interest in intellectual pursuits. In their own day the writings of these authors made little if any difference to the social,

J.M.W. Turner, *Melrose Abbey*, 1822. The lines in the lower left corner are (slightly misquoted) from Canto 2 of Sir Walter Scott's long poem *The Lay of the Last Minstrel* (1805): "If thou would'st view fair Melrose aright, / Go visit it by the pale moonlight."

legal, and economic position of women, who remained little more than property in the eyes of the law for many more years. But over the longer term their impact was considerable; Wollstonecraft and the Bluestockings laid the intellectual foundations for the social and political progress of women that would slowly be achieved over the next 200 years and more.

It would be a mistake to think of women writers of the Romantic period as solely concerned with women's rights and with the stereotypical "female arenas" of education and religion, however. Much of the writing by women in this period is as rich, strong, and plangent as anything produced by their male counterparts. Mary Robinson, for example—famous first as an actress and mistress of the Prince of Wales, then as a successful poet and novelist—earned the admiration of both Wordsworth and Coleridge (who called her "an undoubted genius"), and preceded them in the writing of poetry concerned with the poor and disenfranchised. In her *Elegiac Sonnets* (1784), Charlotte Smith displayed all the power, control, and skill at incisive self-examination that has come to be associated with the male Romantics. Poet Felicia Hemans rivaled (indeed, perhaps surpassed) Byron in popularity. Playwright Joanna Baillie, famous for producing works that, as she put it, "delineate the progress of the higher passions in the human breast," was considered by Walter Scott to be "the best dramatic writer since the days of Shakespeare."

One area of common ground for almost all Romantic writers, male and female, was a strong interest in the "Imagination," the creative power by which an individual took the raw material of the physical world and transformed it into art. Although "Imagination" was recognized as being distinct from religious inspiration, descriptions of imaginative or poetic power often took on strong religious overtones, as in Blake's assertion that "One Power alone makes a Poet—Imagination The Divine Vision." Coleridge, Blake, and Wordsworth were all deeply invested in the notion of the poet as *vates*, or prophet. And the imagination was seen as invested with moral as well as prophetic power. Like earlier ages (but unlike our own), the Romantics saw the realms of the aesthetic and the moral as being closely bound up with each other. But whereas earlier ages had tended to see literature as expressing truths emanating from elsewhere, and to see the ethical element of literature as inhering in its ability to illustrate virtues and vices, and point out moral lessons, the leading Romantics tended to locate the moral element not only of literature but of life itself in the imagination, and tended to see the imagination as embodying truth as well as morality. "The great instrument of moral good," wrote Shelley in his *Defense of Poetry*, "is the imagination," while Keats proclaimed that "what the imagination seizes as beauty must be the truth."[1] More broadly, a belief took root among poets (the great male Romantic poets in particular) that the aesthetic and imaginative truths of poetry were possessed of a transcendent status, a status that placed such insights above the historical or scientific truths of the ordinary world.

Another of the several oppositions that animates the literature of the Romantic period is that between sense and sensibility—a tension with parallels to that between reason and emotion in the intellectual landscape of any age, but also one possessing elements particular to the late eighteenth and early nineteenth centuries. In this era the terms "sentiment," "sentimentality," "sentimentalism" and "sensibility" were all widely used (and to some extent overlapped in meaning), but none more so than "sensibility." The concept of "sensibility" entailed strong emotional responsiveness—life and literary work animated by powerful feeling. Indeed, it was frequently associated with emotional excess: when Jane Austen describes Marianne's "excess of sensibility" in *Sense and Sensibility*, she is using the notion of sensibility in ways that would have been familiar to any late eighteenth- or early nineteenth-century reader:

> She was sensible and clever; but eager in every thing; her sorrows, her joys, could have no moderation. She was generous, amiable, interesting: she was every thing but prudent. The resemblance between her and her mother was strikingly great. Elinor saw, with concern, the excess of her sister's sensibility; but by Mrs. Dashwood it was valued and cherished.

[1] Keats's notion of the value of "negative capability—that is, when a man is capable of being in uncertainties, mysteries, doubts, without any irritable reaching after fact and reason," destabilizes in interesting ways the connections that he and other Romantics drew between morality and the imagination, and between the imagination and truth.

It may well be that most educated Britons of the period privileged sense over sensibility in very much the way that Austen appears to do. But it is also true that the feelings associated with the Romantic sensibility—above all, as they were expressed in poetry—became the de-fining passions of the age. And the poetry of sensibility carried intellectual as well as aesthetic force; for a considerable period it stood in the vanguard of the movement for social and political change.

That is not to say that the distinction separating poets of sensibility from the rest was entirely clear; far from it. Rather in the way that competing factions today will sometimes each accuse the other of being controlled by their emotions rather than their reason, many in the late eighteenth century tried to situate sensibility in a natural alliance with political views they opposed. Anti-Jacobins suggested there was a natural affinity between the supposed excesses of sensibility and those of political radicalism, while radicals often portrayed sensibility as associated with reactionary political views. In truth, the language of sensibility was used by both sides.

Also among the oppositions that occur throughout the literature of the Romantic period are the natural and the artificial, and the original and the imitative. If "artificial" is taken simply to mean "human-made," of course, the distinction between the natural and the artificial is purely a matter of physical process. But "artificial" and "natural" as matters of taste and of style have more fluid meanings. As the culture of sentiment and of sensibility grew over the course of the eighteenth century, "artificial" came to be used less and less frequently to mean "displaying special art or skill" and more and more frequently to mean "contrived, shaped in a way not spontaneous or natural," or even "not expressive of reality." The divide between natural and artificial was felt to connect with that between "novelty" of thought and expression—"originality," as we would call it—and the "servility" of the stale or overly imitative. Whereas the Neoclassical poets had proudly imitated classical models, often devoting themselves to translations of Classical works into English poetry, Romantic writers—and the leading Romantic poets in particular—had little interest in seeing the work of earlier eras as models to be imitated. They might admire the poets of earlier eras, they might be inspired by them (by Shakespeare and by Milton above all), they might aspire to similar glory, but they had no interest in taking the same path to glory. If not entirely for the first time, then certainly to an unprecedented degree, originality came in the Romantic period to be seen as a criterion of poetic achievement in the Romantic period. Even at the beginning of the period we find judgments on poetic worth being made largely on the grounds of the originality the verse displays. A 1791 assessment of a volume of Robinson's poetry, for example, sets up an opposition between the original and the natural—two qualities often assumed to normally accompany each other:

> The attempt at originality is in all pursuits laudable. Invention is a noble attribute of the mind. But the danger is, lest, by pursuing it too intensely, we deviate so far from ease and nature, that the real object of Poetry, that of touching the heart, be lost.

A more familiar set of oppositions involving the natural and the artificial, the "original" and the imitative, is put forward by William Hazlitt in his *The Spirit of the Age* (1825), as he assesses at the end of the Romantic period the place of Wordsworth in the poetry and the intellectual life of the age:

> His popular, inartificial style gets rid (at a blow) of all the trappings of verse, of all the high places of poetry: "the cloud-capt towers, the solemn temples, the gorgeous palaces," are swept to the ground.... All the traditions of learning, all the superstitions of age, are obliterated and effaced. We begin *de novo* on a *tabula rasa* of poetry ... He chooses to have his subject a foil to his invention, to owe nothing but to himself.... Taught by political opinions to say to the vain pomp and glory of the world, "I hate ye," seeing the path of classical and artificial poetry blocked up by the cumbrous ornaments of style and turgid common-places, so that nothing more could be achieved in that direction but by the most ridiculous bombast or the tamest servility, he has ... struck into the sequestered vale of humble life, sought out the muse among sheep-cotes and hamlets, and the peasant's mountain-haunts, has discarded all the tinsel pageantry of verse, and endeavored (not in vain) to ... add the charm of novelty to the familiar.

In passages such as this one, we may see the paradigms according to which the literature of the Romantic period is still largely seen being articulated even before the period had ended. On the one side the natural, the spontaneous, the original, fresh and new; on the other the artificial, the studied, the imitative, the tired, and traditional. On the one side imagination and sensibility, on the other excessive rationalism. On the one side a passion for freedom—especially, aesthetic freedom and freedom of the spirit; on the other restraint, reaction, oppression. On the one side, in short, the Romantic; on the other the Classical, the neoclassical, the conservative.

If this set of oppositions often bears some correspondence to reality, it is important to recognize that the correspondence is just as often loose and unreliable. Romantic literature, and the Romantic period itself, is filled with unexpected parallels, with surprising evolutions, with unexpected paradoxes, with outright contradictions. The Della Cruscans and their followers, for example—poets of sensibility who in the late 1780s and early 1790s took the lead in exuberantly embracing revolutionary freedom in the wake of the French Revolution—have often been taken to task for the supposed artificiality of their verse. Wordsworth, usually seen as the great poet of a natural world set apart from the oppressive workings of the human-made world of cities and factories, writes in 1833 that "Steamboats, Viaducts, and Railways" … Nature doth embrace / Her lawful offspring in Man's art." Coleridge, who in the early 1790s felt strongly the attractions of sensibility and planned to establish a community in Pennsylvania founded on revolutionary democratic ideals, became in later life as dismissive of sensibility as he was of revolutionary fervor. Byron, the paradigmatic Romantic figure, professed to reject many of the impulses at the core of the Romantic Movement; in "To Romance" (1807) he vows to leave the realms of romance "for those of truth:"

> Romance! disgusted with deceit,
> Far from thy motley court I fly,
> Where Affectation holds her seat,
> And sickly Sensibility. …

Keats, for his part, is perhaps at his most enthusiastic when he exclaims not over Nature or freedom but over the experience of Classical literature ("On First Looking into Chapman's Homer") and Classical art ("On Seeing the Elgin Marbles," "Ode on a Grecian Urn"). The distinctions that are often made in attempts to define the essence of the Romantic, in short, often become elusive or indistinct when it comes to particulars—and can be downright misleading. Throughout most of the nineteenth and twentieth centuries, literary critics and theorists tended to accept very much at face value the Romantics' self-representations of the nature and importance of their work; for the past generation or more those self-representations have been more and more frequently problematized, and more and more widely challenged.

There have been few challenges, however, to the view that this was a period of revolutionary developments—or to the notion that at the center of those developments (so far as English literature is concerned) was an extraordinary body of verse. Looking back in 1832 Letitia Landon was among those who identified poetry as a particular locus of change:

> Already there is a wide gulf between the last century and the present. In religion, in philosophy, in politics, in manners, there as passed a great change; but in none has been worked a greater change than in poetry, whether as regards the art itself, or the general feeling towards it.

Poetic ambition was in itself central to the spirit of Romanticism. When they spoke of the confident outpouring of Romantic verse, Romantic poets did not hesitate to compare their own work to that of the great poets of the past—and to feel themselves capable of such greatness. "I would sooner fail than not be among the greatest," wrote Keats.

The tendencies of our own age, when poetry is usually taken in small doses and the lyric mode predominates, sometimes lead modern readers to place far less emphasis than did the Romantics themselves on their longer works. The shorter poems of the Romantic canon (among them Blake's "The Tyger," Wordsworth's "Ode: Intimations of Immortality," Coleridge's "Dejection: An Ode," Byron's "She Walks in Beauty," Shelley's "To a Skylark" and Keats's odes and sonnets) are justly celebrated, and Wordsworth and Coleridge's *Lyrical Ballads* is rightly seen as the era's most significant single volume of literature. But if these retain pride of place it is important to give full notice too to the vast range of the ambitions of the Romantic poets—ambitions that found their fullest expression in extended poetic work. Blake's long prophetic poems charted new territory for English verse, both in the poetry itself and in his unique marriage of the verbal and the visual. Robinson's more substantial works include the long sonnet sequence *Sapho and Phaon* and the series of longer poems on related themes that were eventually published as the sequence *The Progress of Liberty*. Over the course of some 50 years Wordsworth reworked his poetic autobiography, *The Prelude*, into an 8,000 line epic. Coleridge's narrative poems "The Rime of the Ancient Mariner" and "Christabel" are works of modest extent by comparison with these—but still long by modern standards. Byron gave extraordinary new life to the epic romance with *Childe Harold*, broke new ground poetically with what he termed the "epic satire" of *Don Juan*, and wrote seven full-length poetic dramas. Shelley's long works encompass not only the complex allegorical drama *Prometheus Unbound* but also the poems "The Mask of Anarchy" and "Adonais" and the poetic drama *The Cenci*. Keats's *Endymion* is another memorable work of epic proportions. And, though Keats abandoned both the original epic-length version of his *Hyperion* and the later *The Fall of Hyperion: A Dream*, what remains of both also constitutes a very substantial poetic achievement. Charlotte Smith's monumental poem of history, nature, and the self, "Beachy Head" (1807) is a landmark in early nineteenth century poetry, while George Crabbe's *The Borough* memorialized village life in meticulous detail. Felicia Hemans remains best-known for her short poems "Casabianca" and "The Homes of England," but her most significant works are the poetic drama *The Siege of Valencia* and the nineteen poems that together comprise *Records of Woman*.

The ambitions of the Romantic poets extended, too, to poetic theory and criticism; to an unprecedented degree the leading poets of the time were also the leading critics and theorists. Wordsworth's "Preface" to the *Lyrical Ballads*, in its various versions, Shelley's *A Defense of Poetry*, Coleridge's scattered but enormously influential body of literary theory and criticism, and the critical insights of Keats's letters, have all long been regarded as central documents in the literature of Romanticism. But other leading writers too wrote perceptively and extensively about literature—among them Barbauld, Landon, and Elizabeth Inchbald.

The novel, dramatic writing, and the essay all flourished alongside poetry in the Romantic period, even if these genres were not accorded the same degree of respect as poetry. Barbauld commented wryly on the situation of the novel in 1810:

> A collection of novels has a better chance of giving pleasure than of commanding respect. Books of this description are condemned to the grave and despised by the fastidious; but their leaves are seldom found unopened, and they occupy the parlour and the dressing-room while productions of higher name are often gathering dust upon the shelf.

Nonetheless, the novel became increasingly popular, and the period saw changes in this form that continue to reverberate even today.

While the Romantic era saw the decline of that mainstay of eighteenth-century prose, the epistolary novel, other forms of prose fiction thrived. James Hogg produced one of the great masterpieces of psychological literature, *The Private Memoirs and Confessions of a Justified Sinner* (1824). Historical novels—especially those celebrating nationhood—became increasingly popular, among them Maria Edgeworth's *Castle Rackrent* (1800), Sydney Owenson's *The Wild Irish Girl* (1806), and Jane Porter's *Scottish Chiefs* (1810). It was Sir Walter Scott, however, who took the genre of the historical novel and made it his own. The single most influential fiction writer of the Romantic period, Scott single-handedly reshaped notions not just of "the historical novel" but of the novel itself. After beginning his career as a highly successful poet, he switched to long fiction in 1814 and produced a succession of extraordinarily popular novels, including *Waverly* (1814), *Rob Roy* (1817), and *Ivanhoe* (1819), the first modern blockbusters. Using his works to explore the ongoing political struggles of the time—the clash between traditionalism and progress, the tempting attractions of an idealized past that is really a cover for abuse and exploitation, the struggles and missteps that characterize the creation of a just society—Scott at the same time created vivid, entirely engrossing characters. Indeed, one hallmark of his writing is his ability to use these fully-realized individuals to give human expression to broad social and political issues.

Scott produced over 25 full length novels, in addition to other works. His use of dialect and his decision to set his works almost exclusively in Scotland validated the language and folklore of regional and marginalized people at a time when "British" was increasingly equated with "English." His use of editorial personae, interlocutors, mediated (sometimes twice-mediated) story presentation, and complexly constructed authorial selves raise questions about the natures of authority and authorship, the difficulty of interpretation, and the concept of truth itself. Scott not only largely created the version of "Scotland" that persists in the modern mind (a land of kilts and clans, with fierce rivalries fought out against a backdrop of misty mountains and purple heather, filled with eccentric but kind-hearted peasants); he also anticipated or pioneered many of the devices associated with modern and post-modern literature.

Many novels of the period, including Scott's, had roots in an earlier form of long prose fiction, the romance. Whereas "romance novel" today denotes a form of pulp fiction focused on romantic love as wish-fulfillment, the tradition of romance literature has its roots in medieval tales of the supernatural, of chivalry, and of courtly love, in which a sense of the extraordinary or the fantastic continually colors the narrative. The genre of romance made its influence felt in several different sorts of literary work in the Romantic era, but none more so than the Gothic. Gothic novels of the late-eighteenth and early-nineteenth centuries typically investigate human responses to supernatural occurrences—things known (thanks to the advances of science and natural history) to be "impossible." These novels tend to feature stereotypical characters and to take place in worlds temporally or geographically distanced. The surrounding landscape is often highly symbolic, reflecting the psychological world of the character that dominates the work, and the heroine's plight (the protagonist is almost without fail a heroine) is usually rendered in often highly expressive rhetoric full of rhapsodic feeling. The structures of Gothic novels frequently embody political and social tensions resulting from the integration of ancient or historical time, preserved in castles or abbeys, into an otherwise modern world. The Gothic setting of Charlotte Smith's *Emmeline, the Orphan of the Castle*, for example, allows Smith to explore social concerns such as English laws of primogeniture and women's social status and identity within the frame of a courtship novel. Her novel illustrates the ways in which the frightening, distorted world of the Gothic could also serve as a forum for social commentary—as it also does in William Godwin's *Caleb Williams* (1794) and in Eliza Fenwick's *Secresy* (1795). Gothic novels such as Matthew Lewis's *The Monk* (1796), Charlotte Dacre's *Zofloya, or The Moor* (1806), Charles Maturin's *Melmoth the Wanderer* (1820), and Anne Radcliffe's series of highly successful Gothic novels, including *The Romance of the Forest* (1791) and *The Mysteries of Udolpho* (1794), welcomed their readers into a world marked by sexual perversity, threatened female virtue, and grotesque sights and experiences. Concerned with revealing what lay repressed or hidden behind the mask of middle-class conformity, the Gothic also often veered into savagery and melodrama, tendencies captured perfectly in the following exchange from *The Vampyre* (1819), by John Polidori, in which a mysterious villain extracts a promise from his traveling companion:

> "Swear!" cried the dying man raising himself with exultant violence. "Swear by all your soul reveres, by all your nature fears, swear that for a year and a day you will not impart your knowledge of my crimes or death to any living being in any way, whatever may happen, or whatever you may see."—His eyes seemed bursting from their sockets; "I swear!" said Aubrey; he sunk laughing upon his pillow, and breathed no more.

If the heightened atmosphere of the gothic novel often veers toward imaginative excess, it can also foster literary art of a high order—as *Frankenstein*, Mary Shelley's famous first novel, amply demonstrates. The story of a "monster" who turns against his creator, Victor Frankenstein, *Frankenstein* is at one level a gripping tale of adventure, written with engaging apparent simplicity. But it is also a text that brings together virtually all the great themes of the era: freedom and oppression; science and nature; society and the individual; knowledge and power; gender and sexuality; dream and reality; creation and destruction; self-deception and self-discovery; death and life; God and the universe.

If one strand of the tradition of romance literature runs through the evolution of the Gothic novel, a very different strand runs through the development of the courtship novel in the Romantic period. From Frances Burney's *Camilla* (1796) to Elizabeth Susan Ferrier's *The Inheritance* (1824), the pages of Romantic fiction are filled with young people who are misguided, thwarted, and ultimately united in love. But no author of the period was as successful with the courtship genre as was Jane Austen. Between 1811 and 1817 her six major novels were published, all of them warmly engaging yet sharply observant and often satirical novels of courtship, social class, and domestic life. Much as her novels do not engage directly or obviously with the large issues of her age, Austen reveals a shrewd awareness of both politics and economics, particularly as they concern women; her novels emphasize the limited possibilities open to women during the period in which she wrote. But within this limited frame Austen provides a vividly three-dimensional picture of the shaping of female character, of the inner world of the emotions as much as the outer world of social behavior. Austen's heroines are preoccupied with wooing, marriage, and the minutiae of income, entailment, and other details of domestic and marital economy, precisely because these dominated and defined the lives of women of the period, while her concentration on "3 or 4 Families in a country village" (as she famously remarked to her niece) draws attention to the geographical and physical constraints imposed on middle and upper class women during this time. Even the happy endings that have delighted generations of Austenites are undercut by the obvious and acknowledged fictionality of the novels (emphasized through authorial asides, direct appeals to the reader, and other devices), by means of which Austen suggests that all happy endings may be mere fictions.

Austen was a skilled stylist as well a keen-eyed social critic, and brought to her novels an unprecedented range of novelistic technique. With *Lady Susan* she proved herself adept at epistolary narrative; with *Sense and Sensibility*, *Pride and Prejudice* and *Emma* she brought new flexibility to the use of the third person narrative voice, demonstrating perfect pitch in a variety of ironic tones, and pioneering the technique now known as free indirect discourse. In this mode of narration the apparently independent third-person narrative voice temporarily assumes the viewpoint of one or more of the characters—or indeed of an entire social class, as is the case with the famous opening to *Pride and Prejudice*: "It is a truth universally acknowledged, that a single man in possession of a good fortune, must be in want of a wife." In her tone Austen is at a great remove from the leading poets of the Romantic period, but in the importance she places on the exercise of moral imagination—both by her characters and through her own narrative style—she is very much at one with the age.

Other Romantic novels sought to reflect the social and political concerns of the world around them in fiction more fully and more directly than did either most Gothic novels or most courtship novels; a number of writers used the novel as a means of challenging prevailing beliefs and mores. Maria Edgeworth's series of Irish novels, *Castle Rackrent* (1800), *Ennui* (1809), *The Absentee* (1812), and *Ormond* (1817), explored the colonial relationship between England and Ireland. William Godwin's *Caleb Williams* (1794) sought to reveal, in the author's words, the "perfidiousness exercised by the powerful members of the community against those who are more privileged than themselves." Hogg's *Private Memoirs* was a powerful indictment of the smug superiority that could be engendered by religious zeal. And Mary Hays's *The Victim of Prejudice*, a passionate tale of a young woman who dares to resist the pressure put upon her to marry the man who has raped her, was among those novels that spoke powerfully of injustice in a male-dominated society. Conservative voices also spoke out loudly through the medium of prose fiction; important anti-Jacobin novels of the period include Jane West's *A Tale of the Times* (1799), Elizabeth Hamilton's *Memoirs of Modern Philosophers* (1800), and Charles Lucas's *The Infernal Quixote* (1801). And a number of novelists used the novel as a means of making politically pointed connections with other parts of the world, whether to cast a critical eye on the course of European imperialism—as in Sydney

Owenson's *The Missionary* (1811)—or to criticize aspects of British society by presenting them through the view of a view of an outsider—as in Hamilton's *Translations of the Letters of a Hindoo Rajah* (1796).

While the novel prospered and evolved, so too did the genre of non-fiction prose. With the rise of the periodical (see "The Business of Literature," below) came the rise of first critical and then more general essays, designed to engage, enlighten, and entertain the reader. William Hazlitt, originally intended for the Church and later an aspiring painter and philosopher, turned his hand to writing and became the most trenchant cultural critic of his time. His works include dramatic, literary, and art criticism, as well as political journalism, general essays, and his famous collection of pieces on important figures of the eighteenth century and the Romantic period, *The Spirit of the Age* (1824). His friend Charles Lamb rivaled Hazlitt's renown as an essayist, although his style was very different. Where Hazlitt used plain language and popular modes of construction to express his points cleanly and carefully, Lamb cultivated a more genteel style, rich in allusions and puns, the prose both thoughtful and rhetorically complex. Together, the two played a central role in the development of the essay during the Romantic period, but they were far from the only practitioners of the art. From Francis Jeffrey, whose pieces in the *Edinburgh Review* made literary criticism an exercise in stylish perspicacity, to Thomas De Quincey, whose psychological probing anticipates Freud, Romantic essay writers came in all shapes and sizes.

In the field of drama, the Romantic period is traditionally seen as an era of great "closet dramas" (plays written not for the stage but for private performance—in a private room or "closet"—or to be read). And, given that the period produced both Byron's powerful verse drama, *Manfred*, his iconoclastic meditation on sin and damnation, *Cain*, and Shelley's mythographic masterpiece, *Prometheus Unbound*, its reputation as a breeding ground for rich, multi-layered private theatricals may fairly be said to be well deserved. Other serious plays— chief among them Joanna Baillie's series of tragedies, collectively entitled *Plays on the Passions* (1798–1812), failed on the stage but were widely read and highly praised as literature. Depicting the passions "in their rise and progress in the heart" was Baillie's intent, and she believed that such drama could have a moral purpose (though she made no transcendent claims for the moral value of the imagination). The drama, in her view, "improves us by the knowledge we acquire of our own minds, from the natural desire we have to look into the thoughts, and observe the behavior of others." Baillie's explorations in psychology harked back to Enlightenment concepts, but her plays also engaged powerfully with the issues of her own day—chief among them the question of women's rights.)

In Byron's view, the distaste many serious writers felt for the public theater in this period was entirely justified:

> When I first entered upon theatrical affairs, I had some idea of writing for the [play] house myself, but soon became a convert to Pope's opinion of that subject. Who would condescend to the drudgery of the stage, and enslave himself to the humours, the caprices, the taste or tastelessness, of the age? Besides, one must write for particular actors, have them continually in one;'s eye, sacrifice character to the personating of it, cringe to some favorite of the public, neither give him too many nor too few lines to spout …

Baillie was rather more charitable, attributing the low tolerance of audiences for serious drama to an escapism borne of a desire to find refuge from the "commercial hurricane" of the age—and locating a good deal of the problem in the poor acoustics and lighting of the theaters of the day:

> The Public have now to choose between what we shall suppose are well-written and well-acted plays, the words of which are not heard, or heard but imperfectly by two-thirds of the audience, while the finer and more pleasing traits of the acting are by a still greater proportion lost altogether; and splendid pantomime, or pieces whose chief object is to produce striking scenic effect, which can be seen and comprehended by the whole.

As both Byron's and Baillie's comments indicate, the theater in this period was, in some sense at least, thriving. People thronged to the theaters, where they saw plays by such popular and prolific playwrights as Hannah Cowley and Elizabeth Inchbald, as well as successful dramas such as Samuel Taylor Coleridge's *Remorse* and Charles Maturin's *Bertram*. The Stage Licensing Act of 1737 meant that in London only two theaters, Covent Garden and Drury Lane (and, in the summer, the Haymarket) were permitted to present "legitimate" drama, but this in no way limited theatrical production. Stage entertainments of all sorts were held in venues from pubs to tents. In cities and provinces outside London, theaters sprang up to meet the demands of an increasing audience: a survey completed in 1804 counted 280 playhouses throughout the nation. The Licensing Act also required the texts of plays to be submitted to the Lord Chamberlain for censorship before performance. As a result, many works intended for the stage were forced into the closet (perhaps the most famous example is Shelley's *The Cenci*, which features not only father-daughter incest but also parricide). Many, however, were not, and a roll call of drama produced between 1780 and 1834 features everything from light comedy to melodramatic tragedy and from pantomimes to operas, as well as spectacles that featured impressive special effects.

THE BUSINESS OF LITERATURE

The thriving literary scene of the period is intimately tied to developments in the worlds of book publishing, book selling, and book marketing. The most influential of these was the rise of the periodical. By the 1760s there were more than 30 periodicals in London alone—monthly journals, quarterly magazines, collections of reviews and essays designed to inform and stimulate their readers. This boom in the periodical press meant increased employment for those who sought to become men and women of letters; the demand for articles often outweighed the supply. For readers and publishers, it meant an ever-growing number of publications in which reviews of the latest books might appear. Published books were expensive—a three-volume novel could cost a total of nine shillings, roughly $40 today—but reviews often printed long extracts, and thus readers could experience the book through the review. Such extracts were also, of course, excellent advertisements for the books under review.

At the same time as the number of periodicals increased, so did ways to obtain books. Between 1740 and 1790 the number of outlets nearly doubled. Most obviously, books could be bought: well-established bookshops flourished in cities all over the nation. In provincial towns and villages, where bookselling was not profitable on its own, literature was often sold side by side with stationery, patent medicines, and even groceries. Because the cost of books put them outside the means of many readers, however, some booksellers began to lend volumes to customers for a small fee. Thus did the circulating library begin. A patron would pay a yearly fee, then borrow books as he or she pleased.

Although both circulating and subscription libraries offered good value for money, they still lay outside the financial resources of those below the lower middle-classes. For these readers, there were other alternatives. Pedlars and hawkers sold street literature that included ballads, sermons, and tracts. Those who could not afford library subscriptions but who wished to read something more than broadsheet ballads or pamphlets often formed book clubs in which a number of people contributed money to buy a single book, which they would then share. After all had read the book, it might well be sold to a local bookseller, and the proceeds put toward the price of a new one. Slightly more formally, in numerous towns and villages the local male elite came together to select and discuss books and pamphlets, usually on a controversial topic of the day. This literature, too, was sold on, often by means of an auction among members at the end of the year.

Perhaps as a result of these efforts in group reading, or perhaps simply because people enjoyed it, reading aloud remained a feature of the Romantic era. The fiction and the non-fiction of the period abound in scenes of communal reading, and the visions that come down to us range from Countess Granville's admission that when her husband read *Don Juan* to her "I roared till I could neither hear nor see," to Henry Austen's description of his sister Jane as one who "read aloud with very great taste and effect. Her own works, probably, were never heard to such advantage as from her own mouth." Writers of the Romantic period were not very far removed from a time when illiteracy was more common than literacy, a time when literature was still

Thomas Rowlandson, *Dr. Syntax and a Bookseller*, 1812.

J. Bluck, after Augustus Charles Pugin, *Ackermann's Art Library* (detail), c. 1812–15. Rudolf Ackermann (1764–1834) moved to London from his native Germany and opened a print shop in London on the Strand in 1795, selling books and artist supplies as well as prints, and exhibiting paintings. He later also began to publish color-plate books, the most notable of which was *The Microcosm of London*, a three-volume set with 104 hand-colored aquatint plates by various artists (including Thomas Rowlandson and Augustus Pugin), published between 1808 and 1811.

an oral art. It is worth bearing in mind that many of them wrote to be read aloud, and many of their works gain luster from being heard.

"ROMANTIC"

Of the six periods into which the history of British literature has long been conventionally divided, the era of Romanticism is by far the briefest, extending over less than forty years. Arguably it is also the most intense, particularly during the years 1789-1815, the era not only of the French Revolution and the Napoleonic Wars but also of the era's most tumultuous literary developments—and most lasting literary achievements.

This was unquestionably an age of contradiction. It was a period in which political consciousness spread through society in unprecedented ways, with a great growth in collective awareness not only among those whose hearts resonated with revolutionary developments on the Continent but also amongst workers, the disenfranchised poor, women, and anti-slavery activists. Yet it was also a time of unprecedented growth in awareness of humans as individuals, of a rights-based political individualism, and of a Romantic individualism of the soul.

Applying a broad title to any literary or historical period is always risky. As much as any group of authors and thinkers may at first appear to have in common, deeper examination always reveals complexities. In addition, literature, like history, does not occur in isolation. One idea bleeds into another; revolutions are often old ideas returning under new names; factions develop, and their members deny that they are in any way related to the members of other factions. In its own time, Romanticism (a label never used by any of its writers, but rather first applied by the Victorians) was very frequently a house divided. "Lakers" like Wordsworth and Southey denounced the "Satanic School" of Shelley and Byron, who in turn produced vicious satires of these elders. "The Cockney School" of Londoners Leigh Hunt and John Keats was derided by critics of the day, while writers now long ignored, such as Felicia Hemans, Samuel Rogers, and Thomas Moore, were lauded for their skill and were extremely popular. The Romantic era gains richness and interest if we view it not as a perfect stream, but as what it was: a thick murmuring torrent of powerful voices that chorused and clashed, that simultaneously sought and struggled. These mingled tones together make up the voice of a movement that changed English literature.

A CHANGING LANGUAGE

Of all the places in which the political clashes of the Romantic period made themselves felt, perhaps the most surprising was in the arena of linguistics. Concern with questions of nationalism and political loyalties reached into the very language of Britain. From 1750 onward, the book market was flooded with pronunciation guides, a deluge inspired by the belief that standardized pronunciation would foster a sense of national unity. In this case, "standard" pronunciation meant the speech of educated urban dwellers. Even as many adhered to the essentially Tory belief that this supposedly standard speech was superior, there grew up a precisely opposite point of view, largely expressed by radical publishers and writers, that in the everyday speech of the common people one might find all that was best and most true about England: honesty, frankness, and English liberty given verbal form. In his 1785 *Classical Dictionary of the Vulgar Tongue*, Francis Grose transcribed and celebrated the speech of commoners in their many regional variations, and in 1818 the radical William Cobbett published his *Grammar of the English Language*, a book which explicitly treated language as a political issue. Cobbett took issue with the "false grammar" that he saw as having been put forward by eighteenth-century authorities such as Samuel Johnson, and attacked the grammatical slips as well as the privileged position of kings and nobles (chapters include "Errors and Nonsense in a King's Speech." He addressed his work to the less privileged classes, whom he believed should be enabled to participate in political discussions—"to assert with effect the rights and liberties of [their] country." As Cobbett saw it, "tyranny has no enemy so formidable as the pen."

Evidence of the Romantic celebration of "common language" can be found throughout the literature of the period. It accounts in part for the huge popularity of Robert Burns—a poet whose greatest effects come from his mixing of standard English with his native Scots dialect. But it finds its most famous expression in the Preface to the 1800 edition of *Lyrical Ballads.* There, Wordsworth writes that

> "men" in "low and rustic life" hourly communicate with the best objects from which the best part of language is originally derived; and because, from their rank in society and the sameness and narrow circle of intercourse, being less under the influence of social vanity they convey their feelings and notions in simple and unelaborated expressions. Accordingly, such language, rising out of repeated experience and regular feelings, is a more permanent, and far more philosophical language …

Even at the time Wordsworth's opinions on this point represented a minority view, and with the passage of time this Romantic belief in the "philosophical language" of "low and rustic life" became less and less widely held. Fifteen years later one finds Wordsworth's collaborator on *Lyrical Ballads,* Coleridge, writing that

> The best part of human language, properly so called, is derived from reflection on the acts of the mind itself. It is formed by a voluntary appropriation of fixed symbols to internal acts, to processes and results of imagination, the greater part of which have no place in the consciousness of the uneducated man…

As the Romantic period slid into the Victorian and the vogue for rustic or uneducated authors passed away, so the point of view represented in Coleridge's remark came to dominate, and "standard" educated English became more and more widely accepted as an ideal to which all should aspire.

Over the course of this period, the varieties of English were to some extent dissolving into the forms of standard English, many regional variations persisted—and the forms of standard English itself were far from unchanging. In pronunciation the most significant change in "standard British English" was the disappearance of the /r/ sound before many consonants, and before a pause, so that in words such as "harm" or "person," for example, the "r" has since the late eighteenth century been flattened into the smooth "hahm" or "pehson" associated with modern "standard English" pronunciation. Interesting geographical variations have developed over this change, however. In Scotland and in Ireland, as in Canada and most of the United States, the "r" has continued to be sounded in such contexts; these varieties of English are referred to by linguists as "rhotic." In Australia, New Zealand, and South Africa, on the other hand, as well as in some parts of the United States, for instance in Massachusetts and some other parts of New England, non-rhotic forms have come to predominate in much the same way as they have in England.

As the rhymes of English poetry reveal, there were also changes in the sounding of some vowels in the late eighteenth century. In the early eighteenth century, for example, Alexander Pope rhymed "tea" with "obey;" rhymes also suggest that "sea" was pronounced in a manner closer to "say" than to "see." By 1797, however, Coleridge was rhyming "sea" with "free;" and by the end of the Romantic period the older pronunciations of such words had almost certainly died out.

Eighteenth century habits of capitalization and punctuation were also largely abandoned during this period. Capitalization and typography had generally been considered the business of the compositor rather than that of the author, and the tendency in the early and mid-eighteenth century had been to capitalize (or sometimes italicize) a wide range of nouns. By the end of the century, patterns of usage were coming to approximate the conventions of modern English.

Paragraphing remained less strongly conventionalized than it is now—many writers tended to start new paragraphs very infrequently—and the conventions for writing direct speech were still unstable, with the practice of using double quotation marks surrounding the exact words spoken starting to become common at the end of the eighteenth century. (The practice of using single rather than double quotation marks did not become common in Britain until later in the nineteenth century, and did not become entirely standardized as British usage until the twentieth century.)

History of the Language and of Print Culture

In an effort to provide for readers a direct sense of the development of the language and of print culture, examples of texts in their original form (and of illustrations) have been provided in each volume. A list of these within the present volume appears below. Overviews of "the business of literature" and of developments in the history of language during this period appear on pages lviii to lxi, and a "Contexts" section on various aspects of "Reading, Writing, Publishing" appears on pages 266–80.

Robert Burns, all poems (1785–99) in original spelling and punctuation, pp. 116–32

William Blake, all poems (1789–94) in original spelling and punctuation, pp. 36–56.

William Blake, *Songs of Innocence and of Experience*, 1789-94, title page for the full work, p. 36; "The Little Black Boy," p. 37; title page for *Songs of Experience*, p. 40; frontispiece, *Songs of Experience*, p. 40; "The Tyger," p. 42. See also the color insert pages.

William Blake, *The Marriage of Heaven and Hell*, 1793, illustrated plates, pp. 52–5.

Samuel Taylor Coleridge, all poems (1795–1836) in original spelling and punctuation, pp. 299–329.

William Blake, illustrations for John Stedman, *Narrative of Five Years' Expedition against the Revolted Negroes of Surinam*, 1796, p. 515.

William Taylor, "Ellenore," 1796, poem in original spelling and punctuation, pp. 152–55.

William Wordsworth, all poems (1798–1850) in original spelling and punctuation, pp. 193–263.

Mary Robinson, "All Alone," 1800, original spelling and punctuation, pp. 64–66.

Jane Austen, *Lady Susan*, passage in original spelling and punctuation, 1805, p. 377.

William Wordsworth, "I wandered lonely as a Cloud," 1807, facsimile of page from *Poems in Two Volumes* with manuscript additions, p. 225.

Thomas Rowlandson, *Dr. Syntax and a Bookseller*, 1812, p. lix.

J. Bluck, *Ackermann's Art Library*, c.1812–15, p. lix.

Felicia Hemans, all poems (1812–29) in original spelling and punctuation, pp. 678–86.

George Gordon, Lord Byron, all poems (1814–23) in original spelling and punctuation, pp. 528–604.

John Keats, all poems (1816–20) in original spelling and punctuation, pp. 701–40.

Maria Edgeworth, *Angelina, or L'Amie Inconnue*, facsimile pages from 1813 edition of *Moral Tales*, pp. 158, 189–90.

John Clare, all poems (1821–48) in original spelling and punctuation, pp. 688–98.

John Brown, *A Memoir of Robert Blincoe*, title page, 1832, p. xlii.

Anna Laetitia Barbauld

1743 – 1825

William Blake admired Anna Laetitia Barbauld's poetry, as did Samuel Taylor Coleridge, who walked forty miles to meet her, and William Wordsworth, who said about the Barbauld poem "Life": "I am not in the habit of grudging people their good things, but I wish I had written those [final] lines." Although born in the provinces, Barbauld became in her own day a leading figure in London literary life. She composed innovative and influential poetry, hymns, children's literature, political pamphlets, essays, and works of literary criticism. She also established herself as a leading educator and political and social activist. By the time of her death, however, her literary reputation had begun to fade, and she was largely forgotten until recent critical work renewed interest in this talented and versatile professional writer.

Anna Laetitia Aiken was born in Leicestershire to Jane Jennings and John Aiken, a nonconformist Presbyterian minister and schoolteacher at the Warrington Dissenting Academy in Yorkshire. Schooled by her father, she was a precocious child who studied the classics early in life. In her late teens she became acquainted with the influential educator and scientist Joseph Priestley and developed a lasting friendship with him and his wife. Barbauld was inspired by Priestley's poetry, and he was impressed by hers; he eventually encouraged her to publish her first volume, *Poems* (1773). This collection of lyrics, hymns, epistles, and mock-heroic poems, published under her birth name, went through five editions in four years and received considerable critical acclaim, *The Monthly Review* calling it a "great accession to the literary world." That same year Barbauld printed *Miscellaneous Pieces in Prose* with her brother, John Aiken (later the editor of a radical journal, *Monthly Magazine*).

Living at her father's school prepared Barbauld to run her own boys' boarding school, which she started with her husband, the dissenting clergyman Rochemont Barbauld, whom she married in 1774. During this period she wrote her popular and influential *Lessons for Children* (1787–88) and *Hymns in Prose for Children* (1787), designed for the very young. Both went through many printings and continued to be read in the United States and England until the close of the century. By 1785 her husband's mental instability required them to close the school (he eventually became violent and later committed suicide), and from this point on, Barbauld committed herself solely to literary work.

In her political pamphlets and essays of the 1790s, Barbauld addressed ethics, education, and political economy, and argued for freedom of religion and conscience—a cause dear to the hearts of Dissenters. She also argued strongly for the abolition of slavery (at a moment when the movement had suffered a setback) in her verse *Epistle to William Wilberforce* (1791); and in the essay *Sins of Government, Sins of Nation* (1793) she derided the British government for its involvement in the war against France. Barbauld then turned to editorial work, producing the first collection of *The Correspondence of Samuel Richardson* (1804), which includes her biography of the author. She also published *The British Novelists* (1810), a fifty-volume collection featuring the work of 28 novelists, both male and female, along with Barbauld's biographical and critical prefaces. In her general introduction to *On the Origin and Progress of Novel-Writing*, she argued for the value of novels for both education and enjoyment. This was pioneering in its recognition of the novel as a serious genre.

In 1812 Barbauld published her final work, the prophetic poem *Eighteen Hundred and Eleven*. Written in a pessimistic tone, the poem traces the cyclical rise and fall of national empires, indicts Britain for its involvement in the war with France, and predicts the fall of the British Empire. At the end of the poem, "Genius" leaves for America, the nation Barbauld suggests will replace Britain as the new empire. The poem elicited widespread criticism for what was deemed its "anti-patriotism." John Wilson Croker's abusive attack in the *Quarterly Review* used to be credited with effectively ending Barbauld's publishing career, but this is not accurate: she continued writing into the 1820s. After her death in 1825 her niece published two collections of her works.

⌘⌘⌘

Washing Day

... and their voice,
Turning again towards childish treble, pipes
And whistles in its sound.[1]

The Muses[2] are turned gossips; they have lost
The buskined step,[3] and clear high-sounding phrase,
Language of gods. Come, then, domestic Muse,
In slipshod measure loosely prattling on
Of farm or orchard, pleasant curds and cream,
Or drowning flies, or shoe lost in the mire
By little whimpering boy, with rueful face;
Come, Muse, and sing the dreaded Washing-Day.
Ye who beneath the yoke of wedlock bend,
With bowed soul, full well ye ken° the day *know*
Which week, smooth sliding after week, brings on
Too soon; for to that day nor peace belongs
Nor comfort; ere the first grey streak of dawn,
The red-armed washers come and chase repose.
Nor pleasant smile, nor quaint device of mirth,
E'er visited that day; the very cat,
From the wet kitchen scared, and reeking hearth,
Visits the parlour, an unwonted° guest. *infrequent*
The silent breakfast meal is soon dispatched
Uninterrupted, save by anxious looks
Cast at the lowering sky, if sky should lower.
From that last evil, O preserve us, heavens!
For should the skies pour down, adieu to all
Remains of quiet; then expect to hear
Of sad disasters—dirt and gravel stains
Hard to efface, and loaded lines at once
Snapped short—and linen-horse° by dog thrown down, *clotheshorse*
And all the petty miseries of life.
Saints have been calm while stretched upon the rack,
And Guatimozin[4] smiled on burning coals;
But never yet did housewife notable
Greet with a smile a rainy washing-day.
But grant the welkin° fair, require not thou *sky*
Who call'st thyself perchance the master there,
Or study swept, or nicely dusted coat,
Or usual 'tendance; ask not, indiscreet,
Thy stockings mended, though the yawning rents
Gape wide as Erebus,[5] nor hope to find
Some snug recess impervious; should'st thou try
The 'customed garden walks, thine eye shall rue
The budding fragrance of thy tender shrubs,
Myrtle or rose, all crushed beneath the weight
Of coarse checked apron, with impatient hand

[1] *and their voice ... sound* Cf. Shakespeare's *As You Like It* 2.7.161–63: "and his big manly voice, / Turning again toward childish treble, pipes / And whistles in his sound."

[2] *Muses* In classical mythology, nine goddesses who presided over learning and the arts.

[3] *buskined step* I.e., tragic mode. Actors in Athenian tragedy wore buskins, or high, thick-soled boots.

[4] *Guatimozin* Cuauhtémoc, the last Aztec emperor (c. 1495–1522), was captured and tortured by Cortés's Spanish conquistadors when they invaded the Aztec capital (now Mexico City).

[5] *Erebus* In Greek mythology, a place below the earth that the dead pass through on their way to Hades, or the underworld.

Twitched off when showers impend: or crossing lines
Shall mar thy musings, as the wet cold sheet
Flaps in thy face abrupt. Woe to the friend
Whose evil stars have urged him forth to claim
On such a day the hospitable rites;
Looks, blank at best, and stinted courtesy,
Shall he receive. Vainly he feeds his hopes
With dinner of roast chicken, savoury pie,
Or tart or pudding:—pudding he nor tart
That day shall eat; nor, though the husband try,
Mending what can't be helped, to kindle mirth
From cheer deficient, shall his consort's brow
Clear up propitious; the unlucky guest
In silence dines, and early slinks away.
I well remember, when a child, the awe
This day struck into me; for then the maids,
I scarce knew why, looked cross, and drove me from
    them;
Nor soft caress could I obtain, nor hope
Usual indulgencies; jelly or creams,
Relic of costly suppers, and set by
For me their petted one; or buttered toast,
When butter was forbid; or thrilling tale
Of ghost, or witch, or murder—so I went
And sheltered me beside the parlour fire:
There my dear grandmother, eldest of forms,
Tended the little ones, and watched from harm,
Anxiously fond, though oft her spectacles
With elfin cunning hid, and oft the pins
Drawn from her ravelled stocking, might have soured
One less indulgent.—
At intervals my mother's voice was heard,
Urging dispatch; briskly the work went on,
All hands employed to wash, to rinse, to wring,
To fold, and starch, and clap, and iron, and plait.[1]
Then would I sit me down, and ponder much
Why washings were. Sometimes through hollow
    bole° *bowl*
Of pipe amused we blew, and sent aloft
The floating bubbles, little dreaming then
To see, Mongolfier,[2] thy silken ball
Ride buoyant through the clouds—so near approach
The sports of children and the toils of men.
Earth, air, and sky, and ocean, hath its bubbles,[3]
And verse is one of them—this most of all.
—1797

Eighteen Hundred and Eleven,[4] A Poem

Still the loud death drum, thundering from afar,
O'er the vext nations pours the storm of war:
To the stern call still Britain bends her ear,
Feeds the fierce strife, the alternate hope and fear;
Bravely, though vainly, dares to strive with fate,
And seeks by turns to prop each sinking state.
Colossal Power[5] with overwhelming force
Bears down each fort of freedom in its course;
Prostrate she lies beneath the despot's sway,
While the hushed nations curse him—and obey.
    Bounteous in vain, with frantic man at strife,
Glad Nature pours the means—the joys of life;
In vain with orange blossoms scents the gale,
The hills with olives clothes, with corn the vale;
Man calls to Famine,[6] nor invokes in vain,
Disease and Rapine° follow in her train; *plunder*
The tramp of marching hosts disturbs the plough,
The sword, not sickle, reaps the harvest now,[7]
And where the soldier gleans the scant supply,
The helpless peasant but retires to die;
No laws his hut from licensed outrage shield,
And war's least horror is the ensanguined° field. *blood-stained*
    Fruitful in vain, the matron counts with pride

[1] *clap* Smooth; *plait* Fold.

[2] *Montgolfier* Montgolfier brothers, from Annonay, France, who invented and launched the first hot-air balloon in 1783.

[3] *Earth … bubbles* Cf. Shakespeare's *Macbeth* 1.3.83: "The earth hath bubbles, as the water has."

[4] *Eighteen Hundred and Eleven* Britain's war with France, begun in 1793, would not end until the Battle of Waterloo in 1815. By 1811, Russia, Austria, and Spain, Britain's allies, had already capitulated to the strength of Napoleon's army; Britain was in financial distress; and King George III had been declared insane.

[5] *Colossal Power* Napoleon Bonaparte (1769–1821), emperor of France.

[6] *Famine* In 1811 there was widespread hunger in Britain and much of Europe due to crop failures in the preceding years, as well as the necessity of providing food for soldiers.

[7] *The sword … now* Napoleon sent his soldiers out unencumbered with baggage; consequently, most of them were starving and were forced to steal food.

The blooming youths that grace her honoured side;
No son returns to press her widow'd hand,
Her fallen blossoms strew a foreign strand.
—Fruitful in vain, she boasts her virgin race,
Whom cultured arts adorn and gentlest grace;
Defrauded of its homage, Beauty mourns,
And the rose withers on its virgin thorns.
Frequent, some stream obscure, some uncouth name
By deeds of blood is lifted into fame;
Oft o'er the daily page some soft one bends
To learn the fate of husband, brothers, friends,
Or the spread map with anxious eye explores,
Its dotted boundaries and penciled shores,
Asks where the spot that wrecked her bliss is found,
And learns its name but to detest the sound.
    And think'st thou, Britain, still to sit at ease,
An island queen amidst thy subject seas,
While the vext billows, in their distant roar,
But soothe thy slumbers, and but kiss thy shore?
To sport in wars, while danger keeps aloof,
Thy grassy turf unbruised by hostile hoof?
So sing thy flatterers; but, Britain, know,
Thou who hast shared the guilt must share the woe.
Nor distant is the hour; low murmurs spread,
And whispered fears, creating what they dread;
Ruin, as with an earthquake shock, is here,
There, the heart-witherings of unuttered fear,
And that sad death, whence most affection bleeds,
Which sickness, only of the soul, precedes.
Thy baseless wealth dissolves in air away,[1]
Like mists that melt before the morning ray:
No more on crowded mart or busy street
Friends, meeting friends, with cheerful hurry greet;
Sad, on the ground thy princely merchants bend
Their altered looks, and evil days portend,
And fold their arms, and watch with anxious breast
The tempest blackening in the distant West.[2]
    Yes, thou must droop; thy Midas dream is o'er;
The golden tide of Commerce leaves thy shore,
Leaves thee to prove the alternate ills that haunt
Enfeebling Luxury and ghastly Want;
Leaves thee, perhaps, to visit distant lands,
And deal the gifts of Heaven with equal hands.
    Yet, O my country, name beloved, revered,
By every tie that binds the soul endeared,
Whose image to my infant senses came
Mixt with Religion's light and Freedom's holy flame!
If prayers may not avert, if 'tis thy fate
To rank amongst the names that once were great,
Not like the dim cold crescent[3] shalt thou fade,
Thy debt to Science and the Muse unpaid;
Thine are the laws surrounding states revere,
Thine the full harvest of the mental year,
Thine the bright stars in Glory's sky that shine,
And arts that make it life to live are thine.
If westward streams the light that leaves thy shores,
Still from thy lamp the streaming radiance pours.
Wide spreads thy race from Ganges[4] to the pole,
O'er half the western world thy accents roll:
Nations beyond the Appalachian hills[5]
Thy hand has planted and thy spirit fills:
Soon as their gradual progress shall impart
The finer sense of morals and of art,
Thy stores of knowledge the new states shall know,
And think thy thoughts, and with thy fancy glow;
Thy Lockes, thy Paleys[6] shall instruct their youth,
Thy leading star direct their search for truth;
Beneath the spreading platan's[7] tent-like shade,
Or by Missouri's rushing waters laid,
"Old father Thames" shall be the poet's theme,
Of Hagley's woods[8] the enamoured virgin dream,
And Milton's tones the raptured ear enthrall,

[1] *Thy baseless wealth ... away* 1810 saw the failure of many British businesses, and in 1811, the country itself was threatened with financial collapse.

[2] *The tempest ... West* Relations had been strained between England and the United States since the French Revolution; Barbauld here foresees the beginning of the War of 1812.

[3] *crescent* Symbol of the Ottoman Empire, which had been in decline throughout the eighteenth and into the nineteenth century.

[4] *Ganges* Sacred river of India.

[5] *Appalachian hills* Mountain range in the eastern United States.

[6] *Lockes ... Paleys* Men as eminent as John Locke and William Paley. John Locke (1632–1704), English philosopher who wrote about political, intellectual, and religious freedom and William Paley (1743–1805), English theologian and moral philosopher, who defended Christianity in many of his texts.

[7] *platan* Plane tree.

[8] *Hagley's woods* Cf. *The Seasons, "Spring,"* in which James Thomson writes about Lord Lyttleton's lush estate in Worcestershire.

Mixt with the roar of Niagara's fall;
In Thomson's glass[1] the ingenuous youth shall learn
A fairer face of Nature to discern;
Nor of the bards that swept the British lyre
Shall fade one laurel, or one note expire.
Then, loved Joanna,[2] to admiring eyes
Thy storied groups in scenic pomp shall rise;
Their high souled strains and Shakespeare's noble rage
Shall with alternate passion shake the stage.
Some youthful Basil[3] from thy moral lay
With stricter hand his fond desires shall sway;
Some Ethwald,[4] as the fleeting shadows pass,
Start at his likeness in the mystic glass;
The tragic Muse resume her just control,
With pity and with terror purge the soul,
While wide o'er transatlantic realms thy name
Shall live in light, and gather all its fame.
 Where wanders Fancy down the lapse of years
Shedding o'er imaged woes untimely tears?
Fond moody Power! as hopes—as fears prevail,
She longs, or dreads, to lift the awful veil,
On visions of delight now loves to dwell,
Now hears the shriek of woe or Freedom's knell:
Perhaps, she says, long ages past away,
And set in western waves our closing day,
Night, Gothic night, again may shade the plains
Where Power is seated, and where Science reigns;
England, the seat of arts, be only known
By the gray ruin and the mouldering stone;
That time may tear the garland from her brow,
And Europe sit in dust, as Asia now.
 Yet then the ingenuous youth whom Fancy fires
With pictured glories of illustrious sires,
With duteous zeal their pilgrimage shall take
From the Blue Mountains,° or Ontario's lake, *in Pennsylvania*
With fond adoring steps to press the sod
By statesmen, sages, poets, heroes trod;
On Isis' banks[5] to draw inspiring air,
From Runnymede[6] to send the patriot's prayer;
In pensive thought, where Cam's slow waters[7] wind,
To meet those shades that ruled the realms of mind;
In silent halls to sculptured marbles bow,
And hang fresh wreaths round Newton's[8] awful brow.
Oft shall they seek some peasant's homely shed,
Who toils, unconscious of the mighty dead,
To ask where Avon's[9] winding waters stray,
And thence a knot of wild flowers bear away;
Anxious enquire where Clarkson,[10] friend of man,
Or all-accomplished Jones[11] his race began;
If of the modest mansion aught remains
Where Heaven and Nature prompted Cowper's[12] strains;
Where Roscoe, to whose patriot breast belong
The Roman virtue and the Tuscan song,
Led Ceres to the black and barren moor
Where Ceres never gained a wreath before:[13]
With curious search their pilgrim steps shall rove
By many a ruined tower and proud alcove,
Shall listen for those strains that soothed of yore
Thy rock, stern Skiddaw, and thy fall, Lodore;[14]
Feast with Dun Edin's° classic brow their sight, *Edinburgh's*
And visit "Melrose by the pale moonlight."[15]
 But who their mingled feelings shall pursue
When London's faded glories rise to view?

[1] *glass* Mirror; i.e., nature as reflected in Thomson's *The Seasons.*

[2] *Joanna* Scottish playwright Joanna Baillie (1762–1851), who was often compared with Shakespeare.

[3] *Basil* Character in Baillie's tragedy *Count Basil* (1798).

[4] *Ethwald* Character in Baillie's tragedy *Ethwald* (1802).

[5] *Isis' banks* Bank of the River Thames at Oxford, known as the Isis.

[6] *Runnymede* Site where King John signed the Magna Carta (1215).

[7] *Cam* River at Cambridge.

[8] *Newton* Sir Isaac Newton (1642–1727), mathematician, physicist, and professor at Cambridge University.

[9] *Avon* River that runs through Stratford, where Shakespeare was born.

[10] *Clarkson* Thomas Clarkson (1760–1846), abolitionist, whose work helped to end the British slave trade in 1807.

[11] *Jones* Sir William Jones (1746–94), judge and scholar, who promoted Asian and Sanskrit studies.

[12] *Cowper* William Cowper (1731–1800), English poet.

[13] *Roscoe … before* William Roscoe (1753–1831), historian and MP, who promoted the use of the moors for agriculture; *Ceres* Roman goddess of agriculture.

[14] *Skiddaw … Lodore* Mountain and waterfall in the Lake District, England.

[15] *Melrose … moonlight* Site of the beautiful Melrose Abbey ruins in the Scottish Borderlands; cf. Sir Walter Scott's *The Lay of the Last Minstrel* 2.1: "If thou woud'st view fair Melrose aright, / Go visit it by the pale moonlight." See also p. xxxiii in the Introduction to this volume.

The mighty city, which by every road,
In floods of people poured itself abroad;
Ungirt by walls, irregularly great,
No jealous drawbridge, and no closing gate;
Whose merchants (such the state which commerce brings)
Sent forth their mandates to dependant kings;
Streets, where the turban'd Moslem, bearded Jew,
And woolly Afric, met the brown Hindu;
Where through each vein spontaneous plenty flowed,
Where Wealth enjoyed, and Charity bestowed.
Pensive and thoughtful shall the wanderers greet
Each splendid square, and still, untrodden street;
Or of some crumbling turret, mined by time,
The broken stairs with perilous step shall climb,
Thence stretch their view the wide horizon round,
By scattered hamlets trace its ancient bound,
And, choked no more with fleets, fair Thames survey
Through reeds and sedge pursue his idle way.
With throbbing bosoms shall the wanderers tread
The hallowed mansions of the silent dead,
Shall enter the long isle and vaulted dome
Where Genius and where Valour find a home;[1]
Awestruck, midst chill sepulchral marbles breathe,
Where all above is still, as all beneath;
Bend at each antique shrine, and frequent turn
To clasp with fond delight some sculptured urn,
The ponderous mass of Johnson's[2] form to greet,
Or breathe the prayer at Howard's[3] sainted feet.
Perhaps some Briton, in whose musing mind
Those ages live which Time has cast behind,
To every spot shall lead his wondering guests
On whose known site the beam of glory rests:
Here Chatham's eloquence in thunder broke,
Here Fox persuaded, or here Garrick[4] spoke;
Shall boast how Nelson, fame and death in view,
To wonted victory led his ardent crew,
In England's name enforced, with loftiest tone,
Their duty—and too well fulfilled his own:[5]
How gallant Moore,[6] as ebbing life dissolved,
But hoped his country had his fame absolved.[7]
Or call up sages whose capacious mind
Left in its course a track of light behind;
Point where mute crowds on Davy's[8] lips reposed,
And Nature's coyest secrets were disclosed;
Join with their Franklin, Priestley's[9] injured name,
Whom, then, each continent shall proudly claim.
Oft shall the strangers turn their eager feet
The rich remains of ancient art to greet,
The pictured walls with critic eye explore,
And Reynolds be what Raphael[10] was before.
On spoils from every clime their eyes shall gaze,
Egyptian granites and the Etruscan vase;
And when midst fallen London, they survey
The stone where Alexander's ashes lay,[11]
Shall own with humbled pride the lesson just
By Time's slow finger written in the dust.
There walks a Spirit o'er the peopled earth,
Secret his progress is, unknown his birth;
Moody and viewless° as the changing wind, *invisible*
No force arrests his foot, no chains can bind;

[1] *vaulted dome … home* St. Paul's Cathedral, home to statues of eminent British men and women.

[2] *Johnson* Samuel Johnson (1709–84), scholar and author of *The Dictionary of the English Language.*

[3] *Howard* John Howard (1726–90), prison reformer and philanthropist.

[4] *Chatham* William Pitt, 1st Earl of Chatham (1708–78), prime minister and famous patriot and orator; *Fox* Charles James Fox (1749–1806), parliamentarian and orator; *Garrick* David Garrick (1717–79), famous English actor and dramatist.

[5] *Nelson … his own* Admiral Horatio Nelson, English war hero, spoke these famous words before he died at the Battle of Trafalgar in 1805: "England expects that every man will do his duty."

[6] *Moore* Sir John Moore (1761–1809), general who led a retreat during the Napoleonic Wars; he saved his troops, but died in the process.

[7] [Barbauld's note] "I hope England will be satisfied," were the last words of General Moore.

[8] *Davy* Sir Humphrey Davy (1778–1829), physicist and chemist, whose lectures were renowned.

[9] *Franklin* Benjamin Franklin (1706–90), American scientist, inventor, and statesman; *Priestley* Joseph Priestley (1733–1804), English scientist and theologian, whose correspondence with Franklin led to Priestley's experimentation with and discoveries regarding electricity; Priestley was persecuted for his support of the French and American Revolutions, which led to his emigration from England to America.

[10] *Reynolds … Raphael* Sir Joshua Reynolds (1723–92), eminent English portrait artist, and Raphael (1483–1520), famous Italian Renaissance painter and architect.

[11] *stone … lay* The British Museum mistakenly believed it had purchased the tomb of Alexander the Great.

Where'er he turns, the human brute awakes,
And, roused to better life, his sordid hut forsakes:
He thinks, he reasons, glows with purer fires,
Feels finer wants, and burns with new desires:
Obedient Nature follows where he leads;
The steaming marsh is changed to fruitful meads;
The beasts retire from man's asserted reign,
And prove his kingdom was not given in vain.
Then from its bed is drawn the ponderous ore,
Then Commerce pours her gifts on every shore.
Then Babel's towers[1] and terraced gardens rise,
And pointed obelisks invade the skies;
The prince commands, in Tyrian purple drest,
And Egypt's virgins weave the linen vest.
Then spans the graceful arch the roaring tide,
And stricter bounds the cultured fields divide.
Then kindles Fancy, then expands the heart,
Then blow° the flowers of Genius and of Art; *blossom*
Saints, Heroes, Sages, who the land adorn,
Seem rather to descend than to be born;
Whilst History, midst the rolls consigned to fame,
With pen of adamant inscribes their name.
    The Genius now forsakes the favoured shore,
And hates, capricious, what he loved before;
Then empires fall to dust, then arts decay,
And wasted realms enfeebled despots sway;
Even Nature's changed; without his fostering smile
Ophir[2] no gold, no plenty yields the Nile;
The thirsty sand absorbs the useless rill,° *stream*
And spotted plagues from putrid fens distill.
In desert solitudes then Tadmor[3] sleeps,
Stern Marius then o'er fallen Carthage weeps;[4]
Then with enthusiast love the pilgrim roves
To seek his footsteps in forsaken groves,
Explores the fractured arch, the ruined tower,
Those limbs disjointed of gigantic power;
Still at each step he dreads the adder's sting,
The Arab's javelin, or the tiger's spring;
With doubtful caution treads the echoing ground,
And asks where Troy or Babylon[5] is found.
    And now the vagrant Power no more detains
The vale of Tempe, or Ausonian plains;[6]
Northward he throws the animating ray,
O'er Celtic nations bursts the mental day:
And, as some playful child the mirror turns,
Now here now there the moving lustre burns;
Now o'er his changeful fancy more prevail
Batavia's dykes than Arno's[7] purple vale,
And stinted suns, and rivers bound with frost,
Than Enna's plains or Baia's[8] viny coast;
Venice the Adriatic weds in vain,
And Death sits brooding o'er Campania's[9] plain;
O'er Baltic shores and through Hercynian groves,[10]
Stirring the soul, the mighty impulse moves;
Art plies his tools, and Commerce spreads her sail,
And wealth is wafted in each shifting gale.
The sons of Odin[11] tread on Persian looms,
And Odin's daughters breathe distilled perfumes;
Loud minstrel bards, in Gothic halls, rehearse
The Runic rhyme, and "build the lofty verse:"[12]
The Muse, whose liquid notes were wont to swell
To the soft breathings of the Aeolian[13] shell,
Submits, reluctant, to the harsher tone,
And scarce believes the altered voice her own.

---

[1] *Babel's towers* Cf. Genesis 11.3–9. The Babylonians attempted to create a tower that would reach heaven; God punished them by giving them different languages and scattering them around the earth.

[2] *Ophir* Cf. 1 Kings 9.28: "And they came to Ophir, and fetched from thence gold."

[3] *Tadmor* Biblical land in ancient Syria.

[4] *Marius ...* weeps Gaius Marius (157–86 BCE), Roman Consul and general who was once called the "savior of Rome"; upon aging and falling from power, he was said to have wept among the ruins of Carthage.

[5] *Troy* Ancient city in Asia Minor, subject of the Trojan War in Homer's *Iliad*; *Babylon* Ancient Mesopotamian city known for its wealth and beauty, destroyed in 689 BCE.

[6] *vale of Tempe* Valley in Greece celebrated by ancient poets for its beauty; *Ausonian plains* Virgil called Italy "Ausonia."

[7] *Batavia* Republic, now the Netherlands; *Arno* River in Italy.

[8] *Enna* Sicilian valley; *Baia* Italian village on the Bay of Naples, celebrated for its spas in Roman times.

[9] *Campania* Italian province whose plains were marshy and malarial.

[10] *Hercynian groves* Black Forest in Germany.

[11] *Odin* Supreme Norse god.

[12] *build the lofty verse* From Milton's *Lycidas* (10–11): "He knew / Himself to sing, and build the lofty rhyme."

[13] *Aeolian* Aeolis is the ancient name of a beautiful coastal region in Asia Minor (now Turkey).

And now, where Caesar saw with proud disdain
The wattled hut and skin of azure stain,[1]
Corinthian columns rear their graceful forms,
And light verandas brave the wintry storms,
While British tongues the fading fame prolong
Of Tully's eloquence and Maro's[2] song.
Where once Bonduca whirled the scythed car,
And the fierce matrons raised the shriek of war,[3]
Light forms beneath transparent muslins float,
And tutored voices swell the artful note.
Light-leaved acacias and the shady plane
And spreading cedar grace the woodland reign;
While crystal walls the tenderer plants confine,
The fragrant orange and the nectared pine;
The Syrian grape there hangs her rich festoons,
Nor asks for purer air, or brighter noons:
Science and Art urge on the useful toil,
New mold a climate and create the soil,
Subdue the rigour of the northern Bear,[4]
O'er polar climes shed aromatic air,
On yielding Nature urge their new demands,
And ask not gifts but tribute at her hands.
London exults:—on London Art bestows
Her summer ices and her winter rose;
Gems of the East her mural crown adorn,
And Plenty at her feet pours forth her horn;[5]
While even the exiles her just laws disclaim,
People a continent, and build a name:
August she sits, and with extended hands
Holds forth the book of life to distant lands.
But fairest flowers expand but to decay;
The worm is in thy core, thy glories pass away;
Arts, arms and wealth destroy the fruits they bring;
Commerce, like beauty, knows no second spring.
Crime walks thy streets, Fraud earns her unblest bread,
O'er want and woe thy gorgeous robe is spread,
And angel charities in vain oppose:
With grandeur's growth the mass of misery grows.
For see,—to other climes the Genius soars,
He turns from Europe's desolated shores;
And lo, even now, midst mountains wrapt in storm,
On Andes' heights he shrouds his awful form;
On Chimborazo's[6] summits treads sublime,
Measuring in lofty thought the march of Time;
Sudden he calls:—"'Tis now the hour!" he cries,
Spreads his broad hand, and bids the nations rise.
La Plata[7] hears amidst her torrents' roar,
Potosi[8] hears it, as she digs the ore:
Ardent, the Genius fans the noble strife,
And pours through feeble souls a higher life,
Shouts to the mingled tribes from sea to sea,
And swears—Thy world, Columbus, shall be free.

—1812

On the Death of the Princess Charlotte[9]

Yes, Britain mourns, as with electric touch
For youth, for love, for happiness destroyed,
Her universal population melts
In grief spontaneous, and hard hearts are moved,
And rough unpolished natures learn to feel
For those they envied, leveled in the dust
By Fate's impartial stroke; and pulpits sound
With vanity and woe to earthly goods,
And urge and dry the tear. Yet one there is
Who midst this general burst of grief remains

[1] *Caesar … stain* Cf. Julius Caesar's *The Gallic Wars* 5.14: "All the Britains, indeed, dye themselves with wood, which occasions a bluish color, and thereby have a more terrible appearance in fight."

[2] *Tully* Marcus Tullius Cicero (106–43 BCE), Roman orator, philosopher, and politician; *Maro* Publius Vergilius Maro, or Virgil (70–19 BCE), Roman poet, author of the *Aeneid*.

[3] *Bonduca … war* Queen of the ancient Iceni Celts, Boadicea (sometimes written as "Bonduca" or "Boudicca") led a massive rebellion against the Romans in about 60 CE; she committed suicide upon the failure of the mission.

[4] *northern Bear* Ursa Minor, a constellation that includes the North Star.

[5] *horn* Horn of plenty, or cornucopia, contains an abundance of the essentials and luxuries of life.

[6] *Chimborazo* Volcanic mountain in Ecuador.

[7] *La Plata* City in Argentina.

[8] *Potosi* City in Bolivia. All three countries were home to movements resistant to colonial rule. The region was famous for its gold deposits.

[9] *Death … Charlotte* The popular Princess Charlotte Augusta (1796–1817), daughter of the Prince of Wales, the future King George IV, died at the age of 21 of complications from childbirth.

In strange tranquility;[1] whom not the stir
And long drawn murmurs of the gathering crowd,
That by his very windows trail the pomp
Of hearse,[2] and blazoned arms, and long array
Of sad funereal rites, nor the loud groans
And deep-felt anguish of a husband's[3] heart,
Can move to mingle with this flood one tear.
In careless apathy, perhaps in mirth
He wears the day. Yet is he near in blood,
The very stem on which this blossom grew,
And at his knees she fondled, in the charm
And grace spontaneous which alone belongs
To untaught infancy. Yet oh forbear!
Nor deem him hard of heart; for awful, struck
By heaven's severest visitation, sad,
Like a scathed oak amidst the forest trees,
Lonely he stands—leaves bud, and shoot, and fall;
He holds no sympathy with living nature
Or time's incessant change. Then, in this hour,
While pensive thought is busy with the woes
And restless cares of poor humanity,
Think then, oh think of him, and breathe one prayer,
From the full tide of sorrow spare one tear
For him who does not weep!
—1819

To a Little Invisible Being Who is Expected Soon to Become Visible

Germ of new life, whose powers expanding slow
For many a moon their full perfection wait,—
Haste, precious pledge of happy love, to go
Auspicious borne through life's mysterious gate.

What powers lie folded in thy curious frame,—
Senses from objects locked, and mind from thought!
How little canst thou guess thy lofty claim
To grasp at all the worlds the Almighty wrought!

And see, the genial season's warmth to share,
Fresh younglings shoot, and opening roses glow!
Swarms of new life exulting fill the air,—
Haste, infant bud of being, haste to blow!° *blossom*

For thee the nurse prepares her lulling songs,
The eager matrons count the lingering day;
But far the most thy anxious parent longs
On thy soft cheek a mother's kiss to lay.

She only asks to lay her burden down,
That her glad arms that burden may resume;
And nature's sharpest pangs her wishes crown,
That free thee living from thy living tomb.

She longs to fold to her maternal breast
Part of herself, yet to herself unknown;
To see and to salute the stranger guest,
Fed with her life through many a tedious moon.

Come, reap thy rich inheritance of love!
Bask in the fondness of a mother's eye!
Nor wit nor eloquence her heart shall move
Like the first accents of thy feeble cry.

Haste, little captive, burst thy prison doors!
Launch on the living world, and spring to light!
Nature for thee displays her various stores,
Opens her thousand inlets of delight.

If charmed verse or muttered prayers had power,
With favouring spells to speed thee on thy way,
Anxious I'd bid my beads° each passing hour, *pray*
Till thy wished smile thy mother's pangs o'erpay.
—1825

---

[1] *one there is ... tranquility* Charlotte's father is said to have openly expressed his disdain of his daughter, linked, no doubt, to his feud with her mother.

[2] *by his windows ... hearse* The Prince of Wales did not attend his daughter's funeral.

[3] *husband* Leopold of Saxe-Coburg, whom Charlotte married in 1816.

Life

Animula, vagula, blandula.[1]

Life! I know not what thou art,
But know that thou and I must part;
And when, or how, or where we met,
I own to me's a secret yet.
But this I know, when thou art fled,
Where'er they lay these limbs, this head,
No clod so valueless shall be,
As all that then remains of me.
O whither, whither dost thou fly,
Where bend unseen thy trackless course,
And in this strange divorce,
Ah, tell where I must seek this compound I?

To the vast ocean of empyreal flame,[2]
From whence thy essence came,
Dost thou thy flight pursue, when freed
From matter's base encumbering weed?
Or dost thou, hid from sight,
Wait, like some spellbound knight,
Through blank oblivious years th'appointed hour,
To break thy trance and reassume thy power?
Yet canst thou without thought or feeling be?
O say what art thou, when no more thou'rt thee?

Life! we've been long together,
Through pleasant and through cloudy weather;
'Tis hard to part when friends are dear;
Perhaps 'twill cost a sigh, a tear;
Then steal away, give little warning,
Choose thine own time;
Say not good night, but in some brighter clime
Bid me good morning.

—1825

[1] *Animula, vagula, blandula* Latin: "Gentle wandering soul companion." From *The Emperor Hadrian to his Soul.*

[2] *ocean of empyreal flame* Empyrean, or highest sphere of heaven; the sphere of fire.

The Rights of Woman[3]

Yes, injured Woman! rise, assert thy right!
Woman! too long degraded, scorned, opprest;
O born to rule in partial° Law's despite, *biased*
Resume thy native empire o'er the breast!

Go forth arrayed in panoply[4] divine;
That angel pureness which admits no stain;
Go, bid proud Man his boasted rule resign,
And kiss the golden sceptre of thy reign.

Go, gird thyself with grace; collect thy store
Of bright artillery glancing from afar;
Soft melting tones thy thundering cannon's roar,
Blushes and fears thy magazine° of war. *storehouse*

Thy rights are empire: urge no meaner claim,—
Felt, not defined, and if debated, lost;
Like sacred mysteries, which withheld from fame,
Shunning discussion, are revered the most.

Try all that wit and art suggest to bend
Of thy imperial foe the stubborn knee;
Make treacherous Man thy subject, not thy friend;
Thou mayst command, but never canst be free.

Awe the licentious, and restrain the rude;
Soften the sullen, clear the cloudy brow:
Be, more than princes' gifts, thy favours sued;—
She hazards all, who will the least allow.

But hope not, courted idol of mankind,
On this proud eminence secure to stay;
Subduing and subdued, thou soon shalt find
Thy coldness soften, and thy pride give way.

Then, then, abandon each ambitious thought,
Conquest or rule thy heart shall feebly move,
In Nature's school, by her soft maxims taught,
That separate rights are lost in mutual love.

—1825

[3] *The Rights of Woman* Cf. Mary Wollstonecraft's *A Vindication of the Rights of Woman* (1792).

[4] *panoply* Lavish ceremonial attire.

Sir William Jones

1746 – 1794

Lawyer, historian, linguist, botanist, civil servant, and literary theorist William Jones had an interest in promoting understanding of and appreciation for Asian languages and cultures that led him to make an original contribution to scholarship unrivalled in his time. Though "Orientalist Jones" is now best remembered for these numerous contributions to Oriental studies, his theories of poetry and poetic inspiration also had an immeasurable influence on the development of the Romantic movement.

Jones showed an early facility with languages, and before entering Oxford University he knew Greek, Latin, Italian, Portuguese, French, and Spanish and had taught himself the Hebrew and Arabic scripts. At Oxford he expanded his study of Arabic while commencing Persian and Turkish. He soon became one of the nation's leading Oriental scholars, and his first published work, a translation into French of the history of Persian conqueror Nadir Shah, was commissioned by the King of Denmark.

Jones's following publications advanced his goals of increasing the study of Asian languages and the printing of Asian writings. *A Grammar of the Persian Language* (1771) is filled with examples that both provide a comprehensive introduction to Persian poetry and illustrate its beauty and sophistication. *Poems, Consisting Chiefly of Translations from the Asiatic Languages* (1772) fed a burgeoning public interest in Oriental culture and became his most popular early work.

Appended to that collection were two groundbreaking essays. In "On the Arts Commonly Called Imitative," Jones rejects Aristotle's thesis that all fine arts rest upon imitation of the natural world. Instead, he said, poetry is "a strong and animated expression of the human passions"—a declaration almost identical to Wordsworth's more famous, though much later, statement in the Preface to *Lyrical Ballads* (1800) that "good poetry is the spontaneous overflow of powerful feelings." Investigating these same ideas, "On the Poetry of the Eastern Nations" posits that the poetry of Asia (which Jones believed was richer and more inventive because in Asia the passions were more freely experienced and described) could provide a refreshing source of inspiration for Western literature. The work that made Jones's reputation as a great classical and Oriental scholar, however, was his treatise on aesthetics, *Poeseos Asiaticae Commentariorum Libri Sex* (1774). Still untranslated from the original Latin (and therefore virtually unknown today), this comprehensive examination of the topics, imagery, and forms of Asian poetry also develops Jones's theories on the nature of poetry's beauty and the emotional and imaginative sources of its inspiration.

In order to earn a living, Jones practiced law in his father's native Wales for nine years, until his legal work and continued Oriental scholarship allowed him to realize his lifelong dream of a post in Asia. In 1783, Jones, recently knighted and married, arrived in Calcutta as the newest judge on the Bengal Supreme Court. There he founded the Asiatic Society of Bengal—the first organized effort to study the history, society, and culture of India—and began learning Sanskrit in order to access Muslim and Hindu laws in their original form.

In *Asiatic Researches*—the journal of the Asiatic Society in which nearly all Jones's work in mythology, literature, linguistics, botany, history, and poetry was printed—Jones continued his work in aesthetics. "Sixth Anniversary Discourse" (1790) and "On the Mystical Poetry of the Persians and Hindus" (1792) expands upon what would later become an essentially Romantic view of poetry as resulting from mystical experience. Jones also began extensive comparative studies of mythology, and Romantic works such as *Kubla Khan* show the influence of Jones's belief in the common origins of all mythology and in a single origin of civilization (though Coleridge's poem takes this locus as Abyssinia, while Jones proposed Iran).

Jones's interest in Indian culture also spurred him to compose nine hymns addressed to aspects of the Hindu god Vishnu. The images in these poems helped to shape the visions of a mystical, resplendent India found in the works of Romantic poets such as Shelley, Byron, and Coleridge. The most famous of the hymns is the "Hymn to Nārāyena" (1785), whose verses, together with the prefatory argument, examine the nature of perception and create an analogy between the poet's act of creation and that of God. In their emphasis on personal experience, creative imagination, spontaneity of thought, and subjectivity, these poems are distinctly Romantic in sensibility.

Jones's studies led to several other groundbreaking developments. While learning Sanskrit he identified common grammatical roots with classical European languages such as Latin and Greek—a discovery that marked the beginnings of Indo-European comparative grammar and of modern linguistics. In his study of Indian history, Jones became the first to identify a point of correspondence between Western and Indian historical times, enabling Western scholars to determine the chronology of India's past in relation to their own. His translation of the Indian dramas *Śakuntā* by Kālidāsa (*The Fatal Ring*, 1799) and *Gīta Govinda* by Jayadeva (1789) ushered in an enthusiasm for Indian culture in Europe.

At the time of his death in India at the age of 47, William Jones had learned nearly 30 languages and made advancements in poetic theory, law, comparative linguistics, religious studies, and history, the full import of which are still being realized today. His influence on future developments in the genre of poetry alone is such that any comprehensive study of Romantic poetry should begin with his work.

⌘⌘⌘

A Hymn to Nārāyena

The Argument

A complete introduction to the following ode would be no less than a full comment on the Vadys[1] and Purāns[2] of the Hindus, the remains of Egyptian and Persian theology, and the tenets of the Ionick and Italick schools; but this is not the place for so vast a disquisition. It will be sufficient here to premise, that the inextricable difficulties attending the vulgar notion of material substances, concerning which

"We know this only, that we nothing know,"

induced many of the wisest among the Ancients, and some of the most enlightened among the Moderns, to believe, that the whole creation was rather an *energy* than a *work*, by which the Infinite Being, who is present at all times in all places, exhibits to the minds of his creatures a set of perceptions, like a wonderful picture or piece of music, always varied, yet always uniform; so that all bodies and their qualities exist, indeed, to every wise and useful purpose, but exist only as far as they are

[1] *Vadys* Vedas, the oldest sacred Hindu texts. They are written in Sanskrit and consist of four collections: the *Rig-Veda*, the *Yajur Veda*, the *Sama Veda*, and the *Atharva Veda*.

[2] *Purans* Purānas, a group of eighteen sacred poetical works, written in Sanskrit, that describe the creation of the worlds and the genealogy of the gods.

perceived; a theory no less pious than sublime, and as different from any principle of Atheism, as the brightest sunshine differs from the blackest midnight. This illusive operation of the deity the Hindu philosophers call Māyā,[1] or deception; and the word occurs in this sense more than once in the commentary on the *Rig Vayd*, by the great Vasishtha,[2] of which Mr. Halhed[3] has given us an admirable specimen.

The first stanza of the hymn represents the sublimest attributes of the Supreme Being, and the three forms, in which they most clearly appear to us, power, wisdom, and goodness, or, in the language of Orpheus and his disciples,[4] love: the second comprises the Indian and Egyptian doctrine of the Divine Essence and Archetypal Ideas; for a distinct account of which the reader must be referred to a noble description in the sixth book of Plato's *Republic*; and the fine explanation of that passage in an elegant discourse by the author of *Cyrus*,[5] from whose learned work a hint has been borrowed for the conclusion of this piece. The third and fourth are taken from the Institutes of Menu,[6] and the eighteenth Puran of Vyāsā,[7] entitled *Srey Bhagawat,* part of which has been translated into Persian, not without elegance, but rather too paraphrastically. From Brehme, or the Great Being, in the neuter gender, is formed Brehmā, in the masculine; and the second word is appropriated to the creative power of the divinity.

The spirit of God, called Nārāyena, or moving on the water, has a multiplicity of other epithets in Sanskrit, the principal of which are introduced, expressly or by allusion, in the fifth stanza; and two of them contain the names of the evil beings, who are feigned to have sprung from the ears of Vishnu: for thus the divine spirit is entitled, when considered as the preserving power: the sixth ascribes the perception of secondary qualities by our senses to the immediate influence of Māyā; and the seventh imputes to her operation the primary qualities of extension and solidity.

The Hymn

Spirit of Spirits, who, through ev'ry part
Of space expanded and of endless time,
Beyond the stretch of lab'ring thought sublime,
Badst uproar into beauteous order start,
Before Heaven was, Thou art:
Ere spheres beneath us rolled or spheres above,
Ere earth in firmamental ether hung,
Thou satst alone; till, through thy mystic love,
Things unexisting to existence sprung,
And grateful descant sung.
What first impelled thee to exert thy might?
Goodness unlimited. What glorious light
Thy pow'r directed? Wisdom without bound.
What proved it first? Oh! guide my fancy right;
Oh! raise from cumbrous ground
My soul in rapture drowned,
That fearless it may soar on wings of fire;
For Thou, who only knowst, Thou only canst inspire.

Wrapt in eternal solitary shade,
Th' impenetrable gloom of light intense,
Impervious, inaccessible, immense,
Ere spirits were infused or forms displayed,
Brehm his own mind surveyed,
As mortal eyes (thus finite we compare
With infinite) in smoothest mirrors gaze:
Swift, at his look, a shape supremely fair
Leaped into being with a boundless blaze,
That fifty suns might daze.
Primeval Maya was the Goddess named,
Who to her sire, with love divine inflamed,
A casket gave with rich ideas filled,
From which this gorgeous universe he framed;
For, when th' Almighty willed

[1] *Maya* Hindu goddess. The positive personification of illusion and unreality.

[2] *Vasishtha* Author of numerous hymns in the *Rig Veda*.

[3] *Mr. Halhed* Nathaniel Halhed (1751–1830), fellow Oxonian and Orientalist. Halhed's *Code of Gentoo Laws* includes a translation of Vasishtha's commentary.

[4] *Orpheus and his disciples* In Greek mythology, Orpheus is a Thracian poet and musician to whom several poems describing religious dogma and philosophical principles are ascribed. According to Orphean cosmology, the creation of the matter of the universe was presided over by Eros (love).

[5] *the author of Cyrus* Author unknown.

[6] *Institutes of Menu* I.e., Manu, a Sanskrit code of laws.

[7] *Vyasa* Sage who is said to have written down and divided the Vedas and assembled the Purānas.

Unnumbered worlds to build,
From unity diversified he sprang,
While gay Creation laughed, and procreant Nature rang.

First an all-potent all-pervading sound
Bade flow the waters—and the waters flowed,
Exulting in their measureless abode,
Diffusive, multitudinous, profound,
Above, beneath, around;
Then o'er the vast expanse primordial wind
Breathed gently, till a lucid bubble rose,
Which grew in perfect shape an egg refined:
Created substance no such lustre shows,
Earth no such beauty knows.
Above the warring waves it danced elate,
Till from its bursting shell with lovely state
A form cerulean fluttered o'er the deep,
Brightest of beings, greatest of the great:
Who, not as mortals steep,
Their eyes in dewy sleep,
But heavenly-pensive on the lotus[1] lay,
That blossomed at his touch and shed a golden ray.

Hail, primal blossom! hail empyreal gem!
Kemel, or Pedma,[2] or whate'er high name
Delight thee, say, what four-formed Godhead came,
With graceful stole and beamy diadem,
Forth from thy verdant stem?
Full-gifted Brehma! Rapt in solemn thought
He stood, and round his eyes fire-darting threw;
But, whilst his viewless origin he sought,
One plain he saw of living waters blue,
Their spring nor saw nor knew.
Then, in his parent stalk again retired,
With restless pain for ages he inquired
What were his pow'rs, by whom, and why conferred:
With doubts perplexed, with keen impatience fired
He rose, and rising heard
Th' unknown all-knowing Word,
"Brehma! no more in vain research persist:
My veil thou canst not move—Go; bid all worlds exist."

Hail, self-existent, in celestial speech
Narayen, from thy watry cradle, named;
Or Venamaly[3] may I sing unblamed,
With flow'ry braids, that to thy sandals reach,
Whose beauties, who can teach?
Or high Peitamber[4] clad in yellow robes
Than sunbeams brighter in meridian glow,
That weave their heaven-spun light o'er circling globes?
Unwearied, lotus-eyed, with dreadful bow,
Dire Evil's constant foe!
Great Pedmanabha,[5] o'er thy cherished world
The pointed Checra,[6] by thy fingers whirled,
Fierce Kytabh shall destroy and Medhu grim[7]
To black despair and deep destruction hurled.
Such views my senses dim.
My eyes in darkness swim:
What eye can bear thy blaze, what utt'rance tell
Thy deeds with silver trump or many-wreathed shell?

Omniscient Spirit, whose all-ruling pow'r
Bids from each sense bright emanations beam;
Glows in the rainbow, sparkles in the stream,
Smiles in the bud, and glistens in the flow'r
That crowns each vernal bow'r;
Sighs in the gale, and warbles in the throat
Of ev'ry bird, that hails the bloomy spring,
Or tells his love in many a liquid note,
Whilst envious artists touch the rival string,
Till rocks and forests ring;
Breathes in rich fragrance from the sandal grove,
Or where the precious musk-deer playful rove;
In dulcet juice from clust'ring fruit distills,
And burns salubrious in the tasteful clove:
Soft banks and verd'rous hills
Thy present influence fills;

[1] *lotus* Aquatic plant associated with fertility and spiritual purity.

[2] *Kemel, or Pedma* Kamalā and Padmā are two epithets of Devi, the primary Hindu goddess, both of which mean "lotus."

[3] *Vanamaly* Vanamālā, called "the one who is a garland of flowers." This and the other names given in this stanza are epithets or incarnations of Vishnu.

[4] *Peitamber* Pītāmbara, or "he who wears yellow silk."

[5] *Pedmanabha* Epithet that means "the one whose navel is the lotus."

[6] *Checra* Chakra, discus or mystic circle, pictured in hands of Hindu gods.

[7] *Fierce Kytabh ... Medhu grim* Kaitabha and Madhu are two demons who sprang from the ears of Lord Vishnu with the intention of slaying Brahma.

In air, in floods, in caverns, woods, and plains;
Thy will inspirits all, thy sov'reign Maya reigns.

Blue crystal vault, and elemental fires,
That in th'ethereal fluid blaze and breathe;
Thou, tossing main, whose snaky branches wreathe
This pensile° orb with intertwisted gyres; *hanging*
Mountains, whose radiant spires
Presumptuous rear their summits to the skies,
And blend their em'rald hue with sapphire light;
Smooth meads and lawns, that glow with varying dyes
Of dew-bespangled leaves and blossoms bright,
Hence! Vanish from my sight:
Delusive pictures! unsubstantial shows!
My soul absorbed one only Being knows,
Of all perceptions one abundant source,
Whence ev'ry object ev'ry moment flows:
Suns hence derive their force,
Hence planets learn their course;
But suns and fading worlds I view no more:
God only I perceive; God only I adore.

—1785

Charlotte Smith

1749 – 1806

As was the case with many early women writers, Charlotte Smith became a published author largely as a result of pressing financial circumstances. She succeeded in providing for herself and her family first through poetry and then through fiction—and became one of the shaping forces of English Romanticism through her writing. Her work enjoyed enormous popularity in her own day; as the nineteenth century advanced, her sentimental style fell out of fashion and her reputation, like that of so many other sentimental writers, waned.

Smith (née Turner) was born into the landed gentry in 1749 in London; her father was a country gentleman in Sussex, to which county Smith remained devoted throughout her life. Charlotte was the second of three children and her mother died giving birth to her brother when she was three years old. Her education was typical for someone of her gender and social class; she attended a fashionable boarding school between the ages of eight and twelve, at which point she left school and entered "society." Her father remarried in 1764 and it was arranged that Charlotte would marry the following year, at the age of 15. Her husband, Benjamin Smith, was the son of a West Indian merchant and was living beyond his means. Her father-in-law died in 1776, leaving a will that attempted to prevent his legacy from being wasted by his wayward son. The document was so complicated, however, that Smith was to spend the rest of her life going to the courts to fight for her children's inheritance. (Her case became well known in London, and it is probably the basis for the law case in Dickens's *Bleak House*.) Benjamin Smith continued his spendthrift ways and was imprisoned for debt in 1783. For a time, Smith and their growing family lived with him in prison.

In 1784, when Smith first turned to writing professionally, she was 25 years old and had nine living children. Desperate for money while her husband was still in prison, she composed *Elegiac Sonnets*. These remarkable sonnets, famous for their melancholy, pessimism, and pathos, represent an important stylistic achievement in their ability to convey a highly personal effect through an understated and impersonal style. This volume was extremely popular, and she later repeatedly rearranged and enlarged the collection. Among the additions were many poems supposedly written by characters in the novels she wrote later. By 1851 her sonnets had gone through 11 editions. Both Wordsworth and Coleridge learned from her, admiring her more in their youth than they were later willing to admit. Both used Smith's work as a model for working out their new style of Romantic self-expression.

More money troubles were to follow for Smith. When her husband was released from prison in 1785, he fled to France to escape his creditors and Smith followed with the family. While in France she discovered Antoine-François Prevost's controversial *Manon Lescaut* and translated it into English.

In 1785 Smith returned to England with her children; she separated from her husband one year later. From this point onward, she was the sole supporter of her family, a position made more difficult by the fact that at this date everything earned by a wife legally belonged to her husband. In 1788 her first novel, *Emmeline*, was published, from then on she published almost a novel a year. Smith drew on the circumstances of her own life for her fiction: she often portrayed women married to cruel or dissolute husbands, and still more often grasping or incompetent lawyers, while scenes from her stay in debtor's prison appear both in *Ethelinde* and in *Marchmont.* If her own life figured frequently in her work, however, so did many of the great public issues of the day; her fiction is sharply critical of empire, the slave trade, the class system, and marriage laws. She was a strong early supporter of the French Revolution, but was also sensitive to the plight of French emigrés in England after the Terror; in 1793 she published the 800-line blank-verse poem *The Emigrants*.

Although she was known primarily as a novelist and, in the later part of her life, as a children's author, she continued to write poetry. In her last years she suffered from arthritis, which made writing difficult. *Beachy Head*, one of her finest poems, was published the year after her death, in 1807. Wordsworth wrote that she was "a lady to whom English verse is under greater obligations than are likely to be either acknowledged or remembered."

⌘⌘⌘

from *Elegiac Sonnets*

1

The partial Muse,[1] has from my earliest hours
Smil'd on the rugged path I'm doom'd to tread,
And still with sportive° hand has snatch'd wild flowers, *playful*
To weave fantastic garlands for my head:
But far, far happier is the lot of those
Who never learn'd her dear delusive art,
Which while it decks the head with many a rose,
Reserves the thorn, to fester in the heart.
For still she bids° soft Pity's melting eye *commands*
Stream o'er the ills she knows not to remove,
Points° every pang, and deepens every sigh *sharpens*
Of mourning friendship, or unhappy love.
Ah! then, how dear° the Muse's favors cost, *expensive*
If those paint sorrow best—who feel it most! [2]

[1] *partial* Favorable, prejudiced; *Muse* Goddess of poetic inspiration, the invocation of which is a tradition going back to Classical antiquity.

[2] [Smith's note] "The well-sung woes shall soothe my pensive ghost; / He best can paint them who shall feel them most." Pope's "Eloisa to Abelard." 366th line.

2

Written at the Close of Spring

The garlands fade that Spring so lately wove,
Each simple flower which she had nursed in dew,
Anemonies,[3] that spangled every grove,
The primrose wan, and hare-bell[4] mildly blue.
No more shall violets linger in the dell,° *wooded valley*
Or purple orchis variegate[5] the plain,
Till Spring again shall call forth every bell,° *flowering plant*
And dress° with humid hands her wreaths again.— *prepare*
Ah! poor Humanity! so frail, so fair,
Are the fond visions of thy early day,
Till tyrant Passion,° and corrosive Care, *suffering*
Bid° all thy fairy colours fade away! Another *orders*
May new buds and flowers shall bring;
Ah! why has happiness—no second Spring?

[3] [Smith's note] Anemonies. *Anemony Nemeroso.* The wood Anemony. [Flowering plant having brilliant blossoms, common to Great Britain.]

[4] *primrose* Wild flowering plant noted for its yellow blossoms; *hare-bell* Wild hyacinth, blue-bell.

[5] *orchis* Orchids; *variegate* Make varied.

11
To Sleep

Come, balmy Sleep! tired Nature's soft resort![1]
On these sad temples all thy poppies[2] shed;
And bid gay dreams, from Morpheus'[3] airy court,
Float in light vision round my aching head![4]
Secure of all thy blessings, partial° Power! *favorable, prejudiced*
On his hard bed the peasant throws him down;
And the poor sea-boy, in the rudest° hour, *most harsh*
Enjoys thee more than he who wears a crown.[5]
Clasp'd in her faithful shepherd's guardian arms,
Well may the village-girl sweet slumbers prove;
And they, O gentle Sleep! still taste thy charms,
Who wake to labour, liberty, and love.
But still thy opiate aid dost thou deny
To calm the anxious breast, to close the streaming eye.

39
To Night

I love thee, mournful, sober-suited° Night! *darkly clothed*
When the faint moon, yet lingering in her wane,
And veil'd in clouds, with pale uncertain light
Hangs o'er the waters of the restless main.° *sea*
In deep depression sunk, the enfeebled mind
Will to the deaf cold elements complain,
And tell the embosom'd grief, however vain,
To sullen[6] surges and the viewless wind.
Tho' no repose on thy dark breast I find,
I still enjoy thee—cheerless as thou art;
For in thy quiet gloom the exhausted heart
Is calm, tho' wretched; hopeless, yet resign'd.
While to the winds and waves its sorrows given,
May reach—tho' lost on earth—the ear of Heaven!

44
Written in the Church-yard at Middleton in Sussex

Press'd by the Moon, mute arbitress° of tides, *female judge*
While the loud equinox[7] its power combines,
The sea no more its swelling surge confines,
But o'er the shrinking land sublimely rides.
The wild blast, rising from the Western cave,
Drives the huge billows from their heaving bed;
Tears from their grassy tombs the village dead,[8]
And breaks the silent sabbath of the grave!
With shells and sea-weed mingled, on the shore
Lo! their bones whiten in the frequent wave;
But vain to them the winds and waters rave;
They hear the warring elements no more:
While I am doom'd—by life's long storm oppress'd,
To gaze with envy, on their gloomy rest.

59
Written September 1791, during a remarkable thunder storm, in which the moon was perfectly clear, while the tempest gathered in various directions near the earth

What awful pageants° crowd the evening sky! *majestic displays*
The low horizon gathering vapours shroud;
Sudden, from many a deep-embattled cloud
Terrific thunders burst, and lightnings fly—
While in serenest azure,° beaming high, *intense blue*
Night's regent,° of her calm pavilion proud, *moon*

---

[1] *balmy* Soothing; *resort* Escape.

[2] *poppies* Opium, which induces sleep, is made from poppies.

[3] *Morpheus* God of sleep and dreams.

[4] [Smith's note] "Float in light vision round the poet's head." Mason. [Cf. line 12 of William Mason's "Elegy V. On the Death of a Lady," (1760).]

[5] [Smith's note] "Wilt thou upon the high and giddy mast / Seal up the ship boy's eyes, and rock his brains / In cradle of the rude impetuous surge?" Shakespeare's *Henry IV* [Cf. *II Henry IV*, 3.1.18–20. Smith here substitutes "impetuous," for the original "imperious."]

[6] *sullen* Make sluggish or slow.

[7] *equinox* Time of year at which the sun crosses the equator, rendering day and night of equal lengths.

[8] [Smith's note] Middleton is a village on the margin of the sea, in Sussex, containing only two or three houses. There were formerly several acres of ground between its small church and the sea, which now, by its continual encroachments, approaches within a few feet of this half-ruined and humble edifice. The wall, which once surrounded the church-yard, is entirely swept away, many of the graves broken up, and the remains of bodies interred washed into the sea; whence human bones are found among the sand and shingles on the shore.

Gilds the dark shadows that beneath her lie,
Unvex'd by all their conflicts fierce and loud.
—So, in unsullied dignity elate,
A spirit conscious of superior worth,
In placid elevation firmly great,
Scorns the vain cares that give Contention birth;
And blest with peace above the shocks of Fate,
Smiles at the tumult of the troubled earth.

70

On being cautioned against walking on an headland overlooking the sea, because it was frequented by a lunatic

Is there a solitary wretch who hies° *hastens*
To the tall cliff, with starting° pace or slow, *fitful*
And, measuring, views with wild and hollow eyes
Its distance from the waves that chide° below; *scold*
Who, as the sea-born gale with frequent sighs
Chills his cold bed upon the mountain turf,
With hoarse, half-utter'd lamentation, lies
Murmuring responses to the dashing surf?
In moody sadness, on the giddy° brink, *dizzying*
I see him more with envy than with fear;
He has no *nice felicities*° that shrink[1] *good fortunes*
From giant horrors; wildly wandering here,
He seems (uncursed with reason) not to know
The depth or the duration of his woe.

74

The Winter Night

"Sleep, that knits up the ravell'd sleeve of care,"[2]
Forsakes me, while the chill and sullen blast,
As my sad soul recalls its sorrows past,
Seems like a summons, bidding me prepare
For the last sleep of death.—Murmuring I hear
The hollow wind around the ancient towers,[3]
While night and silence reign; and cold and drear
The darkest gloom of Middle Winter lours;° *scowls*
But wherefore° fear existence such as mine, *why*
To change for long and undisturb'd repose?
Ah! when this suffering being I resign,
And o'er my miseries the tomb shall close,
By her,[4] whose loss in anguish I deplore,
I shall be laid, and feel that loss no more!

84

To the Muse[5]

Wilt thou forsake me who in life's bright May
Lent warmer lustre to the radiant morn;
And even o'er Summer scenes by tempests torn,
Shed with illusive light the dewy ray
Of pensive pleasure?—Wilt thou, while the day
Of saddening Autumn closes, as I mourn
In languid, hopeless sorrow, far away
Bend° thy soft step, and never more return?— *aim*
Crush'd to the earth, by bitterest anguish pressed,
From my faint eyes thy graceful form recedes;
Thou canst not heal an heart like mine that bleeds;
But, when in quiet earth that heart shall rest,
Haply° may'st thou one sorrowing vigil keep, *by chance*
Where Pity and Remembrance bend° and weep![6] *kneel*
—1784–97

Beachy Head

On thy stupendous summit, rock sublime!
That o'er the channel rear'd, half way at sea
The mariner at early morning hails,[7]
I would recline; while Fancy° should go forth, *imagination*
And represent the strange and awful hour
Of vast concussion; when the Omnipotent[8]

[1] [Smith's note] "'This delicate felicity that shrinks / When rocking winds are loud." Walpole. [Horace Walpole (1717–97); these lines are untraced.]

[2] [Smith's note] Shakespeare. [Cf. *Macbeth* 2.2.36.]

[3] [Smith's note] These lines were written in a residence among ancient public buildings.

[4] *her* Smith's daughter, Anna Augusta (d. 1795). Cf. Smith's "Sonnet 65," not included in this anthology.

[5] *Muse* Goddess of poetic inspiration, the invocation of whom is a tradition going back to Classical antiquity.

[6] [Smith's note] "Where melancholy friendship bends and weeps." Thomas Gray. [Cf. "Epitaph on Sir William Williams," line 12. by Thomas Gray (1716–42).]

[7] [Smith's note] In crossing the Channel from the coast of France, Beachy-Head is the first land made.

[8] *concussion* Violent shaking; *Omnipotent* God.

Stretch'd forth his arm, and rent the solid hills,
Bidding the impetuous main flood° rush between *sea*
The rifted shores, and from the continent
Eternally divided this green isle.
Imperial lord of the high southern coast!
From thy projecting head-land I would mark[1]
Far in the east the shades of night disperse,
Melting and thinned, as from the dark blue wave
Emerging, brilliant rays of arrowy light
Dart from the horizon; when the glorious sun
Just lifts above it his resplendent orb.
Advances now, with feathery silver touched,
The rippling tide of flood; glisten the sands,
While, inmates of the chalky clefts that scar
Thy sides precipitous, with shrill harsh cry,
Their white wings glancing in the level beam,
The terns, and gulls, and tarrocks, seek their food,[2]
And thy rough hollows echo to the voice
Of the gray choughs, and ever restless daws,[3]
With clamour, not unlike the chiding hounds,
While the lone shepherd, and his baying dog,
Drive to thy turfy° crest his bleating flock. *grassy*

The high meridian of the day° is past, *noon*
And Ocean now, reflecting the calm Heaven,
Is of cerulean° hue; and murmurs low *sky blue*
The tide of ebb, upon the level sands.
The sloop,[4] her angular canvas shifting still,
Catches the light and variable airs° *breezes*
That but a little crisp the summer sea,
Dimpling its tranquil surface.

Afar off,
And just emerging from the arch immense
Where seem to part the elements, a fleet
Of fishing vessels stretch their lesser sails;
While more remote, and like a dubious spot
Just hanging in the horizon, laden deep,
The ship of commerce richly freighted, makes
Her slower progress, on her distant voyage,
Bound to the orient° climates, where the sun *eastern*
Matures the spice within its odorous shell,
And, rivalling the gray worm's filmy toil,° *silk making*
Bursts from its pod the vegetable down;[5]
Which in long turban'd wreaths, from torrid heat
Defends the brows of Asia's countless castes.
There the Earth hides within her glowing breast
The beamy adamant,[6] and the round pearl
Enchased in rugged covering;[7] which the slave,
With perilous and breathless toil, tears off
From the rough sea-rock, deep beneath the waves.
These are the toys of Nature; and her sport
Of little estimate in Reason's eye:
And they who reason, with abhorrence see
Man, for such gauds and baubles,[8] violate
The sacred freedom of his fellow man—
Erroneous estimate! As Heaven's pure air,
Fresh as it blows on this aërial height,
Or sound of seas upon the stony strand,° *shore*
Or inland, the gay harmony of birds,
And winds that wander in the leafy woods;
Are to the unadulterate° taste more worth *uncorrupted*
Than the elaborate harmony, brought out
From fretted stop, or modulated airs[9]
Of vocal science.—So the brightest gems,
Glancing resplendent on the regal crown,
Or trembling in the high born beauty's ear,
Are poor and paltry,° to the lovely light *insignificant, trivial*
Of the fair star,° that as the day declines, *Venus*
Attendant on her queen, the crescent moon,
Bathes her bright tresses in the eastern wave.
For now the sun is verging to the sea,
And as he westward sinks, the floating clouds
Suspended, move upon the evening gale,

---

1 *mark* Observe.

2 [Smith's note] Terns. *Sterna hirundo*, or Sea Swallow. Gulls. *Larus canus*. Tarrocks. *Larus tridactylus*. [All varieties of sea birds.]

3 [Smith's note] Gray choughs. *Corvus Graculus*, Cornish Choughs, or, as these birds are called by the Sussex people, Saddle-backed Crows, build in great numbers on this coast. [*daws* Small crow-like birds.]

4 *sloop* Small, single-masted sailing vessel.

5 [Smith's note] Cotton. *Gossypium herbaceum*.

6 [Smith's note] Diamonds, the hardest and most valuable of precious stones. For the extraordinary exertions of the Indians in diving for the pearl oysters, see the account of the pearl fisheries in Percival's *View of Ceylon*.

7 *Enchased* Ornamented or inlaid decoration.

8 *gauds … baubles* Insignificant but showy trinkets or toys.

9 *fretted stop* Ridges set across the fingerboard of a stringed instrument; *modulated airs* Harmonic melodies varying in pitch and/or tone, here referring specifically to vocal melodies.

And gathering round his orb, as if to shade
The insufferable brightness, they resign
Their gauzy whiteness; and more warm'd, assume
All hues of purple. There, transparent gold
Mingles with ruby tints, and sapphire gleams,
And colours, such as Nature through her works
Shows only in the ethereal canopy.° *heavens*
Thither aspiring Fancy fondly soars,
Wandering sublime thro' visionary vales,
Where bright pavilions rise, and trophies,[1] fann'd
By airs celestial; and adorn'd with wreaths
Of flowers that bloom amid elysian bowers.[2]
Now bright, and brighter still the colours glow,
Till half the lustrous orb within the flood
Seems to retire: the flood reflecting still
Its splendor, and in mimic° glory drest; *imitating*
Till the last ray shot upward, fires the clouds
With blazing crimson; then in paler light,
Long lines of tenderer radiance, lingering yield
To partial darkness; and on the opposing side
The early moon distinctly rising, throws
Her pearly brilliance on the trembling tide.

The fishermen, who at set seasons pass
Many a league[3] off at sea their toiling night,
Now hail their comrades, from their daily task
Returning; and make ready for their own,
With the night tide commencing:—The night tide
Bears a dark vessel on, whose hull° and sails *body*
Mark her a coaster[4] from the north. Her keel
Now ploughs the sand; and sidelong now she leans,
While with loud clamours her athletic crew
Unload her; and resounds the busy hum
Along the wave-worn rocks. Yet more remote,
Where the rough cliff hangs beetling° *overhanging*
 o'er its base,
All breathes repose; the water's rippling sound
Scarce heard; but now and then the sea-snipe's[5] cry
Just tells that something living is abroad;
And sometimes crossing on the moonbright line,
Glimmers the skiff,[6] faintly discern'd awhile,
Then lost in shadow.

Contemplation here,
High on her throne of rock, aloof may sit,
And bid recording Memory unfold
Her scroll voluminous—bid her retrace
The period, when from Neustria's hostile shore[7]
The Norman launch'd his galleys,[8] and the bay
O'er which that mass of ruin[9] frowns even now
In vain and sullen menace, then received
The new invaders; a proud martial race,
Of Scandinavia[10] the undaunted sons,

[1] *trophies* Structure erected, usually on a battlefield, to commemorate a victory.

[2] *elysian* Having the qualities of the Elysium, the resting place of the blessed after death in Greek mythology; *bowers* Wooded enclosures.

[3] *league* Measurement of distance roughly equal to three miles.

[4] *coaster* Ship that sails along the coast, especially one trading from port to port in the same country.

[5] [Smith's note] In crossing the Channel this bird is heard at night, uttering a short cry, and flitting along near the surface of the waves. The sailors call it the Sea Snipe; but I can find no species of sea bird of which this is the vulgar name. A bird so called inhabits the Lake of Geneva.

[6] *skiff* Open boat with flat bottom, having a squared stern and pointed bow.

[7] *Neustria's … shore* Neustria was the western Frankish kingdom from c. 6 CE to 8 CE. After the ninth century, the name was applied to Normandy, the area of northwestern France.

[8] *The Norman* William the Conqueror, the king who led the Norman invasion of England and conquered the country at the historic Battle of Hastings in 1066; *galleys* Large medieval ships used in war or commerce.

[9] [Smith's note] Pevensey Castle.

[10] [Smith's note] The Scandinavians (modern Norway, Sweden, Denmark, Lapland, &c.) and other inhabitants of the north, began towards the end of the 8th century to leave their inhospitable climate in search of the produce of more fortunate countries.

The North-men made inroads on the coasts of France; and carrying back immense booty, excited their compatriots to engage in the same piratical voyages: and they were afterwards joined by numbers of necessitous and daring adventurers from the coasts of Provence and Sicily.

In 844, these wandering innovators had a great number of vessels at sea; and again visiting the coasts of France, Spain, and England, the following year they penetrated even to Paris: and the unfortunate Charles the Bald, King of France, purchased at a high price the retreat of the banditti he had no other means of repelling.

These successful expeditions continued for some time; till Rollo [First Duke of Normandy (c. 860–932 CE), ancestor of William the Conqueror], otherwise Raoul, assembled a number of followers, and after a descent on England, crossed the Channel, and made himself master of Rouen, which he fortified. Charles the Simple [Charles III

Whom Dogon, Fier-a-bras, and Humfroi led
To conquest: while Trinacria to their power
Yielded her wheaten garland; and when thou,
Parthenope! within thy fertile bay
Receiv'd the victors—

In the mailed ranks
Of Normans landing on the British coast
Rode Taillefer; and with astounding voice
Thunder'd the war song daring Roland sang
First in the fierce contention: vainly brave,
One not inglorious struggle England made—
But failing, saw the Saxon heptarchy[1]
Finish for ever.—Then the holy pile,[2]
Yet seen upon the field of conquest, rose,
Where to appease heaven's wrath for so much blood,
The conqueror bade unceasing prayers ascend,
And requiems[3] for the slayers and the slain.
But let not modern Gallia form from hence[4]
Presumptuous hopes, that ever thou again,
Queen of the isles!° shalt crouch to foreign arms. *England*
The enervate sons of Italy may yield;
And the Iberian, all his trophies torn
And wrapp'd in Superstition's monkish weed,° *monastic clothing*
May shelter his abasement, and put on
Degrading fetters.[5] Never, never thou!
Imperial mistress of the obedient sea;
But thou, in thy integrity secure,
Shalt now undaunted meet a world in arms.

England! 'twas where this promontory rears
Its rugged brow above the channel wave,
Parting the hostile nations,[6] that thy fame,
Thy naval fame was tarnish'd, at what time
Thou, leagued with the Batavian, gavest to France[7]

---

of France (879–929 CE)], unable to contend with Rollo, offered to resign to him some of the northern provinces, and to give him his daughter in marriage. Neustria, since called Normandy, was granted to him, and afterwards Brittany. He added the more solid virtues of the legislator to the fierce valour of the conqueror—converted to Christianity, he established justice, and repressed the excesses of his Danish subjects, till then accustomed to live only by plunder. His name became the signal for pursuing those who violated the laws; as well as the cry of Haro, still so usual in Normandy. The Danes and Francs produced a race of men celebrated for their valour; and it was a small party of these that in 983, having been on a pilgrimage to Jerusalem, arrived on their return at Salerno, and found the town surrounded by Mahometans [Islamic soldiers], whom the Salernians were bribing to leave their coast. The Normans represented to them the baseness and cowardice of such submission; and notwithstanding the inequality of their numbers, they boldly attacked the Saracen [Islamic] camp, and drove the infidels to their ships. The prince of Salerno, astonished at their successful audacity, would have loaded them with the marks of his gratitude; but refusing every reward, they returned to their own country, from whence, however, other bodies of Normans passed into Sicily (anciently called Trinacria); and many of them entered into the service of the Emperor of the East [Basil II (976–1025 CE), of the Eastern Roman, or Byzantine Empire], others of the Pope [either Pope Benedict VII or Pope XIV], and the Duke of Naples was happy to engage a small party of them in defence of his newly founded duchy. Soon afterwards three brothers of Coutance [Coutances, a district in Normandy], the sons of Tancred de Hauteville [Norman noble illustrious for the deeds of his sons], Guilllaume Fier-a-bras [William Iron-Arm (d. 1046 CE)], Drogon [d. 1051 CE], and Humfroi [d. 1057 CE], joining the Normans established at Aversa, became masters of the fertile island of Sicily; and Robert Guiscard [another of de Hauteville's sons, Guiscard (1015–1085 CE) was the most successful and well-known of the Normans who conquered southern Italy] joining them, the Normans became sovereigns both of Sicily and Naples (Parthenope). How William, the natural son of Robert, duke of Normandy, possessed himself of England, is too well known to be repeated here. William sailing from St. Valori, landed in the bay of Pevensey; and at the place now called Battle, met the English forces under Harold [Harold II (c. 1022–1066), King of England killed at the Battle of Hastings]: an esquire (*ecuyer*) called Taillefer, mounted on an armed horse, led on the Normans, singing in a thundering tone the war song of Rollo. He threw himself among the English, and was killed on the first onset. In a marsh not far from Hastings, the skeletons of an armed man and horse were found a few years since, which are believed to have belonged to the Normans, as a party of their horse, deceived in the nature of the ground, perished in the morass.

[1] *Saxon heptarchy* Seven kingdoms of the Anglo-Saxons: Northumbria, Mercia, Kent, East Anglia, Wessex (West Saxons), Essex (East Saxons) and Sussex (South Saxons).

[2] [Smith's note] Battle Abbey was raised by the Conqueror, and endowed with an ample revenue, that masses might be said night and day for the souls of those who perished in battle.

[3] *requiems* Masses for the deceased.

[4] *Gallia* France; *hence* This reason.

[5] *The enervate … fetters* By the time Smith wrote *Beachy Head*, Napoleon (1769–1821) had already established his Empire, conquering both Italy and the Iberian Peninsula (Spain and Portugal).

[6] *hostile nations* France and England, who had almost constantly been at violent odds since the Norman Conquest through the end of the Hundred Years' War.

[7] [Smith's note] In 1690, King William being then in Ireland, Tourville, the French admiral, arrived on the coast of England. His fleet consisted of seventy-eight large ships, and twenty-two fire-ships. Lord Torrington, the English admiral, lay at St. Helens, with only

One day of triumph—triumph the more loud,
Because even then so rare. Oh! well redeem'd,
Since, by a series of illustrious men,
Such as no other country ever rear'd,
To vindicate her cause. It is a list
Which, as Fame echoes it, blanches° the cheek *makes pale*
Of bold Ambition; while the despot feels
The extorted sceptre tremble in his grasp.

From even the proudest roll[1] by glory fill'd,
How gladly the reflecting mind returns
To simple scenes of peace and industry,
Where, bosom'd° in some valley of the hills *enclosed*
Stands the lone farm; its gate with tawny ricks[2]
Surrounded, and with granaries and sheds,
Roof'd with green mosses, and by elms and ash
Partially shaded; and not far remov'd
The hut of sea-flints° built; the humble home *sea stones*
Of one, who sometimes watches on the heights,[3]
When hid in the cold mist of passing clouds,
The flock, with dripping fleeces, are dispers'd
O'er the wide down; then from some ridged point
That overlooks the sea, his eager eye
Watches the bark° that for his signal waits *small ship*
To land its merchandise:—Quitting for this
Clandestine traffic his more honest toil,
The crook° abandoning, he braves himself *shepherd's staff*
The heaviest snow-storm of December's night,
When with conflicting winds the ocean raves,
And on the tossing boat, unfearing mounts
To meet the partners of the perilous trade,
And share their hazard. Well it were for him,
If no such commerce of destruction known,
He were content with what the earth affords
To human labour; even where she seems
Reluctant most. More happy is the hind,° *farm laborer*
Who, with his own hands rears on some black moor,
Or turbary,[4] his independent hut
Cover'd with heather, whence the slow white smoke
Of smouldering peat[5] arises——A few sheep,
His best possession, with his children share
The rugged shed when wintry tempests blow;
But, when with Spring's return the green blades rise
Amid the russet heath,[6] the household live
Joint tenants of the waste° throughout the day, *uncultivated wilderness*
And often, from her nest, among the swamps,
Where the gemm'd sun-dew grows, or fring'd buck-bean,[7]
They scare the plover,[8] that with plaintive cries
Flutters, as sorely wounded, down the wind.
Rude,° and but just remov'd from savage life *common, rustic*
Is the rough dweller among scenes like these,
(Scenes all unlike the poet's[9] fabling dreams
Describing Arcady[10])—But he is free;
The dread that follows on illegal acts
He never feels; and his industrious mate
Shares in his labour. Where the brook is traced

---

forty English and a few Dutch ships; and conscious of the disadvantage under which he should give battle, he ran up between the enemy's fleet and the coast, to protect it. The Queen's council, dictated to by Russell, persuaded her to order Torrington to venture a battle. The order Torrington appears to have obeyed reluctantly: his fleet now consisted of twenty-two Dutch and thirty-four English ships. Evertson, the Dutch admiral, was eager to obtain glory; Torrington, more cautious, reflected on the importance of the stake. The consequence was, that the Dutch rashly sailing on were surrounded, and Torrington, solicitous to recover this false step, placed himself with difficulty between the Dutch and the French; but three Dutch ships were burnt, two of their admirals killed, and almost all their ships disabled. The English and the Dutch declining a second engagement, retire towards the mouth of the Thames. The French, from ignorance of the coast, and misunderstanding among each other, failed to take all the advantage they might have done of this victory.

[1] *roll* Rolled parchment (scroll) generally used for official documents, in this case likely a chronicle.

[2] *ricks* Bales of hay or grain.

[3] [Smith's note] The shepherds and laborers of this tract of country, a hardy and athletic race of men, are almost universally engaged in the contraband trade, carried on for the coarsest and most destructive spirits, with the opposite coast. When no other vessel will venture to sea, these men hazard their lives to elude the watchfulness of the Revenue officers, and to secure their cargoes.

[4] *turbary* Area of land from whence turf can be harvested for fuel.

[5] *peat* Moss found in bogs and swamps that is used for fuel.

[6] *heath* Open, uncultivated ground.

[7] [Smith's note] Sun-dew. *Drosera rotundifolia.* [Botanical found in boggy areas, which secretes dew-like drops of liquid;] buck-bean *Menyanthes trifoliatum.* [Pinkish-white flowered water plant.]

[8] [Smith's note] plover *Tringa vanellus.* [Water bird.]

[9] *poet's* Sir Philip Sidney (1554–86), prominent Elizabethan poet who wrote the prose romance *Arcadia.*

[10] *Arcady* Ideal land of the pastoral tradition.

By crowding osiers, and the black coot[1] hides
Among the plashy° reeds, her diving brood, *boggy*
The matron wades; gathering the long green rush[2]
That well prepar'd hereafter lends its light
To her poor cottage, dark and cheerless else
Thro' the drear hours of Winter. Otherwhile
She leads her infant group where charlock[3] grows
"Unprofitably gay,"[4] or to the fields,
Where congregate the linnet° and the finch, *song bird*
That on the thistles, so profusely spread,
Feast in the desert; the poor family
Early resort, extirpating[5] with care
These, and the gaudier mischief of the ground;
Then flames the high rais'd heap; seen afar off
Like hostile war-fires flashing to the sky.[6]
Another task is theirs: On fields that show
As° angry Heaven had rain'd sterility, *as if*
Stony and cold, and hostile to the plough,
Where clamouring loud, the evening curlew[7] runs
And drops her spotted eggs among the flints;
The mother and the children pile the stones
In rugged pyramids;—and all this toil
They patiently encounter; well content
On their flock bed to slumber undisturb'd
Beneath the smoky roof they call their own.
Oh! little knows the sturdy hind, who stands
Gazing, with looks where envy and contempt
Are often strangely mingled, on the car° *carriage*
Where prosperous Fortune sits; what secret care
Or sick satiety is often hid,
Beneath the splendid outside: *He* knows not
How frequently the child of Luxury
Enjoying nothing, flies from place to place

[1] *osiers* Willow trees; [Smith's note] coot *Fulita aterrima.* [Swimming bird.]

[2] *rush* Water rush dried and used for light.

[3] *charlock* Field mustard.

[4] [Smith's note] "With blossom'd furze, unprofitably gay." Goldsmith. [Cf. *The Deserted Village*, line 194 by Oliver Goldsmith (1728–74).]

[5] *extirpating* Removing by pulling up by the roots.

[6] [Smith's note] The Beacons formerly lighted up the hills to give notice of the approach of an enemy. These signals would still be used in case of alarm, if the Telegraph [system of semaphore signals] now substituted could not be distinguished on account of fog or darkness.

[7] [Smith's note] Curlew *Charandrius oedienemus.* [Shore bird.]

In chase of pleasure that eludes his grasp;
And that content is e'en less found by him,
Than by the labourer, whose pick-axe smooths
The road before his chariot; and who doffs
What *was* an hat; and as the train pass on,
Thinks how one day's expenditure, like this,
Would cheer him for long months, when to his toil
The frozen earth closes her marble breast.

Ah! who *is* happy? Happiness! a word
That like false fire, from marsh effluvia[8] born,
Misleads the wanderer, destin'd to contend
In the world's wilderness, with want or woe
Yet *they* are happy, who have never ask'd
What good or evil means. The boy
That on the river's margin gaily plays,
Has heard that Death is there—He knows not Death,
And therefore fears it not; and venturing in
He gains a bullrush, or a minnow—then,
At certain peril, for a worthless prize,
A crow's, or raven's nest, he climbs the boll° *trunk*
Of some tall pine; and of his prowess proud,
Is for a moment happy. Are *your* cares,
Ye who despise him, never worse applied?
The village girl is happy, who sets forth
To distant fair, gay in her Sunday suit,
With cherry colour'd knots,[9] and flourish'd shawl,
And bonnet newly purchas'd. So is he
Her little brother, who his mimic drum
Beats, till he drowns her rural lovers' oaths
Of constant faith, and still increasing love;
Ah! yet a while, and half those oaths believ'd,
Her happiness is vanish'd; and the boy
While yet a stripling,° finds the sound he lov'd *inexperienced youth*
Has led him on, till he has given up
His freedom, and his happiness together.
I once was happy, when while yet a child,
I learn'd to love these upland solitudes,
And, when elastic as the mountain air,
To my light spirit, care was yet unknown
And evil unforeseen:—Early it came,
And childhood scarcely passed, I was condemned,
A guiltless exile, silently to sigh,

[8] *false fire* Hovering phosphorescence created by gases in swampy areas; *effluvia* Emissions (usually vapor or gas).

[9] *knots* I.e., of ribbon.

While Memory, with faithful pencil, drew
The contrast; and regretting, I compar'd
With the polluted smoky atmosphere
And dark and stifling streets, the southern hills
That to the setting Sun, their graceful heads
Rearing, o'erlook the frith, where Vecta[1] breaks
With her white rocks, the strong impetuous tide,
When western winds the vast Atlantic urge
To thunder on the coast—Haunts[2] of my youth!
Scenes of fond day dreams, I behold ye yet!
Where 'twas so pleasant by thy northern slopes
To climb the winding sheep-path, aided oft
By scatter'd thorns: whose spiny branches bore
Small woolly tufts, spoils of the vagrant lamb
There seeking shelter from the noon-day sun;
And pleasant, seated on the short soft turf,
To look beneath upon the hollow way[3]
While heavily upward mov'd the labouring wain,° *wagon*
And stalking slowly by, the sturdy hind
To ease his panting team, stopp'd with a stone
The grating wheel.

Advancing higher still
The prospect° widens, and the village church *view*
But little, o'er the lowly roofs around
Rears its gray belfry, and its simple vane;
Those lowly roofs of thatch[4] are half conceal'd
By the rude arms of trees, lovely in spring,[5]
When on each bough, the rosy-tinctur'd bloom
Sits thick, and promises autumnal plenty.
For even those orchards round the Norman farms,
Which as their owners mark the promis'd fruit,
Console them for the vineyards of the south,
Surpass not these.

Where woods of ash, and beech,
And partial copses, fringe the green hill foot,
The upland shepherd rears his modest home,
There wanders by, a little nameless stream
That from the hill wells forth, bright now and clear,
Or after rain with chalky mixture gray,
But still refreshing in its shallow course,
The cottage garden; most for use design'd,
Yet not of beauty destitute. The vine
Mantles the little casement; yet the briar[6]
Drops fragrant dew among the July flowers;
And pansies rayed, and freak'd° and mottled pinks *flecked*
Grow among balm, and rosemary and rue:[7]
There honeysuckles flaunt, and roses blow[8]
Almost uncultured:° Some with dark green leaves *uncultivated*
Contrast their flowers of pure unsullied° white; *spotlessly pure*
Others, like velvet robes of regal state
Of richest crimson, while in thorny moss
Enshrined and cradled, the most lovely, wear
The hues of youthful beauty's glowing cheek.
With fond regret I recollect e'en now
In Spring and Summer, what delight I felt
Among these cottage gardens, and how much
Such artless nosegays,° knotted with a rush *small bouquets*
By village housewife or her ruddy° maid, *rosy*
Were welcome to me; soon and simply pleas'd.

An early worshipper at Nature's shrine,
I loved her rudest scenes—warrens, and heaths,
And yellow commons,° and birch-shaded hollows, *common lands*
And hedge rows, bordering unfrequented lanes
Bowered with wild roses, and the clasping woodbine[9]
Where purple tassels of the tangling vetch[10]
With bittersweet, and bryony inweave,[11]

[1] *frith* Firth, narrow sea inlet; [Smith's note] Vecta. The Isle of Wight [island in the English Channel, off the south-central coast], which breaks the force of the waves when they are driven by south-west winds against this long and open coast. It is somewhere described as "Vecta shouldering the Western Waves."

[2] *Haunts* Places frequently visited.

[3] *hollow way* Path through a gorge.

[4] *thatch* Plant stalks used for roofing.

[5] [Smith's note] Every cottage in this country has its orchard; and I imagine that not even those of Herefordshire, or Worcestershire, exhibit a more beautiful prospect, when the trees are in bloom, and the "Primavera candida e vermiglia" [Cf. Petrarch's Sonnet 310, line 4 ("Pure and rosy spring")], is every where so enchanting.

[6] *Mantles* Dresses; *casement* Window sash opening outwards; *briar* Small shrub or tree with hardy wooden roots.

[7] *balm … rue* Culinary and medicinal herbs.

[8] *blow* Bloom, blossom.

[9] *woodbine* Climbing vine, such as the honeysuckle.

[10] [Smith's note] Vetch. *Vicia sylvatica.* [Plant with tendrils ending in small flowers of various colors.]

[11] [Smith's note] Bittersweet. *Solanum dulcamara.* [Common shrub.]; Bryony. *Bryonia alba.* [Tendril-bearing vine.]

And the dew fills the silver bindweed's[1] cups—
I loved to trace the brooks whose humid banks
Nourish the harebell, and the freckled pagil;[2]
And stroll among o'ershadowing woods of beech,
Lending in Summer, from the heats of noon
A whispering shade; while haply there reclines
Some pensive lover of uncultur'd flowers,
Who, from the tumps[3] with bright green mosses clad,
Plucks the wood sorrel,[4] with its light thin leaves,
Heart-shaped, and triply folded; and its root
Creeping like beaded coral; or who there
Gathers, the copse's pride, anémones,[5]
With rays like golden studs on ivory laid
Most delicate: but touch'd with purple clouds,
Fit crown for April's fair but changeful brow.

Ah! hills so early loved! in fancy still
I breathe your pure keen air; and still behold
Those widely spreading views, mocking alike
The Poet and the Painter's utmost art.
And still, observing objects more minute,
Wondering remark the strange and foreign forms
Of sea-shells; with the pale calcareous° soil *chalky*
Mingled, and seeming of resembling substance.[6]
Tho' surely the blue Ocean (from the heights
Where the downs westward trend,[7] but dimly seen)
Here never roll'd its surge. Does Nature then
Mimic, in wanton° mood, fantastic shapes *unruly*
Of bivalves, and inwreathed volutes,[8] that cling
To the dark sea-rock of the wat'ry world?
Or did this range of chalky mountains, once
Form a vast basin, where the Ocean waves
Swell'd fathomless? What time these fossil shells,
Buoy'd° on their native-element, were thrown *floated*
Among the imbedding calx:[9] when the huge hill
Its giant bulk heaved, and in strange ferment
Grew up a guardian barrier, 'twixt the sea
And the green level of the sylvan weald.° *upland*

Ah! very vain is Science' proudest boast,
And but a little light its flame yet lends
To its most ardent votaries;[10] since from whence
These fossil forms are seen, is but conjecture,
Food for vague theories, or vain dispute,
While to his daily task the peasant goes,
Unheeding such inquiry; with no care
But that the kindly change of sun and shower,
Fit for his toil the earth he cultivates.
As little recks° the herdsman of the hill, *cares*
Who on some turfy knoll,° idly reclined, *small hill*
Watches his wether° flock; that deep beneath *castrated ram*
Rest the remains of men, of whom is left[11]
No traces in the records of mankind,
Save what these half obliterated mounds
And half fill'd trenches doubtfully impart
To some lone antiquary;[12] who on times remote,
Since which two thousand years have roll'd away,

---

[1] [Smith's note] Bindweed. *Convolvulus sepium.* [Trailing or twining weedy plant with cup-shaped blossoms.]

[2] [Smith's note] harebell. *Hyacinthus non scriptus.* [Plant having bell-shaped white or blue flowers.] Pagil. *Primula veris.* [Primrose.]

[3] *tumps* Hillocks.

[4] [Smith's note] Sorrel. *Oxalis acetosella.* [Culinary herb having a sour taste.]

[5] [Smith's note] Anémonies. *Anémone nemorosa.* [Flowering plant having brilliant blossoms, common to Great Britain.] It appears to be settled on late and excellent authorities, that this word should not be accented on the second syllable, but on the penultima [second to last]. I have however ventured the more known accentuation, as more generally used, and suiting better the nature of my verse.

[6] [Smith's note] Among the crumbling chalk I have often found shells, some quite in a fossil state and hardly distinguishable from chalk. Others appeared more recent; cockles, muscles, and periwinkles, I well remember, were among the number; and some whose names I do not know. A great number were like those of small land snails. It is now many years since I made these observations. The appearance of sea-shells so far from the sea excited my surprise, though I then knew nothing of natural history. I have never read any of the late theories of the earth, nor was I ever satisfied with the attempts to explain many of the phenomena which call forth conjecture in those books I happened to have had access to on this subject.

[7] *downs* Chalky uplands of south and southwest England; *westward trend* Move in a westerly direction.

[8] *bivalves* Mollusks, such as oysters and clams, having two hinged shells; *volutes* Mollusks with spiral-shaped shells, such as conchs.

[9] *calx* Residue remaining after a metal or mineral has been burned.

[10] *votaries* Persons bound by solemn oaths, usually to religious orders.

[11] [Smith's note] These Downs are not only marked with traces of encampments, which from their forms are called Roman or Danish; but there are numerous tumuli [burial mounds] among them. Some of which having been opened a few years ago, were supposed by a learned antiquary to contain the remains of the original natives of the country.

[12] *antiquary* Recorder of antiquities.

Loves to contemplate. He perhaps may trace,
Or fancy he can trace, the oblong square
Where the mail'd legions, under Claudius,[1] rear'd
The rampire, or excavated fossé[2] delved;
What time the huge unwieldly Elephant[3]
Auxiliary reluctant, hither led,
From Afric's forest glooms and tawny sands,
First felt the Northern blast, and his vast frame
Sunk useless; whence in after ages found,
The wondering hinds, on those enormous bones

[1] [Smith's note] That the legions of Claudius [10 BCE–54 CE] were in this part of Britain appears certain. Since this emperor received the submission of Cantii, Atrebates, Irenobates, and Regni [Celtic tribes in pre-Roman Britain], in which latter denomination were included the people of Sussex.

[2] *rampire* Ramparts or barriers; *fossé* Ditch.

[3] [Smith's note] In the year 1740, some workmen digging in the park at Burton in Sussex, discovered, nine feet below the surface, the teeth and bones of an elephant; two of the former were seven feet eight inches in length. There were besides these, tusks, one of which broke in removing it, a grinder not at all decayed, and a part of the jaw-bone, with bones of the knee and thigh, and several others. Some of them remained very lately at Burton House, the seat of John Biddulph, Esq. Others were in possession of the Rev. Dr. Langrish, minister of Petworth at that period, who was present when some of these bones were taken up, and gave it as his opinion, that they had remained there since the universal deluge [Biblical flood of Noah's time]. The Romans under the Emperor Claudius probably brought elephants into Britain. Milton, in the second book of his History, in speaking of the expedition, says that "he [who waiteth ready with a huge preparation, as if not safe enough amidst the flower of all his Romans,] like a great eastern king, with armed elephants, marched [marches] through Gallia." This is given on the authority of Dion Cassius, in his Life of the Emperor Claudius. It has therefore been conjectured, that the bones found at Burton might have been those of one of these elephants, who perished there soon after its landing; or dying on the high downs, one of which, called Duncton Hill, rises immediately above Burton Park, the bones might have been washed down by the torrents of rain, and buried deep in the soil. They were not found together, but scattered at some distance from each other. The two tusks were twenty feet apart. I had often heard of the elephant's bones at Burton, but never saw them; and I have no books to refer to. I think I saw, in what is now called the National Museum at Paris, the very large bones of an elephant, which were found in North America: though it is certain that this enormous animal is never seen in its natural state, but in the countries under the torrid zone of the old world. I have, since making this note, been told that the bones of the rhinoceros and hippopotamus have been found in America.

Gaz'd; and in giants[4] dwelling on the hills
Believed and marvell'd—
Hither, Ambition, come!
Come and behold the nothingness of all
For which you carry thro' the oppressed Earth,
War, and its train° of horrors—see where tread *retinue*
The innumerous hoofs of flocks above the works
By which the warrior sought to register
His glory, and immortalize his name—
The pirate Dane,[5] who from his circular camp
Bore in destructive robbery, fire and sword
Down thro' the vale, sleeps unremember'd here;
And here, beneath the green sward,° rests alike *meadow*
The savage native,[6] who his acorn meal
Shar'd with the herds, that ranged the pathless woods;
And the centurion, who on these wide hills
Encamping, planted the Imperial Eagle.° *Roman flag*
All, with the lapse of Time, have passed away,
Even as the clouds, with dark and dragon shapes,
Or like vast promontories crown'd with towers,
Cast their broad shadows on the downs: then sail
Far to the northward, and their transient gloom
Is soon forgotten.

But from thoughts like these,
By human crimes suggested, let us turn
To where a more attractive study courts
The wanderer of the hills; while shepherd girls
Will from among the fescue[7] bring him flowers,
Of wonderous mockery; some resembling bees
In velvet vest, intent on their sweet toil,[8]

[4] [Smith's note] The peasants believe that the large bones sometimes found belonged to giants, who formerly lived on the hills. The devil also has a great deal to do with the remarkable forms of hill and vale: the Devil's Punch Bowl, the Devil's Leaps, and the Devil's Dyke, are names given to deep hollows, or high and abrupt ridges, in this and the neighboring county.

[5] [Smith's note] The incursions of the Danes were for many ages the scourge of this island.

[6] [Smith's note] The Aborigines of this country lived in woods, unsheltered but by trees and caves; and were probably as truly savage as any of those who are now termed so.

[7] [Smith's note] The grass called Sheep's Fescue, (*Festuca ovina*) clothes these Downs with the softest turf.

[8] [Smith's note] *Ophrys apifera,* Bee Ophrys, or Orchis found plentifully on the hills, as well as the next.

While others mimic flies,[1] that lightly sport
In the green shade, or float along the pool,
But here seem perch'd upon the slender stalk,
And gathering honey dew. While in the breeze
That wafts the thistle's plumed seed along,
Blue bells wave tremulous. The mountain thyme[2]
Purples the hassock of the heaving mole,[3]
And the short turf is gay with tormentil,[4]
And bird's foot trefoil, and the lesser tribes
Of hawkweed;[5] spangling it with fringed stars.—
Near where a richer tract of cultur'd land
Slopes to the south; and burnished by the sun,
Bend in the gale of August, floods of corn;
The guardian of the flock, with watchful care,[6]
Repels by voice and dog the encroaching sheep—
While his boy visits every wired trap[7]
That scars the turf; and from the pit-falls takes
The timid migrants,[8] who from distant wilds,
Warrens, and stone quarries, are destined thus
To lose their short existence. But unsought
By Luxury yet, the Shepherd still protects
The social bird,[9] who from his native haunts
Of willowy current, or the rushy pool,
Follows the fleecy crowd, and flirts and skims,
In fellowship among them.

Where the knoll
More elevated takes the changeful winds,
The windmill rears its vanes; and thitherward
With his white load,° the master travelling, *grain*
Scares the rooks° rising slow on whispering wings, *crows*
While o'er his head, before the summer sun
Lights up the blue expanse, heard more than seen,
The lark sings matins;° and above the clouds *morning worship*
Floating, embathes his spotted breast in dew.
Beneath the shadow of a gnarled thorn,
Bent by the sea blast,[10] from a seat of turf
With fairy nosegays strewn, how wide the view![11]
Till in the distant north it melts away,
And mingles indiscriminate with clouds:
But if the eye could reach so far, the mart
Of England's capital, its domes and spires
Might be perceived—Yet hence the distant range
Of Kentish hills,[12] appear in purple haze;

[1] [Smith's note] *Ophrys muscifera.* Fly Orchis. Linnaeus, misled by the variations to which some of this tribe are really subject, has perhaps too rashly esteemed all those which resemble insects, as forming only one species, which he terms Ophrys insectifera. See *English Botany* [written by James Sowerby in 36 volumes from 1791 to 1814].

[2] [Smith's note] Blue bells. *Campanula rotundifolia.* Mountain thyme. *Thymus serpyllum.* "It is a common notion, that the flesh of sheep which feed upon aromatic plants, particularly wild thyme, is superior in flavour to other mutton. The truth is, that sheep do not crop these aromatic plants, unless now and then by accident, or when they are first turned on hungry to downs, heaths, or commons; but the soil and situations favourable to aromatic plants, produce a short sweet pasturage, best adapted to feeding sheep, whom nature designed for mountains, and not for turnip grounds and rich meadows. The attachment of bees to this, and other aromatic plants, is well known." Martyn's Miller [Thomas Martyn's edition of Philip Miller's *The Gardener's and Botanist's Dictionary*, 1797–1807].

[3] *hassock … mole* Clump of grass thrust up by the tunneling of a mole.

[4] [Smith's note] tormentil. *Tormentilla reptans.* [Plant with yellow flowers and bitter roots.]

[5] [Smith's note] Bird's foot trefoil. *Trifolium ornithopoides.* [Plant having claw-shaped pods.] hawkweed. *Hieracium,* many sorts. [Hairy plants having dandelion-like blossoms.]

[6] [Smith's note] The downs, especially to the south, where they are less abrupt, are in many places under the plough; and the attention of the shepherds is there particularly required to keep the flocks from trespassing.

[7] [Smith's note] Square holes cut in the turf, into which a wire noose is fixed, to catch Wheatears. Mr. White [*The Natural History of Selbourne* (1789)] says, that these birds (*Motacilla oenanthe*) are never taken beyond the river Adur, and Beding Hill; but this is certainly a mistake.

[8] [Smith's note] These birds are extremely fearful, and on the slightest appearance of a cloud, run for shelter to the first rut, or heap of stone, that they see.

[9] [Smith's note] The Yellow Wagtail. *Motacilla flava.* It frequents the banks of rivulets in winter, making its nest in meadows and corn-fields. But after the breeding season is over, it haunts downs and sheepwalks, and is seen constantly among the flocks, probably for the sake of the insects it picks up. In France the shepherds call it *La Bergeronette,* and say it often gives them, by its cry, notice of approaching danger.

[10] [Smith's note] The strong winds from the south-west occasion almost all the trees, which on these hills are exposed to it, to grow the other way.

[11] [Smith's note] So extensive are some of the views from these hills, that only the want of power in the human eye to travel so far, prevents London itself being discerned. Description falls so infinitely short of the reality, that only here and there, distinct features can be given.

[12] [Smith's note] A scar of chalk in a hill beyond Sevenoaks in Kent, is very distinctly seen of a clear day.

And nearer, undulate the wooded heights,
And airy summits, that above the mole[1]
Rise in green beauty; and the beacon'd ridge
Of Black-down[2] shagg'd with heath, and swelling rude
Like a dark island from the vale; its brow
Catching the last rays of the evening sun
That gleam between the nearer park's old oaks,
Then lighten up the river, and make prominent
The portal, and the ruin'd battlements[3]
Of that dismantled fortress; rais'd what time
The Conqueror's° successors fiercely fought, *William I*
Tearing with civil feuds the desolate land.
But now a tiller of the soil dwells there,
And of the turret's loop'd and rafter'd halls
Has made an humbler homestead—Where he sees,
Instead of armed foemen, herds that graze
Along his yellow meadows; or his flocks
At evening from the upland driv'n to fold—

In such a castellated mansion once
A stranger chose his home; and where hard by
In rude disorder fallen, and hid with brushwood
Lay fragments gray of towers and buttresses,
Among the ruins, often he would muse—
His rustic meal soon ended, he was wont° *accustomed*
To wander forth, listening the evening sounds
Of rushing milldam,[4] or the distant team,
Or night-jar, chasing fern-flies:[5] the tir'd hind
Pass'd him at nightfall, wondering he should sit
On the hill top so late: they from the coast
Who sought bye paths with their clandestine
load,° *smugglers*
Saw with suspicious doubt, the lonely man
Cross on their way: but village maidens thought
His senses injur'd; and with pity say
That he, poor youth! must have been cross'd in love—
For often, stretch'd upon the mountain turf
With folded arms, and eyes intently fix'd
Where ancient elms and firs obscured a grange,° *farm*
Some little space within the vale below,
They heard him, as complaining of his fate,
And to the murmuring wind, of cold neglect
And baffled hope he told.—The peasant girls
These plaintive sounds remember, and even now
Among them may be heard the stranger's songs.

Were I a Shepherd on the hill
And ever as the mists withdrew
Could see the willows of the rill° *brook*
Shading the footway to the mill
Where once I walk'd with you—

And as away Night's shadows sail,
And sounds of birds and brooks arise,
Believe, that from the woody vale
I hear your voice upon the gale
In soothing melodies;

And viewing from the Alpine height,
The prospect dress'd in hues of air,
Could say, while transient colours bright

[1] [Smith's note] The hills about Dorking in Surrey; over almost the whole extent of which county the prospect extends; *mole* Cliffs leading down to sea.

[2] [Smith's note] This is an high ridge, extending between Sussex and Surrey. It is covered with heath, and has almost always a dark appearance. On it is a telegraph.

[3] [Smith's note] In this country there are several of the fortresses or castles built by Stephen of Blois [British king (r. 1135–54)], in his contention for the kingdom, with the daughter of Henry the First, the Empress Matilda. Some of these are now converted into farm houses.

[4] *milldam* Dam erected in a stream in order to power a mill.

[5] [Smith's note] Dr. Aikin remarks, I believe, in his essay "On the Application of Natural History to the Purposes of Poetry [1777]," how many of our best poets have noticed the same circumstance, the hum of the Dor Beetle (*Scaraboeus stercorarius*) among the sounds heard by the evening wanderer. I remember only one instance in which the more remarkable, though by no means uncommon noise, of the Fern Owl, or Goatsucker, is mentioned. It is called the Night Hawk, the Jar Bird, the Churn Owl, and the Fern Owl, from its feeding on the *Scaraboeus solstitialis*, or Fern Chafer, which it catches while on the wing with its claws, the middle toe of which is long and curiously serrated, on purpose to hold them. It was this bird that was intended to be described in the Forty-second Sonnet [Smith's *Sonnets*]. I was mistaken in supposing it as visible in November; it is a migrant, and leaves this country in August. I had often seen and heard it, but I did not then know its name or history. It is called Goatsucker (*Caprimulgus*), from a strange prejudice taken against it by the Italians, who assert that it sucks their goats; and the peasants of England still believe that a disease in the backs of their cattle, occasioned by a fly, which deposits its eggs under the skin, and raises a boil, sometimes fatal to calves, is the work of this bird, which they call a Puckeridge. Nothing can convince them that their beasts are not injured by this bird, which they therefore hold in abhorrence."

Touch'd the fair scene with dewy light,
'Tis, that *her* eyes are there!

I think, I could endure my lot
And linger on a few short years,
And then, by all but you forgot,
Sleep, where the turf that clothes the spot
May claim some pitying tears.

For 'tis not easy to forget
One, who thro' life has lov'd you still,
And you, however late, might yet
With sighs to Memory giv'n, regret
The Shepherd of the Hill.

Yet otherwhile it seem'd as if young Hope
Her flattering pencil gave to Fancy's hand,
And in his wanderings, rear'd to sooth his soul
Ideal bowers of pleasure—Then, of Solitude
And of his hermit life, still more enamour'd,
His home was in the forest; and wild fruits
And bread sustain'd him. There in early spring
The Barkmen[1] found him, e'er° the sun arose; *before*
There at their daily toil, the Wedgecutters[2]
Beheld him thro' the distant thicket move.
The shaggy dog following the truffle hunter,[3]
Bark'd at the loiterer; and perchance at night
Belated villagers from fair or wake,
While the fresh night-wind let the moonbeams in
Between the swaying boughs, just saw him pass,
And then in silence, gliding like a ghost
He vanish'd! Lost among the deepening gloom.—
But near one ancient tree, whose wreathed roots
Form'd a rude couch, love-songs and scatter'd rhymes,
Unfinish'd sentences, or half erased,
And rhapsodies like this, were sometimes found—

Let us to woodland wilds repair
While yet the glittering night-dews seem
To wait the freshly-breathing air,
Precursive° of the morning beam, *preparatory*
That rising with advancing day,
Scatters the silver drops away.

An elm, uprooted by the storm,
The trunk with mosses gray and green,
Shall make for us a rustic form,
Where lighter grows the forest scene;
And far among the bowery° shades, *leafy*
Are ferny lawns and grassy glades.

Retiring May to lovely June
Her latest garland now resigns;
The banks with cuckoo-flowers[4] are strewn,
The woodwalks blue with columbines,[5]
And with its reeds, the wandering stream
Reflects the flag-flower's[6] golden gleam.

There, feathering down the turf to meet,
Their shadowy arms the beeches spread,
While high above our sylvan seat,
Lifts the light ash its airy head;
And later leaved, the oaks between
Extend their bows of vernal° green. *spring-like*

The slender birch its paper rind
Seems offering to divided love,
And shuddering even without a wind
Aspens, their paler foliage move,
As if some spirit of the air
Breath'd a low sigh in passing there.

The Squirrel in his frolic mood,
Will fearless bound among the boughs;

[1] [Smith's note] As soon as the sap begins to rise, the trees intended for felling are cut and barked [bark is removed from the trees], at which time the men who are employed in that business pass whole days in the woods.

[2] [Smith's note] The wedges used in ship-building are made of beech wood, and great numbers are cut every year in the woods near the Downs.

[3] [Smith's note] Truffles [rare exotic mushrooms growing underground] are found under the beech woods, by means of small dogs trained to hunt them by the scent.

[4] [Smith's note] Cuckoo-flowers. *Lychnis dioica.* Shakespeare describes the Cuckoo buds as being yellow [Cf. *Love's Labour's Lost* 5.2.894]. He probably meant the numerous Ranunculi, or March marigolds (*Caltha palustris*), which so gild the meadows in Spring; but poets have never been botanists. The Cuckoo flower is the *Lychnis floscuculi.*

[5] [Smith's note] Columbines. *Aquilegia vulgaris.* [Plant with showy blooms featuring variously colored petals surrounded by hollow spurs.]

[6] [Smith's note] Flag-flower. *Iris pseudacorus.*

Yaffils[1] laugh loudly thro' the wood,
And murmuring ring-doves tell their vows;
While we, as sweetest woodscents rise,
Listen to woodland melodies.

And I'll contrive a sylvan room
Against the time of summer heat,
Where leaves, inwoven in Nature's loom,
Shall canopy our green retreat;
And gales that "close the eye of day"[2]
Shall linger, e'er they die away.

And when a sear[3] and sallow hue
From early frost the bower receives,
I'll dress the sand rock cave for you,
And strew the floor with heath and leaves,
That you, against the autumnal air
May find securer shelter there.

The Nightingale will then have ceas'd
To sing her moonlight serenade;
But the gay bird with blushing breast,[4]
And Woodlarks[5] still will haunt the shade,
And by the borders of the spring
Reed-wrens[6] will yet be carolling.

The forest hermit's lonely cave
None but such soothing sounds shall reach,
Or hardly heard, the distant wave
Slow breaking on the stony beach;
Or winds, that now sigh soft and low,
Now make wild music as they blow.

And then, before the chilling North
The tawny foliage falling light,
Seems, as it flits along the earth,
The footfall of the busy Sprite,[7]
Who wrapt in pale autumnal gloom,
Calls up the mist-born Mushroom.

Oh! could I hear your soft voice there,
And see you in the forest green
All beauteous as you are, more fair
You'd look, amid the sylvan scene,
And in a wood-girl's simple guise,
Be still more lovely in mine eyes.

Ye phantoms of unreal delight,
Visions of fond delirium born!
Rise not on my deluded sight,
Then leave me drooping and forlorn
To know, such bliss can never be,
Unless Amanda loved like me.

The visionary, nursing dreams like these,
Is not indeed unhappy. Summer woods
Wave over him, and whisper as they wave,
Some future blessings he may yet enjoy.
And as above him sail the silver clouds,
He follows them in thought to distant climes,
Where, far from the cold policy of this,
Dividing him from her he fondly loves,
He, in some island of the southern sea,[8]
May haply build his cane-constructed[9] bower
Beneath the bread-fruit,[10] or aspiring palm,
With long green foliage rippling in the gale.
Oh! let him cherish his ideal bliss—
For what is life, when Hope has ceas'd to strew
Her fragile flowers along its thorny way?
And sad and gloomy are his days, who lives

1 [Smith's note] Yaffils. Woodpeckers (*Picus*); three or four species in Britain.

2 [Smith's note] "And [Thy] liquid notes that close the eye of day." Milton [from Sonnet 1, "O nightingale," line 5.] The idea here meant to be conveyed is one of the evening wind, so welcome after a hot day of Summer, and which appears to soothe and lull all nature into tranquillity.

3 *sear* Sere, dry.

4 [Smith's note] The Robin, (*Motacilla rubecula*), which is always heard after other songsters have ceased to sing.

5 [Smith's note] The Woodlark (*Alauda nemorosa*) sings very late.

6 [Smith's note] Reed-wrens (*Motacilla arundinacea*) sing all the summer and autumn, and are often heard during the night.

7 *Sprite* Elusive mythical woodland creature.

8 [Smith's note] An allusion to the visionary delights of the newly discovered islands [those in the West Indies, such as Tahiti], where it was at first believed men lived in a state of simplicity and happiness; but where, as later enquiries have ascertained, that exemption from toil, which the fertility of their country gives them, produces the grossest vices; and a degree of corruption that late navigators think will end in the extirpation of the whole people in a few years.

9 *cane-constructed* Built of cane, the thin flexible stems from bamboo and rattan.

10 *bread-fruit* Evergreen tree having large edible fruits.

Of Hope abandon'd!

Just beneath the rock
Where Beachy overpeers the channel wave,
Within a cavern mined by wintry tides
Dwelt one,[1] who long disgusted with the world
And all its ways, appear'd to suffer life
Rather than live; the soul-reviving gale,
Fanning the bean-field, or the thymy heath,
Had not for many summers breathed on him;
And nothing mark'd to him the season's change,
Save that more gently rose the placid sea,
And that the birds which winter on the coast
Gave place to other migrants; save that the fog,
Hovering no more above the beetling cliffs
Betray'd not then the little careless sheep[2]
On the brink grazing, while their headlong fall
Near the lone Hermit's flint-surrounded home,
Claim'd unavailing pity; for his heart
Was feelingly alive to all that breath'd;
And outraged as he was, in sanguine[3] youth,
By human crimes, he still acutely felt
For human misery.

Wandering on the beach,
He learn'd to augur° from the clouds of heaven, *predict*
And from the changing colours of the sea,
And sullen murmurs of the hollow cliffs,
Or the dark porpoises,[4] that near the shore
Gambol'd° and sported on the level brine *leapt playfully*
When tempests were approaching: then at night
He listen'd to the wind; and as it drove
The billows with o'erwhelming vehemence
He, starting from his rugged couch, went forth
And hazarding a life, too valueless,
He waded thro' the waves, with plank or pole,
Towards where the mariner in conflict dread
Was buffeting for life the roaring surge;
And now just seen, now lost in foaming gulfs,
The dismal gleaming of the clouded moon
Show'd the dire peril. Often he had snatch'd
From the wild billows, some unhappy man
Who liv'd to bless the hermit of the rocks.
But if his generous cares were all in vain,
And with slow swell the tide of morning bore
Some blue swol'n cor'se° to land; the pale recluse *corpse*
Dug in the chalk a sepulchre—above
Where the dank sea-wrack[5] mark'd the utmost tide,
And with his prayers perform'd the obsequies° *funeral rites*
For the poor helpless stranger.

One dark night
The equinoctial wind blew south by west,
Fierce on the shore;—the bellowing cliffs were shook
Even to their stony base, and fragments fell
Flashing and thundering on the angry flood.
At day-break, anxious for the lonely man,
His cave the mountain shepherds visited,
Tho' sand and banks of weeds had chok'd their way—
He was not in it; but his drowned cor'se
By the waves wafted, near his former home
Receiv'd the rites of burial. Those who read
Chisel'd within the rock, these mournful lines,
Memorials of his sufferings, did not grieve,
That dying in the cause of charity
His spirit, from its earthly bondage freed,
Had to some better region fled for ever.

—1807

[1] [Smith's note] In a cavern almost immediately under the cliff called Beachy Head, there lived, as the people of the country believed, a man of the name of Darby, who for many years had no other abode than this cave, and subsisted almost entirely on shell-fish. He had often administered assistance to ship-wrecked mariners; but venturing into the sea on this charitable mission during a violent equinoctial storm, he himself perished. As it is above thirty years since I heard this tradition of parson Darby (for so I think he was called), it may now perhaps be forgotten.

[2] [Smith's note] Sometimes in thick weather the sheep feeding on the summit of the cliff miss their footing, and are killed by the fall.

[3] *sanguine* Cheerfully optimistic.

[4] [Smith's note] Dark porpoises. *Delphinus phocoena.*

[5] *sea-wrack* Shipwreck.

William Blake

1757 – 1827

"I labor upwards into futurity," etched William Blake onto the back of one of the copper plates which constituted the "tablets" of his visionary art. A poet and artist whose work was sorely undervalued during his own lifetime, Blake recognized that his was a genius before its time. The mysterious and powerful poetry that he crafted to convey his vision would eventually be recognized as having revolutionary significance; for the past century or more Blake has been recognized as a great poet of the Romantic era.

Blake was born one November evening in 1757 above his parents' hosiery shop in the Soho district of London. James and Catherine Blake, religious Dissenters whose non-compromising beliefs were those of a growing number of tradespeople, allowed their son to pursue a program of self study that saved him from being schooled under the institutional authorities he instinctively abhorred. Although his parents were generally indulgent, there are hints that Blake balked even under their natural expressions of authority. He received a thrashing for declaring he had seen the face of God, and was accused of lying when he reported passing a tree bespangled with angels. Since his family could not afford the expense of artistic training, he was apprenticed at fourteen to a highly respected engraver, with whom he lived for seven years while learning the trade which would thereafter earn him his living

During the period of his apprenticeship, Blake began writing the poems that were eventually collected in *Poetical Sketches* (1783)—the only volume of his verse originally printed by letter-press rather than by the "illuminated" methods he later originated. Of his parents and three siblings, Blake retained lasting affection only for his younger brother, Robert. Blake claimed to communicate daily with the spirit of Robert after his early death from tuberculosis. Indeed, the unique style of relief etching or "Illuminated Printing" which Blake later devised was imparted, he claimed, by Robert in a visitation. Etching words backwards into copper plates so that they would reverse to normal upon printing, Blake in 1788 produced his first illuminated texts with "All Religions Are One" and "There is No Natural Religion." It was a defining moment for him, one in which words and images converged into an indivisible and prophetic expression. He soon applied his new method of printing to a larger project, the poetic and pictorial depiction of a young soul descending into the realm of matter, recounted in *The Book of Thel*.

Blake's words and designs "interanimate each other," in the words of one critic; a master of color, he, at times, achieved unearthly effects in his hand-tinted books, of which no two copies were exactly the same. Rather than reflecting the tones of the natural world, Blake's color—and indeed the vividness of his verse—aim towards the supernatural. Similarly, what separates his poetry from that of contemporaries, such as Wordsworth and Coleridge is his lack of interest in "painting Nature." For Blake, the true aim of art was to tune the senses and the imaginative faculties to the higher pitch of a spiritual reality, not to the natural world. For this reason, Blake detested what he called the "muddy" colors, nuanced shade work, and secular sensibilities of an artist such as Rembrandt, while revering the determined outlines, bright colors and unequivocal contrasts of light and dark achieved by High Renaissance painters such as Michelangelo and Raphael.

The bold, declarative and (to some modern eyes) exaggerated style which Blake admired in painting is paralleled in many of his literary preferences. His work has close associations with the declamatory traditions of prophecy, of the aphorism, of the political pamphlet, and of the proverb. *The Marriage of Heaven and Hell* (1790) contains some of his most chiseled epigrams: "The cut worm forgives the plow" and "The tigers of wrath are wiser than the horses of instruction." The Bible was a tremendous imaginative reserve upon which he drew all of his life. He admired Dante, Milton, Spenser, and Shakespeare, supplied commissioned designs for editions of Milton's *L'Allegro, Il Penseroso, Paradise Lost,* and *Paradise Regained,* and left behind an unfinished series of watercolors illustrating Dante's work. He was also influenced by the architecture and sepulchral art of Westminster Abbey and by the literary gothic of Edward Young's *Night Thoughts* and Robert Blair's *The Grave,* versions of which he illustrated. If he was in many respects an outsider to his own culture, Blake was fully a man of the times in his love of the popular "forgeries" of James Macpherson (author of the "Ossian" poems) and Thomas Chatterton, as well as in his enjoyment of works of Gothic fiction such as Ann Radcliffe's *The Mysteries of Udolpho* (1794).

On at least two occasions Blake struck out to earn a reputation as an artist in his own right. The first occasion came at the end of his apprenticeship, when he submitted a portfolio to the Royal Academy of Arts (under the presidency of Sir Joshua Reynolds—and was accepted into the Academy. Yet he failed to emerge out of obscurity, and was forced to set up an engraver's shop. For twenty years Blake would resign himself to the grueling schedule of a copy engraver, recognized only by a few of his friends as a formidably original artist, and almost wholly overlooked as a poet. In 1809, energized by a gallery showing of works by Dürer, Michelangelo, Giulio Romano, and others, Blake renewed his association with the Royal Academy to launch a solo exhibition of his own work. With the exception of a caustic review or two, the public remained unmoved by—possibly unready for—the idiosyncratic light Blake cast upon subjects such as "The Body of Abel found by Adam and Eve."

Blake found his soul mate in Catherine Boucher, the illiterate daughter of a market gardener. He taught her to read and trained her in the preparation of copper plates, the hand coloring of prints, and the stitching of pages into bound copies. Catherine was evidently a submissive, devoted wife, and some have denigrated Blake's traditional and even misogynist approach to marriage, citing his pronouncement that "the female ... lives from the light of the male." At the same time, however, Blake approved of the arguments for sexual equality made by Mary Wollstonecraft in *A Vindication of the Rights of Woman* (1793). Blake radically proposed that carnal pleasure was a portal to the divine. In *Visions of the Daughters of Albion* (1793), Blake abjures sexual domination and celebrates "the moment of desire!" in a manner highly unconventional at the time. Visitors to the Blake home reported coming across the couple reading naked in a garden house in their back yard, enjoying the innocence of their private Eden and rejecting the narratives of shame and the Fall.

The rewriting of the Biblical drama of the Creation and Fall that underlies nearly all of Blake's work was influenced by radical Dissenters who celebrated nudity as a symbol of unfallen humanity. Blake was also influenced by the mystical systems of Emmanuel Swedenborg and Jacob Boehme, and tapped into veins of esoteric knowledge related to the cabbalistic teachings of the Freemasons, the Rosicrucians, and Paracelsus. He also had associations with decidedly non-mystical political movements that were bravely calling for democratic reforms at a time when the English monarchy was intent on quashing sympathizers with American War of Independence and the French Revolution.

Blake never fully participated in an organized movement of any kind, be it religious or political. His was "a voice crying in the wilderness," an unsystematizable voice urging men and women to realize their "human form divine." Unwilling to conform to any system not of his own creation, Blake's language grew increasingly esoteric and opaque in later major prophecies such as *The Four Zoas, Milton* (1804) and *Jerusalem* (1804–20).

One vision that Blake explores over and over again is that of an earthly Eden triumphing over forces of repression. This is the common theme of *The French Revolution* (1791), *America: A Prophecy* (1793), *Europe: A Prophecy* (1794), and *The Book of Urizen* (1794). When Blake summons Albion, figure of the human form divine in *Jerusalem*, to "Awake!" he is calling for a spiritual revolution in which humanity awakens to the knowledge that the republic of heaven is immanent.

Blake imagined the spiritual dimensions of the geography of London in particularly vivid detail. That the material double of his holy city was corrupt lends a sharp edge to Blake's vision. As one Blake biographer writes, "it was a time when mobs and rioters often controlled large areas of the city; there were riots by sailors, silk-weavers, coal-heavers, hatters, glass-grinders....and bloody demonstrations over the price of bread." The biting simplicity of "The Chimney Sweeper" and "The Little Black Boy" in Blake's *Songs of Innocence and of Experience* (1789–94) are testimony to his acute sensitivity to the realities of poverty and exploitation that accompanied the "dark satanic mills" of the industrial revolution.

In this London, Blake admitted to living in fear that his artistic vision and eccentric tendency to converse with angels and ghosts would land him in trouble with the authorities—a fear horribly realized in 1803. The Blakes had been generously invited by William Hayley, an eminent poet and wealthy patron of the arts, to live in a country cottage at Felpham. One day a drunken private in the Royal Dragoons, John Scofield, fell into a heated argument with Blake at his garden gate. Blake physically evicted the abusive soldier from the premises. Scofield subsequently accused Blake of making seditious remarks against the Crown, an offense punishable by death. Hayley generously paid for his friend's bail and his defense, and Blake was eventually acquitted, to the thunderous approval of the court. However, the incident stamped itself upon his sensitive mind; he raised it to mythological proportions in the convoluted poetic symbology of *Jerusalem*, where the Law is figured as the nauseous region of "Bowlahoola," while Scofield and his cohorts appear as "ministers of evil."

As the culture around him placed increasing faith in the physical laws of natural science, Blake's insistence on the incorruptible coordinates of imaginative truth cast him as an increasing oddity. Many of Blake's contemporaries considered him insane. London was shifting to a secular orientation under the rise of industrial culture. Against the grain of the times, Blake continued producing labor-intensive printings of illuminated books, none of which proved to be a commercial success. Only twenty-eight copies of *Songs of Innocence and of Experience* are known to exist, sixteen of *The Book of Thel*, nine of *The Marriage of Heaven and Hell*, and five of *Jerusalem*.

In his last years, just as he had reconciled himself to poverty and obscurity, Blake attracted the first following he had ever enjoyed, a small group of painters called "the Ancients." Charles Lamb and a few other writers of the period also expressed admiration, but the glimmerings of a full-fledged "Blake industry" did not appear until years after his death, when his art and poetry were discovered by Dante Gabriel Rossetti and the Pre-Raphaelites. Rossetti and, later, William Butler Yeats edited volumes of Blake's poems, and appreciation grew of his powerful poetic as well as painterly achievements. By the middle of the twentieth century, academics around the world were devoting themselves to the scholarly study of Blake's work, which was also exerting a profound influence on the literary and popular culture of the time. Blake was an inspiration to the generation of Beat poets clustered around Allen Ginsberg and to many in the 'sixties counterculture who took up his call to open the "doors of perception" (words straight from *The Marriage of Heaven and Hell*), trying everything from the hallucinogenic drugs proposed by Aldous Huxley, to communal living and free love, to approximate his visionary universe. The future had finally caught up with William Blake.

⌘⌘⌘

from *Songs of Innocence and of Experience* *Showing the Two Contrary States of the Human Soul*

Title page, *Songs of Innocence and of Experience.*

from *Songs of Innocence*

Introduction

Piping down the valleys wild
Piping songs of pleasant glee
On a cloud I saw a child.
And he laughing said to me.

'Pipe a song about a Lamb:'
So I piped with merry chear.[1]
'Piper pipe that song again'
So I piped, he wept to hear.

'Drop thy pipe thy happy pipe
Sing thy songs of happy chear.'
So I sung the same again,
While he wept with joy to hear

'Piper sit thee down and write
In a book that all may read—'
So he vanish'd from my sight
And I pluck'd a hollow reed

And I made a rural pen,
And I stain'd the water clear,
And I wrote my happy songs
Every child may joy to hear
—1789

The Ecchoing Green

The Sun does arise,
And make happy the skies.
The merry bells ring
To welcome the Spring.
The sky-lark and thrush,
The birds of the bush,
Sing louder around,
To the bells chearful sound.
While our sports shall be seen
On the Ecchoing Green.
Old John with white hair
Does laugh away care,
Sitting under the oak,
Among the old folk.
They laugh at our play,
And soon they all say.
'Such such were the joys.
When we all girls & boys,
In our youth-time were seen.
On the Ecchoing Green.'

[1] *chear* The usual practice of this anthology regarding modernization of spelling and punctuation has not been followed in the case of Blake; his idiosyncrasies have been retained.

Till the little ones weary
No more can be merry
The sun does descend,
And our sports have an end:
Round the laps of their mothers.
Many sisters and brothers,
Like birds in their nest,
Are ready for rest:
And sport no more seen,
On the darkening Green.
—1789

The Lamb

Little Lamb who made thee
Dost thou know who made thee
Gave thee life & bid thee feed.
By the stream & o'er the mead;
Gave thee clothing of delight,
Softest clothing wooly bright;
Gave thee such a tender voice,
Making all the vales rejoice;
 Little Lamb who made thee
 Dost thou know who made thee

 Little Lamb I'll tell thee,
 Little Lamb I'll tell thee:
He is called by thy name,
For he calls himself a Lamb:

He is meek & he is mild,[1]
He became a little child:
I a child & thou a lamb,
We are called by his name.
 Little Lamb God bless thee
 Little Lamb God bless thee.
—1789

[1] *He ... mild* Cf. Charles Wesley, "Gentle Jesus, meek and mild."

"The Little Black Boy."

The Little Black Boy

My mother bore me in the southern wild,
And I am black, but O! my soul is white.
White as an angel is the English child:
But I am black as if bereav'd of light.

My mother taught me underneath a tree
And sitting down before the heat of day.
She took me on her lap and kissed me.
And pointing to the east began to say.

'Look on the rising sun! there God does live
And gives his light. and gives his heat away.
And flowers and trees and beasts and men receive
Comfort in morning joy in the noon day.

'And we are put on earth a little space.
That we may learn to bear the beams of love.
And these black bodies and this sun-burnt face
Is but a cloud, and like a shady grove.

'For when our souls have learn'd the heat to bear
The cloud will vanish we shall hear his voice.
Saying: "come out from the grove my love & care,
And round my golden tent like lambs rejoice."'

Thus did my mother say and kissed me.
And thus I say to little English boy.
When I from black and he from white cloud free,
And round the tent of God like lambs we joy:

Ill shade him from the heat till he can bear.
To lean in joy upon our fathers knee
And then Ill stand and stroke his silver hair.
And be like him and he will then love me.
—1789

The Chimney Sweeper [1]

When my mother died I was very young,
And my father sold me while yet my tongue,
Could scarcely cry 'weep weep weep weep.'[2]
So your chimneys I sweep & in soot I sleep.[3]

Theres little Tom Dacre who cried when his head
That curl'd like a lambs back, was shav'd. so I said.
'Hush Tom never mind it, for when your head's bare.
You know that the soot cannot spoil your white hair.'

And so he was quiet, & that very night.
As Tom was a sleeping he had such a sight,
That thousands of sweepers Dick, Joe Ned & Jack
Were all of them lock'd up in coffins of black,

And by came an Angel who had a bright key,
And he open'd the coffins & set them all free.
Then down a green plain leaping laughing they run
And wash in a river and shine in the Sun.[4]

Then naked & white, all their bags left behind.
They rise upon clouds, and sport in the wind.
And the Angel told Tom if he'd be a good boy.
He'd have God for his father & never want joy.

And so Tom awoke and we rose in the dark
And got with our bags & our brushes to work.
Tho' the morning was cold, Tom was happy & warm.
So if all do their duty, they need not fear harm.
—1789

The Divine Image

To Mercy Pity Peace and Love,
All pray in their distress:
And to these virtues of delight
Return their thankfulness.

For Mercy Pity Peace and Love.
Is God our father dear:
And Mercy Pity Peace and Love.
Is Man his child and care.

For Mercy has a human heart
Pity a human face:
And Love, the human form divine.
And Peace, the human dress.

Then every man of every clime,
That prays in his distress,
Prays to the human form divine
Love Mercy Pity Peace.

And all must love the human form,
In heathen, turk or jew.[5]

---

[1] *The Chimney Sweeper* Children were often forced to climb up chimneys to clean them—a filthy, dangerous, and unhealthy job. A law ameliorating their working conditions was passed in 1788, but it was rarely enforced.

[2] *weep … weep* The child is attempting to say "sweep," the chimney-sweeper's street cry. The act of 1788 should have prevented the apprenticing of children younger than eight.

[3] *in soot I sleep* The sweeps used their bags of soot as blankets.

[4] *And wash … Sun* The act of 1788 called for weekly washings for sweeps.

[5] *heathen … jew* Cf. Isaac Watts, "Praise for the Gospel": "Lord, I ascribe it to thy Grace / And not to Chance, as others do, / That I was born of *Christian* Race, / And not a *Heathen*, or a *Jew*." Whereas Watt's emphasis had been on the theological underpinnings for a hierarchy of birth that took for granted the inferiority of other races and religions, Blake's emphasis is on loving even those whom his society despises.

Where Mercy, Love & Pity dwell,
There God is dwelling too.
—1789

Holy Thursday [1]

Twas on a Holy Thursday their innocent faces clean
The children walking two & two in red & blue & green[2]
Grey headed beadles[3] walkd before with wands as white as snow
Till into the high dome of Pauls they like Thames waters flow

O what a multitude they seemd these flowers of London town
Seated in companies they sit with radiance all their own
The hum of multitudes was there but multitudes of lambs
Thousands of little boys & girls raising their innocent hands

Now like a mighty wind they raise to heaven the voice of song
Or like harmonious thunderings the seats of heaven among
Beneath them sit the aged men wise guardians of the poor
Then cherish pity, lest you drive an angel from your door[4]
—1789

Infant Joy

I have no name
I am but two days old.—'
What shall I call thee?
'I happy am
Joy is my name,—'
Sweet joy befall thee!

Pretty joy!
Sweet joy but two days old,
Sweet joy I call thee;
Thou dost smile.
I sing the while
Sweet joy befall thee.
—1789

Nurse's Song

When the voices of children are heard on the green
And laughing is heard on the hill,
My heart is at rest within my breast
And every thing else is still

'Then come home my children, the sun is gone down
And the dews of night arise
Come come leave off play. and let us away
Till the morning appears in the skies.'

'No no let us play, for it is yet day
And we cannot go to sleep
Besides in the sky, the little birds fly
And the hills are all coverd with sheep'

'Well well go & play till the light fades away
And then go home to bed'
The little ones leaped & shouted & laugh'd
And all the hills ecchoed.
—1789

[1] *Holy Thursday* Each year since 1782, the 6,000 children in London's charity schools had been brought to St. Paul's Cathedral for an annual service of thanks-giving. Though "Holy Thursday" is the name given to Ascension Day, these services always occurred on a Thursday, usually in May, but never on Ascension Day.

[2] *in ... green* The school uniforms.

[3] *beadles* Officials.

[4] *cherish ... door* Cf. Hebrews 13.2, "Be not forgetful to entertain strangers; for thereby some have entertained angels unawares."

Title page, *Songs of Experience.*

from *Songs of Experience*

Introduction

Hear the voice of the Bard!
Who Present, Past, & Future sees
Whose ears have heard,
The Holy Word,

That walk'd among the ancient trees.[1]
Calling[2] the lapsed Soul
And weeping in the evening dew:
That[3] might controll
The starry pole;
And fallen fallen light renew!

Frontispiece, *Songs of Experience.*

[1] *Holy Word … trees* Cf. Genesis 3.8: "And they heard the voice of the Lord God walking in the garden in the cool of the day: and Adam and his wife hid themselves from the presence of the Lord God amongst the trees of the garden."

[2] *Calling* The subject here is ambiguous, and could either be the bard or the Holy Word.

[3] *That* Most likely the referent here is the lapsèd soul, but it may also be the Holy Word.

O Earth, O Earth return!
Arise from out the dewy grass;
Night is worn,
And the morn
Rises from the slumberous mass.

'Turn away no more:
Why wilt thou turn away
The starry floor[1]
The watry shore
Is giv'n thee till the break of day.'
—1794

The Clod & the Pebble

Love seeketh not Itself to please.
Nor for itself hath any care;
But for another gives its ease.
And builds a Heaven in Hells despair.'

So sang a little Clod of Clay.
Trodden with the cattles feet:
But a Pebble of the brook.
Warbled out these metres meet.

'Love seeketh only Self to please,
To bind another to Its delight;
Joys in anothers loss of ease,
And builds a Hell in Heavens despite.'[2]
—1794

Holy Thursday

Is this a holy thing to see.
In a rich and fruitful land,
Babes reducd to misery.
Fed with cold and usurous hand?[3]

Is that trembling cry a song?
Can it be a song of joy?
And so many children poor?
It is a land of poverty!

And their sun does never shine.
And their fields are bleak & bare.
And their ways are fill'd with thorns
It is eternal winter there.

For where-e'er the sun does shine.
And where-e'er the rain does fall:
Babe can never hunger there,
Nor poverty the mind appall.
—1794

The Chimney Sweeper

A little black thing among the snow:
Crying 'weep, weep,' in notes of woe!
'Where are thy father & mother? say?'
'They are both gone up to the church to pray.

'Because I was happy upon the heath.
And smil'd among the winters snow:
They clothed me in the clothes of death.
And taught me to sing the notes of woe.

'And because I am happy & dance & sing.
They think they have done me no injury:
And are gone to praise God & his Priest & King
Who make up a heaven of our misery.'
—1794

The Sick Rose

O Rose thou art sick.
The invisible worm.
That flies in the night
In the howling storm:

Has found out thy bed
Of crimson joy:

[1] *starry floor* The sky, the floor of heaven.

[2] *builds ... despite* In Milton's *Paradise Lost* (1.254–55), Satan declares, "The mind is its own place, and in itself / Can make a Heaven of Hell, a Hell of Heaven."

[3] *usurous hand* I.e., the hand of someone engaged in lending money at interest.

And his dark secret love
Does thy life destroy.
—1794

The Fly

Little Fly
Thy summers play.
My thoughtless hand
Has brush'd away.

Am not I
A fly like thee?[1]
Or art not thou
A man like me?

For I dance
And drink & sing:
Till some blind hand
Shall brush my wing.

If thought is life
And strength & breath:
And the want
Of thought is death;[2]

Then am I
A happy fly,
If I live,
Or if I die.
—1794

The Tyger

Tyger Tyger, burning bright,
In the forests of the night;
What immortal hand or eye.
Could frame thy fearful symmetry?

In what distant deeps or skies.
Burnt the fire of thine eyes?

[1] *Am … thee* Cf. Shakespeare, *King Lear* 4.1.36–37: "As flies to wanton boys, are we to the gods, / They kill us for their sport."

[2] *If thought…death* Cf. René Descartes's statement "Cogito, ergo sum" ("I think, therefore I am").

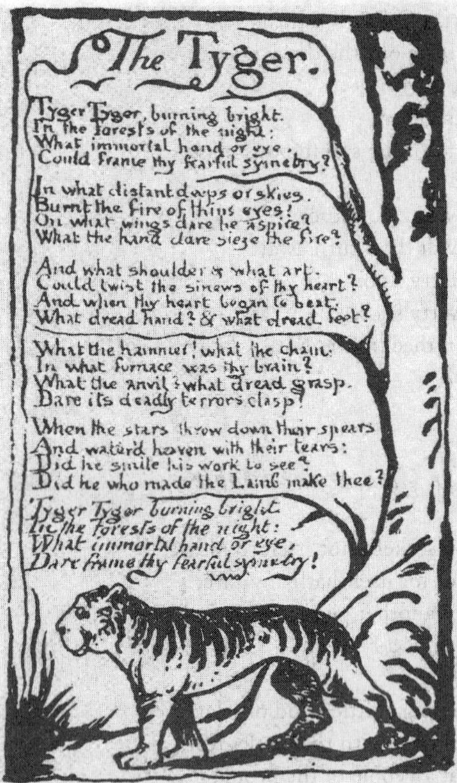

On what wings dare he aspire?[3]
What the hand. dare seize the fire?[4]

And what shoulder, & what art,
Could twist the sinews of thy heart?
And when thy heart began to beat,
What dread hand? & what dread feet?

What the hammer? what the chain,
In what furnace was thy brain?
What the anvil? what dread grasp.
Dare its deadly terrors clasp!

When the stars threw down the spears[5]
And water'd heaven with their tears:

[3] *what … aspire* In Greek mythology, Icarus fashioned wings of wax and feathers; these melted when he attempted to fly too close to the sun.

[4] *What … fire* Prometheus stole fire from heaven to give to humans.

[5] *threw down the spears* Either in surrender or as an act of rebellion —it is uncertain which.

Did he smile his work to see?
Did he who made the Lamb make thee?[1]

Tyger Tyger burning bright,
In the forests of the night:
What immortal hand or eye.
Dare frame thy fearful symmetry?
—1794

Ah! Sun-Flower

Ah Sun-flower! weary of time,
Who countest the steps of the Sun:
Seeking after that sweet golden clime
Where the travellers journey is done.

Where the Youth pined away with desire,
And the pale Virgin shrouded in snow:
Arise from their graves and aspire.
Where my Sun-flower wishes to go.
—1794

The Garden of Love

I went to the Garden of Love.
And saw what I never had seen:
A Chapel was built in the midst,
Where I used to play on the green.[2]

And the gates of this Chapel were shut,
And 'Thou shalt not'[3] writ over the door;
So I turn'd to the Garden of Love,
That so many sweet flowers bore.

And I saw it was filled with graves,
And tomb-stones where flowers should be:
And Priests in black gowns. were walking their rounds,
And binding with briars.[4] my joys & desires.
—1794

London

I wander thro' each charter'd[5] street,
Near where the charter'd Thames does flow,
And mark in every face I meet
Marks of weakness, marks of woe.

In every cry of every Man,
In every Infants cry of fear.
In every voice; in every ban.
The mind-forg'd manacles I hear

How the Chimney-sweepers cry
Every blackning Church appalls.
And the hapless Soldiers sigh
Runs in blood down Palace walls

But most thro' midnight streets I hear
How the youthful Harlots curse[6]
Blasts the new born Infants tear[7]
And blights with plagues the Marriage hearse.
—1794

The Human Abstract

Pity would be no more.
If we did not make somebody Poor:
And Mercy no more could be.
If all were as happy as we;

And mutual fear brings peace;
Till the selfish loves increase.

---

[1] *Did he ... thee* Tigers are not mentioned in the Bible.

[2] *A Chapel ... green* Possibly a reference to the erection of a chapel on South Lambeth Green in 1793.

[3] *Thou shalt not* The phrase that introduces most of the Ten Commandments (Exodus 20.3–17).

[4] *binding with briars* Prior to the nineteenth century, binding graves with briars was a common practice.

[5] *charter'd* Privileged, licensed. While charters grant freedoms, they often do so for a select minority (such as merchants) and thereby simultaneously oppress the majority.

[6] *Harlots curse* Referring both to the oaths she utters and the venereal diseases she spreads.

[7] *Blasts ... tear* A reference to the blindness caused in infants if they contract certain venereal diseases (such as gonorrhea) from the mother.

Then Cruelty knits a snare,
And spreads his baits with care.

He sits down with holy fears,
And waters the ground with tears;
Then Humility takes its root
Underneath his foot.

Soon spreads the dismal shade
Of Mystery over his head;
And the Catterpiller and Fly.
Feed on the Mystery.

And it bears the fruit of Deceit.
Ruddy and sweet to eat;
And the Raven his nest has made
In its thickest shade.

The Gods of the earth and sea.
Sought thro' Nature to find this Tree
But their search was all in vain:
There grows one in the Human Brain
—1794

Infant Sorrow

My mother groand! my father wept.
Into the dangerous world I leapt:
Helpless, naked. piping loud;
Like a fiend hid in a cloud.

Struggling in my fathers hands:
Striving against my swadling bands:
Bound and weary I thought best
To sulk upon my mothers breast.
—1794

A Poison Tree[1]

I was angry with my friend;
I told my wrath, my wrath did end.
I was angry with my foe:
I told it not, my wrath did grow.

And I waterd it in fears,
Night & morning with my tears:
And I sunned it with smiles,
And with soft deceitful wiles.

And it grew both day and night.
Till it bore an apple bright.
And my foe beheld it shine,
And he knew that it was mine.

And into my garden stole.
When the night had veild the pole;
In the morning glad I see.
My foe outstretchd beneath the tree.
—1794

[plate 1][2]

The Marriage of Heaven and Hell[3]

[plate 2]

The Argument[4]

Rintrah[5] roars & shakes his fires in the burdend air;
Hungry clouds swag[6] on the deep

Once meek, and in a perilous path,
The just man kept his course along
The vale of death.
Roses are planted where thorns grow,
And on the barren heath
Sing the honey bees.

Then the perilous path was planted:
And a river, and a spring

[1] *the Poison Tree* Another version of this poem is entitled "Christian Forbearance."

[2] *[plate 1]* The illustrated plates are reproduced below on pp. 52–55.

[3] *Marriage ... Hell* Blake combines the titles of two works by the Swedish visionary Emanuel Swedenborg (1688–1772), *A Treatise Concerning Heaven and Hell, and of the Wonderful Things Therein, as Heard and Seen by Emanuel Swedenborg* (1758, trans. 1784) and *Conjugial Love* (1768, trans. 1790).

[4] *Argument* For the imagery of "The Argument," Cf. Isaiah 5.1–7, 7.23–25, 35.1–10.

[5] *Rintrah* The character of Rintrah, a prophet and herald, reappears in Blake's *Europe a Prophecy* (1794) as well as in his *Milton*.

[6] *swag* Sag, hang heavily.

On every cliff and tomb;
And on the bleached bones[1]
Red clay[2] brought forth.

Till the villain left the paths of ease,
To walk in perilous paths, and drive
The just man into barren climes.

Now the sneaking serpent walks
In mild humility.
And the just man rages in the wilds
Where lions roam.

Rintrah roars & shakes his fires in the burdend air;
Hungry clouds swag on the deep.

[Plate 3]

As a new heaven is begun, and it is now thirty-three years since its advent: the Eternal Hell revives.[3] And lo! Swedenborg is the Angel sitting at the tomb; his writings are the linen clothes folded up. Now is the dominion of Edom,[4] & the return of Adam into Paradise; see Isaiah XXXIV & XXXV chap.[5]

Without Contraries is no progression. Attraction and Repulsion, Reason and Energy, Love and Hate, are necessary to Human existence.

From these contraries spring what the religious call Good & Evil. Good is the passive that obeys Reason Evil is the active springing from Energy.

Good is Heaven. Evil is Hell.

[Plate 4]

The Voice of the Devil

All Bibles or sacred codes have been the causes of the following errors.

1. That Man has two real existing principles Viz: a Body & a Soul.

2. That Energy. calld Evil. is alone from the Body. & that Reason. calld Good. is alone from the soul.

3. That God will torment Man in Eternity for following his Energies.

But the following Contraries to these are True

1. Man has no Body distinct from his soul for that calld Body is a portion of soul discernd by the five Senses, the chief inlets of Soul in this age

2. Energy is the only life and is from the Body and Reason is the bound or outward circumference of Energy.

3. Energy is Eternal Delight

[Plate 5]

Those who restrain desire, do so because theirs is weak enough to be restrained; and the restrainer or reason usurps its place & governs the unwilling.

And being restrained it by degrees becomes passive till it is only the shadow of desire.

The history of this is written in *Paradise Lost*.[6] & the Governor or Reason is call'd Messiah.

And the original Archangel or possessor of the command of the heavenly host, is calld the Devil or Satan and his children are call'd Sin & Death[7]

But in the Book of Job Miltons Messiah is call'd Satan.

For this history has been adopted by both parties

It indeed appear'd to Reason as if Desire was cast out, but the Devils account is, that the Messiah [Plate 6] fell. & formed a heaven of what he stole from the Abyss[8]

[1] *bleached bones* Cf. Ezekiel 37.1–11, in which Ezekiel sees life resurrected from a valley of bones.

[2] *Red clay* Since God created Adam from "the dust of the ground" (Genesis 2.8), "Adam" is sometimes said to mean "red clay" in Hebrew.

[3] *As a … revives* Swedenborg had predicted that the Last Judgment would occur in 1757, coincidentally the year of Blake's birth. In 1790, the "now" of the poem, Blake is 33, Christ's age when He was crucified and rose again.

[4] *Edom* Cf. Genesis 27.40, in which "Edom" is another name for "Esau," whose brother Jacob stole his inheritance. Like "Adam," "Edom" suggests redness.

[5] *Isaiah XXXIV & XXXV* Prophecies of divine vengeance and restoration, respectively.

[6] *Paradise Lost* The rest of this section contains Blake's own reading of Milton's epic.

[7] *Sin & Death* Cf. *Paradise Lost* 2.746–814, in which the birth of Satan's daughter, Sin, and the son of their incestuous union, Death, are described.

[8] *It … Abyss* *Paradise Lost* 6.824ff. describes God's defeat of Satan, originally the Archangel Lucifer, and Satan's expulsion from heaven, along with his rebel faction.

This is shewn in the Gospel, where he prays to the Father to send the comforter[1] or Desire that Reason may have Ideas to build on, the Jehovah of the Bible being no other than he who dwells in flaming fire Know that after Christs death, he became Jehovah.

But in Milton; the Father is Destiny, the Son, a Ratio[2] of the five senses. & the Holy Ghost, Vacuum!

Note. The reason Milton wrote in fetters when he wrote of Angels & God, and at liberty when of Devils & Hell, is because he was a true Poet and of the Devils party without knowing it.

A Memorable Fancy[3]

As I was walking among the fires of hell, delighted with the enjoyments of Genius; which to Angels look like torment and insanity. I collected some of their Proverbs: thinking that as the sayings used in a nation. mark its character, so the Proverbs of Hell, shew the nature of Infernal wisdom better than any description of buildings or garments

When I came home; on the abyss of the five senses. where a flat sided steep frowns over the present world. I saw a mighty Devil folded in black clouds, hovering on the sides of the rock, with corroding [Plate 7] fires[4] he wrote the following sentence now percieved by the minds of men, & read by them on earth.

How do you know but ev'ry Bird that cuts the airy way,
Is an immense world of delight, clos'd by your
senses five?[5]

Proverbs of Hell[6]

In seed time learn, in harvest teach, in winter enjoy.
Drive your cart and your plow over the bones of the dead.
The road of excess leads to the palace of wisdom.
Prudence is a rich ugly old maid courted by Incapacity.
He who desires but acts not, breeds pestilence.
The cut worm forgives the plow.
Dip him in the river who loves water.
A fool sees not the same tree that a wise man sees.
He whose face gives no light, shall never become a star.
Eternity is in love with the productions of time.
The busy bee has no time for sorrow.
The hours of folly are measur'd by the clock, but of wisdom: no clock can measure.
All wholsom food is caught without a net or a trap.
Bring out number weight, & measure in a year of dearth
No bird soars too high. if he soars with his own wings.
A dead body. revenges not injuries.
The most sublime act is to set another before you.
If the fool would persist in his folly he would become wise
Folly is the cloke of knavery.
Shame is Prides cloke.

[Plate 8]

Prisons are built with stones of Law, Brothels with bricks of Religion.
The pride of the peacock is the glory of God.
The lust of the goat is the bounty of God.
The wrath of the lion is the wisdom of God.
The nakedness of woman is the work of God.
Excess of sorrow laughs. Excess of joy weeps.
The roaring of lions, the howling of wolves, the raging of the stormy sea, and the destructive sword. are portions of eternity too great for the eye of man.
The fox condemns the trap, not himself.
Joys impregnate. Sorrows bring forth.
Let man wear the fell of the lion. woman the fleece of the sheep.
The bird a nest. the spider a web. man friendship.

[1] *he prays … comforter* In John 14.16–17, Christ says He will pray to the Father to give mankind another comforter, the Holy Ghost.

[2] *Ratio* Sum.

[3] *Memorable Fancy* Blake's "Memorable Fancies" are modeled on the "Memorable Relations" in which Swedenborg recounts his visionary experiences.

[4] *corroding fires* A reference to Blake's use of acids to etch the copper plates from which he printed his poems. More extended accounts of the printing process occur on plates 14 and 15.

[5] *How do … five* Cf. Thomas Chatterton, *Bristowe Tragedie, or the Dethe of Syr Charles Bawdin* (1768): "How dydd I know that ev'ry darte / That cutte the airie waie / Myghte nott find passage toe my harte / And close myne eyes for aie?" (133–36).

[6] *Proverbs of Hell* A diabolical version of the Old Testament's Book of Proverbs.

The selfish smiling fool & the sullen frowning fool. shall be both thought wise. that they may be a rod.
What is now proved was once only imagin'd.
The rat, the mouse, the fox, the rabbet; watch the roots, the lion. the tyger. the horse. the elephant. watch the fruits.
The cistern contains: the fountain overflows
One thought. fills immensity.
Always be ready to speak your mind, and a base man will avoid you.
Every thing possible to be believ'd is an image of truth.
The eagle never lost so much time as when he submitted to learn of the crow.

[Plate 9]

The fox provides for himself. but God provides for the lion.
Think in the morning. Act in the noon, Eat in the evening, Sleep in the night,
He who has sufferd you to impose on him knows you.
As the plow follows words, so God rewards prayers.
Thy tygers of wrath are wiser than the horses of instruction
Expect poison. from the standing water.
You never know what is enough unless you know what is more than enough.
Listen to the fools reproach! it is a kingly title!
The eyes of fire, the nostrils of air, the mouth of water, the beard of earth.
The weak in courage is strong in cunning.
The apple tree never asks the beech how he shall grow, nor the lion the horse, how he shall take his prey.
The thankful reciever bears a plentiful harvest.
If others had not been foolish, we should be so.
The soul of sweet delight, can never be defil'd,
When thou seest an Eagle. thou seest a portion of Genius. lift up thy head!
As the caterpiller chooses the fairest leaves to lay her eggs on. so the priest lays his curse on the fairest joys.
To create a little flower is the labour of ages.
Damn. braces. Bless relaxes.
The best wine is the oldest. the best water the newest.
Prayers plow not! Praises reap not!
Joys laugh not! Sorrows weep not!

[Plate 10]

The head Sublime, the heart Pathos, the genitals Beauty. the hands & feet Proportion.
As the air to a bird or the sea to a fish, so is contempt to the contemptible.
The crow wish'd every thing was black, the owl, that every thing was white.
Exuberance is Beauty.
If the lion was advised by the fox. he would be cunning.
Improvent makes strait roads, but the crooked roads without Improvement. are roads of Genius.
Sooner murder an infant in its cradle than nurse unacted desires
Where man is not nature is barren.
Truth can never be told so as to be understood. and not be believ'd.
Enough! or Too much

[Plate 11]

The ancient Poets animated all sensible objects with Gods or Geniuses, calling them by the names and adorning them with the properties of woods, rivers, mountains, lakes, cities, nations, and whatever their enlarged & numerous senses could perceive.

And particularly they studied the genius of each city & country. placing it under its mental deity.

Till a system was formed, which some took advantage of & enslav'd the vulgar by attempting to realize or abstract the mental deities from their objects: thus began Priesthood.

Choosing forms of worship from poetic tales.

And at length they pronounced that the Gods had ordered such things.

Thus men forgot that All deities reside in the human breast.

[Plate 12]

A Memorable Fancy

The Prophets Isaiah and Ezekiel dined with me, and I asked them how they dared so roundly to assert. that God spoke to them; and whether they did not think at the time, that they would be misunderstood, & so be the cause of imposition.

Isaiah answer'd. 'I saw no God. nor heard any, in a finite organical perception; but my senses discover'd the infinite in every thing, and as I was then perswaded. & remain confirm'd; that the voice of honest indignation is the voice of God, I cared not for consequences but wrote'

Then I asked: 'does a firm perswasion that a thing is so, make it so?'

He replied, 'All poets believe that it does. & in ages of imagination this firm perswasion removed mountains; but many are not capable of a firm perswasion of any thing'

Then Ezekiel said. The philosophy of the east taught the first principles of human perception some nations held one principle for the origin & some another, we of Israel taught that the Poetic Genius (as you now call it) was the first principle and all the others merely derivative, which was the cause of our despising the Priests & Philosophers of other countries, and prophecying that all Gods [Plate 13] would at last be proved to originate in ours & to be the tributaries of the Poetic Genius, it was this. that our great poet King David desired so fervently & invokes so patheticly, saying by this he conquers enemies & governs kingdoms; and we so loved our God. that we cursed in his name all the deities of surrounding nations, and asserted that they had rebelled; from these opinions the vulgar came to think that all nations would at last be subject to the jews.

'This' said he, 'like all firm perswasions, is come to pass, for all nations believe the jews code and worship the jews god, and what greater subjection can be'

I heard this with some wonder, & must confess my own conviction. After dinner I ask'd Isaiah to favour the world with his lost works, he said none of equal value was lost. Ezekiel said the same of his.

I also asked Isaiah what made him go naked and barefoot three years? he answered, 'the same that made our friend Diogenes the Grecian.'[1]

I then asked Ezekiel. why he eat dung, & lay so long on his right & left side?[2] he answered. 'the desire of raising other men into a perception of the infinite this the North American tribes practise, & is he honest who resists his genius or conscience. only for the sake of present ease or gratification?'

[Plate 14]

The ancient tradition that the world will be consumed in fire at the end of six thousand years[3] is true. as I have heard from Hell.

For the cherub with his flaming sword is hereby commanded to leave his guard at tree of life, and when he does, the whole creation will be consumed, and appear infinite. and holy whereas it now appears finite & corrupt.

This will come to pass by an improvement of sensual enjoyment.

But first the notion that man has a body distinct from his soul, is to be expunged; this I shall do, by printing in the infernal method, by corrosives, which in Hell are salutary and medicinal, melting apparent surfaces away, and displaying the infinite which was hid.[4]

If the doors of perception were cleansed every thing would appear to man as it is, infinite.

For man has closed himself up, till he sees all things thro' narrow chinks of his cavern.[5]

[Plate 15]

[1] *Diogenes the Grecian* Founder of the Cynic school of philosophers, who advocated and practiced a lifestyle of extreme simplicity. In Isaiah 20.2–3, Isaiah is commanded by the Lord to walk "naked and barefoot" for three years.

[2] *why ... side* As he was instructed by the Lord in Ezekiel 4.4–6.

[3] *The ancient ... years* In Genesis 8.21, just after the Flood, God promises not to destroy the world again. The New Testament, however, contains several prophecies that it will be destroyed, this time by fire (Luke 12.49, 2 Peter 3.5–7). The traditional figure of six thousand years seems to have been obtained by combining the six days it took to make the world (Genesis 1) and the idea "that one day is with the Lord as a thousand years" (2 Peter 3.8).

[4] *this I ... hid* In conventional etching, only the lines of the design are burned away by the acid, the rest of the plate being protected by an acid-proof substance such as wax. In Blake's relief etching process, however, almost the whole surface of the plate is burned away, leaving the lines in relief.

[5] *chinks ... cavern* Cf. the allegory of the cave in Plato, *Republic*, and the image of the camera obscura in John Locke (1632–1704), *An Essay Concerning Human Understanding*.

A Memorable Fancy

I was in a Printing House in Hell & saw the method in which knowledge is transmitted from generation to generation

In the first chamber was a Dragon-Man. clearing away the rubbish from a caves mouth; within, a number of Dragons were hollowing the cave,

In the second chamber was a Viper folding round the rock & the cave, and others adorning it with gold silver and precious stones

In the third chamber was an Eagle with wings and feathers of air, he caused the inside of the cave to be infinite, around were numbers of Eagle like men, who built palaces in the immense cliffs.

In the fourth chamber were Lions of flaming fire raging around & melting the metals into living fluids.

In the fifth chamber were Unnam'd forms, which cast the metals into the expanse.

There they were reciev'd by Men who occupied the sixth chamber, and took the forms of books & were arranged in libraries.

[Plate 16]

The Giants who formed this world into its sensual existence and now seem to live in it in chains, are in truth. the causes of its life & the sources of all activity, but the chains are, the cunning of weak and tame minds. which have power to resist energy. according to the proverb, the weak in courage is strong in cunning.

Thus one portion of being, is the Prolific. the other, the Devouring; to the devourer it seems as if the producer was in his chains, but it is not so, he only takes portions of existence and fancies that the whole.

But the Prolific would cease to be Prolific unless the Devourer as a sea received the excess of his delights.

Some will say, 'Is not God alone the Prolific?' I answer, 'God only Acts & Is. in existing beings or Men.'

These two classes of men are always upon earth. & they should be enemies; whoever tries [Plate 17] to reconcile them seeks to destroy existence.

Religion is an endeavour to reconcile the two.

Note. Jesus Christ did not wish to unite but to seperate them, as in the Parable of sheep and goats![1] & he says 'I came not to send Peace but a Sword.'[2]

Messiah or Satan or Tempter was formerly thought to be one of the Antediluvians[3] who are our Energies.

A Memorable Fancy

An Angel came to me and said. 'O pitiable foolish young man! O horrible! O dreadful state! consider the hot burning dungeon thou art preparing for thyself to all eternity, to which thou art going in such career.'

I said. 'perhaps you will be willing to shew me my eternal lot & we will contemplate together upon it and see whether your lot or mine is most desirable'

So he took me thro' a stable & thro a church & down into the church vault at the end of which was a mill; thro' the mill; we went. and came to a cave. down the winding cavern we groped our tedious way till a void boundless as a nether sky appeard beneath us & we held by the roots of trees and hung over this immensity, but I said,' if you please we will commit ourselves to this void, and see whether providence is here also, if you will not I will?' but he answerd. 'do not presume O young-man but as we here remain behold thy lot which will soon appear when the darkness passes away'

So I remained with him sitting in the twisted [Plate 18] root of an oak. he was suspended in a fungus which hung with the head downward into the deep;

By degrees we beheld the infinite Abyss, fiery as the smoke of a burning city; beneath us at an immense distance was the sun, black but shining round it were fiery tracks on which revolv'd vast spiders. crawling after their prey; which flew or rather swum in the infinite deep, in the most terrific shapes of animals sprung from corruption. & the air was full of them, & seemd composed of them; these are Devils. and are called Powers of the air, I now asked my companion which was my eternal lot? he said, 'between the black & white spiders'

---

1 *Parable ... goats* Cf. Matthew 25.32–46. God divides the nations "as a shepherd divideth his sheep from his goats," placing the sheep, who are to be saved, on his right hand, and the goats, who are damned, on his left.

2 *I ... Sword* From Matthew 10.34.

3 *Antediluvians* Those who existed before the Flood.

But now, from between the black & white spiders a cloud and fire burst and rolled thro' the deep blackning all beneath, so that the nether deep grew black as a sea & rolled with a terrible noise: beneath us was nothing now to be seen but a black tempest, till looking east between the clouds & the waves. we saw a cataract of blood mixed with fire and not many stones throw from us appeard and sunk again the scaly fold of a monstrous serpent at last to the east, distant about three degrees[1] appeard a fiery crest above the waves slowly it reared like a ridge of golden rocks till we discoverd two globes of crimson fire. from which the sea fled away in clouds of smoke, and now we saw, it was the head of Leviathan,[2] his forehead was divided into streaks of green & purple like those on a tygers forehead: soon we saw his mouth & red gills hang just above the raging foam tinging the black deep with beams of blood, advancing toward [Plate 19] us with all the fury of a spiritual existence.

My friend the Angel climb'd up from his station into the mill; I remain'd alone, & then this appearance was no more, but I found myself sitting on a pleasant bank beside a river by moon light hearing a harper who sung to the harp. & his theme was, 'The man who never alters his opinion is like standing water, & breeds reptiles of the mind.'

But I arose. and sought for the mill, & there I found my Angel, who surprised asked me, how I escaped?

I answerd. 'All that we saw was owing to your metaphysics: for when you ran away, I found myself on a bank by moonlight hearing a harper, But now we have seen my eternal lot, shall I shew you yours?' he laughd at my proposal; but I by force suddenly caught him in my arms, & flew westerly thro' the night, till we were elevated above the earths shadow: then I flung myself with him directly into the body of the sun, here I clothed myself in white,[3] & taking in my hand Swedenborgs volumes sunk from the glorious clime, and passed all the planets till we came to saturn, here I staid to rest & then leap'd into the void. between saturn & the fixed stars.[4]

'Here' said I! 'is your lot, in this space, if space it may be calld,' Soon we saw the stable and the church, & I took him to the altar and open'd the Bible, and lo! it was a deep pit, into which I descended driving the Angel before me, soon we saw seven houses of brick,[5] one we entred; in it were a [Plate 20] number of monkeys. baboons, & all of that species chaind by the middle, grinning and snatching at one another. but witheld by the shortness of their chains; however I saw that they sometimes grew numerous, and then the weak were caught by the strong and with a grinning aspect, first coupled with & then devourd, by plucking off first one limb and then another till the body was left a helpless trunk. this after grinning & kissing it with seeming fondness they devourd too; and here & there I saw one savourily picking the flesh off his own tail; as the stench terribly annoyd us both we went into the mill, & I in my hand brought the skeleton of a body, which in the mill was Aristotles Analytics.[6]

So the Angel said: 'thy phantasy has imposed upon me & thou oughtest to be ashamed.'

I answerd: 'we impose on one another, & it is but lost time to converse with you whose works are only Analytics.'

Opposition is True Friendship

[Plate 21]

I have always found that Angels have the vanity to speak of themselves as the only wise; this they do with a confident insolence sprouting from systematic reasoning;

Thus Swedenborg boasts that what he writes is new; tho' it is only the Contents or Index of already publish'd books

[1] *three degrees* Paris is three degrees east of London.

[2] *Leviathan* The beast Leviathan is described in Job 4.1, Psalms 104.26, Isaiah 27.1, Revelation 11.7, 12.9, 13.2, 20.1–3. Blake may also be thinking of Thomas Hobbes's *Leviathan; or, The Matter, Form, and Power of a Commonwealth, Ecclesiastical and Civil.*

[3] *clothed … white* Cf. Revelation 7.9, in which those who have been redeemed are clothed in white when they appear before Christ's throne.

[4] *void … stars* In the Ptolemaic world system, Saturn was the outermost planet, and bordered on the sphere of the fixed stars.

[5] *seven … brick* John addresses the book of Revelation to the "seven churches which are in Asia" (Revelation 1.4).

[6] *Analytics* Aristotle's two treatises on logic.

A man carried a monkey about for a shew. & because he was a little wiser than the monkey, grew vain. and conceiv'd himself as much wiser than seven men. It is so with Swedenborg; he shews the folly of churches & exposes hypocrites, till he imagines that all are religious. & himself the single [Plate 22] one on earth that ever broke a net.

Now hear a plain fact: Swedenborg has not written one new truth: Now hear another: he has written all the old falshoods.

And now hear the reason. He conversed with Angels who are all religious. & conversed not with Devils who all hate religion, for he was incapable thro' his conceited notions.

Thus Swedenborgs writings are a recapitulation of all superficial opinions, and an analysis of the more sublime. but no further.

Have now another plain fact: Any man of mechanical talents may from the writings of Paracelsus or Jacob Behmen,[1] produce ten thousand volumes of equal value with Swedenborg's. and from those of Dante or Shakespear. an infinite number.

But when he has done this, let him not say that he knows better than his master, for he only holds a candle in sunshine.

A Memorable Fancy

Once I saw a Devil in a flame of fire. who arose before an Angel that sat on a cloud. and the Devil uttered these words.

'The worship of God is. Honouring his gifts in other men, each according to his genius. and loving the [Plate 23] greatest men best, those who envy or calumniate great men hate God, for there is no other God.'

The Angel hearing this became almost blue but mastering himself he grew yellow, & at last white pink & smiling, and then replied,

'Thou Idolater, is not God One? & is not he visible in Jesus Christ? and has not Jesus Christ given his sanction to the law of ten commandments and are not all other men fools. sinners, & nothings?'

The Devil answer'd; 'bray a fool in a morter with wheat. yet shall not his folly be beaten out of him:[2] if Jesus Christ is the greatest man. you ought to love him in the greatest degree; now hear how he has given his sanction to the law of ten commandments: did he not mock at the sabbath,[3] and so mock the sabbaths God? murder those who were murderd because of him?[4] turn away the law from the woman taken in adultery?[5] steal the labor of others to support him?[6] bear false witness when he omitted making a defence before Pilate?[7] covet when he pray'd for his disciples, and when he bid them shake off the dust of their feet against such as refused to lodge them?[8] I tell you, no virtue can exist without breaking these ten commandments: Jesus was all virtue, and acted from im pulse.[Plate 24] not from rules.'

When he had so spoken: I beheld the Angel who stretched out his arms embracing the flame of fire & he was consumed and arose as Elijah.[9]

Note. This Angel, who is now become a Devil, is my particular friend: we often read the Bible together in its infernal or diabolical sense which the world shall have if they behave well

I have also: The Bible of Hell:[10] which the world shall have whether they will or no.

One Law for the Lion & Ox is Oppression

—1793

[1] *Paracelsus* Philippus Aureolus, Theophrastus Bombastus von Hohenheim (1493–1541), Swiss physician and alchemist; *Behmen* Jakob Boehme (1575–1624), German mystic.

[2] *bray ... him* Proverbs 27.22. This devil can quote scripture to his purpose; *Bray* Crush.

[3] *mock ... sabbath* In Exodus 20.8–11; Matthew 12.8–12; Mark 2.27, 3.2–4; Luke 14.3–5; John 5.16.

[4] *murder ... him* In Exodus 20.13; see the martyrdom of Stephen (Acts 7.58–60).

[5] *turn ... adultery* In Exodus 20.14; John 8.3–11.

[6] *steal ... him* Cf. Exodus 20.15; Matthew 26.6–13.

[7] *bear ... Pilate* Cf. Exodus 20.16; Matthew 27.11–14; Mark 15.2–5.

[8] *covet ... them* Cf. Exodus 20.17; Matthew 10.14, Luke 9.5.

[9] *who ... Elijah* Cf. 2 Kings 2.11: "There appeared a chariot of fire, and ... Elijah went up by a whirlwind into heaven."

[10] *Bible of Hell* A reference to Blake's own work. In addition to the Proverbs of Hell (plates 7–10), this bible is sometimes said to include such later works as *The [First] Book of Urizen*, *The Book of Ahania*, and *The Book of Los* (1794–95).

THE
MARRIAGE
of
HEAVEN
and
HELL

1

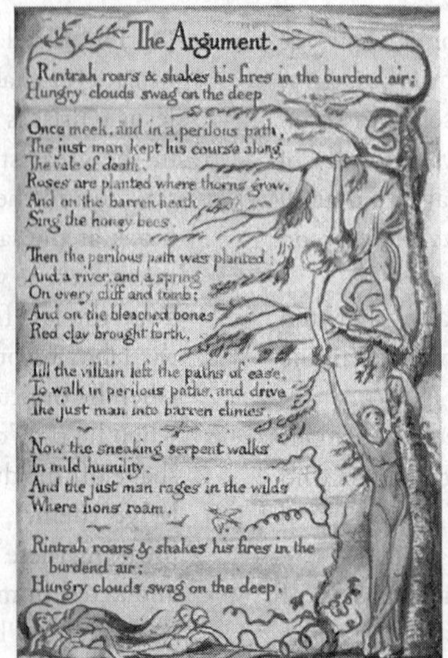

The Argument.

Rintrah roars & shakes his fires in the burdend air;
Hungry clouds swag on the deep

Once meek, and in a perilous path,
The just man kept his course along
The vale of death.
Roses are planted where thorns grow,
And on the barren heath
Sing the honey bees.

Then the perilous path was planted:
And a river, and a spring
On every cliff and tomb;
And on the bleached bones
Red clay brought forth.

Till the villain left the paths of ease,
To walk in perilous paths, and drive
The just man into barren climes.

Now the sneaking serpent walks
In mild humility,
And the just man rages in the wilds
Where lions roam.

Rintrah roars & shakes his fires in the burdend air;
Hungry clouds swag on the deep.

2

3

As a new heaven is begun, and it is now thirty-three years since its advent: the Eternal Hell revives. And lo! Swedenborg is the Angel sitting at the tomb; his writings are the linen clothes folded up. Now is the dominion of Edom, & the return of Adam into Paradise; see Isaiah XXXIV & XXXV Chap:

Without Contraries is no progression. Attraction and Repulsion, Reason and Energy, Love and Hate, are necessary to Human existence.

From these contraries spring what the religious call Good & Evil. Good is the passive that obeys Reason Evil is the active springing from Energy.

Good is Heaven. Evil is Hell.

3

The voice of the Devil

All Bibles or sacred codes, have been the causes of the following Errors.

1. That Man has two real existing principles Viz: a Body & a Soul.

2. That Energy, calld Evil, is alone from the Body, & that Reason, calld Good, is alone from the Soul.

3. That God will torment Man in Eternity for following his Energies.

But the following Contraries to these are True

1. Man has no Body distinct from his Soul for that calld Body is a portion of Soul discernd by the five Senses, the chief inlets of Soul in this age.

2. Energy is the only life and is from the Body and Reason is the bound or outward circumference of Energy.

3. Energy is Eternal Delight.

4

Those who restrain desire, do so because theirs is weak enough to be restrained; and the restrainer or Reason usurps its place & governs the unwilling.

And being restraind it by degrees becomes passive till it is only the shadow of desire.

The history of this is written in Paradise Lost. & the Governor or Reason is calld Messiah.

And the original Archangel or possessor of the command of the heavenly host, is calld the Devil or Satan and his children are calld Sin & Death

But in the Book of Job Miltons Messiah is calld Satan.

For this history has been adopted by both parties

It indeed appeard to Reason as if Desire was cast out. but the Devils account is that the Messi-

5

ah fell. & formed a heaven of what he stole from the Abyss

This is shewn in the Gospel, where he prays to the Father to send the comforter or Desire that Reason may have Ideas to build on, the Jehovah of the Bible being no other than he who dwells in flaming fire. Know that after Christs death, he became Jehovah.

But in Milton; the Father is Destiny, the Son, a Ratio of the five senses. & the Holy-ghost, Vacuum!

Note. The reason Milton wrote in fetters when he wrote of Angels & God, and at liberty when of Devils & Hell, is because he was a true Poet and of the Devils party without knowing it

A Memorable Fancy

As I was walking among the fires of hell, delighted with the enjoyments of Genius; which to Angels look like torment and insanity. I collected some of their Proverbs; thinking that as the sayings used in a nation, mark its character, so the Proverbs of Hell shew the nature of Infernal wisdom better than any description of buildings or garments.

When I came home; on the abyss of the five senses where a flat sided steep frowns over the present world. I saw a mighty Devil folded in black clouds hovering on the sides of the rock, with corro-

6

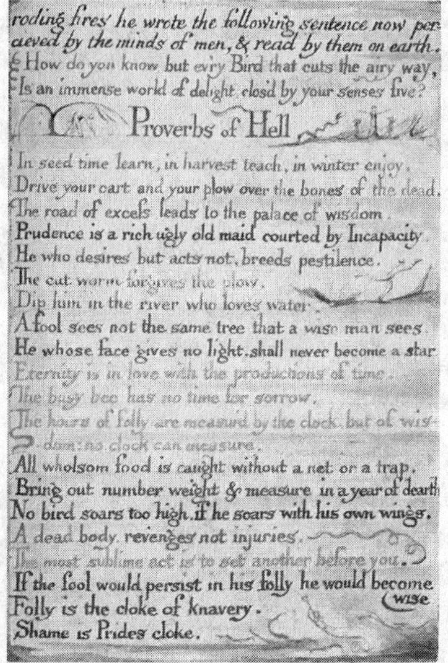
roding fires he wrote the following sentence now perceived by the minds of men, & read by them on earth.
How do you know but evry Bird that cuts the airy way,
Is an immense world of delight, closd by your senses five?
Proverbs of Hell
In seed time learn, in harvest teach, in winter enjoy.
Drive your cart and your plow over the bones of the dead.
The road of excess leads to the palace of wisdom.
Prudence is a rich ugly old maid courted by Incapacity.
He who desires but acts not, breeds pestilence.
The cut worm forgives the plow.
Dip him in the river who loves water.
A fool sees not the same tree that a wise man sees.
He whose face gives no light, shall never become a star.
Eternity is in love with the productions of time.
The busy bee has no time for sorrow.
The hours of folly are measurd by the clock, but of wisdom: no clock can measure.
All wholsom food is caught without a net or a trap.
Bring out number weight & measure in a year of dearth.
No bird soars too high, if he soars with his own wings.
A dead body, revenges not injuries.
The most sublime act is to set another before you.
If the fool would persist in his folly he would become wise
Folly is the cloke of knavery.
Shame is Prides cloke.

7

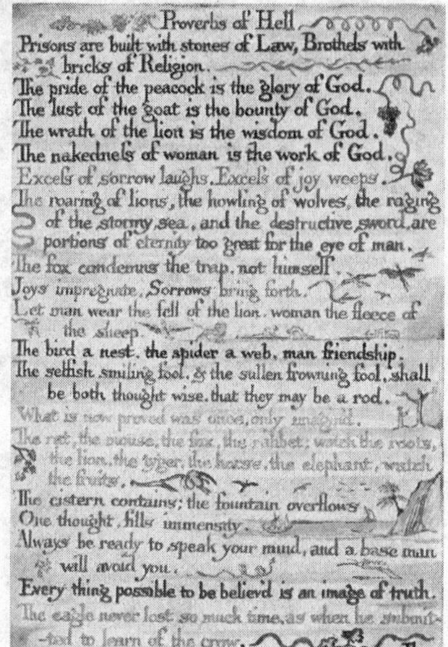
Proverbs of Hell
Prisons are built with stones of Law, Brothels with bricks of Religion.
The pride of the peacock is the glory of God.
The lust of the goat is the bounty of God.
The wrath of the lion is the wisdom of God.
The nakedness of woman is the work of God.
Excess of sorrow laughs. Excess of joy weeps.
The roaring of lions, the howling of wolves, the raging of the stormy sea, and the destructive sword, are portions of eternity too great for the eye of man.
The fox condemns the trap, not himself.
Joys impregnate. Sorrows bring forth.
Let man wear the fell of the lion, woman the fleece of the sheep.
The bird a nest, the spider a web, man friendship.
The selfish smiling fool, & the sullen frowning fool, shall be both thought wise, that they may be a rod.
What is now proved was once, only imagind.
The rat, the mouse, the fox, the rabbet; watch the roots, the lion, the tyger, the horse, the elephant, watch the fruits.
The cistern contains: the fountain overflows.
One thought, fills immensity.
Always be ready to speak your mind, and a base man will avoid you.
Every thing possible to be believd is an image of truth.
The eagle never lost so much time, as when he submitted to learn of the crow.
The

8

Proverbs of Hell
The fox provides for himself, but God provides for the lion.
Think in the morning, Act in the noon, Eat in the evening, Sleep in the night.
He who has sufferd you to impose on him knows you.
As the plow follows words, so God rewards prayers.
The tygers of wrath are wiser than the horses of instruction.
Expect poison from the standing water.
You never know what is enough unless you know what is more than enough.
Listen to the fools reproach! it is a kingly title!
The eyes of fire, the nostrils of air, the mouth of water, the beard of earth.
The weak in courage is strong in cunning.
The apple tree never asks the beech how he shall grow, nor the lion, the horse; how he shall take his prey.
The thankful reciever bears a plentiful harvest.
If others had not been foolish, we should be so.
The soul of sweet delight, can never be defild.
When thou seest an Eagle, thou seest a portion of Genius, lift up thy head!
As the catterpiller chooses the fairest leaves to lay her eggs on, so the priest lays his curse on the fairest joys.
To create a little flower is the labour of ages.
Damn, braces: Bless relaxes.
The best wine is the oldest, the best water the newest.
Prayers plow not! Praises reap not!
Joys laugh not! Sorrows weep not!
The

9

Proverbs of Hell
The head Sublime, the heart Pathos, the genitals Beauty, the hands & feet Proportion.
As the air to a bird or the sea to a fish, so is contempt to the contemptible.
The crow wishd every thing was black, the owl, that every thing was white.
Exuberance is Beauty.
If the lion was advised by the fox, he would be cunning.
Improvent makes strait roads, but the crooked roads without Improvement, are roads of Genius.
Sooner murder an infant in its cradle than nurse unacted desires.
Where man is not nature is barren.
Truth can never be told so as to be understood and not be believd.
Enough! or Too much.

10

The ancient Poets animated all sensible objects with Gods or Geniuses, calling them by the names and adorning them with the properties of woods, rivers, mountains, lakes, cities, nations, and whatever their enlarged & numerous senses could percieve.
And particularly they studied the genius of each city & country, placing it under its mental deity.
Till a system was formed, which some took advantage of & enslavd the vulgar by attempting to realize or abstract the mental deities from their objects: thus began Priesthood.
Choosing forms of worship from poetic tales.
And at length they pronouncd that the Gods had orderd such things.
Thus men forgot that All deities reside in the human breast.

11

A Memorable Fancy.
The Prophets Isaiah and Ezekiel dined with me, and I asked them how they dared so roundly to assert, that God spoke to them; and whether they did not think at the time, that they would be misunderstood, & so be the cause of imposition.
Isaiah answerd, I saw no God, nor heard any, in a finite organical perception; but my senses discoverd the infinite in every thing, and as I was then perswaded, & remain confirmd; that the voice of honest indignation is the voice of God, I cared not for consequences but wrote.
Then I asked: does a firm perswasion that a thing is so, make it so?
He replied, All poets believe that it does, & in ages of imagination this firm perswasion removed mountains; but many are not capable of a firm perswasion of any thing.
Then Ezekiel said, The philosophy of the east taught the first principles of human perception some nations held one principle for the origin & some another, we of Israel taught that the Poetic Genius (as you now call it) was the first principle and all the others merely derivative, which was the cause of our despising the Priests & Philosophers of other countries, and prophecying that all Gods would

12

would at last be proved, to originate in ours & to be the tributaries of the Poetic Genius; it was this. that our great poet King David desired so fervently & invokes so patheticly, saying by this he conquers enemies & governs kingdoms: and we so loved our God. that we cursed in his name all the deities of surrounding nations, and asserted that they had rebelled; from these opinions the vulgar came to think that all nations would at last be subject to the jews.

This said he, like all firm perswasions, is come to pass, for all nations believe the jews code and worship the jews god, and what greater subjection can be

I heard this with some wonder, & must confess my own conviction. After dinner I askd Isaiah to favour the world with his lost works, he said none of equal value was lost. Ezekiel said the same of his.

I also asked Isaiah what made him go naked and barefoot three years? he answerd, the same that made our friend Diogenes the Grecian.

I then asked Ezekiel. why he eat dung, & lay so long on his right & left side? he answerd. the desire of raising other men into a perception of the infinite this the North American tribes practise. & is he honest who resists his genius or conscience. only for the sake of present ease or gratification?

13

The ancient tradition that the world will be consumed in fire at the end of six thousand years is true. as I have heard from Hell.

For the cherub with his flaming sword is hereby commanded to leave his guard at tree of life, and when he does, the whole creation will be consumed, and appear infinite. and holy whereas it now appears finite & corrupt.

This will come to pass by an improvement of sensual enjoyment.

But first the notion that man has a body distinct from his soul, is to be expunged; this I shall do, by printing in the infernal method, by corrosives, which in Hell are salutary and medicinal, melting apparent surfaces away, and displaying the infinite which was hid.

If the doors of perception were cleansed every thing would appear to man as it is: infinite

For man has closed himself up, till he sees all things thro' narrow chinks of his cavern.

14

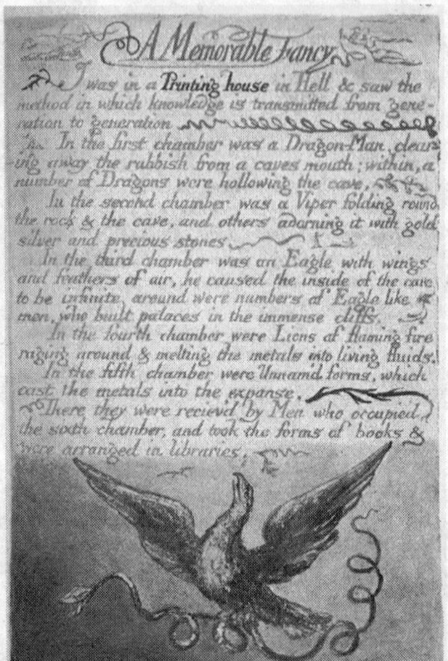

A Memorable Fancy

I was in a Printing house in Hell & saw the method in which knowledge is transmitted from generation to generation.

In the first chamber was a Dragon-Man, clearing away the rubbish from a caves mouth; within, a number of Dragons were hollowing the cave,

In the second chamber was a Viper folding round the rock & the cave, and others adorning it with gold silver and precious stones.

In the third chamber was an Eagle with wings and feathers of air, he caused the inside of the cave to be infinite, around were numbers of Eagle like men, who built palaces in the immense cliffs.

In the fourth chamber were Lions of flaming fire raging around & melting the metals into living fluids.

In the fifth chamber were Unnamd forms, which cast the metals into the expanse.

There they were reciev'd by Men who occupied the sixth chamber, and took the forms of books & were arranged in libraries.

15

The Giants who formed this world into its ensual existence and now seem to live in it n chains; are in truth. the causes of its life s the sources of all activity, but the chains re, the cunning of weak and tame minds. which ave power to resist energy. according to the pro rb, the weak in courage is strong in cunning.

Thus one portion of being, is the Prolific. the ther. the Devouring: to the devourer it seems as f the producer was in his chains, but it is not so, e only takes portions of existence and fancies hat the whole.

But the Prolific would cease to be Prolific nless the Devourer as a sea recieved the excess f his delights.

Some will say, Is not God alone the Prolific? answer, God only Acts & Is, in existing beings r Men.

These two classes of men are always upon arth. & they should be enemies; whoever tries to

16

to reconcile them seeks to destroy existence.

Religion is an endeavour to reconcile the two.

Note. Jesus Christ did not wish to unite but to seperate them, as in the Parable of sheep and goats! & he says I came not to send Peace but a Sword.

Messiah or Satan or Tempter was formerly thought to be one of the Antediluvians who are our Energies.

A Memorable Fancy

An Angel came to me and said. O pitiable foolish young man! O horrible! O dreadful state! consider the hot burning dungeon thou art preparing for thyself to all eternity, to which thou art going in such career.

I said. perhaps you will be willing to shew me my eternal lot & we will contemplate together upon it and see whether your lot or mine is most desirable

So he took me thro' a stable & thro' a church & down into the church vault at the end of which was a mill: thro' the mill we went, and came to a cave. down the winding cavern we groped our tedious way till a void boundless as a nether sky appeard beneath us & we held by the roots of trees and hung over this immensity; but I said, if you please we will commit ourselves to this void, and see whether providence is here also, if you will not I will? but he answerd. do not presume O young-man but as we here remain behold thy lot which will soon appear when the darkness passes away

So I remaind with him sitting in the twisted

17

root of an oak. he was suspended in a fungus which hung with the head downward into the deep:

By degrees we beheld the infinite Abyss, fiery as the smoke of a burning city; beneath us at an immense distance was the sun, black but shining round it were fiery tracks on which revolvd vast spiders, crawling after their prey; which flew or rather swum in the infinite deep, in the most terrific shapes of animals sprung from corruption. & the air was full of them, & seemd composed of them; these are Devils. and are called Powers of the air, I now asked my companion which was my eternal lot? he said, between the black & white spiders

But now, from between the black & white spiders a cloud and fire burst and rolled thro the deep blackning all beneath, so that the nether deep grew black as a sea & rolled with a terrible noise: beneath us was nothing now to be seen but a black tempest, till looking east between the clouds & the waves, we saw a cataract of blood mixed with fire and not many stones throw from us appeard and sunk again the scaly fold of a monstrous serpent. at last to the east, distant about three degrees appeard a fiery crest above the waves. slowly it reared like a ridge of golden rocks till we discoverd two globes of crimson fire, from which the sea fled away in clouds of smoke, and now we saw, it was the head of Leviathan. his forehead was divided into streaks of green & purple like those on a tygers forehead: soon we saw his mouth & red gills hang just above the raging foam tinging the black deep with beams of blood, advancing toward us

18

us with all the fury of a spiritual existence.

My friend the Angel climb'd up from his station into the mill; I remaind alone, & then this appearance was no more, but I found myself sitting on a pleasant bank beside a river by moon light hearing a harper who sung to the harp. & his theme was, The man who never alters his opinion is like standing water, & breeds reptiles of the mind.

But I arose, and sought for the mill, & there I found my Angel, who surprised asked me, how I escaped?

I answerd. All that we saw was owing to your metaphysics: for when you ran away, I found myself on a bank by moonlight hearing a harper, But now we have seen my eternal lot, shall I shew you yours? he laughd at my proposal: but I by force suddenly caught him in my arms, & flew westerly thro' the night, till we were elevated above the earths shadow: then I flung myself with him directly into the body of the sun, here I clothed myself in white, & taking in my hand Swedenborgs volumes sunk from the glorious clime, and passed all the planets till we came to saturn, here I staid to rest & then leap'd into the void, between saturn & the fixed stars.

Here said I! is your lot, in this space, if space it may be calld, Soon we saw the stable and the church, & I took him to the altar and opend the Bible, and lo! it was a deep pit, into which I descended driving the Angel before me, soon we saw seven houses of brick, one we enterd; in it were a num

19

number of monkeys, baboons, & all of that species chaind by the middle, grinning and snatching at one another, but witheld by the shortness of their chains; however I saw that they sometimes grew numerous, and then the weak were caught by the strong and with a grinning aspect, first coupled with & then devourd, by plucking off first one limb and then another till the body was left a helpless trunk. this after grinning & kissing it with seeming fondness they devourd too; and here & there I saw one savourily picking the flesh off of his own tail; as the stench terribly annoyd us both we went into the mill, & I in my hand brought the skeleton of a body, which in the mill was Aristotles Analytics.

So the Angel said: thy phantasy has imposed upon me & thou oughtest to be ashamed.

I answerd: we impose on one another, & it is but lost time to converse with you whose works are only Analytics

20

I have always found that Angels have the vanity to speak of themselves as the only wise; this they do with a confident insolence sprouting from systematic reasoning;

Thus Swedenborg boasts that what he writes is new; tho' it is only the Contents or Index of already publish'd books

A man carried a monkey about for a shew, & because he was a little wiser than the monkey, grew vain, and concievd himself as much wiser than seven men. It is so with Swedenborg; he shews the folly of churches & exposes hypocrites, till he imagines that all are religious, & himself the single one

21

one on earth that ever broke a net.

Now hear a plain fact: Swedenborg has not written one new truth: Now hear another: he has written all the old falshoods.

And now hear the reason. He conversed with Angels who are all religious, & conversed not with Devils who all hate religion, for he was incapable thro' his conceited notions.

Thus Swedenborgs writings are a recapitulation of all superficial opinions, and an analysis of the more sublime, but no further.

Have now another plain fact: Any man of mechanical talents may from the writings of Paracelsus or Jacob Behmen, produce ten thousand volumes of equal value with Swedenborgs. and from those of Dante or Shakespear, an infinite number.

But when he has done this, let him not say that he knows better than his master, for he only holds a candle in sunshine.

A Memorable Fancy

Once I saw a Devil in a flame of fire, who arose before an Angel that sat on a cloud, and the Devil utterd these words.

The worship of God is. Honouring his gifts in other men each according to his genius. and loving the great-

22

greatest men best, those who envy or calumniate great men hate God, for there is no other God.

The Angel hearing this became almost blue but mastering himself he grew yellow, & at last white pink & smiling, and then replied,

Thou Idolater, is not God One? & is not he visible in Jesus Christ? and has not Jesus Christ given his sanction to the law of ten commandments and are not all other men fools, sinners, & nothings?

The Devil answerd; bray a fool in a morter with wheat, yet shall not his folly be beaten out of him: if Jesus Christ is the greatest man, you ought to love him in the greatest degree; now hear how he has given his sanction to the law of ten commandments: did he not mock at the sabbath, and so mock the sabbaths God? murder those who were murderd because of him? turn away the law from the woman taken in adultery? steal the labor of others to support him? bear false witness when he omitted making a defence before Pilate? covet when he pray'd for his disciples, and when he bid them shake off the dust of their feet against such as refused to lodge them? I tell you, no virtue can exist without breaking these ten commandments: Jesus was all virtue, and acted from im-pulse

23

pulse: not from rules.

When he had so spoken: I beheld the Angel who stretched out his arms embracing the flame of fire & he was consumed and arose as Elijah.

Note. This Angel, who is now become a Devil, is my particular friend: we often read the Bible together in its infernal or diabolical sense which the world shall have if they behave well.

I have also: The Bible of Hell: which the world shall have whether they will or no.

24

IN CONTEXT

"A Most Extraordinary Man"

Contemporary documents provide a vivid sense of the degree to which Blake was an extraordinary original. Following are excerpts from a letter written by Charles Lamb to Bernard Barton in 1824, and from a biography by John Thomas Smith of the sculptor Joseph Nollekens, in which Smith published as part of a supplement recollections of Blake, whom he had been acquainted with for some 40 years.

from Charles Lamb, Letter to Bernard Barton,[1] 15 May 1824

Dear B.B.,

... Blake is a real name, I assure you, and a most extraordinary man, if he be still living. He is the Robert Blake whose wild designs accompany a splendid folio edition of the Night Thoughts, which you may have seen, in one of which he pictures the parting of soul and body by a solid mass of human form floating off, God knows how, from a lumpish mass (facsimile to itself) left behind on the dying bed. He paints in water colours, marvellous strange pictures, visions of his brain which he asserts that he has seen. They have great merit. He has *seen* the old Welch bards on Snowdon[2]—he has seen the Beautifullest, the Strongest, and the Ugliest Man, left alone from the Massacre of the Britons by the Romans, and has painted them from memory (I have seen his paintings) and asserts them to be as good as the figures of Raphael and Angelo, but not better, as they had precisely the same retro-visions and prophetic visions with himself. The painters in oil (which he will have it that neither of them practised) he affirms to have been the ruin of art, and affirms that all the while he was engaged in his water-paintings, Titian[3] was disturbing him, Titian the Ill Genius of Oil Painting. His pictures, one in particular, the Canterbury Pilgrims (far above Stothard's),[4] have great merit, but hard, dry, yet with grace. He has written a catalogue of them, with a most spirited criticism on Chaucer, but mystical and full of vision. His poems have been sold hitherto only in manuscript. I never read them, but a friend at my desire procured the Sweep Song. There is one to a Tiger, which I have heard recited, beginning

> Tiger Tiger burning bright
> Thro' the deserts of the night—

[1] *Bernard Barton* Barton had seen a copy of Blake's "The Chimney Sweeper" when Lamb submitted it for publication as part of a project undertaken by the Society for Ameliorating the Condition of Infant Chimney-Sweepers. Barton assumed "Blake" to be a pseudonym of Lamb's. Here Lamb corrects him, though he also gets Blake's first name wrong (Robert was the name of Blake's brother) and confuses Blake's *Night Thoughts* engravings with his engravings for Robert Blair's poem *The Grave*.

[2] *Snowdon* Mountain in northern Wales, under which, according to legend, Arthur and his knights lie sleeping.

[3] *Titian* Italian painter of the sixteenth century.

[4] *Stothard* London painter and engraver.

which is glorious. But alas! I have not the book, for the man is flown, whither I know not, to Hades, or a mad house—but I must look on him as one of the most extraordinary persons of the age....

Yours ever truly,

C.L.

from John Thomas Smith, *Nollekens and His Times* (1828)[1]

Much about this time,[2] Blake wrote many other songs, to which he also composed tunes. These he would occasionally sing to his friends; and though, according to his confession, he was entirely unacquainted with the science of music, his ear was so good that his tunes were sometimes most singularly beautiful, and were noted down by musical professors. As for his later poetry, if it may be so called, attached to his plates, though it was certainly in some parts enigmatically curious as to its application, yet it was not always wholly uninteresting; and I have unspeakable pleasure in being able to state that, though I admit he did not for the last forty years attend any place of divine worship, yet he was not a freethinker,[3] as some invidious detractors have thought proper to assert, nor was he ever in any degree irreligious. Through life, his Bible was every thing with him....

In his choice of subjects, and in his designs in art, perhaps no man had higher claim to originality, nor ever drew with a closer adherence to his own conception; and from what I knew of him, and have heard related by his friends, I most firmly believe few artists have been guilty of less plagiarisms than he. It is true, I have seen him admire and heard him expatiate upon the beauties of Marcantonio and of Albert Dürer;[4] but I verily believe not with any view of borrowing an idea....

After his marriage, which took place at Battersea, and which proved a mutually happy one, he instructed his *beloved,* for so he most frequently called his Kate, and allowed her, till the last moment of his practice, to take off his proof impressions and print his works, which she did most carefully, and ever delighted in the task: nay, she became a draughtswoman; and as a convincing proof that she and her husband were born for each other's comfort, she not only entered cheerfully into his views, but, what is curious, possessed a similar power of imbibing ideas, and has produced drawings equally original, and, in some respects, interesting.

Blake's peace of mind, as well as that of his Catherine, was much broken by the death of their brother Robert,[5] who was a most amicable link in their happiness; and, as a proof how much Blake respected him, whenever he beheld him in his visions, he implicitly attended to his opinion and advice as to his future projected works. I should have stated that Blake was supereminently endowed with the power of disuniting all other thoughts from his mind whenever he wished to indulge in thinking of any particular subject; and so firmly did he believe, by this abstracting power, that the objects of his compositions were before him in his mind's eye, that he frequently believed them to be speaking to him. This I shall now illustrate by the following narrative.

Blake, after deeply perplexing himself as to the mode of accomplishing the publication of his illustrated songs, without their being subject to the expense of letter-press, his brother Robert stood before him in one of his visionary imaginations, and so decidedly directed him in the way in which

---

[1] *Nollekens ... Times* Smith added memoirs of other noted artists such as Blake to his biography of portrait sculptor Joseph Nollekens.

[2] *this time* Around 1780.

[3] *freethinker* One who refuses to allow his or her reason to be dominated by religious faith.

[4] *Marcantonio* Marcantonio Raimondi, a sixteenth-century Italian engraver known for his skill at reproducing pieces of artwork in prints, and for his method of cross-hatching to produce the appearance of depth; *Albert Dürer* Sixteenth-century printmaker and art theorist from Nuremberg.

[5] *death ... Robert* In 1787.

he ought to proceed, that he immediately followed his advice by writing his poetry, and drawing his marginal subjects of embellishments in outline, upon the copper-plate with an impervious liquid, and then eating the plain parts or lights away with aquafortis considerably below them, so that the outlines were left as a stereotype. The plates in this state were then printed in any tint that he wished, to enable him or Mrs. Blake to colour the marginal figures up by hand in imitation of drawings....

Blake and his wife were known to have lived so happily together, that they might unquestionably have been registered at Dunmow.[1] "Their hopes and fears were to each other known," and their days and nights were passed in each other's company, for he always painted, drew, engraved and studied in the same room where they grilled, boiled, stewed, and slept; and so steadfastly attentive was he to his beloved tasks, that for the space of two years he had never once been out of his house; and his application was often so incessant that in the middle of the night he would, after thinking deeply upon a particular subject, leap from his bed and write for two hours or more; and for many years he made a constant practice of lighting the fire and putting on the kettle for breakfast before his Kate awoke.

During his last illness, which was occasioned by the gall mixing with his blood, he was frequently bolstered-up in his bed to complete his drawings, for his intended illustration of Dante; an author so great a favourite with him, that though he agreed with Fuseli and Flaxman[2] in thinking Carey's translation superior to all others, yet, at the age of sixty-three years, he learned the Italian language purposely to enjoy Dante in the highest possible way. For this intended work, he produced seven engraved plates of an imperial quarto size, and nearly one hundred finished drawings of a size considerably larger; which will do equal justice to his wonderful mind, and the liberal heart of their possessor, who engaged him upon so delightful a task at a time when few persons would venture to give him employment, and whose kindness softened, for the remainder of his life, his lingering bodily sufferings, which he was seen to support with the most Christian fortitude.

On the day of his death, August 12th, 1827, he composed and uttered songs to his Maker so sweetly to the ear of his Catherine, that when she stood to hear him, he, looking upon her most affectionately, said, 'My beloved, they are not mine—no—they are not mine.' He expired at six in the evening, with the most cheerful serenity. Some short time before his death, Mrs. Blake asked him where he should like to be buried, and whether he would have the dissenting minister, or the clergyman of the Church of England, to read the service. His answers were, that as far as his own feelings were concerned, they might bury him where she pleased, adding that as his father, mother, aunt, and brother were buried in Bunhill row, perhaps it would be better to lie there, but as to service, he should wish for that of the Church of England.

---

[1] *Dunmow* To this day, the village of Dunmow awards a side of bacon every four years to any couple who can prove that they have lived in complete harmony for a year and a day.

[2] *Fuseli and Flaxman* Henry Fuseli (1741–1825), a painter and art critic, and John Flaxman, an English sculptor and designer (1755–1826).

Mary Robinson

1758 – 1800

Mary Robinson was the author of an extraordinary body of work—groundbreaking poetry, important novels and plays, and influential works of prose non-fiction. Increasingly, she is coming to be recognized as one of the most important writers of the Romantic period. To some extent her genius was recognized in her own time (admirers of her poetry included Samuel Coleridge and William Wordsworth) and certainly her work enjoyed considerable popularity. But both during her lifetime and for several succeeding generations interest in her personal life far exceeded interest in her literary work. The wife of a husband so profligate that he at one point forced his entire family into debtors' prison, Robinson became an independent woman who supported herself through writing and acting. Eventually she also became the acknowledged mistress of some of the leading men of the day, including the future king of England. Inevitably, her independent behavior became fuel for gossip—but her battle to support herself also provided fuel for her non-fiction writings that argued against the subordination of women.

Mary Darby was born in Bristol in 1758, the third of five children. Her father was a naval captain who soon deserted the family, supporting them only sporadically thereafter. Their strained finances led to an irregular education for the young girl. She was taught some Latin, French, and Italian, and for a time she attended school. She was forced to help support the family by teaching English in a school her mother had opened. In 1774, at the age of 15, she was duped into marrying Thomas Robinson, whom she believed to be a man of means. It was only after the marriage had taken place that she found out that he was the illegitimate son of a man who had made no promises to leave him any inheritance. Robinson was in serious financial straits, and the couple had to flee London to Wales to escape his creditors. It was there that their daughter Mary was born later that year. Creditors soon caught up with them, however, forcing the family to reside in King's Bench prison for 15 months. While in prison Robinson began composing poetry, in part to raise funds. The resulting volume, *Captivity, A Poem* (1775), prompted the Duchess of Devonshire to become her patron.

On her release Robinson began to work in the theater to support herself. She made her acting debut as Shakespeare's Juliet and was on the stage for four years, garnering considerable fame. She also began to write for the stage and in 1778 played a role in one of her own plays, *The Lucky Escape*. In 1779, she became known as "the exquisite Perdita" for her role in *A Winter's Tale*. After seeing her performance, the young Prince of Wales requested an audience and soon was insisting she become his mistress (she was then separated from her husband). During this period of her life she was more notorious for her relationship with the Prince than she was renowned for her writing, and the press and cartoonists had a field day with the very public affair: "The Perdita is a prodigious fine clean bottomed vessel, and had taken many prizes during her cruise, particularly the Florizel [i.e., the Prince], a most valuable ship belonging to the Crown, but which was immediately released, after taking out the cargo."

Robinson became the mistress of other men—most notably Banastre Tarleton, a distinguished but dissolute officer—in subsequent years, and she returned to writing to support herself. In the early 1790s she published a substantial amount of non-fiction prose, two books of poetry, several plays, and six novels, supporting herself, her mother, and her young daughter (and often Tarleton) on the proceeds. Novels such as *Vancenza* (1792), *The Widow* (1794), *Angelina* (1796), and *Walsingham* (1797) were lucrative and popular, and went through many editions as well as translations into German and French.

Robinson's poetry came to be seen as embodying the characteristics of the Della Cruscan movement. Here is how those characteristics were described in a July 1791 notice reviewing Robinson's first volume of poems in the *Critical Review*:

> Within a very few years, a race of versifiers has sprung up, determined to claim ... the merit of novelty in expression, in unusual figure and striking combination. Rejecting the accustomed modes of description and phraseology, these fastidious writers seem fond of introducing uncommon terms and ideas, to provoke attention and excite admiration.

It is an interesting reflection of the times that these comments were intended to be taken as highly *critical* of the Della Cruscan School. Subsequent generations, when they did not ignore the Della Cruscans altogether, also tended to deride them for what was claimed to be a tendency toward poetic extravagance and emotional excess. Not all eras respond negatively to "novelty in expression, in unusual figure and striking combination," however, and the theatricality of Della Cruscan verse has in recent years begun to excite critical interest and admiration rather than ridicule. Moreover, it has increasingly come to be recognized that, above and beyond the element of theatricality in Robinson's verse, the feelings conveyed by it are powerful and convincing; she is among the leading poets of sensibility—of intelligent feeling and of intellect.

Nowhere in Robinson's poetry is that union more powerfully expressed than in her 1796 volume *Sappho and Phaon*, a sequence of 44 sonnets that offer an expressive treatment of the story of the legendary Greek poet from the Island of Lesbos who fell desperately in love with Phaon and leapt from a cliff to her death after he abandoned her. The sequence provides an extended passionate discourse on the themes of reason and passion, love and art.

Robinson's last collection was a volume she described as consisting "of Tales, serious and gay, on a variety of subjects in the manner of Wordsworth's Lyrical Ballads." There are indeed close links between the two volumes; Robinson's "All Alone" parallels Wordsworth's "We Are Seven," her "Golfre" parallels Coleridge's "Rime of the Ancient Mariner," and so on. It would be a mistake, however, to regard the tales merely as derivative. Less bucolic than those of Wordsworth, they are more closely in touch with life's often grim realities. They are also in some respects more political; certainly "The Negro Girl" is a notable expression of abolitionist as well as of romantic sentiment. Robinson's strongest political statements, however, were on the subject of gender equality. In *A Letter to the Women of England of England, on the Injustice of the Marital Insubordination* (1791, published originally under the pseudonym Anne Francis Randall), she argued strongly and persuasively against the oppression of women through marriage.

Robinson suffered ill health in her last 15 years, and although she published *Lyrical Tales* in 1800, by the spring she was too ill to write, and she died later that year. Her unfinished memoirs were published by her daughter after her death.

⌘⌘⌘

January, 1795

1

Pavement slip'ry; people sneezing;
Lords in ermine, beggars freezing;
Nobles, scarce the wretched heeding;
Gallant soldiers—fighting!—bleeding!

2

Lofty mansions, warm and spacious;
Courtiers, cringing and voracious:
Titled gluttons, dainties carving;
Genius, in a garret, starving!

3

Wives, who laugh at passive spouses;
Theatres, and meeting-houses;
Balls, where simp'ring misses languish;
Hospitals, and groans of anguish.

4

Arts and sciences bewailing;
Commerce drooping, credit failing!
Placemen,[1] mocking subjects loyal;
Separations; weddings royal!

5

Authors, who can't earn a dinner;
Many a subtle° rogue, a winner! *crafty*
Fugitives, for shelter seeking,
Misers hoarding, tradesmen breaking!

6

Ladies gambling, night and morning;
Fools, the works of genius scorning!
Ancient dames for girls mistaken,
Youthful damsels—quite forsaken!

7

Some in luxury delighting;
More in talking than in fighting;
Lovers old, and beaux decrepit;
Lordlings, empty and insipid.

8

Poets, painters, and musicians;
Lawyers, doctors, politicians;
Pamphlets, newspapers, and odes,
Seeking fame, by diff'rent roads.

9

Taste and talents quite deserted;
All the laws of Truth perverted;
Arrogance o'er merit soaring!
Merit, silently deploring!

10

Gallant souls with empty purses;
Gen'rals, only fit for nurses!
Schoolboys, smit with martial spirit,
Taking place of vet'ran merit!

11

Honest men, who can't get place;
Knaves, who show unblushing faces;
Ruin hasten'd, peace retarded!
Candour spurn'd, and art° rewarded. *artifice*

—1795

from *Sappho and Phaon: In a Series of Legitimate Sonnets, with Thoughts on Poetical Subjects, and Anecdotes of the Grecian Poetess*

4

Why, when I gaze on Phaon's[2] beauteous eyes,
Why does each thought in wild disorder stray?
Why does each fainting faculty decay,
And my chill'd breast in throbbing tumults rise?
Mute, on the ground my lyre neglected lies,
The Muse forgot, and lost the melting lay;[3]
My down-cast looks, my faltering lips betray,

[1] *Placemen* Men appointed to positions of power, often because of self-interested motives.

[2] *Phaon* Boatman with whom Sappho was said to be in love.

[3] *melting lay* Touching song.

That stung by hopeless passion, Sappho[1] dies!
Now, on a bank of cypress[2] let me rest;
Come, tuneful maids, ye pupils of my care,[3]
Come, with your dulcet numbers soothe my breast;
And, as the soft vibrations float on air,
Let pity waft my spirit to the blest,
To mock the barb'rous triumphs of despair!

12

Now, o'er the tessellated pavement[4] strew
Fresh saffron, steep'd in essence of the rose,
While down yon agate column gently flows
A glitt'ring streamlet of ambrosial[5] dew!
My Phaon smiles! the rich carnation's hue,
On his flush'd cheek in conscious lustre glows,
While o'er his breast enamour'd Venus[6] throws
Her starry mantle of celestial blue!
Breathe soft, ye dulcet flutes, among the trees
Where clust'ring boughs with golden citron twine;
While slow vibrations, dying on the breeze,
Shall soothe his soul with harmony divine!
Then let my form his yielding fancy seize,
And all his fondest wishes, blend with mine.

18

Why art thou chang'd? O Phaon! tell me why?
Love flies reproach, when passion feels decay;
Or, I would paint the raptures of that day,
When, in sweet converse, mingling sigh with sigh,
I mark'd the graceful languor of thine eye
As on a shady bank entranc'd we lay:
O! Eyes! whose beamy radiance stole away
As stars fade trembling from the burning sky!
Why art thou chang'd? dear source of all my woes?
Though dark my bosom's tint, through ev'ry vein
A ruby tide of purest lustre flows,
Warm'd by thy love, or chill'd by thy disdain;
And yet no bliss this sensate being knows;
Ah! why is rapture so allied to pain?

30

O'er the tall cliff that bounds the billowy main
Shad'wing the surge that sweeps the lonely strand,° *shore*
While the thin vapours break along the sand,
Day's harbinger unfolds the liquid plain.
The rude sea murmurs, mournful as the strain
That love-lorn minstrels strike with trembling hand,
While from their green beds rise the Siren band[7]
With tongues aerial° to repeat my pain! *ethereal*
The vessel rocks beside the pebbly shore,
The foamy curls its gaudy trappings lave;° *wash*
Oh! Bark[8] propitious! bear me gently o'er,
Breathe soft, ye winds; rise slow, O! swelling wave!
Lesbos;[9] these eyes shall meet thy sands no more:
I fly, to seek my lover, or my grave!

37

When, in the gloomy mansion of the dead,
This with'ring heart, this faded form shall sleep:
When these fond[10] eyes, at length shall cease to weep,
And earth's cold lap receive this fev'rish head:
Envy shall turn away, a tear to shed,
And Time's obliterating pinions° sweep *feathers*
The spot, where poets shall their vigils keep,
To mourn and wander near my freezing bed!
Then, my pale ghost, upon th' Elysian shore,[11]
Shall smile, releas'd from ev'ry mortal care;
While, doom'd love's victim to repine° no more, *complain*

[1] *Sappho* In Roman legend, the poet Sappho (630 BCE) was Phaon's lover. When he rejected her, she threw herself off a cliff and into the sea and drowned.

[2] *cypress* Cypress was a symbol of mourning.

[3] *tuneful maids … care* According to legend, Sappho was head of a girls' school.

[4] *tessellated pavement* Paving stones arranged like a mosaic.

[5] *ambrosial* Ambrosia is the drink of the gods.

[6] *Venus* Roman goddess of love.

[7] *Siren band* Mythological sea nymphs who lured sailors to their deaths with their enchanting singing.

[8] *Bark* Small ship.

[9] *Lesbos* Island in the Aegean sea; home of Sappho.

[10] *fond* Infatuated, foolish.

[11] *Elysian shore* In Greek mythology, Elysium was a section of the underworld where virtuous souls went after death.

My breast shall bathe in endless rapture there!
Ah! no! my restless shade would still deplore,
Nor taste that bliss, which Phaon did not share.
—1796

The Haunted Beach

Upon a lonely desert beach
Where the white foam was scatter'd,
A little shed uprear'd its head
Though lofty barks[1] were shatter'd.
The seaweeds gathering near the door,
A sombre path display'd;
And, all around, the deafening roar,
Re-echo'd on the chalky shore,
By the green billows° made. *waves*

Above, a jutting cliff was seen
Where sea birds hover'd, craving;
And all around, the crags were bound
With weeds, forever waving.
And here and there, a cavern wide
Its shad'wy jaws display'd;
And near the sand, at ebb of tide,
A shiver'd mast was seen to ride
Where the green billows stray'd.

And often, while the morning wind
Stole o'er the summer ocean,
The moonlight scene was all serene,
The waters scarce in motion:
Then, while the smoothly slanting sand
The tall cliff wrapp'd in shade,
The fisherman beheld a band
Of spectres,° gliding hand in hand, *ghosts*
Where the green billows play'd.

And pale their faces were, as snow,
And sullenly they wander'd;
And to the skies, with hollow eyes
They look'd, as tho' they ponder'd.
And sometimes from their hammock shroud,[2]
They dismal howlings made,
And while the blast blew strong and loud
The clear moon mark'd the ghastly crowd,
Where the green billows play'd!

And then, above the haunted hut
The curlews,[3] screaming, hover'd;
And the low door with furious roar
The frothy breakers cover'd.
For, in the fisherman's lone shed
A murder'd man was laid,
With ten wide gashes on his head
And deep was made his sandy bed
Where the green billows played.

A shipwreck'd mariner was he,
Doom'd from his home to sever;
Who swore to be thro' wind and sea
Firm and undaunted ever!
And when the wave resistless roll'd,
About his arm he made
A packet rich of Spanish gold,
And, like a British sailor, bold,
Plung'd where the billows play'd!

The spectre band, his messmates brave
Sunk in the yawning ocean,
While to the mast he lash'd him fast
And brav'd the storm's commotion.
The winter moon, upon the sand
A silv'ry carpet made,
And mark'd the sailor reach the land,
And mark'd his murd'rer wash his hand
Where the green billows play'd.

And since that hour the fisherman
Has toil'd, and toil'd in vain!
For all the night, the moony light
Gleams on the specter'd main!
And when the skies are veil'd in gloom,

[1] *barks* Small ships.

[2] *hammock shroud* Hammocks were used as shrouds to bury corpses at sea.

[3] *curlews* Long-legged seabirds, similar to sandpipers.

The murd'rer's liquid way
Bounds o'er the deeply yawning tomb,
And flashing fires the sands illume,
Where the green billows play!

Full thirty years his task has been,
Day after day, more weary;
For heav'n design'd his guilty mind
Should dwell on prospects dreary.
Bound by a strong and mystic chain,
He has not power to stray;
But destin'd mis'ry to sustain,
He wastes, in solitude and pain,
A loathsome life away.

—1800

All Alone

I

Ah! wherefore by the Church-yard side,
Poor little LORN ONE, dost thou stray?
Thy wavy locks but thinly hide
The tears that dim thy blue-eye's ray;
And wherefore dost thou sigh, and moan,
And weep, that thou art left alone?

II

Thou art not left alone, poor boy,
The Trav'ller stops to hear thy tale;
No heart, so hard, would thee annoy!
For tho' thy mother's cheek is pale
And withers under yon grave stone,
Thou art not, Urchin, left alone.

III

I know thee well! thy yellow hair
In silky waves I oft have seen;
Thy dimpled face, so fresh and fair,
Thy roguish smile, thy playful mien
Were all to me, poor Orphan, known,
Ere Fate had left thee—all alone!

IV

Thy russet coat is scant, and torn,
Thy cheek is now grown deathly pale!
Thy eyes are dim, thy looks forlorn,
And bare thy bosom meets the gale;
And oft I hear thee deeply groan,
That thou, poor boy, art left alone.

V

Thy naked feet are wounded sore
With naked thorns, that cross thy daily road;
The winter winds around thee roar,
The church-yard is thy bleak abode;
Thy pillow now, a cold grave stone—
And there thou lov'st to grieve—alone!

VI

The rain has drench'd thee, all night long;
The nipping frost thy bosom froze;
And still, the yew-tree shades among,
I heard thee sigh thy artless woes;
I heard thee, till the day-star shone
In darkness weep—and weep alone!

VII

Oft have I seen thee, little boy,
Upon thy lovely mother's knee;
For when she liv'd—thou wert her joy,
Though now a mourner thou must be!
For she lies low, where yon grave-stone
Proclaims, that thou art left alone.

VIII

Weep, weep no more; on yonder hill
The village bells are ringing, gay;
The merry reed, and brawling rill° *stream*
Call thee to rustic sports away.
Then wherefore weep, and sigh, and moan,
A truant from the throng—alone?

IX

"I cannot the green hill ascend,
I cannot pace the upland mead;
I cannot in the vale attend,
To hear the merry-sounding reed:
For all is still, beneath yon stone,
Where my poor mother's left alone!

original spelling

original spelling

X

I cannot gather gaudy flowers
To dress the scene of revels loud—
I cannot pass the ev'ning hours
Among the noisy village croud—
For, all in darkness, and alone
My mother sleeps, beneath yon stone.

XI

See how the stars begin to gleam
The sheep-dog barks, 'tis time to go;—
The night-fly hums, the moonlight beam
Peeps through the yew-trees' shadowy row -
It falls upon the white grave-stone,
Where my dear mother sleeps alone.—

XII

O stay me not, for I must go
The upland path in haste to tread;
For there the pale primroses grow
They grow to dress my mother's bed.—
They must, ere peep of day, be strown,
Where she lies mould'ring all alone.

original spelling

XIII

My father o'er the stormy sea
To distant lands was borne away,
And still my mother stay'd with me
And wept by night and toil'd by day.
And shall I ever quit the stone
Where she is left, to sleep alone.

XIV

My father died, and still I found
My mother fond and kind to me;
I felt her breast with rapture bound
When first I prattled on her knee—
And then she blest my infant tone
And little thought of yon grave-stone.

XV

No more her gentle voice I hear,
No more her smile of fondness see;
Then wonder not I shed the tear
She would have DIED, to follow me!
And yet she sleeps beneath yon stone
And I STILL LIVE—to weep alone.

XVI

The playful kid, she lov'd so well
From yon high clift was seen to fall;
I heard, afar, his tink'ling bell—
Which seem'd in vain for aid to call—
I heard the harmless suff'rer moan,
And griev'd that he was left alone.

XVII

Our faithful dog grew mad, and died,
The lightning smote our cottage low—
We had no resting-place beside
And knew not whither we should go—
For we were poor,—and hearts of stone
Will never throb at mis'ry's groan.

original spelling

XVIII

My mother still surviv'd for me,
She led me to the mountain's brow,
She watch'd me, while at yonder tree
I sat, and wove the ozier[1] bough;
And oft she cried, "fear not, MINE OWN!
Thou shalt not, BOY, be left ALONE."

XIX

The blast blew strong, the torrent rose
And bore our shatter'd cot° away; *hut*
And, where the clear brook swiftly flows—
Upon the turf at dawn of day,
When bright the sun's full lustre shone,
I wander'd, FRIENDLESS—and ALONE!"

XX

Thou art not, boy, for I have seen
Thy tiny footsteps print the dew.
And while the morning sky serene
Spread o'er the hill a yellow hue,
I heard thy sad and plaintive moan,
Beside the cold sepulchral stone.

[1] *ozier* Willow tree with flexible branches, frequently used for basket weaving.

original spelling

XXI

And when the summer noontide hours
With scorching rays the landscape spread,
I mark'd thee, weaving fragrant flow'rs
To deck thy mother's silent bed!
Nor, at the church-yard's simple stone,
Wert, thou, poor Urchin, left alone.

XXII

I follow'd thee, along the dale
And up the woodland's shad'wy way:
I heard thee tell thy mournful tale
As slowly sunk the star of day:
Nor, when its twinkling light had flown,
Wert thou a wand'rer, all alone.

XXIII

"O! yes, I was! and still shall be
A wand'rer, mourning and forlorn;
For what is all the world to me—
What are the dews and buds of morn?
Since she, who left me sad, alone
In darkness sleeps, beneath yon stone!

XXIV

No brother's tear shall fall for me,
For I no brother ever knew;
No friend shall weep my destiny
For *friends* are scarce, and *tears* are few;
None do *I* see, save on this stone
Where I will stay, and weep alone!

XXV

My Father never will return,
He rests beneath the sea-green wave;
I have no kindred left, to mourn
When I am hid in yonder grave!
Not one! to dress with flow'rs the stone;—
Then— *surely,* I AM LEFT ALONE!"

—1800

London's Summer Morning

Who has not wak'd to list° the busy sounds *hear*
Of summer's morning, in the sultry smoke
Of noisy London? On the pavement hot
The sooty chimney-boy, with dingy face
And tatter'd covering, shrilly bawls his trade,
Rousing the sleepy housemaid. At the door
The milk-pail rattles, and the tinkling bell
Proclaims the dustman's[1] office; while the street
Is lost in clouds impervious. Now begins
The din of hackney-coaches,[2] wagons, carts;
While tinmen's shops, and noisy trunk-makers,
Knife-grinders, coopers, squeaking cork-cutters,
Fruit-barrows, and the hunger-giving cries
Of vegetable vendors, fill the air.
Now ev'ry shop displays its varied trade,
And the fresh-sprinkled pavement cools the feet
Of early walkers. At the private door
The ruddy house-maid twirls the busy mop,
Annoying the smart 'prentice,° or neat girl *apprentice*
Tripping with band-box[3] lightly. Now the sun
Darts burning splendor on the glitt'ring pane,
Save where the canvas awning throws a shade
On the gay merchandise. Now, spruce and trim,
In shops (where beauty smiles with industry)
Sits the smart damsel; while the passenger
Peeps through the window, watching ev'ry charm.
Now pastry dainties catch the eyes minute
Of humming insects, while the slimy snare
Waits to enthral them. Now the lamp-lighter
Mounts the slight ladder, nimbly venturous,
To trim the half-fill'd lamp; while at his feet
The pot-boy[4] yells discordant! All along
The sultry pavement, the old-clothes-man cries
In tone monotonous, and side-long views
The area for his traffic: now the bag
Is slyly open'd, and the half-worn suit
(Sometimes the pilfer'd treasure of the base

[1] *dustman* Garbage collector.

[2] *hackney-coaches* Horse-drawn carriages for hire.

[3] *band-box* Box for collars, hats, gloves, and other items.

[4] *pot-boy* Boy employed by a tavern to bring beer to customers at their tables.

Domestic spoiler)[1] for one half its worth,
Sinks in the green abyss. The porter now
Bears his huge load along the burning way;
And the poor poet wakes from busy dreams,
To paint the summer morning.
—1804

from *A Letter to the Women of England*

Custom, from the earliest periods of antiquity, has endeavoured to place the female mind in the subordinate ranks of intellectual sociability. WOMAN has ever been considered as a lovely and fascinating part of the creation, but her claims to mental equality have not only been questioned, by envious and interested sceptics; but, by a barbarous policy in the other sex, considerably depressed, for want of liberal and classical cultivation. I will not expatiate largely on the doctrines of certain philosophical sensualists, who have aided in this destructive oppression, because an illustrious British female, (whose death has not been sufficiently lamented, but to whose genius posterity will render justice) has already written volumes in vindication of *The Rights of Woman*.[2] But I shall endeavour to prove that, under the present state of mental subordination, universal knowledge is not only benumbed and blighted, but true happiness, originating in enlightened manners, retarded in its progress. Let WOMAN once assert her proper sphere, unshackled by prejudice, and unsophisticated by vanity; and pride (the noblest species of pride), will establish her claims to the participation of power, both mentally and corporeally. …

In what is woman inferior to man? In some instances, but not always, in corporeal strength; in activity of mind, she is his equal. Then, by this rule, if she is to endure oppression in proportion as she is deficient in muscular power *only*, through all the stages of animation the weaker should give precedence to the stronger. Yet we should find a Lord of the Creation with a puny frame, reluctant to confess the superiority of a lusty peasant girl whom nature had endowed with that bodily strength of which luxury had bereaved him.

The question is simply this: is woman persecuted and oppressed because she is the *weaker* creature? Supposing that to be the order of Nature, let me ask these human despots whether a woman of strong mental and corporeal powers is born to yield obedience, merely because she is a woman, to those shadows of mankind who exhibit the effeminacy of women united with the mischievous foolery of monkeys? I remember once to have heard one of those modern Hannibals[3] confess that he had changed his regiments three times because the regimentals were unbecoming.

If woman be the weaker creature, why is she employed in laborious avocations? Why compelled to endure the fatigue of household drudgery; to scrub, to scour, to labour, both late and early, while the powdered lackey only waits at the chair, or behind the carriage of his employer? Why are women, in many parts of the kingdom, permitted to follow the plough; to perform the laborious business of the dairy; to work in our manufactories; to wash, to brew, and to bake, while men are employed in measuring lace and ribands; folding gauzes; composing artificial bouquets; fancying feathers, and mixing cosmetics for the preservation of beauty? I have seen, and every inhabitant of the metropolis may, during the summer season, behold strong Welsh girls carrying on their heads strawberries, and other fruits from the vicinity of London to Covent-Garden market, in heavy loads which they repeat three, four, and five times, daily, for a very small pittance; while the male domestics of our nobility are revelling in luxury, to which even their lords are strangers. Are women thus compelled to labour, because they are of the weaker sex? In my travels some years since through France and Germany, I often remember having seen stout girls, from the age of seventeen to twenty-five, employed in

[1] *base / Domestic spoiler* Unscrupulous thieving servant.

[2] [Robinson's note] The writer of this letter, though avowedly of the same school, disdains the drudgery of servile imitation. The same subject may be argued in a variety of ways; and though this letter may not display the philosophical reasoning with which "The Rights of Woman" abounded; it is not less suited to the purpose. For it requires a *legion of Wollstonecrafts* to undermine the poisons of prejudice and malevolence. [See chapter 2 of Mary Wollstonecraft's *A Vindication of the Rights of Woman* for a discussion of the dangers male philosophies posed to women.]

[3] *Hannibal* Fearless Carthaginian general of the Second Punic War.

the most fatiguing and laborious avocations; such as husbandry,[1] watering horses, and sweeping the public streets. Were they so devoted to toil because they were the weaker creatures? and would not a modern *petit maître*[2] have fainted beneath the powerful grasp of one of these rustic or domestic Amazons?[3] ...

It is not by precept but by example that conviction strikes deeply into the thinking mind. Man is supposed to be the more wise and more rational creature; his faculties are more liberally expanded by classical education; he is supposed to be more enlightened by an unlimited intercourse with society. He is permitted to assert the dignity of his character, to punish those who assail his reputation, and to assume a superiority over all his fellow creatures. He is not accountable to any mortal for the actions of his life; he may revel in the follies, indulge the vices of his superior nature. He pursues the pleasures or the eccentricities of his imagination with an avidity insatiable, and he perpetually proves that human passions subjugate him to the degradations of human frailty; while woman, the *weaker* animal, she whose enjoyments are limited, whose education, knowledge, and actions are circumscribed by the potent rule of prejudice, she is expected to *resist* temptation; to be invincible in fortitude, strong in prescient and reflecting powers, subtle in the defence of her own honor, and forbearing under all the conflicts of the passions. Man first degrades, and then deserts her. Yet, if driven by famine, insult, shame, and persecution, she rushes forth like the wolf for prey; if, like Millwood, she finds it "necessary to be rich" in this sordid, selfish world,[4] she is shunned, abhorred, condemned to the very lowest scenes of vile debasement; to exist in misery, or to perish unlamented. No kindred breast will pity her misfortunes; no pious tear embalm her ashes: she rushes into the arms of death as her last, her only, asylum from the monsters who have destroyed her.

Woman is destined to pursue no path in which she does not find an enemy. If she is liberal, generous, careless of wealth, friendly to the unfortunate, and bountiful to persecuted merit, she is deemed prodigal, and over-much profuse; all the good she does, every tear she steals from the downcast eye of modest worth, every sigh she converts into a throb of joy, in grateful bosoms, is, by the world, forgotten; while the ingenuous liberality of her soul excites the imputation of folly and extravagance. If, on the contrary, she is wary, shrewd, thrifty, economical, and eager to procure and to preserve the advantages of independence, she is condemned as narrow-minded, mean, unfeeling, artful, mercenary, and base: in either case she is exposed to censure. If liberal, unpitied; if sordid, execrated! In a few words, a generous woman is termed a fool; a prudent one, a miser. ...

Had fortune enabled me, I would build an university for women, where they should be politely, and at the same time classically, educated; the depth of their studies should be proportioned to their mental powers; and those who were incompetent to the labours of knowledge should be dismissed after a fair trial of their capabilities and allotted to the more humble paths of life, such as domestic and useful occupations. The wealthy part of the community who neglected to educate their female offspring at this seminary of learning should pay a fine, which should be appropriated to the maintenance of the unportioned scholars. In half a century there would be a sufficient number of learned women to fill all the departments of the university, and those who excelled in an eminent degree should receive honorary medals, which they should wear as an Order of Literary Merit.

O! my unenlightened country-women! Read, and profit, by the admonition of Reason. Shake off the trifling, glittering shackles which debase you. Resist those fascinating spells, which, like the petrifying torpedo,[5] fasten on your mental faculties. Be less the

[1] *husbandry* Farming; agricultural labor.

[2] *petit maître* French: little master, i.e., dandy, fop.

[3] *Amazons* Mythical race of female warriors.

[4] *if... world* Reference to George Lillo's play *The London Merchant* (1731), in which Millwood seduces a young merchant's apprentice and convinces him first to steal money from his master, and then to kill his uncle and steal his fortune for her. In Act 4, she explains her actions by saying, "My soul disdained, and yet disdains, dependence and contempt. Riches, no matter by what means obtained, I saw secured the worst of men from both. I found it, therefore, necessary to be rich, and to that end I summoned all my arts."

[5] *torpedo* Type of flat fish now more commonly referred to as the electric ray.

slaves of vanity, and more the converts of Reflection. Nature has endowed you with personal attractions: she has also given you the mind capable of expansion. Seek not the visionary triumph of universal conquest; know yourselves equal to greater, nobler, acquirements: and by prudence, temperance, firmness, and reflection, subdue that prejudice which has, for ages past, been your inveterate enemy. Let your daughters be liberally, classically, philosophically, and usefully educated; let them speak and write their opinions freely; let them read and think like rational creatures, adapt their studies to their strength of intellect, expand their minds, and purify their hearts, by teaching them to feel their mental equality with their imperious rulers. By such laudable exertions you will excite the noblest emulation; you will explode the superstitious tenets of bigotry and fanaticism, confirm the intuitive immortality of the soul, and give them that genuine glow of conscious virtue which will grace them to posterity.

There are men who affect to think lightly of the literary productions of women: and yet no works of the present day are so universally read as theirs. The best novels that have been written since those of Smollett, Richardson, and Fielding[1] have been produced by women; and their pages have not only been embellished with the interesting events of domestic life, portrayed with all the elegance of phraseology and all the refinement of sentiment, but with forcible and eloquent political, theological, and philosophical reasoning. To the genius and labours of some enlightened British women posterity will also be indebted for the purest and best translations from the French and German languages. I need not mention Mrs. Dobson, Mrs. Inchbald, Miss Plumptre,[2] &c., &c. Of the more profound researches in the dead languages, we have many female classics of the first celebrity: Mrs. Carter, Mrs. Thomas (late Miss Parkhurst), Mrs. Francis, the Hon. Mrs. Damer, &c., &c.[3]

Of the drama, the wreath of fame has crowned the brows of Mrs. Cowley, Mrs. Inchbald, Miss Lee, Miss Hannah More,[4] and others of less celebrity. Of biography, Mrs. Dobson, Mrs. Thicknesse, Mrs. Piozzi, Mrs. Montagu, Miss Helen Williams, have given specimens highly honourable to their talents.[5] Poetry has unquestionably risen high in British literature from the productions of female pens; for many English women have produced such original and beautiful compositions that the first critics and scholars of the age have wondered, while they applauded.

—1799

[1] *Smollett* Tobias Smollett (1721–71); *Richardson* Samuel Richardson (1689–1761); *Fielding* Henry Fielding (1707–54).

[2] *Mrs. … Plumtree* Three well-known translators: Susannah Dobson (?–1795) is known primarily for her *Life of Petrarch* (1775), translated from Jacques de Sade's original French. Elizabeth Inchbald (1753–1821) and Ann Plumptre both translated August von Kotzebue's German plays.

[3] *Mrs. Carter … Damer* Elizabeth Carter (1717–1806) and Anne Francis were translators of classic Greek and Hebrew texts, respectively, while Anne Seymour Damer (1748–1828) was a famous sculptor and the niece of Horace Walpole.

[4] *Cowley … More Cowley* Hannah Cowley (1743–1809); *Inchbald* Elizabeth Inchbald (1753–1821); *Lee* Sophia Lee (1750–1824); *More* Hannah More (1745–1833).

[5] *Of biography … talents* Susannah Dobson (?–1795) translated Jacques de Sade's *Life of Petrarch*; Ann Ford Thicknesse (1737–1824) wrote *Sketches of the Lives and Writings of the Ladies of France* (1778); Hester Lynch Thrale Piozzi (1741–1821) was best known for her *Anecdotes of the Late Samuel Johnson* (1786); Elizabeth Montagu (1720–1800) published *An Essay on the Writing and Genius of Shakespeare* (1769); and Helen Maria Williams (1761–1827) wrote *Memoirs of M. and Mme. Du Fossé.*

Mary Wollstonecraft

1759 – 1797

When Mary Wollstonecraft died in 1797 she was a literary celebrity. The most recognized female political writer of her day, Wollstonecraft tackled issues such as women and education, human rights, the "unnatural distinctions" of class, and the relationship between the sexes. Her prominent public profile was, however, severely diminished five months after her death when William Godwin published his *Memoirs of the Author of a Vindication of the Rights of Woman*. Godwin, who was Wollstonecraft's husband and intellectual companion, included controversial details of her sexual and emotional history in his book, which shocked many of her admirers. Her reputation was restored to some extent by the women's rights movement in the second half of the nineteenth century, and the women's movement of the 1970s elevated her to the status of a feminist icon. Even those who do not associate themselves with feminism now acknowledge Wollstonecraft as an important writer and thinker of the late eighteenth century—and *A Vindication of the Rights of Woman* as a core text in the Western tradition.

Wollstonecraft was born in London on 27 April 1759 to Elizabeth Dixon and Edward Wollstonecraft; she was the eldest daughter among seven children. The Wollstonecrafts were a middle-class, modestly prosperous family whose fortunes went into a gradual decline. Edward attempted to transform himself into a gentleman farmer, moving the family to Epping, Barking, and finally to Beverley in Yorkshire. These moves exacerbated the family's financial difficulties. As well, Wollstonecraft's father was a violent man. As a child, Wollstonecraft frequently intervened in her father's outbursts in order to try to protect her mother. For solace and respite, she turned to her close friend, Jane Arden. Arden's father, John, was a teacher and philosopher who encouraged Wollstonecraft's self-education and provided her with access to his library.

When Mary was 15 the Wollstonecrafts moved to Hoxton, on the outskirts of London. Here, Wollstonecraft was befriended by her next-door neighbors, the Reverend and Mrs. Clare. They became her surrogate family and were responsible for introducing her to Fanny Blood, with whom she would develop an intensely passionate and possibly romantic friendship. Years later, Wollstonecraft described her connection to Blood as "a friendship so fervent, as for years to have constituted the ruling passion of my mind." Blood became the model for Ann in Wollstonecraft's autobiographical novel, *Mary, A Fiction*.

In 1778, Wollstonecraft made the decision to leave home and earn her own living. Now 19, she took a job as a paid companion to a Mrs. Dawson, a widow in Bath. When her mother became ill in 1781, however, Mary returned to London to nurse her. After months of pain, Elizabeth Wollstonecraft died and Mary took up residence with the Bloods. Shortly afterwards Wollstonecraft's sister Eliza married Meredith Bishop, a well-to-do shipwright. After Eliza gave birth to a daughter in 1783, she fell into a deep postpartum depression that Wollstonecraft attributed to Bishop's cruelty. Wanting to rescue her sister, Wollstonecraft convinced Eliza to run away from her husband and child. (At the time, children legally belonged to the father.) Bishop eventually gave up his attempts to bring his wife back, and their daughter died just days before her first birthday.

Wollstonecraft soon realized that she and Eliza would need to find their own source of financial support. In 1784, together with Fanny Blood, they opened a school at Newington Green, north of London. Here, Wollstonecraft met Richard Price, a preacher and a leader of the Dissenters. His congregation was a Unitarian-like group whose political positions on freedom and equality influenced Wollstonecraft's developing ideas. In 1785, Fanny Blood left Newington Green to marry her long-time suitor, Hugh Skeys, in Lisbon. Wollstonecraft joined them several months later when she heard that Fanny was having trouble with her first pregnancy, but despite her efforts both Fanny and her child died a few days after the birth. Wollstonecraft returned to London where her school's financial problems had worsened during her absence. To raise money, she wrote her first book, *Thoughts on the Education of Daughters*. Joseph Johnson, a leading radical bookseller (that is, publisher) and a fellow Dissenter, published the book in 1787. The book's modest success was not enough to save the school, but it did establish Wollstonecraft in the debate on women's education.

Following the collapse of the school, Wollstonecraft became a governess to the Kingsborough family in Ireland, but it was not a happy development; she was doubtless drawing on experience when she later wrote that governesses "are not always treated in a manner calculated to render them respectable in the eyes of their pupils." She did, however, exert an apparently life-long influence on one of her pupils, who grew up to be a public champion of women's rights. Wollstonecraft soon fell into a depression that was diagnosed as nervous fever. She continued writing, though, beginning work on *Mary: A Fiction*. When she was dismissed from her position as governess, still within the year 1787, she returned to London and convinced Johnson to publish *Mary*. He also hired her as a reviewer for the *Analytical Review*, a monthly progressive periodical. Through her reviews she became an influential voice in the decade of ferment that was coming. Through Johnson, Wollstonecraft met Henry Fuseli, an artist and self-described genius. Although Fuseli was married, Wollstonecraft felt he was her soulmate and they soon began an affair.

Wollstonecraft embraced the start of the French Revolution with excitement. When Edmund Burke published his *Reflections on the Revolution in France* (1790), a treatise that attacked revolutionary ideas, Johnson urged Wollstonecraft to write a reply. She quickly crafted *A Vindication of the Rights of Man*, published anonymously less than a month after the appearance of Burke's book. A few weeks later, a second edition was published under her name, and this solidified her reputation as a radical. In early 1792, she became famous throughout Europe when her new book, *A Vindication of the Rights of Woman*, was published. Written in only six weeks, *A Vindication* presented the case for universal rights, social equality, and women's economic independence. As Wollstonecraft pointed out, the refusal of those who had espoused revolutionary principles of equality to extend rights to women represented a betrayal of those supposedly universal principles.

Eager to obtain first-hand knowledge about the Revolution, and just as eager to escape her deteriorating affair with Fuseli, Wollstonecraft traveled to France in December 1792. There she met Gilbert Imlay, an American and a fellow radical whose lover she soon became. When she discovered she was pregnant, Imlay registered her at the American Embassy as his wife, even though they were not married, so that she could claim the protection of American citizenship. In May 1794, she gave birth to a daughter whom she called Fanny, and two months later Imlay returned to England, leaving mother and child alone. Wollstonecraft's *An Historical and Moral View of the French Revolution* was published in London later that year.

Wollstonecraft's relationship with Imlay was strained, and when she returned to London in April 1795 she discovered he had been unfaithful. Distraught, she attempted suicide but was prevented by him. As a way of distancing himself from her, as well as tracking some bothersome financial losses, Imlay sent her (with Fanny) to Scandinavia on a business trip. She returned to England in September to find him living with another woman. Outraged and increasingly depressed, Wollstonecraft attempted suicide a second time by jumping off Putney Bridge into the Thames. This time, fishers pulled her out of the water.

In January 1796, Wollstonecraft published *Letters Written during a Short Residence in Sweden, Norway, and Denmark*. The book was highly successful, and the praise she received on its publication helped to restore her sense of purpose and mental health. In March, she met Imlay for the final time, and in April she began to write her next novel, *Maria, or The Wrongs of Woman*. In that month she also began a relationship with William Godwin, a leading radical writer and political philosopher to whom she had been introduced by Johnson a few years earlier. They planned a serious mutual commitment without the form of a marriage service, but when Wollstonecraft became pregnant they decided to marry for the sake of the baby. Their marriage on 29 March 1797 caused something of a scandal when it was revealed that Wollstonecraft had never been formally married to Imlay. On 30 August 1797, she gave birth to a daughter, Mary, later to become the wife of Percy Shelley and the author of *Frankenstein*. Only 38 years old, Wollstonecraft died on 10 September from complications resulting from the childbirth. Godwin was left with her manuscripts, and in 1798 published her *Posthumous Works* (which he naively expected to cement her fame) along with his controversial biography.

⌘⌘⌘

from *A Vindication of the Rights of Woman*

Introduction

After considering the historic page, and viewing the living world with anxious solicitude,[1] the most melancholy emotions of sorrowful indignation have depressed my spirits, and I have sighed when obliged to confess that either nature has made a great difference between man and man, or that the civilization which has hitherto taken place in the world has been very partial.[2] I have turned over various books written on the subject of education, and patiently observed the conduct of parents and the management of schools; but what has been the result? A profound conviction that the neglected education of my fellow-creatures is the grand source of the misery I deplore; and that women, in particular, are rendered weak and wretched by a variety of concurring[3] causes, originating from one hasty conclusion. The conduct and manners of women, in fact, evidently prove that their minds are not in a healthy state; for, like the flowers which are planted in too rich a soil, strength and usefulness are sacrificed to beauty; and the flaunting leaves, after having pleased a fastidious eye, fade, disregarded on the stalk, long before the season when they ought to have arrived at maturity. One cause of this barren blooming I attribute to a false system of education, gathered from the books written on this subject by men who, considering females rather as women than human creatures, have been more anxious to make them alluring mistresses than affectionate wives and rational mothers; and the understanding of the sex has been so bubbled[4] by this specious[5] homage that the civilized women of the present century, with a few exceptions, are only anxious to inspire love, when they ought to cherish a nobler ambition, and by their abilities and virtues exact respect.

In a treatise, therefore, on female rights and manners, the works which have been particularly written for their improvement must not be overlooked; especially when it is asserted, in direct terms, that the minds of women are enfeebled by false refinement; that the books of instruction, written by men of genius, have had the same tendency as more frivolous productions; and that,

[1] *solicitude* Concern.

[2] *partial* Biased.

[3] *concurring* Occurring together.

[4] *bubbled* Deluded, fooled.

[5] *specious* Superficially plausible yet misleading.

in the true style of Mahometanism,[1] they are treated as a kind of subordinate beings, and not as a part of the human species, when improvable reason is allowed to be the dignified distinction which raises men above the brute creation, and puts a natural sceptre in a feeble hand.

Yet, because I am a woman, I would not lead my readers to suppose that I mean violently to agitate the contested question respecting the equality or inferiority of the sex; but as the subject lies in my way, and I cannot pass it over without subjecting the main tendency of my reasoning to misconstruction, I shall stop a moment to deliver, in a few words, my opinion. In the government of the physical world it is observable that the female in point of strength is, in general, inferior to the male. This is the law of nature; and it does not appear to be suspended or abrogated[2] in favour of woman. A degree of physical superiority cannot, therefore, be denied—and it is a noble prerogative! But not content with this natural pre-eminence, men endeavour to sink us still lower, merely to render us alluring objects for a moment; and women, intoxicated by the adoration which men, under the influence of their senses, pay them, do not seek to obtain a durable interest in their hearts, or to become the friends of the fellow creatures who find amusement in their society.

I am aware of an obvious inference—from every quarter have I heard exclamations against masculine women; but where are they to be found? If by this appellation men mean to inveigh[3] against their ardour in hunting, shooting, and gaming,[4] I shall most cordially join in the cry; but if it be against the imitation of manly virtues, or, more properly speaking, the attainment of those talents and virtues, the exercise of which ennobles the human character, and which raise females in the scale of animal being when they are comprehensively termed mankind—all those who view them with a philosophic eye must, I should think, wish with me that they may every day grow more and more masculine.

[1] *Mahometanism* Archaic term for Islam.

[2] *abrogated* Repealed, abolished.

[3] *inveigh* Denounce.

[4] *gaming* Gambling.

This discussion naturally divides the subject. I shall first consider women in the grand light of human creatures who, in common with men, are placed on this earth to unfold their faculties; and afterwards I shall more particularly point out their peculiar designation.

I wish also to steer clear of an error which many respectable writers have fallen into; for the instruction which has hitherto been addressed to women has rather been applicable to ladies, if the little indirect advice that is scattered through Sandford and Merton[5] be excepted; but, addressing my sex in a firmer tone, I pay particular attention to those in the middle class because they appear to be in the most natural state. Perhaps the seeds of false-refinement, immorality, and vanity have ever been shed by the great. Weak, artificial beings, raised above the common wants and affections of their race in a premature unnatural manner, undermine the very foundation of virtue, and spread corruption through the whole mass of society! As a class of mankind they have the strongest claim to pity; the education of the rich tends to render them vain and helpless, and the unfolding mind is not strengthened by the practice of those duties that dignify the human character. They only live to amuse themselves, and by the same law that in nature invariably produces certain effects, they soon only afford barren amusement.

But as I purpose taking a separate view of the different ranks of society, and of the moral character of women in each, this hint is, for the present, sufficient; and I have only alluded to the subject because it appears to me to be the very essence of an introduction to give a cursory account of the contents of the work it introduces.

My own sex, I hope, will excuse me if I treat them like rational creatures, instead of flattering their fascinating graces and viewing them as if they were in a state of perpetual childhood, unable to stand alone. I earnestly wish to point out in what true dignity and human

[5] *Sandford and Merton* Thomas Day (1748–89), English poet, philanthropist, political essayist, and author of *The History of Sandford and Merton* (1783), a children's novel that gives expression to Day's educational theories, which are based on the work of Jean-Jacques Rousseau. Highly didactic, the novel contrasts the corrupt, conventional education of spoiled Tommy Merton, son of a Jamaican plantation owner, with the natural education of virtuous Harry Sandford, son of an honest farmer.

happiness consists: I wish to persuade women to endeavour to acquire strength, both of mind and body, and to convince them that the soft phrases, susceptibility of heart, delicacy of sentiment, and refinement of taste are almost synonymous with epithets of weakness, and that those beings who are only the objects of pity and that kind of love, which has been termed its sister, will soon become objects of contempt.

Dismissing then those pretty feminine phrases, which the men condescendingly use to soften our slavish dependence, and despising that weak elegancy of mind, exquisite sensibility, and sweet docility of manners supposed to be the sexual characteristics of the weaker vessel, I wish to show that elegance is inferior to virtue; that the first object of laudable ambition is to obtain a character as a human being, regardless of the distinction of sex; and that secondary views should be brought to this simple touchstone.

This is a rough sketch of my plan; and should I express my conviction with the energetic emotions that I feel whenever I think of the subject, the dictates of experience and reflection will be felt by some of my readers. Animated by this important object, I shall disdain to cull[1] my phrases or polish my style: I aim at being useful, and sincerity will render me unaffected; for, wishing rather to persuade by the force of my arguments than dazzle by the elegance of my language, I shall not waste my time in rounding periods,[2] or in fabricating the turgid bombast of artificial feelings, which, coming from the head, never reach the heart. I shall be employed about things, not words—and, anxious to render my sex more respectable members of society, I shall try to avoid that flowery diction which has slid from essays into novels, and from novels into familiar letters and conversation.

These pretty superlatives, dropping glibly from the tongue, vitiate[3] the taste and create a kind of sickly delicacy that turns away from simple unadorned truth; and a deluge of false sentiments and over-stretched feelings, stifling the natural emotions of the heart, render the domestic pleasures insipid that ought to sweeten the exercise of those severe duties that educate a rational and immortal being for a nobler field of action.

The education of women has, of late, been more attended to than formerly; yet they are still reckoned a frivolous sex, and ridiculed or pitied by the writers who endeavour by satire or instruction to improve them. It is acknowledged that they spend many of the first years of their lives in acquiring a smattering of accomplishments; meanwhile strength of body and mind are sacrificed to libertine[4] notions of beauty, to the desire of establishing themselves—the only way women can rise in the world—by marriage. And this desire making mere animals of them, when they marry they act as such children may be expected to act: they dress, they paint,[5] and nickname God's creatures.[6] Surely these weak beings are only fit for a seraglio![7] Can they be expected to govern a family with judgment, or take care of the poor babes whom they bring into the world?

If then it can be fairly deduced from the present conduct of the sex, from the prevalent fondness for pleasure—which takes place of ambition and those nobler passions that open and enlarge the soul—that the instruction which women have hitherto received has only tended, with the constitution of civil society, to render them insignificant objects of desire—mere propagators of fools! If it can be proved that in aiming to accomplish them without cultivating their understandings they are taken out of their sphere of duties, and made ridiculous and useless when the short-lived bloom of beauty is over,[8] I presume that rational men will excuse me for endeavouring to persuade them to become more masculine and respectable.

---

[1] *cull* Choose carefully.

[2] *rounding periods* Crafting graceful sentences.

[3] *vitiate* Render impure, corrupt.

[4] *libertine* Licentious.

[5] *paint* I.e., wear makeup.

[6] *they dress … God's creatures* From Shakespeare's *Hamlet* 3.1.142–46: "I have heard of your paintings, well enough. God hath given you one face, and you make yourselves another. You jig and amble, and you lisp, you nickname God's creatures and make your wantonness your ignorance."

[7] *seraglio* Harem.

[8] [Wollstonecraft's note] A lively writer, I cannot recollect his name, asks what business women turned of forty have to do in the world? [Wollstonecraft is perhaps referring to a remark made by a libertine character in Frances Burney's *Evelina*, Lord Merton.]

Indeed the word masculine is only a bugbear:[1] there is little reason to fear that women will acquire too much courage or fortitude, for their apparent inferiority with respect to bodily strength must render them, in some degree, dependent on men in the various relations of life; but why should it be increased by prejudices that give a sex to virtue and confound simple truths with sensual reveries?

Women are, in fact, so much degraded by mistaken notions of female excellence that I do not mean to add a paradox when I assert that this artificial weakness produces a propensity to tyrannize, and gives birth to cunning, the natural opponent of strength, which leads them to play off those contemptible infantine airs that undermine esteem even whilst they excite desire. Let men become more chaste and modest, and if women do not grow wiser in the same ratio, it will be clear that they have weaker understandings. It seems scarcely necessary to say that I now speak of the sex in general. Many individuals have more sense than their male relatives; and as nothing preponderates[2] where there is a constant struggle for an equilibrium without[3] it has naturally more gravity, some women govern their husbands without degrading themselves because intellect will always govern.

Chapter 2

The Prevailing Opinion of a Sexual Character Discussed

To account for, and excuse, the tyranny of man, many ingenious arguments have been brought forward to prove that the two sexes, in the acquirement of virtue, ought to aim at attaining a very different character: or, to speak explicitly, women are not allowed to have sufficient strength of mind to acquire what really deserves the name of virtue. Yet it should seem, allowing them to have souls, that there is but one way appointed by Providence to lead mankind to either virtue or happiness.

If then women are not a swarm of ephemeron[4] triflers, why should they be kept in ignorance under the specious name of innocence? Men complain, and with reason, of the follies and caprices[5] of our sex, when they do not keenly satirize our headstrong passions and grovelling vices. Behold, I should answer, the natural effect of ignorance! The mind will ever be unstable that has only prejudices to rest on, and the current will run with destructive fury when there are no barriers to break its force. Women are told from their infancy, and taught by the example of their mothers, that a little knowledge of human weakness, justly termed cunning, softness of temper, outward obedience, and a scrupulous attention to a puerile kind of propriety, will obtain for them the protection of man; and should they be beautiful, every thing else is needless for, at least, twenty years of their lives.

Thus Milton describes our first frail mother; though when he tells us that women are formed for softness and sweet attractive grace,[6] I cannot comprehend his meaning; unless, in the true Mahometan strain, he meant to deprive us of souls and insinuate that we were beings only designed by sweet attractive grace, and docile blind obedience, to gratify the senses of man when he can no longer soar on the wing of contemplation.

How grossly do they insult us who thus advise us only to render ourselves gentle, domestic brutes! For instance, the winning softness so warmly, and frequently, recommended that governs by obeying. What childish expressions, and how insignificant is the being—can it be an immortal one?—who will condescend to govern by such sinister methods! "Certainly," says Lord Bacon, "man is of kin to the beasts by his body; and if he be not of kin to God by his spirit, he is a base and ignoble creature!"[7] Men, indeed, appear to me to act in a very unphilosophical manner when they

[1] *bugbear* Imaginary creature invoked to cause fear.

[2] *preponderates* Weighs more, predominates.

[3] *without* Unless.

[4] *ephemeron* Short-lived.

[5] *caprices* Whims, fancies.

[6] *Milton … grace* John Milton contrasts Adam and Eve, the first man and woman, in *Paradise Lost* (1667): "For contemplation he and valour formed, / For softness she and sweet attractive grace" (4.297–98).

[7] *Certainly … creature* Francis Bacon (1561–1626), English philosopher and statesman, author of *Essays or Counsels Civil and Moral* (1625). The quotation is from Essay 16, "Of Atheism."

try to secure the good conduct of women by attempting to keep them always in a state of childhood. Rousseau[1] was more consistent when he wished to stop the progress of reason in both sexes, for if men eat of the tree of knowledge,[2] women will come in for a taste; but, from the imperfect cultivation which their understandings now receive, they only attain a knowledge of evil.

Children, I grant, should be innocent; but when the epithet is applied to men, or women, it is but a civil term for weakness. For if it be allowed that women were destined by Providence to acquire human virtues and, by the exercise of their understandings, that stability of character which is the firmest ground to rest our future hopes upon, they must be permitted to turn to the fountain of light, and not forced to shape their course by the twinkling of a mere satellite.[3] Milton, I grant, was of a very different opinion; for he only bends to the indefeasible[4] right of beauty, though it would be difficult to render two passages, which I now mean to contrast, consistent. But into similar inconsistencies are great men often led by their senses.

> To whom thus Eve with *perfect beauty* adorn'd.
> My Author and Disposer, what thou bidst
> *Unargued* I obey; so God ordains;
> God *is thy law, thou mine*: to know no more
> Is Woman's *happiest* knowledge and her *praise*.[5]

These are exactly the arguments that I have used to children; but I have added, "Your reason is now gaining strength, and, until it arrives at some degree of maturity, you must look up to me for advice—then you ought to think and only rely on God."

Yet in the following lines Milton seems to coincide with me when he makes Adam thus expostulate[6] with his Maker.

> Hast thou not made me here thy substitute,
> And these inferior far beneath me set?
> Among *unequals* what society
> Can sort, what harmony or true delight?
> Which must be mutual, in proportion due
> Giv'n and receiv'd; but in *disparity*
> The one intense, the other still remiss
> Cannot well suit with either, but soon prove
> Tedious alike: of *fellowship* I speak
> Such as I seek, fit to participate
> All rational delight—[7]

In treating, therefore, of the manners of women, let us, disregarding sensual arguments, trace what we should endeavour to make them in order to co-operate, if the expression be not too bold, with the supreme Being.

By individual education, I mean—for the sense of the word is not precisely defined—such an attention to a child as will slowly sharpen the senses, form the temper, regulate the passions as they begin to ferment, and set the understanding to work before the body arrives at maturity; so that the man may only have to proceed, not to begin, the important task of learning to think and reason.

To prevent any misconstruction, I must add that I do not believe that a private education can work the wonders which some sanguine[8] writers have attributed to it. Men and women must be educated, in a great degree, by the opinions and manners of the society they live in. In every age there has been a stream of popular opinion that has carried all before it, and given a family character, as it were, to the century. It may then fairly be inferred that until society be differently constituted, much cannot be expected from education. It is, however, sufficient for my present purpose to assert that whatever effect circumstances have on the abilities, every being may become virtuous by the exercise of its own reason; for if but one being was created with vicious inclinations that is positively bad, what can save us from

[1] *Rousseau* Jean-Jacques Rousseau (1712–78), Geneva born philosopher, composer and essayist.

[2] *tree of knowledge* In Genesis 2:17, God forbids Adam and Eve to eat of the tree of the knowledge of good and evil; tempted by the serpent, Eve disobeys and Adam follows suit.

[3] *satellite* Subordinate, secondary planet orbiting round a larger one.

[4] *indefeasible* Incapable of being defeated.

[5] *To whom ... praise* Milton, *Paradise Lost*, 4.634–38. [Wollstonecraft's italics.]

[6] *expostulate* Remonstrate, argue.

[7] *Hast ... delight* Milton, *Paradise Lost*, 8.381–91. [Wollstonecraft's italics.]

[8] *sanguine* Cheerfully optimistic.

atheism? Or, if we worship a God, is not that God a devil?

Consequently, the most perfect education, in my opinion, is such an exercise of the understanding as is best calculated to strengthen the body and form the heart. Or, in other words, to enable the individual to attain such habits of virtue as will render it independent. In fact, it is a farce to call any being virtuous whose virtues do not result from the exercise of its own reason. This was Rousseau's opinion respecting men:[1] I extend it to women, and confidently assert that they have been drawn out of their sphere by false refinement and not by an endeavour to acquire masculine qualities. Still the regal homage which they receive is so intoxicating that until the manners of the times are changed and formed on more reasonable principles, it may be impossible to convince them that the illegitimate power, which they obtain by degrading themselves, is a curse, and that they must return to nature and equality if they wish to secure the placid satisfaction that unsophisticated affections impart. But for this epoch we must wait—wait, perhaps, until kings and nobles, enlightened by reason, and preferring the real dignity of man to childish state, throw off their gaudy hereditary trappings: and if then women do not resign the arbitrary power of beauty, they will prove that they have less mind than man.

I may be accused of arrogance; still I must declare what I firmly believe: that all the writers who have written on the subject of female education and manners from Rousseau to Dr. Gregory[2] have contributed to render women more artificial, weak characters than they would otherwise have been; and, consequently, more useless members of society. I might have expressed this conviction in a lower key, but I am afraid it would have been the whine of affectation and not the faithful expression of my feelings, of the clear result which experience and reflection have led me to draw. When I come to that division of the subject, I shall advert[3] to the passages that I more particularly disapprove of in the works of the authors I have just alluded to; but it is first necessary to observe that my objection extends to the whole purport[4] of those books, which tend, in my opinion, to degrade one half of the human species and render women pleasing at the expense of every solid virtue.

Though, to reason on Rousseau's ground, if man did attain a degree of perfection of mind when his body arrived at maturity, it might be proper, in order to make a man and his wife one, that she should rely entirely on his understanding; and the graceful ivy, clasping the oak that supported it, would form a whole in which strength and beauty would be equally conspicuous. But, alas! Husbands, as well as their helpmates, are often only overgrown children; nay, thanks to early debauchery, scarcely men in their outward form—and if the blind lead the blind,[5] one need not come from heaven to tell us the consequence.

Many are the causes that, in the present corrupt state of society, contribute to enslave women by cramping their understandings and sharpening their senses. One, perhaps, that silently does more mischief than all the rest is their disregard of order.

To do every thing in an orderly manner is a most important precept which women, who generally speaking receive only a disorderly kind of education, seldom attend to with that degree of exactness that men, who from their infancy are broken into method, observe. This negligent kind of guess-work—for what other epithet can be used to point out the random exertions of a sort of instinctive common sense, never brought to the test of reason?—prevents their generalizing matters of fact: so they do today what they did yesterday, merely because they did it yesterday.

This contempt of the understanding in early life has more baneful[6] consequences than is commonly supposed; for the little knowledge which women of strong minds attain is, from various circumstances, of a more desultory[7] kind than the knowledge of men, and it is acquired more by sheer observations on real life than

[1] *Rousseau's … men* Jean-Jacques Rousseau, *Émile* (1762), Book One.

[2] *Dr. Gregory* John Gregory (1724–73), Scottish physician, author of *A Father's Legacy to His Daughters* (1774), an influential conduct book for young women.

[3] *advert* Take notice.

[4] *purport* Intention.

[5] *blind lead the blind* Matthew 15:14: "And if the blind lead the blind, both shall fall into the ditch."

[6] *baneful* Destructive, poisonous.

[7] *desultory* Irregular, unmethodical.

from comparing what has been individually observed with the results of experience generalized by speculation. Led by their dependent situation and domestic employments more into society, what they learn is rather by snatches; and as learning is with them, in general, only a secondary thing, they do not pursue any one branch with that persevering ardour necessary to give vigour to the faculties and clearness to the judgment. In the present state of society, a little learning is required to support the character of a gentleman; and boys are obliged to submit to a few years of discipline. But in the education of women, the cultivation of the understanding is always subordinate to the acquirement of some corporeal accomplishment; even while enervated[1] by confinement and false notions of modesty, the body is prevented from attaining that grace and beauty which relaxed half-formed limbs never exhibit. Besides, in youth their faculties are not brought forward by emulation; and having no serious scientific study, if they have natural sagacity it is turned too soon on life and manners. They dwell on effects, and modifications, without tracing them back to causes; and complicated rules to adjust behaviour are a weak substitute for simple principles.

As a proof that education gives this appearance of weakness to females, we may instance the example of military men who are, like them, sent into the world before their minds have been stored with knowledge or fortified by principles. The consequences are similar; soldiers acquire a little superficial knowledge, snatched from the muddy current of conversation, and, from continually mixing with society, they gain what is termed a knowledge of the world; and this acquaintance with manners and customs has frequently been confounded[2] with a knowledge of the human heart. But can the crude fruit of casual observation, never brought to the test of judgment, formed by comparing speculation and experience, deserve such a distinction? Soldiers, as well as women, practice the minor virtues with punctilious[3] politeness. Where is then the sexual difference when the education has been the same? All the difference that I can discern arises from the superior advantage of liberty, which enables the former to see more of life.

It is wandering from my present subject, perhaps, to make a political remark; but, as it was produced naturally by the train of my reflections, I shall not pass it silently over.

Standing armies can never consist of resolute, robust men; they may be well-disciplined machines, but they will seldom contain men under the influence of strong passions or with very vigorous faculties. And as for any depth of understanding, I will venture to affirm that it is as rarely to be found in the army as amongst women; and the cause, I maintain, is the same. It may be further observed that officers are also particularly attentive to their persons, fond of dancing, crowded rooms, adventures, and ridicule.[4] Like the fair sex, the business of their lives is gallantry. They were taught to please, and they only live to please. Yet they do not lose their rank in the distinction of sexes, for they are still reckoned superior to women, though in what their superiority consists, beyond what I have just mentioned, it is difficult to discover.

The great misfortune is this: that they both acquire manners before morals, and a knowledge of life before they have, from reflection, any acquaintance with the grand ideal outline of human nature. The consequence is natural; satisfied with common nature, they become a prey to prejudices, and taking all their opinions on credit, they blindly submit to authority. So that, if they have any sense, it is a kind of instinctive glance that catches proportions and decides with respect to manners, but fails when arguments are to be pursued below the surface, or opinions analyzed.

May not the same remark be applied to women? Nay, the argument may be carried still further, for they are both thrown out of a useful station by the unnatural distinctions established in civilized life. Riches and hereditary honours have made ciphers[5] of women to

[1] *enervated* Mentally weakened.

[2] *confounded* Disordered, confused.

[3] *punctilious* Carefully polite.

[4] [Wollstonecraft's note] Why should women be censured with petulant acrimony, because they seem to have a passion for a scarlet coat? Has not education placed them more on a level with soldiers than any other class of men? [See Jonathan Swift's "The Furniture of a Woman's Mind."]

[5] *ciphers* Neutral symbols which can change the value of other numbers depending on their position.

give consequence to the numerical figure; and idleness has produced a mixture of gallantry and despotism into society which leads the very men who are the slaves of their mistresses to tyrannize over their sisters, wives, and daughters. This is only keeping them in rank and file, it is true. Strengthen the female mind by enlarging it and there will be an end to blind obedience; but, as blind obedience is ever sought for by power, tyrants and sensualists are in the right when they endeavour to keep women in the dark, because the former only want slaves, and the latter a play-thing. The sensualist, indeed, has been the most dangerous of tyrants, and women have been duped by their lovers, as princes by their ministers, whilst dreaming that they reigned over them.

I now principally allude to Rousseau, for his character of Sophia[1] is, undoubtedly, a captivating one, though it appears to me grossly unnatural; however, it is not the superstructure but the foundation of her character, the principles on which her education was built, that I mean to attack; nay, warmly as I admire the genius of that able writer, whose opinions I shall often have occasion to cite, indignation always takes place of admiration, and the rigid frown of insulted virtue effaces the smile of complacency, which his eloquent periods are wont to raise when I read his voluptuous reveries. Is this the man who, in his ardour for virtue, would banish all the soft arts of peace and almost carry us back to Spartan discipline?[2] Is this the man who delights to paint the useful struggles of passion, the triumphs of good dispositions, and the heroic flights which carry the glowing soul out of itself? How are these mighty sentiments lowered when he describes the pretty foot and enticing airs of his little favourite! But, for the present, I wave the subject, and, instead of severely reprehending[3] the transient effusions of overweening[4] sensibility, I shall only observe that whoever has cast a benevolent eye on society must often have been gratified by the sight of humble mutual love, not dignified by sentiment, or strengthened by a union in intellectual pursuits. The domestic trifles of the day have afforded matters for cheerful converse, and innocent caresses have softened toils which did not require great exercise of mind or stretch of thought: yet, has not the sight of this moderate felicity excited more tenderness than respect? An emotion similar to what we feel when children are playing, or animals sporting,[5] whilst the contemplation of the noble struggles of suffering merit has raised admiration and carried our thoughts to that world where sensation will give place to reason.

Women are, therefore, to be considered either as moral beings, or so weak that they must be entirely subjected to the superior faculties of men.

Let us examine this question. Rousseau declares that a woman should never, for a moment, feel herself independent, that she should be governed by fear to exercise her natural cunning, and made a coquettish slave in order to render her a more alluring object of desire, a sweeter companion to man whenever he chooses to relax himself.[6] He carries the arguments, which he pretends to draw from the indications of nature, still further and insinuates that truth and fortitude, the corner stones of all human virtue, should be cultivated with certain restrictions, because, with respect to the female character, obedience is the grand lesson which ought to be impressed with unrelenting rigour.

What nonsense! When will a great man arise with sufficient strength of mind to puff away the fumes which pride and sensuality have thus spread over the subject! If women are by nature inferior to men, their virtues must be the same in quality, if not in degree, or virtue is a relative idea; consequently, their conduct should be founded on the same principles and have the

[1] *Sophia* Character in Jean-Jacques Rousseau, *Émile*, Book Five.

[2] *Spartan discipline* The militaristic Greek city-state of Sparta was infamous for its harsh laws, outlined in Plutarch's account of Lycurgus (*Lives*), which controlled nearly every aspect of the lives of its citizens.

[3] *reprehending* Finding fault with.

[4] *overweening* Arrogant.

[5] [Wollstonecraft's note] Similar feelings has Milton's pleasing picture of paradisiacal happiness ever raised in my mind; yet, instead of envying the lovely pair, I have, with conscious dignity, or Satanic pride, turned to hell for sublimer objects. In the same style, when viewing some noble monument of human art, I have traced the emanation of the Deity in the order I admired, till, descending from that giddy height, I have caught myself contemplating the grandest of all human sights;—for fancy quickly placed, in some solitary recess, an outcast of fortune, rising superior to passion and discontent.

[6] *Rousseau … himself* See Jean-Jacques Rousseau, *Émile*, Book Five.

same aim.

Connected with man as daughters, wives, and mothers, their moral character may be estimated by their manner of fulfilling those simple duties; but the end, the grand end of their exertions should be to unfold their own faculties and acquire the dignity of conscious virtue. They may try to render their road pleasant, but ought never to forget, in common with man, that life yields not the felicity which can satisfy an immortal soul. I do not mean to insinuate that either sex should be so lost in abstract reflections or distant views as to forget the affections and duties that lie before them, and are, in truth, the means appointed to produce the fruit of life; on the contrary, I would warmly recommend them, even while I assert that they afford most satisfaction when they are considered in their true, sober light.

Probably the prevailing opinion, that woman was created for man,[1] may have taken its rise from Moses's poetical story;[2] yet, as very few, it is presumed, who have bestowed any serious thought on the subject ever supposed that Eve was, literally speaking, one of Adam's ribs,[3] the deduction must be allowed to fall to the ground; or, only be so far admitted as it proves that man, from the remotest antiquity, found it convenient to exert his strength to subjugate his companion, and his invention to show that she ought to have her neck bent under the yoke because the whole creation was only created for his convenience or pleasure.

Let it not be concluded that I wish to invert the order of things; I have already granted that, from the constitution of their bodies, men seem to be designed by Providence to attain a greater degree of virtue. I speak collectively of the whole sex; but I see not the shadow of a reason to conclude that their virtues should differ in respect to their nature. In fact, how can they, if virtue has only one eternal standard? I must, therefore, if I reason consequentially, as strenuously maintain that they have the same simple direction as that there is a God.

It follows then that cunning should not be opposed to wisdom, little cares to great exertions, or insipid softness, varnished over with the name of gentleness, to that fortitude which grand views alone can inspire.

I shall be told that woman would then lose many of her peculiar graces, and the opinion of a well-known poet might be quoted to refute my unqualified assertion. For Pope[4] has said, in the name of the whole male sex:

> Yet ne'er so sure our passion to create,
> As when she touch'd the brink of all we hate.[5]

In what light this sally[6] places men and women, I shall leave to the judicious to determine; meanwhile I shall content myself with observing that I cannot discover why, unless they are mortal, females should always be degraded by being made subservient to love or lust.

To speak disrespectfully of love is, I know, high treason against sentiment and fine feelings; but I wish to speak the simple language of truth, and rather to address the head than the heart. To endeavour to reason love out of the world would be to out Quixote Cervantes[7] and equally offend against common sense; but an endeavour to restrain this tumultuous passion, and to prove that it should not be allowed to dethrone superior powers, or to usurp the sceptre which the understanding should ever coolly wield, appears less wild.

Youth is the season for love in both sexes; but in those days of thoughtless enjoyment, provision should be made for the more important years of life when reflection takes place of sensation. But Rousseau, and most of the male writers who have followed his steps,

---

1 *woman ... man* Genesis 2.18–25: "And the Lord God said, It is not good that the man should be alone; I will make him an helpmeet for him" (Genesis 2:18).

2 *Moses's ... story* I.e., Genesis. Moses was believed to be the author of the Pentateuch, the first five books of the Bible: Genesis, Exodus, Leviticus, Numbers, and Deuteronomy.

3 *Adam's ribs* "And the Lord God caused a deep sleep to fall upon Adam, and he slept: and he took one of his ribs, and closed up the flesh instead thereof; And the rib, which the Lord God had taken from man, made he a woman, and brought her unto the man" (Genesis 2.22–23).

4 *Pope* Alexander Pope (1688–1744), English poet and satirist.

5 *Yet ... hate* Alexander Pope, "Epistle II: To a Lady (Of the Characters of Women)," from "Epistles to Several Persons," *Works*, 51–52 (1735).

6 *sally* Sudden attack on an enemy.

7 *out Quixote Cervantes* I.e., even more than the hero of Cervantes's picaresque novel, *Don Quixote*, be determined to carry out a lofty albeit impossible goal.

have warmly inculcated[1] that the whole tendency of female education ought to be directed to one point: to render them pleasing.

Let me reason with the supporters of this opinion who have any knowledge of human nature: do they imagine that marriage can eradicate the habitude of life? The woman who has only been taught to please will soon find that her charms are oblique sunbeams, and that they cannot have much effect on her husband's heart when they are seen every day, when the summer is passed and gone. Will she then have sufficient native energy to look into herself for comfort and cultivate her dormant faculties? Or, is it not more rational to expect that she will try to please other men; and, in the emotions raised by the expectation of new conquests, endeavour to forget the mortification her love or pride has received? When the husband ceases to be a lover—and the time will inevitably come—her desire of pleasing will then grow languid, or become a spring of bitterness; and love, perhaps, the most evanescent of all passions, gives place to jealousy or vanity.

I now speak of women who are restrained by principle or prejudice; such women, though they would shrink from an intrigue with real abhorrence, yet, nevertheless, wish to be convinced by the homage of gallantry that they are cruelly neglected by their husbands; or, days and weeks are spent in dreaming of the happiness enjoyed by congenial souls until their health is undermined and their spirits broken by discontent. How then can the great art of pleasing be such a necessary study? It is only useful to a mistress; the chaste wife, and serious mother, should only consider her power to please as the polish of her virtues, and the affection of her husband as one of the comforts that render her task less difficult and her life happier. But, whether she be loved or neglected, her first wish should be to make herself respectable, and not to rely for all her happiness on a being subject to like infirmities with herself.

The worthy Dr. Gregory fell into a similar error. I respect his heart, but entirely disapprove of his celebrated *Legacy to his Daughters*.

He advises them to cultivate a fondness for dress,[2] because a fondness for dress, he asserts, is natural to them. I am unable to comprehend what either he or Rousseau mean when they frequently use this indefinite term. If they told us that in a pre-existent state the soul was fond of dress, and brought this inclination with it into a new body, I should listen to them with a half smile, as I often do when I hear a rant about innate elegance. But if he only meant to say that the exercise of the faculties will produce this fondness—I deny it. It is not natural; but arises, like false ambition in men, from a love of power.

Dr. Gregory goes much further; he actually recommends dissimulation,[3] and advises an innocent girl to give the lie to her feelings, and not dance with spirit, when gaiety of heart would make her feel eloquent without making her gestures immodest. In the name of truth and common sense, why should not one woman acknowledge that she can take more exercise than another? Or, in other words, that she has a sound constitution; and why, to damp innocent vivacity, is she darkly to be told that men will draw conclusions which she little thinks of? Let the libertine draw what inference he pleases; but I hope that no sensible mother will restrain the natural frankness of youth by instilling such indecent cautions. Out of the abundance of the heart the mouth speaketh;[4] and a wiser than Solomon[5] hath said that the heart should be made clean, and not trivial ceremonies observed,[6] which it is not very difficult to fulfil with scrupulous exactness when vice reigns in the heart.

Women ought to endeavour to purify their heart; but can they do so when their uncultivated understandings make them entirely dependent on their senses for employment and amusement, when no noble pursuit sets them above the little vanities of the day, or enables them to curb the wild emotions that agitate a reed over

---

[1] *inculcated* Taught through force or persistence.

[2] *fondness for dress* Gregory, *A Father's Legacy to his Daughters*, 55–57.

[3] *dissimulation* Concealment, feigning; Gregory, *A Father's Legacy to his Daughters*, 57–58.

[4] *Out of … speaketh* Matthew 12.34: "O generation of vipers, how can ye, being evil, speak good things? For out of the abundance of the heart the mouth speaketh."

[5] *a wiser than Solomon* I.e., Jesus; see Luke 11.31.

[6] *the heart … observed* Matthew 23.25: "Woe unto you, scribes and Pharisees, hypocrites! For ye make clean the outside of the cup and of the platter, but within they are full of extortion and excess."

which every passing breeze has power? To gain the affections of a virtuous man is affectation necessary? Nature has given woman a weaker frame than man; but, to ensure her husband's affections, must a wife—who, by the exercise of her mind and body whilst she was discharging the duties of a daughter, wife, and mother, has allowed her constitution to retain its natural strength, and her nerves a healthy tone—is she, I say, to condescend to use art and feign a sickly delicacy in order to secure her husband's affection? Weakness may excite tenderness and gratify the arrogant pride of man; but the lordly caresses of a protector will not gratify a noble mind that pants for and deserves to be respected. Fondness is a poor substitute for friendship!

In a seraglio, I grant that all these arts are necessary; the epicure[1] must have his palate tickled or he will sink into apathy; but have women so little ambition as to be satisfied with such a condition? Can they supinely[2] dream life away in the lap of pleasure, or the languor of weariness, rather than assert their claim to pursue reasonable pleasures and render themselves conspicuous by practising the virtues which dignify mankind? Surely she has not an immortal soul who can loiter life away, merely employed to adorn her person, that she may amuse the languid hours, and soften the cares of a fellow-creature who is willing to be enlivened by her smiles and tricks when the serious business of life is over.

Besides, the woman who strengthens her body and exercises her mind will, by managing her family and practising various virtues, become the friend and not the humble dependent of her husband; and if she, by possessing such substantial qualities, merit his regard, she will not find it necessary to conceal her affection, nor to pretend to an unnatural coldness of constitution to excite her husband's passions. In fact, if we revert to history, we shall find that the women who have distinguished themselves have neither been the most beautiful nor the most gentle of their sex.

Nature, or, to speak with strict propriety, God, has made all things right; but man has sought him out many inventions to mar the work. I now allude to that part of Dr. Gregory's treatise where he advises a wife never to let her husband know the extent of her sensibility or affection.[3] Voluptuous precaution, and as ineffectual as absurd. Love, from its very nature, must be transitory. To seek for a secret that would render it constant would be as wild a search as for the philosopher's stone, or the grand panacea:[4] and the discovery would be equally useless, or rather pernicious, to mankind. The most holy band of society is friendship. It has been well said, by a shrewd satirist, "that rare as true love is, true friendship is still rarer."[5]

This is an obvious truth, and the cause, not lying deep, will not elude a slight glance of inquiry.

Love, the common passion in which chance and sensation take place of choice and reason, is, in some degree, felt by the mass of mankind; for it is not necessary to speak, at present, of the emotions that rise above or sink below love. This passion, naturally increased by suspense and difficulties, draws the mind out of its accustomed state and exalts the affections; but the security of marriage, allowing the fever of love to subside, a healthy temperature is thought insipid only by those who have not sufficient intellect to substitute the calm tenderness of friendship, the confidence of respect, instead of blind admiration and the sensual emotions of fondness.

This is, must be, the course of nature—friendship or indifference inevitably succeeds love—and this constitution seems perfectly to harmonize with the system of government which prevails in the moral world. Passions are spurs to action and open the mind; but they sink into mere appetites, become a personal and momentary gratification, when the object is gained and the satisfied mind rests in enjoyment. The man who had some virtue whilst he was struggling for a crown often becomes a voluptuous tyrant when it graces his brow; and, when the lover is not lost in the husband, the dotard,[6] a prey

[1] *epicure* One devoted to physical pleasures.

[2] *supinely* Indolently, literally on one's back.

[3] *never to let ... affection* Gregory, *A Father's Legacy to his Daughters*, 87–88.

[4] *wild a search ... panacea* Alchemists believed in the existence of a philosopher's stone, a substance which could turn base metals into gold, as well as a grand panacea, a medicine that could cure all illnesses.

[5] *that rare ... rarer* François de La Rochefoucauld (1613–80), French essayist, author of *Réflexions; ou Sentences et maximes morales* (1665).

[6] *dotard* Senile person.

to childish caprices and fond jealousies, neglects the serious duties of life, and the caresses which should excite confidence in his children are lavished on the overgrown child, his wife.

In order to fulfil the duties of life, and to be able to pursue with vigour the various employments which form the moral character, a master and mistress of a family ought not to continue to love each other with passion. I mean to say that they ought not to indulge those emotions which disturb the order of society and engross the thoughts that should be otherwise employed. The mind that has never been engrossed by one object wants vigour—if it can long be so, it is weak.

A mistaken education, a narrow, uncultivated mind, and many sexual prejudices tend to make women more constant than men; but, for the present, I shall not touch on this branch of the subject. I will go still further and advance, without dreaming of a paradox, that an unhappy marriage is often very advantageous to a family, and that the neglected wife is, in general, the best mother. And this would almost always be the consequence if the female mind were more enlarged: for it seems to be the common dispensation[1] of Providence that what we gain in present enjoyment should be deducted from the treasure of life—experience; and that when we are gathering the flowers of the day and revelling in pleasure, the solid fruit of toil and wisdom should not be caught at the same time. The way lies before us, we must turn to the right or left; and he who will pass life away in bounding from one pleasure to another must not complain if he acquire neither wisdom nor respectability of character.

Supposing, for a moment, that the soul is not immortal, and that man was only created for the present scene; I think we should have reason to complain that love, infantine fondness, ever grew insipid and palled upon the sense. Let us eat, drink, and love, for tomorrow we die,[2] would be, in fact, the language of reason, the morality of life; and who but a fool would part with a reality for a fleeting shadow? But, if awed by observing the improbable powers of the mind, we disdain to confine our wishes or thoughts to such a comparatively mean field of action that only appears grand and important, as it is connected with a boundless prospect and sublime hopes, what necessity is there for falsehood in conduct, and why must the sacred majesty of truth be violated to detain a deceitful good that saps the very foundation of virtue? Why must the female mind be tainted by coquettish arts to gratify the sensualist and prevent love from subsiding into friendship, or compassionate tenderness, when there are not qualities on which friendship can be built? Let the honest heart show itself, and reason teach passion to submit to necessity; or, let the dignified pursuit of virtue and knowledge raise the mind above those emotions which rather embitter than sweeten the cup of life when they are not restrained within due bounds.

I do not mean to allude to the romantic passion which is the concomitant[3] of genius. Who can clip its wing? But that grand passion not proportioned to the puny enjoyments of life is only true to the sentiment and feeds on itself. The passions which have been celebrated for their durability have always been unfortunate. They have acquired strength by absence and constitutional melancholy—the fancy has hovered round a form of beauty dimly seen—but familiarity might have turned admiration into disgust; or, at least, into indifference, and allowed the imagination leisure to start fresh game. With perfect propriety, according to this view of things, does Rousseau make the mistress of his soul, Eloisa, love St. Preux[4] when life was fading before her; but this is no proof of the immortality of the passion.

Of the same complexion is Dr. Gregory's advice respecting delicacy of sentiment,[5] which he advises a woman not to acquire if she have determined to marry. This determination, however, perfectly consistent with his former advice, he calls indelicate, and earnestly persuades his daughters to conceal it, though it may govern their conduct—as if it were indelicate to have

[1] *dispensation* Divine ordering of the world.

[2] *Let us … die* Isaiah 22.13.

[3] *concomitant* Accompaniment.

[4] *Eloisa … St. Preux* Eloisa/Julie is the heroine of Rousseau's epistolary novel *Julie, ou, La Nouvelle Héloïse* (1761). Julie falls in love with her tutor, St. Preux, but is forced to marry her father's friend, Wolmar. St. Preux and Julie meet again many years later, and Julie ultimately admits on her deathbed that she has never stopped loving him.

[5] *advice … sentiment* Gregory, *A Father's Legacy to His Daughters,* 116–119.

the common appetites of human nature.

Noble morality!, and consistent with the cautious prudence of a little soul that cannot extend its views beyond the present minute division of existence. If all the faculties of woman's mind are only to be cultivated as they respect her dependence on man; if, when a husband be obtained, she have arrived at her goal and, meanly proud, rests satisfied with such a paltry crown, let her grovel contentedly, scarcely raised by her employments above the animal kingdom; but if, struggling for the prize of her high calling, she look beyond the present scene, let her cultivate her understanding without stopping to consider what character the husband may have whom she is destined to marry. Let her only determine, without being too anxious about present happiness, to acquire the qualities that ennoble a rational being, and a rough inelegant husband may shock her taste without destroying her peace of mind. She will not model her soul to suit the frailties of her companion, but to bear with them: his character may be a trial, but not an impediment to virtue.

If Dr. Gregory confined his remark to romantic expectations of constant love and congenial feelings, he should have recollected that experience will banish what advice can never make us cease to wish for, when the imagination is kept alive at the expense of reason.

I own it frequently happens that women who have fostered a romantic, unnatural delicacy of feeling waste their lives in imagining how happy they should have been with a husband who could love them with a fervid increasing affection every day, and all day. But they might as well pine married as single—and would not be a jot more unhappy with a bad husband than longing for a good one. That a proper education or, to speak with more precision, a well stored mind would enable a woman to support a single life with dignity, I grant; but that she should avoid cultivating her taste lest her husband should occasionally shock it, is quitting a substance for a shadow. To say the truth, I do not know of what use is an improved taste if the individual be not rendered more independent of the casualties of life; if new sources of enjoyment, only dependent on the solitary operations of the mind, are not opened. People of taste, married or single, without distinction, will ever be disgusted by various things that touch not less observing minds. On this conclusion the argument must not be allowed to hinge; but in the whole sum of enjoyment is taste to be denominated a blessing?

The question is whether it procures most pain or pleasure? The answer will decide the propriety of Dr. Gregory's advice, and show how absurd and tyrannical it is thus to lay down a system of slavery; or to attempt to educate moral beings by any other rules than those deduced from pure reason, which apply to the whole species.

Gentleness of manners, forbearance, and long-suffering are such amiable Godlike qualities[1] that in sublime poetic strains the Deity has been invested with them; and, perhaps, no representation of his goodness so strongly fastens on the human affections as those that represent him abundant in mercy and willing to pardon.[2] Gentleness, considered in this point of view, bears on its front all the characteristics of grandeur combined with the winning graces of condescension;[3] but what a different aspect it assumes when it is the submissive demeanour of dependence, the support of weakness that loves, because it wants protection, and is forbearing, because it must silently endure injuries, smiling under the lash at which it dare not snarl. Abject as this picture appears, it is the portrait of an accomplished woman, according to the received opinion of female excellence, separated by specious reasoners from human excellence. Or, they kindly restore the rib and make one moral being of a man and woman—not forgetting to give her all the "submissive charms."

How women are to exist in that state where there is to be neither marrying nor giving in marriage,[4] we are not told. For though moralists have agreed that the tenor[5] of life seems to prove that man is prepared by

---

[1] *Gentleness ... long-suffering* Galatians 5.22–23: "But the fruit of the Spirit is love, joy, peace, longsuffering, gentleness, goodness, faith, meekness, temperance: against such there is no law."

[2] *abundant ... pardon* Isaiah 55.7. "Let the wicked forsake his way, and the unrighteous man his thoughts: and let him return unto the Lord, and he will have mercy upon him; and to our God, for he will abundantly pardon."

[3] *condescension* Gracious behavior shown to a social inferior.

[4] *neither ... marriage* Matthew 22.30: "For in the resurrection they neither marry, nor are given in marriage, but are as the angels of God in heaven."

[5] *tenor* Continuous meaning.

various circumstances for a future state, they constantly concur in advising woman only to provide for the present. Gentleness, docility, and a spaniel-like affection are, on this ground, consistently recommended as the cardinal virtues of the sex; and, disregarding the arbitrary economy of nature, one writer has declared that it is masculine for a woman to be melancholy. She was created to be the toy of man, his rattle, and it must jingle in his ears whenever, dismissing reason, he chooses to be amused.

To recommend gentleness, indeed, on a broad basis is strictly philosophical. A frail being should labour to be gentle. But when forbearance confounds right and wrong, it ceases to be a virtue; and, however convenient it may be found in a companion, that companion will ever be considered as an inferior and only inspire a vapid tenderness, which easily degenerates into contempt. Still, if advice could really make a being gentle, whose natural disposition admitted not of such a fine polish, something towards the advancement of order would be attained; but if, as might quickly be demonstrated, only affectation be produced by this indiscriminate counsel, which throws a stumbling-block in the way of gradual improvement and true melioration[1] of temper, the sex is not much benefited by sacrificing solid virtues to the attainment of superficial graces, though for a few years they may procure the individuals regal sway.

As a philosopher, I read with indignation the plausible epithets which men use to soften their insults; and, as a moralist, I ask what is meant by such heterogeneous associations as fair defects, amiable weaknesses, &c.? If there be but one criterion of morals, but one archetype for man, women appear to be suspended by destiny, according to the vulgar tale of Mahomet's coffin;[2] they have neither the unerring instinct of brutes, nor are allowed to fix the eye of reason on a perfect model. They were made to be loved, and must not aim at respect, lest they should be hunted out of society as masculine.

But to view the subject in another point of view. Do passive, indolent women make the best wives? Confining our discussion to the present moment of existence, let us see how such weak creatures perform their part. Do the women who, by the attainment of a few superficial accomplishments, have strengthened the prevailing prejudice merely contribute to the happiness of their husbands? Do they display their charms merely to amuse them? And have women, who have early imbibed notions of passive obedience, sufficient character to manage a family or educate children? So far from it that, after surveying the history of woman, I cannot help agreeing with the severest satirist, considering the sex as the weakest as well as the most oppressed half of the species. What does history disclose but marks of inferiority, and how few women have emancipated themselves from the galling yoke of sovereign man? So few that the exceptions remind me of an ingenious conjecture respecting Newton: that he was probably a being of a superior order accidentally caged in a human body.[3] Following the same train of thinking, I have been led to imagine that the few extraordinary women who have rushed in eccentrical directions out of the orbit prescribed to their sex were male spirits, confined by mistake in female frames. But if it be not philosophical to think of sex when the soul is mentioned, the inferiority must depend on the organs; or the heavenly fire, which is to ferment the clay, is not given in equal portions.

But avoiding, as I have hitherto done, any direct comparison of the two sexes collectively, or frankly acknowledging the inferiority of woman, according to the present appearance of things, I shall only insist that men have increased that inferiority until women are almost sunk below the standard of rational creatures. Let their faculties have room to unfold, and their virtues to gain strength, and then determine where the whole sex must stand in the intellectual scale. Yet let it be remembered that for a small number of distinguished women I do not ask a place.

It is difficult for us purblind[4] mortals to say to what height human discoveries and improvements may arrive when the gloom of despotism subsides, which makes us

[1] *melioration* Betterment.

[2] *Mahomet's coffin* It was believed that Mohammed's coffin was suspended in mid-air at his tomb in Medina, Saudi Arabia.

[3] *Newton ... body* Newton and his scientific discoveries were held in extremely high regard during the eighteenth century; consider, for example, Pope's *Epitaph. Intended for Sir Isaac Newton, In Westminster-Abbey* (1730): "Nature and nature's laws lay hid in night; / God said 'Let Newton be' and all was light."

[4] *purblind* Imperfectly sighted.

stumble at every step; but, when morality shall be settled on a more solid basis, then, without being gifted with a prophetic spirit, I will venture to predict that woman will be either the friend or slave of man. We shall not, as at present, doubt whether she is a moral agent or the link which unites man with brutes. But, should it then appear that, like the brutes, they were principally created for the use of man, he will let them patiently bite the bridle and not mock them with empty praise; or, should their rationality be proved, he will not impede their improvement merely to gratify his sensual appetites. He will not, with all the graces of rhetoric, advise them to submit implicitly their understanding to the guidance of man. He will not, when he treats of[1] the education of women, assert that they ought never to have the free use of reason, nor would he recommend cunning and dissimulation to beings who are acquiring, in like manner as himself, the virtues of humanity.

Surely there can be but one rule of right, if morality has an eternal foundation; and whoever sacrifices virtue, strictly so called, to present convenience, or whose duty it is to act in such a manner,[2] lives only for the passing day and cannot be an accountable creature.

The poet then should have dropped his sneer when he says:

> If weak women go astray,
> The stars are more in fault than they.[3]

For that they are bound by the adamantine[4] chain of destiny is most certain, if it be proved that they are never to exercise their own reason, never to be independent, never to rise above opinion, or to feel the dignity of a rational will that only bows to God—and often forgets that the universe contains any being but itself and the model of perfection to which its ardent gaze is turned—to adore attributes that, softened into virtues, may be imitated in kind, though the degree overwhelms the enraptured mind.

If, I say, for I would not impress by declamation when Reason offers her sober light, if they be really capable of acting like rational creatures, let them not be treated like slaves, or like the brutes who are dependent on the reason of man when they associate with him; but cultivate their minds, give them the salutary, sublime curb of principle, and let them attain conscious dignity by feeling themselves only dependent on God. Teach them, in common with man, to submit to necessity, instead of giving, to render them more pleasing, a sex to morals.

Further, should experience prove that they cannot attain the same degree of strength of mind, perseverance, and fortitude, let their virtues be the same in kind, though they may vainly struggle for the same degree; and the superiority of man will be equally clear, if not clearer; and truth, as it is a simple principle, which admits of no modification, would be common to both. Nay, the order of society as it is at present regulated would not be inverted, for woman would then only have the rank that reason assigned her, and arts could not be practised to bring the balance even, much less to turn it.

These may be termed Utopian dreams—thanks to that Being who impressed them on my soul and gave me sufficient strength of mind to dare to exert my own reason until, becoming dependent only on him for the support of my virtue, I view, with indignation, the mistaken notions that enslave my sex.

I love man as my fellow; but his sceptre, real or usurped, extends not to me, unless the reason of an individual demands my homage; and even then the submission is to reason, and not to man. In fact, the conduct of an accountable being must be regulated by the operations of its own reason, or on what foundation rests the throne of God?

It appears to me necessary to dwell on these obvious truths because females have been insulated, as it were; and, while they have been stripped of the virtues that should clothe humanity, they have been decked with artificial graces that enable them to exercise a short-lived tyranny. Love, in their bosoms, takes the place of every nobler passion; their sole ambition is to be fair, to raise emotion instead of inspiring respect; and this ignoble desire, like the servility in absolute monarchies, destroys all strength of character. Liberty is the mother of virtue, and if women be, by their very constitution, slaves, and not allowed to breathe the sharp invigorating air of

[1] *treats of* Discourses on.

[2] *to act in such a manner* I.e., to sacrifice duty to convenience.

[3] *If weak ... they* "Hans Carvel" (1700) by Matthew Prior.

[4] *adamantine* Unbreakable.

freedom, they must ever languish like exotics, and be reckoned beautiful flaws in nature.

As to the argument respecting the subjection in which the sex has ever been held, it retorts on[1] man. The many have always been enthralled by the few; and monsters, who scarcely have shown any discernment of human excellence, have tyrannized over thousands of their fellow-creatures. Why have men of superior endowments submitted to such degradation? For is it not universally acknowledged that kings, viewed collectively, have ever been inferior, in abilities and virtue, to the same number of men taken from the common mass of mankind—yet have they not, and are they not still treated with a degree of reverence that is an insult to reason? China is not the only country where a living man has been made a God.[2] Men have submitted to superior strength to enjoy with impunity[3] the pleasure of the moment; women have only done the same, and therefore until it is proved that the courtier, who servilely resigns the birthright of a man, is not a moral agent, it cannot be demonstrated that woman is essentially inferior to man because she has always been subjugated.

Brutal force has hitherto governed the world; and that the science of politics is in its infancy is evident from philosophers scrupling to give the knowledge most useful to man that determinate distinction.

I shall not pursue this argument any further than to establish an obvious inference: that as sound politics diffuse liberty, mankind, including woman, will become more wise and virtuous.

Chapter 3

The Same Subject Continued

… I wish to sum up what I have said in a few words, for I here throw down my gauntlet and deny the existence of sexual virtues, not excepting modesty. For man and woman, truth—if I understand the meaning of the word—must be the same; yet for the fanciful female character, so prettily drawn by poets and novelists demanding the sacrifice of truth and sincerity, virtue becomes a relative idea, having no other foundation than utility, and of that utility men pretend arbitrarily to judge, shaping it to their own convenience.

Women, I allow, may have different duties to fulfil; but they are human duties, and the principles that should regulate the discharge of them, I sturdily maintain, must be the same.

To become respectable, the exercise of their understanding is necessary; there is no other foundation for independence of character. I mean explicitly to say that they must only bow to the authority of reason instead of being the modest slaves of opinion.

In the superior ranks of life how seldom do we meet with a man of superior abilities, or even common acquirements? The reason appears to me clear: the state they are born in was an unnatural one. The human character has ever been formed by the employments that the individual, or class, pursues; and if the faculties are not sharpened by necessity, they must remain obtuse. The argument may fairly be extended to women; for, seldom occupied by serious business, the pursuit of pleasure gives that insignificancy to their character which renders the society of the great so insipid. The same want of firmness, produced by a similar cause, forces them both to fly from themselves to noisy pleasures, and artificial passions, until vanity takes place of every social affection, and the characteristics of humanity can scarcely be discerned. Such are the blessings of civil governments, as they are at present organized, that wealth and female softness equally tend to debase mankind and are produced by the same cause; but allowing women to be rational creatures, they should be incited to acquire virtues which they may call their own, for how can a rational being be ennobled by any thing that is not obtained by its own exertions?

—1792

[1] *retorts on* Answers back.

[2] *China … God* See A *Discourse on the Love of our Country* (1789) by Richard Price (1723–91), English philosopher and writer.

[3] *impunity* Safety from punishment.

IN CONTEXT

Contemporary Reviews of *A Vindication of the Rights of Woman*

Early reviews of *The Vindication of the Rights of Woman* divided largely along party lines. Reviewers from the *Analytic Review* and the *Monthly Review*, for example, praised the work while more conservative papers such as the *Critical Review*, the *General Magazine* and the *Gentleman's Magazine* attacked it. Excerpts from the *Analytic Review* and the *Critical Review* are reprinted below.

from *Analytical Review* 12 (1792)

... It is with some reluctance that for the present we take our leave of this singular, and, on the whole, excellent production. The subjects which it investigates, are of the utmost importance to human nature, and we should be wanting in our engagements, and in our duty, if we passed it over too slightly. This circumstance makes it necessary to defer the further analysis to a future Review, when we shall proceed to the remaining topics of this volume.

It might have been supposed that Mrs. W. had taken advantage of the popular topic of the "Rights of Man" in calling her work "A Vindication of the Rights of Woman," had she not already published a work, one of the first answers that appeared to Mr. Burke, under the title of "A Vindication of the Rights of Man." But in reality the present work is an elaborate *treatise* of *female education*. The lesser wits will probably affect to make themselves merry at the title and apparent object of this publication; but we have no doubt if even her contemporaries should fail to do her justice, posterity will compensate the defect; and have no hesitation in declaring, that if the bulk of the great truths which this publication contains were reduced to practice, the nation would be better, wiser and happier, than it is upon the wretched, trifling, useless and absurd system of education which is now prevalent.

from *Critical Review* 4 (1792)

One of the strictest proofs in mathematical demonstrations, is the reducing the questions to an absurdity; by allowing, for instance, that the proposition is not true, and then showing that this would lead to the most obvious inconsistencies. Miss Wollstonecraft has converted this method of proceeding with the same success: reasoning on the boasted principles of the Rights of Man, she finds they lead very clearly to the object of her work, a Vindication of the Rights of Woman; and, by the absurdity of many of her conclusions, shows, while we admit the reasoning, that the premises must be, in some respects, fallacious.

> Dismissing then those pretty feminine phrases, which the men condescendingly use to soften our slavish dependence, and despising that weak elegancy of mind, exquisite sensibility, and sweet docility of manners, supposed to be the sexual characteristics of the weaker vessel, I wish to shew that elegance is inferior to virtue, that the first object of laudable ambition is to obtain a character as a human being, regardless of the distinction of sex; and that secondary views should be brought to this simple touchstone.

This is the outline of her plan; but before she proceeds to show that this change would be suitable, useful, advantageous, it will be first necessary to prove that there is no sexual distinction of character; that the female mind is equally fitted for the more arduous mental operations; that women are equally able to pursue the toilsome road of minute, laborious, investigation; that their judgments are equally sound, their resolution equally strong. After this is done, the benefit derived must be considered; and, when all are strong, to whom must the weaker operations belong? The female Plato will find it unsuitable to "the dignity of her virtue" to dress the child, and descend to the disgusting offices of a nurse: the new Archimedes will measure the shirts by means of the altitude taken by a quadrant; and the young lady, instead of studying the softer and more amiable arts of pleasing, must contend with her lover for superiority of mind, for greater dignity of virtue; and before she condescends to become his wife, must prove herself his equal or superior.—It may be fancy, prejudice, or obstinacy, we contend not for a name, but we are infinitely better pleased with the present system; and, in truth, dear young lady, for by the appellation sometimes prefixed to your name we must suppose you to be young, endeavour to attain "the weak elegancy of mind," the "sweet docility of manners," "the exquisite sensibility," the former ornaments of your sex; we are certain you will be more pleasing, and we dare pronounce that you will be infinitely happier. Mental superiority is not an object worth contending for, if happiness be the aim. But, as this is the first female combatant in the new field of the Rights of Woman, if we smile only, we shall be accused of wishing to decline the contest; if we content ourselves with paying a compliment to her talents, it will be styled inconsistent with "true dignity," and as showing that we want to continue the "slavish dependence."—We must contend then with this new Atalanta; and who knows whether, in this modern instance, we may not gain two victories by the contest? There is more than one bachelor in our corps; and, if we should succeed, Miss Wollstonecraft may take her choice.

This work is dedicated to M. Talleyrand-Perigord, late bishop of Autun, who, in his treatise on National Education, does not seem to be perfectly convinced that the rights of man extend to woman; yet in France the diffusion of knowledge, our author asserts, is greater than in any other European nation, on account of the more unreserved communication between the sexes, though what the ladies have gained in knowledge they seem confessedly to have lost in delicacy. The following passage we must transcribe, for we confess we do not fully understand it.

> Contending for the rights of woman, my main argument is built on this simple principle, that if she be not prepared by education to become the companion of man, she will stop the progress of knowledge, for truth must be common to all, or it will be inefficacious with respect to its influence on general practice. And how can woman be expected to co-operate unless she know why she ought to be virtuous! unless freedom strengthen her reason till she comprehend her duty, and see in what manner it is connected with her real good? If children are to be educated to understand the true principle of patriotism, their mother must be a patriot; and the love of mankind, from which an orderly train of virtues spring, can only be produced by considering the moral and civil interest of mankind; but the education and situation of woman, at present, shuts her out from such investigations.
>
> In this work I have produced many arguments, which to me were conclusive, to prove that the prevailing notion respecting a sexual character was subversive of morality, and I have contended, that to render the human body and mind more perfect, chastity must more universally prevail, and that chastity will never be respected in the male world till the person of a woman is not, as it were, idolized, when little virtue or sense embellish it with the grand traces of mental beauty, or the interesting simplicity of affection.

The first sentence is erroneous in fact and in reasoning: it is contradicted by the experience of ages, the practice of different nations. The second sentence is a curious one—How can she be supposed to co-operate (we *suppose* in the progress of knowledge) unless she know why she ought to be *virtuous?* Virtuous! Here must be some mistake: what has virtue to do with the progress of knowledge? As to freedom, strengthening the reason, &c. we see no occasion for metaphysical investigation on this subject: that virtue is connected with prosperity and happiness, and vice with misfortune and misery, she might learn, not from Locke, but the New Testament. The concluding sentence of the first paragraph is still more strange. Patriotism may be very properly instilled by a *father,* and we must beg leave to differ in opinion from this lady in another point: we are confident, from frequent and extensive observation, no arguments can confute the opinion that we have formed, and we must still persist in thinking, that the education and situation of women, *at present,* really and effectually *inspire* the *love* of *mankind.* We do believe with Miss Wollstonecraft, that chastity will be respected more, when the person of a woman ceases to be idolized, and the grand traces of mental beauty are principally conspicuous....

from *Maria; or The Wrongs of Woman*

Chapter 5

"My Father," said Jemima, "seduced my mother, a pretty girl, with whom he lived fellow-servant; and she no sooner perceived the natural, the dreaded consequence, than the terrible conviction flashed on her— that she was ruined. Honesty, and a regard for her reputation, had been the only principles inculcated by her mother; and they had been so forcibly impressed that she feared shame more than the poverty to which it would lead. Her incessant importunities[1] to prevail upon my father to screen her from reproach by marrying her, as he had promised in the fervour of seduction, estranged him from her so completely that her very person became distasteful to him; and he began to hate, as well as despise me, before I was born.

"My mother, grieved to the soul by his neglect, and unkind treatment, actually resolved to famish herself and injured her health by the attempt; though she had not sufficient resolution to adhere to her project, or renounce it entirely. Death came not at her call; yet sorrow, and the methods she adopted to conceal her condition, still doing the work of a house-maid, had such an effect on her constitution that she died in the wretched garret where her virtuous mistress had forced her to take refuge in the very pangs of labour; though my father, after a slight reproof,[2] was allowed to remain in his place—allowed by the mother of six children who, scarcely permitting a footstep to be heard during her month's indulgence,[3] felt no sympathy for the poor wretch denied every comfort required by her situation.

"The day my mother died, the ninth after my birth, I was consigned to the care of the cheapest nurse my father could find; who suckled her own child at the same time, and lodged as many more as she could get in two cellar-like apartments.

"Poverty, and the habit of seeing children die off her hands, had so hardened her heart that the office of a mother did not awaken the tenderness of a woman; nor were the feminine caresses which seem a part of the rearing of a child ever bestowed on me. The chicken has a wing to shelter under; but I had no bosom to nestle in, no kindred warmth to foster me. Left in dirt, to cry with cold and hunger till I was weary, and sleep without ever being prepared by exercise, or lulled by kindness to rest, could I be expected to become any thing but a weak and rickety babe? Still, in spite of neglect, I continued to exist, to learn to curse existence her countenance grew ferocious as she spoke, and the treatment that rendered me miserable seemed to sharpen my wits. Confined then in a damp hovel, to rock the cradle of the succeed-

[1] *importunities* Attempts to get attention.

[2] *reproof* Rebuke.

[3] *during her month's indulgence* I.e., during the period when she herself had been recovering after childbirth.

ing tribe, I looked like a little old woman, or a hag shriveling into nothing. The furrows of reflection and care contracted the youthful cheek, and gave a sort of supernatural wildness to the ever-watchful eye. During this period, my father had married another fellow-servant, who loved him less and knew better how to manage his passion than my mother. She likewise proving with child, they agreed to keep a shop: my stepmother—if, being an illegitimate offspring, I may venture thus to characterize her—having obtained a sum of a rich relation for that purpose.

"Soon after her lying-in,[1] she prevailed on my father to take me home, to save the expense of maintaining me, and of hiring a girl to assist her in the care of the child. I was young, it was true, but appeared a knowing little thing and might be made handy. Accordingly I was brought to her house; but not to a home—for a home I never knew. Of this child, a daughter, she was extravagantly fond; and it was a part of my employment to assist to spoil her, by humouring all her whims and bearing all her caprices. Feeling her own consequence before she could speak, she had learned the art of tormenting me, and if I ever dared to resist, I received blows, laid on with no compunctious hand,[2] or was sent to bed dinnerless, as well as supperless. I said that it was a part of my daily labour to attend this child with the servility of a slave; still it was but a part. I was sent out in all seasons, and from place to place, to carry burdens far above my strength, without being allowed to draw near the fire, or ever being cheered by encouragement or kindness. No wonder then, treated like a creature of another species, that I began to envy, and at length to hate, the darling of the house. Yet, I perfectly remember that it was the caresses, and kind expressions of my stepmother, which first excited my jealous discontent. Once, I cannot forget it, when she was calling in vain her wayward child to kiss her, I ran to her, saying, 'I will kiss you, ma'am!'; and how did my heart, which was in my mouth, sink, what was my debasement of soul, when pushed away with—'I do not want you, pert thing!' Another day, when a new gown had excited the highest good humour, and she uttered the appropriate *dear,* addressed unexpectedly to me, I thought I could never do enough to please her; I was all alacrity,[3] and rose proportionably in my own estimation.

"As her daughter grew up, she was pampered with cakes and fruit, while I was, literally speaking, fed with the refuse of the table, with her leavings. A liquorish tooth[4] is, I believe, common to children, and I used to steal any thing sweet that I could catch up with a chance of concealment. When detected, she was not content to chastise me herself at the moment, but, on my father's return in the evening (he was a shopman), the principal discourse was to recount my faults, and attribute them to the wicked disposition which I had brought into the world with me, inherited from my mother. He did not fail to leave the marks of his resentment on my body, and then solaced himself by playing with my sister. I could have murdered her at those moments. To save myself from these unmerciful corrections, I resorted to falsehood, and the untruths which I sturdily maintained were brought in judgment against me, to support my tyrant's inhuman charge of my natural propensity to vice. Seeing me treated with contempt, and always being fed and dressed better, my sister conceived a contemptuous opinion of me that proved an obstacle to all affection; and my father, hearing continually of my faults, began to consider me as a curse entailed[5] on him for his sins: he was therefore easily prevailed on to bind me apprentice to one of my step-mother's friends, who kept a slop shop[6] in Wapping.[7] I was represented (as it was said) in my true colours; but she 'warranted,'[8] snapping her fingers, 'that she should break my spirit or heart.'

"My mother replied, with a whine, 'that if any body could make me better, it was such a clever woman as herself; though, for her own part, she had tried in vain, but good nature was her fault.'

"I shudder with horror when I recollect the treatment I had now to endure. Not only under the lash of my task-mistress, but the drudge of the maid, appren-

[1] *lying-in* Period of rest following childbirth.

[2] *compunctious hand* I.e., Jemima was beaten without pity, or indeed any concern.

[3] *alacrity* Readiness.

[4] *liquorish tooth* Sweet tooth, i.e., fondness for sweets.

[5] *entailed* Irrevocably attached.

[6] *slop shop* Shop that sold inexpensive, ready-made clothing.

[7] *Wapping* District of east London.

[8] *warranted* Guaranteed.

tices, and children, I never had a taste of human kindness to soften the rigour of perpetual labour. I had been introduced as an object of abhorrence into the family; as a creature of whom my step-mother, though she had been kind enough to let me live in the house with her own child, could make nothing. I was described as a wretch whose nose must be kept to the grinding stone—and it was held there with an iron grasp. It seemed indeed the privilege of their superior nature to kick me about like the dog or cat. If I were attentive, I was called fawning, if refractory,[1] an obstinate mule, and like a mule I received their censure on my loaded back. Often has my mistress, for some instance of forgetfulness, thrown me from one side of the kitchen to the other, knocked my head against the wall, spit in my face, with various refinements on barbarity that I forbear to enumerate, though they were all acted over again by the servant, with additional insults, to which the appellation of *bastard* was commonly added with taunts or sneers. But I will not attempt to give you an adequate idea of my situation, lest you, who probably have never been drenched with the dregs of human misery, should think I exaggerate.

"I stole now—from absolute necessity—bread; yet whatever else was taken, which I had it not in my power to take, was ascribed to me. I was the filching cat, the ravenous dog, the dumb brute who must bear all; for if I endeavoured to exculpate[2] myself, I was silenced without any enquiries being made, with 'Hold your tongue, you never tell truth.' Even the very air I breathed was tainted with scorn; for I was sent to the neighbouring shops with Glutton, Liar, or Thief written on my forehead. This was, at first, the most bitter punishment; but sullen pride, or a kind of stupid desperation, made me, at length, almost regardless of the contempt which had wrung from me so many solitary tears at the only moments when I was allowed to rest.

"Thus was I the mark of cruelty till my sixteenth year; and then I have only to point out a change of misery, for a period I never knew. Allow me first to make one observation. Now I look back, I cannot help attributing the greater part of my misery to the misfortune of having been thrown into the world without the grand support of life—a mother's affection. I had no one to love me, or to make me respected, to enable me to acquire respect. I was an egg dropped on the sand; a pauper by nature, hunted from family to family, who belonged to nobody—and nobody cared for me. I was despised from my birth, and denied the chance of obtaining a footing for myself in society. Yes; I had not even the chance of being considered as a fellow-creature—yet all the people with whom I lived, brutalized as they were by the low cunning of trade, and the despicable shifts of poverty, were not without bowels,[3] though they never yearned for me. I was, in fact, born a slave, and chained by infamy[4] to slavery during the whole of existence, without having any companions to alleviate it by sympathy, or teach me how to rise above it by their example....

"At sixteen, I suddenly grew tall, and something like comeliness[5] appeared on a Sunday, when I had time to wash my face and put on clean clothes. My master had once or twice caught hold of me in the passage; but I instinctively avoided his disgusting caresses. One day however, when the family were at a Methodist meeting, he contrived to be alone in the house with me, and by blows—yes, blows and menaces—compelled me to submit to his ferocious desire; and, to avoid my mistress's fury, I was obliged in future to comply, and skulk to my loft at his command, in spite of increasing loathing.

"The anguish which was now pent up in my bosom seemed to open a new world to me: I began to extend my thoughts beyond myself and grieve for human misery, until I discovered, with horror—ah! what horror!—that I was with child. I know not why I felt a mixed sensation of despair and tenderness, excepting that, ever called a bastard, a bastard appeared to me an object of the greatest compassion in creation.

"I communicated this dreadful circumstance to my master, who was almost equally alarmed at the intelligence; for he feared his wife and public censure at the meeting. After some weeks of deliberation had elapsed, I in continual fear that my altered shape would be noticed, my master gave me a medicine in a phial which

[1] *refractory* Stubborn, non-compliant.

[2] *exculpate* Clear oneself from blame.

[3] *bowels* Heart, compassion.

[4] *infamy* Scandalous reputation.

[5] *comeliness* Beauty.

he desired me to take, telling me, without any circumlocution,[1] for what purpose it was designed. I burst into tears, I thought it was killing myself—yet was such a self as I worth preserving? He cursed me for a fool, and left me to my own reflections. I could not resolve to take this infernal potion; but I wrapped it up in an old gown, and hid it in a corner of my box.

"Nobody yet suspected me, because they had been accustomed to view me as a creature of another species. But the threatening storm at last broke over my devoted head—never shall I forget it! One Sunday evening when I was left, as usual, to take care of the house, my master came home intoxicated, and I became the prey of his brutal appetite. His extreme intoxication made him forget his customary caution, and my mistress entered and found us in a situation that could not have been more hateful to her than me. Her husband was 'pot-valiant,'[2] he feared her not at the moment, nor had he then much reason, for she instantly turned the whole force of her anger another way. She tore off my cap, scratched, kicked, and buffeted me until she had exhausted her strength, declaring, as she rested her arm, 'that I had wheedled[3] her husband from her. But, could any thing better be expected from a wretch whom she had taken into her house out of pure charity?' What a torrent of abuse rushed out, until, almost breathless, she concluded with saying, 'that I was born a strumpet;[4] it ran in my blood, and nothing good could come to those who harboured me.'

"My situation was, of course, discovered, and she declared that I should not stay another night under the same roof with an honest family. I was therefore pushed out of doors, and my trumpery[5] thrown after me, when it had been contemptuously examined in the passage lest I should have stolen any thing.

"Behold me then in the street, utterly destitute! Whither could I creep for shelter? To my father's roof I had no claim when not pursued by shame—now I shrunk back as from death from my mother's cruel reproaches, my father's execrations.[6] I could not endure to hear him curse the day I was born, though life had been a curse to me. Of death I thought, but with a confused emotion of terror, as I stood leaning my head on a post and starting at every footstep, lest it should be my mistress coming to tear my heart out. One of the boys of the shop passing by heard my tale, and immediately repaired to his master to give him a description of my situation; and he touched the right key—the scandal it would give rise to if I were left to repeat my tale to every enquirer. This plea came home to his reason, who had been sobered by his wife's rage, the fury of which fell on him when I was out of her reach, and he sent the boy to me with half-a-guinea,[7] desiring him to conduct me to a house where beggars, and other wretches, the refuse of society, nightly lodged.

"This night was spent in a state of stupefaction, or desperation. I detested mankind, and abhorred myself.

"In the morning I ventured out, to throw myself in my master's way, at his usual hour of going abroad. I approached him, he 'damned me for a b——, declared I had disturbed the peace of the family, and that he had sworn to his wife never to take any more notice of me.' He left me; but, instantly returning, he told me that he should speak to his friend, a parish-officer,[8] to get a nurse for the brat I laid to him; and advised me, if I wished to keep out of the house of correction, not to make free with his name.

"I hurried back to my hole, and, rage giving place to despair, sought for the potion that was to procure abortion and swallowed it, with a wish that it might destroy me at the same time that it stopped the sensations of new-born life, which I felt with indescribable emotion. My head turned round, my heart grew sick, and in the horrors of approaching dissolution,[9] mental anguish was swallowed up. The effect of the medicine

[1] *circumlocution* Indirect speaking.

[2] *pot-valiant* Courageous due to the affects of alcohol.

[3] *wheedled* Seduced by flattery or gentle coaxing.

[4] *strumpet* Derogatory term for a woman who has a number of sexual partners.

[5] *trumpery* Worthless clothing goods.

[6] *execrations* Expressions of intense loathing.

[7] *half-a-guinea* Gold coin.

[8] *parish-officer* General term for person holding any one of several elected positions within a parish, including churchwarden, surveyor, overseer of the poor, constable, etc.; overseers of the poor set and collected poor rates, as well as administering benefits to those in need.

[9] *dissolution* Death.

was violent, and I was confined to my bed several days; but, youth and a strong constitution prevailing, I once more crawled out to ask myself the cruel question, 'Whither I should go?' I had but two shillings[1] left in my pocket, the rest had been expended, by a poor woman who slept in the same room, to pay for my lodging and purchase the necessaries of which she partook.

"With this wretch I went into the neighbouring streets to beg, and my disconsolate appearance drew a few pence from the idle, enabling me still to command a bed; until, recovering from my illness, and taught to put on my rags to the best advantage, I was accosted from different motives, and yielded to the desire of the brutes I met with the same detestation that I had felt for my still more brutal master. I have since read in novels of the blandishments[2] of seduction, but I had not even the pleasure of being enticed into vice.

"I shall not," interrupted Jemima, "lead your imagination into all the scenes of wretchedness and depravity which I was condemned to view, or mark the different stages of my debasing misery. Fate dragged me through the very kennels[3] of society: I was still a slave, a bastard, a common property. Become familiar with vice, for I wish to conceal nothing from you, I picked the pockets of the drunkards who abused me; and proved by my conduct that I deserved the epithets with which they loaded me at moments when distrust ought to cease.

"Detesting my nightly occupation, though valuing, if I may so use the word, my independence, which only consisted in choosing the street in which I should wander, or the roof, when I had money, in which I should hide my head, I was some time before I could prevail on myself to accept of a place in a house of ill fame[4] to which a girl, with whom I had accidentally conversed in the street, had recommended me. I had been hunted almost into a fever by the watchmen[5] of the quarter of the town I frequented; one, whom I had unwittingly offended, giving the word to the whole pack. You can scarcely conceive the tyranny exercised by these wretches: considering themselves as the instruments of the very laws they violate, the pretext which steels their conscience hardens their heart. Not content with receiving from us, outlaws of society (let other women talk of favours), a brutal gratification gratuitously as a privilege of office, they extort a tithe[6] of prostitution, and harass with threats the poor creatures whose occupation affords not the means to silence the growl of avarice. To escape from this persecution, I once more entered into servitude.

"A life of comparative regularity restored my health; and— do not start[7]—my manners were improved in a situation where vice sought to render itself alluring, and taste was cultivated to fashion the person, if not to refine the mind. Besides, the common civility of speech, contrasted with the gross vulgarity to which I had been accustomed, was something like the polish of civilization. I was not shut out from all intercourse[8] of humanity. Still I was galled[9] by the yoke of service, and my mistress often flying into violent fits of passion made me dread a sudden dismission, which I understood was always the case. I was therefore prevailed on, though I felt a horror of men, to accept the offer of a gentleman, rather in the decline of years, to keep his house, pleasantly situated in a little village near Hampstead.[10]

"He was a man of great talents, and of brilliant wit; but, a worn-out votary of voluptuousness,[11] his desires became fastidious in proportion as they grew weak, and the native tenderness of his heart was undermined by a vitiated[12] imagination. A thoughtless career of libertinism[13] and social enjoyment had injured his health to such a degree that, whatever pleasure his conversation afforded me (and my esteem was ensured by proofs of the generous humanity of his disposition), the being his

1 *shillings* Coins of small value.

2 *blandishments* Flattering words.

3 *kennels* Gutters.

4 *house of ill-fame* Brothel.

5 *watchmen* Before the Police Act of 1839, men were formally appointed to guard city and town streets from sunset to sunrise.

6 *tithe* Tenth of one's earnings.

7 *do not start* I.e., do not be startled, shocked.

8 *intercourse* Social interaction or communication.

9 *galled* Irritated, chafed.

10 *Hampstead* North London suburb.

11 *votary of voluptuousness* Person devoted to sensuality.

12 *vitiated* Rendered impure, soiled.

13 *libertinism* Unrestrained, licentious conduct.

mistress was purchasing it at a very dear rate. With such a keen perception of the delicacies of sentiment, with an imagination invigorated by the exercise of genius, how could he sink into the grossness of sensuality!

"But, to pass over a subject which I recollect with pain, I must remark to you, as an answer to your often-repeated question—'Why my sentiments and language were superior to my station?'—that I now began to read, to beguile[1] the tediousness of solitude, and to gratify an inquisitive, active mind. I had often, in my childhood, followed a ballad-singer to hear the sequel of a dismal story, though sure of being severely punished for delaying to return with whatever I was sent to purchase. I could just spell and put a sentence together, and I listened to the various arguments, though often mingled with obscenity, which occurred at the table where I was allowed to preside: for a literary friend or two frequently came home with my master to dine and pass the night. Having lost the privileged respect of my sex, my presence, instead of restraining, perhaps gave the reins to their tongues; still I had the advantage of hearing discussions from which, in the common course of life, women are excluded.

"You may easily imagine that it was only by degrees that I could comprehend some of the subjects they investigated, or acquire from their reasoning what might be termed a moral sense. But my fondness of reading increasing, and my master occasionally shutting himself up in this retreat for weeks together to write, I had many opportunities of improvement. At first, considering money ("I was right!" exclaimed Jemima, altering her tone of voice) as the only means, after my loss of reputation, of obtaining respect, or even the toleration of humanity, I had not the least scruple to secrete a part of the sums entrusted to me, and to screen myself from detection by a system of falsehood. But, acquiring new principles, I began to have the ambition of returning to the respectable part of society, and was weak enough to suppose it possible. The attention of my unassuming instructor, who, without being ignorant of his own powers, possessed great simplicity of manners, strengthened the illusion. Having sometimes caught up hints for thought from my untutored remarks, he often led me to discuss the subjects he was treating, and would read to me his productions, previous to their publication, wishing to profit by the criticism of unsophisticated feeling. The aim of his writings was to touch the simple springs of the heart; for he despised the would-be oracles, the self-elected philosophers, who fright away fancy while sifting each grain of thought to prove that slowness of comprehension is wisdom.

"I should have distinguished this as a moment of sunshine, a happy period in my life, had not the repugnance the disgusting libertinism of my protector inspired daily become more painful. And, indeed, I soon did recollect it as such with agony, when his sudden death (for he had recourse to the most exhilarating cordials to keep up the convivial tone of his spirits) again threw me into the desert of human society. Had he had any time for reflection, I am certain he would have left the little property in his power to me: but, attacked by the fatal apoplexy[2] in town, his heir, a man of rigid morals, brought his wife with him to take possession of the house and effects before I was even informed of his death—'to prevent,' as she took care indirectly to tell me, 'such a creature as she supposed me to be from purloining[3] any of them, had I been apprized of the event in time.'

"The grief I felt at the sudden shock the information gave me, which at first had nothing selfish in it, was treated with contempt, and I was ordered to pack up my clothes; and a few trinkets and books, given me by the generous deceased, were contested, while they piously hoped, with a reprobating[4] shake of the head, 'that God would have mercy on his sinful soul!' With some difficulty, I obtained my arrears of wages; but asking—such is the spirit-grinding consequence of poverty and infamy—for a character[5] for honesty and economy, which God knows I merited, I was told by this—why must I call her woman?—'that it would go against her conscience to recommend a kept mistress.' Tears started in my eyes, burning tears; for there are situations in which a wretch is humbled by the contempt they are conscious they do not deserve.

[1] *beguile* Charm away.

[2] *apoplexy* Stroke.

[3] *purloining* Stealing.

[4] *reprobating* Condemning.

[5] *character* I.e., formal reference from an employer.

"I returned to the metropolis; but the solitude of a poor lodging was inconceivably dreary after the society I had enjoyed. To be cut off from human converse, now I had been taught to relish it, was to wander a ghost among the living. Besides, I foresaw, to aggravate the severity of my fate, that my little pittance would soon melt away. I endeavoured to obtain needlework; but, not having been taught early, and my hands being rendered clumsy by hard work, I did not sufficiently excel to be employed by the ready-made linen shops when so many women, better qualified, were suing[1] for it. The want of a character prevented my getting a place; for, irksome as servitude would have been to me, I should have made another trial had it been feasible. Not that I disliked employment, but the inequality of condition to which I must have submitted. I had acquired a taste for literature during the five years I had lived with a literary man, occasionally conversing with men of the first abilities of the age; and now to descend to the lowest vulgarity was a degree of wretchedness not to be imagined unfelt. I had not, it is true, tasted the charms of affection, but I had been familiar with the graces of humanity.

"One of the gentlemen, whom I had frequently dined in company with while I was treated like a companion, met me in the street and enquired after my health. I seized the occasion, and began to describe my situation; but he was in haste to join, at dinner, a select party of choice spirits; therefore, without waiting to hear me, he impatiently put a guinea into my hand, saying, 'It was a pity such a sensible woman should be in distress—he wished me well from his soul.'

"To another I wrote, stating my case and requesting advice. He was an advocate for unequivocal sincerity; and had often, in my presence, descanted[2] on the evils which arise in society from the despotism of rank and riches.

"In reply, I received a long essay on the energy of the human mind with continual allusions to his own force of character. He added, 'That the woman who could write such a letter as I had sent him could never be in want of resources, were she to look into herself and exert her powers; misery was the consequence of indolence, and, as to my being shut out from society, it was the lot of man to submit to certain privations.'[3]

"How often have I heard," said Jemima, interrupting her narrative, "in conversation, and read in books, that every person willing to work may find employment? It is the vague assertion, I believe, of insensible[4] indolence when it relates to men; but, with respect to women, I am sure of its fallacy, unless they will submit to the most menial bodily labour; and even to be employed at hard labour is out of the reach of many whose reputation misfortune or folly has tainted.

"How writers, professing to be friends to freedom and the improvement of morals, can assert that poverty is no evil, I cannot imagine."

"No more can I," interrupted Maria, "yet they even expatiate[5] on the peculiar happiness of indigence,[6] though in what it can consist, excepting in brutal rest, when a man can barely earn a subsistence, I cannot imagine. The mind is necessarily imprisoned in its own little tenement; and, fully occupied by keeping it in repair, has not time to rove abroad for improvement. The book of knowledge is closely clasped against those who must fulfill their daily task of severe manual labour or die; and curiosity, rarely excited by thought or information, seldom moves on the stagnate lake of ignorance."

"As far as I have been able to observe," replied Jemima, "prejudices, caught up by chance, are obstinately maintained by the poor to the exclusion of improvement; they have not time to reason or reflect to any extent, or minds sufficiently exercised to adopt the principles of action, which form perhaps the only basis of contentment in every station."

"And independence," said Darnford, "they are necessarily strangers to, even the independence of despising their persecutors. If the poor are happy, or can be happy, *things are very well as they are.* And I cannot conceive on what principle those writers contend for a change of system who support this opinion. The authors on the other side of the question are much more consis-

[1] *suing* Asking, applying.

[2] *descanted* Commented on.

[3] *privations* Absence of comforts.

[4] *insensible* Incapable of feeling.

[5] *expatiate* Write or speak copiously on a subject.

[6] *indigence* Poverty.

tent who grant the fact; yet, insisting that it is the lot of the majority to be oppressed in this life, kindly turn them over to another, to rectify the false weights and measures of this, as the only way to justify the dispensations of Providence.[1] I have not," continued Darnford, "an opinion more firmly fixed by observation in my mind than that, though riches may fail to produce proportionate happiness, poverty most commonly excludes it by shutting up all the avenues to improvement."

"And as for the affections," added Maria, with a sigh, "how gross,[2] and even tormenting do they become, unless regulated by an improving mind! The culture of the heart ever, I believe, keeps pace with that of the mind. But pray go on," addressing Jemima, "though your narrative gives rise to the most painful reflections on the present state of society."

"Not to trouble you," continued she, "with a detailed description of all the painful feelings of unavailing[3] exertion, I have only to tell you that at last I got recommended to wash in a few families, who did me the favour to admit me into their houses without the most strict enquiry, to wash from one in the morning till eight at night for eighteen or twenty-pence a day. On the happiness to be enjoyed over a washing-tub I need not comment; yet you will allow me to observe that this was a wretchedness of situation peculiar to my sex. A man with half my industry, and, I may say, abilities, could have procured a decent livelihood and discharged some of the duties which knit mankind together; whilst I, who had acquired a taste for the rational—nay, in honest pride let me assert it, the virtuous enjoyments of life—was cast aside as the filth of society. Condemned to labour, like a machine, only to earn bread, and scarcely that, I became melancholy and desperate.

"I have now to mention a circumstance which fills me with remorse, and fear it will entirely deprive me of your esteem. A tradesman became attached to me, and visited me frequently, and I at last obtained such a power over him that he offered to take me home to his house. Consider, dear madam, I was famishing: wonder not that I became a wolf! The only reason for not taking me home immediately was the having a girl in the house with child by him; and this girl, I advised him—yes, I did! Would I could forget it!—to turn out of doors: and one night he determined to follow my advice. Poor wretch! She fell upon her knees, reminded him that he had promised to marry her, that her parents were honest! What did it avail? She was turned out.

"She approached her father's door in the skirts of London, listened at the shutters, but could not knock. A watchman had observed her go and return several times—Poor wretch! (The remorse Jemima spoke of seemed to be stinging her to the soul, as she proceeded.)

"She left it, and, approaching a tub where horses were watered, she sat down in it, and, with desperate resolution, remained in that attitude[4]—till resolution was no longer necessary!

"I happened that morning to be going out to wash, anticipating the moment when I should escape from such hard labour. I passed by, just as some men, going to work, drew out the stiff, cold corpse—let me not recall the horrid moment! I recognized her pale visage; I listened to the tale told by the spectators, and my heart did not burst. I thought of my own state, and wondered how I could be such a monster! I worked hard; and, returning home, I was attacked by a fever. I suffered both in body and mind. I determined not to live with the wretch. But he did not try[5] me; he left the neighbourhood. I once more returned to the wash tub.

"Still this state, miserable as it was, admitted of aggravation. Lifting one day a heavy load, a tub fell against my shin and gave me great pain. I did not pay much attention to the hurt until it became a serious wound, being obliged to work as usual or starve. But, finding myself at length unable to stand for any time, I thought of getting into an hospital. Hospitals, it should seem (for they are comfortless abodes for the sick), were expressly endowed for the reception of the friendless; yet I, who had on that plea a right to assistance, wanted the recommendation of the rich and respectable, and was several weeks languishing for admittance; fees were demanded on entering; and, what was still more unrea-

[1] *dispensations of Providence* Providential management of the world.

[2] *gross* Unrefined, lacking sensitivity.

[3] *unavailing* Of no avail, no use or hope.

[4] *attitude* Posture, bodily position.

[5] *try* Put to the test.

sonable, security for burying me—that expense not coming into the letter of the charity. A guinea was the stipulated sum—I could as soon have raised a million; and I was afraid to apply to the parish for an order, lest they should have passed me I knew not whither.[1] The poor woman at whose house I lodged, compassionating[2] my state, got me into the hospital; and the family where I received the hurt sent me five shillings, three and six-pence of which I gave at my admittance—I know not for what.

"My leg grew quickly better; but I was dismissed before my cure was completed because I could not afford to have my linen washed to appear decently, as the virago[3] of a nurse said, when the gentlemen (the surgeons) came. I cannot give you an adequate idea of the wretchedness of an hospital; everything is left to the care of people intent on gain. The attendants seem to have lost all feeling of compassion in the bustling discharge of their offices; death is so familiar to them that they are not anxious to ward it off. Everything appeared to be conducted for the accommodation of the medical men and their pupils, who came to make experiments on the poor for the benefit of the rich. One of the physicians, I must not forget to mention, gave me half-a-crown, and ordered me some wine, when I was at the lowest ebb. I thought of making my case known to the lady-like matron;[4] but her forbidding countenance prevented me. She condescended to look on the patients, and make general enquiries, two or three times a week; but the nurses knew the hour when the visit of ceremony would commence, and every thing was as it should be.

"After my dismission, I was more at a loss than ever for a subsistence, and, not to weary you with a repetition of the same unavailing attempts, unable to stand at the washing-tub, I began to consider the rich and poor as natural enemies, and became a thief from principle. I could not now cease to reason, but I hated mankind. I despised myself, yet I justified my conduct. I was taken, tried, and condemned to six months' imprisonment in a house of correction. My soul recoils with horror from the remembrance of the insults I had to endure until, branded with shame, I was turned loose in the street, penniless. I wandered from street to street until, exhausted by hunger and fatigue, I sunk down senseless at a door where I had vainly demanded a morsel of bread. I was sent by the inhabitant to the work-house, to which he had surlily bid me go, saying, he 'paid enough in conscience to the poor' when, with parched tongue, I implored his charity. If those well-meaning people who exclaim against beggars were acquainted with the treatment the poor receive in many of these wretched asylums, they would not stifle so easily involuntary sympathy by saying that they have all parishes to go to, or wonder that the poor dread to enter the gloomy walls. What are the common run of workhouses but prisons, in which many respectable old people, worn out by immoderate labour, sink into the grave in sorrow to which they are carried like dogs!"

Alarmed by some indistinct noise, Jemima rose hastily to listen, and Maria, turning to Darnford, said, "I have indeed been shocked beyond expression when I have met a pauper's funeral. A coffin carried on the shoulders of three or four ill-looking wretches, whom the imagination might easily convert into a band of assassins hastening to conceal the corpse and quarrelling about the prey on their way. I know it is of little consequence how we are consigned to the earth;[5] but I am led by this brutal insensibility, to what even the animal creation appears forcibly to feel, to advert to[6] the wretched, deserted manner in which they died."

"True," rejoined Darnford, "and until the rich will give more than a part of their wealth, until they will give time and attention to the wants of the distressed, never let them boast of charity. Let them open their hearts, and not their purses, and employ their minds in the service if they are really actuated by humanity; or charitable institutions will always be the prey of the

[1] *I was afraid ... whither* One applied for poor relief from the parish in which one was last legally settled; terms of legal settlement included being born into a parish, renting property of a certain value, working for over a year and a day, serving an apprenticeship of seven years or more, marrying into the parish, etc. If one applied for poor relief without meeting the settlement requirements, one would be sent back to a parish in which one did.

[2] *compassionating* Having compassion for.

[3] *virago* Bold woman, scold.

[4] *matron* Woman in charge of the nurses.

[5] *how we are consigned to the earth* I.e., how we are buried.

[6] *advert to* Pay attention to.

lowest order of knaves."

Jemima returning, seemed in haste to finish her tale. "The overseer farmed[1] the poor of different parishes, and out of the bowels of poverty was wrung the money with which he purchased this dwelling, as a private receptacle for madness. He had been a keeper at a house of the same description, and conceived that he could make money much more readily in his old occupation. He is a shrewd—shall I say it?—villain. He observed something resolute in my manner, and offered to take me with him and instruct me how to treat the disturbed minds he meant to entrust to my care. The offer of forty pounds a year, and to quit a workhouse, was not to be despised, though the condition of shutting my eyes and hardening my heart was annexed[2] to it.

"I agreed to accompany him; and four years have I been attendant on many wretches, and"—she lowered her voice—"the witness of many enormities.[3] In solitude my mind seemed to recover its force, and many of the sentiments which I imbibed in the only tolerable period of my life returned with their full force. Still, what should induce me to be the champion for suffering humanity? Who ever risked any thing for me? Who ever acknowledged me to be a fellow-creature?"

Maria took her hand, and Jemima, more overcome by kindness than she had ever been by cruelty, hastened out of the room to conceal her emotions.

Darnford soon after heard his summons, and, taking leave of him, Maria promised to gratify his curiosity, with respect to herself, at the first opportunity.

—1798

[1] *farmed* Contracted out care or maintenance for a fee.

[2] *annexed* Included as a condition.

[3] *enormities* Gross breaches of law or morals.

WOMEN AND SOCIETY

CONTEXTS

In the later eighteenth century, women's education and social status became a topic of heated debate among philanthropists, political and educational theorists, and many middle- and upper-class parents. As the first excerpt in this section, from William Blackstone's *Commentaries on the Laws of England*, shows, women's identity in marriage was subsumed under that of their husbands—as it was subsumed under that of their fathers before marriage. Women could not conduct business, own property (unless widowed), reject their fathers' choice of husbands for them, or choose to divorce their husbands. Without legal status they had no representation in Parliament; the idea of female suffrage was one entertained by only the most radical thinkers.

A common concern voiced by educational theorists at the time was that the fashion of educating women in "accomplishments" would help them to attract a husband but would not equip them to fulfill their roles as capable wives or mothers. Instead, many began to stress moral, religious, and domestic training. While more radical feminists, such as Mary Wollstonecraft, insisted that changes in gender roles and assumptions about female nature were essential to improving the status of women, these ideas were not generally accepted. Nevertheless, many of those who supported traditional notions of female roles and behavior advocated education reform along similar lines—insisting that practical education for women would benefit society as a whole. The excerpts printed here from Catharine Macaulay's *Letters on Education*, a series of letters to a fictional friend, Hortensia, criticize the idea that women's education "should be of an opposite kind to that of males." The weaknesses that were typically considered natural in women were a result of education and situation only, she argues, and women should not accept this assumption of inferiority. She proposes one standard of rational conduct by which both sexes should be judged and attacks traditional gender ideologies and the often-praised female art of "coquetry," by which women attempt to manipulate men. These ideas align Macaulay with Wollstonecraft, who was deeply influenced by the work, and later praised Macaulay in her *Vindication of the Rights of Woman* (1792). Others were less sympathetic, however; upon publication, Macaulay's *Letters* made her the subject of many personal attacks. In general, the work was more influential in France than in England.

The next excerpt is taken from French novelist and playwright Olympe de Gouge's *The Rights of Woman*, a piece with many similarities to Wollstonecraft's work of the following year. De Gouge's pamphlet also emphasizes the importance of female education and professional opportunities to the betterment of society and compares women's situation with that of slaves, demonstrating the corrupting effect on men of such arbitrary power over both groups. Even in France such views were considered too revolutionary, and de Gouges was sent to the guillotine during the French Revolution. The newspaper of the Committee of Public Safety declared upon her death, "She wanted to be a statesman, and it seems the law has punished this conspiratress for having forgotten the virtues befitting her sex."

A more conservative approach to female education is exemplified in novelist Maria Edgeworth and her father Richard Lovell Edgeworth's *Practical Education*, excerpted here, which emphasizes moral education (as opposed to the acquisition of accomplishments). Conservative thinkers such as the Edgeworths tended to advocate women's training in "traditional female virtues" of modesty, piety, and obedience; such an education consisted of instruction in domestic duties and Christian principles.

Quaker philanthropist Priscilla Wakefield's *Reflections on the Present Condition of the Female Sex* proceeds along similar lines, positing that women will be better able to fulfill their roles as wives and mothers if given opportunities for education and professional advancement. She also helps to bring to public attention the plight of many genteel women faced with social and economic difficulties while lacking the skills or opportunities that would enable them to help themselves.

Hannah More's *Strictures on the Modern System of Female Education*, excerpted here, advocates separate spheres for men and women and emphasizes the education of young women in Christian virtue, morality, and rational education in practical matters. Like most conservative thinkers, More believed that social divisions of class and gender were ordained by God and should not be challenged. Though her ideas for the education of women are, practically speaking, similar to Wollstonecraft's, More insisted on female subordination to men.

Reverend Richard Polwhele's poem "The Unsexed Females" was part of the backlash against thinkers such as Macaulay and Wollstonecraft that occurred at the turn of the century, following a decade of debate initiated by those two women's works. While Polwhele's poem celebrates women he sees as modestly virtuous, it depicts Wollstonecraft and her followers as unnatural, anti-Christian women driven by a godless "Reason." His poem contains numerous footnotes (most of which are included here) that extend and amplify his arguments.

The final piece excerpted here, William Thompson and Anna Wheeler's *Appeal of One Half of the Human Race*, challenges those utilitarians who overlooked women in their search for universal happiness, as did many of Thompson and Wheeler's fellow reformers. It also argues for female suffrage and takes issue with the misogynist belief that women's interests are best represented by those of their husbands. Written primarily by Thompson but with key passages by Wheeler, the *Appeal* extends many of the ideas developed by Wollstonecraft in her *Vindications of the Rights of Woman*. It examines the faults in the economic system that help to create the social iniquities Wollstonecraft examines, and extends Wollstonecraft's comparison of women to slaves, comparing the status of plantation laborers in the New World and of Turkish harem-slaves with that of Englishwomen.

⌘⌘⌘

from William Blackstone, *Commentaries on the Laws of England* (1765), Book 1, Chapter 15

Of Husband and Wife

By marriage, the husband and wife are one person in law: that is, the very being or legal existence of the woman is suspended during the marriage, or at least is incorporated and consolidated into that of the husband, under whose wing, protection, and *cover* she performs everything; and is therefore called in our law-French[1] a *feme-covert*; is said to be a *covert-baron*, or under the protection and influence of her husband, her *baron*, or lord; and her condition during her marriage is called her *coverture*. Upon this principle, of a union of person in husband and wife, depend almost all the legal rights, duties, and disabilities that either of them acquire by the marriage. I speak not at present of the rights of property, but of such as are merely *personal*. For this reason, a man cannot grant anything to his wife, or enter into covenant with her; for the grant would be to suppose her separate existence, and to covenant with her would be only to covenant with himself. And therefore it is also generally true that all compacts made between husband and wife when single are voided by the intermarriage. A woman indeed may be attorney for her husband; for that implies no separation from, but is rather a representation of, her lord. And a husband may also bequeath anything to his wife by will; for that cannot take effect

[1] *law-French* Corrupt dialect of Norman French used in English law books until the reign of Edward III (1327–77).

till the coverture is determined[1] by his death. The husband is bound to provide his wife with necessaries by law, as much as himself; and if he contracts debts for them, he is obliged to pay them: but for anything besides necessaries he is not chargeable. Also, if a wife elopes, and lives with another man, the husband is not chargeable even for necessaries—at least if the person who furnishes them is sufficiently apprized of her elopement. If the wife be indebted before marriage, the husband is bound afterwards to pay the debt; for he has adopted her and her circumstances together. If the wife be injured in her person or her property, she can bring no action for redress without her husband's concurrence, and in his name as well as her own; neither can she be sued without making the husband a defendant....

These are the chief legal effects of marriage during the coverture, upon which we may observe that even the disabilities which the wife lies under are for the most part intended for her protection and benefit. So great a favourite is the female sex of the laws of England.[2]

from Catharine Macaulay, *Letters on Education* (1790)

from LETTER 21, MORALS MUST BE TAUGHT ON IMMUTABLE PRINCIPLES

... In order to take from public sentiment a reproach which leaves a deep stain on the human character, and to correct many irregularities, and even enormities, which arise from incorrect systems of ethics, it ought to be the first care of education to teach virtue on immutable principles, and to avoid that confusion which must arise from confounding the laws and customs of society with those obligations which are founded on correct principles of equity. But as you have had patience to go through my whole plan of education, from infancy to manhood, it is but fair that I should attend to your objections, and examine whether my plan is founded on error, or on the principles of reason and truth. Know then, good Hortensia, that I have given similar rules for male and female education, on the following grounds of reasoning.

First, That there is but one rule of right for the conduct of all rational beings; consequently that true virtue in one sex must be equally so in the other, whenever a proper opportunity calls for its exertion, and, *vice versa*, what is vice in one sex cannot have a different property when found in the other.

Secondly, that true wisdom, which is never found at variance with rectitude, is as useful to women as to men, because it is necessary to the highest degree of happiness, which can never exist with ignorance.

Lastly, that as on our first entrance into another world our state of happiness may possibly depend on the degree of perfection we have attained in this, we cannot justly lessen, in one sex or the other, the means by which perfection, that is another word for wisdom, is acquired.

It would be paying you a bad compliment, Hortensia, were I to answer all the frivolous objections which prejudice has framed against the giving a learned education to women; for I know of no learning worth having that does not tend to free the mind from error and enlarge our stock of useful knowledge. Thus much it may be proper to observe, that those hours which are spent in studious retirement by learned women will not in all probability intrude so much on the time for useful avocation as the wild and spreading dissipations of the present day; that levity and ignorance will always be found in opposition to what is useful and graceful in life; and that the contrary may be expected from a truly enlightened understanding. However, Hortensia, to throw some illustration on what I have advanced on this subject, it may be necessary to show you that all those vices and imperfections which have been generally regarded as inseparable from the female character do not in any manner proceed from sexual causes, but are entirely the effects of situation and education. But these observations must be left to further discussion.

---

[1] *determined* Terminated.

[2] *So great ... England* Not until 1870, with the Married Woman's Property Act, did women gain the right to retain their earnings. In 1882 amendments to this Act allowed them to keep personal property that they brought to or acquired during a marriage. They also finally gained a legal identity separate from their husbands', and could then enter into legal contracts and seek restitution in courts.

from LETTER 22, NO CHARACTERISTIC DIFFERENCE IN SEX

… It must be confessed that the virtues of the males among the human species, though mixed and blended with a variety of vices and errors, have displayed a bolder and a more consistent picture of excellence than female nature has hitherto done. It is on these reasons that when we compliment the appearance of a more than ordinary energy in the female mind, we call it masculine; and hence it is that Pope has elegantly said "a perfect woman's but a softer man."[1] And if we take in the consideration that there can be but one rule of moral excellence for beings made of the same materials, organized after the same manner, and subjected to similar laws of nature, we must either agree with Mr. Pope, or we must reverse the proposition, and say that "a perfect man is a woman formed after a coarser mold." The difference that actually does subsist between the sexes is too flattering for men to be willingly imputed to accident; for what accident occasions, wisdom might correct, and it is better, says Pride, to give up the advantages we might derive from the perfection of our fellow associates than to own that nature has been just in the equal distribution of her favours. These are the sentiments of the men; but mark how readily they are yielded to by the women—not from humility, I assure you, but merely to preserve with character those fond vanities on which they set their hearts. No; suffer them to idolize their persons, to throw away their life in the pursuit of trifles, and to indulge in the gratification of the meaner passions, and they will heartily join in the sentence of their degradation.

Among the most strenuous asserters of a sexual difference in character, Rousseau[2] is the most conspicuous, both on account of that warmth of sentiment which distinguishes all his writings, and the eloquence of his compositions: but never did enthusiasm and the love of paradox, those enemies to philosophical disquisition, appear in more strong opposition to plain sense than in Rousseau's definition of this difference. He sets out with a supposition that Nature intended the subjection of the one sex to the other; that consequently there must be an inferiority of intellect in the subjected party; but as man is a very imperfect being, and apt to play the capricious tyrant, Nature, to bring things nearer to an equality, bestowed on the woman such attractive graces, and such an insinuating address, as to turn the balance on the other scale. Thus Nature, in a giddy mood, recedes from her purposes, and subjects prerogative to an influence which must produce confusion and disorder in the system of human affairs. Rousseau saw this objection, and in order to obviate it he has made up a moral person of the union of the two sexes, which, for contradiction and absurdity, outdoes every metaphysical riddle that was ever formed in the schools. In short, it is not reason, it is not wit; it is pride and sensuality that speak in Rousseau, and, in this instance, has lowered the man of genius to the licentious pedant.

But whatever might be the wise purpose intended by Providence in such a disposition of things, certain it is that some degree of inferiority, in point of corporal strength, seems always to have existed between the two sexes; and this advantage, in the barbarous ages of mankind, was abused to such a degree as to destroy all the natural rights of the female species and reduce them to a state of abject slavery. What accidents have contributed in Europe to better their condition would not be to my purpose to relate, for I do not intend to give you a history of women; I mean only to trace the sources of their peculiar foibles and vices, and these I firmly believe to originate in situation and education only: for so little did a wise and just Providence intend to make the condition of slavery an unalterable law of female nature, that in the same proportion as the male sex have consulted the interest of their own happiness, they have relaxed in their tyranny over women; and such is their use in the system of mundane creation, and such their natural influence over the male mind, that were these advantages properly exerted, they might carry every point of any importance to their honour and happiness. However, till that period arrives in which women will

[1] *a perfect … man* Reference to Alexander Pope, "Epistle 2: To a Lady, on the Characters of Women" (1735), lines 271–72: "Heaven, when it strives to polish all it can / Its last best work, but forms a softer man."

[2] *Rousseau* In his *Émile* (1762), French philosopher Jean-Jacques Rousseau argues that female children should be educated, but should be taught to remain subordinate and submissive to men.

act wisely, we will amuse ourselves in talking of their follies.

The situation and education of women, Hortensia, is precisely that which must necessarily tend to corrupt and debilitate both the powers of mind and body. From a false notion of beauty and delicacy, their system of nerves is depraved before they come out of their nursery; and this kind of depravity has more influence over the mind, and consequently over morals, than is commonly apprehended. But it would be well if such causes only acted towards the debasement of the sex; their moral education is, if possible, more absurd than their physical. The principles and nature of virtue, which is never properly explained to boys, is kept quite a mystery to girls. They are told, indeed, that they must abstain from those vices which are contrary to their personal happiness, or they will be regarded as criminals, both by God and man; but all the higher parts of rectitude, everything that ennobles our being, and that renders us both innoxious and useful, is either not taught, or is taught in such a manner as to leave no proper impression on the mind. This is so obvious a truth that the defects of female education have ever been a fruitful topic of declamation for the moralist; but not one of this class of writers have laid down any judicious rules for amendment. Whilst we still retain the absurd notion of a sexual excellence, it will militate against the perfecting a plan of education for either sex. The judicious Addison animadverts on the absurdity of bringing a young lady up with no higher idea of the end of education than to make her agreeable to a husband, and confining the necessary excellence for this happy acquisition to the mere graces of person.[1]

Every parent and tutor may not express himself in the same manner as is marked out by Addison; yet certain it is that the admiration of the other sex is held out to women as the highest honour they can attain; and whilst this is considered as their *summum bonum*,[2] and the beauty of their persons the chief *desideratum*[3] of men, Vanity and its companion Envy must taint, in their characters, every native and every acquired excellence. Nor can you, Hortensia, deny that these qualities, when united to ignorance, are fully equal to the engendering and rivetting all those vices and foibles which are peculiar to the female sex—vices and foibles which have caused them to be considered, in ancient times, as beneath cultivation, and in modern days have subjected them to the censure and ridicule of writers of all descriptions, from the deep thinking philosopher to the man of ton and gallantry, who, by the by,[4] sometimes distinguishes himself by qualities which are not greatly superior to those he despises in women....

from Olympe de Gouges, *The Rights of Woman* (1791)[5]

Man, are you able to be just? It is a woman who asks you the question; you will not take that right, at least, away from her. Tell me: what has given you the sovereign power to oppress my sex? your strength? your talents? Observe the Creator in His wisdom; survey nature in all its grandeur, to which you seem to want to compare yourself, and give me, if you dare, an example of this tyrannical power. Go back to the animals, consult the elements, study the vegetables, cast a glance, finally, over all the modifications of organized matter; and submit to the evidence when I give you the means to; search, excavate, and distinguish the sexes, if you can, in the government of nature. Everywhere you will find them mingled, everywhere they cooperate as a harmonious consort in this immortal masterpiece.

Man alone has dressed up this exception as a principle. Bizarre, blind, bloated with sciences and degenerated, in this age of enlightenment and wisdom, into the crassest ignorance, he wants to rule like a despot over a sex which has received all the intellectual faculties; he pretends to rejoice in the revolution, and to claim his rights to equality, in order to say no more about it.

[1] *judicious Addison ... person* Reference to an article in *Spectator* No. 66 (16 May 1711) actually written by Richard Steele; *animadverts* Comments critically.

[2] *summum bonum* Latin: greatest good.

[3] *desideratum* Latin: thing desired.

[4] *by the by* Incidentally; as a side issue.

[5] *The Rights of Woman* Translated from the French by D.L. Macdonald.

DECLARATION OF THE RIGHTS OF WOMAN AND OF THE FEMALE CITIZEN.

To be decreed by the National Assembly in its last sessions or in that of the next legislature.

PREAMBLE.

The mothers, daughters, sisters, representatives of the nation, demand to be formed into a national assembly. Considering that ignorance, neglect, or contempt of the rights of woman are the sole causes of public misfortunes and the corruption of governments, have resolved to set forth in a solemn declaration the natural, inalienable, and sacred rights of woman, that this declaration, being constantly present to all the members of the body social, may ever remind them of their rights and their duties; that the acts of the power of women, and those of the power of men, being capable of being every moment compared with the end of all political institutions, may be more respected; that the claims of the female citizens, founded hereafter on simple and incontestable principles, may always tend to the maintenance of the constitution and of good morals, and to the general happiness.

Accordingly, the sex that is as superior in beauty as in courage, in the sufferings of maternity, recognizes and declares, in the presence and under the auspices of the Supreme Being, the following Rights of Woman and of the Female Citizen.

FIRST ARTICLE.

Woman is born free and remains equal to man in rights. Social distinctions can only be founded on common utility.

2

The end of all political association is the preservation of the natural and imprescriptible[1] rights of woman and of man: these rights are liberty, property, security, and above all resistance to oppression.

3

The principle of all sovereignty resides essentially in the Nation, which is nothing more than the union of woman and man: no body, no individual, can exercise an authority which does not emanate expressly from it.

4

Liberty and justice consist in rendering to others all that belongs to them; thus the exercise of the natural rights of woman has no other limits than the perpetual tyranny that man opposes to it; these limits should be reformed by the laws of nature and of reason.

5

The laws of nature and of reason prohibit all actions hurtful to society: nothing that is not prohibited by these laws, wise and divine, may be hindered, nor may anyone be compelled to do what they do not enjoin.

6

The law should be the expression of the general will; all the female and male citizens should concur personally, or by their representatives, in its formation; it should be the same for all: all the female and all the male citizens, being equal in its eyes, should be equally admissible to all honours, positions, and public employments, according to their capacities, and without any other distinctions than those of their virtues and their talents.

7

No woman is exempt; she is accused, arrested, and detained in cases determined by the law. Women, like men, obey this rigorous law.

8

The law should impose only those penalties which are strictly and evidently necessary, and no one can be punished except by virtue of a law established and promulgated previously to the offense and legally applied to women.

9

Whenever a woman is declared guilty, all rigour is exercised by the law.

[1] *imprescriptible* That cannot legally be taken away.

10

No one should be molested for their opinions, even fundamental ones; woman has the right to mount the scaffold; she should equally have the right to mount the tribune,[1] provided that her actions do not disturb the public order established by the law.

11

The free communication of thoughts and opinions is one of the most precious rights of woman, since this liberty ensures that fathers acknowledge their children. Every female citizen may therefore say freely, I am the mother of a child who belongs to you, without a barbarous prejudice to force her to conceal the truth, provided she is held responsible for the abuse of this liberty in the cases determined by the law.

12

The good of the majority is necessary in order to secure the rights of woman and the female citizen; this security should be instituted for the advantage of all, and not for the particular good of those women to whom it is entrusted.

13

For the maintenance of the public force, and for the expenses of government, the contributions of woman and man are equal; she takes part in all the drudgery, in all the laborious tasks; she should therefore take the same part in the distribution of positions, of employments, of commissions, of honours, and of business.

14

The female and male citizens have the right to determine, by themselves or by their representatives, the necessity of public contributions. The female citizens cannot enjoy this right except by being allowed an equal share, not only in wealth, but also in public administration, and by being allowed to determine the amount, the basis, the collection, and the duration of taxation.

15

The mass of women, united for the purposes of taxation with that of men, has the right to demand of all its public agents an account of their administration.

16

Every society in which the security of rights is not assured, and the separation of powers is not determined, has no constitution; the constitution is null and void if the majority of the individuals who make up the nation has not cooperated in drawing it up.

17

Property belongs to both sexes, individually or collectively; it is everyone's inviolable and sacred right; as it is a true patrimony of nature, no one may be deprived of it, except when public necessity, legally ascertained, evidently demands it, and on condition of a previously established and just indemnity.

from Maria Edgeworth and Richard Lovell Edgeworth, *Practical Education* (1798)

Prudence and Economy

In the education of girls we must teach them much more caution than is necessary to boys: their prudence must be more the result of reasoning than of experiment; they *must* trust to the experience of others; they cannot always have recourse to what *ought to be*, they must adapt themselves to what is. They cannot rectify the material mistakes in their conduct. Timidity, a certain tardiness of decision, and reluctance to act in public situations are not considered as defects in a woman's character; her pausing prudence does not to a man of discernment denote imbecility, but appears to him the graceful auspicious characteristic of female virtue. There is always more probability that women should endanger their own happiness by precipitation than by forbearance.

Promptitude of choice is seldom expected from the female sex; they should avail themselves of the leisure that is permitted to them for reflection. "Begin nothing of which you have not well considered the end," was the piece of advice for which the Eastern Sultan paid a purse of gold, the price set upon it by a sage. The monarch did not repent of his purchase. This maxim should be engraved upon the memory of our female pupils by the

[1] *tribune* Raised platform or dais for addressing an assembly.

repeated lessons of education. We should even in trifles avoid every circumstance which can tend to make girls venturesome, which can encourage them to trust to their good fortune, instead of relying on their own prudence....

In the choice of friends, and on all matters of taste, young women should be excited to reason about their own feelings. "There is no reasoning about taste," is a pernicious maxim; if there was more reasoning, there would be disputation upon this subject. If women questioned their own minds, or allowed their friends to question them concerning the reasons of their "preferences and aversions," there would not probably be so many love matches, and so few love marriages. It is in vain to expect that young women should begin to reason miraculously, at the very moment that reason is wanted in the guidance of their conduct. We should also observe that women are called upon for the exertion of their prudence at an age when young men are scarcely supposed to possess that virtue; therefore women should be more early, and more carefully educated for the purpose. The important decisions of a woman's life are often made before she is twenty; a man does not come upon the theatre of public life, where most of his prudence is shown, till he is much older.

from Priscilla Wakefield, *Reflections on the Present Condition of the Female Sex; With Suggestions for Its Improvement* (1798)

from Chapter 3

The Necessity of Women Being Educated for the Exercise of Lucrative Employments Shown, and the Absurdity of a Woman Honourably Earning a Support Being Excluded from Society, Exposed

In the education of females, the same view actuates every rank: an advantageous settlement on marriage is the universal prize, for which parents of all classes enter their daughters upon the lists; and partiality or self-complacency assures to every competitor the most flattering prospect of success. To this one point tends the principal part of female instruction; for the promotion of this design, their best years for improvement are sacrificed to the attainment of attractive qualities, showy superficial accomplishments, polished manners, and, in one word, the whole science of pleasing, which is cultivated with unceasing assiduity as an object of the most essential importance.

The end is laudable, and deserving of every effort that can be exerted to secure it; a happy marriage may be estimated among the rarest felicities of human life, but it may be doubted whether the means used to accomplish it are adequate to the purpose, as the making a first impression is by no means effectual to determine the preference of a wise man. It is not then sufficient that a girl be qualified to excite admiration; her own happiness, and that of the man to whom she devotes the remainder of her days, depend upon her possession of those virtues, which alone can preserve lasting esteem and confidence.

The offices of a wife are very different from those of the mere pageant of a ballroom; and as their nature is more exalted, the talents they require are of a more noble kind: something far beyond the elegant trifler is wanted in a companion for life. A young woman is very ill-adapted to enter into the most solemn of social contracts who is not prepared, by her education, to become the participator of her husband's cares, the consoler of his sorrows, his stimulator to every praiseworthy undertaking, his partner in the labours and vicissitudes of life, the faithful and economical manager of his affairs, the judicious superintendant of his family, the wife and affectionate mother of his children, the preserver of his honour, his chief counsellor, and, to sum up all, the chosen friend of his bosom. If a modern female education be not calculated to produce these effects, as few surely will judge it to be, who reflect upon its tendency, it is incompetent to that very purpose, which is confessedly its main object, and must therefore be deemed imperfect, and require reformation....

from Chapter 6

Lucrative Employments for the First and Second Classes Suggested ... With Strictures on a Theatrical Life

Transitions in private life from affluence to poverty, like the sable pageantry of death, from their frequency produce no lasting impressions on the beholders. Unexpected misfortunes befall an acquaintance who has been caressed in the days of prosperity: the change is lamented, and she is consoled by the visits of her friends, in the first moments of affliction; she sinks gradually into wretchedness; she becomes obscure, and is forgotten.... A few remarks upon the nature of those employments which are best adapted to the higher classes of the sex, when reduced to necessitous circumstances, may, perhaps, afford useful hints to those who are languishing under the pressure of misfortune, and induce abler pens to treat a subject hitherto greatly neglected.

Numerous difficulties arise in the choice of occupations for the purpose. They must be such as are neither laborious nor servile, and they must of course be productive, without requiring a capital.

For these reasons, pursuits which require the exercise of intellectual rather than bodily powers are generally the most eligible.

Literature affords a respectable and pleasing employment for those who possess talents and an adequate degree of mental cultivation. For although the emolument is precarious, and seldom equal to a maintenance, yet if the attempt be tolerably successful, it may yield a comfortable assistance in narrow circumstances and beguile many hours, which might otherwise be passed in solitude or unavailing regret. The fine arts offer a mode of subsistence congenial to the delicacy of the most refined minds, and they are peculiarly adapted, by their elegance, to the gratification of taste. The perfection of every species of painting is attainable by women, from the representation of historic facts to the minute execution of the miniature portrait, if they will bestow sufficient time and application for the acquisition of the principles of the art, in the study of those models which have been the means of transmitting the names and character of so many men to the admiration of posterity. The successful exercise of this imitative art requires invention, taste, and judgment: in the two first, the sex are allowed to excel, and the last may be obtained by a perseverance in examining, comparing, and reflecting upon the works of those masters who have copied nature in her most graceful forms....

The stage is a profession to which many women of refined manners and a literary turn of mind have had recourse. Since it has been customary for females to assume dramatic characters, there appears to have been full as great a proportion of women who have attained celebrity among those who have devoted themselves to a theatrical life, as of the other sex—a fact which argues that there is no inequality of genius in the sexes for the imitative arts. The observation may operate as a stimulant to women to those pursuits which are less objectionable than the stage, which is not mentioned for the purpose of recommending it, but of proving that the abilities of the female sex are equal to nobler labours than are usually undertaken by women. The profession of an actress is indeed most unsuitable to the sex in every point of view, whether it be considered with respect to the courage requisite to face an audience, or the variety of situations incident to it, which expose moral virtue to the most severe trials. Let the daughters of a happier destiny, whilst they lament the evils to which some of their sex are exposed, remember those unpropitious circumstances that have cast them into a line of life in which it is scarcely possible to preserve that purity of sentiment and conduct which characterizes female excellence. When their errors are discussed, let the harsh voice of censure be restrained by the reflection that she who has made the greatest advances towards perfection might have fallen, had she been surrounded by the same influences.

That species of agriculture which depends upon skill in the management of the nursery ground, in rearing the various kinds of shrubs and flowers for the supply of gentlemen's gardens and pleasure grounds, would supply an elegant means of support to those women who are able to raise a capital for carrying on a work of that magnitude. Ornamental gardening, and the laying out of pleasure grounds and parks with the improvement of natural landscape, one of the refinements of modern times, may likewise afford an eligible maintenance to some of those females who, in the days of their prosperity, displayed their taste in the embellishment of the own domains.

The presiding over seminaries for female education is likewise a suitable employment for those whose minds

The most renowned actress of the day was Sarah Siddons (1755–1831), born into the theatrical family of Roger Kemble. Siddons's most famous role was that of Lady Macbeth, which she first played in 1785. Above left is a detail from a painting (c. 1790) of her playing the role opposite her brother; at right is George Henry Harlow's *Sarah Siddons in the Scene of Lady Macbeth Sleepwalking* (1814). Siddons's farewell stage performance had been as Lady Macbeth in 1812.

have been enlarged by liberal cultivation, whilst the under parts of that profession may be more suitably filled by persons whose early views have been contracted within narrower limits. After all that can be suggested by general remarks, the different circumstances of individuals must decide the profession most convenient to them. But it is a consolatory reflection that amidst the daily vicissitudes of human life, from which no rank is exempt, there are resources from which aid may be drawn, without derogating from the true dignity of a rational being.

from Richard Polwhele, "The Unsexed Females: a Poem, Addressed to the Author of *The Pursuits of Literature*"[1] (1798)

Survey with me, what ne'er our fathers saw,
A female band despising Nature's law,[2]
As "proud defiance"[3] flashes from their arms,
And vengeance smothers all their softer charms.
I shudder at the new unpictured scene,
Where unsexed woman vaunts the imperious
mien;° *bearing*
Where girls, affecting to dismiss the heart,
Invoke the Proteus of petrific art;[4]
With equal ease, in body or in mind,
To Gallic freaks or Gallic faith resigned,
The crane-like neck, as Fashion bids, lay bare,
Or frizzle,[5] bold in front, their borrowed hair;
Scarce by a gossamery film carest,
Sport,[6] in full view, the meretricious° breast;[7] *whorish*
Loose the chaste cincture,[8] where the graces shone,
And languished all the Loves, the ambrosial zone;
As lordly domes inspire dramatic rage,
Court prurient Fancy to the private stage;
With bliss botanic[9] as their bosoms heave,
Still pluck forbidden fruit, with mother Eve,
For puberty in sighing florets pant,
Or point the prostitution of a plant;
Dissect[10] its organ of unhallowed lust,

[1] *the Author … Literature* Thomas James Mathias, whose extremely popular satirical poem *The Pursuits of Literature* (1794–97) reacted against radical politics, particularly against feminists such as Mary Wollstonecraft. Polwhele draws on Mathias's comment in the poem's preface that "our *unsexed* female writers now instruct, or confuse, us and themselves, in the labyrinth of politics, or turn us wild with Gallic frenzy" (i.e., ideas inspired by the French Revolution).

[2] [Polwhele's note] Nature is the grand basis of all laws human and divine: and the woman who has no regard to nature, either in decoration of her person or the culture of her mind, will soon "walk after the flesh in the lust of uncleanness, and despise government." [Polwhele quotes from 2 Peter 2.10.]

[3] [From Polwhele's note] "A troop came next, who crowns and armour wore / And proud defiance in their looks they bore" Pope. The Amazonian band—the female Quixotes of the new philosophy are here too justly characterised.… [Polwhele quotes Alexander Pope's "The Temple of Fame" (1711), lines 342–43. *Amazons* Members of a legendary race of warrior women from Scythia; *Quixotes* Idealists, dreamers. "Female Quixotes" refers more specifically to Charlotte Lennox's famous novel of 1752, *The Female Quixote*.]

[4] *Proteus* God who could change shape at will; *petrific* Able to turn to stone, or to turn something else to stone.

[5] *frizzle* Curl in small curls.

[6] [From Polwhele's note] To "sport a face" is a cant phrase in one of our universities, by which is meant an impudent obtrusion of a man's person in company. It is not applicable, perhaps, to the open bosom—a fashion which we have never invited or sanctioned.

[7] [Polwhele's note] The fashions of France, which have been always imitated by the English, were, heretofore, unexceptionable in a moral point of view; since, however ridiculous or absurd, they were innocent. But they have now their source among prostitutes—among women of the most abandoned character. …

[8] *cincture* Girdle for the waist, sometimes surrounding the breasts as well.

[9] [Polwhele's note] Botany has lately become a fashionable amusement with the ladies. But how the study of the sexual system can accord with female modesty, I am not able to comprehend. I had at first, written, "More eager for illicit knowledge pant, / With lustful boys anatomise a plant; / The virtues of its dust prolific speak, / Or point its pistil with unblushing cheek." I have, several times, seen boys and girls botanizing together.

[10] [Polwhele's note] Miss Wollstonecraft does not blush to say, in an introduction to a book designed for the use of young ladies, that, "in order to lay the axe at the root of corruption, it would be proper to familiarize the sexes to an unreserved discussion of those topics which are generally avoided in conversation from a principle of false delicacy; and that it would be right to speak of the organs of generation as freely as we mention our eyes or our hands." To such language our botanizing girls are doubtless familiarized; and they are in a fair way of becoming worthy disciples of Miss W. If they do not take heed to their ways, they will soon exchange the blush of modesty for the bronze of impudence. [Polwhele refers to Mary Wollstonecraft's "Introductory Address to Parents," from her

And fondly gaze the titillating dust;
With liberty's sublimer views expand,
And o'er the wreck of kingdoms[1] sternly stand;
And, frantic, midst the democratic storm,
Pursue, Philosophy! thy phantom-form.[2]
Far other is the female shape and mind,
By modest luxury heightened and refined;
Those limbs, that figure, though by Fashion[3] graced,
By Beauty polished, and adorned by Taste;
That soul, whose harmony perennial flows,
In Music trembles, and in Color glows;
Which bids sweet Poesy reclaim the praise
With faery light to gild fastidious days,
From sullen clouds relieve domestic care,
And melt in smiles the withering frown of war.
Ah! once the female Muse,[4] to *Nature* true,
The unvalued store from *Fancy*, *Feeling* drew;
Won, from the grasp of woe, the roseate hours,
Cheered life's dim vale, and strewed the grave with
flowers.
But lo! where, pale amidst the wild,[5] she draws
Each precept cold from sceptic Reason's[6] vase;
Pours with rash arm the turbid stream along,
And in the foaming torrent whelms the throng.[7] …
See Wollstonecraft, whom no decorum checks,
Arise, the intrepid champion of her sex;
O'er humbled man assert the sovereign claim,
And slight the timid blush[8] of virgin fame.

from Hannah More, *Strictures on the Modern System of Female Education, With a View of the Principles and Conduct Prevalent among Women of Rank and Fortune* (1799)

from VOLUME 1, CHAPTER 4, COMPARISON OF THE MODE OF FEMALE EDUCATION IN THE LAST AGE WITH THE PRESENT AGE

A young lady may excel in speaking French and Italian, may repeat a few passages from a volume of extracts; play like a professor, and sing like a siren;[9] have her dressing-room decorated with her own drawings, tables, stands, screens, and cabinets; nay, she may dance like Sempronia[10] herself, and yet may have been very

Elements of Morality, For the Use of Children (1792), but he misrepresents her argument, which is that children can be discouraged from masturbating by being taught about the sexual organs and by having explained to them "the noble use which they were designed for." In her *Vindication of the Rights of Woman* (1792) she also argues that the study of botany can be consistent with female modesty.]

[1] [Polwhele's note] The female advocates of democracy in this country, though they have had no opportunity of imitating the French ladies in their acts of atrocious cruelty, have yet assumed a stern serenity in the contemplation of those savage excesses. "To express their abhorrence of royalty, they (the French ladies) threw away the character of their sex, and bit the amputated limbs of their murdered countrymen. I say this on the authority of a young gentleman who saw it. I am sorry to add that the relation, accompanied with looks of horror and disgust, only provoked a contemptuous smile from an illuminated British fair-one." See Robison—p.219. [John Robison's *Proofs of a Conspiracy Against All the Religions and Governments of Europe* (1797).]

[2] [From Polwhele's note] Philosophism, the false image of philosophy.…

[3] [Polwhele's note] I admit that we are quickly reconciled to the fashion of the day, and often consider it as graceful, if it offends not against delicacy.

[4] *Muse* One of nine daughters of Zeus and Mnemosyne, each of whom presided over and provided inspiration for an aspect of arts and sciences.

[5] [Polwhele's note] "A wild, where flowers and weeds promiscuous shoot; / A garden tempting with forbidden fruit" Pope. [From Alexander Pope's *Essay on Man* (1733) 1.7–8.]

[6] [Polwhele's note] A troubled stream only can proceed from the vase of skepticism; if it be not "the broken cistern that will hold no water" [from Jeremiah 2.13].

[7] [Polwhele's note] "Raging waves, foaming out their own shame"—St. Jude. Such were those infamous publications of Paine and others, which, like the torrents of December, threatened to sweep all before them—to overwhelm the multitude. [Polwhele quotes from Jude 1.13 and refers to Thomas Paine's *The Rights of Man* (1791–92), his reply to an attack on the French Revolutionaries by Edmund Burke.]

[8] [Polwhele's note] That Miss Wollstonecraft was a sworn enemy to the blushes, I need not remark. But many of my readers, perhaps, will be astonished to hear that at several of our boarding schools for young ladies, a blush incurs a penalty.

[9] *siren* Mythical creature, part woman and part bird, whose enchanted songs were said to lure sailors to their destruction.

[10] *Sempronia* Infamous woman of ancient Rome, known for her loose morals, who was said to have taken part in Cataline's conspiracy to overthrow the government in 63 BCE. According to Roman

badly educated. I am far from meaning to set no value whatever on any or all of these qualifications; they are all of them elegant, and many of them properly tend to the perfecting of a polite education. These things, in their measure and degree, may be done, but there are others which should not be left undone. Many things are becoming, but "one thing is needful." Besides, as the world seems to be fully apprized of the value of whatever tends to embellish life, there is less occasion here to insist on its importance.

But, though a well bred young lady may lawfully learn most of the fashionable arts, yet it does not seem to be the true end of education to make women of fashion dancers, singers, players, painters, actresses, sculptors, gilders, varnishers, engravers, and embroiderers. Most men are commonly destined to some profession, and their minds are consequently turned each to its respective object. Would it not be strange if they were called out to exercise their profession, or to set up their trade, with only a little general knowledge of the trades of all other men, and without any previous definite application to their own peculiar calling? The profession of ladies, to which the bent of their instruction should be turned, is that of daughters, wives, mothers, and mistresses of families. They should be therefore trained with a view to these several conditions, and be furnished with a stock of ideas and principles, and qualifications ready to be applied and appropriated, as occasion may demand, to each of these respective situations: for though the arts which merely embellish life must claim admiration, yet when a man of sense comes to marry, it is a companion whom he wants, and not an artist. It is not merely a creature who can paint, and play, and dress, and dance; it is a being who can comfort and counsel him; one who can reason and reflect, and feel, and judge, and discourse, and discriminate; one who can assist him in his affairs, lighten his cares, soothe his sorrows, strengthen his principles, and educate his children.

historian Sallust, Sempronia "had greater skill in lyre playing and dancing than there is any need for a respectable woman to acquire. There was nothing that she set a smaller value on than seemliness and chastity."

from Volume 1, Chapter 6, On the Early Forming of Habits. On the Necessity of Forming the Judgment to Direct those Habits

An early habitual restraint is peculiarly important to the future character and happiness of women. They should when very young be inured to contradiction. Instead of hearing their bon-mots[1] treasured up and repeated to the guests till they begin to think it dull when they themselves are not the little heroine of the theme, they should be accustomed to receive but little praise for their vivacity or their wit, though they should receive just commendation for their patience, their industry, their humility, and other qualities which have more worth than splendour. They should be led to distrust their own judgment; they should learn not to murmur at expostulation, but should be accustomed to expect and to endure opposition. It is a lesson with which the world will not fail to furnish them, and they will not practice it the worse for having learnt it the sooner. It is of the last importance to their happiness in life that they should early acquire a submissive temper and a forbearing spirit. They must even endure to be thought wrong sometimes when they cannot but feel they are right. And while they should be anxiously aspiring to do well, they must not expect always to obtain the praise of having done so. But while a gentle demeanor is inculcated, let them not be instructed to practise gentleness merely on the low ground of its being decorous and feminine, and pleasing, and calculated to attract human favour; but let them be carefully taught to cultivate it on the high principle of obedience to Christ.

from William Thompson and Anna Wheeler, *Appeal of One Half the Human Race, Women, Against the Pretensions of the Other Half, Men, To Retain Them in Political, and Thence in Civil And Domestic Slavery* (1825)

from Introductory Letter to Mrs. Wheeler

With you I would equally elevate both sexes. Really enlightened women, disdaining equally the

[1] *bon-mots* French: witticisms.

submissive tricks of the slave and the caprices of the despot, breathing freely only in the air of the esteem of equals, and of mutual, *unbought*, *uncommanded* affection, would find it difficult to meet with associates worthy of them in men as now formed, full of ignorance and vanity, priding themselves on a *sexual* superiority, entirely independent of any merit, any superior qualities, or pretensions to them, claiming respect from the strength of their arm and the lordly faculty of producing beards attached by nature to their chins! No: unworthy of, as incapable of appreciating, the delight of the society of such women, are the great majority of the existing race of men. The pleasures of mere animal appetite, the pleasures of commanding (the prettier and more helpless the slave, the greater these pleasures of the brute) are the only pleasures which the majority of men seek for from women, are the only pleasures which their education and the hypocritical system of morals with which they have been necessarily imbued, permit them to expect....

Even under the present arrangements of society, founded as they all are on the basis of individual competition, nothing could be more easy than to put the *rights* of women, political and civil, on a perfect equality with those of men. It is only to abolish all prohibitory and exclusive laws—statute or what are called "common"—the remnants of the barbarous customs of our ignorant ancestors; particularly the horrible and odious inequality and indissolubility of that disgrace of civilization, the present marriage code. Women then might exert in a free career with men their faculties of mind and body, to whatever degree developed, in pursuit of happiness by means of exertion, as men do. But this would not raise women to an equality of happiness with men: their rights might be equal, but not their happiness, because unequal powers under free competition must produce unequal effects.

In truth, the system of the most enlightened of the school of those reformers called political economists is still founded on exclusions. Its basis is too narrow for human happiness. A more comprehensive system, founded on equal benevolence, on the true development of the principle of Utility,[1] is wanting. Let the *competitive* political economists be satisfied with the praise of causing the removal of some of the rubbish of ignorant restrictions, under the name of laws, impeding the development of human exertion in the production of wealth. To build up a new fabric of social happiness, comprehending equally the interests of all existing human beings, has never been contemplated by them, and is altogether beyond the scope of their little theories; aiming at the utmost at increasing the number of what they style the happy middling orders, but leaving the great bulk of human beings to eternal ignorance and toil, requited by the mere means of prolonging from day to day an unhealthy and precarious existence. To a new science, the *social science*, or the science of promoting human happiness, that of political economy, or the mere science of producing wealth by individual competition, must give way.

from PART 2

As soon as adult daughters become wives, their civil rights disappear; they fall back again, and remain all their lives—should their owners and directors live so long—into the state of children or idiots, the passive property of their owners; protected by the law in some few respects only, like other slaves, from the excessive abuse of despotic power.

Woman is then compelled, in marriage, by the possession of superior strength on the part of men, by the want of knowledge, skill, and wealth, by the positive, cruel, partial, and cowardly enactments of law, by the terrors of superstition, by the mockery of a pretended vow of obedience, and to crown all, and as the result of all, by the force of an unrelenting, unreasoning, unfeeling public opinion, to be the literal unequivocal *slave* of the man who may be styled her husband. I say emphatically the slave; for a slave is a person whose actions and earnings, instead of being under his own control, liable only to equal laws, to public opinion, and to his own calculations, under these, of his own interest, are under the arbitrary control of any other human being, by whatever name called. This is the essence of slavery, and what distinguishes it from freedom. A domestic, a civil, a political slave, in the plain unsophisticated sense of the word—in no metaphorical sense—is

[1] *principle of Utility* Central principle of utilitarianism, an ethical theory developed by Jeremy Bentham and others.

every married woman. No matter with what wealth she may be surrounded, with what dainties she may be fed, with what splendor of trappings adorned, with what voluptuousness her corporeal, mental, or moral sweets may be gathered; that high prerogative of human nature, the faculty of self-government, the basis of intellectual development, without which no moral conduct can exist, is to her wanting.... Till laws afford married women the same protection against the restraints and violence of the men to whom they are married, that they affect to afford them against all other individuals; till they afford them the same protection against the restraints and violence of their husbands, that their husbands enjoy against their caprices and violence, the social condition of the civilized wife will remain more completely slavish than that of the female slave of the West Indies....

Be consistent, men! Ye stronger half of the race, be at length rational! Three or four thousand years have worn threadbare your vile cloak of hypocrisy. Even women, your poor, weak, contented slaves, at whose impotence of penetration, the result of your vile exclusions, you have been accustomed to laugh, begin to see through it and to shudder at the loathsomeness beneath. Cast aside this tattered cloak before it leaves you naked and exposed. Clothe yourselves with the new garments of sincerity. Be rational human beings, not mere male sexual creatures. Cast aside the ferocious brute of your nature: give up the pleasures of the brute, those of mere lust and command, for the pleasures of the rational being. So shall you enjoy the love of your *equals*, enlightened, benevolent, graceful, like yourselves, founded on an appreciation of your real merits: so shall you be happy. For the intercourse of the *bought* prostitute, or of the *commanded* household slave, you shall have full and equal participation in the compounded and associated pleasures of sense, intellect, and benevolence. To the highest enjoyments of which your nature is susceptible, there is no shorter road than the simple road of equal justice....

Women of England! women, in whatever country ye breathe—wherever ye breathe, degraded—awake! Awake to the contemplation of the happiness that awaits you when all your faculties of mind and body shall be fully cultivated and developed; when every path in which ye can exercise those improved faculties shall be laid open and rendered delightful to you, even as to them who now ignorantly enslave and degrade you....

Robert Burns

1759 – 1796

There is a riddle among certain linguists: "What is the difference between a language and a dialect?" Answer: "A language is a dialect that has an army and a navy." The point is well taken and the enduring popularity of the British language across the planet no doubt is connected to the huge successes of the British navy in the last two and a half centuries. But when we sing Robert Burns's "Auld Lang Syne" on New Year's Eve we repeat a dialect piece that made good without the backing of an army or a navy. No doubt the distinctive resonance of Burns's Ayrshire dialect has helped to make the words of "Auld Lang Syne" memorable, but its popularity also rests on the degree to which it speaks the language of the heart, conveying a strong sense of mortality and of the blessings of memory itself.

Burns was born in Ayrshire, a county in southwestern Scotland, and spent his early years laboring with his father, a tenant-farmer who died in 1784. Intending to accept a position on a plantation in Jamaica, Burns gave up on this scheme when his first volume of poems, *Poems, Chiefly in the Scottish Dialect* (1786), brought him instant acclaim and the means to a more comfortable life. The Scottish dialect in which he wrote was descended from the Northumbrian dialect of Old English and had been known originally as "Inglis." In the eighteenth century it came to be called "Scots." Mostly gathered in Edinburgh, the champions of the Scottish Enlightenment attempted to be equally fluent in Scots and English. Burns owes his reputation as "Heaven-taught plowman" to his ear for his Scots dialect, but he also knew how to write using English diction.

In some of his best poems, broad Scots and formal English alternate—indeed, nearly overlap. Burns's most famous narrative poem, the mock-heroic "Tam o'Shanter," is one in which we may see and hear the double-fluency of the poet, his broad Scots dialect giving way to "pure English." Many readers, both in Burns's time and in our own, have felt some relief when the poetry gives us a brief shower of "pure English." But by not forsaking the richness of his dialect, Burns was helping to ensure his future status as Scotland's national poet—and dealing a blow to the class prejudice against him that was always present, despite the Edinburgh aristocracy's celebration of him when *Poems* first appeared.

Burns's *Poems* became known as the "Kilmarnock edition," after the place in which the book was published. Already at twenty-seven, Burns had written his most famous poems, and he spent much of the rest of his short life helping to formalize an oral tradition in Scotland, contributing many of the works collected in James Johnson's *The Scots Musical Museum* and in George Thomson's *Select Collection of Original Scottish Airs*. Although never a wealthy man, Burns refused any money for his contribution to this work.

Burns's reputation as a lover for a time rivaled his fame as a poet. Having fathered several illegitimate children, he finally settled down in 1788 with a former lover, Jean Armour, in the town of Dumfries, where he received a commission as an excise (tax) officer. Thereafter he seems to have become a good family man and to have enjoyed relative prosperity in the last years of his life. Burns's love songs often express both his love of women and his feeling for his craft, as in "Green grow the rashes": "Auld nature swears, the lovely dears / Her noblest work she classes, O: / Her prentice han' she tries on man, / An' then she made the lasses, O." Burns also collected all the bawdy songs he inherited and invented in *The Merry Muses of Caledonia*, published shortly after his death (and subjected to expurgation and suppression ever since).

A rebel in religion (he chafed against his strict Calvinist upbringing, although he attended church his entire life) and a sympathizer with the revolutions in America and France, Burns often wrote politically-charged poems. In "Robert Bruce's March to Bannockburn" (popularly known as "Scots, wha hae"), for example, we hear a war-cry for emancipation: "Lay the proud usurpers low! / Tyrants fall in every foe! / Liberty's in every blow! / Let us do, or die!" Burns could also see the world from the lowliest, humblest places, even to the point of reckoning the mischief and malice of plowing up a field mouse from its home and seeing the calamity from the mouse's point of view ("To a Mouse").

Burns drew heavily on oral tradition, using the ballad form to produce what many consider his masterpiece: "Love and Liberty: A Cantata," commonly known as "The Jolly Beggars" (published posthumously in 1799). The cantata is a series of songs sung by a group of vagabonds, who recall past events in their lives. Burns was strongly influenced by his literary predecessors—perhaps most notably the Scottish Chaucerians of the fifteenth and sixteenth centuries (Gavin Douglas, William Dunbar), and the eighteenth-century Scottish poets Allan Ramsay and Robert Fergusson, whose work supplied him with materials and forms for his comprehensive refashioning of the lyric tradition in Scotland.

Burns was only thirty-seven when he died from an attack of rheumatic fever in 1796, on the day that his wife gave birth to the couple's ninth child. He was buried in St. Michael's Churchyard, Dumfries, Scotland, but his remains were later moved to a mausoleum. Scottish people around the world continue to celebrate Burns's birthday each year on 25 January.

⌘⌘⌘

To a Mouse, On Turning Her Up in Her Nest with the Plough

Wee, sleekit, cowrin, tim'rous beastie,
　O, what a panic's in thy breastie!
Thou need na start awa sae hasty,
　Wi' bickerin' brattle![1]
I wad be laith° to rin an' chase thee, *loathe*
　Wi' murd'ring pattle!° *plough spade*

I'm truly sorry man's dominion
Has broken nature's social union,
An' justifies that ill opinion,
　Which makes thee startle,
At me, thy poor, earth-born companion,
　An' fellow mortal!

I doubt na, whyles,° but thou may thieve; *at times*
What then? poor beastie, thou maun° live! *must*
A daimen icker in a thrave[2]
　'S a sma' request;
I'll get a blessin wi' the lave,° *rest*
　An' never miss't!

Thy wee-bit housie, too, in ruin!
It's silly wa's° the win's are strewin! *walls*
An' naething, now, to big° a new ane, *build*
　O' foggage° green! *moss*
An' bleak December's winds ensuin,
　Baith snell° an' keen! *bitter*

Thou saw the fields laid bare an' waste,
An's weary winter comin fast,
An' cozie here, beneath the blast,
　Thou thought to dwell,

[1] *bickerin' brattle* Hurrying scurry.

[2] *A daimen icker in a thrave* The odd ear in 24 sheaves of corn.

Till crash! the cruel coulter° past *plow blade*
Out thro' thy cell.

That wee-bit heap o' leaves an' stibble,
Has cost thee monie a weary nibble!
Now thou's turn'd out, for a' thy trouble,
But° house or hald,° *without / belongings*
To thole° the winter's sleety dribble, *bear*
An' cranreuch° cauld! *hoar frost*

But, Mousie, thou art no thy lane,[1]
In proving foresight may be vain:
The best-laid schemes o' mice an' men
Gang aft agley,[2]
An' lea'e us nought but grief an' pain,
For promis'd joy!

Still thou art blest, compar'd wi' me!
The present only toucheth thee:
But, Och! I backward cast my e'e
On prospects drear!
An' forward, tho' I canna see,
I guess an' fear!
—1785

The Fornicator

Ye jovial boys who love the joys,
The blissful joys of lovers;
Yet dare avow with dauntless brow,
When th'bony lass discovers;
I pray draw near and lend an ear,
And welcome in a frater,° *brother*
For I've lately been on quarantine,
A proven Fornicator.

Before the congregation wide
I pass'd the muster fairly,
My handsome Betsey by my side,
We gat our ditty° rarely; *sermon*
But my downcast eye by chance did spy
What made my lips to water,
Those limbs so clean where I, between
Commenc'd a Fornicator.

With rueful face and signs of grace
I pay'd the buttock–hire,[3]
The night was dark and thro the park
I could not but convoy her;
A parting kiss, what could I less,
My vows began to scatter,
My Betsey fell—lal de dal lal lal,
I am a Fornicator.

But for her sake this vow I make,
And solemnly I swear it,
That while I own a single crown,
She's welcome for to share it;
And my roguish boy his mother's joy,
And the darling of his pater, *father*
For him I boast my pains and cost,
Although a Fornicator.

Ye wenching blades whose hireling jades° *prostitutes*
Have tipt ye off blue–joram,[4]
I tell ye plain, I do disdain
To rank ye in the quorum;
But a bony lass upon the grass
To teach her esse mater,[5]
And no reward but for regard,
O that's a Fornicator.

Your warlike kings and heroes bold,
Great captains and commanders;
Your mighty Caesars fam'd of old,
And conquering Alexanders;
In fields they fought and laurels[6] bought
And bulwarks strong did batter,
But still they grac'd our noble list
And ranked Fornicator!!!
—1785

[1] *no thy lane* Not alone.

[2] *Gang aft agley* Go oft awry.

[3] *buttock-hire* Church fine charged to fornicators.

[4] *tipt ye off blue-joram* Given you the pox.

[5] *esse mater* Latin: to be a mother.

[6] *laurels* Leaves of the bay laurel tree were once a symbol of victory in battle.

Halloween

Yes! let the rich deride, the proud disdain,
The simple pleasure of the lowly train;
To me more dear, congenial to my heart,
One native charm, than all the gloss of art.[1]
—GOLDSMITH

1

Upon that night, when fairies light
On Cassilis Downans[2] dance,
Or owre the lays, in splendid blaze,
On sprightly coursers° prance; *horses*
Or for Colean° the rout is ta'en, *a cavern*
Beneath the moon's pale beams;
There, up the cove, to stray an' rove,
Amang the rocks and streams
To sport that night.

2

Amang the bonie winding banks,
Where Doon rins, wimplin,[3] clear;
Where Bruce[4] ance rul'd the martial ranks,
An' shook his Carrick[5] spear;
Some merry, friendly, countra-folks
Together did convene,
To burn their nits, an' pou[6] their stocks,
An' haud° their Halloween *hold*
Fu' blythe° that night. *merry*

3

The lasses feat,° an' cleanly neat, *well-dressed*
Mair braw° than when they're fine; *handsome*
Their faces blythe, fu' sweetly kythe,° *displayed*
Hearts leal,° an' warm, an' kin':° *loyal / kind*
The lads sae trig,° wi' wooer-babs *neat*
Weel-knotted on their garten;[7]
Some unco blate,[8] an' some wi' gabs° *mouths*
Gar° lasses' hearts gang startin *cause*
Whiles fast at night.

4

Then, first an' foremost, thro' the kail,
Their stocks maun° a' be sought ance;° *must / once*
They steek° their een,° and grape an' wale *close / eyes*
For muckle anes,[9] an' straught anes.
Poor hav'rel° Will fell aff the drift,[10] *half-wit*
An' wandered thro' the bow-kail, *cabbage*
An' pou't° for want o' better shift° *pulled / choice*
A runt° was like a sow-tail *cabbage*
Sae bow't° that night. *bent*

5

Then, straught or crooked, yird° or nane,° *earth / none*
They roar an' cry a' throu'ther;° *recklessly*
The vera wee-things, toddlin, rin,
Wi' stocks out owre their shouther:
An' gif° the custock's sweet or sour, *if / kale-stock*
Wi' joctelegs° they taste them; *pocketknives*
Syne° coziely, aboon° the door, *then / above*
Wi' cannie care, they've plac'd them
To lie that night.

6

The lassies staw frae[11] 'mang them a,'
To pou their stalks o' corn;
But Rab slips out, an' jinks° about, *dodges*
Behint the muckle° thorn: *great*
He grippit Nelly hard and fast:
Loud skirl'd° a' the lasses; *shrieked*
But her tap-pickle[12] maist° was lost, *most*

---

[1] *Yes!... art* From Oliver Goldsmith's *The Deserted Village* (1770) 251–54.

[2] *Cassilis Downans* Small hills in Ayrshire County, Scotland.

[3] *Doon rins, wimplin* The river Doon runs, winding.

[4] *Bruce* Scottish hero Robert the Bruce (1274–1329).

[5] *Carrick* District in Ayrshire.

[6] *nits* Nuts; *pou* Pull.

[7] *wooer-babs ... garten* Garters worn in a particular way in order to announce that the wearer is wooing the person he is visiting.

[8] *unco blate* Extremely shy.

[9] *They steek ... anes* They shut their eyes, and grope and choose / For big ones.

[10] *fell aff the drift* Wandered away.

[11] *staw frae* Steal from.

[12] *tap-pickle* Grain at the top of the stalk.

What kiutlan° in the fause-house[1] *fondling*
Wi' him that night.

7

The auld guid-wife's° weel-hoordit° nits *landlady's / hoarded*
Are round an' round divided,
An' mony lads an' lasses' fates
Are there that night decided:
Some kindle couthie° side by side, *comfortably*
And burn thegither° trimly; *together*
Some start awa wi' saucy pride,
An' jump out owre the chimlie° *chimney*
Fu' high that night.

8

Jean slips in twa, wi' tentie° e'e; *watchful*
Wha 'twas, she wadna tell;
But this is Jock, an' this is me,
She says in to hersel':
He bleez'd owre her, an' she owre him,
As they wad never mair part:
Till fuff! he started up the lum,° *chimney*
An' Jean had e'en a sair° heart *sore*
To see't that night.

9

Poor Willie, wi' his bow-kail runt,
Was brunt° wi' primsie° Mallie; *burned / prim*
An' Mary, nae doubt, took the drunt,[2]
To be compar'd to Willie:
Mall's nit lap° out, wi' pridefu' fling, *leaped*
An' her ain fit,[3] it brunt it;
While Willie lap, and swore by jing,
'Twas just the way he wanted
To be that night.

10

Nell had the fause-house in her min',
She pits hersel an' Rob in;
In loving bleeze they sweetly join,
Till white in ase° they're sobbin: *ash*
Nell's heart was dancin at the view;
She whisper'd Rob to leuk for't:
Rob, stownlins,° prie'd° her bonie mou', *stealthily / kissed*
Fu' cozie in the neuk° for't, *nook*
Unseen that night.

11

But Merran sat behint their backs,
Her thoughts on Andrew Bell:
She lea'es them gashin at their cracks,[4]
An' slips out-by hersel';
She thro' the yard the nearest taks,
An' for the kiln she goes then,
An' darklins[5] grapit for the bauks,
And in the blue-clue[6] throws then,
Right fear't that night.

12

An' ay she win't,° an' ay she swat°— *wound / sweated*
I wat° she made nae jaukin;° *know / dawdling*
Till something held within the pat,
Good Lord! but she was quaukin!
But whether 'twas the deil himsel,
Or whether 'twas a bauk-en',° *beam end*
Or whether it was Andrew Bell,
She did na wait on talkin
To spier that night. *inquire*

13

Wee Jenny to her graunie says,
"Will ye go wi' me, graunie?
I'll eat the apple at the glass,
I gat frae uncle Johnie":
She fuff't° her pipe wi' sic a lunt,[7] *puffed*
In wrath she was sae vap'rin,
She notic't na an aizle° brunt *hot ember*
Her braw, new, worset apron
Out thro' that night.

[1] *fause-house* Hollow in a large stack of corn stalks, created for drying the corn.

[2] *took the drunt* Sulked.

[3] *ain fit* Own foot.

[4] *gashin at their cracks* Gossiping.

[5] *darklins grapit for the bauks* In the darkness grabbed for the beams.

[6] *clue* Clew; ball of yarn.

[7] *lunt* Smoke column.

14

"Ye little skelpie-limmer's face!° *naughty girl's*
I daur you try sic sportin,
As seek the foul thief° ony place, *devil*
For him to spae° your fortune: *tell*
Nae doubt but ye may get a sight!
Great cause ye hae to fear it;
For mony a ane has gotten a fright,
An' liv'd an' died deleerit,° *delirious*
On sic° a night. *such*

15

"Ae hairst° afore the Sherra-moor, *harvest*
I mind't as weel's yestreen—
I was a gilpey° then, I'm sure *young girl*
I was na past fyfteen:
The simmer had been cauld an' wat,
An' stuff was unco green;
An' eye a rantin kirn[1] we gat,
An' just on Halloween
It fell that night.

16

"Our stibble-rig° was Rab M'Graen, *chief harvester*
A clever, sturdy fallow;
His sin° gat Eppie Sim wi' wean,° *son / child*
That lived in Achmacalla:
He gat hemp-seed, I mind° it weel, *remember*
An'he made unco light o't;
But mony a day was by himsel,'
He was sae sairly frighted
That vera night."

17

Then up gat fechtin° Jamie Fleck, *fighting*
An' he swoor by his conscience,
That he could saw° hemp-seed a peck; *sow*
For it was a' but nonsense:
The auld guidman raught° down the pock,° *reached / bag*
An' out a handfu' gied° him; *gave*
Syne bad[2] him slip frae' mang the folk,
Sometime when nae ane see'd him,
An' try't that night.

[1] *rantin kirn* Boisterous party.

[2] *Syne bad* Soon bade.

18

He marches thro' amang the stacks,
Tho' he was something sturtin;° *frightened*
The graip° he for a harrow taks, *pitchfork*
An' haurls° at his curpin:[3] *drags*
And ev'ry now an' then, he says,
"Hemp-seed I saw thee,
An' her that is to be my lass
Come after me, an' draw thee
As fast this night."

19

He wistl'd up Lord Lennox' March
To keep his courage cherry;
Altho' his hair began to arch,
He was sae fley'd° an' eerie: *terrified*
Till presently he hears a squeak,
An' then a grane an' gruntle;
He by his shouther gae a keek,° *glance*
An' tumbled wi' a wintle *somersault*
Out-owre that night.

20

He roar'd a horrid murder-shout,
In dreadfu' desperation!
An' young an' auld come rinnin out,
An' hear the sad narration:
He swoor 'twas hilchin° Jean M'Craw, *limping*
Or crouchie° Merran Humphie— *hunchbacked*
Till stop! she trotted thro' them a';
And wha was it but grumphie° *a pig*
Asteer that night!

21

Meg fain° wad to the barn gaen,° *gladly / have gone*
To winn° three wechts° o' naething; *winnow / sieves*
But for to meet the deil her lane,[4]
She pat but little faith in:
She gies the herd° a pickle° nits, *shepherd / few*
An' twa red cheekit apples,
To watch, while for the barn she sets,
In hopes to see Tam Kipples
That vera night.

[3] *at his curpin* Behind him (at his buttocks).

[4] *her lane* Alone.

22

She turns the key wi' cannie thraw,[1]
An'owre the threshold ventures;
But first on Sawnie° gies a ca', *Sandy*
Syne baudly in she enters:
A ratton° rattl'd up the wa', *rat*
An' she cry'd Lord preserve her!
An' ran thro' midden-hole° an' a', *dung pile*
An' pray'd wi' zeal and fervour,
Fu' fast that night.

23

They hoy't° out Will, wi' sair advice; *urged*
They hecht° him some fine braw ane; *promised*
It chanc'd the stack he faddom't thrice
Was timmer-propt° for thrawin: *propped up*
He taks a swirlie auld moss-oak
For some black, grousome carlin;° *witch*
An' loot a winze,[2] an' drew a stroke,
Till skin in blypes° cam haurlin *shreds*
Aff's nieves° that night. *fists*

24

A wanton widow Leezie was,
As cantie° as a kittlen;° *lively / kitten*
But och! that night, amang the shaws,° *woods*
She gat a fearfu' settlin!
She thro' the whins,° an' by the cairn, *gorse bushes*
An' owre the hill gaed scrievin;° *running swiftly*
Whare three lairds' lan's met at a burn,
To dip her left sark°-sleeve in, *shirt*
Was bent that night.

25

Whiles owre a linn° the burnie° plays, *waterfall / brook*
As thro' the glen it wimpl't;
Whiles round a rocky scar° it strays, *cliff*
Whiles in a wiel° it dimpl't; *eddy*
Whiles glitter'd to the nightly rays,
Wi' bickerin,' dancin' dazzle;
Whiles cookit° underneath the braes, *hidden*
Below the spreading hazel
Unseen that night.

26

Amang the brachens, on the brae,
Between her an' the moon,
The deil, or else an outler quey,[3]
Gat up an' ga'e a croon:
Poor Leezie's heart maist lap the hool;[4]
Near lav'rock°-height she jumpit, *lark*
But mist a fit, an' in the pool
Out-owre the lugs° she plumpit, *ears*
Wi' a plunge that night.

27

In order, on the clean hearth-stane,
The luggies° three are ranged; *wooden dishes*
An' ev'ry time great care is ta'en
To see them duly changed:
Auld uncle John, wha wedlock's joys
Sin' Mar's-year[5] did desire,
Because he gat the toom° dish thrice, *empty*
He heav'd them on the fire
In wrath that night.

28

Wi' merry sangs, an' friendly cracks,
I wat they did na weary;
And unco tales, an' funnie jokes—
Their sports were cheap an' cheery:
Till butter'd sowens,[6] wi' fragrant lunt,° *steam*
Set a' their gabs a-steerin;[7]
Syne, wi' a social glass o' strunt,° *liquor*
They parted aff careerin
Fu' blythe that night.

—1786

[1] *cannie thraw* Careful turn.

[2] *loot a winze* Cursed.

[3] *outler quey* Cows in the field.

[4] *maist lap the hool* Almost jumped out of her skin.

[5] *Mar's-year* 1715, the year of the Jacobite Rebellion.

[6] *butter'd sowens* Puddings.

[7] *gabs a-steerin* Tongues wagging.

Address to the De'il[1]

O Prince, O chief of many throned pow'rs,
That led th'embattled Seraphim to war—[2]
MILTON

O Thou, whatever title suit thee!
Auld Hornie, Satan, Nick, or Clootie,° *Hoofie*
Wha in yon cavern grim an' sooty
Closed under hatches,
Spairges about the brunstane cootie,[3]
To scaud° poor wretches! *scald*

Hear me, auld Hangie,° for a wee, *hangman*
An' let poor, damned bodies bee;
I'm sure sma' pleasure it can gie,
Ev'n to a de'il,
To skelp° an' scaud poor dogs like me, *strike*
An' hear us squeel!

Great is thy pow'r, an' great thy fame;
Far ken'd,° an' noted is thy name; *known*
An' tho' yon lowan heugh's[4] thy hame,
Thou travels far;
An' faith! thou's neither lag° nor lame, *slow*
Nor blate° nor scaur.° *shy / scared*

Whyles,° ranging like a roaring lion, *sometimes*
For prey, a' holes an' corners tryin;
Whyles, on the strong-wing'd tempest flyin,
Tirlan the kirks;[5]
Whyles, in the human bosom pryin,
Unseen thou lurks.

I've heard my rev'rend Graunie° say, *grandmother*
In lanely° glens ye like to stray; *lonely*
Or where auld, ruined castles, gray,
Nod to the moon,
Ye fright the nightly wand'rer's way,
Wi' eldritch croon.[6]

When twilight did my Graunie summon,
To say her pray'rs, douse,° honest woman, *grave*
Aft 'yont° the dyke she's heard you bumman° *beyond / humming*
Wi' eerie drone;
Or, rustling, thro' the boortries° coman, *elder shrubs*
Wi' heavy groan.

Ae dreary, windy, winter night,
The stars shot down wi' sklentan° light, *slanting*
Wi' you, mysel, I gat a fright
Ayont the lough;° *lake*
Ye, like a rash-buss,[7] stood in sight,
Wi' waving sugh:° *sound*

The cudgel in my nieve° did shake, *fist*
Each bristl'd hair stood like a stake,
When wi' an eldritch, stoor,° quaick, quaick, *hoarse*
Amang the springs,
Awa ye squatter'd° like a drake, *fluttered*
On whistling wings.

Let warlocks grim, an' wither'd hags,
Tell, how wi' you, on ragweed nags,[8]
They skim the muirs° an' dizzy crags, *moors*
Wi' wicked speed;
And in kirk-yards renew their leagues,
Owre howcket° dead. *dug up*

Thence, countra° wives, wi' toil an' pain, *country*
May plunge an' plunge the kirn° in vain; *churn*
For och! the yellow treasure's taen,° *taken*
By witching skill;
An' dawtit, twal-pint Hawkie's gane
As yell's the bill.[9]

---

1 *De'il* Devil.

2 *O Prince ... war* From *Paradise Lost* 1.128–9.

3 *Spairges ... cootie* Splashes about the brimstone vat.

4 *lowan heugh* Flaming pit.

5 *Tirlan the kirks* Unroofing the churches.

6 *eldrich croon* Ghastly moan.

7 *rash-buss* Bunch of rushes.

8 *ragweed nags* Broomsticks.

9 *dawtit ... bill* Pampered twelve-pint cow's gone / As milkless as the bull.

Thence, mystic knots mak great abuse,
On young guidmen,° fond, keen an' croose;° *husbands / spirited*
When the best warklum° i' the house, *tool*
By cantraip° wit, *enchanted*
Is instant made no worth a louse,
Just at the bit.° *final moment*

When thowes° dissolve the snawy hoord,° *thaws / hoard*
An' float the jinglan° icy boord,° *crackling / shore*
Then, water-kelpies haunt the foord,[1]
By your direction,
An' nighted trav'llers are allur'd
To their destruction.

An' aft your moss-traversing spunkies° *will-o'-the-wisps*
Decoy the wight° that late an' drunk is; *person*
The bleezan,° curst, mischievous monkies *blazing*
Delude his eyes,
Till in some miry slough he sunk is,
Ne'er mair to rise.

When Masons'[2] mystic word an' grip,
In storms an' tempests raise you up,
Some cock, or cat, your rage maun° stop, *must*
Or, strange to tell!
The youngest brother ye wad whip
Aff straught to H-ll.

Lang syne[3] in Eden's bonie yard,
When youthfu' lovers first were pair'd,
An' all the soul of love they shar'd,
The raptured hour,
Sweet on the fragrant, flow'ry swaird,° *surface*
In shady bow'r:

Then you, ye auld, snick°-drawing dog! *latch*
Ye cam to Paradise incog,° *disguised*
An' play'd on a man a cursed brogue,° *trick*
(Black be your fa'!)
An' gied° the infant warld a shog,° *gave / shock*
'Maist° ruin'd a.' *almost*

D'ye mind that day, when in a bizz,° *flurry*
Wi' reeket duds, an' reestet gizz,[4]
Ye did present your smoutie phiz[5]
'Mang better folk,
An' sklented on the man of Uz[6]
Your spitefu' joke?

An' how ye gat him i' your thrall,
An' brak him out o' house an' hal',
While scabs an' botches° did him gall, *tumor*
Wi' bitter claw,
An' lows'd° his ill-tongu'd, wicked scawl[7] *loosed*
Was warst ava?[8]

But a' your doings to rehearse,
Your wily snares an' fechtin° fierce, *fighting*
Sin' that day Michael did you pierce,[9]
Down to this time,
Wad ding° a' Lallan° tongue, or Erse, *overcome / Lowland*
In prose or rhyme.

An' now, auld cloots, I ken ye're thinkan,
A certain bardie's° rantin, drinkin, *poet's*
Some luckless hour will send him linkan,° *running*
To your black pit;
But faith! he'll turn a corner jinkan,° *ducking*
An' cheat you yet.

But fare you weel, auld Nickie-ben!° *Devil*
O wad ye tak a thought an' men'!° *mend*
Ye aiblins° might—I dinna ken— *perhaps*
Still hae a stake[10]—
I'm wae° to think upo' yon den, *sad*
Ev'n for your sake.

—1786

---

[1] *water-kelpies ... foord* Water spirits haunt the rivers.

[2] *Masons* Freemasons; members of an organization, formerly of stone masons, with secret codes and rites.

[3] *Lang syne* Long ago.

[4] *reeket ... gizz* Smoky clothes and singed face.

[5] *smoutie phiz* Dirty face.

[6] *man of Uz* Job, the man of Uz, was a righteous man who lost everything when God and Satan challenged his faith. See Job 1.1.

[7] *scawl* Scolding wife.

[8] *warst ava* Worst of all.

[9] *Michael did you pierce* See Milton's *Paradise Lost* 6.321–5, in which Satan stabs the angel Michael with a sword.

[10] *hae a stake* Have a chance.

Flow gently, sweet Afton[1]

Flow gently, sweet Afton, among thy green braes!° *banks*
Flow gently, I'll sing thee a song in thy praise!
My Mary's asleep by thy murmuring stream—
Flow gently, sweet Afton, disturb not her dream!

Thou stock–dove whose echo resounds thro' the glen,
Ye wild whistling blackbirds in yon thorny den,
Thou green–crested lapwing, thy screaming forbear—
I charge you, disturb not my slumbering fair!

How lofty, sweet Afton, thy neighbouring hills,
Far mark'd with the courses of clear, winding rills!° *brooks*
There daily I wander, as noon rises high,
My flocks and my Mary's sweet cot° in my eye. *cottage*

How pleasant thy banks and green valleys below,
Where wild in the woodlands the primroses blow;
There oft, as mild ev'ning weeps over the lea,
The sweet–scented birk° shades my Mary and me. *birch*

Thy crystal stream, Afton, how lovely it glides,
And winds by the cot where my Mary resides!
How wanton thy waters her snowy feet lave,° *wash*
As, gathering sweet flowerets, she stems thy clear wave.

Flow gently, sweet Afton, among thy green braes!
Flow gently, sweet river, the theme of my lays!° *song*
My Mary's asleep by thy murmuring stream—
Flow gently, sweet Afton, disturb not her dream!
—1792

Ae Fond Kiss[2]

Ae° fond kiss, and then we sever; *one*
Ae fareweel, alas, forever!
Deep in heart-wrung tears I'll pledge thee,
Warring sighs and groans I'll wage thee.

[1] *Afton* River that runs through southwestern Scotland.

[2] *Ae Fond Kiss* Burns wrote this love song for Nancy McLehose (the two called each other "Sylvander" and "Clarinda"), when she left England to reunite with her husband in Jamaica.

Who shall say that Fortune grieves him,
While the star of hope she leaves him?
Me, nae cheerful twinkle lights me;
Dark despair around benights me.

I'll ne'er blame my partial fancy,
Naething could resist my Nancy:
But to see her was to love her;
Love but her, and love forever.
Had we never lov'd sae kindly,
Had we never lov'd sae blindly,
Never met—or never parted,
We had ne'er been brokenhearted.

Fare-thee-weel, thou first and fairest!
Fare-thee-weel, thou best and dearest!
Thine be ilka° joy and treasure, *every*
Peace, Enjoyment, Love and Pleasure!
Ae fond kiss, and then we sever!
Ae fareweel, alas, forever!
Deep in heart-wrung tears I'll pledge thee,
Warring sighs and groans I'll wage thee.
—1792

Robert Bruce's March To Bannockburn[3]

Scots, wha hae° wi' Wallace[4] bled, *who have*
Scots, wham° Bruce has aften led, *whom*
Welcome to your gory bed,
  Or to victorie!

Now's the day, and now's the hour;
See the front o' battle lour;° *threaten*
See approach proud Edward's power—
  Chains and slaverie!

Wha will be a traitor knave?
Wha can fill a coward's grave?

[3] *Robert Bruce … Bannockburn* In 1314, Robert the Bruce, King of the Scots, fought successfully for a free Scotland in a battle against the English under Edward I at Bannockburn.

[4] *Wallace* Sir William Wallace led numerous battles against the English under King Edward I.

Wha sae base as be a slave?
Let him turn and flee!

Wha, for Scotland's King and Law,
Freedom's sword will strongly draw,
Free–man stand, or Free–man fa',
Let him on wi' me!

By Oppression's woes and pains!
By your Sons in servile chains!
We will drain our dearest veins,
But they shall be free!

Lay the proud usurpers low!
Tyrants fall in every foe!
Liberty's in every blow!—
Let us Do or Die!

—1795

A Man's A Man For A' That

Is there for honest poverty
That hings° his head, an' a'° that; *hangs / all*
The coward slave—we pass him by,
We dare be poor for a' that!
For a' that, an' a' that.
Our toils obscure an' a' that,
The rank is but the guinea's stamp,
The Man's the gowd° for a' that. *gold*

What though on hamely° fare we dine, *simple*
Wear hoddin grey,[1] an' a that;
Gie° fools their silks, and knaves their wine; *give*
A Man's a Man for a' that:
For a' that, and a' that,
Their tinsel show, an' a' that;
The honest man, tho' e'er sae° poor, *so*
Is king o' men for a' that.

Ye see yon birkie,[2] ca'd° "a lord," *called*
Wha struts, an' stares, an' a' that;
Tho' hundreds worship at his word,
He's but a coof° for a' that: *fool*
For a' that, an' a' that,
His ribband,° star,[3] an' a' that: *ribbon*
The man o' independent mind
He looks an' laughs at a' that.

A prince can mak a belted knight,
A marquis, duke, an' a' that;
But an honest man's aboon° his might, *above*
Gude faith, he mauna fa'[4] that!
For a' that, an' a' that,
Their dignities an' a' that;
The pith° o' sense, an' pride o' worth, *importance*
Are higher rank than a' that.

Then let us pray that come it may,
As come it will for a' that,
That sense and worth, o'er a' the earth,
Shall bear the gree,[5] an' a' that.
For a' that, an' a' that,
It's coming yet for a' that,
That Man to Man, the world o'er,
Shall brithers be for a' that.

—1795

Comin' thro' the Rye

Chorus

O, Jenny's a' weet,[6] poor body,
Jenny's seldom dry;
She draigl't[7] a' her petticoatie
Comin thro' the rye!

Comin thro' the rye, poor body,
Comin thro' the rye,
She draigl't a' her petticoatie,
Comin thro' the rye!

[1] *hodden grey* Coarse, woolen peasant cloth.

[2] *birkie* Conceited, swaggering fellow.

[3] *ribband, star* Emblems of nobility.

[4] *mauna fa' that* Musn't have that befall him.

[5] *bear the gree* Have the victory.

[6] *a' weet* All wet.

[7] *draigl't* Dragged; dragged through the mud.

Gin° a body meet a body *suppose*
Comin thro' the rye,
Gin a body kiss a body,
Need a body cry?

Gin a body meet a body
Comin thro' the glen,
Gin a body kiss a body,
Need the warld ken°? *know*

CHORUS

O, Jenny's a' weet, poor body,
Jenny's seldom dry;
She draigl't a' her petticoatie
Comin thro' the rye!

—1796

A Red, Red Rose

O, my luve's like a red, red rose,
That's newly sprung in June;
O, my luve's like the melodie,
That's sweetly play'd in tune.

As fair art thou, my bonie lass,
So deep in luve am I;
And I will luve thee still, my dear,
Till a' the seas gang° dry. *go*

Till a' the seas gang dry, my dear,
And the rocks melt wi' the sun;
And I will luve thee still, my dear,
While the sands o' life shall run.

And fare thee weel, my only luve!
And fare thee weel, a while!
And I will come again, my luve,
Tho' 'twere ten thousand mile!

—1796

Auld Lang Syne[1]

Should auld acquaintance be forgot,
And never brought to mind?
Should auld acquaintance be forgot,
And auld lang syne!

CHORUS

For auld lang syne, my dear,
For auld lang syne.
We'll tak a cup o' kindness yet,
For auld lang syne.

And surely ye'll be° your pint stowp![2] *raise*
And surely I'll be mine!
And we'll tak a cup o' kindness yet,
For auld lang syne.

CHORUS

We twa° hae run about the braes,° *two / hills*
And pou'd° the gowans fine; *pulled / daisies*
But we've wander'd mony a weary fit,° *foot*
Sin'° auld lang syne. *since*

CHORUS

We twa hae paidl'd in the burn,° *stream*
Frae morning sun till dine;
But seas between us braid° hae roar'd *broad*
Sin'° auld lang syne. *since*

CHORUS

And there's a hand, my trusty fiere!° *friend*
And gie's° a hand o' thine! *give us*
And we'll tak a right gude willie-waught,[3]
For auld lang syne.

CHORUS

—1796

---

[1] *Auld Lang Syne* Times long since passed.

[2] *stowp* Drinking glass.

[3] *gude willie-waught* Hearty glass of draught beer.

Love and Liberty. A Cantata[1]

RECITATIVO

When lyart° leaves bestrow the yird,° *decayed / ground*
Or wavering like the bauckie-bird,° *bat*
Bedim cauld Boreas' blast;[2]
When hailstanes drive wi' bitter skyte,° *lash*
And infant frosts begin to bite,
In hoary cranreuch[3] drest;
Ae night at e'en a merry core° *corps*
O' randie, gangrel° bodies, *vagrant*
In Poosie Nansie's[4] held the splore,° *drinking spree*
To drink their orra duddies;[5]
Wi' quaffing an' laughing,
They ranted an' they sang,
Wi' jumping an' thumping,
The vera girdle[6] rang,

First, neist° the fire, in auld red rags, *next*
Ane sat, weel brac'd wi' mealy bags,[7]
And knapsack a' in order;
His doxy° lay within his arm; *wench*
Wi' usquebae° an' blankets warm *whiskey*
She blinkit on her sodger;
An' aye he gies the tozie drab[8]
The tither skelpin'[9] kiss,
While she held up her greedy gab,° *mouth*
Just like an aumous° dish; *alms*
Ilk° smack still, did crack still, *each*
Just like a cadger's[10] whip;
Then staggering an' swaggering
He roar'd this ditty up—

AIR

I am a son of Mars[11] who have been in many wars,
And show my cuts and scars wherever I come;
This here was for a wench, and that other in a trench,
When welcoming the French at the sound of the drum.
Lal de daudle, &c.

My 'prenticeship I past where my leader breath'd his last,
When the bloody die was cast on the heights of Abram:[12]
And I served out my trade when the gallant game was play'd,
And the Moro[13] low was laid at the sound of the drum.

I lastly was with Curtis[14] among the floating batt'ries,
And there I left for witness an arm and a limb;
Yet let my country need me, with Elliot[15] to head me,
I'd clatter on my stumps at the sound of a drum.

And now tho' I must beg, with a wooden arm and leg,
And many a tatter'd rag hanging over my bum,
I'm as happy with my wallet, my bottle, and my callet,° *whore*
As when I used in scarlet to follow a drum.

What tho' with hoary locks, I must stand the winter shocks,
Beneath the woods and rocks oftentimes for a home,

[1] *Love and Liberty. A Cantata* Commonly known by the title "The Jolly Beggars."

[2] *Boreas' blast* North wind (Boreas is the Greek god of the north wind).

[3] *hoary cranreuch* Hoar frost.

[4] *Poosie Nansie's* Scottish tavern where Burns found the inspiration for *The Jolly Beggars*.

[5] *orra duddies* Extra rags.

[6] *vera girdle* Very griddle.

[7] *weel brac'd wi' mealy bags* Well fed with porridge.

[8] *tozie drab* Drunken slut.

[9] *tither skelpin'* Other smacking.

[10] *cadger* Salesman who traveled with a horse and cart.

[11] *Mars* Roman god of war.

[12] *heights of Abram* In 1759, British general James Wolfe's troops won the Battle of the Plains of Abraham against the French in Quebec; Wolfe and the opposing general, Montcalm, both died in the battle.

[13] *Moro* El Moro was a castle on the island of Santiago, Cuba, which was stormed by the British in 1762.

[14] *Curtis* Rear Admiral Sir Roger Curtis, who took part in the battle of 1782 against the Spanish off the waters of Gibraltar.

[15] *Elliot* Sir George Augustus Elliot, who also helped defend Gibraltar.

When the t'other bag I sell, and the t'other bottle tell,
I could meet a troop of hell, at the sound of a drum.

RECITATIVO

He ended; and the kebars° sheuk, *rafters*
Aboon° the chorus roar; *above*
While frighted rattons° backward leuk, *rats*
An' seek the benmost° bore: *innermost*
A fairy fiddler frae the neuk,
He skirl'd out, *Encore!*
But up arose the martial chuck,° *camp whore*
An' laid the loud uproar.

AIR

I once was a maid, tho' I cannot tell when,
And still my delight is in proper young men;
Some one of a troop of dragoons was my daddie,
No wonder I'm fond of a sodger laddie,
Sing, lal de lal, &c.

The first of my loves was a swaggering blade,
To rattle the thundering drum was his trade;
His leg was so tight, and his cheek was so ruddy,
Transported I was with my sodger laddie.

But the godly old chaplain left him in the lurch;
The sword I forsook for the sake of the church:
He ventur'd the soul, and I risked the body,
'Twas then I proved false to my sodger laddie.

Full soon I grew sick of my sanctified sot,
The regiment at large for a husband I got;
From the gilded spontoon° to the fife I was ready, *weapon*
I asked no more but a sodger laddie.

But the peace it reduc'd me to beg in despair,
Till I met old boy in a Cunningham fair,
His rags regimental, they flutter'd so gaudy,
My heart it rejoic'd at a sodger laddie.

And now I have liv'd—I know not how long,
And still I can join in a cup and a song;
But whilst with both hands I can hold the glass steady,
Here's to thee, my hero, my sodger laddie.

RECITATIVO

Poor Merry-Andrew,[1] in the neuk,
Sat guzzling wi' a tinkler-hizzie;° *tinker-hussy*
They mind't na wha the chorus teuk,
Between themselves they were sae busy:
At length, wi' drink an' courting dizzy,
He stoiter'd° up an' made a face; *staggered*
Then turn'd an' laid a smack on Grizzie,
Syne° tun'd his pipes wi' grave grimace. *then*

AIR

Sir Wisdom's a fool when he's fou;° *drunk*
Sir Knave is a fool in a session;
He's there but a 'prentice I trow,° *trust*
But I am a fool by profession.

My grannie she bought me a beuk,
An' I held° awa to the school; *went*
I fear I my talent misteuk,
But what will ye hae of a fool?

For drink I would venture my neck;
A hizzie's the half of my craft;
But what could ye other expect
Of ane that's avowedly daft?

I ance was tied up like a stirk,° *young cow*
For civilly swearing and quaffin;[2]
I ance was abus'd i' the kirk,° *church*
For towsing a lass i' my daffin.[3]

Poor Andrew that tumbles for sport,
Let naebody name wi' a jeer;
There's even, I'm tauld, i' the Court
A tumbler ca'd the Premier.

Observ'd ye yon reverend lad
Mak faces to tickle the mob;
He rails at our mountebank[4] squad—
It's rivalship just i' the job.

---

[1] *Merry-Andrew* Clown, joker, buffoon.

[2] *quaffin* Drinking large amounts of alcohol.

[3] *towsing a lass i' my daffin* Literally, disheveling a woman in merriment; obliquely, having sex out of wedlock.

[4] *mountebank* Itinerant seller of supposed remedies.

And now my conclusion I'll tell,
For faith I'm confoundedly dry;
The chiel° that's a fool for himsel', *young boy*
Guid Lord! he's far dafter than I.

Recitativo

Then niest° outspak a raucle carlin,[1] *next*
Wha kent fu' weel to cleek° the sterlin;° *steal / money*
For mony a pursie she had hooked,
An' had in mony a well been douked;° *ducked*
Her love had been a Highland laddie,
But weary fa' the waefu' woodie!° *dolt*
Wi' sighs an' sobs she thus began
To wail her braw° John Highlandman. *handsome*

Air

A Highland lad my love was born,
The Lalland° laws he held in scorn; *Lowland*
But he still was faithfu' to his clan,
My gallant, braw John Highlandman.

Chorus

Sing hey my braw John Highlandman!
Sing ho my braw John Highlandman!
There's not a lad in a' the lan'
Was match for my John Highlandman.

With his philibeg° an' tartan plaid, *kilt*
An' guid claymore° down by his side, *sword*
The ladies' hearts he did trepan,° *entrap*
My gallant, braw John Highlandman.
Sing hey, &c.

We ranged a' from Tweed to Spey,
An' liv'd like lords an' ladies gay;
For a Lalland face he feared none—
My gallant, braw John Highlandman.
Sing hey, &c.

They banish'd him beyond the sea.
But ere the bud was on the tree,
Adown my cheeks the pearls ran,
Embracing my John Highlandman.
Sing hey, &c.

But, och! they catch'd him at the last,
And bound him in a dungeon fast:
My curse upon them every one,
They've hang'd my braw John Highlandman!
Sing hey, &c.

And now a widow, I must mourn
The pleasures that will ne'er return:
The comfort but a hearty can,
When I think on John Highlandman.
Sing hey, &c.

Recitativo

A pigmy scraper wi' his fiddle,
Wha us'd at trystes° an' fairs to driddle. *markets / dawdle*
Her strappin limb and gausy° middle *plump*
(He reach'd nae higher)
Had hol'd his heartie like a riddle,
An' blawn't° on fire. *blown it*

Wi' hand on hainch, and upward e'e,
He croon'd his gamut, one, two, three,
Then in an arioso key,
The wee Apollo[2]
Set off wi' allegretto glee
His giga° solo. *jig*

Air

Let me ryke° up to dight° that tear, *reach / wipe*
An' go wi' me an' be my dear;
An' then your every care an' fear
May whistle owre the lave° o't. *rest*

Chorus

I am a fiddler to my trade,
An' a' the tunes that e'er I played,
The sweetest still to wife or maid,
Was whistle owre the lave o't.

At kirns° an' weddins we'se be there, *harvest feasts*
An' O sae nicely's we will fare!
We'll bowse° about till Daddie Care *drink*
Sing whistle owre the lave o't.
I am, &c.

[1] *raucle carlin* Stout hag.

[2] *Apollo* Greek god of music.

Sae merrily's the banes° we'll pyke,° *bones / pick*
An' sun oursel's about the dyke;
An' at our leisure, when ye like,
We'll whistle owre the lave o't.
I am, &c.

But bless me wi' your heav'n o' charms,
An' while I kittle° hair on thairms,[1] *tickle*
Hunger, cauld, an' a' sic° harms, *such*
May whistle owre the lave o't.
I am, &c.

RECITATIVO

Her charms had struck a sturdy caird,° *tinker*
As weel as poor gut-scraper;
He taks the fiddler by the beard,
An' draws a roosty° rapier— *rusty*
He swoor, by a' was swearing worth,
To speet° him like a pliver,° *pierce / plover*
Unless he would from that time forth
Relinquish her forever.

Wi' ghastly e'e° poor tweedle-dee *eye*
Upon his hunkers° bended, *haunches*
An' pray'd for grace wi' ruefu' face,
An' so the quarrel ended.
But tho' his little heart did grieve
When round the tinkler prest her,
He feign'd to snirtle° in his sleeve, *snicker*
When thus the caird address'd her:

AIR

My bonie lass, I work in brass,
A tinkler is my station:
I've travell'd round all Christian ground
In this my occupation;
I've taen the gold, an' been enrolled
In many a noble squadron;
But vain they search'd when off I march'd
To go an' clout° the cauldron. *patch*

Despise that shrimp, that wither'd imp,
With a' his noise an' cap'rin;
An' take a share with those that bear
The budget° and the apron! *pouch*
And by that stowp!° my faith an' houp, *cup*
And by that dear Kilbaigie![2]
If e'er ye want, or meet wi' scant,
May I ne'er weet° my craigie.° *wet / throat*

RECITATIVO

The caird prevail'd—th' unblushing fair
In his embraces sunk;
Partly wi' love o'ercome sae sair,
An' partly she was drunk:
Sir Violino, with an air
That show'd a man o' spunk,
Wish'd unison between the pair,
An' made the bottle clunk
To their health that night.

But hurchin° Cupid shot a shaft, *urchin*
That play'd a dame a shavie°— *trick*
The fiddler rak'd her, fore and aft,
Behint the chicken cavie.° *coop*
Her lord, a wight° of Homer's craft, *creature*
Tho' limpin wi' the spavie,[3]
He hirpl'd° up, an' lap° like daft, *limped / leapt*
An' shor'd° them Dainty Davie[4] *offered*
O' boot[5] that night.

He was a care-defying blade[6]
As ever Bacchus[7] listed!
Tho' Fortune sair upon him laid,
His heart, she ever miss'd it.
He had no wish but—to be glad,
Nor want but—when he thirsted;
He hated nought but—to be sad,
An' thus the muse suggested
His sang that night.

[1] *hair on thairms* Fiddle strings.

[2] *Kilbaigie* Brand of whiskey.

[3] *spavie* Tumorous bone disease.

[4] *Dainty Davie* Lovemaking; Dainty Davie is the subject of a Scottish song about David Williamson, who was said to have been given refuge by the Laird of Cherrytrees. The Laird hid the man in his daughter's bed, and the girl was later discovered to be pregnant.

[5] *O' boot* For free.

[6] *blade* Good-natured fellow.

[7] *Bacchus* Roman god of wine.

AIR

I am a Bard of no regard,
Wi' gentle folks an' a' that;
But Homer—like, the glowrin byke,° *crowd*
Frae town to town I draw that.

CHORUS

For a' that, an' a' that,
An' twice as muckle's° a' that; *much*
I've lost but ane, I've twa behin,'
I've wife eneugh for a' that.

I never drank the Muses'[1] stank,° *pool*
Castalia's[2] burn,° an' a' that; *brewing water*
But there it streams an' richly reams,
My Helicon[3] I ca' that.
For a' that, &c.

Great love I bear to a' the fair,
Their humble slave an' a' that;
But lordly will, I hold it still
A mortal sin to thraw° that. *thwart*
For a' that, &c.

In raptures sweet, this hour we meet,
Wi' mutual love an' a' that;
But for how lang the flie may stang,
Let inclination law that.
For a' that, &c.

Their tricks an' craft hae put me daft,
They've taen me in, an' a' that;
But clear your decks, and here's—"The Sex!"
I like the jads° for a' that. *young ladies*

CHORUS

For a' that, an' a' that,
An' twice as muckle's a' that;
My dearest bluid,° to do them guid, *blood*
They're welcome till't° for a' that. *to it*

RECITATIVO

So sang the bard — and Nansie's wa's
Shook with a thunder of applause,
Re-echo'd from each mouth!
They toom'd° their pocks,° they pawn'd their duds, *emptied / pockets*
They scarcely left to co'er their fuds,° *behinds*
To quench their lowin drouth:[4]
Then owre again, the jovial thrang
The poet did request
To lowse his pack an' wale° a sang, *choose*
A ballad o' the best;
He rising, rejoicing,
Between his twa Deborahs,[5]
Looks round him, an' found them
Impatient for the chorus.

AIR

See the smoking bowl before us,
Mark our jovial ragged ring!
Round and round take up the chorus,
And in raptures let us sing—

CHORUS

A fig for those by law protected!
Liberty's a glorious feast!
Courts for cowards were erected,
Churches built to please the priest.

What is title, what is treasure,
What is reputation's care?
If we lead a life of pleasure,
'Tis no matter how or where!
A fig for, &c.

With the ready trick and fable,
Round we wander all the day;
And at night in barn or stable,
Hug our doxies° on the hay. *mistresses*
A fig for, &c.

[1] *Muses* In Greek mythology, the nine daughters of Zeus and Mnemosyne, each of whom presided over and provided inspiration for an aspect of learning or the arts.

[2] *Castalia* Spring on Mount Parnassus that was sacred to the Muses.

[3] *Helicon* Mountain dedicated to the Muses.

[4] *lowin drouth* Burning thirst.

[5] *twa Deborahs* The two Deborahs of the Bible.

Does the train-attended carriage
  Thro' the country lighter rove?
Does the sober bed of marriage
  Witness brighter scenes of love?
    A fig for, &c.

Life is all a variorum,[1]
  We regard not how it goes;
Let them cant about decorum,
  Who have character to lose.
    A fig for, &c.

Here's to budgets, bags and wallets!
  Here's to all the wandering train.
Here's our ragged brats and callets,° *strumpets*
  One and all cry out, Amen!

    A fig for those by law protected!
      Liberty's a glorious feast!
    Courts for cowards were erected,
      Churches built to please the priest.

—1799

[1] *variorum* Changing scene, variation.

Joanna Baillie

1762 – 1851

Although an important and influential figure in her lifetime, Joanna Baillie, like many women writers of the Romantic era, subsequently fell into obscurity. Only recently has critical and scholarly attention returned to her writing. Her plays had been held in particularly high regard; Sir Walter Scott called her "the best dramatic writer whom Britain has produced since the days of Shakespeare and Massinger." Baillie also produced an important work of literary criticism—she included an "Introductory Discourse" to her *Plays on the Passions* (1798) (published the same year as Wordsworth's famous "Preface" to *Lyrical Ballads*), in which she analyzed Enlightenment drama and critiqued its discourse of tragedy.

Joanna Baillie was born in 1762 to Dorothea Hunter and James Baillie, a Presbyterian minister, in Lanarkshire, Scotland. Her mother was known as a good storyteller, a talent that Baillie picked up at an early age. Despite this interest, she shunned reading until she was ten years old, preferring to spend her time outdoors. In 1768 she left the rural area in which she was born when her father was transferred to a church in Hamilton, a nearby town on the banks of the Clyde River.

Baillie was sent to boarding school in Glasgow in 1772. Four years later the rest of her family joined her when her father was hired as Professor of Divinity at the University of Glasgow. At boarding school, she proved herself to be a vivacious and outgoing young woman, studying music, visual art, mathematics, and reading. In addition to her studies, she was active in the school's artistic life, helping to stage plays. The family returned to Lanarkshire when her father died in 1778. While her brother Matthew left to study at Oxford, Baillie pursued her own studies privately. (Universities would remain a male preserve in England until the mid-nineteenth century.) Home was to be the realm for her work and career throughout the rest of her life.

In 1784 the family moved again, this time to London. There Baillie began to publish, releasing a small book in 1790 entitled *Poems: Wherein it is Attempted to Describe Certain Views of Nature*. She published *Poems* anonymously, as was common for women writers at the time. The book had little impact, but Baillie's plays proved much more successful. She wrote mainly closet dramas—plays intended to be read, not performed. Nevertheless, some of her plays did make it to the stage, and were acted by prominent actors such as John Kemble, Sarah Siddons, and Edmund Kean. In 1798 the first of her six-volume *A Series of Plays* (now commonly referred to as *Plays on the Passions*) was published. The volume, composed of three plays, was the beginning of an investigation into the strongest human passions: love, fear, hatred, and jealousy. Each passion was to be the subject of one comedy and one tragedy.

Count Basil, a meditation on love, is a tragedy about a man caught between his responsibilities as a military general and his love for a woman—*The Tryal* is its comic counterpart. The third play, and arguably her most distinguished work, is *De Montfort*, a meditation on hatred. The "Introductory Discourse" to the volume is an important piece of early Romantic literary criticism. In it, Baillie argues for a grounded, psychologically based treatment of dramatic characters, urging authors not to rely on overblown rhetoric or scenes of extreme emotion to convey the passions of their characters.

Baillie published the first volume of *A Series of Plays* anonymously, and there was considerable public discussion over the identity of the author. Most readers immediately assumed that the author was male (although several women—Hester Thrale, for one—guessed otherwise); the plays were widely attributed to Sir Walter Scott and later the "Introductory Discourse" to Baillie's brother, Matthew. At the time, many took as an article of faith Voltaire's dictum that "the composition of a tragedy requires *testicles*." It was with reference to this notion that Byron remarked in admiration of her work: "Lord knows what Joanna Baillie does—I suppose she borrows them." She went on to release five further volumes in the series under her own name, in 1802, 1812, and 1836.

Many prominent literary figures of the time came to visit Baillie, including Lord Byron, William Wordsworth, Maria Edgeworth, and Sir Walter Scott. Through her friendship with Scott, Baillie had the opportunity to return to Scotland in 1807 and 1820. The visit had a profound affect on her writing. She began to use a Scottish idiom in some of her work, and chose to include Scottish figures such as William Wallace and Lady Grisell Baillie (a possible ancestor) in her *Metrical Legends of Exalted Characters* (1821).

In later life, Baillie's writing became more reflective and often addressed religious matters, as in *A View of the General Tenor of the New Testament Regarding the Nature and Dignity of Jesus Christ* (1831). Baillie's last volume of work, *The Dramatic and Poetical Works of Joanna Baillie*, was published a few weeks before her death, at the age of 88, in 1851.

⌘⌘⌘

A Mother to Her Waking Infant

Now in thy dazzling half-op'd eye,
Thy curled nose, and lip awry,
Thy up-hoist arms, and noddling head,
And little chin with crystal spread,
Poor helpless thing! what do I see,
That I should sing of thee?

From thy poor tongue no accents come,
Which can but rub thy toothless gum:
Small understanding boast thy face,
Thy shapeless limbs nor step, nor grace:
A few short words thy feats may tell,
And yet I love thee well.

When sudden wakes the bitter shriek,
And redder swells thy little cheek;
When rattled keys thy woe beguile,
And through the wet eye gleams the smile,
Still for thy weakly self is spent
Thy little silly plaint.° *complaint*

But when thy friends are in distress,
Thou'lt laugh and chuckle ne'er the less;
Nor e'en with sympathy be smitten,
Tho' all are sad but thee and kitten;
Yet little varlet° that thou art, *rascal*
Thou twitchest at the heart.

Thy rosy cheek so soft and warm;
Thy pinky hand, and dimpled arm;
Thy silken locks that scantly peep,
With gold-tipped ends, where circle deep
Around thy neck in harmless grace
So soft and sleekly hold their place,
Might harder hearts with kindness fill,
And gain our right good will.

Each passing clown° bestows his blessing, *rustic*
Thy mouth is worn with old wives' kissing:
E'en lighter looks the gloomy eye
Of surly sense, when thou art by;
And yet I think whoe'er they be,
They love thee not like me.

Perhaps when time shall add a few
Short years to thee, thou'lt love me too.
Then wilt thou through life's weary way
Become my sure and cheering stay:
Wilt care for me, and be my hold,° *protector*
When I am weak and old.

Thou'lt listen to my lengthened tale,
And pity me when I am frail—
But see, the sweepy° spinning fly *sweeping*
Upon the window takes thine eye.
Go to thy little senseless play—
Thou dost not heed my lay.° *song*

—1790

A Child to His Sick Grandfather

Grand-dad, they say you're old and frail,
Your stocked[1] legs begin to fail:
Your knobbed stick (that was my horse)
Can scarce support your bended corse;° *body*
While back to wall, you lean so sad,
I'm vexed to see you, dad.

You used to smile, and stroke my head,
And tell me how good children did;
But now I wot° not how it be, *know*
You take me seldom on your knee;
Yet ne'ertheless I am right glad
To sit beside you, dad.

How lank and thin your beard hangs down!
Scant are the white hairs on your crown:
How wan° and hollow are your cheeks! *unhealthy*
Your brow is rough with crossing breaks;
But yet, for all his strength is fled,
I love my own old dad.

The housewives round their potions brew,
And gossips come to ask for you:
And for your weal° each neighbour cares, *well-being*
And good men kneel, and say their pray'rs:
And ev'rybody looks so sad,
When you are ailing, dad.

You will not die, and leave us then?
Rouse up and be our dad again.
When you are quiet and laid in bed,
We'll doff our shoes and softly tread;
And when you wake we'll aye° be near, *always*
To fill old dad his cheer.

When through the house you shift your stand,
I'll lead you kindly by the hand:
When dinner's set, I'll with you bide,
And aye be serving by your side:
And when the weary fire burns blue,
I'll sit and talk with you.

I have a tale both long and good,
About a partlet° and her brood; *hen*
And cunning greedy fox, that stole,
By dead of midnight through a hole,
Which slyly to the hen-roost led—
You love a story, dad?

And then I have a wond'rous tale
Of men all clad in coats of mail,
With glitt'ring swords—you nod, I think?
Your fixed eyes begin to wink:
Down on your bosom sinks your head:
You do not hear me, dad.

—1790

[1] *stocked* Dressed in stockings.

Thunder

Spirit of strength! To whom in wrath 'tis given,
To mar the earth and shake its vasty dome,
Behold the somber robes whose gathering folds,
Thy secret majesty conceal. Their skirts
Spread on mid air move slow and silently,
O'er noon-day's beam thy sultry shroud is cast,
Advancing clouds from every point of heaven,
Like hosts of gathering foes in pitchy° volumes, *dark*
Grandly dilated, clothe the fields of air,
And brood aloft o'er the empurpled earth.

Spirit of strength! It is thy awful hour;
The wind of every hill is laid to rest,
And far o'er sea and land deep silence reigns.

Wild creatures of the forest homeward hie,° *hurry*
And in their dens with fear unwonted cower;
Pride in the lordly palace is put down,
While in his humble cot° the poor man sits *cottage*
With all his family round him hushed and still,
In awful expectation. On his way
The traveller stands aghast and looks to heaven.
On the horizon's verge thy lightning gleams,
And the first utterance of thy deep voice
Is heard in reverence and holy fear.

From nearer clouds bright burst more vivid gleams,
As instantly in closing darkness lost;
Pale sheeted flashes cross the wide expanse
While over boggy moor or swampy plain,
A steaming cataract° of flame appears, *waterfall*
To meet a nether fire from earth cast up,
Commingling terribly; appalling gloom
Succeeds, and lo! the rifted center pours
A general blaze, and from the war of clouds,
Red, writhing falls the embodied bolt of heaven.
Then swells the rolling peal, full, deep'ning, grand,
And in its strength lifts the tremendous roar,
With mingled discord, rattling, hissing, growling;
Crashing like rocky fragments downward hurled,
Like the upbreaking of a ruined world,
In awful majesty the explosion bursts
Wide and astounding o'er the trembling land.
Mountain, and cliff, repeat the dread turmoil,
And all to man's distinctive senses known,
Is lost in the immensity of sound.
Peal after peal, succeeds with waning strength,
And hushed and deep each solemn pause between.

Upon the lofty mountain's side
The kindled forest blazes wide;
Huge fragments of the rugged steep
Are tumbled to the lashing deep;
Firm rooted in his cloven rock,
Crashing falls the stubborn oak.
The lightning keen in wasteful ire
Darts fiercely on the pointed spire,
Rending in twain the iron-knit stone,
And stately towers to earth are thrown.
No human strength may brave the storm,
Nor shelter screen the shrinking form,
Nor castle wall its fury stay,
Nor massy° gate impede its way: *solid*
It visits those of low estate,
It shakes the dwellings of the great,
It looks athwart the vaulted tomb,
And glares upon the prison's gloom.
Then dungeons black in unknown light,
Flash hideous on the wretches' sight,
And strangely groans the downward cell,
Where silence deep is wont to dwell.

Now eyes, to heaven up-cast, adore,
Knees bend that never bent before,
The stoutest hearts begin to fail,
And many a manly face is pale;
Benumbing fear awhile up-binds,
The palsied action of their minds,
Till waked to dreadful sense they lift their eyes,
And round the stricken corse° shrill shrieks of horror rise. *body*

Now rattling hailstones, bounding as they fall
To earth, spread motley[1] winter o'er the plain,
Receding peals sound fainter on the ear,
And roll their distant grumbling far away:
The lightning doth in paler flashes gleam,
And through the rent° cloud, silvered with his rays, *torn*
The sun on all this wild affray looks down,
As, high enthroned above all mortal ken,° *perception*
A higher Power beholds the strife of men.
—1790

A Winter Day

The cock, warm roosting 'midst his feathered dames
Now lifts his beak and snuffs the morning air,
Stretches his neck and claps his heavy wings,

[1] *motley* Many-colored, variegated in appearance.

Gives three hoarse crows, and glad his task is done;
Low, chuckling, turns himself upon the roost,
Then nestles down again amongst his mates.
The lab'ring hind,° who on his bed of straw, *servant*
Beneath his home-made coverings, coarse, but warm,
Locked in the kindly arms of her who spun them,
Dreams of the gain that next year's crop should bring;
Or at some fair disposing° of his wool, *sale*
Or by some lucky and unlooked-for bargain,
Fills his skin purse with heaps of tempting gold,
Now wakes from sleep at the unwelcome call,
And finds himself but just the same poor man
As when he went to rest.
He hears the blast against his window beat,
And wishes to himself he were a lord,
That he might lie a-bed.
He rubs his eyes, and stretches out his arms;
Heigh ho! Heigh ho! He drawls with gaping mouth,
Then most unwillingly creeps out of bed,
And without looking-glass puts on his clothes.
With rueful face he blows the smothered fire,
And lights his candle at the red'ning coal;
First sees that all be right amongst his cattle,
Then hies° him to the barn with heavy tread, *goes*
Printing his footsteps on the new fall'n snow.
From out the heap of corn he pulls his sheaves,
Dislodging the poor red-breast° from his shelter, *robin*
Where all the live-long night he slept secure;
But now affrighted, with uncertain flight
He flutters round the walls, to seek some hole,
At which he may escape out to the frost.
And now the flail, high whirling o'er his head,
Descends with force upon the jumping sheave,
Whilst every rugged wall, and neighb'ring cot° *cottage*
Re-echoes back the noise of his strokes.

The fam'ly cares call next upon the wife
To quit her mean° but comfortable bed. *simple*
And first she stirs the fire, and blows the flame,
Then from her heap of sticks, for winter stored,
An armful brings; loud crackling as they burn,
Thick fly the red sparks upward to the roof,
While slowly mounts the smoke in wreathy clouds.
On goes the seething pot with morning cheer,
For which some little wishful hearts await,
Who, peeping from the bed-clothes, spy, well pleased,
The cheery light that blazes on the wall,
And bawl for leave to rise.
Their busy mother knows not where to turn,
Her morning work comes now so thick upon her.
One she must help to tie his little coat,
Unpin his cap, and seek another's shoe.
When all is o'er, out to the door they run,
With new combed sleeky hair, and glist'ning cheeks,
Each with some little project in his head.
One on the ice must try his new soled shoes:
To view his well-set trap another hies,
In hopes to find some poor unwary bird
(No worthless prize) entangled in his snare;
While one, less active, with round rosy face,
Spreads out his purple fingers to the fire,
And peeps, most wishfully, into the pot.

But let us leave the warm and cheerful house,
To view the bleak and dreary scene without,
And mark the dawning of a winter day.
For now the morning vapour, red and grumly,° *dense*
Rests heavy on the hills; and o'er the heav'ns
Wide spreading forth in lighter gradual shades,
Just faintly colours the pale muddy sky.
Then slowly from behind the southern hills,
Enlarged and ruddy looks the rising sun,
Shooting his beams askance the hoary waste,
Which gild the brow of ev'ry swelling height,
And deepen every valley with a shade.
The crusted window of each scattered cot,
The icicles that fringe the thatched roof,
The new swept slide upon the frozen pool,
All lightly glance, new kindled with his rays;
And e'en the rugged face of scowling Winter
Looks somewhat gay. But for a little while
He lifts his glory o'er the bright'ning earth,
Then hides his head behind a misty cloud.

The birds now quit their holes and lurking sheds,
Most mute and melancholy, where through night
All nestling close to keep each other warm,
In downy sleep they had forgot their hardships;
But not to chant and carol in the air,
Or lightly swing upon some waving bough,

And merrily return each other's notes;
No; silently they hop from bush to bush,
Yet find no seeds to stop their craving want,
Then bend their flight to the low smoking cot,
Chirp on the roof, or at the window peck,
To tell their wants to those who lodge within.
The poor lank° hare flies homeward to his den, *thin*
But little burthened with his nightly meal
Of withered greens grubbed from the farmer's garden;
A poor and scanty portion snatched in fear;
And fearful creatures, forced abroad by want,
Are now to ev'ry enemy a prey.

The husbandman lays bye his heavy flail,
And to the house returns, where on him wait
His smoking breakfast and impatient children;
Who, spoon in hand, and longing to begin,
Towards the door cast many a weary look
To see their dad come in.
Then round they sit, a cheerful company,
All eagerly begin, and with heaped spoons
Besmear from ear to ear their rosy cheeks.
The faithful dog stands by his master's side
Wagging his tail, and looking in his face;
While humble puss pays court to all around,
And purrs and rubs them with her furry sides;
Nor goes this little flattery unrewarded.
But the laborious sit not long at table;
The grateful father lifts his eyes to heav'n
To bless his God, whose ever bounteous hand
Him and his little ones doth daily feed;
Then rises satisfied to work again.

The cheerful rousing noise of industry
Is heard, with varied sounds, through all the village.
The humming wheel, the thrifty housewife's tongue,
Who scolds to keep her maidens at their work,
Rough grating cards,[1] and voice of squalling children
Issue from every house.
But hark! The sportsman from the neighb'ring hedge
His thunder sends! Loud bark each village cur;° *dog*
Up from her wheel each curious maiden starts,
And hastens to the door, whilst matrons chide,
Yet run to look themselves, in spite of thrift,[2]
And all the little town is in a stir.

Strutting before, the cock leads forth his train,
And, chuckling near the barn among the straw,
Reminds the farmer of his morning's service;
His grateful master throws a lib'ral handful;
They flock about it, whilst the hungry sparrows
Perched on the roof, look down with envious eye,
Then, aiming well, amidst the feeders light,
And seize upon the feast with greedy bill,
Till angry partlets° peck them off the field. *hens*
But at a distance, on the leafless tree,
All woebegone, the lonely blackbird sits;
The cold north wind ruffles his glossy feathers;
Full oft' he looks, but dare not make approach;
Then turns his yellow bill to peck his side,
And claps his wings close to his sharpened breast.
The wand'ring fowler, from behind the hedge,
Fastens his eye upon him, points his gun,
And firing wantonly as at a mark,
E'en lays him low in that same cheerful spot
Which oft' hath echoed with his ev'ning's song.

The day now at its height, the pent-up kine° *cattle*
Are driven from their stalls to take the air.
How stupidly they stare! and feel how strange!
They open wide their smoking mouths to low,
But scarcely can their feeble sound be heard;
Then turn and lick themselves, and step by step
Move dull and heavy to their stalls again.
In scattered groups the little idle boys
With purple fingers, moulding in the snow
Their icy ammunition, pant for war;
And drawing up in opposite array,
Send forth a mighty shower of well aimed balls,
Whilst little heroes try their growing strength,
And burn to beat the en'my off the field.
Or on the well worn ice in eager throngs,
Aiming their race, shoot rapidly along,
Trip up each other's heels, and on the surface
With knotted shoes, draw many a chalky line.

[1] *cards* Wool combs for carding, or dressing, raw material such as wool before it can be woven.

[2] *thrift* I.e., in spite of their commitment to their work, their ideas of household economy would suggest to them that they stay busy and avoid idling or gossip.

Untired of play, they never cease their sport
Till the faint sun has almost run his course,
And threat'ning clouds, slow rising from the north,
Spread grumly darkness o'er the face of heav'n;
Then, by degrees, they scatter to their homes,
With many a broken head and bloody nose,
To claim their mothers' pity, who, most skilful,
Cures all their troubles with a bit of bread.

The night comes on apace—
Chill blows the blast, and drives the snow in wreaths.
Now ev'ry creature looks around for shelter,
And, whether man or beast, all move alike
Towards their several° homes; and happy they *different*
Who have a house to screen them from the cold!
Lo, o'er the frost a rev'rend form advances!
His hair white as the snow on which he treads,
His forehead marked with many a care-worn furrow,
Whose feeble body, bending o'er a staff,
Still show that once it was the seat of strength,
Though now it shakes like some old ruined tow'r.
Clothed indeed, but not disgraced with rags,
He still maintains that decent dignity
Which well becomes those who have served their country.
With tott'ring steps he to the cottage moves:
The wife within, who hears his hollow cough,
And patt'ring of his stick upon the threshold,
Sends out her little boy to see who's there.
The child looks up to view the stranger's face,
And seeing it enlightened with a smile,
Holds out his little hand to lead him in.
Roused from her work, the mother turns her head,
And sees them, not ill-pleased.
The stranger whines not with a piteous tale,
But only asks a little, to relieve
A poor old soldier's wants.
The gentle matron brings the ready chair,
And bids him sit, to rest his wearied limbs,
And warm himself before her blazing fire.
The children, full of curiosity,
Flock round, and with their fingers in their mouths,
Stand staring at him; whilst the stranger, pleased,
Takes up the youngest boy upon his knee.
Proud of its seat, it wags its little feet,
And prates,° and laughs, and plays with his white locks. *chatters*
But soon the soldier's face lays off its smiles;
His thoughtful mind is turned on other days,
When his own boys were wont to play around him,
Who now lie distant from their native land
In honourable, but untimely graves.
He feels how helpless and forlorn he is,
And bitter tears gush from his dim-worn eyes.
His toilsome daily labour at an end,
In comes the wearied master of the house,
And marks with satisfaction his old guest,
With all his children round.
His honest heart is filled with manly kindness;
He bids him stay, and share their homely meal,
And take with them his quarters for the night.
The weary wanderer thankfully accepts,
And, seated with the cheerful family,
Around the plain but hospitable board,
Forgets the many hardships he has passed.

When all are satisfied, about the fire
They draw their seats, and form a cheerful ring.
The thrifty housewife turns her spinning wheel;
The husband, useful even in his rest,
A little basket weaves of willow twigs,
To bear her eggs to town on market days;
And work but serves t'enliven conversation.
Some idle neighbours now come straggling in,
Draw round their chairs, and widen out the circle.
Without a glass the tale and jest go round;
And every one, in his own native way,
Does what he can to cheer the merry group.
Each tells some little story of himself,
That constant subject upon which mankind,
Whether in court or country, love to dwell.
How at a fair he saved a simple clown° *rustic*
From being tricked in buying of a cow;
Or laid a bet upon his horse's head
Against his neighbour's, bought for twice his price,
Which failed not to repay his better skill:
Or on a harvest day, bound in an hour
More sheaves of corn than any of his fellows,
Though ne'er so keen, could do in twice the time.
But chief the landlord, at his own fire-side,

Doth claim the right of being listened to;
Nor dares a little bawling tongue be heard,
Though but in play, to break upon his story.
The children sit and listen with the rest;
And should the youngest raise its little voice,
The careful mother, ever on the watch,
And always pleased with what her husband says,
Gives it a gentle tap upon the fingers,
Or stops its ill timed prattle with a kiss.
The soldier next, but not unasked, begins,
And tells in better speech what he has seen;
Making his simple audience to shrink
With tales of war and blood. They gaze upon him,
And almost weep to see the man so poor,
So bent and feeble, helpless and forlorn,
That oft' has stood undaunted in the battle
Whilst thund'ring cannons shook the quaking earth,
And showering bullets hissed around his head.
With little care they pass away the night,
Till time draws on when they should go to bed;
Then all break up, and each retires to rest
With peaceful mind, nor torn with vexing cares,
Nor dancing with the unequal beat of pleasure.

But long accustomed to observe the weather,
The labourer cannot lay him down in peace
Till he has looked to mark what bodes the night.
He turns the heavy door, thrusts out his head,
Sees wreathes of snow heaped up on ev'ry side,
And black and grumly all above his head,
Save when a red gleam shoots along the waste
To make the gloomy night more terrible.
Loud blows the northern blast—
He hears it hollow grumbling from afar,
Then, gath'ring strength, roll on with doubled might,
And break in dreadful bellowings o'er his head;
Like pithless saplings bend the vexed trees,
And their wide branches crack. He shuts the door,
And, thankful for the roof that covers him,
Hies him to bed.
—1790

Song, Woo'd and Married and A'[1]

(*Version taken from an old song of that name.*)

The bride she is winsome and bonny,
Her hair it is snooded[2] sae° sleek, *so*
And faithfu' and kind is her Johnny,
Yet fast fa' the tears on her cheek.
New pearlins[3] are cause of her sorrow,
New pearlins and plenishing[4] too,
The bride that has a' to borrow,
Has e'en right mickle ado.[5]
Woo'd and married and a'!
Woo'd and married and a'!
Is na' she very weel aff
To be woo'd and married at a'?

Her mither then hastily spak,
"The lassie is glakit° wi' pride; *giddy*
In my pouch I had never a plack[6]
On the day when I was a bride.
E'en tak' to your wheel, and be clever,
And draw out your thread in the sun;
The gear[7] that is gifted, it never
Will last like the gear that is won.
Woo'd and married and a'!
Wi' havins° and tocher° sae sma'! *shelter / dowry*
I think ye are very weel aff,
To be woo'd and married at a'!"

"Toot, toot!" quo'° her grey-headed faither, *quoth*
"She's less o' a bride than a bairn,° *child*
She's ta'en like a cout° frae° the heather, *colt / from*
Wi' sense and discretion to learn.
Half husband, I trow,° and half daddy, *trust*
As humour inconstantly leans,
The chiel° maun° be patient and steady, *young man / must*

[1] *A'* All.

[2] *snooded* Bound by a ribbon.

[3] *pearlins* Lace trimmings.

[4] *plenishing* Bride's contribution to the setting up of a new household.

[5] *right … ado* Great amount to do.

[6] *plack* Small coin worth four pennies.

[7] *gear* Household goods, possessions.

That yokes wi' a mate in her teens.
A kerchief sae douce° and sae neat, *pleasant*
O'er her locks that the winds used to blaw!
I'm baith° like to laugh and to greet,° *both / cry*
When I think o' her married at a'!"

Then out spak' the wily bridegroom,
Weel° waled° were his wordies, I *well / chosen*
ween,° *think*
"I'm rich, though my coffer be toom,° *empty*
Wi' the blinks o' your bonny blue een.° *eyes*
I'm prouder o' thee by my side,
Though thy ruffles or ribbons be few,
Than Kate o' the Croft[1] were my bride,
Wi' purfles[2] and pearlins enow.
Dear, and dearest of ony!
Ye're woo'd and buikit[3] and a'!
And do ye think scorn o' your Johnny,
And grieve to be married at a'?"

She turned, and she blushed, and she smiled,
And she looket sae bashfully down;
The pride o' her heart was beguiled,
And she played wi' the sleeves o' her gown;
She twirled the tag° o' her lace, *end*
And she nippet° her boddice sae blue, *pinched*
Syne° blinket sae sweet in his face, *then*
And aff like a maukin° she flew. *hare*
Woo'd and married and a'!
Wi' Johnny to roose° her and a'! *praise*
She thinks hersel very weel aff,
To be woo'd and married at a'.

—1840

[1] *Croft* Small agricultural landholding. "Kate O' the Croft" would thus be a girl whose family held some property, unlike the bride of this poem.

[2] *purfles* Embroidered details at the edge of a garment.

[3] *buikit* Registered, recorded.

from *Plays on the Passions*[4]

Introductory Discourse

It is natural for a writer, who is about to submit his works to the public, to feel a strong inclination, by some preliminary address, to conciliate the favour of his reader, and dispose him, if possible, to peruse them with a favourable eye. I am well aware, however, that his endeavours are generally fruitless: in his situation our hearts revolt from all appearance of confidence, and we consider his diffidence as hypocrisy. Our own word is frequently taken for what we say of ourselves, but very rarely for what we say of our works. Were these three plays, which this small volume contains, detached pieces only, and unconnected with others that do not yet appear, I should have suppressed this inclination altogether, and have allowed my reader to begin what is before him, and to form what opinion of it his taste or his humour might direct, without any previous trespass upon his time or his patience. But they are part of an extensive design; of one which, as far as my information goes, has nothing exactly similar to it in any language; of one which a whole life time will be limited enough to accomplish; and which has, therefore, a considerable chance of being cut short by that hand which nothing can resist.

Before I explain the plan of this work, I must make a demand upon the patience of my reader, whilst I endeavour to communicate to him those ideas regarding human nature, as they in some degree affect almost every species of moral writings, but particularly the dramatic, that induced me to attempt it; and, as far as my judgment enabled me to apply them, has directed me in the execution of it.

From that strong sympathy which most creatures, but the human above all, feel for others of their kind, nothing has become so much an object of man's curiosity as man himself. We are all conscious of this within ourselves, and so constantly do we meet with it in others, that like every circumstance of continually repeated occurrence, it thereby escapes observation.

[4] *Plays on the Passions* This volume, first published in 1798, included *Count Basil: A Tragedy* and *The Tryal: A Comedy*, as well as *De Montfort: A Tragedy*.

Every person who is not deficient in intellect, is more or less occupied in tracing, amongst the individuals he converses with, the varieties of understanding and temper which constitute the characters of men; and receives great pleasure from every stroke of nature that points out to him those varieties. This is, much more than we are aware of, the occupation of children, and of grown people also, whose penetration is but lightly esteemed; and that conversation which degenerates with them into trivial and mischievous tattling takes its rise not infrequently from the same source that supplies the rich vein of the satirist and the wit. That eagerness so universally shown for the conversation of the latter, plainly enough indicates how many people have been occupied in the same way with themselves. Let any one, in a large company, do or say what is strongly expressive of his peculiar character, or of some passion or humour of the moment, and it will be detected by almost every person present. How often may we see a very stupid countenance animated with a smile, when the learned and the wise have betrayed some native feature of their own minds! And how often will this be the case when they have supposed it to be concealed under a very sufficient disguise! From this constant employment of their minds, most people, I believe, without being conscious of it, have stored up in idea the greater part of those strong marked varieties of human character, which may be said to divide it into classes; and in one of those classes they involuntarily place every new person they become acquainted with.

I will readily allow that the dress and the manners of men, rather than their characters and disposition, are the subjects of our common conversation, and seem chiefly to occupy the multitude. But let it be remembered that it is much easier to express our observations upon these. It is easier to communicate to another how a man wears his wig and cane, what kind of house he inhabits, and what kind of table he keeps, than from what slight traits in his words and actions we have been led to conceive certain impressions of his character: traits that will often escape the memory, when the opinions that were founded upon them remain. Besides, in communicating our ideas of the characters of others, we are often called upon to support them with more expense of reasoning than we can well afford, but our observations on the dress and appearance of men seldom involve us in such difficulties. For these and other reasons too tedious to mention, the generality of people appear to us more trifling than they are, and I may venture to say that, but for this sympathetic curiosity towards others of our kind, which is so strongly implanted within us, the attention we pay to the dress and the manners of men would dwindle into an employment as insipid as examining the varieties of plants and minerals is to one who understands not natural history.

In our ordinary intercourse with society, this sympathetic propensity of our minds is exercised upon men, under the common occurrences of life, in which we have often observed them. Here vanity and weakness put themselves forward to view, more conspicuously than the virtues: here men encounter those smaller trials, from which they are not apt to come off victorious; and here, consequently, that which is marked with the whimsical and ludicrous will strike us most forcibly, and make the strongest impression on our memory. To this sympathetic propensity of our minds, so exercised, the genuine and pure comic of every composition, whether drama, fable, story, or satire is addressed.

If man is an object of so much attention to man, engaged in the ordinary occurrences of life, how much more does he excite his curiosity and interest when placed in extraordinary situations of difficulty and distress? It cannot be any pleasure we receive from the sufferings of a fellow creature which attracts such multitudes of people to a public execution, though it is the horror we conceive for such a spectacle that keeps so many more away. To see a human being bearing himself up under such circumstances, or struggling with the terrible apprehensions which such a situation impresses must be the powerful incentive which makes us press forward to behold what we shrink from, and wait with trembling expectation for what we dread. For though few at such a spectacle can get near enough to distinguish the expression of face or the minuter parts of a criminal's behaviour, yet from a considerable distance will they eagerly mark whether he steps firmly; whether the motions of his body denote agitation or calmness; and if the wind does but ruffle his garment, they will, even from that change upon the outline of his distant figure, read some expression connected with his dreadful situation. Though there is a greater proportion of people in whom this strong curiosity will be overcome by other dispositions and motives, though there are many more who will stay away from such a sight than will go to it, yet there are very few who will not be eager to converse with a person who has beheld it, and to learn, very minutely, every circumstance connected with it, except the very act itself of inflicting death. To lift up the roof of his dungeon, like the *Diable boiteux*,[1] and look upon a criminal the night before he suffers, in his still hours of privacy, when all that disguise, which respect for the opinion of others, the strong motive by which even the lowest and wickedest of men still continue to be moved, would present an object to the mind of every person, not withheld from it by great timidity of character, more powerfully attractive than almost any other.

Revenge, no doubt, first began amongst the savages of America that dreadful custom of sacrificing their prisoners of war. But the perpetration of such hideous cruelty could never have become a permanent national custom, but for this universal desire in the human mind to behold man in every situation, putting forth his strength against the current of adversity, scorning all bodily anguish, or struggling with those feelings of nature, which, like a beating stream, will oft times burst through the artificial barriers of pride. Before they begin those terrible rites they treat their prisoner kindly; and it cannot be supposed that men, alternately enemies and friends to so many neighbouring tribes in manners and appearance like themselves, should so strongly be actuated by a spirit of public revenge. This custom, therefore, must be considered as a grand and terrible game, which every tribe plays against another, where they try not the strength of the arm, the swiftness of the feet, nor the acuteness of the eye, but the fortitude of the soul. Considered in this light, the excess of cruelty exercised upon their miserable victim, in which every hand is described as ready to inflict its portion of pain, and every head ingenious in the contrivance of it, is no longer to be wondered at. To put into his measure of misery one agony less would be, in some degree, betraying the honour of their nation; would be doing a species of injustice to every hero of their own tribe who had already sustained it, and to those who might be called upon to do so; amongst whom each of these savage tormentors has his chance of being one, and has prepared himself for it from his childhood. Nay, it would be a species of injustice to the haughty victim himself, who would scorn to purchase his place amongst the heroes of his nation, at an easier price than his undaunted predecessors.

Amongst the many trials to which the human mind is subjected, that of holding intercourse,[2] real or imaginary, with the world of spirits, of finding itself alone with a being terrific and awful, whose nature and power are unknown, has been justly considered as one of the most severe. The workings of nature in this situation, we all know, have ever been the object of our most eager enquiry. No man wishes to see the ghost himself, which would certainly procure him the best information on the subject, but every man wishes to see one who believes that he sees it, in all the agitation and wildness of that species of terror. To gratify this curiosity how many people have dressed up hideous apparitions to frighten the timid and superstitious! And have done it at the risk of destroying their happiness or understanding forever. For the instances of intellect being destroyed by this kind of trial are more numerous, perhaps, in proportion to the few who have undergone it than by any other.

How sensible are we of this strong propensity within us when we behold any person under the pressure of great and uncommon calamity! Delicacy and respect for the afflicted will indeed make us turn ourselves aside from observing him, and cast down our eyes in his presence; but the first glance we direct to him will involuntarily be one of the keenest observation, how hastily soever it may be checked; and often will a returning look of enquiry mix itself by stealth with our sympathy and reserve.

But it is not in situations of difficulty and distress alone that man becomes the object of this sympathetic curiosity; he is no less so when the evil he contends with arises in his own breast, and no outward circumstance connected with him either awakens our attention or our pity. What human creature is there, who can behold a being like himself under the violent agitation of those

[1] *Diable boiteux* 1707 novel by Alain René Lesage, in which the devil removes the roofs of houses in order to show a student the vices that are occurring within.

[2] *intercourse* Conversation.

passions which all have, in some degree, experienced, without feeling himself most powerfully excited by the sight? I say, all have experienced; for the bravest man on earth knows what fear is as well as the coward, and will not refuse to be interested for one under the dominion of this passion, provided there be nothing in the circumstances attending it to create contempt. Anger is a passion that attracts less sympathy than any other, yet the unpleasing and distorted features of an angry man will be more eagerly gazed upon by those who are no wise concerned with his fury or the objects of it than the most amiable placid countenance in the world. Every eye is directed to him, every voice hushed to silence in his presence. Even children will leave off their gambols[1] as he passes, and gaze after him more eagerly than the gaudiest equipage.[2] The wild tossings of despair; the gnashing of hatred and revenge; the yearnings of affection, and the softened mien[3] of love; all that language of the agitated soul, which every age and nation understands, is never addressed to the dull nor inattentive.

It is not merely under the violent agitations of passion, that man so rouses and interests us; even the smallest indications of an unquiet mind, the restless eye, the muttering lip, the half-checked exclamation, and the hasty start, will set our attention as anxiously upon the watch, as the first distant flashes of a gathering storm. When some great explosion of passion bursts forth, and some consequent catastrophe happens, if we are at all acquainted with the unhappy perpetrator, how minutely will we endeavour to remember every circumstance of his past behaviour! And with what avidity[4] will we seize upon every recollected word or gesture that is in the smallest degree indicative of the supposed state of his mind, at the time when they took place. If we are not acquainted with him, how eagerly will we listen to similar recollections from another! Let us understand, from observation or report, that any person harbours in his breast concealed from the world's eye some powerful rankling passion of what kind soever it may be; we will observe every word, every motion, every look, even the distant gait of such a man, with a constancy and attention bestowed upon no other. Nay, should we meet him unexpectedly on our way, a feeling will pass across our minds as though we found ourselves in the neighbourhood of some secret and fearful thing. If invisible, would we not follow him into his lonely haunts, into his closet, into the midnight silence of his chamber? There is, perhaps, no employment which the human mind will with so much avidity pursue as the discovery of concealed passion, as the tracing the varieties and progress of a perturbed soul.

It is to this sympathetic curiosity of our nature, exercised upon mankind in great and trying occasions and under the influence of the stronger passions when the grand, the generous, the terrible attract our attention far more than the base and depraved, that the high and powerfully tragic, of every composition, is addressed.

This propensity is universal. Children begin to show it very early; it enters into many of their amusements, and that part of them too, for which they show the keenest relish. It tempts them many times, as well as the mature in years, to be guilty of tricks, vexations, and cruelty; yet God Almighty has implanted it within us, as well as all our other propensities and passions, for wise and good purposes. It is our best and most powerful instructor. From it we are taught the proprieties and decencies of ordinary life, and are prepared for distressing and difficult situations. In examining others we know ourselves. With limbs untorn, with head unsmitten, with senses unimpaired by despair, we know what we ourselves might have been on the rack, on the scaffold, and in the most afflicting circumstances of distress. Unless when accompanied with passions of the dark and malevolent kind, we cannot well exercise this disposition without becoming more just, more merciful, more compassionate; and as the dark and malevolent passions are not the predominant inmates of the human breast, it hath produced more deeds—many more—of kindness than of cruelty. It holds up for our example a standard of excellence, which, without its assistance, our inward consciousness of what is right and becoming might never have dictated. It teaches us, also, to respect ourselves, and our kind; for it is a poor mind, indeed, that from this employment of its faculties learns not to dwell upon the noble view of human nature rather than the mean.

[1] *gambols* Games.

[2] *equipage* Carriage and horses, with attendants.

[3] *mien* Here, expression of the face.

[4] *avidity* Ardent desire.

Universal, however, as this disposition undoubtedly is, with the generality of mankind it occupies itself in a passing and superficial way. Though a native trait of character or of passion is obvious to them as well as to the sage, yet to their minds it is but the visitor of a moment; they look upon it singly and unconnected. And though this disposition, even so exercised, brings instruction as well as amusement, it is chiefly by storing up in their minds those ideas to which the instructions of others refer, that it can be eminently useful. Those who reflect and reason upon what human nature holds out to their observation, are comparatively but few. No stroke of nature which engages their attention stands insulated and alone. Each presents itself to them with many varied connections; and they comprehend not merely the immediate feeling which gave rise to it, but the relation of that feeling to others which are concealed. We wonder at the changes and caprices of men; they see in them nothing but what is natural and accountable. We stare upon some dark catastrophe of passion, as the Indians did upon an eclipse of the moon; they, conceiving the track of ideas through which the impassioned mind has passed, regard it like the philosopher who foretold the phenomenon. Knowing what situation of life he is about to be thrown into, they perceive in the man, who, like Hazael,[1] says, "is thy servant a dog that he should do this thing?" the foul and ferocious murderer. A man of this contemplative character partakes, in some degree, of the entertainment of the Gods, who were supposed to look down upon this world and the inhabitants of it, as we do upon a theatrical exhibition; and if he is of a benevolent disposition, a good man struggling with and triumphing over adversity will be to him also the most delightful spectacle. But though this eagerness to observe their fellow creatures in every situation leads not the generality of mankind to reason and reflect, and those strokes of nature which they are so ready to remark, stand single and unconnected in their minds, yet they may be easily induced to do both; and there is no mode of instruction which they will so eagerly pursue as that which lays open before them in a more enlarged and connected view than their individual observations are capable of supplying, the varieties of the human mind. Above all, to be well exercised in this study will fit a man more particularly for the most important situations of life. He will prove for it the better judge, the better magistrate, the better advocate; and as a ruler or conductor of other men, under every occurring circumstance, he will find himself the better enabled to fulfill his duty, and accomplish his designs. He will perceive the natural effect of every order that he issues upon the minds of his soldiers, his subjects, or his followers, and he will deal to others judgment tempered with mercy; that is to say truly just, for justice appears to us severe only when it is imperfect.

In proportion as moral writers of every class have exercised within themselves this sympathetic propensity of our nature, and have attended to it in others, their works have been interesting and instructive. They have struck the imagination more forcibly, convinced the understanding more clearly, and more lastingly impressed the memory. If unseasoned with any reference to this, the fairy bowers[2] of the poet, with all his gay images of delight, will be admired and forgotten; the important relations of the historian, and even the reasonings of the philosopher will make a less permanent impression.

The historian points back to the men of other ages, and from the gradually clearing mist in which they are first discovered, like the mountains of a far distant land, the generations of the world are displayed to our mind's eye in grand and regular procession. But the transactions of men become interesting to us only as we are made acquainted with men themselves. Great and bloody battles are to us battles fought in the moon if it is not impressed upon our minds, by some circumstances attending them, that men subject to like weaknesses and passions with ourselves were the combatants.[3] The

[1] *Hazael* King of Damascus. The quotation is his response to Elisha's prophecy that he will commit atrocities on the people of Israel. See 2 Kings 8.11–13.

[2] *bowers* Dwellings.

[3] [Baillie's note] Let two great battles be described to us with all the force and clearness of the most able pen. In the first let the most admirable exertions of military skill in the General, and the most unshaken courage in the soldiers, gain over an equal or superiour number of brave opponents a compleat and glorious victory. In the second let the General be less scientifick, and the soldiers less dauntless. Let them go into the field for a cause that is dear to them, and fight with the ardour which such motives inspire; till discouraged with the many deaths around them, and the renovated pressure

establishments of policy make little impression upon us if we are left ignorant of the beings whom they affected. Even a very masterly drawn character will but slightly imprint upon our memory the great man it belongs to, if, in the account we receive of his life, those lesser circumstances are entirely neglected, which do best of all point out to us the dispositions and tempers of men. Some slight circumstance characteristic of the particular turn of a man's mind, which at first sight seems but little connected with the great events of his life, will often explain some of those events more clearly to our understanding than the minute details of ostensible policy. A judicious selection of those circumstances which characterize the spirit of an associated mob, paltry and ludicrous as some of them may appear, will oftentimes convey to our minds a clearer idea why certain laws and privileges were demanded and agreed to than a methodical explanation of their causes. A historian who has examined human nature himself, and likewise attends to the pleasure which developing and tracing it does ever convey to others, will employ our understanding as well as our memory with his pages; and if this is not done, he will impose upon the latter a very difficult task, in retaining what she is concerned with alone.

In argumentative and philosophical writings, the effect which the author's reasoning produces on our minds depends not entirely on the justness of it. The images and examples that he calls to his aid to explain and illustrate his meaning will very much affect the attention we are able to bestow upon it, and consequently the quickness with which we shall apprehend, and the force with which it will impress us. These are selected from animated and unanimated nature, from the habits, manners, and characters of men; and though that image or example, whatever it may be in itself which brings out his meaning most clearly, ought to be preferred before every other, yet of two equal in this respect, that which is drawn from the most interesting source will please us the most at the time, and most lastingly take hold of our minds. An argument supported with vivid and interesting illustration will long be remembered when many equally important and clear are forgotten; and a work where many such occur will be held in higher estimation by the generality of men than one its superior, perhaps, in acuteness, perspicuity, and good sense.

Our desire to know what men are in the closet as well as the field, by the blazing hearth, and at the social board,[1] as well as in the council and the throne, is very imperfectly gratified by real history; romance writers, therefore, stepped boldly forth to supply the deficiency, and tale writers and novel writers of many descriptions followed after. If they have not been very skilful in their delineations of nature, if they have represented men and women speaking and acting as men and women never did speak or act, if they have caricatured both our virtues and our vices, if they have given us such pure and unmixed, or such heterogeneous combinations of character as real life never presented, and yet have pleased and interested us, let it not be imputed to the dullness of man in discerning what is genuinely natural in himself. There are many inclinations belonging to us, besides this great master propensity of which I am treating. Our love of the grand, the beautiful, the novel, and above all of the marvellous, is very strong; and if we are richly fed with what we have a good relish for, we may be weaned to forget our native and favourite aliment.[2] Yet we can never so far forget it, but that we will cling to, and acknowledge it again, whenever it is presented before us. In a work abounding with the marvellous and unnatural, if the author has anyhow stumbled upon an unsophisticated genuine stroke of nature, we will immediately perceive and be delighted with it, though we are foolish enough to admire at the

of the foe, some unlooked-for circumstance, trifling in itself, strikes their imagination at once; they are visited with the terrours of nature; their national pride, the honour of soldiership is forgotten; they fly like a fearful flock. Let some beloved chief then stop forth, and call upon them by the love of their country, by the memory of their valiant fathers, by every thing that kindles in the bosom of man the high and generous passions: they stop; they gather round him; and goaded by shame and indignation, returning again to the charge, with the fury of wild beasts rather than the courage of soldiers, bear down every thing before them. Which of these two battles will interest us the most? and which of them shall we remember the longest? The one will stand forth in the imagination of the reader like a rock of the desert, which points out to the far-removed traveller the country through which he has passed, when its lesser objects are obscured in the distance; whilst the other leaves no traces behind it, but in the minds of the scientifick in war.

[1] *social board* Table.

[2] *aliment* Food.

same time all the nonsense with which it is surrounded. After all the wonderful incidents, dark mysteries, and secrets revealed, which eventful novel so liberally presents to us; after the beautiful fairy ground, and even the grand and sublime scenes of nature with which descriptive novel so often enchants us; those works which most strongly characterize human nature in the middling and lower classes of society, where it is to be discovered by stronger and more unequivocal marks, will ever be the most popular. For though great pains have been taken in our higher sentimental novels to interest us in the delicacies, embarrassments, and artificial distresses of the more refined part of society, they have never been able to cope in the public opinion with these. The one is a dressed and beautiful pleasure ground, in which we are enchanted for a while, amongst the delicate and unknown plants of artful cultivation, the other is a rough forest of our native land: the oak, the elm, the hazel, and the bramble are there, and amidst the endless varieties of its paths we can wander for ever. Into whatever scenes the novelist may conduct us, what objects soever he may present to our view, still is our attention most sensibly awake to every touch faithful to nature, still are we upon the watch for every thing that speaks to us of ourselves.

The fair field of what is properly called poetry is enriched with so many beauties that in it we are often tempted to forget what we really are, and what kind of beings we belong to. Who in the enchanted regions of simile, metaphor, allegory and description, can remember the plain order of things in this everyday world? From heroes whose majestic forms rise like a lofty tower, whose eyes are lightning, whose arms are irresistible, whose course is like the storms of heaven, bold and exalted sentiments we will readily receive, and will not examine them very accurately by that rule of nature which our own breast prescribes to us. A shepherd whose sheep, with fleeces of the purest snow, browse the flowery herbage of the most beautiful valleys, whose flute is ever melodious, and whose shepherdess is ever crowned with roses, whose every care is love, will not be called very strictly to account for the loftiness and refinement of his thoughts. The fair nymph, who sighs out her sorrows to the conscious and compassionate wilds, whose eyes gleam like the bright drops of heaven, whose loose tresses stream to the breeze, may say what she pleases with impunity. I will venture, however, to say, that amidst all this decoration and ornament, all this loftiness and refinement, let one simple trait of the human heart, one expression of passion genuine and true to nature be introduced, and it will stand forth alone in the boldness of reality, whilst the false and unnatural around it fades away upon every side, like the rising exhalations of the morning. With admiration, and often with enthusiasm, we proceed on our way through the grand and the beautiful images, raised to our imagination by the lofty epic muse, but what even here are those things that strike upon the heart, that we feel and remember? Neither the descriptions of war, the sound of the trumpet, the clanging of arms, the combat of heroes, nor the death of the mighty, will interest our minds like the fall of the feeble stranger, who simply expresses the anguish of his soul, at the thoughts of that far-distant home which he must never return to again, and closes his eyes, amongst the ignoble and forgotten; like the timid stripling[1] goaded by the shame of reproach, who urges his trembling steps to the fight, and falls like a tender flower before the first blast of winter. How often will some simple picture of this kind be all that remains upon our minds of the terrific and magnificent battle, whose description we have read with admiration! How comes it that we relish so much the episodes of an heroic poem? It cannot merely be that we are pleased with a resting-place, where we enjoy the variety of contrast; for were the poem of the simple and familiar kind, and an episode after the heroic style introduced into it, ninety readers out of an hundred would pass over it altogether. Is it not that we meet such a story, so situated, with a kind of sympathetic good will, as in passing through a country of castles and of palaces, we should pop unawares upon some humble cottage, resembling the dwellings of our own native land, and gaze upon it with affection. The highest pleasures we receive from poetry, as well as from the real objects which surround us in the world, are derived from the sympathetic interest we all take in beings like ourselves; and I will even venture to say, that were the grandest scenes which can enter into the imagination of man, presented to our view, and all reference to man com-

[1] *stripling* Adolescent.

pletely shut out from our thoughts, the objects that composed it would convey to our minds little better than dry ideas of magnitude, colour, and form; and the remembrance of them would rest upon our minds like the measurement and distances of the planets.

If the study of human nature then is so useful to the poet, the novelist, the historian, and the philosopher, of how much greater importance must it be to the dramatic writer? To them it is a powerful auxiliary, to him it is the centre and strength of the battle. If characteristic views of human nature enliven not their pages, there are many excellencies with which they can, in some degree, make up for the deficiency; it is what we receive from them with pleasure rather than demand. But in his works no richness of invention, harmony of language, nor grandeur of sentiment will supply the place of faithfully delineated nature. The poet and the novelist may represent to you their great characters from the cradle to the tomb. They may represent them in any mood or temper, and under the influence of any passion which they see proper, without being obliged to put words into their mouths, those great betrayers of the feigned and adopted. They may relate every circumstance however trifling and minute, that serves to develop their tempers and dispositions. They tell us what kind of people they intend their men and women to be, and as such we receive them. If they are to move us with any scene of distress, every circumstance regarding the parties concerned in it, how they looked, how they moved, how they sighed, how the tears gushed from their eyes, how the very light and shadow fell upon them, is carefully described, and the few things that are given them to say along with all this assistance must be very unnatural indeed if we refuse to sympathize with them. But the characters of the drama must speak directly for themselves. Under the influence of every passion, humour, and impression, in the artificial veilings of hypocrisy and ceremony, in the openness of freedom and confidence, and in the lonely hour of meditation they speak. He who made us hath placed within our breast a judge that judges instantaneously of every thing they say. We expect to find them creatures like ourselves; and if they are untrue to nature, we feel that we are imposed upon, as though the poet had introduced to us for brethren creatures of a different race, beings of another world.

As in other works deficiency in characteristic truth may be compensated by excellencies of a different kind. In the drama characteristic truth will compensate every other defect. Nay, it will do what appears a contradiction; one strong genuine stroke of nature will cover a multitude of sins even against nature herself. When we meet in some scene of a good play a very fine stroke of this kind, we are apt to become so intoxicated with it, and so perfectly convinced of the author's great knowledge of the human heart, that we are unwilling to suppose that the whole of it has not been suggested by the same penetrating spirit. Many well-meaning enthusiastic critics have given themselves a great deal of trouble in this way, and have shut their eyes most ingeniously against the fair light of nature for the very love of it. They have converted, in their great zeal, sentiments palpably false, both in regard to the character and situation of the persons who utter them, sentiments which a child or a clown[1] would detect, into the most skilful depictments of the heart. I can think of no stronger instance to show how powerfully this love of nature dwells within us.

Formed as we are with these sympathetic propensities in regard to our own species, it is not at all wonderful that theatrical exhibition has become the grand and favourite amusement of every nation into which it has been introduced. Savages will, in the wild contortions of a dance, shape out some rude story expressive of character or passion, and such a dance will give more delight to his companions than the most artful exertions of agility. Children in their gambols will make out a mimic representation of the manners, characters, and passions of grown men and women, and such a pastime will animate and delight them much more than a treat of the daintiest sweetmeats, or the handling of the gaudiest toys. Eagerly as it is enjoyed by the rude[2] and the young, to the polished and the ripe in years it is still the most interesting amusement. Our taste for it is durable as it is universal. Independently of those circumstances which first introduced it, the world would not have long been without it. The progress of society would soon have brought it forth; and men in the whimsical decora-

[1] *clown* Rustic, country dweller.

[2] *rude* Uneducated.

tions of fancy would have displayed the characters and actions of their heroes, the folly and absurdity of their fellow-citizens, had no Priests of Bacchus[1] ever existed.

In whatever age or country the drama might have its rise, tragedy would have been the first-born of its children. For every nation has its great men, and its great events upon record; and to represent their own forefathers struggling with those difficulties, and braving those dangers, of which they have heard with admiration, and the effects of which they still perhaps experience would certainly have been the most animating subject for the poet and the most interesting for his audience, even independently of the natural inclination we all so universally show for scenes of horror and distress, of passion and heroic exertion. Tragedy would have been the first child of the drama, for the same reasons that have made heroic ballad, with all its battles, murders and disasters, the earliest poetical compositions of every country.

We behold heroes and great men at a distance, unmarked by those small but distinguishing features of the mind, which give a certain individuality to such an infinite variety of similar beings, in the near and familiar intercourse of life. They appear to us from this view like distant mountains, whose dark outlines we trace in the clear horizon, but the varieties of whose roughened sides, shaded with heath and brushwood, and seamed with many a cleft, we perceive not. When accidental anecdote reveals to us any weakness or peculiarity belonging to them, we start upon it like a discovery. They are made known to us in history only, by the great events they are connected with, and the part they have taken in extraordinary or important transactions. Even in poetry and romance, with the exception of some love story interwoven with the main events of their lives, they are seldom more intimately made known to us. To tragedy it belongs to lead them forward to our nearer regard, in all the distinguishing varieties which nearer inspection discovers; with the passions, the humours, the weaknesses, the prejudices of men. It is for her to present to us the great and magnanimous hero, who appears to our distant view as a superior being, as a God, softened down with those smaller frailties and imperfections which enable us to glory in and claim kindred to his virtues. It is for her to exhibit to us the daring and ambitious man, planning his dark designs, and executing his bloody purposes, marked with those appropriate characteristics, which distinguish him as an individual of that class, and agitated with those varied passions, which disturb the mind of man when he is engaged in the commission of such deeds. It is for her to point out to us the brave and impetuous warrior struck with those visitations of nature, which, in certain situations, will unnerve the strongest arm, and make the boldest heart tremble. It is for her to show the tender, gentle, and unassuming mind animated with that fire which, by the provocation of circumstances, will give to the kindest heart the ferocity and keenness of a tiger. It is for her to present to us the great and striking characters that are to be found amongst men, in a way which the poet, the novelist, and the historian can but imperfectly attempt. But above all, to her, and to her only it belongs to unveil to us the human mind under the dominion of those strong and fixed passions, which, seemingly unprovoked by outward circumstances, will from small beginnings brood within the breast, till all the better dispositions, all the fair gifts of nature are borne down before them. Those passions which conceal themselves from the observation of men, which cannot unbosom themselves even to the dearest friend, and can often times only give their fullness vent in the lonely desert, or in the darkness of midnight. For who hath followed the great man into his secret closet, or stood by the side of his nightly couch, and heard those exclamations of the soul which heaven alone may hear, that the historian should be able to inform us? And what form of story, what mode of rehearsed speech will communicate to us those feelings, whose irregular bursts, abrupt transitions, sudden pauses, and half-uttered suggestions, scorn all harmony of measured verse, all method and order of relation? …

How little credit soever, upon perusing these plays, the reader may think me entitled to in regard to the execution of the work, he will not, I flatter myself, deny me some credit in regard to the plan. I know of no series of plays, in any language, expressly descriptive of the different passions; and I believe there are few plays existing in which the display of one strong passion is the chief business of the drama, so written that they could properly make part of such a series. I do not think that

[1] *Priests of Bacchus* I.e., Baccants, or revelers.

we should, from the works of various authors, be able to make a collection which would give us any thing exactly of the nature of that which is here proposed. If the reader, in perusing it, perceives that the abilities of the author are not proportioned to the task which is imposed upon them, he will wish in the spirit of kindness rather than of censure, as I most sincerely do, that they had been more adequate to it. However, if I perform it ill, I am still confident that this (pardon me if I call it noble) design will not be suffered to fall to the ground, some one will arise after me who will do it justice; and there is no poet, possessing genius for such a work, who will not at the same time possess that spirit of justice and of candour, which will lead him to remember me with respect.

I have now only to thank my reader, whoever he may be, who has followed me through the pages of this discourse, for having had the patience to do so. May he, in going through what follows (a wish the sincerity of which he cannot doubt) find more to reward his trouble than I dare venture to promise him; and for the pains he has already taken, and that, which he intends to take for me, I request that he will accept of my grateful acknowledgments.

—1798

William Taylor

1765 – 1836

In 1796, William Taylor of Norwich published the first English translation of Gottfried Augustus Burger's *Lenore* (1773), thereby introducing the English literary establishment, and particularly the Romantic poets Wordsworth, Coleridge, and Southey, to the German tradition of Gothic poetry. The ballad, entitled "Lenora," appeared in the second issue of *Monthly Magazine*, edited by John Aikin, brother to Anna Letitia Barbauld. Along with it were a commendatory article on Burger and two further translations: *The Lass of Fair Wone* (later reworked by Wordsworth and published as "The Thorn," 1798) and *The Chase*. Taylor printed the poem by itself not long after as *Ellenore*, the version included in this anthology. Though the poem did not see print until 1796, it had been circulating in manuscript form since 1790, most likely among Norwich literary circles. It was not, however, until Barbauld gave a reading of the poem to a literary audience at Edinburgh in 1794 that the work excited widespread literary interest. The famous poet's reading of the ghostly ballad stirred and inspired the audience; before long, six subsequent versions had appeared, including one penned by Walter Scott (*William and Helen*, 1796). Taylor's 1796 German translations, which spoke to the increasing literary interest in the supernatural, initiated a new trend of Gothic balladry among the Romantic poets.

Born in Norwich, 1765, Taylor was raised by his father to be a businessman. He began his formal education at the Palgrave, Suffolk boarding school run by Anna Letitia Barbauld and her husband, Rochemont Barbauld (Taylor later called Barbauld "the mother of his mind"). There Taylor met the poet Frank Sayers, whose *Poetical Works* he edited in 1828. Upon completing his education at Suffolk, Taylor embarked on a series of travels on the Continent; his father's business partner accompanied him and taught him how to conduct foreign correspondence. It was during these travels that Taylor first came into contact with German literature and culture. From Belgium, where he lived throughout 1781, he wrote to his father that he preferred English prose and German poetry. A year later in Germany, Taylor met J.W. Goëthe, the translation of whose *Iphigenia in Tauris* was published in 1793. By the end of 1782 he had returned to Norwich, where literary endeavors gave over to business affairs.

Until his father's business closed in 1791, Taylor remained in charge of foreign correspondence. Also during this time, he was active in radical politics and belonged to several political groups that looked to revolutionary France as "the land of liberty." With the dissolution of his father's business, Taylor turned to building his literary career and wrote several critical essays. William Taylor translated Gothold Ephraim Lessing's *Nathan the Wise* in 1790 (published 1805), and later produced an English version of Christopher Martin Wieland's *Dialogues of the Gods* (1795), and a collection of French and German prose translations under the title *Tales of Yore* (1810). His *Historic Survey of German Poetry* (1828–30) in three volumes was to be the culmination of his career; by the time it appeared, however, the Gothic craze had waned and interest in German poetry had somewhat subsided.

As a critic, Taylor wrote for the *Monthly Magazine*, the *Monthly Review*, the *Annual Review*, the *Critical Review*, and the *Athenaeum* in a critical career that spanned the years 1793 to 1827. During these years he formed a close friendship with Southey and was an acquaintance of Thomas Paine.

Taylor's *Ellenore* diverges from its German original by setting the action not during the Seven Years' War but in the time of the Crusades (a move Scott follows in his version). The ballad tells the story of the young Ellenore, who questions God's mercy when her lover does not return from the war. When William finally does return, the lovers embark on a night ride to their wedding altar—a ride that is quickly transformed into a ghostly gallop through a graveyard. The macabre ending of the ballad serves as a moral indictment of Ellenore's lack of faith, but the poem's religious message had little to do with its appeal. The story of doomed lovers and the imagery of the charnel house, graveyard, and phantom spoke to the Gothic tastes of the time.

From the end of the eighteenth century through the early decades of the 1800s, Taylor relied on his pen for his income. His last publication, *A Memoir of the late Philip Meadows Martineau, Surgeon* appeared in 1831, marking the end of a nearly forty-year literary career. Not long after, in 1836, Taylor died, unmarried, in Norwich.

⌘⌘⌘

Ellenore

At break of day from frightful dreams
Upstarted Ellenore:
"My William, art thou slayn," she sayde,[1]
"Or dost thou love no more?"

He went abroade with Richard's host[2]
The paynim° foes to quell; *pagan*
But he no word to her had writt,
An° he were sick or well. *whether*

With blore° of trump and thump of drum *blowing*
His fellow-soldyers come,
Their helms bedeckt with oaken boughs,
They seeke their long'd-for home.

And evry road and evry lane
Was full of old and young
To gaze at the rejoycing band,
To haile with gladsom toung.

"Thank God!" their wives and children sayde,
"Welcome!" the brides did saye;
But grief or kiss gave Ellenore
To none upon that daye.

And when the soldiers all were bye,
She tore her raven hair,
And cast herself upon the growne,° *ground*
In furious despair.

[1] *slayn, she sayde* Taylor consciously employs archaisms throughout this poem; for that reason, original spelling and punctuation have in this case been retained.

[2] *Richard's host* Army of Richard I of England (1157–99), one of the leaders of the Third Crusade.

Her mother ran and lyfte her up,
And clasped her in her arm,
"My child, my child, what dost thou ail?
God shield thy life from harm!"

"O mother, mother! William's gone
What's all besyde to me?
There is no mercie, sure, above!
All, all were spar'd but he!"

"Kneele downe, thy paternoster[3] saye,
'T will calm thy troubled spright:° *spirit*
The Lord is wise, the Lord is good;
What He hath done is right."

"O mother, mother! saye not so;
Most cruel is my fate:
I prayde, and prayde; but watte avaylde?
'T is now, alas! too late."

"Our Heavenly Father, if we praye,
Will help a suffring child:
Go take the holy sacrament;
So shall thy grief grow mild."

"O mother, what I feele within,
No sacrament can staye;
No sacrament can teche the dead
To bear the sight of daye."

"May-be, among the heathen folk
Thy William false doth prove,

[3] *paternoster* Latin for "our father"; the Lord's Prayer.

And put away his faith and troth,
And take another love.

"Then wherefor sorrowe for his loss?
Thy moans are all in vain:
But when his soul and body parte,
His falsehode brings him pain."

"O mother, mother! gone is gone:
My hope is all forlorn;
The grave my only safeguard is—
O had I ne'er been born!

"Go out, go out, my lamp of life;
In grizely darkness die:
There is no mercie, sure, above.
Forever let me lie."

"Almighty God! O do not judge
My poor unhappy child;
She knows not what her lips pronounce,
Her anguish makes her wild.

"My girl, forget thine earthly woe,
And think on God and bliss;
For so, at least shall not thy soul
Its heavenly bridegroom[1] miss."

"O mother, mother! what is bliss,
And what the fiendis° cell? *devil's*
With him 'tis heaven any where,
Without my William, hell.

"Go out, go out, my lamp of life,
In endless darkness die:
Without him I must loathe the earth,
Without him scorn the skie."

And so despair did rave and rage
Athwarte° her boiling veins; *along*
Against the Providence of God
She hurlde her impious strains.

She bet° her breast, and wrung her hands, *beat*
And rollde her tearless eye,

From rise of morn, til the pale stars
Again orespread the skye.

When harke! abroade she herde the tramp
Of nimble-hoofed steed;
She herde a knight with clank alighte,
And climbe the stair in speed.

And soon she herde a tinkling hand,
That twirled at the pin;
And thro her door, that opened not,
These words were breathed in.

"What ho! what ho! thy door undo;
Art watching or asleepe?
My love, dost yet remember me,
And dost thou laugh or weepe?"

"Ah! William here so late at night!
Oh! I have wachte and wak'd:
Whense art thou come? For thy return
My heart has sorely ak'd."

"At midnight only we may ride;
I come ore land and see:
I mounted late, but soone I go;
Aryse, and come with mee."

"O William, enter first my bowre,° *bedroom*
And give me one embrace:
The blasts° athwarte the hawthorn hiss; *gales*
Awayte a little space."

"Tho blasts athwarte the hawthorn hiss,
I may not harbour here;
My spurs are sett, my courser° pawes, *swift horse*
My hour of flight is nere.

"All as thou lyest upon thy couch,
Aryse, and mount behinde;
To-night we'le ride a thousand miles,
The bridal bed to finde."

"How, ride to-night a thousand miles?
Thy love thou dost bemock:
Eleven is the stroke that still
Rings on within the clock."

[1] *heavenly bridegroom* I.e., Christ.

"Looke up; the moon is bright, and we
Outstride the earthly men:
I'le take thee to the bridal bed,
And night shall end but then."

"And where is then thy house, and home,
And bridal bed so meet?"° *fitting*
"'Tis narrow, silent, chilly, low,
Six planks, one shrouding sheet."

"And is there any room for me,
Wherein that I may creepe?'
'There's room enough for thee and me,
Wherein that we may sleepe.

"All as thou lyest upon thy couch,
Aryse, no longer stop;
The wedding-guests thy coming wayte,
The chamber-door is ope."° *open*

All in her sarke,[1] as there she lay,
Upon his horse she sprung;
And with her lily hands so pale
About her William clung.

And hurry-skurry off they go,
Unheeding wet or dry;
And horse and rider snort and blow,
And sparkling pebbles fly.

How swift the flood, the mead,° the wood, *meadow*
Aright, aleft, are gone!
The bridges thunder as they pass,
But earthly sowne° is none. *sound*

Tramp, tramp, across the land they speede;
Splash, splash, across the see:
"Hurrah! the dead can ride apace;
Dost fear to ride with me?

"The moon is bright, and blue the night;
Dost quake the blast to stem?
Dost shudder, mayd, to seeke the dead?"
"No, no, but what of them?"

[1] *sarke* Night dress.

How glumly sownes yon dirgy song!
Night-ravens flappe the wing.
What knell doth slowly tolle ding dong?
The psalms of death who sing?

Forth creeps a swarthy funeral train,
A corse is on the biere;[2]
Like croke of todes from lonely moores,
The chauntings° meete the eere. *chantings*

"Go, beare her corse when midnight's past,
With song, and tear, and wail;
I've gott my wife, I take her home,
My hour of wedlock hail!

"Leade forth, O clark, the chaunting quire,[3]
To swell our spousal-song:
Come, preest, and reade the blessing soone;
For our dark bed we long."

The bier is gon, the dirges hush;
His bidding all obaye,
And headlong rush thro briar and bush,
Beside his speedy waye.

Halloo! halloo! how swift they go,
Unheeding wet or dry;
And horse and rider snort and blow,
And sparkling pebbles fly.

How swift the hill, how swift the dale,
Aright, aleft, are gon!
By hedge and tree, by thorp° and town, *village*
They gallop, gallop on.

Tramp, tramp, across the land they speede;
Splash, splash, across the see:
"Hurrah! the dead can ride apace;
Dost feare to ride with mee?

[2] *corse* Corpse; *biere* Platform used to convey a body to the grave.

[3] *clark* I.e., clerk. Layman who performs various offices in cathedrals, churches, or chapels. In the Prayer-book of 1549 clerks were identified as choir-men; *quire* Choir.

"Look up, look up, an airy crew
 In roundel dances° reele: *round dances*
The moon is bright, and blue the night,
 Mayst dimly see them wheele.

"Come to, come to, ye ghostly crew,
 Come to, and follow me,
And daunce for us the wedding daunce,
 When we in bed shall be."

And brush, brush, brush, the ghostly crew,
 Came wheeling ore their heads,
All rustling like the witherd leaves
 That wide the whirlwind spreads.

Halloo! halloo! away they go,
 Unheeding wet or dry;
And horse and rider snort and blow,
 And sparkling pebbles fly.

And all that in the moonshyne lay,
 Behind them fled afar;
And backward scudded° overhead *hurried*
 The skie and every star.

Tramp, tramp, across the land they speede;
 Splash, splash, across the see:
"Hurrah! the dead can ride apace;
 Dost fear to ride with mee?

"I weene° the cock prepares to crowe; *think*
 The sand[1] will soone be run:
I snuffe the early morning air;
 Downe, downe! our work is done.

"The dead, the dead can ride apace:
 Our wed-bed here is fit:° *ready*
Our race is ridde, our journey ore,
 Our endless union knit."

And lo! an yron-grated gate
 Soon biggens to their view:
He crackde his whyppe; the locks, the bolts,
 Cling, clang! asunder flew.

They passe, and 'twas on graves they trodde;
 "'Tis hither we are bound:"
And many a tombstone ghastly white
 Lay in the moonshyne round.

And when he from his steed alytte,
 His armure, black as cinder,
Did moulder, moulder all awaye,
 As were it made of tinder.

His head became a naked skull;
 Nor hair nor eyne° had he: *eye*
His body grew a skeleton,
 Whilome so blithe of ble.[2]

And at his dry and boney heel
 No spur was left to bee;
And in his witherd hand you might
 The scythe and hour-glass[3] see.

And lo! his steed did thin to smoke,
 And charnel-fires[4] outbreathe;
And pal'd, and bleachde, then vanishde quite
 The mayd from underneathe.

And hollow howlings hung in air,
 And shrekes from vaults arose:
Then knew the mayd she might no more
 Her living eyes unclose.

But onward to the judgment-seat,
 Thro' mist and moonlight dreare,
The ghostly crew their flight persewe,
 And hollowe° in her eare: *shout*

"Be patient; though thyne heart should breke,
 Arrayne not Heaven's decree;
Thou nowe art of thy bodie reft,° *bereft*
 Thy soul forgiven bee!"

—1796

---

[1] *sand* I.e., in an hour-glass.

[2] *Whilome … ble* Once so beautiful a color.

[3] *scythe and hour-glass* Carried by Death.

[4] *charnel-fires* Fires in mortuaries, said to be produced by the undead.

MARIA EDGEWORTH

1768 – 1849

A leading female Irish intellectual, novelist and essayist Maria Edgeworth produced works whose popularity rivaled those of Walter Scott and Jane Austen. Her social novels, which often espoused strong moral values, gained critical attention for their frank treatment of female characters, their experimentations with form, and the questions of nationality and gender that they raised. Edgeworth's writing, both literary and political, shows her as an early champion of Irish independence and the education of women.

The second of twenty-one children by four wives, Maria Edgeworth was born in England but remained for most of her life in Ireland on the estate of her father, Richard Lovell Edgeworth. Maria received little of her father's attentions until 1782, when the family returned from England to Edgeworthstown, where Maria helped her father with estate business and began to forge a professional and intellectual partnership with him that would last the remainder of his life.

In 1795 Edgeworth brought out her first publication, *Letters to Literary Ladies,* a series of letters about the importance of educating women—a subject of personal importance to Edgeworth, who was responsible for the education of thirteen of her younger siblings. The following year she continued her work on education by publishing *The Parent's Assistant*, a series of moral stories and a play for children. *Moral Tales for Young People* (1801), designed for older children, provided a further series of tales, this time in a less didactic narrative mode. Edgeworth and her father produced a series of *Essays on Practical Education* (1798).

Edgeworth became a literary success with her first novel, *Castle Rackrent, An Hibernian Tale taken from the Facts and from the Manners of the Irish Squires Before the Year 1782* (1800), which she published anonymously; only after its success did she reveal her authorship. In the novel Edgeworth uses details from her own experiences dealing with tenants not only to give color to her narrative, but also to show the stark, unpleasant realities of life under the Irish administration. In her "Preface" to *Castle Rackrent*, Edgeworth defends the unique blending of memoir, history, and biography that results:

> We are surely justified in this eager desire to collect the most minute facts relative to the domestic lives, not only of the great and good, but even of the worthless and insignificant, since it is only by a comparison of their actual happiness or misery in the privacy of domestic life, that we can form a just estimate of the real reward of virtue, or the real punishment of vice.

The novel's pedestrian narrator, Thady Quirk, makes good on this claim, detailing in a highly idiomatic style the lives, manners, and facts regarding the Rackrent family. Another novel, *Belinda*, written in a similar style, followed in 1801.

As a result of their joint literary success, father and daughter began to move in the world of literati. In 1802, the Edgeworths visited Brussels and Paris, where Maria received—and declined—a proposal of marriage from a Swedish count, Edelcrantz. Her sense of duty to her family prevailed and she returned to Edgeworthstown in 1803, where her father encouraged her writings, sometimes (though it is uncertain to what extent) providing plots and characters, and inserting passages of his own. Her novels continued to earn handsome royalties, particularly the six-volume *Tales of Fashionable Life*. *The Absentee* (1812) and *Ormond* (1817), like *Castle Rackrent*, depict the rituals and routines of Irish life. Edgeworth's friend Sir Walter Scott, author of *Waverley* (which Edgeworth's novel *The Absentee* inspired him to publish), said his purpose was "in some distant degree to emulate the admirable Irish portraits drawn by Miss Edgeworth."

In 1817 her father died, and Maria completed his *Memoirs* on his behalf, though they were not especially well received. In 1826 she resumed the management of the family estates in Ireland on behalf of her brother, but she continued to write. Among her later works were her *Helen* (1834), her last novel, and *Orlandino* (1848), a story that she sold at the end of the great famine to "earn a little money for our parish poor."

The popularity of Edgeworth's writings declined in the Victorian era, particularly in Ireland, where cultural nationalism was on the rise, and she remained a largely neglected writer until the latter part of the twentieth century. *Castle Rackrent*, however, has always remained an influential work. In Thady Quirk, Edgeworth created one of the first "low" characters to take over the narration of a lengthy novel, an experiment in point-of-view that had enormous implications for the development of both British and American novels.

⌘⌘⌘

Angelina; Or, L'amie Inconnue[1]

Chapter I

"But, my dear Lady Di, indeed you should not let this affair prey so continually upon your spirits," said Miss Burrage, in the condoling tone of a humble companion—"you really have almost fretted yourself into a nervous fever. I was in hopes that change of air, and change of scene, would have done every thing for you, or I never would have consented to your leaving London; for you know your ladyship's always better in London than anywhere else. And I'm sure your ladyship has thought and talked of nothing but this sad affair since you came to Clifton."

"I confess," said Lady Diana Chillingworth, "I deserve the reproaches of my friends for giving way to my sensibility, as I do, upon this occasion: but I own I cannot help it. Oh, what will the world say! What will the world say! The world will lay all the blame upon *me*; yet I'm sure I'm the last, the very last person that ought to be blamed."

"Assuredly," replied Miss Burrage, "nobody can blame your ladyship; and nobody will, I am persuaded. The blame will all be thrown where it ought to be, upon the young lady herself."

"If I could but be convinced of that," said her ladyship, in a tone of great feeling; "such a young creature, scarcely sixteen, to take such a step! I am sure I wish to Heaven her father had never made me her guardian. I confess, I was most exceedingly imprudent, out of regard to her family, to take under my protection such a self-willed, unaccountable, romantic girl. Indeed, my dear," continued Lady Diana Chillingworth, turning to her sister, Lady Frances Somerset, "it was you that misled me. You remember you used to tell me that Anne Warwick had such great abilities—"

"That I thought it a pity they had not been well directed," said Lady Frances.

"And such generosity of temper, and such warm affections—" said Lady Di.

"That I regretted their not having been properly cultivated."

[1] *L'amie Inconnue* French: the unknown friend.

MORAL TALES,

BY MISS EDGEWORTH.

IN THREE VOLUMES.

VOL. II.

CONTAINING

THE GOOD AUNT,

AND

ANGELINA.

SIXTH EDITION.

LONDON:
PRINTED FOR J. JOHNSON AND CO.,
ST. PAUL'S CHURCH-YARD.
1813.

Title page of the 1813 edition of *Moral Tales*. See pages 189–90 for other facsimile pages.

"I confess, Miss Warwick was never a great favourite of mine," said Miss Burrage; "but now that she has lost her best friend—"

"She is likely to find a great number of enemies," said Lady Frances.

"She has been her own enemy, poor girl! I am sure I pity her," replied Miss Burrage; "but, at the same time, I must say that ever since she came to my Lady Di Chillingworth's, she has had good advice enough."

"Too much, perhaps; which is worse than too little," thought Lady Frances.

"Advice!" repeated Lady Di Chillingworth. "Why, as to that, my conscience, I own, acquits me there; for, to be sure, no young person of her age, or of any age, had ever more advice, or more *good* advice, than Miss Warwick had from me; I thought it my duty to advise her, and advise her I did from morning till night, as Miss Burrage very well knows, and will do me the justice, I hope, to say in all companies."

"*That* I shall certainly make it a principle to do," said Miss Burrage. "I am sure it would surprise and grieve you, Lady Frances, to hear the sort of foolish, imprudent things that Miss Warwick, with all her abilities, used to say. I recollect—"

"Very possibly," replied Lady Frances; "but why should we trouble ourselves to recollect all the foolish, imprudent things which this poor girl may have said? This unfortunate elopement is a sufficient proof of her folly and imprudence. With whom did she go off?"

"With nobody," cried Lady Diana—"there's the wonder."

"With nobody! Incredible! She had certainly some admirer, some lover, and she was afraid, I suppose, to mention the business to you."

"No such thing, my dear: there is no love at all in the case; indeed, for my part, I cannot in the least comprehend Miss Warwick, nor ever could. She used, every now and then, to begin and talk to me some nonsense about her hatred of the forms of the world, and her love of liberty, and I know not what; and then she had some female correspondent, to whom she used to write folio sheets,[1] twice a week, I believe; but I could never see any of these letters. Indeed, in town, you know, I could not possibly have leisure for such things; but Miss Burrage, I fancy, has one of the letters, if you have any curiosity to see it. Miss Burrage can tell you a great deal more of the whole business than I can; for you know, in London, engaged as I always was, with scarcely a moment ever to myself, how could I attend to all Anne Warwick's oddities? I protest I know nothing of the matter, but that, one morning, Miss Warwick was nowhere to be found, and my maid brought me a letter, of one word of which I could not make sense: the letter was found on the young lady's dressing-table, according to the usual custom of eloping heroines. Miss Burrage, do show Lady Frances the letters—you have them somewhere—and tell my sister all you know of the matter; for I declare, I'm quite tired of it; besides, I shall be wanted at the card-table."

Lady Diana Chillingworth went to calm her sensibility at the card-table, and Lady Frances turned to Miss Burrage for further information.

"All I know," said Miss Burrage, "is that one night I saw Miss Warwick putting a lock of frightful hair into a locket, and I asked her whose it was. 'My amiable Araminta's,' said Miss Warwick. 'Is she pretty?' said I. 'I have never seen her,' said Miss Warwick, 'but I will show you a charming picture of her mind!'—and she put this long letter into my hand. I'll leave it with your ladyship, if you please; it is a good, or rather a bad hour's work to read it."

"*Araminta*!" exclaimed Lady Frances, looking at the signature of the letter—"this is only a nom de guerre,[2] I suppose."

"Heaven knows!" answered Miss Burrage; "but Miss Warwick always signed her epistles Angelina, and her unknown friend's were always signed Araminta. I do suspect that Araminta, whoever she is, was the instigator of this elopement."

"I wish," said Lady Frances, examining the postmark of the letter, "I wish that we could find out where Araminta lives; we might then, perhaps, recover this poor Miss Warwick before the affair is talked of in the world—before her reputation is injured."

"It would certainly be a most desirable thing," said Miss Burrage; "but Miss Warwick has such odd notions that I question whether she will ever behave like other

[1] *folio sheets* I.e., large sheets of paper.

[2] *nom de guerre* French: literally, "name of war," i.e., assumed name.

people; and, for my part, I cannot blame Lady Diana Chillingworth for giving her up. She is one of those young ladies whom it is scarcely possible to manage by common sense."

"It is certainly true," said Lady Frances, "that young women of Miss Warwick's superior abilities require something more than *common* sense to direct them properly. Young ladies who think of nothing but dress, public amusements, and forming what they call high connections, are undoubtedly most easily managed, by the fear of what the world will say of them; but Miss Warwick appeared to me to have higher ideas of excellence; and I therefore regret that she should be totally given up by her friends."

"It is Miss Warwick who has given up her friends," said Miss Burrage, with a mixture of embarrassment and sarcasm in her manner; "it is Miss Warwick who has given up her friends; not Miss Warwick's friends who have given up Miss Warwick."

The letter from the "amiable Araminta," which Miss Burrage left for the perusal of Lady Frances Somerset, contained three folio sheets, of which, it is hoped, the following abridgment will be sufficiently ample to satisfy the curiosity even of those who are lovers of long letters:

"Yes, my Angelina! our hearts are formed for that higher species of friendship, of which common souls are inadequate to form an idea, however their fashionable puerile lips may, in the intellectual inanity of their conversation, profane the term. Yes, my Angelina, you are right—every fibre of my frame, every energy of my intellect, tells me so. I read your letter by moonlight! The air balmy and pure as my Angelina's thoughts! The river silently meandering!—The rocks!—The woods!—Nature in all her majesty. Sublime confidante! sympathizing with my supreme felicity. And shall I confess to you, friend of my soul! that I could not refuse myself the pleasure of reading to my Orlando[1] some of those passages in your last, which evince so powerfully the superiority of that understanding, which, if I mistake not strangely, is formed to combat, in all its Proteus[2] forms, the system of social slavery? With what soul-rending eloquence does my Angelina describe the solitariness, the *isolation* of the heart she experiences in a crowded metropolis! With what emphatic energy of inborn independence does she exclaim against the family phalanx of her aristocratic persecutors! Surely—surely she will not he intimidated from 'the settled purpose of her soul' by the phantom-fear of worldly censure! The garnish-tinselled wand of fashion has waved in vain in the illuminated halls of folly-painted pleasure; my Angelina's eyes have withstood, yes, without a blink, the dazzling enchantment. And will she—no, I cannot, I will not think so for an instant—will she now submit her understanding, spell-bound, to the soporific charm of nonsensical words, uttered in an awful tone by that potent enchantress, *Prejudice*?—The declamation, the remonstrances of self-elected judges of right and wrong, should be treated with deserved contempt by superior minds, who claim the privilege of thinking and acting for themselves. The words *ward* and *guardian* appall my Angelina! But what are legal technical formalities, what are human institutions, to the view of shackle-scorning Reason! Oppressed, degraded, enslaved, must our unfortunate sex forever submit to sacrifice their rights, their pleasures, their *will*, at the altar of public opinion; whilst the shouts of interested priests, and idle spectators, raise the senseless enthusiasm of the self-devoted victim, or drown her cries in the truth-extorting moment of agonizing nature! You will not perfectly understand, perhaps, to what these last exclamations of your Araminta allude: But, chosen friend of my heart! when we meet—and oh, let that be quickly!—my cottage longs for the arrival of my unsophisticated Angelina!—when we meet you shall know all—your Araminta, too, has had her sorrows—Enough of this!—But her Orlando has a heart, pure as the infantine god of love could, in his most perfect mood, delight at once to wound, and own—joined to an understanding—shall I say it?—worthy to judge of your Araminta's. And will not my sober-minded Angelina prefer, to all that palaces can afford, such society in a cottage? I shall reserve for my next the description of a cottage, which I have in my eye, within view of——; but I will not anticipate. Adieu, my amiable Angelina. I enclose, as you desire, a lock of my hair.

[1] *Orlando* Traditional name for romance hero.

[2] *Proteus* Greek sea-god, who was able to change shape at will.

Ever, unalterably, your affectionate, though almost heart-broken,

ARAMINTA.

April, 1800.—*Angelina Bower!*
So let me christen my cottage!"

What effect this letter may have on *sober-minded* readers in general can easily be guessed; but Miss Warwick, who was little deserving of this epithet, was so charmed with the sound of it, that it made her totally to forget to judge of her amiable Araminta's mode of reasoning. "Garnish-tinselled wands"—"shackle-scorning Reason"—"isolation of the heart"—"soul-rending eloquence"—with "rocks and woods, and a meandering river—balmy air—moonlight— Orlando—energy of intellect—a cottage—and a heart-broken friend," made, when all mixed together, strange confusion in Angelina's imagination. She neglected to observe that her Araminta was, in the course of two pages, "almost heart-broken" and in the possession of "supreme felicity." Yet Miss Warwick, though she judged so like a simpleton, was a young woman of considerable abilities: her want of what the world calls common sense arose from certain mistakes in her education. She had passed her childhood with a father and mother who cultivated her literary taste, but who neglected to cultivate her judgment: her reading was confined to works of imagination; and the conversation which she heard was not calculated to give her any knowledge of realities. Her parents died when she was about fourteen, and she then went to reside with Lady Diana Chillingworth, a lady who placed her whole happiness in living in a certain circle of high company in London. Miss Warwick saw the follies of the society with which she now mixed; she felt insupportable ennui from the want of books and conversation suited to her taste; she heard with impatience Lady Diana's dogmatical advice; observed, with disgust, the meanness[1] of her companion, Miss Burrage, and felt with triumph the superiority of her own abilities. It was in this situation of her mind that Miss Warwick happened, at a circulating library, to meet with a new novel, called *The Woman of Genius.* The character of Araminta, the heroine, charmed her beyond measure; and having been informed, by the preface, that the story was founded on facts in the life of the authoress herself, she longed to become acquainted with her, and addressed a letter to "The Woman of Genius," at her publisher's. The letter was answered in a highly flattering, and, consequently, very agreeable style, and the correspondence continued for nearly two years; till, at length, Miss W. formed a strong desire to see her unknown friend. The ridicule with which Miss Burrage treated every thing, and every idea, that was not sanctioned by fashion, and her total want of any taste for literature, were continually contrasted, in Miss Warwick's mind, with the picture she had formed of her Araminta. Miss Burrage, who dreaded, though certainly without reason, that she might be supplanted in the good graces of Lady Diana, endeavoured by every petty means in her power to disgust her young rival with the situation in which she was placed. She succeeded beyond her hopes. Miss Warwick determined to accept of her unknown friend's invitation to Angelina Bower—a charming romantic cottage in South Wales, where, according to Araminta's description, she might pass her halcyon[2] days in tranquil, elegant retirement. It was not difficult for our heroine, though unused to deception, to conceal her project from Lady Diana Chillingworth, who was much more observant of the appearance of her protégée in public than interested about what passed in her mind in private. Miss Warwick quitted her ladyship's house without the least difficulty, and the following is the letter which our heroine left upon her dressing-table. Under all the emphatic words, according to the custom of some letter-writers, were drawn emphatic lines.

"Averse as I am to every thing that may have the appearance of a clandestine transaction, I have, however, found myself under the necessity of leaving your ladyship's house, without imparting to you my intentions. Confidence and sympathy go hand in hand, nor can either be *commanded* by the voice of authority. Your ladyship's opinions and mine, upon *all* subjects, differ so *essentially,* that I could never hope for your approbation, either of my *sentiments* or my conduct. It is my *unalterable determination* to *act* and *think* upon every occasion for myself; though I am well aware that they who start out of the common track, either in words or

[1] *meanness* Inferiority.

[2] *halcyon* Peaceful; undisturbed.

action, are exposed to the ridicule and persecution of vulgar or illiberal minds. They who venture to carry the *first* torch into *unexplored* or *unfrequented* passages in the mine of truth are exposed to the most imminent danger. Rich, however, are the treasures of the place, and cowardly the soul that hesitates! But I forget myself.

"It may be necessary to inform your ladyship that, disgusted with the frivolity of what is called fashionable life, and *unable* to *live* without the higher pleasures of friendship, I have chosen for my asylum the humble, tranquil cottage of a female friend, whose tastes, whose principles, have long been known to me: whose *genius* I admire! whose *virtues* I revere! whose example I *emulate*!

"Though I do not condescend to use the fulsome language of *a mean dependant*, I am not forgetful of the kindness I have received from your ladyship. It has not been without a *painful* struggle that I have broken my bonds asunder—the bonds of what is *falsely* called *duty*: *spontaneous* gratitude ever will have full, *indisputable*, *undisputed* power over the *heart* and *understanding* of

ANNE-ANGELINA WARWICK

"P.S. It will be in vain to attempt to discover the place of my retreat. All I ask is to be left in peace, to enjoy, in my retirement, *perfect felicity*."

CHAPTER 2

Full of her hopes of finding "perfect felicity" in her retreat at Angelina Bower, exulting in the idea of the courage and magnanimity with which she had escaped from her "aristocratic persecutors," our heroine pursued her journey to South Wales.

She had the misfortune—and it is a great misfortune to a young lady of her way of thinking—to meet with no difficulties or adventures, nothing interesting upon her journey. She arrived, with inglorious safety, at Cardiff. The inn at Cardiff was kept by a landlady of the name of Hoel. "Not high-born Hoel.[1] Alas!" said Angelina to herself, when the name was screamed in her hearing by a waiter, as she walked into the inn. "Vocal no more to high-born Hoel's harp, or soft Llewellynn's lay!" A harper was sitting in the passage, and he tuned his harp to catch her attention as she passed. "A harp! O play for me some plaintive air!" The harper followed her into a small parlour.

"How delightful," said Miss Warwick, who, in common with other heroines, had the habit of talking to herself; or, to use more dignified terms, who had the habit of indulging in soliloquy—"how delightful to taste at last the air of Wales. But 'tis a pity 'tis not North instead of South Wales, and Conway[2] instead of Cardiff Castle."

The harper, after he had finished playing a melancholy air, exclaimed, "That was but a melancholy ditty, miss—we'll try a merrier." And he began—

"Of a noble race was Shenkin."[3]

"No more," cried Angelina, stopping her ears; "no more, barbarous man! You break the illusion."

"Break the what?" said the harper to himself; "I thought, miss, that tune would surely please you; for it is a favourite one in these parts."

"A favourite with Welsh squires, perhaps," said our heroine; "but, unfortunately, *I* am not a Welsh squire, and have no taste for your 'Bumper Squire Jones.'"[4]

The man tuned his harp sullenly. "I'm sorry for it, miss," said he: "more's the pity, I can't please you better!"

Angelina cast upon him a look of contempt. "He no way fills my idea of a bard! an ancient and immortal bard! He has no soul—fingers without a soul! No 'master's hand,' or 'prophet's fire!' No 'deep sorrows!' No 'sable garb of woe!' No loose beard, or hoary hair, 'streaming like a meteor to the troubled air!' 'No haggard eyes!' Heigho!"[5]

"It is time for me to be going," said the harper, who began to think, by the young lady's looks and manners, that she was not in her right understanding. "It is time for me to be going; the gentlemen above in the Dolphin

[1] *high-born Hoel* Reference to Thomas Gray's poem "The Bard: A Pindaric Ode" (1757) lines 27–28: "Vocal no more, since Cambria's fatal day, / To high-born Hoel's harp, or soft Llewellyn's lay."

[2] *Conway* Setting of Gray's poem.

[3] *Of ... Shenkin* Popular Welsh melody.

[4] *Bumper Squire Jones* Popular Irish tune.

[5] *master's hand ... eyes* All references to Gray's "The Bard"; *Heigho* Expression of disappointment or weariness.

will be ready for me."

"A mere modern harper! He is not even blind," Angelina said to herself, as he examined the shilling which she gave him. "Begone, for Heaven's sake!" added she, aloud, as he left the room, and "leave me, leave me to repose."

She threw up the sash, to taste the evening air; but scarcely had she begun to repeat a sonnet to her Araminta—scarcely had she repeated the first two lines—

> "Hail, far-famed, fairest, unknown friend,
> Our sacred silent sympathy of soul,"

when a little ragged Welsh boy, who was playing with his companions in a field at the back of Cardiff Inn, espied her, gave the signal to his playfellows, and immediately they all came running up to the window at which Angelina was standing, and with one loud shrill chorus of "Gi' me ha'penny! Gi' me ha'penny! Gi' me one ha'penny!" interrupted the sonnet. Angelina threw out some money to the boys, though she was provoked by their interruption: her donation was, in the true spirit of a heroine, much greater than the occasion required; and the consequence was that these urchins, by spreading the fame of her generosity through the town of Cardiff, collected a Lilliputian[1] mob of petitioners, who assailed Angelina with fresh vehemence. Not a moment's peace, not a moment for poetry or reverie would they allow her: so that she was impatient for her chaise[2] to come to the door. Her Araminta's cottage was but six miles distant from Cardiff; and to speak in due sentimental language, every moment that delayed her long-expected interview with her beloved unknown friend appeared to her an age.

"And what would you be pleased to have for supper, ma'am?" said the landlady. "We have fine Tenby[3] oysters, ma'am; and, if you'd like a Welsh rabbit—"

"Tenby oysters! Welsh rabbits!" repeated Angelina, in a disdainful tone. "Oh, detain me not in this cruel manner! I want no Tenby oysters, I want no Welsh rabbits; only let me be gone—I am all impatience to see a dear friend. Oh, if you have any feeling, any humanity, detain me not!" cried she, clasping her hands.

Miss Warwick had an ungovernable propensity to make a display of sensibility; a fine theatrical scene upon every occasion; a propensity which she had acquired from novel-reading. It was never more unluckily displayed than in the present instance; for her audience and spectators, consisting of the landlady, a waiter, and a Welsh boy, who just entered the room with a knife-tray in his hand, were all more inclined to burst into rude laughter than to join in gentle sympathy. The chaise did not come to the door one moment sooner than it would have done without this pathetic wringing of the hands. As soon as Angelina drove from the door, the landlady's curiosity broke forth—

"Pray tell me, Hugh Humphries," said Mrs. Hoel, turning to the postilion,[4] who drove Angelina from Newport, "pray, now, does not this seem strange, that such a young lady as this should be travelling about in such wonderful haste? I believe, by her flighty airs, she is upon no good errand—and I would have her to know, at any rate, that she might have done better than to sneer, in that way, at Mrs. Hoel of Cardiff and her Tenby oysters, and her Welsh rabbit. Oh, I'll make her repent her *pe*haviour to Mrs. Hoel, of Cardiff. 'Not high-born Hoel,' forsooth! How does she know that, I should be glad to hear? The Hoels are as high born, I'll venture to say, as my young miss herself, I've a notion! and would scorn, moreover, to have a runaway lady for a relation of theirs. Oh, she shall learn to repent her disrespects to Mrs. Hoel, of Cardiff. I *pe*lieve she shall soon meet herself in the public newspapers—her eyes, and her nose, and her hair, and her inches, and her description at full length she shall see—and her friends shall see it too—and maybe they shall thank, and maybe they shall reward handsomely Mrs. Hoel, of Cardiff."

Whilst the angry Welsh landlady was thus forming projects of revenge for the contempt with which she imagined that her high birth and her Tenby oysters had been treated, Angelina pursued her journey towards the cottage of her unknown friend, forming charming pictures, in her imagination, of the manner in which her

---

[1] *Lilliputian* From Jonathan Swift's *Gulliver's Travels*, referring to a race of small people.

[2] *chaise* Light open carriage.

[3] *Tenby* Town on the Welsh coast.

[4] *postilion* One who rides the near horse of a carriage or post-chaise.

amiable Araminta would start, and weep, and faint, perhaps, with joy and surprise, at the sight of her Angelina. It was a fine moonlight night—an unlucky circumstance, for the by-road which led to Angelina Bower was so narrow and bad that if the night had been dark, our heroine must infallibly have been overturned, and this overturn would have been a delightful incident in the history of her journey; but Fate ordered it otherwise. Miss Warwick had nothing to lament but that her delicious reveries were interrupted, for several miles, by the Welsh postilion's expostulations with his horses.

"Good Heavens!" exclaimed she, "cannot the man hold his tongue? His uncouth vociferations distract me! So fine a scene, so placid the moonlight—but there is always something that is not in perfect unison with one's feelings."

"Miss, if you please, you must light[1] here, and walk for a matter of a quarter of a mile, for I can't drive up to the house door, because there is no carriage-road down the lane; but if you be pleased, I'll go on before you—my horses will stand quite quiet here—and I'll knock the folks up[2] for you, miss."

"Folks!—Oh, don't talk to me of knocking folks up," cried Angelina, springing out of the carriage "stay with your horses, man, I beseech you. You shall be summoned when you are wanted—I choose to walk up to the cottage alone."

"As you please, miss," said the postilion; "only *hur* had better take care of the dogs."

This last piece of sage counsel was lost upon our heroine; she heard it not—she was "rapt into future times."[3]

"By moonlight will be our first interview—just as I had pictured to myself—but can this be the cottage? It does not look quite so romantic as I expected—but 'tis the dwelling of my Araminta—Happy, thrice happy moment! Now for our secret signal—I am to sing the first, and my unknown friend the second part of the same air."

Angelina then began to sing the following stanza—

O waly[4] waly up the bank,
And waly waly down the brae,[5]
And waly waly yon burn side,[6]
Where I and my love were wont to gae.[7]

She sung and paused, in expectation of hearing the second part from her amiable Araminta—but no voice was heard.

"All is hushed," said Angelina—"ever tranquil be her slumbers! Yet I must waken her—her surprise and joy at seeing me thus will be so great!—by moonlight too!"

She knocked at the cottage window—still no answer.

"All silent as night!" said she—

When not a breath disturbs the deep serene,
And not a cloud o'ercasts the solemn scene."[8]

Angelina, as she repeated these lines, stood with her back to the cottage window: the window opened, and a Welsh servant girl put out her head; her night-cap, if cap it might be called which shape had none, was half off, her black hair streamed over her shoulders, and her face was the face of vulgar, superstitious amazement.

"Oh, 'tis our old ghost of Nelly Gwynn, all in white, walking and saying her prayers packwards[9]—I heard 'em quite plain, as I hope to preathe," said the terrified girl to herself; and, shutting the window with a trembling hand, she hastened to waken an old woman, who slept in the same room with her. Angelina, whose patience was by this time exhausted, went to the door of the cottage, and shook it with all her force. It rattled loud, and a shrill scream was heard from within.

"A scream!" cried Angelina; "Oh, my Araminta! All is hushed again." Then raising her voice, she called as loudly as she could at the window—"My Araminta! my unknown friend! be not alarmed, 'tis your Angelina."

[1] *light* Alight; get out of the carriage.

[2] *knock … up* Wake up.

[3] *rapt … times* Cf. Alexander Pope's *Pastorals* 4: "Rapt into future times, the bard begun: A virgin shall conceive, a virgin bear a son!"

[4] *waly* Expression of lamentation.

[5] *brae* Hillside.

[6] *burn side* Ground at the side of a brook ("burn").

[7] *gae* Go.

[8] *When … scene* Pope's translation of Homer's *The Iliad*, from Bk. 8, 200–01.

[9] *packwards* Welsh habits of pronunciation are broadly satirized in Edgeworth's narrative.

The door opened slowly and softly, and a slip-shod beldam[1] peeped out, leaning upon a stick; the head of Betty Williams appeared over the shoulder of this sibyl; Angelina was standing, in a pensive attitude, listening at the cottage window. At this instant the postilion, who was tired of waiting, came whistling up the lane; he carried a trunk on his back, and a bag in his hand. As soon as the old woman saw him, she held up her stick, exclaiming—

"A man! a man! a ropper and murterer! Cot save us! and keep the door fast polted." They shut the door instantly.

"What is all this?" said Angelina, with dignified composure.

"A couple of fools, I take it, miss, who are afraid and in tred of roppers," said the postilion; "put I'll make 'em come out, I'll be pound, plockheads." So saying, he went to the door of Angelina Bower, and thundered and kicked at it, speaking all the time very volubly in Welsh. In about a quarter of an hour he made them comprehend that Angelina was a young lady come to visit their mistress: then they came forth curtsying.

"My name's Betty Williams," said the girl, who was tying a clean cap under her chin. "Welcome to Llanwaetur, miss!—pe pleased to excuse our keeping hur waiting, and polting the toor, and taking hur for a ghost and a ropper—put we know who you are now—the young lady from London, that we have been told to expect."

"Oh, then, I have been expected; all's right—and my Araminta, where is she? where is she?"

"Welcome to Llanwaetur, welcome to Llaawaetur, and Cot pless hur pretty face," said the old woman, who followed Betty Williams out of the cottage.

"Hur's my grandmother, miss," said Betty.

"Very likely—but let me see my Araminta," cried Angelina; "cruel woman! where is she, I say?"

"Cot pless hur!—Cot pless hur pretty face," repeated the old woman, curtsying.

"My grandmother's as deaf as a post, miss—don't mind her; she can't tell Inglis well, put I can—who would you pe pleased to have?"

"In plain English, then—the lady who lives in this cottage."

"Our Miss Hodges?"

This odious name of Hodges provoked Angelina, who was so used to call her friend Araminta that she had almost forgotten her real name.

"Oh, miss," continued Betty Williams, "Miss Hodges has gone to Pristol for a few days."

"Gone! how unlucky! my Araminta gone!"

"Put Miss Hodges will pe pack on Tuesday—Miss Hodges did not expect hur till Thursday—put her ped is very well aired—pe pleased to walk in, and light hur a candle, and get hur a night-cap."

"Heigho! must I sleep again without seeing my Araminta! Well, but I shall sleep in a cottage for the first time in my life—

The swallow twittering from the straw-built shed."[2]

At this moment, Angelina, forgetting to stoop, hit herself a violent blow as she was entering Angelina Bower—the roof of which, indeed, "was too low for so lofty a head." A headache came on which kept her awake the greatest part of the night. In the morning she set about to explore the cottage; it was nothing like the species of elegant retirement of which she had drawn such a charming picture in her imagination. It consisted of three small bedchambers, which were more like what she had been used to call closets; a parlour, the walls of which were, in many places, stained with damp; and a kitchen which smoked. The scanty, moth-eaten furniture of the rooms was very different from the luxury and elegance to which Angelina had been accustomed in the apartments of Lady Diana Chillingworth. Coarse and ill-dressed was the food which Betty Williams with great bustle and awkwardness served up to her guest; but Angelina was no epicure. The first dinner which she ate on wooden trenchers[3] delighted her; the second, third, fourth, and fifth, appeared less and less delectable; so that by the time she had boarded one week at her cottage, she was completely convinced that

[1] *beldam* Grandmother; aged woman.

[2] *The swallow … shed* Thomas Gray, "Elegy Written in a Country Churchyard" (1751), line 18.

[3] *trenchers* Plates.

"A scrip with herbs and fruit supplied,
And water from the spring,"[1]

though delightful to Goldsmith's Hermit, are not quite so satisfactory in actual practice as in poetic theory; at least to a young lady who had been habituated to all the luxuries of fashionable life. It was in vain that our heroine repeated

"Man wants but little here below:"[2]

she found that even the want[3] of double refined sugar, of green tea and Mocha coffee, was sensibly felt. Hour after hour, and day after day, passed with Angelina in anxious expectation of her Araminta's return home. Her time hung heavy upon her hands, for she had no companion with whom she could converse; and one odd volume of Rousseau's *Eloise*, and a few well-thumbed German plays, were the only books which she could find in the house. There was, according to Betty Williams's report, "a vast sight of books in a press,[4] along with some tablecloths," but Miss Hodges had the key of this press in her pocket. Deprived of the pleasures both of reading and conversation, Angelina endeavoured to amuse herself by contemplating the beauties of nature. There were some wild, solitary walks in the neighbourhood of Angelina Bower; but though our heroine was delighted with these, she wanted, in her rambles, some kindred soul to whom she might exclaim—"How charming is solitude!" The day after her arrival in Wales, she wrote a long letter to Araminta, which Betty Williams undertook to send by a careful lad, a particular friend of her own, who would deliver it, without fail, into Miss Hodges's own hands, and who would engage to bring an answer by three o'clock the next day. The careful lad did not return till four days afterward, and he then could give no account of his mission, except that he had left the letter at Bristol with a particular friend of his own, who would deliver it, without fail, into Miss Hodges's own hands, if he could meet with her. The post seems to be the last expedient which a heroine ever thinks of for the conveyance of her letters; so that, if we were to judge from the annals of romance, we should infallibly conclude there was no such thing as a post-office in England. On the sixth day of her abode at this comfortless cottage, the possibility of sending a letter to her friend by the post occurred to Angelina, and she actually discovered that there was a post office at Cardiff. Before she could receive an answer to this epistle, a circumstance happened which made her determine to abandon her present retreat. One evening she rambled out to a considerable distance from the cottage, and it was long after sunset ere she recollected that it would be necessary to return homewards before it grew dark. She mistook her way at last, and following a sheep-path down the steep side of a mountain, she came to a point at which she apparently could neither advance nor recede. A stout Welsh farmer, who was counting his sheep in a field at the top of the mountain, happened to look down its steep side in search of one of his flock that was missing: the farmer saw something white at a distance below him, but there was a mist—it was dusk in the evening—and whether it were a woman, or a sheep, he could not be certain. In the hope that Angelina was his lost sheep, he went to her assistance, and though, upon a nearer view, he was disappointed in finding that she was a woman, yet he had the humanity to hold out his stick to her, and he helped her up by it with some difficulty. One of her slippers fell off as she scrambled up the hill—there was no recovering it; her other slipper, which was of the thinnest kid leather, was cut through by the stones; her silk stockings were soon stained with the blood of her tender feet; and it was with real gratitude that she accepted the farmer's offer to let her pass the night at his farmhouse, which was within view. Angelina Bower was, according to his computation, about four miles distant, as well, he said, as he could judge of the place she meant by her description: she had unluckily forgotten that the common name of it was Llanwaetur. At the farmer's house she was, at first, hospitably received by a tight-looking woman; but she had not been many minutes seated before she found herself the object of much curiosity and suspicion. In one corner of the room, at a small round table, with a jug of ale before him, sat a man who looked like the

[1] *A scrip ... spring* From Oliver Goldsmith's "The Hermit" (1766), lines 27–28.

[2] *Man ... below* Also from "The Hermit," line 31.

[3] *want* Lack.

[4] *press* Large cupboard.

picture of a Welsh squire: a candle had just been lighted for his worship, for he was a magistrate, and a great man, in those parts, for he could read the newspaper, and his company was, therefore, always welcome to the farmer, who loved to hear the news, and the reader was paid for his trouble with good ale, which he loved even better than literature.

"What news, Mr. Evans?" said the farmer.

"What news?" repeated Mr. Evans, looking up from his paper with a sarcastic smile. "Why, news that might not be altogether so agreeable to the whole of this good company; so 'tis best to keep it to ourselves."

"Every thing's agreeable to me, I'm sure," said the farmer—"every thing's agreeable to me in the way of news."

"And to me, not excepting politics, which you gentlemen always think so polite," said the farmer's wife, "to keep to yourselves; but, you recollect, I was used to politics when I lived with my uncle at Cardiff; not having, though a farmer's wife, always lived in the country, as you see, ma'am—nor being quite illiterate. Well, Mr. Evans, let us have it. What news of the fleets?"[1]

Mr. Evans made no reply, but pointed out a passage in the newspaper to the farmer, who leant over his shoulder, in vain endeavouring to spell and put it together: his smart wife, whose curiosity was at least equal to her husband's, ran immediately to peep at the wonderful paragraph, and she read aloud the beginning of an advertisement:

"Suspected to have strayed, or eloped, from her friends or relations, a young lady, seemingly not more than sixteen years of age, dressed in white, with a straw hat, blue eyes, light hair."

Angelina coloured so deeply whilst this was read, and the description so exactly suited with her appearance, that the farmer's wife stopped short; the farmer fixed his eyes upon her; and Mr. Evans cleared his throat several times with much significance. A general silence ensued; at last the three heads nodded to one another across the round table; the farmer whistled and walked out of the room; his wife fidgeted at a buffet, in which she began to arrange some cups and saucers; and, after a few minutes, she followed her husband. Angelina took up the newspaper, to read the remainder of the advertisement. She could not doubt that it was meant for her when she saw that it was dated the very day of her arrival at the inn at Cardiff, and signed by the landlady of the inn, Mrs. Hoel. Mr. Evans swallowed the remainder of his ale, and then addressed Angelina in these words:

"Young lady, it is plain to see you know when the cap fits: now, if you'll take my advice, you'll not make the match you have in your eye; for, though a lord's son, he is a great gambler. I dined with one that has dined with him not long ago. My son, who has a living near Bristol, knows a great deal—more about you than you'd think; and 'tis my advice to you, which I wouldn't be at the trouble of giving if you were not as pretty as you are, to go back to your relations; for he'll never marry you, and marriage to be sure is your object. I have no more to say, but only this—I shall think it my duty, as a magistrate, to let your friends know as soon as possible where you are, coming under my cognizance as you do; for a vagabond, in the eye of the law, is a person—"

Angelina had not patience to listen to any more of this speech; she interrupted Mr. Evans with a look of indignation, assured him that he was perfectly unintelligible to her, and walked out of the room with great dignity. Her dignity made no impression upon the farmer or his wife, who now repented having offered her a night's lodging in their house: in the morning they were as eager to get rid of her as she was impatient to depart. Mr. Evans insisted upon seeing her safe home, evidently for the purpose of discovering precisely where she lived. Angelina saw that she could no longer remain undisturbed in her retreat, and determined to set out immediately in quest of her unknown friend at Bristol. Betty Williams, who had a strong desire to have a jaunt to Bristol, a town which she had never seen but once in her life, offered to attend Miss Warwick, assuring her that she perfectly well knew the house where Miss Hodges always lodged. Her offer was accepted; and what adventures our heroine met with in Bristol, and what difficulties she encountered before she discovered her Araminta, will be seen in the next chapter.

[1] *news of the fleet* Arrivals and departures of merchant vessels as well as news of the navy.

Chapter 3

Angelina went by water from Cardiff to Bristol; the water was rather rough, and, as she was unused to the motion of a vessel, she was both frightened and sick. She spent some hours very disagreeably, and without even the sense of acting like a heroine to support her spirits. It was late in the evening before she arrived at the end of her voyage: she was landed on the quay at Bristol. No hackney-coach was to he had, and she was obliged to walk to the bush.[1] To find herself in the midst of a bustling, vulgar crowd, by whom she was unknown, but not unnoticed, was new to Miss Warwick. Whilst she was with Lady Diana Chillingworth, she had always been used to see crowds make way for her; she was now surprised to feel herself jostled in the streets by passengers who were all full of their own affairs, hurrying different ways in pursuit of objects which probably seemed to them as important as the search for an unknown friend appeared to Angelina.

Betty Williams's friend's friend, the careful lad who was to deliver the letter to Miss Hodges, was a waiter at the bush. Upon inquiry, it was found that he had totally forgotten his promise: Angelina's letter was, after much search, found in a bottle-drainer, so much stained with port wine that it was illegible. The man answered with the most provoking nonchalance, when Angelina reproached him for his carelessness, "That, indeed, no such person as Miss Hodges was to be found: that nobody he could meet with had ever heard the name." They who are extremely enthusiastic suffer continually from the total indifference of others to their feelings; and young people can scarcely conceive the extent of this indifference until they have seen something of the world. Seeing the world does not *always* mean seeing a certain set of company in London.

Angelina, the morning after her arrival at the Bush, took a hackney-coach,[2] and left the care of directing the coachman to Betty Williams, who professed to have a perfect knowledge of Bristol. Betty desired the man to drive to the drawbridge; and, at the sound of the word drawbridge, various associations of ideas with the drawbridges of ancient times were called up in Miss Warwick's imagination. How different was the reality from her castles in the air! She was roused from her reverie by the voices of Betty Williams and the coachman.

"Where *will* I drive ye to, I ask you?" said the coachman, who was an Irishman: "*Will* I stand all day upon the drawbridge stopping the passage?"

"Trive on a step, and I will get out and see apout me," said Betty: "I know the look of the house as well as I know any thing."

Betty got out of the coach and walked up and down the street, looking at the houses like one bewildered.

"Bad luck to you! For a Welsh woman as you are," exclaimed the coachman, jumping down from the box, "will I lave the young lady standing in the streets all day alone for you to be making a fool this way of us both? Sorrow take me now! If I do—"

"Pless us, pe not in a pet or a pucker, or how shall I recollect any body or any thing. Cood! Cood! Stand you there while I just say over my alphabet: a, p, c, t, e, f, g, h, i, k, 1, m, n, o, b. It was some name which begins with *p*, and ends with a *t*, I pelieve."

"Here's a pretty direction, upon my troth; some name which begins with a *p*, and ends with a *t*," cried the coachman; and after he had uttered half a score of Hibernian[3] execrations upon the Welsh woman's folly, he with much good nature went along with her to read the names on the street doors. "Here's a name now that's the very thing for you—here's Pushit now. Was the name Pushit? Ricollict yourself, my good girl, was that your name?"

"Pushit! Oh, yes, I am sure, and pelieve it was Pushit—Mrs. Pushit's house, Pristol, where our Miss Hodges lodges alway."

"Mrs. Pushit—but this is quite another man; I tell you this is Sir John—Faith now we are in luck," continued the coachman—"here's another p just at hand; here's Mrs. Puffit; sure she begins with a p, and ends with a t, and is a milliner[4] into the bargain? So sure enough I'll engage the young lady lodges here. Puffit—Hey? Ricollict now, and don't be looking as if you'd just been pulled out of your sleep, and had never been in a Christian town before now."

[1] *bush* Tavern.

[2] *hackney-coach* Rented coach, for six persons.

[3] *Hibernian* Irish.

[4] *milliner* Maker and seller of women's clothing.

"Pless us, Cot pless us!" said the Welsh girl, who was quite overpowered by the Irishman's flow of words—and she was on the point of having recourse, in her own defence, to her native tongue, in which she could have matched either male or female in fluency; but, to Angelina's great relief, the dialogue between the coachman and Betty Williams ceased. The coachman drew up to Mrs. Puffit's; but, as there was a handsome carriage at the door, Miss Warwick was obliged to wait in her hackney-coach some time longer. The handsome carriage belonged to Lady Frances Somerset. By one of those extraordinary coincidences which sometimes occur in real life, but which are scarcely believed to be natural when they are related in books, Miss Warwick happened to come to this shop at the very moment when the persons she most wished to avoid were there. Whilst the dialogue between Betty Williams and the hackney-coachman was passing, Lady Diana Chillingworth and Miss Burrage were seated in Mrs. Puffit's shop: Lady Diana was extremely busy bargaining with the milliner; for, though rich, and a woman of quality, her ladyship piqued herself upon making the cheapest bargains in the world.

"Your la'ship did not look at this eight and twenty shilling lace," said Mrs. Puffit; "'tis positively the cheapest thing your la'ship ever saw. Jessie! the laces in the little blue band-box.[1] Quick! for my Ladi Di. Quick!"

"But it is out of my power to stay to look at any thing more now," said Lady Diana; "and yet," whispered she to Miss Burrage, "when one does go out a shopping, one certainly likes to bring home a bargain."

"Certainly; but Bristol's not the place for bargains," said Miss Burrage; "you will find nothing tolerable, I assure you, my dear Lady Di, at Bristol."

"Why, my dear," said her ladyship, "were you ever at Bristol before? How comes it that I never heard that you were at Bristol before? Where were you, child?"

"At the Wells, at the Wells, ma'am," replied Miss Burrage, and she turned pale and red in the space of a few seconds; but Lady Diana, who was very near-sighted, was holding her head so close to the blue band-box full of lace that she could not see the changes in her companion's countenance. The fact was that Miss Burrage was born and bred in Bristol, where she had several relations who were not in high life, and by whom she consequently dreaded to be claimed. When she first met Lady Diana Chillingworth at Buxton, she had passed herself upon her for one of the Burrages of Dorsetshire, and she knew that if her ladyship was to discover the truth, she would cast her off with horror. For this reason, she had done every thing in her power to prevent Lady Di from coming to Clifton; and for this reason she now endeavoured to persuade her that nothing tolerable could be met with at Bristol.

"I am afraid, Lady Di, you will be late at Lady Mary's," said she.

"Look at this lace, child, and give me your opinion—eight-and-twenty shillings, Mrs. Puffit, did you say?"

"Eight-and-twenty, my lady—and I lose by every yard I sell at that price. Ma'am, you see," said Mrs. Puffit, appealing to Miss Burrage, "'tis real Valenciennes,[2] you see."

"I see 'tis horrid dear,"[3] said Miss Burrage: then in a whisper to Lady Di she added, "at Miss Trentham's at the Wells, your ladyship will meet with such bargains!"

Mrs. Puffit put her lace upon the alabaster neck of the large doll which stood in the middle of her shop. "Only look, my lady—only see, ma'am, how beautiful becoming 'tis to the neck, and sets off a dress too, you know, ma'am. And (turning to Miss Burrage) eight-and-twenty, you know, ma'am, is really nothing for any lace you'd wear; but more particularly for real Valenciennes, which can scarce be had *real*, for love or money, since the French Rev*or*lution. Real Valenciennes! and will wear and wash, and wash and wear—not that your ladyship minds that—for ever and ever, and is such a bargain, and so becoming to the neck, especially to ladies of your la'ship's complexion."

"Well, I protest, I believe, Burrage, I don't know what to say, my dear—hey?"

"I'm told," whispered Miss Burrage, "that Miss Trentham's to have a lace raffle at the Wells next week."

"A raffle?" cried Lady Di, turning her back immediately upon the doll and the lace.

[1] *band-box* Box for storing hats, collars, etc.

[2] *Valenciennes* Lace manufactured in the French town of that name.

[3] *dear* Expensive.

"Well," cried Mrs. Puffit, "instead of eight say seven-and-twenty shillings, Miss Burrage, for old acquaintance sake."

"Old acquaintance!" exclaimed Miss Burrage: "la! Mrs. Puffit, I don't remember ever being twice in your shop all the time I was at the Wells before."

"No, ma'am," replied Mrs. Puffit, with a malicious smile—"but when you *was* living on Saint Augustin's Back."

"Saint Augustin's Back, my dear!" exclaimed Lady Diana Chillingworth, with a look of horror and amazement.

Miss Burrage, laying down a bank-note on the counter, made a quick and expressive sign to the milliner to hold her tongue.

"Dear Mrs. Puffit," cried she, "you certainly mistake me for some other strange person. Lady Di, now I look at it with my glass, this lace is very fine, I must agree with you, and not dear, by any means, for real Valenciennes: cut me off three yards of this lace—I protest there's no withstanding it, Lady Di."

"Three yards at eight-and-twenty—here, Jesse," said Mrs. Puffit. "I beg your pardon, ma'am, for my mistake; I supposed it was some other lady of the same name; there are so many Burrages. *Only* three yards did you say, ma'am?"

"Nay, I don't care if you give me four. I'm of the Burrages of Dorsetshire."

"A very good family, those Burrages of Dorsetshire, as any in England," said Lady Di—"and put up twelve yards of this for me, Mrs. Puffit."

"Twelve at eight-and-twenty—yes, my lady—very much obliged to your ladyship—much obliged to you, Miss Burrage. Here, Jesse, this to my Lady Di. Chillingworth's carriage." Jesse called at the shop-door, in a shrill voice, to a black servant of Lady Frances Somerset—"Mr. Hector, Mr. Hector! Sir, pray put this parcel into the carriage for Lady Diana Chillingworth."

Angelina, who was waiting in her hackney-coach, started; she could scarcely believe that she heard the name rightly—but an instant afterwards the voice of Lady Diana struck her ear, and she sunk back in great agitation. However, neither Miss Burrage nor Lady Di saw her; they got into their carriage and drove away.

Angelina was so much alarmed that she could scarcely believe that the danger was past when she saw the carriage at the furthest end of the street.

"Wouldn't you be pleased to 'light, ma'am?" said Jesse. "We don't bring things to the door."

"Who have we here?" cried Mrs. Puffit; "who have we here?"

"Only some folks out of a hack,[1] that was kept waiting, and couldn't draw up whilst my Lady Di's carriage was at the door," said Jesse.

"A good pretty girl, the foremost," said Mrs. Puffit. "But, in the name of wonder, what's that odd fish coining behind her?"

"A queer-looking pair, in good truth!" said Jesse.

Angelina seated herself and gave a deep sigh. "Ribands, if you please, ma'am," said she to Mrs. Puffit. "I must," thought she, "ask for something before I ask for my Araminta."

"Ribands—yes, ma'am—what sort? Keep an eye upon the glass," whispered the milliner to her shop girl, as she stooped behind the counter for a drawer of ribands—"keep an eye on the glass, Jesse—a girl of the town, I take it. What colour, ma'am?"

"Blue—'cerulean blue.' Here, child," said Angelina, turning to Betty Williams, "here's a riband for you."

Betty Williams did not hear, for Betty was fascinated by the eyes of the great doll, opposite to which she stood fixed.

"Lord, what a fine lady! and how hur stares at Betty Williams!" thought she: "I wish hur would take her eyes off me."

"Betty! Betty Williams! a riband for you," cried Angelina in a louder tone.

Betty started—"Miss! a riband!" She ran forward, and, in pushing by the doll, threw it backward: Mrs. Puffit caught it in her arms, and Betty, stopping short, curtsied, and said to the doll—"Peg pardon, miss—peg pardon, miss—tit I hurt you?—peg pardon. Pless us! 'tis a toll, and no woman, I teclare."

The milliner and Jesse now burst into uncontrollable, and, as Angelina feared, "unextinguishable laughter." Nothing is so distressing to a sentimental heroine as ridicule: Miss Warwick perceived that she had her share of that which Betty Williams excited; and she who imagined herself to be capable of "combating, in all its

[1] *hack* I.e., hackney carriage.

Proteus forms, the system of social slavery," was unable to withstand the laughter of a milliner and her 'prentice.

"Do you please to want anything else, ma'am?" said Mrs. Puffit in a saucy tone—"Rouge, perhaps?"

"I wish to know, madam," said Angelina, "whether a lady of the name of Hodges does not lodge here?"

"A lady of the name of Hodges! No, ma'am—I'm very particular about lodgers—no such lady ever lodged with me. Jesse! to the door—quick!—Lady Mary Tasselton's carriage."

Angelina hastily rose and departed. Whilst Jesse ran to the door, and whilst Mrs. Puffit's attention was fixed upon Lady Mary Tasselton's carriage, Betty Williams twitched from off the doll's shoulders the remainder of the piece of Valenciennes lace which had been left there. "Since hur's only wood, I'll make free," said she to herself, and she carried off the lace unobserved.

Angelina's impatience to find her Araminta was increased by the dread of meeting Lady Di Chillingworth in every carriage that passed, and in every shop where she might call. At the next house at which the coachman stopped, the words *Dinah Plait, relict*[1] *of Jonas Plait, cheesemonger,* were written in large letters over the shop door. Angelina thought she was in no danger of meeting her ladyship here, and she alighted. There was no one in the shop but a child of seven years old; he could not understand well what Angelina or Betty said, but he ran to call his aunt. Dinah Plait was at dinner; and when the child opened the door of the parlour, there came forth such a savoury smell that Betty Williams, who was extremely hungry, could not forbear putting her head in to see what was upon the table.

"Pless hur! heggs and pacon and toasted cheese—Cot pless hur!" exclaimed Betty.

"Aunt Dinah," said the child, "here are two women in some great distress, they told me—and astray and hungry."

"In some great distress, and astray and hungry?—then let them in here, child, this minute."

There was seated at a small table, in a perfectly neat parlour, a Quaker whose benevolent countenance charmed Angelina the moment she entered the room.

"Pardon this intrusion," said she.

"Friend, thou art welcome," said Dinah Plait, and her looks said so more expressively than her words. An elderly man rose, and, leaving the corkscrew in the half-drawn cork of a bottle of cider, he set a chair for Angelina and withdrew to the window.

"Be seated, and eat, for verily thou seemest to be hungry," said Mrs. Plait to Betty Williams, who instantly obeyed, and began to eat like one that had been half famished.

"And now, friend, thy business, thy distress—what is it?" said Dinah, turning to Angelina: "so young to have sorrows."

"I had best take myself away," said the elderly gentleman who stood at the window—"I had best take myself away, for miss may not like to speak before me—though she might, for that matter."

"Where is the gentleman going?" said Miss Warwick; "I have but one short question to ask, and I have nothing to say that need—"

"I dare say, young lady, you can have nothing to say that you need be ashamed of, only people in distress don't like so well to speak before third folks, I *guess*—though, to say the truth, I have never known, by my own experience, what it was to be in much distress since I came into the world—but I hope I am not the more hard-hearted for that—for I can guess, I say, pretty well, how those in distress feel when they come to speak. Do as you would be done by is my maxim till I can find a better—so I take myself away, leaving my better part behind me, if it will be of any service to you, madam."

As he passed by Miss Warwick, he dropped his purse into her lap, and he was gone before she could recover from her surprise.

"Sir! Madam!" cried she, rising hastily, "here has been some strange mistake—I am not a beggar—I am much, very much obliged to you, but—"

"Nay, keep it, friend, keep it," said Dinah Plait, pressing the purse upon Angelina; "John Barker is as rich as a Jew,[2] and as generous as a prince. Keep it, friend, and you'll oblige both him and me—'tis dangerous in this world for one so young and so pretty as you

[1] *relict* Widow.

[2] *rich as a Jew* Jews had long been prevented from entering most "respectable" professions, but had been allowed to work in some of the less respectable fields of commerce and finance; the success of some Jews in these fields was frequently caricatured, and often resented.

are to be in *great distress*; so be not proud." "I am not proud," said Miss Warwick, drawing her purse from her pocket; "but my distress is not of a pecuniary nature—Convince yourself—I am in distress only for a friend, *an unknown* friend."

"Touched in her brain, I doubt,"[1] thought Dinah.

"Coot ale!" exclaimed Betty Williams—"Coot heggs and pacon."

"Does a lady of the name of Araminta—Miss Hodges, I mean—lodge here?" said Miss Warwick.

"Friend, I do not let lodgings; and I know of no such person as Miss Hodges."

"Well, I swear hur name, the coachman told me, did begin with a p, and end with a t," cried Betty Williams, "or I would never have let him knock at hur toor."

"Oh, my Araminta! my Araminta!" exclaimed Angelina, turning up her eyes towards heaven—"when, oh when shall I find thee? I am the most unfortunate person upon earth."

"Had not hur petter eat a hegg, and a pit of pacon? here's one pit left," said Betty: "hur must be hungry, for 'tis two o'clock past, and we preakfasted at nine—hur must be hungry;" and Betty pressed her *to try the pacon*; but Angelina put it away, or, in the proper style, motioned the bacon from her.

"I am in no want of food," cried she, rising: "happy they who have no conception of any but corporeal sufferings. Farewell, madam! May the sensibility of which your countenance is so strongly expressive never be a source of misery to you!" And with that depth of sigh which suited the close of such a speech, Angelina withdrew.

"If I could but have felt her pulse," said Dinah Plait to herself, "I could have prescribed something that, maybe, would have done her good, poor distracted thing! Now it was well done of John Barker to leave this purse for her—but how is this?—poor thing! she's not fit to be trusted with money—here she has left her own purse full of guineas."

Dinah ran immediately to the house door, in hopes of being able to catch Angelina; but the coach had turned down into another street, and was out of sight. Mrs. Plait sent for her constant counsellor, John Barker, to deliberate on the means of returning the purse. It should be mentioned, to the credit of Dinah's benevolence, that, at the moment when she was interrupted by the entrance of Betty Williams and Angelina, she was hearing the most flattering things from a person who was not disagreeable to her: her friend, John Barker, was a rich hosier who had retired from business; and who, without any ostentation, had a great deal of real feeling and generosity. But the fastidious taste of *fine*, or sentimental readers, will probably be disgusted by our talking of the feelings and generosity of a hosier and a cheesemonger's widow. It belongs to a certain class of people to indulge in the luxury of sentiment: we shall follow our heroine, therefore, who, both from her birth and education, is properly qualified to have—"exquisite feelings."

The next house at which Angelina stopped to search for her amiable Araminta was at Mrs. Porett's academy for young ladies.

"Yes, ma'am, Miss Hodges is here—Pray walk into this room, and you shall see the young lady immediately." Angelina burst into the room instantly, exclaiming—"Oh, my Araminta! have I found you at last?" She stopped short, a little confounded at finding herself in a large room full of young ladies who were dancing reels, and who all stood still at one and the same instant, and fixed their eyes upon her, struck with astonishment at her theatrical entrée and exclamation.

"Miss Hodges!" said Mrs. Porett—and a little girl of seven years old came forward: "Here, ma'am," said Mrs. Porett to Angelina, "here is Miss Hodges."

"Not *my* Miss Hodges! not my Araminta! alas!" "No, ma'am," said the little girl; "I am only Letty Hodges." Several of her companions now began to titter. "These girls," said Angelina to herself, "take me for a fool;" and, turning to Mrs. Porett, she apologized for the trouble she had given, in language as little romantic as she could condescend to use.

"Tid you bid me, miss, wait in the coach, or the passage?" cried Betty Williams, forcing her way in at the door, so as almost to push down the dancing-master, who stood with his back to it. Betty stared round, and dropped curtsy after curtsy, whilst the young ladies laughed and whispered, and whispered and laughed; and the words, odd—vulgar—strange—who is she?—what is she?—reached Miss Warwick.

[1] *doubt* Believe.

"This Welsh girl," thought she, "is my torment. Wherever I go she makes me share the ridicule of her folly."

Clara Hope, one of the young ladies, saw and pitied Angelina's confusion.

"Gif over, an ye[1] have any gude nature—gif over your whispering and laughing," said Clara to her companions. "Ken ye not ye make her so bashful, she'd fain hide her face wi' her twa hands."[2]

But it was in vain that the good-natured Clara Hops remonstrated: her companions could not forbear tittering as Betty Williams, upon Miss Warwick's laying the blame of the mistake on her, replied in a strong Welsh accent—

"I will swear almost the name was Porett or Plait, where our Miss Hodges tid always lodge in Pristol. Porett, or Plait, or Puffit, or some of her names that pekin with a p and ent with a t."

Angelina, quite *overpowered*, shrunk back as Betty bawled out her vindication, and she was yet more confused when Monsieur Richelet, the dancing-master, at this unlucky instant came up to her, and with an elegant bow said, "It is not difficult to see by her air that mademoiselle dances superiorly. Mademoiselle vould she do me de plaisir—de honneur[3] to dance one minuet?"

"Oh, if she would but dance!" whispered some of the group of young ladies.

"Excuse me, sir," said Miss Warwick.

"Not a minuet? Den a minuet de la cour,[4] a cotillon, or contredanse,[5] or reel; vatever mademoiselle please vill do us honneur."

Angelina, with a mixture of impatience and confusion, repeated, "Excuse me, sir—I am going—I interrupt—I beg I may not interrupt."

"A coot morrow to you all, creat and small," said Betty Williams, curtsying awkwardly at the door as she went out before Miss Warwick.

The young ladies were now diverted so much beyond the bounds of decorum, that Mrs. Porett was obliged to call them to order.

"Oh, my Araminta, what scenes have I gone through! to what derision have I exposed myself for your sake!" said our heroine to herself.

Just as she was leaving the dancing-room, she was stopped short by Betty Williams, who, with a face of terror, exclaimed, "'Tis a poy in the hall that I tare not pass for my lifes; he has a pasket full of pees in his hand, and I cannot apide pees, ever since one tay when I was a chilt and was stung on the nose by a pee. The poy in the hall has a pasketful of pees, ma'am," said Betty, with an imploring accent, to Mrs. Porett.

"A basketful of bees!" said Mrs. Porett, laughing: "Oh, you are mistaken: I know what the boy has in his basket—they are only flowers; they are not bees: you may safely go by them."

"Put I saw pees with my own eyes," persisted Betty.

"Only a basketful of the bee orchis,[6] which I commissioned a little boy to bring from St. Vincent's rocks for my young botanists," said Mrs. Porett to Angelina: "you know the flower is so like a bee, that at first sight you might easily mistake it." Mrs. Porett, to convince Betty Williams that she had no cause for fear, went on before her into the hall; but Betty still hung back, crying—

"It is a pasket full of pees! I saw the pees with my own eyes."

The noise she made excited the curiosity of the young ladies in the dancing-room: they looked out to see what was the matter.

"Oh, 'tis the wee-wee French prisoner boy, with the bee orchises for us—there, I see him standing in the hall," cried Clara Hope, and instantly she ran, followed by several of her companions, into the hall.

"You see that they are not bees," said Mrs. Porett to Betty Williams, as she took several of the flowers in her hand. Betty, half convinced, yet half afraid, moved a few steps into the hall.

"You have no cause for dread," said Clara Hope; "poor boy, he has nought in his basket that can hurt any body."

Betty Williams's heavy foot was now set upon the

---

[1] *an ye* If you.

[2] *Ken ye … hands* Do you not know that you make her so bashful that she would rather hide her face with her two hands?

[3] *plaisir—de honneur* French: the pleasure—the honor.

[4] *de la cour* French: of the court.

[5] *contredanse* French: country dance.

[6] *orchis* Orchid.

train of Clara's gown, and, as the young lady sprang forwards, her gown, which was of thin muslin, was torn so as to excite the commiseration of all her young companions.

"What a terrible rent! and her best gown!" said they. "Poor Clara Hope!"

"Pless us! peg pardon, miss!" cried the awkward, terrified Betty; "peg pardon, miss!"

"Pardon's granted," said Clara; and whilst her companions stretched out her train, deploring the length and breadth of her misfortune, she went on speaking to the little French boy. "Poor wee boy! 'tis a sad thing to be in a strange country, far away from one's ane ane kin and happy hame—poor wee thing," said she, slipping some money into his hand.

"What a heavenly countenance!" thought Angelina, as she looked at Clara Hope: "Oh, that my Araminta may resemble her!"

"Plait il[1]—take vat you vant—tank you," said the little boy, offering to Clara Hope his basket of flowers, and a small box of trinkets, which he held in his hand.

"Here's a many pretty toys—who'll buy?" cried Clara, turning to her companions.

The young ladies crowded round the box and the basket.

"Is he in distress?" said Angelina; "perhaps I can be of some use to him!" and she put her hand into her pocket to feel for her purse.

"He's a very honest, industrious little boy," said Mrs. Porett, "and he supports his parents by his active ingenuity."

"And, Louis, is your father sick still?" continued Clara Hope to the poor boy.

"Bien malade! bien malade! very sick! very sick!" said he.

The unaffected language of real feeling and benevolence is easily understood, and is never ridiculous; even in the broken English of little Louis, and the broad Scotch tone of Clara, it was both intelligible and agreeable.

Angelina had been for some time past feeling in her pocket for her purse.

"'Tis gone—certainly gone!" she exclaimed: "I've lost it! lost my purse! Betty, do you know any thing of it? I had it at Mrs. Plait's! What shall I do for this poor little fellow? This trinket is of gold!" said she, taking from her neck a locket. "Here, my little fellow, I have no money to give you, take this—nay, you must, indeed."

"Tanks! tanks! bread for my poor fader! joy! joy!—too much joy! too much!"

"You see you were wrong to laugh at her," whispered Clara Hope to her companions: "I liked her lukes from the first."

Natural feeling, at this moment, so entirely occupied and satisfied Angelina that she forgot her sensibility for her unknown friend; and it was not till one of the children observed the lock of hair in her locket that she recollected her accustomed cant of—

"*Oh, my Araminta! my amiable Araminta!* could I part with that hair, more precious than gold?"

"Pless us!" said Betty; "put, if she has lost her purse, who shall pay for the coach, and what will become of our tinners?"

Angelina silenced Betty Williams with peremptory dignity.

Mrs. Porett, who was a good and sensible woman, and who had been interested for our heroine by her good-nature to the little French boy, followed Miss Warwick as she left the room.

"Let me detain you but for a few minutes," said she, opening the door of a little study. "You have nothing to fear from any impertinent curiosity on my part; but, perhaps, I may be of some assistance to you." Miss Warwick could not refuse to be detained a few minutes by so friendly a voice.

"Madam, you have mentioned the name of Araminta several times since you came into this house," said Mrs. Porett, with something of embarrassment in her manner, for she was afraid of appearing impertinent. "I know, or at least I knew, a lady who writes under that name, and whose real name is Hodges."

"Oh, a thousand, thousand thanks!" cried Angelina: "tell me, where can I find her?"

"Are you acquainted with her? You seem to be a stranger, young lady, in Bristol. Are you acquainted with Miss Hodges's *whole* history?"

"Yes, her *whole* history; every feeling of her soul; every thought of her mind!" cried Angelina, with enthusiasm. "We have corresponded for two years past."

[1] *Plait il* French: it pleases?

Mrs. Porett smiled. "It is not always possible," said she, "to judge of ladies by their letters. I am not inclined to believe *above half* what the world says, according to Lord Chesterfield's[1] allowance for scandalous stories; but it may be necessary to warn you, as you seem very young, that—"

"Madam," cried Angelina, "young as I am, I know that superior genius and virtue are the inevitable objects of scandal. It is in vain to detain me further."

"I am truly sorry for it," said Mrs. Porett; "but, perhaps, you will allow me to tell you, that—"

"No, not a word; not a word more will I hear," cried our heroine; and she hurried out of the house, and threw herself into the coach. Mrs. Porett contrived, however, to make Betty Williams hear that the most probable means of gaining any intelligence of Miss Hodges would be to inquire for her at the shop of Mr. Beatson, who was her printer. To Mr. Beatson's they drove—though Betty professed that she was half unwilling to inquire for Miss Hodges from any one whose name did not begin with a p, and end with a t.

"What a pity it is," said Mrs. Porett, when she returned to her pupils—"what a pity it is that this young lady's friends should permit her to go about in a hackney-coach, with such a strange, vulgar servant girl as that! She is too young to know how quickly, and often how severely, the world judges by appearances. Miss Hope, now we talk of appearances, you forget that your gown is torn, and you do not know, perhaps, that your friend, Lady Frances Somerset—"

"Lady Frances Somerset!" cried Clara Hope—"I luve to hear her very name."

"For which reason you interrupt me the moment I mention it—I have a great mind not to tell you—that Lady Frances Somerset has invited you to go to the play with her tonight: *The Merchant of Venice, and the Adopted Child.*"

"Gude-natured Lady Frances Somerset, I'm sure an' if Clara Hope had been your adopted child twenty times over, you could not have been more kind to her *nor* you have been. No, not had she been your ane countrywoman, and of your ane clan and all for the same reasons that make some neglect and look down upon her—because Clara is not meikle[2] rich, and is far away from her ane ane friends. Gude Lady Frances Somerset! Clara Hope luves you in her heart, and she's as blythe[3] wi' the thought o' ganging to see you as if she were going to dear Inverary."[4]

It is a pity, for the sake of our story, that Miss Warwick did not stay a few minutes longer at Mrs. Porett's, that she might have heard this eulogium on Lady Frances Somerset, and might have, a second time in one day, discovered that she was on the very brink of meeting with the persons she most dreaded to see; but, however temptingly romantic such an incident would have been, we must, according to our duty as faithful historians, deliver a plain unvarnished tale.[5]

Miss Warwick arrived at Mr. Beatson's, and as soon as she had pronounced the name of Hodges, the printer called to his devil[6] for a parcel of advertisements, which he put into her hand; they were proposals for printing by subscription a new novel—*The Sorrows of Araminta*.

"Oh, my Araminta! my amiable Araminta! have I found you at last?—*The Sorrows of Araminta, a novel, in nine volumes*—Oh, charming!—*together with a tragedy on the same plan*—Delightful!—*Subscriptions received at Joseph Beatson's, printer and bookseller; and by Rachael Hodges*—Odious name!—*at Mrs. Bertrand's.*"

"*Bartrand*!—There now *you*, do ye hear that? the lady lives at Mrs. Bartrand's: how will you make out now that Bartrand begins with a p, and ends with a t, now?" said the hackney-coachman to Betty, who was standing at the door.

"Pertrant! Why," cried Betty, "what would you have?"

"Silence! O silence!" said Miss Warwick; and she continued reading—"*Subscriptions received at Mrs. Bertrand's.*"

"Pertrant, you hear, plockhead, you Irishman!" cried Betty Williams.

"Bartrand—you have no ears, Welshwoman as you

[1] *Lord Chesterfield* Philip Dormer Stanhope, 4th Earl of Chesterfield, noted politician, wit, and orator (1694–1773).

[2] *meikle* Very.

[3] *blythe* Glad; happy.

[4] *Inverary* Inverary, Scotland.

[5] *plain … tale* Cf. Shakespeare's *Othello*, "I will a round unvarnish'd tale deliver" (1.3.90).

[6] *devil* Errand-boy; apprentice.

are!" retorted Terence O'Grady.

"Subscription two guineas, for the *Sorrows of Araminta*," continued our heroine; but, looking up, she saw Betty Williams and the hackney-coachman making menacing faces and gestures at one another.

"Fight it out in the passage, for Heaven's sake!" said Angelina; "if you must fight, fight out of my sight."

"For shame, before the young lady!" said Mr. Beatson, holding the hackney-coachman: "have done disputing so loud."

"I've done, but she is wrong," cried Terence.

"I've done, put he is wrong," said Betty.

Terence was so much provoked by the Welshwoman that he declared he would not carry her a step further in his coach—that his beasts were tired, and that he must be paid his fare, for that he neither could nor would wait any longer. Betty Williams was desired by Angelina to pay him. She hesitated; but after being assured by Miss Warwick that the debt should be punctually discharged in a few hours, she acknowledged that she had silver enough "in a little box at the bottom of her pocket;" and, after much fumbling, she pulled out a snuff-box, which, she said, had been given to her by her "creat crandmother." Whilst she was paying the coachman, the printer's devil observed one end of a piece of lace hanging out of her pocket; she had, by accident, pulled it out along with the snuff-box.

"And was this your great grandmother's too?" said the printer's devil, taking hold of the lace.

Betty started. Angelina was busy making inquiries from the printer, and she did not see or hear what was passing close to her: the coachman was intent upon the examination of his shillings. Betty, with great assurance, reproved the printer's devil for touching such lace with his plack fingers.

"'Twas not my crandmother's—'tis the young lady's," said she: "let it pe, pray—look how you have placked it, and marked it, with plack fingers."

She put the stolen lace hastily into her pocket, and immediately went out, as Miss Warwick desired, to call another coach.

Before we follow our heroine to Mrs. Bertrand's, we must beg leave to go, and, if we can, to transport our readers with us to Lady Frances Somerset's house at Clifton.

CHAPTER 4

"Well, how I am to get up this hill again, Heaven knows!" said Lady Diana Chillingworth, who had been prevailed upon to walk down Clifton Hill to the Wells.[1] "Heigho! That sister of mine, Lady Frances, walks, and talks, and laughs, and admires the beauties of nature till I'm half dead."

"Why, indeed, Lady Frances Somerset, I must allow," said Miss Burrage, "is not the fittest companion in the world for a person of your ladyship's nerves; but then it is to be hoped that the glass of water which you have just taken fresh at the pump will be of service, provided the racketing to Bristol to the play don't counteract it, and undo all again."

"How I dread going into that Bristol playhouse!" said Miss Burrage to herself—"some of my precious relations may be there to claim me. My aunt Dinah—God bless her for a starched Quaker—wouldn't be seen at a play, I'm sure—so she's safe—but the odious sugar-baker's daughters might be there, dizened out;[2] and between the acts their great tall figures might rise in judgment against me—spy me out—stare and curtsy—pop—pop—pop at me without mercy, or bawl out across the benches, 'Cousin Burrage! Cousin Burrage!' And Lady Diana Chillingworth to hear it! Oh, I should sink into the earth."

"What amusement," continued Miss Burrage, addressing herself to Lady Di, "what amusement Lady Frances Somerset can find at a Bristol playhouse, and at this time of the year too, is to me really unaccountable."

"I do suppose," replied Lady Diana, "that my sister goes only to please that child (Clara Hope, I think they call her)—not to please me, I'm sure; but what is she doing all this time in the pump-room?[3] Does she know we are waiting for her? Oh, here she comes. Frances, I am half dead."

"Half dead, my dear! well, here is something to bring you to life again," said Lady Frances: "I do believe I have found out Miss Warwick."

1 *Wells* The medicinal springs at Clifton, a spa near Bristol.

2 *dizened out* Decked out; adorned with finery.

3 *pump-room* Room in which medicinal waters are pumped in spas such as Clifton or Bath.

"I am sure, my dear, *that* does not revive me—I've been almost plagued to death with her already," said Lady Diana.

"There's no living in this world without plagues of some sort or other—but the pleasure of doing good makes one forget them all: here, look at this advertisement, my dear," said Lady Frances: "a gentleman whom I have just met with in the pump-room was reading it in the newspaper when I came in, and a whole knot of scandal-mongers were settling who it could possibly be. One snug little man, a Welsh curate, I believe, was certain it was the bar-maid of an inn at Bath, who is said to have inveigled a young nobleman into matrimony. I left the Welshman in the midst of a long story, about his father and a young lady who lost her shoe on the Welsh mountains, and I ran away with the paper to bring it to you."

Lady Diana received the paper with an air of reluctance.

"Was not I very fortunate to meet with it?" said Lady Frances.

"I protest I see no good fortune in the business, from beginning to end."

"Ah, because you are not come to the end yet—look— 'tis from Mrs. Hoel, of the inn at Cardiff, and, by the date, she must have been there last week."

"Who—Mrs. Hoel?"

"Miss Warwick, my dear—I beg pardon for my pronoun—but do read this—eyes—hair—complexion—age—size—it certainly must be Miss Warwick."

"And what then?" said Lady Di, with provoking coldness, walking on towards home.

"Why, then, my dear, you know we can go to Cardiff tomorrow morning, find the poor girl, and, before any body knows any thing of the matter, before her reputation is hurt, or you blamed, before any harm can happen, convince the girl of her folly and imprudence, and bring her back to you and common sense."

"To common sense, and welcome, if you can; but not to me."

"Not to you! Nay, but, my dear, what will become of her?"

"Nay, but, my dear Frances, what will the world say?"

"Of her?"

"Of me."

"My dear Di, shall I tell you what the world would say?"

"No, Lady Frances, I'll tell *you* what the world would say—that Lady Diana Chillingworth's house was an asylum for runaways."

"An asylum for nonsense! I beg your pardon, sister—but it always provokes me to see a person afraid to do what they think right, because, truly, 'the world will say it is wrong.' What signifies the uneasiness we may suffer from the idle blame or tittle-tattle of the day, compared with the happiness of a young girl's whole life, which is at stake?"

"Oh, Lady Frances, that is spoken like yourself—I love you in my heart—that's right! that's right!" thought Clara Hope.

Lady Diana fell back a few paces, that she might consult one whose advice she always found agreeable to her own opinions.

"In my opinion," whispered Miss Burrage to Lady Diana, "you are right, quite right, to have nothing more to do with the *happiness* of a young lady who has taken such a step."

They were just leaving St. Vincent's Parade when they heard the sound of music upon the walk by the river side, and they saw a little boy there, seated at the foot of a tree, playing on the guitar, and singing—

> "J'ai quitté mon pays et mes amis,
> Pour jouer de la guitare,
> Qui va clin, clin, qui va clin, clin,[1]
> Qui va clin, clin, clin, clin."

"Ha! my wee wee friend," said Clara Hope, "are you here? I was just thinking of you, just wishing for you. By gude luck, have you the weeny locket about you that the young lady gave you this morning? The weeny locket, my bonny boy?"

"Plait-il?" said little Louis.

"He *don't* understand one word," said Miss Burrage, laughing sarcastically, "he don't understand one word of all your *bonnys,* and *wee wees* and *weenies,* Miss Hope;

[1] *J'ai ... clin* French: "I've left my country and my friends, / To play the guitar, / Which goes clin, clin, which goes clin, clin."

he, unfortunately, don't understand broad Scotch, and maybe he mayn't be so great a proficient as you are in *boarding-school* French; but I'll try if he can understand *me*, if you'll tell me what you want."

"Such a trinket as this," said Clara, showing a locket which hung from her neck.

"Ah oui—yes, I comprehend now," cried the boy, taking from his coat-pocket a small case of trinkets—"la voila!—here is vat de young lady did give me—good young lady!" said Louis, and he produced the locket.

"I declare," exclaimed Miss Burrage, catching hold of it, "'tis Miss Warwick's locket! I'm sure of it—here's the motto—I've read it, and laughed at it twenty times—L'Amie Inconnue."

"When I heard you all talking just now about that description of the young lady in the newspaper, I cude not but fancy," said Clara Hope, "that the lady whom I saw this morning must be Miss Warwick."

"Saw—where?" cried Lady Frances, eagerly.

"At Bristol—at our academy—at Mrs. Porett's," said Clara; "but mark me, she is not there now—I do not ken where she may be now."

"Moi je sais![1]—I do know de demoiselle did stop in a coach at one house; I was in de street—I can show you de house."

"Can you so, my good little fellow? Then let us begone directly," said Lady Frances.

"You'll excuse me, sister," said Lady Di.

"Excuse you! *I* will, but *the world* will not. You'll be abused, sister, shockingly abused."

This assertion made more impression upon Lady Di Chillingworth than could have been made either by argument or entreaty.

"One really does not know how to act—people take so much notice of every thing that is said and done by persons of a certain rank: if you think that I shall be so much abused—I absolutely do not know what to say."

"But I thought," interposed Miss Burrage, "that Lady Frances was going to take you to the play tonight, Miss Hope?"

"Oh, never heed the play—never heed the play, or Clara Hope—never heed taking me to the play: Lady Frances is going to do a better thing.—Come on, my bonny boy," said she to the little French boy, who was following them.

[1] *Moi je sais* French: Me, I know.

We must now return to our heroine, whom we left on her way to Mrs. Bertrand's. Mrs. Bertrand kept a large confectionary and fruit shop in Bristol.

"Please to walk through this way, ma'am—Miss Hodges is above stairs—she shall be apprized directly—Jenny! run upstairs," said Mrs. Bertrand to her maid—"run upstairs, and tell Miss Hodges here's a young lady wants to see her in a great hurry—You'd best sit down, ma'am," continued Mrs. Bertrand to Angelina, "till the girl has been up with the message."

"Oh, my Araminta! how my heart beats!" exclaimed Miss Warwick.

"How my mouth waters!" cried Betty Williams, looking round at the fruit and confectionaries.

"Would you, ma'am, be pleased," said Mrs. Bertrand, "to take a glass of ice this warm evening? cream-ice, or water-ice, ma'am? pineapple or strawberry ice?" As she spoke, Mrs. Bertrand held a salver covered with ices toward Miss Warwick; but apparently she thought that it was not consistent with the delicacy of friendship to think of eating or drinking when she was thus upon the eve of her first interview with her Araminta. Betty Williams, who was of a different nature from our heroine, saw the salver recede with excessive surprise and regret; she stretched out her hand after it, and seized a glass of raspberry-ice; but no sooner had she tasted it than she made a frightful face and let the glass fall, exclaiming—"Pless us! 'tis not as good as cooseberry fool." Mrs. Bertrand next offered her a cheesecake, which Betty ate voraciously.

"She's actually a female Sancho Panza!" thought Angelina: her own more striking resemblance to the female Quixote[2] never occurred to our heroine—so blind are we to our own failings.

"Who is the young lady?" whispered the mistress of the fruit shop to Betty Williams, whilst Miss Warwick was walking—we should say *pacing*—up and down the room, in *anxious solicitude, and evident agitation.*

"Hur's a young lady," replied Betty, stopping to take a mouthful of cheesecake between every member of her

[2] *female Sancho ... Quixote* Reference to Spanish novelist Miguel de Cervantes's novel *Don Quixote* (1615), in which the hero—whose romantic ideals and beliefs come directly from romance novels—travels the world with his companion, Sancho Panza.

sentence, "a young lady—that has—lost hur—"

"Her heart—so I thought."

"Hur purse!" said Betty, with an accent which showed that she thought this the more serious loss of the two.

"Her purse! That's bad indeed—you pay for your own cheesecake and raspberry-ice, and for the glass that you broke," said Mrs. Bertrand.

"Put hur has a great deal of money in hur trunk, I pelieve, at Llanwaetur," said Betty.

"Surely Miss Hodges does not know I am here," cried Miss Warwick—"her Angelina!"

"Ma'am, she'll be down immediately, I do suppose," said Mrs. Bertrand. "What was it you pleased called for—angelica,[1] ma'am, did you say? At present we are quite out, I'm ashamed to say, of angelica, ma'am—Well, child," continued Mrs. Bertrand to her maid, who was at this moment seen passing by the back door of the shop in great haste.

"Ma'am—anan," said the maid, turning back her cap from off her ear.

"Anan! deaf doll! didn't you hear me tell you to tell Miss Hodges a lady wanted to speak to her in a great hurry?"

"No, mam," replied the girl, who spoke in the broad Somersetshire dialect: "I heard you zay, *up to Miss Hodges*; zoo I thought it was the bottle o'brandy, and zoo I took alung with the tea-kettle—but I'll go up again now, and zay miss bes in a hurry, az she zays."

"Brandy!" repeated Miss Warwick, on whom the word seemed to make a great impression.

"Pranty, ay, pranty," repeated Betty Williams—"our Miss Hodges always takes pranty in her teas at Llanwaetur."

"Brandy! Then she can't be my Araminta."

"Oh, the very same, and no other; you are quite right, ma'am," said Mrs. Bertrand, "if you mean the same that is publishing the novel, ma'am—*The Sorrows of Araminta*—for the reason I know so much about it is that I take in the subscriptions, and distributed the *pur*posals."

Angelina had scarcely time to believe or disbelieve what she heard before the maid returned with, "Mam, Mizz Hodges haz hur best love to you, mizz—and please to walk up—There be two steps; please to have a care, or you'll break your neck."

Before we introduce Angelina to her "unknown friend," we must relate the conversation which was actually passing between the amiable Araminta and her Orlando, whilst Miss Warwick was waiting in the fruit shop. Our readers will be so good as to picture to themselves a woman with a face and figure which seemed to have been intended for a man, with a voice and gesture capable of setting even man, "imperial man," at defiance—such was Araminta. She was, at this time, sitting cross-legged in an arm-chair at a tea-table, on which, beside the tea equipage, was a medley of things of which no prudent tongue or pen would undertake to give a correct inventory. At the feet of this fair lad, kneeling on one knee, was a thin, subdued, simple-looking Quaker of the name of Nathaniel Gazabo.

"But now, Natty," said Miss Hodges, in a voice more masculine than her looks, "you understand the conditions—If I give you my hand, and make you my husband, it is upon condition that you never contradict any of my opinions: do you promise me that?"

"Yea, verily," replied Nat.

"And you promise to leave me entirely at liberty to act, as well as to think, in all things as my own independent understanding shall suggest?"

"Yea, verily," was the man's response.

"And you will be guided by me in all things?"

"Yea, verily."

"And you will love and admire me all your life, as much as you do now?"

"Yea, verily."

"Swear," said the unconscionable woman.

"Nay, verily," replied the meekest of men, "I cannot swear, my Rachel, being a Quaker; but I will affirm."

"Swear, swear," cried the lady, in an imperious tone, "or I will never be your Araminta."

"I swear," said Nat Gazabo, in a timid voice.

"Then, Natty, I consent to be Mrs. Hodges Gazabo. Only remember always to call me your dear Araminta."

"My dear Araminta! Thus," said he, embracing her, "thus let me thank thee, my dear Araminta!"

It was in the midst of these thanks that the maid interrupted the well-matched pair with the news that a

[1] *angelica* Candied angelica, a confection made from the plant of that name.

young lady was below, who was in a great hurry to see Miss Hodges.

"Let her come," said Miss Hodges; "I suppose it is only one of the Miss Carvers—Don't stir, Nat; it will vex her to see you kneeling to me—don't stir, I say—"

"Where is she? Where is my Araminta?" cried Miss Warwick as the maid was trying to open the outer passage-door for her, which had a bad lock.

"Get up, get up, Natty; and get some fresh water in the tea-kettle—quick!" cried Miss Hodges, and she began to clear away some of the varieties of literature, &c, which lay scattered about the room. Nat, in obedience to her commands, was making his exit with all possible speed, when Angelina entered, exclaiming—

"My amiable Araminta! My unknown friend!"

"My Angelina! My charming Angelina!" cried Miss Hodges.

Miss Hodges was not the sort of person our heroine expected to see—and to conceal the panic with which the first sight of her unknown friend struck her disappointed imagination, she turned back to listen to the apologies which Nat Gazabo was pouring forth about his awkwardness and the tea-kettle.

"Turn, Angelina, ever dear!" cried Miss Hodges, with the tone and action of a bad actress who is rehearsing an embrace—"Turn, Angelina, ever dear! Thus, thus let us meet, to part no more."

"But her voice is so loud," said Angelina to herself, "and her looks so vulgar, and there is such a smell of brandy! How unlike the elegant delicacy I had expected in my unknown friend!" Miss Warwick involuntarily shrunk from the stifling embrace.

"You are overpowered, my Angelina—lean on me," said her Araminta.

Nat Gazabo re-entered with the tea-kettle—

"Here's *boiling* water, and we'll have fresh tea in a trice—the young lady's over-tired, seemingly—Here's a chair, miss, here's a chair," cried Nat. Miss Warwick *sunk* upon the chair: Miss Hodges seated herself beside her, continuing to address her in a theatrical tone.

"This moment is bliss unutterable! My kind, my noble-minded Angelina, thus to leave all your friends for your Araminta!"—suddenly changing her voice—"Set the tea-kettle, Nat!"

"Who is this Nat, I wonder?" thought Miss Warwick. "Well, and tell me," said Miss Hodges, whose attention was awkwardly divided between the ceremonies of making tea and making speeches—"and tell me, my Angelina—That's water enough, Nat—and tell me, my Angelina, how did you find me out?"

"With some difficulty, indeed, *my Araminta*." Miss Warwick could hardly pronounce the words.

"So kind, so noble-minded," continued Miss Hodges—"and did you receive my last letter—three sheets? And how did you contrive—Stoop the kettle, *do*, Nat."

"Oh, this odious Nat! How I wish she would send him away!" thought Miss Warwick.

"And tell me, my Araminta—my Angelina I mean—how did you contrive your elopement—and how did you escape from the eye of your aristocratic Argus[1]—how did you escape from all your unfeeling persecutors? Tell me, tell me all your adventures, my Angelina! Butter the toast, Nat," said Miss Hodges, who was cutting bread and butter, which she did not do with the celebrated grace of Charlotte, in the *Sorrows of Werter*.[2]

"I'll tell you all, my Araminta," whispered Miss Warwick, "when we are by ourselves."

"Oh, never mind Nat," whispered Miss Hodges.

"Couldn't you tell him," rejoined Miss Warwick, "that he need not wait any longer?"

"*Wait*, my dear! Why, what do you take him for?"

"Why, is not he your footman?" whispered Angelina.

"My footman!—Nat!" exclaimed Miss Hodges, bursting out a laughing, "My Angelina took you for my footman."

"Good heavens! What is he?" said Angelina, in a low voice.

"Verily," said Nat Gazabo, with a sort of bashful simple laugh, "verily, I am the humblest of her servants."

"And does my Angelina—spare my delicacy," said Miss Hodges—"does my Angelina not remember, in any of my long letters, the name of—Orlando!—There he stands."

[1] *Argus* Many-eyed creature of Greek mythology, in one account commanded by Hera, Zeus's wife, to watch over Zeus's mistress Io.

[2] *Charlotte ... Sorrows of Werter* Heroine of novel by German writer Johann Wolfgang van Goethe (1774).

"Orlando! Is this gentleman your Orlando, of whom I have heard so much?"

"He! he! he!" simpered Nat. "I am Orlando, of whom you have heard so much; and she (pointing to Miss Hodges)—she is, tomorrow morning, God willing, to be Mistress Hodges Gazabo."

"Mrs. Hodges Gazabo, my Araminta!" said Angelina, with astonishment which she could not suppress.

"Yes, my Angelina: so end "The Sorrows of Araminta" —Another cup? Do I make the tea too sweet?" said Miss Hodges, whilst Nat handed the bread and butter to the ladies officiously.

"The man looks like a fool," thought Miss Warwick.

"Set down the bread and butter and be quiet, Nat—Then, as soon as the wedding is over, we fly, my Angelina, to our charming cottage in Wales—there may we bid defiance to the storms of fate—

'The world forgetting, by the world forgot.'"

"That," said Angelina, "'is the blameless vestal's lot':[1] but you forget that you are to be married, my Araminta; and you forget that, in your letter of three folio sheets, you said not one word to me of this intended marriage."

"Nay, my dear, blame me not for a want of confidence, that my heart disclaims," said Miss Hodges: "from the context of my letters, you must have suspected the progress my Orlando had made in my affections; but, indeed, I should not have brought myself to decide apparently so precipitately, had it not been for the opposition, the persecution of my friends —I was determined to show them that I know, and can assert, my right to think and act, upon all occasions, for myself."

Longer, much longer, Miss Hodges, spoke in the most peremptory voice; but whilst she was declaiming on her favourite topic, her Angelina was "revolving in her altered mind" the strange things which she had seen and heard in the course of the last half-hour; every thing appeared to her in a new light; when she compared the conversation and conduct of Miss Hodges with the sentimental letters of her Araminta; when she compared Orlando in description to Orlando in reality, she could scarcely believe her senses: accustomed as she had been to elegance of manners, the vulgarity and awkwardness of Miss Hodges shocked and disgusted her beyond measure. The disorder, and—for the words must be said—slatternly dirty appearance of her Araminta's dress, and of every thing in her apartment, were such as would have made a hell of heaven; and the idea of spending her life in a cottage with Mrs. Hodges Gazabo and Nat overwhelmed our heroine with the double fear of wretchedness and ridicule.

"Another cup of tea, my Angelina?" said Miss Hodges, when she had finished her tirade against her persecutors—that is to say, her friends, "another cup, my Angelina?—do, after your journey and fatigue, take another cup."

"No more, I thank you."

"Then reach me that tragedy, Nat—you know—"

"Your own tragedy, is it, my dear?" said he.

"Ah, Nat, now! you never can keep a secret," said Miss Hodges. "I wanted to have surprised my Angelina."

"I am surprised!" thought Angelina—"oh, how much surprised!"

"I have a motto for our cottage here somewhere," said Miss Hodges, turning over the leaves of her tragedy—"but I'll keep that till tomorrow—since tomorrow's the day sacred to love and friendship."

Nat, by way of showing his joy in a becoming manner, rubbed his hands and hummed a tune. His mistress frowned and bit her lips; but the signals were lost upon him, and he sung out, in an exulting tone—

When the lads of the village so merrily, ah!
Sound their tabours,[2] I'll hand thee along.

"Fool! Dolt! Idiot!" cried his Araminta, rising furious—"out of my sight!" Then, sinking down upon the chair, she burst into tears and threw herself into the arms of her pale, astonished Angelina. "Oh, my Angelina!" she exclaimed, "I am the most ill-matched! most unfortunate! most wretched of women!"

[1] *The world ... lot* Cf. Alexander Pope's "Eloisa to Abelard" (1717): "How happy is the blameless vestal's lot! / The world forgetting, by the world forgot" (207–08).

[2] *tabours* Drums.

"Don't be frighted, miss," said Nat; "she'll come to again presently—'tis only *her way.*" As he spoke, he poured out a bumper[1] of brandy and, kneeling, presented it to his mistress. "'Tis the only thing in life does her good," continued he, "in this sort of fits."

"Heavens, what a scene!" said Miss Warwick to herself—"and the woman so heavy, I can scarce support her weight—and is this *my unknown friend*?"

How long Miss Hodges would willingly have continued to sob upon Miss Warwick's shoulder, or how long that shoulder could possibly have sustained her weight, is a mixed problem in physics and metaphysics, which must for ever remain unsolved: but suddenly a loud scream was heard. Miss Hodges started up—the door was thrown open, and Betty Williams rushed in, crying loudly—"Oh, shave me! shave me! for the love of Cot, shave me, miss!" and, pushing by the swain,[2] who held the unfinished glass of brandy in his hand, she threw herself on her knees at the feet of Angelina.

"Gracious me!" exclaimed Nat, "whatever you are, you need not push one so."

"What now, Betty Williams? is the wench mad or drunk?" cried Miss Hodges.

"We are to have a mad scene next, I suppose," said Miss Warwick, calmly—"I am prepared for every thing, after what I have seen."

Betty Williams continued crying bitterly, and wringing her hands—"Oh, shave me this once, miss! 'tis the first thing of the kind I ever tid, inteet, inteet! Oh, shave me this once—I tid not know it was worth so much as a shilling, and that I could be hanged, inteet—and I—"

Here Betty was interrupted by the entrance of Mrs. Puffit, the milliner, the printer's devil, and a stern-looking man, to whom Mrs. Puffit, as she came in, said, pointing to Betty Williams and Miss Warwick, "There they are—do your duty, Mr. Constable: I'll swear to my lace."

"And I'll swear to my black thumbs," said the printer's devil. "I saw the lace hanging out of her pocket, and there's the marks of my fingers upon it, Mr. Constable."

"Fellow!" cried Miss Hodges, taking the constable by the arm, "this is my apartment, into which no minion of the law has a right to enter; for, in England, every man's house is his castle."

"I know that as well as you do, *madam*!" said the constable; "but I make it a principle to do nothing without a warrant—here's my warrant."

"Oh, shave me! the lace is hers inteet!" cried Betty Williams, pointing to Miss Warwick. "Oh, miss is my mistress inteet—"

"Come, mistress or miss, then, you'll be pleased to come along with me," said the constable, seizing hold of Angelina—"like mistress, like maid."

"Villain! unfeeling villain! Oh, unhand my Angelina, or I shall die! I shall die!" exclaimed Araminta, falling into the arms of Nat Gazabo, who immediately held the replenished glass of brandy to her lips—"Oh, my Angelina, my Angelina!"

Struck with horror at her situation, Miss Warwick shrunk from the grasp of the constable and leaned motionless on the back of a chair.

"Come, my angel, as they call you, I think—the lady there has brandy enough, if you want spirits—all the fits and faintings in Christendom won't serve you now. I'm used to the tricks o' the trade. The law must take its course; and if you can't walk, I must carry you."

"Touch me at your peril! I am innocent," said Angelina.

"Innocent—innocence itself! Pure, spotless, injured innocence!" cried Miss Hodges. "I shall die! I shall die! I shall die on the spot! Barbarous, barbarous villain!"

Whilst Miss Hodges spoke, the ready Nat poured out a fresh glass of that restorative, which he always had ready for cases of life and death; and she screamed and sipped, and sipped and screamed, as the constable took up Angelina in his arms and carried her towards the door.

"Mrs. Innocence," said the man, "you shall see whom you shall see."

Mrs. Puffit opened the door; and, to the utter astonishment of every body present, Lady Diana Chillingworth entered the room, followed by Lady Frances Somerset and Mrs. Bertrand. The constable set down Angelina. Miss Hodges set down the glass of brandy. Mrs. Puffit curtsied. Betty Williams stretched

[1] *bumper* Full cup.

[2] *swain* Country gallant; lover.

out her arms to Lady Diana, crying, "Shave me! shave me this once!" Miss Warwick hid her face with her hands.

"Only my Valenciennes lace, that has been found in that girl's pocket, and—" said Mrs. Puffit.

Lady Diana Chillingworth turned away with indescribable haughtiness, and, addressing herself to her sister, said, "Lady Frances Somerset, you would not, I presume, have Lady Diana Chillingworth lend her countenance to such a scene as this—I hope, sister, that you are satisfied now." As she said these words, her ladyship walked out of the room.

"Never was further from being satisfied in my life," said Lady Frances.

"If you look at this, my lady," said the constable, holding out the lace, "you'll soon be satisfied as to what sort of a young lady *that* is."

"Oh, you mistake the young lady," said Mrs. Bertrand, and she whispered to the constable. "Come away: you may be sure you'll be satisfied—we shall all be satisfied, handsomely, all in good time. Don't let the *delinquency* there on her knees," added she aloud, pointing to Betty Williams—"don't let the *delinquency* there on her knees escape."

"Come along, mistress," said the constable, pulling up Betty Williams from her knees. "But I say the law must have its course, if I am not satisfied."

"Oh, I am confident," said Mrs. Puffit, the milliner, "we shall all be satisfied, no doubt; but Lady Di Chillingworth knows my Valenciennes lace, and Miss Burrage too, for they did me this morning the honour—"

"Will you do me the favour," interrupted Lady Frances Somerset, "to leave us, good Mrs. Puffit, for the present? Here is some mistake—the less noise we make about it the better. You shall be satisfied."

"Oh, your ladyship—I'm sure, I'm confident—I sha'n't utter another syllable—nor never would have articulated a syllable about the lace (though Valenciennes, and worth thirty guineas if it is worth a farthing), had I had the least intimacy or suspicion the young lady was your la'ship's protégée. I sha'n't, at any rate, utter another syllable."

Mrs. Puffit, having glibly run off this speech, left the room, and carried in her train the constable and Betty Williams, the printer's devil, and Mrs. Bertrand, the woman of the house.

Miss Warwick, whose confusion during this whole scene was excessive, stood without power to speak or move.

"Thank God, they are gone!" said Lady Frances; and she went to Angelina, and taking her hands gently from before her face, said, in a soothing tone, "Miss Warwick, your friend, Lady Frances Somerset, you cannot think that she suspects—"

"La, dear, no!" cried Nat Gazabo, who had now sufficiently recovered from his fright and amazement to be able to speak: "Dear heart! Who could go for to suspect such a thing? But they made such a bustle and noise, they quite flabbergasted me, so *maany* on them in this small room. Please to sit down, my lady. Is there any thing I can do?"

"If you could have the goodness, sir, to leave us for a few minutes," said Lady Frances, in a polite, persuasive manner—"if you could have the goodness, sir, to leave us for a few minutes."

Nat, who was not *always* spoken to by so gentle a voice, smiled, bowed, and was retiring, when Miss Hodges came forward with an air of defiance: "Aristocratic insolence!" exclaimed she: "Stop, Nat—stir not a foot, at your peril, at the word of command of any of the privileged orders upon earth—stir not a foot, at your peril, at the behest of any titled *She* in the universe! Madam, or my lady—or by whatever other name more high, more low, you choose to be addressed—this is my husband."

"Very probably, madam," said Lady Frances, with an easy calmness, which provoked Miss Hodges to a louder tone of indignation.

"Stir not a foot, at your peril, Nat," cried she. "I will defend him, I say, madam, against every shadow, every penumbra of aristocratic insolence."

"As you and he think proper, madam," replied Lady Frances. "'Tis easy to defend the gentleman against shadows."

Miss Hodges marched up and down the room with her arms folded. Nat stood stock still.

"The woman," whispered Lady Frances to Miss Warwick, "is either mad or drunk—or both; at all events we shall be better in another room." As she spoke, she drew Miss Warwick's arm within hers. "Will you allow aristocratic insolence to pass by you, sir?" said she to Nat Gazabo, who stood like a statue in the doorway—he edged himself aside.

"And is this your independence of soul, my Angelina?" cried Araminta, setting her back to the door, so as effectually to prevent her from passing—"and is this your independence of soul, my Angelina—thus, thus tamely to submit, to resign yourself again to your unfeeling, proud, prejudiced, intellect-lacking persecutors?"

"This lady is *my friend*, madam," said Angelina, in as firm and tranquil a tone as she could command, for she was quite terrified by her Araminta's violence.

"Take your choice, my dear; stay or follow me, as you think best," said Lady Frances.

"Your friend!" pursued the oratorical lady, detaining Miss Warwick with a heavy hand: "Do you feel the force of the word? *Can* you feel it, as I once thought you could? Your friend! Am not *I* your friend, your best friend, my Angelina? Your own Araminta, your amiable Araminta, your *unknown friend?*"

"My *unknown* friend, indeed!" said Angelina. Miss Hodges let go her struggling hand, and Miss Warwick that instant followed Lady Frances, who, having effected her retreat, had by this time gained the staircase.

"Gone!" cried Miss Hodges; "then never will I see or speak to her more. Thus I whistle her off, and let her down the wind to prey at fortune."

"Gracious heart! what quarrels," said Nat, "and doings, the night before our wedding day!"

We leave this well-matched pair to their happy prospects of conjugal union and equality.

Lady Frances, who perceived that Miss Warwick was scarcely able to support herself, led her to a sofa, which she luckily saw through the half-open door of a drawing-room at the head of the staircase.

"To be taken for a thief! Oh, to what have I exposed myself!" said Miss Warwick.

"Sit down, my dear, now we are in a room where we need not fear interruption—sit down, and don't tremble like an aspen leaf," said Lady Frances Somerset, who saw that at this moment reproaches would have been equally unnecessary and cruel.

Unused to be treated with judicious kindness, Angelina's heart was deeply touched by it, and she opened her whole mind to Lady Frances, with the frankness of a young person conscious of her own folly, not desirous to apologize or extenuate, but anxious to regain the esteem of a friend.

"To be sure, my dear, it was, as you say, rather foolish to set out in quest of an *unknown friend*," said Lady Frances, after listening to the confessions of Angelina. "And why, after all, was it necessary to have an elopement?"

"Oh, madam, I am sensible of my folly—I had long formed a project of living in a cottage in Wales—and Miss Burrage described Wales to me as a terrestrial paradise."

"Miss Burrage! Then why did she not go to paradise along with you?" said Lady Frances.

"I don't know—she was so much attached to Lady Di Chillingworth, she said, she could never think of leaving her: she charged me never to mention the cottage scheme to Lady Di, who would only laugh at it. Indeed, Lady Di was almost always out whilst we were in London, or dressing, or at cards, and I could seldom speak to her, especially about cottages; and I wished for a friend, to whom I could open my whole heart, and whom I could love and esteem, and who should have the same tastes and notions with myself."

"I am sorry that last condition is part of your definition of a friend," said Lady Frances, smiling; "for I will not swear that my notions are the same as yours, but yet I think you would have found me as good a friend as this Araminta of yours. Was it necessary to perfect felicity to have *an unknown friend*?"

"Ah! there was my mistake," said Miss Warwick. "I had read Araminta's writings, and they speak so charmingly of friendship and felicity, that I thought 'Those best can paint them who can feel them most.'"

"No uncommon mistake," said Lady Frances.

"But I am fully sensible of my folly," said Angelina.

"Then there is no occasion to say any more about it at present—tomorrow, as you like romances, we'll read *Arabella, or the Female Quixote*;[1] and you shall tell me which, of all your acquaintance, the heroine resembles most. And in the mean time, as you seem to have

[1] *Arabella … Quixote* *The Female Quixote, or the Adventures of Arabella* (1752), by English author Charlotte Lennox.

satisfied your curiosity about your *unknown friend*, will you come home with me?"

"Oh, madam," said Angelina, with emotion, "your goodness—"

"But we have not time to talk of my goodness yet—stay—let me see—yes, it will be best that it should be known that you are with us as soon as possible—for there is a thing, my dear, of which, perhaps, you are not fully sensible—of which you are too young to be fully sensible—that, to people who have nothing to do or to say, scandal is a necessary luxury of life; and that, by such a step as you have taken, you have given room enough for scandal-mongers to make you and your friends completely miserable."

Angelina burst into tears—though a sentimental lady, she had not yet acquired the art of *bursting into tears* upon every trifling occasion. Hers were tears of real feeling. Lady Frances was glad to see that she had made a sufficient impression upon her mind; but she assured Angelina that she did not intend to torment her with useless lectures and reproaches. Lady Frances Somerset understood the art of giving advice rather better than Lady Diana Chillingworth.

"*I* do not mean, my dear," said Lady Frances, "to make you miserable for life—but I mean to make an impression upon you that may make you prudent and happy for life. So don't cry till you make your eyes so red as not to be fit to be seen at the play tonight, where they must—positively—be seen."

"But Lady Diana is below," said Miss Warwick: "I am ashamed and afraid to see her again."

"It will be difficult, but I hope not impossible, to convince my sister," said Lady Frances, "that you clearly understand that you have been a simpleton; but that a simpleton of sixteen is more an object of mercy than a simpleton of sixty—so my verdict is—Guilty; but recommended to mercy."

By this mercy Angelina was more touched than she could have been by the most severe reproaches.

Chapter 5

Whilst the preceding conversation was passing, Lady Diana Chillingworth was in Mrs. Bertrand's fruit-shop, occupied with her smelling-bottle and Miss Burrage. Clara Hope was there also, and Mrs. Puffit, the milliner, and Mrs. Bertrand, who was assuring her ladyship that not a word of the affair about the young lady and the lace should go out of her house.

"Your la'ship need not be in the least uneasy," said Mrs. Bertrand, "for I have satisfied the constable, and satisfied every body; and the constable allows Miss Warwick's name was not mentioned in the warrant; and as to the servant girl, she's gone before the magistrate, who, of course, will send her to the house of correction; but that will no ways implicate the young lady, and nothing shall transpire from this house detrimental to the young lady, who is under your la'ship's protection. And I'll tell your la'ship how Mrs. Puffit and I have settled to tell the story: with your ladyship's approbation, I shall say—"

"Nothing, if you please," said her ladyship, with more than her usual haughtiness. "The young lady to whom you allude is under Lady Frances Somerset's protection, not mine; and whatever you do or say, I beg that in this affair the name of Lady Diana Chillingworth may not be used."

She turned her back upon the disconcerted milliner as she finished this speech, and walked to the furthest end of the long room, followed by the constant flatterer of all her humours, Miss Burrage.

The milliner and Mrs. Bertrand now began to console themselves for the mortification they had received from her ladyship's pride, and for the insolent forgetfulness of her companion, by abusing them both in a low voice. Mrs. Bertrand began with, "Her ladyship's so touchy and so proud; she's as high as the moon, and higher."

"Oh, all the Chillingworths, by all accounts, are so," said Mrs. Puffit; "but then, to he sure, they have a right to be so if any body has, for they certainly are real high-born people. But I can't tolerate to see some people, that aren't no ways born nor entitled to it, give themselves such airs as some people do. Now, there's that Miss Burrage, that pretends not to know me, ma'am."

"And me, ma'am—just the same. Such provoking assurance—I that knew her from this high."

"On St. Augustin's Back, you know," said Mrs. Puffit.

"On St. Augustin's Back, you know," echoed Mrs.

Bertrand.

"So I told her this morning, ma'am," said Mrs. Puffit.

"And so I told her this evening, ma'am, when the three Miss Herrings came in to give me a call in their way to the play; girls that she used to walk with, ma'am, for ever and ever in the green, you know."

"Yes; and that she was always glad to drink tea with, ma'am, when asked, you know," said Mrs. Puffit.

"Well, ma'am," pursued Mrs. Bertrand, "here she had the impudence to pretend not to know them. She takes up her glass—my Lady Di herself couldn't have done it better, and squeezes up her ugly face this way, pretending to be nearsighted, though she can see as well as you or I can."

"Such airs! *She* near-sighted!" said Mrs. Puffit: "what will the world come to!"

"Oh, I wish her pride may have a fall," resumed the provoked milliner, as soon as she had breath. "I dare to say now she wouldn't know her own relations if she was to meet them; I'd lay any wager she would not vouchsafe a curtsy to that good old John Barker, the friend of her father, you know, who gave up to this Miss Burrage I don't know how many hundreds of pounds that were due to him, or else miss wouldn't have had a farthing in the world; yet now, I'll be bound, she'd forget this as well as St. Augustin's Back, and wouldn't know John Barker from Abraham; and I don't doubt that she'd pull out her glass at her aunt Dinah, because she is a cheesemonger's widow."

"Oh no," said Mrs. Bertrand, "she couldn't have the baseness to be near-sighted to good Dinah Plait, that bred her up and was all in all to her."

Just as Mrs. Bertrand finished speaking, into the fruit-shop walked the very persons of whom she had been talking—Dinah Plait and Mr. Barker.

"Mrs. Dinah Plait, I declare!" exclaimed Mrs. Bertrand.

"I never was so glad to see you, Mrs. Plait and Mr. Barker, in all my days," said Mrs. Puffit.

"Why you should be so particularly glad to see me, Mrs. Puffit, I don't know," said Mr. Barker, laughing; "but I'm not surprised Dinah Plait should be a welcome guest wherever she goes, especially with a purse full of guineas in her hand."

"Friend Bertrand," said Dinah Plait, producing a purse which she held under her cloak, "I am come to restore this purse to its rightful owner: after a great deal of trouble, John Barker (who never thinks it a trouble to do good) hath traced her to your house."

"There is a young lady here, to be sure," said Mrs. Bertrand, "but you can't see her just at present, for she is talking on *petticlar* business with my Lady Frances Somerset above stairs."

"'Tis well," said Dinah Plait: "I would willingly restore this purse, not to the young creature herself, but to some of her friends—for I fear she is not quite in a right state of mind. If I could see any of the young lady's friends."

"Miss Burrage," cried Mrs. Bertrand, in a tone of voice so loud that she could not avoid hearing it, "are not you one of the young lady's friends?"

"What young lady's friend?" replied Miss Burrage, without stirring from her seat.

"Miss Burrage, here's a purse for a young lady," said Mrs. Puffit.

"A purse for whom? Where?" said Miss Burrage, at last deigning to rise and come out of her recess.

"There, ma'am," said the milliner. "Now for her glass!" whispered Mrs. Puffit to Mrs. Bertrand. And, exactly as it had been predicted, Miss Burrage eyed her aunt Dinah through her glass, pretending not to know her. "The purse is not mine," said she, coolly: "I know nothing of it—nothing."

"Hetty!" exclaimed her aunt; but as Miss Burrage still eyed her through her glass with unmoved invincible assurance, Dinah thought that, however strong the resemblance, she was mistaken. "No, it can't be Hetty. I beg pardon, madam," said she, "but I took you for—Did not I hear you say the name of Burrage, friend Puffit?"

"Yes, Burrage; one of the Burrages of Dorsetshire," said the milliner, with malicious archness.

"One of the Burrages of Dorsetshire: I beg pardon. But did you ever see such a likeness, friend Barker, to my poor niece, Hetty Burrage?"

Miss Burrage, who overheard these words, immediately turned her back upon her aunt. "A grotesque statue of starch—one of your Quakers, I think, they call themselves: Bristol is full of such primitive figures," said

Miss Burrage to Clara Hope, and she walked back to the recess and to Lady Di.

"So like, voice and all, to my poor Hester," said Dinah Plait, and she wiped the tears from her eyes. "Though Hetty has neglected me so of late, I have a tenderness for her; we cannot but have some for our own relations."

"Grotesque or not, 'tis a statue that seems to have a heart, and a gude one," said Clara Hope.

"I wish we could say the same of every body," said Mrs. Bertrand.

All this time, old Mr. Barker, leaning on his cane, had been silent: "Burrage of Dorsetshire!" said he; "I'll soon see whether she be or no; for Hetty has a wart on her chin that I cannot forget, let her forget whom and what she pleases."

Mr. Barker, who was a plain-spoken, determined man, followed the young lady to the recess; and, after looking her full in the face, exclaimed in a loud voice, "Here's the wart!—'tis Hetty!"

"Sir!—wart!—man!—Lady Di!" cried Miss Burrage, in accents of the utmost distress and vexation.

Mr. Barker, regardless of her frowns and struggles, would by no means relinquish her hand; but leading, or rather pulling her forwards, he went on with barbarous steadiness: "Dinah," said he, "'tis your own niece. Hetty, 'tis your own aunt, that bred you up! What, struggle—Burrage of Dorsetshire!"

"There certainly," said Lady Diana Chillingworth in a solemn tone, "is a conspiracy, this night, against my poor nerves. These people, amongst them, will infallibly surprise me to death. What is the matter now? Why do you drag the young lady, sir? She came here with *me*, sir—with Lady Diana Chillingworth; and, consequently, she is not a person to be insulted."

"Insult her!" said Mr. Barker, whose sturdy simplicity was not to be baffled or disconcerted either by the cunning of Miss Burrage or by the imposing manner and awful name of Lady Diana Chillingworth. "Insult her! why, 'tis she insults us; she won't know us."

"How should Miss Burrage know you, sir, or any body here?" said Lady Diana, looking round as if upon beings of a species different from her own.

"How should she know her own aunt that bred her up?" said the invincible John Barker, "and me who have had her on my knee a hundred times, giving her barley-sugar till she was sick?"

"Sick! I am sure you make me sick," said Lady Diana. "Sir, that young lady is one of the Burrages of Dorsetshire, as good a family as any in England."

"Madam," said John Barker, replying in a solemnity of tone equal to her ladyship's, "that young lady is one of the Burrages of Bristol, drysalters;[1] niece to Dinah Plait, who is widow to a man who was, in his time, as honest a cheesemonger as any in England."

"Miss Burrage! My God!—don't you speak!" cried Lady Diana in a voice of terror.

"The young lady is bashful, my lady, among strangers," said Mrs. Bertrand.

"Oh, Hester Burrage, is this kind of thee?" said Dinah Plait, with an accent of mixed sorrow and affection; "but thou art my niece, and I forgive thee."

"A cheesemonger's niece!" cried Lady Diana with horror; "how have I been deceived! But this is the consequence of making acquaintance at Buxton, and those watering-places: I've done with her, however. Lord bless me! Here comes my sister, Lady Frances! Good heavens! My dear," continued her ladyship, going to meet her sister, and drawing her into the recess at the farthest end of the room, "here are more misfortunes—misfortunes without end. What will the world say? Here's this Miss Burrage—take no more notice of her, sister; she's an impostor; who do you think she turns out to be? Daughter to a drysalter, niece to a cheesemonger! Only conceive!—a person that has been going about with *me* everywhere! What will the world say?"

"That it is very imprudent to have *unknown friends*, my dear," replied Lady Frances. "The best thing you can possibly do is to say nothing about the matter, and to receive this penitent ward of yours without reproaches; for if you talk of her *unknown friends*, the world will certainly talk of yours."

Lady Diana drew back with haughtiness when her sister offered to put Miss Warwick's hands into hers; but she condescended to say, after an apparent struggle with herself, "I am happy to hear, Miss Warwick, that you have returned to your senses. Lady Frances takes you under her protection, I understand; at which, for all our

[1] *drysalters* Dealers in dyes and chemicals.

sakes, I rejoice; and I have only one piece of advice, Miss Warwick, to give you—"

"Keep it till after the play, my dear Diana," whispered Lady Frances; "it will have more effect."

"The play! Bless me!" said Lady Diana, "why, you have contrived to make Miss Warwick fit to be seen, I protest. But, after all I have gone through tonight, how can I appear in public? My dear, this Miss Burrage's business has given me such a shock—such nervous affections!"

"Nervous affections! Some people, I do believe, have none but nervous affections," thought Lady Frances.

"Permit me," said Mrs. Dinah Plait, coming up to Lady Frances and presenting Miss Warwick's purse—"permit me, as thou seemest to be a friend to this young lady, to restore to thee her purse, which she left by mistake at my house this forenoon. I hope she is better, poor thing!"

"She *is* better, and I thank you for her, madam," said Lady Frances, who was struck with the obliging manner and benevolent countenance of Dinah Plait, and who did not think herself contaminated by standing in the same room with the widow of a cheesemonger.

"Let me thank you myself, madam," said Angelina; "I am perfectly in my senses *now*, I can assure you; and I shall never forget the kindness which you and this benevolent gentleman showed me when you thought I was in real distress."

"Some people are more grateful than other people," said Mrs. Puffit, looking at Miss Burrage, who in mortified, sullen silence, followed the aunt and the benefactor of whom she was ashamed, and who had reason to be ashamed of her.

We do not imagine that our readers can be much interested for a young lady who was such a compound of pride and meanness; we shall therefore only add that her future life was spent on St. Augustin's Back, where she made herself at once as ridiculous and as unhappy as she deserved to be.

As for our heroine, under the friendly and judicious care of Lady Frances Somerset, she acquired that which is more useful to the possessor than genius—good sense. Instead of rambling over the world in search of an *unknown friend*, she attached herself to those of whose worth she received proofs more convincing than a letter of three folio sheets, stuffed with sentimental nonsense. In short, we have now, in the name of Angelina Warwick, the pleasure to assure all those whom it may concern, that it is possible for a young lady of sixteen to cure herself of the affectation of sensibility and the folly of romance.

—1801

IN CONTEXT

Edgeworth's *Moral Tales*

Reproduced here in facsimile form are several pages from the 1813 edition of Edgeworth's three-volume *Moral Tales* (1813). The corresponding text with modernized spelling and punctuation appears on pages 157–59 above. The notation "H2" at the foot of the page reproduced below is a printer's mark designed to facilitate keeping the signatures of the book in their proper order during the binding process (this page occurs at the beginning of a signature).

ANGELINA;

OR,

L'AMIE INCONNUE.

CHAPTER I.

"BUT my dear lady Di., indeed you should not let this affair prey so continually upon your spirits," said miss Burrage, in the condoling tone of an humble companion.—"You really have almost fretted yourself into a nervous fever.—I was in hopes, that change of air, and change of scene, would have done every thing for you, or I never would have consented to your leaving London; for you know your ladyship's always better in London than any where else.—And I'm sure your ladyship has thought and talked of nothing but this sad affair since you came to Clifton."

"I confess," said lady Diana Chillingworth, "I deserve the reproaches of my friends for giving way to my sensibility as I do, upon this occasion: but I own I

H 2

cannot help it—Oh, what will the world say! What will the world say!—The world will lay all the blame upon *me*; yet I'm sure I'm the last, the very last person, that ought to be blamed."

"Assuredly," replied miss Burrage, "nobody can blame your ladyship; and nobody will, I am persuaded.—The blame will all be thrown where it ought to be, upon the young lady herself."

"If I could but be convinced of that," said her ladyship in a tone of great feeling; "such a young creature, scarcely sixteen, to take such a step!—I am sure I wish to Heaven her father had never made me her guardian.—I confess, I was most exceedingly imprudent, out of regard to her family, to take under my protection such a self-willed, unaccountable romantic girl.—Indeed, my dear," continued lady Diana Chillingworth, turning to her sister, lady Frances Somerset, "it was you, that misled me. You remember, you used to tell me, that Anne Warwick had such great abilities!——"

"That I thought it a pity they had not been well directed," said lady Frances.

"And such generosity of temper, and such warm affections!" said lady Di.—

"That I regretted their not having been properly cultivated."

"I confess, miss Warwick was never a

great favourite of mine," said miss Burrage,—"but now that she has lost her best friend——"

"She is likely to find a great number of enemies," said lady Frances.

"She has been her own enemy, poor girl! I am sure, I pity her," replied miss Burrage; "but, at the same time, I must say, that ever since she came to my lady Di. Chillingworth's, she has had good advice enough."

"Too much, perhaps; which is worse than too little," thought lady Frances.

"Advice!" repeated lady Di. Chillingworth, "why, as to that, my conscience, I own, acquits me there; for to be sure, no young person of her age, or of any age, had ever more advice, or more *good* advice, than miss Warwick had from me; I thought it my duty to advise her, and advise her I did from morning till night, as miss Burrage very well knows, and will do me the justice, I hope, to say in all companies."

"*That* I shall certainly make it a principle to do," said miss Burrage. "I am sure it would surprise and grieve you, lady Frances, to hear the sort of foolish, imprudent things, that miss Warwick, with all her abilities, used to say. I recollect——"

"Very possibly," replied lady Frances;

William Wordsworth

1770 – 1850

Since about 1815, William Wordsworth has been acknowledged as a central figure in the English Romantic Movement. *Lyrical Ballads*, produced in conjunction with Samuel Taylor Coleridge though largely Wordsworth's project, marks a decisive break with the formalism and neo-classicism of eighteenth-century literature. It became the touchstone of a new literary sensibility that gave its faith to the benevolence of feeling, and of the vehicle it associated most with feeling: a poetry of sincerity. And it established the idea of Nature as the measure by which to judge whether a poem's expression of feeling was genuine or not.

Wordworth's poems respond powerfully to the major developments of his day—including the French Revolution, war, and industrialization. That response, however, was marked by many tensions and contradictions. It is the play of those contradictions that give such weight and continued authority to Wordsworth's work.

Wordsworth was born in the Lake District of England, in West Cumberland, and spent his boyhood absorbing the natural beauty around him. The death of his mother when he was eight, and of his father only five years later, unsettled the lives of William and his four siblings. Their situation was worsened by the fact that the only substantial legacy their father left was a sum owed to him by his employer, Lord Lonsdale, who withheld the money until his death in 1802. Along with his three brothers, William was sent to school at Hawkshead. His sister Dorothy—later his muse, confidante, and secretary—found herself shifting among various relatives.

At Hawkshead Wordsworth and his brothers boarded at the home of Ann Tyson, who became a surrogate mother to Wordsworth, encouraging his love of nature and tolerating his habit of roaming the countryside. Wordsworth paid close attention to and frequently conversed with the town's working people. His observations would inform the representation of many of the humble rural characters who appear in his poetry. Leaving the Lake District for the first time in 1787, he entered St. John's College, Cambridge. During this period he made two walking tours with his friend Robert Jones, first through France and the Alps during a crucial period of the French Revolution, and later through Wales (excursions described in Books Six and Fourteen respectively of the 1850 *Prelude*).

These adventures quickened Wordsworth's belief in the healing powers of nature and of his own responsive imagination, and they also awakened radical sentiments. While traveling in France in 1791–1792 he was swept up in the heady excitement that followed the French Revolution (1789). Young Wordsworth also fell in love with Annette Vallon, whose politics (Royalist) and religion (Catholic) he did not share, and they produced a daughter, Caroline, out of wedlock. Too poor to remain in France, which was now at war with England, Wordsworth returned to his country a divided man, his disillusionment growing as France fell into a Reign of Terror.

Financial concerns fed Wordsworth's doubts about his political convictions and his choice of vocation. In 1795, however, Wordsworth received a legacy of £900 from a friend, Raisley Calvert, whom he had nursed through his final illness. With this sum, and a rent-free cottage in Alfoxden provided by other friends, Wordsworth was able to set up housekeeping with his sister Dorothy, with his friend Coleridge not far away at Nether Stowey. (Describing his relationship with Coleridge in an 1832 letter to a friend, Wordsworth declared, "He and my beloved sister are the two beings to whom my intellect is most indebted.") Long walks and talks with Coleridge resulted in an extraordinary literary collaboration, *Lyrical Ballads, with a few other poems* (1798), a slender, anonymously-published volume that opens with Coleridge's literary ballad "The Rime of the Ancient Mariner" and closes with Wordsworth's blank-verse meditation, "Lines, Composed a Few Miles Above Tintern Abbey." The volume sought to combat what the authors saw as the increasingly marginal position of the poet in society, and the overly artificial language on which poetry relied.

As Coleridge and Wordsworth had expected, critics attacked the tone and subject matter of the volume. In the *Preface to the Second Edition* (1800)—perhaps the most famous poetic manifesto in the language—Wordsworth explained and defended the decision he made "to choose incidents and situations from common life, and to relate or describe them, throughout, as far as was possible, in a selection of language really used by men." In poems such as "Michael" and "The Brothers" (added to the 1800 edition of *Lyrical Ballads*), Wordsworth shows the strength and dignity with which the Lake District's inhabitants endure hardship, living in harmony with the natural world, removed from the taint of urban superficiality. Wordsworth was thus in an important sense what he is often taken to be, a "poet of nature." But his main object was not to depict directly "the beautiful and permanent forms of nature" but rather to explore how "the passions of men are incorporated with" such forms, and to depict the "ennobling interchange" between the natural world and the mental world. It is the mind, ultimately, that was Wordsworth's "haunt, and the main region of my song."

After a brief, inhospitable stay in Germany in 1798–99, during which Wordsworth wrote the "Lucy" poems (the identity of "Lucy" is unknown) and Coleridge assimilated German philosophy, Wordsworth and his sister returned to England and took up residence at Dove Cottage in Grasmere. Here Dorothy kept journals that have since become famous in their own right, and Wordsworth composed some of his finest lyrics, including "Resolution and Independence," "The Solitary Reaper" (a memorial of his walking tour through Scotland), and *Ode: Intimations of Immortality from Recollections of Early Childhood*, all of which were later published in his *Poems, in Two Volumes* (1807).

In 1802, Wordsworth married a childhood friend, Mary Hutchinson, and began a period of relative tranquility and poetic fruitfulness, although these years were not without grief and disappointment. By 1812, two of his five children were dead, his brother John had been lost at sea, his friendship with Coleridge (whose health was deteriorating as his opium addiction deepened) had become strained, and *Poems, in Two Volumes* had suffered damaging reviews.

Then in 1814 Wordsworth published *The Excursion*, a long blank-verse meditation that was a forecast and first installment of his planned epic, *The Recluse*. The book was poorly reviewed, even ridiculed. Nevertheless, Wordworth by this time had gained a growing audience of devoted admirers, and his reputation from this low point began to establish itself firmly.

Like *The Excursion*, *The Prelude*, which Wordsworth had begun in 1799, was intended as a subsidiary piece that would be incorporated into *The Recluse*. He completed a two-book version of *The Prelude* in 1799 and a much expanded thirteen-book poem in 1805. He then continued to revise the poem for the rest of his life. This epic in blank verse—which Coleridge, upon hearing it, declared a "prophetic Lay"—describes the growth of the poet's mind from earliest memories to adulthood. By the end of his journey in the poem, Wordsworth reaffirms both providential design and the revolutionary potential of the imagination. *The Prelude* is a great, long lesson showing "how the mind of Man becomes / A thousand times more beautiful than the earth / On which he dwells."

In 1813, the Wordsworth household left Dove Cottage for the more expansive environs of Rydal Mount. There the poet, his beloved sister, and his wife lived out their days. The move was made possible by Wordsworth's improved financial situation, the result of a literary patronage granted by Lord Lonsdale and a position as Stamp Distributor for Westmorland. In the eyes of the younger generation (including Percy Shelley, Lord Byron, and Robert Browning), the patronage and the government position seemed to transform the once radical poet into a hypocritical and complacent hireling. As they saw it, Wordsworth had abandoned his early commitment to be the voice of the disenfranchised and the poor. Increasingly skeptical of external revolutions and political agitation, Wordsworth saw himself not as having abandoned his ideals but rather as having internalized—or spiritualized—his commitment to truth and liberty.

During his middle and old age Wordsworth wrote numerous sonnets, including *Ecclesiastical Sketches* (1822), inspired by his brother Christopher, a clergyman and scholar. Having begun as a poetic and political revolutionary, he ended his life an iconic figure of the early Victorian era. Queen Victoria crowned him her Poet Laureate in 1843, and admirers flocked to the Lake District to seek him out in his home. The influence of his poetic style remained strong until well into the twentieth century, and Victorian writers of prose and poetry alike—including Tennyson, Charles Dickens, George Eliot, and Elizabeth Gaskell—acknowledged their debt to the life he had breathed into ways of thinking about nature, poetic feeling, and the human imagination.

⌘⌘⌘

from *Lyrical Ballads, 1798*

ADVERTISEMENT

It is the honourable characteristic of Poetry that its materials are to be found in every subject which can interest the human mind. The evidence of this fact is to be sought, not in the writings of Critics, but in those of Poets themselves.

The majority of the following poems are to be considered as experiments. They were written chiefly with a view to ascertain how far the language of conversation in the middle and lower classes of society is adapted to the purposes of poetic pleasure. Readers accustomed to the gaudiness and inane phraseology of many modern writers, if they persist in reading this book to its conclusion, will perhaps frequently have to struggle with feelings of strangeness and awkwardness: they will look round for poetry, and will be induced to enquire by what species of courtesy these attempts can be permitted to assume that title. It is desirable that such readers, for their own sakes, should not suffer the solitary word Poetry, a word of very disputed meaning, to stand in the way of their gratification; but that, while they are perusing this book, they should ask themselves if it contains a natural delineation of human passions, human characters, and human incidents; and if the answer be favourable to the author's wishes, that they should consent to be pleased in spite of that most dreadful enemy to our pleasures, our own pre-established codes of decision.

Readers of superior judgment may disapprove of the style in which many of these pieces are executed. It must be expected that many lines and phrases will not exactly suit their taste. It will perhaps appear to them that, wishing to avoid the prevalent fault of the day, the author has sometimes descended too low, and that many of his expressions are too familiar, and not of sufficient dignity. It is apprehended that the more conversant the reader is with our elder writers, and with those in modern times who have been the most successful in painting manners and passions, the fewer complaints of this kind will he have to make.

An accurate taste in poetry, and in all the other arts, Sir Joshua Reynolds[1] has observed, is an acquired talent, which can only be produced by severe thought, and a long continued intercourse with the best models of composition. This is mentioned not with so ridiculous a purpose as to prevent the most inexperienced reader from judging for himself; but merely to temper the

[1] *Sir Joshua Reynolds* Renowned portrait and history painter, and first President of the Royal Academy (1723–92).

rashness of decision, and to suggest that if poetry be a subject on which much time has not been bestowed, the judgment may be erroneous, and that in many cases it necessarily will be so.

The tale of Goody Blake and Harry Gill is founded on a well-authenticated fact which happened in Warwickshire. Of the other poems in the collection, it may be proper to say that they are either absolute inventions of the author, or facts which took place within his personal observation or that of his friends. The poem of the Thorn, as the reader will soon discover, is not supposed to be spoken in the author's own person: the character of the loquacious narrator will sufficiently show itself in the course of the story. The Rime of the Ancyent Marinere was professedly written in imitation of the style, as well as of the spirit of the elder poets; but with a few exceptions, the Author believes that the language adopted in it has been equally intelligible for these three last centuries. The lines entitled Expostulation and Reply, and those which follow, arose out of conversation with a friend who was somewhat unreasonably attached to modern books of moral philosophy.

We Are Seven

A simple child, dear brother Jim,
That lightly draws its breath,
And feels its life in every limb,
What should it know of death?

I met a little cottage girl,
She was eight years old, she said;
Her hair was thick with many a curl
That cluster'd round her head.

She had a rustic, woodland air,
And she was wildly clad;
Her eyes were fair, and very fair
—Her beauty made me glad.

"Sisters and brothers, little maid,
How many may you be?"

"How many? seven in all," she said,
And wondering looked at me.

"And where are they, I pray you tell?"
She answered, "Seven are we,
And two of us at Conway[1] dwell,
And two are gone to sea.

"Two of us in the church-yard lie,
My sister and my brother,
And in the church-yard cottage, I
Dwell near them with my mother."

"You say that two at Conway dwell,
And two are gone to sea,
Yet you are seven; I pray you tell
Sweet Maid, how this may be?"

Then did the little Maid reply,
"Seven boys and girls are we;
Two of us in the church-yard lie,
Beneath the church-yard tree."

"You run about, my little maid,
Your limbs they are alive;
If two are in the church-yard laid,
Then ye are only five."

"Their graves are green, they may be seen,"
The little Maid replied,
"Twelve steps or more from my mother's door,
And they are side by side.

"My stockings there I often knit,
My 'kerchief there I hem;
And there upon the ground I sit—
I sit and sing to them.

"And often after sunset, Sir,
When it is light and fair,
I take my little porringer,[2]
And eat my supper there.

---

[1] *Conway* Seaport of southern Wales.

[2] *porringer* Small metal or earthenware basin from which broth or porridge is eaten.

"The first that died was little Jane;
In bed she moaning lay,
Till God released her of her pain,
And then she went away.

"So in the church-yard she was laid,
And all the summer dry,
Together round her grave we played,
My brother John and I.

"And when the ground was white with snow,
And I could run and slide,
My brother John was forced to go,
And he lies by her side."

"How many are you then," said I,
If they two are in Heaven?"
The little Maiden did reply,
"O Master! we are seven."

"But they are dead; those two are dead!
Their spirits are in heaven!"
'Twas throwing words away; for still
The little Maid would have her will,
And said, "Nay, we are seven!"
—1798

Lines Written in Early Spring

I heard a thousand blended notes,
While in a grove I sat reclined,
In that sweet mood when pleasant thoughts
Bring sad thoughts to the mind.

To her fair works did nature link
The human soul that through me ran;
And much it griev'd my heart to think
What man has made of man.

Through primrose-tufts, in that sweet bower,
The periwinkle trail'd its wreathes;
And 'tis my faith that every flower
Enjoys the air it breathes.

The birds around me hopp'd and play'd:
Their thoughts I cannot measure,
But the least motion which they made,
It seem'd a thrill of pleasure.

The budding twigs spread out their fan,
To catch the breezy air;
And I must think, do all I can,
That there was pleasure there.

If I these thoughts may not prevent,
If such be of my creed the plan,
Have I not reason to lament
What man has made of man?
—1798

The Thorn[1]

1

There is a thorn;° it looks so old, *thorn bush*
In truth you'd find it hard to say,
How it could ever have been young,
It looks so old and grey.
Not higher than a two-years' child,
It stands erect this aged thorn;
No leaves it has, no thorny points;
It is a mass of knotted joints,
A wretched thing forlorn.
It stands erect, and like a stone
With lichens it is overgrown.

2

Like rock or stone, it is o'ergrown
With lichens to the very top,
And hung with heavy tufts of moss,
A melancholy crop:
Up from the earth these mosses creep,
And this poor thorn they clasp it round

[1] [Wordsworth's note] Arose from my observing, on the ridge of Quantock Hill, on a stormy day a thorn which I had often passed in calm and bright weather without noticing it. I said to myself, "Cannot I by some invention do as much to make this Thorn permanently an impressive object as the storm has made it to my eyes at this moment?"

So close, you'd say that they were bent
With plain and manifest intent,
To drag it to the ground;
And all had joined in one endeavour
To bury this poor thorn for ever.

3

High on a mountain's highest ridge,
Where oft the stormy winter gale
Cuts like a scythe, while through the clouds
It sweeps from vale to vale;
Not five yards from the mountain-path,
This thorn you on your left espy;
And to the left, three yards beyond,
You see a little muddy pond
Of water, never dry;
I've measured it from side to side:
'Tis three feet long, and two feet wide.

4

And close beside this aged thorn,
There is a fresh and lovely sight,
A beauteous heap, a hill of moss,
Just half a foot in height.
All lovely colours there you see,
All colours that were ever seen,
And mossy network too is there,
As if by hand of lady fair
The work had woven been,
And cups,° the darlings of the eye, *blossoms*
So deep is their vermilion° dye. *red*

5

Ah me! what lovely tints are there!
Of olive-green and scarlet bright,
In spikes, in branches, and in stars,
Green, red, and pearly white.
This heap of earth o'ergrown with moss,
Which close beside the thorn you see,
So fresh in all its beauteous dyes,
Is like an infant's grave in size
As like as like can be:
But never, never any where,
An infant's grave was half so fair.

6

Now would you see this aged thorn,
This pond and beauteous hill of moss,
You must take care and choose your time
The mountain when to cross.
For oft there sits, between the heap
That's like an infant's grave in size,
And that same pond of which I spoke,
A woman in a scarlet cloak,
And to herself she cries,
"Oh misery! oh misery!
"Oh woe is me! oh misery!"

7

At all times of the day and night
This wretched woman thither goes,
And she is known to every star,
And every wind that blows;
And there beside the thorn she sits
When the blue day-light's in the skies,
And when the whirlwind's on the hill,
Or frosty air is keen and still,
And to herself she cries,
"Oh misery! oh misery!
Oh woe is me! oh misery!"

8

"Now wherefore thus, by day and night,
In rain, in tempest, and in snow,
Thus to the dreary mountain-top
Does this poor woman go?
And why sits she beside the thorn
When the blue day-light's in the sky,
Or when the whirlwind's on the hill,
Or frosty air is keen and still,
And wherefore does she cry?
Oh wherefore? wherefore? tell me why
Does she repeat that doleful cry?"

9

I cannot tell; I wish I could;
For the true reason no one knows,
But if you'd gladly view the spot,
The spot to which she goes;
The heap that's like an infant's grave,

The pond—and thorn, so old and grey;
Pass by her door—'tis seldom shut—
And if you see her in her hut,
Then to the spot away!
I never heard of such as dare
Approach the spot when she is there.

10

"But wherefore to the mountain-top
Can this unhappy woman go,
Whatever star is in the skies,
Whatever wind may blow?"
Nay rack your brain—'tis all in vain,
I'll tell you every thing I know;
But to the thorn, and to the pond
Which is a little step beyond,
I wish that you would go:
Perhaps when you are at the place
You something of her tale may trace.

11

I'll give you the best help I can:
Before you up the mountain go,
Up to the dreary mountain-top,
I'll tell you all I know.
'Tis now some two and twenty years,
Since she (her name is Martha Ray)
Gave with a maiden's true good will
Her company to Stephen Hill;
And she was blithe and gay,
And she was happy, happy still
Whene'er she thought of Stephen Hill.

12

And they had fix'd the wedding-day,
The morning that must wed them both;
But Stephen to another maid
Had sworn another oath;
And with this other maid to church
Unthinking Stephen went—
Poor Martha! on that woeful day
A cruel, cruel fire, they say,
Into her bones was sent:
It dried her body like a cinder,
And almost turn'd her brain to tinder.[1]

13

They say, full six months after this,
While yet the summer leaves were green,
She to the mountain-top would go,
And there was often seen.
'Tis said, a child was in her womb,
As now to any eye was plain;
She was with child, and she was mad,
Yet often she was sober sad
From her exceeding pain.
Oh me! ten thousand times I'd rather
That he had died, that cruel father!

14

Sad case for such a brain to hold
Communion with a stirring child!
Sad case, as you may think, for one
Who had a brain so wild!
Last Christmas when we talked of this,
Old Farmer Simpson did maintain,
That in her womb the infant wrought
About its mother's heart, and brought
Her senses back again:
And when at last her time drew near,
Her looks were calm, her senses clear.

15

No more I know, I wish I did,
And I would tell it all to you;
For what became of this poor child
There's none that ever knew:
And if a child was born or no,
There's no one that could ever tell;
And if 'twas born alive or dead,
There's no one knows, as I have said,
But some remember well,
That Martha Ray about this time
Would up the mountain often climb.

[1] *tinder* Dry, flammable substance that will take fire from a spark.

16

And all that winter, when at night
The wind blew from the mountain-peak,
'Twas worth your while, though in the dark,
The church-yard path to seek:
For many a time and oft were heard
Cries coming from the mountain-head,
Some plainly living voices were,
And others, I've heard many swear,
Were voices of the dead:
I cannot think, whate'er they say,
They had to do with Martha Ray.

17

But that she goes to this old thorn,
The thorn which I've described to you,
And there sits in a scarlet cloak,
I will be sworn is true.
For one day with my telescope,
To view the ocean wide and bright,
When to this country first I came,
Ere I had heard of Martha's name,
I climbed the mountain's height:
A storm came on, and I could see
No object higher than my knee.

18

'Twas mist and rain, and storm and rain,
No screen, no fence could I discover,
And then the wind! in faith, it was
A wind full ten times over.
I looked around, I thought I saw
A jutting crag, and off I ran,
Head-foremost, through the driving rain,
The shelter of the crag to gain,
And, as I am a man,
Instead of jutting crag, I found
A woman seated on the ground.

19

I did not speak—I saw her face,
Her face it was enough for me;
I turned about and heard her cry,
"O misery! O misery!"
And there she sits, until the moon
Through half the clear blue sky will go,
And when the little breezes make
The waters of the pond to shake,
As all the country know,
She shudders and you hear her cry,
"Oh misery! oh misery!"

20

"But what's the thorn? and what's the pond?
And what's the hill of moss to her?
And what's the creeping breeze that comes
The little pond to stir?"
I cannot tell; but some will say
She hanged her baby on the tree,
Some say she drowned it in the pond,
Which is a little step beyond,
But all and each agree,
The little babe was buried there,
Beneath that hill of moss so fair.

21

I've heard the scarlet moss is red
With drops of that poor infant's blood;
But kill a new-born infant thus!
I do not think she could.
Some say, if to the pond you go,
And fix on it a steady view,
The shadow of a babe you trace,
A baby and a baby's face,
And that it looks at you;
Whene'er you look on it, 'tis plain
The baby looks at you again.

22

And some had sworn an oath that she
Should be to public justice brought;
And for the little infant's bones
With spades they would have sought.
But then the beauteous hill of moss
Before their eyes began to stir;
And for full fifty yards around,
The grass it shook upon the ground;
But all do still aver
The little babe is buried there,
Beneath that hill of moss so fair.

23

I cannot tell how this may be,
But plain it is, the thorn is bound
With heavy tufts of moss, that strive
To drag it to the ground.
And this I know, full many a time,
When she was on the mountain high,
By day, and in the silent night,
When all the stars shone clear and bright,
That I have heard her cry,
"Oh misery! oh misery!
"Oh woe is me! oh misery!"
—1798

Expostulation and Reply

"Why William, on that old grey stone,
Thus for the length of half a day,
Why William, sit you thus alone,
And dream your time away?

"Where are your books? that light bequeath'd
To beings else forlorn and blind!
Up! Up! and drink the spirit breath'd
From dead men to their kind.

"You look round on your mother earth,
As if she for no purpose bore you;
As if you were her first-born birth,
And none had lived before you!"

One morning thus, by Esthwaite lake,[1]
When life was sweet I knew not why,
To me my good friend Matthew spake,
And thus I made reply.

"The eye it cannot choose but see,
We cannot bid the ear be still;
Our bodies feel, where'er they be,
Against, or with our will.

"Nor less I deem that there are powers,
Which of themselves our minds impress,
That we can feed this mind of ours,
In a wise passiveness.

"Think you, mid all this mighty sum
Of things for ever speaking,
That nothing of itself will come,
But we must still be seeking?

"—Then ask not wherefore, here, alone,
Conversing as I may,
I sit upon this old grey stone,
And dream my time away."
—1798

[1] *Esthwaite lake* Located at Hawkshead (in England's Lake District), where Wordsworth attended grammar school.

The Tables Turned

An Evening Scene on the Same Subject

Up! up! my friend, and clear your looks,
Why all this toil and trouble?
Up! up! my friend, and quit your books,
Or surely you'll grow double.[2]

The sun above the mountain's head,
A freshening lustre mellow,
Through all the long green fields has spread,
His first sweet evening yellow.

Books! 'tis a dull and endless strife,
Come, hear the woodland linnet,
How sweet his music; on my life
There's more of wisdom in it.

And hark! how blithe the throstle° sings! *thrush*
And he is no mean preacher;
Come forth into the light of things,
Let Nature be your teacher.

She has a world of ready wealth,
Our minds and hearts to bless—

[2] *double* Doubled over.

Spontaneous wisdom breathed by health,
Truth breathed by cheerfulness.

One impulse from a vernal wood
May teach you more of man;
Of moral evil and of good,
Than all the sages can.

Sweet is the lore which nature brings;
Our meddling intellect
Mishapes the beauteous forms of things
—We murder to dissect.

Enough of science and of art;
Close up these barren leaves;
Come forth, and bring with you a heart
That watches and receives.
—1798

Lines Written a Few Miles above Tintern Abbey

On Revisiting the Banks of the Wye during a Tour, July 13, 1798[1]

Five years have passed; five summers, with the length
Of five long winters! and again I hear
These waters, rolling from their mountain-springs
With a sweet inland murmur.[2] Once again
Do I behold these steep and lofty cliffs,
Which on a wild secluded scene impress
Thoughts of more deep seclusion; and connect
The landscape with the quiet of the sky.
The day is come when I again repose
Here, under this dark sycamore, and view
These plots of cottage-ground, these orchard-tufts,
Which, at this season, with their unripe fruits,
Among the woods and copses lose themselves,
Nor, with their green and simple hue, disturb
The wild green landscape. Once again I see
These hedge-rows, hardly hedge-rows, little lines
Of sportive wood run wild; these pastoral farms
Green to the very door; and wreaths of smoke
Sent up, in silence, from among the trees,
With some uncertain notice, as might seem,
Of vagrant dwellers in the houseless woods,
Or of some hermit's cave, where by his fire
The hermit sits alone.

Though absent long,
These forms of beauty have not been to me,
As is a landscape to a blind man's eye:
But oft, in lonely rooms, and 'mid the din
Of towns and cities, I have owed to them,
In hours of weariness, sensations sweet,
Felt in the blood, and felt along the heart,
And passing even into my purer mind
With tranquil restoration—feelings too
Of unremembered pleasure; such, perhaps,
As may have had no trivial influence
On that best portion of a good man's life;
His little, nameless, unremembered acts
Of kindness and of love. Nor less, I trust,
To them I may have owed another gift,
Of aspect more sublime; that blessed mood,
In which the burthen of the mystery,
In which the heavy and the weary weight
Of all this unintelligible world
Is lighten'd—that serene and blessed mood,
In which the affections gently lead us on,
Until, the breath of this corporeal frame,
And even the motion of our human blood
Almost suspended, we are laid asleep
In body, and become a living soul:
While with an eye made quiet by the power
Of harmony, and the deep power of joy,
We see into the life of things.

If this
Be but a vain belief, yet, oh! how oft,
In darkness, and amid the many shapes
Of joyless day-light; when the fretful stir

[1] [Wordsworth's note] No poem of mine was composed under circumstances more pleasant for me to remember than this. I began it upon leaving Tintern, after crossing the Wye, and concluded it just as I was entering Bristol in the evening, after a ramble of 4 or 5 days, with my sister. Not a line of it was altered, and not any part of it was written down till I reached Bristol.

[2] [Wordsworth's note] The river is not affected by the tides a few miles above Tintern.

Unprofitable, and the fever of the world,
Have hung upon the beatings of my heart,
How oft, in spirit, have I turned to thee
O sylvan Wye! Thou wanderer through the woods,
How often has my spirit turned to thee!
And now, with gleams of half-extinguish'd thought,
With many recognitions dim and faint,
And somewhat of a sad perplexity,
The picture of the mind revives again:
While here I stand, not only with the sense
Of present pleasure, but with pleasing thoughts
That in this moment there is life and food
For future years. And so I dare to hope
Though changed, no doubt, from what I was, when first
I came among these hills; when like a roe° *deer*
I bounded o'er the mountains, by the sides
Of the deep rivers, and the lonely streams,
Wherever nature led; more like a man
Flying from something that he dreads, than one
Who sought the thing he loved. For nature then
(The coarser pleasures of my boyish days,
And their glad animal movements all gone by)
To me was all in all. I cannot paint
What then I was. The sounding cataract
Haunted me like a passion: the tall rock,
The mountain, and the deep and gloomy wood,
Their colours and their forms, were then to me
An appetite: a feeling and a love,
That had no need of a remoter charm,
By thought supplied, or any interest
Unborrowed from the eye. That time is past,
And all its aching joys are now no more,
And all its dizzy raptures. Not for this
Faint[1] I, nor mourn nor murmur: other gifts
Have followed, for such loss, I would believe,
Abundant recompence. For I have learned
To look on nature, not as in the hour
Of thoughtless youth, but hearing oftentimes
The still, sad music of humanity,
Not harsh nor grating, though of ample power
To chasten and subdue. And I have felt
A presence that disturbs me with the joy
Of elevated thoughts; a sense sublime
Of something far more deeply interfused,
Whose dwelling is the light of setting suns,
And the round ocean, and the living air,
And the blue sky, and in the mind of man,
A motion and a spirit, that impels
All thinking things, all objects of all thought,
And rolls through all things. Therefore am I still
A lover of the meadows and the woods,
And mountains; and of all that we behold
From this green earth; of all the mighty world
Of eye and ear, both what they half create,
And what perceive; well pleased to recognize
In nature and the language of the sense,
The anchor of my purest thoughts, the nurse,
The guide, the guardian of my heart, and soul
Of all my moral being.

Nor, perchance,
If I were not thus taught, should I the more
Suffer my genial° spirits to decay: *creative*
For thou art with me, here, upon the banks
Of this fair river; thou, my dearest Friend,[2]
My dear, dear Friend, and in thy voice I catch
The language of my former heart, and read
My former pleasures in the shooting lights
Of thy wild eyes. Oh! yet a little while
May I behold in thee what I was once,
My dear, dear Sister! And this prayer I make,
Knowing that Nature never did betray
The heart that loved her; 'tis her privilege,
Through all the years of this our life, to lead
From joy to joy: for she can so inform
The mind that is within us, so impress
With quietness and beauty, and so feed
With lofty thoughts, that neither evil tongues,
Rash judgments, nor the sneers of selfish men,
Nor greetings where no kindness is, nor all
The dreary intercourse of daily life,
Shall e'er prevail against us, or disturb
Our cheerful faith that all which we behold
Is full of blessings. Therefore let the moon
Shine on thee in thy solitary walk;
And let the misty mountain winds be free

[1] *Faint* Lose heart; grow weak.

[2] *my dearest Friend* I.e., Dorothy Wordsworth, Wordsworth's sister.

To blow against thee: and in after years,
When these wild ecstasies shall be matured
Into a sober pleasure, when thy mind
Shall be a mansion for all lovely forms,
Thy memory be as a dwelling-place
For all sweet sounds and harmonies; Oh! then,
If solitude, or fear, or pain, or grief,
Should be thy portion, with what healing thoughts
Of tender joy wilt thou remember me,
And these my exhortations! Nor, perchance,
If I should be, where I no more can hear
Thy voice, nor catch from thy wild eyes these gleams
Of past existence, wilt thou then forget
That on the banks of this delightful stream
We stood together; and that I, so long
A worshipper of Nature, hither came,
Unwearied in that service: rather say
With warmer love, oh! with far deeper zeal
Of holier love. Nor wilt thou then forget,
That after many wanderings, many years
Of absence, these steep woods and lofty cliffs,
And this green pastoral landscape, were to me
More dear, both for themselves, and for thy sake.
—1798

from *Lyrical Ballads, 1800, 1802*

Preface[1]

The first Volume of these Poems has already been submitted to general perusal. It was published as an experiment, which, I hoped, might be of some use to ascertain how far, by fitting to metrical arrangement a selection of the real language of men in a state of vivid sensation, that sort of pleasure and that quantity of pleasure may be imparted, which a Poet may rationally endeavour to impart.

I had formed no very inaccurate estimate of the probable effect of those Poems: I flattered myself that they who should be pleased with them would read them with more than common pleasure: and, on the other hand, I was well aware that by those who should dislike them they would be read with more than common dislike. The result has differed from my expectation in this only, that I have pleased a greater number than I ventured to hope I should please.

For the sake of variety, and from a consciousness of my own weakness, I was induced to request the assistance of a Friend,[2] who furnished me with the Poems of the *Ancient Mariner*, the *Foster-Mother's Tale*, the *Nightingale*, and the Poem entitled *Love*. I should not, however, have requested this assistance, had I not believed that the Poems of my Friend would in a great measure have the same tendency as my own, and that, though there would be found a difference, there would be found no discordance in the colours of our style; as our opinions on the subject of poetry do almost entirely coincide.

Several of my Friends are anxious for the success of these Poems from a belief that, if the views with which they were composed were indeed realized, a class of Poetry would be produced, well adapted to interest mankind permanently, and not unimportant in the multiplicity, and in the quality of its moral relations: and on this account they have advised me to prefix a systematic defence of the theory upon which the poems were written. But I was unwilling to undertake the task, because I knew that on this occasion the Reader would look coldly upon my arguments, since I might be suspected of having been principally influenced by the selfish and foolish hope of *reasoning* him into an approbation of these particular Poems: and I was still more unwilling to undertake the task, because, adequately to display my opinions, and fully to enforce my arguments, would require a space wholly disproportionate to the nature of a preface. For to treat the subject with the clearness and coherence of which I believe it susceptible, it would be necessary to give a full account of the present state of the public taste in this country, and to determine how far this taste is healthy or depraved; which, again, could not be determined without pointing out in what manner language and the human mind act and re-act on each other, and without retracing the revolutions, not of literature alone, but likewise of society itself. I have therefore altogether declined to

[1] *Preface* This preface first appeared in the 1800 edition of *Lyrical Ballads*, and was revised for the 1802 edition.

[2] *Friend* Samuel Taylor Coleridge (1772–1834). Coleridge gives his account of their plan in his *Biographia Literaria*, chapter 14.

enter regularly upon this defence; yet I am sensible that there would be some impropriety in abruptly obtruding upon the Public, without a few words of introduction, Poems so materially different from those upon which general approbation is at present bestowed.

It is supposed, that by the act of writing in verse an Author makes a formal engagement that he will gratify certain known habits of association; that he not only thus apprizes the Reader that certain classes of ideas and expressions will be found in his book, but that others will be carefully excluded. This exponent or symbol held forth by metrical language must in different areas of literature have excited very different expectations: for example, in the age of Catullus, Terence, and Lucretius and that of Statius or Claudian;[1] and in our own country, in the age of Shakespeare and Beaumont and Fletcher, and that of Donne and Cowley, or Dryden, or Pope.[2] I will not take upon me to determine the exact import of the promise which by the act of writing in verse an Author, in the present day, makes to his Reader; but, I am certain, it will appear to many persons that I have not fulfilled the terms of an engagement thus voluntarily contracted. They who have been accustomed to the gaudiness and inane phraseology of many modern writers, if they persist in reading this book to its conclusion, will, no doubt, frequently have to struggle with feelings of strangeness and awkwardness: they will look round for poetry, and will be induced to inquire by what species of courtesy these attempts can be permitted to assume that title. I hope therefore the Reader will not censure me if I attempt to state what I have proposed to myself to perform; and also (as far as the limits of a preface will permit) to explain some of the chief reasons which have determined me in the choice of my purpose: that at least he maybe spared any unpleasant feeling of disappointment, and that I myself may be protected from the most dishonorable accusation which can be brought against an Author, namely, that of an indolence which prevents him from endeavouring to ascertain what is his duty, or, when his duty is ascertained, prevents him from performing it.

The principal object, then, which I proposed to myself in these Poems was to choose incidents and situations from common life, and to relate or describe them, throughout, as far as was possible, in a selection of language really used by men; and, at the same time, to throw over them a certain colouring of imagination, whereby ordinary things should be presented to the mind in an unusual way; and, further, and above all, to make these incidents and situations interesting by tracing in them, truly though not ostentatiously, the primary laws of our nature: chiefly as far as regards the manner in which we associate ideas in a state of excitement. Low and rustic life was generally chosen because, in that condition, the essential passions of the heart find a better soil in which they can attain their maturity, are less under restraint, and speak a plainer and more emphatic language; because in that condition of life our elementary feelings co-exist in a state of greater simplicity, and, consequently, may be more accurately contemplated, and more forcibly communicated; because the manners of rural life germinate from those elementary feelings; and, from the necessary character of rural occupations, are more easily comprehended, and are more durable; and lastly, because in that condition the passions of men are incorporated with the beautiful and permanent forms of nature. The language, too, of these men is adopted (purified indeed from what appear to be its real defects, from all lasting and rational causes of dislike or disgust) because such men hourly communicate with the best objects from which the best part of language is originally derived; and because, from their rank in society and the sameness and narrow circle of their intercourse, being less under the influence of social vanity they convey their feelings and notions in simple and unelaborated expressions. Accordingly, such a language, arising out of repeated experience and regular feelings, is a more permanent, and a far more philosophical language, than that which is frequently substituted for it by Poets, who think that they are conferring honour upon themselves and their art, in proportion as they separate themselves from the sympathies of men,

[1] *Catullus, Terence, and Lucretius* Roman poets of the first and second centuries BCE; *Statius or Claudian* Roman epic poets of the first and fourth centuries CE, respectively.

[2] *Shakespeare and Beaumont and Fletcher* The age of Renaissance drama, during which Shakespeare, Francis Beaumont, and John Fletcher wrote; *Donne and Cowley* John Donne and Abraham Cowley, poets of the seventeenth century; *Dryden* John Dryden, Poet Laureate during the Restoration (1660–1700); *Pope* Alexander Pope, a major poet of the eighteenth century.

and indulge in arbitrary and capricious habits of expression, in order to furnish food for fickle tastes, and fickle appetites, of their own creation.[1]

I cannot, however, be insensible of the present outcry against the triviality and meanness both of thought and language, which some of my contemporaries have occasionally introduced into their metrical compositions; and I acknowledge that this defect, where it exists, is more dishonorable to the Writer's own character than false refinement or arbitrary innovation, though I should contend at the same time that it is far less pernicious in the sum of its consequences. From such verses the Poems in these volumes will be found distinguished at least by one mark of difference, that each of them has a worthy *purpose*. Not that I mean to say that I always began to write with a distinct purpose formally conceived; but I believe that my habits of meditation have so formed my feelings, as that my descriptions of such objects as strongly excite those feelings will be found to carry along with them a *purpose.* If in this opinion I am mistaken, I can have little right to the name of a Poet. For all good poetry is the spontaneous overflow of powerful feelings: but though this be true, Poems to which any value can be attached, were never produced on any variety of subjects but by a man who, being possessed of more than usual organic sensibility, had also thought long and deeply. For our continued influxes of feeling are modified and directed by our thoughts, which are indeed the representatives of all our past feelings; and, as by contemplating the relation of these general representatives to each other we discover what is really important to men, so, by the repetition and continuance of this act, our feelings will be connected with important subjects, till at length, if we be originally possessed of much sensibility, such habits of mind will be produced, that, by obeying blindly and mechanically the impulses of those habits, we shall describe objects, and utter sentiments, of such a nature and in such connection with each other, that the understanding of the being to whom we address ourselves, if he be in a healthful state of association, must necessarily be in some degree enlightened, and his affections ameliorated.

I have said that each of these poems has a purpose. I have also informed my Reader what this purpose will be found principally to be: namely to illustrate the manner in which our feelings and ideas are associated in a state of excitement. But, speaking in language somewhat more appropriate, it is to follow the fluxes and refluxes of the mind when agitated by the great and simple affections of our nature. This object I have endeavoured in these short essays to attain by various means; by tracing the maternal passion through many of its more subtle windings, as in the poems of the *Idiot Boy* and the *Mad Mother*; by accompanying the last struggles of a human being, at the approach of death, cleaving in solitude to life and society, as in the Poem of the *Forsaken Indian*; by showing, as in the Stanzas entitled *We Are Seven,* the perplexity and obscurity which in childhood attend our notion of death, or rather our utter inability to admit that notion; or by displaying the strength of fraternal, or to speak more philosophically, of moral attachment when early associated with the great and beautiful objects of nature, as in *The Brothers*; or, as in the *Incident of Simon Lee*, by placing my Reader in the way of receiving from ordinary moral sensations another and more salutary impression than we are accustomed to receive from them. It has also been part of my general purpose to attempt to sketch characters under the influence of less impassioned feelings, as in the *Two April Mornings*, *The Fountain*, *The Old Man Travelling*, *The Two Thieves*, &c., characters of which the elements are simple, belonging rather to nature than to manners, such as exist now, and will probably always exist, and which from their constitution may be distinctly and profitably contemplated. I will not abuse the indulgence of my Reader by dwelling longer upon this subject; but it is proper that I should mention one other circumstance which distinguishes these Poems from the popular Poetry of the day; it is this, that the feeling therein developed gives importance to the action and situation, and not the action and situation to the feeling. My meaning will be rendered perfectly intelligible by referring my Reader to the Poems entitled *Poor Susan* and the *Childless Father*, particularly to the last Stanza of the latter Poem.

I will not suffer a sense of false modesty to prevent

[1] [Wordsworth's note] It is worth while here to observe that the affecting parts of Chaucer are almost always expressed in language pure and universally intelligible even to this day.

me from asserting that I point my Reader's attention to this mark of distinction, far less for the sake of these particular Poems than from the general importance of the subject. The subject is indeed important! For the human mind is capable of being excited without the application of gross and violent stimulants; and he must have a very faint perception of its beauty and dignity who does not know this, and who does not further know that one being is elevated above another, in proportion as he possesses this capability. It has therefore appeared to me that to endeavour to produce or enlarge this capability is one of the best services in which, at any period, a Writer can be engaged; but this service, excellent at all times, is especially so at the present day. For a multitude of causes, unknown to former times, are now acting with a combined force to blunt the discriminating powers of the mind, and unfitting it for all voluntary exertion to reduce it to a state of almost savage torpor. The most effective of these causes are the great national events which are daily taking place,[1] and the increasing accumulation of men in cities, where the uniformity of their occupations produces a craving for extraordinary incident, which the rapid communication of intelligence hourly gratifies. To this tendency of life and manners the literature and theatrical exhibitions of the country have conformed themselves. The invaluable works of our elder writers, I had almost said the works of Shakespeare and Milton, are driven into neglect by frantic novels, sickly and stupid German Tragedies, and deluges of idle and extravagant stories in verse.[2] When I think upon this degrading thirst after outrageous stimulation, I am almost ashamed to have spoken of the feeble effort with which I have endeavoured to counteract it; and, reflecting upon the magnitude of the general evil, I should be oppressed with no dishonorable melancholy, had I not a deep impression of certain inherent and indestructible qualities of the human mind, and likewise of certain powers in the great and permanent objects that act upon it which are equally inherent and indestructible; and did I not further add to this impression a belief that the time is approaching when the evil will be systematically opposed, by men of greater powers, and with far more distinguished success.

Having dwelt thus long on the subjects and aim of these Poems, I shall request the Reader's permission to apprize him of a few circumstances relating to their *style*, in order, among other reasons, that I may not be censured for not having performed what I never attempted. The Reader will find that personifications of abstract ideas rarely occur in these volumes; and, I hope, are utterly rejected as an ordinary device to elevate the style, and raise it above prose. I have proposed to myself to imitate, and, as far as is possible, to adopt, the very language of men; and assuredly such personifications do not make any natural or regular part of that language. They are, indeed, a figure of speech occasionally prompted by passion, and I have made use of them as such; but I have endeavoured utterly to reject them as a mechanical device of style, or as a family language which Writers in metre seem to lay claim to by prescription. I have wished to keep my Reader in the company of flesh and blood, persuaded that by so doing I shall interest him. I am, however, well aware that others who pursue a different track may interest him likewise; I do not interfere with their claim, I only wish to prefer a different claim of my own. There will also be found in these volumes little of what is usually called poetic diction; I have taken as much pains to avoid it as others ordinarily take to produce it; this I have done for the reason already alleged, to bring my language near to the language of men, and further, because the pleasure which I have proposed to myself to impart is of a kind very different from that which is supposed by many persons to be the proper object of poetry. I do not know how without being culpably particular I can give my Reader a more exact notion of the style in which I wished these poems to be written than by informing him that I have at all times endeavoured to look steadily at my subject; consequently, I hope that there is in these Poems little falsehood of description, and that my ideas are expressed in language fitted to their respective importance. Something I must have gained by this practice, as it is friendly to one property of all good poetry, namely, good sense;

[1] *great national ... place* I.e., the wars against France and the Irish rebellion.

[2] *frantic novels ... verse* References to popular Gothic novels of the time, such as Matthew Gregory Lewis's *The Monk* (1796) and the novels of Ann Radcliffe, and to the German sentimental melodramas translated and staged during the 1780s.

but it has necessarily cut me off from a large portion of phrases and figures of speech which from father to son have long been regarded as the common inheritance of Poets. I have also thought it expedient to restrict myself still further, having abstained from the use of many expressions, in themselves proper and beautiful, but which have been foolishly repeated by bad Poets, till such feelings of disgust are connected with them as it is scarcely possible by any art of association to overpower.

If in a Poem there should be found a series of lines, or even a single line, in which the language, though naturally arranged and according to the strict laws of metre, does not differ from that of prose, there is a numerous class of critics, who, when they stumble upon these prosaisms, as they call them, imagine that they have made a notable discovery, and exult over the Poet as over a man ignorant of his own profession. Now these men would establish a canon of criticism which the Reader will conclude he must utterly reject, if he wishes to be pleased with these volumes. And it would be a most easy task to prove to him that not only the language of a large portion of every good poem, even of the most elevated character, must necessarily, except with reference to the metre, in no respect differ from that of good prose, but likewise that some of the most interesting parts of the best poems will be found to be strictly the language of prose, when prose is well written. The truth of this assertion might be demonstrated by innumerable passages from almost all the poetical writings, even of Milton himself. I have not space for much quotation; but, to illustrate the subject in a general manner, I will here adduce a short composition of Gray,[1] who was at the head of those who by their reasonings have attempted to widen the space of separation betwixt Prose and Metrical composition, and was more than any other man curiously elaborate in the structure of his own poetic diction.

> In vain to me the smiling mornings shine,
> And reddening Phoebus[2] lifts his golden fire:
> The birds in vain their amorous descant join,
> Or cheerful fields resume their green attire:
> These ears alas! for other notes repine;
> *A different object do these eyes require;*
> *My lonely anguish melts no heart but mine;*
> *And in my breast the imperfect joys expire;*
> Yet Morning smiles the busy race to cheer,
> And new-born pleasure brings to happier men;
> The fields to all their wonted tribute bear;
> To warm their little loves the birds complain.
> *I fruitless mourn to him that cannot hear*
> *And weep the more because I weep in vain.*

It will easily be perceived that the only part of this Sonnet which is of any value is the lines printed in Italics: it is equally obvious that, except in the rhyme, and in the use of the single word "fruitless" for fruitlessly, which is so far a defect, the language of these lines does in no respect differ from that of prose.

By the foregoing quotation I have shown that the language of Prose may yet be well adapted to Poetry; and I have previously asserted that a large portion of the language of every good poem can in no respect differ from that of good Prose. I will go further. I do not doubt that it may be safely affirmed that there neither is, nor can be, any essential difference between the language of prose and metrical composition....

I ask what is meant by the word Poet? What is a Poet? To whom does he address himself? And what language is to be expected from him? He is a man speaking to men: a man, it is true, endued with more lively sensibility, more enthusiasm and tenderness, who has a greater knowledge of human nature, and a more comprehensive soul, than are supposed to be common among mankind; a man pleased with his own passions and volitions, and who rejoices more than other men in the spirit of life that is in him; delighting to contemplate similar volitions and passions as manifested in the goings-on of the Universe, and habitually impelled to create them where he does not find them. To these qualities he has added a disposition to be affected more than other men by absent things as if they were present; an ability of conjuring up in himself passions, which are indeed far from being the same as those produced by real events, yet (especially in those parts of the general sympathy which are pleasing and delightful) do more nearly resemble the passions produced by real events than any thing which, from the motions of their own

[1] *Gray* Thomas Gray (1716–71). Wordsworth quotes his *Sonnet on the Death of Richard West.*

[2] *Phoebus* Apollo, god of the sun and of poetry.

minds merely, other men are accustomed to feel in themselves; whence, and from practice, he has acquired a greater readiness and power in expressing what he thinks and feels, and especially those thoughts and feelings which, by his own choice, or from the structure of his own mind, arise in him without immediate external excitement.

But, whatever portion of this faculty we may suppose even the greatest Poet to possess, there cannot be a doubt but that the language which it will suggest to him must, in liveliness and truth, fall far short of that which is uttered by men in real life, under the actual pressure of those passions, certain shadows of which the Poet thus produces, or feels to be produced, in himself. However exalted a notion we would wish to cherish of the character of a Poet, it is obvious that, while he describes and imitates passions, his situation is altogether slavish and mechanical, compared with the freedom and power of real and substantial action and suffering. So that it will be the wish of the Poet to bring his feelings near to those of the persons whose feelings he describes—nay, for short spaces of time, perhaps, to let himself slip into an entire delusion, and even confound and identify his own feelings with theirs; modifying only the language which is thus suggested to him, by a consideration that he describes for a particular purpose, that of giving pleasure. Here, then, he will apply the principle on which I have so much insisted, namely, that of selection; on this he will depend for removing what would otherwise be painful or disgusting in the passion; he will feel that there is no necessity to trick out or to elevate nature: and, the more industriously he applies this principle, the deeper will be his faith that no words which his fancy or imagination can suggest will be to be compared with those which are the emanations of reality and truth....

It is not, then, in the dramatic parts of composition that we look for this distinction of language; but still it may be proper and necessary where the Poet speaks to us in his own person and character. To this I answer by referring my Reader to the description which I have before given of a Poet. Among the qualities which I have enumerated as principally conducting to form a Poet, is implied nothing differing in kind from other men, but only in degree. The sum of what I have there said is that the Poet is chiefly distinguished from other men by a greater promptness to think and feel without immediate external excitement, and a greater power in expressing such thoughts and feelings as are produced in him in that manner. But these passions and thoughts and feelings are the general passions and thoughts and feelings of men. And with what are they connected? Undoubtedly with our moral sentiments and animal sensations, and with the causes which excite these; with the operations of the elements and the appearances of the visible universe; with storm and sunshine, with the revolutions of the seasons, with cold and heat, with loss of friends and kindred, with injuries and resentments, gratitude and hope, with fear and sorrow. These, and the like, are the sensations and objects which the Poet describes, as they are the sensations of other men, and the objects which interest them. The Poet thinks and feels in the spirit of the passions of men. How, then, can his language differ in any material degree from that of all other men who feel vividly and see clearly? It might be *proved* that it is impossible. But supposing that this were not the case, the Poet might then be allowed to use a peculiar language when expressing his feelings for his own gratification, or that of men like himself. But Poets do not write for Poets alone, but for men. Unless therefore we are advocates for that admiration which depends upon ignorance, and that pleasure which arises from hearing what we do not understand, the Poet must descend from this supposed height, and, in order to excite rational sympathy, he must express himself as other men express themselves. To this it may be added, that while he is only selecting from the real language of men, or, which amounts to the same thing, composing accurately in the spirit of such selection, he is treading upon safe ground, and we know what we are to expect from him. Our feelings are the same with respect to metre; for, as it may be proper to remind the Reader, the distinction of metre is regular and uniform, and not like that which is produced by what is usually called poetic diction, arbitrary, and subject to infinite caprices upon which no calculation whatever can be made. In the one case, the Reader is utterly at the mercy of the Poet respecting what imagery or diction he may choose to connect with the passion, whereas, in the other, the metre obeys certain laws, to which the Poet and Reader both willingly submit because they are certain, and because no interference is made by them with the passion but such as the concurring testimony of ages has shown to heighten and improve the pleasure which co-exists with it.

It will now be proper to answer an obvious question, namely, why, professing these opinions, have I written in verse? To this, in addition to such answer as is included in what I have already said, I reply in the first place, because, however I may have restricted myself, there is still left open to me what confessedly constitutes the most valuable object of all writing whether in prose or verse, the great and universal passions of men, the most general and interesting of their occupations, and the entire world of nature, from which I am at liberty to supply myself with endless combinations of forms and imagery. Now, supposing for a moment that whatever is interesting in these objects may be as vividly described in prose, why am I to be condemned, if to such description I have endeavoured to superadd the charm which, by the consent of all nations, is acknowledged to exist in metrical language? To this, by such as are unconvinced by what I have already said, it may be answered that a very small part of the pleasure given by Poetry depends upon the metre, and that it is injudicious to write in metre, unless it be accompanied with the other artificial distinctions of style with which metre is usually accompanied, and that by such deviation more will be lost from the shock which will be thereby given to the Reader's associations than will be counterbalanced by any pleasure which he can derive from the general power of numbers. In answer to those who still contend for the necessity of accompanying metre with certain appropriate colours of style in order to the accomplishment of its appropriate end, and who also, in my opinion, greatly under-rate the power of metre in itself, it might perhaps, as far as relates to these Poems, have been almost sufficient to observe that poems are extant, written upon more humble subjects, and in a more naked and simple style than I have aimed at, which poems have continued to give pleasure from generation to generation. Now, if nakedness and simplicity be a defect, the fact here mentioned affords a strong presumption that poems somewhat less naked and simple are capable of affording pleasure at the present day; and, what I wished *chiefly* to attempt, at present, was to justify myself for having written under the impression of this belief.

But I might point out various causes why, when the style is manly, and the subject of some importance, words metrically arranged will long continue to impart such a pleasure to mankind as he who is sensible of the extent of that pleasure will be desirous to impart. The end of Poetry is to produce excitement in co-existence with an overbalance of pleasure. Now, by the supposition, excitement is an unusual and irregular state of the mind; ideas and feelings do not in that state succeed each other in accustomed order. But, if the words by which this excitement is produced are in themselves powerful, or the images and feelings have an undue proportion of pain connected with them, there is some danger that the excitement may be carried beyond its proper bounds. Now the co-presence of something regular, something to which the mind has been accustomed in various moods and in a less excited state, cannot but have great efficacy in tempering and restraining the passion by an intertexture of ordinary feeling, and of feeling not strictly and necessarily connected with the passion. This is unquestionably true, and hence, though the opinion will at first appear paradoxical, from the tendency of metre to divest language in a certain degree of its reality, and thus to throw a sort of half consciousness of unsubstantial existence over the whole composition, there can be little doubt but that more pathetic situations and sentiments—that is, those which have a greater proportion of pain connected with them—may be endured in metrical composition, especially in rhyme, than in prose. The metre of the old Ballads is very artless; yet they contain many passages which would illustrate this opinion, and, I hope, if the following Poems be attentively perused, similar instances will be found in them....

I have said that Poetry is the spontaneous overflow of powerful feelings: it takes its origin from emotion recollected in tranquillity: the emotion is contemplated till by a species of reaction the tranquillity gradually disappears, and an emotion, kindred to that which was before the subject of contemplation, is gradually produced, and does itself actually exist in the mind. In this mood successful composition generally begins, and in a mood similar to this it is carried on; but the emotion, of whatever kind and in whatever degree, from various causes is qualified by various pleasures, so that in describing any passions whatsoever, which are voluntarily described, the mind will upon the whole be in a state of enjoyment. Now, if Nature be thus cautious in preserving in a state of enjoyment a being thus employed, the Poet ought to profit by the lesson thus held forth to him, and ought especially to take care that whatever passions he communicates to his Reader, those passions, if his Reader's mind be sound and vigorous, should always be accompanied with an overbalance of pleasure. Now the music of harmonious metrical language, the sense of difficulty overcome, and the blind association of pleasure which has been previously received from works of rhyme or metre of the same or similar construction, an indistinct perception perpetually renewed of language closely resembling that of real life, and yet, in the circumstance of metre, differing from it so widely, all these imperceptibly make up a complex feeling of delight, which is of the most important use in tempering the painful feeling which will always be found intermingled with powerful descriptions of the deeper passions. This effect is always produced in pathetic and impassioned poetry; while, in lighter compositions, the ease and gracefulness with which the Poet manages his numbers[1] are themselves confessedly a principal source of the gratification of the Reader. I might perhaps include all which it is *necessary* to say upon this subject by affirming what few persons will deny, that, of two descriptions, either of passions, manners, or characters, each of them equally well executed, the one in prose and the other in verse, the verse will be read a hundred times where the prose is read once. We see that Pope, by the power of verse alone, has contrived to render the plainest common sense interesting, and even frequently to invest it with the appearance of passion....

I know that nothing would have so effectually contributed to further the end which I have in view as to have shown of what kind the pleasure is, and how that pleasure is produced, which is confessedly produced by metrical composition essentially different from that which I have here endeavoured to recommend: for the Reader will say that he has been pleased by such composition; and what can I do more for him? The power of any art is limited; and he will suspect that, if I propose to furnish him with new friends, it is only upon condition of his abandoning his old friends. Besides, as I have said, the Reader is himself conscious of the pleasure which he has received from such composition, composition to which he has peculiarly attached the endearing name of Poetry; and all men feel an habitual gratitude, and something of an honorable bigotry for the objects which have long continued to please them: we not only wish to be pleased, but to be pleased in that particular way in which we have been accustomed to be pleased. There is a host of arguments in these feelings; and I should be the less able to combat them successfully, as I am willing to allow that, in order entirely to enjoy the Poetry which I am recommending, it would be necessary to give up much of what is ordinarily enjoyed. But, would my limits have permitted me to point out how this pleasure is produced, I might have removed many obstacles, and assisted my Reader in perceiving that the powers of language are not so limited as he may suppose; and that it is possible that poetry may give other enjoyments, of a purer, more lasting, and more exquisite nature. This part of my subject I have not altogether neglected; but it has been less my present aim to prove that the interest excited by some other kinds of poetry is less vivid, and less worthy of the nobler powers of the mind, than to offer reasons for presuming that, if the object which I have proposed to myself were adequately attained, a species of poetry would be produced which is genuine poetry; in its nature well adapted to interest mankind permanently, and likewise important in the multiplicity and quality of its moral relations.

From what has been said, and from a perusal of the Poems, the Reader will be able clearly to perceive the object which I have proposed to myself: he will determine how far I have attained this object; and, what is a much more important question, whether it be worth attaining; and upon the decision of these two questions will rest my claim to the approbation of the public.
—1800, 1802

[1] *numbers* Meter.

[*There was a Boy*]

There was a Boy, ye knew him well, ye Cliffs
And Islands of Winander![1] many a time,
At evening, when the stars began
To move along the edges of the hills,
Rising or setting, would he stand alone,
Beneath the trees, or by the glimmering lake,
And there, with fingers interwoven, both hands
Press'd closely palm to palm and to his mouth
Uplifted, he, as through an instrument,
Blew mimic hootings to the silent owls
That they might answer him. And they would shout
Across the wat'ry vale and shout again
Responsive to his call, with quivering peals,
And long halloos, and screams, and echoes loud
Redoubled and redoubled, a wild scene
Of mirth and jocund din. And, when it chanced
That pauses of deep silence mock'd his skill,
Then, sometimes, in that silence, while he hung
Listening, a gentle shock of mild surprise
Has carried far into his heart the voice
Of mountain torrents, or the visible scene
Would enter unawares into his mind
With all its solemn imagery, its rocks,
Its woods, and that uncertain heaven, receiv'd
Into the bosom of the steady lake.
Fair are the woods, and beauteous is the spot,
The vale where he was born: the Church-yard hangs
Upon a slope above the village school,[2]
And there along that bank when I have pass'd
At evening, I believe, that near his grave
A full half-hour together I have stood,
Mute—for he died when he was ten years old.
—1800

[1] *Winander* Windermere, the largest lake in England's Lake District.

[2] *the village school* Hawkshead Grammar School in Esthwaite.

[*Strange fits of passion I have known*][3]

Strange fits of passion I have known,
And I will dare to tell,
But in the Lover's ear alone,
What once to me befell.

When she I lov'd, was strong and gay
And like a rose in June,
I to her cottage bent my way,
Beneath the evening moon.

Upon the moon I fix'd my eye,
All over the wide lea;° *meadow*
My horse trudg'd on, and we drew nigh
Those paths so dear to me.

And now we reach'd the orchard plot,
And, as we climb'd the hill,
Towards the roof of Lucy's cot° *cottage*
The moon descended still.

In one of those sweet dreams I slept,
Kind Nature's gentlest boon!
And, all the while, my eyes I kept
On the descending moon.

My horse mov'd on; hoof after hoof
He rais'd and never stopp'd:
When down behind the cottage roof
At once the planet dropp'd.

What fond and wayward thoughts will slide
Into a Lover's head—
"O mercy!" to myself I cried,
"If Lucy should be dead!"[4]
—1800

[3] *Strange ... known* This and the following two lyrics are part of a group of five lyrics now commonly called the "Lucy poems," all of which were composed during the winter of 1798–9, when Wordsworth and his sister were in Germany. The identity of Lucy is unknown (if she existed at all); she is not the Lucy of Wordsworth's poem *Lucy Gray* (1800). Some critics believe that in these poems Wordsworth attempts to express his feelings for his sister.

[4] *If ... dead* In an earlier manuscript version, another stanza followed: "I told her this: her laughter light / Is ringing in my ears;/ And when I think upon that night / My eyes are dim with tears."

Song [She dwelt among th'untrodden ways]

She dwelt among th'untrodden ways
Beside the springs of Dove,[1]
A Maid whom there were none to praise
And very few to love.

A violet by a mossy stone
Half-hidden from the Eye!
—Fair, as a star when only one
Is shining in the sky.

She *liv'd* unknown, and few could know
When Lucy ceas'd to be;
But she is in her Grave, and Oh!
The difference to me.

—1800

[A slumber did my spirit seal] [2]

A slumber did my spirit seal,
I had no human fears:
She seem'd a thing that could not feel
The touch of earthly years.

No motion has she now, no force
She neither hears nor sees
Roll'd round in earth's diurnal° course *daily*
With rocks and stones and trees!

—1800

[1] *Dove* Name of numerous rivers in England, one of which is in the Lake District.

[2] *A slumber ... seal* Of this poem, Coleridge wrote to a friend in April 1799: "Some months ago Wordsworth transmitted to me a most sublime epitaph. ... Whether it had any reality, I cannot say. Most probably, in some gloomier moment he had fancied the moment in which his sister might die."

Lucy Gray [3]

Oft I had heard of Lucy Gray,
And when I cross'd the Wild,
I chanc'd to see at break of day
The solitary child.

No Mate, no comrade Lucy knew;
She dwelt on a wide Moor,
The sweetest Thing that ever grew
Beside a human door!

You yet may spy the Fawn at play,
The Hare upon the Green;
But the sweet face of Lucy Gray
Will never more be seen.

"To-night will be a stormy night,
You to the Town must go,
And take a lantern, Child, to light
Your Mother thro' the snow."

"That, Father! will I gladly do;
'Tis scarcely afternoon—
The Minster°-clock has just struck two, *church*
And yonder is the Moon!"

At this the Father rais'd his hook,
And snapp'd a faggot-band;[4]
He plied his work, and Lucy took
The lantern in her hand.

Not blither° is the mountain roe, *more merry*
With many a wanton° stroke *frolicsome*

[3] *Lucy Gray* Based on an account of a drowned girl told to Wordsworth by his sister. In his note, Wordsworth says that after the girl had become lost in a snowstorm, "her footsteps were traced by her parents to the middle of the lock of a canal, and no other vestige of her, backward or forward, could be traced. The body, however, was found in the canal. The way in which the incident was treated and the spiritualizing of the character might furnish hints for consulting the imaginative influences which I have endeavoured to throw over common life with Crabbe's matter of fact style of treating subjects of the same kind." (Wordsworth refers to the poet George Crabbe [1754–1832].)

[4] *faggot-band* Cord for binding a bundle of firewood.

Her feet disperse the powd'ry snow,
That rises up like smoke.

The storm came on before its time,
She wander'd up and down,
And many a hill did Lucy climb:
But never reach'd the Town.

The wretched Parents all that night
Went shouting far and wide;
But there was neither sound nor sight
To serve them for a guide.

At day-break on a hill they stood
That overlook'd the Moor;
And thence they saw the Bridge of Wood,
A furlong[1] from their door.

And now they homeward turn'd, and cry'd
"In Heaven we all shall meet!"
When in the snow the Mother spied
The print of Lucy's feet.

Then downward from the steep hill's edge
They track'd the footmarks small;
And through the broken hawthorn-hedge,
And by the long stone-wall;

And then an open field they cross'd,
The marks were still the same;
They track'd them on, nor ever lost,
And to the Bridge they came.

They follow'd from the snowy bank
Those footmarks, one by one,
Into the middle of the plank,
And further there were none.

Yet some maintain that to this day
She is a living Child,
That you may see sweet Lucy Gray
Upon the lonesome Wild.

[1] *furlong* Measurement equal to 220 yards, or one eighth of a mile.

O'er rough and smooth she trips along,
And never looks behind;
And sings a solitary song
That whistles in the wind.
—1800

Nutting

It seems a day,
(I speak of one from many singled out)
One of those heavenly days which cannot die,
When forth I sallied from our cottage-door,
And with a wallet° o'er my shoulder slung, *knapsack*
A nutting crook[2] in hand, I turn'd my steps
Towards the distant woods, a Figure quaint,
Trick'd out in proud disguise of Beggar's weeds° *garments*
Put on for the occasion, by advice
And exhortation of my frugal Dame.[3]
Motley accoutrements! of power to smile
At thorns, and brakes,° and brambles, and, in truth, *thickets*
More ragged than need was. Among the woods,
And o'er the pathless rocks, I forc'd my way
Until, at length, I came to one dear nook
Unvisited, where not a broken bough
Droop'd with its wither'd leaves, ungracious sign
Of devastation, but the hazels rose
Tall and erect, with milk-white clusters hung,
A virgin scene!—A little while I stood,
Breathing with such suppression of the heart
As joy delights in; and with wise restraint
Voluptuous, fearless of a rival, eyed
The banquet, or beneath the trees I sat
Among the flowers, and with the flowers I play'd;
A temper known to those, who, after long
And weary expectation, have been bless'd
With sudden happiness beyond all hope.
—Perhaps it was a bower beneath whose leaves
The violets of five seasons re-appear
And fade, unseen by any human eye,

[2] *nutting crook* Hooked instrument for gathering nuts.

[3] *my frugal Dame* Ann Tyson, at whose house Wordsworth boarded during his school years.

Where fairy water-breaks[1] do murmur on
For ever, and I saw the sparkling foam,
And with my cheek on one of those green stones
That, fleec'd with moss, beneath the shady trees,
Lay round me scatter'd like a flock of sheep,
I heard the murmur and the murmuring sound,
In that sweet mood when pleasure loves to pay
Tribute to ease, and, of its joy secure
The heart luxuriates with indifferent things,
Wasting its kindliness on stocks° and stones, *stumps*
And on the vacant air. Then up I rose,
And dragg'd to earth both branch and bough, with crash
And merciless ravage; and the shady nook
Of hazels, and the green and mossy bower
Deform'd and sullied, patiently gave up
Their quiet being: and unless I now
Confound my present feelings with the past,
Even then, when from the bower I turn'd away,
Exulting, rich beyond the wealth of kings
I felt a sense of pain when I beheld
The silent trees and the intruding sky.

Then, dearest Maiden![2] move along these shades
In gentleness of heart with gentle hand
Touch—for there is a Spirit in the woods.
—1800

Michael

Wordsworth said this pastoral poem is founded on two real incidents, one of "the son of an old couple having become dissolute, and run away from his parents" and the other of "an old shepherd having been seven years in building up a sheepfold in a solitary valley." In combining these tales, he said in a letter to Thomas Poole, "I have attempted to give a picture of a man of strong mind and lively sensibility, agitated by two of the most powerful affections of the human heart—parental affection and the love of property, landed property, including the feelings of inheritance, home, and personal and family independence." As in his poem *Brothers*, Wordsworth writes "with a view to show that men who do not wear fine clothes can feel deeply" and attempts "to draw a picture of the domestic affections, as I know they exist among a class of men who are now almost confined to the north of England. They are small independent proprietors of land, here called 'states-men,' men of respectable education, who daily labor on their own little properties. The domestic affections will always be strong amongst men who live in a country not crowded with population; if these men are placed above poverty.... Their little tract of land serves as a kind of permanent rallying point for their domestic feelings, as a tablet on which they are written, which makes them objects of memory in a thousand instances, when they would otherwise be forgotten."

Michael, A Pastoral Poem

If from the public way you turn your steps
Up the tumultuous brook of Green-head Gill,[3]
You will suppose that with an upright path
Your feet must struggle; in such bold ascent
The pastoral Mountains front you, face to face.
But, courage! for beside that boisterous Brook
The mountains have all open'd out themselves,
And made a hidden valley of their own.
No habitation can be seen; but such
As journey thither find themselves alone
With a few sheep, with rocks and stones, and kites[4]
That overhead are sailing in the sky.

It is in truth an utter solitude,
Nor should I have made mention of this Dell
But for one object which you might pass by,
Might see and notice not. Beside the brook
There is a straggling heap of unhewn stones!
And to that place a story appertains,

[1] *water-breaks* Places where the water flow is broken by underlying rocks.

[2] *Maiden* In a longer manuscript draft of the poem, a passage originally intended to lead up to "Nutting" describes a maiden named Lucy ravaging a bower.

[3] *Gill* Steep, narrow valley with a stream running through it. Green-head Gill is near Wordsworth's cottage at Grasmere.

[4] *kites* Small falcon-like birds of prey.

Which, though it be ungarnish'd with events,
Is not unfit, I deem, for the fire-side,
Or for the summer shade. It was the first,
The earliest of those tales that spake to me
Of Shepherds, dwellers in the valleys, men
Whom I already lov'd, not verily
For their own sakes, but for the fields and hills
Where was their occupation and abode.
And hence this Tale, while I was yet a boy
Careless of books, yet having felt the power
Of Nature, by the gentle agency
Of natural objects led me on to feel
For passions that were not my own, and think
At random and imperfectly indeed
On man; the heart of man and human life.
Therefore, although it be a history
Homely and rude, I will relate the same
For the delight of a few natural hearts,
And with yet fonder feeling, for the sake
Of youthful Poets, who among these Hills
Will be my second self when I am gone.

Upon the Forest-side in Grasmere Vale
There dwelt a Shepherd, Michael was his name,
An old man, stout of heart, and strong of limb.
His bodily frame had been from youth to age
Of an unusual strength: his mind was keen
Intense and frugal, apt for all affairs,
And in his Shepherd's calling he was prompt
And watchful more than ordinary men.
Hence he had learn'd the meaning of all winds,
Of blasts of every tone, and often-times
When others heeded not, He heard the South[1]
Make subterraneous music, like the noise
Of Bagpipers on distant Highland hills;
The Shepherd, at such warning, of his flock
Bethought him, and he to himself would say
The winds are now devising work for me!
And truly at all times the storm, that drives
The Traveller to a shelter, summon'd him
Up to the mountains: he had been alone
Amid the heart of many thousand mists
That came to him and left him on the heights.
So liv'd he till his eightieth year was pass'd.
And grossly that man errs, who should suppose
That the green Valleys, and the Streams and Rocks
Were things indifferent to the Shepherd's thoughts.
Fields, where with cheerful spirits he had breath'd
The common air; the hills, which he so oft
Had climb'd with vigorous steps; which had impress'd
So many incidents upon his mind
Of hardship, skill or courage, joy or fear;
Which like a book preserv'd the memory
Of the dumb animals, whom he had sav'd,
Had fed or shelter'd, linking to such acts,
So grateful in themselves, the certainty
Of honorable gains; these fields, these hills
Which were his living Being, even more
Than his own Blood—what could they less? had laid
Strong hold on his affections, were to him
A pleasurable feeling of blind love,
The pleasure which there is in life itself.

He had not passed his days in singleness.
He had a Wife, a comely Matron, old
Though younger than himself full twenty years.
She was a woman of a stirring life
Whose heart was in her house: two wheels she had
Of antique form, this large for spinning wool,
That small for flax, and if one wheel had rest,
It was because the other was at work.
The Pair had but one Inmate in their house,
An only Child, who had been born to them
When Michael telling° o'er his years began *counting*
To deem that he was old, in Shepherd's phrase,
With one foot in the grave. This only son,
With two brave sheep dogs tried in many a storm,
The one of an inestimable worth,
Made all their Household. I may truly say,
That they were as a proverb in the vale
For endless industry. When day was gone,
And from their occupations out of doors
The Son and Father were come home, even then
Their labour did not cease, unless when all
Turn'd to their cleanly supper-board,[2] and there
Each with a mess of pottage[3] and skimm'd milk,
Sat round their basket pil'd with oaten cakes,

[1] *South* South wind.

[2] *supper-board* Table.

[3] *pottage* Stew of vegetables, and sometimes meat, boiled in water.

And their plain home-made cheese. Yet when their meal
Was ended, LUKE (for so the Son was nam'd)
And his old Father, both betook themselves
To such convenient work, as might employ
Their hands by the fire-side; perhaps to card[1]
Wool for the House-wife's spindle, or repair
Some injury done to sickle, flail,[2] or scythe,
Or other implement of house or field.
Down from the ceiling by the chimney's edge,
Which in our ancient uncouth country style
Did with a huge projection overbrow° *overhang*
Large space beneath, as duly as the light
Of day grew dim, the House-wife hung a lamp;
An aged utensil, which had perform'd
Service beyond all others of its kind.
Early at evening did it burn and late,
Surviving Comrade of uncounted Hours
Which going by from year to year had found
And left the Couple neither gay perhaps
Nor cheerful, yet with objects and with hopes
Living a life of eager industry.
And now, when LUKE was in his eighteenth year,
There by the light of this old lamp they sat,
Father and Son, while late into the night
The House-wife plied her own peculiar work,
Making the cottage thro' the silent hours
Murmur as with the sound of summer flies.
Not with a waste of words, but for the sake
Of pleasure, which I know that I shall give
To many living now, I of this Lamp
Speak thus minutely: for there are no few
Whose memories will bear witness to my tale.
The Light was famous in its neighbourhood,
And was a public Symbol of the life,
The thrifty Pair had liv'd. For, as it chanc'd,
Their Cottage on a plot of rising ground
Stood single, with large prospect North and South,
High into Easedale, up to Dunmal-Raise,
And Westward to the village near the Lake.
And from this constant light so regular
And so far seen, the House itself by all
Who dwelt within the limits of the vale,
Both old and young, was nam'd The Evening Star.
Thus living on through such a length of years,
The Shepherd, if he lov'd himself, must needs
Have lov'd his Help-mate; but to Michael's heart
This Son of his old age was yet more dear—
Effect which might perhaps have been produc'd
By that instinctive tenderness, the same
Blind Spirit, which is in the blood of all,
Or that a child, more than all other gifts,
Brings hope with it, and forward-looking thoughts,
And stirrings of inquietude, when they
By tendency of nature needs must fail.
From such, and other causes, to the thoughts
Of the old Man his only Son was now
The dearest object that he knew on earth.
Exceeding was the love he bare to him,
His Heart and his Heart's joy! For oftentimes
Old Michael, while he was a babe in arms,
Had done him female service, not alone
For dalliance and delight, as is the use
Of Fathers, but with patient mind enforc'd
To acts of tenderness; and he had rock'd
His cradle with a woman's gentle hand.

And in a later time, ere yet the Boy
Had put on Boy's attire, did Michael love,
Albeit of a stern unbending mind,
To have the young one in his sight, when he
Had work by his own door, or when he sat
With sheep before him on his Shepherd's stool,
Beneath that large old Oak, which near their door
Stood, and from its enormous breadth of shade
Chosen for the Shearer's covert from the sun,
Thence in our rustic dialect was call'd
The CLIPPING° TREE, a name which yet it bears. *shearing*
There, while they two were sitting in the shade,
With others round them, earnest all and blithe,
Would Michael exercise his heart with looks
Of fond correction and reproof bestow'd
Upon the child, if he disturb'd the sheep
By catching at their legs, or with his shouts
Scar'd them, while they lay still beneath the shears.
And when by Heaven's good grace the Boy grew up
A healthy Lad, and carried in his cheek
Two steady roses that were five years old,

[1] *card* Comb out impurities.

[2] *flail* Tool for threshing corn.

Then Michael from a winter coppice[1] cut
With his own hand a sapling, which he hoop'd
With iron, making it throughout in all
Due requisites a perfect Shepherd's Staff,
And gave it to the Boy; wherewith equipp'd
He as a Watchman oftentimes was plac'd
At gate or gap, to stem or turn the flock,
And to his office prematurely call'd
There stood the urchin, as you will divine,
Something between a hindrance and a help,
And for this cause not always, I believe,
Receiving from his Father hire of praise.
Though nought was left undone which staff, or voice,
Or looks, or threatening gestures, could perform.
But soon as Luke, full ten years old, could stand
Against the mountain blasts, and to the heights,
Not fearing toil, nor length of weary ways,
He with his Father daily went, and they
Were as companions, why should I relate
That objects which the Shepherd loved before
Were dearer now? that from the Boy there came
Feelings and emanations, things which were
Light to the sun and music to the wind;
And that the Old Man's heart seemed born again?
Thus in his Father's sight the Boy grew up:
And now when he had reached his eighteenth year,
He was his comfort and his daily hope.

While this good household thus were living on
From day to day, to Michael's ear there came
Distressful tidings. Long before the time
Of which I speak, the Shepherd had been bound
In surety for his Brother's Son, a man
Of an industrious life, and ample means,
But unforeseen misfortunes suddenly
Had press'd upon him, and old Michael now
Was summon'd to discharge the forfeiture,
A grievous penalty, but little less
Than half his substance. This un-look'd for claim
At the first hearing, for a moment took
More hope out of his life than he supposed
That any old man ever could have lost.
As soon as he had gather'd so much strength
That he could look his trouble in the face,
It seem'd that his sole refuge was to sell
A portion of his patrimonial fields.
Such was his first resolve; he thought again,
And his heart fail'd him. "Isabel," said he,
Two evenings after he had heard the news,
"I have been toiling more than seventy years,
And in the open sunshine of God's love
Have we all liv'd, yet if these fields of ours
Should pass into a Stranger's hand, I think
That I could not lie quiet in my grave.
Our lot is a hard lot; the Sun itself
Has scarcely been more diligent than I,
And I have liv'd to be a fool at last
To my own family. An evil Man
That was, and made an evil choice, if he
Were false to us; and if he were not false,
There are ten thousand to whom loss like this
Had been no sorrow. I forgive him—but
'Twere better to be dumb than to talk thus.
When I began, my purpose was to speak
Of remedies and of a cheerful hope.
Our Luke shall leave us, Isabel; the land
Shall not go from us, and it shall be free,[2]
He shall possess it, free as is the wind
That passes over it. We have, thou knowest,
Another Kinsman, he will be our friend
In this distress. He is a prosperous man,
Thriving in trade, and Luke to him shall go,
And with his Kinsman's help and his own thrift,
He quickly will repair this loss, and then
May come again to us. If here he stay,
What can be done? Where every one is poor
What can be gain'd?" At this, the old man paus'd,
And Isabel sat silent, for her mind
Was busy, looking back into past times.
There's Richard Bateman, thought she to herself,[3]
He was a parish-boy[4]—at the church-door
They made a gathering for him, shillings, pence,
And halfpennies, wherewith the Neighbours bought
A Basket, which they fill'd with Pedlar's wares,

[1] *coppice* Thicket of small trees.

[2] *free* I.e., not mortgaged.

[3] [Wordsworth's note] The story alluded to here is well known in the country. The chapel is called Ings Chapel and is on the road leading from Kendal to Ambleside.

[4] *parish-boy* Youth cared for and supported by the parish.

And with this Basket on his arm, the Lad
Went up to London, found a Master there,
Who out of many chose the trusty Boy
To go and overlook his merchandise
Beyond the seas, where he grew wond'rous rich,
And left estates and monies to the poor,
And at his birth-place built a Chapel, floor'd
With Marble, which he sent from foreign lands.
These thoughts, and many others of like sort,
Pass'd quickly thro' the mind of Isabel,
And her face brighten'd. The Old Man was glad,
And thus resum'd. "Well! Isabel, this scheme
These two days has been meat and drink to me.
Far more than we have lost is left us yet.
—We have enough—I wish indeed that I
Were younger, but this hope is a good hope.
—Make ready Luke's best garments, of the best
Buy for him more, and let us send him forth
To-morrow, or the next day, or to-night:
—If he could go, the Boy should go to-night."

Here Michael ceas'd, and to the fields went forth
With a light heart. The House-wife for five days
Was restless morn and night, and all day long
Wrought on with her best fingers to prepare
Things needful for the journey of her Son.
But Isabel was glad when Sunday came
To stop her in her work; for, when she lay
By Michael's side, she for the last two nights
Heard him, how he was troubled in his sleep:
And when they rose at morning she could see
That all his hopes were gone. That day at noon
She said to Luke, while they two by themselves
Were sitting at the door, "Thou must not go,
We have no other Child but thee to lose,
None to remember—do not go away,
For if thou leave thy Father he will die."
The Lad made answer with a jocund voice,
And Isabel, when she had told her fears,
Recover'd heart. That evening her best fare
Did she bring forth, and all together sat
Like happy people round a Christmas fire.
Next morning Isabel resum'd her work,
And all the ensuing week the house appear'd
As cheerful as a grove in Spring: at length
The expected letter from their Kinsman came,
With kind assurances that he would do
His utmost for the welfare of the Boy,
To which requests were added that forthwith
He might be sent to him. Ten times or more
The letter was read over; Isabel
Went forth to shew it to the neighbours round:
Nor was there at that time on English land
A prouder heart than Luke's. When Isabel
Had to her house return'd, the Old Man said,
"He shall depart to-morrow." To this word
The House-wife answered, talking much of things
Which, if at such short notice he should go,
Would surely be forgotten. But at length
She gave consent, and Michael was at ease.

Near the tumultuous brook of Green-head Gill,
In that deep Valley, Michael had design'd
To build a Sheep-fold,[1] and, before he heard
The tidings of his melancholy loss,
For this same purpose he had gathered up
A heap of stones, which close to the brook side
Lay thrown together, ready for the work.
With Luke that evening thitherward he walk'd;
And soon as they had reach'd the place he stopp'd,
And thus the Old Man spake to him. "My Son,
To-morrow thou wilt leave me; with full heart
I look upon thee, for thou art the same
That wert a promise to me ere thy birth,
And all thy life hast been my daily joy.
I will relate to thee some little part
Of our two histories; 'twill do thee good
When thou art from me, even if I should speak
Of things thou canst not know of.——After thou
First cam'st into the world, as it befalls
To new-born infants, thou didst sleep away
Two days, and blessings from thy Father's tongue
Then fell upon thee. Day by day pass'd on,
And still I lov'd thee with encreasing love.
Never to living ear came sweeter sounds
Than when I heard thee by our own fire-side
First uttering without words a natural tune,
When thou, a feeding babe, didst in thy joy
Sing at thy Mother's breast. Month follow'd month,

[1] *Sheep-fold* Stone-walled pen for sheep.

And in the open fields my life was pass'd
And in the mountains, else I think that thou
Hadst been brought up upon thy father's knees.
—But we were playmates, Luke; among these hills,
As well thou know'st, in us the old and young
Have play'd together, nor with me didst thou
Lack any pleasure which a boy can know."

Luke had a manly heart; but at these words
He sobb'd aloud; the Old Man grasp'd his hand,
And said, "Nay, do not take it so—I see
That these are things of which I need not speak.
—Even to the utmost I have been to thee
A kind and a good Father: and herein
I but repay a gift which I myself
Receiv'd at others hands, for, though now old
Beyond the common life of man, I still
Remember them who lov'd me in my youth.
Both of them sleep together: here they liv'd
As all their Forefathers had done, and when
At length their time was come, they were not loth
To give their bodies to the family mold.
I wish'd that thou should'st live the life they liv'd.
But 'tis a long time to look back, my Son,
And see so little gain from sixty years.
These fields were burthen'd° when they came to me; *mortgaged*
'Till I was forty years of age, not more
Than half of my inheritance was mine.
I toil'd and toil'd; God bless'd me in my work,
And 'till these three weeks past the land was free.
—It looks as if it never could endure
Another Master. Heaven forgive me, Luke,
If I judge ill for thee, but it seems good
That thou should'st go." At this the Old Man paus'd,
Then, pointing to the Stones near which they stood,
Thus, after a short silence, he resum'd:
"This was a work for us, and now, my Son,
It is a work for me. But, lay one Stone—
Here, lay it for me, Luke, with thine own hands.
Nay, Boy, be of good hope: we both may live
To see a better day. At eighty-four
I still am strong and stout; do thou thy part,
I will do mine. I will begin again
With many tasks that were resign'd to thee;
Up to the heights, and in among the storms,
Will I without thee go again, and do
All works which I was wont to do alone,
Before I knew thy face. Heaven bless thee, Boy!
Thy heart these two weeks has been beating fast
With many hopes—it should be so—yes—yes—
I knew that thou could'st never have a wish
To leave me, Luke, thou hast been bound to me
Only by links of love, when thou art gone
What will be left to us! But, I forget
My purposes. Lay now the corner-stone,
As I requested, and hereafter, Luke,
When thou art gone away, should evil men
Be thy companions, let this Sheep-fold be
Thy anchor and thy shield; amid all fear
And all temptation, let it be to thee
An emblem of the life thy Fathers liv'd,
Who, being innocent, did for that cause
Bestir them in good deeds. Now, fare thee well—
When thou return'st, thou in this place wilt see
A work which is not here, a covenant
'Twill be between us—but whatever fate
Befall thee, I shall love thee to the last,
And bear thy memory with me to the grave."

The Shepherd ended here; and Luke stoop'd down,
And as his Father had requested, laid
The first stone of the Sheep-fold; at the sight
The Old Man's grief broke from him, to his heart
He press'd his Son, he kissed him and wept;
And to the House together they return'd.
Next morning, as had been resolv'd, the Boy
Began his journey, and when he had reach'd
The public Way, he put on a bold face;
And all the Neighbours as he pass'd their doors
Came forth, with wishes and with farewell pray'rs,
That follow'd him 'till he was out of sight.
A good report did from their Kinsman come,
Of Luke and his well-doing; and the Boy
Wrote loving letters, full of wond'rous news,
Which, as the House-wife phrased it, were throughout
The prettiest letters that were ever seen.
Both parents read them with rejoicing hearts.
So, many months pass'd on: and once again
The Shepherd went about his daily work

With confident and cheerful thoughts; and now
Sometimes when he could find a leisure hour
He to that valley took his way, and there
Wrought at the Sheep-fold. Meantime Luke began
To slacken in his duty, and at length
He in the dissolute city gave himself
To evil courses: ignominy and shame
Fell on him, so that he was driven at last
To seek a hiding-place beyond the seas.

There is a comfort in the strength of love;
'Twill make a thing endurable, which else
Would break the heart: Old Michael found it so.
I have convers'd with more than one who well
Remember the Old Man, and what he was
Years after he had heard this heavy news.
His bodily frame had been from youth to age
Of an unusual strength. Among the rocks
He went, and still look'd up upon the sun,
And listen'd to the wind; and as before
Perform'd all kinds of labour for his Sheep,
And for the land his small inheritance.
And to that hollow Dell from time to time
Did he repair, to build the Fold of which
His flock had need. 'Tis not forgotten yet
The pity which was then in every heart
For the Old Man—and 'tis believ'd by all
That many and many a day he thither went,
And never lifted up a single stone.

There, by the Sheep-fold, sometimes was he seen
Sitting alone, with that his faithful Dog,
Then old, beside him, lying at his feet.
The length of full seven years from time to time
He at the building of this Sheep-fold wrought,
And left the work unfinished when he died.

Three years, or little more, did Isabel,
Survive her Husband: at her death the estate
Was sold, and went into a Stranger's hand.
The Cottage which was nam'd The Evening Star
Is gone, the ploughshare has been through the ground
On which it stood; great changes have been wrought
In all the neighbourhood, yet the Oak is left
That grew beside their Door; and the remains
Of the unfinished Sheep-fold may be seen
Beside the boisterous brook of Green-head Gill.
—1800

[*I Griev'd for Buonaparté*][1]

I griev'd for Buonaparté, with a vain
And an unthinking grief! the vital blood
Of that Man's mind what can it be? What food
Fed his first hopes? What knowledge could *He* gain?
'Tis not in battles that from youth we train
The Governor who must be wise and good,
And temper with the sternness of the brain
Thoughts motherly, and meek as womanhood.
Wisdom doth live with children round her knees:
Books, leisure, perfect freedom, and the talk
Man holds with week-day man in the hourly walk
Of the mind's business: these are the degrees
By which true Sway doth mount; this is the stalk
True Power doth grow on; and her rights are these.
—1802

Ode to Duty

Stern Daughter of the Voice of God![2]
O Duty! if that name thou love
Who art a Light to guide, a Rod
To check the erring, and reprove;
Thou, who art victory and law
When empty terrors overawe;
From vain temptations dost set free;
From strife and from despair; a glorious ministry.

There are who ask not if thine eye
Be on them; who, in love and truth,
Where no misgiving is, rely
Upon the genial° sense° of youth: *natural / vitality*

[1] *I ... Buonaparté* According to Dorothy Wordsworth, this sonnet was composed in 1802, the year that Napoleon Buonaparte declared himself First Consul of France for life.

[2] *Stern ... God* Cf. Milton, *Paradise Lost* 9.652–54: "God so commanded, and left that Command / Sole Daughter of His voice; the rest, we live / Law to ourselves, our Reason is our Law."

Glad Hearts! without reproach or blot;
Who do thy work, and know it not:
May joy be theirs while life shall last!
And Thou, if they should totter, teach them to stand
fast!

Serene will be our days and bright,
And happy will our nature be,
When love is an unerring light,
And joy its own security.
And bless'd are they who in the main
This faith, even now, do entertain:
Live in the spirit of this creed;
Yet find that other strength, according to their need.

I, loving freedom, and untried;
No sport of every random gust,
Yet being to myself a guide,
Too blindly have reposed my trust:
Resolved that nothing e'er should press
Upon my present happiness,
I shoved unwelcome tasks away;
But thee I now would serve more strictly, if I may.

Through no disturbance of my soul,
Or strong compunction in me wrought,
I supplicate for thy control;
But in the quietness of thought:
Me this uncharter'd freedom tires;
I feel the weight of chance desires:
My hopes no more must change their name,
I long for a repose that ever is the same.

Yet not the less would I throughout
Still act according to the voice
Of my own wish; and feel past doubt
That my submissiveness was choice:
Not seeking in the school of pride
For "precepts over dignified,"
Denial and restraint I prize
No farther than they breed a second Will more wise.

Stern Lawgiver! yet thou dost wear
The Godhead's most benignant grace;
Nor know we anything so fair
As is the smile upon thy face:
Flowers laugh before thee on their beds;
And Fragrance in thy footing treads;
Thou dost preserve the Stars from wrong;
And the most ancient Heavens, through Thee are fresh
and strong.

To humbler functions, awful Power!
I call thee: I myself commend
Unto thy guidance from this hour;
Oh! let my weakness have an end!
Give unto me, made lowly wise,
The spirit of self-sacrifice;
The confidence of reason give;
And in the light of truth thy Bondman let me live!
—1807

Resolution and Independence

There was a roaring in the wind all night;
The rain came heavily and fell in floods;
But now the sun is rising calm and bright;
The birds are singing in the distant woods;
Over his own sweet voice the Stock-dove° *wild pigeon*
broods;
The Jay makes answer as the Magpie chatters;
And all the air is fill'd with pleasant noise of waters.

All things that love the sun are out of doors;
The sky rejoices in the morning's birth;
The grass is bright with rain-drops; on the moors
The Hare is running races in her mirth;
And with her feet she from the plashy[1] earth
Raises a mist; which, glittering in the sun,
Runs with her all the way, wherever she doth run.

I was a Traveller then upon the moor;
I saw the Hare that rac'd about with joy;
I heard the woods, and distant waters, roar;
Or heard them not, as happy as a Boy:
The pleasant season did my heart employ:

[1] *plashy* Having many puddles or pools of water; wet.

My old remembrances went from me wholly;
And all the ways of men, so vain and melancholy.

But, as it sometimes chanceth, from the might
Of joy in minds that can no farther go,
As high as we have mounted in delight
In our dejection do we sink as low,
To me that morning did it happen so;
And fears, and fancies, thick upon me came;
Dim sadness, and blind thoughts I knew not nor could
name.

I heard the Sky-lark singing in the sky;
And I bethought me of the playful Hare:
Even such a happy Child of earth am I;
Even as these blissful Creatures do I fare;
Far from the world I walk, and from all care;
But there may come another day to me,
Solitude, pain of heart, distress, and poverty.

My whole life I have liv'd in pleasant thought,
As if life's business were a summer mood;
As if all needful things would come unsought
To genial faith, still rich in genial good;
But how can He expect that others should
Build for him, sow for him, and at his call
Love him, who for himself will take no heed at all?

I thought of Chatterton,[1] the marvellous Boy,
The sleepless Soul that perish'd in its pride;
Of Him who walk'd in glory and in joy
Behind his plough, upon the mountain-side:[2]
By our own spirits are we deified;
We Poets in our youth begin in gladness;
But thereof comes in the end despondency and
madness.

Now, whether it were by peculiar grace,
A leading from above, a something given,
Yet it befel, that, in this lonely place,
When up and down my fancy thus was driven,
And I with these untoward thoughts had striven,
I saw a Man before me unawares:
The oldest man he seem'd that ever wore grey hairs.

My course I stopped as soon as I espied
The Old Man in that naked wilderness:
Close by a Pond, upon the further side,
He stood alone: a minute's space I guess
I watch'd him, he continuing motionless:
To the Pool's further margin then I drew;
He being all the while before me full in view.

As a huge Stone is sometimes seen to lie
Couch'd on the bald top of an eminence;
Wonder to all who do the same espy
By what means it could thither come, and whence;
So that it seems a thing endued with sense:
Like a Sea-beast crawl'd forth, which on a shelf
Of rock or sand reposeth, there to sun itself.

Such seem'd this Man, not all alive nor dead,
Nor all asleep; in his extreme old age:
His body was bent double, feet and head
Coming together in their pilgrimage;
As if some dire constraint of pain, or rage
Of sickness felt by him in times long past,
A more than human weight upon his frame had cast.

Himself he propp'd, his body, limbs, and face,
Upon a long grey Staff of shaven wood:
And, still as I drew near with gentle pace,
Beside the little pond or moorish flood
Motionless as a Cloud the Old Man stood;
That heareth not the loud winds when they call;
And moveth altogether, if it move at all.

At length, himself unsettling, he the Pond
Stirred with his Staff, and fixedly did look
Upon the muddy water, which he conn'd,° *studied*
As if he had been reading in a book:
And now such freedom as I could I took;
And, drawing to his side, to him did say,
"This morning gives us promise of a glorious day."

[1] *Chatterton* Poet Thomas Chatterton (1752–70), who, after failing to make a living as a poet in London, poisoned himself at the age of seventeen.

[2] *Him who … mountain-side* Scottish poet Robert Burns (1759–96), known as "the Ploughman Poet" because of his farming background.

A gentle answer did the Old Man make,
In courteous speech which forth he slowly drew:
And him with further words I thus bespake,
"What kind of work is that which you pursue?
This is a lonesome place for one like you."
He answer'd me with pleasure and surprise;
And there was, while he spake, a fire about his eyes.

His words came feebly, from a feeble chest,
Yet each in solemn order follow'd each,
With something of a lofty utterance drest;
Choice word, and measured phrase; above the reach
Of ordinary men; a stately speech!
Such as grave Livers[1] do in Scotland use,
Religious men, who give to God and Man their dues.

He told me that he to this pond had come
To gather Leeches,[2] being old and poor:
Employment hazardous and wearisome!
And he had many hardships to endure:
From Pond to Pond he roam'd, from moor to moor,
Housing, with God's good help, by choice or chance:
And in this way he gain'd an honest maintenance.

The old Man still stood talking by my side;
But now his voice to me was like a stream
Scarce heard; nor word from word could I divide;
And the whole Body of the man did seem
Like one whom I had met with in a dream;
Or like a Man from some far region sent;
To give me human strength, and strong admonishment.

My former thoughts return'd: the fear that kills;
The hope that is unwilling to be fed;
Cold, pain, and labour, and all fleshly ills;
And mighty Poets in their misery dead.
And now, not knowing what the Old Man had said,
My question eagerly did I renew,
"How is it that you live, and what is it you do?"

He with a smile did then his words repeat;
And said that, gathering Leeches, far and wide
He travelled; stirring thus about his feet
The waters of the Ponds where they abide.
"Once I could meet with them on every side;
But they have dwindled long by slow decay;
Yet still I persevere, and find them where I may."

While he was talking thus, the lonely place,
The Old Man's shape, and speech, all troubled me:
In my mind's eye I seem'd to see him pace
About the weary moors continually,
Wandering about alone and silently.
While I these thoughts within myself pursued,
He, having made a pause, the same discourse renewed.

And soon with this he other matter blended,
Cheerfully uttered, with demeanour kind,
But stately in the main; and, when he ended,
I could have laugh'd myself to scorn, to find
In that decrepit Man so firm a mind.
"God," said I, "be my help and stay° secure; *support*
I'll think of the Leech-gatherer on the lonely moor."
—1807

Composed upon Westminster Bridge Sept. 3, 1803[3]

Earth has not any thing to show more fair:
Dull would he be of soul who could pass by
A sight so touching in its majesty:
This City now doth like a garment wear
This beauty of the morning; silent, bare,
Ships, towers, domes, theatres, and temples lie
Open unto the fields, and to the sky;
All bright and glittering in the smokeless air.
Never did sun more beautifully steep
In his first splendor valley, rock, or hill;
Ne'er saw I, never felt, a calm so deep!

[1] *grave Livers* I.e., those who live seriously.

[2] *Leeches* Used at this time by doctors for drawing the blood of patients. A leech gatherer would find leeches by standing in shallow water and allowing them to attach themselves to his legs.

[3] *Composed ... 1803* Wordsworth misremembered the date of composition, which was actually (according to Dorothy Wordsworth's *Grasmere Journals*) July 1802, when Wordsworth set out for a brief trip to France, where his former lover Annette Vallon lived with their daughter, Caroline.

The river glideth at his own sweet will:
Dear God! the very houses seem asleep;
And all that mighty heart is lying still!
—1807

[*The world is too much with us*]

The world is too much with us; late and soon,
Getting and spending, we lay waste our powers:
Little we see in nature that is ours;
We have given our hearts away, a sordid boon!
The Sea that bares her bosom to the moon;
The Winds that will be howling at all hours
And are up-gathered now like sleeping flowers;
For this, for every thing, we are out of tune;
It moves us not. Great God! I'd rather be
A Pagan suckled in a creed outworn;
So might I, standing on this pleasant lea,
Have glimpses that would make me less forlorn;
Have sight of Proteus coming from the sea;
Or hear old Triton blow his wreathed horn.[1]
—1807

[*It is a beauteous Evening*]

It is a beauteous Evening, calm and free;
The holy time is quiet as a Nun
Breathless with adoration; the broad sun
Is sinking down in its tranquillity;
The gentleness of heaven is on the Sea:
Listen! the mighty Being is awake
And doth with his eternal motion make
A sound like thunder—everlastingly.
Dear Child! dear Girl![2] that walkest with me here,
If thou appear'st untouch'd by solemn thought,
Thy nature is not therefore less divine:
Thou liest in Abraham's bosom[3] all the year;
And worshipp'st at the Temple's inner shrine,
God being with thee when we know it not.
—1807

London
1802[4]

Milton! thou should'st be living at this hour:
England hath need of thee: she is a fen
Of stagnant waters: altar, sword, and pen,
Fireside, the heroic wealth of hall and bower,
Have forfeited their ancient English dower
Of inward happiness. We are selfish men;
Oh! raise us up, return to us again;
And give us manners, virtue, freedom, power.
Thy soul was like a Star and dwelt apart:
Thou hadst a voice whose sound was like the sea;
Pure as the naked heavens, majestic, free,
So didst thou travel on life's common way,
In cheerful godliness; and yet thy heart
The lowliest duties on itself did lay.
—1807

The Solitary Reaper[5]

Behold her, single in the field,
Yon solitary Highland Lass!
Reaping and singing by herself;
Stop here, or gently pass!
Alone she cuts, and binds the grain,
And sings a melancholy strain;
O listen! for the Vale profound
Is overflowing with the sound.

---

[1] *Proteus* Shape-changing sea god; *Triton* Sea god with the head and torso of a man and the tail of a fish. He was usually depicted blowing on a conch shell.

[2] *Dear … Girl* Wordsworth's daughter Caroline.

[3] *Abraham's bosom* The resting place for souls bound for heaven. See Luke 16.22: "And it came to pass, that the beggar died, and was carried by the angels into Abraham's bosom."

[4] *London, 1802* Written immediately after Wordsworth's return from France, when he was struck by the differences between his native country and France after the Revolution. Milton died in 1674.

[5] *The Solitary Reaper* Suggested by the following passage in Thomas Wilkinson's *Tours to the British Mountains* (1824): "Passed a female who was reaping alone: she sung in Erse [a Gaelic language] as she bended over her sickle; the sweetest human voice I ever heard: her strains were tenderly melancholy, and felt delicious, long after they were heard no more."

No Nightingale did ever chaunt
So sweetly to reposing bands
Of Travellers in some shady haunt,
Among Arabian Sands:
No sweeter voice was ever heard
In spring-time from the Cuckoo-bird,
Breaking the silence of the seas
Among the farthest Hebrides.

Will no one tell me what she sings?
Perhaps the plaintive numbers° flow *verses*
For old, unhappy, far-off things,
And battles long ago:
Or is it some more humble lay,
Familiar matter of today?
Some natural sorrow, loss, or pain,
That has been, and may be again!

Whate'er the theme, the Maiden sang
As if her song could have no ending;
I saw her singing at her work,
And o'er the sickle bending;
I listen'd till I had my fill:
And, as I mounted up the hill,
The music in my heart I bore,
Long after it was heard no more.
—1807

[*My heart leaps up*]

My heart leaps up when I behold
A Rainbow in the sky:
So was it when my life began;
So is it now I am a Man;
So be it when I shall grow old,
Or let me die!
The Child is Father of the Man;
And I could wish my days to be
Bound each to each by natural piety.
—1804

IN CONTEXT

"I Wandered Lonely as a Cloud": Stages in the Life of a Poem

The earliest version of this poem was composed in 1804 and first published in 1807. It was evidently inspired by an entry in Dorothy Wordsworth's journal from two years earlier, describing a scene at Glencoyne Bay, Ullswater, seen by Dorothy and William on their way back to Grasmere after a long ramble. Appearing below are the scene as described by Dorothy in the journal; William's first version of the poem; a facsimile copy of the page in the copy of *Poems in Two Volumes* in which William began to compose an additional stanza to the poem; a transcription of his handwritten jottings; and William's revised version, with the added stanza and some other changes (which was not published until 1815).

from Dorothy Wordsworth, *Grasmere Journal* (Thursday, 15 April 1802)

When we were in the woods beyond Gowbarrow park we saw a few daffodils close to the water side. We fancied that the lake had floated the seeds ashore and that the little colony had so sprung up. But as we went along there were more and yet more and at last under the boughs of the trees, we saw that there was a long belt of them along the shore, about the breadth of a country turnpike road. I never saw daffodils so beautiful they grew among the mossy stones about and about them, some rested their heads upon these stones as on a pillow for weariness and the rest tossed and reeled and danced and seemed as if they verily laughed with the wind that blew upon them over the lake, they looked so gay ever glancing ever changing. This wind blew directly over the lake to them. There was here and there a little knot and a few stragglers a few yards higher up but they were so few as not to disturb the simplicity and unity and life of that one busy highway.

[*I wandered lonely as a Cloud*]

I wandered lonely as a Cloud
That floats on high o'er Vales and Hills,
When all at once I saw a crowd
A host of dancing Daffodils;
Along the Lake, beneath the trees,
Ten thousand dancing in the breeze.

The waves beside them danced, but they
Outdid the sparkling waves in glee—
A Poet could not but be gay
In such a laughing company:
I gazed—and gaz'd—but little thought
What wealth the show to me had brought:

For oft when on my couch I lie
In vacant or in pensive mood,
They flash upon that inward eye
Which is the bliss of solitude,
And then my heart with pleasure fills,
And dances with the Daffodils.
—1807

I wandered lonely as a Cloud
That floats on high o'er Vales and Hills,
When all at once I saw a crowd
A host of dancing Daffodills;
Along the Lake, beneath the trees,
Ten thousand dancing in the breeze.

The waves beside them danced, but they
Outdid the sparkling waves in glee:—
A Poet could not but be gay
In such a laughing company:
I gaz'd—and gaz'd—but little thought
What wealth the shew to me had brought:

VOL. II. D

I wandered lonely as a cloud[1]

l
A host of golden Daffodi ls
Beside
~~Along~~ the Lake beneath the trees
vernal
All dancing ~~dancing~~ in the breeze
Continuous
ed
~~Close crowd ing, [?like]~~
~~As numerous~~ ‸ as the stars that shine
and twinkle
on
At midnight, in the milky way
a
They stretch'd in never ending line
Along the margin of a bay
Ten thousand saw I at a glance
Tossing their heads in spritely dance

[*I wandered lonely as a Cloud*]

I wandered lonely as a cloud
That floats on high o'er vales and hills,
When all at once I saw a crowd,
A host, of golden daffodils;
Beside the lake, beneath the trees,
Fluttering and dancing in the breeze.

Continuous as the stars that shine
And twinkle on the milky way,
They stretched in never-ending line
Along the margin of a bay:
Ten thousand saw I at a glance,
Tossing their heads in sprightly dance.

The waves beside them danced, but they
Outdid the sparkling waves in glee:
A poet could not but be gay,
In such a jocund company;
I gazed—and gazed—but little thought
What wealth the show to me had brought:

For oft, when on my couch I lie
In vacant or in pensive mood,
They flash upon that inward eye
Which is the bliss of solitude;
And then my heart with pleasure fills,
And dances with the daffodils.
—1815

[1] *I wandered … cloud* Transcription of Wordsworth's manuscript (see previous page for facsimile).

Elegiac Stanzas

Suggested by a Picture of Peele Castle, in a Storm, painted by Sir George Beaumont[1]

I was thy Neighbour once, thou rugged Pile!° *castle*
Four summer weeks I dwelt in sight of thee:
I saw thee every day; and all the while
Thy Form was sleeping on a glassy sea.

So pure the sky, so quiet was the air!
So like, so very like, was day to day!
Whene'er I look'd, thy Image still was there;
It trembled, but it never pass'd away.

How perfect was the calm! it seem'd no sleep;
No mood, which season takes away, or brings:
I could have fancied that the mighty Deep
Was even the gentlest of all gentle Things.

Ah! THEN, if mine had been the Painter's hand,
To express what then I saw; and add the gleam,
The light that never was, on sea or land,
The consecration, and the Poet's dream;

I would have planted thee, thou hoary Pile!
Amid a world how different from this!
Beside a sea that could not cease to smile;
On tranquil land, beneath a sky of bliss:

Thou shouldst have seem'd a treasure-house, a mine
Of peaceful years; a chronicle of heaven—
Of all the sunbeams that did ever shine
The very sweetest had to thee been given.

A Picture had it been of lasting ease,
Elysian[2] quiet, without toil or strife;
No motion but the moving tide, a breeze,
Or merely silent Nature's breathing life.

Such, in the fond delusion of my heart,
Such Picture would I at that time have made:
And seen the soul of truth in every part;
A faith, a trust, that could not be betray'd.

So once it would have been—'tis so no more;
I have submitted to a new control:
A power is gone, which nothing can restore;
A deep distress hath humaniz'd my Soul.

Not for a moment could I now behold
A smiling sea and be what I have been:
The feeling of my loss will ne'er be old;
This, which I know, I speak with mind serene.

Then, Beaumont, Friend! who would have been the Friend,
If he had lived, of Him whom I deplore,° *mourn*
This Work of thine I blame not, but commend;
This sea in anger, and that dismal shore.

Oh 'tis a passionate Work!—yet wise and well;
Well chosen is the spirit that is here;
That Hulk which labours in the deadly swell,
This rueful sky, this pageantry of fear!

And this huge Castle, standing here sublime,
I love to see the look with which it braves,
Cased in the unfeeling armour of old time,
The light'ning, the fierce wind, and trampling waves.

Farewell, farewell the Heart that lives alone,
Hous'd in a dream, at distance from the Kind![3]
Such happiness, wherever it be known,
Is to be pitied; for 'tis surely blind.

[1] *Suggested by ... Beaumont* In 1794, Wordsworth spent a month in Rampside, Lancashire, which is located across the Morecambe Bay from the Furness Peninsula, where the ruins of Peele Castle stand. In 1806 he saw the two pictures of this castle that had been painted by Sir George Beaumont, a landscape painter who was Wordsworth's friend and patron. Wordsworth's youngest brother, a captain with the East India Company, drowned when his ship sank off the Bill of Portland in February 1805.

[2] *Elysian* Blissful. Referring to Elysium, where, according to classical mythology, the blessed reside after death.

[3] *Kind* Human race.

But welcome fortitude, and patient cheer,
And frequent sights of what is to be born!
Such sights, or worse, as are before me here.
Not without hope we suffer and we mourn.
—1807

Ode

[*Intimations of Immortality*]

In an 1843 letter to Isabella Fenwick, Wordsworth explained the experiences from his own life on which this ode is based, saying, "Nothing was more difficult for me in childhood than to admit the notion of death as a state applicable to my own being.… I used to brood over the stories of Enoch and Elijah, and almost to persuade myself that, whatever might become of others, I should be translated, in something of the same way, to heaven. With a feeling congenial to this, I was often unable to think of external things as having external existence, and I communed with all that I saw as something not apart from, but inherent in, my own immaterial nature. Many times while going to school have I grasped at a wall or tree to recall myself from this abyss of idealism to the reality. At that time I was afraid of such processes. In later periods of life I have deplored, as we have all reason to do, a subjugation of an opposite character, and have rejoiced over the remembrances, as is expressed in the lines—

> Obstinate questionings
> Of sense and outward things,
> Fallings from us, vanishings; etc."[1]

Wordsworth wrote the first four stanzas of the poem in 1802, and two years elapsed before he completed the poem in 1804. In 1815 he changed the title to "Ode: Intimations of Immortality from Recollections of Early Childhood," its more common title today. He also replaced the Latin epigram from Virgil with the last three lines from "My heart leaps up": "The Child is Father to the Man: / And I could wish my days to be / Bound each to each by natural piety."

[1] *Obstinate … etc.* Lines 141–43.

Ode

[*Intimations of Immortality* from *Recollections of Early Childhood*]

Paulo majora canamus.[2]

There was a time when meadow, grove, and stream,
The earth, and every common sight,
To me did seem
Apparelled in celestial light,
The glory and the freshness of a dream.
It is not now as it has been of yore;—
Turn wheresoe'er I may,
By night or day,
The things which I have seen I now can see no more.

The Rainbow comes and goes,
And lovely is the Rose,
The Moon doth with delight
Look round her when the heavens are bare;
Waters on a starry night
Are beautiful and fair;
The sunshine is a glorious birth;
But yet I know, where'er I go,
That there hath passed away a glory from the earth.

Now, while the Birds thus sing a joyous song,
And while the young Lambs bound
As to the tabor's[3] sound,
To me alone there came a thought of grief:
A timely utterance gave that thought relief,
And I again am strong.
The Cataracts blow their trumpets from the steep,
No more shall grief of mine the season wrong;
I hear the Echoes through the mountains throng,

[2] *Paulo majora canamus* Latin: "Let us sing of loftier things." From Virgil's Fourth Eclogue.

[3] *tabor* Small drum.

The Winds come to me from the fields of sleep,
And all the earth is gay,
Land and sea
Give themselves up to jollity,
And with the heart of May
Doth every Beast keep holiday,
Thou Child of Joy
Shout round me, let me hear thy shouts, thou happy
Shepherd Boy!

Ye blessed Creatures, I have heard the call
Ye to each other make; I see
The heavens laugh with you in your jubilee;
My heart is at your festival,
My head hath it's coronal,° *wreath*
The fullness of your bliss, I feel—I feel it all.
Oh evil day! if I were sullen
While Earth herself is adorning,
This sweet May-morning,
And the Children are pulling,
On every side,
In a thousand valleys far and wide,
Fresh flowers; while the sun shines warm,
And the Babe leaps up on his mother's arm:—
I hear, I hear, with joy I hear!
—But there's a Tree, of many one,
A single Field which I have looked upon,
Both of them speak of something that is gone:
The Pansy at my feet
Doth the same tale repeat:
Whither is fled the visionary gleam?
Where is it now, the glory and the dream?

Our birth is but a sleep and a forgetting:
The Soul that rises with us, our life's Star,
Hath had elsewhere it's setting,
And cometh from afar:
Not in entire forgetfulness,
And not in utter nakedness,
But trailing clouds of glory do we come
From God, Who is our home:
Heaven lies about us in our infancy!
Shades of the prison-house begin to close
Upon the growing Boy,
But he beholds the light, and whence it flows,
He sees it in his joy;
The Youth, who daily farther from the East
Must travel, still is Nature's Priest,
And by the vision splendid
Is on his way attended;
At length the Man perceives it die away,
And fade into the light of common day.

Earth fills her lap with pleasures of her own;
Yearnings she hath in her own natural kind,
And, even with something of a Mother's mind,
And no unworthy aim,
The homely° Nurse doth all she can *simple*
To make her Foster-child, her Inmate Man,
Forget the glories he hath known,
And that imperial palace whence he came.
Behold the Child among his new-born blisses,
A four year's Darling of a pigmy size!
See, where 'mid work of his own hand he lies,
Fretted by sallies of his Mother's kisses,
With light upon him from his Father's eyes!
See, at his feet, some little plan or chart,
Some fragment from his dream of human life,
Shaped by himself with newly-learned art;
A wedding or a festival,
A mourning or a funeral;
And this hath now his heart,
And unto this he frames his song:
Then will he fit his tongue
To dialogues of business, love, or strife;
But it will not be long
Ere this be thrown aside,
And with new joy and pride
The little Actor cons another part,
Filling from time to time his "humourous stage"[1]
With all the Persons, down to palsied Age,
That Life brings with her in her Equipage;

---

[1] *humourous stage* From Elizabethan poet Samuel Daniel's *Musophilus* (1599), in reference to the different character types (defined by their dominant temperaments, or "humors") depicted in Renaissance drama.

As if his whole vocation
Were endless imitation.

Thou, whose exterior semblance doth belie
Thy Soul's immensity;
Thou best Philosopher, who yet dost keep
Thy heritage, thou Eye among the blind,
That, deaf and silent, read'st the eternal deep,
Haunted for ever by the eternal mind—
Mighty Prophet! Seer blest!
On whom those truths do rest,
Which we are toiling all our lives to find;
Thou, over whom thy Immortality
Broods like the Day, a Master o'er a Slave,
A Presence which is not to be put by;
To whom the grave
Is but a lonely bed without the sense or sight
Of day or the warm light,
A place of thought where we in waiting lie;
Thou little Child, yet glorious in the might
Of untamed pleasures, on thy Being's height,
Why with such earnest pains dost thou provoke
The Years to bring the inevitable yoke,
Thus blindly with thy blessedness at strife?
Full soon thy Soul shall have her earthly freight,
And custom lie upon thee with a weight,
Heavy as frost, and deep almost as life!

O joy! that in our embers
Is something that doth live,
That nature yet remembers
What was so fugitive!
The thought of our past years in me doth breed
Perpetual benedictions: not indeed
For that which is most worthy to be blest;
Delight and liberty, the simple creed
Of Childhood, whether fluttering or at rest,
With new-born hope for ever in his breast:—
Not for these I raise
The song of thanks and praise;
But for those obstinate questionings
Of sense and outward things,
Fallings from us, vanishings;
Blank misgivings of a Creature
Moving about in worlds not realized,[1]
High instincts, before which our mortal Nature
Did tremble like a guilty Thing surprised:
But for those first affections,
Those shadowy recollections,
Which, be they what they may,
Are yet the fountain light of all our day,
Are yet a master light of all our seeing;
Uphold us, cherish us, and make
Our noisy years seem moments in the being
Of the eternal Silence: truths that wake,
To perish never;
Which neither listlessness, nor mad endeavour,
Nor Man nor Boy,
Nor all that is at enmity with joy,
Can utterly abolish or destroy!
Hence, in a season of calm weather,
Though inland far we be,
Our Souls have sight of that immortal sea
Which brought us hither,
Can in a moment travel thither,
And see the Children sport upon the shore,
And hear the mighty waters rolling evermore.

Then, sing ye Birds, sing, sing a joyous song!
And let the young Lambs bound
As to the tabor's sound!
We in thought will join your throng,
Ye that pipe and ye that play,
Ye that through your hearts to day
Feel the gladness of the May!
What though the radiance which was once so bright
Be now for ever taken from my sight,
Though nothing can bring back the hour
Of splendour in the grass, of glory in the flower;
We will grieve not, rather find
Strength in what remains behind,
In the primal sympathy
Which having been must ever be,
In the soothing thoughts that spring

[1] *realized* Seeming real.

Out of human suffering,
In the faith that looks through death,
In years that bring the philosophic mind.

And oh ye Fountains, Meadows, Hills, and Groves,
Think not of any severing of our loves!
Yet in my heart of hearts I feel your might;
I only have relinquished one delight
To live beneath your more habitual sway.
I love the Brooks which down their channels fret,
Even more than when I tripped lightly as they;
The innocent brightness of a new-born Day
Is lovely yet;
The Clouds that gather round the setting sun
Do take a sober colouring from an eye
That hath kept watch o'er man's mortality;
Another race hath been, and other palms[1] are won.
Thanks to the human heart by which we live,
Thanks to its tenderness, its joys, and fears,
To me the meanest flower that blows can give
Thoughts that do often lie too deep for tears.
—1807

from *The Excursion*

[*The Ruined Cottage*]

This excerpt is taken from Wordsworth's nine-book epic *The Excursion, Being a Portion of The Recluse, A Poem* (1814). It was intended as the second part of the tripartite *The Recluse*, which was never completed, and *The Excursion* was the only part of the poem published during Wordsworth's lifetime. *The Prelude* was planned as an autobiographical introduction to the project. The portion from *The Excursion* reprinted here is from the end of Book 1, which is titled "The Wanderer," and was originally conceived and written as a poem entitled "The Ruined Cottage."

Of the character of the Wanderer (the principal character of the poem), Wordsworth says, "Had I been born in a class which would have deprived me of what is called a liberal education, it is not unlikely that, being strong in body, I should have taken to a way of life such as that in which my Pedlar passed the greater part of his days. At all events, I am here called upon freely to acknowledge that the character I have represented in his person is chiefly an idea of what I fancied my own character might have become in his circumstances," combined with observations of such figures encountered in his own youth.

[1] *palms* Prizes. (In ancient Greece, palm branches or wreaths were often awarded to the winners of foot races.)

from *The Excursion*

[*The Ruined Cottage*]

SUPINE the Wanderer lay,
His eyes as if in drowsiness half shut,
The shadows of the breezy elms above
Dappling his face. He had not heard my steps
As I approached; and near him did I stand
Unnotic'd in the shade, some minutes' space.
At length I hailed him, seeing that his hat
Was moist with water-drops, as if the brim
Had newly scooped a running stream. He rose,
And ere the pleasant greeting that ensued
Was ended, "'Tis," said I, "a burning day;
My lips are parched with thirst, but you, I guess,
Have somewhere found relief." He, at the word,
Pointing towards a sweet-briar, bade me climb
The fence hard by, where that aspiring shrub
Looked out upon the road. It was a plot
Of garden-ground run wild, its matted weeds
Marked with the steps of those, whom, as they pass'd
The gooseberry trees that shot in long lank slips,
Or currants hanging from their leafless stems
In scanty strings, had tempted to o'erleap
The broken wall. I looked around, and there,
Where two tall hedge-rows of thick alder boughs
Joined in a cold damp nook, espied a Well
Shrouded with willow-flowers and plumy fern.
My thirst I slaked, and from the cheerless spot
Withdrawing, straightway to the shade returned
Where sat the Old Man on the Cottage bench;

And, while, beside him, with uncovered head,
I yet was standing, freely to respire,
And cool my temples in the fanning air,
Thus did he speak. "I see around me here
Things which you cannot see: we die, my Friend,
Nor we alone, but that which each man loved
And prized in his peculiar nook of earth
Dies with him, or is changed; and very soon
Even of the good is no memorial left.
—The Poets, in their elegies and songs
Lamenting the departed, call the groves,
They call upon the hills and streams to mourn,
And senseless rocks; nor idly; for they speak,
In these their invocations, with a voice
Obedient to the strong creative power
Of human passion. Sympathies there are
More tranquil, yet perhaps of kindred birth,
That steal upon the meditative mind,
And grow with thought. Beside yon Spring I stood,
And eyed its waters till we seemed to feel
One sadness, they and I. For them a bond
Of brotherhood is broken: time has been
When, every day, the touch of human hand
Dislodged the natural sleep that binds them up
In mortal stillness; and they minister'd
To human comfort. As I stooped to drink,
Upon the slimy foot-stone I espied
The useless fragment of a wooden bowl,
Green with the moss of years; a pensive sight
That moved my heart!—recalling former days
When I could never pass that road but She
Who lived within these walls, at my approach,
A Daughter's welcome gave me; and I loved her
As my own child. O Sir! the good die first,
And they whose hearts are dry as summer dust
Burn to the socket. Many a Passenger
Hath blessed poor Margaret for her gentle looks,
When she upheld the cool refreshment drawn
From that forsaken Spring; and no one came
But he was welcome; no one went away
But that it seemed she loved him. She is dead,
The light extinguished of her lonely Hut,
The Hut itself abandoned to decay,
And She forgotten in the quiet grave!

"I speak," continued he, "of One whose stock
Of virtues bloom'd beneath this lowly roof.
She was a Woman of a steady mind,
Tender and deep in her excess of love,
Not speaking much, pleased rather with the joy
Of her own thoughts: by some especial care
Her temper had been framed, as if to make
A Being—who by adding love to peace
Might live on earth a life of happiness.
Her wedded Partner lacked not on his side
The humble worth that satisfied her heart:
Frugal, affectionate, sober, and withal
Keenly industrious. She with pride would tell
That he was often seated at his loom,
In summer, ere the Mower was abroad
Among the dewy grass—in early spring,
Ere the last Star had vanished. They who passed
At evening, from behind the garden fence
Might hear his busy spade, which he would ply,
After his daily work, until the light
Had failed, and every leaf and flower were lost
In the dark hedges. So their days were spent
In peace and comfort; and a pretty Boy
Was their best hope—next to the God in Heaven.

Not twenty years ago, but you I think
Can scarcely bear it now in mind, there came
Two blighting seasons when the fields were left
With half a harvest. It pleased heaven to add
A worse affliction in the plague of war;
This happy Land was stricken to the heart!
A Wanderer then among the Cottages
I, with my freight of winter raiment, saw
The hardships of that season; many rich
Sank down, as in a dream, among the poor;
And of the poor did many cease to be
And their place knew them not. Meanwhile abridg'd
Of daily comforts, gladly reconciled
To numerous self-denials, Margaret

Went struggling on through those calamitous years
With cheerful hope: but ere the second autumn
Her life's true Help-mate on a sick-bed lay,
Smitten with perilous fever. In disease
He lingered long; and when his strength return'd,
He found the little he had stored, to meet
The hour of accident or crippling age,
Was all consumed. Two children had they now,
One newly born. As I have said, it was
A time of trouble; shoals of Artisans
Were from their daily labour turn'd adrift
To seek their bread from public charity,
They, and their wives and children—happier far
Could they have lived as do the little birds
That peck along the hedges, or the Kite[1]
That makes his dwelling on the mountain Rocks!

A sad reverse it was for him who long
Had filled with plenty, and possess'd in peace,
This lonely Cottage. At the door he stood,
And whistled many a snatch of merry tunes
That had no mirth in them; or with his knife
Carved uncouth figures on the heads of sticks—
Then, not less idly, sought, through every nook
In house or garden, any casual work
Of use or ornament; and with a strange,
Amusing, yet uneasy novelty,
He blended, where he might, the various tasks
Of summer, autumn, winter, and of spring.
But this endured not; his good humour soon
Became a weight in which no pleasure was:
And poverty brought on a petted° mood *sulky*
And a sore temper: day by day he drooped,
And he would leave his work—and to the Town,
Without an errand, would direct his steps,
Or wander here and there among the fields.
One while he would speak lightly of his Babes,
And with a cruel tongue: at other times
He toss'd them with a false unnatural joy:
And 'twas a rueful thing to see the looks
Of the poor innocent children. "Every smile,"
Said Margaret to me, here beneath these trees,
"Made my heart bleed."

At this the Wanderer paused;
And, looking up to those enormous Elms,
He said, "'Tis now the hour of deepest noon.—
At this still season of repose and peace,
This hour, when all things which are not at rest
Are cheerful; while this multitude of flies
Is filling all the air with melody;
Why should a tear be in an Old Man's eye?
Why should we thus, with an untoward mind,
And in the weakness of humanity,
From natural wisdom turn our hearts away,
To natural comfort shut our eyes and ears,
And, feeding on disquiet, thus disturb
The calm of nature with our restless thoughts?"

He spake with somewhat of a solemn tone:
But, when he ended, there was in his face
Such easy cheerfulness, a look so mild,
That for a little time it stole away
All recollection, and that simple Tale
Passed from my mind like a forgotten sound.
A while on trivial things we held discourse,
To me soon tasteless. In my own despite
I thought of that poor Woman as of one
Whom I had known and loved. He had rehearsed
Her homely Tale with such familiar power,
With such an active countenance, an eye
So busy, that the things of which he spake
Seemed present; and, attention now relax'd,
There was a heart-felt chillness in my veins.—
I rose; and, turning from the breezy shade,
Went forth into the open air, and stood
To drink the comfort of the warmer sun.
Long time I had not staid, ere, looking round
Upon that tranquil Ruin, I return'd,
And begged of the Old Man that, for my sake,
He would resume his story.—

He replied,
"It were a wantonness, and would demand
Severe reproof, if we were Men whose hearts
Could hold vain dalliance with the misery

[1] *Kite* Small bird of prey of the falcon family.

Even of the dead; contented thence to draw
A momentary pleasure, never marked
By reason, barren of all future good.
But we have known that there is often found
In mournful thoughts, and always might be found,
A power to virtue friendly; were't not so,
I am a Dreamer among men, indeed
An idle Dreamer! 'Tis a common Tale,
An ordinary sorrow of Man's life,
A tale of silent suffering, hardly clothed
In bodily form. But, without further bidding,
I will proceed—
                                        While thus it fared with them,
To whom this Cottage, till those hapless years,
Had been a blessed home, it was my chance
To travel in a Country far remote.
And glad I was, when, halting by yon gate
That leads from the green lane, once more I saw
These lofty elm-trees. Long I did not rest:
With many pleasant thoughts I cheer'd my way
O'er the flat Common. Having reached the door
I knock'd—and, when I entered with the hope
Of usual greeting, Margaret looked at me
A little while; then turn'd her head away
Speechless, and sitting down upon a chair
Wept bitterly. I wist° not what to do, *knew*
Or how to speak to her. Poor Wretch! at last
She rose from off her seat, and then—O Sir!
I cannot *tell* how she pronounced my name.
With fervent love, and with a face of grief
Unutterably helpless, and a look
That seemed to cling upon me, she enquired
If I had seen her Husband. As she spake
A strange surprise and fear came to my heart,
Nor had I power to answer ere she told
That he had disappear'd—not two months gone.
He left his House: two wretched days had pass'd,
And on the third, as wistfully she rais'd
Her head from off her pillow, to look forth,
Like one in trouble, for returning light,
Within her chamber-casement she espied
A folded paper, lying as if placed
To meet her waking eyes. This tremblingly
She open'd—found no writing, but therein
Pieces of money carefully enclosed,
Silver and gold. "I shuddered at the sight,"
Said Margaret, "for I knew it was his hand
Which placed it there; and ere that day was ended,
That long and anxious day! I learned from One
Sent hither by my Husband to impart
The heavy news—that he had joined a Troop
Of Soldiers, going to a distant Land.
—He left me thus—he could not gather heart
To take a farewell of me; for he fear'd
That I should follow with my Babes, and sink
Beneath the misery of that wandering Life."

This Tale did Margaret tell with many tears:
And when she ended I had little power
To give her comfort, and was glad to take
Such words of hope from her own mouth as served
To cheer us both—but long we had not talked
Ere we built up a pile of better thoughts,
And with a brighter eye she look'd around
As if she had been shedding tears of joy.
We parted. 'Twas the time of early spring;
I left her busy with her garden tools;
And well remember, o'er that fence she looked,
And, while I paced along the foot-way path,
Called out, and sent a blessing after me,
With tender cheerfulness; and with a voice
That seem'd the very sound of happy thoughts.

I roved o'er many a hill and many a dale,
With my accustomed load; in heat and cold,
Through many a wood, and many an open ground,
In sunshine and in shade, in wet and fair,
Drooping, or blithe of heart, as might befall;
My best companions now the driving winds,
And now the "trotting brooks" and whispering trees,
And now the music of my own sad steps,
With many a short-lived thought that pass'd between,
And disappeared. I journey'd back this way
Towards the wane of Summer; when the wheat
Was yellow; and the soft and bladed grass
Springing afresh had o'er the hay-field spread

Its tender verdure. At the door arrived,
I found that she was absent. In the shade,
Where now we sit, I waited her return.
Her Cottage, then a cheerful Object, wore
Its customary look—only, I thought,
The honeysuckle, crowding round the porch,
Hung down in heavier tufts: and that bright weed,
The yellow stone-crop, suffered to take root
Along the window's edge, profusely grew,
Blinding the lower panes. I turned aside,
And strolled into her garden. It appeared
To lag behind the season, and had lost
Its pride of neatness. From the border lines
Composed of daisy and resplendent thrift,[1]
Flowers straggling forth had on those paths encroached
Which they were used to deck: Carnations, once
Prized for surpassing beauty, and no less
For the peculiar pains they had required,
Declined their languid heads—without support.
The cumbrous bind-weed, with its wreaths and bells,
Had twined about her two small rows of peas,
And dragged them to the earth.—Ere this an hour
Was wasted.—Back I turned my restless steps,
And, as I walked before the door, it chanced
A Stranger passed; and, guessing whom I sought,
He said that she was used to ramble far.
The sun was sinking in the west; and now
I sat with sad impatience. From within
Her solitary Infant cried aloud;
Then, like a blast that dies away self-stilled,
The voice was silent. From the bench I rose;
But neither could divert nor soothe my thoughts.
The spot, though fair, was very desolate—
The longer I remained more desolate.
And, looking round, I saw the corner stones,
Till then unnotic'd, on either side the door
With dull red stains discolour'd, and stuck o'er
With tufts and hairs of wool, as if the Sheep,
That fed upon the Common, thither came
Familiarly; and found a couching-place
Even at her threshold. Deeper shadows fell
From these tall elms; the Cottage-clock struck eight;
I turned, and saw her distant a few steps.
Her face was pale and thin, her figure too
Was changed. As she unlocked the door, she said,
"It grieves me you have waited here so long,
But, in good truth, I've wandered much of late,
And, sometimes—to my shame I speak—have need
Of my best prayers to bring me back again."
While on the board she spread our evening meal,
She told me, interrupting not the work
Which gave employment to her listless hands,
That she had parted with her elder Child;
To a kind Master on a distant farm
Now happily apprenticed—"I perceive
You look at me, and you have cause; to-day
I have been travelling far; and many days
About the fields I wander, knowing this
Only, that what I seek I cannot find.
And so I waste my time: for I am changed;
And to myself," said she, "have done much wrong,
And to this helpless Infant. I have slept
Weeping, and weeping I have waked; my tears
Have flowed as if my body were not such
As others are; and I could never die.
But I am now in mind and in my heart
More easy; and I hope," said she, "that heaven
Will give me patience to endure the things
Which I behold at home." It would have grieved
Your very soul to see her; Sir, I feel
The story linger in my heart: I fear
'Tis long and tedious; but my spirit clings
To that poor Woman—so familiarly
Do I perceive her manner, and her look,
And presence, and so deeply do I feel
Her goodness, that, not seldom, in my walks
A momentary trance comes over me;
And to myself I seem to muse on One
By sorrow laid asleep; or borne away,
A human being destined to awake
To human life, or something very near
To human life, when he shall come again
For whom she suffered. Yes, it would have grieved
Your very soul to see her: evermore

[1] *thrift* Common plant that bears pink, white, or purple flowers.

Her eyelids drooped, her eyes were downward cast;
And, when she at her table gave me food,
She did not look at me. Her voice was low,
Her body was subdued. In every act
Pertaining to her house affairs, appeared
The careless stillness of a thinking mind
Self-occupied; to which all outward things
Are like an idle matter. Still she sighed,
But yet no motion of the breast was seen,
No heaving of the heart. While by the fire
We sate together, sighs came on my ear,
I knew not how, and hardly whence they came.

Ere my departure to her care I gave,
For her Son's use, some tokens of regard,
Which with a look of welcome she received;
And I exhorted her to have her trust
In God's good love, and seek his help by prayer.
I took my staff, and, when I kissed her babe
The tears stood in her eyes. I left her then
With the best hope and comfort I could give;
She thanked me for my wish;—but for my hope
Methought she did not thank me.
I returned,
And took my rounds along this road again
Ere on its sunny bank the primrose flower
Peeped forth, to give an earnest of the Spring.
I found her sad and drooping; she had learned
No tidings of her Husband; if he lived
She knew not that he lived; if he were dead
She knew not he was dead. She seem'd the same
In person and appearance; but her House
Bespake a sleepy hand of negligence.
The floor was neither dry nor neat, the hearth
Was comfortless, and her small lot of books,
Which, in the Cottage window, heretofore
Had been piled up against the corner panes
In seemly order, now, with straggling leaves
Lay scattered here and there, open or shut,
As they had chanced to fall. Her Infant Babe
Had from its Mother caught the trick of grief,
And sighed among its playthings. Once again
I turned towards the garden gate, and saw,
More plainly still, that poverty and grief
Were now come nearer to her: weeds defaced
The harden'd soil, and knots of wither'd grass;
No ridges there appeared of clear black mold,
No winter greenness; of her herbs and flowers,
It seemed the better part were gnawed away
Or trampled into earth; a chain of straw,
Which had been twined about the slender stem
Of a young apple-tree, lay at its root;
The bark was nibbled round by truant Sheep.
—Margaret stood near, her Infant in her arms,
And, noting that my eye was on the tree,
She said, "I fear it will be dead and gone
Ere Robert come again." Towards the House
Together we returned; and she enquired
If I had any hope: but for her Babe
And for her little orphan Boy, she said,
She had no wish to live, that she must die
Of sorrow. Yet I saw the idle loom
Still in its place; his Sunday garments hung
Upon the self-same nail; his very staff
Stood undisturbed behind the door. And when,
In bleak December, I retraced this way,
She told me that her little Babe was dead,
And she was left alone. She now, released
From her maternal cares, had taken up
The employment common through these Wilds,
and gain'd
By spinning hemp a pittance for herself;
And for this end had hired a neighbour's Boy
To give her needful help. That very time
Most willingly she put her work aside,
And walked with me along the miry road
Heedless how far; and, in such piteous sort
That any heart had ached to hear her, begged
That, wheresoe'er I went, I still would ask
For him whom she had lost. We parted then,
Our final parting; for from that time forth
Did many seasons pass ere I return'd
Into this tract again.
Nine tedious years;
From their first separation, nine long years,
She lingered in unquiet widowhood;

A Wife and Widow. Needs must it have been
A sore heart-wasting! I have heard, my Friend,
That in yon arbour oftentimes she sat
Alone, through half the vacant Sabbath-day,
And if a dog passed by she still would quit
The shade, and look abroad. On this old Bench
For hours she sate; and evermore her eye
Was busy in the distance, shaping things
That made her heart beat quick. You see that path,
Now faint—the grass has crept o'er its grey line;
There, to and fro, she paced through many a day
Of the warm summer, from a belt of hemp
That girt her waist, spinning the long drawn thread
With backward steps. Yet ever as there pass'd
A man whose garments showed the Soldier's red,
Or crippled Mendicant in Sailor's garb,
The little Child who sate to turn the wheel
Ceas'd from his task; and she with faltering voice
Made many a fond enquiry; and when they,
Whose presence gave no comfort, were gone by,
Her heart was still more sad. And by yon gate,
That bars the Traveller's road, she often stood,
And when a stranger Horseman came, the latch
Would lift, and in his face look wistfully;
Most happy, if, from aught discovered there
Of tender feeling, she might dare repeat
The same sad question. Meanwhile her poor Hut
Sank to decay: for he was gone—whose hand,
At the first nipping of October frost,
Closed up each chink, and with fresh bands of straw
Chequered the green-grown thatch. And so she lived
Through the long winter, reckless and alone;
Until her House by frost, and thaw, and rain,
Was sapped; and while she slept the nightly damps
Did chill her breast; and in the stormy day
Her tattered clothes were ruffled by the wind;
Even at the side of her own fire. Yet still
She loved this wretched spot, nor would for worlds
Have parted hence; and still that length of road,
And this rude bench, one torturing hope endeared,
Fast rooted at her heart: and here, my Friend,
In sickness she remained; and here she died,
Last human Tenant of these ruined Walls."

The Old Man ceased: he saw that I was moved;
From that low Bench, rising instinctively
I turn'd aside in weakness, nor had power
To thank him for the Tale which he had told,
I stood, and leaning o'er the Garden wall,
Reviewed that Woman's sufferings; and it seemed
To comfort me while with a Brother's love
I bless'd her—in the impotence of grief.
At length towards the Cottage I returned
Fondly, and traced with interest more mild,
That secret spirit of humanity
Which, 'mid the calm oblivious tendencies
Of Nature, 'mid her plants, and weeds, and flowers,
And silent overgrowings, still survived.
The Old Man, noting this, resumed, and said,
"My Friend! enough to sorrow you have given,
The purposes of wisdom ask no more;
Be wise and cheerful; and no longer read
The forms of things with an unworthy eye.
She sleeps in the calm earth, and peace is here.
I well remember that those very plumes,
Those weeds, and the high spear-grass on that wall,
By mist and silent rain-drops silver'd o'er,
As once I passed, did to my heart convey
So still an image of tranquillity,
So calm and still, and looked so beautiful
Amid the uneasy thoughts which filled my mind,
That what we feel of sorrow and despair
From ruin and from change, and all the grief
The passing shows of Being leave behind,
Appeared an idle dream, that could not live
Where meditation was. I turned away
And walked along my road in happiness."

He ceased. Ere long the sun declining shot
A slant and mellow radiance, which began
To fall upon us, while beneath the trees
We sat on that low Bench: and now we felt,
Admonished thus, the sweet hour coming on.
A linnet warbled from those lofty elms,
A thrush sang loud, and other melodies,
At distance heard, peopled the milder air.
The Old Man rose, and, with a sprightly mien° *countenance*

Of hopeful preparation, grasped his Staff:
Together casting then a farewell look
Upon those silent walls, we left the Shade;
And, ere the Stars were visible, had reached
A Village Inn—our Evening resting-place.
—1814

Surprised by Joy

Surprised by joy—impatient as the Wind
I turned to share the transport—Oh! with whom
But Thee,[1] deep buried in the silent tomb,
That spot which no vicissitude can find?
Love, faithful love, recalled thee to my mind—
But how could I forget thee? Through what power,
Even for the least division of an hour,
Have I been so beguiled as to be blind
To my most grievous loss?—That thought's return
Was the worst pang that sorrow ever bore,
Save one, one only, when I stood forlorn,
Knowing my heart's best treasure was no more;
That neither present time, nor years unborn
Could to my sight that heavenly face restore.
—1815

[1] *Thee* Catherine, the Wordsworths's daughter, who died in June 1812 at the age of three.

Mutability[2]

From low to high doth dissolution climb,
And sink from high to low, along a scale
Of awful° notes, whose concord shall not fail; *awe-inspiring*
A musical but melancholy chime,
Which they can hear who meddle not with crime,
Nor avarice, nor over-anxious care.
Truth fails not; but her outward forms that bear
The longest date do melt like frosty rime,
That in the morning whitened hill and plain
And is no more; drop like the tower sublime
Of yesterday, which royally did wear
His crown of weeds, but could not even sustain
Some casual shout that broke the silent air,
Or the unimaginable touch of Time.
—1822

Steamboats, Viaducts, and Railways

Motions and Means, on land and sea at war
With old poetic feeling, not for this,
Shall ye, by Poets even, be judged amiss!
Nor shall your presence, howsoe'er it mar
The loveliness of Nature, prove a bar
To the Mind's gaining that prophetic sense
Of future change, that point of vision whence
May be discovered what in soul ye are.
In spite of all that beauty may disown
In your harsh features, Nature doth embrace
Her lawful offspring in Man's art; and Time,
Pleased with your triumphs o'er his brother Space,
Accepts from your bold hands the proffered crown
Of hope, and smiles on you with cheer sublime.
—1835

[2] *Mutability* From *Ecclesiastical Sonnets*, a sequence of poems dealing with the history of the Church of England.

In Context

Visual Depictions of "Man's Art"

While one artistic tradition emphasized the "harsh features" of the products of the industrial revolution, many painters in the first half of the nineteenth century depicted such subjects as viaducts and railways in ways which suggested that, like Wordsworth, they saw these as nature's "lawful offspring."

John Sell Cotman, *Chirk Aqueduct* (1806–07).
The aqueduct, built between 1796 and 1801, is 70 feet high.

J.M.W. Turner, *Rain, Steam and Speed* (1844).

The Prelude

Wordsworth first began this blank-verse epic poem—generally regarded as his crowning achievement—in 1798, as a preface to his projected masterpiece, *The Recluse*, a philosophical poem that was never completed. Throughout his life Wordsworth referred to *The Prelude* simply as "the poem on my life," "the poem on the growth of my mind," or "the poem to Coleridge." It was his wife, Mary, who, publishing the piece a few months after his death, gave it the title by which it is now known.

The history of *The Prelude* is a long and complex one, spanning over forty years of revisions that saw several preliminary versions before the final, fourteen-book poem was completed in 1839. Wordsworth began *The Prelude* in 1798, during a lonely, cold winter in Germany, during which he and his sister Dorothy struggled with homesickness. This first part, which deals with Wordsworth's early childhood, and a second part describing his adolescence (composed after Wordsworth's return to England in 1799) formed the two books of the 1799 *Prelude*.

Wordsworth returned to *The Prelude* again in 1804, expanding the piece to five books that covered his life through his residence at Cambridge. After completing this version, Wordsworth began envisioning the project as a poem of epic proportions that would re-examine his life and convictions. In the expanded version of thirteen books, Wordsworth revisits France of the 1790s in his imagination, reliving those painful years and showing how, in the face of disappointment at the failure of the French Revolution and the growth of tyranny in Europe, he was restored through his ties with nature. This version, completed in May of 1805, begins with echoes of Milton's *Paradise Lost* as Wordsworth describes his vision of the fallen world in which he began his quest to develop his poetic imagination. Still spanning Wordsworth's childhood and maturity, the work no longer proceeds chronologically, but instead moves continuously between past and present as the poet recollects events and then examines their effects on his development. By the poem's end, he emerges from these events transformed and with his poetic sensibilities fully developed.

Wordsworth continued to revise *The Prelude* until 1839, when Dora Wordsworth (the poet's daughter) prepared a beautiful copy of the poem in its fourteen-book version. When *The Prelude* was first released in 1850, critics were often puzzled as to how it should be classified. In part, the poem is a familiar verse epistle to Coleridge and a testament to the power of friendship. At the same time, it is a personal narrative of spiritual journey. Yet the prophetic narrator and the deliberate parallels with other epics elevate the work above the merely personal and provide a representative story of a naive English adolescent who, maturing during the aftermath of a failed revolution, learns to celebrate his heritage.

It was not until the twentieth century that the earlier 1798 and 1805 versions of *The Prelude* were discovered. Both of these have since received much independent critical attention and have been seen by some critics as superior to the final version.

The Two-Part Prelude of 1799

FIRST PART

Was it for this
That one, the fairest of all rivers, loved
To blend his murmurs with my Nurse's song,
And from his alder[1] shades, and rocky falls,
And from his fords and shallows, sent a voice
That flowed along my dreams? For this didst thou
O Derwent, travelling over the green plains
Near my "sweet birth-place,"[2] didst thou beauteous Stream
Make ceaseless music through the night and day,
Which with its steady cadence tempering
Our human waywardness, composed my thoughts
To more than infant softness, giving me,
Among the fretful dwellings of mankind,
A knowledge, a dim earnest of the calm
Which Nature breathes among the fields and groves?
Beloved Derwent! fairest of all Streams!
Was it for this that I, a four year's child,
A naked Boy, among thy silent pools
Made one long bathing of a summer's day?
Basked in the sun, or plunged into thy streams,
Alternate, all a summer's day, or coursed
Over the sandy fields, and dashed the flowers
Of yellow grunsel,[3] or when crag and hill,
The woods and distant Skiddaw's[4] lofty height
Were bronzed with a deep radiance, stood alone,
A naked Savage in the thunder shower?
And afterwards, 'twas in a later day
Though early, when upon the mountain-slope
The frost and breath of frosty wind had snapped
The last autumnal crocus, 'twas my joy

John "Warwick" Smith, *Ulls-water in Paterdale*, 1792–95.

[1] *alder* Tree resembling a birch and usually found in wet places.

[2] *sweet birthplace* From Coleridge's *Frost at Midnight* (1798). Wordsworth's childhood home was in Cockermouth, Cumblerland, through which the Derwent River flows.

[3] *grunsel* Groundsel, a common weed.

[4] *Skiddaw* Mountain east of Cockermouth.

To wander half the night among the cliffs
And the smooth hollows, where the woodcocks ran
Along the moonlight turf. In thought and wish,
That time, my shoulder all with springes° hung, *snares*
I was a fell destroyer. Gentle Powers!
Who give us happiness and call it peace!
When scudding on from snare to snare I plied
My anxious visitation, hurrying on,
Still hurrying hurrying onward, how my heart
Panted; among the scattered yew-trees, and the crags
That looked upon me, how my bosom beat
With expectation. Sometimes strong desire,
Resistless, overpowered me, and the bird
Which was the captive of another's toils[1]
Became my prey; and when the deed was done
I heard among the solitary hills
Low breathings coming after me, and sounds
Of undistinguishable motion, steps
Almost as silent as the turf they trod.

Nor less, in spring-time, when on southern banks
The shining sun had from his knot of leaves
Decoyed the primrose-flower, and when the vales
And woods were warm, was I a rover then
In the high places, on the lonesome peaks,
Among the mountains and the winds. Though mean
And though inglorious were my views, the end° *result*
Was not ignoble. Oh, when I have hung
Above the raven's nest, by knots of grass,
Or half-inch fissures in the slipp'ry rock,
But ill sustained, and almost, as it seemed,
Suspended by the blast which blew amain,° *violently*
Shouldering the naked crag, oh at that time,
While on the perilous ridge I hung alone,
With what strange utterance did the loud dry wind
Blow through my ears! the sky seemed not a sky
Of earth, and with what motion moved the clouds!

The mind of man is fashioned and built up
Even as a strain of music: I believe
That there are spirits, which, when they would form
A favored being, from his very dawn
Of infancy do open out the clouds
As at the touch of lightning, seeking him
With gentle visitation; quiet Powers!
Retired and seldom recognized, yet kind,
And to the very meanest not unknown;
With me, though rarely, in my early days
They communed: others too there are who use,
Yet haply aiming at the self-same end,
Severer interventions, ministry
More palpable, and of their school was I.

They guided me: one evening, led by them,
I went alone into a Shepherd's boat,
A skiff that to a willow-tree was tied
Within a rocky cave, its usual home;
The moon was up, the lake was shining clear
Among the hoary mountains: from the shore
I pushed, and struck the oars, and struck again
In cadence, and my little Boat moved on
Just like a man who walks with stately step
Though bent on speed. It was an act of stealth
And troubled pleasure; not without the voice
Of mountain-echoes did my boat move on,
Leaving behind her still on either side
Small circles glittering idly in the moon
Until they melted all into one track
Of sparkling light. A rocky steep uprose
Above the cavern of the willow tree,
And now, as suited one who proudly rowed
With his best skill, I fixed a steady view
Upon the top of that same craggy ridge,
The bound of the horizon, for behind
Was nothing—but the stars and the grey sky.
—She was an elfin pinnace;[2] twenty times
I dipped my oars into the silent lake,
And, as I rose upon the stroke, my Boat
Went heaving through the water, like a swan—
When from behind that rocky steep, till then
The bound of the horizon, a huge Cliff,
As if with voluntary power instinct,° *imbued*
Upreared its head: I struck, and struck again,
And, growing still in stature, the huge cliff
Rose up between me and the stars, and still

[1] *toils* Meaning both "snares" and "labor."

[2] *pinnace* Small boat.

With measured motion, like a living thing,
Strode after me. With trembling hands I turned,
And through the silent water stole my way
Back to the cavern of the willow-tree.
There, in her mooring-place I left my bark,
And through the meadows homeward went with grave
And serious thoughts: and after I had seen
That spectacle, for many days my brain
Worked with a dim and undetermined sense
Of unknown modes of being: in my thoughts
There was a darkness, call it solitude
Or blank desertion; no familiar shapes
Of hourly objects, images of trees,
Of sea or sky, no colours of green fields:
But huge and mighty forms, that do not live
Like living men, moved slowly through my mind
By day, and were the trouble of my dreams.
    Ah! not in vain ye Beings of the hills!
And ye that walk the woods and open heaths
By moon or star-light, thus from my first dawn
Of childhood did ye love to intertwine
The passions that build up our human soul,
Not with the mean and vulgar° works of man, *ordinary*
But with high objects, with eternal things,
With life and nature, purifying thus
The elements of feeling and of thought,
And sanctifying by such discipline
Both pain and fear, until we recognise
A grandeur in the beatings of the heart.
    Nor was this fellowship vouchsafed to me
With stinted kindness. In November days,
When vapours, rolling down the valleys, made
A lonely scene more lonesome, among woods
At noon, and 'mid the calm of summer nights
When by the margin of the trembling lake
Beneath the gloomy hills I homeward went
In solitude, such intercourse was mine.
    And in the frosty season when the sun
Was set, and, visible for many a mile,
The cottage windows through the twilight blazed,
I heeded not the summons: clear and loud
The village clock tolled six; I wheeled about
Proud and exulting like an untired horse
That cares not for its home.— All shod with steel
We hissed along the polished ice, in games
Confederate, imitative of the chase
And woodland pleasures, the resounding horn,
The pack loud bellowing, and the hunted hare.
So through the darkness and the cold we flew,
And not a voice was idle: with the din,
Meanwhile, the precipices rang aloud,
The leafless trees and every icy crag
Tinkled like iron, while the distant hills
Into the tumult sent an alien sound
Of melancholy not unnoticed while the stars,
Eastward, were sparkling clear, and in the west
The orange sky of evening died away.
    Not seldom from the uproar I retired
Into a silent bay, or sportively
Glanced sideway leaving the tumultuous throng
To cut across the shadow° of a star *reflection*
That gleamed upon the ice: and oftentimes
When we had given our bodies to the wind
And all the shadowy banks on either side
Came sweeping through the darkness, spinning still
The rapid line of motion, then at once
Have I, reclining back upon my heels,
Stopped short; yet still the solitary cliffs
Wheeled by me, even as if the earth had rolled
With visible motion her diurnal° round; *daily*
Behind me did they stretch in solemn train
Feebler and feebler, and I stood and watched
Till all was tranquil as a summer sea.
    Ye Powers of earth! ye Genii of the springs!
And ye that have your voices in the clouds
And ye that are Familiars of the lakes
And of the standing pools, I may not think
A vulgar hope was yours when ye employed
Such ministry, when ye through many a year
Thus by the agency of boyish sports
On caves and trees, upon the woods and hills,
Impressed upon all forms the characters° *signs*
Of danger or desire, and thus did make
The surface of the universal earth
With meanings of delight, of hope and fear,
Work° like a sea. *seethe*

Not uselessly employed
I might pursue this theme through every change
Of exercise and sport to which the year
Did summon us in its delightful round.
We were a noisy crew: the sun in heaven
Beheld not vales more beautiful than ours
Nor saw a race in happiness and joy
More worthy of the fields where they were sown.
I would record with no reluctant voice
Our home amusements by the warm peat fire
At evening, when with pencil, and with slate
In square divisions parcelled out, and all
With crosses and with cyphers scribbled o'er,[1]
We schemed and puzzled, head opposed to head
In strife too humble to be named in verse,
Or round the naked table, snow-white deal,° *pine*
Cherry or maple, sat in close array
And to the combat—Lu or Whist[2]—led on
A thick-ribbed army, not as in the world
Discarded and ungratefully thrown by
Even for the very service they had wrought,
But husbanded through many a long campaign.
Oh with what echoes on the board they fell—
Ironic diamonds, hearts of sable hue,
Queens gleaming through their splendour's last decay,
Knaves wrapt in one assimilating gloom,
And Kings indignant at the shame incurr'd
By royal visages. Meanwhile abroad
The heavy rain was falling, or the frost
Raged bitterly with keen and silent tooth,
And interrupting the impassioned game
Oft from the neighbouring lake the splitting ice
While it sank down towards the water sent
Among the meadows and the hills its long
And frequent yellings, imitative some
Of wolves that howl along the Bothnic main.[3]
Nor with less willing heart would I rehearse
The woods of autumn and their hidden bowers
With milk-white clusters hung; the rod and line,
True symbol of the foolishness of hope,
Which with its strong enchantment led me on
By rocks and pools where never summer-star
Impressed its shadow, to forlorn cascades
Among the windings of the mountain-brooks;
The kite, in sultry calms from some high hill
Sent up, ascending thence till it was lost
Among the fleecy clouds, in gusty days
Launched from the lower grounds, and suddenly
Dash'd headlong—and rejected by the storm.
All these and more with rival claims demand
Grateful acknowledgement. It were a song
Venial,° and such as if I rightly judge *pardonable*
I might protract unblamed; but I perceive
That much is overlooked, and we should ill
Attain our object if from delicate fears
Of breaking in upon the unity
Of this my argument I should omit
To speak of such effects as cannot here
Be regularly classed, yet tend no less
To the same point, the growth of mental power
And love of Nature's works.
Ere I had seen
Eight summers (and 'twas in the very week
When I was first transplanted to thy vale,
Beloved Hawkshead![4] when thy paths, thy shores
And brooks were like a dream of novelty
To my half-infant mind) I chanced to cross
One of those open fields which, shaped like ears,
Make green peninsulas on Esthwaite's lake.
Twilight was coming on, yet through the gloom
I saw distinctly on the opposite shore
Beneath a tree and close by the lake side
A heap of garments, as if left by one
Who there was bathing: half an hour I watched
And no one owned them: meanwhile the calm lake
Grew dark with all the shadows on its breast,
And now and then a leaping fish disturbed
The breathless stillness. The succeeding day

[1] *With crosses … o'er* Echo of Milton, *Paradise Lost* 8.83: "With centric and eccentric scribbled o'er." Here Wordsworth uses this heroic diction to describe a game of tick-tack-toe.

[2] *Lu or Whist* Popular card games. The "thick-ribbed army" of the next line is the pack of cards made of thick "card-board."

[3] *Bothnic main* Baltic Sea.

[4] *Hawkshead* Where Wordsworth attended grammar school.

There came a company, and in their boat
Sounded with iron hooks and with long poles.
At length the dead man 'mid that beauteous scene
Of trees, and hills, and water, bolt upright
Rose with his ghastly face.[1] I might advert
To numerous accidents in flood or field,
Quarry or moor, or 'mid the winter snows,
Distresses and disasters, tragic facts
Of rural history that impressed my mind
With images, to which in following years
Far other feelings were attached, with forms
That yet exist with independent life
And, like their archetypes, know no decay.
    There are in our existence spots of time
Which with distinct pre-eminence retain
A fructifying virtue,[2] whence, depressed
By trivial occupations and the round
Of ordinary intercourse, our minds
(Especially the imaginative power)
Are nourished, and invisibly repaired.
Such moments chiefly seem to have their date
In our first childhood. I remember well
('Tis of an early season that I speak,
The twilight of rememberable life)
While I was yet an urchin, one who scarce
Could hold a bridle, with ambitious hopes
I mounted, and we rode towards the hills;
We were a pair of horsemen: honest James[3]
Was with me, my encourager and guide.
We had not travelled long ere some mischance
Disjoined me from my comrade, and through fear
Dismounting, down the rough and stony moor
I led my horse and, stumbling on, at length
Came to a bottom where in former times
A man, the murderer of his wife, was hung
In irons; mouldered° was the gibbet[4] mast, *decayed*
The bones were gone, the iron and the wood,
Only a long green ridge of turf remained
Whose shape was like a grave. I left the spot,
And, reascending the bare slope, I saw
A naked pool that lay beneath the hills,
The beacon on the summit, and more near
A girl who bore a pitcher on her head
And seemed with difficult steps to force her way
Against the blowing wind. It was in truth
An ordinary sight but I should need
Colours and words that are unknown to man
To paint the visionary dreariness
Which, while I looked all round for my lost guide,
Did, at that time, invest the naked pool,
The beacon on the lonely eminence,
The woman and her garments vexed and tossed
By the strong wind. Nor less I recollect
(Long after, though my childhood had not ceased)
Another scene which left a kindred power
Implanted in my mind.
                                        One Christmas time,
The day before the holidays began,
Feverish, and tired and restless, I went forth
Into the fields, impatient for the sight
Of those three horses which should bear us home,
My Brothers and myself. There was a crag,
An eminence which from the meeting point
Of two highways ascending overlooked
At least a long half-mile of those two roads,
By each of which the expected steeds might come,
The choice uncertain. Thither I repaired
Up to the highest summit; 'twas a day
Stormy, and rough, and wild, and on the grass
I sat, half-sheltered by a naked wall;
Upon my right hand was a single sheep,
A whistling hawthorn on my left, and there,
Those two companions at my side, I watched
With eyes intensely straining as the mist
Gave intermitting prospects of the wood
And plain beneath. Ere I to school returned
That dreary time, ere I had been ten days

[1] *At length ... face* In June 1779, shortly after Wordsworth arrived at Hawkshead, a schoolmaster from a neighboring village drowned while swimming in Esthwaite Water.

[2] *fructifying virtue* I.e., power to make fruitful.

[3] *honest James* Most likely the family's servant.

[4] *gibbet* Upright post from which the bodies of criminals were hung for display after execution.

A dweller in my Father's house, he died,[1]
And I and my two Brothers, orphans then,
Followed his body to the grave. The event
With all the sorrow which it brought appeared
A chastisement, and when I called to mind
That day so lately passed when from the crag
I looked in such anxiety of hope,
With trite reflections of morality
Yet with the deepest passion I bowed low
To God, who thus corrected my desires;
And afterwards the wind, and sleety rain,
And all the business of the elements,
The single sheep, and the one blasted tree,
And the bleak music of that old stone wall,
The noise of wood and water, and the mist
Which on the line of each of those two roads
Advanced in such indisputable shapes,
All these were spectacles and sounds to which
I often would repair, and thence would drink
As at a fountain, and I do not doubt
That in this later time when storm and rain
Beat on my roof at midnight, or by day
When I am in the woods, unknown to me
The workings of my spirit thence are brought.
Nor sedulous° to trace *diligent*
How Nature by collateral° interest *indirect*
And by extrinsic passion peopled first
My mind with forms, or beautiful or grand,
And made me love them, may I well forget
How other pleasures have been mine, and joys
Of subtler origin, how I have felt
Not seldom, even in that tempestuous time,
Those hallowed and pure motions of the sense
Which seem in their simplicity to own
An intellectual charm, that calm delight
Which, if I err not, surely must belong
To those first-born affinities that fit
Our new existence to existing things
And in our dawn of being constitute
The bond of union betwixt life and joy.
Yes, I remember when the changeful earth
And twice five seasons on my mind had stamped
The faces of the moving year, even then,
A Child, I held unconscious intercourse
With the eternal Beauty, drinking in
A pure organic pleasure from the lines
Of curling mist or from the level plain
Of waters coloured by the steady clouds.
The sands of Westmoreland, the creeks and bays
Of Cumbria's[2] rocky limits, they can tell
How when the sea threw off his evening shade
And to the Shepherd's hut beneath the crags
Did send sweet notice of the rising moon,
How I have stood to images like these
A stranger, linking with the spectacle
No body of associated forms
And bringing with me no peculiar sense
Of quietness or peace, yet I have stood
Even while my eye has moved o'er three long leagues
Of shining water, gathering, as it seemed,
Through the wide surface of that field of light
New pleasure, like a bee among the flowers.
Thus often in those fits of vulgar joy
Which through all seasons on a child's pursuits
Are prompt attendants, 'mid that giddy bliss
Which like a tempest works along the blood
And is forgotten, even then I felt
Gleams like the flashing of a shield; the earth
And common face of Nature spake to me
Rememberable things: sometimes, 'tis true,
By quaint associations, yet not vain
Nor profitless if haply° they impressed *by chance*
Collateral[3] objects and appearances,
Albeit lifeless then, and doomed to sleep
Until maturer seasons called them forth
To impregnate and to elevate the mind.
——And if the vulgar joy by its own weight
Wearied itself out of the memory,
The scenes which were a witness of that joy
Remained, in their substantial lineaments
Depicted on the brain, and to the eye

[1] *ere I … died* Wordsworth's father died on December 30, 1783. His mother had died five years earlier.

[2] *Westmoreland … Cumbria* Counties of the Lake District.

[3] *Collateral* I.e., indirect, lying aside from the main interests of the poet.

Were visible, a daily sight: and thus
By the impressive agency of fear,
By pleasure and repeated happiness,
So frequently repeated, and by force
Of obscure feelings representative
Of joys that were forgotten, these same scenes
So beauteous and majestic in themselves,
Though yet the day was distant, did at length
Become habitually dear, and all
Their hues and forms were by invisible links
Allied to the affections.
                                        I began
My story early, feeling, as I fear,
The weakness of a human love for days
Disowned by memory, ere the birth of spring
Planting my snow-drops among winter snows.
Nor will it seem to thee, my Friend,[1] so prompt
In sympathy, that I have lengthened out
With fond and feeble tongue a tedious tale.
Meanwhile my hope has been that I might fetch
Reproaches from my former years, whose power
May spur me on, in manhood now mature,
To honourable toil. Yet, should it be
That this is but an impotent desire,
That I by such inquiry am not taught
To understand myself, nor thou to know
With better knowledge how the heart was framed
Of him thou lovest, need I dread from thee
Harsh judgements if I am so loath to quit
Those recollected hours that have the charm
Of visionary things,[2] and lovely forms
And sweet sensations that throw back our life
And make our infancy a visible scene
On which the sun is shining?

Second Part

Thus far my Friend, have we retraced the way
Through which I travelled when I first began
To love the woods and fields: the passion yet
Was in its birth, sustained as might befall
By nourishment that came unsought, for still
From week to week, from month to month, we lived
A round of tumult: duly° were our games *fittingly*
Prolonged in summer till the day-light failed;
No chair remained before the doors, the bench
And threshold steps were empty, fast asleep
The labourer and the old man who had sat
A later lingerer, yet the revelry
Continued and the loud uproar: at last
When all the ground was dark, and the huge clouds
Were edged with twinkling stars, to bed we went
With weary joints and with a beating mind.
Ah! is there one who ever has been young
And needs a monitory voice to tame
The pride of virtue and of intellect,
And is there one, the wisest and the best
Of all mankind, who does not sometimes wish
For things which cannot be, who would not give,
If so he might, to duty and to truth
The eagerness of infantine desire?
A tranquillizing spirit presses now
On my corporeal frame, so wide appears
The vacancy between me and those days
Which yet have such self-presence in my heart
That sometimes when I think of them I seem
Two consciousnesses, conscious of myself
And of some other being. A grey stone
Of native rock, left midway in the square
Of our small market-village, was the home
And centre of these joys, and when, returned
After long absence, thither I repaired,
I found that it was split and gone to build
A smart assembly-room that perked and flared
With wash and rough-cast,[3] elbowing the ground
Which had been ours. But let the fiddle scream
And be ye happy! yet I know, my Friends,
That more than one of you will think with me
Of those soft starry nights and that old dame
From whom the stone was named, who there had sat
And watched her table with its huckster's wares,

[1] *my Friend* Coleridge.

[2] *visionary things* Things seen in the imagination.

[3] *smart assembly-room* Hawkshead Town Hall, built in 1790; *wash* Whitewash; *roughcast* Plaster made of lime and gravel.

Assiduous, for the length of sixty years.
—We ran a boisterous race, the year span round
With giddy motion. But the time approached
That brought with it a regular desire
For calmer pleasures, when the beauteous scenes
Of nature were collaterally attached
To every scheme of holiday delight
And every boyish sport, less grateful° else *pleasing*
And languidly pursued.
When summer came
It was the pastime of our afternoons
To beat along the plain of Windermere
With rival oars; and the selected bourn° *goal*
Was now an island musical with birds
That sang for ever, now a sister isle
Beneath the oak's umbrageous° covert sown *shady*
With lilies of the valley like a field,
And now a third small island[1] where remained
An old stone table and one mouldered cave,
A hermit's history. In such a race,
So ended, disappointment could be none,
Uneasiness, or pain, or jealousy;
We rested in the shade all pleased alike,
Conquered and conqueror. Thus our selfishness
Was mellowed down, and thus the pride of strength
And the vain-glory of superior skill
Were interfused with objects which subdued
And tempered them, and gradually produced
A quiet independence of the heart.
And to my Friend who knows me I may add,
Unapprehensive of reproof, that hence
Ensued a diffidence and modesty,
And I was taught to feel, perhaps too much,
The self-sufficing power of solitude.
No delicate viands sapped our bodily strength;
More than we wished we knew the blessing then
Of vigorous hunger, for our daily meals
Were frugal, Sabine fare![2] and then exclude
A little weekly stipend, and we lived
Through three divisions of the quartered year
In penniless poverty. But now to school
Returned from the half-yearly holidays,
We came with purses more profusely filled,
Allowance which abundantly sufficed
To gratify the palate with repasts
More costly than the Dame of whom I spake,
That ancient woman, and her board° supplied, *table*
Hence inroads into distant vales, and long
Excursions far away among the hills;
Hence rustic dinners on the cool green ground
Or in the woods or by a river-side
Or fountain,° festive banquets that provoked *spring*
The languid action° of a natural scene *effect*
By pleasure of corporeal appetite.
Nor is my aim neglected if I tell
How twice in the long length of those half-years
We from our funds perhaps with bolder hand
Drew largely, anxious for one day at least
To feel the motion of the galloping steed;
And with the good old Innkeeper in truth
I needs must say that sometimes we have used
Sly subterfuge, for the intended bound
Of the day's journey was too distant far
For any cautious man, a Structure famed
Beyond its neighbourhood, the antique walls
Of a large Abbey[3] with its fractured arch,
Belfry, and images, and living trees,
A holy scene! Along the smooth green turf
Our horses grazed: in more than inland peace
Left by the winds that overpass the vale
In that sequestered ruin trees and towers
Both silent, and both motionless alike,
Hear all day long the murmuring sea that beats
Incessantly upon a craggy shore.
Our steeds remounted, and the summons given,
With whip and spur we by the Chantry[4] flew
In uncouth race, and left the cross-legged Knight
And the stone Abbot, and that single wren

[1] *third small island* Island of Lady Holm, where a chapel dedicated to the Virgin Mary was formerly located.

[2] *Sabine fare* I.e., like the meals prepared at the Sabine Farm of the poet Horace; farm fare.

[3] *a large Abbey* Furness Abbey, located about twenty miles south of Hawkshead.

[4] *Chantry* Chapel which has been endowed for daily masses to be sung for the donor.

Which one day sang so sweetly in the nave
Of the old church that, though from recent showers
The earth was comfortless, and touched by faint
Internal breezes from the roofless walls
The shuddering ivy dripped large drops, yet still
So sweetly 'mid the gloom the invisible bird
Sang to itself that there I could have made
My dwelling-place, and lived for ever there
To hear such music. Through the walls we flew
And down the valley, and, a circuit made
In wantonness of heart, through rough and smooth
We scampered homeward. O ye rocks and streams
And that still spirit of the evening air,
Even in this joyous time I sometimes felt
Your presence, when with slackened step we breathed[1]
Along the sides of the steep hills, or when,
Lightened by gleams of moonlight from the sea,
We beat with thundering hoofs the level sand.
    There was a row of ancient trees, since fallen,
That on the margin of a jutting land
Stood near the lake of Coniston and made
With its long boughs above the water stretched
A gloom through which a boat might sail along
As in a cloister. An old Hall[2] was near,
Grotesque and beautiful, its gavel° end *gable*
And huge round chimneys to the top o'ergrown
With fields of ivy. Thither we repaired,
'Twas even a custom with us, to the shore
And to that cool piazza. They who dwelt
In the neglected mansion-house supplied
Fresh butter, tea-kettle, and earthen-ware,
And chafing-dish with smoking coals, and so
Beneath the trees we sat in our small boat
And in the covert eat° our delicate meal *ate*
Upon the calm smooth lake. It was a joy
Worthy the heart of one who is full grown
To rest beneath those horizontal boughs
And mark the radiance of the setting sun,
Himself unseen, reposing on the top
Of the high eastern hills. And there I said,
That beauteous sight before me, there I said
(Then first beginning in my thoughts to mark
That sense of dim similitude which links
Our moral feelings with external forms)
That in whatever region I should close
My mortal life I would remember you,
Fair scenes! that dying I would think on you,
My soul would send a longing look to you:
Even as that setting sun while all the vale
Could nowhere catch one faint memorial gleam
Yet with the last remains of his last light
Still lingered, and a farewell lustre threw
On the dear mountain-tops where first he rose.
    'Twas then my fourteenth summer, and these words
Were uttered in a casual access
Of sentiment, a momentary trance
That far outran the habit of my mind.
    Upon the eastern shore of Windermere,
Above the crescent of a pleasant bay,
There was an Inn,[3] no homely-featured shed,
Brother of the surrounding cottages,
But 'twas a splendid place, the door beset
With chaises, grooms, and liveries, and within
Decanters, glasses, and the blood-red wine.
In ancient times, or ere the Hall[4] was built
On the large island, had the dwelling been
More worthy of a poet's love, a hut
Proud of its one bright fire and sycamore shade.
But though the rhymes were gone which once inscribed
The threshold, and large golden characters
On the blue-frosted sign-board had usurped
The place of the old Lion in contempt
And mockery of the rustic painter's hand,
Yet to this hour the spot to me is dear
With all its foolish pomp. The garden lay
Upon a slope surmounted by the plain
Of a small bowling-green; beneath us stood
A grove, with gleams of water through the trees
And over the tree-tops; nor did we want
Refreshment, strawberries and mellow cream,

[1] *breathed* I.e., let our horses catch their breath.

[2] *old Hall* Coniston Hall, built in 1580.

[3] *an Inn* White Lion, at Bowness.

[4] *the Hall* Built on Belle Isle in Lake Windermere in the early 1780s.

And there through half an afternoon we played
On the smooth platform, and the shouts we sent
Made all the mountains ring. But ere the fall
Of night, when in our pinnace we returned
Over the dusky lake, and to the beach
Of some small island steered our course with one,
The minstrel of our troop, and left him there
And rowed off gently while he blew his flute
Alone upon the rock—oh then the calm
And dead still water lay upon my mind
Even with a weight of pleasure, and the sky,
Never before so beautiful, sank down
Into my heart and held me like a dream.
    Thus day by day my sympathies increased
And thus the common range of visible things
Grew dear to me: already I began
To love the sun, a Boy I loved the sun
Not, as I since have loved him, as a pledge
And surety of my earthly life, a light
Which while I view I feel I am alive,
But for this cause, that I had seen him lay
His beauty on the morning hills, had seen
The western mountain touch his setting orb
In many a thoughtless hour, when from excess
Of happiness my blood appeared to flow
With its own pleasure and I breathed with joy.
And from like feelings, humble though intense,
To patriotic and domestic love
Analogous, the moon to me was dear,
For I would dream away my purposes
Standing to look upon her while she hung
Midway between the hills as if she knew
No other region but belonged to thee,
Yea, appertained by a peculiar right
To thee and thy grey huts,[1] my native vale.
    Those incidental charms which first attached
My heart to rural objects day by day
Grew weaker, and I hasten on to tell
How nature, intervenient[2] till this time
And secondary, now at length was sought
For her own sake. But who shall parcel out
His intellect by geometric rules,
Split like a province into round and square;
Who knows the individual hour in which
His habits were first sown, even as a seed;
Who that shall point as with a wand and say,
This portion of the river of my mind
Came from yon fountain? Thou, my Friend, art one
More deeply read in thy own thoughts, no slave
Of that false secondary power by which
In weakness we create distinctions, then
Believe our puny boundaries are things
Which we perceive and not which we have made.
To thee, unblinded by these outward shows,
The unity of all has been revealed,
And thou wilt doubt with me, less aptly skilled
Than many are to class the cabinet
Of their sensations and in voluble phrase
Run through the history and birth of each
As of a single independent thing.
Hard task to analyse a soul in which
Not only general habits and desires
But each most obvious and particular thought,
Not in a mystical and idle sense
But in the words of reason deeply weighed,
Hath no beginning.
                                Bless'd the infant Babe
(For with my best conjectures I would trace
The progress of our being) blest the Babe
Nursed in his Mother's arms, the Babe who sleeps
Upon his Mother's breast, who when his soul
Claims manifest kindred with an earthly soul
Doth gather passion from his Mother's eye!
Such feelings pass into his torpid life
Like an awakening breeze, and hence his mind
Even in the first trial of its powers
Is prompt and watchful, eager to combine
In one appearance all the elements
And parts of the same object, else detached
And loath to coalesce. Thus day by day
Subjected to the discipline of love
His organs and recipient faculties
Are quickened, are more vigorous, his mind spreads

[1] *grey huts* Grey stone cottages.

[2] *intervenient* Coming between; incidental.

Tenacious of the forms which it receives.
In one beloved presence, nay, and more,
In that most apprehensive habitude[1]
And those sensations which have been derived
From this beloved presence, there exists
A virtue which irradiates and exalts
All objects through all intercourse of sense.
No outcast he, bewildered and depressed:
Along his infant veins are interfused
The gravitation and the filial bond
Of nature that connect him with the world.
Emphatically such a being lives
An inmate of this *active* universe;
From nature largely he receives, nor so
Is satisfied but largely gives again,
For feeling has to him imparted strength,
And powerful in all sentiments of grief,
Of exultation, fear and joy, his mind,
Even as an agent of the one great mind,
Creates, creator and receiver both,
Working but in alliance with the works
Which it beholds. Such verily is the first
Poetic spirit of our human life,
By uniform control of after years
In most abated and suppressed, in some
Through every change of growth or of decay
Preeminent till death.
From early days,
Beginning not long after that first time
In which, a Babe, by intercourse of touch
I held mute dialogues with my Mother's heart,
I have endeavoured to display the means
Whereby this infant sensibility,
Great birth-right of our being, was in me
Augmented and sustained. Yet is a path
More difficult before me, and I fear
That in its broken windings we shall need
The Chamois'[2] sinews and the Eagle's wing:
For now a trouble came into my mind
From obscure causes. I was left alone
Seeking this visible world, nor knowing why:
The props of my affections were removed[3]
And yet the building stood as if sustained
By its own spirit. All that I beheld
Was dear to me, and from this cause it came
That now to Nature's finer influxes° *influences*
My mind lay open, to that more exact
And intimate communion which our hearts
Maintain with the minuter properties
Of objects which already are beloved,
And of those only. Many are the joys
Of youth, but oh! what happiness to live
When every hour brings palpable access
Of knowledge, when all knowledge is delight,
And sorrow is not there. The seasons came
And every season brought a countless store
Of modes and temporary qualities
Which but for this most watchful power of love
Had been neglected, left a register
Of permanent relations, else unknown:
Hence life, and change, and beauty, solitude
More active even than "best society,"[4]
Society made sweet as solitude
By silent inobtrusive sympathies
And gentle agitations of the mind
From manifold distinctions, difference
Perceived in things where to the common eye
No difference is: and hence from the same source
Sublimer joy; for I would walk alone
In storm and tempest or in starlight nights
Beneath the quiet heavens, and at that time
Would feel whate'er there is of power in sound
To breathe an elevated mood by form
Or image unprofaned: and I would stand
Beneath some rock listening to sounds that are
The ghostly language of the ancient earth
Or make their dim abode in distant winds.
Thence did I drink the visionary power.
I deem not profitless these fleeting moods

[1] *apprehensive habitude* Disposition most suited to learning.

[2] *Chamois* Antelope found in the mountains of Europe.

[3] *The props … removed* Wordsworth's mother died just before his eighth birthday.

[4] *best society* See Milton, *Paradise Lost* 9.249: "For solitude sometimes is the best society."

Of shadowy exaltation, not for this,
That they are kindred to our purer mind
And intellectual life, but that the soul
Remembering how she felt, but what she felt
Remembering not, retains an obscure sense
Of possible sublimity to which
With growing faculties she doth aspire,
With faculties still growing, feeling still
That whatsoever point they gain, they still
Have something to pursue.
And not alone
In grandeur and in tumult, but no less
In tranquil scenes, that universal power
And fitness in the latent qualities
And essences of things, by which the mind
Is moved with feelings of delight, to me
Came strengthened with a superadded soul,
A virtue not its own. My morning walks
Were early; oft before the hours of school
I travelled round our little lake, five miles
Of pleasant wandering, happy time more dear
For this, that one was by my side, a Friend
Then passionately loved;[1] with heart how full
Will he peruse these lines, this page, perhaps
A blank to other men, for many years
Have since flowed in between us, and, our minds
Both silent to each other, at this time
We live as if those hours had never been.
Nor seldom did I lift our cottage latch
Far earlier, and before the vernal° thrush *spring-time*
Was audible, among the hills I sat
Alone upon some jutting eminence
At the first hour of morning when the vale
Lay quiet in an utter solitude.
How shall I trace the history, where seek
The origin of what I then have felt?
Oft in those moments such a holy calm
Did overspread my soul that I forgot
The agency of sight, and what I saw
Appeared like something in myself—a dream,
A prospect° in my mind. 'Twere long to tell *view*
What spring and autumn, what the winter-snows
And what the summer-shade, what day and night,
The evening and the morning, what my dreams
And what my waking thoughts supplied, to nurse
That spirit of religious love in which
I walked with nature. But let this at least
Be not forgotten, that I still retained
My first creative sensibility,
That by the regular action of the world
My soul was unsubdued. A plastic° power *formative*
Abode with me, a forming hand, at times
Rebellious, acting in a devious mood,
A local spirit of its own, at war
With general tendency, but for the most
Subservient strictly to the external things
With which it communed. An auxiliar light
Came from my mind which on the setting sun
Bestowed new splendour, the melodious birds,
The gentle breezes, fountains that ran on
Murmuring so sweetly in themselves, obeyed
A like dominion, and the midnight storm
Grew darker in the presence of my eye.
Hence my obeisance, my devotion hence,
And *hence* my transport.° *exaltation*
Nor should this perchance
Pass unrecorded, that I still° had loved *always*
The exercise and produce of a toil
Than analytic industry to me
More pleasing, and whose character, I deem,
Is more poetic, as resembling more
Creative agency: I mean to speak
Of that interminable building reared
By observation of affinities
In objects where no brotherhood exists
To common minds. My seventeenth year was come,
And whether from this habit rooted now
So deeply in my mind, or from excess
Of the great social principle of life
Coercing all things into sympathy,
To unorganic natures I transferred
My own enjoyments, or, the power of truth
Coming in revelation, I conversed
With things that really are. I at this time

---

[1] *Friend ... loved* John Fleming, also mentioned in *The Vale of Esthwaite* (1785-87).

Saw blessings spread around me like a sea.
Thus did my days pass on, and now at length
From Nature and her overflowing soul
I had received so much that all my thoughts
Were steeped in feeling; I was only then
Contented when with bliss ineffable
I felt the sentiment of being spread
O'er all that moves, and all that seemeth still,
O'er all that, lost beyond the reach of thought
And human knowledge, to the human eye
Invisible, yet liveth to the heart,
O'er all that leaps, and runs, and shouts and sings
Or beats the gladsome air, o'er all that glides
Beneath the wave, yea, in the wave itself
And mighty depth of waters: wonder not
If such my transports were, for in all things
I saw one life and felt that it was joy.
One song they sang, and it was audible,
Most audible then when the fleshly ear,
O'ercome by grosser prelude of that strain,
Forgot its functions, and slept undisturbed.
If this be error, and another faith
Find easier access to the pious mind,
Yet were I grossly destitute of all
Those human sentiments which make this earth
So dear, if I should fail with grateful voice
To speak of you, ye mountains! and ye lakes
And sounding cataracts! ye mists and winds
That dwell among the hills where I was born.
If, in my youth, I have been pure in heart,
If, mingling with the world, I am content
With my own modest pleasures, and have lived
With God and Nature communing, removed
From little enmities and low desires,
The gift is yours: if in these times[1] of fear,
This melancholy waste° of hopes o'erthrown, *wasteland*
If, 'mid indifference and apathy
And wicked exultation, when good men
On every side fall off we know not how
To selfishness disguised in gentle names
Of peace, and quiet, and domestic love,
Yet mingled, not unwillingly, with sneers
On visionary minds, if in this time
Of dereliction and dismay I yet
Despair not of our nature, but retain
A more than Roman confidence, a faith
That fails not, in all sorrow my support,
The blessing of my life, the gift is yours,
Ye Mountains! thine, O Nature! thou hast fed
My lofty speculations, and in thee
For this uneasy heart of ours I find
A never-failing principle of joy
And purest passion.
Thou, my Friend, wast reared
In the great city 'mid far other scenes,[2]
But we, by different roads, at length have gained
The self-same bourne. And from this cause to thee
I speak unapprehensive of contempt,
The insinuated scoff of coward tongues,
And all that silent language which so oft
In conversation betwixt man and man
Blots from the human countenance all trace
Of beauty and of love. For thou hast sought
The truth in solitude, and thou art one,
The most intense of Nature's worshippers,
In many things my brother, chiefly here
In this my deep devotion.
Fare thee well!
Health and the quiet of a healthful mind
Attend thee! seeking oft the haunts of men
But yet more often living with thyself
And for thyself, so haply shall thy days
Be many and a blessing to mankind.
—1799

[1] *in these times* I.e., following the failure of the French Revolution. Many radicals were recanting. In a 1799 letter to Wordsworth, Coleridge asks him to write something about those who "have thrown up all hopes of the amelioration of mankind, and are sinking into an almost epicurean selfishness, disguising the same under the soft titles of domestic attachment and contempt for visionary *philosophes*."

[2] *Thou … scenes* See Coleridge, *Frost at Midnight* 51–52: "For I was reared / In the great city, pent 'mid cloisters dim."

from *The Fourteen-Book Prelude*

from BOOK FIRST

INTRODUCTION, CHILDHOOD, AND SCHOOL-TIME

O there is blessing in this gentle Breeze,
A visitant that, while he fans my cheek,
Doth seem half-conscious of the joy he brings
From the green fields, and from yon azure sky.
Whate'er his mission, the soft breeze can come
To none more grateful than to me; escaped
From the vast City,[1] where I long have pined
A discontented Sojourner—Now free,
Free as a bird to settle where I will.
What dwelling shall receive me? in what vale
Shall be my harbour? underneath what grove
Shall I take up my home? and what clear stream
Shall with its murmur lull me into rest?
The earth is all before me:[2] with a heart
Joyous, nor scared at its own liberty,
I look about; and should the chosen guide
Be nothing better than a wandering cloud,
I cannot miss my way. I breathe again;
Trances of thought and mountings of the heart
Come fast upon me: it is shaken off,
That burthen of my own unnatural self,
The heavy weight of many a weary day
Not mine, and such as were not made for me.
Long months of peace (if such bold word accord
With any promises of human life),
Long months of ease and undisturbed delight
Are mine in prospect; whither shall I turn,
By road or pathway, or through trackless field,
Up hill or down, or shall some floating thing
Upon the River point me out my course?
Dear Liberty! Yet what would it avail,
But for a gift that consecrates the joy?
For I, methought, while the sweet breath of heaven
Was blowing on my body, felt, within,
A correspondent breeze, that gently moved
With quickening virtue, but is now become
A tempest, a redundant° energy, *abounding*
Vexing its own creation. Thanks to both,
And their congenial powers that, while they join
In breaking up a long continued frost,
Bring with them vernal° promises, the hope *spring-time*
Of active days urged on by flying hours;
Days of sweet leisure taxed with patient thought
Abstruse, nor wanting punctual service high,
Matins and vespers, of harmonious verse!
Thus far, O Friend! did I, not used to make
A present joy the matter of a Song,
Pour forth, that day, my soul in measured strains,
That would not be forgotten, and are here
Recorded: to the open fields I told
A prophecy: poetic numbers° came *verses*
Spontaneously, to clothe in priestly robe
A renovated Spirit singled out,
Such hope was mine, for holy services:
My own voice cheered me, and, far more, the mind's
Internal echo of the imperfect sound;
To both I listened, drawing from them both
A cheerful confidence in things to come.
Content, and not unwilling now to give
A respite to this passion, I paced on
With brisk and eager steps; and came at length
To a green shady place where down I sat
Beneath a tree, slackening my thoughts by choice,
And settling into gentler happiness.
'Twas Autumn, and a clear and placid day,
With warmth, as much as needed, from a sun
Two hours declined towards the west, a day
With silver clouds, and sunshine on the grass,
And, in the sheltered and the sheltering grove,
A perfect stillness. Many were the thoughts
Encouraged and dismissed, till choice was made
Of a known Vale[3] whither my feet should turn,
Nor rest till they had reached the very door
Of the one Cottage which methought I saw.
No picture of mere memory ever looked

[1] *the vast City* London.

[2] *The earth … me* See Milton, *Paradise Lost* 12.646. Milton writes that following the expulsion of Adam and Eve from Eden, "The world was all before them."

[3] *a known Vale* Grasmere, where Wordsworth and his sister moved in 1799.

So fair; and while upon the fancied scene
I gazed with growing love, a higher power
Than Fancy gave assurance of some work
Of glory, there forthwith to be begun,
Perhaps too there performed.[1] Thus long I mused,
Nor e'er lost sight of what I mused upon,
Save where, amid the stately grove of Oaks,
Now here—now there—an acorn, from its cup
Dislodged, through sere leaves rustled, or at once
To the bare earth dropped with a startling sound.
From that soft couch I rose not, till the sun
Had almost touched the horizon; casting then
A backward glance upon the curling cloud
Of city smoke, by distance ruralized,
Keen as a Truant or a Fugitive,
But as a Pilgrim resolute, I took,
Even with the chance equipment of that hour,
The road that pointed tow'rd the chosen Vale.
It was a splendid evening: and my Soul
Once more made trial of her strength, nor lacked
Eolian visitations;[2] but the harp
Was soon defrauded, and the banded host
Of harmony dispersed in straggling sounds;
And lastly utter silence! "Be it so;
Why think of any thing but present good?"
So, like a Home-bound Labourer, I pursued
My way, beneath the mellowing sun, that shed
Mild influence;[3] nor left in me one wish
Again to bend the sabbath of that time[4]
To a servile yoke. What need of many words?
A pleasant loitering journey, through three days
Continued, brought me to my hermitage.
I spare to tell of what ensued, the life
In common things—the endless store of things
Rare, or at least so seeming, every day
Found all about me in one neighbourhood;
The self-congratulation,[5] and from morn
To night unbroken cheerfulness serene.
But speedily an earnest longing rose
To brace myself to some determined aim,
Reading or thinking; either to lay up
New stores, or rescue from decay the old
By timely interference: and therewith
Came hopes still higher, that with outward life
I might endue some airy fantasies
That had been floating loose about for years;
And to such Beings temperately deal forth
The many feelings that oppressed my heart.
That hope hath been discouraged; welcome light
Dawns from the East, but dawns—to disappear
And mock me with a sky that ripens not
Into a steady morning: if my mind,
Remembering the bold promise of the past,
Would gladly grapple with some noble theme,
Vain is her wish: where'er she turns, she finds
Impediments from day to day renewed.
And now it would content me to yield up
Those lofty hopes awhile for present gifts
Of humbler industry. But, O dear Friend!
The Poet, gentle Creature as he is,
Hath, like the Lover, his unruly times,
His fits when he is neither sick nor well,
Though no distress be near him but his own
Unmanageable thoughts: his mind, best pleas'd
While she, as duteous as the Mother Dove,
Sits brooding,[6] lives not always to that end,
But, like the innocent Bird, hath goadings on
That drive her, as in trouble, through the groves:
With me is now such passion, to be blamed
No otherwise than as it lasts too long.
When, as becomes a Man who would prepare
For such an arduous Work, I through myself
Make rigorous inquisition, the report
Is often cheering; for I neither seem

[1] *some work ... performed* Wordsworth's poem *The Recluse*, intended to be his major work but never completed.

[2] *Eolian visitations* Influences that act on his soul as winds act on an Aeolian harp, which makes music when touched by a breeze.

[3] *influence* I.e., astrological influence, exerted by the stars over human life.

[4] *sabbath ... time* Time of rest.

[5] *self-congratulation* Self-rejoicing.

[6] *While she ... brooding* See *Paradise Lost* 1.21–2, in which the narrator invokes the Holy Spirit, who, at the time of Creation, "Dovelike satst brooding on the vast Abyss / And madst it pregnant."

To lack that first great gift, the vital Soul,
Nor general Truths, which are themselves a sort
Of Elements and Agents, Under-powers,
Subordinate helpers of the living Mind:
Nor am I naked of external things,
Forms, images, nor numerous other aids
Of less regard, though won perhaps with toil,
And needful to build up a Poet's praise.
Time, place, and manners° do I seek, and these *habits*
Are found in plenteous store, but no where such
As may be singled out with steady choice:
No little band of yet remembered names
Whom I in perfect confidence might hope
To summon back from lonesome banishment,
And make them dwellers in the hearts of men
Now living, or to live in future years.
Sometimes the ambitious Power of choice, mistaking
Proud spring-tide swellings for a regular sea,
Will settle on some British theme, some old
Romantic Tale by Milton left unsung:[1]
More often turning to some gentle place
Within the groves of Chivalry, I pipe
To Shepherd Swains,° or seated, harp in hand, *lovers*
Amid reposing knights by a River side
Or fountain, listen to the grave reports
Of dire enchantments faced, and overcome
By the strong mind, and Tales of warlike feats
Where spear encountered spear, and sword with sword
Fought, as if conscious of the blazonry
That the shield bore, so glorious was the strife;
Whence inspiration for a song that winds
Through ever changing scenes of votive quest,[2]
Wrongs to redress, harmonious tribute paid
To patient courage and unblemished truth,
To firm devotion, zeal unquenchable,
And Christian meekness hallowing faithful loves.[3]
Sometimes, more sternly moved, I would relate
How vanquished Mithridates northward passed,
And, hidden in the cloud of years, became
Odin, the Father of a Race by whom
Perished the Roman Empire;[4] how the friends
And followers of Sertorius,[5] out of Spain
Flying, found shelter in the Fortunate Isles;
And left their usages, their arts, and laws
To disappear by a slow gradual death;
To dwindle and to perish, one by one,
Starved in those narrow bounds: but not the soul
Of Liberty, which fifteen hundred years
Survived, and, when the European came
With skill and power that might not be withstood,
Did, like a pestilence, maintain its hold,
And wasted down by glorious death that Race
Of natural Heroes; or I would record
How, in tyrannic times, some high-souled Man,
Unnamed among the chronicles of Kings,
Suffered in silence for truth's sake: or tell
How that one Frenchman,[6] through continued force
Of meditation on the inhuman deeds
Of those who conquered first the Indian isles,
Went, single in his ministry, across
The Ocean—not to comfort the Oppressed,
But, like a thirsty wind, to roam about,
Withering the Oppressor: how Gustavus sought
Help at his need in Dalecarlia's mines:[7]

[1] *some old ... unsung* In *Paradise Lost* 9.24–41, Milton writes that he chose to compose a Biblical rather than a romantic epic.

[2] *votive quest* Quest undertaken as the result of a vow.

[3] *And Christian ... loves* Reference to Spenser's *Faerie Queene*, line 9: "Fierce warres and faithful loves shall moralize my song."

[4] *How vanquished ... Empire* Mithridates was a king of Pontus who was defeated by the Romans in 66 BCE. In *Decline and Fall of the Roman Empire* (1776–1788), Edward Gibbon associates the story of King Mithridates's downfall with the tale of Odin, a Goth chieftain who marched towards Rome and who hoped that his descendants would defeat the conquering Romans.

[5] *Sertorius* Roman general and ally of Mithridates who conquered much of Spain but was assassinated in 72 BCE. His followers were said to have emigrated to the Canary Island (the "Fortunate Isles") to escape the Romans, and to have survived there until the fifteenth century, when they were defeated by the invading Spaniards.

[6] [Wordsworth's note] Dominique de Gourges, a French gentleman who went in 1569 to Florida to avenge the massacre of the French by the Spaniards there.

[7] *Gustavus ... mines* Gustavus Vasa led a successful revolt in Sweden against the ruling Danes after gaining support in the mining town of Dalecarlia.

How Wallace[1] fought for Scotland, left the name
Of Wallace to be found, like a wild flower,
All over his dear Country, left the deeds
Of Wallace, like a family of Ghosts,
To people the steep rocks and river banks,
Her natural sanctuaries, with a local soul
Of independence and stern liberty.
Sometimes it suits me better to invent
A Tale from my own heart, more near akin
To my own passions, and habitual thoughts,
Some variegated Story, in the main
Lofty, but the unsubstantial Structure melts
Before the very sun that brightens it,
Mist into air dissolving! Then, a wish,
My last and favourite aspiration, mounts,
With yearning, tow'rds some philosophic Song
Of Truth that cherishes our daily life;
With meditations passionate, from deep
Recesses in man's heart, immortal verse
Thoughtfully fitted to the Orphean lyre;[2]
But from this awful° burthen I full soon *awe-inspiring*
Take refuge, and beguile myself with trust
That mellower years will bring a riper mind
And clearer insight. Thus my days are passed
In contradiction; with no skill to part
Vague longing, haply bred by want of power,
From paramount impulse—not to be withstood;
A timorous capacity from prudence;
From circumspection, infinite delay.
Humility and modest awe themselves
Betray me, serving often for a cloak
To a more subtle selfishness; that now
Locks every function up in blank° reserve,° *total / inaction*
Now dupes me, trusting to an anxious eye
That with intrusive restlessness beats off
Simplicity, and self-presented truth.
Ah! better far than this, to stray about
Voluptuously,° through fields and rural walks, *luxuriously*
And ask no record of the hours, resigned
To vacant musing, unreproved neglect
Of all things, and deliberate holiday:
Far better never to have heard the name
Of zeal and just ambition, than to live
Baffled and plagued by a mind that every hour
Turns recreant to her task, takes heart again,
Then feels immediately some hollow thought
Hang like an interdict° upon her hopes. *prohibition*
This is my lot; for either still I find
Some imperfection in the chosen theme;
Or see of absolute accomplishment
Much wanting, so much wanting, in myself
That I recoil and droop, and seek repose
In listlessness from vain perplexity;
Unprofitably travelling toward the grave,
Like a false Steward who hath much received,
And renders nothing back.[3] …

from BOOK FIFTH

BOOKS

… Hitherto,
In progress through this Work, my mind hath looked
Upon the speaking face of earth and heaven
As her prime Teacher, intercourse with man
Established by the sovereign Intellect
Who through that bodily Image hath diffused,
As might appear to the eye of fleeting Time,
A deathless Spirit. Thou also, Man! hast wrought,
For commerce of thy nature with herself,
Things that aspire to unconquerable life:
And yet we feel, we cannot choose but feel
That they must perish. Tremblings of the heart
It gives, to think that our immortal being
No more shall need such garments; and yet Man,
As long as he shall be the Child of earth,
Might almost "weep to have"[4] what he may lose,

[1] *Wallace* William Wallace, Scottish hero who fought for the freedom of his country but was executed by Edward I in 1305.

[2] *Orphean lyre* Lyre of Orpheus, the poet of Greek myth who could charm all living things with his music.

[3] *false Steward … back* Reference to the parable of the false steward in Matthew 25.14–30, who wastes what his lord gives him.

[4] *weep to have* See Shakespeare's Sonnet 64, lines 13–14: "This thought [of the destruction caused by time] is as a death, which cannot choose / But weep to have that which it fears to lose."

Nor be himself extinguished; but survive
Abject, depressed, forlorn, disconsolate.
A thought is with me sometimes, and I say—
Should the whole frame of earth by inward throes
Be wrenched, or fire come down from far to scorch
Her pleasant habitations, and dry up
Old Ocean in his bed, left singed and bare,
Yet would the living Presence still subsist
Victorious; and composure would ensue,
And kindlings like the morning—presage sure
Of day returning, and of life revived.
But all the meditations of mankind,
Yea, all the adamantine° hold° of truth, *indestructible / fortresses*
By reason built, or passion, which itself
Is highest reason in a soul sublime;
The consecrated works of Bard and Sage,
Sensuous or intellectual, wrought by men,
Twin labourers, and heirs of the same hopes;
Where would they be? Oh! why hath not the Mind
Some element to stamp her image on
In nature somewhat nearer to her own?
Why, gifted with such powers to send abroad
Her spirit, must it lodge in shrines so frail?
One day, when from my lips a like complaint
Had fallen in presence of a studious friend,
He with a smile made answer that in truth
'Twas going far to seek disquietude,
But, on the front of his reproof, confessed
That he himself had oftentimes given way
To kindred hauntings. Whereupon I told
That once in the stillness of a summer's noon,
While I was seated in a rocky cave
By the sea-side, perusing, so it chanced,
The famous history of the errant Knight
Recorded by Cervantes,[1] these same thoughts
Beset me, and to height unusual rose,
While listlessly I sat, and, having closed
The Book, had turned my eyes tow'rd the wide Sea.
On Poetry, and geometric truth,
And their high privilege of lasting life,
From all internal injury exempt,
I mused; upon these chiefly: and, at length,
My senses yielding to the sultry air,
Sleep seized me, and I passed into a dream.
I saw before me stretched a boundless plain,
Of sandy wilderness, all blank and void;
And as I looked around, distress and fear
Came creeping over me, when at my side,
Close at my side, an uncouth Shape appeared
Upon a Dromedary, mounted high.
He seemed an Arab of the Bedouin Tribes:
A Lance he bore, and underneath one arm
A Stone; and, in the opposite hand, a Shell
Of a surpassing brightness. At the sight
Much I rejoiced, not doubting but a Guide
Was present, one who with unerring skill
Would through the desert lead me; and while yet
I looked, and looked, self-questioned what this freight
Which the New-comer carried through the Waste
Could mean, the Arab told me that the Stone
(To give it in the language of the Dream)
Was Euclid's Elements;[2] "and this," said he,
"This other," pointing to the Shell, "this book
Is something of more worth"; and, at the word,
Stretched forth the Shell, so beautiful in shape,
In color so resplendent, with command
That I should hold it to my ear. I did so—
And heard, that instant, in an unknown tongue,
Which yet I understood, articulate sounds,
A loud prophetic blast of harmony—
An Ode, in passion uttered, which foretold
Destruction to the Children of the Earth,
By Deluge now at hand. No sooner ceased
The Song than the Arab with calm look declared
That all would come to pass, of which the voice
Had given forewarning, and that he himself
Was going then to bury those two Books:
The One that held acquaintance with the stars,
And wedded Soul to Soul in purest bond
Of Reason, undisturbed by space or time:
Th'other, that was a God, yea many Gods,

[1] *famous history … Cervantes* Miguel de Cervantes's *Don Quixote* (1605).

[2] *Euclid's Elements* Foundational geometry textbook by third century BCE Greek mathematician Euclid.

Had voices more than all the winds, with power
To exhilarate the Spirit, and to soothe,
Through every clime, the heart of human kind.
While this was uttering, strange as it may seem,
I wondered not, although I plainly saw
The One to be a Stone, the Other a Shell,
Nor doubted once but that they both were Books;
Having a perfect faith in all that passed.
Far stronger now grew the desire I felt
To cleave unto this Man; but when I prayed
To share his enterprize, he hurried on,
Reckless° of me: I followed, not unseen, *heedless*
For oftentimes he cast a backward look,
Grasping his twofold treasure. Lance in rest,
He rode, I keeping pace with him; and now
He to my fancy had become the Knight
Whose tale Cervantes tells; yet not the Knight,
But was an Arab of the desert, too,
Of these was neither, and was both at once.
His countenance, meanwhile, grew more disturbed,
And looking backwards when he looked, mine eyes
Saw, over half the wilderness diffused,
A bed of glittering light: I asked the cause.
"It is," said he, "the waters of the Deep
Gathering upon us"; quickening then the pace
Of the unwieldy Creature he bestrode,
He left me; I called after him aloud—
He heeded not; but with his twofold charge
Still in his grasp, before me, full in view,
Went hurrying o'er the illimitable Waste
With the fleet waters of a drowning World
In chase of him; whereat I waked in terror;
And saw the Sea before me, and the Book,
In which I had been reading, at my side.
Full often, taking from the world of Sleep
This Arab Phantom, which I thus beheld,
This semi-Quixote, I to him have given
A substance, fancied him a living man,
A gentle Dweller in the desert, crazed
By love and feeling, and internal thought
Protracted among endless solitudes;
Have shaped him, in the oppression of his brain,
And so equipped, wandering upon this quest!
Nor have I pitied him; but rather felt
Reverence was due to a Being thus employed;
And thought that, in the blind and awful lair
Of such a madness, reason did lie couched.
Enow° there are on earth to take in charge *enough*
Their Wives, their Children, and their virgin Loves,
Or whatsoever else the heart holds dear;
Enow to stir for these—yea, will I say,
Contemplating in soberness the approach
Of an event so dire, by signs, in earth
Or heaven, made manifest—that I could share
That maniac's fond anxiety, and go
Upon like errand. Oftentimes, at least,
Me hath such strong entrancement overcome,
When I have held a volume in my hand,
Poor earthly casket of immortal Verse,
Shakespeare, or Milton, Labourers divine! …
Here must we pause; this only let me add,
From heart-experience, and in humblest sense
Of modesty, that he, who, in his youth,
A daily Wanderer among woods and fields,
With living Nature hath been intimate,
Not only in that raw unpractised time
Is stirred to ecstasy, as others are,
By glittering verse; but, further, doth receive,
In measure only dealt out to himself,
Knowledge and increase of enduring joy
From the great Nature that exists in works
Of mighty Poets. Visionary Power
Attends the motions of the viewless° winds *invisible*
Embodied in the mystery of words:
There darkness makes abode, and all the host
Of shadowy things work endless changes there,
As in a mansion like their proper home.
Even forms and substances are circumfused
By that transparent veil with light divine;
And, through the turnings intricate of verse,
Present themselves as objects recognized,
In flashes, and with glory not their own.
Thus far a scanty record is deduced
Of what I owed to Books in early life;
Their later influence yet remains untold;
But as this work was taking in my mind

Proportions that seemed larger than had first
Been meditated, I was indisposed
To any further progress, at a time
When these acknowledgments were left unpaid.

from BOOK SIXTH

CAMBRIDGE, AND THE ALPS[1]

... 'Tis not my present purpose to retrace
That variegated journey step by step;
A march it was of military speed,
And earth did change her images and forms
Before us, fast as clouds are changed in heaven.
Day after day, up early and down late,
From hill to vale we dropped—from vale to hill
Mounted—from province on to province swept—
Keen hunters in a chase of fourteen weeks,
Eager as birds of prey, or as a Ship
Upon the stretch when winds are blowing fair.
Sweet coverts did we cross of pastoral life,
Enticing Valleys, greeted them and left
Too soon, while yet the very flash and gleam
Of salutation were not passed away.
Oh! sorrow for the Youth who could have seen
Unchastened, unsubdued, unawed, unraised
To patriarchal dignity of mind
And pure simplicity of wish and will,
Those sanctified Abodes of peaceful Man;
Pleased (though to hardship born, and compassed round
With danger, varying as the seasons change),
Pleased with his daily tasks, or, if not pleased,
Contented, from the moment that the Dawn,
Ah! surely not without attendant gleams
Of soul-illumination, calls him forth
To industry, by glistenings flung on rocks
Whose evening shadows lead him to repose.
Well might a Stranger look with bounding heart
Down on a green Recess, the first I saw
Of those deep haunts, an aboriginal Vale,
Quiet, and lorded over, and possessed
By naked huts, wood-built and sown like tents,
Or Indian Cabins over the fresh lawns
And by the river side. That very day,
From a bare ridge we also first beheld
Unveiled the summit of Mont Blanc, and grieved
To have a soulless image on the eye
Which had usurped upon a living thought
That never more could be. The wondrous Vale
Of Chamouny[2] stretched far below, and soon
With its dumb° cataracts, and streams of ice, *unheard*
A motionless array of mighty waves,
Five rivers broad and vast, made rich amends,
And reconciled us to realities.
There small birds warble from the leafy trees,
The eagle soars high in the element;
There doth the Reaper bind the yellow sheaf,
The Maiden spread the hay-cock[3] in the sun,
While Winter like a well-tamed lion walks,
Descending from the Mountain to make sport
Among the Cottages by beds of flowers.
Whate'er in this wide circuit we beheld,
Or heard, was fitted to our unripe state
Of intellect and heart. With such a book
Before our eyes we could not choose but read
Lessons of genuine brotherhood, the plain
And universal reason of mankind,
The truths of Young and Old. Nor, side by side
Pacing, two social Pilgrims, or alone
Each with his humour,° could we fail to abound *disposition*
In dreams and fictions pensively composed,
Dejection taken up for pleasure's sake,
And gilded sympathies; the willow[4] wreath,
And sober posies° of funereal flowers *bouquets*
Gathered, among those solitudes sublime,
From formal gardens of the Lady Sorrow,
Did sweeten many a meditative hour.
Yet still in me with those soft luxuries
Mixed something of stern mood, an under thirst

[1] *from ... Alps* In this passage Wordsworth describes his journey through the Alps, along the Simplon Pass, with Robert Jones, a fellow Cambridge student.

[2] *Vale of Chamouny* Valley located at the foot of Mont Blanc. (The modern spelling is Chamonix.)

[3] *hay-cock* Conical pile of hay.

[4] *willow* Symbol of sadness.

Of vigor seldom utterly allayed.
And from that source how different a sadness
Would issue, let one incident make known.
When from the Vallais we had turned, and
  climb° *climbed*
Along the Simplon's steep and rugged road,
Following a band of Muleteers, we reached
A halting-place where all together took
Their noon-tide meal. Hastily rose our Guide,
Leaving *us* at the Board; awhile we lingered,
Then paced the beaten downward way that led
Right to a rough stream's edge and there broke off.
The only track now visible was one
That from the torrent's further brink held forth
Conspicuous invitation to ascend
A loft mountain. After brief delay
Crossing the unbridged stream, that road we took
And clomb with eagerness, till anxious fears
Intruded, for we failed to overtake
Our Comrades gone before. By fortunate chance,
While every moment added doubt to doubt,
A Peasant met us, from whose mouth we learned
That to the Spot which had perplexed us first
We must descend, and there should find the road,
Which in the stony channel of the Stream
Lay a few steps, and then along its banks;
And that our future course, all plain to sight,
Was downwards, with the current of that Stream.
Loth to believe what we so grieved to hear,
For still we had hopes that pointed to the clouds,
We questioned him again, and yet again;
But every word that from the Peasant's lips
Came in reply, translated by our feelings,
Ended in this, *that we had crossed the Alps*. . .

from BOOK THIRTEENTH
SUBJECT CONCLUDED

From Nature doth emotion come, and moods
Of calmness equally are Nature's gift:
This is her glory; these two attributes
Are sister horns[1] that constitute her strength.
Hence Genius, born to thrive by interchange
Of peace and excitation,° finds in her *stimulus*
His best and purest friend, from her receives
That energy by which he seeks the truth,
From her that happy stillness of the mind
Which fits him to receive it, when unsought.
  Such benefit the humblest intellects
Partake of, each in their degree: 'tis mine
To speak of what myself have known and felt.
Smooth task! for words find easy way, inspired
By gratitude and confidence in truth.
Long time in search of knowledge did I range
The field of human life, in heart and mind
Benighted, but the dawn beginning now
To reappear, 'twas proved that not in vain
I had been taught to reverence a Power
That is the visible quality and shape
And image of right reason,[2] that matures
Her processes by steadfast laws, gives birth
To no impatient or fallacious hopes,
No heat of passion or excessive zeal,
No vain conceits, provokes to no quick turns
Of self-applauding intellect—but trains
To meekness, and exalts by humble faith;
Holds up before the mind, intoxicate
With present objects, and the busy dance
Of things that pass away, a temperate show
Of objects that endure; and by this course
Disposes her, when over-fondly set
On throwing off incumbrances, to seek
In Man, and in the frame of social life,
Whate'er there is desireable and good
Of kindred permanence, unchanged in form
And function, or through strict vicissitude
Of life and death revolving. Above all
Were re-established now those watchful thoughts
Which (seeing little worthy or sublime
In what the Historian's pen so much delights
To blazon, Power and Energy detached
From moral purpose) early tutored me
To look with feelings of fraternal love

[1] *horns* Symbols of strength in the Old Testament.

[2] *right reason* Type of reason that is in accordance with natural law.

Upon the unassuming things that hold
A silent station in this beauteous world.
Thus moderated, thus composed, I found
Once more in Man an object of delight,
Of pure imagination, and of love;
And, as the horizon of my mind enlarged,
Again I took the intellectual eye
For my Instructor, studious more to see
Great Truths, than touch and handle little ones.
Knowledge was given accordingly; my trust
Became more firm in feelings that had stood
The test of such a trial; clearer far
My sense of excellence—of right and wrong:
The promise of the present time retired
Into its true proportion; sanguine° schemes, *hopeful*
Ambitious projects, pleased me less; I sought
For present good in life's familiar face,
And built thereon my hopes of good to come.
With settling judgments now of what would last
And what must disappear, prepared to find
Presumption, folly, madness, in the Men
Who thrust themselves upon the passive world
As Rulers of the world, to see in these,
Even when the public welfare is their aim,
Plans without thought, or built on theories
Vague and unsound, and having brought the Books
Of modern Statists[1] to their proper test,
Life, human life with all its sacred claims
Of sex and age, and heaven-descended rights
Mortal, or those beyond the reach of death;
And having thus discerned how dire a thing
Is worshipped in that Idol proudly named
"The Wealth of Nations,"[2] where alone that wealth
Is lodged, and how encreased; and having gained
A more judicious knowledge of the worth
And dignity of individual Man,
No composition of the brain, but Man
Of whom we read, the Man whom we behold
With our own eyes—I could not but enquire,
Not with less interest than heretofore,
But greater, though in Spirit more subdued,
Why is this glorious Creature to be found
One only in ten thousand? What one is,
Why may not millions be? What bars are thrown
By Nature in the way of such a hope?
Our animal appetites, and daily wants,
Are these obstructions insurmountable?
If not, then others vanish into air.
"Inspect the basis of the social Pile:
Enquire," said I, "how much of mental Power
And genuine virtue they possess who live
By bodily toil, labour exceeding far
Their due proportion, under all the weight
Of that injustice which upon ourselves
Ourselves entail." Such estimate to frame
I chiefly looked (what need to look beyond?)
Among the natural Abodes of men,
Fields with their rural works, recalled to mind
My earliest notices,° with these compared *observations*
The observations made in later youth,
And to that day continued.—For the time
Had never been when throes of mightiest Nations
And the world's tumult unto me could yield,
How far soe'er transported and possessed,
Full measure of content; but still I craved
An intermingling of distinct regards° *sights*
And truths of individual sympathy
Nearer ourselves. Such often might be gleaned
From the great City, else it must have proved
To me a heart-depressing wilderness;
But much was wanting; therefore did I turn
To you, ye pathways, and ye lonely roads;
Sought you enriched with every thing I prized,
With human kindness and simple joys....

from BOOK FOURTEENTH

CONCLUSION

In one of those Excursions (may they ne'er
Fade from remembrance!), through the Northern

[1] *Statists* Political theorists.

[2] *The ... Nations* Adam Smith's *Inquiry into the Nature and Cause of the Wealth of Nations* (1776), an economic treatise.

tracts
Of Cambria ranging with a youthful Friend,[1]
I left Bethgellert's huts at couching-time,
And westward took my way, to see the sun
Rise from the top of Snowdon. To the door
Of a rude Cottage at the Mountain's base
We came, and roused the Shepherd who attends
The adventurous Stranger's steps, a trusty Guide;
Then, cheered by short refreshment, sallied forth.
—It was a close, warm, breezeless summer night,
Wan, dull, and glaring,° with a dripping fog *rainy*
Low-hung and thick, that covered all the sky.
But, undiscouraged, we began to climb
The mountain-side. The mist soon girt us round,
And, after ordinary Travellers' talk
With our Conductor, pensively we sank
Each into commerce with his private thoughts:
Thus did we breast the ascent, and by myself
Was nothing either seen or heard that checked
Those musings or diverted, save that once
The Shepherd's Lurcher,[2] who, among the crags,
Had to his joy unearthed a Hedgehog, teased
His coiled-up Prey with barkings turbulent.
This small adventure, for even such it seemed
In that wild place, and at the dead of night,
Being over and forgotten, on we wound
In silence as before. With forehead bent
Earthward, as if in opposition set
Against an enemy, I panted up
With eager pace, and no less eager thoughts.
Thus might we wear a midnight hour away,
Ascending at loose distance each from each,
And I, as chanced, the foremost of the Band:
When at my feet the ground appeared to brighten,
And with a step or two seemed brighter still;
Nor was time given to ask, or learn, the cause;
For instantly a light upon the turf
Fell like a flash; and lo! as I looked up,
The Moon hung naked in a firmament
Of azure without cloud, and at my feet
Rested a silent sea of hoary mist.
A hundred hills their dusky backs upheaved
All over this still Ocean; and beyond,
Far, far beyond, the solid vapours stretched,
In Headlands, tongues, and promontory shapes,
Into the main Atlantic, that appeared
To dwindle, and give up his majesty,
Usurped upon far as the sight could reach.
Not so the ethereal Vault; encroachment none
Was there, nor loss; only the inferior stars
Had disappeared, or shed a fainter light
In the clear presence of the full-orbed Moon;
Who, from her sovereign elevation, gazed
Upon the billowy ocean, as it lay
All meek and silent, save that through a rift
Not distant from the shore whereon we stood,
A fixed, abysmal, gloomy breathing-place,
Mounted the roar of waters—torrents—streams
Innumerable, roaring with one voice!
Heard over earth and sea, and in that hour,
For so it seemed, felt by the starry heavens.
When into air had partially dissolved
That Vision, given to Spirits of the night,
And three chance human Wanderers, in calm thought
Reflected, it appeared to me the type
Of a majestic Intellect, its acts
And its possessions, what it has and craves,
What in itself it is, and would become.
There I beheld the emblem of a Mind
That feeds upon infinity, that broods
Over the dark abyss, intent to hear
Its voices issuing forth to silent light
In one continuous stream; a mind sustained
By recognitions of transcendent power
In sense, conducting to ideal form;
In soul, of more than mortal privilege.
One function, above all, of such a mind
Had Nature shadowed there, by putting forth,
'Mid circumstances awful and sublime,

[1] *In one ... Friend* This trip was a walking tour through North Wales (Cambria) with Robert Jones, the same friend with whom he crossed the Alps. In this passage, they ascend Mount Snowdon, the highest peak in Wales, from the village of Bethgellert.

[2] *Lurcher* Rabbit-hunting dog.

That mutual domination which she loves
To exert upon the face of outward things,
So moulded, joined, abstracted; so endowed
With interchangeable supremacy,
That Men least sensitive see, hear, perceive,
And cannot choose but feel. The power which all
Acknowledge when thus moved, which Nature thus
To bodily sense exhibits, is the express
Resemblance of that glorious faculty[1]
That higher minds bear with them as their own.
This is the very spirit in which they deal
With the whole compass of the universe:
They, from their native selves, can send abroad
Kindred mutations; for themselves create
A like existence; and whene'er it dawns
Created for them, catch it—or are caught
By its inevitable mastery,
Like angels stopped upon the wing by sound
Of harmony from heaven's remotest spheres.
Them the enduring and the transient both
Serve to exalt; they build up greatest things
From least suggestions; ever on the watch,
Willing to work and to be wrought upon,
They need not extraordinary calls
To rouse them, in a world of life they live;
By sensible impressions not enthralled,
But, by their quickening impulse, made more prompt
To hold fit converse with the spiritual world,
And with the generations of mankind
Spread over time, past, present, and to come,
Age after age, till Time shall be no more.
Such minds are truly from the Deity,
For they are powers; and hence the highest bliss
That flesh can know is theirs—the consciousness
Of whom they are, habitually infused
Through every image, and through every thought,
And all affections by communion raised
From earth to heaven, from human to divine.
Hence endless occupation for the Soul,
Whether discursive or intuitive;
Hence cheerfulness for acts of daily life,
Emotions which best foresight need not fear,
Most worthy then of trust when most intense:
Hence, amid ills that vex, and wrongs that crush
Our hearts, if here the words of Holy Writ[2]
May with fit reverence be applied, that peace
Which passeth understanding[3]—that repose
In moral judgements which from this pure source
Must come, or will by Man be sought in vain....
 Oh! yet a few short years of useful life,
And all will be complete, thy race be run,
Thy monument of glory will be raised;
Then, though, too weak to tread the ways of truth,
This Age fall back to old idolatry,
Though Men return to servitude as fast
As the tide ebbs, to ignominy and shame
By Nations sink together, we shall still
Find solace—knowing what we have learnt to know,
Rich in true happiness if allowed to be
Faithful alike in forwarding a day
Of firmer trust, joint laborers in the Work
(Should Providence such grace to us vouchsafe)
Of their deliverance, surely yet to come.
Prophets of Nature, we to them will speak
A lasting inspiration, sanctified
By reason, blest by faith: what we have loved
Others will love, and we will teach them how,
Instruct them how the mind of Man becomes
A thousand times more beautiful than the earth
On which he dwells, above this Frame of things
(Which 'mid all revolutions in the hopes
And fears of Men doth still remain unchanged)
In beauty exalted, as it is itself
Of quality and fabric more divine.
—1850

[1] *that glorious faculty* I.e., imagination.

[2] *Holy Writ* Scripture.

[3] *that peace ... understanding* See Philippians 4.7: "That peace of God, which passeth all understanding."

Reading, Writing, Publishing

Contexts

During the Romantic period, questions concerning the definition of literature and the nature of its role in society pervaded print culture. Among the topics debated were definitions of intellectual property, the ways in which dissemination of texts should be encouraged or restrained, and the extent to which literature could effect social or political reform. For many, particularly in light of the French Revolution, literature was felt to hold a radical potential to change the world.

Some questioned whether women or members of the laboring classes should be allowed access to political tracts, and feared that less educated or discerning minds could be easily swayed by the persuasive rhetoric of radicals. Daniel Isaac Eaton was among those whom they feared; he had been tried nine times for publishing or writing radical texts and on one occasion had been sentenced to eighteen months in jail. Here he satirizes the anti-revolutionaries' fear of the power of the press and the government's desire to control the circulation of potentially seditious material through legislation and taxes. Eaton's weekly magazine, *Politics for the People* (1793–95), was an important and popular organ of radical journalism; when he was placed in the pillory in 1812 for printing the third part of *Age of Reason*, he was cheered by a large crowd.

Thomas Spence, whose poem on the theme of repression appears next, was also well acquainted with the accusation of libel. He had been arrested four times and imprisoned twice between 1792 and 1794 alone. In the poem reproduced here, his parenthetical denials cleverly serve to protect him from such charges while simultaneously articulating radical criticism of the monarchy and aristocracy. The poem following Spence's, by an anonymous author, uses the sort of animal analogies that were commonly relied upon in political satire at the time. By exploiting traditional moral fables, writers could create poems that were clearly understood by their readers, yet were ambiguous enough to allow their authors to disavow any subversive intent.

The piece that follows emphasizes the importance of literature to revolutionary efforts. While Eaton had mocked anti-radicals' fear of the press, the anonymous author of "On the Characteristics of Poetry" links the feelings excited by poetry to powerful political action, and even to military victory.

The period was what John Stuart Mill called "a reading age"; there were more readers than ever before, and publishing was becoming a major industry. While many viewed this development as beneficial to society, others feared a proliferation of trivial works that would neither improve the minds of readers nor encourage them to pick up more challenging works. If too many books were produced each year for any one person to read, how could people hope to peruse them all and decide which were most worthy of their attention? Voicing a common fear, the anonymous correspondent to the *Monthly Magazine* whose letter is excerpted here claims that the proliferation of writers has led to a decline in literary standards and a decreased appreciation for writers of true genius. In the piece following, Samuel Pratt proposes an effective solution to this problem in the form of literary journals, whose writers can together provide readers with a balanced critical appraisal. In a slightly later article, Isaac D'Israeli proposes another solution in the form of changes to copyright laws that would reward authors of true genius rather than benefitting only the "booksellers" (publishers), who in his view sought to publish trivial works of mass appeal.

Hannah More, in *Strictures on the Modern System of Female Education*, examines what she sees as the negative effects of the abundant novels and other "alluring little works" on the morals and intellects of young women. In a later excerpt, prolific novelist Anna Laetitia Barbauld, in her introduction to her edition of *The British Novelists*, celebrates the novel's ability to divert and entertain, a characteristic more important to the average reader than moral instruction.

During this period, literature was often celebrated as a vehicle for debate, and reading was frequently a communal activity accompanied by discussion and reflection. In this manner, readers—particularly young or less educated ones—were trained to read critically. Two adaptations of Shakespeare stressed the importance of reading as a family activity. Thomas Bowdler's highly successful ten-volume *Family Shakespeare* (whose name became a component of a verb, "to bowdlerize," referring to the removal of "inappropriate" material from a literary work) did not add any new material to the original texts, but omitted "those words and expressions … which cannot with propriety be read aloud in a family." He was also careful to alter the representation of those events that might not be suitable for younger readers. Ophelia's suicide in *Hamlet*, for example, is presented as an accidental drowning. Charles and Mary Lamb's *Tales from Shakespeare*, which recasts the plays as prose stories for younger audiences, allowed children to gain exposure to Shakespeare's plays and to discuss them with older family members, helping them gain a fuller appreciation for the plays when they were read later in life.

In the final two excerpts, John Stuart Mill and William Hazlitt express opposing views on the future of British literature and culture. Hazlitt takes a more positive view of the commodification of literature, accepting what he sees as inevitable, while Mill predicts the downfall of a culture whose integrity he feared would soon be undermined by commercial society.

⌘⌘⌘

from Daniel Isaac Eaton, *The Pernicious Effects of the Art of Printing Upon Society, Exposed* (1793)

Before this diabolical art was introduced among men, there was social order. … In the times we are speaking of (the Golden Age), the feudal system prevailed—a system replete with blessings—by it the different orders of society were kept perfectly distinct and separate—there were kings, barons, priests, yeomanry, villains[1] or slaves; and they were, I believe, with regard to rank and power, in the order in which I have named them. The villains, or lowest class, were what Mr. Burke so elegantly terms the *Swinish Multitude*,[2] but of rights or privileges as men they had not an idea; we may with propriety style them the Jackals of the times: they tilled the earth, and performed all manual labour; but in return, their superiors allowed them sufficient of the produce for subsistence—permitted them to take some rest, in order that they might be strong. To bear hardship and fatigue took from them the trouble of thinking—indeed, from the very prudent manner in which they were brought up, I will not say educated, they were little capable of thought, of course exempt from the mental fatigues of study and reflections. The Scriptures having declared gold to be the root of every evil, they were very humanely prevented from possessing any. As to religion, the clergy taught them as much as they thought necessary, and they were without doubt the best judges, being in general good scholars.…

Since printing has been employed as the medium of diffusing sentiments, &c. government has become more difficult—the governors are frequently and insolently called upon to give an account of the national treasure,

[1] *villains* I.e., villeins, serfs or peasants.

[2] *Mr. Burke … multitude* Edmund Burke, probably in reference to a particular faction of extremists (rather than all members of the working classes), said that if learning were removed from the hierarchical social order in which it had originated, it would be "cast into the mire, and trodden down under the hoofs of a swinish multitude." Reformers took this comment as proof of the arrogance and superiority with which conservatives regarded the people.

its expenditure, &c.—and if they are in any respect tardy, or should circumstances render evasion necessary, it is astonishing, with what boldness some men will dare to revile and insult them.

The lower orders begin to have ideas of rights, as men—to think that one man is as good as another; that society is at present founded upon false principles; that hereditary honours and distinctions are absurd, unjust, and oppressive; that abilities and morals only should recommend to the first officers in a state; that no regard should be paid to rank and titles; that instruction, sufficient to qualify a man for being a member of society, is a debt due to every individual, and that it is the duty of every state to take care that he receive it; that every man has a right to a share in the government, either in his own person, or that of his representative, and that no portion of his property or labour ought to be taxed without his consent, given either by himself, or representative; that everyone should contribute to the support of the state in proportion to his ability, and that all partial exactions are oppressive; that laws should be the same to all, and that no one, whatever may be his rank or station, should be allowed to offend them with impunity; that freedom of speech is the equal right of all, and that the rich have no right to dictate to the poor what sentiments they shall adopt on any subject, or in any wise[1] prevent investigation and inquiry. This, with a great deal more such stuff, is called the rights of man—blessed fruits of the art of printing—the scum of the earth, the swinish multitude, talking of their rights! and insolently claiming, nay, almost demanding, that political liberty shall be the same to all—to the high and the low, the rich and the poor—what audacity!—what unparalleled effrontery!—it ought to meet correction. With similar mistaken notions of liberty, even many women are infatuated; and the press, that grand prolific source of evil, that fruitful mother of mischief, has already favoured the public with several female productions on this very popular subject—one in particular, called *Rights of Women*,[2] and in which, as one of their rights, a share in legislation is claimed and asserted —gracious heaven! to what will this fatal delusion lead, and in what will it terminate! ...

For all these, and numberless other evils, the natural consequence of a diffusion of knowledge and science, some remedy must be found; the present administration have made some trifling feeble attempts to check their progress, such as additional duties upon advertisements and newspapers, which almost preclude cheap publications—of the same nature I suppose the late tax upon paper to be—but these remedies are totally inadequate, at least they will be so exceedingly slow in their operation, that the present race have but little prospect of living to see any of their good effects.

To rid ourselves of such a monster, some strong efficient measure must be had recourse to, something that will strike at the root, and have an almost instantaneous effect—such a one, I think, I can point out.

Let all printing presses be committed to the flames, all letter foundries be destroyed, schools and seminaries of learning abolished, dissenters of every denominations double and treble taxed, all discourse upon government and religion prohibited, political clubs and associations of every kind suppressed—excepting those formed for the express purpose of supporting government—and lastly, issue a proclamation against reading, and burn all private libraries. To carry some part of this plan into execution, it will be necessary to employ spies and informers, which by many (Jacobins and Republicans) are thought to be signs either of a weak or wicked and corrupt government; they say that governors, conscious of acting for the public good, of having it only in view in all their measure, would scorn using such unworthy and dishonourable means. I cannot be of this opinion, but am confident that if the measures I have proposed be but speedily adopted, and rigorously pursued, the happiest consequences would soon be experienced; all the wild, idle theories with which men are at present disturbed, would soon vanish—the lower orders would mind their work, become tractable and docile, and perhaps in less than half a century that desirable state of ignorance and darkness, which formerly prevailed, might again restore to this Island that happy state of society with which it once was blessed.

[1] *wise* Way.

[2] *Rights of Women* Mary Wollstonecraft's *Vindication of the Rights of Woman* (1792).

Thomas Spence, "Examples of Safe Printing," from *Pig's Meat*,[1] Volume 2 (1794)

To prevent misrepresentation in these prosecuting times, it seems necessary to publish every thing relating to tyranny and oppression, though only among brutes, in the most guarded manner.

The following are meant as specimens:

That tyger, or that other salvage wight° *savage creature*
Is so exceeding furious and fell,° *fierce*
As WRONG,
[*Not meaning our most gracious sovereign*
Lord the King, or the Government of this
country]
when it hath arm'd himself with might;
Not fit 'mong men that do with reason mell,° *mix*
But 'mong wild beasts and salvage woods to dwell;
Where still the stronger
[*Not meaning the great men of this country*]
doth the weak devour,
And they that most in boldness do excell,
Are dreaded most, and feared by their power.
—E. Spencer[2]

Joshua,[3] "Sonnet: The Lion," from *Moral and Political Magazine*, Volume 1 (1796)

Why grace we the stern lion with the name
That marks the chiefs of Europe? More of use
To man's assistance do the kine° produce; *cattle*
For bulk, behold the elephant's huge frame!
For agile beauty see the stately horse.
King of the forest HE, and doomed to reign,
Like earthly monarch, o'er the Lybian plain
For fierce pre-eminence in brutal force:
Before his tyrant rage the fleet° horse flies, *swift*
The patient sheep avoids him, or he dies.
Stern bloody beast! they named thee well: thy right
Is to this royal title just and good;
Thou gain'dst it by thy savage joy in fight,
Thy brutal fury, and thy thirst for blood.

[1] *Pig's Meat* The title is a reference to Burke's term "swinish multitude," which many radical writers adopted as an ironic definition of the working classes.

[2] *E. Spencer* I.e., Renaissance poet Edmund Spenser (1552?–99), whom the poet imitates in order to create historical distance from the referents of the poem.

[3] *Joshua* Biblical lieutenant of Moses who led the Israelites to victory over the Canaanites (see Joshua 1–12).

from Anonymous, "On the Characteristics of Poetry" No. 2, from *Monthly Magazine* (1797)

In the course of our last discussion, we seemed to be unanimously of opinion that the grand characteristic, the *sine qua non*[4] of poetry, consists in its capacity of pressing the mind with the most vivid pictures. Indeed, the maxim *ut pictura poesis*[5] is amply illustrated whenever poetry is in any shape the subject of investigation. The terms of the painter's art then insensibly creep into the discourse and model our phraseology.

Pursuing, then, this idea, we may perhaps lay it down as the grand and leading end of poetry to make a strong and lively impression on the feelings. In her operations she hurries us far beyond the reach of the voice of sober judgment, and captivates by exciting the aid of the passions. Here, then, we see the cause of the mighty energy of verse, nor wonder at the efficaciousness that has been ascribed to the Muses.[6] For how easily are mankind guided by those that possess the happy art of awakening or allaying their feelings. Though all unconscious of being under the guidance of another, they turn obedient to the rein. They are roused to insurrection, or moderated to peace, by him who can touch, with a skilful hand, the master springs that regulate the motions of their minds. When Brutus ascends the rostrum, the words of truth and soberness are heard, and plain integrity convinces the judgment.

[4] *sine qua non* Latin: indispensable attribute.

[5] *ut pictura poetis* Latin: "As is painting, so is poetry" (from Horace, *Ars Poetica*).

[6] *Muses* Nine daughters of Zeus and Mnemosyne, each of whom presided over and provided inspiration for an aspect of the arts and sciences.

But, when Anthony displays the bloody robe, and points to the wounds of Caesar, reminding the people that this was once their darling benefactor, the multitude are melted to sorrow, and at last roused from pity to fury and revenge.[1]

Here, then, this essay might, perhaps, with propriety, have been closed. But I must rely upon your candour for the admission of a few more observations, which may, perhaps, tend to illustrate the point to which this enquiry has led us:

The end of poetry, it is said, is an impression upon the feelings. But as there is an intimate connection between feeling and action, so that where the one appears, the other "follows hard upon," if the foregoing observations be true, we may expect to find that the actions of mankind are, in some measure, influenced by the Muses.

And if we look to the simpler ages of society, when we can best distinguish the grand outlines of the human character, where the springs that actuate the conduct of man are, in a manner, bared for inspection, we shall find this to have been the case. In the infancy of states, poetry is a method equally captivating and efficacious of forming the dispositions of the people, and kindling in their hearts that love of glory which is their country's safeguard and defence. Whether we look to the cold regions of Scandinavia, or the delicious clime of Greece, we find that when society has made a certain progress, mankind are strongly influenced by a love of song, and listen, with raptured attention, to the strains that record the tale of other times, and the deeds of heroes of old. They listen till they imbibe the enthusiasm of warfare, and in the day of battle, the hero's arm has not unfrequently been nerved by the rough energy of the early bard.…

But, indeed, what occasion have we to search into the dust of antiquity for examples of the influence of verse upon human conduct? The transactions of our own times may teach us that as strong feelings generate poetic language, so poetic language inspires the mind with at least a temporary enthusiasm, and thus impels to action. In this country, the fervour or loyalty has of late been blown into a blaze, and for this event the parties interested are not a little indebted to the assistance of the Muses. And when the Marseillaise Hymn[2] echoed through the ranks of the French army at the field of Jemappe,[3] we need not wonder that "the spear of liberty was wielded with classic grace," and that the energy of heroism was communicated with the sound.

[1] *Brutus* One of the men who assassinated Julius Caesar, who had become dictator of Rome for life; *Anthony* Marc Antony, consul who, after Caesar's assassination, aroused the mob against the conspirators, causing them to be driven from the city.

from Anonymous, Letter to the *Monthly Magazine* (24 October 1798)

Sir,

Literature is either less cultivated, or less valued in these days than it was in those of our ancestors, for certainly learning does not *now* receive the honours it *then* did. That it is less cultivated, cannot, I think, with any truth be asserted, because the present is denominated a learned age. It must be the universality then, with which it is diffused throughout society, that renders it less valuable—as articles grow cheap, not in proportion to their insignificancy, but their abundance. Great talents, indeed, in any condition of civilized society must inevitably confer a certain degree of power, inasmuch as they render their possessors either useful or formidable; but scarcely any literary attainments would, I apprehend, raise a writer in these days to the same degree of eminence and request as Petrarch, Erasmus, and Politiano[4] enjoyed in their respective times. We have now amongst us many scholars of great erudition (Parr, Wakefield, Professors Porson and White,[5] &c.

[2] *Marseillaise Hymn* Composed by Claude Joseph Rouget de Lisle on 24 April 1792, "the Marseillaise" celebrated freedom and human rights and became a rallying cry for the French Revolutionaries. It was declared the French national anthem in 1795.

[3] *field of Jemappe* Where a Revolutionary victory occurred in 1792.

[4] *Petrarch* Francesco Petrarch, Italian poet and Humanist of the fourteenth century, famous for his sonnets; *Erasmus* Desidero Erasmus, Dutch Humanist (1466–1536); *Politiano* Italian poet Angelo Poliziano (1454–95), who also served as professor of Greek and Latin at the University of Florence.

[5] *Parr* Samuel Parr (1747–1825), a Latin scholar, schoolmaster, minister, and vocal Whig supporter; *Wakefield* Gilbert Wakefield (1756–1801), a Biblical scholar and religious and political controversialist who also produced an edition of Virgil's *Georgics* (1788);

&c.), men of distinguished abilities; yet I much question, as haughty as kings were under the feudal system, if any of the princes in being would contend with the same eagerness for their favour, as we learn the various sovereigns of Europe did for that of Petrarch or Erasmus.

It has been questioned by some whether the number of publications, which are annually poured upon the world, have contributed in any proportionable ratio to the increase of literature? In my opinion, they have *not.* To a liberal and cultivated mind there is certainly no indulgence equal to the luxury of books; but, in works of learning, may not the facilities of information be increased, until the powers of application and retention be diminished? After admitting that the present is a learned age, it may appear singular to doubt whether it affords[1] individuals as profoundly learned (at least, as far as Latin and Greek go), as some who flourished in the fifteenth and sixteenth centuries.

From these remarks, I would not be understood as wishing to make invidious comparisons between the learning of different ages, or to depreciate that of our own. Upon a fair investigation, there can be no doubt, I think, to which side the scale of general literature would incline. My object simply is, to show the different direction which letters take, and the different patronage they obtain, in different periods of society. Indeed, learning may more properly be said to *lead* than to *follow* the course of the world: since, though it may, at first, bend to the spirit of the age, it will in the end assuredly direct and govern it. The general stock of genius is, perhaps, always pretty equal; the opportunities of improving it, and the support it receives, vary with the times. Petrarch and Erasmus were caressed by popes and princes; Butler, Otway, and Chatterton,[2] not much inferior in merit, were absolutely starved; and Johnson,[3] whose moral works were calculated to delight and improve the age, lived long in distress, and at length received a scanty pension. In some ages, and upon some occasions, it must be admitted, a genius darts upon the world with intellectual powers that no industry, in the common course of things, can hope to equal. But this is a *particular* case, and is generally compensated some other way. If former times have enjoyed works of more fancy, and sublimity of imagination, than are given to us, we, in return, possess more useful acquisitions. If they have had their Spenser, Tasso, and Shakespeare, we boast Newton, Locke, and Johnson.[4] Science, taste, and correction are indeed the characteristics of the present day. Everything is refined; everything is grand. We are actually misers in luxury and taste, and have left nothing for posterity. "*Venimus ad summum fortunae*"[5]—We learn our Greek from the Pursuits of Literature,[6] and our morality from Parissot, and I do not see how we are to be outdone either in learning or in dress.

I remain, Sir, &c., &c.

Ausonius[7]

Professors Porson and White Richard Porson (1759–1808), Greek professor at Cambridge, and Gilbert White (1720–93), noted naturalist.

[1] *affords* Is capable of yielding.

[2] *Butler, Otway, and Chatterton* Satirical poet Samuel Butler (1612–80), tragic dramatist Thomas Otway (1652–85), and young poet Thomas Chatterton (1752–70) all lived in dire poverty.

[3] *Johnson* Samuel Johnson (1709–84), lexicographer, poet, and author of the journals *The Rambler* and *The Idler*. He struggled for financial security until 1762, when he was granted a pension for his work on the *Dictionary*.

[4] *Spenser* English poet Edmund Spenser (c. 1552–99), author of *The Faerie Queene*; *Tasso* Italian poet Torquato Tasso (1544–95); *Locke* Philosopher John Locke (1632–1704); *Newton* Mathematician and natural philosopher Sir Isaac Newton (1642–1727).

[5] *"Venimus ... fortunae"* Latin: "We have come to the height of fortune" (Horace, *Epistles* 2.1).

[6] *Pursuits of Literature* Four-part satirical poem by Thomas James Mathias concerning the nature of literature. Its publication (1794–97) aroused much debate.

[7] *Ausonius* I.e., the author's pseudonym, referring to the Latin poet Dicimius Magmus Ausonius (c. 310–c. 393).

from Samuel Pratt, *Gleanings in England: Descriptive of the Countenance, Mind, and Character of the Country* (1799)

There cannot be a doubt but that while the liberty of the press, as to the freedom of publication, shall be sacred—and on this side of licentiousness, it ought to be uncontrolled—it is equally just that the sense and nonsense which indiscriminately issue from the immense vehicle of communication should be subject to vigilant examination, otherwise the whole world would be over-run with abortions of the mind. We want the assistance of some guides who will take upon themselves the trouble of separating the good from the bad and wade through the troubled deep of literature in order, if we may be permitted a continuation of the figure, to collect the pearls and gems, and to describe the useless weeds, whether swimming on the surface or lying at the muddy bottom. A stupendous labour if we consider the great disproportion betwixt the former and the latter. Applying this to the case in point, and it is by no means inapposite, a reader unused to such arduous undertakings can image to himself no task so overwhelming as that of being left unaided to search for instruction in the mass of productions which are every year piled, mountain high, before him.... For this reason, it would be proper that there should be some professional inspectors to direct our choice, even were literary excellence and defect nearly equal. But when the average is on a ratio of at least ninety in the hundred in the scale of compositions *deadweight*, there is not, perhaps, any office so necessary as his, who, with patient circumspection, will examine the great account betwixt wisdom and folly, and settle the balance.

It is not, therefore, possible to conceive a more useful institution than that of a literary journal, when conducted with various ability and inflexible justice; nor can it be denied that a great variety of articles, in every branch of literature, have been analysed on these principles, and a due proportion of good has thence resulted to the community.

We have to boast, even at this day, of great and noble critics; and from most, indeed, in all of our literary journals, we find substantial evidence of unimpeachable judgement and unwarped integrity. It is not, however, to be expected that any human association composed of many members should be conducted on principles uniformly sagacious and correct. Were they to write apart, and consult together ultimately, there must even then often be a clash of sentiment, a dissonance of opinion.

Yet I am persuaded the critics above-described are the very persons who must reprobate the virulences[1] and regret the errors for which they are made responsible. The literary body cannot be supposed to separate, or seem to move a limb independently—much less to commit themselves, and confederate against each other, by deploring the want of candour in some of their colleagues, and of capacity in others. Thus from their not being associated by congeniality, or chosen by consent—and yet under a kind of compact to hold together, and by the good faith that should be preserved in all treaties, bound to support one another in the way of a common cause—the errors, incongruities, adulations, and virulences, which are observed occasionally to disfigure their journals, attach indiscriminately to all.

from Hannah More, *Strictures on the Modern System of Female Education* (1799)

from CHAPTER 8, "ON FEMALE STUDY"

Will it not be ascribed to a captious singularity, if I venture to remark that real knowledge and real piety, though they may have gained in many instances, have suffered in others from that profusion of little, amusing, sentimental books with which the youthful library overflows? Abundance has its dangers as well as scarcity. In the first place, may not the multiplicity of these alluring little works increase the natural reluctance to those more dry and uninteresting studies, of which, after all, the rudiments of every part of learning *must* consist? And, secondly, is there not some danger (though there are many honourable exceptions) that some of those engaging narratives may serve to infuse into the youthful heart a sort of spurious goodness, a confidence of virtue, a parade of charity? And that the benevolent actions with the recital of which they abound, when they are not made to flow from any source but *feeling*, may tend to inspire a self-complacency, a self-gratulation, a "stand by, for I am holier than thou?" May not the success with which the good deeds of the little heroes are uniformly crowned, the invariable reward which is made the instant concomi-

[1] *virulences* Incidences of bitter hostility or antagonism.

tant of well-doing, furnish the young reader with false views of the condition of life, and the nature of the divine dealings with men? May they not help to suggest a false standard of morals, to infuse a love of popularity and an anxiety for praise, in the place of that simple and unostentatious rule of doing whatever good we do *because it is the will of God*? The universal substitution of this principle would tend to purify the worldly morality of many a popular little story. And there are few dangers which good parents will more carefully guard against than that of giving their children a mere political piety—that sort of religion which just goes to make people more respectable, and to stand well with the world; a religion which is to save appearances without inculcating realities; a religion which affects to "preach peace and good will to men," but which forgets to give "glory to God in the highest."[1]

There is a certain precocity of mind which is much helped on by these superficial modes of instruction; for frivolous reading will produce its correspondent effect in much less time than books of solid instruction; the imagination being liable to be worked upon, and the feelings to be set a going, much faster than the understanding can be opened and the judgment enlightened. A talent for conversation should be the result of instruction, not its precursor: it is a golden fruit when suffered to ripen gradually on the tree of knowledge; but if forced in the hot-bed of a circulating library, it will turn out worthless and vapid in proportion as it was artificial and premature. Girls who have been accustomed to devour a multitude of frivolous books will converse and write with a far greater appearance of skill, as to style and sentiment, at twelve or fourteen years old, than those of a more advanced age who are under the discipline of severer studies; but the former having early attained to that low standard which had been held out to them, become stationary; while the latter, quietly progressive, are passing through just gradations to a higher strain of mind; and those who early begin with talking and writing like women, commonly end with thinking and acting like children.

... Who are those ever-multiplying authors that with unparalleled fecundity are overstocking the world with their quick-succeeding progeny? They are NOVEL-WRITERS, the easiness of whose productions is at once the cause of their own fruitfulness, and of the almost infinitely numerous race of imitators to whom they give birth. Such is the frightful facility of this species of composition, that every raw girl, while she reads, is tempted to fancy that she can also write. And as Alexander, on perusing the *Iliad*, found by congenial sympathy the image of Achilles stamped on his own ardent soul, and felt himself the hero he was studying; and as Correggio, on first beholding a picture which exhibited the perfection of the graphic art, prophetically felt all his own future greatness, and cried out in rapture, "And I, too, am a painter!"[2] so a thorough-paced novel-reading Miss, at the close of every tissue of hackneyed adventures, feels within herself the stirring impulse of corresponding genius, and triumphantly exclaims, "And I, too, am an author!" The glutted imagination soon overflows with the redundance of cheap sentiment and plentiful incident, and by a sort of arithmetical proportion is enabled by the perusal of any three novels to produce a fourth; till every fresh production, like the prolific progeny of Banquo, is followed by "Another, and another, and another!"[3] Is a lady, however destitute of talents, education, or knowledge of the world, whose studies have been completed by a circulating library, in any distress of mind? the writing a novel suggests itself as the best soother of her sorrows! Does she labour under any depression of circumstances? writing a novel occurs as the readiest receipt for mending them! and she solaces her imagination with the conviction that the subscription which has been extorted by her importunity, or given to her necessities, has been offered as a homage to her genius; and this confidence instantly levies a fresh contribution for a succeeding work. Capacity and cultivation are so little taken into the account, that writing a book seems to be now considered as the only sure resource which the idle and the illiterate have always in their power.

[1] *preach peace ... the highest* Quotations from Luke 2.14.

[2] *Alexander ... ardent soul* Reference to a famous anecdote recounting Alexander the Great's sympathy with Achilles, the Greek hero of Homer's *Iliad*; *Correggio* Italian Renaissance painter Antonio Allegri (c. 1494–1534), called Correggio after his birthplace.

[3] *prolific progeny ... another* See *Macbeth* 4.1, in which Macbeth is frustrated by a vision of a nearly endless line of Banquo's royal heirs.

from Charles and Mary Lamb, "Preface," *Tales from Shakespeare* (1807)[1]

The following tales are meant to be submitted to the young reader as an introduction to the study of Shakespeare, for which purpose his words are used whenever it seemed possible to bring them in; and in whatever has been added to give them the regular form of a connected story, diligent care has been taken to select such words as might least interrupt the effect of the beautiful English tongue in which he wrote: therefore, words introduced into our language since his time have been as far as possible avoided.

In those tales which have been taken from the tragedies, the young readers will perceive, when they come to see the source from which these stories are derived, that Shakespeare's own words, with little alteration, recur very frequently in the narrative as well as in the dialog; but in those made from the comedies the writers found themselves scarcely ever able to turn his words into the narrative form: therefore it is feared that, in them, dialogue has been made use of too frequently for young people not accustomed to the dramatic form of writing. But this fault, if it be a fault, has been caused by an earnest wish to give as much of Shakespeare's own words as possible; and if the "he said" and "she said," the question and the reply, should sometimes seem tedious to their young ears, they must pardon it, because it was the only way in which could be given to them a few hints and little foretastes of the great pleasure which awaits them in their elder years, when they come to the rich treasures from which these small and valueless coins are extracted; pretending to no other merit than as faint and imperfect stamps of Shakespeare's matchless image. Faint and imperfect images they must be called, because the beauty of his language is too frequently destroyed by the necessity of changing many of his excellent words into words far less expressive of his true sense, to make it read something like prose; and even in some few places, where his blank verse is given unaltered, as hoping from its simple plainness to cheat the young reader into the belief that they are reading prose, yet still, his language being transplanted from its own natural soil and wild poetic garden, it must want much of its native beauty.

It has been wished to make these tales easy reading for very young children. To the utmost of their ability the writers have constantly kept this in mind; but the subjects of most of them made this a very difficult task. It was no easy matter to give the histories of men and women in terms familiar to the apprehension of a very young mind. For young ladies too, it has been the intention chiefly to write; because boys being generally permitted the use of their fathers' libraries at a much earlier age than girls are, they frequently have the best scenes of Shakespeare by heart before their sisters are permitted to look into this manly book; and, therefore, instead of recommending these tales to the perusal of young gentlemen who can read them so much better in the originals, their kind assistance is rather requested in explaining to their sisters such parts as are hardest for them to understand. And when they have helped them to get over the difficulties, then perhaps they will read to them (carefully selecting what is proper for a young sister's ear) some passage which has pleased them in one of these stories, in the very words of the scene from which it is taken; and it is hoped they will find that the beautiful extracts, the select passages, they may choose to give their sisters in this way will be much better relished and understood from their having some notion of the general story from one of these imperfect abridgments; which, if they be fortunately so done as to prove delightful to any of the young readers, it is hoped that no worse effect will result than to make them wish themselves a little older, that they may be allowed to read the plays at full length (such a wish will be neither peevish nor irrational). When time and leave of judicious friends shall put them into their hands, they will discover in such of them as are here abridged (not to mention almost as many more, which are left untouched) many surprising events and turns of fortune, which for their infinite variety could not be contained in this little book, besides a world of sprightly and

[1] *Tales from Shakespeare* This first appeared under Charles's name. He had written the first half of the preface and adapted some of the tragedies, while Mary had completed the rest of the collection.

cheerful characters, both men and women, the humour of which it was feared would be lost if it were attempted to reduce the length of them....

from an advertisement in *The Times* for Thomas Bowdler's *The Family Shakespeare* (15 December 1818)

Bowdler's work gained little attention upon publication until, in 1812, two literary journals, *Blackwood's Magazine* and the *Edinburgh Review*, began a literary debate over the merits and achievements of Bowdler's work. The controversy sparked sales, making the work a sudden bestseller.

Entire New School Books, and New Editions, published by Longman, Hunt, Rees, Orme, and Brown, London,

1. THE FAMILY SHAKESPEARE; in which nothing is added to the original text; but those words and expressions are omitted which cannot with propriety be read aloud in a family. By THOMAS BOWDLER, Esq....

"My great objects in this undertaking are to remove from the writings of Shakespeare some defects which diminish their value, and at the same to present to the public an edition of his plays, which the parent, the guardian, and the instructor of youth may place without fear in the hands of the pupil; and from which the pupil may derive instruction as well as pleasure; may improve his moral principles while he refines his taste; and, without incurring the danger of being hurt with any indelicacy of expression, may learn, in the fate of Macbeth, that even a kingdom is dearly purchased, if virtue be the price of acquisition."—Preface.

Anna Laetitia Barbauld, "On the Origin and Progress of Novel-Writing" (1810)[1]

A collection of novels has a better chance of giving pleasure than of commanding respect. Books of this description are condemned by the grave, and despised by the fastidious; but their leaves are seldom found unopened, and they occupy the parlour and the dressing-room while productions of higher name are often gathering dust upon the shelf. It might not perhaps be difficult to show that this species of composition is entitled to a higher rank than has been generally assigned it. Fictitious adventures, in one form or other, have made a part of the polite literature of every age and nation. These have been grafted upon the actions of their heroes; they have been interwoven with their mythology; they have been moulded upon the manners of the age—and, in return, have influenced the manners of the succeeding generation by the sentiments they have infused and the sensibilities they have excited.

If the end and object of this species of writing be asked, many no doubt will be ready to tell us that its object is to call in fancy to the aid of reason, to deceive the mind into embracing truth under the guise of fiction:

Cosi a l'egro fanciul porgiamo aspersi
Di soave licor gli orli del vaso,
Succhi amari, ingannato in tanto ei beve,
E da l'inganno suo vita riceve,[2]

with such-like reasons equally grave and dignified. For my own part, I scruple not to confess that when I take up a novel my end and object is entertainment; and as I suspect that to be the case with most readers, I hesitate not to say that entertainment is their legitimate end and object. To read the productions of wit and genius is a very high pleasure to all persons of taste, and the avidity

[1] *On the ... Writing* From the introduction to Barbauld's fifty-volume edition of *The British Novelists*.

[2] *Cosi a ... riceve* Italian: "So when the draught we give to the sick child, / The vessel's edge we touch with syrup sweet; / Cheated, he swift drinks down the bitter brew, / And from the cheat receives his life anew" (from Torquato Tasso's *Gerusalemme Liberata*, 1575).

with which they are read by all such shows sufficiently that they are calculated to answer this end. Reading is the cheapest of pleasures: it is a domestic pleasure. Dramatic exhibitions give a more poignant delight, but they are seldom enjoyed in perfection, and never without expense and trouble. Poetry requires in the reader a certain elevation of mind and a practiced ear. It is seldom relished unless a taste be formed for it pretty early. But the humble novel is always ready to enliven the gloom of solitude, to soothe the languor of debility and disease, to win the attention from pain or vexatious occurrences, to take man from himself (at many seasons the worst company he can be in), and, while the moving picture of life passes before him, to make him forget the subject of his own complaints. It is pleasant to the mind to sport in the boundless regions of possibility; to find relief from the sameness of everyday occurrences by expatiating amidst brighter skies and fairer fields; to exhibit love that is always happy, valour that is always successful; to feed the appetite for wonder by a quick succession of marvelous events; and to distribute, like a ruling Providence, rewards and punishments which fall just where they ought to fall.

It is sufficient, therefore, as an end, that these writings add to the innocent pleasures of life; and if they do no harm, the entertainment they give is a sufficient good. We cut down the tree that bears no fruit, but we ask nothing of a flower beyond its scent and its colour. The unpardonable sin in a novel is dullness: however grave or wise it may be, if its author possesses no powers of amusing, he has no business to write novels; he should employ his pen in some more serious part of literature.

from Isaac D'Israeli, *The Case of Authors Stated, Including the History of Literary Property* (1812)

Johnson has dignified the booksellers as "the patrons of literature,"[1] which was generous in that great author, who had written well and lived but ill all his life on that patronage. Eminent booksellers, in their constant intercourse with the most enlightened class of the community, that is, with the best authors and the best readers, partake of the intelligence around them; their great capitals, too, are productive of good and evil in literature; useful when they carry on great works, and pernicious when they sanction indifferent ones. Yet are they but commercial men. A trader can never be deemed a patron, for it would be romantic to purchase what is not saleable; and where no favour is conferred, there is no patronage.

Authors continue poor, and booksellers become opulent; an extraordinary result! Booksellers are not agents for authors, but proprietors of their works, so that the perpetual revenues of literature are solely in the possession of the trade.[2]

Is it then wonderful that even successful authors are indigent? They are heirs to fortunes, but by a strange singularity they are disinherited at their birth; for, on the publication of their works, these cease to be their own property. Let that natural property be secured, and a good book would be an inheritance, a leasehold or a freehold, as you choose it; it might at least last out a generation, and descend to the author's blood, were they permitted to live on their father's glory, as in all other property they do on his industry....

The verbal and tasteless lawyers, not many years past, with legal metaphysics wrangled like the schoolmen,[3] inquiring of each other, "whether the *style* and *ideas* of an author were tangible things; or if these were *property*, how is *possession* to be taken, or any act of *occupancy* made on mere intellectual *ideas*." Nothing, said they, can be an object of property but which has a corporeal substance; the air and the light, to which they compared an author's ideas, are common to all; ideas in

[1] *Johnson ... literature* According to James Boswell's *Life of Samuel Johnson* (1791), the lexicographer and author (whose father was a bookseller) referred to his publisher ("bookseller") as his "patron" in a letter to a friend. Johnson is also recorded as having said mockingly to the Earl of Chesterfield (the *Dictionary*'s intended patron, with whom Johnson had quarreled), "Is not a patron, my lord, one who looks with unconcern on a man struggling for life in the water and when he has reached ground encumbers him with help?"

[2] *Authors continue ... trade* The Statute of Anne (1710), generally considered the first copyright act, granted copyright protection to authors or proprietors for a fixed period of fourteen years. The law generally protected publishers rather than authors.

[3] *schoolmen* I.e., the Scholastics, adherents of the Scholastic philosophy.

the MS[1] state were compared to birds in a cage; while the author confines them in his own dominion, none but he has a right to let them fly; but the moment he allows the bird to escape from his hand, it is no violation of property in anyone to make it his own. And to prove that there existed no property after publication, they found an analogy in the gathering of acorns, or in seizing on a vacant piece of ground; and thus degrading that most refined piece of art formed in the highest state of society, a literary production, they brought us back to a state of nature, and seem to have concluded that literary property was purely ideal; a phantom which, as its author could neither grasp nor confine to himself, he must entirely depend on the public benevolence for his reward.[2]

The ideas, that is, the work of an author, are "tangible things." "There are works," to quote the words of a near and dear relative, "which require great learning, great industry, great labour, and great capital, in their preparation. They assume a palpable form. You may fill warehouses with them, and freight ships; and the tenure by which they are held is superior to that of all other property, for it is original. It is tenure which does not exist in a doubtful title; which does not spring from any adventitious circumstances; it is not found, it is not purchased, it is not prescriptive—it is original; so it is the most natural of all titles, because it is the most simple and least artificial. It is paramount and sovereign, because it is a tenure by creation."[3]

There were indeed some more generous spirits and better philosophers fortunately found on the same bench; and the identity of a literary composition was resolved into its sentiments and language, besides what was more obviously valuable to some persons, the print and paper. On this slight principle was issued the profound award which accorded a certain term of years to any work, however immortal. They could not diminish the immortality of a book, but only its reward. In all the litigations respecting literary property, authors were little considered—except some honourable testimonies due to genius, from the sense of Willes, and the eloquence of Mansfield.[4] Literary property was still disputed, like the rights of a parish common. An honest printer, who could not always write grammar, had the shrewdness to make a bold effort in this scramble, and perceiving that even by this last favourable award all literary property would necessarily centre with the booksellers, now stood forward for his own body—the printers. This rough advocate observed that "a few persons who call themselves *booksellers*, about the number of *twenty-five*, have kept the *monopoly of books and copies* in their hands, to the entire exclusion of all others, but more especially to the *printers*, whom they have always held it a rule never to let become purchasers in *copy*." Not a word for the *authors*! As for them, they were doomed by both parties as the fat oblation: they indeed sent forth some meek bleatings; but what were authors, between judges, booksellers, and printers? The sacrificed among the sacrificers....

As the matter now stands, let us address an arithmetical age—but my pen hesitates to bring down my subject to an argument fitted to "these coster-monger times."[5] On the present principle of literary property, it results that an author disposes of a leasehold property of twenty-eight years, often for less than the price of one year's purchase! How many living authors are the sad witnesses of this fact, who, like so many Esaus, have sold their inheritance for a meal![6] I leave the whole school of Adam Smith to calm their calculating emotions concerning "that unprosperous race of men" (sometimes

[1] *MS* I.e., manuscript.

[2] [D'Israeli's note] Sir James Burrows's Reports on Literary Property.

[3] [D'Israeli's note] *Mirror of Parliament*, 3529. [*Mirror of Parliament* was a journal, founded by Sir John Barrow in 1828, that aimed to provide a record of Parliamentary debates.]

[4] *Willes* Sir John Willes (1685–1761), who was the presiding judge in several copyright cases, and who believed that authors had a right to their intellectual property; *Mansfield* William Murray, first Earl of Mansfield (1705–93), a judge who upheld authors' perpetual common-law rights to their literary property in the influential copyright case *Millar v. Taylor* (1769, overturned in *Donaldson v. Beckett*, 1774).

[5] [D'Israeli's note] A coster-monger, or Costard-monger, is "A dealer in apples, which are so called because they are shaped like a costard, i.e., a man's head."—*Stevens*. Johnson explains the phrase eloquently: "In these times when the prevalence of trade has produced that meanness that rates the merit of everything by money."

[6] *Esaus ... meal* Cf. Hebrews 12.16: "Lest there be any fornicator, or profane person, as Esau, who for one morsel of meat sold his birthright."

this master-seer calls them "unproductive") "commonly called *men of letters*," who are pretty much in the situation which lawyers and physicians would be in, were these, as he tells us, in that state when "*a scholar* and *a beggar* seem to have been very nearly *synonymous terms*"[1]—and this melancholy fact that man of genius discovered, without the feather of his pen brushing away a tear from his lid—without one spontaneous and indignant groan!

Authors may exclaim, "we ask for justice, not charity." They would not need to require any favour, nor claim any other than that protection which an enlightened government, in its wisdom and its justice, must bestow. They would leave to the public disposition the sole appreciation of their works; their book must make its own fortune; a bad work may be cried up, and a good work may be cried down; but Faction will soon lose its voice, and Truth acquire one. The cause we are pleading is not the calamities of indifferent writers, but of those whose utility or whose genius long survives that limited term which has been so hardly wrenched from the penurious hand of verbal lawyers. Every lover of literature, and every votary of humanity has long felt indignant at that sordid state and all those secret sorrows to which men of the finest genius, or of sublime industry, are reduced and degraded in society. Johnson himself, who rejected that perpetuity of literary property which some enthusiasts seemed to claim at the time the subject was undergoing the discussion of the judges, is, however, for extending the copyright to a *century*. Could authors secure this, their natural right, literature would acquire a permanent and a nobler reward; for great authors would then be distinguished by the very profits they would receive from that obscure multitude whose common disgraces they frequently participate, notwithstanding the superiority of their own genius....

Authors now submit to have a shorter life than their own celebrity. While the book markets of Europe are supplied with the writings of English authors, and they have a wider diffusion in America than at home, it seems a national ingratitude to limit the existence of works for their authors to a short number of years, and then to seize on their possession for ever.

William Hazlitt, "A Review of *The St. James Chronicle, The Morning Chronicle, The Times, The New Times, The Courier*, &c., *Cobbett's Weekly Journal, The Examiner, The Observer, The Gentleman's Magazine, The New Monthly Magazine, The London*, &c. &c.," from *The Edinburgh Review* (1823)

Literature formerly was a sweet Heremitress,[2] who fed on the pure breath of Fame in silence and in solitude, far from the madding strife, in sylvan shade or cloistered hall, she trimmed her lamp or turned her hourglass, pale with studious care, and aiming only to "make the age to come her own!"[3] She gave her life to the perfecting some darling work, and bequeathed it, dying, to posterity! Vain hope, perhaps; but the hope itself was fruition—calm, serene, blissful, unearthly! Modern literature, on the contrary, is a gay Coquette, fluttering, fickle, vain; followed by a train of flatterers; besieged by a crowd of pretenders; courted, she courts again; receives delicious praise, and dispenses it; is impatient for applause; pants for the breath of popularity; renounces eternal fame for a newspaper puff; trifles with all sorts of arts and sciences; coquettes with fifty accomplishments—*mille ornatus habet, mille decenter*[4]—is the subject of polite conversation; the darling of private parties; the go-between in politics; the directress of fashion; the polisher of manners; and, like her winged prototype in Spenser,

> "Now this now that, she tasteth tenderly,"[5]

[1] *Adam Smith ... terms* Reference to Adam Smith's *Wealth of Nations*, Book 1, Chapter 10, in which Smith discusses "that unprosperous race of men commonly called men of letters." He says these writers were generally educated for the Church, and then failed for some reason to take holy orders. "They have generally, therefore, been educated at the public expense, and their numbers are everywhere so great as commonly to reduce the price of their labor to a very paltry recompense."

[2] *Heremitress* I.e., female hermit.

[3] *make the ... own* Cf. Abraham Cowley, "The Motto" (1656), line 2.

[4] *mille ... decenter* Latin: "She has a thousand trifling things, a thousand things which are fitting to her." Reference to a quotation from the work of Roman elegiac poet Tibullus (c. 55–c. 19 BCE).

[5] *Now this ... tenderly* From Edmund Spenser's "Muiopotmos, or The Fate of the Butterflie" (1590).

glitters, flutters, buzzes, spawns, dies—and is forgotten! But the very variety and superficial polish show the extent and height to which knowledge has been accumulated, and the general interest taken in letters.

To dig to the bottom of a subject through so many generations of authors is now impossible: the concrete mass is too voluminous and vast to be contained in any single head; and therefore, we must have essences and samples as substitutes for it. We have collected a superabundance of raw materials: the grand *desideratum*[1] now is, to fashion and render them portable. Knowledge is no longer confined to the few: the object therefore is, to make it accessible and attractive to the many. The *Monachism*[2] of literature is at an end; the cells of learning are thrown open and let in the light of universal day. We can no longer be churls of knowledge, ascetics in pretension. We must yield to the spirit of change (whether for the better or worse); and "to beguile the time, look like the time."[3] A modern author may (without much imputation of his wisdom) declare for a short life and a merry one. He may be a little gay, thoughtless, and dissipated. Literary immortality is now let on short leases, and he must be contented to succeed by rotation. A scholar of the olden time had resources, had consolations to support him under many privations and disadvantages. A light (that light which penetrates the most clouded skies) cheered him in his lonely cell, in the most obscure retirement; and, with the eye of faith, he could see the meanness of his garb exchanged for the wings of the Shining Ones, and the wedding-garment of the Spouse. Again, he lived only in the contemplation of old books and old events; and the remote and future became habitually present to his imagination, like the past. He was removed from low, petty vanity by the nature of his studies, and could wait patiently for his reward till after death. We exist in the bustle of the world, and cannot escape from the notice of our contemporaries. We must please to live, and therefore should live to please. We must look to the public for support. Instead of solemn testimonies from the learned, we require the smiles of the fair and the polite. If princes scowl upon us, the broad shining face of the people may turn to us with a favorable aspect. Is not this life (too) sweet? Would we change it for the former if we could? But the great point is that *we cannot*! Therefore, let reviews[4] flourish—let magazines increase and multiply—let the daily and weekly newspapers live forever! We are optimists in literature, and hold, with certain limitations that in this respect, whatever is, is right![5]

from John Stuart Mill, "The Present State of Literature" (16 November 1827)[6]

It is the demand, in literature as in most other things, which calls forth the supply.… Assuming, therefore, as an indisputable truth, that the writers of every age are for the most part what the readers make them, it becomes important to the present question to consider who formed the reading public formerly, and who compose it now. The present age is very remarkably distinguished from all other ages by the number of persons who can read, and, what is of more consequence, by the number who do. Our working classes have learned to read, and our idle classes have learned to find pleasure in reading, and to devote a part of that time to it which they formerly spent in amusements of a grosser kind. That human nature will be a gainer, and that in a high degree, by this change, no one can be more firmly convinced than I am—but it will perhaps be found that the benefit lies rather in the ultimate than in the immediate effects. Reading is necessary, but no wise or even sensible man was ever made by reading alone. The proper use of reading is to be subservient to thinking. It is by those who read to think that knowledge is advanced, prejudices dispelled, and the physical and moral condition of mankind is improved. I cannot, however, perceive that the general diffusion (so remarkable in our own day) of the taste for reading has yet been accompanied by any marked increase in taste for the

1 *desideratum* Latin: thing desired.

2 *Monachism* Monasticism.

3 *to beguile … like the time* From Shakespeare's *Macbeth* 1.5.62–63.

4 *reviews* I.e., literary journals or periodicals.

5 *whatever … right* Reference to Alexander Pope's *Essay on Man* (1733), Epistle 1, line 294: "One truth is clear: whatever is, is right."

6 *The Present … 1827* From a speech delivered to the London Debating Society.

severer exercises of the intellect; that such will one day be its effect, may fairly be presumed, but it has not yet declared itself: and it is to the immense multiplication in the present day of those who read but do not think, that I should be disposed to ascribe what I view as the degeneracy of our literature.

In former days the literati and the learned formed a class apart, and few concerned themselves with literature and philosophy except those who had leisure and inclination to form their philosophical opinions by study and meditation, and to cultivate their literary taste by the assiduous perusal of the most approved models. Those whose sole occupation was pleasure did not seek it in books, but in the gaieties of a court, or in field sports and debauchery. The public for which authors wrote was a small but, to a very considerable degree, an instructed public; and their suffrages were only to be gained by thinking to a certain extent profoundly and by writing well. The authors who were then in highest reputation are chiefly those to whom we now look back as the ablest thinkers and best writers of their time. No doubt there were many blockheads among the reading public in those days, as well as in our own, and the blockheads often egregiously misplaced their admiration, as blockheads are wont, but the applause of the blockheads was not then the object aimed at even by those who obtained it, and they did not constitute so large and so influential a class of readers as to tempt any writer of talent to lay himself out for their admiration. If an author failed of obtaining the suffrages of men of knowledge and taste, it was for want of powers, not from the misapplication of them. The case is now altered. We live in a refined age, and there is a corresponding refinement in our amusements. It is now the height of *mauvais ton*[1] to be drunk, neither is it any longer considered decorous among gentlemen that the staple of their conversation should consist of bawdy. Reading has become one of the most approved and fashionable methods of killing time, and the number of persons who have skimmed the surface of literature is far greater than at any previous period of our history. Our writers therefore find that the greatest success is now to be obtained by writing for the many, and endeavouring all they can to bring themselves down to the level of the many, both in their matter and in the manner of expressing it.

[1] *mauvais ton* French: bad form.

Dorothy Wordsworth

1771 – 1855

When Ernest de Selincourt published Dorothy Wordsworth's journals in 1933, he called her "the most distinguished of English writers who never wrote a line for the general public." Although her more famous brother William did publish a few of her poems, Dorothy Wordsworth never considered herself an author; she wrote journals of daily life in England and travels to Scotland and Europe simply for the "pleasure" they gave William. William did indeed derive immense pleasure from his sister's work, and he consulted her journals for recollections and inspiration for many of his poems. But Dorothy's exquisite observations on nature, her keen eye and ear for the details of the appearance and speech-patterns of the local populace—and her incisive sense of their harsh economic conditions and ingenious survival strategies—make her writings valuable in their own right. For Virginia Woolf, an ardent admirer of Wordsworth's work, the journals have in them "the suggestive power which is the gift of the poet rather than of the naturalist, the power which, taking only the simplest facts, so orders them that the whole scene comes before us, heightened and composed, the lake in its quiet, the hills in their splendour."

Dorothy Wordsworth was born on Christmas Day of 1771 to John Wordsworth, an attorney, and Ann (née Cookson), in Cockermouth, Cumberland, in the Lake District of England. Her mother died when Wordsworth was only six, and her father sent her to Yorkshire to live with relatives. She rarely saw her father again up to the day he, too, suffered an untimely death. Her childhood was spent happily among aunts and cousins, but at age fifteen she was sent to live with her stern grandparents; in the nine years she lived there she longed for the company of her four brothers. Her dream of living with William was realized when in 1795 he was bequeathed a legacy by a college friend, allowing the two siblings to secure a home together in Dorset in southwestern England. They were never again parted until William's death 55 years later.

The two made the acquaintance of Samuel Taylor Coleridge while in Somerset, and soon after that they moved to Alfoxden House to be nearer him. The bond the triad created was powerful, "three persons with one soul," according to Coleridge. This friendship marked the beginning of an intensely creative time for Coleridge and for William Wordsworth, culminating in their "*annus mirabilis*" that yielded the *Lyrical Ballads*. This alliance was productive for Dorothy Wordsworth, as well. She began her Alfoxden journal (the earliest that has survived) in 1798, chiefly for the enjoyment of her brother, who took great delight in reading and sometimes writing his own poems in her journals. Her sensitive descriptions of farm workers, beggars, leech gatherers, and a myriad of other characters, as well her vivid images of rural scenes, were also an invaluable resource for William, who would use them to spark his memory when he later "recollected in tranquility" an event the two had experienced. According to Woolf, "Dorothy stored the mood in prose, and later William came and bathed in it and made it into poetry." When the Wordsworths moved to Dove Cottage in the Lake District, Dorothy wrote in her Grasmere journal (1800–03): "I never saw daffodils so beautiful they grew among the mossy stones about and about them, some rested their heads upon these stones as on a pillow for weariness and the rest tossed and reeled and danced and seemed as if they verily laughed with the wind...., they looked so gay ever glancing ever changing." These words became the inspiration for William's description of daffodils in his poem "I Wandered Lonely as a Cloud."

Wordsworth remained with her brother in Grasmere even after his marriage in 1802. The two continued to take many excursions together, which she recorded in various travel journals. Her writing was curtailed in 1829, when she suffered the first of a series of ailments that eventually debilitated her both physically and mentally. By June of 1835 she was an invalid from some kind of dementia said to be caused by arteriosclerosis. She remained so, albeit with brief periods of lucidity, for the following two decades, but she was cared for lovingly by those whom she had once tended. She died in 1855, outliving her beloved William by five years. Wordsworth's poems, letters, journals, and travelogues were published long after her death. Once valued mainly as a resource for their insights into the poetry of the Lake Poets, they are valued today for their descriptive power. Their author, according to Coleridge, possessed an "eye watchful in minutest observation of nature—and her taste a perfect electrometer—it bends, protrudes, and draws in at subtlest beauties and most recondite faults."

⌘⌘⌘

from *The Grasmere Journal*

May 14 1800 Wm. & John[1] set off into Yorkshire after dinner at ½ past 2 o'clock—cold pork in their pockets. I left them at the turning of the Low Wood bay[2] under the trees. My heart was so full that I could hardly speak to W. when I gave him a farewell kiss. I sat a long time upon a stone at the margin of the lake, and after a flood of tears my heart was easier. The lake looked to me I knew not why dull and melancholy, the weltering[3] on the shores seemed a heavy sound. I walked as long as I could amongst the stones of the shore. The wood rich in flowers. A beautiful yellow, palish yellow flower, that looked thick round and double, and smelt very sweet—I supposed it was a ranunculus—crowfoot, the grassy-leaved rabbit-toothed white flower, strawberries, geranium—scentless violet, anemones two kinds, orchises, primroses. The heckberry very beautiful as a low shrub. The crab coming out. Met a blind man driving a very large beautiful bull and a cow—he walked with two sticks. Came home by Clappersgate. The valley very green, many sweet views up to Rydale head when I could juggle away the fine houses, but they disturbed me even more than when I have been happier—one beautiful view of the bridge, without Sir Michael's.[4] Sat down very often, though it was cold. I resolved to write a journal of the time till W. and J. return, and I set about keeping my resolve because I will not quarrel with myself, and because I shall give Wm. pleasure by it when he comes home again. At Rydale a woman of the village, stout and well-dressed, begged a halfpenny—she had never she said done it before—but these hard times! Arrived at home with a bad headache, set some slips of privet.[5] The evening cold had a fire—my face now flame-coloured. It is nine o'clock—I shall soon go to bed. A young woman begged at the door—she had come from Manchester on Sunday morn with two shillings and a slip of paper which she supposed a bank note—it was a cheat. She had buried her husband and three children within a year and a half—all in one grave—burying very dear—paupers all put in one place—20 shillings paid for as much ground as will bury a man—a grave stone to be put over it or the right will be lost—11/6[6] each time the ground is opened. Oh! that I had a letter from William!

[1] *Wm. & John* Dorothy Wordsworth's brothers, William (often written as "Wm." or "W.") and John.

[2] *Low Wood bay* In the Lake District, where Dorothy and William Wordsworth lived.

[3] *weltering* Tumbling (of waves).

[4] *bridge, without Sir Michael's* Pelter Bridge, beyond Sir Michael le Fleming's castle.

[5] *privet* Common hedge plant.

[6] *11/6* Eleven shillings and sixpence.

Friday 3rd October. Very rainy all the morning—little Sally[1] learning to mark. Wm. walked to Ambleside after dinner. I went with him part of the way—he talked much about the object of his essay for the second volume of LB.[2] I returned expecting the Simpsons—they did not come. I should have met Wm. but my teeth ached and it was showery and late—he returned after 10. Amos Cottle's[3] death in the morning Post. Wrote to S. Lowthian.[4]

N.B.[5] When Wm. and I returned from accompanying Jones we met an old man almost double—he had on a coat thrown over his shoulders above his waistcoat and coat. Under this he carried a bundle and had an apron on and a night cap. His face was interesting. He had dark eyes and a long nose—John who afterwards met him at Wythburn took him for a Jew. He was of Scotch parents but had been born in the army. He had had a wife "and a good woman and it pleased God to bless us with ten children"—all these were dead but one of whom he had not heard for many years, a sailor—his trade was to gather leeches but now leeches are scarce and he had not strength for it—he lived by begging and was making his way to Carlisle where he should buy a few godly books to sell. He said leeches were very scarce partly owing to this dry season, but many years they have been scarce—he supposed it owing to their being much sought after, that they did not breed fast, and were of slow growth. Leeches were formerly 2/6 100; they are now 30/. He had been hurt in driving a cart his leg broke his body driven over his skull fractured—he felt no pain till he recovered from his first insensibility. It was then late in the evening—when the light was just going away.

[1] *little Sally* Sally Ashburner, daughter of the Wordsworths' neighbor.

[2] *LB Lyrical Ballads,* written with Samuel Taylor Coleridge (1798); William Wordsworth wrote a lengthy preface to the second edition, published in 1800.

[3] *Amos Cottle's* Cottle was a poet, translator, and a member of the "Lake School," which included W. Wordsworth, Coleridge, and Southey; his brother, Joseph Cottle, was a poet and the publisher of Coleridge and W. Wordsworth's *Lyrical Ballads.*

[4] *S. Lowthian* Sally, one of Wordsworth's father's domestic staff.

[5] *NB Nota bene*: Note well (Latin); i.e., important note.

Saturday 11th A fine October morning—sat in the house working all the morning. Wm. composing—Sally Ashburner learning to mark. After dinner we walked up Greenhead Gill in search of a sheepfold. We went by Mr. Ollif's and through his woods. It was a delightful day and the views looked excessively cheerful and beautiful chiefly that from Mr. Oliff's field where our house is to be built. The colours of the mountains soft and rich, with orange fern. The cattle pasturing upon the hilltops kites[6] sailing as in the sky above our heads—sheep bleating and in lines and chains and patterns scattered over the mountains. They come down and feed on the little green islands in the beds of the torrents and so may be swept away. The sheepfold is falling away it is built nearly in the form of a heart unequally divided. Look down the brook and see the drops rise upwards and sparkle in the air, at the little falls, the higher sparkles the tallest. We walked along the turf of the mountain till we came to a cattle track—made by the cattle which come upon the hills. We drank tea at Mr. Simpson's returned at about nine—a fine mild night.

[November, 1801]

Tuesday 24th A rainy morning. We all were well except that my head ached a little and I took my breakfast in bed. I read a little of Chaucer, prepared the goose for dinner, and then we all walked out—I was obliged to return for my fur tippet and spenser[7] it was so cold. We had intended going to Easedale but we shaped our course to Mr. Gell's[8] cottage. It was very windy and we heard the wind everywhere about us as we went along the lane but the walls sheltered us—John Green's house looked pretty under Silver How[9]—as we were going along we were stopped at once, at the distance perhaps of 50 yards from our favorite birch tree. It was yielding to the gusty wind with all its tender twigs, the sun shone upon it and it glanced in the wind like a flying sunshiny shower—it was a tree in shape with stem and branches but it was like a spirit of water. The sun went in and it resumed its purplish appearance the twigs still yielding

[6] *kites* Birds (of prey).

[7] *tippet and spenser* Shawl and jacket.

[8] *Mr. Gell's* Anthropologist Sir William Gell's.

[9] *Silver How* Hill near Grasmere.

to the wind but not so visibly to us. The other birch trees that were near it looked bright and cheerful—but it was a creature by its own self among them. We could not get into Mr. Gell's grounds—the old tree fallen from its undue exaltation above the gate. A shower came on when we were at Benson's. We went through the wood—it became fair, there was a rainbow which spanned the lake from the island house to the foot of Bainriggs. The village looked populous and beautiful. Catkins[1] are coming out palm trees budding—the alder with its plum coloured buds. We came home over the stepping stones—the lake was foamy with white waves. I saw a solitary butter flower[2] in the wood. *I* found it not easy to get over the stepping stones—reached home at dinner time. Sent Peggy Ashburner some goose. She sent me some honey—with a thousand thanks—"alas the gratitude of men has &c."[3] I went in to set her right about this and sat a while with her. She talked about Thomas's having sold his land—"Ay" says she, "I said many a time "he's not come fra London to buy our land however." Then she told me with what pains and industry they had made up their taxes interest &c. &c. — how they all got up at 5 o'clock in the morning to spin and Thomas carded,[4] and that they had paid off a hundred pound of the interest. She said she used to take such pleasure in the cattle and sheep— "Oh how pleased I used to be when they fetched them down, and when I had been a bit poorly I would gang[5] out upon a hill and look ower t' fields and see them and it used to do me so much good you cannot think"—Molly said to me when I came in "poor body! She's very ill but one does not know how long she may last. Many a fair face may gang before her." We sat by the fire without work for some time then Mary[6] read a poem of Daniel[7] upon learning. After tea Wm. read Spenser now and then a little aloud to us. We were making his waistcoat. We had a note from Mrs. C.[8] with bad news from poor C. very ill. William walked to John's grove—I went to meet him—moonlight but it rained. I met him before I had got as far as John Batys—he had been surprized and terrified by a sudden rushing of winds which seemed to bring earth sky and lake together, as if the whole were going to enclose him in—he was glad that he was in a high road.

In speaking of our walk on Sunday evening the 22nd November I forgot to notice one most impressive sight—it was the moon and the moonlight seen through hurrying driving clouds immediately behind the stone man upon the top of the hill on the forest side. Every tooth and every edge of rock was visible, and the man stood like a giant watching from the roof of a lofty castle. The hill seemed perpendicular from the darkness below it. It was a sight that I could call to mind at any time it was so distinct.

Friday 27th Snow upon the ground thinly scattered. It snowed after we got up and then the sun shone and it was very warm though frosty—now the sun shines sweetly. A woman came who was travelling with her husband—he had been wounded and was going with her to live at Whitehaven. She had been at Ambleside the night before, offered 4d at the Cock for a bed—they sent her to one Harrison's where she and her husband had slept upon the hearth and bought a pennyworth of chips for a fire. Her husband was gone before very lame. "Aye" says she, "I was once an officer's wife I, as you see me now. My first husband married me at Appleby. I had 18£ a year for teaching a school and because I had no fortune his father turned him out of doors. I have been in the West Indies—I lost the use of this finger. Just before he died he came to me and said he must bid farewell to his dear children and me—I had a muslin gown on like yours—I seized hold of his coat as he went from me and slipped the joint of my finger—he was shot directly. I came to London and married this man. He was clerk to Judge Chambray, that man that's going on the road now. If he, Judge Chambray, had been at

[1] *Catkins* Cylindrical buds on birch and willow trees.

[2] *butter flower* Buttercup.

[3] *"alas ... &c."* From William Wordsworth's "Simon Lee" 95–96: "I've heard of hearts unkind, kind deeds / With coldness still returning; / Alas! the gratitude of men / Hath oftener left me mourning."

[4] *carded* Combed the wool.

[5] *gang* Go.

[6] *Mary* Mary Hutchison, Wordsworth's friend and William's future wife; Wordsworth often refers to her as MH in the journals.

[7] *Daniel* Samuel Daniel (1562–1619).

[8] *Mrs. C.* Mrs. Coleridge.

Kendal he would given us a guinea or two and made nought of it, for he is very generous."

Before dinner we set forward to walk intending to return to dinner. But as we had got as far as Rydale Wm. thought he would go on to Mr. Luffs. We accompanied him under Loughrigg, and parted near the stepping stones—it was very cold. Mary and I walked quick home. There was a fine gleam of sunshine upon the eastern side of Ambleside vale. We came up the old road and turning round we were struck with the appearance. Mary wrote to her aunt. We expected the Simpsons. I was sleepy and weary and went to bed—before tea. It came on wet in the evening and was very cold. We expected letters from C. and Sara[1]—Sara's came by the boy. But none from C.—a sad disappointment. We did not go to meet Wm. as we had intended—Mary was at work at Wm's warm waistcoat.

[December]

Tuesday 22nd Still thaw. I washed my head. Wm. and I went to Rydale for letters—the road was covered with dirty snow, rough and rather slippery. We had a melancholy letter from C. for he had been very ill, though he was better when he wrote. We walked home almost without speaking—Wm. composed a few lines of the Pedlar.[2] We talked about Lamb's tragedy[3] as we went down the White Moss. We stopped a long time in going to watch a little bird with a salmon coloured breast—a white cross or T upon its wings, and a brownish back with faint stripes. It was pecking the scattered dung upon the road—it began to peck at the distance of 4 yards from us and advanced nearer and nearer till it came within the length of Wm's stick without any apparent fear of us. As we came up the White Moss we met an old man, who I saw was a beggar by his two bags hanging over his shoulder, but from a half laziness, half indifference and a wanting to *try* him if he would speak I let him pass. He said nothing, and my heart smote me. I turned back and said You are begging? "Ay" says he—I gave him a halfpenny. William, judging from his appearance joined in I suppose you were a Sailor? "Ay" he replied, "I have been fifty-seven years at sea, twelve of them on board a man-of-war[4] under Sir Hugh Palmer." Why have you not a pension? "I have no pension, but I could have got into Greenwich hospital[5] but all my officers are dead." He was seventy-five years of age, had a freshish colour in his cheeks, grey hair, a decent hat with a binding round the edge, the hat worn brown and glossy, his shoes were small thin shoes low in the quarters, pretty good—they had belonged to a gentleman. His coat was blue, frock shaped coming over his thighs, it had been joined up at the seams behind with paler blue to let it out, and there were three bell-shaped patches of darker blue behind where the buttons had been. His breeches were either of fustian[6] or grey cloth, with strings hanging down, whole and tight and he had a checked shirt on, and a small coloured handkerchief tied round his neck. His bags were hung over each shoulder and lay on each side of him, below his breast. One was brownish and of coarse stuff, the other was white with meal[7] on the outside, and his blue waistcoat was whitened with meal. In the coarse bag I guessed he put his scraps of meat &c. He walked with a slender stick decently stout, but his legs bowed outwards. We overtook old Fleming at Rydale, leading his little Dutchman-like grandchild along the slippery road. The same pace seemed to be natural to them both, the old man and the little child, and they went hand in hand, the grandfather cautious, yet looking proud of his charge. He had two patches of new cloth at the shoulder blades of his faded claret coloured coat, like eyes at each shoulder, not worn elsewhere. I found Mary at home in her riding-habit all her clothes being put up. We were very sad about Coleridge. Wm. walked further. When he came home he cleared a path to the necessary[8]—called me out to see it but before we got there a whole housetop full of snow had fallen from the roof upon the path and it echoed in the ground beneath like a dull

[1] *C. and Sara* Samuel Taylor Coleridge and Sara Hutchinson, sister of William Wordsworth's future wife.

[2] *the Pedlar* "The Pedlar," a poem by William Wordsworth that was eventually incorporated into *The Excursion.*

[3] *Lamb's tragedy* Charles Lamb's play *John Woodvil* (1802).

[4] *man-of-war* Warship.

[5] *Greenwich hospital* Royal Naval Hospital, i.e., home for pensioned seamen.

[6] *fustian* Coarse cloth made of cotton and linen.

[7] *meal* Grain ground to a powder, like flour.

[8] *necessary* Outdoor toilet.

beating upon it. We talked of going to Ambleside after dinner to borrow money of Luff, but we thought we would defer our visit to Eusemere a day. Half the seaman's nose was reddish as if he had been in his youth somewhat used to drinking, though he was not injured by it. We stopped to look at the stone seat at the top of the hill. There was a white cushion upon it round at the edge like a cushion and the rock behind looked soft as velvet, of a vivid green and so tempting! The snow too looked as soft as a down cushion. A young foxglove, like a star in the centre. There were a few green lichens about it and a few withered brackens of fern here and there and upon the ground near. All else was a thick snow—no foot mark to it, not the foot of a sheep. When we were at Thomas Ashburner's on Sunday Peggy talked about the Queen of Patterdale. She had been brought to drinking by her husband's unkindness and avarice. She was formerly a very nice tidy woman. She had taken to drinking but "that was better than if she had taken to something worse" (by this I suppose she meant killing herself). She said that her husband used to be out all night with other women and she used to hear him come in in the morning for they never slept together—"Many a poor body a wife like me, has had a working heart for her, as much stuff as she had." We sat snugly round the fire. I read to them the Tale of Custance and the Syrian Monarch, also some of the Prologues. It is the Man of Lawes Tale.[1] We went to bed early. It snowed and thawed.

[1802]

Monday Morning 8th February 1802. It was very windy and rained very hard all the morning. William worked at his poem and I read a little in Lessing[2] and the grammar. A chaise[3] came past to fetch Ellis the carrier[4] who had hurt his head. After dinner (i.e. we set off at about ½ past 4) we went towards Rydale for letters. It was a "*Cauld Clash*"[5]—the rain had been so cold that it hardly melted the snow. We stopped at Park's to get some straw in William's shoes. The young mother was sitting by a bright wood fire with her youngest child upon her lap and the other two sat on each side of the chimney. The light of the fire made them a beautiful sight, with their innocent countenances, their rosy cheeks and glossy curling hair. We sat and talked about poor Ellis, and our journey over the Hawes.[6] It had been reported that we came over in the night. Willy told us of three men who were once lost in crossing that way in the night—they had carried a lantern with them—the lantern went out at the tarn[7] and they all perished. Willy had seen their cloaks drying at the public house in Patterdale the day before their funeral. We walked on very wet through the clashy cold roads in bad spirits at the idea of having to go as far as Rydale, but before we had come again to the shore of the lake, we met our patient, bow-bent friend with his little wooden box at his back. "Where are you going?" said he, "To Rydale for letters"—"I have two for you in my box." We lifted up the lid and there they lay—poor fellow, he straddled and pushed on with all his might but we soon outstripped him far away when we had turned back with our letters. We were very thankful that we had not to go on, for we should have been sadly tired. In thinking of this I could not help comparing lots with him! He goes at that slow pace every morning, and after having wrought a hard day's work returns at night, however weary he may be, takes it all quietly, and though perhaps he neither feels thankfulness, nor pleasure when he eats his supper, and has no luxury to look forward to but falling asleep in bed, yet I daresay he neither murmurs nor thinks it hard. He seems mechanized to labour. We broke the seal of Coleridge's letter, and I had light enough just to see that he was not ill. I put it in my pocket but at the top of the White Moss I took it to my bosom, a safer place for it. The night was wild. There was a strange mountain lightness when we were at the top of the White Moss. I have often observed it there in the evenings, being between the two valleys. There is

[1] *Tale of Custance … Man of Lawes Tale* From Geoffrey Chaucer's *The Canterbury Tales.*

[2] *Lessing* German author and critic Gotthold Ephraim Lessing (1729–81).

[3] *chaise* Light open carriage.

[4] *carrier* I.e., common carrier, a hired parcel delivery person.

[5] *"Cauld Clash"* Scottish phrase meaning a cold blow.

[6] *the Hawes* Grisedale Pass.

[7] *tarn* Small mountain lake.

more of the sky there than any other place. It has a strange effect sometimes along with the obscurity of evening or night. It seems almost like a peculiar *sort* of light. There was not much wind till we came to John's Grove, then it roared right out of the grove, all the trees were tossing about. C's letter somewhat damped us, it spoke with less confidence about France.[1] William wrote to him. The other letter was from Montagu with 8£. William was very unwell, tired when he had written, he went to bed, and left me to write to M.H., Montagu and Calvert, and Mrs. Coleridge. I had written in his letter to Coleridge. We wrote to Calvert to beg him not to fetch us on Sunday. Wm left me with a *little* peat fire—it grew less—I wrote on and was starved.[2] At 2 o'clock I went to put my letters under Fletcher's door. I never felt such a cold night. There was a strong wind and it froze very hard. I collected together all the clothes I could find (for I durst not go into the pantry for fear of waking William). At first when I went to bed I seemed to be warm, I suppose because the cold air which I had just left no longer touched my body, but I soon found that I was mistaken. I could not sleep from sheer cold. I had baked pies and bread in the morning. Coleridge's letter contained prescriptions.

NB The moon came out suddenly when we were at John's Grove and "a star or two beside."[3]

[18 March]

Thursday A very fine morning. The sun shone but it was far colder than yesterday. I felt myself weak, and William charged me not to go to Mrs. Lloyds—I seemed indeed, to myself unfit for it but when he was gone I thought I would get the visit over if I could—so I ate a beefsteak thinking it would strengthen me, so it did, and I went off—I had a very pleasant walk. Rydale vale was full of life and motion. The wind blew briskly and the lake was covered all over with bright silver waves that were there each the twinkling of an eye, then others rose up and took their place as fast as they went away. The rocks glittered in the sunshine, the crows and the ravens were busy, and the thrushes and little birds sang—I went through the fields, and sat ½ an hour afraid to pass a cow. The cow looked at me and I looked at the cow and whenever I stirred the cow gave over eating. I was not very much tired when I reached Lloyds—I walked in the garden. Charles is all for agriculture. Mrs. L. in her kindest way. A parcel came in from Birmingham, with Lamb's play for us and for C. They came with me as far as Rydale. As we came along Ambleside vale in the twilight—it was a grave evening—there was something in the air that compelled me to serious thought—the hills were large, closed in by the sky. It was nearly dark when I parted from the Lloyds that is, night was come on and the moon was overcast. But as I climbed Moss the moon came out from behind a mountain mass of black clouds—O the unutterable darkness of the sky and the earth below the moon! and the glorious brightness of the moon itself! There was a vivid sparkling streak of light at this end of Rydale water but the rest was very dark and Loughrigg fell and Silver How were white and bright as if they were covered with hoar frost. The moon retired again and appeared and disappeared several times before I reached home. Once there was no moonlight to be seen but upon the island house and the promontory of the island where it stands, "That needs must be a holy place" &c.—&c. I had many very exquisite feelings when I saw this lowly building in the waters among the dark and lofty hills, with that bright soft light upon it—it made me more than half a poet. I was tired when I reached home. I could not sit down to reading and tried to write verses but alas! I gave up expecting William and went soon to bed. Fletcher's carts came home late.

[April]

Thursday 15th It was a threatening misty morning—but mild. We set off after dinner from Eusemere—Mrs. Clarkson went a short way with us but turned back. The wind was furious, and we thought we must have returned. We first rested in the large boat-house, then under a furze bush[4] opposite Mr. Clarkson's—saw the plough going in the field. The wind seized our breath

[1] *it spoke … France* Regarding plans for the Wordsworths and Coleridges to move to France.

[2] *starved* Frozen.

[3] *"a star or two beside"* From Coleridge's "The Rime of the Ancient Mariner," Part IV.

[4] *furze bush* Common evergreen shrub.

the lake was rough. There was a boat by itself floating in the middle of the Bay below Water Millock—We rested again in the Water Millock lane. The hawthorns are black and green, the birches here and there greenish but there is yet more of purple to be seen on the Twigs. We got over into a field to avoid some cows—people working, a few primroses by the roadside, woodsorrel flowers, the anemone, scentless violets, strawberries, and that starry yellow flower which Mrs. C. calls pile wort. When we were in the woods beyond Gowbarrow park we saw a few daffodils close to the water-side; we fancied that the lake had floated the seeds ashore and that the little colony had so sprung up. But as we went along there were more and yet more and at last under the boughs of the trees, we saw that there was a long belt of them along the shore, about the breadth of a country turnpike road. I never saw daffodils so beautiful they grew among the mossy stones about and about them, some rested their heads upon these stones as on a pillow for weariness and the rest tossed and reeled and danced and seemed as if they verily laughed with the wind that blew upon them over the lake, they looked so gay ever glancing ever changing. This wind blew directly over the lake to them. There was here and there a little knot and a few stragglers a few yards higher up but they were so few as not to disturb the simplicity and unity and life of that one busy highway. We rested again and again. The bays were stormy and we heard the waves at different distances and in the middle of the water like the sea—rain came on, we were wet when we reached Luffs but we called in. Luckily all was cheerless and gloomy so we faced the storm—we *must* have been wet if we had waited—put on dry clothes at Dobson's. I was very kindly treated by a young woman, the landlady looked sour but it is her way. She gave us a goodish supper, excellent ham and potatoes. We paid 7/ when we came away. William was sitting by a bright fire when I came downstairs. He soon made his way to the library piled up in a corner of the window. He brought out a volume of Enfield's Speaker,[1] another miscellany, and an odd volume of Congreve's plays.[2] We had a glass of warm rum and water—we enjoyed ourselves and wished for Mary. It rained and blew when we went to bed. NB deer in Gowbarrow park like to skeletons.

[May]

Tuesday May 4th William had slept pretty well and though he went to bed nervous and jaded in the extreme, he rose refreshed. I wrote the Leech Gatherer[3] for him which he had begun the night before and of which he wrote several stanzas in bed this Monday morning. It was very hot, we called at Mr. Simpson's door as we passed but did not go in. We rested several times by the way, read and repeated the Leech Gatherer. We were almost melted before we ere at the top of the hill. We saw Coleridge on the Wytheburn side of the water, he crossed the beck[4] to us. Mr. Simpson was fishing there. William and I ate a luncheon, then went on towards the waterfall. It is a glorious wild solitude under that lofty purple crag. It stood upright by itself. Its own self and its shadow below, one mass—all else was sunshine. We went on further. A bird at the top of the crags was flying round and round and looked in thinness and transparency, shape and motion, like a moth. We climbed the hill but looked in vain for a shade except at the foot of the great waterfall, and there we did not like to stay on account of the loose stones above our heads. We came down and rested upon a moss covered rock, rising out of the bed of the river. There we lay ate our dinner and stayed there till about 4 o'clock or later—Wm. and C. repeated and read verses. I drank a little brandy and water and was in heaven. The stag's horn is very beautiful and fresh springing upon the fells. Mountain ashes, green. We drank tea at a farm house. The woman had not a pleasant countenance, but was civil enough. She had a pretty boy a year old whom she suckled. We parted from Coleridge at Sara's crag after having looked at the letters which C. carved in the morning. I kissed them all. Wm. deepened the T with C's penknife. We sat afterwards on the wall, seeing the sun go down and the reflections in the still water. C. looked well and parted from us cheerfully, hopping up upon the side stones. On the rays we met a woman with 2 little girls one in her arms the other about 4 years old walking by

[1] *Enfield's Speaker* William Enfield's *The Speaker; or Miscellaneous Pieces, selected from the Best English Writers.*

[2] *Congreve's plays* Plays of William Congreve (1670–1729).

[3] *wrote the Leech Gatherer* Transcribed William's poem "Resolution and Independence."

[4] *beck* Stream.

her side, a pretty little thing, but half starved. She had on a pair of slippers that had belonged to some gentleman's child, down at the heels, but it was not easy to keep them on—but, poor thing! young as she was, she walked carefully with them. Alas too young for such cares and such travels. The mother when we accosted her told us that her husband had left her and gone off with another woman and how she "*pursued*" them. Then her fury kindled and her eyes rolled about. She changed again to tears. She was a Cockermouth woman—30 years of age a child at Cockermouth when I was—I was moved and gave her a shilling, I believe 6^{d} more than I ought to have given. We had the crescent moon with the "auld moon in her arms"[1]—We rested often:—always upon the bridges. Reached home at about 10 o'clock. The Lloyds had been here in our absence. We went soon to bed. I repeated verses to William while he was in bed—he was soothed and I left him. "This is the Spot"[2] over and over again.

[July]

Tuesday 26th Market day streets dirty, very rainy, did not leave Hull till 4 o'clock, and left Barton at about 6—rained all the way—almost—a beautiful village at the foot of a hill with trees—a gentleman's house converted into a lady's boarding school. We had a woman in bad health in the coach, and took in a lady and her daughter—supped at Lincoln. Duck and peas, and cream cheese—paid 2/-. We left Lincoln on Wednesday morning 27th July at six o'clock it rained heavily and we could see nothing but the ancientry of some of the buildings as we passed along. The night before, however, we had seen enough to make us regret this. The minster[3] stands at the edge of a hill, overlooking an immense plain. The country very flat as we went along—the day mended—We went to see the outside of the minster while the passengers were dining at Peterborough—the west end very grand. The little girl who was a great scholar, and plainly her mothers favorite though she had a large family at home had bought The Farmer's Boy.[4] She said it was written by a man without education and was very wonderful.

On Thursday morning, 29th, we arrived in London. Wm. left me at the inn—I went to bed &c. &c. &c. After various troubles and disasters we left London on Saturday morning at ½ past 5 or 6, the 31st of July (I have forgot which) we mounted the Dover coach at Charing Cross. It was a beautiful morning. The city, St. Paul's, with the river and a multitude of little boats, made a most beautiful sight as we crossed Westminster Bridge. The houses were not overhung by their cloud of smoke and they were spread out endlessly, yet the sun shone so brightly with such a pure light that there was even something like the purity of one of nature's own grand spectacles. We rode on cheerfully now with the Paris Diligence[5] before us, now behind—we walked up the steep hills, beautiful prospects everywhere, till we even reached Dover. At first the rich populous wide spreading woody country about London, then the river Thames, ships sailing, chalk cliffs, trees, little villages. Afterwards Canterbury, situated on a plain, rich and woody, but the city and cathedral disappointed me. Hop grounds on each side of the road some miles from Canterbury, then we came to a common, the race ground, an elevated plain, villages among trees in the bed of a valley at our right, and rising above this valley, green hills scattered over with wood—neat gentlemen's houses—one white house almost hid with green trees which we longed for and the parsons house as neat a place as could be which would just have suited Coleridge. No doubt we might have found one for Tom Hutchinson and Sara and a good farm too. We halted at a halfway house—fruit carts under the shade of trees, seats for guests, a tempting place to the weary traveller. Still as we went along the country was beautiful, hilly, with cottages lurking under the hills and their little plots of hop ground like vineyards. It was a bad hop-year—a woman on the top of the coach said to me "it is a sad thing for the poor people for the hop-gathering is the women's harvest, there is employment about the hops both for women and children." We saw the castle of Dover and the sea beyond four or five miles before we reached D. We looked at it through a long vale, the

1 *"auld moon in her arms"* From the popular ballad "Sir Patrick Spens"; Coleridge also quoted this line in "Dejection: An Ode."

2 *"This is the Spot"* From a poem by Dorothy Wordsworth, never published in her lifetime.

3 *minster* Monastery church.

4 *The Farmer's Boy* By Robert Bloomfield.

5 *Diligence* Coach.

castle being upon an eminence, as it seemed at the end of this vale which opened to the sea. The country now became less fertile but near Dover it seemed more rich again. Many buildings stand on the flat fields, sheltered with tall trees. There is one old chapel that might have been there just in the same state in which it now is, when this vale was as retired and as little known to travellers, as our own Cumberland mountain wilds 30 years ago. There was also a very old building on the other side of the road which had a strange effect among the many new ones that are springing up everywhere. It seemed odd that it could have kept itself pure in its ancientry among so many upstarts. It was near dark when we reached Dover. We were told that the packet[1] was about to sail, so we went down to the Customhouse in half an hour, had our luggage examined &c. &c. and then we drank tea, with the honorable Mr. Knox and his tutor. We arrived at Calais at 4 o'clock on Sunday morning the 31st of July. We stayed in the vessel till ½ past 7. Then Wm. went for letters, at about ½ past 8 or 9. We found out Annette and C.[2] chez Madame Avril dans la Rue de la Tête d'or. We lodged opposite two ladies in tolerably decent-sized rooms but badly furnished, and with large store of bad smells and dirt in the yard, and all about. The weather was very hot. We walked by the seashore almost every evening with Annette and Caroline or Wm. and I alone. I had a bad cold and could not bathe at first but William did. It was a pretty sight to see as we walked upon the sands when the tide was low, perhaps a hundred people bathing about ¼ of a mile distant from us, and we had delightful walks after the heat of the day was passed away—seeing far off in the west the coast of England like a cloud crested with Dover Castle, which was but like the summit of the cloud—the evening star and the glory of the sky. The reflections in the water were more beautiful than the sky itself, purple waves brighter than precious stones forever melting away upon the sands. The fort, a wooden building, at the entrance of the harbour at Calais, when the evening twilight was coming on, and we could not see anything of the building but its shape which was far more distinct than in perfect daylight, seemed to be reared upon pillars of ebony, between which pillars the sea was seen in the most beautiful colours that can be conceived. Nothing in romance was ever half so beautiful. Now came in view as the evening star sank down and the colours of the west faded away the two lights of England, lighted up by Englishmen in our country, to warn vessels of rocks or sands. These we used to see from the pier when we could see no other distant objects but the clouds the sky and the sea itself. All was dark behind. The town of Calais seemed deserted of the light of heaven, but there was always light, and life, and joy upon the sea. One night, though, I shall never forget, the day had been very hot, and William and I walked alone together upon the pier—the sea was gloomy for there was a blackness over all the sky except when it was overspread with lightning which often revealed to us a distant vessel. Near us the waves roared and broke against the pier, and as they broke and as they travelled towards us, they were interfused with greenish fiery light. The more distant sea always black and gloomy. It was, also beautiful on the calm hot nights to see the little Boats row out of harbour with wings of fire and the sail boats with the fiery track which they cut as they went along and which closed up after them with a hundred thousand sparkles balls shootings, and streams of glowworm light. Caroline was delighted.

On Sunday the 29th of August we left Calais at 12 o'clock in the morning and landed at Dover at 1 on Monday the 30th. I was sick all the way. It was very pleasant to me when we were in harbour at Dover to breathe the fresh air, and to look up and see the stars among the ropes of the vessel. The next day was very hot. We both bathed and sat upon the Dover cliffs and looked upon France with many a melancholy and tender thought. We could see the shores almost as plain as if it were but an English lake. We mounted the coach at ½ past 4 and arrived in London at 6 the 30th August. It was misty and we could see nothing. We stayed in London till Wednesday the 22nd of September, and arrived at Gallow Hill on Friday 24th September. Mary first met us in the avenue. She looked so fat and well that we were made very happy by the sight of her—then came Sara, and last of all Joanna. Tom was forking corn[3]

[1] *packet* Boat originally used to carry mail (packets).

[2] *Annette and C.* Annette Vallon, with whom William Wordsworth had had an affair when he visited France in his youth, and their daughter, Caroline.

[3] *corn* Grain.

standing upon the corn cart. We dressed ourselves immediately and got tea—the garden looked gay with asters and sweet peas—I looked at everything with tranquillity and happiness but I was ill both on Saturday and Sunday and continued to be poorly most of the time of our stay. Jack and George came on Friday evening 1st October. On Saturday 2nd we rode to Hackness, William Jack George and Sara single, I behind Tom.[1] On Sunday 3rd Mary and Sara were busy packing. On Monday 4th October 1802, my brother William was married to Mary Hutchinson. I slept a good deal of the night and rose fresh and well in the morning—at a little after 8 o'clock I saw them go down the avenue towards the church. William had parted from me upstairs. I gave him the wedding ring—with how deep a blessing! I took it from my forefinger where I had worn it the whole of the night before—he slipped it again onto my finger and blessed me fervently. When they were absent my dear little Sara prepared the breakfast. I kept myself as quiet as I could, but when I saw the two men running up the walk, coming to tell us it was over, I could stand it no longer and threw myself on the bed where I lay in stillness, neither hearing or seeing anything, till Sara came upstairs to me and said "They are coming." This forced me from the bed where I lay and I moved I knew not how straight forward, faster than my strength could carry me till I met my beloved William and fell upon his bosom. He and John Hutchinson led me to the house and there I stayed to welcome my dear Mary. As soon as we had breakfasted we departed. It rained when we set off. Poor Mary was much agitated when she parted from her brothers and sisters and her home. Nothing particular occurred till we reached Kirby. We had sunshine and showers, pleasant talk, love and cheerfulness. We were obliged to stay two hours at K. while the horses were feeding. We wrote a few lines to Sara and then walked out, the sun shone and we went to the churchyard, after we had put a letter into the post office for the York Herald. We sauntered about and read the gravestones. There was one to the memory of 5 children, who had all died within 5 years, and the longest lived had only lived 4 years. There was another stone erected to the memory of an unfortunate woman (as we supposed, by a stranger). The verses engraved upon it expressed that she had been neglected by her relations and counselled the readers of those words to look within and recollect their own frailties. We left Kirby at about ½ past 2. There is not much variety of prospect from K. to Helmsely but the country is very pleasant, being rich and woody, and Helmsely itself stands very sweetly at the foot of the rising grounds of Duncombe Park which is scattered over with tall woods and lifting itself above the common buildings of the town stands Helmsely Castle, now a ruin, formerly inhabited by the gay Duke of Buckingham. Every foot of the road was, of itself interesting to us, for we had travelled along it on foot Wm. and I when we went to fetch our dear Mary, and had sat upon the turf by the roadside more than once. Before we reached Helmsely our driver told us that he could not take us any further, so we stopped at the same inn where we had slept before. My heart danced at the sight of its cleanly outside, bright yellow walls, casements overshadowed with jasmine and its low, double gavel-ended front. We were not shown into the same parlour where Wm. and I were, it was a small room with a drawing over the chimney piece which the woman told us had been bought at a sale. Mary and I warmed ourselves at the kitchen fire—we then walked into the garden, and looked over a gate up to the old ruin which stands at the top of a mount, and round about it the moats are grown up into soft green cradles, hollows surrounded with green grassy hillocks and these are overshadowed by old trees, chiefly ashes. I prevailed upon William to go up with me to the ruins. We left Mary sitting by the kitchen fire. The sun shone, it was warm and very pleasant. One part of the castle seems to be inhabited. There was a man mowing nettles in the open space which had most likely once been the castle court. There is one gateway exceedingly beautiful—children were playing upon the sloping ground. We came home by the street. After about an hour's delay we set forward again, had an excellent driver who opened the gates so dexterously that the horses never stopped. Mary was very much delighted with the view of the castle from the point where we had seen it before. I was pleased to see again the little path which we had walked upon, the gate I had climbed over, and the road down which we had seen the two little boys drag a log of wood, and a team

[1] *Jack George and Sara ... Tom* Mary Hutchinson's siblings.

of horses struggle under the weight of a great load of timber. We had felt compassion for the poor horses that were under the governance of oppressive and ill-judging drivers, and for the poor boys who seemed of an age to have been able to have dragged the log of wood merely out of the love of their own activity, but from poverty and bad food they panted for weakness and were obliged to fetch their father from the town to help them. Duncombe House looks well from the road—a large building, though I believe only 2 thirds of the original design are completed. We rode down a very steep hill to Ryvaux valley, with woods all round us. We stopped upon the bridge to look at the abbey and again when we had crossed it. Dear Mary had never seen a ruined abbey before except Whitby. We recognized the cottages, houses, and the little valleys as we went along. We walked up a long hill, the road carrying us up the cleft or valley with woody hills on each side of us. When we *went* to G.H.[1] I had walked down this valley alone. Wm. followed me. It was not dark evening when we passed the little public house,[2] but before we had crossed the Hambledon hills and reached the point overlooking Yorkshire it was quite dark. We had not wanted, however, fair prospects before us, as we drove along the flat plain of the high hill, far far off us, in the western sky, we saw shapes of castles, ruins among groves, a great, spreading wood, rocks, and single trees, a minster with its tower unusually distinct, minarets in another quarter, and a round Grecian temple also—the colours of the sky of a bright grey and the forms of a sober grey, with a dome. As we descended the hill there was no distinct view, but of a great space, only near us, we saw the wild and (as the people say) bottomless tarn in the hollow at the side of the hill. It seemed to be made visible to us only by its own light, for all the hill about us was dark. Before we reached Thirsk we saw a light before us which we at first thought was the moon, then lime kilns, but when we drove into the market place it proved a large bonfire with lads dancing round it, which is a sight I dearly love. The inn was like an illuminated house—every room full. We asked the cause, and were told by the girl that it was "Mr. John Bell's Birthday, that he had heired his estate." The landlady was very civil. She did not recognise the despised foot-travellers. We rode nicely in the dark, and reached Leming Lane at 11 o'clock. I am always sorry to get out of a chaise when it is night. The people of the house were going to bed and we were not very well treated though we got a hot supper. We breakfasted the next morning and set off at about ½ past 8 o'clock. It was a cheerful sunny morning. We soon turned out of Leming Lane and passed a nice village with a beautiful church. We had a few showers, but when we came to the green fields of Wensley, the sun shone upon them all, and the Eure in its many windings glittered as it flowed along under the green slopes of Middleham and Middleham Castle. Mary looked about for her friend Mr. Place, and thought she had him sure on the contrary side of the vale from that on which we afterwards found that he lived. We went to a new built house at Leyburn, the same village where Wm. and I had dined with George Hutchinson on our road to Grasmere 2 years and ¾ ago, but not the same house. The landlady was very civil, giving us cake and wine but the horses being out we were detained at least 2 hours and did not set off till 2 o'clock. We paid for 35 miles, i.e. to Sedbergh, but the landlady did not encourage us to hope to get beyond Hawes. A shower came on just after we left the inn. While the rain beat against the windows we ate our dinners which M. and W. heartily enjoyed—I was not quite well. When we passed through the village of Wensly my heart was melted away with dear recollections, the bridge, the little waterspout the steep hill the church. They are among the most vivid of my own inner visions, for they were the first objects that I saw after we were left to ourselves, and had turned our whole hearts to Grasmere as a home in which we were to rest. The vale looked most beautiful each way. To the left the bright silver stream inlaid the flat and very green meadows, winding like a serpent. To the right we did not see it so far, it was lost among trees and little hills. I could not help observing as we went along how much more *varied* the prospects of Wensley Dale are in the summer time than I could have thought possible in the winter. This seemed to be in great measure owing to the trees being in leaf, and forming groves, and screens, and thence little openings upon recesses and concealed retreats which in winter only made a part of the one

[1] *G.H.* George Hutchinson.

[2] *public house* Tavern.

great vale. The *beauty* of the summertime here as much excels that of the winter as the variety, owing to the excessive greenness of the fields, and the trees in leaf half concealing, and where they do not conceal, softening the hard bareness of the limey white roofs. One of our horses seemed to grow a little restive as we went through the first village, a long village on the side of a hill. It grew worse and worse, and at last we durst not go on any longer. We walked a while, and then the post-boy[1] was obliged to take the horse out and go back for another. We seated ourselves again snugly in the post chaise. The wind struggled about us and rattled the window and gave a gentle motion to the chaise, but we were warm and at our ease within. Our station was at the top of a hill, opposite Bolton Castle, the Eure flowing beneath. William has since wrote a sonnet on this our imprisonment—Hard was thy durance Queen compared with ours.[2] Poor Mary! Wm. fell asleep, lying upon my breast and I upon Mary. I lay motionless for a long time, but I was at last obliged to move. I became very sick and continued so for some time after the boy brought the horse to us. Mary had been a little sick but it soon went off. We had a sweet ride till we came to a public house on the side of a hill where we alighted and walked down to see the waterfalls. The sun was not set, and the woods and fields were spread over with the yellow light of evening, which made their greenness a thousand times more green. There was too much water in the river for the beauty of the falls, and even the banks were less interesting than in winter. Nature had entirely got the better in her struggles against the giants who first cast the mould of these works; for indeed it is a place that did not in winter remind one of God, but one could not help feeling as if there had been the agency of some "Mortal Instruments"[3] which nature had been struggling against without making a perfect conquest. There was something so wild and new in this feeling, knowing as we did in the inner man that God alone had laid his hand upon it that I could not help regretting the want of it, besides it is a pleasure to a real lover of nature to give winter all the glory he can, for summer *will* make its own way, and speak its own praises. We saw the pathway which Wm. and I took at the close of evening, the path leading to the rabbit warren where we lost ourselves. The farm with its holly hedges was lost among the green hills and hedgerows in general, but we found it out and were glad to look at it again. When William had left us to seek the waterfalls Mary and I were frightened by a cow. At our return to the inn we found new horses and a new driver, and we went on nicely to Hawes where we arrived before it was quite dark. Mary and I got tea, and William had a partridge and mutton chops and tarts for his supper. Mary sat down with him. We had also a shilling's worth of negus[4] and Mary made me some broth for all which supper we were only charged 2/-. I could not sit up long. I vomited, and took the broth and then slept sweetly. We rose at 6 o'clock—a rainy morning. We had a good breakfast and then departed. There was a very pretty view about a mile from Hawes, where we crossed a bridge, bare, and very green fields with cattle, a glittering stream cottages, a few ill-grown trees, and high hills. The sun shone now. Before we got upon the bare hills there was a hunting lodge on our right exactly like Greta Hill, with fir plantations about it. We were very fortunate in the day, gleams of sunshine passing clouds, that travelled with their shadows below them. Mary was much pleased with Garsdale. It was a dear place to William and me. We noted well the public-house (Garsdale Hall) where we had baited and drunk our pint of ale, and afterwards the mountain which had been adorned by Jupiter[5] in his glory when we were here before. It was midday when we reached Sedbergh, and *market* day. We were in the same room where we had spent the evening together in our road to Grasmere. We had a pleasant ride to Kendal, where we arrived at about 2 o'clock—the day favored us—M. and I went to see the house where dear Sara had lived, then went to seek Mr. Bousfield's shop but we found him not—he had sold all his goods the day before. We then went to the

[1] *post-boy* Boy who "rides post," i.e., a person who rides the leading horse and acts as guide or coachman.

[2] *Hard … with ours* Mary, Queen of Scots was imprisoned at Bolton Castle for six months in 1568–69. In 1817 William Wordsworth published "Lament of Mary Queen of Scots: On the Eve of a New Year," which dealt with the queen's imprisonment and execution.

[3] *"Mortal Instruments"* From Shakespeare's *Julius Caesar* 2.1 and W. Wordsworth's *The Borderers* 2.3.

[4] *negus* Hot drink made with wine or port.

[5] *Jupiter* Supreme Roman deity.

pot woman's and bought 2 jugs and a dish, and some paper at Pennington's. When we came to the inn William was almost ready for us. The afternoon was not cheerful but it did not rain till we came near Windermere. I am always glad to see Stavely. It is a place I dearly love to think of—the first mountain village that I came to with Wm. when we first began our pilgrimage together. Here we drank a bason of milk at a public house, and here I washed my feet in the brook and put on a pair of silk stockings by Wm's advice. Nothing particular occurred till we reached Ing's chapel—the door was open and we went in. It is a neat little place, with a marble floor and marble communion table with a painting over it of the last supper, and Moses and Aaron on each side. The woman told us that "they had painted them as near as they could by the dresses as they are described in the Bible," and gay enough they are. The marble had been sent by Richard Bateman from Leghorn. The woman told us that a man had been at her house a few days before who told her he had helped to bring it down the Red Sea and she had believed him gladly. It rained very hard when we reached Windermere. We sat in the rain at Wilcock's to change horses, and arrived at Grasmere at about 6 o'clock on Wednesday Evening, the 6th of October 1802. Molly was overjoyed to see us,—for my part I cannot describe what I felt, and our dear Mary's feelings would I dare say not be easy to speak of. We went by candle light into the garden and were astonished at the growth of the brooms, Portugal laurels, &c. &c. &c.—The next day, Thursday, we unpacked the boxes. On Friday 8th we baked bread, and Mary and I walked, first upon the hill side, and then in John's Grove, then in view of Rydale, the first walk that I had taken with my sister.

—1897 (WRITTEN 1800–02)

Grasmere—A Fragment

Peaceful our valley, fair and green,
And beautiful her cottages,
Each in its nook, its sheltered hold,
Or underneath its tuft of trees
Many and beautiful they are;
But there is *one* that I love best,
A lowly shed, in truth, it is,
A brother of the rest.

Yet when I sit on rock or hill,
Down looking on the valley fair,
That cottage with its clustering trees
Summons my heart; it settles there.

Others there are whose small domain
Of fertile fields and hedgerows green
Might more seduce a wanderer's mind
To wish that *there* his home had been.

Such wish be his! I blame him not,
My fancies they perchance are wild
—I love that house because it is
The very mountains' child.

Fields hath it of its own, green fields,
But they are rocky steep and bare;
Their fence is of the mountain stone,
And moss and lichen flourish there.

And when the storm comes from the north
It lingers near that pastoral spot,
And, piping through the mossy walls,
It seems delighted with its lot.

And let it take its own delight;
And let it range the pastures bare;
Until it reach that group of trees,
—It may not enter there!

A green unfading grove it is,
Skirted with many a lesser tree,
Hazel and holly, beech and oak,
A bright and flourishing company.

Precious the shelter of those trees;
They screen the cottage that I love;

The sunshine pierces to the roof,
And the tall pine-trees tower above.

When first I saw that dear abode,
It was a lovely winter's day:
After a night of perilous storm
The west wind ruled with gentle sway;

A day so mild, it might have been
The first day of the gladsome spring;
The robins warbled, and I heard
One solitary throstle° sing. *song thrush*

A stranger, Grasmere, in thy vale,
All faces then to me unknown,
I left my sole companion-friend
To wander out alone.

Lured by a little winding path,
I quitted soon the public road,
A smooth and tempting path it was,
By sheep and shepherds trod.

Eastward, towards the lofty hills,
This pathway led me on
Until I reached a stately rock,
With velvet moss o'ergrown.

With russet oak and tufts of fern
Its top was richly garlanded;
Its sides adorned with eglantine° *fragrant rose*
Bedropped with hips° of glossy red. *rose berries*

There, too, in many a sheltered chink
The foxglove's broad leaves flourished fair,
And silver birch whose purple twigs
Bend to the softest breathing air.

Beneath that rock my course I stayed,
And, looking to its summit high,
"Thou wear'st," said I, "a splendid garb,
Here winter keeps his revelry."

"Full long a dweller on the plains,
I grieved when summer days were gone;
No more I'll grieve; for Winter here
Hath pleasure gardens of his own.

What need of flowers? The splendid moss
Is gayer than an April mead°; *meadow*
More rich its hues of various green,
Orange, and gold, and glittering red."

—Beside that gay and lovely rock
There came with merry voice
A foaming streamlet glancing by;
It seemed to say "Rejoice!"

My youthful wishes all fulfilled,
Wishes matured by thoughtful choice,
I stood an inmate of this vale
How *could* I but rejoice?

—1892 (WRITTEN 1805)

Thoughts on My Sick-bed

And has the remnant of my life
Been pilfered of this sunny spring?
And have its own prelusive° sounds *introductory*
Touched in my heart no echoing string?

Ah! say not so—the hidden life
Couchant° within this feeble frame *lying*
Hath been enriched by kindred gifts,
That, undesired, unsought-for, came

With joyful heart in youthful days
When fresh each season in its round
I welcomed the earliest celandine° *yellow flower*
Glittering upon the mossy ground;

With busy eyes I pierced the lane
In quest of known and *un*known things,

—The primrose a lamp on its fortress rock,
The silent butterfly spreading its wings,

The violet betrayed by its noiseless breath,
The daffodil dancing in the breeze,
The carolling thrush, on his naked perch,
Towering above the budding trees.

Our cottage-hearth no longer our home,
Companions of nature were we,
The stirring, the still, the loquacious, the mute—
To all we gave our sympathy.

Yet never in those careless days
When spring-time in rock, field, or bower
Was but a fountain of earthly hope
A promise of fruits and the *splendid* flower.

No! then I never felt a bliss
That might with *that* compare
Which, piercing to my couch of rest,
Came on the vernal° air. *springtime*

When loving friends an offering brought,
The first flowers of the year,
Culled from the precincts of our home,
From nooks to memory dear.

With some sad thoughts the work was done,
Unprompted and unbidden,
But joy it brought to my *hidden* life,
To consciousness no longer hidden.

I felt a power unfelt before,
Controlling weakness, languor, pain;
It bore me to the terrace walk
I trod the hills again;—

No prisoner in this lonely room,
I *saw* the green banks of the Wye,
Recalling thy prophetic words,
Bard, brother, friend from infancy![1]

No need of motion, or of strength,
Or even the breathing air:
—I thought of nature's loveliest scenes;
And with memory I was there.

—1978 (WRITTEN 1832)

[1] *recalling … infancy* Wordsworth is referring to her brother William's poem "Lines Composed a Few Miles above Tintern Abbey."

Samuel Taylor Coleridge

1772 – 1834

Samuel Taylor Coleridge is one of the most important figures of English Romanticism. Over the course of a few years, when in his mid-twenties, he composed poems that continue to be regarded as central to the English canon, among them "The Rime of the Ancient Mariner," "Frost at Midnight," and the fragment "Kubla Khan." Hhe wrote few poems for the last thirty-five years of his life, as he was undermined by procrastination and an addiction to opium. Nonetheless, Coleridge's story is in the end one of success. His poetry has remained fresh and affecting for generations of readers, and his later philosophical writing earned him a place as one of the most profound thinkers of the nineteenth century.

Born in 1772, Coleridge was the youngest son of the vicar of Ottery St. Mary, the Rev. John Coleridge, and his wife, Anna Bowdon. He was a voracious reader with a mind that he described as "habituated to *the Vast*." When his father died, his mother arranged for nine-year-old Samuel to be sent to Christ's Hospital in London, a school founded to educate the promising sons of the poor. Although he received an excellent education at Christ's, Coleridge remained ambivalent about the school long after he left, continuing to feel injured by the fact that he had been a "charity boy."

In 1791, Coleridge entered Jesus College, Cambridge, where his intellectual abilities and academic success were matched only by his facility in running up debts and his increasing despair at his financial situation. He eventually attempted to escape his financial problems by enlisting (under the name Silas Tomkyn Comberbache), but he was rescued by his brother George from both the army and financial distress. In 1794 he met Robert Southey, then an Oxford undergraduate, and the two recognized a shared interest in poetry and radical political ideas. They hatched a plan to found a communitarian settlement in Pennsylvania to be run under a system they called "Pantisocracy." Both the plan and the friendship, however, foundered over the question of what role women and servants should play (Coleridge insisted on a completely egalitarian community; Southey did not). In his early exuberance for the scheme Coleridge became engaged to Sara Fricker, the sister of Southey's fiancée, and he felt bound to honor the commitment even though his feeling for her quickly waned. They married in 1795 but after a brief period of happiness they became progressively more miserable, finally separating in 1807. The marriage produced four children.

Coleridge began a short-lived liberal periodical in 1796 called *The Watchman.* He also published his first poetic collection, *Poems on Various Subjects*, which contained the poem that would later be titled "The Eolian Harp." Almost destitute, he was saved by a yearly pension granted him by Tom and Josiah Wedgwood, sons of the famous potter. The following year he met William Wordsworth and began a troubled but lifelong friendship, the first fruit of which was the joint volume *Lyrical Ballads,* which opened with Coleridge's "The Rime of the Ancyent Marinere" (revised and retitled in 1816). Shortly afterward he accompanied Wordsworth and his sister Dorothy to Germany, where he immersed himself in German philosophy.

Returning to England in 1799, Coleridge joined Wordsworth in the Lake District. Here he met Sara Hutchinson, Wordsworth's future sister-in-law, and became infatuated with her. The relationship between the two remained platonic, but it magnified Coleridge's estrangement from his wife, and the situation was made worse by his increasing dependence on laudanum, the liquid form of opium. From 1802 onward Coleridge spent only brief periods with his family. In 1804 he set off for Malta, where he took a post in the British government. From this time forth he became progressively more conservative, eventually going so far as to deny entirely his early liberal leanings. After a year and a half he returned to England penniless.

From 1808 to 1818, Coleridge intermittently delivered lectures with topics that ranged from German philosophy to current educational controversies. The highlight was a series he gave on Shakespeare and Milton, which displayed all the brilliance of his critical skills. Although frequently sidetracked onto other topics, he also offered incisive analyses of aspects of Shakespeare's plays, from a consideration of love in *Romeo and Juliet* to an anatomization of Hamlet's paradoxical psychology. He ended the series with a masterful examination of *Paradise Lost*.

Coleridge's great talents as a poet lay in his ability to combine Gothicism with complex psychological presentation and to delineate the mind as it explored itself and its relation to the larger world. His more uncanny poems, such as "The Rime of the Ancient Mariner," are haunting both because they excite tension in the reader and because the psychological complexity of the characters and relationships brings to life what might otherwise be clichéd sensationalism. Poems such as "Frost at Midnight" mingle contemplation and description to produce a richly interrelated whole, a style which influenced not only Wordsworth (specifically in "Tintern Abbey"), but poets to the present day.

From the first Coleridge was interested in newspaper writing, in which he could comment on immediate social and cultural issues. The most important of his journalistic ventures was *The Friend* (1809–10), a weekly newspaper he largely wrote himself. In 1813 his drama, *Remorse,* was staged at the Drury Lane Theatre. Three years later he took up residence in Highgate with the family of the young doctor James Gillman. He asked to stay for a month; he remained for the rest of his life. The situation offered a stable environment, and Coleridge began publishing regularly. His Gothic ballad ,"Christabel," long known to other writers through private recitation (and an influence on Walter Scott's "The Lay of the Last Minstrel" and Lord Byron's "The Siege of Corinth"), was published in a collection with "Kubla Khan" and "The Pains of Sleep" in 1816, through Byron's enthusiastic support. Soon afterward Coleridge published *Sybilline Leaves*, a collection of his previous poems (including a newly revised *Ancient Mariner* with a marginal gloss) and the long work *Biographia Literaria*.

Although at times rambling and discursive, *Biographia Literaria* is a major literary and philosophical work. Its first volume is autobiographical, detailing (among other events) Coleridge's education and his first involvement with Wordsworth. This volume also begins to delve into literary analysis as, for example, in the famous passage in Chapter 13, in which Coleridge differentiates between imagination and fancy, defining the qualities of each and declaring imagination superior. The second volume consists almost entirely of literary criticism, both formal and philosophical, much of it focusing on Wordsworth's poetry. In both volumes, Coleridge anatomizes both poetry and poetic production, considering not only formal elements but also the psychology of the creative process.

Coleridge's genius and importance were gradually acknowledged by a considerable number of his contemporaries, and the "Sage of Highgate" began to be viewed as an important thinker. This opinion was cemented by the publication of *Aids to Reflection* (1825), which stressed the role of the personal in Christian faith, and *On the Constitution of Church and State* (1830), which emphasized the importance of national culture and defined the class of intellectuals needed to protect it. This latter book in particular had a profound influence on such authors as Matthew Arnold and Thomas Carlyle.

From 1832 onward Coleridge became increasingly ill, although this did not prevent him from helping to prepare *Poetical Works* (1834), a collection of his poetry—he died shortly after its publication. *Table Talk*, a posthumously-published collection of his remarks on miscellaneous topics, appeared the following year.

⌘⌘⌘

The Eolian Harp[1]

Composed at Clevedon, Somersetshire

My pensive Sara![2] thy soft cheek reclined
Thus on mine arm, most soothing sweet it is
To sit beside our Cot,° our Cot o'ergrown *cottage*
With white-flower'd Jasmin, and the broad-leav'd Myrtle,
(Meet emblems they of Innocence and Love!)
And watch the clouds, that late were rich with light,
Slow saddening round, and mark the star of eve
Serenely brilliant (such should Wisdom be)
Shine opposite! How exquisite the scents
Snatch'd from yon bean-field! and the world *so* hush'd!
The stilly murmur of the distant Sea
Tells us of silence.

And that simplest Lute,
Placed length-ways in the clasping casement, hark!
How by the desultory breeze caress'd,
Like some coy maid half yielding to her lover,
It pours such sweet upbraiding, as must needs
Tempt to repeat the wrong! And now, its strings
Boldlier swept, the long sequacious° notes *unvarying*
Over delicious surges sink and rise,
Such a soft floating witchery of sound
As twilight Elfins make, when they at eve
Voyage on gentle gales from Fairy-Land,
Where Melodies round honey-dropping flowers,
Footless and wild, like birds of Paradise,[3]
Nor pause, nor perch, hovering on untam'd wing!
O! the one Life within us and abroad,
Which meets all motion and becomes its soul,
A light in sound, a sound-like power in light,
Rhythm in all thought, and joyance every where—
Methinks, it should have been impossible
Not to love all things in a world so fill'd;
Where the breeze warbles, and the mute still air
Is Music slumbering on her instrument.
And thus, my Love! as on the midway slope
Of yonder hill I stretch my limbs at noon,
Whilst through my half-clos'd eye-lids I behold
The sunbeams dance, like diamonds, on the main,
And tranquil muse upon tranquillity;
Full many a thought uncall'd and undetain'd,
And many idle flitting phantasies,
Traverse my indolent and passive brain,
As wild and various, as the random gales
That swell and flutter on this subject Lute!
And what if all of animated nature
Be but organic Harps diversely fram'd,
That tremble into thought, as o'er them sweeps
Plastic and vast, one intellectual breeze,
At once the Soul of each, and God of all?
But thy more serious eye a mild reproof
Darts, O belovéd Woman! nor such thoughts
Dim and unhallow'd dost thou not reject,
And biddest me walk humbly with my God.
Meek Daughter in the family of Christ!
Well hast thou said and holily disprais'd
These shapings of the unregenerate mind;
Bubbles that glitter as they rise and break
On vain Philosophy's aye-babbling spring.
For never guiltless may I speak of Him,
The Incomprehensible! save when with awe
I praise Him, and with Faith that inly *feels*;
Who with His saving mercies healéd me,
A sinful and most miserable man,
Wilder'd and dark, and gave me to possess
Peace, and this Cot, and thee, heart-honour'd Maid!
—1795

[1] *Eolian Harp* Musical instrument named after Æolus, Greek god of the winds; the music of the harp is created by exposure to the wind passing through it.

[2] *Sara* Sara Fricker, whom Coleridge had recently wed.

[3] *birds of Paradise* New Guinean birds of brilliant plumage, thought by Europeans to have no feet.

Fears In Solitude

Written in April 1798, During the Alarm of An Invasion[4]

A green and silent spot, amid the hills,
A small and silent dell! O'er stiller place

[4] *Invasion* By the French, who threatened an attack on Wales.

No singing sky-lark ever poised himself.
The hills are heathy, save that swelling slope,
Which hath a gay and gorgeous covering on,
All golden with the never-bloomless furze,° *evergreen shrub*
Which now blooms most profusely: but the dell,
Bathed by the mist, is fresh and delicate
As vernal corn-field, or the unripe flax,
When, through its half-transparent stalks, at eve,
The level sunshine glimmers with green light.
O! 'tis a quiet spirit-healing nook!
Which all, methinks, would love; but chiefly he,
The humble man, who, in his youthful years,
Knew just so much of folly, as had made
His early manhood more securely wise!
Here he might lie on fern or withered heath,
While from the singing lark (that sings unseen
The minstrelsy that solitude loves best),
And from the sun, and from the breezy air,
Sweet influences trembled o'er his frame;
And he, with many feelings, many thoughts,
Made up a meditative joy, and found
Religious meanings in the forms of Nature!
And so, his senses gradually wrapt
In a half sleep, he dreams of better worlds,
And dreaming hears thee still, O singing lark,
That singest like an angel in the clouds!

My God! it is a melancholy thing
For such a man, who would full fain preserve
His soul in calmness, yet perforce must feel
For all his human brethren—O my God!
It weighs upon the heart, that he must think
What uproar and what strife may now be stirring
This way or that way o'er these silent hills—
Invasion, and the thunder and the shout,
And all the crash of onset; fear and rage,
And undetermined conflict—even now,
Even now, perchance, and in his native isle:
Carnage and screams beneath this blessed sun!
We have offended, O! my countrymen!
We have offended very grievously,
And have been tyrannous. From east to west
A groan of accusation pierces Heaven!
The wretched plead against us; multitudes
Countless and vehement, the sons of God,
Our brethren! like a cloud that travels on,
Steamed up from Cairo's swamps of pestilence,
Even so, my countrymen! have we gone forth
And borne to distant tribes slavery and pangs,
And, deadlier far, our vices, whose deep taint
With slow perdition murders the whole man,
His body and his soul! Meanwhile, at home,
All individual dignity and power
Engulfed in Courts, Committees, Institutions,
Associations and Societies,
A vain, speech-mounting, speech-reporting Guild,
One Benefit-Club for mutual flattery,
We have drunk up, demure as at a grace,
Pollutions from the brimming cup of wealth;
Contemptuous of all honourable rule,
Yet bartering freedom and the poor man's life
For gold, as at a market! The sweet words
Of Christian promise, words that even yet
Might stem destruction, were they wisely preached,
Are muttered o'er by men, whose tones proclaim
How flat and wearisome they feel their trade:
Rank scoffers some, but most too indolent
To deem them falsehoods, or to know their truth.
O! blasphemous! the Book of Life is made
A superstitious instrument, on which
We gabble o'er the oaths we mean to break,
For all must swear[1]—all and in every place,
College and wharf, council and justice-court;
All, all must swear, the briber and the bribed,
Merchant and lawyer, senator and priest,
The rich, the poor, the old man and the young;
All, all make up one scheme of perjury,
That faith doth reel; the very name of God
Sounds like a juggler's charm; and bold with joy,
Forth from his dark and lonely hiding-place,
(Portentous sight!) the owlet Atheism,
Sailing on obscene wings athwart the noon,
Drops his blue-fringéd lids, and holds them close,
And hooting at the glorious sun in Heaven,
Cries out, "Where is it?"

Thankless too for peace,
(Peace long preserved by fleets and perilous seas)

[1] *all must swear* According to the Test and Corporation Acts, all public officials were required to swear allegiance to the Church of England. (Thus there would be no Catholics, Nonconformists, or Jews in office.)

Secure from actual warfare, we have loved
To swell the war-whoop, passionate for war!
Alas! for ages ignorant of all
Its ghastlier workings, (famine or blue plague,
Battle, or siege, or flight thro' wintry snows,)
We, this whole people, have been clamorous
For war and bloodshed; animating sports,
The which we pay for as a thing to talk of,
Spectators and not combatants! No guess
Anticipative of a wrong unfelt,
No speculation on contingency,
However dim and vague, too vague and dim
To yield a justifying cause; and forth,
(Stuffed out with big preamble, holy names,
And adjurations° of the God in Heaven,) *appeal*
We send our mandates for the certain death
Of thousands and ten thousands! Boys and girls,
And women, that would groan to see a child
Pull off an insect's leg, all read of war,
The best amusement for our morning meal!
The poor wretch, who has learnt his only prayers
From curses, who knows scarcely words enough
To ask a blessing from his Heavenly Father,
Becomes a fluent phraseman, absolute
And technical in victories and defeats,
And all our dainty terms for fratricide;
Terms which we trundle smoothly o'er our tongues
Like mere abstractions, empty sounds to which
We join no feeling and attach no form!
As if the soldier died without a wound;
As if the fibres of this godlike frame
Were gored without a pang; as if the wretch,
Who fell in battle, doing bloody deeds,
Passed off to Heaven, translated and not killed;
As though he had no wife to pine for him,
No God to judge him! Therefore, evil days
Are coming on us, O my countrymen!
And what if all-avenging Providence,
Strong and retributive, should make us know
The meaning of our words, force us to feel
The desolation and the agony
Of our fierce doings?

Spare us yet awhile,
Father and God! O! spare us yet awhile!
Oh! let not English women drag their flight
Fainting beneath the burthen of their babes,
Of the sweet infants, that but yesterday
Laughed at the breast! Sons, brothers, husbands, all
Who ever gazed with fondness on the forms
Which grew up with you round the same fire-side,
And all who ever heard the sabbath-bells
Without the infidel's scorn, make yourselves pure!
Stand forth! be men! repel an impious foe,
Impious and false, a light yet cruel race,
Who laugh away all virtue, mingling mirth
With deeds of murder; and still promising
Freedom, themselves too sensual to be free,
Poison life's amities, and cheat the heart
Of faith and quiet hope, and all that soothes,
And all that lifts the spirit! Stand we forth;
Render them back upon the insulted ocean,
And let them toss as idly on its waves
As the vile sea-weed, which some mountain-blast
Swept from our shores! And oh! may we return
Not with a drunken triumph, but with fear,
Repenting of the wrongs with which we stung
So fierce a foe to frenzy!

I have told,
O Britons! O my brethren! I have told
Most bitter truth, but without bitterness.
Nor deem my zeal or factious or mistimed;
For never can true courage dwell with them,
Who, playing tricks with conscience, dare not look
At their own vices. We have been too long
Dupes of a deep delusion! Some, belike,
Groaning with restless enmity, expect
All change from change of constituted power;
As if a Government had been a robe,
On which our vice and wretchedness were tagged
Like fancy-points and fringes, with the robe
Pulled off at pleasure. Fondly these attach
A radical causation to a few
Poor drudges of chastising Providence,
Who borrow all their hues and qualities
From our own folly and rank wickedness,
Which gave them birth and nursed them. Others, meanwhile,
Dote with a mad idolatry; and all

Who will not fall before their images,
And yield them worship, they are enemies
Even of their country!

Such have I been deemed.—
But, O dear Britain! O my Mother Isle!
Needs must thou prove a name most dear and holy
To me, a son, a brother, and a friend,
A husband, and a father! who revere
All bonds of natural love, and find them all
Within the limits of thy rocky shores.
O native Britain! O my Mother Isle!
How shouldst thou prove aught else but dear and holy
To me, who from thy lakes and mountain-hills,
Thy clouds, thy quiet dales, thy rocks and seas,
Have drunk in all my intellectual life,
All sweet sensations, all ennobling thoughts,
All adoration of the God in nature,
All lovely and all honourable things,
Whatever makes this mortal spirit feel
The joy and greatness of its future being?
There lives nor form nor feeling in my soul
Unborrowed from my country! O divine
And beauteous island! thou hast been my sole
And most magnificent temple, in the which
I walk with awe, and sing my stately songs,
Loving the God that made me!—

May my fears,
My filial fears, be vain! and may the vaunts
And menace of the vengeful enemy
Pass like the gust, that roared and died away
In the distant tree: which heard, and only heard
In this low dell, bowed not the delicate grass.

But now the gentle dew-fall sends abroad
The fruit-like perfume of the golden furze:
The light has left the summit of the hill,
Though still a sunny gleam lies beautiful,
Aslant the ivied beacon. Now farewell,
Farewell, awhile, O soft and silent spot!
On the green sheep-track, up the heathy hill,
Homeward I wind my way; and lo! recalled
From bodings that have well-nigh wearied me,
I find myself upon the brow, and pause
Startled! And after lonely sojourning
In such a quiet and surrounded nook,
This burst of prospect, here the shadowy main,
Dim tinted, there the mighty majesty
Of that huge amphitheatre of rich
And elmy fields, seems like society—
Conversing with the mind, and giving it
A livelier impulse and a dance of thought!
And now, belovéd Stowey![1] I behold
Thy church-tower, and, methinks, the four huge elms
Clustering, which mark the mansion of my friend;
And close behind them, hidden from my view,
Is my own lowly cottage, where my babe
And my babe's mother dwell in peace! With light
And quickened footsteps thitherward I tend,
Remembering thee, O green and silent dell!
And grateful, that by nature's quietness
And solitary musings, all my heart
Is softened, and made worthy to indulge
Love, and the thoughts that yearn for human kind.
—1798

Frost at Midnight

The Frost performs its secret ministry,
Unhelped by any wind. The owlet's cry
Came loud—and hark, again! loud as before.
The inmates of my cottage, all at rest,
Have left me to that solitude, which suits
Abstruser musings: save that at my side
My cradled infant slumbers peacefully.
'Tis calm indeed! so calm, that it disturbs
And vexes meditation with its strange
And extreme silentness. Sea, hill, and wood,
This populous village! Sea, and hill, and wood,
With all the numberless goings-on of life,
Inaudible as dreams! the thin blue flame
Lies on my low-burnt fire, and quivers not;
Only that film,[2] which fluttered on the grate,

[1] *Stowey* Nether Stowey, a village in Somerset where Coleridge lived for a few years.

[2] [Coleridge's note] In all parts of the kingdom these films are called *strangers* and supposed to portend the arrival of some absent friend.

Still flutters there, the sole unquiet thing.
Methinks, its motion in this hush of nature
Gives it dim sympathies with me who live,
Making it a companionable form,
Whose puny flaps and freaks the idling Spirit
By its own moods interprets, every where
Echo or mirror seeking of itself,
And makes a toy of Thought.

But O! how oft,
How oft, at school, with most believing mind,
Presageful, have I gazed upon the bars,
To watch that fluttering *stranger*! and as oft
With unclosed lids, already had I dreamt
Of my sweet birth-place, and the old church-tower,
Whose bells, the poor man's only music, rang
From morn to evening, all the hot Fair-day,
So sweetly, that they stirred and haunted me
With a wild pleasure, falling on mine ear
Most like articulate sounds of things to come!
So gazed I, till the soothing things, I dreamt,
Lulled me to sleep, and sleep prolonged my dreams!
And so I brooded all the following morn,
Awed by the stern preceptor's° face, mine eye *teacher's*
Fixed with mock study on my swimming book:
Save if the door half opened, and I snatched
A hasty glance, and still my heart leaped up,
For still I hoped to see the *stranger's* face,
Townsman, or aunt, or sister more beloved,
My play-mate when we both were clothed alike!

Dear Babe, that sleepest cradled by my side,
Whose gentle breathings, heard in this deep calm,
Fill up the interspersèd vacancies
And momentary pauses of the thought!
My babe so beautiful! it thrills my heart
With tender gladness, thus to look at thee,
And think that thou shalt learn far other lore,
And in far other scenes! For I was reared
In the great city, pent 'mid cloisters dim,
And saw nought lovely but the sky and stars.
But *thou*, my babe! shalt wander like a breeze
By lakes and sandy shores, beneath the crags
Of ancient mountain, and beneath the clouds,
Which image in their bulk both lakes and shores
And mountain crags: so shalt thou see and hear
The lovely shapes and sounds intelligible
Of that eternal language, which thy God
Utters, who from eternity doth teach
Himself in all, and all things in himself.
Great universal Teacher! he shall mould
Thy spirit, and by giving make it ask.

Therefore all seasons shall be sweet to thee,
Whether the summer clothe the general earth
With greenness, or the redbreast sit and sing
Betwixt the tufts of snow on the bare branch
Of mossy apple-tree, while the nigh thatch
Smokes in the sun-thaw; whether the eave-drops fall
Heard only in the trances of the blast,
Or if the secret ministry of frost
Shall hang them up in silent icicles,
Quietly shining to the quiet Moon.
—1798

from *The Rime of the Ancyent Marinere, in Seven Parts*[1]

Argument

How a Ship having passed the Line was driven by Storms to the cold Country towards the South Pole; and how from thence she made her course to the Tropical Latitude of the Great Pacific Ocean; and of the strange things that befell; and in what manner the Ancyent Marinere came back to his own Country.

Part I

It is an ancyent Marinere,
And he stoppeth one of three:
"By thy long grey beard and thy glittering eye,
"Now wherefore stoppest thou me?

"The Bridegroom's doors are open'd wide,
"And I am next of kin;

[1] *The Rime … Parts* This is an excerpt from the version of the poem first published in Wordsworth and Coleridge's *Lyrical Ballads* (1798).

"The Guests are met, the Feast is set—
"May'st hear the merry din."

But still he holds the wedding-guest—
There was a Ship, quoth he—
"Nay, if thou'st got a laughsome tale,
"Marinere! Come with me."

He holds him with his skinny hand,
Quoth he, there was a Ship—
"Now get thee hence, thou grey-beard Loon!
"Or my Staff shall make thee skip."[1]

He holds him with his glittering eye—
The wedding-guest stood still,
And listens like a three year's child;
The Marinere hath his will.[2]

The wedding-guest sate on a stone,
He cannot chuse but hear:
And thus spake on that ancyent man,
The bright-eyed Marinere.

The Ship was cheer'd, the Harbour clear'd—
Merrily did we drop
Below the Kirk,° below the Hill, *church*
Below the Light-house top.

The Sun came up upon the left,
Out of the Sea came he:
And he shone bright, and on the right
Went down into the Sea.

Higher and higher every day,
Till over the mast at noon—
The wedding-guest here beat his breast,
For he heard the loud bassoon.

The Bride hath pac'd into the Hall,
Red as a rose is she;
Nodding their heads before her goes
The merry Minstralsy.

The wedding-guest he beat his breast,
Yet he cannot chuse but hear:
And thus spake on that ancyent Man,
The bright-eyed Marinere.

Listen, Stranger! Storm and Wind,
A Wind and Tempest strong!
For days and weeks it play'd us freaks—
Like Chaff we drove along.

Listen, Stranger! Mist and Snow,
And it grew wond'rous cauld:
And Ice mast-high came floating by
As green as Emerauld.

And thro' the drifts the snowy clifts
Did send a dismal sheen;
Ne shapes of men ne beasts we ken—
The Ice was all between.

The Ice was here, the Ice was there,
The Ice was all around:
It crack'd and growl'd, and roar'd and howl'd—
Like noises of a swound!

At length did cross an Albatross,
Thorough the Fog it came;
And an° it were a Christian Soul, *as though*
We hail'd it in God's name.

The Marineres gave it biscuit-worms,
And round and round it flew:
The Ice did split with a Thunder-fit;
The Helmsman steer'd us thro.'

And a good south wind sprung up behind,
The Albatross did follow;
And every day for food or play
Came to the Marinere's hollo!

In mist or cloud on mast or shroud
It perch'd for vespers nine,

[1] *my staff shall make thee skip* Cf. Shakespeare's *King Lear* 5.3.275–76: "[W]ith my good biting falchion [sword] / I would have made them skip."

[2] *And listens ... will* Wordsworth claimed to have composed these two lines.

Whiles all the night thro' fog-smoke white
Glimmer'd the white moon-shine.

"God save thee, ancyent Marinere!
"From the fiends that plague thee thus—
"Why look'st thou so?"—with my Cross-bow
I shot the Albatross.

—1798

The Rime of the Ancient Mariner

In Seven Parts[1]

Facile credo, plures esse Naturas invisibiles quam visibiles in rerum universitate. Sed horum omnium familiam quis nobis enarrabit? et gradus et cognationes et discrimina et singulorum munera? Quid agunt? quæ loca habitant? Harum rerum notitiam semper ambivit ingenium humanum, nunquam attigit. Juvat, interea, non diffiteor, quandoque in animo, tanquam in Tabulâ, majoris et melioris mundi imaginem contemplari: ne mens assuefecta hodiernæ vitæ minutiis se contrahat nimis, & tota subsidat in pusillas cogitationes. Sed veritati interea invigilandum est, modusque servandus, ut certa ab incertis, diem a nocte, distinguamus.—T. Burnet. *Archaeol. Phil.* p. 68.[2]

PART I

An ancient Mariner meeteth three Gallants bidden to a wedding-feast, and detaineth one.

It is an ancient Mariner,
And he stoppeth one of three.
"By thy long grey beard and glittering eye,
Now wherefore stopp'st thou me?
"The Bridegroom's doors are opened wide,
And I am next of kin;
The guests are met, the feast is set:
May'st hear the merry din."

He holds him with his skinny hand,
"There was a ship," quoth he.
"Hold off! unhand me, grey-beard loon!"
Eftsoons[3] his hand dropt he.

The wedding-guest is spellbound by the eye of the old sea-faring man, and constrained to hear his tale.

He holds him with his glittering eye—
The Wedding-Guest stood still,
And listens like a three years' child:
The Mariner hath his will.

The Wedding-Guest sat on a stone:
He cannot choose but hear;
And thus spake on that ancient man,
The bright-eyed Mariner.

The Mariner tells how the ship sailed southward with a good wind and fair weather, till it reached the line.

"The ship was cheered, the harbour cleared,
Merrily did we drop
Below the kirk,[4] below the hill,
Below the lighthouse top.

"The Sun came up upon the left,
Out of the sea came he!
And he shone bright, and on the right
Went down into the sea.

Higher and higher every day,
Till over the mast at noon—"
The Wedding-Guest here beat his breast,
For he heard the loud bassoon.

The wedding-guest heareth the bridal music; but the mariner continueth his tale.

The bride hath paced into the hall
Red as a rose is she;
Nodding their heads before her goes
The merry minstrelsy.

The Wedding-Guest he beat his breast,
Yet he cannot choose but hear;

[1] *The Rime ... Parts* This version of the poem was published in 1817.

[2] *Facile ... distinguamus* From Thomas Burnet's *Archaeologiae Philosophicae* (1692), translated by Mead and Foxton (1736): "I can easily believe, that there are more invisible than visible beings in the universe. But who will declare to us the family of all these, and acquaint us with the agreements, differences, and peculiar talents which are to be found among them? It is true, human wit has always desired a knowledge of these things, though it has never yet attained it. I will own that it is very profitable, sometimes to contemplate in the mind, as in a draught, the image of the greater and better world, lest the soul being accustomed to the trifles of this present life, should contract itself too much, and altogether rest in mean cogitations, but, in the meantime, we must take care to keep to the truth, and observe moderation, that we may distinguish certain from uncertain things, and day from night."

[3] *Eftsoons* At once.

[4] *kirk* Church.

And thus spake on that ancient man,
The bright-eyed Mariner.

The ship drawn by a storm toward the south pole.

"And now the STORM-BLAST came, and he
Was tyrannous and strong:
He struck with his o'ertaking wings,
And chased us south along.

With sloping masts and dipping prow,
As who pursued with yell and blow
Still treads the shadow of his foe,
And forward bends his head,
The ship drove fast, loud roared the blast,
And southward aye we fled.

And now there came both mist and snow,
And it grew wondrous cold:
And ice, mast-high, came floating by,
As green as emerald.

The land of ice, and of fearful sounds, where no living thing was to be seen.

And through the drifts the snowy clifts
Did send a dismal sheen:
Nor shapes of men nor beasts we ken[1]—
The ice was all between.

The ice was here, the ice was there,
The ice was all around:
It cracked and growled, and roared and howled,
Like noises in a swound![2]

Till a great sea-bird, called the Albatross, came through the snow-fog, and was received with great joy and hospitality.

At length did cross an Albatross,
Thorough the fog it came;
As if it had been a Christian soul,
We hailed it in God's name.

It ate the food it ne'er had eat,
And round and round it flew.
The ice did split with a thunder-fit;
The helmsman steered us through!

And lo! the Albatross proveth a bird of good omen, and followeth the ship as it returned northward, through fog and floating ice.

And a good south wind sprung up behind;
The Albatross did follow,
And every day, for food or play,
Came to the Mariner's hollo!

In mist or cloud, on mast or shroud,
It perched for vespers nine;[3]
Whiles all the night, through fog-smoke white,
Glimmered the white Moon-shine."

The ancient Mariner inhospitably killed the pious bird of good omen.

"God save thee, ancient Mariner!
From the fiends, that plague thee thus!—
Why look'st thou so?"—"With my cross-bow
I shot the ALBATROSS.

PART 2

The Sun now rose upon the right:
Out of the sea came he,
Still hid in mist, and on the left
Went down into the sea.

And the good south wind still blew behind,
But no sweet bird did follow,
Nor any day for food or play
Came to the mariners' hollo!

His ship mates cry out against the ancient Mariner, for killing the bird of good luck.

And I had done a hellish thing,
And it would work 'em woe:
For all averred, I had killed the bird
That made the breeze to blow.
Ah wretch! said they, the bird to slay,
That made the breeze to blow!

But when the fog cleared off, they justify the same—and thus make themselves accomplices in the crime.

Nor dim nor red, like God's own head,
The glorious Sun uprist:
Then all averred, I had killed the bird
That brought the fog and mist.
'Twas right, said they, such birds to slay,
That bring the fog and mist.

The fair breeze continues;

The fair breeze blew, the white foam flew,
The furrow followed free;
We were the first that ever burst
Into that silent sea.

[1] *ken* Recognize.

[2] *swound* Swoon.

[3] *vespers nine* I.e., nine evenings. Vespers are evening prayer.

Down dropt the breeze, the sails dropt down,
'Twas sad as sad could be;
And we did speak only to break
The silence of the sea!

The ship enters the Pacific Ocean and sails northward, even till it reaches the Line.

The ship hath been suddenly becalmed.

All in a hot and copper sky,
The bloody Sun, at noon,
Right up above the mast did stand,
No bigger than the Moon.

Day after day, day after day,
We stuck, nor breath nor motion;
As idle as a painted ship
Upon a painted ocean.

And the Albatross begins to be avenged.

Water, water, every where,
And all the boards did shrink;
Water, water, every where,
Nor any drop to drink.

The very deep did rot: O Christ!
That ever this should be!
Yea, slimy things did crawl with legs
Upon the slimy sea.

A spirit has followed them; one of the invisible inhabitants of this planet, neither departed souls nor angels; concerning whom the learned Jew, Josephus, and the Platonic Constantinopolitan, Michael Psellus, may be consulted, and there is no climate or element without one or more.

About, about, in reel and rout
The death-fires[1] danced at night;
The water, like a witch's oils,
Burnt green, and blue and white.

And some in dreams assuréd were
Of the Spirit that plagued us so;
Nine fathom deep he had followed us
From the land of mist and snow.

And every tongue, through utter drought,
Was withered at the root;
We could not speak, no more than if
We had been choked with soot.

The shipmates in their sore distress, would fain throw the whole guilt on the ancient Mariner: in sign whereof they hang the dead sea-bird round his neck.

Ah! well a-day! what evil looks
Had I from old and young!
Instead of the cross, the Albatross
About my neck was hung.

[1] *death-fires* Possibly luminescent plankton.

PART 3

There passed a weary time. Each throat
Was parched, and glazed each eye.
A weary time! a weary time!
How glazed each weary eye,
When looking westward, I beheld
A something in the sky.

The ancient Mariner beholdeth a sign in the element afar off.

At first it seemed a little speck,
And then it seemed a mist;
It moved and moved, and took at last
A certain shape, I wist.

A speck, a mist, a shape, I wist!
And still it neared and neared:
And as if it dodged a water-sprite,
It plunged and tacked and veered.

As its nearer approach, it seemeth him to be a ship; and at a dear ransom he freeth his speech from the bonds of thirst.

With throat unslacked, with black lips baked,
We could nor laugh nor wail;
Through utter drought all dumb we stood!
I bit my arm, I sucked the blood,
And cried, A sail! a sail!

A flash of joy.

With throat unslacked, with black lips baked,
Agape they heard me call:
Gramercy![2] they for joy did grin,
And all at once their breath drew in,
As they were drinking all.

And horror follows. For can it be a *ship* that comes onward without wind or tide?

See! see! (I cried) she tacks no more!
Hither to work us weal;[3]
Without a breeze, without a tide,
She steadies with upright keel!

The western wave was all a-flame.
The day was well nigh done!
Almost upon the western wave
Rested the broad bright Sun;
When that strange shape drove suddenly
Betwixt us and the Sun.

[2] *Gramercy* Grant mercy, i.e., may God reward you in His mercy.

[3] *us weal* Will benefit us.

It seemeth him but the skeleton of a ship.

And straight the Sun was flecked with bars,
(Heaven's Mother send us grace!)
As if through a dungeon-grate he peered
With broad and burning face.

And its ribs are seen as bars on the face of the setting Sun. The spectre-woman and her death-mate, and no other board the skeleton-ship.

Alas! (thought I, and my heart beat loud)
How fast she nears and nears!
Are those *her* sails that glance in the Sun,
Like restless gossameres?

Are those *her* ribs through which the Sun
Did peer, as through a grate?
And is that Woman all her crew?
Is that a DEATH? and are there two?
Is DEATH that woman's mate?

Like vessel, like crew! Death and Life-in-Death have diced for the ship's crew, and she (the latter) winneth the ancient Mariner.

Her lips were red, *her* looks were free,
Her locks were yellow as gold:
Her skin was as white as leprosy,
The Night-mare LIFE-IN-DEATH was she,
Who thicks man's blood with cold.

The naked hulk alongside came,
And the twain were casting dice;
"The game is done! I've won! I've won!"
Quoth she, and whistles thrice.

No twilight within the courts of the sun.

The Sun's rim dips; the stars rush out:
At one stride comes the dark;
With far-heard whisper, o'er the sea,
Off shot the spectre-bark.

At the rising of the Moon,

We listened and looked sideways up!
Fear at my heart, as at a cup,
My life-blood seemed to sip!
The stars were dim, and thick the night,
The steersman's face by his lamp gleamed white;
From the sails the dews did drip—
Till clomb above the eastern bar
The hornéd Moon, with one bright star
Within the nether tip.

One after another,

One after one, by the star-dogged Moon
Too quick for groan or sigh,
Each turned his face with a ghastly pang,
And cursed me with his eye.

His ship-mates drop down dead.

Four times fifty living men,
(And I heard nor sigh nor groan)
With heavy thump, a lifeless lump,
They dropped down one by one.

But Life-in-Death begins her work on the ancient Mariner.

The souls did from their bodies fly,—
They fled to bliss or woe!
And every soul, it passed me by,
Like the whiz of my cross-bow!

PART 4

The wedding-guest feareth that a spirit is talking to him;

"I fear thee, ancient Mariner!
I fear thy skinny hand!
And thou art long, and lank, and brown,
As is the ribbed sea-sand.[1]

I fear thee and thy glittering eye,
And thy skinny hand, so brown."—

But the ancient Mariner assureth him of his bodily life, and proceedeth to relate his horrible penance.

Fear not, fear not, thou Wedding-Guest!
This body dropt not down.

Alone, alone, all, all alone,
Alone on a wide wide sea!
And never a saint took pity on
My soul in agony.

He despiseth the creatures of the calm,

The many men, so beautiful!
And they all dead did lie:
And a thousand thousand slimy things
Lived on; and so did I.

And envieth that *they* should live, and so many lie dead.

I looked upon the rotting sea,
And drew my eyes away;
I looked upon the rotting deck,
And there the dead men lay.

I looked to heaven, and tried to pray;
But or ever a prayer had gusht,
A wicked whisper came, and made
My heart as dry as dust.

---

[1] [Coleridge's note] For the two last lines of this stanza, I am indebted to Mr. WORDSWORTH. It was on a delightful walk from Nether Stowey to Dulverton, with him and his sister, in the Autumn of 1797, that this Poem was planned, and in part composed.

I closed my lids, and kept them close,
And the balls like pulses beat;
For the sky and the sea, and the sea and the sky
Lay like a load on my weary eye,
And the dead were at my feet.

The cold sweat melted from their limbs,
Nor rot nor reek did they:
The look with which they looked on me
Had never passed away.

But the curse liveth for him in the eye of the dead men.

An orphan's curse would drag to hell
A spirit from on high;
But oh! more horrible than that
Is the curse in a dead man's eye!
Seven days, seven nights, I saw that curse,
And yet I could not die.

In his loneliness and fixedness, he yearneth towards the journeying Moon, and the stars that still sojourn, yet still move onwards; and every where the blue sky belongs to them, and is their appointed rest, and their native country, and their own natural homes, which they enter unannounced, as lords that are certain expected, and yet there is a silent joy at their arrival.

The moving Moon went up the sky,
And no where did abide:
Softly she was going up,
And a star or two beside—

Her beams bemocked the sultry main,
Like April hoar-frost spread;
But where the ship's huge shadow lay,
The charméd water burnt alway
A still and awful red.

By the light of the Moon he beholdeth God's creatures of the great calm.

Beyond the shadow of the ship,
I watched the water-snakes:
They moved in tracks of shining white,
And when they reared, the elfish light
Fell off in hoary flakes.

Within the shadow of the ship
I watched their rich attire:
Blue, glossy green, and velvet black,
They coiled and swam; and every track
Was a flash of golden fire.

Their beauty and their happiness.

O happy living things! no tongue
Their beauty might declare:
A spring of love gushed from my heart,
And I blessed them unaware:

He blesseth them in his heart.

Sure my kind saint took pity on me,
And I blessed them unaware.

The spell begins to break.

The selfsame moment I could pray;
And from my neck so free
The Albatross fell off, and sank
Like lead into the sea.

PART 5

Oh sleep! it is a gentle thing,
Beloved from pole to pole!
To Mary Queen the praise be given!
She sent the gentle sleep from Heaven,
That slid into my soul.

By grace of the holy Mother, the ancient Mariner is refreshed with rain.

The silly[1] buckets on the deck,
That had so long remained,
I dreamt that they were filled with dew;
And when I awoke, it rained.

My lips were wet, my throat was cold,
My garments all were dank;
Sure I had drunken in my dreams,
And still my body drank.

I moved, and could not feel my limbs:
I was so light—almost
I thought that I had died in sleep,
And was a blesséd ghost.

He heareth sounds, and seeth strange sights and commotions in the sky and the elements.

And soon I heard a roaring wind:
It did not come anear;
But with its sound it shook the sails,
That were so thin and sere.

The upper air burst into life!
And a hundred fire-flags sheen,
To and fro they were hurried about!
And to and fro, and in and out,
The wan stars danced between.

And the coming wind did roar more loud,
And the sails did sigh like sedge;

[1] *silly* Simple.

And the rain poured down from one black cloud;
The Moon was at its edge.

The thick black cloud was cleft, and still
The Moon was at its side:
Like waters shot from some high crag,
The lightning fell with never a jag,
A river steep and wide.

The bodies of the ship's crew are inspirited, and the ship moves on;

The loud wind never reached the ship,
Yet now the ship moved on!
Beneath the lightning and the Moon
The dead men gave a groan.

They groaned, they stirred, they all uprose,
Nor spake, nor moved their eyes;
It had been strange, even in a dream,
To have seen those dead men rise.

The helmsman steered, the ship moved on;
Yet never a breeze up-blew;
The mariners all 'gan work the ropes,
Where they were wont to do;
They raised their limbs like lifeless tools—
We were a ghastly crew.

The body of my brother's son
Stood by me, knee to knee:
The body and I pulled at one rope,
But he said nought to me.

But not by the souls of the men, nor by dæmons of earth or middle air, but by a blessed troop of angelic spirits, sent down by the invocation of the guardian saint.

"I fear thee, ancient Mariner!"
Be calm, thou Wedding-Guest!
'Twas not those souls that fled in pain,
Which to their corses[1] came again,
But a troop of spirits blest:

For when it dawned—they dropped their arms,
And clustered round the mast;
Sweet sounds rose slowly through their mouths,
And from their bodies passed.

Around, around, flew each sweet sound,
Then darted to the Sun;
Slowly the sounds came back again,
Now mixed, now one by one.

Sometimes a-dropping from the sky
I heard the sky-lark sing;
Sometimes all little birds that are,
How they seemed to fill the sea and air
With their sweet jargoning!

And now 'twas like all instruments,
Now like a lonely flute;
And now it is an angel's song,
That makes the heavens be mute.

It ceased; yet still the sails made on
A pleasant noise till noon,
A noise like of a hidden brook
In the leafy month of June,
That to the sleeping woods all night
Singeth a quiet tune.

Till noon we quietly sailed on,
Yet never a breeze did breathe:
Slowly and smoothly went the ship,
Moved onward from beneath.

The lonesome spirit from the south-pole carries on the ship as far as the line, in obedience to the angelic troop, but still requireth vengeance.

Under the keel nine fathom deep,
From the land of mist and snow,
The spirit slid: and it was he
That made the ship to go.
The sails at noon left off their tune,
And the ship stood still also.

The Sun, right up above the mast,
Had fixed her to the ocean:
But in a minute she 'gan stir,
With a short uneasy motion—
Backwards and forwards half her length
With a short uneasy motion.

Then like a pawing horse let go,
She made a sudden bound:
It flung the blood into my head,
And I fell down in a swound.

[1] *corses* Corpses.

How long in that same fit I lay,
I have not to declare;
But ere my living life returned,
I heard and in my soul discerned
Two voices in the air.

The Polar Spirit's fellow-dæmons, the invisible inhabitants of the element, take part in his wrong; and two of them relate, one to the other, that penance long and heavy for the ancient Mariner hath been accorded to the Polar Spirit, who returned southward.

"Is it he?" quoth one, "Is this the man?
By Him who died on cross,
With his cruel bow he laid full low
The harmless Albatross.

The spirit who bideth by himself
In the land of mist and snow,
He loved the bird that loved the man
Who shot him with his bow."

The other was a softer voice,
As soft as honey-dew:
Quoth he, "The man hath penance done,
And penance more will do."

PART 6

FIRST VOICE

"But tell me, tell me! speak again,
Thy soft response renewing—
What makes that ship drive on so fast?
What is the ocean doing?"

SECOND VOICE

"Still as a slave before his lord,
The ocean hath no blast;
His great bright eye most silently
Up to the Moon is cast—

If he may know which way to go;
For she guides him smooth or grim.
See, brother, see! how graciously
She looketh down on him."

FIRST VOICE

"But why drives on that ship so fast,
Without or wave or wind?"

SECOND VOICE

"The air is cut away before,
And closes from behind.

The Mariner hath been cast into a trance; for the angelic power causeth the vessel to drive northward, faster than human life could endure.

Fly, brother, fly! more high, more high!
Or we shall be belated:
For slow and slow that ship will go,
When the Mariner's trance is abated."

The super-natural motion is retarded; the Mariner awakes, and his penance begins anew.

I woke, and we were sailing on
As in a gentle weather:
'Twas night, calm night, the Moon was high;
The dead men stood together.

All stood together on the deck,
For a charnel-dungeon fitter:[1]
All fixed on me their stony eyes,
That in the Moon did glitter.

The pang, the curse, with which they died,
Had never passed away:
I could not draw my eyes from theirs,
Nor turn them up to pray.

The curse is finally expiated.

And now this spell was snapt: once more
I viewed the ocean green,
And looked far forth, yet little saw
Of what had else been seen—

Like one, that on a lonesome road
Doth walk in fear and dread,
And having once turned round, walks on,
And turns no more his head;
Because he knows, a frightful fiend
Doth close behind him tread.

But soon there breathed a wind on me,
Nor sound nor motion made:
Its path was not upon the sea,
In ripple or in shade.

It raised my hair, it fanned my cheek
Like a meadow-gale of spring—

[1] *charnel-dungeon* Mortuary; house of death.

It mingled strangely with my fears,
Yet it felt like a welcoming.

Swiftly, swiftly flew the ship,
Yet she sailed softly too:
Sweetly, sweetly blew the breeze—
On me alone it blew.

And the ancient Mariner beholdeth his native country.

Oh! dream of joy! is this indeed
The light-house top I see?
Is this the hill? is this the kirk?
Is this mine own countree?

We drifted o'er the harbour-bar,
And I with sobs did pray—
O let me be awake, my God!
Or let me sleep alway.

The harbour-bay was clear as glass,
So smoothly was it strewn!
And on the bay the moonlight lay,
And the shadow of the Moon.

The rock shone bright, the kirk no less,
That stands above the rock:
The moonlight steeped in silentness
The steady weathercock.

The angelic spirits leave the dead bodies,

And the bay was white with silent light,
Till rising from the same,
Full many shapes, that shadows were,
In crimson colours came.

And appear in their own forms of light.

A little distance from the prow
Those crimson shadows were:
I turned my eyes upon the deck—
Oh, Christ! what saw I there!

Each corse lay flat, lifeless and flat,
And, by the holy rood!
A man all light, a seraph-man,[1]
On every corse there stood.

This seraph-band, each waved his hand:
It was a heavenly sight!
They stood as signals to the land,
Each one a lovely light;

This seraph-band, each waved his hand,
No voice did they impart—
No voice; but oh! the silence sank
Like music on my heart.

But soon I heard the dash of oars,
I heard the Pilot's cheer;
My head was turned perforce away
And I saw a boat appear.

The Pilot and the Pilot's boy,
I heard them coming fast:
Dear Lord in Heaven! it was a joy
The dead men could not blast.

I saw a third—I heard his voice:
It is the Hermit good!
He singeth loud his godly hymns
That he makes in the wood.
He'll shrieve[2] my soul, he'll wash away
The Albatross's blood.

PART 7

The Hermit of the Wood.

This Hermit good lives in that wood
Which slopes down to the sea.
How loudly his sweet voice he rears!
He loves to talk with marineres
That come from a far countree.

He kneels at morn, and noon, and eve—
He hath a cushion plump:
It is the moss that wholly hides
The rotted old oak-stump.

The skiff-boat neared: I heard them talk,
"Why, this is strange, I trow![3]
Where are those light so many and fair,
That signal made but now?"

[1] *rood* Cross; *seraph-man* Angel.

[2] *shrieve* Give absolution to.

[3] *trow* Believe.

"Strange, by my faith!" the Hermit said—
"And they answered not our cheer!
The planks look warped! and see those sails,
How thin they are and sere!
I never saw aught like to them,
Unless perchance it were

Approacheth the ship with wonder.

Brown skeletons of leaves that lag
My forest-brook along;
When the ivy-tod[1] is heavy with snow,
And the owlet whoops to the wolf below,
That eats the she-wolf's young."

"Dear Lord! it hath a fiendish look—
(The Pilot made reply)
I am a-feared"—"Push on, push on!"
Said the Hermit cheerily.

The boat came closer to the ship,
But I nor spake nor stirred;
The boat came close beneath the ship,
And straight a sound was heard.

Under the water it rumbled on,
Still louder and more dread:
It reached the ship, it split the bay;
The ship went down like lead.

The ship suddenly sinketh.

Stunned by that loud and dreadful sound,
Which sky and ocean smote,
Like one that hath been seven days drowned
My body lay afloat;
But swift as dreams, myself I found
Within the Pilot's boat.

The ancient Mariner is saved in the Pilot's boat.

Upon the whirl, where sank the ship,
The boat spun round and round;
And all was still, save that the hill
Was telling of the sound.

I moved my lips—the Pilot shrieked
And fell down in a fit;
The holy Hermit raised his eyes,
And prayed where he did sit.

I took the oars: the Pilot's boy,
Who now doth crazy go,
Laughed loud and long, and all the while
His eyes went to and fro.
"Ha! ha!" quoth he, "full plain I see,
The Devil knows how to row."

And now, all in my own countree,
I stood on the firm land!
The Hermit stepped forth from the boat,
And scarcely he could stand.

"O shrieve me, shrieve me, holy man!"
The Hermit crossed his brow.
"Say quick," quoth he, "I bid thee say—
What manner of man art thou?"

The ancient Mariner earnestly entreateth the Hermit to shrieve him; and the penance of life falls on him.

Forthwith this frame of mine was wrenched
With a woful agony,
Which forced me to begin my tale;
And then it left me free.

Since then, at an uncertain hour,
That agony returns;
And till my ghastly tale is told,
This heart within me burns.

And ever and anon throughout his future life an agony constraineth him to travel from land to land.

I pass, like night, from land to land;
I have strange power of speech;
That moment that his face I see,
I know the man that must hear me:
To him my tale I teach.

What loud uproar bursts from that door!
The wedding-guests are there:
But in the garden-bower the bride
And bride-maids singing are:
And hark the little vesper bell,
Which biddeth me to prayer!

O Wedding-Guest! this soul hath been
Alone on a wide wide sea:
So lonely 'twas, that God Himself
Scarce seemèd there to be.

[1] *ivy-tod* Bush.

O sweeter than the marriage-feast,
'Tis sweeter far to me,
To walk together to the kirk
With a goodly company!—

To walk together to the kirk,
And all together pray,
While each to his great Father bends,
Old men, and babes, and loving friends
And youth and maidens gay!

And to teach by his own example, love and reverence to all things that God made and loveth.

Farewell, farewell! but this I tell
To thee, thou Wedding-Guest!
He prayeth well, who loveth well
Both man and bird and beast.

He prayeth best, who loveth best
All things both great and small;
For the dear God who loveth us,
He made and loveth all."

The Mariner, whose eye is bright,
Whose beard with age is hoar,[1]
Is gone: and now the Wedding-Guest
Turned from the bridegroom's door.

He went like one that hath been stunned,
And is of sense forlorn:
A sadder and a wiser man,
He rose the morrow morn.
—1817

IN CONTEXT

The Origin of "The Rime of the Ancient Mariner"

Almost twenty years after the first publication of "The Rime of the Ancient Mariner," Coleridge gave the following account of the poem's origin and composition in Chapter 14 of *Biographia Literaria* (1817):

During the first year that Mr. Wordsworth and I were neighbours, our conversations turned frequently on the two cardinal points of poetry, the power of exciting the sympathy of the reader by a faithful adherence to the truth of nature, and the power of giving the interest of novelty by the modifying colours of imagination. The sudden charm, which accidents of light and shade, which moonlight or sunset diffused over a known and familiar landscape, appeared to represent the practicability of combining both. These are the poetry of nature. The thought suggested itself (to which of us I do not recollect) that a series of poems might be composed of two sorts. In the one, the incidents and agents were to be, in part at least supernatural; and the excellence aimed at was to consist in the interesting of the affections by the dramatic truth of such emotions, as would naturally accompany such situations, supposing them real. And real in *this* sense they have been to every human being who, from whatever source of delusion, has at any time believed himself under supernatural agency. For the second class, subjects were to be chosen from ordinary life; the characters and incidents were to be such, as will be found in every village and its vicinity where there is a meditative and feeling mind to seek after them, or to notice them, when they present themselves. In this idea originated the plan of the *Lyrical Ballads*; in which it was agreed, that my endeavours should be directed to persons and characters supernatural, or at least romantic; yet so as to transfer from our inward nature a human interest and a semblance of truth sufficient to procure for these shadows of imagination that willing suspension of disbelief for the moment, which constitutes poetic faith. Mr. Wordsworth, on the other hand, was to propose to himself as his object, to give the charm of novelty

[1] *hoar* White, as with frost (hoarfrost).

to things of every day, and to excite a feeling analogous to the supernatural, by awakening the mind's attention from the lethargy of custom, and directing it to the loveliness and the wonders of the world before us; an inexhaustible treasure, but for which, in consequence of the film of familiarity and selfish solicitude we have eyes, yet see not, and hearts that neither feel or understand. With this view I wrote "The Ancient Mariner," and was preparing among other poems, "The Dark Ladie," and the "Christabel" in which I should have more nearly realized my ideal than I had done in my first attempt.

A letter from the Rev. Alexander Dyce to Hartley Coleridge (published 1852) quoted Wordsworth as saying the following about the poem's inception:

"The Ancient Mariner" was founded on a strange dream, which a friend of Coleridge had, who fancied he saw a skeleton ship, with figures in it. We had both determined to write some poetry for a monthly magazine, the profits of which were to defer the expenses of a little excursion we were to make together. "The Ancient Mariner" was intended for this periodical, but was too long. I had very little share in the composition of it, for I soon found the style of Coleridge and myself would not assimilate. Beside the lines (in the fourth part) "And thou art long, and lank, and brown, / As in the ribbed sea-sand—" I wrote the stanza (in the first part) "He holds him with his glittering eye— / The Wedding-Guest stood still, / And listens like a three-years child: / The Mariner hath his will" and four or five lines more in different parts of the poem, which I could not now point out. The idea of shooting an albatross was mine; for I had been reading *Shelvocke's Voyages*, which probably Coleridge never saw. I also suggested the reanimation of the dead bodies, to work the ship.

The Lime-Tree Bower My Prison[1]

Addressed to Charles Lamb,
Of the India House, London

Well, they are gone, and here must I remain,
This lime-tree bower my prison! I have lost
Beauties and feelings, such as would have been
Most sweet to my remembrance even when age
Had dimm'd mine eyes to blindness! They, meanwhile,
Friends, whom I never more may meet again,
On springy heath, along the hill-top edge,
Wander in gladness, and wind down, perchance,
To that still roaring dell, of which I told;
The roaring dell, o'erwooded, narrow, deep,
And only speckled by the mid-day sun;
Where its slim trunk the ash from rock to rock
Flings arching like a bridge;—that branchless ash,
Unsunn'd and damp, whose few poor yellow leaves
Ne'er tremble in the gale, yet tremble still,
Fann'd by the water-fall! and there my friends
Behold the dark green file of long lank weeds,[2]
That all at once (a most fantastic sight!)
Still nod and drip beneath the dripping edge
Of the blue clay-stone.

Now, my friends emerge
Beneath the wide wide Heaven—and view again
The many-steepled tract magnificent
Of hilly fields and meadows, and the sea,
With some fair bark, perhaps, whose sails light up
The slip of smooth clear blue betwixt two Isles

[1] [Coleridge's note] In the June of 1797 some long-expected friends [Charles Lamb and William and Dorothy Wordsworth] paid a visit to the author's cottage; and on the morning of their arrival, he met with an accident, which disabled him from walking during the whole time of their stay. One evening, when they had left him for a few hours, he composed the following lines in the garden-bower.

[2] [Coleridge's note] The *Asplenium Scolopendrium*, called in some countries the Adder's Tongue, in others the Hart's Tongue, but Withering gives the Adder's Tongue as the trivial name of the *Ophioglossum* only.

Of purple shadow! Yes! they wander on
In gladness all; but thou, methinks, most glad,
My gentle-hearted Charles! for thou hast pined
And hunger'd after Nature, many a year,
In the great City pent, winning thy way
With sad yet patient soul, through evil and pain
And strange calamity![1] Ah! slowly sink
Behind the western ridge, thou glorious Sun!
Shine in the slant beams of the sinking orb,
Ye purple heath-flowers! richlier burn, ye clouds!
Live in the yellow light, ye distant groves!
And kindle, thou blue Ocean! So my friend
Struck with deep joy may stand, as I have stood,
Silent with swimming sense; yea, gazing round
On the wide landscape, gaze till all doth seem
Less gross than bodily; and of such hues
As veil the Almighty Spirit, when yet he makes
Spirits perceive his presence.

A delight
Comes sudden on my heart, and I am glad
As I myself were there! Nor in this bower,
This little lime-tree bower, have I not mark'd
Much that has sooth'd me. Pale beneath the blaze
Hung the transparent foliage; and I watch'd
Some broad and sunny leaf, and lov'd to see
The shadow of the leaf and stem above
Dappling its sunshine! And that walnut-tree
Was richly ting'd, and a deep radiance lay
Full on the ancient ivy, which usurps
Those fronting elms, and now, with blackest mass
Makes their dark branches gleam a lighter hue
Through the late twilight: and though now the bat
Wheels silent by, and not a swallow twitters,
Yet still the solitary humble-bee
Sings in the bean-flower! Henceforth I shall know
That Nature ne'er deserts the wise and pure;
No plot so narrow, be but Nature there,
No waste so vacant, but may well employ
Each faculty of sense, and keep the heart
Awake to Love and Beauty! and sometimes
'Tis well to be bereft of promis'd good,
That we may lift the soul, and contemplate
With lively joy the joys we cannot share.
My gentle-hearted Charles! when the last rook
Beat its straight path along the dusky air
Homewards, I blest it! deeming its black wing
(Now a dim speck, now vanishing in light)
Had cross'd the mighty Orb's dilated glory,
While thou stood'st gazing; or, when all was still,
Flew creeking o'er thy head, and had a charm[2]
For thee, my gentle-hearted Charles, to whom
No sound is dissonant which tells of Life.
—1800

[1] *strange calamity* Charles Lamb's sister Mary, who suffered from periods of insanity, had fatally stabbed their mother.

[2] [Coleridge's note] Some months after I had written this line, it gave me pleasure to find that Bartram had observed the same circumstance of the Savanna Crane. "When these Birds move their wings in flight, their strokes are slow, moderate and regular; and even when at a considerable distance or high above us, we plainly hear the quill-feathers: their shafts and webs upon one another creek as the joints or working of a vessel in a tempestuous sea."

Christabel

Preface

The first part of the following poem was written in the year 1797, at Stowey, in the county of Somerset. The second part, after my return from Germany, in the year 1800, at Keswick, Cumberland. Since the latter date, my poetic powers have been, till very lately, in a state of suspended animation. But as, in my very first conception of the tale, I had the whole present to my mind, with the wholeness, no less than with the liveliness of a vision; I trust that I shall be able to embody in verse the three parts yet to come, in the course of the present year.

It is probable that if the poem had been finished at either of the former periods, or if even the first and second part had been published in the year 1800, the impression of its originality would have been much greater than I dare at present expect. But for this, I have only my own indolence to blame. The dates are mentioned for the exclusive purpose of precluding charges of plagiarism or servile imitation from myself. For there is among us a set of critics, who seem to hold, that every possible thought and image is traditional; who have no notion that there are such things as fountains in the world, small as well as great; and who would therefore charitably derive every rill[1] they behold flowing from a perforation made in some other man's tank. I am confident however, that as far as the present poem is concerned, the celebrated poets whose writings I might be suspected of having imitated,[2] either in particular passages, or in the tone and the spirit of the whole, would be among the first to vindicate me from the charge, and who, on any striking coincidence, would permit me to address them in this doggerel version of two monkish Latin hexameters:

> 'Tis mine and it is likewise yours,
> But an if this will not do;
> Let it be mine, good friend! for I
> Am the poorer of the two.

I have only to add, that the metre of the Christabel is not, properly speaking, irregular, though it may seem so from its being founded on a new principle: namely, that of counting in each line the accents, not the syllables. Though the latter may vary from seven to twelve, yet in each line the accents will be found to be only four. Nevertheless this occasional variation in the number of syllables is not introduced wantonly, or for the mere ends of convenience, but in correspondence with some transition in the nature of the imagery or passion.

Part I

'Tis the middle of night by the castle clock,
And the owls have awakened the crowing cock;
Tu—whit!—Tu—whoo!
And hark, again! the crowing cock,
How drowsily it crew.

Sir Leoline, the Baron rich,
Hath a toothless mastiff bitch;
From her kennel beneath the rock
She maketh answer to the clock,
Four for the quarters, and twelve for the hour;
Ever and aye,° by shine and shower, *always*
Sixteen short howls, not over loud;
Some say, she sees my lady's shroud.

Is the night chilly and dark?
The night is chilly, but not dark.
The thin gray cloud is spread on high,
It covers but not hides the sky.
The moon is behind, and at the full;
And yet she looks both small and dull.
The night is chill, the cloud is gray:
'Tis a month before the month of May,
And the Spring comes slowly up this way.

The lovely lady, Christabel,
Whom her father loves so well,
What makes her in the wood so late,
A furlong from the castle gate?
She had dreams all yesternight
Of her own betrothéd knight;
And she in the midnight wood will pray
For the weal° of her lover that's far away. *well-being*

She stole along, she nothing spoke,
The sighs she heaved were soft and low,
And naught was green upon the oak
But moss and rarest misletoe:[3]
She kneels beneath the huge oak tree,
And in silence prayeth she.

The lady sprang up suddenly,
The lovely lady, Christabel!
It moaned as near, as near can be,
But what it is she cannot tell.—
On the other side it seems to be,
Of the huge, broad-breasted, old oak tree.

The night is chill; the forest bare;
Is it the wind that moaneth bleak?
There is not wind enough in the air
To move away the ringlet curl
From the lovely lady's cheek—
There is not wind enough to twirl

[1] *rill* Brook.

[2] *celebrated poets … imitated* Lord Byron and Sir Walter Scott, both of whom had read "Christabel" in manuscript form and had been influenced by it in their own subsequent writings.

[3] *mistletoe* Plant considered sacred in ancient Britain when found growing on oak trees.

The one red leaf, the last of its clan,
That dances as often as dance it can,
Hanging so light, and hanging so high,
On the topmost twig that looks up at the sky.

Hush, beating heart of Christabel!
Jesu, Maria, shield her well!
She folded her arms beneath her cloak,
And stole to the other side of the oak.
What sees she there?

There she sees a damsel bright,
Dressed in a silken robe of white,
That shadowy in the moonlight shone:
The neck that made that white robe wan,
Her stately neck, and arms were bare;
Her blue-veined feet unsandal'd were,
And wildly glittered here and there
The gems entangled in her hair.
I guess, 'twas frightful there to see
A lady so richly clad as she—
Beautiful exceedingly!

Mary mother, save me now!
(Said Christabel,) And who art thou?

The lady strange made answer meet,
And her voice was faint and sweet:—
Have pity on my sore distress,
I scarce can speak for weariness:
Stretch forth thy hand, and have no fear!
Said Christabel, How camest thou here?
And the lady, whose voice was faint and sweet,
Did thus pursue her answer meet:—

My sire is of a noble line,
And my name is Geraldine:
Five warriors seized me yestermorn,
Me, even me, a maid forlorn:
They choked my cries with force and fright,
And tied me on a palfrey° white. *saddle horse*
The palfrey was as fleet as wind,
And they rode furiously behind.
They spurred amain,° their steeds were white: *forcefully*
And once we crossed the shade of night.
As sure as Heaven shall rescue me,
I have no thought what men they be;
Nor do I know how long it is
(For I have lain entranced, I wis°) *know*
Since one, the tallest of the five,
Took me from the palfrey's back,
A weary woman, scarce alive.
Some muttered words his comrades spoke:
He placed me underneath this oak;
He swore they would return with haste;
Whither they went I cannot tell—
I thought I heard, some minutes past,
Sounds as of a castle bell.
Stretch forth thy hand (thus ended she),
And help a wretched maid to flee.

Then Christabel stretched forth her hand,
And comforted fair Geraldine:
O well, bright dame! may you command
The service of Sir Leoline;
And gladly our stout° chivalry *fierce*
Will he send forth and friends withal
To guide and guard you safe and free
Home to your noble father's hall.

She rose: and forth with steps they passed
That strove to be, and were not, fast.
Her gracious stars the lady blest,
And thus spake on sweet Christabel:
All our household are at rest,
The hall is silent as the cell;
Sir Leoline is weak in health,
And may not well awakened be,
But we will move as if in stealth,
And I beseech your courtesy,
This night, to share your couch with me.

They crossed the moat, and Christabel
Took the key that fitted well;
A little door she opened straight,
All in the middle of the gate;
The gate that was ironed within and without,
Where an army in battle array had marched out.

The lady sank, belike through pain,
And Christabel with might and main
Lifted her up, a weary weight,
Over the threshold of the gate:
Then the lady rose again,
And moved, as she were not in pain.

So free from danger, free from fear,
They crossed the court: right glad they were.
And Christabel devoutly cried
To the Lady by her side,
Praise we the Virgin all divine
Who hath rescued thee from thy distress!
Alas, alas! said Geraldine,
I cannot speak for weariness.
So free from danger, free from fear,
They crossed the court: right glad they were.

Outside her kennel, the mastiff old
Lay fast asleep, in moonshine cold.
The mastiff old did not awake,
Yet she an angry moan did make!
And what can ail the mastiff bitch?
Never till now she uttered yell
Beneath the eye of Christabel.
Perhaps it is the owlet's scritch:
For what can aid the mastiff bitch?

They passed the hall, that echoes still
Pass as lightly as you will!
The brands° were flat, the brands were dying, *burning logs*
Amid their own white ashes lying;
But when the lady passed, there came
A tongue of light, a fit of flame;
And Christabel saw the lady's eye,
And nothing else saw she thereby,
Save the boss of the shield of Sir Leoline tall,
Which hung in a murky old niche in the wall.
O softly tread, said Christabel,
My father seldom sleepeth well.

Sweet Christabel her feet doth bare,
And jealous of the listening air
They steal their way from stair to stair,
Now in glimmer, and now in gloom,
And now they pass the Baron's room,
As still as death, with stifled breath!
And now have reached her chamber door;
And now doth Geraldine press down
The rushes of the chamber floor.

The moon shines dim in the open air,
And not a moonbeam enters here.
But they without its light can see
The chamber carved so curiously,
Carved with figures strange and sweet,
All made out of the carver's brain,
For a lady's chamber meet:° *suitable*
The lamp with twofold silver chain
Is fastened to an angel's feet.

The silver lamp burns dead and dim;
But Christabel the lamp will trim.
She trimmed the lamp, and made it bright,
And left it swinging to and fro,
While Geraldine, in wretched plight,
Sank down upon the floor below.

O weary lady, Geraldine,
I pray you, drink this cordial wine!
It is a wine of virtuous powers;
My mother made it of wild flowers.

And will your mother pity me,
Who am a maiden most forlorn?
Christabel answered—Woe is me!
She died the hour that I was born.
I have heard the gray-haired friar tell
How on her death-bed she did say,
That she should hear the castle-bell
Strike twelve upon my wedding-day.
O mother dear! that thou wert here!
I would, said Geraldine, she were!

But soon with altered voice, said she—
"Off, wandering mother! Peak and pine!
I have power to bid thee flee."
Alas! what ails poor Geraldine?
Why stares she with unsettled eye?
Can she the bodiless dead espy?

And why with hollow voice cries she,
"Off, woman, off! this hour is mine—
Though thou her guardian spirit be,
Off, woman, off! 'tis given to me."

Then Christabel knelt by the lady's side,
And raised to heaven her eyes so blue—
Alas! said she, this ghastly ride—
Dear lady! it hath wildered you!
The lady wiped her moist cold brow,
And faintly said, "'tis over now!"

Again the wild-flower wine she drank:
Her fair large eyes 'gan glitter bright,
And from the floor whereon she sank,
The lofty lady stood upright:
She was most beautiful to see,
Like a lady of a far countrée.

And thus the lofty lady spake—
"All they who live in the upper sky,
Do love you, holy Christabel!
And you love them, and for their sake
And for the good which me befell,
Even I in my degree will try,
Fair maiden, to requite you well.
But now unrobe yourself; for I
Must pray, ere yet in bed I lie."

Quoth Christabel, So let it be!
And as the lady bade, did she.
Her gentle limbs did she undress
And lay down in her loveliness.

But through her brain of weal and woe
So many thoughts moved to and fro,
That vain it were her lids to close;
So half-way from the bed she rose,
And on her elbow did recline
To look at the lady Geraldine.

Beneath the lamp the lady bowed,
And slowly rolled her eyes around;
Then drawing in her breath aloud,
Like one that shuddered, she unbound
The cincture° from beneath her breast: *girdle*
Her silken robe, and inner vest,
Dropt to her feet, and full in view,
Behold! her bosom, and half her side—
A sight to dream of, not to tell!
O shield her! shield sweet Christabel!

Yet Geraldine nor speaks nor stirs;
Ah! what a stricken look was hers!
Deep from within she seems half-way
To lift some weight with sick assay,° *attempt*
And eyes the maid and seeks delay;
Then suddenly as one defied
Collects herself in scorn and pride,
And lay down by the Maiden's side!—
And in her arms the maid she took,
    Ah wel-a-day!
And with low voice and doleful look
These words did say:
"In the touch of this bosom there worketh a spell,
Which is lord of thy utterance, Christabel!
Thou knowest to-night, and wilt know to-morrow
This mark of my shame, this seal of my sorrow;
    But vainly thou warrest,
        For this is alone in
    Thy power to declare,
        That in the dim forest
    Thou heard'st a low moaning,
And found'st a bright lady, surpassingly fair;
And didst bring her home with thee in love and in
    charity,
To shield her and shelter her from the damp air."

The Conclusion To Part I

It was a lovely sight to see
The lady Christabel, when she
Was praying at the old oak tree.
        Amid the jaggéd shadows
        Of mossy leafless boughs,
        Kneeling in the moonlight,
        To make her gentle vows;
Her slender palms together prest,
Heaving sometimes on her breast;

Her face resigned to bliss or bale°— *grief*
Her face, oh call it fair not pale,
And both blue eyes more bright than clear.
Each about to have a tear.

With open eyes (ah, woe is me!)
Asleep, and dreaming fearfully,
Fearfully dreaming, yet, I wis,
Dreaming that alone, which is—
O sorrow and shame! Can this be she,
The lady, who knelt at the old oak tree?
And lo! the worker of these harms,
That holds the maiden in her arms,
Seems to slumber still and mild,
As a mother with her child.

A star hath set, a star hath risen,
O Geraldine! since arms of thine
Have been the lovely lady's prison.
O Geraldine! one hour was thine—
Thou'st had thy will! By tairn° and rill, *mountain pool*
The night-birds all that hour were still.
But now they are jubilant anew,
From cliff and tower, tu—whoo! tu—whoo!
Tu—whoo! tu—whoo! from wood and fell!° *hill*

And see! the lady Christabel
Gathers herself from out her trance;
Her limbs relax, her countenance
Grows sad and soft; the smooth thin lids
Close o'er her eyes; and tears she sheds—
Large tears that leave the lashes bright!
And oft the while she seems to smile
As infants at a sudden light!

Yea, she doth smile, and she doth weep,
Like a youthful hermitess,
Beauteous in a wilderness,
Who, praying always, prays in sleep.
And, if she move unquietly,
Perchance, 'tis but the blood so free
Comes back and tingles in her feet.
No doubt, she hath a vision sweet.
What if her guardian spirit 'twere,
What if she knew her mother near?
But this she knows, in joys and woes,
That saints will aid if men will call:
For the blue sky bends over all!

Part 2

Each matin° bell, the Baron saith, *morning*
Knells us back to a world of death.
These words Sir Leoline first said,
When he rose and found his lady dead:
These words Sir Leoline will say
Many a morn to his dying day!

And hence the custom and law began
That still at dawn the sacristan,° *church sexton*
Who duly pulls the heavy bell,
Five and forty beads° must tell° *rosary beads / count*
Between each stroke—a warning knell,
Which not a soul can choose but hear
From Bratha Head to Wyndermere.[1]

Saith Bracy the bard, So let it knell!
And let the drowsy sacristan
Still count as slowly as he can!
There is no lack of such, I ween,° *suppose*
As well fill up the space between.
In Langdale Pike and Witch's Lair,
And Dungeon-ghyll so foully rent,
With ropes of rock and bells of air
Three sinful sextons' ghosts are pent,
Who all give back, one after t'other,
The death-note to their living brother;
And oft too, by the knell offended,
Just as their one! two! three! is ended,
The devil mocks the doleful tale
With a merry peal from Borodale.

The air is still! through mist and cloud
That merry peal comes ringing loud;
And Geraldine shakes off her dread,
And rises lightly from the bed;
Puts on her silken vestments white,

[1] *Bratha Head ... Wyndermere* In the Lake District.

And tricks her hair in lovely plight,[1]
And nothing doubting of her spell
Awakens the lady Christabel.
"Sleep you, sweet lady Christabel?
I trust that you have rested well."

And Christabel awoke and spied
The same who lay down by her side—
O rather say, the same whom she
Raised up beneath the old oak tree!
Nay, fairer yet! and yet more fair!
For she belike hath drunken deep
Of all the blessedness of sleep!
And while she spake, her looks, her air
Such gentle thankfulness declare,
That (so it seemed) her girded vests
Grew tight beneath her heaving breasts.
"Sure I have sinn'd!" said Christabel,
"Now heaven be praised if all be well!"
And in low faltering tones, yet sweet,
Did she the lofty lady greet
With such perplexity of mind
As dreams too lively leave behind.

So quickly she rose, and quickly arrayed
Her maiden limbs, and having prayed
That He, who on the cross did groan,
Might wash away her sins unknown,
She forthwith led fair Geraldine
To meet her sire, Sir Leoline.

The lovely maid and the lady tall
Are pacing both into the hall,
And pacing on through page and groom,
Enter the Baron's presence-room.

The Baron rose, and while he prest
His gentle daughter to his breast,
With cheerful wonder in his eyes
The lady Geraldine espies,
And gave such welcome to the same,
As might beseem so bright a dame!

But when he heard the lady's tale,
And when she told her father's name,
Why waxed Sir Leoline so pale,
Murmuring o'er the name again,
Lord Roland de Vaux of Tryermaine?

Alas! they had been friends in youth;
But whispering tongues can poison truth;
And constancy lives in realms above;
And life is thorny; and youth is vain;
And to be wroth with one we love,
Doth work like madness in the brain.
And thus it chanced, as I divine,
With Roland and Sir Leoline.
Each spake words of high disdain
And insult to his heart's best brother:
They parted—ne'er to meet again!
But never either found another
To free the hollow heart from paining—
They stood aloof, the scars remaining,
Like cliffs which had been rent asunder;
A dreary sea now flows between;—
But neither heat, nor frost, nor thunder,
Shall wholly do away, I ween,
The marks of that which once hath been.

Sir Leoline, a moment's space,
Stood gazing on the damsel's face:
And the youthful Lord of Tryermaine
Came back upon his heart again.

O then the Baron forgot his age,
His noble heart swelled high with rage;
He swore by the wounds in Jesu's side,
He would proclaim it far and wide
With trump and solemn heraldry,
That they, who thus had wronged the dame,
Were base as spotted infamy!
"And if they dare deny the same,
My herald shall appoint a week,
And let the recreant traitors seek
My tourney° court—that there and then *tournament*
I may dislodge their reptile souls
From the bodies and forms of men!"
He spake: his eye in lightning rolls!
For the lady was ruthlessly seized; and he kenned° *recognized*
In the beautiful lady the child of his friend!

[1] *plight* I.e., plait, or braid.

And now the tears were on his face,
And fondly in his arms he took
Fair Geraldine, who met the embrace,
Prolonging it with joyous look.
Which when she viewed, a vision fell
Upon the soul of Christabel,
The vision of fear, the touch and pain!
She shrunk and shuddered, and saw again—
(Ah, woe is me! Was it for thee,
Thou gentle maid! such sights to see?)

Again she saw that bosom old,
Again she felt that bosom cold,
And drew in her breath with a hissing sound:
Whereat the Knight turned wildly round,
And nothing saw, but his own sweet maid
With eyes upraised, as one that prayed.

The touch, the sight, had passed away,
And in its stead that vision blest,
Which comforted her after-rest.
While in the lady's arms she lay,
Had put a rapture in her breast,
And on her lips and o'er her eyes
Spread smiles like light!
With new surprise,
"What ails then my belovéd child?"
The Baron said—His daughter mild
Made answer, "All will yet be well!"
I ween, she had no power to tell
Aught else: so mighty was the spell.

Yet he, who saw this Geraldine,
Had deemed her sure a thing divine:
Such sorrow with such grace she blended,
As if she feared she had offended
Sweet Christabel, that gentle maid!
And with such lowly tones she prayed,
She might be sent without delay
Home to her father's mansion.
"Nay!
Nay, by my soul!" said Leoline.
"Ho! Bracy the bard, the charge be thine!
Go thou, with music sweet and loud,
And take two steeds with trappings proud,
And take the youth whom thou lov'st best
To bear thy harp, and learn thy song,
And clothe you both in solemn vest,
And over the mountains haste along,
Lest wandering folk, that are abroad,
Detain you on the valley road.

"And when he has crossed the Irthing flood,
My merry bard! he hastes, he hastes
Up Knorren Moor, through Halegarth Wood,
And reaches soon that castle good
Which stands and threatens Scotland's wastes.

"Bard Bracy! bard Bracy! your horses are fleet,
Ye must ride up the hall, your music so sweet,
More loud than your horses' echoing feet!
And loud and loud to Lord Roland call,
Thy daughter is safe in Langdale hall!
Thy beautiful daughter is safe and free—
Sir Leoline greets thee thus through me!
He bids thee come without delay
With all thy numerous array
And take thy lovely daughter home:
And he will meet thee on the way
With all his numerous array
White with their panting palfreys' foam:
And, by mine honour! I will say,
That I repent me of the day
When I spake words of fierce disdain
To Roland de Vaux of Tryermaine!—
—For since that evil hour hath flown,
Many a summer's sun hath shone;
Yet ne'er found I a friend again
Like Roland de Vaux of Tryermaine."

The lady fell, and clasped his knees,
Her face upraised, her eyes o'erflowing;
And Bracy replied, with faltering voice,
His gracious hail on all bestowing!—
"Thy words, thou sire of Christabel,
Are sweeter than my harp can tell;
Yet might I gain a boon° of thee, *request*
This day my journey should not be,
So strange a dream hath come to me,
That I had vowed with music loud

To clear yon wood from thing unblest,
Warned by a vision in my rest!
For in my sleep I saw that dove,
That gentle bird, whom thou dost love,
And call'st by thy own daughter's name—
Sir Leoline! I saw the same
Fluttering, and uttering fearful moan,
Among the green herbs in the forest alone.
Which when I saw and when I heard,
I wonder'd what might ail the bird;
For nothing near it could I see,
Save the grass and herbs underneath the old tree.

"And in my dream methought I went
To search out what might there be found;
And what the sweet bird's trouble meant,
That thus lay fluttering on the ground.
I went and peered, and could descry
No cause for her distressful cry;
But yet for her dear lady's sake
I stooped, methought, the dove to take,
When lo! I saw a bright green snake
Coiled around its wings and neck.
Green as the herbs on which it couched,
Close by the dove's its head it crouched;
And with the dove it heaves and stirs,
Swelling its neck as she swelled hers!
I woke; it was the midnight hour,
The clock was echoing in the tower;
But though my slumber was gone by,
This dream it would not pass away—
It seems to live upon my eye!
And thence I vowed this self-same day,
With music strong and saintly song
To wander through the forest bare,
Lest aught unholy loiter there."

Thus Bracy said: the Baron, the while,
Half-listening heard him with a smile;
Then turned to Lady Geraldine,
His eyes made up of wonder and love;
And said in courtly accents fine,
"Sweet maid, Lord Roland's beauteous dove,
With arms more strong than harp or song,
Thy sire and I will crush the snake!"
He kissed her forehead as he spake,
And Geraldine in maiden wise,
Casting down her large bright eyes,
With blushing cheek and courtesy fine
She turned her from Sir Leoline;
Softly gathering up her train,
That o'er her right arm fell again;
And folded her arms across her chest,
And couched her head upon her breast,
And looked askance at Christabel—
Jesu, Maria, shield her well!

A snake's small eye blinks dull and shy;
And the lady's eyes they shrunk in her head,
Each shrunk up to a serpent's eye,
And with somewhat of malice, and more of dread,
At Christabel she looked askance!—
One moment—and the sight was fled!
But Christabel in dizzy trance
Stumbling on the unsteady ground
Shuddered aloud, with a hissing sound;
And Geraldine again turned round,
And like a thing, that sought relief,
Full of wonder and full of grief,
She rolled her large bright eyes divine
Wildly on Sir Leoline.

The maid, alas! her thoughts are gone,
She nothing sees—no sight but one!
The maid, devoid of guile and sin,
I know not how, in fearful wise,
So deeply had she drunken in
That look, those shrunken serpent eyes,
That all her features were resigned
To this sole image in her mind:
And passively did imitate
That look of dull and treacherous hate!
And thus she stood, in dizzy trance,
Still picturing that look askance
With forced unconscious sympathy
Full before her father's view—
As far as such a look could be
In eyes so innocent and blue!

And when the trance was o'er, the maid
Paused awhile, and inly prayed:
Then falling at the Baron's feet,
"By my mother's soul do I entreat
That thou this woman send away!"
She said: and more she could not say:
For what she knew she could not tell,
O'er-mastered by the mighty spell.

Why is thy cheek so wan and wild,
Sir Leoline? Thy only child
Lies at thy feet, thy joy, thy pride,
So fair, so innocent, so mild;
The same, for whom thy lady died!
O by the pangs of her dear mother
Think thou no evil of thy child!
For her, and thee, and for no other,
She prayed the moment ere she died:
Prayed that the babe for whom she died,
Might prove her dear lord's joy and pride!
That prayer her deadly pangs beguiled,
Sir Leoline!
And wouldst thou wrong thy only child,
Her child and thine?

Within the Baron's heart and brain
If thoughts, like these, had any share,
They only swelled his rage and pain,
And did but work confusion there.
His heart was cleft with pain and rage,
His cheeks they quivered, his eyes were wild,
Dishonored thus in his old age;
Dishonored by his only child,
And all his hospitality
To the wronged daughter of his friend
By more than woman's jealousy
Brought thus to a disgraceful end—
He rolled his eye with stern regard
Upon the gentle minstrel bard,
And said in tones abrupt, austere—
"Why, Bracy! dost thou loiter here?
I bade thee hence!" The bard obeyed;
And turning from his own sweet maid,
The agéd knight, Sir Leoline,
Led forth the lady Geraldine!

The Conclusion to Part 2

A little child, a limber elf,
Singing, dancing to itself,
A fairy thing with red round cheeks,
That always finds, and never seeks,
Makes such a vision to the sight
As fills a father's eyes with light;
And pleasures flow in so thick and fast
Upon his heart, that he at last
Must needs express his love's excess
With words of unmeant bitterness.
Perhaps 'tis pretty to force together
Thoughts so all unlike each other;
To mutter and mock a broken charm,
To dally with wrong that does no harm.
Perhaps 'tis tender too and pretty
At each wild word to feel within
A sweet recoil of love and pity.
And what, if in a world of sin
(O sorrow and shame should this be true!)
Such giddiness of heart and brain
Comes seldom save from rage and pain,
So talks as it's most used to do.
—1801

Dejection: An Ode[1]

Late, late yestreen I saw the new Moon,
With the old Moon in her arms;
And I fear, I fear, my Master dear!
We shall have a deadly storm.
"Ballad of Sir Patrick Spence"[2]

1

Well! If the Bard was weather-wise, who made
The grand old ballad of Sir Patrick Spence,
This night, so tranquil now, will not go hence
Unroused by winds, that ply a busier trade

[1] *Dejection: An Ode* Coleridge originally wrote this poem as a verse letter to Sara Hutchinson (Wordsworth's future sister-in-law), with whom he had fallen in love.

[2] *Ballad of Sir Patrick Spence* Anonymous; published in Thomas Percy's *Reliques of Ancient English Poetry* (1765).

Than those which mould yon cloud in lazy flakes,
Or the dull sobbing draft, that moans and rakes
Upon the strings of this Æolian lute,[1]
Which better far were mute.
For lo! the New-moon winter-bright!
And overspread with phantom light,
(With swimming phantom light o'erspread
But rimmed and circled by a silver thread)
I see the old Moon in her lap, foretelling
The coming-on of rain and squally blast.
And oh! that even now the gust were swelling,
And the slant night-shower driving loud and fast!
Those sounds which oft have raised me, whilst they awed,
And sent my soul abroad,
Might now perhaps their wonted° impulse give, *usual*
Might startle this dull pain, and make it move and live!

2

A grief without a pang, void, dark, and drear,
A stifled, drowsy, unimpassioned grief,
Which finds no natural outlet, no relief,
In word, or sigh, or tear—
O Lady! in this wan and heartless mood,
To other thoughts by yonder throstle° woo'd, *song-thrush*
All this long eve, so balmy and serene,
Have I been gazing on the western sky,
And its peculiar tint of yellow green:
And still I gaze—and with how blank an eye!
And those thin clouds above, in flakes and bars,
That give away their motion to the stars;
Those stars, that glide behind them or between,
Now sparkling, now bedimmed, but always seen:
Yon crescent Moon, as fixed as if it grew
In its own cloudless, starless lake of blue;
I see them all so excellently fair,
I see, not feel, how beautiful they are!

3

My genial spirits fail;
And what can these avail
To lift the smothering weight from off my breast?
It were a vain endeavour,
Though I should gaze for ever
On that green light that lingers in the west:
I may not hope from outward forms to win
The passion and the life, whose fountains are within.

4

O Lady! we receive but what we give,
And in our life alone does Nature live:
Ours is her wedding-garment, ours her shroud!
And would we aught behold, of higher worth,
Than that inanimate cold world allowed
To the poor loveless ever-anxious crowd,
Ah! from the soul itself must issue forth
A light, a glory, a fair luminous cloud
Enveloping the Earth—
And from the soul itself must there be sent
A sweet and potent voice, of its own birth,
Of all sweet sounds the life and element!

5

O pure of heart! thou need'st not ask of me
What this strong music in the soul may be!
What, and wherein it doth exist,
This light, this glory, this fair luminous mist,
This beautiful and beauty-making power.
Joy, virtuous Lady! Joy that ne'er was given,
Save to the pure, and in their purest hour,
Life, and Life's effluence, cloud at once and shower,
Joy, Lady! is the spirit and the power,
Which wedding Nature to us gives in dower
A new Earth and new Heaven,
Undreamt of by the sensual and the proud—
Joy is the sweet voice, Joy the luminous cloud—
We in ourselves rejoice!
And thence flows all that charms or ear or sight,
All melodies the echoes of that voice,
All colours a suffusion from that light.

6

There was a time when, though my path was rough,
This joy within me dallied with distress,
And all misfortunes were but as the stuff
Whence Fancy made me dreams of happiness:
For hope grew round me, like the twining vine,
And fruits, and foliage, not my own, seemed mine.

[1] *Æolian lute* Musical instrument named after Æolus, Greek god of the winds; the music of the lute, or, rather, harp, is made by exposure to the wind passing through it.

But now afflictions bow me down to earth:
Nor care I that they rob me of my mirth;
But oh! each visitation
Suspends what nature gave me at my birth,
My shaping spirit of Imagination.
For not to think of what I needs must feel,
But to be still and patient, all I can;
And haply by abstruse research to steal
From my own nature all the natural man—
This was my sole resource, my only plan:
Till that which suits a part infects the whole,
And now is almost grown the habit of my soul.

7

Hence, viper thoughts, that coil around my mind,
Reality's dark dream!
I turn from you, and listen to the wind,
Which long has raved unnoticed. What a scream
Of agony by torture lengthened out
That lute sent forth! Thou Wind, that rav'st without,
Bare crag, or mountain-tairn,[1] or blasted tree,
Or pine-grove whither woodman never clomb,
Or lonely house, long held the witches' home,
Methinks were fitter instruments for thee,
Mad Lutanist! who in this month of showers,
Of dark-brown gardens, and of peeping flowers,
Mak'st Devils' yule, with worse than wintry song,
The blossoms, buds, and timorous leaves among.
Thou Actor, perfect in all tragic sounds!
Thou mighty Poet, e'en to frenzy bold!
What tell'st thou now about?
'Tis of the rushing of an host in rout,
With groans, of trampled men, with smarting wounds—
At once they groan with pain, and shudder with the cold!
But hush! there is a pause of deepest silence!
And all that noise, as of a rushing crowd,
With groans, and tremulous shudderings—all is over—
It tells another tale, with sounds less deep and loud!
A tale of less affright,
And tempered with delight,
As Otway's[2] self had framed the tender lay,—
'Tis of a little child
Upon a lonesome wild,
Not far from home, but she hath lost her way:
And now moans low in bitter grief and fear,
And now screams loud, and hopes to make her mother hear.

8

'Tis midnight, but small thoughts have I of sleep:
Full seldom may my friend such vigils keep!
Visit her, gentle Sleep! with wings of healing,
And may this storm be but a mountain-birth,
May all the stars hang bright above her dwelling,
Silent as though they watched the sleeping Earth!
With light heart may she rise,
Gay fancy, cheerful eyes,
Joy lift her spirit, joy attune her voice;
To her may all things live, from the pole to pole,
Their life the eddying of her living soul!
O simple spirit, guided from above,
Dear Lady! friend devoutest of my choice,
Thus mayest thou ever, evermore rejoice.
—1802

[1] [Coleridge's note] Tairn is a small lake, generally if not always applied to the lakes up in the mountains and which are the feeders of those in the valleys. This address to the Storm-wind will not appear extravagant to those who have heard it at night and in a mountainous country.

[2] *Otway* Thomas Otway (1652–85), English playwright known for his tragedies.

Work Without Hope

Lines Composed 21st February 1825

All Nature seems at work. Slugs leave their lair—
The bees are stirring—birds are on the wing—
And Winter slumbering in the open air,
Wears on his smiling face a dream of Spring!
And I the while, the sole unbusy thing,
Nor honey make, nor pair, nor build, nor sing.

Yet well I ken° the banks where amaranths[3] blow, *recognize*
Have traced the fount whence streams of nectar flow.
Bloom, O ye amaranths! bloom for whom ye may,
For me ye bloom not! Glide, rich streams, away!

[3] *amaranths* Imaginary flowers, the blossoms of which never fade.

With lips unbrightened, wreathless brow, I stroll:
And would you learn the spells that drowse my soul?
Work without hope draws nectar in a sieve,
And Hope without an object cannot live.
—1828

Kubla Khan

Or, A Vision in a Dream. A Fragment[1]

In Xanadu did Kubla Khan
A stately pleasure-dome decree:
Where Alph, the sacred river, ran
Through caverns measureless to man
Down to a sunless sea.
So twice five miles of fertile ground
With walls and towers were girdled round:
And there were gardens bright with sinuous rills,° *brooks*
Where blossomed many an incense-bearing tree;
And here were forests ancient as the hills,
Enfolding sunny spots of greenery.

But oh! that deep romantic chasm which slanted
Down the green hill athwart a cedarn cover!
A savage place! as holy and enchanted
As e'er beneath a waning moon was haunted
By woman wailing for her demon-lover!
And from this chasm, with ceaseless turmoil seething,
As if this earth in fast thick pants were breathing,
A mighty fountain momently was forced:
Amid whose swift half-intermitted burst
Huge fragments vaulted like rebounding hail,
Or chaffy grain beneath the thresher's flail:
And 'mid these dancing rocks at once and ever
It flung up momently the sacred river.
Five miles meandering with a mazy° motion *labyrinthine*
Through wood and dale the sacred river ran,
Then reached the caverns measureless to man,
And sank in tumult to a lifeless ocean:
And 'mid this tumult Kubla heard from far
Ancestral voices prophesying war!
The shadow of the dome of pleasure
Floated midway on the waves;
Where was heard the mingled measure
From the fountain and the caves.
It was a miracle of rare device,
A sunny pleasure-dome with caves of ice!

[1] [Coleridge's note] The following fragment is here published at the request of a poet [Lord Byron] of great and deserved celebrity, and as far as the Author's own opinions are concerned, rather as a psychological curiosity, than on the ground of any supposed poetic merits.

In the summer of the year 1797, the Author, then in ill health, had retired to a lonely farmhouse between Porlock and Linton, on the Exmoor confines of Somerset and Devonshire. In consequence of a slight indisposition [dysentery], an anodyne [opium] had been prescribed, from the effects of which he fell asleep in his chair at the moment that he was reading the following sentence, or words of the same substance, in *Purchas's Pilgrimage* [i.e., *Purchas his Pilgrimage* (1613, 1614, 1617, 1626)]: "Here the Khan Kubla commanded a palace to be built, and a stately garden thereunto. And thus ten miles of fertile ground were inclosed with a wall." The author continued for about three hours in a profound sleep, at least of the external senses, during which time he has the most vivid confidence, that he could not have composed less than from two to three hundred lines, if that indeed can be called composition in which all the images rose up before him as things, with a parallel production of the correspondent expressions, without any sensation or consciousness of effort. On awaking he appeared to himself to have a distinct recollection of the whole, and taking his pen, ink, and paper, instantly and eagerly wrote down the lines that are here preserved. At this moment he was unfortunately called out by a person on business from Porlock, and detained by him above an hour, and on his return to his room, found to his no small surprise and mortification, that though he still retained some vague and dim recollection of the general purpose of the vision, yet, with the exception of some eight or ten scattered lines and images, all the rest had passed away like the images on the surface of a stream into which a stone has been cast, but, alas! without the after restoration of the latter!

Then all the charm
Is broken—all that phantom-world so fair
Vanishes, and a thousand circlets spread,
And each mis-shape the other. Stay awhile,
Poor youth! who scarcely dar'st lift up thine eyes—
The stream will soon renew its smoothness, soon
The visions will return! And lo, he stays,
And soon the fragments dim of lovely forms
Come trembling back, unite, and now once more
The pool becomes a mirror.

[from Coleridge's "The Picture, or the Lover's Resolution" (1802) 69–78]

Yet from the still surviving recollections in his mind, the Author has frequently purposed to finish for himself what had been originally, as it were, given to him. Σαμερον αδιον ασω [from Theocritus's *Idyll* 1.145]: but the tomorrow is yet to come.

As a contrast to this vision, I have annexed a fragment of a very different character [Coleridge's poem "The Pains of Sleep"], describing with equal fidelity the dream of pain and disease.

A damsel with a dulcimer
In a vision once I saw:
It was an Abyssinian maid,
And on her dulcimer she played,
Singing of Mount Abora.
Could I revive within me
Her symphony and song,
To such a deep delight 'twould win me,
That with music loud and long,
I would build that dome in air,
That sunny dome! those caves of ice!
And all who heard should see them there,
And all should cry, Beware! Beware!
His flashing eyes, his floating hair!
Weave a circle round him thrice,
And close your eyes with holy dread,
For he on honey-dew hath fed,
And drunk the milk of Paradise.

—1816 (written 1798)

Epitaph

Stop, Christian passerby!—Stop, child of God,
And read with gentle breast. Beneath this sod
A poet lies, or that which once seem'd he.
O, lift one thought in prayer for S.T.C.;
That he who many a year with toil of breath
Found death in life, may here find life in death!
Mercy for praise—to be forgiven for[1] fame
He ask'd, and hoped, through Christ. Do thou the same!

—1833

On Donne's Poetry

With Donne,[2] whose muse on dromedary trots,
Wreathe iron pokers into true-love knots;
Rhyme's sturdy cripple, fancy's maze and clue,
Wit's forge and fire-blast, meaning's press and screw.

—1836

[1] [Coleridge's note] "For" in the sense of "instead of."

[2] *Donne* English poet John Donne (1572–1631).

from *Lectures and Notes On Literature*

[Definition of Poetry]

Readers may be divided into four classes:

1. Sponges, who absorb all they read, and return it nearly in the same state, only a little dirtied.

2. Sand-glasses, who retain nothing, and are content to get through a book for the sake of getting through the time.

3. Strain-bags, who retain merely the dregs of what they read.

4. Mogul diamonds, equally rare and valuable, who profit by what they read, and enable others to profit by it also.

from Notes on *Lear*

Of all Shakespeare's plays *Macbeth* is the most rapid, *Hamlet* the slowest, in movement. *Lear* combines length with rapidity—like the hurricane and the whirlpool, absorbing while it advances. It begins as a stormy day in summer, with brightness; but that brightness is lurid, and anticipates the tempest.…

It is well worth notice, that *Lear* is the only serious performance of Shakespeare the interest and situations of which are derived from the assumption of a gross improbability; whereas Beaumont and Fletcher's tragedies are, almost all, founded on some out-of-the-way accident or exception to the general experience of mankind. But observe the matchless judgement of Shakespeare! First, improbable as the conduct of Lear is, in the first scene, yet it was an old story, rooted in the popular faith—a thing taken for granted already, and consequently without any of the *effects* of improbability. Secondly, it is merely the canvas to the characters and passions, a mere *occasion*—not (as in Beaumont and Fletcher) perpetually recurring, as the cause and *sine qua non*[3] of the incidents and emotions. Let the first scene of *Lear* have been lost, and let it be only understood that a fond father had been duped by hypocritical professions of love and duty on the part of two daughters to disinherit a third, previously, and deservedly, more dear to

[3] *sine qua non* Latin: literally, without which not; i.e., something essential.

him, and all the rest of the tragedy would retain its interest undiminished, and be perfectly intelligible. The *accidental* is nowhere the groundwork of the passions, but the κάθολου,[1] that which in all ages has been and ever will be close and native to the heart of man—parental anguish from filial ingratitude, the genuineness of worth, tho' coffered in bluntness, the vileness of smooth iniquity....

from [On the English Language]

The language, that is to say the particular tongue, in which Shakespeare wrote, cannot be left out of consideration. It will not be disputed, that one language may possess advantages which another does not enjoy; and we may state with confidence, that English excels all other languages in the number of its practical words. The French may bear the palm in the names of trades, and in military and diplomatic terms. Of the German it may be said, that, exclusive of many mineralogical words, it is incomparable in its metaphysical and psychological force.... Italian is the sweetest and softest language; Spanish the most majestic. All these have their peculiar faults; but I never can agree that any language is unfit for poetry, although different languages, from the condition and circumstances of the people, may certainly be adapted to one species of poetry more than to another.

Take the French as an example. It is, perhaps, the most perspicuous[2] and pointed language in the world, and therefore best fitted for conversation, for the expression of light and airy passion, attaining its object by peculiar and felicitous turns of phrase, which are evanescent, and, like the beautifully coloured dust on the wings of a butterfly, must not be judged by the test of touch. It appears as if it were all surface and had no substratum, and it constantly most dangerously tampers with morals, without positively offending decency. As the language for what is called modern genteel comedy all others must yield to French.

... Italian, though sweet and soft, is not deficient in force and dignity....

But in English I find that which is possessed by no other modern language, and which, as it were, appropriates it to the drama. It is a language made out of many, and it has consequently many words, which originally had the same meaning; but in the progress of society those words have gradually assumed different shades of meaning. Take any homogeneous language, such as German, and try to translate into it the following lines:

> But not to one, in this benighted age,
> Is that diviner inspiration given,
> That burns in Shakespeare's or in Milton's page,
> The pomp and prodigality of heaven.
>
> Gray's "Stanzas to Bentley"[3]

In German it would be necessary to say "the pomp and *spend-thriftness* of heaven," because the German has not, as we have, one word with two such distinct meanings, one expressing the nobler, the other the baser idea of the same action.

The monosyllabic character of English enables us, besides, to express more meaning in a shorter compass than can be done in any other language.

[Mechanic Vs. Organic Form]

Are the plays of Shakespeare works of rude uncultivated genius, in which the splendour of the parts compensates, if aught can compensate, for the barbarous shapelessness and irregularity of the whole? ... Or is the form equally admirable with the matter, the judgment of the great poet not less deserving of our wonder than his genius? Or to repeat the question in other words, is Shakespeare a great dramatic poet on account only of those beauties and excellencies which he possesses in common with the ancients, but with diminished claims to our love and honour to the full extent of his difference from them? Or are these very differences additional proofs of poetic wisdom, at once results and symbols of living power as contrasted with lifeless mechanism, of free and rival

[1] κάθολου Greek: universal, general. Coleridge here contrasts the idea of universal or general characteristics (common to all people) with those that are "accidental," particular, or specific to certain people in certain times and places. (Cf. Aristotle's *Poetics*, in which he discusses the universal versus the accidental in history and poetry.)

[2] *perspicuous* Transparent.

[3] *Gray's ... Bentley* I.e., Thomas Gray's "Stanzas to Mr. Bentley."

originality as contradistinguished from servile imitation, or more accurately, a blind copying of effects instead of a true imitation of the essential principles? Imagine not I am about to oppose genius to rules. No! the comparative value of these rules is the very cause to be tried. The spirit of poetry, like all other living powers, must of necessity circumscribe itself by rules, were it only to unite power with beauty. It must embody in order to reveal itself; but a living body is of necessity an organized one—and what is organization but the connection of parts to a whole, so that each part is at once end and means! This is no discovery of criticism; it is a necessity of the human mind—and all nations have felt and obeyed it, in the invention of meter and measured sounds as the vehicle and involucrum[1] of poetry, itself a fellow growth from the same life, even as the bark is to the tree.

No work of true genius dare want its appropriate form; neither indeed is there any danger of this. As it must not, so neither can it, be lawless! For it is even this that constitutes its genius—the power of acting creatively under laws of its own origination. How then comes it that … whole nations have combined in unhesitating condemnation of our great dramatist, as a sort of African nature, fertile in beautiful monsters, as a wild heath where islands of fertility look greener from the surrounding waste, where the loveliest plants now shine out among unsightly weeds and now are choked by their parasitic growth, so intertwined that we cannot disentangle the weed without snapping the flower.… The true ground of the mistake, as has been well remarked by a continental critic,[2] lies in the confounding mechanical regularity with organic form. The form is mechanic when on any given material we impress a predetermined form, not necessarily arising out of the properties of the material, as when to a mass of wet clay we give whatever shape we wish it to retain when hardened. The organic form, on the other hand, is innate; it shapes as it develops itself from within, and the fullness of its development is one and the same with the perfection of its outward form. Such is the life, such the form. Nature, the prime genial artist, inexhaustible in diverse powers, is equally inexhaustible in forms. Each exterior is the physiognomy of the being within, its true image reflected and thrown out from the concave mirror. And even such is the appropriate excellence of her chosen poet, of our own Shakespeare, himself a nature humanized, a genial understanding directing self-consciously a power and an implicit wisdom deeper than consciousness.

—1811–12

[1] *involucrum* Outer membrane.

[2] *a continental critic* German art and literary critic August Wilhelm Schlegel (1767–1845).

from *Biographia Literaria; or Biographical Sketches of my Literary Life and Opinions*

from CHAPTER 1
Reception of the Author's First Publication

… In 1794, when I had barely passed the verge of manhood, I published a small volume of juvenile poems. They were received with a degree of favour, which young as I was, I well know was bestowed on them not so much for any positive merit, as because they were considered buds of hope, and promises of better works to come. The critics of that day, the most flattering, equally with the severest, concurred in objecting to them: obscurity, a general turgidness of diction, and a profusion of new coined double epithets.[3]

[3] [Coleridge's note] The authority of Milton and Shakespeare may be usefully pointed out to young authors. In the *Comus* and other early poems of Milton there is a superfluity of double epithets, while in the *Paradise Lost* we find very few, in the *Paradise Regained* scarce any. The same remark holds almost equally true of the *Love's Labour Lost, Romeo and Juliet, Venus and Adonis,* and *Lucrece*, compared with the *Lear, Macbeth, Othello*, and *Hamlet* of our great dramatist. The rule for the admission of double epithets seems to be this: either that they should be already denizens of our language, such as blood-stained, terror-stricken, self-applauding, or when a new epithet, or one found in books only, is hazarded, that it, at least, be one word, not two words made one by mere virtue of the printer's hyphen. A language which, like the English, is almost without cases, is indeed in its very genius unfitted for compounds. If a writer, every time a compounded word suggests itself to him, would seek for some other mode of expressing the same sense, the chances are always greatly in favour of his finding a better word. *Ut tanquam scopulum sic fugias insolens verbum*, is the wise advice of Caesar to the Roman orators, and the precept applies with double force to the writers in our own language. But it must not be forgotten that the same Caesar wrote a treatise for the purpose of reforming the ordinary language by

... From that period to the date of the present work I have published nothing, with my name, which could by any possibility have come before the board of anonymous criticism. Even the three or four poems, printed with the works of a friend, as far as they were censured at all, were charged with the same or similar defects, though I am persuaded not with equal justice: with an excess of ornament, in addition to strained and elaborate diction. (*Vide*[1] *the criticisms on the "Ancient Mariner" in the Monthly and Critical Reviews of the first volume of the* Lyrical Ballads.) May I be permitted to add, that, even at the early period of my juvenile poems, I saw and admitted the superiority of an austerer, and more natural style, with an insight not less clear, than I at present possess. My judgement was stronger, than were my powers of realizing its dictates; and the faults of my language, though indeed partly owing to a wrong choice of subjects, and the desire of giving a poetic colouring to abstract and metaphysical truths, in which a new world then seemed to open upon me, did yet, in part likewise, originate in unfeigned diffidence of my own comparative talent....

The Effect of Contemporary Writers on Youthful Minds

... Among those with whom I conversed, there were, of course, very many who had formed their taste, and their notions of poetry, from the writings of Mr. Pope[2] and his followers: or to speak more generally, in that school of French poetry, condensed and invigorated by English understanding, which had predominated from the last century. I was not blind to the merits of this school, yet as from inexperience of the world and consequent want of sympathy with the general subjects of these poems, they gave me little pleasure, I doubtless undervalued the *kind*, and with the presumption of youth withheld from its masters the legitimate name of poets. I saw, that the excellence of this kind consisted in just and acute observations on men and manners in an artificial state of society, as its matter and substance: and in the logic of wit, conveyed in smooth and strong epigrammatic couplets, as its *form*. Even when the subject was addressed to the fancy, or the intellect, as in *The Rape of the Lock*, or *The Essay on Man*—nay, when it was a consecutive narration, as in that astonishing product of matchless talent and ingenuity, Pope's Translation of the *Iliad*—still a *point* was looked for at the end of each second line, and the whole was as it were a sorites,[3] or, if I may exchange a logical for a grammatical metaphor, a *conjunction disjunctive*, of epigrams.[4] Meantime the matter and diction seemed to me characterized not so much by poetic thoughts, as by thoughts *translated* into the language of poetry.

... I was ... led to a conjecture, which, many years afterwards was recalled to me from the same thought having been started in conversation, but far more ably, and developed more fully, by Mr. Wordsworth; namely, that this style of poetry, which I have characterised above, as translations of prose thoughts into poetic language, had been kept up by, if it did not wholly arise from, the custom of writing Latin verses, and the great importance attached to these exercises, in our public schools. Whatever might have been the case in the fifteenth century, when the use of the Latin tongue was. so general among learned men, that Erasmus[5] is said to have forgotten his native language; yet in the present day it is not to be supposed, that a youth can *think* in Latin, or that he can have any other reliance on the force or fitness of his phrases, but the authority of the writer from whence he has adopted them. Consequently he must first prepare his thoughts, and then pick out, from Virgil, Horace, Ovid,[6] or perhaps more compendiously from his *Gradus*,[7] halves and quarters of lines, in which to embody them....

bringing it to a greater accordance with the principles of logic or universal grammar.

[1] *Vide* Latin: see.

[2] *Mr. Pope* British poet Alexander Pope (1688–1744). It is to his work that Coleridge proceeds to refer.

[3] *sorites* Type of argument in which the predicate of one thesis becomes the subject of the next.

[4] *conjunctive disjunctive, of epigrams* Connecting and disconnecting, in poems that seem to lead up to one point and then turn at the end to make another.

[5] *Erasmus* Dutch author, priest, and scholar (1466?–1536), who translated many classics into Greek and Latin.

[6] *Virgil, Horace, Ovid* Roman poets.

[7] *Gradus* Latin dictionary of verse (*Gradus ad Parnassum*) used to aid in composition.

Bowles's Sonnets

... Our genuine admiration of a great poet is a continuous *undercurrent* of feeling; it is everywhere present, but seldom anywhere as a separate excitement. I was wont boldly to affirm, that it would be scarcely more difficult to push a stone out from the pyramids with the bare hand, than to alter a word, or the position of a word, in Milton or Shakespeare (in their most important works at least), without making the author say something else, or something worse, than he does say. One great distinction, I appeared to myself to see plainly, between, even the characteristic faults of our elder poets, and the false beauty of the moderns. In the former, from Donne to Cowley,[1] we find the most fantastic out-of-the-way thoughts, but in the most pure and genuine mother English; in the latter, the most obvious thoughts, in language the most fantastic and arbitrary. Our faulty elder poets sacrificed the passion, and passionate flow of poetry, to the subtleties of intellect, and to the starts of wit; the moderns to the glare and glitter of a perpetual, yet broken and heterogeneous imagery, or rather to an amphibious something, made up, half of image, and half of abstract meaning. The one sacrificed the heart to the head; the other both heart and head to point and drapery.

The reader must make himself acquainted with the general style of composition that was at that time deemed poetry, in order to understand and account for the effect produced on me by the *Sonnets*, the "Monody at Matlock," and the "Hope," of Mr. Bowles;[2] for it is peculiar to original genius to become less and less *striking*, in proportion to its success in improving the taste and judgement of its contemporaries. The poems of West indeed had the merit of chaste and manly diction, but they were cold, and, if I may so express it, only *dead-coloured*; while in the best of Warton's there is a stiffness, which too often gives them the appearance of imitations from the Greek. Whatever relation therefore of cause or impulse Percy's collection of ballads[3] may bear to the most *popular* poems of the present day; yet in the more sustained and elevated style, of the then living poets, Bowles and Cowper[4] were, to the best of my knowledge, the first who combined natural thoughts with natural diction; the first who reconciled the heart with the head....

[1] *Donne ... Cowley* English poets of the early seventeenth century.

[2] *Mr. Bowles* William Lisle Bowles (1762–1850), English poet and literary critic, who published a collection of his sonnets in 1789.

[3] *Percy's collection of ballads* Reverend Thomas Percy's *Reliques of Ancient English Poetry* (1765).

from Chapter 4
Mr. Wordsworth's Earlier Poems

... During the last year of my residence at Cambridge, I became acquainted with Mr. Wordsworth's first publication entitled *Descriptive Sketches*,[5] and seldom, if ever, was the emergence of an original poetic genius above the literary horizon more evidently announced. In the form, style, and manner of the whole poem, and in the structure of the particular lines and periods, there is an harshness and acerbity connected and combined with words and images all aglow, which might recall those products of the vegetable world, where gorgeous blossoms rise out of the hard and thorny rind and shell, within which the rich fruit was elaborating. The language was not only peculiar and strong, but at times knotty and contorted, as by its own impatient strength, while the novelty and struggling crowd of images, acting in conjunction with the difficulties of the style, demanded always a greater closeness of attention than poetry (at all events, than descriptive poetry) has a right to claim. It not seldom therefore justified the complaint of obscurity. In the following extract I have sometimes fancied that I saw an emblem of the poem itself, and of the author's genius as it was then displayed.

[4] [Coleridge's note] Cowper's *Task* was published some time before the *Sonnets* of Mr. Bowles; but I was not familiar with it till many years afterwards. The vein of satire which runs through that excellent poem, together with the somber hue of its religious opinions, would probably, *at that time*, have prevented its laying any strong hold on my affections. The love of nature seems to have led Thompson to a cheerful religion; and a gloomy religion to have led Cowper to a love of nature. The one would carry his fellow men along with him into nature; the other flies to nature from his fellow men. In chastity of diction, however, and the harmony of blank verse, Cowper leaves Thompson immeasurably below him; yet still I feel the latter to have been the *born poet*.

[5] *Descriptive Sketches* Published 1793 and again in 1815 in an altered version.

'Tis storm; and hid in mist from hour to hour,
All day the floods a deepening murmur pour;
The sky is veiled, and every cheerful sight:
Dark is the region as with coming night;
And yet what frequent bursts of overpowering light!
Triumphant on the bosom of the storm,
Glances the fire-clad eagle's wheeling form;
Eastward, in long perspective glittering, shine
The wood-crowned cliffs that o'er the lake recline;
Wide o'er the Alps a hundred streams unfold,
At once to pillars turned that flame with gold;
Behind his sail the peasant strives to shun
The West, that burns like one dilated sun,
Where in a mighty crucible expire
The mountains, glowing hot, like coals of fire.[1]

The poetic psyche, in its process to full development, undergoes as many changes as its Greek namesake, the butterfly.[2] And it is remarkable how soon genius clears and purifies itself from the faults and errors of its earliest products; faults which, in its earliest compositions, are the more obtrusive and confluent, because as heterogeneous elements, which had only a temporary use, they constitute the very *ferment*, by which themselves are carried off. Or we may compare them to some diseases, which must work on the humours, and be thrown out on the surface, in order to secure the patient from their future recurrence. I was in my twenty-fourth year, when I had the happiness of knowing Mr. Wordsworth personally, and while memory lasts, I shall hardly forget the sudden effect produced on my mind, by his recitation of a manuscript poem, which still remains unpublished,[3] but of which the stanza, and tone of style were the same as those of "The Female Vagrant" as originally printed in the first volume of the *Lyrical Ballads*. There was here, no mark of strained thought, or forced diction, no crowd or turbulence of imagery; and, as the poet hath himself well described in his lines "on revisiting the Wye,"[4] manly reflection, and human associations had given both variety, and an additional interest to natural objects, which in the passion and appetite of the first love they had seemed to him neither to need or permit. The occasional obscurities, which had risen from an imperfect control over the resources of his native language, had almost wholly disappeared, together with that worse defect of arbitrary and illogical phrases, at once hackneyed, and fantastic, which hold so distinguished a place in the *technique* of ordinary poetry, and will, more or less, alloy the earlier poems of the truest genius, unless the attention has been specifically directed to their worthlessness and incongruity.[5] I did not perceive anything particular in the mere style of the poem alluded to during its recitation, except indeed such difference as was not separable from the thought and manner; and the Spenserian stanza, which always, more or less, recalls to the reader's mind Spenser's own style, would doubtless have authorized, in my then opinion, a more frequent descent to the phrases of ordinary life, than could without an ill effect have been hazarded in the heroic couplet. It was not however the freedom from

[1] *'Tis storm ... fire* From "Descriptive Sketches Taken During a Pedestrian Tour in the Alps" (1815).

[2] [Coleridge's note] The fact that in Greek Psyche is the common name for the soul, and the butterfly is thus alluded to in the following stanzas from an unpublished poem ["The Butterfly" (1817)] of the author:

The butterfly the ancient Grecians made
The soul's fair emblem, and its only name—
But of the soul, escaped the slavish trade
Of mortal life! For in this earthly frame
Our's is the reptile's lot, much toil, much blame,
Manifold motions making little speed,
And to deform and kill the things, whereon we feed.

[3] *manuscript ... unpublished* "Guilt and Sorrow; or, Incidents Upon Salisbury Plain" (1842; written 1793-94).

[4] *"on revisiting the Wye"* From Wordsworth's "Lines Composed a Few Miles Above Tintern Abbey," 77–94.

[5] [Coleridge's note] Mr. Wordsworth, even in his two earliest, "An Evening Walk" and the "Descriptive Sketches," is more free from this latter defect than most of the young poets his contemporaries. It may, however, be exemplified, together with the harsh and obscure construction, in which he more often offended, in the following lines:

'Mid stormy vapours ever driving by,
Where ospreys, cormorants, and herons cry;
Where hardly given the hopeless waste to cheer,
Denied the bread of life, the foodful ear,
Dwindles the pear on autumn's latest spray,
And *apple sickens* pale in summer's ray;
Ev'n here content has fixed her smiling reign
With independence, child of high disdain.

I hope, I need not say, that I have quoted these lines for no other purpose than to make my meaning fully understood. It is to be regretted that Mr. Wordsworth has not republished these two poems entire.

false taste, whether as to common defects, or to those more properly his own, which made so unusual an impression on my feelings immediately, and subsequently on my judgement. It was the union of deep feeling with profound thought; the fine balance of truth in observing, with the imaginative faculty in modifying the objects observed; and above all the original gift of spreading the tone, the *atmosphere*, and with it the depth and height of the ideal world around forms, incidents, and situations, of which, for the common view, custom had bedimmed all the lustre, had dried up the sparkle and the dew drops. "To find no contradiction in the union of old and new; to contemplate the Ancient of days and all his works with feelings as fresh, as if all had then sprang forth at the first creative fiat;[1] characterizes the mind that feels the riddle of the world, and may help to unravel it. To carry on the feelings of childhood into the powers of manhood; to combine the child's sense of wonder and novelty with the appearances, which every day for perhaps forty years had rendered familiar;

> With sun and moon and stars throughout the year,
> And man and woman;[2]

this is the character and privilege of genius, and one of the marks which distinguish genius from talents. And therefore is it the prime merit of genius and its most unequivocal mode of manifestation, so to represent familiar objects as to awaken in the minds of others a kindred feeling concerning them and that freshness of sensation which is the constant accompaniment of mental, no less than of bodily, convalescence. Who has not a thousand times seen snow fall on water? Who has not watched it with a new feeling, from the time that he has read Burns' comparison of sensual pleasure

> To snow that falls upon a river
> A moment white—then gone for ever![3]

In poems, equally as in philosophic disquisitions, genius produces the strongest impressions of novelty, while it rescues the most admitted truths from the impotence caused by the very circumstance of their universal admission. Truths of all others the most awful and mysterious, yet being at the same time of universal interest, are too often considered as so true, that they lose all the life and efficiency of truth, and lie bedridden in the dormitory of the soul, side by side with the most despised and exploded errors."—The Friend,[4] p. 76, No. 5.

This excellence, which in all Mr. Wordsworth's writings is more or less predominant, and which constitutes the character of his mind, I no sooner felt, than I sought to understand. Repeated meditations led me first to suspect (and a more intimate analysis of the human faculties, their appropriate marks, functions, and effects matured my conjecture into full conviction) that fancy and imagination were two distinct and widely different faculties, instead of being, according to the general belief, either two names with one meaning, or, at furthest, the lower and higher degree of one and the same power. It is not, I own, easy to conceive a more apposite translation of the Greek *Phantasia* than the Latin Imaginatio; but it is equally true that in all societies there exists an instinct of growth, a certain collective, unconscious good sense working progressively to desynonymize[5] those words originally of the same

[1] *fiat* Command.

[2] *With sun ... woman* Milton's sonnet "To Mr. Cyriack Skinner upon his Blindness" (1655) actually reads: "Of sun or moon or star throughout the year, / Or man or woman."

[3] *To snow ... for ever!* Robert Burns's "Tam O'Shanter" (1791) reads: "Or like the snow falls in the river, / A moment white—then melts for ever."

[4] [Coleridge's note] As "The Friend" was printed on stampt sheets, and sent only by the poet to a very limited number of subscribers, the author has felt less objection to quote from it, though a work of his own. To the public at large indeed it is the same as a volume in manuscript.

[5] [Coleridge's note] This is effected either by giving to the one word a general, and to the other an exclusive use; as "to put on the back" and "to indorse;" or by an actual distinction of meanings as "naturalist," and "physician"; or by difference of relation as "I" and "Me"; (each of which the rustics of our different provinces still use in all the cases singular of the first personal pronoun). Even the mere difference, or corruption, in the *pronunciation* of the same word, if it have become general, will produce a new word with a distinct signification; thus "property" and "propriety"; the latter of which, even to the time of Charles II was the *written* word for all the senses of both. Thus too "mister" and "master" both hasty pronunciations of the same word "magister," "mistress," and "miss," "if," and "give," &c. &c. There is a sort of *minim immortal* among the *animalcula infusoria* which has not naturally either birth, or death, absolute beginning, or absolute end: for at a certain period a small point

meaning, which the conflux of dialects had supplied to the more homogeneous languages, as the Greek and German: and which the same cause, joined with accidents of translation from original works of different countries, occasion in mixed languages like our own. The first and most important point to be proved is, that two conceptions perfectly distinct are confused under one and the same word, and (this done) to appropriate that word exclusively to one meaning, and the synonym (should there be one) to the other. But if (as will be often the case in the arts and sciences) no synonym exists, we must either invent or borrow a word. In the present instance the appropriation has already begun, and been legitimated in the derivative adjective: Milton had a highly *imaginative*, Cowley a very *fanciful* mind. If therefore I should succeed in establishing the actual existences of two faculties generally different, the nomenclature would be at once determined. To the faculty by which I had characterized Milton, we should confine the term *imagination*; while the other would be contra-distinguished as *fancy*. Now were it once fully ascertained, that this division is no less grounded in nature, than that of delirium from mania, or Otway's

> Lutes, lobsters, seas of milk, and ships of amber,[1]

from Shakespeare's

> What! have his daughters brought him to this pass?[2]

or from the preceding apostrophe to the elements; the theory of the fine arts, and of poetry in particular, could not, I thought, but derive some additional and important light. It would in its immediate effects furnish a torch of guidance to the philosophical critic; and ultimately to the poet himself. In energetic minds, truth soon changes by domestication into power; and from directing in the discrimination and appraisal of the product, becomes influencive in the production. To admire on principle, is the only way to imitate without loss of originality....

from CHAPTER 11

An affectionate exortation to those who in early life feel themselves disposed to become authors

... With no other privilege than that of sympathy and sincere good wishes, I would address an affectionate exhortation to the youthful literati, grounded on my own experience. It will be but short; for the beginning, middle, and end converge to one charge: NEVER PURSUE LITERATURE AS A TRADE. With the exception of one extraordinary man, I have never known an individual, least of all an individual of genius, healthy or happy without a *profession*, i.e., some *regular* employment, which does not depend on the will of the moment, and which can be carried on so far *mechanically* that an average quantum only of health, spirits, and intellectual exertion are requisite to its faithful discharge. Three hours of leisure, unannoyed by any alien anxiety, and looked forward to with delight as a change and recreation, will suffice to realize in literature a larger product of what is truly *genial*, than weeks of compulsion. Money, and immediate reputation form only an arbitrary and accidental end of literary labour. The *hope* of increasing them by any given exertion will often prove a stimulant to industry; but the *necessity* of acquiring them will in all works of genius convert the stimulant into a *narcotic*. Motives by excess reverse their very nature, and instead of exciting, stun and stupify the mind. For it is one contradistinction of genius from talent, that its predominant end is always comprized in the means; and this is one of the many points which establish an analogy between genius and virtue. Now though talents may exist without genius, yet as genius cannot exist, certainly not manifest itself, without talents, I would advise every scholar, who feels the genial

appears on its back, which deepens and lengthens till the creature divides into two, and the same process recommences in each of the halves now become integral. This may be a fanciful, but it is by no means a bad emblem of the formation of words, and may facilitate the conception, how immense a nomenclature may be organized from a few simple sounds by rational beings in a social state. For each new application, or excitement of the same sound, will call forth a different sensation, which cannot but affect the pronunciation. The after recollection of the sound, without the same vivid sensation, will modify it still further; till at length all trace of the original likeness is worn away.

[1] *Lutes ... amber* From Thomas Otway's play *Venice Preserved* (1682) 5.2.; Otway's version has the word "laurel" replacing "lobster."

[2] *What! ... pass?* From *King Lear* 3.4.65.

power working within him, so far to make a division between the two, as that he should devote his *talents* to the acquirement of competence in some known trade or profession, and his genius to objects of his tranquil and unbiased choice; while the consciousness of being actuated in both alike by the sincere desire to perform his duty, will alike ennoble both. My dear young friend (I would say), "Suppose yourself established in any honourable occupation. From the manufactory or counting-house, from the law-court, or from having visited your last patient, you return at evening,

> Dear tranquil time, when the sweet sense of home
> Is sweetest—[1]

to your family, prepared for its social enjoyments, with the very countenances of your wife and children brightened, and their voice of welcome made doubly welcome, by the knowledge that, as far as *they* are concerned, you have satisfied the demands of the day by the labour of the day. Then, when you retire into your study, in the books on your shelves you revisit so many venerable friends with whom you can converse. Your own spirit scarcely less free from personal anxieties than the great minds, that in those books are still living for you! Even your writing desk with its blank paper and all its other implements will appear as a chain of flowers, capable of linking your feelings as well as thoughts to events and characters past or to come; not a chain of iron which binds you down to think of the future and the remote by recalling the claims and feelings of the peremptory present. But why should I say *retire*? The habits of active life and daily intercourse with the stir of the world will tend to give you such self-command, that the presence of your family will be no interruption. Nay, the social silence, or undisturbing voices of a wife or sister will be like a restorative atmosphere, or soft music which moulds a dream without becoming its object. If facts are required to prove the possibility of combining weighty performances in literature with full and independent employment, the works of Cicero and Xenophon among the ancients; of Sir Thomas Moore, Bacon, Baxter, or to refer at once to later and contemporary instances, Darwin and Roscoe,[2] are at once decisive of the question."

[1] *Dear ... sweetest* From Coleridge's "To William Wordsworth," 96–97.

from Chapter 13

On the Imagination, or Esemplastic[3] Power

The IMAGINATION then I consider either as primary, or secondary. The primary IMAGINATION I hold to be the living Power and prime Agent of all human Perception, and as a repetition in the finite mind of the eternal act of creation in the infinite I AM. The secondary I consider as an echo of the former, co-existing with the conscious will, yet still as identical with the primary in the *kind* of its agency, and differing only in *degree,* and in the *mode* of its operation. It dissolves, diffuses, dissipates, in order to re-create; or where this process is rendered impossible, yet still at all events it struggles to idealize and to unify. It is essentially *vital,* even as all objects (as objects) are essentially fixed and dead.

FANCY, on the contrary, has no other counters to play with, but fixities and definites. The Fancy is indeed no other than a mode of Memory emancipated from the order of time and space; and blended with, and modified by that empirical phenomenon of the will, which we express by the word CHOICE. But equally with the ordinary memory it must receive all its materials ready made from the law of association.

Whatever more than this, I shall think it fit to declare concerning the powers and privileges of the imagination in the present work, will be found in the critical essay on the uses of the Supernatural in poetry and the principles that regulate its introduction, which the reader will find prefixed to the poem of *The Ancient Mariner.*

[2] *Cicero* Roman orator, philosopher, and statesman of the first century BCE; *Xenophon* Greek historian (c. 430 BCE–c. 355 BCE); *Sir Thomas More* English statesman (1478–1535); More was eventually beatified by the Catholic Church; *Bacon* Francis Bacon (1561–1626), English philosopher and statesman; *Baxter* Clergyman Richard Baxter (1615–91); *Darwin* Erasmus Darwin (1731–1802), physician, botanist, and author of *The Botanic Garden* (1789); *Roscoe* William Rosco (1753–1831), English lawyer, historian, and MP. All of those mentioned are also authors.

[3] *Esemplastic* Word coined by Coleridge to mean "moulded into unity."

CHAPTER 14
Occasion of the Lyrical Ballads

During the first year that Mr. Wordsworth and I were neighbours, our conversations turned frequently on the two cardinal points of poetry, the power of exciting the sympathy of the reader by a faithful adherence to the truth of nature, and the power of giving the interest of novelty by the modifying colours of imagination. The sudden charm, which accidents of light and shade, which moonlight or sunset diffused over a known and familiar landscape, appeared to represent the practicability of combining both. These are the poetry of nature. The thought suggested itself (to which of us I do not recollect) that a series of poems might be composed of two sorts. In the one, the incidents and agents were to be, in part at least, supernatural; and the excellence aimed at was to consist in the interesting of the affections by the dramatic truth of such emotions, as would naturally accompany such situations, supposing them real. And real in *this* sense they have been to every human being who, from whatever source of delusion, has at any time believed himself under supernatural agency. For the second class, subjects were to be chosen from ordinary life; the characters and incidents were to be such, as will be found in every village and its vicinity, where there is a meditative and feeling mind to seek after them, or to notice them, when they present themselves.

In this idea originated the plan of the *Lyrical Ballads*, in which it was agreed, that my endeavours should be directed to persons and characters supernatural, or at least romantic; yet so as to transfer from our inward nature a human interest and a semblance of truth sufficient to procure for these shadows of imagination that willing suspension of disbelief for the moment, which constitutes poetic faith. Mr. Wordsworth, on the other hand, was to propose to himself as his object, to give the charm of novelty to things of every day, and to excite a feeling analogous to the supernatural, by awakening the mind's attention from the lethargy of custom, and directing it to the loveliness and the wonders of the world before us; an inexhaustible treasure, but for which in consequence of the film of familiarity and selfish solicitude we have eyes, yet see not, ears that hear not, and hearts that neither feel nor understand.[1]

With this view I wrote *The Ancient Mariner*, and was preparing among other poems, the "Dark Ladie," and the "Christabel," in which I should have more nearly realized my ideal, than I had done in my first attempt. But Mr. Wordsworth's industry had proved so much more successful, and the number of his poems so much greater, that my compositions, instead of forming a balance, appeared rather an interpolation of heterogeneous matter. Mr. Wordsworth added two or three poems written in his own character, in the impassioned, lofty, and sustained diction, which is characteristic of his genius. In this form the *Lyrical Ballads* were published; and were presented by him, as an *experiment*, whether subjects, which from their nature rejected the usual ornaments and extra-colloquial style of poems in general, might not be so managed in the language of ordinary life as to produce the pleasurable interest, which it is the peculiar business of poetry to impart. To the second edition he added a preface of considerable length, in which notwithstanding some passages of apparently a contrary import, he was understood to contend for the extension of this style to poetry of all kinds, and to reject as vicious and indefensible all phrases and forms of style that were not included in what he (unfortunately, I think, adopting an equivocal expression) called the language of *real* life. From this preface, prefixed to poems in which it was impossible to deny the presence of original genius, however mistaken its direction might be deemed, arose the whole long continued controversy. For from the conjunction of perceived power with supposed heresy I explain the inveteracy[2] and in some instances, I grieve to say, the acrimonious passions, with which the controversy has been conducted by the assailants.

Had Mr. Wordsworth's poems been the silly, the childish things, which they were for a long time described as being; had they been really distinguished from the compositions of other poets merely by meanness of language and inanity of thought; had they indeed contained nothing more than what is found in the

[1] *we have eyes ... understand* Cf. Isaiah 6.9: "Hear ye indeed, but understand not; and see ye indeed, but perceive not." See also Matthew 13.13–14.

[2] *inveteracy* Deeply rooted prejudice.

parodies and pretended imitations of them; they must have sunk at once, a dead weight, into the slough of oblivion, and have dragged the preface along with them. But year after year increased the number of Mr. Wordsworth's admirers. They were found too not in the lower classes of the reading public, but chiefly among young men of strong sensibility and meditative minds; and their admiration (inflamed perhaps in some degree by opposition) was distinguished by its intensity, I might almost say, by its *religious* fervour. These facts, and the intellectual energy of the author, which was more or less consciously felt, where it was outwardly and even boisterously denied, meeting with sentiments of aversion to his opinions, and of alarm at their consequences, produced an eddy of criticism, which would of itself have borne up the poems by the violence with which it whirled them round and round. With many parts of this preface in the sense attributed to them and which the words undoubtedly seem to authorise, I never concurred; but on the contrary objected to them as erroneous in principle, and as contradictory (in appearance at least) both to other parts of the same preface, and to the author's own practice in the greater number of the poems themselves. Mr. Wordsworth in his recent collection[1] has, I find, degraded this prefatory disquisition to the end of his second volume, to be read or not at the reader's choice. But he has not, as far as I can discover, announced any change in his poetic creed. At all events, considering it as the source of a controversy, in which I have been honoured, more than I deserve, by the frequent conjunction of my name with his, I think it expedient to declare once for all, in what points I coincide with his opinions, and in what points I altogether differ. But in order to render myself intelligible I must previously, in as few words as possible, explain my ideas, first, of a POEM; and secondly, of POETRY itself, in *kind*, and in *essence*.

The office of philosophical *disquisition* consists in just *distinction*; while it is the privilege of the philosopher to preserve himself constantly aware, that distinction is not division. In order to obtain adequate notions of any truth, we must intellectually separate its distinguishable parts; and this is the technical *process* of philosophy. But having so done, we must then restore them in our conceptions to the unity, in which they actually co-exist; and this is the *result* philosophy. A poem contains the same elements as a prose composition; the difference therefore must consist in different combination of them, in consequence of a different object proposed. According to the difference of the object will be the difference of the combination. It is possible, that the object may be merely to facilitate the recollection of any given facts or observations by artificial arrangement; and the composition will be a poem, merely because it is distinguished from prose by metre, or by rhyme, or by both conjointly. In this, the lowest sense, a man might attribute the name of a poem to the well known enumeration of the days in the several months;

Thirty days hath September,
April, June, and November, &c.

and others of the same class and purpose. And as a particular pleasure is found in anticipating the recurrence of sounds and quantities, all compositions that have this charm superadded, whatever be their contents, *may* be entitled poems.

So much for the superficial *form*. A difference of object and contents supplies an additional ground of distinction. The immediate purpose may be the communication of truths; either of truth absolute and demonstrable, as in works of science; or of facts experienced and recorded, as in history. Pleasure, and that of the highest and most permanent kind, may *result* from the *attainment* of the end; but it is not itself the immediate end. In other works the communication of pleasure may be the immediate purpose; and though truth, either moral or intellectual, ought to be the *ultimate* end, yet this will distinguish the character of the author, not the class to which the work belongs. Blest indeed is that state of society, in which the immediate purpose would be baffled by the perversion of the proper ultimate end; in which no charm of diction or imagery could exempt the Bathyllus even of an Anacreon, or the

[1] *recent collection* Two volumes entitled *Poems by William Wordsworth* (1815).

Alexis of Virgil,[1] from disgust and aversion! But the communication of pleasure may be the immediate object of a work not metrically composed; and that object may have been in a high degree attained, as in novels and romances. Would then the mere superaddition of metre, with or without rhyme, entitle *these* to the name of poems? The answer is, that nothing can permanently please, which does not contain in itself the reason why it is so, and not otherwise. If metre be superadded, all other parts must be made consonant with it. They must be such, as to justify the perpetual and distinct attention to each part, which an exact correspondent recurrence of accent and sound are calculated to excite. The final definition then, so deduced, may be thus worded. A poem is that species of composition, which is opposed to works of science, by proposing for its *immediate* object pleasure, not truth; and from all other species (having *this* object in common with it) it is discriminated by proposing to itself such delight from the *whole*, as is compatible with a distinct gratification from each component *part*.

Controversy is not seldom excited in consequence of the disputants attaching each a different meaning to the same word; and in few instances has this been more striking, than in disputes concerning the present subject. If a man chooses to call every composition a poem, which is rhyme, or measure, or both, I must leave his opinion uncontroverted. The distinction is at least competent to characterize the writer's intention. If it were subjoined, that the whole is likewise entertaining or affecting, as a tale, or as a series of interesting reflections, I of course admit this as another fit ingredient of a poem, and an additional merit. But if the definition sought for be that of a *legitimate* poem, I answer, it must be one, the parts of which mutually support and explain each other; all in their proportion harmonizing with, and supporting the purpose and known influences of metrical arrangement. The philosophic critics of all ages coincide with the ultimate judgment of all countries, in equally denying the praises of a just poem, on the one hand, to a series of striking lines or distichs,[2] each of which absorbing the whole attention of the reader to itself disjoins it from its context, and makes it a separate whole, instead of an harmonizing part; and on the other hand, to an unsustained composition, from which the reader collects rapidly the general result unattracted by the component parts. The reader should be carried forward, not merely or chiefly by the mechanical impulse of curiosity, or by a restless desire to arrive at the final solution; but by the pleasurable activity of mind excited by the attractions of the journey itself. Like the motion of a serpent, which the Egyptians made the emblem of intellectual power; or like the path of sound through the air; at every step he pauses and half recedes, and from the retrogressive movement collects the force which again carries him onward. *Præcipitandus est liber spiritus*,[3] says Petronius Arbiter most happily. The epithet, *liber*,[4] here balances the preceding verb; and it is not easy to conceive more meaning condensed in fewer words.

But if this should be admitted as a satisfactory character of a poem, we have still to seek for a definition of poetry. The writings of Plato, and Bishop Taylor, and the *Theoria Sacra* of Burnet,[5] furnish undeniable proofs that poetry of the highest kind may exist without metre, and even without the contra-distinguishing objects of a poem. The first chapter of Isaiah (indeed a very large proportion of the whole book) is poetry in the most emphatic sense; yet it would be not less irrational than strange to assert, that pleasure, arid not truth, was the immediate object of the prophet. In short, whatever *specific* import we attach to the word, poetry, there will be found involved in it, as a necessary consequence;, that a poem of any length neither can be, or ought to be, all poetry. Yet if an harmonious whole is to be produced, the remaining parts must be preserved *in keeping* with the poetry; and this can be no otherwise effected than by such a studies selection and artificial arrangement, as will partake of *one*, though not a *peculiar*, property of poetry. And this again can be no

[1] *Ballythus ... Virgil* Both Virgil and Anacreon wrote homoerotic poems. In this period, homosexuality was viewed unfavorably, in a way that we now consider prejudiced and unfair.

[2] *distichs* Poetic couplets.

[3] *Præcipitandus est liber spiritus* Latin: from the *Satyricon*: "The free spirit must be hurried along."

[4] *liber* Free.

[5] *Bishop Taylor* English theologian and author Jeremy Taylor (1613–67); *Burnet* English cleric and author Thomas Burnet (1635–1715), who wrote *Sacred Theory of the Earth*.

other than the property of exciting a more continuous and equal attention, than the language of prose aims at, whether colloquial or written.

My own conclusions on the nature of poetry, in the strictest use of the word, have been in part anticipated in the preceding disquisition on the fancy and imagination. What is poetry? is so nearly the same question with, what is a poet? that the answer to the one is involved in the solution of the other. For it is a distinction resulting from the poetic genius itself, which sustains and modifies the images, thoughts, and emotions of the poet's own mind. The poet, described in *ideal* perfection, brings the whole soul of man into activity, with the subordination of its faculties to each other, according to their relative worth and dignity. He diffuses a tone, and spirit of unity, that blends, and (as it were) *fuses*, each into each, by that synthetic and magical power, to which we have exclusively appropriated the name of imagination. This power, first put in action by the will and understanding, and retained under their irremissive, though gentle and unnoticed, controul (*laxis effertur habenis*)[1] reveals itself in the balance or reconciliation of opposite or discordant qualities: of sameness, with difference; of the general, with the concrete; the idea, with the image; the individual, with the representative; the sense of novelty and freshness, with old and familiar objects; a more than usual state of emotion, with more than usual order; judgement ever awake and steady self-possession, with enthusiasm and feeling profound or vehement; and while it blends and harmonizes the natural and the artificial, still subordinates art to nature; the manner to the matter; and our admiration of the poet to our sympathy with the poetry. "Doubtless," as Sir John Davies observes of the soul (and his words may with slight alteration be applied, and even more appropriately to the poetic IMAGINATION):

Doubtless this could not be, but that she turns
Bodies to spirit by sublimation strange,
As fire converts to fire the things it burns,
As we our food into our nature change.

From their gross matter she abstracts their forms,
And draws a kind of quintessence from things;
Which to her proper nature she transforms
To bear them light, on her celestial wings.

Thus does she, when from individual states
She doth abstract the universal kinds;
Which then re-clothed in divers names and fates
Steal access through our senses to our minds.[2]

Finally, GOOD SENSE is the BODY of poetic genius, FANCY , its DRAPERY, MOTION its LIFE, and IMAGINATION the SOUL that is everywhere, and in each; and forms all into one graceful and intelligent whole.

from Chapter 17
Examination of the Tenets Peculiar to Mr. Wordsworth

As far then as Mr. Wordsworth in his preface contended, and most ably contended, for a reformation in our poetic diction, as far as he has evinced the truth of passion, and the *dramatic* propriety of those figures and metaphors in the original poets, which stript of their justifying reasons, and converted into mere artifices of connection or ornament, constitute the characteristic falsity in the poetic style of the moderns; and as far as he has, with equal acuteness and clearness, pointed out the process in which this change was effected, and the resemblances between that state into which the reader's mind is thrown by the pleasurable confusion of thought from an unaccustomed bain[3] of words and images; and that state which is induced by the natural language of empassioned feeling; he undertook a useful task, and deserves all praise, both for the attempt and for the execution....

My own differences from certain supposed parts of Mr. Wordsworth's theory ground themselves on the assumption, that his words had been rightly interpreted, as purporting that the proper diction for poetry in general consists altogether in a language taken, with due exceptions, from the mouths of men in real life, a

[1] *laxis effertur habenis* Latin: moved forward with loosened rein.

[2] *Doubtless ... soul* Adapted from "Nosce Teipsum: Of Human Knowledge" (1599).

[3] *bain* Vessel for water.

language which actually constitutes the natural conversation of men under the influence of natural feelings. My objection is, first, that in *any* sense this rule is applicable only to *certain* classes of poetry; secondly, that even to these classes it is not applicable, except in such a sense, as hath never by any one (as far as I know or have read) been denied or doubted; and lastly, that as far as, and in that degree in which it is *practicable*, yet as a *rule* it is useless, if not injurious, and therefore either need not, or ought not to be practised. The poet informs his reader, that he had generally chosen *low and rustic* life; but not *as* low and rustic, or in order to repeat that pleasure of doubtful moral effect, which persons of elevated rank and of superior refinement oftentimes derive from a happy *imitation* of the rude unpolished manners and discourse of their inferiors. For the pleasure so derived may be traced to three exciting causes. The first is the naturalness, in *fact*, of the things presented. The second is the apparent naturalness of the *representation*, as raised and qualified by an imperceptible infusion of the author's own knowledge and talent, which infusion does, indeed, constitute it an *imitation* as distinguished from a mere *copy*. The third cause may be found in the reader's conscious feeling of his superiority awakened by the contrast presented to him; even as for the same purpose the kings and great barons of yore retained, sometimes *actual* clowns and fools, but more frequently shrewd and witty fellows in that *character*. These, however, were not Mr. Wordsworth's objects. *He* chose low and rustic life, "because in that condition the essential passions of the heart find a better soil, in which they can attain their maturity, are less under restraint, and speak a plainer and more emphatic language; because in that condition of life our elementary feelings coexist in a state of greater simplicity, and consequently may be more accurately contemplated, and more forcibly communicated; because the manners of rural life germinate from those elementary feelings; and from the necessary character of rural occupations are more easily comprehended, and are more durable; and lastly, because in that condition the passions of men are incorporated with the beautiful and permanent forms of nature."[1]

Now it is clear to me, that in the most interesting of the poems, in which the author is more or less dramatic, as the "Brothers," "Michael," "Ruth," the "Mad Mother," &c. the persons introduced are by no means taken *from low or rustic life* in the common acceptation of those words; and it is not less clear, that the sentiments and language, as far as they can be conceived to have been really transferred from the minds and conversation of such persons, are attributable to causes and circumstances not necessarily connected with "their occupations and abode." The thoughts, feelings, language, and manners of the shepherd-farmers in the vales of Cumberland and Westmoreland, as far as they are actually adopted in those poems, may be accounted for from causes, which will and do produce the same results in *every* state of life, whether in town or country. As the two principal I rank that INDEPENDENCE, which raises a man above servitude, or daily toil for the profit of others, yet not above the necessity of industry and a frugal simplicity of domestic life; and the accompanying unambitious, but solid and religious EDUCATION, which has rendered few books familiar, but the Bible, and the liturgy or hymn book. To this latter cause, indeed, which is so far *accidental*, that it is the blessing of particular countries and a particular age, not the product of particular places or employments, the poet owes the shew of probability, that his personages might really feel, think, and talk with any tolerable resemblance to his representation. It is an excellent remark of Dr. Henry More's (*Enthusiasmus triumphatus*, Sec. xxxv) that "a man of confined education, but of good parts, by constant reading of the Bible will naturally form a more winning and commanding rhetoric than those that are learned; the intermixture of tongues and of artificial phrases debasing *their* style."

It is, moreover, to be considered that to the formation of healthy feelings, and a reflecting mind, *negations* involve impediments not less formidable, than sophistication intermixture. I am convinced, that for the human soul to prosper in rustic life, a certain vantage-ground is prerequisite. It is not every man, that is likely to be improved by a country life or by country labours.

[1] *"because … nature"* From Wordsworth's "Preface" to *Lyrical Ballads* (1800).

Education, or original sensibility, or both, must pre-exist, if the changes, forms, and incidents of nature are to prove a sufficient stimulant. And where these are not sufficient, the mind contracts and hardens by want of stimulants; and the man becomes selfish, sensual, gross, hard-hearted. Let the management of the POOR LAWS in Liverpool, Manchester, or Bristol be compared with the ordinary dispensation of the poor rates in agricultural villages, where the *farmers* are the overseers and guardians of the poor.... [The] result would engender more than skepticism concerning the desirable influences of low and rustic life in and for itself....

If then I am compelled to doubt the theory, by which the choice of *characters* was to be directed, not only *a priori*,[1] from grounds of reason, but both from the few instances in which the poet himself *need* be supposed to have been governed by it, and from the comparative inferiority of those instances; still more must I hesitate in my assent to the sentence which immediately follows the former citation; and which can neither admit as particular fact, or a general rule. "The language too of these men is adopted (purified indeed from what appear to be its real defects, from all lasting and rational causes of dislike or disgust) because such men hourly communicate with the best objects from which the best part of language is originally derived; and because, from their rank in society, and the sameness and narrow circle of their intercourse, being less under the action of social vanity, they convey their feelings and notions in simple and unelaborated expressions."[2] To this I reply; that a rustic's language, purified from all provincialism and grossness, and so far reconstructed as to be made consistent with the rules of grammar which are in essence no other than the laws of universal logic, applied to psychological materials will not differ from the language of any other man of commonsense, however learned or refined he may be, except as far as the notions, which the rustic has to convey, are fewer and more indiscriminate. This will become still clearer, if we add the consideration (equally important though less obvious) that the rustic, from the more imperfect development of his faculties, and from the lower state of their cultivation, aims almost solely to convey *insulated facts*, either those of his scanty experience or his traditional belief; while the educated man chiefly seeks to discover and express those *connections* of things, or those relative *hearings* of fact to fact, from which some more or less general law is deducible. For *facts* are valuable to a wise man, chiefly as they lead to the discovery of the indwelling *law*, which is the true *being* of things, the sole solution of their modes of existence, and in the knowledge of which consists our dignity and our power....

Here let me be permitted to remind the reader, that the positions, which I controvert, at contained in the sentences—"*a selection of the* REAL *language of men*"—"*the language of these men* (i.e, men in low and rustic life) I *propose to myself to imitate, and as far as possible, to adopt the very language of men*." "*Between the language of prose and that of metrical composition, there neither is, nor can be any essential difference*."[3] It is against these exclusively, that my opposition is directed.

I object, in the very first instance, to an equivocation in the use of the word "real." Every man's language varies, according to the extent of his knowledge, the activity of his faculties, and the depth or quickness of his feelings. Every man's language has, first, its *individualities*; secondly, the common properties of the *class* to which he belongs; and thirdly, words and phrases of *universal* use. The language of Hooker,[4] Bacon, Bishop Taylor, and Burke,[5] differ from the common language of the learned class only by the superior number and novelty of the thoughts and relations which they had to convey. The language of Algernon Sidney differs not at all from that, which every well educated gentleman would wish to write, and (with due allowances for the undeliberateness, and less connected train, of thinking natural and proper to conversation) such as he would wish to talk. Neither one or the other differ half as much from the general language of cultivated society, as

[1] *a priori* Latin: without direct experience.

[2] *"The language ... expressions"* From Wordsworth's "Preface" to *Lyrical Ballads* (1800).

[3] *"a selection ... difference"* From Wordsworth's "Preface" to *Lyrical Ballads* (1800).

[4] *Hooker* English clergyman and theologian Richard Hooker (1554–1600).

[5] *Burke* British statesman and political writer Edmund Burke (1729–97).

the language of Mr. Wordsworth's homeliest composition differs from that of a common peasant. For "real" therefore, we must substitute *ordinary*, or *lingua communis*.[1] And this, we have proved, is no more to be found in the phraseology of low and rustic life, than in that of any other class. Omit the peculiarities of each, and the result of course must be common to all. And assuredly the omissions and changes to be made in the language of rustics, before it could be transferred to any species of poem, except the drama or other professed imitation, are at least as numerous and weighty, as would be required in adapting to the same purpose the ordinary language of tradesmen and manufacturers. Not to mention, that the language so highly extolled by Mr. Wordsworth varies in every county, nay in every village, according to the accidental character of the clergyman, the existence or non-existence of schools; or even, perhaps, as the exciseman, publican, or barber happen to be, or not to be, zealous politicians, and readers of the weekly newspaper *pro bono publico*.[2] Anterior to cultivation the lingua communis of every country, as Dante has well observed, exists everywhere in parts, and nowhere as a whole.

Neither is the case rendered at all more tenable by the addition of the words, "*in a state of excitement.*" For the nature of a man's words, when he is strongly affected by joy, grief, or anger, must necessarily depend on the number and quality of the general truths, conceptions and images, and of the words expressing them, with which his mind had been previously stored. For the property of passion is not to *create*; but to set in increased activity. At least, whatever new connections of thought or images, or (which is equally, if not more than equally, the appropriate effect of strong excitement) whatever generalizations of truth or experience, the heat of passion may produce; yet the terms of their conveyance must have pre-existed in his former conversations, and are only collected and crowded together by the unusual stimulation. It is indeed very possible to adopt in a poem the unmeaning repetitions, habitual phrases, and other blank counters, which an unfurnished or confused understanding interposes at short intervals, in order to keep hold of his subject which is still slipping from him, and to give him time for recollection; or in mere aid of vacancy, as in the scanty companies of a country stage the same player pops backwards and forwards, in order to prevent the appearance of empty spaces, in the procession of *Macbeth*, or *Henry VIII*. But what assistance to the poet, or ornament to the poem, these can supply, I am at a loss to conjecture. Nothing assuredly can differ either in origin or in mode more widely from the *apparent* tautologies[3] of intense and turbulent feeling, in which the passion is greater and of longer endurance, than to be exhausted or satisfied by a single representation of the image or incident exciting it. Such repetitions I admit to be a beauty of the highest kind; as illustrated by Mr. Wordsworth himself from the song of Deborah. "*At her feet he bowed, he fell, he lay down; at her feet he bowed, he fell; where he bowed, there he fell down dead.*"[4]

—1817

from *Table Talk*

[On Various Shakespearean Characters]

Othello must not be conceived as a negro, but a high and chivalrous Moorish chief. Shakespeare learned the spirit of the character from the Spanish poetry, which was prevalent in England in his time. Jealousy does not strike me as the point in his passion; I take it to be rather an agony that the creature, whom he had believed angelic, with whom he had garnered up his heart, and whom he could not help still loving, should be proved impure and worthless. It was the struggle *not* to love her. It was a moral indignation and regret that virtue should so fall: "But yet the *pity* of it, Iago!—O Iago! the *pity* of it, Iago!" In addition to this, his honour was concerned: Iago would not have succeeded but by hinting that his honour was compromised. There is no ferocity in Othello; his mind is majestic and composed. He deliberately determines to die, and speaks his last speech with a view of showing his attachment to the

[1] *lingua communis* Latin: common language.

[2] *pro bono publico* Latin: for the good of the public.

[3] *tautologies* Repetitions.

[4] *"At her feet ... dead"* From Wordsworth's note to "The Thorn" (1798).

Venetian state, though it had superseded him.

Schiller has the material sublime; to produce an effect, he sets you a whole town on fire, and throws infants with their mothers into the flames, or locks up a father in an old tower. But Shakespeare drops a handerchief, and the same or greater effects follow.

Lear is the most tremendous effort of Shakespeare as a poet; Hamlet as a philosopher or meditator; and Othello is the union of the two. There is something gigantic and unformed in the former two; but in the latter, everything assumes its due place and proportion, and the whole mature powers of his mind are displayed in admirable equilibrium.

I have often told you that I do not think there is any jealousy, properly so called, in the character of Othello. There is no predisposition to suspicion, which I take to be an essential term in the definition of the word. Desdemona very truly told Emilia that he was not jealous, that is, of a jealous habit, and he says so as truly of himself. Iago's suggestions, you see, are quite new to him; they do not correspond with any thing of a like nature previously in his mind. If Desdemona had, in fact, been guilty, no one would have thought of calling Othello's conduct that of a jealous man. He could not act otherwise than he did with the lights he had; whereas jealousy can never be strictly right. See how utterly unlike Othello is to Leontes, in *The Winter's Tale*, or even to Leonatus, in *Cymbeline*! The jealousy of the first proceeds from an evident trifle, and something like hatred is mingled with it; and the conduct of Leonatus in accepting the wager, and exposing his wife to the trial, denotes a jealous temper already formed.

Hamlet's character is the prevalence of the abstracting and generalizing habit over the practical. He does not want courage, skill, will, or opportunity; but every incident sets him thinking; and it is curious, and, at the same time, strictly natural, that Hamlet, who all the play seems reason itself, should be impelled, at last, by mere accident, to effect his object. I have a smack of Hamlet myself, if I may say so.

[The Ancient Mariner]

Mrs. Barbauld[1] once told me that she admired the Ancient Mariner very much, but that there were two faults in it—it was improbable, and had no moral. As for the probability, I owned that that might admit some question; but as to the want of a moral, I told her that in my own judgement the poem had too much; and that the only or chief fault, if I might say so, was the obtrusion[2] of the moral sentiment so openly on the reader as a principle or cause of action in a work of such pure imagination. It ought to have had no more moral than the Arabian Nights' tale of the merchant's sitting down to eat dates by the side of a well, and throwing the shells aside, and lo! a genie starts up, and says he *must* kill the aforesaid merchant, *because* one of the date-shells had, it seems, put out the eye of the genie's son.

I took the thought of "*grinning for joy*," in that poem, from poor Burnett's remark to me, when we had climbed to the top of Plinlimmon, and were nearly dead with thirst. We could not speak from the constriction, till we found a little puddle under a stone. He said to me, "You grinned like an idiot!" He had done the same.

[On Borrowing]

A poet ought not to pick nature's pocket: let him borrow, and so borrow as to repay by the very act of borrowing. Examine nature accurately, but write from recollection; and trust more to your imagination than to your memory.

[On Metre]

Really, the metre of some of the modern poems I have read, bears about the same relation to metre properly understood, that dumb bells do to music; both are for exercise, and pretty severe too, I think.

---

[1] *Mrs. Barbauld* Poet Anna Laetitia Barbauld (1743–1825).

[2] *obtrusion* Imposition.

[On Women]

"Most women have no character at all," said Pope,[1] and meant it for satire. Shakespeare, who knew man and woman much better, saw that it, in fact, was the perfection of woman to be characterless.

Every one wishes a Desdemona or Ophelia for a wife—creatures who, though they may not always understand you, do always feel you, and feel with you.

[On Corrupt Language]

I regret to see that vile and barbarous vocable *talented*, stealing out of the newspapers into the leading reviews and most respectable publications of the day. Why not *shillinged, farthinged, tenpenced*, &c.? The formation of a participle passive from a noun is a license that nothing but a very peculiar felicity can excuse. If mere convenience is to justify such attempts upon the idiom, you cannot stop till the language becomes, in the proper sense of the word, corrupt. Most of these pieces of slang come from America.

[On Milton]

In the *Paradise Lost*—indeed, in every one of his poems —it is Milton himself whom you see; his Satan, his Adam, his Raphael, almost his Eve—are all John Milton; and it is a sense of this intense egotism that gives me the greatest pleasures in reading Milton's works. The egotism of such a man is a revelation of spirit.

[The Three Most Perfect Plots]

What a master of composition Fielding[2] was! Upon my word, I think the *Oedipus Tyrannus, The Alchymist*, and *Tom Jones* the three most perfect plots ever planned. And how charming, how wholesome, Fielding always is! To take him up after Richardson[3] is like emerging from a sick-room heated by stoves into an open lawn on a breezy day in May.

—1836

[1] *Most women … Pope* From "Epistle II: To a Lady," 2.

[2] *Fielding* Henry Fielding, English novelist and playwright (1797–54).

[3] *Richardson* Samuel Richardson, English novelist (1689–1761).

India and the Orient

CONTEXTS

From the early sixteenth century to the middle of the nineteenth, the story of the British connection with India is very largely the story of the United Company of Merchants of England Trading to the East Indies (less formally, the British East India Company), which in 1600 acquired from the Crown a monopoly on trading rights between England and the East Indies. The power of the company was at first quite limited—the Dutch and Portuguese were already established in the region, and the Dutch in particular were successful in preventing English incursions on their trading rights in the Malay Archipelago. But in 1612, after a military victory by the forces of the Indian Mughal Empire over the Portuguese, the English began to acquire substantial trading privileges in India, and an English presence began to be established on the subcontinent. In the 1750s, Robert Clive led the British in a military campaign that resulted in the defeat of the French East India Company and the acquisition for Britain of the state of Bengal. Through a variety of arrangements with local rulers, British control began to extend over much of India—and many British traders and adventurers ("nabobs," as they came to be called) began to amass large fortunes, often with what appeared to be very little effort.

Beginning in the late eighteenth century, British involvement in India began to be attended by considerable controversy. The actions of the nabobs lent a frequently disreputable air to British involvement in India, and eventually Clive himself was charged with having engaged in corrupt practices during his tenure as Governor of Bengal. In 1773 he was acquitted (suffering from poor health as well as a damaged reputation, he committed suicide the following year), but in the same year Parliament took measures through the East India Act to place tighter controls on activities in India, including the appointment for the first time of a Governor-General as the representative of the Crown.

The first Governor-General, Warren Hastings, was eventually accused of corruption too—specifically, of bribery and a variety of high-handed extra-legal dealings with local rulers. In Hastings's case, matters were complicated by the patronage he gave to (and the support he received from) "Orientalists" such as William Jones and Charles Hamilton, who were endeavoring to build among the British a knowledge of, and appreciation for, the languages, literatures, and cultures of the East. To Edmund Burke and many other critics of Hastings, the Governor-General's admiration for Indian culture and his high-handed behavior as an administrator were not unconnected; in Burke's view Hastings had adopted a "geographical morality"—what today might be referred to as moral relativism.

Hastings was impeached and tried on a variety of charges, and arguments over the case divided much of Britain; again like Clive, he was eventually acquitted (in 1795). Over the course of the next half-century, British rule in India was largely purged both of the taint of corruption and of the taint of Orientalism among its administrators. In 1833, control of the East India Company was transferred to the Crown, and in 1858, following the Indian Mutiny, Britain assumed direct administration of many of her Indian "possessions"; the East India Company was disbanded. British imperial rule over India, however, would not end until after World War Two.

The cultural influence of Orientalism also continued through the nineteenth century and into the twentieth. Whereas the Occident—the West—represented all that was familiar culturally, the Orient came in many minds to represent the exotic, "the Other." This influential concept, advanced in the 1940s by Simone de Beauvoir in the context of gender, was applied in the 1970s by Edward

Said and others to cultural divides: "The Orient is … the place of Europe's grandest and richest and oldest colonies, the source of its civilizations and languages, its cultural contestant, and one of its deepest and most recurring images of the Other." Said also influentially adapted the word "Orientalist," applying it not only as a term specific to a group of Westerners studying, promoting and (in Said's view) usually misrepresenting the cultures of the Orient, but also much more broadly:

> Taking the late eighteenth century as a very roughly defined starting point, Orientalism can be discussed and analyzed as the corporate institution for dealing with the Orient—dealing with it by making statements about it, authorizing views of it, describing it, by teaching it, settling it, ruling over it: in short, Orientalism as a Western style for dominating, restructuring, and having authority over the Orient.

As Said wrote in his groundbreaking 1978 work, *Orientalism*, Western representations of the Orient, though typically grounded in the material realities of imperialism, have tended to be composed of projections of western aspirations, fears, and desires; they tend to tell us more about the West than about their purported subject.

Much as there is a core of ethnocentrism in Western attitudes towards the Orient, such attitudes have also exhibited considerable complexity. Intellectual and cultural pioneers such as Jones may finally have been trapped by the limitations of their own culture, but their lives were devoted to the attempt to transcend such limitations. Undifferentiated exoticism may be a dominant motif in the Orientalist imagination, but Orientalists such as Jones and Elizabeth Hamilton were intent on establishing meaningful distinctions among cultures and peoples. Often, lines of prejudice or of cultural chauvinism cut across expected patterns—as, for example, when Macaulay supports his case for a quintessentially imperialist project (of making English the universal language of instruction in 1830s India) through a strenuous defense of the capabilities of the colonized, arguing (against those who would denigrate the native peoples of India) that Indians are in fact entirely "competent to discuss political or scientific questions with fluency and precision in the English language." As such cases suggest, Orientalism is often of as much interest for the ironies and contradictions within it as it is for the powerful hold it exerted for so long on the British imagination.

⌘⌘⌘

from Sir William Jones, "A Discourse on the Institution of a Society for Inquiring into the History, Civil and Natural, the Antiquities, Arts, Sciences and Literature of Asia" (1784)

The speech from which these excerpts are taken was delivered not long after Jones's arrival in Calcutta in 1783. The Asiatic Society of Bengal was founded in 1784.

Gentlemen

When I was at sea last August, on my voyage to this country, which I had long and ardently desired to visit, I found one evening, on inspecting the observations of the day, that India lay before us, and Persia on our left, whilst a breeze from Arabia blew nearly on our stern. A situation so pleasing in itself, and to me so new, could not fail to awaken a train of reflections in a mind, which had early been accustomed to contemplate with delight the eventful histories and agreeable fictions of this eastern world.…

It is your design, I conceive, to take an ample space for your learned investigations, bounding them only by the geographical limits of Asia; so that, considering Hindustan as a centre, and turning your eyes in idea to the North, you have on your right, many important kingdoms in the Eastern peninsula, the ancient and wonderful empire of China with all her Tartarian dependencies, and that of Japan, which the cluster of precious islands, in which many singular curiosities have too long been concealed: before you lies that prodigious chain of mountains, which formerly perhaps were a barrier against the violence of the sea, and beyond them the very interesting country of Tibet, … : on your left are the beautiful and celebrated provinces of Iran or Persia, the unmeasured, and perhaps unmeasurable deserts of Arabia, and the once flourishing kingdom of Yemen, with the pleasant isles that the Arabs have subdued or colonized; and farther westward, the Asiatic dominions of the Turkish sultans, whose moon seems approaching rapidly to its wane. By this great circumference, the field of your useful researches will be enclosed; but, since Egypt had unquestionably an old connection with this country, … you may not be displeased occasionally to follow the streams of Asiatic learning a little beyond its natural boundary; and, if it be necessary or convenient, that a short name or epithet be given to our society, in order to distinguish it in the world, that of *Asiatic* appears both classical and proper, whether we consider the place or the object of the institution, and preferable to *Oriental,* which is in truth a word merely relative, and, though commonly used in Europe, conveys no very distinct idea.

If now it be asked, what are the intended objects of our inquiries within these spacious limits, we answer, MAN and NATURE; whatever is performed by the one, or produced by the other.…

Agreeably to this analysis, you will investigate whatever is rare in the stupendous fabrick of nature, will correct the geography of Asia by new observations and discoveries; will trace the annals, and even traditions, of those nations, who from time to time have peopled or desolated it; and will bring to light their various forms of government, with their institutions civil and religious; you will examine their improvements and methods in arithmetic and geometry, in trigonometry, … mechanics, optics, astronomy, and general physics; their systems of morality, grammar, rhetoric, and dialectic; their skill in … medicine, and their advancement, whatever it may be, in anatomy and chemistry. To this you will add researches into their agriculture, manufactures, trade; and, whilst your inquire with pleasure into their music, architecture, painting, and poetry, will not neglect those inferior arts, by which the comforts and even elegances of social life are supplied or improved. You may observe, that I have omitted their languages, the diversity and difficulty of which are a sad obstacle to the progress of useful knowledge; but I have ever considered languages as the mere instruments of real learning, and think them improperly confounded with learning itself: the attainment of them is, however, indispensably necessary.…

Let us, if you please, for the present, have weekly evening meetings in this hall, for the purpose of hearing original papers read on such subjects as fall within the circle of our inquiries. Let all curious and learned men be invited to send their tracts to our secretary, for which they ought immediately to receive our thanks; and if, towards the end of each year, we should be supplied with a sufficiency of valuable materials to fill a volume, let us present our Asiatic miscellany to the literary world.…

One thing only, as essential your dignity, I recommend with earnestness, on no account to admit a new member, who has not expressed a voluntary desire to become so; and in that case, you will not require, I suppose, any other qualification than a love of knowledge, and a zeal for the promotion of it.

Your institution, I am persuaded, will ripen of itself, and your meetings will be amply supplied with interesting and amusing papers, as soon as the object of your inquiries shall be generally known.

Edmund Burke and the Impeachment of Warren Hastings

Hastings had been appointed Governor of Bengal in 1772, and Governor-General of Bengal (with authority over Madras and Bombay) the following year, with the passage of the East India Company Act. He resigned in 1785 and impeachment proceedings against him began in 1786. Hastings was finally acquitted of all charges in 1794.

from Edmund Burke, Speech on the Impeachment of Warren Hastings (15–19 February, 1788)

My lords, we contend that Mr. Hastings, as a British Governor, ought to govern upon British principles.… We call for that spirit of equity, that spirit of justice, that spirit of safety, that spirit of protection, that spirit of lenity,[1] which ought to characterize every British subject in power; and upon these, and these principles only, he will be tried.

But he has told your lordships in his defence, that actions in Asia do not bear the same moral qualities as the same actions would bear in Europe.... And having stated at large what he means by saying that the same actions have not the same qualities in Asia and in Europe, ... [he and others] have formed a plan of geographical morality, by which the duties of men in public and in private situations are not to be governed by their relations to the great governor of the universe, or by their relations to men, but by climates, degrees of longitude and latitude, parallels not of life but of latitudes; as if, when you have crossed the equinoctial line, all the virtues die, as they say some animals die when they cross the line; as if there were a kind of baptism, like that practised by seamen, by which they unbaptize themselves of all that they learned in Europe, and commence a new order and system of things.

This geographical morality we do protest against.... We think it necessary, in justification of ourselves, to declare that the laws of morality are the same everywhere, and that there is no action which would pass for an action of extortion, of peculation,[2] of bribery, and of oppression, in England that is not an act of extortion, of peculation, of bribery and oppression, in Europe, Asia, Africa, and all the world over....

Mr. Hastings comes before your lordships not as a British Governor answering to a British tribunal, but as a subahdar.[3] ... He says, "I had an arbitrary power to exercise; I exercised it. Slaves I found the people; slaves they are. They are so by their constitution; and if they are, I did not make it for them. I was unfortunately bound to exercise this arbitrary power, and accordingly I did exercise it. It was disagreeable to me, but I did exercise it, and no other power can be exercised in that country."

Think of an English Governor tried before you as a British subject, and yet declaring that he governed upon the principles of arbitrary power! This plea is, that he did govern there upon arbitrary and despotic, and, as he supposes, Oriental principles....

[1] *lenity* Mildness, mercy.

[2] *peculation* Appropriation of public funds.

[3] *subahdar* Governor of an Indian province.

If your lordships will permit, me, I will state one of the many places in which he has avowed these principles as the basis and foundation of all his conduct:

> The sovereignty which they assumed, it fell to my lot, very unexpectedly, to exert; and whether or not such power or powers of that nature were delegated to me by any provisions of any Act of Parliament, I confess myself too little of a lawyer to pronounce. I only know that the acceptance of the sovereignty of Benares, etc.[4] is not acknowledged or admitted by any Act of Parliament; and yet, by the particular interference of the majority of the council, the Company[5] is clearly and indisputably seized of[6] that sovereignty.

... Now, if your lordships will suffer the laws to be broken by those that are not of the long robe, I am afraid those of the long robe will have none to punish but those of their own profession. Mr. Hastings, therefore, goes to a law which he knows better, that is, the law of arbitrary power and force, if it deserves to be called by any such name. "If therefore," says he,

> the sovereignty of Benares, as ceded to us by the Vizier,[7] have any rights whatever annexed to it, and be not a mere empty word without meaning, those rights must be such as are held, countenanced, and established, by the law, custom, and usage, of the Mogul Empire,[8] and not by the provisions of any British Act of Parliament hitherto enacted. Those rights, and none other, I have been the involuntary instrument of enforcing. And if any future Act of Parliament shall positively, or by implication, tend to annihilate those very rights or their exertion, as I

[4] *the sovereignty of Benares, etc.* In many areas of India during the colonial period British control was indirect and/or less than precisely defined, with local authorities retaining a degree of real authority. Among these was the Hindu holy city of Benares (now Varanasi) on the banks of the Ganges River.

[5] *Company* British East India Company.

[6] *seized of* Made aware of.

[7] *Vizier* Governor (a term used particularly in Islamic-controlled areas).

[8] *Mogul Empire* The Mogul (or Mughal) Empire was founded in 1526, and for several centuries thereafter extended across much of the Indian subcontinent; the Mughals, originating in what is now Turkey and Persia, were followers of Islam. The last remnants of the Mughal Empire were dissolved by the British in 1857.

> have exerted them, I much fear that the boasted sovereignty of Benares, … will be found a burden instead of a benefit, a heavy clog rather than a precious gem to its present possessors.…
>
> Every part of Hindustan has been constantly exposed to … [anarchy, confusion, and] similar disadvantages ever since the Mohammedan conquests.[1] The Hindus, who never incorporated with their conquerors, were kept in order only by the strong hand of power. … Rebellion itself is the parent and promoter of despotism. Sovereignty in India implies nothing else; for I know not how we can form an estimate of its powers but from its visible effects, and those are everywhere the same from Kabul to Assam. The whole history of Asia is nothing more than precedents to prove the invariable exercise of arbitrary power. To all this I strongly alluded in the minutes I delivered in Council when the treaty with the new Vizier was on foot[2] in 1775.… I knew that, from the history of Asia, and from the very nature of mankind, the subjects of a despotic empire are always vigilant for the moment to rebel, and the sovereign is ever jealous I of rebellious intentions.… "The mean[3] and depraved state of a mere zemindar"[4] is … this very dependence above-mentioned on a despotic government, this very proneness to shake off his allegiance, and this very exposure to continual danger from his sovereign's jealousy, which are consequent on the political state of Hindustanic governments.

My lords, you have now heard the principles upon which Mr. Hastings governs the part of Asia subjected to the British Empire. You have heard his opinion of "the mean and depraved state" of those who are subject to it. You have heard his lecture upon arbitrary power, which he states to be the constitution of Asia. Do your lordships really think that the nation would bear, that any human creature would bear, to hear an English governor defend himself upon such principles? "I know," says he, "the constitution of Asia only from its practices." Will your lordships ever bear the corrupt practices of mankind made the principles of government? It will be your pride and glory to teach men that they are to confirm their practices to principles, and not to draw their principles from the corrupt practices of any man whatever. Was there ever heard, or could it be conceived, that a man would dare to mention the practices of all the villains, all the mad usurpers, all the thieves and robbers, in Asia, that he should gather them all up, and form the whole mass of abuses into one code and call it the duty of a British governor? I believe that till this time so audacious a thing was never attempted by mankind.

[1] *Mohammedan conquests* Islamic forces first conquered large areas of the Indian subcontinent between the 7th and the 12th centuries CE.

[2] *on foot* Afoot; being discussed as a possibility or being negotiated.

[3] *mean* Impoverished.

[4] *zemindar* At this time, Indian landholder paying rent to the British government.

from Warren Hastings, Address in His Defence (2 June 1791)

My Lords, in the course of this trial, my accusers, to excite a popular odium against me, have called me the abettor or usurper of arbitrary power. I certainly did not use the words arbitrary power in the sense which has been imputed to me. The language, it is true, was not my own, for I was indebted for that part of my Defence to the assistance of a friend; but this I can aver, that nothing more was meant by arbitrary power than discretionary power. I considered myself and Council as invested with that discretionary power which commanders-in-chief have over their armies, which the Legislature has lately conferred, in a greater extent, on Lord Cornwallis,[5] singly, and which all Governments have in their legislative capacity over the property of their subjects. I never considered that my will or caprice was to be the guide to my conduct; but that I was responsible for the use of the authority with which I was invested to those who had conferred it on me.

My Lords, let me be tried by this rule—did I act prudently and consistently with the interest of my superiors and of the people whom I governed? Whatever may be your Lordships' opinion upon this question, I can with a safe conscience declare to all the world that my intentions were perfectly upright, and biased by no selfish considerations whatever.…

Were I therefore for a moment to suppose that the acts with which I am charged and which I so commu-

[5] *Lord Cornwallis* Charles Cornwallis, 1st Marquis Cornwallis (1738–1805), leader of the British forces for much of the American Revolutionary War, and Governor-General of India from 1786–93.

nicated—for I communicated all—to the court of Directors, were intrinsically wrong, yet from such proofs it is evident that I thought them right; and therefore the worst that could be said of them, as they could affect me, is, that they were errors of judgment....

Two great sources of revenue, opium and salt, were of my creation. The first, which I am accused for not having made more productive, amounts at this time yearly to the net income of 120,000 pounds sterling. The last—and all my colleagues in the Council refused to share with me in the responsibility attendant upon a new system—to the yearly net income of above 800,000 pounds.

To sum up all—I maintained the provinces of my immediate administration in a state of peace, plenty, and security, when every other member of the British empire was involved in external wars or civil tumult.

In a dreadful season of famine, which visited all the neighbouring states of India during three successive years, I repressed it in its first approach to the countries of the British dominion, and by timely and continued regulations prevented its return....

And, lastly, I raised the collective annual income of the Company's possessions under my administration from three to five millions sterling—not of temporary and forced exaction, but of an easy, continued, and still existing production—the surest evidence of a good government, improving agriculture and increased population.

To the Commons of England, in whose name I am arraigned for desolating the provinces of their dominion in India, I dare to reply, that they are—and their representatives annually persist in telling them so—the most flourishing of all the states in India. It was I who made them so. The valour of others acquired—I enlarged and gave shape and consistency to—the dominion which you hold there. I preserved it. I sent forth its armies with an effectual but an economical hand, through unknown and hostile regions, to the support of your other possessions—to the retrieval of one from degradation and dishonour, and of the other from utter loss and subjection.

from Elizabeth Hamilton, *Translations of the Letters of a Hindoo Rajah* (1796)

Hamilton's novel falls within a substantial eighteenth-century tradition of satirizing British society by imagining it through the fresh perspective of foreign eyes. But it is also an important document in the history of British Orientalistm—not least of all for the distinctions Hamilton draws between India's two religions.

That part of Asia, known to Europeans by the name of Hindoostan, extends from the mountains of Thibet on the north, to the sea on the south, and from the river Indus on the west, to the Barampooter on the east, comprehending, within its limits, a variety of provinces, many of which have been famous, from the earliest ages, for the salubrity of their climate, the richness of their productions, and the fertility of their soil. Of this country, the Hindoos are the aborigines. Over the origin of this celebrated people, Time has cast the impenetrable mantle of oblivion. Their own annals trace it back to a period so remote, so far beyond the date of European chronology, as to be rejected by European pride. The magnificent proofs of ancient grandeur, however, which are still to be found, and which have been sought for with the most successful assiduity, by many of our countrymen in India, give the most irrefragable testimony of the antiquity of their empire, and seem to confirm the assertion of its historians, "that its duration is not to be paralleled by the history of any other portion of the human race." To account for this extraordinary degree of permanency, we must direct our attention, not to the barriers formed by nature around their territories, but to those internal causes arising from the *nature of their Government, their Laws, Religion, moral Prejudices,* and established manners.

The ancient government, throughout Hindoostan, appears to have been a federative union of the various states, each governed by its own Rajah, or Chief, but subjected, in a sort of feudal vassalage, to the sovereignty of the supreme Emperor, who was head of the whole.

The manner in which the Rajahs of the Hindoos exercised the rights of dominion over their people, bears so little analogy to that practised by the petty sovereigns of such European states as are placed in circumstances nearly similar; that it would be doing the greatest injustice to the amiable and benevolent character of the Hindoos, to bring them into comparison. *There* the right of sovereignty bore the mild aspect of parental authority. The Prince considered the people in the light of children, whom he was appointed by Heaven to protect and cherish; and the affection of the subject for the Prince, under whose auspices he enjoyed the blessings of freedom, and tranquility, was heightened by esteem for his virtues, into the most inviolable attachment....

An abhorrence of the shedding of blood, is a principle which pervades the whole of the Hindoo religion, but the Bramins observe it in the strictest degree. They eat nothing that has life in it: their food consisting entirely of fruit and vegetables, and their only luxury being the milk of the cow, an animal for whose species they have a particular veneration. Not only every act of hostility, but even every method of defence is, to them, strictly prohibited; submitting to violence with unresisting patience and humility, they leave it to God, and their Rajahs, to avenge whatever injuries they may sustain.

The separation of the different castes from each other is absolute and irreversible; it forms the fundamental principle of their laws, and the slightest breach of it never fails to incur universal reprobation.

Thus those sources of disquiet, which have held most of the empires of the earth in a state of perpetual agitation, were unknown to the peaceful children of Brahma. The turbulence of ambition, the emulations of envy, and the murmurs of discontent, were equally unknown to a people, where each individual, following the occupation, and walking in the steps of his fathers, considered it as his primary duty to keep in the situation that he firmly believed to have been marked out for him by the hand of Providence.

In the spirit of the religion of the Hindoos, a still more efficient cause, of the durability of their state, presents itself to our view. Original in its nature, and absolute in its decrees, its precepts induce a total seclusion from the rest of mankind. Far, however, from disturbing those who are of a different faith, by endeavours to convert them, it does not even admit of proselytes to its own. Though tenacious of their own doctrines, in a degree that is unexampled in the history of any other religion, the most fervent zeal in the most pious Hindoos, leads them neither to hate, nor despise, nor pity such as are of a different belief, nor does it suffer them to consider others as less favoured by the Almighty than themselves. This spirit of unbounded toleration proceeded in a natural course from the sublime and exalted notions of the Deity, taught by the Bramins, and every where to be met with in their writings, and which are only equalled in that Gospel "which brought life and immortality to light." ...

Under the banners of their religion, the irascible passions were never ranged. "He, my servant," says Krishna, speaking in the person of the Deity, "He, my servant, is dear to me, who is *free from enmity,* merciful, and exempt from pride and selfishness, and who is the same in pain and in pleasure, patient of wrongs, contented, and whose mind is fixed on me alone."

I shall conclude this account of the notions of the Deity, entertained by the Hindoos, with the first stanza of that beautiful Hymn to Narryána, or the Spirit of God exerted in Creation, translated by the elegant pen of Sir William Jones.

Spirit of Spirits! who through every part,
Of space expanded, and of endless time,
Beyond the stretch of lab'ring thought sublime,
Bad'st uproar into beauteous order start,
Before Heaven was, Thou art:
Ere spheres beneath us roll'd, or spheres above,
Ere Earth in firmamental ether hung,
Thou sat'st alone, till through thy mystic love,
Things unexisting to existence sprung,
And grateful descant sung,
What first impell'd Thee to exert thy might?
Goodness unlimited.—What glorious light
Thy powers directed? Wisdom without bound
What prov'd it first? Oh! guide my fancy right,
Oh raise from cumb'rous ground
My soul, in rapture drown'd,
That fearless it may soar on wings of fire;
For Thou, who only know'st, Thou only canst inspire.

... A further view of their religious system may be necessary, and will, perhaps, be sufficient to elucidate another characteristic feature of the Hindoos, which has forcibly struck all who have had an opportunity of observing them. The patience evinced by this mild and gentle race under the severest suffering, and the indifference with which they view the approach of death, which has been severally assigned to constitutional apathy, to their mode of living, and to the delicate texture of their bodies, may perhaps be equally accounted for, from their firm and steadfast belief in a future state. This belief, indeed, is darkened by many errors. They believe that the human soul must be purified by suffering, and that it is not till after having undergone this expiatory discipline through a series of different bodies, that it becomes worthy of admission to eternal happiness. The evils inflicted upon the seemingly inoffensive, is attributed by them as a punishment for crimes committed in a pre-existent state. Revolting from the idea of eternal punishment, as incompatible with the justice and goodness of their Creator, they believe that the souls of the wicked, after having been for a time confined in Narekha (the infernal regions) are sent back upon the stage of life, to animate the bodies of the inferior creation, till by various chastisements and transmigrations in these probationary states, every vicious inclination is sufficiently corrected to admit of their reception into the regions of perfection and happiness....

The reader of sensibility, will, it is hoped, pardon a digression, into which the writer has been betrayed, by feelings of which they know the power and influence, and from which she hastily returns, to remark that the happiness enjoyed by the Hindoos under the mild and auspicious government of their native Princes, and preserved, without any material interruption, through such a mighty period of revolving time, as staggers the belief of the ever-fluctuating nations of Europe, was at length doomed to see its overthrow effected, by the resistless fury of fanatic zeal.

The imposter of Mecca had established, as one of the principles of his doctrine, the merit of extending it, either by persuasion, or the sword, to all parts of the earth. How steadily this injunction was adhered to by his followers, and with what success it was pursued, is well known to all, who are in the least conversant in history.

The same overwhelming torrent, which had inundated the greater part of Africa, burst its way into the very heart of Europe, and covered many kingdoms of Asia with unbounded desolation; directed its baleful course to the flourishing provinces of Hindoostan. Here these fierce and hardy adventurers, whose only improvement had been in the science of destruction, who added the fury of fanaticism to the ravages of war, found the great end of their conquests opposed, by obstacles which neither the ardour of their persevering zeal, nor savage barbarity could surmount. Multitudes were sacrificed by the cruel hand of religious persecution, and whole countries were deluged in blood, in the vain hope, that by the destruction of a part, the remainder might be persuaded, or terrified into the profession of Mahommadenism: but all these sanguinary efforts were ineffectual; and at length being fully convinced, that though they might extirpate, they could never hope to convert, any number of the Hindoos, they relinquished the impracticable idea, with which they had entered upon their career of conquest, and contented themselves with the acquirement of the civil dominion and almost universal empire of Hindoostan.

In these provinces, where the Mussulman jurisdiction was fully established, Mussulman courts of justice were erected. The laws which the Hindoos had for numberless ages been accustomed to revere, as of divine authority, were set aside, and all causes judged and decided by the standard of Mussulman jurisprudence; an evil which appeared to the unhappy Hindoo more formidable than the extortions of avarice, or the devastations of cruelty. Nor was the effect of these latter passions unfelt, the peculiar punishment of forfeiting their caste, which is attached by their law to the most temporary and seemingly trivial deviation from its precepts, and which involves in it the dreadful consequences of irremediable alienation and irreversible proscription, was converted by their Mahommedan rulers into a lucrative source of oppression. Superstition combined with avarice to invent the means of inflicting this dreadful chastisement, and fines, without mercy, were exacted by those bigoted and venal judges.

By the same merciless conquerors, their commerce was impeded by every clog which avaricious and unfeeling power could invent to obstruct it. Neither the mild and tolerating spirit of the religion of the Hindoos, nor the gentle and inoffensive manners of its votaries, were sufficient to protect them from the intolerant zeal and brutal antipathy of their Mahommedan invaders. In the effusions of their barbarous enthusiasm, the temples of the Hindoos ornamented with all the ingenuity and skill for which they were celebrated, were utterly demolished, and the monuments of their ancient splendour every where destroyed.

from Anonymous, "Review of *Translations of the Letters of a Hindoo Rajah*," from *The Analytical Review* (October 1796)

The author of these letters seems to have taken the hint of conveying her sentiments to the public in the present form, from Montesquieu's and Lord Lyttelton's *Persian Letters*, Goldsmith's *Citizen of the World*, the *Turkish Spy*, &c. It might be invidious to draw comparisons, but we confess, with pleasure, we have received entertainment from the perusal of this lively and amusing little work.

The writer displays, both in the letters and preliminary dissertation on Hindoo mythology, history, and literature, considerable knowledge of India affairs: but it is doubtful, whether the generality of readers will perfectly accord with her in opinion, respecting the happy change which the long-suffering Hindoos have experienced under the dominion of Great Britain. Many, it may be, will be rather inclined to believe, that, however mitigated in some respects by the more tolerant principles of the British Legislature, on the subjects of law and religion; these injured people have merely *changed masters,* and one species of oppression for another. The interference of foreign states in the internal government of nations is generally equivocal in its motives, and always mischievous in its tendency. A simple, commercial intercourse would perhaps have been attended with more beneficial consequences to both countries. The compliments which are paid by our author to Governor Hastings, to whom her production is dedicated, will be adjudged by the reader, either as just, or the grateful language of private obligation or friendship, according to his own preconceived opinions on the subject. We expected from the title of this work, to find the follies and vices of our contemporaries satirised by the fictitious Indian prince, nor were we disappointed: a vein of ingenious pleasantry runs through it, mingled with a number of judicious, and sensible observations, on various subjects, especially on the female mind and manners....

Tipu Sultan and the British

The following documents illustrate the elliptical fashion in which communications and negotiations between the British and local rulers often proceeded.

from *Letter from Tipu Sultan to the Governor General* (received 13 February, 1799)

I have been much gratified by the agreeable receipt of your Lordship's two friendly letters, the first brought by a Camel-man, the last by a *Harkara,*[1] and understood their contents. The letter of the Prince, in station like Jamshed; with angels as his guards, with troops numerous as the stars; the sun illumining the world of the heaven of empire and dominion; the luminary giving splendour to the universe of the firmament of glory and power; the Sultan of the sea and the land; the King of Rome (i.e. the Grand Signior) be his Empire and his power perpetual; addressed to me, which reached you through the British Envoy and which you transmitted has arrived. Being frequently disposed to make excursions and hunt, I am accordingly proceeding upon a hunting excursion; you will be pleased to despatch Major Doveton (about whose coming your friendly pen has repeatedly written) slightly attended (or unattended).

Always continue to gratify me by friendly letters, notifying your welfare.

from *Declaration of the Right Honourable the Governor-General-in-Council* (22 February 1799)

The strict principles of self-defence would have justified the Allies ... in making an immediate attack upon the territories of Tipu Sultan; but even the happy intelligence of the glorious success of the British fleet at the mouths of the Nile, did not abate the anxious desire of the Allies to maintain the relations of amity and peace with Tipu Sultan; they attempted by a moderate representation, to recall him to a sense of his obligations, and of the genuine principles of prudence and policy; and they employed every effort to open the channels of negotiation and to facilitate the means of amicable accommodation....

[1] *Harkara* Soldier.

Tipu Sultan declined, by various evasions and subterfuges, this friendly and moderate advance on the part of the Allies, and he manifested an evident disposition to reject the means of pacific accommodation, by suddenly breaking up, in the month of December, the conferences, which had commenced with respect to the districts of Amerah and Souleah, and by interrupting the intercourse between his subjects and those of the Company on their respective frontiers. On the 9th of January 1799, the Governor-General, being arrived at Fort St. George (notwithstanding these discouraging circumstances in the conduct of Tipu Sultan) renewed with increased earnestness the expression of His Lordship's anxious desire to despatch an Ambassador to the Sultan.

The Governor-General expressly solicited the Sultan to reply within one day to this letter; and as it involved no proposition either injurious to the rights, dignity, or honour of the Sultan, or in any degree novel or complicated, either in form or substance, it could not require a longer consideration, the Governor-General waited with the utmost solicitude for an answer to the reasonable and distinct proposition contained in his letter of the 9th January, 1799.

Tipu Sultan, however, who must have received the said letter before the 17th of January, remained silent, although the Governor-General had plainly apprised the Prince, that dangerous consequences would result from delay. In the meanwhile the season for military operations had already advanced to so late a period, as to render a speedy decision indispensible to the security of the Allies.

Under these circumstances on the 3rd of February (twelve days having elapsed from the period, when an answer might have been received from Seringapatam to the Governor-General's letter of the 9th of January). His Lordship declared to the Allies, that the necessary measures must now be adopted without delay for securing such advantages, as should place the common safety of the Allies beyond the reach of the insincerity of Tipu Sultan and the violence of the French. *With this view the Governor-General, on the 3rd of February, issued orders to the British Armies to march and signified to the Commander of His Majesty's squadron that the obstinate silence of the Sultan must be considered as a rejection of the proposed negotiation.*

At length, on the 13th of February a letter from Tipu Sultan reached the Governor-General in which the Sultan signifies to His Lordship "that being frequently disposed to hunt, he was accordingly proceeding upon a hunting excursion," adding "that the Governor-General would be pleased to despatch Major Doveton to him, unattended." The Allies will not dwell on the peculiar phrases of this letter; but it must be evident in all the States of India that the answer of the Sultan has been deferred to this late period of the season with no other view than to preclude the Allies by insidious delays from the benefit of those advantages, which their combined military operations would enable them to secure....

The Allies cannot suffer Tipu Sultan to profit by his own studied and systematic delay, nor to impede such a disposition of their military and naval force as shall appear best calculated to give effect to their just views.

Bound by the sacred obligations of public faith professing the most amicable disposition and undisturbed in the possession of those dominions secured to him by Treaty, Tipu Sultan wantonly violated the relations of amity and peace and compelled the Allies to arm in defence of their rights, their happiness and their honour.

For a period of three months he obstinately rejected every pacific overture, in the hourly expectation of receiving that succour, which he had eagerly solicited for the prosecution of his favourite purposes of ambition and revenge; disappointed in his hopes of immediate vengeance, and conquest, he now resorts to subterfuge and procrastination; and by a tardy, reluctant, and insidious acquiescence in a proposition, which he had so long and repeatedly declined, he endeavours to frustrate the precautions of the Allies, and to protract every effectual operation, until some change of circumstance and of season shall revive his expectations of disturbing the tranquillity of India, by favouring the irruption of a French Army.

The Allies are equally prepared to repel his violence and to counteract his artifices and delays. The Allies are, therefore, resolved to place their army in such a position as shall afford adequate protection against any artifice or insincerity and shall preclude the return of that danger which has so lately menaced their possessions. The Allies, however, retaining an anxious desire to effect an adjustment with Tipu Sultan, Lieutenant General Harris,

Commander-in-Chief of His Majesty's and the Honourable Company's Forces on the Coast of Coromandel and Malabar, is authorized to receive any Embassy which Tipu Sultan may despatch to the Headquarters of the British Army and to concert a treaty on such conditions, as appear to the Allies to be indispensibly necessary for the establishment of a secure and permanent peace.

By order of the Right Honourable the Governor-General.

(Fort St. George: February 22, 1799)

from Mary Robinson, "The Lascar" (1800)

Robinson (1758–1800), one of the leading poets of her day, often wrote verse dramatizing the plight of the downtrodden. Following are the opening stanzas of a twenty-six stanza poem that appeared in Robinson's 1800 volume *Lyrical Tales.*

The Lascar[1]

1

"Another day, Ah! me, a day
Of dreary Sorrow is begun!
And still I loathe the temper'd ray,
And still I hate the sickly Sun!
Far from my Native Indian shore,
I hear our wretched race deplore;
I mark the smile of taunting Scorn,
And curse the hour, when I was born!
I weep, but no one gently tries
To stop my tear, or check my sighs;
For, while my heart beats mournfully,
Dear Indian home, I sigh for Thee!

2

Since, gaudy Sun! I see no more
Thy hottest glory gild the day;
Since, sever'd from my burning shore,
I waste the vapid hours away;
O! darkness come! come, deepest gloom!
Shroud the young Summer's op'ning bloom;
Burn, temper'd Orb, with fiercer beams
This northern world! and drink the streams
That thro' the fertile valleys glide
To bathe the feasted Fiends of Pride!
Or, hence, broad Sun! extinguish'd be!
For endless night encircles Me!

3

What is, to me, the City gay?
And what, the board profusely spread?
I have no home, no rich array,
No spicy feast, no downy bed!
I, with the dogs am doom'd to eat,
To perish in the peopled street,
To drink the tear of deep despair;
The scoff and scorn of fools to bear!
I sleep upon a bed of stone,
I pace the meadows, wild, alone!
And if I curse my fate severe,
Some Christian Savage mocks my tear!

4

Shut out the Sun, O! pitying Night!
Make the wide world my silent tomb!
O'ershade this northern, sickly light,
And shroud me, in eternal gloom!
My Indian plains, now smiling glow,
There stands my Parent's hovel low,
And there the tow'ring aloes rise
And fling their perfumes to the skies!
There the broad palm Trees covert lend,
There Sun and Shade delicious blend;
But here, amid the blunted ray,
Cold shadows hourly cross my way!

5

Was it for this, that on the main
I met the tempest fierce and strong,
And steering o'er the liquid plain,
Still onward, press'd the waves among?
Was it for this, the LASCAR brave
Toil'd, like a wretched Indian Slave;
Preserv'd your treasures by his toil,
And sigh'd to greet this fertile soil?
Was it for this, to beg, to die,
Where plenty smiles, and where the
Sky Sheds cooling airs; while fev'rish pain,
Maddens the famish'd LASCAR'S brain?

[1] *Lascar* East Indian sailor.

6

Oft, I the stately Camel led,
And sung the short-hour'd night away;
And oft, upon the top-mast's head,
Hail'd the red Eye of coming day.
The Tanyan's back my mother bore;
And oft the wavy Ganges' roar
Lull'd her to rest, as on she past—
'Mid the hot sands and burning blast!
And oft beneath the Banyan tree
She sat and fondly nourish'd me;
And while the noontide hour past slow,
I felt her breast with kindness glow.

7

Where'er I turn my sleepless eyes,
No cheek so dark as mine, I see;
For Europe's Suns, with softer dyes
Mark Europe's favour'd progeny!
Low is my stature, black my hair,
The emblem of my Soul's despair!
My voice no dulcet cadence flings,
To touch soft pity's throbbing strings!
Then wherefore cruel Briton, say,
Compel my aching heart to stay?
To-morrow's Sun—may rise, to see—
The famish'd LASCAR, blest as thee!"

The Pavilion at Brighton, viewed from the east. Located on the coast of England, directly south of London, the Pavilion is one of the most prominent expressions of the early nineteenth-century taste for Oriental exoticism. A property belonging to the Prince Regent (later George IV), the Pavilion was transformed by architect John Nash over the years 1815–23 into an "Indian style" palace.

from Thomas Macaulay, *Minute on Indian Education* (1835)

Macaulay (1800–59) served from 1834–37 on the Supreme Council of India. His arguments concerning Indian education—and concerning the supremacy of English language literature and culture—marked a turning point in imperial administration.

It does not appear to me that the Act of Parliament can, by any art of construction, be made to bear the meaning which has been assigned to it. It contains nothing about the particular languages or sciences which are to be studied. A sum is set apart "for the revival and promotion of literature and the encouragement of the learned natives of India, and for the introduction and promotion of a knowledge of the sciences among the inhabitants of the British territories." It is argued, or rather taken for granted, that by literature the Parliament can have only meant Arabic and Sanscrit literature, that they never would have given the honourable appellation of a "learned native" to a native who was familiar with the poetry of Milton, the metaphysics of Locke, and the physics of Newton; but that they meant to designate by that name only such persons as might have studied in the sacred books of the Hindoos all the usages of cusa-grass, and all the mysteries of absorption into the Deity. This does not appear to be a very satisfactory interpretation. To take a parallel case; suppose that the Pacha of Egypt, a country once superior in knowledge to the nations of Europe, but now sunk far below them, were to appropriate a sum for the purpose sum for the purpose of "reviving and promoting literature, and encouraging learned natives of Egypt," would anybody infer that he meant the youth of his pachalic to give years to the study of hieroglyphics, to search into all the doctrines disguised under the fable of Osiris, and to ascertain with all possible accuracy the ritual with which cats and onions were anciently adored? Would he be justly charged with inconsistency, if, instead of employing his young subjects in deciphering obelisks, he were to order them to be instructed in the English and French languages, and in all the sciences to which those languages are the chief keys? …

We now come to the gist of the matter. We have a fund to be employed as Government shall direct for the intellectual improvement of the people of this country. The simple question is, what is the most useful way of employing it?

All parties seem to be agreed on one point, that the dialects commonly spoken among the natives of this part of India contain neither literary nor scientific information, and are, moreover so poor and rude that, until they are enriched from some other quarter, it will not be easy to translate any valuable work into them. It seems to be admitted on all sides that the intellectual improvement of those classes of the people who have the means of pursuing higher studies can at present be effected only by means of some language not vernacular amongst them.

What, then, shall that language be? One half of the Committee maintain that it should be the English. The other half strongly recommend the Arabic and Sanscrit. The whole question seems to me to be, which language is the best worth knowing?

I have no knowledge of either Sanscrit or Arabic. But I have done what I could to form a correct estimate of their value. I have read translations of the most celebrated Arabic and Sanscrit works. I have conversed both here and at home with men distinguished by their proficiency in the Eastern tongues. I am quite ready to take the Oriental learning at the valuation of the Orientalists themselves. I have never found one among them who could deny that a single shelf of a good European library was worth the whole native literature of India and Arabia. The intrinsic superiority of the Western literature is, indeed, fully admitted by those members of the Committee who support the Oriental plan of education.

It will hardly be disputed, I suppose, that the department of literature in which the Eastern writers stand highest is poetry. And I certainly never met with any Orientalist who ventured to maintain that the Arabic and Sanscrit poetry could be compared to that of the great European nations. But, when we pass from works of imagination to works in which facts are recorded and general principles investigated, the superiority of the Europeans becomes absolutely immeasurable. It is, I believe, no exaggeration to say, that all the historical information which has been collected from all the books written in the Sanscrit language is less valuable than what may be found in the most paltry abridgments used at preparatory schools in England. In every branch of physical or moral philosophy the relative position of the two nations is nearly the same.

How, then, stands the case? We have to educate a people who cannot at present be educated by means of their mother-tongue. We must teach them some foreign language. The claims of our own language it is hardly necessary to recapitulate. It stands preeminent even among the languages of the West. It abounds with works of imagination not inferior to the noblest which Greece has bequeathed to us; with models of every species of eloquence; with historical compositions, which, considered merely as narratives, have seldom been surpassed, and which, considered as vehicles of ethical and political instruction, have never been equalled; with just and lively representations of human life and human nature; with the most profound speculations on metaphysics, morals, government, jurisprudence, and trade; with full and correct information respecting every experimental science which tends to preserve the health, to increase the comfort, or to expand the intellect of man. Whoever knows that language, has ready access to all the vast intellectual wealth, which all the wisest nations of the earth have created and hoarded in the course of ninety generations. It may safely be said that the literature now extant in that language is of far greater value than all the literature which three hundred years ago was extant in all the languages of the world together. Nor is this all. In India, English is the language spoken by the ruling class. It is spoken by the higher class of natives at the seats of Government. It is likely to become the language of commerce throughout the seas of the East. It is the language of two great European communities which are rising, the one in the south of Africa, the other in Australasia; communities which are every year becoming more important, and more closely connected with our Indian Empire. Whether we look at the intrinsic value of our literature, or at the particular situation of this country, we shall see the strongest reason to think that, of all foreign tongues, the English tongue is that which would be the most useful to our native subjects....

It is taken for granted by the advocates of Oriental learning that no native of this country can possibly attain more than a mere smattering of English. They do not attempt to prove this; but they perpetually insinuate it. They designate the education which their opponents recommend as a mere spelling-book education. They assume it as undeniable, that the question is between a profound knowledge of Hindoo and Arabian literature and science on the one side, and a superficial knowledge of the rudiments of English on the other. This is not merely an assumption, but an assumption contrary to all reason and experience. We know that foreigners of all nations do learn our language sufficiently to have access to all the most abstruse knowledge which it contains, sufficiently to relish even the more delicate graces of our most idiomatic writers. There are in this very town natives who are quite competent to discuss political or scientific questions with fluency and precision in the English language. I have heard the very question on which I am now writing discussed by native gentlemen with a liberality and an intelligence which would do credit to any member of the Committee of Public Instruction. Indeed, it is unusual to find, even in the literary circles of the continent, any foreigner who can express himself in English with so much facility and correctness as we find in many Hindoos. Nobody, I suppose, will contend that English is so difficult to a Hindoo as Greek to an Englishman. Yet an intelligent English youth, in a much smaller number of years than our unfortunate pupils pass at the Sanscrit college, becomes able to read, to enjoy, and even to imitate, not unhappily, the composition of the best Greek authors. Less than half the time which enables an English youth to read Herodotus and Sophocles ought to enable a Hindoo to read Hume and Milton....

In one point I fully agree with the gentlemen to whose general views I am opposed. I feel, with them, that it is impossible for us, with our limited means, to attempt to educate the body of the people. We must at present do our best to form a class who may be interpreters between us and the millions whom we govern; a class of persons, Indian in blood and colour, but English in taste, in opinions, in morals, and in intellect. To that class we may leave it to refine the vernacular dialects of the country, to enrich those dialects with terms of science borrowed from the Western nomenclature, and to render them by degrees fit vehicles for conveying knowledge to the great mass of the population.

Roger Fenton, *Frank Dillon in Near Eastern Dress*, 1858.

Roger Fenton, Orientalist Studies (1858)

The images reproduced below are from a series of approximately fifty photographs by the renowned Victorian photographer Roger Fenton (1819–69). Fenton himself did not spend time in the East other than during the Crimean War. Evidently Fenton consulted the English landscape painter Frank Dillon as he prepared to take the series of photos; Dillon, who had traveled extensively in Egypt in 1854–55, appears in many of the images. The identity of the young woman who appears in many of the photographs is not known; she is widely assumed to have been a professional model.

Roger Fenton, *Nubian Water Carrier*, 1858.

Roger Fenton, *Pasha and Bayadère*, 1858.

Roger Fenton, *Orientalist Group*, 1858.

Roger Fenton, *Reclining Odalisque*, 1858.

from Col. Henry Yule and A.C. Burnell, *Hobson-Jobson: A Glossary of Colloquial Anglo-Indian Words and Phrases, and of Kindred Terms, Etymological, Historical, Geographical, and Discursive* (1886)

Yule and Burnell's guide was re-issued in a revised edition in 1903, and remained in use well into the twentieth century. Like the *Oxford English Dictionary* (on which work began in 1884), Yule and Burnell provide for each word a historical selection of illustrative quotations.

BUNGALOW, s. The most usual class of house occupied by Europeans in the interior of India: being on one story, and covered by a pyramidal roof, which in the normal bungalow is of thatch, but may be of tiles without impairing its title to be called a *bungalow*. Most of the houses of officers in Indian cantonments are of this character. In reference to the style of the house, *bungalow* is sometimes employed in contradistinction to the (usually more pretentious) *pucka house*; by which latter term is implied a masonry house with a terraced roof.

HOBSON-JOBSON, s. A native festal excitement … but especially the Moharram ceremonies. This phrase may be taken as a typical one of the most highly assimilated class of Anglo-Indian *argot*, and we have ventured to borrow from it a concise alternative title for this Glossary. It is peculiar to the British soldier and his surroundings, with whom it probably originated, and with whom it is by no means obsolete, as we once supposed. My friend Major John Trotter tells me that he has repeatedly heard it used by British soldiers in the Punjab; and has heard it also from a regimental Moonshee. It is in fact an Anglo-Saxon version of the wailings of the Mahommedans as they beat their breasts in the procession of the *Moharram*—"Ya Hasan! Ya Hosain!" It is to be remembered that these observances are *in India* by no means confined to Shi'as. Except at Lucknow and Murshidabad, the great majority of Mahommedans in the country are professed Sunnis. Yet here is a statement of the facts from an unexceptionable authority:

"The commonalty of the Mussulmans, and especially the women, have more regard for the memory of Hasan and Hussein, than for that of Muhammad and his khalifs. The heresy of making Ta'ziyas (see TAZEFA) on the anniversary of the two latter imáms, is most common throughout India: so much so that opposition to it is ascribed by the ignorant to blasphemy. This example is followed by many of the Hindus, especially the Mahrattas. The Muharram is celebrated throughout the Dekhan and Malwa, with greater enthusiasm than in other parts of India. Grand preparations are made in every town on the occasion, as if for a festival of rejoicing, rather than of observing the rites of mourning, as they ought. The observance of this custom has so strong a hold on the mind of the commonalty of the Mussulmans that they believe Muhammadanism to depend merely on keeping the memory of the imáms in the above manner." *Mir Shahamat Ali*, in *J.R. As. Soc.* xiii. 369.

NABÓB, s. … a deputy, and was applied in a singular sense to a delegate of the supreme chief, viz. to a Viceroy or supreme chief, viz. to a Viceroy or chief Governor under the Great Mogul *e.g.* the *Nawâb* of Surat, the *Namâb* of Oudh, the *Nawâb* of Arcot, the *Nawâb Nazim* of Bengal. From this use it became a title of rank without necessarily having any office attached. It is now a title occasionally conferred, like a peerage, on Mohammedan gentlemen of distinction and good service, as *Râî* and *Râjâ* are upon Hindus.

Nabob is used in two ways: (a) simply as a corruption and representative of *Nawâb*. We get it direct from the Port. *nabâbo,* see quotation from Bluteau below. (b) It began to be applied in the 18th century, when the transactions of Clive made the epithet familiar in England, to Anglo-Indians who returned with fortunes from the East; and Foote's play of "The Nabob" (*Nábob)* (1768) aided in giving general currency to the word in this sense.

1742 "We have had a great man called the Nabob (who is the next person in dignity to the Great Mogul) to visit the Governor.… His lady, with all her women attendants, came the night before him. All the guns fired round the fort upon her arrival, as well as upon his; *he* and *she* are Moors, whose women are never seen by any man upon earth except their husbands."—Letter from Madras in *Mrs. Delany's Life,* ii. 169.

1743 "Every governor of a fort, and every commander of a district had assumed the title of Nabob ... one day after having received the homage of several of these little lords, Nizam ul muluck said that he had that day seen no less than eighteen Nabobs in the Carnatic."—*Orme,* Reprint, Bk. i.

1783 "The office given to a young man going to India is of trifling consequence. But he that goes out an insignificant boy, in a few years returns a great Nabob. Mr. Hastings says he has two hundred and fifty of that kind of raw material, who expect to be speedily manufactured into the merchantlike quality I mention." *Burke, Speech on Fox's E. I. Bill,* in *Works and Con.,* ed. 1852, iii. 506.

1848 "Isn't he very rich?" said Rebecca.

"'They say all Indian Nabobs are enormously rich.'"—*Vanity Fair,* ed. 1867, i. 17.

PUNDIT, s. ... "a learned man." Properly a man learned in Sanskrit lore. The Pundit of the Supreme Court was a Hindu Law-Officer, whose duty it was to advise the English Judges when needful on questions of Hindu Law. The office became extinct on the constitution of the "High Court," superseding the Supreme Court and Sudder Court, under the Queen's Letters Patent of May 14, 1862.

In the Mahratta and Telegu countries, the word *Pandit* is usually pronounced *Pant* (in English colloquial *Punt)*; but in this form it has, as with many other Indian words in like case, lost its original significance, and become a mere personal title, familiar in Mahratta history, *e.g.* the Nânâ Dhundo*pant* of evil fame.

Within the last 30 or 35 years the term has acquired in India a peculiar application to the natives trained in the use of instruments, who have been employed beyond the British Indian frontier in surveying regions inaccessible to Europeans. This application originated in the fact that two of the earliest men to be so employed, the explorations by one of whom acquired great celebrity, were masters of village schools in our Himâlayan provinces. And the title *Pundit* is popularly employed there much as *Dominie* used to be in Scotland. The *Pundit* who brought so much fame on the title was the late Nain Singh.

1785 "I can no longer bear to be at the mercy of our pundits, who deal out Hindu law as they please; and make it at reasonable rates, when they cannot find it ready made."—Letter of *Sir W. Jones,* in Mem. by *Ld. Teignmouth,* 1807, ii. 67.

1798 "... the most learned of the Pundits or Bramin lawyers, were called up from different parts of Bengal."—*Raynal, Hist,* i. 42.

1877 "Colonel Y—Since Nain Singh's absence from this country precludes my having the pleasure of handing to him in person, this, the Victoria or Patron's Medal, which has been awarded to him, ... I beg to place it in your charge for transmission to the Pundit."—*Address* by *Sir R. Alcock,* Prest. R. Geog. Soc., May 28.

Mary Tighe

1772 – 1810

Mary Tighe's reputation rests on a single long poem—*Psyche*—but that one poem exerted significant influence on the poetry of the Romantic period, and is now increasingly being recognized as a work of great beauty and considerable importance.

Daughter of Theodosia Tighe Blachford, an Irish aristocrat, and the Reverend William Blachford (who died shortly after her birth), Mary Tighe was born in Dublin on 9 October 1772. Her mother believed in advanced education for women and dedicated herself to the schooling of Mary and her brother, John. Tutors were retained for music and drawing; Mary and John copied out and memorized poems; they both learned to translate French authors. Mary eventually married her first cousin, Henry Tighe of Woodstock, County Wicklow. They spent their first eight years of marriage engaged in an active social life in London, but she was not in love with her husband and they had no children.

In 1801, the Tighes returned to Ireland, where Mary composed *Psyche*; or *The Legend of Love*, a reworking of the myth of Cupid and Psyche based on Apuleius and written in Spenserian stanzas. Tighe professed to have pictured innocent love, such as the purest bosom might confess, but the poem is a masterpiece of decorously sublimated Eros, sensual as well as sensuous in its lush imagery. The poem was printed privately in 1805; it was not published until 1811, a year after she died, and it was an immediate success. The poem went into a fourth edition within one year. Both Shelley and Keats were impressed by the poem, and the latter's "Ode to Psyche" (1819) clearly owes a debt of gratitude to the precursor poem; as Wordsworth observed, it is hard to imagine that Keats could have composed the "first of his great Odes ... without [Tighe] coming to mind." Other admirers of Tighe's poem included Thomas Moore and Felicia Hemans, who was moved to write two poems about Tighe after visiting her grave. But Tighe's work was largely forgotten in the Victorian period, and remained so for most of the next hundred years; only in the late twentieth century did the very considerable aesthetic virtues of her poetry begin again to be acknowledged.

As early as 1804, Tighe began to show signs of tuberculosis. Although she was counseled to leave England for more a hospitable climate, she repaired instead to her native Dublin, where she died on March 24, 1810, at the age of thirty-seven. Among her literary remains is a 2,451-page manuscript of a novel called *Selena*, a novel of intrigue and vengeance that includes a precursor to the Byronic hero in the handsomely dissipated Lord Dallamore. It is for *Psyche*, however, that she continues to be remembered.

⌘⌘⌘

from *Psyche;*[1] *or The Legend of Love*

Sonnet Addressed to My Mother

Oh, thou! whose tender smile most partially
Hath ever blessed thy child: to thee belong
The graces which adorn my first wild song,
If aught of grace it knows: nor thou deny
Thine ever prompt attention to supply.
But let me lead thy willing ear along,
Where virtuous love still bids the strain prolong
His innocent applause; since from thine eye
The beams of love first charmed my infant breast,
And from thy lip Affection's soothing voice
That eloquence of tenderness expressed,
Which still my grateful heart confessed divine:
Oh! ever may its accents sweet rejoice
The soul which loves to own whate'er it has is thine!

Psyche

Let not the rugged brow the rhymes accuse,
Which speak of gentle knights and ladies fair,
Nor scorn the lighter labours of the muse,
Who yet, for cruel battles would not dare
The low-strung chords of her weak lyre prepare:
But loves to court repose in slumbery lay,
To tell of goodly bowers and gardens rare,
Of gentle blandishments and amorous play,
And all the lore of love, in courtly verse essay.

And ye whose gentle hearts in thraldom held
The power of mighty Love already own,
When you the pains and dangers have beheld,
Which erst your lord hath for his Psyche known,
For all your sorrows this may well atone,
That he you serve the same hath suffered;
And sure, your fond applause the tale will crown
In which your own distress is pictured,
And all that weary way which you yourselves must tread.

Most sweet would to my soul the hope appear,
That sorrow in my verse a charm might find,
To smooth the brow long bent with bitter cheer,
Some short distraction to the joyless mind
Which grief, with heavy chain, hath fast confined
To sad remembrance of its happier state;
For to myself I ask no boon more kind
Than power another's woes to mitigate,
And that soft soothing art which anguish can abate.

And thou, sweet sprite,° whose sway doth far extend, *spirit*
Smile on the mean historian of thy fame!
My heart in each distress and fear befriend,
Nor ever let it feel a fiercer flame
Than innocence may cherish free from blame,
And hope may nurse, and sympathy may own;
For, as thy rights I never would disclaim,
But true allegiance offered to thy throne,
So may I love but one, by one belov'd alone.

That anxious torture may I never feel,
Which, doubtful, watches o'er a wandering heart.
Oh! who that bitter torment can reveal,
Or tell the pining anguish of that smart!
In those affections may I ne'er have part,
Which easily transferred can learn to rove:
No, dearest Cupid! when I feel thy dart,
For thy sweet Psyche's sake may no false love
The tenderness I prize lightly from me remove!

Canto I

Much wearied with her long and dreary way,
And now with toil and sorrow well nigh spent,
Of sad regret and wasting grief the prey,
Fair Psyche through untrodden forests went,
To lone shades uttering oft a vain lament.
And oft in hopeless silence sighing deep,

[1] *Psyche* Mortal daughter of royalty in Greek and Roman mythology. When Venus, goddess of beauty, saw that Psyche's beauty eclipsed her own, she ordered her son Cupid, winged god of love, to punish the beautiful virgin. Rather than obeying Venus's orders, Cupid became Psyche's anonymous lover, visiting her in the dark of night and ordering her not to investigate his identity. Psyche's sisters eventually persuaded her to unmask her lover. She lit a lamp but in doing so dropped some oil upon Cupid, wakening him, whereupon he abandoned her. She then wandered in search of him and was forced to perform daunting tasks for Venus. Eventually Cupid took pity upon her and made her his immortal wife.

As she her fatal error did repent,
While dear remembrance bade her ever weep,
And her pale cheek in ceaseless showers of sorrow steep.

'Mid the thick covert of that woodland shade,
A flowery bank there lay undressed by art,
But of the mossy turf spontaneous made;
Here the young branches shot their arms athwart,
And wove the bower so thick in every part,
That the fierce beams of Phœbus[1] glancing strong
Could never through the leaves their fury dart;
But the sweet creeping shrubs that round it throng,
Their loving fragrance mix, and trail their flowers along.

And close beside a little fountain played,
Which through the trembling leaves all joyous shone,
And with the cheerful birds sweet music made,
Kissing the surface of each polished stone
As it flowed past; sure as her favourite throne
Tranquillity might well esteem the bower,
The fresh and cool retreat have called her own,
A pleasant shelter in the sultry hour,
A refuge from the blast, and angry tempest's power.

Wooed by the soothing silence of the scene
Here Psyche stood, and looking round, lest aught
Which threatened danger near her might have been,
Awhile to rest her in that quiet spot
She laid her down, and piteously bethought
Herself on the sad changes of her fate,
Which in so short a space so much had wrought,
And now had raised her to such high estate,
And now had plunged her low in sorrow desolate.

Oh! how refreshing seemed the breathing wind
To her faint limbs! and while her snowy hands
From her fair brow her golden hair unbind,
And of her zone° unloose the silken bands, *belt*
More passing bright unveiled her beauty stands;
For faultless was her form as beauty's queen,
And every winning grace that Love demands,
With mild attempered° dignity was seen *balanced*
Play o'er each lovely limb, and deck her angel mien.° *face*

[1] *beams of Phœbus* Sunbeams. Phoebus is Phoebus Apollo, the god of the sun.

from Canto 2

Illumined bright now shines the splendid dome,
Melodious accents her arrival hail:
But not the torches' blaze can chase the gloom,
And all the soothing powers of music fail;
Trembling she seeks her couch with horror pale,
But first a lamp conceals in secret shade,
While unknown terrors all her soul assail.
Thus half their treacherous counsel is obeyed,
For still her gentle soul abhors the murderous blade.

And now, with softest whispers of delight,
Love welcomes Psyche still more fondly dear;
Not unobserved, though hid in deepest night,
The silent anguish of her secret fear.
He thinks that tenderness excites the tear
By the late image of her parents' grief,
And half offended seeks in vain to cheer,
Yet, while he speaks, her sorrows feel relief,
Too soon more keen to sting from this suspension brief!

…

Allowed to settle on celestial eyes
Soft Sleep exulting now exerts his sway,
From Psyche's anxious pillow gladly flies
To veil those orbs, whose pure and lambent ray
The powers of heaven submissively obey.
Trembling and breathless then she softly rose
And seized the lamp, where it obscurely lay,
With hand too rashly daring to disclose
The sacred veil which hung mysterious o'er her woes.

Twice, as with agitated step she went,
The lamp expiring shone with doubtful gleam,
As though it warned her from her rash intent:
And twice she paused, and on its trembling beam
Gazed with suspended breath, while voices seem
With murmuring sound along the roof to sigh;
As one just waking from a troublous dream,
With palpitating heart and straining eye,
Still fixed with fear remains, still thinks the danger nigh.

Oh, daring Muse! wilt thou indeed essay
To paint the wonders which that lamp could shew?° *show*
And canst thou hope in living words to say

The dazzling glories of that heavenly view?
Ah! well I ween,° that if with pencil true *think*
That splendid vision could be well exprest,
The fearful awe imprudent Psyche knew
Would seize with rapture every wondering breast,
When Love's all potent charms divinely stood confest.

All imperceptible to human touch,
His wings display celestial essence light,
The clear effulgence of the blaze is such,
The brilliant plumage shines so heavenly bright
That mortal eyes turn dazzled from the sight;
A youth he seems in manhood's freshest years;
Round his fair neck, as clinging with delight,
Each golden curl resplendently appears,
Or shades his darker brow, which grace majestic wears.

Or o'er his guileless front the ringlets bright
Their rays of sunny lustre seem to throw,
That front than polished ivory more white!
His blooming cheeks with deeper blushes glow
Than roses scattered o'er a bed of snow:
While on his lips, distilled in balmy dews,
(Those lips divine that even in silence know
The heart to touch) persuasion to infuse
Still hangs a rosy charm that never vainly sues.

The friendly curtain of indulgent sleep
Disclosed not yet his eyes' resistless sway,
But from their silky veil there seemed to peep
Some brilliant glances with a softened ray,
Which o'er his features exquisitely play,
And all his polished limbs suffuse with light.
Thus through some narrow space the azure day
Sudden its cheerful rays diffusing bright,
Wide darts its lucid beams, to gild the brow of night.

His fatal arrows and celestial bow
Beside the couch were negligently thrown,
Nor needs the god his dazzling arms, to show
His glorious birth, such beauty round him shone
As sure could spring from Beauty's self alone;
The bloom which glowed o'er all of soft desire,
Could well proclaim him Beauty's cherished son;
And Beauty's self will oft these charms admire,
And steal his witching smile, his glance's living fire.

Speechless with awe, in transport strangely lost
Long Psyche stood with fixed adoring eye;
Her limbs immoveable, her senses tossed
Between amazement, fear, and ecstasy,
She hangs enamoured o'er the Deity.
Till from her trembling hand extinguished falls
The fatal lamp—He starts—and suddenly
Tremendous thunders echo through the halls,
While ruin's hideous crash bursts o'er the affrighted walls.

Dread horror seizes on her sinking heart,
A mortal chillness shudders at her breast,
Her soul shrinks fainting from death's icy dart,
The groan scarce uttered dies but half expressed,
And down she sinks in deadly swoon oppressed:
But when at length, awaking from her trance,
The terrors of her fate stand all confessed,
In vain she casts around her timid glance,
The rudely frowning scenes her former joys enhance.

No traces of those joys, alas, remain!
A desert solitude alone appears.
No verdant shade relieves the sandy plain,
The wide spread waste no gentle fountain cheers,
One barren face the dreary prospect wears;
Nought through the vast horizon meets her eye
To calm the dismal tumult of her fears,
No trace of human habitation nigh,
A sandy wild beneath, above a threatening sky.

—1805

Jane Austen

1775 – 1817

Jane Austen is considered to be one of the finest novelists in the English language. Her six major novels, along with her shorter fictional works, juvenilia, and surviving correspondence, share a keenness of wit and irony of observation that have ensured her continued popularity among scholars and general readers alike into the twenty-first century. Her fiction scrutinizes the manners and the behavior of ordinary women of the emergent middle-class in Georgian England, who need to negotiate between feeling and duty, personal desire and social expectation. As Sir Walter Scott, the most famous novelist of Austen's time, commented in reviewing her favorably in the influential *Quarterly Review,* her writing bears "that exquisite touch which renders ordinary commonplace things and characters interesting." Her work was not as highly esteemed in the middle decades of the nineteenth century, but her popularity rose in the 1870s, and her life and work have for generations been the subject of what is often called an "industry," both scholarly and popular.

Jane Austen was born at Steventon, Hampshire, the sixth child in a family of seven, and the younger of two daughters. Her father, the Reverend George Austen, was a spirited and cultivated man who allowed his daughters free access to his extensive library. Educated mostly at home, she read broadly, including novels by Frances Burney, Laurence Sterne, Henry Fielding, and Samuel Richardson, whose *Sir Charles Grandison* was a particular favorite. Owing in part to the proximity of the boys' school run by Austen's parents from the Steventon Rectory, the household in which Austen grew up was busy and lively, and its members enjoyed and encouraged each others' literary and theatrical pursuits. The young Jane Austen's imagination was fed by family theatricals directed and performed by her elder siblings and cousins for friends and neighbors. Austen's biographer, Claire Tomalin, speculates that the young Jane may have played a minor role in the family production of Richard Brinsley Sheridan's *The Rivals* before she was ten years old. Most importantly, Austen was encouraged to read aloud from her early writing, and her family delighted in the comic stories and burlesques she produced in her teenage years. Fictions such as *Lesley Castle* and *Love & Freindship* (sic), the latter written when Austen was 14, are filled with impertinent and riotous humor, indecorous behavior on the part of young women, and an already astute sense of generic convention. Her father was particularly supportive of her writing: at the front of a notebook he had given her, in which she had composed her *History of England,* a juvenile parody of popular histories, George Austen inscribed the following appreciation: "Effusions of Fancy by a very Young Lady Consisting of Tales in a Style entirely new."

Austen lived a quiet country life among a wide network of relations, friends and neighbors, an ideal context in which to hone the skills in social observation that informed her writing. She never married, although she had at least two admirers, and even accepted a proposal of marriage in 1802 (retracting her acceptance the following day). In 1795–96 she wrote an epistolary sketch called "Elinor and Marianne," which went through several rewrites in subsequent years before taking its final form as *Sense and Sensibility*. This became Austen's first published work (1811), selling out by 1813 and receiving positive reviews. Three other novels were published in quick succession: *Pride and Prejudice* in 1813, *Mansfield Park* in 1814, and *Emma* in 1816. *Pride and Prejudice*, whose first title was "First Impressions," had initially been rejected in 1797 by the publisher Thomas Cadell, who did not even read the manuscript before returning it. When it finally did appear, *Pride and Prejudice* was an instant hit, and it has since become one of the most widely-read novels in the English language. Much of its success is due to the appeal of its heroine, Elizabeth Bennet, whose intelligence, feeling, and independence of thought Austen conveys through sparkling dialogue and pioneering use of narrative techniques that provide for flexibility of viewpoint.

The composition of Austen's major works can be divided into two distinct periods. By 1800 she had written three full-length novels, none of them published. Then followed a ten-year silence: the Austens' decision to quit the family home at Steventon and move to Bath, taking Jane and her elder sister Cassandra with them, meant a break in Austen's writing routine. The family moved often in the next several years, and with the death of several friends and family members in this period, most importantly her father in 1805, Austen seems to have experienced a depression that prevented her from writing. Tomalin points out how easily Austen's existing manuscripts in this decade could have been lost or destroyed. With her settlement at Chawton Cottage in Hampshire late in 1808 with her mother and sister, Austen again found the time and space to write, and it was here that she revised "Elinor and Marianne" into *Sense and Sensibility*, and wrote *Mansfield Park*, *Emma*, and *Persuasion*.

Two of Austen's six major novels were published posthumously in 1818. *Northanger Abbey* had been written under the title "Susan" in 1798–99 and sold to the publisher Richard Crosby in 1803 for the low sum of ten pounds. Although he placed advertisements for the book, he never printed it, and refused to turn over the manuscript or copyright at her request in 1809. *Persuasion*, written in 1815-16, was Austen's last completed novel. Some readers find in it a tone of melancholy, which might be attributable to the fact that she was suffering from illness when it was completed. It is also unique among her major works as the only novel for which any manuscript material survives. Many of her letters were also destroyed by her elder sister Cassandra Austen after her death. The Austen sisters were extremely close, sparing no confidence in their correspondence with each other. Many of Austen's surviving letters to her sister are characterized by harshly honest observations of others' foibles.

Lady Susan stands between Austen's juvenilia and her major work in several respects. She probably wrote most of it in 1794–95, revising and adding its abrupt conclusion by 1805, thus putting its date of composition between her last known juvenile writing and her first draft of what would become *Sense and Sensibility*. More importantly, *Lady Susan* seems to bring many of the impulses of Austen's juvenile writing to a head while displaying a sophistication that anticipates her mature work. Many critics have pointed out the novel's debt in both theme and form to the mid-eighteenth-century fiction and Restoration drama Austen grew up on, with its sexual frankness and cynical tone. The novel is in several respects anomalous in the Austen canon: it is her only mature fiction written in the epistolary form, and its eponymous heroine is a female rake—a sexual predator—who openly uses her sexual power to dominate others. Although Austen seems to have become frustrated with the limitations of the epistolary form, eventually abandoning it altogether in her adult writing, in *Lady Susan* it allows the author a moral detachment from the story's action: one is never quite sure whether Austen approved of or deplored her heroine's rebellion against accepted models of proper femininity. *Lady Susan* remained unpublished until 1871, when Austen's nephew James Austen-Leigh included it in his *Memoir of Jane Austen*.

Austen wrote fiction at a moment when women were getting their work into print in ever greater numbers, yet faced relentless pressure to think and behave in ways that militated against their attaining, or expressing, social power and authority. Although by 1816 Austen was a critical and popular success (whose most illustrious fan was the Prince Regent himself), she wore her success lightly, famously referring in a letter of that year to her nephew to the "little bit (two inches wide) of Ivory on which I work with so fine a brush." Perhaps the best known description of Austen's writing, the statement has been read by critics as both a disclaimer and a sly celebration of "women's" writing and the domestic novel. But perhaps not too much should be made of a comment made in a spirit of playful banter with a teenager. By the time she wrote this letter she was already seriously ill. She was working on a new novel around this time—*Sanditon*—but it was never finished. Jane Austen died of an undetermined illness on 18 July 1817, and was buried at Winchester Cathedral.

⌘⌘⌘

Lady Susan

Letter 1

Lady Susan Vernon to Mr. Vernon

Langford, December

My dear brother,

I can no longer refuse myself the pleasure of profiting by your kind invitation when we last parted, of spending some weeks with you at Churchill, and therefore if quite convenient to you and Mrs. Vernon to receive me at present, I shall hope within a few days to be introduced to a sister whom I have so long desired to be acquainted with. My kind friends here are most affectionately urgent with me to prolong my stay, but their hospitable and cheerful dispositions lead them too much into society for my present situation and state of mind; and I impatiently look forward to the hour when I shall be admitted into your delightful retirement. I long to be made known to your dear little children, in whose hearts I shall be very eager to secure an interest. I shall soon have occasion for all my fortitude, as I am on the point of separation from my own daughter. The long illness of her dear father prevented my paying her that attention which duty and affection equally dictated, and I have but too much reason to fear that the governess to whose care I consigned her, was unequal to the charge. I have therefore resolved on placing her at one of the best private schools in town, where I shall have an opportunity of leaving her myself, in my way to you. I am determined, you see, not to be denied admittance at Churchill. It would indeed give me most painful sensations to know that it were not in your power to receive me.

Your most obliged and affectionate sister,
Susan Vernon

Letter 2

Lady Susan to Mrs. Johnson

Langford

You were mistaken, my dear Alicia, in supposing me fixed at this place for the rest of the winter. It grieves me to say how greatly you were mistaken, for I have seldom spent three months more agreeably than those which have just flown away. At present nothing goes smoothly. The females of the family are united against me. You foretold how it would be, when I first came to Langford; and Manwaring is so uncommonly pleasing that I was not without apprehensions myself. I remember saying to myself as I drove to the house, "I like this man; pray Heaven no harm come of it!" But I was determined to be discreet, to bear in mind my being only four months a widow, and to be as quiet as possible—and I have been so; my dear creature, I have admitted no one's attentions but Manwaring's, I have avoided all general flirtation whatever, I have distinguished no creature besides of all the numbers resorting hither, except Sir James Martin, on whom I bestowed a little notice in order to detach him from Miss Manwaring. But if the world could know my motive *there,* they would honour me. I have been called an unkind mother, but it was the sacred impulse of maternal affection, it was the advantage of my daughter that led me on; and if that daughter were not the greatest simpleton on earth, I might have been rewarded for my exertions as I ought. Sir James did make proposals to me for Frederica—but Frederica, who was born to be the torment of my life, chose to set herself so violently against the match, that I thought it better to lay aside the scheme for the present. I have more than once repented that I did not marry him myself, and were he but one degree less contemptibly weak I certainly should, but I must own myself rather romantic in that respect, and that riches only, will not satisfy me. The event of all this is very provoking. Sir James is gone, Maria highly incensed, and Mrs. Manwaring insupportably jealous; so jealous in short, and so enraged against me, that in the fury of her temper I should not be surprised at her appealing to her guardian if she had the liberty of addressing him—but there your husband stands my friend, and the kindest, most amiable action of his life was his throwing her off forever on her marriage. Keep up his resentment therefore I charge you. We are now in a sad state; no house was ever more altered; the whole family are at war, and Manwaring scarcely dares speak to me. It is time for me to be gone; I have therefore determined on leaving them, and shall spend I hope a comfortable day with you in town within this week. If I am as little in favour with Mr. Johnson as ever, you must come to me at No. 10, Wigmore St.—but I hope this may not be the case, for as Mr. Johnson with all his faults is a man to whom that great word "Respectable" is always given, and I am known to be so intimate with his wife, his slighting me has an awkward look. I take town in my way to that insupportable spot, a country village, for I am really going to Churchill. Forgive me my dear friend, it is my last resource. Were there another place in England open to me, I would prefer it. Charles Vernon is my aversion, and I am afraid of his wife. At Churchill, however, I must remain till I have something better in view. My young lady accompanies me to town, where I shall deposit her under the care of Miss Summers in Wigmore Street, till she becomes a little more reasonable. She will make good connections there, as the girls are all of the best families. The price is immense, and much beyond what I can ever attempt to pay.

Adieu. I will send you a line, as soon as I arrive in town.

Yours ever,

Susan Vernon

Letter 3

MRS. VERNON TO LADY DE COURCY

Churchill

My dear mother,

I am very sorry to tell you that it will not be in our power to keep our promise of spending the Christmas with you; and we are prevented that happiness by a circumstance which is not likely to make us any amends. Lady Susan in a letter to her brother, has declared her intention of visiting us almost immediately—and as such a visit is in all probability merely an affair of convenience, it is impossible to conjecture its length. I was by no means prepared for such an event, nor can I now account for her ladyship's conduct. Langford appeared so exactly the place for her in every respect, as well from the elegant and expensive style of living there, as from her particular attachment to Mrs. Manwaring, that I was very far from expecting so speedy a distinction,[1] though I always imagined from her increasing friendship for us since her husband's death, that we should at some future period be obliged to receive her. Mr. Vernon I think was a great deal too kind to her, when he was in Staffordshire. Her behaviour to him, independent of her general character, has been so inexcusably artful[2] and ungenerous since our marriage was first in agitation, that no one less amiable and mild than himself could have overlooked it at all; and though as his brother's widow and in narrow circumstances it was proper to render her pecuniary assistance, I cannot help thinking his pressing invitation to her to visit us at Churchill perfectly unnecessary. Disposed however as he always is to think the best of every one, her display of grief, and professions of regret, and general resolutions of prudence were sufficient to soften his heart, and make him really confide in her sincerity. But as for myself, I am still unconvinced; and plausibly as her ladyship has now written, I cannot make up my mind, till I better understand her real meaning in coming to us. You may guess therefore my dear Madam, with what feelings I look forward to her arrival. She will have occasion for all those attractive powers for which she

[1] *from expecting so speedy a distinction* From expecting to be favored [by the announcement of an impending visit] so quickly.

[2] *artful* Crafty, deceitful.

is celebrated, to gain any share of my regard; and I shall certainly endeavour to guard myself against their influence, if not accompanied by something more substantial. She expresses a most eager desire of being acquainted with me, and makes very generous mention of my children, but I am not quite weak enough to suppose a woman who has behaved with inattention if not unkindness to her own child, should be attached to any of mine. Miss Vernon is to be placed at a school in town before her mother comes to us, which I am glad of, for her sake and my own. It must be to her advantage to be separated from her mother; and a girl of sixteen who has received so wretched an education would not be a very desirable companion here. Reginald has long wished I know to see this captivating Lady Susan, and we shall depend on his joining our party soon. I am glad to hear that my father continues so well, and am, with best love etc.,

Catherine Vernon

Letter 4

MR. DE COURCY TO MRS. VERNON

Parklands

My dear sister,

I congratulate you and Mr. Vernon on being about to receive into your family, the most accomplished coquette in England. As a very distinguished flirt, I have always been taught to consider her; but it has lately fallen in my way to hear some particulars of her conduct at Langford, which prove that she does not confine herself to that sort of honest flirtation which satisfies most people, but aspires to the more delicious gratification of making a whole family miserable. By her behaviour to Mr. Manwaring, she gave jealousy and wretchedness to his wife, and by her attentions to a young man previously attached to Mr. Manwaring's sister, deprived an amiable girl of her lover. I learnt all this from a Mr. Smith now in this neighbourhood—I have dined with him at Hurst and Wilford—who is just come from Langford, where he was a fortnight in the house with her ladyship, and who is therefore well qualified to make the communication.

What a woman she must be! I long to see her, and shall certainly accept your kind invitation, that I may form some idea of those bewitching powers which can do so much—engaging at the same time and in the same house the affections of two men who were neither of them at liberty to bestow them—and all this, without the charm of youth. I am glad to find that Miss Vernon does not come with her mother to Churchill, as she has not even manners to recommend her, and according to Mr. Smith's account, is equally dull and proud. Where pride and stupidity unite, there can be no dissimulation worthy notice, and Miss Vernon shall be consigned to unrelenting contempt; but by all that I can gather, Lady Susan possesses a degree of captivating deceit which must be pleasing to witness and detect. I shall be with you very soon, and am

Your affectionate brother Reginald De Courcy

Letter 5

LADY SUSAN TO MRS. JOHNSON

Churchill

I received your note, my dear Alicia, just before I left town, and rejoice to be assured that Mr. Johnson suspected nothing of your engagement the evening before; it is undoubtedly better to deceive him entirely; since he will be stubborn, he must be tricked. I arrived here in safety, and have no reason to complain of my reception from Mr. Vernon; but I confess myself not equally satisfied with the conduct of his lady. She is perfectly well bred indeed, and has the air of a woman of fashion, but her manners are not such as can persuade me of her being prepossessed in my favour. I wanted her to be delighted at seeing me—I was as amiable as possible on the occasion—but all in vain—she does not like me. To be sure, when we consider that I *did* take some pains to prevent my brother-in-law's marrying her, this want of cordiality is not very surprising—and yet it shows an illiberal and vindictive spirit to resent a project which influenced me six years ago, and which never succeeded at last. I am sometimes half disposed to repent that I did not let Charles buy Vernon Castle when we were obliged to sell it, but it was a trying circumstance, especially as the sale took place exactly at the time of his marriage—and everybody ought to respect the delicacy of those feelings, which could not endure that my husband's dignity should be lessened by his younger brother's having possession of the family estate. Could matters have been so arranged as to prevent the necessity of our leaving the Castle, could we have lived with Charles and kept him single, I should have been very far from persuading my husband to dispose of it elsewhere; but Charles was then on the point of marrying Miss De Courcy, and the event has justified me. Here are children in abundance, and what benefit could have accrued to me from his purchasing Vernon? My having prevented it, may perhaps have given his wife an unfavourable impression—but where there is a disposition to dislike a motive will never be wanting; and as to money-matters, it has not withheld him from being very useful to me. I really have a regard for him, he is so easily imposed on!

The house is a good one, the furniture fashionable, and everything announces plenty and elegance. Charles is very rich I am sure; when a man has once got his name in a banking house he rolls in money. But they do not know what to do with their fortune, keep very little company, and never go to town[1] but on business. We shall be as stupid as possible. I mean to win my sister-in-law's heart through her children; I know all their names already, and am going to attach myself with the greatest sensibility to one in particular, a young Frederic, whom I take on my lap and sigh over for his dear uncle's sake.

Poor Manwaring! I need not tell you how much I miss him—how perpetually he is in my thoughts. I found a dismal letter from him on my arrival here, full of complaints of his wife and sister, and lamentations on the cruelty of his fate. I passed off the letter as his wife's, to the Vernons, and when I write to him, it must be under cover to you.

Yours ever, S.V.

Letter 6

MRS. VERNON TO MR. DE COURCY

Churchill

Well, my dear Reginald, I have seen this dangerous creature, and must give you some description of her, though I hope you will soon be able to form your own judgement. She is really excessively pretty. However you may choose to question the allurements of a lady no longer young, I must for my own part declare that I have seldom seen so lovely a woman as Lady Susan. She is delicately fair, with fine grey eyes and dark eyelashes; and from her appearance one would not suppose her more than five and twenty, though she must in fact be ten years older. I was certainly not disposed to admire her, though always hearing she was beautiful; but I cannot help feeling that she possesses an uncommon union of symmetry, brilliancy and grace. Her address to me was so gentle, frank and even affectionate, that if I had not known how much she has always disliked me for marrying Mr. Vernon, and that we had never met before, I should have imagined her an attached friend. One is apt I believe to connect assurance of manner with coquetry, and to expect that an impudent address will necessarily attend an impudent mind; at least I was myself prepared for an improper degree of confidence in Lady Susan; but her countenance is absolutely sweet, and her voice and manner winningly mild. I am sorry it is so, for what is this but deceit? Unfortunately, one knows her too well. She is clever and agreeable, has all that knowledge of the world which makes conversation easy, and talks very well, with a happy command of language, which is too often used I believe to make black appear white. She has already almost persuaded me of her being warmly attached to her daughter, though I have so long been convinced of the contrary. She speaks of her with so much tenderness and anxiety, lamenting so bitterly the neglect of her education, which she represents however as wholly unavoidable, that I am forced to recollect how many successive springs her ladyship spent in town, while her daughter was left in Staffordshire to the care of servants or a governess very little better, to prevent my believing whatever she says.

If her manners have so great an influence on my resentful heart, you may guess how much more strongly they operate on Mr. Vernon's generous temper. I wish I could be as well satisfied as he is, that it was really her choice to leave Langford for Churchill; and if she had not stayed three months there before she discovered that her friends' manner of living did not suit her situation or feelings, I might have believed that concern for the loss of such a husband as Mr. Vernon, to whom her own behaviour was far from unexceptionable, might for a time make her wish for retirement. But I cannot forget the

[1] *to town* To London.

length of her visit to the Manwarings, and when I reflect on the different mode of life which she led with them, from that to which she must now submit, I can only suppose that the wish of establishing her reputation by following, though late, the path of propriety, occasioned her removal from a family where she must in reality have been particularly happy. Your friend Mr. Smith's story however cannot be quite true, as she corresponds regularly with Mrs. Manwaring; at any rate it must be exaggerated; it is scarcely possible that two men should be so grossly deceived by her at once.

Yours etc., Catherine Vernon

Letter 7

LADY SUSAN TO MRS. JOHNSON

Churchill

My dear Alicia,

You are very good in taking notice of Frederica, and I am grateful for it as a mark of your friendship; but as I cannot have a doubt of the warmth of that friendship, I am far from exacting so heavy a sacrifice. She is a stupid girl, and has nothing to recommend her. I would not therefore on any account have you encumber one moment of your precious time by sending her to Edward St., especially as every visit is so many hours deducted from the grand affair of education, which I really wish to be attended to, while she remains with Miss Summers. I want her to play and sing with some portion of taste, and a good deal of assurance, as she has my hand and arm, and a tolerable voice. I was so much indulged in my infant years that I was never obliged to attend to anything, and consequently am without those accomplishments which are necessary to finish a pretty woman. Not that I am an advocate for the prevailing fashion of acquiring a perfect knowledge in all the languages, arts, and sciences; it is throwing time away; to be mistress of French, Italian, German, music, singing, drawing etc., will gain a woman some applause, but will not add one lover to her list. Grace and manner after all are of the greatest importance. I do not mean therefore that Frederica's acquirements should be more than superficial, and I flatter myself that she will not remain long enough at school to understand anything thoroughly. I hope to see her the wife of Sir James within a twelvemonth. You know on what I ground my hope, and it is certainly a good foundation, for school must be very humiliating to a girl of Frederica's age; and by the bye, you had better not invite her any more on that account, as I wish her to find her situation as unpleasant as possible. I am sure of Sir James at any time, and could make him renew his application by a line. I shall trouble you meanwhile to prevent his forming any other attachment when he comes to town; ask him to your house occasionally, and talk to him about Frederica that he may not forget her.

Upon the whole I commend my own conduct in this affair extremely, and regard it as a very happy mixture of circumspection and tenderness. Some mothers would have insisted on their daughter's accepting so great an offer on the first overture, but I could not answer it to myself to force Frederica into a marriage from which her heart revolted; and instead of adopting so harsh a measure, merely propose to make it her own choice by rendering her life thoroughly uncomfortable till she does accept him. But enough of this tiresome girl.

You may well wonder how I contrive to pass my time here—and for the first week, it was most insufferably dull. Now however, we begin to mend; our party is enlarged by Mrs. Vernon's brother, a handsome young man, who promises me some amusement. There is something about him that rather interests me, a sort of sauciness, of familiarity which I shall teach him to correct. He is lively and seems clever, and when I have inspired him with greater respect for me than his sister's kind offices have implanted, he may be an agreeable flirt. There is exquisite pleasure in subduing an insolent spirit, in making a person pre-determined to dislike, acknowledge one's superiority. I have disconcerted him already by my calm reserve; and it shall be my endeavour to humble the pride of these self-important De Courcys still lower, to convince Mrs. Vernon that her sisterly cautions have been bestowed in vain, and to persuade Reginald that she has scandalously belied me. This project will serve at least to amuse me, and prevent my feeling so acutely this dreadful separation from you and all whom I love. Adieu.

Yours ever,

S. Vernon

Letter 8

MRS. VERNON TO LADY DE COURCY

Churchill

My dear mother,

You must not expect Reginald back again for some time. He desires me to tell you that the present open weather induces him to accept Mr. Vernon's invitation to prolong his stay in Sussex that they may have some hunting together. He means to send for his horses immediately, and it is impossible to say when you may see him in Kent. I will not disguise my sentiments on this change from you, my dear Madam, though I think you had better not communicate them to my father, whose excessive anxiety about Reginald would subject him to an alarm which might seriously affect his health and spirits. Lady Susan has certainly contrived in the space of a fortnight to make my brother like her. In short, I am persuaded that his continuing here beyond the time originally fixed for his return, is occasioned as much by a degree of fascination towards her, as by the wish of hunting with Mr. Vernon, and of course I cannot receive that pleasure from the length of his visit which my brother's company would otherwise give me. I am indeed provoked at the artifice of this unprincipled woman. What stronger proof of her dangerous abilities can be given, than this perversion of Reginald's judgement, which when he entered the house was so decidedly against her? In his last letter he actually gave me some particulars of her behaviour at Langford, such as he received from a gentleman who knew her perfectly well, which if true must raise abhorrence against her, and which Reginald himself was entirely disposed to credit. His opinion of her, I am sure, was as low as of any woman in England, and when he first came it was evident that he considered her as one entitled neither to delicacy nor respect, and that he felt she would be delighted with the attentions of any man inclined to flirt with her.

Her behaviour I confess has been calculated to do away with such an idea, I have not detected the smallest impropriety in it—nothing of vanity, of pretension, of levity—and she is altogether so attractive, that I should not wonder at his being delighted with her, had he known nothing of her previous to this personal acquaintance; but against reason, against conviction, to be so well pleased with her as I am sure he is, does really astonish me. His admiration was at first very strong, but no more than was natural; and I did not wonder at his being struck by the gentleness and delicacy of her manners; but when he has mentioned her of late, it has been in terms of more extraordinary praise, and yesterday he actually said, that he could not be surprised at any effect produced on the heart of man by such loveliness and such abilities; and when I lamented in reply the badness of her disposition, he observed that whatever might have been her errors, they were to be imputed to her neglected education and early marriage, and that she was altogether a wonderful woman.

This tendency to excuse her conduct, or to forget it in the warmth of admiration vexes me; and if I did not know that Reginald is too much at home at Churchill to need an invitation for lengthening his visit, I should regret Mr. Vernon's giving him any.

Lady Susan's intentions are of course those of absolute coquetry, or a desire of universal admiration. I cannot for a moment imagine that she has anything more serious in view, but it mortifies me to see a young man of Reginald's sense duped by her at all. I am etc.,

Catherine Vernon

Letter 9

MRS. JOHNSON TO LADY SUSAN

Edward St.

My dearest friend,

I congratulate you on Mr. De Courcy's arrival, and advise you by all means to marry him; his father's estate is we know considerable, and I believe certainly entailed. Sir Reginald is very infirm, and not likely to stand in your way long. I hear the young man well spoken of, and though no one can really deserve you my dearest Susan, Mr. De Courcy may be worth having. Manwaring will storm of course, but you may easily pacify him. Besides, the most scrupulous point of honour could not require you to wait for his emancipation. I have seen Sir James—he came to town for a few days last week, and called several times in Edward Street. I talked to him about you and your daughter, and he is so far from having forgotten you, that I am sure he would marry either of you with pleasure. I gave him hopes of Frederica's relenting, and told him a great deal of her improvements.

I scolded him for making love to Maria Manwaring; he protested that he had been only in joke, and we both laughed heartily at her disappointment, and in short were very agreeable. He is as silly as ever.—

Yours faithfully,
Alicia

Letter 10[1]
LADY SUSAN TO MRS. JOHNSON
Churchill

I am obliged to you, my dear friend, for your advice respecting Mr. De Courcy, which I know was given with the full conviction of its expediency, tho' I am not quite determined on following it. I cannot easily resolve on anything so serious as Marriage; especially as I am not at present in want of money, & might perhaps, till the old Gentleman's death, be very little benefited by the match. It is true that I am vain enough to beleive it within my reach. I have made him sensible of my power, & can now enjoy the pleasure of triumphing over a Mind prepared to dislike me, & prejudiced against all my past actions. His sister, too, is, I hope, convinced how little the ungenerous representations of any one to the disadvantage of another will avail when opposed to the immediate influence of Intellect & Manner. I see plainly that she is uneasy at my progress in the good opinion of her Brother, & conclude that nothing will be wanting on her part to counteract me; but having once made him doubt the justice of her opinion of me, I think I may defy her. It has been delightful to me to watch his advances towards intimacy, especially to observe his altered manner in consequence of my repressing by the calm dignity of my deportment his insolent approach to direct familiarity. My conduct has been equally guarded from the first, & I never behaved less like a Coquette in the whole course of my Life, tho' perhaps my desire of dominion was never more decided. I have subdued him entirely by sentiment & serious conversation, & made him, I may venture to say, at least *half* in Love with me, without the semblance of the most commonplace flirtation. Mrs. Vernon's consciousness of deserving every sort of revenge that it can be in my power to inflict for her ill-offices could alone enable her to perceive that I am actuated by any design in behaviour so gentle & unpretending. Let her think & act as she chuses, however. I have never yet found that the advice of a Sister could prevent a young Man's being in love if he chose it. We are advancing now towards some kind of confidence, & in short are likely to be engaged in a sort of platonic friendship. On *my* side you may be sure of its never being more, for if I were not already as much attached to another person as I can be to any one, I should make a point of not bestowing my affection on a Man who had dared to think so meanly of me.

Reginald has a good figure, & is not unworthy the praise you have heard given him, but is still greatly inferior to our friend at Langford. He is less polished, less insinuating than Manwaring, & is comparatively deficient in the power of saying those delightful things which put one in good humour with oneself & all the world. He is quite agreable enough, however, to afford me amusement, & to make many of those hours pass very pleasantly which would otherwise be spent in endeavouring to overcome my sister-in-law's reserve, & listening to her Husband's insipid talk.

Your account of Sir James is most satisfactory, & I mean to give Miss Frederica a hint of my intentions very soon.—Yours, &c.,

S. VERNON.

Letter 11
MRS. VERNON TO LADY DE COURCY

I really grow quite uneasy, my dearest mother, about Reginald, from witnessing the very rapid increase of Lady Susan's influence. They are now on terms of the most particular friendship, frequently engaged in long

[1] *Letter 10* Though the manuscript of *Lady Susan* was completed circa 1805, it was not published until 1871, when it appeared as part of Edward Austen-Leigh's *Memoir* (Austen had left her manuscript untitled; the title was provided by Austen-Leigh). Not surprisingly, then, the original text is illustrative of spelling and punctuation practices that were common in the very late eighteenth and very early nineteenth centuries. Spelling had still not been regularized (particularly in such matters as "i before e"); something of the eighteenth century habit of capitalizing abstract nouns (such as "intellect" and "manner") remained; and the ampersand ("&") was frequently used in place of "and."

original spelling

original spelling

conversations together, and she has contrived by the most artful coquetry to subdue his judgement to her own purposes. It is impossible to see the intimacy between them, so very soon established, without some alarm, though I can hardly suppose that Lady Susan's views extend to marriage. I wish you could get Reginald home again, under any plausible pretence. He is not at all disposed to leave us, and I have given him as many hints of my father's precarious state of health, as common decency will allow me to do in my own house. Her power over him must now be boundless, as she has entirely effaced all his former ill-opinion, and persuaded him not merely to forget, but to justify her conduct. Mr. Smith's account of her proceedings at Langford, where he accused her of having made Mr. Manwaring and a young man engaged to Miss Manwaring distractedly in love with her, which Reginald firmly believed when he came to Churchill, is now he is persuaded only a scandalous invention. He has told me so in a warmth of manner which spoke his regret at having ever believed the contrary himself.

How sincerely do I grieve that she ever entered this house! I always looked forward to her coming with uneasiness—but very far was it, from originating in anxiety for Reginald. I expected a most disagreeable companion to myself, but could not imagine that my brother would be in the smallest danger of being captivated by a woman with whose principles he was so well acquainted, and whose character he so heartily despised. If you can get him away, it will be a good thing.

Yours affectionately,

Catherine Vernon

Letter 12
SIR REGINALD DE COURCY TO HIS SON

Parklands

I know that young men in general do not admit of any enquiry even from their nearest relations, into affairs of the heart; but I hope my dear Reginald that you will be superior to such as allow nothing for a father's anxiety, and think themselves privileged to refuse him their confidence and slight his advice. You must be sensible that as an only son and the representative of an ancient family, your conduct in life is most interesting to your connections. In the very important concern of marriage especially, there is everything at stake; your own happiness, that of your parents, and the credit of your name. I do not suppose that you would deliberately form an absolute engagement of that nature without acquainting your mother and myself, or at least without being convinced that we should approve your choice; but I cannot help fearing that you may be drawn in by the lady who has lately attached you, to a marriage, which the whole of your family, far and near, must highly reprobate.[1]

Lady Susan's age is itself a material objection, but her want of character is one so much more serious, that the difference of even twelve years becomes in comparison of small account. Were you not blinded by a sort of fascination, it would be ridiculous in me to repeat the instances of great misconduct on her side, so very generally known. Her neglect of her husband, her encouragement of other men, her extravagance and dissipation were so gross and notorious, that no one could be ignorant of them at the time, nor can now have forgotten them. To our family, she has always been represented in softened colours by the benevolence of Mr. Charles Vernon; and yet in spite of his generous endeavours to excuse her, we know that she did, from the most selfish motives, take all possible pains to prevent his marrying Catherine.

My years and increasing infirmities make me very desirous, my dear Reginald, of seeing you settled in the world. To the fortune of your wife, the goodness of my own, will make me indifferent; but her family and character must be equally unexceptionable. When your choice is so fixed as that no objection can be made to either, I can promise you a ready and cheerful consent; but it is my duty to oppose a match, which deep art only could render probable, and must in the end make wretched.

It is possible that her behaviour may arise only from vanity, or a wish of gaining the admiration of a man whom she must imagine to be particularly prejudiced against her; but it is more likely that she should aim at something farther. She is poor, and may naturally seek an alliance which may be advantageous to herself. You know your own rights, and that it is out of my power to prevent

[1] *reprobate* Disapprove of.

your inheriting the family estate. My ability of distressing you during my life, would be a species of revenge to which I should hardly stoop under any circumstances. I honestly tell you my sentiments and intentions. I do not wish to work on your fears, but on your sense and affection. It would destroy every comfort of my life, to know that you were married to Lady Susan Vernon. It would be the death of that honest pride with which I have hitherto considered my son, I should blush to see him, to hear of him, to think of him.

I may perhaps do no good, but that of relieving my own mind, by this letter; but I felt it my duty to tell you that your partiality for Lady Susan is no secret to your friends, and to warn you against her. I should be glad to hear your reasons for disbelieving Mr. Smith's intelligence; you had no doubt of its authenticity a month ago.

If you can give me your assurance of having no design beyond enjoying the conversation of a clever woman for a short period, and of yielding admiration only to her beauty and abilities without being blinded by them to her faults, you will restore me to happiness; but if you cannot do this, explain to me at least what has occasioned so great an alteration in your opinion of her.

I am etc.,

Reginald De Courcy

Letter 13

LADY DE COURCY TO MRS. VERNON

Parklands

My dear Catherine,

Unluckily I was confined to my room when your last letter came, by a cold which affected my eyes so much as to prevent my reading it myself, so I could not refuse your father when he offered to read it to me, by which means he became acquainted to my great vexation with all your fears about your brother. I had intended to write to Reginald myself, as soon as my eyes would let me, to point out as well as I could the danger of an intimate acquaintance with so artful a woman as Lady Susan, to a young man of his age and high expectations. I meant moreover to have reminded him of our being quite alone now, and very much in need of him to keep up our spirits these long winter evenings. Whether it would have done any good, can never be settled now; but I am excessively vexed that Sir Reginald should know anything of a matter which we foresaw would make him so uneasy. He caught all your fears the moment he had read your letter, and I am sure has not had the business out of his head since; he wrote by the same post to Reginald, a long letter full of it all, and particularly asking for an explanation of what he may have heard from Lady Susan to contradict the late shocking reports. His answer came this morning, which I shall enclose to you, as I think you will like to see it; I wish it was more satisfactory, but it seems written with such a determination to think well of Lady Susan, that his assurances as to marriage etc., do not set my heart at ease. I say all I can however to satisfy your father, and he is certainly less uneasy since Reginald's letter. How provoking it is, my dear Catherine, that this unwelcome guest of yours, should not only prevent our meeting this Christmas, but be the occasion of so much vexation and trouble. Kiss the dear children for me.

Your affectionate mother,

C. De Courcy

Letter 14

MR. DE COURCY TO SIR REGINALD

Churchill

My dear Sir,

I have this moment received your letter, which has given me more astonishment than I ever felt before. I am to thank my sister I suppose, for having represented me in such a light as to injure me in your opinion, and give you all this alarm. I know not why she should choose to make herself and her family uneasy by apprehending an event, which no one but herself, I can affirm, would ever have thought possible. To impute such a design to Lady Susan would be taking from her every claim to that excellent understanding which her bitterest enemies have never denied her; and equally low must sink my pretensions to common-sense, if I am suspected of matrimonial views in my behaviour to her. Our difference of age must be an insuperable objection, and I entreat you my dear Sir to quiet your mind, and no longer harbour a suspicion which cannot be more injurious to your own peace than to our understandings.

I can have no view in remaining with Lady Susan

than to enjoy for a short time (as you have yourself expressed it) the conversation of a woman of high mental powers. If Mrs. Vernon would allow something to my affection for herself and her husband in the length of my visit, she would do more justice to us all; but my sister is unhappily prejudiced beyond the hope of conviction against Lady Susan. From an attachment to her husband which in itself does honour to both, she cannot forgive those endeavours at preventing their union, which have been attributed to selfishness in Lady Susan. But in this case, as well as in many others, the world has most grossly injured that lady, by supposing the worst, where the motives of her conduct have been doubtful.

Lady Susan had heard something so materially to the disadvantage of my sister, as to persuade her that the happiness of Mr. Vernon, to whom she was always much attached, would be absolutely destroyed by the marriage. And this circumstance, while it explains the true motive of Lady Susan's conduct, and removes all the blame which has been so lavished on her, may also convince us how little the general report of any one ought to be credited, since no character however upright, can escape the malevolence of slander. If my sister in the security of retirement, with as little opportunity as inclination to do evil, could not avoid censure, we must not rashly condemn those who living in the world and surrounded with temptation, should be accused of errors which they are known to have the power of committing.

I blame myself severely for having so easily believed the scandalous tales invented by Charles Smith to the prejudice of Lady Susan, as I am now convinced how greatly they have traduced her. As to Mrs. Manwaring's jealousy, it was totally his own invention; and his account of her attaching Miss Manwaring's lover was scarcely better founded. Sir James Martin had been drawn in by that young lady to pay her some attention, and as he is a man of fortune, it was easy to see that her views extended to marriage. It is well known that Miss Manwaring is absolutely on the catch for a husband, and no one therefore can pity her, for losing by the superior attractions of another woman, the chance of being able to make a worthy man completely miserable. Lady Susan was far from intending such a conquest, and in finding how warmly Miss Manwaring resented her lover's defection, determined, in spite of Mr. and Mrs. Manwaring's most earnest entreaties, to leave the family. I have reason to imagine that she did receive serious proposals from Sir James, but her removing from Langford immediately on the discovery of his attachment, must acquit her on that article, with every mind of common candour. You will, I am sure my dear Sir, feel the truth of this reasoning, and will hereby learn to do justice to the character of a very injured woman.

I know that Lady Susan in coming to Churchill was governed only by the most honourable and amiable intentions. Her prudence and economy are exemplary, her regard for Mr. Vernon equal even to *his* deserts, and her wish of obtaining my sister's good opinion merits a better return than it had received. As a mother she is unexceptionable.[1] Her solid affection for her child is shown by placing her in hands, where her education will be properly attended to; but because she has not the blind and weak partiality of most mothers, she is accused of wanting[2] maternal tenderness. Every person of sense however will know how to value and commend her well directed affection, and will join me in wishing that Frederica Vernon may prove more worthy than she has yet done, of her mother's tender care.

I have now my dear Sir, written my real sentiments of Lady Susan; you will know from this letter, how highly I admire her abilities, and esteem her character; but if you are not equally convinced by my full and solemn assurance that your fears have been most idly created, you will deeply mortify and distress me.—I am etc.,

R. De Courcy

Letter 15

MRS. VERNON TO LADY DE COURCY

Churchill

My dear mother,

I return you Reginald's letter, and rejoice with all my heart that my father is made easy by it. Tell him so, with my congratulations; but between ourselves, I must own it has only convinced *me* of my brother's having no present intention of marrying Lady Susan—not that he is in no

[1] *she is unexceptionable* It would be impossible to take exception to her behavior in this regard.

[2] *wanting* Lacking.

danger of doing so three months hence. He gives a very plausible account of her behaviour at Langford, I wish it may be true, but his intelligence must come from herself, and I am less disposed to believe it, than to lament the degree of intimacy subsisting between them, implied by the discussion of such a subject.

I am sorry to have incurred his displeasure, but can expect nothing better while he is so very eager in Lady Susan's justification. He is very severe against me indeed, and yet I hope I have not been hasty in my judgement of her. Poor woman! though I have reasons enough for my dislike, I can not help pitying her at present as she is in real distress, and with too much cause. She had this morning a letter from the lady with whom she has placed her daughter, to request that Miss Vernon might be immediately removed, as she had been detected in an attempt to run away. Why, or whither she intended to go, does not appear; but as her situation seems to have been unexceptionable, it is a sad thing and of course highly afflicting to Lady Susan.

Frederica must be as much as sixteen, and ought to know better, but from what her mother insinuates I am afraid she is a perverse girl. She has been sadly neglected however, and her mother ought to remember it.

Mr. Vernon set off for town as soon as she had determined what should be done. He is if possible to prevail on Miss Summers to let Frederica continue with her, and if he cannot succeed, to bring her to Churchill for the present, till some other situation can be found for her. Her ladyship is comforting herself meanwhile by strolling along the shrubbery with Reginald, calling forth all his tender feelings I suppose on this distressing occasion. She has been talking a great deal about it to me, she talks vastly well, I am afraid of being ungenerous or I should say she talks too well to feel so very deeply. But I will not look for faults. She may be Reginald's wife. Heaven forbid it! - but why should I be quicker sighted than anybody else? Mr. Vernon declares that he never saw deeper distress than hers, on the receipt of the letter—and is his judgement inferior to mine?

She was very unwilling that Frederica should be allowed to come to Churchill, and justly enough, as it seems a sort of reward to behaviour deserving very differently. But it was impossible to take her any where else, and she is not to remain here long.

"It will be absolutely necessary", said she, "as you my dear sister must be sensible, to treat my daughter with some severity while she is here—a most painful necessity, but I will endeavour to submit to it. I am afraid I have been too often indulgent, but my poor Frederica's temper could never bear opposition well. You must support and encourage me—you must urge the necessity of reproof, if you see me too lenient."

All this sounds very reasonable. Reginald is so incensed against the poor silly girl! Surely it is not to Lady Susan's credit that he should be so bitter against her daughter; his idea of her must be drawn from the mother's description.

Well, whatever may be his fate, we have the comfort of knowing that we have done our utmost to save him. We must commit the event to an Higher Power. Yours ever etc.,

Catherine Vernon

Letter 16

LADY SUSAN TO MRS. JOHNSON

Churchill

Never my dearest Alicia, was I so provoked in my life as by a letter this morning from Miss Summers. That horrid girl of mine has been trying to run away.—I had not a notion of her being such a little devil before; she seemed to have all the Vernon milkiness; but on receiving the letter in which I declared my intentions about Sir James, she actually attempted to elope; at least, I cannot otherwise account for her doing it. She meant I suppose to go to the Clarkes in Staffordshire, for she has no other acquaintance. But she shall be punished, she shall have him. I have sent Charles to town to make matters up if he can, for I do not by any means want her here. If Miss Summers will not keep her, you must find me out another school, unless we can get her married immediately. Miss S. writes word that she could not get the young lady to assign any cause for her extraordinary conduct, which confirms me in my own private explanation of it.

Frederica is too shy I think, and too much in awe of me, to tell tales; but if the mildness of her uncle should get anything from her, I am not afraid. I trust I shall be able to make my story as good as hers. If I am vain of anything, it is of my eloquence. Consideration and esteem as surely follow command of language, as admiration waits on beauty. And here I have opportunity enough for the exercise of my talent, as the chief of my time is spent in conversation. Reginald is never easy unless we are by ourselves, and when the weather is tolerable, we pace the shrubbery for hours together. I like him on the whole very well, he is clever and has a good deal to say, but he is sometimes impertinent and troublesome. There is a sort of ridiculous delicacy about him which requires the fullest explanation of whatever he may have heard to my disadvantage, and is never satisfied till he thinks he has ascertained the beginning and end of everything.

This is *one* sort of love—but I confess it does not particularly recommend itself to me. I infinitely prefer the tender and liberal spirit of Manwaring, which impressed with the deepest conviction of my merit, is satisfied that whatever I do must be right; and look with a degree of contempt on the inquisitive and doubting fancies of that heart which seems always debating on the reasonableness of its emotions. Manwaring is indeed beyond compare superior to Reginald—a superior in everything but the power of being with me. Poor fellow! he is quite distracted by jealousy, which I am not sorry for, as I know no better support of love. He has been teasing me to allow of his coming into this country, and lodging somewhere near me *incog.*—but I forbid anything of the kind. Those women are inexcusable who forget what is due to themselves and the opinion of the world.

S. Vernon

Letter 17

MRS. VERNON TO LADY DE COURCY

Churchill

My dear mother,

Mr. Vernon returned on Thursday night, bringing his niece with him. Lady Susan had received a line from him by that day's post informing her that Miss Summers had absolutely refused to allow of Miss Vernon's continuance in her Academy. We were therefore prepared for her arrival, and expected them impatiently the whole evening. They came while we were at tea, and I never saw any creature look so frightened in my life as Frederica when she entered the room.

Lady Susan who had been shedding tears before and showing great agitation at the idea of the meeting, received her with perfect self-command, and without betraying the least tenderness of spirit. She hardly spoke to her, and on Frederica's bursting into tears as soon as we were seated, took her out of the room and did not return for some time; when she did, her eyes looked very red, and she was as much agitated as before. We saw no more of her daughter.

Poor Reginald was beyond measure concerned to see his fair friend in such distress, and watched her with so much tender solicitude that I, who occasionally caught her observing his countenance with exultation, was quite out of patience. This pathetic representation lasted the whole evening, and so ostentatious and artful a display had entirely convinced me that she did in fact feel nothing.

I am more angry with her than ever since I have seen her daughter. The poor girl looks so unhappy that my heart aches for her. Lady Susan is surely too severe, because Frederica does not seem to have the sort of temper to make severity necessary. She looks perfectly timid, dejected and penitent.

She is very pretty, though not so handsome as her mother, nor at all like her. Her complexion is delicate, but neither so fair, nor so blooming as Lady Susan's— and she has quite the Vernon cast of countenance, the oval face and mild dark eyes, and there is peculiar sweetness in her look when she speaks either to her uncle or me, for as we behave kindly to her, we have of course engaged her gratitude. Her mother has insinuated that her temper is untractable, but I never saw a face less indicative of any evil disposition than hers; and from what I now see of the behaviour of each to the other, the invariable severity of Lady Susan, and the silent dejection of Frederica, I am led to believe as heretofore that the former has no real love for her daughter and has never done her justice, or treated her affectionately.

I have not yet been able to have any conversation with my niece; she is shy, and I think I can see that some pains are taken to prevent her being much with me. Nothing satisfactory transpires as to her reason for running away.

Her kindhearted uncle you may be sure, was too fearful of distressing her, to ask many questions as they travelled. I wish it had been possible for me to fetch her instead of him; I think I should have discovered the truth in the course of a thirty mile journey.

The small pianoforte has been removed within these few days at Lady Susan's request, into her dressing room, and Frederica spends great part of the day there; *practising* it is called, but I seldom hear any noise when I pass that way. What she does with herself there I do not know, there are plenty of books in the room, but it is not every girl who has been running wild the first fifteen years of her life, that can or will read. Poor creature! the prospect from her window is not very instructive, for that room overlooks the lawn you know with the shrubbery on one side, where she may see her mother walking for an hour together, in earnest conversation with Reginald. A girl of Frederica's age must be childish indeed, if such things do not strike her. Is it not inexcusable to give such an example to a daughter? Yet Reginald still thinks Lady Susan the best of mothers— still condemns Frederica as a worthless girl! He is convinced that her attempt to run away, proceeded from no justifiable cause, and had no provocation. I am sure I cannot say that it *had,* but while Miss Summers declares that Miss Vernon showed no sign of obstinacy or perverseness during her whole stay in Wigmore St. till she was detected in this scheme, I cannot so readily credit what Lady Susan has made him and wants to make me believe, that it was merely an impatience of restraint, and a desire of escaping from the tuition of masters which brought on the plan of an elopement. Oh! Reginald, how is your judgement enslaved! He scarcely dares even allow her to be handsome, and when I speak of her beauty, replies only that her eyes have no brilliancy.

Sometimes he is sure that she is deficient in understanding, and at others that her temper only is in fault. In short when a person is always to deceive, it is impossible to be consistent. Lady Susan finds it necessary for her own justification that Frederica should be to blame, and probably has sometimes judged it expedient to accuse her of ill-nature and sometimes to lament her want of sense. Reginald is only repeating after her ladyship.

I am etc.,

Catherine Vernon

Letter 18

FROM THE SAME TO THE SAME

Churchill

My dear Madam,

I am very glad to find that my description of Frederica Vernon has interested you, for I do believe her truly deserving of our regard, and when I have communicated a notion that has recently struck me, your kind impression in her favour will I am sure be heightened. I cannot help fancying that she is growing partial to my brother, I so very often see her eyes fixed on his face with a remarkable expression of pensive admiration! He is certainly very handsome—and yet more—there is an openness in his manner that must be highly prepossessing, and I am sure she feels it so. Thoughtful and pensive in general her countenance always brightens with a smile when Reginald says anything amusing; and let the subject be ever so serious that he may be conversing on, I am much mistaken if a syllable of his uttering, escape her.

I want to make him sensible of all this, for we know the power of gratitude on such a heart as his; and could Frederica's artless affection detach him from her mother, we might bless the day which brought her to Churchill. I think my dear Madam, you would not disapprove of her as a daughter. She is extremely young to be sure, has had a wretched education and a dreadful example of levity in her mother; but yet I can pronounce her disposition to be excellent, and her natural abilities very good.

Though totally without accomplishment, she is by no means so ignorant as one might expect to find her, being fond of books and spending the chief of her time in reading. Her mother leaves her more to herself now than she *did,* and I have her with me as much as possible, and have taken great pains to overcome her timidity. We are very good friends, and though she never opens her lips before her mother, she talks enough when alone with me, to make it clear that if properly treated by Lady Susan she would always appear to much greater advantage. There cannot be a more gentle, affectionate heart, or more obliging manners, when acting without restraint. Her little cousins are all very fond of her.

Yours affectionately,

Catherine Vernon

Letter 19

LADY SUSAN TO MRS. JOHNSON

Churchill

You will be eager I know to hear something farther of Frederica, and perhaps may think me negligent for not writing before. She arrived with her uncle last Thursday fortnight, when of course I lost no time in demanding the reason of her behaviour, and soon found myself to have been perfectly right in attributing it to my own letter. The purport of it frightened her so thoroughly that with a mixture of true girlish perverseness and folly, without considering that she could not escape from my authority by running away from Wigmore Street, she resolved on getting out of the house, and proceeding directly by the stage to her friends the Clarkes, and had really got as far as the length of two streets in her journey, when she was fortunately missed, pursued, and overtaken.

Such was the first distinguished exploit of Miss Frederica Susanna Vernon, and if we consider that it was achieved at the tender age of sixteen we shall have room for the most flattering prognostics of her future renown. I am excessively provoked however at the parade of propriety which prevented Miss Summers from keeping the girl; and it seems so extraordinary a piece of nicety, considering what are my daughter's family connections, that I can only suppose the lady to be governed by the fear of never getting her money. Be that as it may, however, Frederica is returned on my hands, and having now nothing else to employ her, is busy in pursuing the plan of romance begun at Langford. She is actually falling in love with Reginald De Courcy. To disobey her mother by refusing an unexceptionable offer is not enough; her affections must likewise be given without her mother's approbation. I never saw a girl of her age bid fairer to be the sport of mankind. Her feelings are tolerably lively, and she is so charmingly artless in their display, as to afford the most reasonable hope of her being ridiculed and despised by every man who sees her.

Artlessness will never do in love matters, and that girl is born a simpleton who has it either by nature or affectation. I am not yet certain that Reginald sees what she is about; nor is it of much consequence; she is now an object of indifference to him, she would be one of contempt were he to understand her emotions. Her beauty is much admired by the Vernons, but it has no effect on him. She is in high favour with her aunt altogether—because she is so little like myself of course. She is exactly the companion for Mrs. Vernon, who dearly loves to be first, and to have all the sense and all the wit of the conversation to herself; Frederica will never eclipse her. When she first came, I was at some pains to prevent her seeing much of her aunt, but I have since relaxed, as I believe I may depend on her observing the rules I have laid down for their discourse.

But do not imagine that with all this lenity, I have for a moment given up my plan of her marriage; no, I am unalterably fixed on that point, though I have not yet quite resolved on the manner of bringing it about. I should not choose to have the business brought forward here, and canvassed by the wise heads of Mr. and Mrs. Vernon; and I cannot just now afford[1] to go to town. Miss Frederica must therefore wait a little.

Yours ever,

S. Vernon

Letter 20

MRS. VERNON TO LADY DE COURCY

Churchill

We have a very unexpected guest with us at present, my dear mother. He arrived yesterday. I heard a carriage at the door as I was sitting with my children while they dined, and supposing I should be wanted left the nursery soon afterwards and was halfway down stairs, when Frederica as pale as ashes came running up, and rushed by me into her own room. I instantly followed, and asked her what was the matter. "Oh!" cried she, "he is come, Sir James is come—and what am I to do?" This was no explanation; I begged her to tell me what she meant. At

[1] *afford* Manage.

that moment we were interrupted by a knock at the door; it was Reginald, who came by Lady Susan's direction to call Frederica down. "It is Mr. De Courcy," said she, colouring violently, "Mama has sent for me, and I must go."

We all three went down together, and I saw my brother examining the terrified face of Frederica with surprise. In the breakfast room we found Lady Susan and a young man of genteel appearance, whom she introduced to me by the name of Sir James Martin, the very person, as you may remember, whom it was said she had been at pains to detach from Miss Manwaring. But the conquest it seems was not designed for herself, or she has since transferred it to her daughter, for Sir James is now desperately in love with Frederica, and with full encouragement from Mama. The poor girl however I am sure dislikes him; and though his person and address are very well, he appears both to Mr. Vernon and me a very weak young man.

Frederica looked so shy, so confused, when we entered the room, that I felt for her exceedingly. Lady Susan behaved with great attention to her visitor, and yet I thought I could perceive that she had no particular pleasure in seeing him. Sir James talked a good deal, and made many civil excuses to me for the liberty he had taken in coming to Churchill, mixing more frequent laughter with his discourse than the subject required; said many things over and over again, and told Lady Susan three times that he had seen Mrs. Johnson a few evenings before. He now and then addressed Frederica, but more frequently her mother. The poor girl sat all this time without opening her lips; her eyes cast down, and her colour varying every instant, while Reginald observed all that passed, in perfect silence.

At length Lady Susan, weary I believe of her situation, proposed walking, and we left the two gentlemen together to put on our pelisses.[1]

As we went upstairs Lady Susan begged permission to attend me for a few moments in my dressing room, as she was anxious to speak with me in private. I led her thither accordingly, and as soon as the door was closed she said, "I was never more surprised in my life than by Sir James's arrival, and the suddenness of it requires some apology to you my dear sister, though to me as a mother, it is highly flattering. He is so warmly attached to my daughter that he could no longer exist without seeing her. Sir James is a young man of an amiable disposition, and excellent character; a little too much of the rattle perhaps, but a year or two will rectify that, and he is in other respects so very eligible a match for Frederica that I have always observed his attachment with the greatest pleasure, and am persuaded that you and my brother will give the alliance your hearty approbation. I have never before mentioned the likelihood of its taking place to any one, because I thought that while Frederica continued at school, it had better not be known to exist; but now, as I am convinced that Frederica, is too old ever to submit to school confinement, and have therefore begun to consider her union with Sir James as not very distant, I had intended within a few days to acquaint yourself and Mr. Vernon with the whole business. I am sure my dear sister, you will excuse my remaining silent on it so long, and agree with me that such circumstances, while they continue from any cause in suspense, cannot be too cautiously concealed. When you have the happiness of bestowing your sweet little Catherine some years hence on a man, who in connection and character is alike unexceptionable, you will know what I feel now; though thank heaven! you cannot have all my reasons for rejoicing in such an event. Catherine will be amply provided for, and not like my Frederica indebted to a fortunate establishment for the comforts of life."

She concluded by demanding my congratulations. I gave them somewhat awkwardly I believe; for in fact, the sudden disclosure of so important a matter took from me the power of speaking with any clearness. She thanked me however most affectionately for my kind concern in the welfare of herself and her daughter, and then said,

"I am not apt to deal in professions,[2] my dear Mrs. Vernon, and I never had the convenient talent of affecting sensations foreign to my heart; and therefore I trust you will believe me when I declare that much as I had heard in your praise before I knew you, I had no idea that I should ever love you as I now do; and must farther say that your friendship towards me is more particularly gratifying, because I have reason to believe that some

[1] *pelisses* Long cloaks.

[2] *professions* Declarations, whether true or false.

attempts were made to prejudice you against me. I only wish that they—whoever they are—to whom I am indebted for such kind intentions, could see the terms on which we now are together, and understand the real affection we feel for each other! But I will not detain you any longer. God bless you, for your goodness to me and my girl, and continue to you all your present happiness."

What can one say of such a woman, my dear mother?—such earnestness, such solemnity of expression!—and yet I cannot help suspecting the truth of everything she said.

As for Reginald, I believe he does not know what to make of the matter. When Sir James first came, he appeared all astonishment and perplexity. The folly of the young man and the confusion of Frederica entirely engrossed him; and though a little private discourse with Lady Susan has since had its effect, he is still hurt I am sure at her allowing of such a man's attentions to her daughter.

Sir James invited himself with great composure to remain here a few days; hoped we would not think it odd, was aware of its being very impertinent, but he took the liberty of a relation, and concluding by wishing with a laugh, that he might be really one soon. Even Lady Susan seemed a little disconcerted by this forwardness; in her heart I am persuaded, she sincerely wishes him gone.

But something must be done for this poor girl, if her feelings are such as both her uncle and I believe them to be. She must not be sacrificed to policy or ambition, she must not be even left to suffer from the dread of it. The girl, whose heart can distinguish Reginald De Courcy, deserves, however he may slight her, a better fate than to be Sir James Martin's wife. As soon as I can get her alone, I will discover the real truth, but she seems to wish to avoid me. I hope this does not proceed from anything wrong, and that I shall not find out I have thought too well of her. Her behaviour before Sir James certainly speaks the greatest consciousness and embarrassment; but I see nothing in it more like encouragement.

Adieu my dear Madam,

Yours etc.,

Catherine Vernon

Letter 21

MISS VERNON TO MR. DE COURCY

Sir,

I hope you will excuse this liberty, I am forced upon it by the greatest distress, or I should be ashamed to trouble you. I am very miserable about Sir James Martin, and have no other way in the world of helping myself but by writing to you, for I am forbidden ever speaking to my uncle or aunt on the subject; and this being the case, I am afraid my applying to you will appear no better than equivocation, and as if I attended only to the letter and not the spirit of Mama's commands, but if you do not take my part, and persuade her to break it off, I shall be half-distracted, for I cannot bear him. No human being but you could have any chance of prevailing with her. If you will therefore have the unspeakable great kindness of taking my part with her, and persuading her to send Sir James away, I shall be more obliged to you than it is possible for me to express. I always disliked him from the first, it is not a sudden fancy I assure you Sir, I always thought him silly and impertinent and disagreeable, and now he is grown worse than ever. I would rather work for my bread than marry him. I do not know how to apologize enough for this letter, I know it is taking so great a liberty, I am aware how dreadfully angry it will make Mama, but I must run the risk. I am Sir, your most humble servant,

F.S.V.

Letter 22

LADY SUSAN TO MRS. JOHNSON

Churchill

This is insufferable! My dearest friend, I was never so enraged before, and must relieve myself by writing to you, who I know will enter into all my feelings. Who should come on Tuesday but Sir James Martin? Guess my astonishment and vexation—for as you well know, I never wished him to be seen at Churchill. What a pity that you should not have known his intentions! Not content with coming, he actually invited himself to remain here a few days. I could have poisoned him; I made the best of it however, and told my story with great success to Mrs.

Vernon who, whatever might be her real sentiments, said nothing in opposition to mine. I made a point also of Frederica's behaving civilly to Sir James, and gave her to understand that I was absolutely determined on her marrying him. She said something of her misery, but that was all. I have for some time been more particularly resolved on the match, from seeing the rapid increase of her affection for Reginald, and from not feeling perfectly secure that a knowledge of that affection might not in the end awaken a return. Contemptible, as a regard founded only on compassion, must make them both, in my eyes, I felt by no means assured that such might not be the consequence. It is true that Reginald had not in any degree grown cool towards me; but yet he had lately mentioned Frederica spontaneously and unnecessarily, and once had said something in praise of her person.

He was all astonishment at the appearance of my visitor; and at first observed Sir James with an attention which I was pleased to see not unmixed with jealousy; but unluckily it was impossible for me really to torment him, as Sir James though extremely gallant to me, very soon made the whole party understand that his heart was devoted to my daughter.

I had no great difficulty in convincing De Courcy when we were alone, that I was perfectly justified, all things considered, in desiring the match; and the whole business seemed most comfortably arranged. They could none of them help perceiving that Sir James was no Solomon, but I had positively forbidden Frederica's complaining to Charles Vernon or his wife, and they had therefore no pretence for interference, though my impertinent sister I believe wanted only opportunity for doing so.

Everything however was going on calmly and quietly; and though I counted the hours of Sir James's stay, my mind was entirely satisfied with the posture of affairs. Guess then what I must feel at the sudden disturbance of all my schemes, and that too from a quarter, whence I had least reason to apprehend it. Reginald came this morning into my dressing room, with a very unusual solemnity of countenance, and after some preface informed me in so many words, that he wished to reason with me on the impropriety and unkindness of allowing Sir James Martin to address my daughter, contrary to her inclination. I was all amazement. When I found that he was not to be laughed out of his design, I calmly required an explanation, and begged to know by what he was impelled, and by whom commissioned to reprimand me. He then told me, mixing in this speech a few insolent compliments and ill-timed expressions of tenderness to which I listened with perfect indifference, that my daughter had acquainted him with some circumstances concerning herself, Sir James, and me, which gave him great uneasiness.

In short, I found that she had in the first place actually written to him, to request his interference, and that on receiving her letter he had conversed with her on the subject of it, in order to understand the particulars and assure himself of her real wishes!

I have not a doubt but that the girl took this opportunity of making downright love[1] to him; I am convinced of it, from the manner in which he spoke of her. Much good, may such love do him! I shall ever despise the man who can be gratified by the passion, which he never wished to inspire, nor solicited the avowal of. I shall always detest them both. He can have no true regard for me, or he would not have listened to her; and she, with her little rebellious heart and indelicate feelings to throw herself into the protection of a young man with whom she had scarcely ever exchanged two words before. I am equally confounded at her impudence and his credulity. How dared he believe what she told him in my disfavour! Ought he not to have felt assured that I must have unanswerable motives for all that I had done! Where was his reliance on my sense or goodness then; where the resentment which true love would have dictated against the person defaming me, that person, too, a chit, a child, without talent or education, whom he had been always taught to despise?

I was calm for some time, but the greatest degree of forbearance may be overcome; and I hope I was afterwards sufficiently keen. He endeavoured, long endeavoured to soften my resentment, but that woman is a fool indeed who while insulted by accusation, can be worked on by compliments. At length he left me, as deeply provoked as myself, and he showed his anger more. I was quite cool,

[1] *making ... love* Expressing romantic affection. (The phrase "making love" did not carry with it any suggestion of sexual activity until the 1960s.)

but he gave way to the most violent indignation. I may therefore expect it will sooner subside; and perhaps his may be vanished forever, while mine will be found still fresh and implacable.

He is now shut up in his apartment, whither I heard him go, on leaving mine. How unpleasant, one would think, must his reflections be! But some people's feelings are incomprehensible. I have not yet tranquillized myself enough to see Frederica. She shall not soon forget the occurrences of this day. She shall find that she has poured forth her tender tale of love in vain, and exposed herself forever to the contempt of the whole world, and the severest resentment of her injured mother.

Yours affectionately,
S. Vernon

Letter 23
MRS. VERNON TO LADY DE COURCY

Churchill

Let me congratulate you, my dearest mother. The affair which has given us so much anxiety is drawing to a happy conclusion. Our prospect is most delightful; and since matters have now taken so favourable a turn, I am quite sorry that I ever imparted my apprehensions to you; for the pleasure of learning that the danger is over, is perhaps dearly purchased by all that you have previously suffered.

I am so much agitated by delight that I can scarcely hold a pen, but am determined to send you a few lines by James, that you may have some explanation of what must so greatly astonish you, as that Reginald should be returning to Parklands.

I was sitting about half an hour ago with Sir James in the breakfast parlour, when my brother called me out of the room. I instantly saw that something was the matter; his complexion was raised, and he spoke with great emotion. You know his eager manner, my dear Madam, when his mind is interested.

"Catherine," said he, "I am going home today. I am sorry to leave you, but I must go. It is a great while since I have seen my father and mother. I am going to send James forward with my hunters immediately, if you have any letter therefore he can take it. I shall not be at home myself till Wednesday or Thursday, as I shall go through London, where I have business. But before I leave you," he continued, speaking in a lower voice and with still greater energy, "I must warn you of one thing. Do not let Frederica Vernon be made unhappy by that Martin. He wants to marry her—her mother promotes the match—but she cannot endure the idea of it. Be assured that I speak from the fullest conviction of the truth of what I say. I know that Frederica is made wretched by Sir James' continuing here. She is a sweet girl, and deserves a better fate. Send him away immediately. He is only a fool—but what her mother can mean, Heaven only knows! Good bye," he added shaking my hand with earnestness—"I do not know when you will see me again. But remember what I tell you of Frederica; you must make it your business to see justice done her. She is an amiable girl, and has a very superior mind to what we have ever given her credit for."

He then left me and ran upstairs. I would not try to stop him, for I knew what his feelings must be; the nature of mine as I listened to him, I need not attempt to describe. For a minute or two I remained in the same spot, overpowered by wonder—of a most agreeable sort indeed; yet it required some consideration to be tranquilly happy.

In about ten minutes after my return to the parlour, Lady Susan entered the room. I concluded of course that she and Reginald had been quarrelling, and looked with anxious curiosity for a confirmation of my belief in her face. Mistress of deceit however she appeared perfectly unconcerned, and after chatting on indifferent subjects for a short time, said to me, "I find from Wilson that we are going to lose Mr. De Courcy. Is it true that he leaves Churchill this morning?" I replied that it was. "He told us nothing of all this last night," said she laughing, "or even this morning at breakfast. But perhaps he did not know it himself. Young men are often hasty in their resolutions—and not more sudden in forming, than unsteady in keeping them. I should not be surprised if he were to change his mind at last, and not go."

She soon afterwards left the room. I trust however my dear mother, that we have no reason to fear an alteration of his present plan; things have gone too far. They must have quarrelled, and about Frederica too. Her calmness astonishes me. What delight will be yours in seeing him again, in seeing him still worthy your esteem, still capable of forming your happiness!

When next I write, I shall be able I hope to tell you that Sir James is gone, Lady Susan vanquished, and Frederica at peace. We have much to do, but it shall be done. I am all impatience to know how this astonishing change was effected. I finish as I began, with the warmest congratulations.

Yours ever,

Catherine Vernon

Letter 24

FROM THE SAME TO THE SAME

Churchill

Little did I imagine my dear mother, when I sent off my last letter, that the delightful perturbation of spirits I was then in, would undergo so speedy, so melancholy a reverse! I never can sufficiently regret that I wrote to you at all. Yet who could have foreseen what has happened? My dear mother, every hope which but two hours ago made me so happy, is vanished. The quarrel between Lady Susan and Reginald is made up, and we are all as we were before. One point only is gained; Sir James Martin is dismissed. What are we now to look forward to? I am indeed disappointed. Reginald was all but gone; his horse was ordered, and almost brought to the door! Who would not have felt safe?

For half an hour I was in momentary expectation of his departure. After I had sent off my letter to you, I went to Mr. Vernon and sat with him in his room, talking over the whole matter. I then determined to look for Frederica, whom I had not seen since breakfast. I met her on the stairs and saw that she was crying.

"My dear aunt," said she, "he is going, Mr. De Courcy is going, and it is all my fault. I am afraid you will be angry, but indeed I had no idea it would end so."

"My love," replied I, "do not think it necessary to apologize to me on that account. I shall feel myself under an obligation to anyone who is the means of sending my brother home; because (recollecting myself) I know my father wants very much to see him. But what is it that you have done to occasion all this?"

She blushed deeply as she answered, "I was so unhappy about Sir James that I could not help—I have done something very wrong, I know—but you have not an idea of the misery I have been in, and Mama had ordered me never to speak to you or my uncle about it,—and—" "You therefore spoke to my brother, to engage *his* interference," said I, wishing to save her the explanation. "No—but I wrote to him. I did indeed. I got up this morning before it was light—I was two hours about it—and when my letter was done, I thought I never should have the courage to give it. After breakfast, however, as I was going to my own room, I met him in the passage, and then as I knew that everything must depend on that moment, I forced myself to give it. He was so good as to take it immediately; I dared not look at him—and ran away directly. I was in such a fright that I could hardly breathe. My dear aunt, you do not know how miserable I have been."

"Frederica," said I, "you ought to have told me all your distresses. You would have found in me a friend always ready to assist you. Do you think that your uncle and I should not have espoused your cause as warmly as my brother?"

"Indeed I did not doubt your goodness," said she, colouring again, "but I thought that Mr. De Courcy could do anything with my mother; but I was mistaken; they have had a dreadful quarrel about it, and he is going. Mama will never forgive me, and I shall be worse off than ever." "No, you shall not," replied I.—"In such a point as this, your mother's prohibition ought not to have prevented your speaking to me on the subject. She has no right to make you unhappy, and she shall not do it. Your applying however to Reginald can be productive only of good to all parties. I believe it is best as it is. Depend upon it that you shall not be made unhappy any longer."

At that moment, how great was my astonishment at seeing Reginald come out of Lady Susan's dressing room. My heart misgave me instantly. His confusion on seeing me was very evident. Frederica immediately disappeared. "Are you going?" said I. "You will find Mr. Vernon in his own room." "No Catherine," replied he. "I am not going. Will you let me speak to you a moment?"

We went into my room. "I find," continued he, his confusion increasing as he spoke, "that I have been acting with my usual foolish impetuosity. I have entirely misunderstood Lady Susan, and was on the point of leaving the house under a false impression of her conduct. There has been some very great mistake—we have been all mistaken I fancy. Frederica does not know her mother—Lady Susan means nothing but her good—but Frederica will not make a friend of her. Lady Susan therefore does not always know what will make her daughter happy. Besides I could have no right to interfere—Miss Vernon was mistaken in applying to me. In short Catherine, everything has gone wrong— but it is now all happily settled. Lady Susan I believe wishes to speak to you about it, if you are at leisure." "Certainly;" replied I, deeply sighing at the recital of so lame a story. I made no remarks however, for words would have been in vain. Reginald was glad to get away, and I went to Lady Susan; curious indeed to hear her account of it.

"Did not I tell you," said she with a smile, "that your brother would not leave us after all?" "You did indeed," replied I very gravely, "but I flattered myself that you would be mistaken." "I should not have hazarded such an opinion," returned she, "if it had not at that moment occurred to me, that his resolution of going might be occasioned by a conversation in which we had been this morning engaged, and which had ended very much to his dissatisfaction from our not rightly understanding each other's meaning. This idea struck me at the moment, and I instantly determined that an accidental dispute in which I might probably be as much to blame as himself, should not deprive you of your brother. If you remember, I left the room almost immediately. I was resolved to lose no time in clearing up these mistakes as far as I could. The case was this. Frederica had set herself violently against marrying Sir James." "And can your ladyship wonder that she should?" cried I with some warmth. "Frederica has an excellent understanding, and Sir James has none." "I am at least very far from regretting it, my dear sister," said she; "on the contrary, I am grateful for so favourable a sign of my daughter's sense. Sir James is certainly under par—his boyish manners make him appear the worse—and had Frederica possessed the penetration, the abilities, which I could have wished in my daughter, or had I ever known her to possess so much as she does, I should not have been anxious for the match." "It is odd that you alone should be ignorant of your daughter's sense." "Frederica never does justice to herself; her manners are shy and childish. She is besides afraid of me; she scarcely loves me. During her poor father's life she was a spoilt child; the severity which it has since been necessary for me to show, has entirely alienated her affection; neither has she any of that brilliancy of intellect, that genius, or vigour of mind which will force itself forward." "Say rather that she has been unfortunate in her education." "Heaven knows, my dearest Mrs. Vernon, how fully I am aware of that; but I would wish to forget every circumstance that might throw blame on the memory of one, whose name is sacred with me."

Here she pretended to cry. I was out of patience with her. "But what," said I, "was your ladyship going to tell me about your disagreement with my brother?" "It originated in an action of my daughter's, which equally marks her want of judgement, and the unfortunate dread of me I have been mentioning. She wrote to Mr. De Courcy." "I know she did. You had forbidden her speaking to Mr. Vernon or me on the cause of her distress; what could she do therefore but apply to my brother?" "Good God," she exclaimed, "what an opinion you must have of me! Can you possibly suppose that I was aware of her unhappiness? That it was my object to make my own child miserable, and that I had forbidden her speaking to you on that subject, from a fear of your interrupting the diabolical scheme? Do you think me destitute of every honest, every natural feeling? Am I capable of consigning her to everlasting misery, whose welfare it is my first earthly duty to promote?" "The idea is horrible. What then was your intention when you insisted on her silence?" "Of what use my dear sister, could be any application to you, however the affair might stand? Why should I subject you to entreaties, which I refused to attend to myself? Neither for your sake, for hers, nor for my own, could such a thing be desirable. Where my own resolution was taken, I could not wish for the interference, however friendly, of another person. I was mistaken, it is true, but I believed myself to be right." "But what was this mistake, to which your ladyship so often alludes? From whence arose so astonishing a misapprehension of your daughter's feelings? Did not you know that she disliked Sir James?" "I knew that he was not absolutely the man she would have chosen. But I was persuaded that her objections to him did not arise from any perception of his deficiency. You must not question me however, my dear sister, too minutely on this point—" continued she, taking me affectionately by the hand. "I honestly own that there is something to conceal. Frederica makes me very unhappy. Her applying to Mr. De Courcy hurt me particularly." "What is it that you mean to infer," said I, "by this appearance of mystery? If you think your daughter at all attached to Reginald, her objecting to Sir James could not less deserve to be attended to, than if the cause of her objecting had been a consciousness of his folly. And why should your ladyship at any rate quarrel with my brother for an interference which you must know, it was not in his nature to refuse, when urged in such a manner?"

"His disposition you know is warm, and he came to expostulate with me, his compassion all alive for this ill-used girl, this heroine in distress! We misunderstood each other. He believed me more to blame than I really was; I considered his interference as less excusable than I now find it. I have a real regard for him, and was beyond expression mortified to find it as I thought so ill bestowed. We were both warm, and of course both to blame. His resolution of leaving Churchill is consistent with his general eagerness; when I understood his intention however, and at the same time began to think that we had perhaps been equally mistaken in each other's meaning, I resolved to have an explanation before it were too late. For any member of your family I must always feel a degree of affection, and I own it would have sensibly hurt me, if my acquaintance with Mr. De Courcy had ended so gloomily. I have now only to say farther, that as I am convinced of Frederica's having a reasonable dislike to Sir James, I shall instantly inform him that he must give up all hope of her. I reproach myself for having ever, though so innocently, made her unhappy on that score. She shall have all the retribution in my power to make; if she values her own happiness as much as I do, if she judge wisely and command herself as she ought, she may now be easy. Excuse me, my dearest sister, for thus trespassing on your time, but I owed it to my own character; and after this explanation I trust I am in no danger of sinking in your opinion."

I could have said "Not much indeed"—but I left her almost in silence. It was the greatest stretch of forbearance I could practise. I could not have stopped myself, had I begun. Her assurance, her deceit—but I will not allow myself to dwell on them; they will strike you sufficiently. My heart sickens within me.

As soon as I was tolerably composed, I returned to the parlour. Sir James's carriage was at the door, and he, merry as usual, soon afterwards took his leave. How easily does her ladyship encourage, or dismiss a lover!

In spite of this release, Frederica still looks unhappy, still fearful perhaps of her mother's anger, and though dreading my brother's departure jealous, it may be, of his staying. I see how closely she observes him and Lady Susan. Poor girl, I have now no hope for her. There is not a chance of her affection being returned. He thinks very differently of her, from what he used to do, he does her some justice, but his reconciliation with her mother precludes every dearer hope.

Prepare my dear Madam, for the worst. The probability of their marrying is surely heightened. He is more securely hers than ever. When that wretched event takes place, Frederica must belong wholly to us.

I am thankful that my last letter will precede this by so little, as every moment that you can be saved from feeling a joy which leads only to disappointment is of consequence.

Yours ever,

Catherine Vernon

Letter 25

LADY SUSAN TO MRS. JOHNSON

Churchill

I call on you, dear Alicia, for congratulations. I am again myself—gay and triumphant. When I wrote to you the other day, I was in truth in high irritation, and with ample cause. Nay, I know not whether I ought to be quite tranquil now, for I have had more trouble in restoring peace than I ever intended to submit to. This Reginald has a proud spirit of his own!—a spirit too, resulting from a fancied sense of superior integrity which is peculiarly insolent. I shall not easily forgive him I assure you. He was actually on the point of leaving Churchill! I had scarcely concluded my last, when Wilson brought me word of it. I found therefore that something must be done, for I did not choose to have my character at the mercy of a man whose passions were so violent and resentful. It would have been trifling with my reputation, to allow of his departing with such an impression in my disfavour; in this light, condescension[1] was necessary.

I sent Wilson to say that I desired to speak with him before he went. He came immediately. The angry emotions which had marked every feature when we last parted, were partially subdued. He seemed astonished at the summons, and looked as if half wishing and half fearing to be softened by what I might say.

If my countenance expressed what I aimed at, it was composed and dignified—and yet with a degree of pensiveness which might convince him that I was not quite happy. "I beg your pardon Sir, for the liberty I have taken in sending to you", said I, "but as I have just learnt your intention of leaving this place today, I feel it my duty to entreat that you will not on my account shorten your visit here, even an hour. I am perfectly aware that after what has passed between us, it would ill suit the feelings of either to remain longer in the same house. So very great, so total a change from the intimacy of friendship, must render any future intercourse the severest punishment; and your resolution of quitting Churchill is undoubtedly in unison with our situation and with those lively feelings which I know you to possess. But at the same time, it is not for me to suffer such a sacrifice, as it must be, to leave relations to whom you are so much attached and are so dear. My remaining here cannot give that pleasure to Mr. and Mrs. Vernon which your society must; and my visit has already perhaps been too long. My removal[2] therefore, which must at any rate take place soon, may with perfect convenience be hastened; and I make it my particular request that I may not in any way be instrumental in separating a family so affectionately attached to each other. Where I go is of no consequence to anyone; of very little to myself; but you are of importance to all your connections." Here I concluded, and I hope you will be satisfied with my speech. Its effect on Reginald justifies some portion of vanity, for it was no less favourable than instantaneous. Oh! How delightful it was, to watch the variations of his countenance while I spoke, to see the struggle between returning tenderness and the remains of displeasure. There is something agreeable in feelings so easily worked on. Not that I would envy him their possession, nor would for the world have such myself, but they are very convenient when one wishes to influence the passions of another. And yet this Reginald, whom a very few words from me softened at once into the utmost submission, and rendered more tractable, more attached, more devoted than ever, would have left me in the first angry swelling of his proud heart, without deigning to seek an explanation!

Humbled as he now is, I cannot forgive him such an instance of pride; and am doubtful whether I ought not to punish him, by dismissing him at once after this our reconciliation, or by marrying and teasing him for ever. But these measures are each too violent to be adopted without some deliberation. At present my thoughts are fluctuating between various schemes. I have many things to compass.[3] I must punish Frederica, and pretty severely too, for her application to Reginald; I must punish him for receiving it so favourably, and for the rest of his conduct. I must torment my sister-in-law for the insolent triumph of her look and manner since Sir James has been dismissed—for in reconciling Reginald to me, I was not able to save that ill-fated young man—and I must make myself amends for the humiliations to which I have stooped within these few days. To effect all this I have various plans. I have also an idea of being soon in town, and whatever may be my determination as to the rest, I shall probably put that project in execution—for London will be always the fairest field of action, however my views may be directed, and at any rate, I shall there be rewarded by your society and a little dissipation for a ten weeks' penance at Churchill.

I believe I owe it to my own character, to complete the match between my daughter and Sir James, after having so long intended it. Let me know your opinion on this point. Flexibility of mind, a disposition easily biased by others, is an attribute which you know I am not very desirous of obtaining; nor has Frederica any claim to the indulgence of her whims, at the expense of her mother's

[1] *condescension* Gracious and considerate behavior.

[2] *removal* Departure.

[3] *compass* Contrive, devise.

inclination. Her idle love for Reginald too; it is surely my duty to discourage such romantic nonsense. All things considered therefore, it seems incumbent on me to take her to town, and marry her immediately to Sir James.

When my own will is effected, contrary to his, I shall have some credit in being on good terms with Reginald, which at present in fact I have not, for though he is still in my power, I have given up the very article by which our quarrel was produced, and at best, the honour of victory is doubtful.

Send me your opinion on all these matters, my dear Alicia, and let me know whether you can get lodgings to suit me within a short distance of you.

Your most attached,

S. Vernon

Letter 26

MRS. JOHNSON TO LADY SUSAN

Edward St.

I am gratified by your reference, and this is my advice; that you come to town yourself without loss of time, but that you leave Frederica behind. It would surely be much more to the purpose to get yourself well established by marrying Mr. De Courcy, than to irritate him and the rest of his family, by making her marry Sir James. You should think more of yourself, and less of your daughter. She is not of a disposition to do you credit in the world, and seems precisely in her proper place, at Churchill with the Vernons; but you are fitted for society, and it is shameful to have you exiled from it. Leave Frederica therefore to punish herself for the plague she has given you, by indulging that romantic tenderheartedness which will always ensure her misery enough; and come yourself to town, as soon as you can.

I have another reason for urging this.

Manwaring came to town last week, and has contrived, in spite of Mr. Johnson, to make opportunities of seeing me. He is absolutely miserable about you, and jealous to such a degree of De Courcy, that it would be highly unadvisable for them to meet at present; and yet if you do not allow him to see you here, I cannot answer for his not committing some great imprudence—such as going to Churchill for instance, which would be dreadful. Besides, if you take my advice, and resolve to marry De Courcy, it will be indispensably necessary for you to get Manwaring out of the way, and you only can have influence enough to send him back to his wife.

I have still another motive for your coming. Mr. Johnson leaves London next Tuesday. He is going for his health to Bath, where if the waters[1] are favourable to his constitution and my wishes, he will be laid up with the gout many weeks. During his absence we shall be able to choose our own society, and have true enjoyment.

I would ask you to Edward St. but that he once forced from me a kind of promise never to invite you to my house. Nothing but my being in the utmost distress for money, could have extorted it from me. I can get you however a very nice drawing-room-apartment in Upper Seymour St., and we may be always together, there or here, for I consider my promise to Mr. Johnson as comprehending only (at least in his absence) your not sleeping in the house.

Poor Manwaring gives me such histories of his wife's jealousy! Silly woman, to expect constancy from so charming a man! But she was always silly; intolerably so, in marrying him at all. She, the heiress of a large fortune, he without a shilling! *One* title I know she might have had, besides Baronet's. Her folly in forming the connection was so great, that though Mr. Johnson was her guardian and I do not in general share his feelings, I never can forgive her.

Adieu,

Yours, Alicia

Letter 27

MRS. VERNON TO LADY DE COURCY

Churchill

This letter, my dear mother, will be brought you by Reginald. His long visit is about to be concluded at last, but I fear the separation takes place too late to do us any good. She is going to town, to see her particular friend, Mrs. Johnson. It was at first her intention that Frederica

[1] *waters* Since Roman times the hot mineral springs at Bath in southwestern Britain have been a destination for those seeking their supposed healing powers.

should accompany her for the benefit of masters, but we overruled her there. Frederica was wretched in the idea of going, and I could not bear to have her at the mercy of her mother. Not all the masters in London could compensate for the ruin of her comfort. I should have feared too for her health, and for everything in short but her principles; *there* I believe she is not to be injured, even by her mother, or all her mother's friends; but with those friends (a very bad set I doubt not) she must have mixed, or have been left in total solitude, and I can hardly tell which would have been worse for her. If she is with her mother, moreover, she must alas! in all probability, be with Reginald—and that would be the greatest evil of all.

Here we shall in time be at peace. Our regular employments, our books and conversation, with exercise, the children, and every domestic pleasure in my power to procure her, will, I trust, gradually overcome this youthful attachment. I should not have a doubt of it, were she slighted for any other woman in the world, than her own mother.

How long Lady Susan will be in town, or whether she returns here again, I know not. I could not be cordial in my invitation; but if she chooses to come, no want of cordiality on my part will keep her away.

I could not help asking Reginald if he intended being in town this winter, as soon as I found that her ladyship's steps would be bent thither; and though he professed himself quite undetermined, there was a something in his look and voice as he spoke, which contradicted his words. I have done with lamentation. I look upon the event as so far decided, that I resign myself to it in despair. If he leaves you soon for London, everything will be concluded.

Yours affectionately,

Catherine Vernon

Letter 28

MRS. JOHNSON TO LADY SUSAN

Edward St.

My dearest friend,

I write in the greatest distress; the most unfortunate event has just taken place. Mr. Johnson has hit on the most effectual manner of plaguing us all. He had heard I imagine by some means or other, that you were soon to be in London, and immediately contrived to have such an attack of the gout, as must at least delay his journey to Bath, if not wholly prevent it. I am persuaded the gout is brought on, or kept off at pleasure; it was the same, when I wanted to join the Hamiltons to the Lakes;[1] and three years ago when I had a fancy for Bath, nothing could induce him to have a gouty symptom.

I have received yours, and have engaged the lodgings in consequence. I am pleased to find that my letter had so much effect on you, and that De Courcy is certainly your own. Let me hear from you as soon as you arrive, and in particular tell me what you mean to do with Manwaring. It is impossible to say when I shall be able to see you. My confinement must be great. It is such an abominable trick, to be ill here, instead of at Bath, that I can scarcely command myself at all. At Bath, his old aunts would have nursed him, but here it all falls upon me—and he bears pain with such patience that I have not the common excuse for losing my temper.

Yours ever,

Alicia

Letter 29

LADY SUSAN TO MRS. JOHNSON

Upper Seymour St.

My dear Alicia,

There needed not this last fit of the gout to make me detest Mr. Johnson; but now the extent of my aversion is not to be estimated. To have you confined, a nurse in his apartment! My dear Alicia, of what a mistake were you guilty in marrying a man of his age!—just old enough to be formal, ungovernable and to have the gout—too old to be agreeable, and too young to die.

I arrived last night about five, and had scarcely swallowed my dinner when Manwaring made his appearance. I will not dissemble what real pleasure his sight afforded me, nor how strongly I felt the contrast between his person and manners, and those of Reginald, to the infinite disadvantage of the latter. For an hour or two, I was even staggered in my resolution of marrying him—and though this was too idle and nonsensical an

[1] *the Lakes* The Lake District in northwestern England, renowned for its scenery, and a popular holiday destination.

idea to remain long on my mind, I do not feel very eager for the conclusion of my marriage, or look forward with much impatience to the time when Reginald according to our agreement is to be in town. I shall probably put off his arrival, under some pretence or other. He must not come till Manwaring is gone.

I am still doubtful at times, as to marriage. If the old man would die, I might not hesitate; but a state of dependance on the caprice of Sir Reginald, will not suit the freedom of my spirit; and if I resolve to wait for that event, I shall have excuse enough at present, in having been scarcely ten months a widow.

I have not given Manwaring any hint of my intention—or allowed him to consider my acquaintance with Reginald as more than the commonest flirtation; and he is tolerably appeased. Adieu till we meet. I am enchanted with my lodgings.

Yours ever,
S. Vernon

Letter 30

LADY SUSAN TO MR. DE COURCY

Upper Seymour St.

I have received your letter; and though I do not attempt to conceal that I am gratified by your impatience for the hour of meeting, I yet feel myself under the necessity of delaying that hour beyond the time originally fixed. Do not think me unkind for such an exercise of my power, or accuse me of instability, without first hearing my reasons. In the course of my journey from Churchill, I had ample leisure for reflection on the present state of our affairs, and every review has served to convince me that they require a delicacy and cautiousness of conduct, to which we have hitherto been too little attentive. We have been hurried on by our feelings to a degree of precipitance which ill accords with the claims of our friends, or the opinion of the world. We have been unguarded in forming this hasty engagement; but we must not complete the imprudence by ratifying it, while there is so much reason to fear the connection would be opposed by those friends on whom you depend.

It is not for us to blame any expectation on your father's side of your marrying to advantage; where possessions are so extensive as those of your family, the wish of increasing them, if not strictly reasonable, is too common to excite surprise or resentment. He has a right to require a woman of fortune in his daughter-in-law, and I am sometimes quarrelling with myself for suffering you to form a connection so imprudent. But the influence of reason is often acknowledged too late by those who feel like me.

I have now been but a few months a widow; and however little indebted to my husband's memory for any happiness derived from him during an union of some years, I cannot forget that the indelicacy of so early a second marriage, must subject me to the censure of the world, and incur what would be still more insupportable, the displeasure of Mr. Vernon. I might perhaps harden myself in time against the injustice of a general reproach; but the loss of his valued esteem, I am as you well know, ill fitted to endure; and when to this, may be added the consciousness of having injured you with your family, how am I to support myself? With feelings so poignant as mine, the conviction of having divided the son from his parents, would make me, even with you, the most miserable of beings.

It will surely therefore be advisable to delay our union, to delay it till appearances are more promising, till affairs have taken a more favourable turn. To assist us in such a resolution, I feel that absence will be necessary. We must not meet. Cruel as this sentence may appear, the necessity of pronouncing it, which can alone reconcile it to myself, will be evident to you when you have considered our situation in the light in which I have found myself imperiously obliged to place it. You may be, you must be well assured that nothing but the strongest conviction of duty, could induce me to wound my own feelings by urging a lengthened separation; and of insensibility to yours, you will hardly suspect me. Again therefore I say that we ought not, we must not yet meet. By a removal for some months from each other, we shall tranquillize the sisterly fears of Mrs. Vernon, who, accustomed herself to the enjoyment of riches, considers fortune as necessary every where, and whose sensibilities are not of a nature to comprehend ours.

Let me hear from you soon, very soon. Tell me that you submit to my arguments, and do not reproach me for using such. I cannot bear reproaches. My spirits are not so high as to need being repressed. I must endeavour to seek amusement abroad, and fortunately many of my friends are in town—among them, the Manwarings. You know how sincerely I regard both husband and wife.

I am ever, faithfully yours,

S. Vernon

Letter 31

LADY SUSAN TO MRS. JOHNSON

Upper Seymour St.

My dear friend,

That tormenting creature Reginald is here. My letter, which was intended to keep him longer in the country, has hastened him to town. Much as I wish him away, however, I cannot help being pleased with such a proof of attachment. He is devoted to me, heart and soul. He will carry this note himself, which is to serve as an introduction to you, with whom he longs to be acquainted. Allow him to spend the evening with you, that I may be in no danger of his returning here. I have told him that I am not quite well, and must be alone—and should he call again there might be confusion, for it is impossible to be sure of servants. Keep him therefore I entreat you in Edward St. You will not find him a heavy companion, and I allow you to flirt with him as much as you like. At the same time do not forget my real interest; say all that you can to convince him that I shall be quite wretched if he remain here; you know my reasons—propriety and so forth. I would urge them more myself, but that I am impatient to be rid of him, as Manwaring comes within half an hour. Adieu.

S.V.

Letter 32

MRS. JOHNSON TO LADY SUSAN

Edward St.

My dear creature,

I am in agonies, and know not what to do, nor what *you* can do. Mr. De Courcy arrived, just when he should not. Mrs. Manwaring had that instant entered the house, and forced herself into her guardian's presence, though I did not know a syllable of it till afterwards, for I was out when both she and Reginald came, or I would have sent him away at all events; but *she* was shut up with Mr. Johnson, while *he* waited in the drawing room for me. She arrived yesterday in pursuit of her husband; but perhaps you know this already from himself. She came to this house to entreat my husband's interference, and before I could be aware of it, everything that you could wish to be concealed, was known to him; and unluckily she had wormed out of Manwaring's servant that he had visited you every day since your being in town, and had just watched him to your door herself! What could I do? Facts are such horrid things! All is by this time known to De Courcy, who is now alone with Mr. Johnson. Do not accuse me; indeed, it was impossible to prevent it. Mr. Johnson has for some time suspected De Courcy of intending to marry you, and would speak with him alone, as soon as he knew him to be in the house.

That detestable Mrs. Manwaring, who for your comfort, had fretted herself thinner and uglier than ever, is still here, and they have been all closeted together. What can be done? If Manwaring is now with you, he had better be gone. At any rate I hope he will plague his wife more than ever. With anxious wishes,

Yours faithfully,

Alicia

Letter 33

LADY SUSAN TO MRS. JOHNSON

Upper Seymour St.

This *eclaircissement*[1] is rather provoking. How unlucky that you should have been from home! I thought myself sure of you at seven. I am undismayed however. Do not torment yourself with fears on my account. Depend upon it, I can make my own story good with Reginald. Manwaring is just gone; he brought me the news of his wife's arrival. Silly woman! what does she expect by such manoeuvres? Yet, I wish she had stayed quietly at Langford.

Reginald will be a little enraged at first, but by tomorrow's dinner, everything will be well again. Adieu.

S.V.

---

[1] *eclaircissement* Clarification (of Lady Susan's behavior).

Letter 34

MR. DE COURCY TO LADY SUSAN

Hotel

I write only to bid you farewell. The spell is removed. I see you as you are. Since we parted yesterday, I have received from indisputable authority, such an history of you as must bring the most mortifying conviction of the imposition I have been under, and the absolute necessity of an immediate and eternal separation from you. You cannot doubt to what I allude; Langford—Langford—that word will be sufficient. I received my information in Mr. Johnson's house, from Mrs. Manwaring herself.

You know how I have loved you, you can intimately judge of my present feelings; but I am not so weak as to find indulgence in describing them to a woman who will glory in having excited their anguish, but whose affection they have never been able to gain.

R. De Courcy

Letter 35

LADY SUSAN TO MR. DE COURCY

Upper Seymour St.

I will not attempt to describe my astonishment on reading the note, this moment received from you. I am bewildered in my endeavours to form some rational conjecture of what Mrs. Manwaring can have told you, to occasion so extraordinary a change in your sentiments. Have I not explained everything to you with respect to myself which could bear a doubtful meaning, and which the ill-nature of the world had interpreted to my discredit ? What can you now have heard to stagger your esteem for me? Have I ever had a concealment from you? Reginald, you agitate me beyond expression. I cannot suppose that the old story of Mrs. Manwaring's jealousy can be revived again, or at least, be listened to again. Come to me immediately, and explain what is at present absolutely incomprehensible. Believe me, the single word of *Langford* is not of such potent intelligence, as to supersede the necessity of more. If we *are* to part, it will at least be handsome to take your personal leave. But I have little heart to jest; in truth, I am serious enough—for to be sunk, though but an hour, in your opinion, is an humiliation to which I know not how to submit. I shall count every moment till your arrival.

S.V.

Letter 36

MR. DE COURCY TO LADY SUSAN

Hotel

Why would you write to me? Why do you require particulars? But since it must be so, I am obliged to declare that all the accounts of your misconduct during the life and since the death of Mr. Vernon which had reached me in common with the world in general, and gained my entire belief before I saw you, but which you by the exertion of your perverted abilities had made me resolve to disallow, have been unanswerably proved to me. Nay, more, I am assured that a connection, of which I had never before entertained a thought, has for some time existed, and still continues to exist between you and the man, whose family you robbed of its peace, in return for the hospitality with which you were received into it! That you have corresponded with him ever since your leaving Langford—not with his wife, but with him—and that he now visits you every day. Can you, dare you deny it? and all this at the time when I was an encouraged, an accepted lover! From what have I not escaped! I have only to be grateful. Far from me be all complaint, and every sigh of regret. My own folly has endangered me, my preservation I owe to the kindness, the integrity of another. But the unfortunate Mrs. Manwaring, whose agonies while she related the past, seemed to threaten her reason—how is she to be consoled?

After such a discovery as this, you will scarcely affect farther wonder at my meaning in bidding you adieu. My understanding is at length restored, and teaches me no less to abhor the artifices which had subdued me, than to despise myself for the weakness, on which their strength was founded.

R. De Courcy

Letter 37

LADY SUSAN TO MR. DE COURCY

Upper Seymour St.

I am satisfied—and will trouble you no more when these few lines are dismissed. The engagement which you were eager to form a fortnight ago, is no longer compatible with your views, and I rejoice to find that the prudent advice of your parents has not been given in vain. Your restoration to peace will, I doubt not, speedily follow this act of filial obedience, and I flatter myself with the hope of surviving my share in this disappointment.

S.V.

Letter 38

MRS. JOHNSON TO LADY SUSAN

Edward St.

I am grieved, though I cannot be astonished at your rupture with Mr. De Courcy; he has just informed Mr. Johnson of it by letter. He leaves London he says to-day. Be assured that I partake in all your feelings, and do not be angry if I say that your intercourse even by letter must soon be given up. It makes me miserable—but Mr. Johnson vows that if I persist in the connection, he will settle in the country for the rest of his life—and you know it is impossible to submit to such an extremity while any other alternative remains.

You have heard of course that the Manwarings are to part; I am afraid Mrs. M. will come home to us again. But she is still so fond of her husband and frets so much about him that perhaps she may not live long.

Miss Manwaring is just come to town to be with her aunt, and they say, that she declares she will have Sir James Martin before she leaves London again. If I were you, I would certainly get him myself. I had almost forgot to give you my opinion of De Courcy, I am really delighted with him, he is full as handsome I think as Manwaring, and with such an open, good-humoured countenance that one cannot help loving him at first sight. Mr. Johnson and he are the greatest friends in the world. Adieu, my dearest Susan. I wish matters did not go so perversely. That unlucky visit to Langford! But I dare say you did all for the best, and there is no defying destiny.

Your sincerely attached,

Alicia

Letter 39

LADY SUSAN TO MRS. JOHNSON

Upper Seymour St.

My dear Alicia,

I yield to the necessity which parts us. Under such circumstances you could not act otherwise. Our friendship cannot be impaired by it; and in happier times, when your situation is as independent as mine, it will unite us again in the same intimacy as ever. For this I shall impatiently wait; and meanwhile can safely assure you that I never was more at ease, or better satisfied with myself and everything about me, than at the present hour. Your husband I abhor—Reginald I despise—and I am secure of never seeing either again. Have I not reason to rejoice? Manwaring is more devoted to me than ever; and were he at liberty, I doubt if I could resist even matrimony offered by him. This event, if his wife live with you, it may be in your power to hasten. The violence of her feelings, which must wear her out, may be easily kept in irritation. I rely on your friendship for this. I am now satisfied that I never could have brought myself to marry Reginald; and am equally determined that Frederica never shall. Tomorrow I shall fetch her from Churchill, and let Maria Manwaring tremble for the consequence. Frederica shall be Sir James's wife before she quits my house. She may whimper, and the Vernons may storm; I regard them not. I am tired of submitting my will to the caprices of others—of resigning my own judgement in deference to those, to whom I owe no duty, and for whom I feel no respect. I have given up too much—have been too easily worked on; but Frederica shall now find the difference.

Adieu, dearest of friends. May the next gouty attack be more favourable. And may you always regard me as unalterably yours,

S. Vernon

Letter 40

LADY DE COURCY TO MRS. VERNON

Parklands

My dear Catherine,

I have charming news for you, and if I had not sent off my letter this morning, you might have been spared the vexation of knowing of Reginald's being gone to town, for he is returned, Reginald is returned, not to ask our consent to his marrying Lady Susan, but to tell us that they are parted forever! He has been only an hour in the house, and I have not been able to learn particulars, for he is so very low, that I have not the heart to ask questions; but I hope we shall soon know all. This is the most joyful hour he has ever given us, since the day of his birth. Nothing is wanting but to have you here, and it is our particular wish and entreaty that you would come to us as soon as you can. You have owed us a visit many long weeks. I hope nothing will make it inconvenient to Mr. Vernon, and pray bring all my grandchildren, and your dear niece is included of course; I long to see her. It has been a sad heavy winter hitherto, without Reginald, and seeing nobody from Churchill; I never found the season so dreary before, but this happy meeting will make us young again. Frederica runs much in my thoughts, and when Reginald has recovered his usual good spirits (as I trust he soon will), we will try to rob him of his heart once more, and I am full of hopes of seeing their hands joined at no great distance.

Your affectionate mother,

C. De Courcy

Letter 41

MRS. VERNON TO LADY DE COURCY

Churchill

My dear Madam,

Your letter has surprised me beyond measure. Can it be true that they are really separated—and for ever? I should be overjoyed if I dared depend on it, but after all that I have seen, how can one be secure? And Reginald really with you! My surprise is the greater, because on Wednesday, the very day of his coming to Parklands, we had a most unexpected and unwelcome visit from Lady Susan, looking all cheerfulness and good humour, and seeming more as if she were to marry him when she got back to town, than as if parted from him for ever. She stayed nearly two hours, was as affectionate and agreeable as ever, and not a syllable, not a hint was dropped of any disagreement or coolness between them. I asked her whether she had seen my brother since his arrival in town—not as you may suppose with any doubt of the fact—but merely to see how she looked. She immediately answered without any embarrassment that he had been kind enough to call on her on Monday, but she believed he had already returned home—which I was very far from crediting.

Your kind invitation is accepted by us with pleasure, and on Thursday next, we and our little ones will be with you. Pray heaven! Reginald may not be in town again by that time!

I wish we could bring dear Frederica too, but I am sorry to add that her mother's errand hither was to fetch her away; and miserable as it made the poor girl, it was impossible to detain her. I was thoroughly unwilling to let her go, and so was her uncle; and all that could be urged, we *did* urge. But Lady Susan declared that as she was now about to fix herself in town for several months, she could not be easy if her daughter were not with her, for masters, etc. Her manner, to be sure, was very kind and proper—and Mr. Vernon believes that Frederica will now be treated with affection. I wish I could think so too!

The poor girl's heart was almost broke at taking leave of us. I charged her to write to me very often, and to remember that if she were in any distress, we should be always her friends. I took care to see her alone, that I might say all this, and I hope made her a little more comfortable. But I shall not be easy till I can go to town and judge of her situation myself.

I wish there were a better prospect than now appears, of the match, which the conclusion of your letter declares your expectation of. At present it is not very likely.

Yours etc.,

Catherine Vernon

CONCLUSION

This correspondence, by a meeting between some of the parties and a separation between the others, could not, to the great detriment of the Post Office revenue, be continued longer. Very little assistance to the state could be derived from the epistolary intercourse of Mrs. Vernon and her niece, for the former soon perceived by the style of Frederica's letters, that they were written under her mother's inspection, and therefore deferring all particular enquiry till she could make it personally in town, ceased writing minutely[1] or often.

Having learnt enough in the meanwhile from her open-hearted brother, of what had passed between him and Lady Susan to sink the latter lower than ever in her opinion, she was proportionably more anxious to get Frederica removed from such a mother, and placed under her own care; and though with little hope of success, was resolved to leave nothing unattempted that might offer a chance of obtaining her sister-in-law's consent to it. Her anxiety on the subject made her press for an early visit to London; and Mr. Vernon, who, as it must have already appeared, lived only to do whatever he was desired, soon found some accommodating business to call him thither. With a heart full of the matter, Mrs. Vernon waited on Lady Susan, shortly after her arrival in town; and she was met with such an easy and cheerful affection as made her almost turn from her with horror. No remembrance of Reginald, no consciousness of guilt, gave one look of embarrassment. She was in excellent spirits, and seemed eager to show at once, by every possible attention to her brother and sister, her sense of their kindness, and her pleasure in their society.

Frederica was no more altered than Lady Susan; the same restrained manners, the same timid look in the presence of her mother as heretofore, assured her aunt of her situation's being uncomfortable, and confirmed her in the plan of altering it. No unkindness however on the part of Lady Susan appeared. Persecution on the subject of Sir James was entirely at an end—his name merely mentioned to say that he was not in London; and in all her conversation she was solicitous only for the welfare and improvement of her daughter, acknowledging in terms of grateful delight that Frederica was now growing every day more and more what a parent could desire.

Mrs. Vernon surprised and incredulous, knew now what to suspect, and without any change in her own views, only feared greater difficulty in accomplishing them. The first hope of anything better was derived from Lady Susan's asking her whether she thought Frederica looked quite as well as she had done at Churchill, as she must confess herself to have sometimes an anxious doubt of London's perfectly agreeing with her.

Mrs. Vernon encouraging the doubt, directly proposed her niece's returning with them into the country. Lady Susan was unable to express her sense of such kindness; yet knew not from a variety of reasons how to part with her daughter; and as, though her own plans were not yet wholly fixed, she trusted it would ere long be in her power to take Frederica into the country herself, concluded by declining entirely to profit by such unexampled attention. Mrs. Vernon however persevered in the offer of it, and though Lady Susan continued to resist, her resistance in the course of a few days seemed somewhat less formidable.

The lucky alarm of an influenza, decided what might not have been decided quite so soon. Lady Susan's maternal fears were then too much awakened for her to think of anything but Frederica's removal from the risk of infection. Above all disorders in the world, she most dreaded influenza for her daughter's constitution. Frederica returned to Churchill with her uncle and aunt, and three weeks afterwards Lady Susan announced her being married to Sir James Martin.

Mrs. Vernon was then convinced of what she had only suspected before, that she might have spared herself all the trouble of urging a removal, which Lady Susan had doubtless resolved on from the first. Frederica's visit was nominally for six weeks; but her mother, though inviting her to return in one or two affectionate letters, was very ready to oblige the whole party by consenting to a prolongation of her stay, and in the course of two months ceased to write of her absence, and in the course of two more, to write to her at all.

Frederica was therefore fixed in the family of her uncle and aunt, till such time as Reginald De Courcy could be talked, flattered and finessed into an affection for her—which, allowing leisure for the conquest of his attachment to her mother, for his abjuring all future attachments and detesting the sex, might be reasonably looked for in the course of a twelvemonth. Three months might have done it in general, but Reginald's feelings were no less lasting than lively.

Whether Lady Susan was, or was not happy in her second choice—I do not see how it can ever be ascertained—for who would take her assurance of it, on either side of the question? The world must judge from

[1] *minutely* Thoroughly.

probability. She had nothing against her, but her husband, and her conscience.

Sir James may seem to have drawn an harder lot than mere folly merited. I leave him therefore to all the pity that anybody can give him. For myself, I confess that I can pity only Miss Manwaring, who coming to town and putting herself to an expense in clothes, which impoverished her for two years, on purpose to secure him, was defrauded of her due by a woman ten years older than herself.

—1871 (WRITTEN 1793–94, 1805)

Pride and Prejudice

Pride and Prejudice, first published in 1813, has remained Austen's most popular novel. The story turns on the marriage prospects of the five daughters of Mr. And Mrs. Bennet; on the affection between the eldest, Jane, and the charming Mr. Bingley; and on the prejudice formed by Jane's sister, Elizabeth, against the proud and distant Mr. Darcy. The novel's famous opening chapters set the tone; they also provide a sense of the characteristic style of Austen's major novels.

from *Pride and Prejudice*

CHAPTER I

It is a truth universally acknowledged, that a single man in possession of a good fortune must be in want of a wife.

However little known the feelings or views of such a man may be on his first entering a neighbourhood, this truth is so well fixed in the minds of the surrounding families that he is considered as the rightful property of some one or other of their daughters.

"My dear Mr. Bennet," said his lady to him one day, "have you heard that Netherfield Park is let at last?"

Mr. Bennet replied that he had not.

"But it is," returned she; "for Mrs. Long has just been here, and she told me all about it."

Mr. Bennet made no answer.

"Do not you want to know who has taken it?" cried his wife impatiently.

"*You* want to tell me, and I have no objection to hearing it."

This was invitation enough.

"Why, my dear, you must know, Mrs. Long says that Netherfield is taken by a young man of large fortune from the north of England; that he came down on Monday in a chaise and four[1] to see the place, and was so much delighted with it that he agreed with Mr. Morris immediately; that he is to take possession before Michaelmas,[2] and some of his servants are to be in the house by the end of next week."

"What is his name?"

"Bingley."

"Is he married or single?"

"Oh! single, my dear, to be sure! A single man of large fortune; four or five thousand a year. What a fine thing for our girls!"

"How so? how can it affect them?"

"My dear Mr. Bennet," replied his wife, "how can you be so tiresome! You must know that I am thinking of his marrying one of them."

"Is that his design in settling here?"

"Design! nonsense, how can you talk so! But it is very likely that he *may* fall in love with one of them, and therefore you must visit him as soon as he comes."

"I see no occasion for that. You and the girls may go, or you may send them by themselves, which perhaps will be still better, for as you are as handsome as any of them, Mr. Bingley might like you the best of the party."

"My dear, you flatter me. I certainly *have* had my share of beauty, but I do not pretend to be anything extraordinary now. When a woman has five grown up daughters, she ought to give over thinking of her own beauty."

"In such cases, a woman has not often much beauty to think of."

"But, my dear, you must indeed go and see Mr. Bingley when he comes into the neighbourhood."

"It is more than I engage for,[3] I assure you."

---

1 *chaise and four* Traveling carriage pulled by four horses.

2 *Michaelmas* The feast of St. Michael, on 29 September.

3 *engage for* Promise to perform.

"But consider your daughters. Only think what an establishment it would be for one of them. Sir William and Lady Lucas are determined to go, merely on that account, for in general you know they visit no newcomers. Indeed you must go, for it will be impossible for *us* to visit him, if you do not."

"You are over scrupulous, surely. I dare say Mr. Bingley will be very glad to see you; and I will send a few lines by you to assure him of my hearty consent to his marrying which ever he chooses of the girls, though I must throw in a good word for my little Lizzy."

"I desire you will do no such thing. Lizzy is not a bit better than the others, and I am sure she is not half so handsome as Jane, nor half so good humoured as Lydia. But you are always giving *her* the preference."

"They have none of them much to recommend them," replied he; "they are all silly and ignorant like other girls, but Lizzy has something more of quickness than her sisters."

"Mr. Bennet, how can you abuse your own children in such a way? You take delight in vexing me. You have no compassion on my poor nerves."

"You mistake me, my dear. I have a high respect for your nerves. They are my old friends. I have heard you mention them with consideration these twenty years at least."

"Ah! you do not know what I suffer."

"But I hope you will get over it, and live to see many young men of four thousand a year come into the neighbourhood."

"It will be no use to us if twenty such should come, since you will not visit them."

"Depend upon it, my dear, that when there are twenty, I will visit them all."

Mr. Bennet was so odd a mixture of quick parts, sarcastic humour, reserve, and caprice, that the experience of three and twenty years had been insufficient to make his wife understand his character. *Her* mind was less difficult to develop. She was a woman of mean[1] understanding, little information, and uncertain temper. When she was discontented she fancied herself nervous. The business of her life was to get her daughters married; its solace was visiting and news.

[1] *mean* Modest.

Chapter 2

Mr. Bennet was among the earliest of those who waited on Mr. Bingley. He had always intended to visit him, though to the last always assuring his wife that he should not go; and till the evening after the visit was paid, she had no knowledge of it. It was then disclosed in the following manner. Observing his second daughter employed in trimming a hat, he suddenly addressed her with,

"I hope Mr. Bingley will like it, Lizzy."

"We are not in a way to know *what* Mr. Bingley likes," said her mother resentfully, "since we are not to visit."

"But you forget, mama," said Elizabeth, "that we shall meet him at the assemblies, and that Mrs. Long has promised to introduce him."

"I do not believe Mrs. Long will do any such thing. She has two nieces of her own. She is a selfish, hypocritical woman, and I have no opinion[2] of her."

"No more have I," said Mr. Bennet; "and I am glad to find that you do not depend on her serving you."

Mrs. Bennet deigned not to make any reply; but unable to contain herself, began scolding one of her daughters.

"Don't keep coughing so, Kitty, for heaven's sake! Have a little compassion on my nerves. You tear them to pieces."

"Kitty has no discretion in her coughs," said her father; "she times them ill."

"I do not cough for my own amusement," replied Kitty fretfully.

"When is your next ball to be, Lizzy?"

"Tomorrow fortnight."[3]

"Aye, so it is," cried her mother, "and Mrs. Long does not come back till the day before; so, it will be impossible for her to introduce him, for she will not know him herself."

"Then, my dear, you may have the advantage of your friend, and introduce Mr. Bingley to *her*."

"Impossible, Mr. Bennet, impossible, when I am not acquainted with him myself; how can you be so teazing?"

[2] *have no opinion of her* I.e., have no great opinion of her; regard her as unworthy.

[3] *Tomorrow fortnight* I.e., a fortnight (two weeks) from tomorrow.

"I honour your circumspection. A fortnight's acquaintance is certainly very little. One cannot know what a man really is by the end of a fortnight. But if *we* do not venture, somebody else will; and after all, Mrs. Long and her nieces must stand their chance; and therefore, as she will think it an act of kindness, if you decline the office, I will take it on myself."

The girls stared at their father. Mrs. Bennet said only, "Nonsense, nonsense!"

"What can be the meaning of that emphatic exclamation?" cried he. "Do you consider the forms of introduction, and the stress that is laid on them, as nonsense? I cannot quite agree with you *there*. What say you, Mary? for you are a young lady of deep reflection I know, and read great books, and make extracts."

Mary wished to say something very sensible, but knew not how.

"While Mary is adjusting her ideas," he continued, "let us return to Mr. Bingley."

"I am sick of Mr. Bingley," cried his wife.

"I am sorry to hear *that*; but why did not you tell me so before? If I had known as much this morning, I certainly would not have called on him. It is very unlucky, but as I have actually paid the visit, we cannot escape the acquaintance now."

The astonishment of the ladies was just what he wished; that of Mrs. Bennet perhaps surpassing the rest; though when the first tumult of joy was over, she began to declare that it was what she had expected all the while. "How good it was in you, my dear Mr. Bennet! But I knew I should persuade you at last. I was sure you loved your girls too well to neglect such an acquaintance. Well, how pleased I am! and it is such a good joke, too, that you should have gone this morning, and never said a word about it till now."

"Now, Kitty, you may cough as much as you choose," said Mr. Bennet; and, as he spoke, he left the room, fatigued with the raptures of his wife.

"What an excellent father you have, girls," said she, when the door was shut. "I do not know how you will ever make him amends for his kindness; or me either, for that matter. At our time of life, it is not so pleasant, I can tell you, to be making new acquaintance every day; but for your sakes, we would do anything. Lydia, my love, though you *are* the youngest, I dare say Mr. Bingley will dance with you at the next ball."

"Oh!" said Lydia stoutly, "I am not afraid; for though I *am* the youngest, I'm the tallest."

The rest of the evening was spent in conjecturing how soon he would return Mr. Bennet's visit, and determining when they should ask him to dinner.

Chapter 3

Not all that Mrs. Bennet, however, with the assistance of her five daughters, could ask on the subject was sufficient to draw from her husband any satisfactory description of Mr. Bingley. They attacked him in various ways: with barefaced questions, ingenious suppositions, and distant surmises; but he eluded the skill of them all, and they were at last obliged to accept the second-hand intelligence of their neighbour Lady Lucas. Her report was highly favourable. Sir William had been delighted with him. He was quite young, wonderfully handsome, extremely agreeable, and to crown the whole, he meant to be at the next assembly with a large party. Nothing could be more delightful! To be fond of dancing was a certain step towards falling in love; and very lively hopes of Mr. Bingley's heart were entertained.

"If I can but see one of my daughters happily settled at Netherfield," said Mrs. Bennet to her husband, "and all the others equally well married, I shall have nothing to wish for."

In a few days Mr. Bingley returned Mr. Bennet's visit, and sat about ten minutes with him in his library. He had entertained hopes of being admitted to a sight of the young ladies, of whose beauty he had heard much; but he saw only the father. The ladies were somewhat more fortunate, for they had the advantage of ascertaining, from an upper window, that he wore a blue coat and rode a black horse.

An invitation to dinner was soon afterwards dispatched; and already had Mrs. Bennet planned the courses that were to do credit to her housekeeping, when an answer arrived which deferred it all. Mr. Bingley was obliged to be in town the following day, and consequently unable to accept the honour of their invitation, &c. Mrs. Bennet was quite disconcerted. She could not imagine what business he could have in town so soon after his arrival in Hertfordshire, and she began to fear that he might be always flying about from one place to another, and never settled at Netherfield as he ought to be. Lady Lucas quieted her fears a little by starting the idea of his being gone to London only to get a large party for the ball; and a report soon followed that Mr. Bingley was to bring twelve ladies and seven gentlemen with him to the assembly. The girls grieved over such a large number of ladies, but were comforted the day before the ball by hearing that, instead of twelve, he had brought only six with him from London, his five sisters and a cousin. And when the party entered the assembly room, it consisted of only five altogether; Mr. Bingley, his two sisters, the husband of the eldest, and another young man.

Mr. Bingley was good looking and gentlemanlike; he had a pleasant countenance, and easy, unaffected manners. His sisters were fine women, with an air of decided fashion. His brother-in-law, Mr. Hurst, merely looked the gentleman; but his friend Mr. Darcy soon drew the attention of the room by his fine, tall person, handsome features, noble mien,[1] and the report which was in general circulation within five minutes after his entrance, of his having ten thousand a year. The gentlemen pronounced him to be a fine figure of a man, the ladies declared he was much handsomer than Mr. Bingley, and he was looked at with great admiration for about half the evening, till his manners gave a disgust which turned the tide of his popularity; for he was discovered to be proud, to be above his company, and above being pleased; and not all his large estate in Derbyshire could then save him from having a most forbidding, disagreeable countenance, and being unworthy to be compared with his friend.

Mr. Bingley had soon made himself acquainted with all the principal people in the room; he was lively and unreserved, danced every dance, was angry that the ball closed so early, and talked of giving one himself at Netherfield. Such amiable qualities must speak for themselves. What a contrast between him and his friend! Mr. Darcy danced only once with Mrs. Hurst and once with Miss Bingley, declined being introduced to any other lady, and spent the rest of the evening in walking about the room, speaking occasionally to one of his own party. His character was decided. He was the proudest, most disagreeable man in the world, and everybody hoped that he would never come there again. Amongst the most violent against him was Mrs. Bennet, whose dislike of his general behaviour was sharpened into particular resentment by his having slighted one of her daughters.

Elizabeth Bennet had been obliged, by the scarcity of gentlemen, to sit down for two dances; and during part of that time, Mr. Darcy had been standing near enough for her to overhear a conversation between him and Mr. Bingley, who came from the dance for a few minutes to press his friend to join it.

"Come, Darcy," said he, "I must have you dance. I hate to see you standing about by yourself in this stupid manner. You had much better dance."

"I certainly shall not. You know how I detest it, unless I am particularly acquainted with my partner. At such an assembly as this, it would be insupportable. Your sisters are engaged, and there is not another woman in the room whom it would not be a punishment to me to stand up with."

"I would not be so fastidious as you are," cried Bingley, "for a kingdom! Upon my honour, I never met with so many pleasant girls in my life as I have this evening; and there are several of them you see uncommonly pretty."

"*You* are dancing with the only handsome girl in the room," said Mr. Darcy, looking at the eldest Miss Bennet.

"Oh! she is the most beautiful creature I ever beheld! But there is one of her sisters sitting down just behind you who is very pretty, and, I dare say, very agreeable. Do let me ask my partner to introduce you."

"Which do you mean?" and turning round, he looked for a moment at Elizabeth, till, catching her eye, he withdrew his own and coldly said, "She is tolerable; but not handsome enough to tempt *me*; and I am in no humour at present to give consequence to young ladies who are slighted by other men. You had better return to your partner and enjoy her smiles, for you are wasting your time with me."

[1] *mien* Bearing.

Mr. Bingley followed his advice. Mr. Darcy walked off, and Elizabeth remained with no very cordial feelings towards him. She told the story however with great spirit among her friends; for she had a lively, playful disposition, which delighted in anything ridiculous.

The evening altogether passed off pleasantly to the whole family. Mrs. Bennet had seen her eldest daughter much admired by the Netherfield party. Mr. Bingley had danced with her twice, and she had been distinguished by his sisters. Jane was as much gratified by this as her mother could be, though in a quieter way. Elizabeth felt Jane's pleasure. Mary had heard herself mentioned to Miss Bingley as the most accomplished girl in the neighbourhood; and Catherine and Lydia had been fortunate enough to be never without partners, which was all that they had yet learnt to care for at a ball. They returned therefore in good spirits to Longbourn, the village where they lived, and of which they were the principal inhabitants. They found Mr. Bennet still up. With a book he was regardless of time; and on the present occasion he had a good deal of curiosity as to the event of an evening which had raised such splendid expectations. He had rather hoped that all his wife's views on the stranger would be disappointed; but he soon found that he had a very different story to hear.

"Oh! my dear Mr. Bennet," as she entered the room, "we have had a most delightful evening, a most excellent ball. I wish you had been there. Jane was so admired, nothing could be like it. Everybody said how well she looked; and Mr. Bingley thought her quite beautiful, and danced with her twice. Only think of *that* my dear; he actually danced with her twice, and she was the only creature in the room that he asked a second time. First of all, he asked Miss Lucas. I was so vexed to see him stand up with her; but, however, he did not admire her at all—indeed, nobody can, you know—and he seemed quite struck with Jane as she was going down the dance. So, he enquired who she was, and got introduced, and asked her for the two next. Then, the two third he danced with Miss King, and the two fourth with Maria Lucas, and the two fifth with Jane again, and the two sixth with Lizzy, and the Boulanger."[1]

[1] *Boulanger* French dance, performed by a circle of couples, in which each person dances briefly with each member of the opposite sex. The boulanger was the closing dance at balls.

"If he had had any compassion for *me*," cried her husband impatiently, "he would not have danced half so much! For God's sake, say no more of his partners. Oh! that he had sprained his ankle in the first dance!"

"Oh! my dear," continued Mrs. Bennet, "I am quite delighted with him. He is so excessively handsome! and his sisters are charming women. I never in my life saw anything more elegant than their dresses. I dare say the lace upon Mrs. Hurst's gown—"

Here she was interrupted again. Mr. Bennet protested against any description of finery. She was therefore obliged to seek another branch of the subject, and related, with much bitterness of spirit and some exaggeration, the shocking rudeness of Mr. Darcy.

"But I can assure you," she added, "that Lizzy does not lose much by not suiting *his* fancy; for he is a most disagreeable, horrid man, not at all worth pleasing. So high and so conceited that there was no enduring him! He walked here, and he walked there, fancying himself so very great! Not handsome enough to dance with! I wish you had been there, my dear, to have given him one of your set downs. I quite detest the man."

CHAPTER 4

When Jane and Elizabeth were alone, the former, who had been cautious in her praise of Mr. Bingley before, expressed to her sister how very much she admired him.

"He is just what a young man ought to be," said she, "sensible, good humoured, lively; and I never saw such happy manners!—so much ease, with such perfect good breeding!"

"He is also handsome," replied Elizabeth, "which a young man ought likewise to be, if he possibly can. His character is thereby complete."

"I was very much flattered by his asking me to dance a second time. I did not expect such a compliment."

"Did not you? *I* did for you. But that is one great difference between us. Compliments always take *you* by surprise, and *me* never. What could be more natural than his asking you again? He could not help seeing that you were about five times as pretty as every other women in the room. No thanks to his gallantry for that. Well, he certainly is very agreeable, and I give you leave to like him. You have liked many a stupider person."

"Dear Lizzy!"

"Oh! you are a great deal too apt, you know, to like people in general. You never see a fault in anybody. All the world are good and agreeable in your eyes. I never heard you speak ill of a human being in my life."

"I would wish not to be hasty in censuring anyone; but I always speak what I think."

"I know you do; and it is *that* which makes the wonder. With *your* good sense, to be honestly blind to the follies and nonsense of others! Affectation of candour is common enough; one meets it everywhere. But to be candid without ostentation or design—to take the good of everybody's character and make it still better, and say nothing of the bad—belongs to you alone. And so, you like this man's sisters too, do you? Their manners are not equal to his."

"Certainly not, at first. But they are very pleasing women when you converse with them. Miss Bingley is to live with her brother and keep his house; and I am much mistaken if we shall not find a very charming neighbour in her."

Elizabeth listened in silence, but was not convinced; their behaviour at the assembly had not been calculated to please in general; and with more quickness of observation and less pliancy of temper than her sister, and with a judgment too unassailed by any attention to herself, she was very little disposed to approve them. They were in fact very fine ladies; not deficient in good humour when they were pleased, nor in the power of being agreeable where they chose it; but proud and conceited. They were rather handsome, had been educated in one of the first private seminaries in town, had a fortune of twenty thousand pounds, were in the habit of spending more than they ought, and of associating with people of rank; and were therefore in every respect entitled to think well of themselves, and meanly of others. They were of a respectable family in the north of England, a circumstance more deeply impressed on their memories than that their brother's fortune and their own had been acquired by trade.

Mr. Bingley inherited property to the amount of nearly an hundred thousand pounds from his father, who had intended to purchase an estate, but did not live to do it. Mr. Bingley intended it likewise, and sometimes made choice of his county; but as he was now provided with a good house and the liberty of a manor, it was doubtful to many of those who best knew the easiness of his temper, whether he might not spend the remainder of his days at Netherfield, and leave the next generation to purchase.

His sisters were very anxious for his having an estate of his own; but though he was now established only as a tenant, Miss Bingley was by no means unwilling to preside at his table, nor was Mrs. Hurst, who had married a man of more fashion than fortune, less disposed to consider his house as her home when it suited her. Mr. Bingley had not been of age two years when he was tempted by an accidental recommendation to look at Netherfield House. He did look at it and into it for half an hour, was pleased with the situation and the principal rooms, satisfied with what the owner said in its praise, and took it immediately.

Between him and Darcy there was a very steady friendship, in spite of a great opposition of character. Bingley was endeared to Darcy by the easiness, openness, ductility of his temper—though no disposition could offer a greater contrast to his own, and though with his own he never appeared dissatisfied. On the strength of Darcy's regard Bingley had the firmest reliance, and of his judgment the highest opinion. In understanding, Darcy was the superior. Bingley was by no means deficient, but Darcy was clever. He was at the same time haughty, reserved, and fastidious, and his manners, though well bred, were not inviting. In that respect his friend had greatly the advantage. Bingley was sure of being liked wherever he appeared; Darcy was continually giving offence.

The manner in which they spoke of the Meryton assembly was sufficiently characteristic. Bingley had never met with pleasanter people or prettier girls in his life; every ody had been most kind and attentive to him, there had been no formality, no stiffness, he had soon felt acquainted with all the room; and as to Miss Bennet, he could not conceive an angel more beautiful. Darcy, on the contrary, had seen a collection of people in whom there was little beauty and no fashion, for none of whom he had felt the smallest interest, and from none received either attention or pleasure. Miss Bennet he acknowledged to be pretty, but she smiled too much.

Mrs. Hurst and her sister allowed it to be so—but still they admired her and liked her, and pronounced her to be a sweet girl, and one whom they should not object to know more of. Miss Bennet was therefore established as a sweet girl, and their brother felt authorised by such commendation to think of her as he chose.

—1811 (WRITTEN 1796-97)

IN CONTEXT

Austen's Letters

Though there is little in the correspondence that has come down to us that sheds direct light on Jane Austen novels, Austen's letters are of considerable interest both in the impressions they give us of the daily life of the time and in comments Austen makes about writing—far more often the writing of others than her own work. The following sampling includes two letters to her sister Cassandra, one to her niece, Anna Austen Lefroy, the latter written in response to her niece having sent her a manuscript, and one to her nephew, James-Edward Austen, who later wrote *A Memoir of Jane Austen.*

Steventon: Monday night [24 December 1798]

My Dear Cassandra,[1]

I have got some pleasant news for you which I am eager to communicate, and therefore begin my letter sooner, though I shall not *send* it sooner than usual.

Admiral Gambier,[2] in reply to my father's application, writes as follows:—"As it is usual to keep young officers in small vessels, it being most proper on account of their inexperience, and it being also a situation where they are more in the way of learning their duty, your son has been continued in the 'Scorpion'; but I have mentioned to the Board of Admiralty his wish to be in a frigate, and when a proper opportunity offers and it is judged that he has taken his turn in a small ship, I hope he will be removed. With regard to your son now in the 'London' I am glad I can give you the assurance that his promotion is likely to take place very soon, as Lord Spencer has been so good as to say he would include him in an arrangement that he proposes making in a short time relative to some promotions in that quarter."[3]

There! I may now finish my letter and go and hang myself, for I am sure I can neither write nor do anything which will not appear insipid to you after this. *Now* I really think he will soon be made, and only wish we could communicate our foreknowledge of the event to him whom it principally concerns.[4] My father has written to Daysh[5] to desire that he will inform us, if he can, when the commission is sent. Your chief wish is now ready to be accomplished; and could Lord Spencer give happiness to Martha[6] at the same time, what a joyful heart he would make of yours!

---

[1] *Cassandra* Austen's elder sister and dear friend.

[2] *Admiral Gambier* James Gambier, first Baron, and Lord of the Admiralty. He was related by marriage to the Austens.

[3] *"As it is usual … in that quarter"* Two of Jane Austen's brothers, Francis-William ("Frank") and Charles-John ("Charles") served in the British Navy.

[4] *him whom it principally concerns* Frank.

[5] *Daysh* George Daysh of the Navy Office.

[6] *Martha* Martha Lloyd, whom Frank married thirty years later (a second marriage).

I have sent the same extract of the sweets of Gambier to Charles, who, poor fellow, though he sinks into nothing but an humble attendant on the hero of the piece, will, I hope, be contented with the prospect held out to him. By what the Admiral says, it appears as if he had been designedly kept in the "Scorpion." But I will not torment myself with conjectures and suppositions; facts shall satisfy me.

Frank had not heard from any of us for ten weeks when he wrote to me on November 12 in consequence of Lord St. Vincent[1] being removed to Gibraltar. When his commission is sent, however, it will not be so long on its road as our letters, because all the Government despatches are forwarded by land to his lordship from Lisbon with great regularity.

I returned from Manydown[2] this morning, and found my mother certainly in no respect worse than when I left her. She does not like the cold weather, but that we cannot help. I spent my time very quietly and very pleasantly with Catherine. Miss Blackford[3] is agreeable enough. I do not want people to be very agreeable, as it saves me the trouble of liking them a great deal. I found only Catherine and her when I got to Manydown on Thursday. We dined together and went together to Worting to seek the protection of Mrs. Clarke, with whom were Lady Mildmay, her eldest son, and a Mr. and Mrs. Hoare.

Our ball was very thin, but by no means unpleasant. There were thirty-one people, and only eleven ladies out of the number, and but five single women in the room. Of the gentlemen present you may have some idea from the list of my partners—Mr. Wood, G. Lefroy, Rice, a Mr. Butcher (belonging to the Temples, a sailor and not of the 11th Light Dragoons), Mr. Temple (not the horrid one of all), Mr. Wm. Orde (cousin to the Kingsclere man), Mr. John Harwood, and Mr. Calland, who appeared as usual with his hat in his hand, and stood every now and then behind Catherine and me to be talked to and abused for not dancing. We teased him, however, into it at last. I was very glad to see him again after so long a separation, and he was altogether rather the genius and flirt of the evening. He inquired after you.

There were twenty dances, and I danced them all, and without any fatigue. I was glad to find myself capable of dancing so much, and with so much satisfaction as I did; from my slender enjoyment of the Ashford balls (as assemblies for dancing) I had not thought myself equal to it, but in cold weather and with few couples I fancy I could just as well dance for a week together as for half an hour. My black cap was openly admired by Mrs. Lefroy, and secretly I imagine by everybody else in the room.

Tuesday. [25 December 1798]—I thank you for your long letter, which I will endeavour to deserve by writing the rest of this as closely as possible. I am full of joy at much of your information; that you should have been to a ball, and have danced at it, and supped with the Prince,[4] and that you should meditate the purchase of a new muslin gown, are delightful circumstances. *I* am determined to buy a handsome one whenever I can, and I am so tired and ashamed of half my present stock, that I even blush at the sight of the wardrobe which contains them. But I will not be much longer libelled by the possession of my coarse spot; I shall turn it into a petticoat very soon. I wish you a merry Christmas, but *no* compliments of the season.

Poor Edward! It is very hard that he, who has everything else in the world that he can wish for, should not have good health too.[5] But I hope with the assistance of stomach complaints, faintnesses, and sicknesses, he will soon be restored to that blessing likewise. If his nervous complaint proceeded from a

---

[1] *Lord St. Vincent* Admiral John Jervis, 1st Earl of St. Vincent, commanded the British fleet in the Mediterranean.

[2] *Manydown* The manor house of the Bigg-Wither family in Wooton St. Lawrence, Hants. Elizabeth, Catherine, and Alethea Bigg were friends of Jane and Cassandra Austen.

[3] *Miss Blackford* The Blachfords (sic) were cousins of the Bigg-Withers'.

[4] *the Prince* Prince William-Frederick, second Duke of Gloucester. Prince William-Frederick was also a Major-General and would have been in Kent because of his military duties.

[5] *Poor Edward! … too* Edward Austen, Jane's brother, was adopted by a cousin, Thomas Knight, and made heir to Knight's three estates.

suppression of something that ought to be thrown out, which does not seem unlikely, the first of these disorders may really be a remedy, and I sincerely wish it may, for I know no one more deserving of happiness without alloy than Edward is.

I cannot determine what to do about my new gown; I wish such things were to be bought ready-made. I have some hopes of meeting Martha at the christening at Deane[1] next Tuesday, and shall see what she can do for me. I want to have something suggested which will give me no trouble of thought or direction.

Again I return to my joy that you danced at Ashford, and that you supped with the Prince. I can perfectly comprehend Mrs. Cage's distress and perplexity. She has all those kind of foolish and incomprehensible feelings which would make her fancy herself uncomfortable in such a party. I love her, however, in spite of all her nonsense. Pray give "t'other Miss Austen's" compliments to Edward Bridges when you see him again.

I insist upon your persevering in your intention of buying a new gown; I am sure you must want one, and as you will have 5*l.* due in a week's time, I am certain you may afford it very well, and if you think you cannot, I will give you the body-lining.

Of my charities to the poor since I came home you shall have a faithful account. I have given a pair of worsted stockings to Mary Hutchins, Dame Kew, Mary Steevens, and Dame Staples; a shift to Hannah Staples, and a shawl to Betty Dawkins; amounting in all to about half a guinea. But I have no reason to suppose that the *Battys* would accept of anything, because I have not made them the offer.

I am glad to hear such a good account of Harriet Bridges; she goes on now as young ladies of seventeen ought to do, admired and admiring, in a much more rational way than her three elder sisters, who had so little of that kind of youth.[2] I dare say she fancies Major Elkington as agreeable as Warren, and if she can think so, it is very well.

I was to have dined at Keane to-day, but the weather is so cold that I am not sorry to be kept at home by the appearance of snow. We are to have company to dinner on Friday: the three Digweeds and James. We shall be a nice silent party, I suppose. Seize upon the scissors as soon as you possibly can on the receipt of this. I only fear your being too late to secure the prize.

The Lords of the Admiralty will have enough of our applications at present, for I hear from Charles that he has written to Lord Spencer[3] himself to be removed. I am afraid his Serene Highness will be in a passion, and order some of our heads to be cut off.

My mother wants to know whether Edward has ever made the hen-house which they planned together. I am rejoiced to hear from Martha that they certainly continue at Ibthorp, and I have just heard that I am sure of meeting Martha at the christening.

You deserve a longer letter than this; but it is my unhappy fate seldom to treat people so well as they deserve … God bless you!

Yours affectionately,

Jane Austen

---

[1] *christening at Deane* That of James-Edward Austen-Leigh, son of Austen's brother James and author of *A Memoir of Jane Austen*.

[2] *Harriet Bridges … that kind of youth* Harriet Bridges' sisters married young, and two of them died young.

[3] *Lord Spencer* George John, Second Earl Spencer, First Lord of the Admiralty 1794–1826.

Rolinda Sharples, *The Cloakroom, Clifton Assembly Rooms* (detail), c. 1815.
This painting conveys a vivid sense of the atmosphere of English social gatherings in the early nineteenth century.

The famous Mrs. Siddons (Sarah Kemble), whom Austen expresses regret at not having seen, is portrayed in this Thomas Rowlandson drawing in rehearsal, with her father, Roger Kemble.

Drawing attributed to Cassandra Austen (sister of Jane), of Austen's niece, Fanny Knight, painting a watercolor, c. 1814.

Sloane St.:[1] Thursday [25 April 1811]

My Dearest Cassandra,

I can return the compliment by thanking you for the unexpected pleasure of *your* letter yesterday, and as I like unexpected pleasure, it made me very happy; and, indeed, you need not apologise for your letter in any respect, for it is all very fine, but not *too* fine, I hope, to be written again, or something like it.

I think Edward will not suffer much longer from heat; by the look of things this morning I suspect the weather is rising into the balsamic north-east. It has been hot here, as you may suppose, since it was so hot with you, but I have not suffered from it at all, nor felt it in such a degree as to make me imagine it would be anything in the country. Everybody has talked of the heat, but I set it all down to London.

I give you joy of our new nephew,[2] and hope if he ever comes to be hanged it will not be till we are too old to care about it. It is a great comfort to have it so safely and speedily over. The Miss Curlings[3] must be hard worked in writing so many letters, but the novelty of it may recommend it to *them*; mine was from Miss Eliza, and she says that my brother[4] may arrive to-day.

No, indeed, I am never too busy to think of S. & S.[5] I can no more forget it than a mother can forget her sucking child; and I am much obliged to you for your inquiries. I have had two sheets to correct, but the last only brings us to Willoughby's first appearance.[6] Mrs. K.[7] regrets in the most flattering manner that she must wait *till* May, but I have scarcely a hope of its being out in June. Henry does not neglect it; he *has* hurried the printer, and says he will see him again to-day. It will not stand still during his absence, it will be sent to Eliza.[8]

The *Incomes* remain as they were, but I will get them altered if I can. I am very much gratified by Mrs. K's interest in it; and whatever may be the event of it as to my credit with her, sincerely wish her curiosity could be satisfied sooner than is now probable. I think she will like my Elinor, but cannot build on anything else.

Our party went off extremely well. There were many solicitudes, alarms, and vexations, beforehand, of course, but at last everything was quite right. The rooms were dressed up with flowers, &c., and looked very pretty. A glass for the mantlepiece was lent by the man who is making their own. Mr. Egerton and Mr. Walter came at half-past five, and the festivities began with a pair of very fine soals.

Yes, Mr. Walter—for he postponed his leaving London on purpose—which did not give much pleasure at the time, any more than the circumstance from which it rose—his calling on Sunday and being asked by Henry to take the family dinner on that day, which he did; but it is all smoothed over now, and she likes him very well.

At half-past seven arrived the musicians in two hackney coaches, and by eight the lordly company began to appear. Among the earliest were George and Mary Cooke, and I spent the greater part of the evening very pleasantly with them. The drawing-room being soon hotter than we liked, we placed ourselves in the connecting passage, which was comparatively cool, and gave us all the advantage of the music at a pleasant distance, as well as that of the first view of every new comer.

---

1 *Sloane St.* Home of Austen's brother Henry-Thomas Austen, in London.

2 *our new nephew* Henry Edgar Austen, second son of Francis-William Austen (Frank).

3 *Miss Curlings* Cousins of Mary Gibson, Frank's wife.

4 *my brother* Frank Austen.

5 *S & S* Austen's novel *Sense and Sensibility.*

6 *Willoughby* The character Willoughby first appears in *Sense and Sensibility* in Book 1, chapter 9.

7 *Mrs. K.* Catherine Knight, who adopted Austen's brother Edward with her husband, Thomas Knight.

8 *Eliza* Henry's wife Eliza.

I was quite surrounded by acquaintances, especially gentlemen; and what with Mr. Hampson, Mr. Seymour, Mr. W. Knatchbull, Mr. Guillemarde, Mr. Cure, a Captain Simpson, brother to *the* Captain Simpson, besides Mr. Walter and Mr. Egerton, in addition to the Cookes, and Miss Beckford, and Miss Middleton, I had quite as much upon my hands as I could do.

Poor Miss B. has been suffering again from her old complaint, and looks thinner than ever. She certainly goes to Cheltenham the beginning of June. We were all delight and cordiality of course. Miss M. seems very happy, but has not beauty enough to figure in London.

Including everybody we were sixty-six— which was considerably more than Eliza had expected, and quite enough to fill the back drawing-room and leave a few to be scattered about in the other and in the passage.

The music was extremely good. It opened (tell Fanny) with "Prike de Parp pirs praise of Prapela"; and of the other glees I remember, "In peace love tunes," "Rosabelle," "The Red Cross Knight," and "Poor Insect."[1] Between the songs were lessons on the harp, or harp and pianoforte together; and the harp-player was Wiepart, whose name seems famous, though new to me. There was one female singer, a short Miss Davis, all in blue, bringing up for the public line, whose voice was said to be very fine indeed; and all the performers gave great satisfaction by doing what they were paid for, and giving themselves no airs. No amateur could be persuaded to do anything.

The house was not clear till after twelve. If you wish to hear more of it, you must put your questions, but I seem rather to have exhausted than spared the subject.

This said Captain Simpson told us, on the authority of some other Captain just arrived from Halifax, that Charles was bringing the "Cleopatra" home, and that she was probably by this time in the Channel; but, as Captain S. was certainly in liquor, we must not quite depend on it. It must give one a sort of expectation, however, and will prevent my writing to him any more. I would rather he should not reach England till I am at home, and the Steventon party gone.

My mother and Martha both write with great satisfaction of Anna's[2] behaviour. She is quite an Anna with variations, but she cannot have reached her last, for that is always the most flourishing and showy; she is at about her third or fourth, which are generally simple and pretty.

Your lilacs are in *leaf*, are in bloom. The horse-chestnuts are quite out, and the elms almost. I had a pleasant walk in Kensington Gardens on Sunday with Henry, Mr. Smith, and Mr. Tilson; everything was fresh and beautiful.

We *did* go to the play after all on Saturday. We went to the Lyceum, and saw the "Hypocrite,"[3] an old play taken from Molière's "Tartuffe," and were well entertained. Dowton and Mathews were the good actors; Mrs. Edwin was the heroine, and her performance is just what it used to be. I have no chance of seeing Mrs. Siddons; she *did* act on Monday, but, as Henry was told by the boxkeeper that he did not think she would, the plans, and all thought of it, were given up. I should particularly have liked seeing her in "Constance,"[4] and could swear at her with little effort for disappointing me.

Henry has been to the Water-Colour Exhibition,[5] which opened on Monday, and is to meet us there again some morning. If Eliza cannot go (and she has a cold at present) Miss Beaty will be invited to be

[1] *"Prike de Parp"* "Strike the Harp," a chorus by Sir Henry Rowley Bishop; *"In peace love tunes"* A glee by J. Attwood; *"Rosabelle"* A glee by John Wall Callcott; *"The Red Cross Knight"* By Callcott; *"Poor Insect"* "The May Fly," by Calcott.

[2] *Anna* James Austen's eldest child, and recipient of the following letter.

[3] *"Hypocrite"* A play by Isaac Bickerstaffe.

[4] *Mrs. Siddons … Constance* I.e., Austen would have liked to have seen the famous actress, Sarah Siddons, in the role of Constance in Shakespeare's *King John*, one of Siddons' greatest triumphs.

[5] *Water-Colour Exhibition* The annual exhibition of the Society of Painters in Watercolours, established in 1805.

my companion. Henry leaves town on Sunday afternoon, but he means to write soon himself to Edward, and will tell his own plans.

The tea is this moment setting out.

Do not have your coloured muslin unless you really want it, because I am afraid I could not send it to the coach without giving trouble here.

Eliza caught her cold on Sunday in our way to the D'Entraigues.[1] The horses actually gibbed on this side of Hyde Park Gate: a load of fresh gravel made it a formidable hill to them, and they refused the collar; I believe there was a sore shoulder to irritate. Eliza was frightened and we got out, and were detained in the evening air several minutes. The cold is in her chest, but she takes care of herself, and I hope it may not last long.

This engagement prevented Mr. Walter's staying late— he had his coffee and went away. Eliza enjoyed her evening very much, and means to cultivate the acquaintance; and I see nothing to dislike in them but their taking quantities of snuff. Monsieur, the old Count, is a very fine-looking man, with quiet manners, good enough for an Englishman, and, I believe, is a man of great information and taste. He has some fine paintings, which delighted Henry as much as the son's music gratified Eliza; and among them a miniature of Philip V of Spain, Louis XIV's grandson, which exactly suited *my* capacity. Count Julien's performance is very wonderful.

We met only Mrs. Latouche and Miss East, and we are just now engaged to spend next Sunday evening at Mrs. L.'s, and to meet the D'Entraigues, but M. le Comte must do without Henry. If he would but speak English, *I* would take to him.

Have you ever mentioned the leaving off tea to Mrs. K.? Eliza has just spoken of it again. The *benefit* she has found from it in sleeping has been very great.

I shall write soon to Catherine to fix my day, which will be Thursday. We have no engagement but for Sunday. Eliza's cold makes quiet advisable. Her party is mentioned in this morning's paper. I am sorry to hear of poor Fanny's state.[2] From *that* quarter, I suppose, is to be the alloy of her happiness. I *will* have no more to say.

Yours affectionately,

J.A.

10–18 August 1814

My Dear Anna,

I am quite ashamed to find that I have never answered some question of yours in a former note. I kept it on purpose to refer to it at a proper time and then forgot it. I like the name "Which is the Heroine" very well, and I daresay shall grow to like it very much in time; but "Enthusiasm" was something so very superior that my common title must appear to disadvantage. I am not sensible of any blunders about Dawlish;[3] the library was pitiful and wretched twelve years ago and not likely to have anybody's publications.... There is no such title as Desborough either among dukes, marquises, earls, viscounts, or barons. These were your inquiries. I will now thank you for your envelope received this morning.... Your Aunt Cass is as well pleased with St. Julian as ever, and I am delighted with the idea of seeing Progillian again.

[1] *the D'Entraigues* The family of Comte Emmanuel-Lewis D'Antraigues, scholar, spy, forger, and double-agent for the French and English governments.

[2] *poor Fanny's state* Austen's sister-in-law Fanny, wife of her brother Charles, was pregnant with her third child. Fanny would give birth four times within six years. She died, aged 24, in childbirth.

[3] *Dawlish* On the south coast of Devon in southwest England.

Wednesday 17.—We have just finished the first of the three books I had the pleasure of receiving yesterday. *I* read it aloud and we are all very much amused, and like the work quite as well as ever. I depend on getting through another book before dinner, but there is really a good deal of respectable reading in your forty-eight pages. I have no doubt six would make a very good-sized volume. You must have been quite pleased to have accomplished so much. I like Lord Portman and his brother very much. I am only afraid that Lord P.'s good nature will make most people like him better than he deserves. The whole family are very good, and Lady Anne, who was your great dread, you have succeeded particularly well with. Bell Griffin is just what she should be. My corrections have not been more important than before; here and there we have thought the sense could be expressed in fewer words, and I have scratched out Sir Thos. from walking with the others to the stables, &c. the very day after breaking his arm; for, though I find your papa *did* walk out immediately after *his* arm was set, I think it can be so little usual as to *appear* unnatural in a book. Lyme will not do. Lyme is towards forty miles from Dawlish and would not be talked of there. I have put Starcross instead. If you prefer Exeter, that must be always safe.[1]

I have also scratched out the introduction between Lord Portman and his brother and Mr. Griffin. A country surgeon (don't tell Mr. C. Lyford) would not be introduced to men of their rank, and when Mr. P. is first brought in, he would not be introduced as the Honourable. That distinction is never mentioned at such times, at least I believe not. Now we have finished the second book, or rather the fifth. I *do* think you had better omit Lady Helena's postscript. To those that are acquainted with "Pride and Prejudice" it will seem an imitation. And your Aunt C. and I both recommend your making a little alteration in the last scene between Devereux F. and Lady Clanmurray and her daughter. We think they press him too much, more than sensible or well-bred women would do; Lady C., at least, should have discretion enough to be sooner satisfied with his determination of not going with them. I am very much pleased with Egerton as yet. I did not expect to like him, but I do, and Susan is a very nice little animated creature; but St. Julian is the delight of our lives. He is quite interesting. The whole of his break off with Lady Helena is very well done. Yes; Russell Square is a very proper distance from Berkeley Square.[2] We are reading the last book. They must be *two* days going from Dawlish to Bath. They are nearly 100 miles apart.

Thursday.— We finished it last night after our return from drinking tea at the Great House. The last chapter does not please us quite so well; we do not thoroughly like the play, perhaps from having had too much of plays in that way lately, and we think you had better not leave England. Let the Portmans go to Ireland; but as you know nothing of the manners there, you had better not go with them. You will be in danger of giving false representations. Stick to Bath and the Foresters. There you will be quite at home.

Your Aunt C. does not like desultory novels, and is rather afraid yours will be too much so, that there will be too frequently a change from one set of people to another, and that circumstances will be introduced of apparent consequence which will lead to nothing. It will not be so great an objection to *me* if it does. I allow much more latitude than she does, and think nature and spirit cover many sins of a wandering story, and people in general do not care so much about it, for your comfort.

I should like to have had more of Devereux. I do not feel enough acquainted with him. You were afraid of meddling with him I dare say. I like your sketch of Lord Clanmurray, and your picture of the

[1] *Lyme ... be safe* Lyme, Dawlish, Starcross, and Exeter are all in Devon, England.

[2] *Russell Square ... Berkeley Square* Addresses in London.

two young girls' enjoyment is very good. I have not noticed St. Julian's serious conversation with Cecilia, but I like it exceedingly. What he says about the madness of otherwise sensible women on the subject of their daughters is worth its weight in gold.

I do not perceive that the language sinks. Pray go on.

J.A.

Chawton, Monday, Dec. 16th [1816].

My Dear E.,[1]—One reason for my writing to you now is, that I may have the pleasure of directing to you Esqre. I give you joy of having left Winchester.[2] Now you may own how miserable you were there; now it will gradually all come out, your crimes and your miseries—how often you went up by the Mail[3] to London and threw away fifty guineas at a tavern, and how often you were on the point of hanging yourself, restrained only, as some ill-natured aspersion upon poor old Winton has it, by the want of a tree within some miles of the city. Charles Knight and his companions passed through Chawton about 9 this morning; later than it used to be. Uncle Henry and I had a glimpse of his handsome face, looking all health and good humour. I wonder when you will come and see us. I know what I rather speculate upon, but shall say nothing. We think uncle Henry in excellent looks. Look at him this moment, and think so too, if you have not done it before; and we have the great comfort of seeing decided improvement in uncle Charles, both as to health, spirits, and appearance. And they are each of them so agreeable in their different way, and harmonise so well, that their visit is thorough enjoyment. Uncle Henry writes very superior sermons.[4] You and I must try to get hold of one or two, and put them into our novels: it would be a fine help to a volume; and we could make our heroine read it aloud on a Sunday evening, just as well as Isabella Wardour, in the "Antiquary,"[5] is made to read the "History of the Hartz Demon" in the ruins of St. Ruth, though I believe, on recollection, Lovell is the reader. By the bye, my dear E., I am quite concerned for the loss your mother mentions in her letter. Two chapters and a half to be missing is monstrous! It is well that *I* have not been at Steventon lately, and therefore cannot be suspected of purloining them: two strong twigs and a half towards a nest of my own would have been something. I do not think however, that any theft of that sort would be really very useful to me. What should I do with your strong, manly, spirited sketches, full of variety and glow? How could I possibly join them on to the little bit (two inches wide) of ivory on which I work with so fine a brush, as produces little effect after much labour?

You will hear from uncle Henry how well Anna is. She seems perfectly recovered. Ben was here on Saturday, to ask uncle Charles and me to dine with them, as to-morrow, but I was forced to decline it, the walk is beyond my strength (though I am otherwise very well), and this is not a season for donkey-carriages; and as we do not like to spare uncle Charles, he has declined it too. *Tuesday.* Ah, ha! Mr. E., I doubt your seeing uncle Henry at Steventon to-day. The weather will prevent your expecting him, I think. Tell your father, with aunt Cass's love and mine, that the pickled cucumbers are extremely good, and tell him also—"tell him what you will." No, don't tell him what you will, but tell him that grandmamma begs him to make Joseph Hall pay his rent, if he can.

[1] *My Dear E.* James-Edward Austen, Jane Austen's nephew and son of her brother James.

[2] *I may have … left Winchester* I.e., having left Winchester, an English public school, Edward is now to be considered a man ("Esquire").

[3] *the Mail* The Mail Coach.

[4] *Uncle Henry … sermons* Henry Austen took Holy Orders and became curate of Chawton at this time.

[5] *"Antiquary"* Sir Walter Scott's novel *The Antiquary* had been published earlier in 1816.

You must not be tired of reading the word *uncle*, for I have not done with it. Uncle Charles thanks your mother for her letter; it was a great pleasure to him to know that the parcel was received and gave so much satisfaction, and he begs her to be so good as to give *three shillings* for him to Dame Staples, which shall be allowed for in the payment of her debt here.

Adieu, Amiable! I hope Caroline behaves well to you.

Yours affectionately,

J. Austen

William Hazlitt
1778 – 1830

William Hazlitt is often placed alongside the major authors of the Romantic era—a remarkable association in that Hazlitt was neither a poet nor a novelist nor a playwright. He was, however, perhaps the most significant essayist of his time, writing with great facility and great energy on literature, on theater, on art, and on politics. Hazlitt won many admirers for the steadfastness of his moral stance and, even more so, for his lively and penetrating prose style; it has sometimes been claimed he changed the nature of criticism, turning it into an art form in itself. His personality was less widely admired, however. With his critical essays and "portraits" of authors, many of them disparaging, many of them passionately argued, Hazlitt made scores of enemies, and was in turn often viciously attacked by the press. According to his contemporary Thomas De Quincey, he "wilfully placed himself in collision from the first with all the interests that were in the sunshine of the world, and of all the persons that were then powerful in England."

Hazlitt came by his rebellious nature honestly: he was born in Maidstone, Kent, into a family of Dissenters, a group of independent thinkers who disagreed with the tenets of the Church of England. His father was an Irish Unitarian minister who outspokenly supported the ideals of the French and American Revolutions and moved his family first to Ireland and then to the new republic of the United States of America in 1783, where he founded its first Unitarian church. In 1787 the family returned to England and settled in Shropshire. When he was 15, Hazlitt was sent to the New Unitarian College in London to train for the ministry, but he eventually realized he had no calling. For a time he followed in his brother John's footsteps and attempted a career as a painter; he ultimately recognized that he could not make a living painting portraits, but his eye for detail would later surface in the literary "portraits" for which he would become famous.

In 1798, Hazlitt made the acquaintance of Samuel Taylor Coleridge and William Wordsworth; years later the two would become the subjects of a charming essay, "My First Acquaintance with Poets" (1823). Hazlitt began to move in literary circles, also becoming friends (and sometimes enemies) with William Godwin, Leigh Hunt, Robert Southey, Percy Bysshe Shelley, Lord Byron, and Charles Lamb (Lamb was one of the few to remain a loyal companion). Hazlitt embarked on a career as a writer himself in 1805, publishing his first book, *An Essay on the Principles of Human Action*. It was followed by various political essays and pamphlets, and in 1808 (also the year in which he began an ill-fated marriage to Sarah Stoddart) Hazlitt began writing for *The Times*. Within a few years he was writing as well for the *Morning Chronicle* and for Leigh Hunt's journal *The Examiner*; in later years the *Edinburgh Review* and *London Magazine* were added to this list. It was for the *London Magazine* that he wrote *Table-Talk* (published in book form in 1821 and 1822), a series of brilliant and sparkling essays.

In 1824 *New Monthly Magazine* began publishing Hazlitt's next series of essays, *The Spirit of the Age*, in which he created memorably biting literary portraits of such contemporary writers as Byron ("he cares little what it is he says, so that he can say it differently from others") and Sir Walter Scott ("his speculative understanding is empty, flaccid, poor, and dead"). Hazlitt established himself as a leading art, literary, and drama critic, and, through his lectures and essays on William Shakespeare, helped spark a revival of Elizabethan theater.

Hazlitt stayed true to his radical roots, and remained an ardent supporter of Napoleon and the principles of the French Revolution (Hazlitt's four-volume *The Life of Napoleon Buonaparte* was published in 1828 and 1830). This spirit caused a rift with many of his fellow writers—most notably with Wordsworth, whose writing Hazlitt would praise, but whom he would publicly accuse of being an "apostate" to the French Revolution, saying that he "turned from his beliefs of his younger days and sold out to the establishment in accepting government jobs, pensions and laurels." For these convictions Hazlitt was blasted by the conservative press, whose recriminations were often scathing (Hazlitt was prompted to bring charges of libel against *Blackwood's Magazine* in 1818).

Hazlitt wrote about an enormous variety of subjects, telling the public, as J.B. Priestley put it in 1960, "what William Hazlitt thought and felt about everything," leaving a legacy of writing that spans 21 volumes. He died of cancer in 1830; although Hazlitt claimed on his death bed that he had led "a happy life," Charles Lamb was the only one of his old friends to attend his funeral. For Hazlitt, however, a life was made happy by the power of one's convictions and the zeal with which one lived out those convictions. "The love of life" was, according to Hazlitt, "the elect not of our enjoyment, but of our passions."

⌘⌘⌘

from *The Spirit of the Age; or Contemporary Portraits*

Mr. Coleridge

The present is an age of talkers, and not of doers; and the reason is, that the world is growing old. We are so far advanced in the Arts and Sciences, that we live in retrospect, and dote on past achievements. The accumulation of knowledge has been so great, that we are lost in wonder at the height it has reached, instead of attempting to climb or add to it; while the variety of objects distracts and dazzles the looker-on. What *niche* remains unoccupied? What path untried? What is the use of doing anything, unless we could do better than all those who have gone before us? What hope is there of this? We are like those who have been to see some noble monument of art, who are content to admire without thinking of rivalling it; or like guests after a feast, who praise the hospitality of the donor "and thank the bounteous Pan"[1]—perhaps carrying away some trifling fragments; or like the spectators of a mighty battle, who still hear its sound afar off, and the clashing of armour and the neighing of the war-horse and the shout of victory is in their ears, like the rushing of innumerable waters!

Mr. Coleridge has "a mind reflecting ages past";[2] his voice is like the echo of the congregated roar of the "dark rearward and abyss" of thought. He who has seen a mouldering tower by the side of a crystal lake, hid by the mist, but glittering in the wave below, may conceive the dim, gleaming, uncertain intelligence of his eye: he who has marked the evening clouds unrolled (a world of vapours), has seen the picture of his mind, unearthly, unsubstantial, with gorgeous tints and ever-varying forms—

> That which was now a horse, even with a thought
> The rack dislimns, and makes it indistinct
> As water is in water.[3]

Our author's mind is (as he himself might express it) *tangential.* There is no subject on which he has not

[1] *"and thank the bounteous Pan"* From John Milton's *A Mask Presented at Ludlow Castle* ("Comus"): "In wanton dance they praise the bounteous Pan" (Greek god of shepherds and flocks).

[2] *"a mind … past"* In an 1818 lecture, Hazlitt also wrote of Shakespeare: "He had 'a mind reflecting ages past' and present."

[3] *That which … water* From Shakespeare's *Antony and Cleopatra* 4.14.9–11.

touched, none on which he has rested. With an understanding fertile, subtle, expansive, "quick, forgetive, apprehensive,"[1] beyond all living precedent, few traces of it will perhaps remain. He lends himself to all impressions alike; he gives up his mind and liberty of thought to none. He is a general lover of art and science, and wedded to no one in particular. He pursues knowledge as a mistress, with outstretched hands and winged speed; but as he is about to embrace her, his Daphne turns— alas! not to a laurel![2] Hardly a speculation has been left on record from the earliest time, but it is loosely folded up in Mr. Coleridge's memory, like a rich, but somewhat tattered piece of tapestry: we might add (with more seeming than real extravagance), that scarce a thought can pass through the mind of man, but its sound has at some time or other passed over his head with rustling pinions. On whatever question or author you speak, he is prepared to take up the theme with advantage—from Peter Abelard down to Thomas Moore,[3] from the subtlest metaphysics to the politics of the *Courier*. There is no man of genius, in whose praise, he descants, but the critic seems to stand above the author, and "what in him is weak, to strengthen, what is low, to raise and support": nor is there any work of genius that does not come out of his hands like an illuminated Missal,[4] sparkling even in its defects. If Mr. Coleridge had not been the most impressive talker of his age, he would probably have been the finest writer; but he lays down his pen to make sure of an auditor, and mortgages the admiration of posterity for the stare of an idler. If he had not been a poet, he would have been a powerful logician; if he had not dipped his wing in the Unitarian controversy,[5] he might have soared to the very summit of fancy. But in writing verse, he is trying to subject the Muse to *transcendental* theories: in his abstract reasoning, he misses his way by strewing it with flowers. All that he has done of moment, he had done twenty years ago: since then, he may be said to have lived on the sound of his own voice. Mr. Coleridge is too rich in intellectual wealth, to need to task himself to any drudgery: he has only to draw the sliders of his imagination, and a thousand subjects expand before him, startling him with their brilliancy, or losing themselves in endless obscurity—

> And by the force of blear illusion,
> They draw him on to his confusion.[6]

What is the little he could add to the stock, compared with the countless stores that lie about him, that he should stoop to pick up a name, or to polish an idle fancy? He walks abroad in the majesty of a universal understanding, eyeing the "rich strond,"[7] or golden sky above him, and "goes sounding on his way," in eloquent accents, uncompelled and free! Persons of the greatest capacity are often those, who for this reason do the least; for surveying themselves from the highest point of view, amidst the infinite variety of the universe, their own share in it seems trifling, and scarce worth a thought, and they prefer the contemplation of all that is, or has been, or can be, to the making a coil about doing what, when done, is no better than vanity. It is hard to concentrate all our attention and efforts on one pursuit, except from ignorance of others; and without this concentration of our faculties, no great progress can be made in any one effort; it does not think the effort worth making. Action is one; but thought is manifold. He whose restless eye glances through the wide compass of nature and art, will not consent to have "his own nothings monstered";[8] but he must do this, before he can give his whole soul to them. The mind, after "letting contemplation have its fill," or

> Sailing with supreme dominion,
> Through the azure deep of air,[9]

sinks down on the ground, breathless, exhausted, power-

[1] *"quick, forgetive, apprehensive"* From Shakespeare's *2 Henry IV*, 4.3.98–99: "Apprehensive, quick, forgetive"; *forgetive* inventive.

[2] *Daphne … laurel* In Greek mythology, a nymph who eluded her pursuer by transforming herself into a laurel tree.

[3] *Peter Abelard* French philosopher and theologian (1079–1142); *Thomas Moore* Irish poet and composer (1779–1852).

[4] *Missal* Roman Catholic prayerbook.

[5] *Unitarian controversy* Coleridge became a Unitarian preacher in 1798; Hazlitt wrote in praise of Coleridge's lay-sermon of 1798.

[6] *And by … confusion* From Shakespeare's *Macbeth* 3.5.28–29.

[7] *"rich strond"* Beach; from Edmund Spenser's *The Faerie Queene* 3.4.2.

[8] *"his own … monstered"* From Shakespeare's *Coriolanus* 3.2.81.

[9] *Sailing … air* From Thomas Gray's *The Progress of Poesy: A Pindaric Ode* 2.116–17.

less, inactive; or if it must have some vent to its feelings, seeks the most easy and obvious; is soothed by friendly flattery, lulled by the murmur of immediate applause, thinks as it were aloud, and babbles in its dreams! A scholar (so to speak) is a more disinterested and abstracted character than a mere author. The first looks at the numberless volumes of a library, and says, "All these are mine": the other points to a single volume (perhaps it may be an immortal one) and says, "My name is written on the back of it." This is a puny and groveling ambition, beneath the lofty amplitude of Mr. Coleridge's mind. No, he revolves in his wayward soul, or utters to the passing wind, or discourses to his own shadow, things mightier and more various!—Let us draw the curtain, and unlock the shrine.

Learning rocked him in his cradle, and while yet a child,

> He lisped in numbers, for the numbers came.[1]

At sixteen he wrote his *Ode on Chatterton*,[2] and he still reverts to that period with delight, not so much as it relates to himself (for that string of his own early promise of fame rather jars than otherwise) but as exemplifying the youth of a poet. Mr. Coleridge talks of himself, without being an egotist, for in him the individual is always merged in the abstract and general. He distinguished himself at school and at the University by his knowledge of the classics, and gained several prizes for Greek epigrams. How many men are there (great scholars, celebrated names in literature) who having done the same thing in their youth, have no other idea all the rest of their lives but of this achievement, of a fellowship and dinner, and who, installed in academic honours, would look down on our author as a mere strolling bard! At Christ's Hospital,[3] where he was brought up, he was the idol of those among his schoolfellows, who mingled with their bookish studies the music of thought and of humanity; and he was usually attended round the cloisters by a group of these (inspiring and inspired) whose hearts, even then, burnt within them as he talked, and where the sounds yet linger to mock ELIA[4] on his way, still turning pensive to the past! One of the finest and rarest parts of Mr. Coleridge's conversation, is when he expatiates on the Greek tragedians (not that he is not well acquainted, when he pleases, with the epic poets, or the philosophers, or orators, or historians of antiquity)—on the subtle reasonings and melting pathos of Euripides, on the harmonious gracefulness of Sophocles, tuning his love-laboured song, like sweetest warblings from a sacred grove; on the high-wrought trumpet-tongued eloquence of Æschylus,[5] whose Prometheus, above all, is like an Ode to Fate, and a pleading with Providence, his thoughts being let loose as his body is chained on his solitary rock, and his afflicted will (the emblem of mortality)

> Struggling in vain with ruthless destiny.[6]

As the impassioned critic speaks and rises in his theme, you would think you heard the voice of the Man hated by the Gods, contending with the wild winds as they roar, and his eye glitters with the spirit of Antiquity!

Next, he was engaged with Hartley's[7] tribes of mind, "etherial braid, thought-woven,"—and he busied himself for a year or two with vibrations and vibratiuncles[8] and the great law of association that binds all things in its mystic chain, and the doctrine of Necessity (the mild teacher of Charity) and the Millennium, anticipative of a life to come—and he plunged deep into the controversy on Matter and Spirit, and, as an escape from Dr.

[1] *He lisped … came* From Alexander Pope's "An Epistle to Dr. Arbuthnot" 128: "I lisped in numbers, for the numbers came."

[2] *Ode on Chatterton* "Monody on the Death of Chatterton."

[3] *Christ's Hospital* Christ's Hospital School for poor boys, founded by Edward VI.

[4] *ELIA* Pen name of essayist Charles Lamb (1775–1834). Lamb's "Elia" essays included a piece on Christ's, where he had been to school with Coleridge.

[5] *Euripides* Greek tragedian (480?–406 BCE), author of *Medea*; *Sophocles* Greek tragedian (496?–406 BCE), author of *Oedipus Rex*; *Æschylus* The father of the Greek tragedy (525–456 BCE), author of *Prometheus Bound*.

[6] *Struggling … destiny* From William Wordsworth's *The Excursion* (1814) 6.557.

[7] *Hartley's* Referring to the theories of David Hartley (1705–57), English physician and materialist philosopher, who believed that all mental phenomena are functions of the brain; Hartley's ideas greatly influenced Coleridge.

[8] *vibratiuncles* Small vibrations.

Priestley's Materialism,[1] where he felt himself imprisoned by the logician's spell, like Ariel in the cloven pine-tree,[2] he became suddenly enamoured of Bishop Berkeley's[3] fairy-world,[4] and used in all companies to build the universe, like a brave poetical fiction, of fine words—and he was deep-read in Malebranche, and in Cudworth's Intellectual System (a huge pile of learning, unwieldy, enormous) and in Lord Brook's hieroglyphic theories, and in Bishop Butler's Sermons, and in the Duchess of Newcastle's fantastic folios, and in Clark and South and Tillotson, and all the fine thinkers and masculine reasoners of that age—and Leibnitz's *Pre-Established Harmony* reared its arch above his head,[5] like the rainbow in the cloud, covenanting[6] with the hopes of man—and then he fell plump, ten thousand fathoms down (but his wings saved him harmless) into the *hortus siccus*[7] of Dissent, where he pared religion down to the standard of reason and stripped faith of mystery, and preached Christ crucified and the Unity of the Godhead, and so dwelt for a while in the spirit with John Huss and Jerome of Prague and Socinus and old John Zisca,[8] and ran through Neal's History of the Puritans, and Calamy's Non-Conformists' Memorial,[9] having like thoughts and passions with them—but then Spinoza[10] became his God, and he took up the vast chain of being in his hand, and the round world became the centre and the soul of all things in some shadowy sense, forlorn of meaning, and around him he beheld the living traces and the sky-pointing proportions of the mighty Pan—but poetry redeemed him from this spectral philosophy, and he bathed his heart in beauty, and gazed at the golden light of heaven, and drank of the spirit of the universe, and wandered at eve by fairy-stream or fountain,

> —When he saw nought but beauty,
> When he heard the voice of that Almighty One
> In every breeze that blew, or wave that murmured—[11]

and wedded with truth in Plato's shade, and in the writings of Proclus and Plotinus saw the ideas of things in the eternal mind, and unfolded all mysteries with the Schoolmen and fathomed the depths of Duns Scotus and Thomas Aquinas, and entered the third heaven with Jacob Behmen, and walked hand in hand with Swedenborg through the pavilions of the New Jerusalem, and sung his faith in the promise and in the word in his *Religious Musings*[12]—and lowering himself from that dizzy

[1] *Dr. Priestley's Materialism* Joseph Priestley's (1733–1804) philosophical theory: all things that exist are composed of matter.

[2] *Ariel ... pine-tree* From Shakespeare's *The Tempest* 1.2.324; the evil witch Sycorax imprisoned the spirit Ariel in a cloven pine tree.

[3] *Bishop Berkeley's* Referring to the theories of George Berkeley (1685–1753), an Anglo-Irish clergyman and idealist philosopher who argued that God thinks everything into existence.

[4] [Hazlitt's note] Mr. Coleridge named his eldest son (the writer of some beautiful sonnets) after Hartley, and the second after Berkeley. The third was called Derwent, after the river of that name. Nothing can be more characteristic of his mind than this circumstance. All his ideas indeed are like a river, flowing on for ever, and still murmuring as it flows, discharging its still waters and still replenished—"And so by many winding nooks it strays, with willing sport to the ocean world!" [*"And so by ... wild ocean"* From Shakespeare's *The Two Gentlemen of Verona* 2.7.31–32.]

[5] *Malebranche* Nicolas Malebranche (1638–1715) was a French Cartesian philosopher who argued that mind and body are separate, but God coordinates the two; *Cudworth* Ralph Cudworth (1617–88) was an English philosopher who argued against atheism and determinism; *Lord Brook* Robert Greville, Lord Brooke (1608–43) was an English philosopher who proposed that all things are emanations from God; *Duchess of Newcastle* Margaret Cavendish (1623–73) was an English author and materialist philosopher who argued that nothing in nature is incorporeal; *Tillotson* John Tillotson (1630–94) was an Archbishop of Canterbury who argued against atheism; *Leibniz* Gottfried Leibniz (1646–1716) was a German mathematician and rationalist philosopher who argued that there is a non-causal relationship between mind and body, and that there is a pre-existing harmony in the world established by God.

[6] *covenanting* Suiting; agreeing.

[7] *hortus siccus* Dry garden.

[8] *John Huss ... John Zisca* Church reformers, most of whom died for their beliefs.

[9] *Neal's ... Memorial* Daniel Neal (1678–1743), English historian; Edmund Calamy (1678–1732), English historian and dissenting minister.

[10] *Spinoza* Dutch determinist philosopher (1632–1677) who argued that God and nature are one and the same.

[11] *When ... murmered* From Coleridge's *Remorse* 4.2.100–02.

[12] *Plato* Greek philosopher (428?–348? BCE) and author of *The Republic*, who argued that all we see in the world is a glimpse of what is ultimately a perfect "form" and that good art stimulates the passions, giving us a vision of the ideal form; *Proclus* Greek philosopher (411–85), Neoplatonist, who argued for the existence of one ultimate, original creator (reality), from whom emanates all existence in lower and lower forms; *Plotinus* Egyptian philosopher

height, poised himself on Milton's wings, and spread out his thoughts in charity with the glad prose of Jeremy Taylor,[1] and wept over Bowles's Sonnets,[2] and studied Cowper's[3] blank verse, and betook himself to Thomson's Castle of Indolence,[4] and sported with the wits of Charles the Second's days and of Queen Anne, and relished Swift's[5] style and that of the John Bull (Arbuthnot's we mean, not Mr. Croker's),[6] and dallied with the British essayists and novelists, and knew all qualities of more modern writers with a learned spirit, Johnson, and Goldsmith, and Junius, and Burke, and Godwin, and the Sorrows of Werter, and Jean Jacques Rousseau, and Voltaire, and Marivaux, and Crebillon, and thousands more—now "laughed with Rabelais[7] in his easy chair" or pointed to Hogarth, or afterwards dwelt on Claude's classic scenes, or spoke with rapture of Raphael,[8] and compared the women at Rome to figures that had walked out of his pictures, or visited the Oratory of Pisa, and described the works of Giotto and Ghirlandaio and Masaccio,[9] and gave the moral of the picture of the Triumph of Death, where the beggars and the wretched invoke his dreadful dart, but the rich and mighty of the earth quail and shrink before it; and in that land of siren sights and sounds, saw a dance of peasant girls, and was charmed with lutes and gondolas,—or wandered into Germany and lost himself in the labyrinths of the Hartz Forest and of the Kantean philosophy, and amongst the cabalistic names of Fichte and Schelling and Lessing,[10] and God knows who—this was long after, but all the former while, he had nerved his heart and filled his eyes with tears, as he hailed the rising orb of liberty, since quenched in darkness and in blood, and had kindled his affections at the blaze of the French Revolution, and sang for joy when the towers of the Bastille[11] and the proud places of the insolent and the oppressor fell, and would have floated his bark, freighted with fondest fancies, across the Atlantic wave with Southey[12] and others to seek for peace and freedom—

(205–270), Neoplatonist, whose theories of emanation postulated the existence of one supreme source that creates the possibility of all other existences; *Duns Scotus* Scottish philosopher and theologian (c. 1266–1308), who argued for the "univocity" or commonality of being that provides our understanding of "essential truths"; *Thomas Aquinas* Italian priest (later made a saint) and philosopher (1225–74), who said that reason can prove the existence of God; *Jacob Behmen* Sometimes spelled Jakob Boehme (1575–1634), German mystic who wrote of a Supreme reality and of humankind's struggle to choose good over evil; *Swedenborg* Emanuel Swedenborg, Swedish theologian, scientist, and philosopher (1688–1772), whose visionary writings gave rise to the Church of the New Jerusalem (or New Church); *Religious Musings* Coleridge's *Religious Musings: a Desultory Poem, written on Christmas Eve in the year of our Lord, 1794.*

[1] *Jeremy Taylor* (1613–67), clergyman.

[2] *Bowles's Sonnets* William Lyle Bowles's (1762–1850) influential *Fourteen Sonnets.*

[3] *Cowper's* Poet William Cowper's (1731–68) verse.

[4] *Thomson's Castle of Indolence* A poem by James Thomson (1700–48).

[5] *Swift's* Jonathan Swift's (1667–1745) satiric style.

[6] *John Bull ... Croker's* John Arbuthnot (1667–1735) wrote *The History of John Bull* (1727), a satire; John Wilson Croker (1780–1857), was a conservative MP, writer, and critic.

[7] *Johnson ... Rabelais Johnson* Samuel Johnson (1709–84); *Goldsmith* Oliver Goldsmith (1728–74); *Junius* A pseudonym for the author of *The Letters of Junius*, satirical polemics on English politics; *Burke* Edmund Burke (1729–97), statesman, orator, and author; *Godwin* William Godwin (1756–1836), radical philosopher; *Sorrows of Werter The Sorrows of Young Werther*, by Johann Wolfgang von Goethe (1749–1832); *Jean Jacques Rousseau* French philosopher (1712–78); *Voltaire* Author and philosopher (1694–1778); *Marivaux* Pierre Carlet de Marivaux (1688–1763), French dramatist; *Crebillon* P.J. de Crébillon (1674–1762), French dramatist; *Rabelais* François Rabelais (1494–1553), writer known for his humorous *La Vie de Gargantua and Pantagruel.*

[8] *Hogarth ... Raphael Hogarth* English artist William Hogarth (1697–1764); *Claude's* Referring to the paintings of Claude Lorraine, Baroque painter (c. 1600–82); *Raphael* Raffaello Sanzi, Italian artist (1483– 1520).

[9] *Giotto ... Masaccio* Giotto di Bondone, Florentine painter and architect (1267–1337); *Ghirlandaio* Domenico Ghirlandio, Florentine painter (1401–27?); *Masaccio* Tommaso Cassai, Florentine painter (1401–27?).

[10] *Kantean philosophy ... Lessing Kantean philosophy* The theories of philosopher Immanuel Kant (1724–1804); *Fichte* J.G. Fichte (1762–1814), German philosopher and follower of Kant; *Schelling* Friedrich W.J. Schelling (1775–1854), German philosopher and follower of Kant; *Lessing* Gotthold Ephraim Lessing (1729–81), German critic and playwright.

[11] *towers of ... Bastille* The Bastille, a French prison, was stormed by the people of Paris on 14 July 1789.

[12] *Southey* Robert Southey (1774–1843), British Poet Laureate from 1813–43, collaborated with Coleridge on political and creative works, and shared an interest in the egalitarian principles of the French Revolution.

In Philarmonia's undivided dale![1]

Alas! "Frailty, thy name is *Genius*!"[2]—What is become of all this mighty heap of hope, of thought, of learning, and humanity? It has ended in swallowing doses of oblivionand in writing paragraphs in the *Courier.*—Such, and so little is the mind of man!

It was not to be supposed that Mr. Coleridge could keep on at the rate he set off; he could not realize all he knew or thought, and less could not fix his desultory ambition; other stimulants supplied the place, and kept up the intoxicating dream, the fever and the madness of his early impressions. Liberty (the philosopher's and the poet's bride) had fallen a victim, meanwhile, to the murderous practices of the hag, Legitimacy. Proscribed by court-hirelings, too romantic for the herd of vulgar politicians, our enthusiast stood at bay, and at last turned on the pivot of a subtle casuistry to the *unclean side:* but his discursive reason would not let him trammel himself into a poet-laureate or stamp-distributor,[3] and he stopped, ere he had quite passed that well-known "bourne from whence no traveller returns"[4]—and so has sunk into torpid, uneasy repose, tantalized by useless resources, haunted by vain imaginings, his lips idly moving, but his heart for ever still, or, as the shattered chords vibrate of themselves, making melancholy music to the ear of memory! Such is the fate of genius in an age, when in the unequal contest with sovereign wrong, every man is ground to powder who is not either a born slave, or who does not willingly and at once offer up the yearnings of humanity and the dictates of reason as a welcome sacrifice to besotted prejudice and loathsome power.

Of all Mr. Coleridge's productions, the *Ancient Mariner* is the only one that we could with confidence put into any person's hands, on whom we wished to impress a favourable idea of his extraordinary powers. Let whatever other objections be made to it, it is unquestionably a work of genius—of wild, irregular, overwhelming imagination, and has that rich, varied movement in the verse, which gives a distant idea of the lofty or changeful tones of Mr. Coleridge's voice. In the *Christabel,* there is one splendid passage on divided friendship. The *Translation of Schiller's Wallenstein* is also a masterly production in its kind, faithful and spirited. Among his smaller pieces there are occasional bursts of pathos and fancy, equal to what we might expect from him; but these form the exception, and not the rule. Such, for instance, is his affecting Sonnet to the author of the Robbers.

Schiller! that hour I would have wish'd to die,
    If through the shudd'ring midnight I had sent
    From the dark dungeon of the tower time-rent,
That fearful voice, a famish'd father's cry—
That in no after-moment aught less vast
    Might stamp me mortal! A triumphant shout
    Black horror scream'd, and all her goblin rout
From the more with'ring scene diminsh'd pass'd.
Ah ! Bard tremendous in sublimity!
    Could I behold thee in thy loftier mood,
Wand'ring at eve, with finely frenzied eye,
    Beneath some vast old tempest-swinging wood!
    Awhile, with mute awe gazing, I would brood,
Then weep aloud in a wild ecstacy.[5]

His Tragedy, entitled *Remorse,* is full of beautiful and striking passages, but it does not place the author in the first rank of dramatic writers. But if Mr. Coleridge's works do not place him in that rank, they injure instead of conveying a just idea of the man, for he himself is certainly in the first class of general intellect.

If our author's poetry is inferior to his conversation, his prose is utterly abortive. Hardly a gleam is to be found in it of the brilliancy and richness of those stores of thought and language that he pours out incessantly, when they are lost like drops of water in the ground. The principal work, in which he has attempted to embody his general views of things, is the FRIEND,[6] of which, though

[1] *In ... dale* From Coleridge's "Monody on the Death of Chatterton" 40.

[2] *"Frailty ... Genius"* From Shakespeare's *Hamlet* 1.2.146, "Frailty, thy name is woman!"

[3] *poet-laureate or stamp-distributor* William Wordsworth, Poet Laureate from 1843–50; when Wordsworth in 1813 took a position with the tax department as the Distributor of Stamps, many proponents of the reform came to believe that he had abandoned progressive causes.

[4] *"bourne ... returns"* From Shakespeare's *Hamlet* 3.1: "The undiscover'd country from whose bourne / No traveller returns."

[5] *Schiller! ... ecstacy* Coleridge's "Effusion" 20, from *Poems on Various Subjects* (1796).

[6] *the FRIEND* Coleridge's *The Friend* was first published in periodical form (1809–10).

it contains some noble passages and fine trains of thought, prolixity and obscurity are the most frequent characteristics.

No two persons can be conceived more opposite in character or genius than the subject of the present and of the preceding sketch. Mr. Godwin, with less natural capacity, and with fewer acquired advantages, by concentrating his mind on some given object, and doing what he had to do with all his might, has accomplished much, and will leave more than one monument of a powerful intellect behind him; Mr. Coleridge, by dissipating his, and dallying with every subject by turns, has done little or nothing to justify to the World or to posterity, the high opinion which all who have ever heard him converse, or known him intimately, with one accord entertain of him. Mr. Godwin's faculties have kept at home, and plied their task in the workshop of the brain, diligently and effectually: Mr. Coleridge's have gossiped their time away, and gadded about from house to house, as if life's business were to melt the hours in listless talk. Mr. Godwin is intent on a subject, only as it concerns himself and his reputation; he works it out as a matter of duty, and discards from his mind whatever does not forward his main object as impertinent and vain. Mr. Coleridge, on the other hand, delights in nothing but episodes and digressions, neglects whatever he undertakes to perform, and can act only on spontaneous impulses, without object or method. "He cannot be constrained by mastery."[1] While he should be occupied with a given pursuit, he is thinking of a thousand other things; a thousand tastes, a thousand objects tempt him, and distract his mind, which keeps open house, and entertains all comers; and after being fatigued and amused with morning calls from idle visitors, finds the day consumed and its business unconcluded. Mr. Godwin, on the contrary, is somewhat exclusive and unsocial in his habits of mind, entertains no company but what he gives his whole time and attention to, and wisely writes over the doors of his understanding, his fancy, and his senses—"No admittance except on business." He has none of that fastidious refinement and false delicacy, which might lead him to balance between the endless variety of modern attainments. He does not throw away his life (nor a single half-hour of it) in adjusting the claims of different accomplishments, and in choosing between them or making himself master of them all. He sets about his task, (whatever it may be) and goes through it with spirit and fortitude. He has the happiness to think an author the greatest character in the world, and himself the greatest author in it. Mr. Coleridge, in writing an harmonious stanza, would stop to consider whether there was not more grace and beauty in a *Pas de trois*,[2] and would not proceed till he had resolved this question by a chain of metaphysical reasoning without end. Not so Mr. Godwin. That is best to him, which he can do best. He does not waste himself in vain aspirations and effeminate sympathies. He is blind, deaf, insensible to all but the trump of Fame. Plays, operas, painting, music, ballrooms, wealth, fashion, titles, lords, ladies, touch him not—all these are no more to him than to the magician in his cell, and he writes on to the end of the chapter, through good report and evil report. *Pingo in eternitatem*[3]—is his motto. He neither envies nor admires what others are, but is contented to be what he is, and strives to do the utmost he can. Mr. Coleridge has flirted with the Muses[4] as with a set of mistresses: Mr. Godwin has been married twice, to Reason and to Fancy, and has to boast no short-lived progeny by each. So to speak, he has *valves* belonging to his mind, to regulate the quantity of gas admitted into it, so that like the bare, unsightly, but well-compacted steam-vessel, it cuts its liquid way, and arrives at its promised end: while Mr. Coleridge's bark, "taught with the little nautilus to sail,"[5] the sport of every breath, dancing to every wave,

> Youth at its prow, and Pleasure at its helm,[6]

flutters its gaudy pennons[7] in the air, glitters in the sun, but we wait in vain to hear of its arrival in the destined

[1] *"He cannot be constrained by mastery"* From Geoffrey Chaucer's *The Canterbury Tales*, "The Franklin's Tale" 764: "Love wol nat been constreyned by maistrye."

[2] *Pas de trois* Dance for three.

[3] *Pingo in eternitatem* Ceaselessly depict.

[4] *Muses* The nine goddesses of classical mythology who inspire learning and the arts.

[5] *"taught … sail"* From Pope's *An Essay on Man: Epistle* (1733–34) 3.177: "Learn of the little Nautilus to sail."

[6] *Youth … helm* From Thomas Gray's *The Bard: A Pindaric Ode* (1757) 2.2.12: "Youth on the prow, and Pleasure at the helm."

[7] *pennons* Banners.

harbour. Mr. Godwin, with less variety and vividness, with less subtlety and susceptibility both of thought and feeling, has had firmer nerves, a more determined purpose, a more comprehensive grasp of his subject, and the results are as we find them. Each has met with his reward: for justice has, after all, been done to the pretensions of each; and we must, in all cases, use means to ends!

It was a misfortune to any man of talent to be born in the latter end of the last century. Genius stopped the way of Legitimacy, and therefore it was to be abated, crushed, or set aside as a nuisance. The spirit of the monarchy was at variance with the spirit of the age. The flame of liberty, the light of intellect was to be extinguished with the sword—or with slander, whose edge is sharper than the sword. The war between power and reason was carried on by the first of these abroad—by the last at home. No quarter was given (then or now) by the Government-critics, the authorised censors of the press, to those who followed the dictates of independence, who listened to the voice of the tempter, Fancy. Instead of gathering fruits and flowers, immortal fruits and amaranthine[1] flowers, they soon found themselves beset not only by a host of prejudices, but assailed with all the engines of power, by nicknames, by lies, by all the arts of malice, interest and hypocrisy, without the possibility of their defending themselves "from the pelting of the pitiless storm,"[2] that poured down upon them from the strong-holds of corruption and authority. The philosophers, the dry abstract reasoners, submitted to this reverse pretty well, and armed themselves with patience "as with triple steel"[3] to bear discomfiture, persecution, and disgrace. But the poets, the creatures of sympathy, could not stand the frowns both of king and people. They did not like to be shut out when places and pensions, when the critic's praises, and the laurel-wreath were about to be distributed. They did not stomach being *sent to Coventry*,[4] and Mr. Coleridge sounded a retreat for them by the help of casuistry, and a musical voice.—"His words were hollow, but they pleased the ear"[5] of his friends of the Lake School, who turned back disgusted and panic-struck from the dry desert of unpopularity, like Hassan the camel driver,

> And curs'd the hour, and curs'd the luckless day,
> When first from Shiraz' walls they bent their way.[6]

They are safely enclosed there, but Mr. Coleridge did not enter with them; pitching his tent upon the barren waste without, and having no abiding place nor city of refuge.[7]

Mr. Wordsworth

Mr. Wordsworth's genius is a pure emanation of the Spirit of the Age. Had he lived in any other period of the world, he would never have been heard of. As it is, he has some difficulty to contend with the hebetude[8] of his intellect, and the meanness of his subject. With him "lowliness is young ambition's ladder":[9] but he finds it a toil to climb in this way the steep of Fame. His homely Muse can hardly raise her wing from the ground, nor spread her hidden glories to the sun. He has "no figures nor no fantasies, which busy *passion* draws in the brains of men":[10] neither the gorgeous machinery of mythologic lore, nor the splendid colours of poetic diction. His style is vernacular: he delivers household truths. He sees nothing loftier than human hopes; nothing deeper than the human heart. This he probes, this he tampers with, this he poises, with all its incalculable weight of thought and feeling, in his hands; and at the same time calms the throbbing pulses of his own heart, by keeping his eye ever

[1] *amaranthine* Everlasting.

[2] *"from ... storm"* From Shakespeare's *King Lear* (1608) 3.4.28–29: "Poor naked wretches, whereso'er you are / That bide the pelting of this pitiless storm."

[3] *"as with triple steel"* From Milton's *Paradise Lost* (1667) 2.569.

[4] *sent to Coventry* Shunned.

[5] *"His words ... ear"* From Milton's *Paradise Lost* 2.112–17: "But all was false and hollow... yet he pleas'd the ear."

[6] *And curs'd ... way* From William Collins's *The Persian Eclogues* 11.3–4: "Eclogue the Second Hassan; or, The Camel Driver" (1742): "Sad was the hour and luckless was the day, / When first from Shiraz' walls I bent my way."

[7] *city of refuge* From Joshua 20.7–9.

[8] *hebetude* Dullness.

[9] *"lowliness ... ladder"* From William Shakespeare's *Julius Caesar* 2.1.231–32.

[10] *"no figures ... men"* From *Julius Caesar* 2.1.231–32; Hazlitt substitutes the word "passion" for "care."

fixed on the face of nature. If he can make the life-blood flow from the wounded breast, this is the living colouring with which he paints his verse: if he can assuage the pain or close up the wound with the balm of solitary musing, or the healing power of plants and herbs and "skyey influences,"[1] this is the sole triumph of his art. He takes the simplest elements of nature and of the human mind, the mere abstract conditions inseparable from our being, and tries to compound a new system of poetry from them; and has perhaps succeeded as well as any one could. "*Nihil humani a me alienum puto*"[2]—is the motto of his works. He thinks nothing low or indifferent of which this can be affirmed: every thing that professes to be more than this, that is not an absolute essence of truth and feeling, he holds to be vitiated, false, and spurious. In a word, his poetry is founded on setting up an opposition (and pushing it to the utmost length) between the natural and the artificial; between the spirit of humanity, and the spirit of fashion and of the world!

It is one of the innovations of the time. It partakes of, and is carried along with, the revolutionary movement of our age: the political changes of the day were the model on which he formed and conducted his poetical experiments. His Muse (it cannot be denied, and without this we cannot explain its character at all) is a levelling one. It proceeds on a principle of equality, and strives to reduce all things to the same standard. It is distinguished by a proud humility. It relies upon its own resources, and disdains external show and relief. It takes the commonest events and objects, as a test to prove that nature is always interesting from its inherent truth and beauty, without any of the ornaments of dress or pomp of circumstances to set it off. Hence the unaccountable mixture of seeming simplicity and real abstruseness in the *Lyrical Ballads*. Fools have laughed at, wise men scarcely understand them. He takes a subject or a story merely as pegs or loops to hang thought and feeling on; the incidents are trifling, in proportion to his contempt for imposing appearances; the reflections are profound, according to the gravity and the aspiring pretensions of his mind.

His popular, inartificial style gets rid (at a blow) of all the trappings of verse, of all the high places of poetry: "the cloud-capt towers, the solemn temples, the gorgeous palaces," are swept to the ground, and "like the baseless fabric of a vision, leave not a wreck behind."[3] All the traditions of learning, all the superstitions of age, are obliterated and effaced. We begin *de novo,* on a *tabula rasa*[4] of poetry. The purple pall, the nodding plume of tragedy are exploded as mere pantomime and trick, to return to the simplicity of truth and nature. Kings, queens, priests, nobles, the altar and the throne, the distinctions of rank, birth, wealth, power, "the judge's robe, the marshal's truncheon, the ceremony that to great ones 'longs,"[5] are not to be found here. The author tramples on the pride of art with greater pride. The Ode and Epode, the Strophe and the Antistrophe,[6] he laughs to scorn. The harp of Homer, the trump of Pindar and of Alcaeus[7] are still. The decencies of costume, the decorations of vanity are stripped off without mercy as barbarous, idle, and Gothic. The jewels in the crisped hair,[8] the diadem[9] on the polished brow are thought meretricious, theatrical, vulgar; and nothing contents his fastidious taste beyond a simple garland of flowers. Neither does he avail himself of the advantages which nature or accident holds out to him. He chooses to have his subject a foil to his invention, to owe nothing but to himself. He gathers manna in the wilderness, he strikes the barren rock for the

[1] *"skyey influences"* Influences of the stars. From Shakespeare's *Measure for Measure* 3.1.9.

[2] *"Nihil … puto"* From Roman playwright Terence (195–159 BCE), "Nothing human is alien to me."

[3] *"the … behind"* From Shakespeare's *The Tempest* 4.1.151–56: "And, like the baseless fabric of this vision, / The cloud-capp'd towers, the gorgeous palaces, / The solemn temples, the great globe itself, / Yea all which it inherit, shall dissolve / And, like this insubstantial pageant faded, / Leave not a rack behind."

[4] *de novo, on a tabula rasa* Anew, on a blank slate.

[5] *"the judge's robe … 'longs"* From Shakespeare's *Measure for Measure* 2.2.59–61: "No ceremony that to great ones 'longs, / Not the king's crown, nor the deputed sword, / The marshal's truncheon, nor the judge's robe."

[6] *The Ode … Antistrophe* *ode* A rhymed lyric poem in the form of an address, with an irregular or varied meter; *epode* Lyric poem composed of couplets, in which a long line is followed by a short line; *strophe* Metrically-structured section of an ode; *antistrophe* Response to strophe.

[7] *The harp … Alcaeus* Homer: ancient Greek poet, author of the *Iliad* and the *Odyssey*; Pindar (518?–c. 438 BCE) and Alcaeus (c. 620– c. 580 BCE): Greek lyric poets.

[8] *jewels in the crisped hair* *Crisped* Wavy. From William Collins's "The Manners: An Ode"; Hazlitt substitutes "the" for "his."

[9] *diadem* Jeweled crown.

gushing moisture. He elevates the mean by the strength of his own aspirations; he clothes the naked with beauty and grandeur from the stores of his own recollections. No cypress grove loads his verse with funeral pomp: but his imagination lends "a sense of joy"

> To the bare trees and mountains bare,
> And grass in the green field.[1]

No storm, no shipwreck startles us by its horrors: but the rainbow lifts it head in the cloud, and the breeze sighs through the withered fern. No sad vicissitude of fate, no overwhelming catastrophe in nature deforms his page: but the dew-drop glitters on the bending flower, the tear collects in the glistening eye.

> Beneath the hills, along the flowery vales,
> The generations are prepared; the pangs,
> The internal pangs, are ready; the dread strife
> Of poor humanity's afflicted will,
> Struggling in vain with ruthless destiny.[2]

As the lark ascends from its low bed on fluttering wing, and salutes the morning skies; so Mr. Wordsworth's unpretending Muse, in russet guise, scales the summits of reflection, while it makes the round earth its footstool, and its home!

Possibly a good deal of this may be regarded as the effect of disappointed views and an inverted ambition. Prevented by native pride and indolence from climbing the ascent of learning or greatness, taught by political opinions to say to the vain pomp and glory of the world, "I hate ye,"[3] seeing the path of classical and artificial poetry blocked up by the cumbrous ornaments of style and turgid *common-places*, so that nothing more could be achieved in that direction but by the most ridiculous bombast or the tamest servility; he has turned back partly from the bias of his mind, partly perhaps from a judicious policy—has struck into the sequestered vale of humble life, sought out the Muse among sheep-cotes and hamlets and the peasant's mountain-haunts, has discarded all the tinsel pageantry of verse, and endeavoured (not in vain) to aggrandise the trivial and add the charm of novelty to the familiar. No one has shown the same imagination in raising trifles into importance: no one has displayed the same pathos in treating of the simplest feelings of the heart. Reserved, yet haughty, having no unruly or violent passions, (or those passions having been early suppressed,) Mr. Wordsworth has passed his life in solitary musing, or in daily converse with the face of nature. He exemplifies in an eminent degree the power of *association*; for his poetry has no other source or character. He has dwelt among pastoral scenes, till each object has become connected with a thousand feelings, a link in the chain of thought, a fibre of his own heart. Every one is by habit and familiarity strongly attached to the place of his birth, or to objects that recall the most pleasing and eventful circumstances of his life. But to the author of the *Lyrical Ballads*, nature is a kind of home; and he may be said to take a personal interest in the universe. There is no image so insignificant that it has not in some mood or other found the way into his heart: no sound that does not awaken the memory of other years.—

> To him the meanest flower that blows can give
> Thoughts that do often lie too deep for tears.[4]

The daisy looks up to him with sparkling eye as an old acquaintance: the cuckoo haunts him with sounds of early youth not to be expressed: a linnet's nest startles him with boyish delight: an old withered thorn is weighed down with a heap of recollections: a grey cloak, seen on some wild moor, torn by the wind, or drenched in the rain, afterwards becomes an object of imagination to him: even the lichens on the rock have a life and being in his thoughts. He has described all these objects in a way and with an intensity of feeling that no one else had done before him, and has given a new view or aspect of nature. He is in this sense the most original poet now living, and the one whose writings could the least be spared: for they have no substitute elsewhere. The vulgar do not read them, the learned, who see all things through books, do

[1] *a sense ... field* From Wordsworth's "To My Sister" 6–8.

[2] *Beneath ... destiny* From *The Excursion* 6.553–57; the first line should read: "Amid the groves, under the shadowy hills."

[3] *vain pomp ... ye* From Shakespeare's *Henry VIII* 3.2.365: "Vain pomp and glory of this world, I hate ye!"

[4] *To him ... tears* From Wordsworth's "Ode: Intimations of Immortality from Recollections of Early Childhood" 11.203; Hazlitt substitutes "him" for "me."

not understand them, the great despise, the fashionable may ridicule them: but the author has created himself an interest in the heart of the retired and lonely student of nature, which can never die. Persons of this class will still continue to feel what he has felt: he has expressed what they might in vain wish to express, except with glistening eye and faultering tongue! There is a lofty philosophic tone, a thoughtful humanity, infused into his pastoral vein. Remote from the passions and events of the great world, he has communicated interest and dignity to the primal movements of the heart of man, and ingrafted his own conscious reflections on the casual thoughts of hinds[1] and shepherds. Nursed amidst the grandeur of mountain scenery, he has stooped to have a nearer view of the daisy under his feet, or plucked a branch of white-thorn from the spray: but in describing it, his mind seems imbued with the majesty and solemnity of the objects around him—the tall rock lifts its head in the erectness of his spirit; the cataract roars in the sound of his verse; and in its dim and mysterious meaning, the mists seem to gather in the hollows of Helvellyn, and the forked Skiddaw[2] hovers in the distance. There is little mention of mountainous scenery in Mr. Wordsworth's poetry; but by internal evidence one might be almost sure that it was written in a mountainous country, from its bareness, its simplicity, its loftiness and its depth!

His later philosophic productions have a somewhat different character. They are a departure from, a dereliction of his first principles. They are classical and courtly. They are polished in style, without being gaudy; dignified in subject, without affectation. They seem to have been composed not in a cottage at Grasmere,[3] but among the half-inspired groves and stately recollections of Cole-Orton.[4] We might allude in particular, for examples of what we mean, to the lines on a Picture by Claude Lorraine,[5] and to the exquisite poem, entitled *Laodamia*. The last of these breathes the pure spirit of the finest fragments of antiquity—the sweetness, the gravity, the strength, the beauty and the languor of death—

> Calm contemplation and majestic pains.[6]

Its glossy brilliancy arises from the perfection of the finishing, like that of careful sculpture, not from gaudy colouring—the texture of the thoughts has the smoothness and solidity of marble. It is a poem that might be read aloud in Elysium,[7] and the spirits of departed heroes and sages would gather round to listen to it! Mr. Wordsworth's philosophic poetry, with a less glowing aspect and less tumult in the veins than Lord Byron's on similar occasions, bends a calmer and keener eye on morality; the impression, if less vivid, is more pleasing and permanent; and we confess it (perhaps it is a want of taste and proper feeling) that there are lines and poems of our author's, that we think of ten times for once that we recur to any of Lord Byron's.[8] Or if there are any of the latter's writings, that we can dwell upon in the same way, that is, as lasting and heart-felt sentiments, it is when laying aside his usual pomp and pretension, he descends with Mr. Wordsworth to the common ground of a disinterested humanity. It may be considered as characteristic of our poet's writings, that they either make no impression on the mind at all, seem mere *nonsense-verses*, or that they leave a mark behind them that never wears out. They either

> Fall blunted from the indurated breast—[9]

without any perceptible result, or they absorb it like a passion. To one class of readers he appears sublime, to another (and we fear the largest) ridiculous. He has probably realised Milton's wish,—"and fit audience found, though few";[10] but we suspect he is not reconciled to the alternative. There are delightful passages in the EXCURSION, both of natural description and of inspired reflection (passages of the latter kind that in the sound of the thoughts and of the swelling language resemble

[1] *hinds* Deer.

[2] *Helvellyn ... Skiddaw* Mountains in England's Lake District.

[3] *Grasmere* Wordsworth's home in the Lake District.

[4] *Cole-Orton* Coleorton, a village in Leicestershire.

[5] *Claude Lorraine* Baroque painter (c. 1600–82).

[6] *Calm ... pains* From "Laodamia" 72: "Calm pleasures there abide—majestic pains."

[7] *Elysium* Paradise.

[8] *Byron's* The poems of George Gordon, Lord Byron (1788–1824).

[9] *Fall ... breast* From Oliver Goldsmith's "The Traveller" 232: "Falls blunted from each indurated heart."

[10] *"and fit ... few"* From Milton's *Paradise Lost* 7.30–1: "govern thou my Song, / Urania, and fit audience find, though few."

heavenly symphonies, mournful *requiems* over the grave of human hopes); but we must add, in justice and in sincerity, that we think it impossible that this work should ever become popular, even in the same degree as the *Lyrical Ballads*. It affects a system without having any intelligible clue to one; and instead of unfolding a principle in various and striking lights, repeats the same conclusions till they become flat and insipid. Mr. Wordsworth's mind is obtuse, except as it is the organ and the receptacle of accumulated feelings; it is not analytic, but synthetic; it is reflecting, rather than theoretical. The EXCURSION, we believe, fell still-born from the press. There was something abortive, and clumsy, and ill-judged in the attempt. It was long and laboured. The personages, for the most part, were low, the fare rustic: the plan raised expectations which were not fulfilled, and the effect was like being ushered into a stately hall and invited to sit down to a splendid banquet in the company of clowns, and with nothing but successive courses of apple-dumplings served up. It was not even *toujours perdrix*![1]

Mr. Wordsworth, in his person, is above the middle size, with marked features, and an air somewhat stately and Quixotic. He reminds one of some of Holbein's heads,[2] grave, saturnine, with a slight indication of sly humour, kept under by the manners of the age or by the pretensions of the person. He has a peculiar sweetness in his smile, and great depth and manliness and a rugged harmony, in the tones of his voice. His manner of reading his own poetry is particularly imposing; and in his favourite passages his eye beams with preternatural lustre, and the meaning labours slowly up from his swelling breast. No one who has seen him at these moments could go away with an impression that he was a "man of no mark or likelihood."[3] Perhaps the comment of his face and voice is necessary to convey a full idea of his poetry. His language may not be intelligible, but his manner is not to be mistaken. It is clear that he is either mad or inspired. In company, even in a *tête-à-tête*,[4] Mr. Wordsworth is often silent, indolent, and reserved. If he is become verbose and oracular of late years, he was not so in his better days. He threw out a bold or an indifferent remark without either effort or pretension, and relapsed into musing again. He shone most (because he seemed most roused and animated) in reciting his own poetry, or in talking about it. He sometimes gave striking views of his feelings and trains of association in composing certain passages; or if one did not always understand his distinctions, still there was no want of interest—there was a latent meaning worth inquiring into, like a vein of ore that one cannot exactly hit upon at the moment, but of which there are sure indications. His standard of poetry is high and severe, almost to exclusiveness. He admits of nothing below, scarcely of any thing above himself. It is fine to hear him talk of the way in which certain subjects should have been treated by eminent poets, according to his notions of the art. Thus he finds fault with Dryden's description of Bacchus in the *Alexander's Feast*, as if he were a mere good-looking youth, or boon companion—

> Flushed with a purple grace, He shows his honest face—[5]

instead of representing the God returning from the conquest of India, crowned with vine-leaves, and drawn by panthers, and followed by troops of satyrs, of wild men and animals that he had tamed. You would think, in hearing him speak on this subject, that you saw Titian's picture of the meeting of *Bacchus and Ariadne*—so classic were his conceptions, so glowing his style. Milton is his great idol, and he sometimes dares to compare himself with him. His sonnets, indeed, have something of the same high-raised tone and prophetic spirit. Chaucer is another prime favourite of his, and he has been at the pains to modernize some of the Canterbury Tales. Those persons who look upon Mr. Wordsworth as a merely puerile writer, must be rather at a loss to account for his strong predilection for such geniuses as Dante and Michelangelo.[6] We do not think our author has any very cordial sympathy with Shakespeare. How should he? Shakespeare was the least of an egotist of any body in the world. He does not much relish the variety and scope of dramatic composition. "He hates those interlocutions between Lucius and Caius." Yet Mr. Wordsworth himself

[1] *toujours perdrix* "Always partridge": too much of the same thing.

[2] *Holbein's heads* The portraits of Hans Holbein (1497–1543).

[3] *"man ... likelihood"* From Shakespeare's *1 Henry IV*, 3.2.45: "A fellow of no mark no likelihood."

[4] *tête-à-tête* Private conversation between two people.

[5] *Flushed ... face* From John Dryden's "Alexander's Feast," 3.5–6.

[6] *Dante* Alighieri Dante (1265–1321); *Michelangelo* Michelangelo Buonarroti (1475–1564).

wrote a tragedy when he was young; and we have heard the following energetic lines quoted from it, as put into the mouth of a person smit with remorse for some rash crime:

—Action is momentary,
The motion of a muscle this way or that;
Suffering is long, obscure, and infinite![1]

Perhaps for want of light and shade, and the unshackled spirit of the drama, this performance was never brought forward. Our critic has a great dislike to Gray, and a fondness for Thomson and Collins. It is mortifying to hear him speak of Pope and Dryden,[2] whom, because they have been supposed to have all the possible excellences of poetry, he will allow to have none. Nothing, however, can be fairer, or more amusing, than the way in which he sometimes exposes the unmeaning verbiage of modern poetry. Thus, in the beginning of Dr. Johnson's *Vanity of Human Wishes*—

Let observation with extensive view
Survey mankind from China to Peru[3]

he says there is a total want of imagination accompanying the words, the same idea is repeated three times under the disguise of a different phraseology: it comes to this—"let *observation*, with extensive *observation, observe mankind*"; or take away the first line, and the second,

Survey mankind from China to Peru.

literally conveys the whole. Mr. Wordsworth is, we must say, a perfect Drawcansir[4] as to prose writers. He complains of the dry reasoners and matter-of-fact people for their want of *passion*; and he is jealous of the rhetorical declaimers and rhapsodists as trenching on the province of poetry. He condemns all French writers (as well of poetry as prose) in the lump. His list in this way is indeed small. He approves of Walton's Angler, Paley,[5] and some other writers of an inoffensive modesty of pretension. He also likes books of voyages and travels, and Robinson Crusoe.[6] In art, he greatly esteems Bewick's woodcuts, and Waterloo's[7] sylvan etchings. But he sometimes takes a higher tone, and gives his mind fair play. We have known him enlarge with a noble intelligence and enthusiasm on Nicolas Poussin's fine landscape-compositions, pointing out the unity of design that pervades them, the superintending mind, the imaginative principle that brings all to bear on the same end; and declaring he would not give a rush for any landscape that did not express the time of day, the climate, the period of the world it was meant to illustrate, or had not this character of *wholeness* in it. His eye also does justice to Rembrandt's[8] fine and masterly effects. In the way in which that artist works something out of nothing, and transforms the stump of a tree, a common figure into an *ideal* object, by the gorgeous light and shade thrown upon it, he perceives an analogy to his own mode of investing the minute details of nature with an atmosphere of sentiment; and in pronouncing Rembrandt to be a man of genius, feels that he strengthens his own claim to the title. It has been said of Mr. Wordsworth, that "he hates conchology, that he hates the Venus of Medicis."[9] But these, we hope, are mere epigrams and *jeux-d'esprit*,[10] as far from truth as they are free from malice; a sort of running satire or critical clenches—

Where one for sense and one for rhyme
Is quite sufficient at one time.[11]

We think, however, that if Mr. Wordsworth had been a more liberal and candid critic, he would have been a more

---

[1] *Action ... infinite!* From Wordsworth's play *The Borderers*: "Action is transitory—a step, a blow, / The motion of a muscle—this way or that— / ... / Suffering is permanent, obscure and dark."

[2] *Gray ... Dryden* Poets Thomas Gray (1716–71), James Thomson (1700–48), William Collins (1721–59), Alexander Pope (1688–1744), John Dryden (1631–1700).

[3] *Let ... Peru* "The Vanity of Human Wishes" 1–2.

[4] *Drawcansir* Bully, from a character in George Villiers's play *The Rehearsal.*

[5] *Walton's Angler* Izaak Walton's *The Compleat Angler* (1653); *Paley* William Paley (1743–1805), philosopher and theologian.

[6] *Robinson Crusoe* Novel by Daniel Defoe (1660–1731).

[7] *Bewick* Thomas Bewick (1753–1828); *Waterloo* Anthonie Waterloo (1610–90).

[8] *Rembrandt* Rembrandt Harmenszoon van Rijn (1606–69).

[9] *"he hates ... Medicis"* Referring to Sandro Botticelli's painting *The Birth of Venus*, in which Venus is standing on a scallop shell.

[10] *jeux-d'esprit* Witticisms.

[11] *Where ... time* From Samuel Butler's *Hudibras* 2.1.29–30: "For one for sense, and one for rhyme, / I think's sufficient at one time."

sterling writer. If a greater number of sources of pleasure had been open to him, he would have communicated pleasure to the world more frequently. Had he been less fastidious in pronouncing sentence on the works of others, his own would have been received more favourably, and treated more leniently. The current of his feelings is deep, but narrow; the range of his understanding is lofty and aspiring rather than discursive. The force, the originality, the absolute truth and identity with which he feels some things, makes him indifferent to so many others. The simplicity and enthusiasm of his feelings, with respect to nature, renders him bigotted and intolerant in his judgments of men and things. But it happens to him, as to others, that his strength lies in his weakness; and perhaps we have no right to complain. We might get rid of the cynic and the egotist, and find in his stead a common place man. We should "take the good the Gods provide us":[1] a fine and original vein of poetry is not one of their most contemptible gifts, and the rest is scarcely worth thinking of, except as it may be a mortification to those who expect perfection from human nature; or who have been idle enough at some period of their lives, to deify men of genius as possessing claims above it. But this is a chord that jars, and we shall not dwell upon it.

Lord Byron we have called, according to the old proverb, "the spoiled child of fortune":[2] Mr. Wordsworth might plead, in mitigation of some peculiarities, that he is "the spoiled child of disappointment." We are convinced, if he had been early a popular poet, he would have borne his honours meekly, and would have been a person of great *bonhommie*[3] and frankness of disposition. But the sense of injustice and of undeserved ridicule sours the temper and narrows the views. To have produced works of genius, and to find them neglected or treated with scorn, is one of the heaviest trials of human patience. We exaggerate our own merits when they are denied by others, and are apt to grudge and cavil[4] at every particle of praise bestowed on those to whom we feel a conscious superiority. In mere self-defence we turn against the world, when it turns against us; brood over the undeserved slights we receive; and thus the genial current of the soul is stopped, or vents itself in effusions of petulance and self-conceit. Mr. Wordsworth has thought too much of contemporary critics and criticism; and less than he ought of the award of posterity, and of the opinion, we do not say of private friends, but of those who were made so by their admiration of his genius. He did not court popularity by a conformity to established models, and he ought not to have been surprised that his originality was not understood as a matter of course. He has *gnawed too much on the bridle*; and has often thrown out crusts to the critics, in mere defiance or as a point of honour when he was challenged, which otherwise his own good sense would have withheld. We suspect that Mr. Wordsworth's feelings are a little morbid in this respect, or that he resents censure more than he is gratified by praise. Otherwise, the tide has turned much in his favour of late years—he has a large body of determined partisans—and is at present sufficiently in request with the public to save or relieve him from the last necessity to which a man of genius can be reduced—that of becoming the God of his own idolatry!

—1825

[1] *"take ... provide us"* From Plautus's play *Rudens* 4.7.3: "If you are wise, be wise; keep what goods the gods provide you."

[2] *"spoiled child of fortune"* From the Latin *"fortunae filius."* After Byron's death in 1824, Thomas Moore wrote: "[Byron] was truly a spoiled child, not merely the spoiled child of his parent, but the spoiled child of nature, the spoiled child of fortune, the spoiled child of fame, the spoiled child of society."

[3] *bonhommie* Pleasant nature.

[4] *cavil* Quibble.

Thomas De Quincey

1785 – 1859

Because he published his first essay in 1821, Thomas De Quincey appears to be a contemporary of Byron, Shelley, and Keats. The sensational title of his most famous work, *Confessions of an English Opium-Eater*, adds to the case for associating him with these later Romantics. For his elegant and introspective style, however, De Quincey is better compared with Wordsworth and Coleridge, the earlier Romantics he so admired, as well as with the other major essayists of his time, Lamb and Hazlitt. Written in installments for one of the magazines popular in the day, *Confessions* was one of the first pieces De Quincey submitted, and it brought him immediate notoriety and success. Citing St. Augustine and Rousseau as predecessors of his autobiographical "impassioned prose," De Quincey at times wrote lovingly about his addiction: "If opium-eating be a sensual pleasure, and if I am bound to confess that I have indulged in it to an excess not yet *recorded* of any other man, it is no less true that I have struggled against this fascinating enthralment with a religious zeal, and have at length accomplished what I never yet heard attributed to any other man—have untwisted, almost to its final links, the accursed chain which fettered me." Whether he ever became unfettered is in question—De Quincey seems to have remained hopelessly addicted his entire adult life—but he went on to write hundreds of essays on subjects as diverse as German philosophy and literature, Shakespearean drama, the French Revolution, economics, Christianity, and the California gold rush.

De Quincey was born in Manchester in 1785 to Elizabeth Penson and Thomas Quincey, a successful linen merchant. One of eight children, he had already experienced the loss of two sisters by the time of his father's early death in 1793. Even though these events made for a troubled childhood, De Quincey gained a reputation as a precocious student and scholar. In 1796 he entered Bath Grammar School, where he became fluent in Latin and Greek despite what he considered his ineffectual teachers. He later wrote that a headmaster once said of his brilliance as a Greek scholar: "[T]hat boy could harangue an Athenian mob better than you and I could address an English one."

In 1802 De Quincey fled the school with the thought of presenting himself to Wordsworth, whose *Lyrical Ballads* he had greatly admired. Instead he embarked on a tour of Wales and eventually arrived in London, hungry and destitute. These years, although difficult, were fodder for some of his most vivid recollections. In the *Confessions,* for example, De Quincey often recalls his relationship with a prostitute named Ann, who had befriended and housed him in London. A year later, he returned to his family and enrolled in Worcester College, Oxford, where he became known as a solitary but brilliant scholar. During his college years he began taking laudanum—the liquid form of opium—for a toothache, and for a number of years his habit was kept under control. In 1807 he once again quit school, this time on the brink of examinations for which he had appeared to be extremely well-prepared.

De Quincey came to know Coleridge during his university years, and through Coleridge he met his idol, Wordsworth. The attraction was such that De Quincey settled in Grasmere in order to be near both poets, eventually moving into Dove Cottage, the Wordsworths' home, when Dorothy and William moved into a larger house. After years of close friendship, De Quincey became estranged from the Wordsworths when his addiction became uncontrollable and when he chose to live out of wedlock with

Margaret Simpson, a local farmer's daughter. The couple married in 1816 after the birth of their son. They eventually had eight children together during their twenty-one years of marriage.

Again destitute, De Quincey moved his family to London and began publishing the *Confessions* anonymously in *The London Magazine*. His "spiritual autobiography" is in part a paean to the glories of opium—"Thou hast the keys of Paradise, oh just, subtle, and mighty opium!"—and in part a record of the nightmares and dream visions he experienced as an addict. (He influenced both Edgar Allan Poe and Charles Baudelaire, not only in their writing, but also in their use of the drug.)

De Quincey had a sense of the importance of dreams and the unconscious that was remarkable for his time. "I feel assured," he wrote in *Confessions*, "that there is no such thing as *forgetting* possible to the mind; a thousand accidents may, and will, interpose a veil between our present consciousness and the secret inscriptions on the mind. Accidents of the same sort will also rend away this veil; but alike, whether veiled or unveiled, the inscription remains forever." De Quincey later penned *Suspiria de Profundis* (1845), a sequel to the *Confessions* in which he wrote about his dreams with considerable psychological acuity; many regard his ideas as precursors to Freud's dream theories.

Although his lifestyle was anything but conservative, the political and moral conservatism of many of his ideas was deep-seated. He was also a talented humorist, as his 1827 essay "On Murder Considered as One of the Fine Arts" well illustrates. De Quincey delineates how "drinking and Sabbath-breaking" and eventual "incivility and procrastination" follows on the "downward path" from murder. "Many a man," De Quincey writes, "dated his ruin from some murder or other that perhaps he thought little of at the time."

In the 1850s De Quincey began compiling the fourteen-volume series *Selections Grave and Gay from Writings Published and Unpublished*, which was completed in 1860, a year after his death. In the words of a review written shortly afterward in London's *Quarterly Review*, "The position of De Quincey in the literature of the present day is remarkable. We might search in vain for a writer who, with equal powers, has made an equally slight impression upon the general public. His style is superb; his powers of reasoning are unsurpassed; his imagination is warm and brilliant, and his humor … delicate." The past few decades have seen a surge of interest in De Quincey and his *Confessions of an English Opium-Eater*, which has struck a chord with many who have similarly experienced isolation and alienation from society.

⌘⌘⌘

Confessions of an English Opium-Eater

To the Reader

I here present you, courteous reader, with the record of a remarkable period in my life; according to my application of it, I trust that it will prove not merely an interesting record, but in a considerable degree useful and instructive. In *that* hope it is that I have drawn it up; and *that* must be my apology for breaking through that delicate and honourable reserve which, for the most part, restrains us from the public exposure of our own errors and infirmities. Nothing, indeed, is more revolting to English feelings than the spectacle of a human being obtruding on our notice his moral ulcers or scars, and tearing away that "decent drapery"[1] which time or indulgence to human frailty may have drawn over them; accordingly, the greater part of *our* confessions (that is, spontaneous and extra-judicial confessions) proceed from demi-reps,[2] adventurers, or swindlers; and for any such acts of gratuitous self-humiliation from those who can be supposed in sympathy with the decent and self-respecting part of society, we must look to French literature, or to that part of the German which is tainted with the spurious and defective sensibility of the French. All this I feel

[1] *"decent drapery"* From Edmund Burke's *Reflections on the Revolution in France* (1790): "All the pleasing illusions … are to be dissolved by this new conquering empire of light and reason. All the decent drapery of life is to be rudely torn off."

[2] *demi-reps* Women of dubious character.

so forcibly, and so nervously am I alive to reproach of this tendency, that I have for many months hesitated about the propriety of allowing this or any part of my narrative to come before the public eye until after my death (when, for many reasons, the whole will be published); and it is not without an anxious review of the reasons for and against this step that I have at last concluded on taking it.

Guilt and misery shrink, by a natural instinct, from public notice; they court privacy and solitude; and even in their choice of a grave will sometimes sequester themselves from the general population of the churchyard, as if declining to claim fellowship with the great family of man, and wishing (in the affecting language of Mr. Wordsworth)

> —humbly to express
> A penitential loneliness.[1]

It is well, upon the whole, and for the interest of us all, that it should be so; nor would I willingly in my own person manifest a disregard of such salutary feelings, nor in act or word do anything to weaken them; but, on the one hand, as my self-accusation does not amount to a confession of guilt, so, on the other, it is possible that, if it *did*, the benefit resulting to others from the record of an experience purchased at so heavy a price might compensate, by a vast overbalance, for any violence done to the feelings I have noticed, and justify a breach of the general rule. Infirmity and misery do not of necessity imply guilt. They approach or recede from shades of that dark alliance, in proportion to the probable motives and prospects of the offender, and the palliations,[2] known or secret, of the offence, in proportion as the temptations to it were potent from the first, and the resistance to it, in act or in effort, was earnest to the last. For my own part, without breach of truth or modesty, I may affirm that my life has been, on the whole, the life of a philosopher; from my birth I was made an intellectual creature, and intellectual in the highest sense my pursuits and pleasures have been, even from my schoolboy days. If opium-eating be a sensual pleasure, and if I am bound to confess that I have indulged in it to an excess not yet *recorded*[3] of any other man, it is no less true that I have struggled against this fascinating enthralment with a religious zeal, and have at length accomplished what I never yet heard attributed to any other man—have untwisted, almost to its final links, the accursed chain which fettered me. Such a self-conquest may reasonably be set off in counterbalance to any kind or degree of self-indulgence. Not to insist that in my case the self-conquest was unquestionable, the self-indulgence open to doubts of casuistry,[4] according as that name shall be extended to acts aiming at the bare relief of pain, or shall be restricted to such as aim at the excitement of positive pleasure.

Guilt, therefore, I do not acknowledge; and if I did, it is possible that I might still resolve on the present act of confession in consideration of the service which I may thereby render to the whole class of opium-eaters. But who are they? Reader, I am sorry to say a very numerous class indeed. Of this I became convinced some years ago by computing at that time the number of those in one small class of English society (the class of men distinguished for talents, or of eminent station) who were known to me, directly or indirectly, as opium-eaters; such, for instance, as the eloquent and benevolent ——,[5] the late Dean of ——, Lord ——, Mr. —— the philosopher, a late Under-Secretary of State (who described to me the sensation which first drove him to the use of opium in the very same words as the Dean of ——, viz.,[6] "that he felt as though rats were gnawing and abrading the coats of his stomach"), Mr. ——, and many others hardly less known, whom it would be tedious to mention. Now, if one class, comparatively so limited, could furnish so many scores of cases (and that within the knowledge of one single inquirer), it was a natural inference that the entire population of England would furnish a proportionable number. The soundness of this inference, however, I doubted, until some facts became known to me which satisfied me

[1] *humbly ... loneliness* From Wordsworth's "The White Doe of Rylstone, or The Fate of the Nortons" (176–77): "[G]uilt, that humbly would express / A penitential loneliness."

[2] *palliations* Concealment or alleviation of symptoms.

[3] [De Quincey's note] "Not yet *recorded*," I say; for there is one celebrated man of the present day, who, if all be true which is reported of him, has greatly exceeded me in quantity. [De Quincey is referring to Samuel Taylor Coleridge.]

[4] *casuistry* Specious rationalization used to determine morality.

[5] *benevolent ——* De Quincey entered the full names in his 1856 revision to the *Confessions*, saying that the editor of the original version deleted the names.

[6] *viz.* I.e., *Le videlicet.* Latin: that is to say.

that it was not incorrect. I will mention two.

(1) Three respectable London druggists, in widely remote quarters of London, from whom I happened lately to be purchasing small quantities of opium, assured me that the number of amateur opium-eaters (as I may term them) was at this time immense; and that the difficulty of distinguishing those persons to whom habit had rendered opium necessary from such as were purchasing it with a view to suicide, occasioned them daily trouble and disputes. This evidence respected London only. But,

(2) —which will possibly surprise the reader more—some years ago, on passing through Manchester, I was informed by several cotton manufacturers that their workpeople were rapidly getting into the practice of opium-eating, so much so, that on a Saturday afternoon the counters of the druggists were strewed with pills of one, two, or three grains, in preparation for the known demand of the evening. The immediate occasion of this practice was the lowness of wages, which at that time would not allow them to indulge in ale or spirits, and wages rising, it may be thought that this practice would cease; but as I do not readily believe that any man having once tasted the divine luxuries of opium will afterwards descend to the gross and mortal enjoyments of alcohol, I take it for granted

That those eat now who never ate before;
And those who always ate, now eat the more.

Indeed, the fascinating powers of opium are admitted even by medical writers, who are its greatest enemies. Thus, for instance, Awsiter, apothecary to Greenwich Hospital, in his "Essay on the Effects of Opium" (published in the year 1763), when attempting to explain why Mead[1] had not been sufficiently explicit on the properties, counteragents, &c., of this drug, expresses himself in the following mysterious terms (φωνάντα συνετοισ[2]): "Perhaps he thought the subject of too delicate a nature to be made common; and as many people might then indiscriminately use it, it would take from that necessary fear and caution which should prevent their experiencing the extensive power of this drug, *for there are many properties in it, if universally known, that would habituate the use, and make it more in request with us than with Turks themselves*, the result of which knowledge," he adds, "must prove a general misfortune." In the necessity of this conclusion I do not altogether concur; but upon that point I shall have occasion to speak at the close of my Confessions, where I shall present the reader with the moral of my narrative.

Preliminary Confessions

These preliminary confessions, or introductory narrative of the youthful adventures which laid the foundation of the writer's habit of opium-eating in afterlife, it has been judged proper to premise, for three several reasons:

1. As forestalling that question, and giving it a satisfactory answer, which else would painfully obtrude itself in the course of the Opium Confessions—"How came any reasonable being to subject himself to such a yoke of misery; voluntarily to incur a captivity so servile, and knowingly to fetter himself with such a sevenfold chain?"—a question which, if not somewhere plausibly resolved, could hardly fail, by the indignation which it would be apt to raise as against an act of wanton folly, to interfere with that degree of sympathy which is necessary in any case to an author's purposes.

2. As furnishing a key to some parts of that tremendous scenery which afterwards peopled the dreams of the opium-eater.

3. As creating some previous interest of a personal sort in the confessing subject, apart from the matter of the confessions, which cannot fail to render the confessions themselves more interesting. If a man "whose talk is of oxen" should become an opium-eater, the probability is that (if he is not too dull to dream at all) he will dream about oxen; whereas, in the case before him, the reader will find that the opium-eater boasteth himself to be a philosopher, and accordingly, that the phantasmagoria of *his* dreams (waking or sleeping, daydreams or night-dreams) is suitable to one who in that character

Humani nihil a se alienum putat.[3]

For amongst the conditions which he deems indispensable to the sustaining of any claim to the title of

[1] *Mead* Dr. Richard Mead (1673–1754), said to be the leading physician of the age, whose patients included Queen Anne and Sir Isaac Newton.

[2] φωνάντα συνετοισ ι Greek: speaking to the wise.

[3] *Humani … putat* Latin: from Terence's *Heautontimorumenos* (163 BCE); translates to: He thinks that nothing that is human is alien to him.

philosopher is not merely the possession of a superb intellect in its *analytic* functions (in which part of the pretensions, however, England can for some generations show but few claimants; at least, he is not aware of any known candidate for this honour who can be styled emphatically *a subtle thinker*, with the exception of Samuel Taylor Coleridge, and in a narrower department of thought with the recent illustrious exception[1] of David Ricardo[2]) but also on such a constitution of the *moral* faculties as shall give him an inner eye and power of intuition for the vision and the mysteries of our human nature: *that* constitution of faculties, in short, which (amongst all the generations of men that from the beginning of time have deployed into life, as it were, upon this planet) our English poets have possessed in the highest degree, and Scottish professors[3] in the lowest.

I have often been asked how I first came to be a regular opium-eater, and have suffered, very unjustly, in the opinion of my acquaintance from being reputed to have brought upon myself all the sufferings which I shall have to record, by a long course of indulgence in this practice purely for the sake of creating an artificial state of pleasurable excitement. This, however, is a misrepresentation of my case. True it is that for nearly ten years I did occasionally take opium for the sake of the exquisite pleasure it gave me; but so long as I took it with this view I was effectually protected from all material bad consequences by the necessity of interposing long intervals between the several acts of indulgence, in order to renew the pleasurable sensations. It was not for the purpose of creating pleasure, but of mitigating pain in the severest degree, that I first began to use opium as an article of daily diet. In the twenty-eighth year of my age a most painful affection of the stomach, which I had first experienced about ten years before, attacked me in great strength. This affection had originally been caused by extremities of hunger, suffered in my boyish days. During the season of hope and redundant happiness which succeeded (that is, from eighteen to twenty-four) it had slumbered; for the three following years it had revived at intervals; and now, under unfavourable circumstances, from depression of spirits, it attacked me with a violence that yielded to no remedies but opium. As the youthful sufferings which first produced this derangement of the stomach were interesting in themselves, and in the circumstances that attended them, I shall here briefly retrace them.

My father died when I was about seven years old, and left me to the care of four guardians. I was sent to various schools, great and small, and was very early distinguished for my classical attainments, especially for my knowledge of Greek. At thirteen I wrote Greek with ease; and at fifteen my command of that language was so great that I not only composed Greek verses in lyric metres, but could converse in Greek fluently and without embarrassment—an accomplishment which I have not since met with in any scholar of my times, and which in my case was owing to the practice of daily reading off the newspapers into the best Greek I could furnish extempore;[4] for the necessity of ransacking my memory and invention for all sorts and combinations of periphrastic expressions as equivalents for modern ideas, images, relations of things, &c., gave me a compass of diction which would never have been called out by a dull translation of moral essays, &c. "That boy," said one of my masters, pointing the attention of a stranger to me, "that boy could harangue an Athenian mob better than you and I could address an English one." He who honoured me with this eulogy was a scholar, "and a ripe and a good one,"[5] and of all my tutors was the only one whom I loved or reverenced. Unfortunately for me (and, as I afterwards learned, to this worthy man's great indignation), I was transferred to the care, first of a blockhead, who was in a perpetual panic lest I should expose his ignorance, and finally to that of a

[1] [De Quincey's note] A third exception might perhaps have been added; and my reason for not adding that exception is chiefly because it was only in his juvenile efforts that the writer whom I allude to [William Hazlitt] expressly addressed hints to philosophical themes; his riper powers having been all dedicated (on very excusable and very intelligible grounds, under the present direction of the popular mind in England) to criticism and the fine arts. This reason apart, however, I doubt whether he is not rather to be considered an acute thinker than a subtle one. It is, besides, a great drawback on his mastery over philosophical subjects that he has obviously not had the advantage of a regular scholastic education: he has not read Plato in his youth (which most likely was only his misfortune), but neither has he read Kant in his manhood (which is his fault).

[2] *David Ricardo* British political economist, author of *On the Principles of Political Economy, and Taxation* (1819).

[3] [De Quincey's note] I disclaim any allusion to *existing* professors, of whom indeed I know only one.

[4] *extempore* Latin: immediately, without preparation or assistance.

[5] *"and a ripe and a good one"* From Shakespeare's *Henry VIII* 4.2: "He was a scholar, and a ripe and good one."

respectable scholar at the head of a great school on an ancient foundation. This man had been appointed to his situation by—— College, Oxford, and was a sound, well-built scholar, but (like most men whom I have known from that college) coarse, clumsy, and inelegant. A miserable contrast he presented, in my eyes, to the Etonian brilliancy of my favourite master; and beside, he could not disguise from my hourly notice the poverty and meagreness of his understanding. It is a bad thing for a boy to be and to know himself far beyond his tutors, whether in knowledge or in power of mind. This was the case, so far as regarded knowledge at least, not with myself only, for the two boys, who jointly with myself composed the first form,[1] were better Grecians than the headmaster, though not more elegant scholars, nor at all more accustomed to sacrifice to the Graces.[2] When I first entered I remember that we read Sophocles; and it was a constant matter of triumph to us, the learned triumvirate of the first form, to see our "Archididascalus"[3] (as he loved to be called) conning[4] our lessons before we went up, and laying a regular train, with lexicon and grammar, for blowing up and blasting (as it were) any difficulties he found in the choruses, whilst *we* never condescended to open our books until the moment of going up, and were generally employed in writing epigrams upon his wig or some such important matter. My two class-fellows were poor, and dependent for their future prospects at the university on the recommendation of the headmaster; but I, who had a small patrimonial property, the income of which was sufficient to support me at college, wished to be sent thither immediately. I made earnest representations on the subject to my guardians, but all to no purpose. One, who was more reasonable and had more knowledge of the world than the rest, lived at a distance; two of the other three resigned all their authority into the hands of the fourth; and this fourth, with whom I had to negotiate, was a worthy man in his way, but haughty, obstinate, and intolerant of all opposition to his will. After a certain number of letters and personal interviews, I found that I had nothing to hope for, not even a compromise of the matter, from my guardian. Unconditional submission was what he demanded, and I prepared myself, therefore, for other measures. Summer was now coming on with hasty steps, and my seventeenth birthday was fast approaching, after which day I had sworn within myself that I would no longer be numbered amongst schoolboys. Money being what I chiefly wanted, I wrote to a woman of high rank, who, though young herself, had known me from a child, and had latterly treated me with great distinction, requesting that she would "lend" me five guineas. For upwards of a week no answer came, and I was beginning to despond, when at length a servant put into my hands a double letter with a coronet on the seal. The letter was kind and obliging. The fair writer was on the seacoast, and in that way the delay had arisen; she enclosed double of what I had asked, and good-naturedly hinted that if I should *never* repay her, it would not absolutely ruin her. Now, then, I was prepared for my scheme. Ten guineas, added to about two which I had remaining from my pocket money, seemed to me sufficient for an indefinite length of time; and at that happy age, if no *definite* boundary can be assigned to one's power, the spirit of hope and pleasure makes it virtually infinite.

It is a just remark of Dr. Johnson's[5] (and, what cannot often be said of his remarks, it is a very feeling one), that we never do anything consciously for the last time (of things, that is, which we have long been in the habit of doing) without sadness of heart. This truth I felt deeply when I came to leave ——, a place which I did not love, and where I had not been happy. On the evening before I left —— forever, I grieved when the ancient and lofty schoolroom resounded with the evening service, performed for the last time in my hearing; and at night, when the muster-roll[6] of names was called over, and mine (as usual) was called first, I stepped forward, and passing the headmaster, who was standing by, I bowed to him, and looked earnestly in his face, thinking to myself, "He is old and infirm, and in this world I shall not see him again." I was right; I never *did* see him again, nor ever shall. He looked at me complacently, smiled good-naturedly, returned my salutation (or rather my valediction), and we parted (though he knew it not) forever. I could not reverence him intellectually, but he had been uniformly kind to me, and had allowed me many indul-

[1] *form* Grade.

[2] *Graces* In Greek mythology, the three sisters who personified grace and beauty.

[3] *"Archididascalus"* From the Greek word meaning "headmaster."

[4] *conning* Studying.

[5] *Dr. Johnson* Samuel Johnson (1709–84), English literary scholar and critic, and author of the *Dictionary of the English Language.*

[6] *muster-roll* Full list.

gences; and I grieved at the thought of the mortification I should inflict upon him.

The morning came which was to launch me into the world, and from which my whole succeeding life has in many important points taken its coloring. I lodged in the headmaster's house, and had been allowed from my first entrance the indulgence of a private room, which I used both as a sleeping room and as a study. At half after three I rose, and gazed with deep emotion at the ancient towers of ——, "drest in earliest light,"[1] and beginning to crimson with the radiant lustre of a cloudless July morning. I was firm and immovable in my purpose, but yet agitated by anticipation of uncertain danger and troubles; and if I could have foreseen the hurricane and perfect hailstorm of affliction which soon fell upon me, well might I have been agitated. To this agitation the deep peace of the morning presented an affecting contrast, and in some degree a medicine. The silence was more profound than that of midnight; and to me the silence of a summer morning is more touching than all other silence, because, the light being broad and strong as that of noonday at other seasons of the year, it seems to differ from perfect day chiefly because man is not yet abroad; and thus the peace of nature and of the innocent creatures of God seems to be secure and deep only so long as the presence of man and his restless and unquiet spirit are not there to trouble its sanctity. I dressed myself, took my hat and gloves, and lingered a little in the room. For the last year and a half this room had been my "pensive citadel": here I had read and studied through all the hours of night, and though true it was that for the latter part of this time I, who was framed for love and gentle affections, had lost my gaiety and happiness during the strife and fever of contention with my guardian, yet, on the other hand, as a boy so passionately fond of books, and dedicated to intellectual pursuits, I could not fail to have enjoyed many happy hours in the midst of general dejection. I wept as I looked round on the chair, hearth, writing table, and other familiar objects, knowing too certainly that I looked upon them for the last time. Whilst I write this it is eighteen years ago, and yet at this moment I see distinctly, as if it were yesterday, the lineaments and expression of the object on which I fixed my parting gaze. It was a picture of the lovely ——, which hung over the mantelpiece, the eyes and mouth of which were so beautiful, and the whole countenance so radiant with benignity and divine tranquillity, that I had a thousand times laid down my pen or my book to gather consolation from it, as a devotee from his patron saint. Whilst I was yet gazing upon it the deep tones of —— clock proclaimed that it was four o'clock. I went up to the picture, kissed it, and then gently walked out and closed the door forever!

* * *

So blended and intertwisted in this life are occasions of laughter and of tears, that I cannot yet recall without smiling an incident which occurred at that time, and which had nearly put a stop to the immediate execution of my plan. I had a trunk of immense weight, for, besides my clothes, it contained nearly all my library. The difficulty was to get this removed to a carrier's: my room was at an aerial elevation in the house, and (what was worse) the staircase which communicated with this angle of the building was accessible only by a gallery, which passed the headmaster's chamber door. I was a favourite with all the servants, and knowing that any of them would screen me and act confidentially, I communicated my embarrassment to a groom of the headmaster's. The groom swore he would do anything I wished, and when the time arrived went upstairs to bring the trunk down. This I feared was beyond the strength of any one man; however, the groom was a man

> Of Atlantean shoulders, fit to bear
> The weight of mightiest monarchies;[2]

and had a back as spacious as Salisbury Plain. Accordingly he persisted in bringing down the trunk alone, whilst I stood waiting at the foot of the last flight in anxiety for the event. For some time I heard him descending with slow and firm steps; but unfortunately, from his trepidation, as he drew near the dangerous quarter, within a few steps of the gallery, his foot slipped, and the mighty burden falling from his shoulders, gained such increase of impetus at each step of the descent, that on reaching the bottom it trundled, or rather leaped, right across, with the noise of twenty devils, against the very bedroom door of the Archididascalus. My first thought was that all was lost, and that my only chance for executing a retreat was to sacrifice my baggage. However, on reflection I determined

[1] *"drest in earliest light"* From Percy Bysshe Shelley's *The Revolt of Islam* (5.43.7–8).

[2] *Of Atlantean ... monarchies* From Milton's *Paradise Lost* (2.306–7).

to abide the issue. The groom was in the utmost alarm, both on his own account and on mine, but, in spite of this, so irresistibly had the sense of the ludicrous in this unhappy contretemps taken possession of his fancy, that he sang out a long, loud, and canorous[1] peal of laughter, that might have wakened the Seven Sleepers.[2] At the sound of this resonant merriment, within the very ears of insulted authority, I could not myself forbear joining in it, subdued to this, not so much by the unhappy *ètourderie*[3] of the trunk, as by the effect it had upon the groom. We both expected, as a matter of course, that Dr. —— would sally, out of his room, for in general, if but a mouse stirred, he sprang out like a mastiff from his kennel. Strange to say, however, on this occasion, when the noise of laughter had ceased, no sound, or rustling even, was to be heard in the bedroom. Dr. —— had a painful complaint, which, sometimes keeping him awake, made his sleep perhaps, when it did come, the deeper. Gathering courage from the silence, the groom hoisted his burden again, and accomplished the remainder of his descent without accident. I waited until I saw the trunk placed on a wheelbarrow and on its road to the carrier's; then, "with Providence my guide,"[4] I set off on foot, carrying a small parcel with some articles of dress under my arm: a favourite English poet in one pocket, and a small 12 mo.[5] volume, containing about nine plays of Euripides,[6] in the other.

It had been my intention originally to proceed to Westmoreland, both from the love I bore to that country and on other personal accounts. Accident, however, gave a different direction to my wanderings, and I bent my steps towards North Wales.

After wandering about for some time in Denbighshire, Merionethshire, and Carnarvonshire, I took lodgings in a small neat house in B——. Here I might have stayed with great comfort for many weeks, for provisions were cheap at B——, from the scarcity of other markets for the surplus produce of a wide agricultural district. An accident, however, in which perhaps no offence was designed, drove me out to wander again. I know not whether my reader may have remarked, but I have often remarked, that the proudest class of people in England (or at any rate the class whose pride is most apparent) are the families of bishops. Noblemen and their children carry about with them, in their very titles, a sufficient notification of their rank. Nay, their very names (and this applies also to the children of many untitled houses) are often, to the English ear, adequate exponents of high birth or descent. Sackville, Manners, Fitzroy, Paulet, Cavendish, and scores of others, tell their own tale. Such persons, therefore, find everywhere a due sense of their claims already established, except among those who are ignorant of the world by virtue of their own obscurity: "Not to know *them*, argues one's self unknown." Their manners take a suitable tone and coloring, and for once they find it necessary to impress a sense of their consequence upon others, they meet with a thousand occasions for moderating and tempering this sense by acts of courteous condescension. With the families of bishops it is otherwise: with them, it is all uphill work to make known their pretensions; for the proportion of the episcopal bench taken from noble families is not at any time very large, and the succession to these dignities is so rapid that the public ear seldom has time to become familiar with them, unless where they are connected with some literary reputation. Hence it is that the children of bishops carry about with them an austere and repulsive air, indicative of claims not generally acknowledged, a sort of *noli me tangere*[7] manner, nervously apprehensive of too familiar approach, and shrinking with the sensitiveness of a gouty man from all contact with the οι πολλοι.[8] Doubtless, a powerful understanding, or unusual goodness of nature, will preserve a man from such weakness, but in general the truth of my representation will be acknowledged; pride, if not of deeper root in such families, appears at least more upon the surface of their manners. This spirit of manners naturally communicates itself to their domestics and other

[1] *canorous* Resonant.

[2] *Seven Sleepers* Cf. Symeon Metaphrastes's legend (as told in "Lives of the Saints") of the seven Christians of Ephesus, who fled to a cave during Decius's persecution of Christians (250 BCE), and there fell asleep for 200 years. This story has been retold in many cultures and is the basis of the tale of Rip Van Winkle.

[3] *ètourderie* French: blunder.

[4] *"with Providence my guide"* From Milton's *Paradise Lost* (12.645–6): "The world was all before them, where to choose / Their place of rest, and Providence their guide."

[5] *12 mo.* Duodecimo (the smallest of the standard book sizes—each page measures 1/12th of a full sheet of paper).

[6] *Euripedes* Greek playwright (c. 480–406 BCE).

[7] *noli me tangere* Latin: touch me not.

[8] οι πολλοι Greek: hoi polloi, common people.

dependants. Now, my landlady had been a lady's maid or a nurse in the family of the Bishop of ——, and had but lately married away and "settled" (as such people express it) for life. In a little town like B——, merely to have lived in the bishop's family conferred some distinction; and my good landlady had rather more than her share of the pride I have noticed on that score. What "my lord" said and what "my lord" did, how useful he was in Parliament and how indispensable at Oxford, formed the daily burden of her talk. All this I bore very well, for I was too good-natured to laugh in anybody's face, and I could make an ample allowance for the garrulity of an old servant. Of necessity, however, I must have appeared in her eyes very inadequately impressed with the bishop's importance, and, perhaps to punish me for my indifference, or possibly by accident, she one day repeated to me a conversation in which I was indirectly a party concerned. She had been to the palace to pay her respects to the family, and, dinner being over, was summoned into the dining room. In giving an account of her household economy she happened to mention that she had let her apartments. Thereupon the good bishop (it seemed) had taken occasion to caution her as to her selection of inmates, "for," said he, "you must recollect, Betty, that this place is in the high road to the Head; so that multitudes of Irish swindlers running away from their debts into England, and of English swindlers running away from their debts to the Isle of Man, are likely to take this place in their route." This advice certainly was not without reasonable grounds, but rather fitted to be stored up for Mrs. Betty's private meditations than specially reported to me. What followed, however, was somewhat worse. "Oh, my lord," answered my landlady (according to her own representation of the matter), "I really don't think this young gentleman is a swindler, because——" "You don't *think* me a swindler?" said I, interrupting her, in a tumult of indignation: "for the future I shall spare you the trouble of thinking about it." And without delay I prepared for my departure. Some concessions the good woman seemed disposed to make; but a harsh and contemptuous expression, which I fear that I applied to the learned dignitary himself, roused her indignation in turn, and reconciliation then became impossible. I was indeed greatly irritated at the bishop's having suggested any grounds of suspicion, however remotely, against a person whom he had never seen; and I thought of letting him know my mind in Greek, which, at the same time that it would furnish some presumption that I was no swindler, would also (I hoped) compel the bishop to reply in the same language, in which case I doubted not to make it appear that if I was not so rich as his lordship, I was a far better Grecian. Calmer thoughts, however, drove this boyish design out of my mind; for I considered that the bishop was in the right to counsel an old servant; that he could not have designed that his advice should be reported to me; and that the same coarseness of mind which had led Mrs. Betty to repeat the advice at all, might have coloured it in a way more agreeable to her own style of thinking than to the actual expressions of the worthy bishop.

I left the lodgings the very same hour, and this turned out a very unfortunate occurrence for me, because, living henceforward at inns, I was drained of my money very rapidly. In a fortnight I was reduced to short allowance; that is, I could allow myself only one meal a day. From the keen appetite produced by constant exercise and mountain air, acting on a youthful stomach, I soon began to suffer greatly on this slender regimen, for the single meal which I could venture to order was coffee or tea. Even this, however, was at length withdrawn; and afterwards, so long as I remained in Wales, I subsisted either on blackberries, hips, haws, &c., or on the casual hospitalities which I now and then received in return for such little services as I had an opportunity of rendering. Sometimes I wrote letters of business for cottagers who happened to have relatives in Liverpool or in London; more often I wrote love letters to their sweethearts for young women who had lived as servants at Shrewsbury or other towns on the English border. On all such occasions I gave great satisfaction to my humble friends, and was generally treated with hospitality; and once in particular, near the village of Llan-y-styndw (or some such name), in a sequestered part of Merionethshire, I was entertained for upwards of three days by a family of young people with an affectionate and fraternal kindness that left an impression upon my heart not yet impaired. The family consisted at that time of four sisters and three brothers, all grown up, and all remarkable for elegance and delicacy of manners. So much beauty, and so much native good breeding and refinement, I do not remember to have seen before or since in any cottage, except once or twice in Westmoreland and Devonshire. They spoke English, an accomplishment not often met with in so many members of one family, especially in villages remote from the high road. Here I wrote, on my first introduction, a letter about prize money,[1] for one of the brothers, who had served on board an English man-of-war,[2] and, more privately, two love letters for two of the sisters. They were both interesting looking girls, and one of uncommon loveliness. In the midst of their confusion and blushes, whilst dictating, or rather giving me general instructions, it did not require any great penetration to discover that what they wished was that their letters should be as kind as was consistent with proper maidenly pride. I contrived so to temper my expressions as to reconcile the gratification of both feelings; and they were as much pleased with the way in which I had expressed their thoughts as (in their simplicity) they were astonished at my having so readily discovered them. The reception one meets with from the women of a family generally determines the tenor of one's whole entertainment. In this case I had discharged my confidential duties as secretary so much to the general satisfaction, perhaps also amusing them with my conversation, that I was pressed to stay with a cordiality which I had little inclination to resist. I slept with the brothers, the only unoccupied bed standing in the apartment of the young women; but in all other points they treated me with a respect not usually paid to purses as light as mine—as if my scholarship were sufficient evidence that I was of "gentle blood." Thus I lived with them for three days and great part of a fourth; and, from the undiminished kindness which they continued to show me, I believe I might have stayed with them up to this time, if their power had corresponded with their wishes. On the last morning, however, I perceived upon their countenances, as they sat at breakfast, the expression of some unpleasant communication which was at hand; and soon after, one of the brothers explained to me that their parents had gone, the day before my arrival, to an annual meeting of Methodists, held at Carnarvon, and were that day expected to return; "and if they should not be so civil as they ought to be," he begged, on the part of all the young people, that I would not take it amiss. The parents returned with churlish faces, and "Dym Sassenach" (no English) in answer to all my addresses. I saw how matters stood; and so, taking an affectionate leave of my kind and interesting young hosts, I went my way; for, though they spoke warmly to their parents in my behalf, and often excused the manner of the old people by saying it was "only their way," yet I easily understood that my talent for writing love letters would do as little to recommend me with two grave sexagenarian Welsh Methodists as my Greek sapphics or alcaics;[3] and what had been hospitality when offered to me with the gracious courtesy of my young friends, would become charity when connected with the harsh demeanour of these old people. Certainly, Mr. Shelley is right in his notions about old age:[4] unless powerfully counteracted by all sorts of opposite agencies, it is a miserable corrupter and blighter to the genial charities of the human heart.

Soon after this I contrived, by means which I must omit for want of room, to transfer myself to London. And now began the latter and fiercer stage of my long sufferings, without using a disproportionate expression I might say, of my agony. For I now suffered, for upwards of sixteen weeks, the physical anguish of hunger in various degrees of intensity, but as bitter perhaps as ever any human being can have suffered who has survived it. I would not needlessly harass my reader's feelings by a detail of all that I endured; for extremities such as these, under any circumstances of heaviest misconduct or guilt, cannot be contemplated, even in description, without a rueful pity that is painful to the natural goodness of the human heart. Let it suffice, at least on this occasion, to say that a few fragments of bread from the breakfast table of one individual (who supposed me to be ill, but did not know of my being in utter want), and these at uncertain intervals, constituted my whole support. During the former part of my sufferings (that is, generally in Wales, and always for the first two months in London) I was houseless, and very seldom slept under a roof. To this constant exposure to the open air I ascribe it mainly that I did not sink under my torments. Latterly, however, when colder and more inclement weather came on, and when, from the length of my sufferings, I had begun to sink into a more languishing condition, it was no doubt fortunate for me that the same person to whose breakfast table I had access, allowed me to sleep in a large unoccupied house of which he was tenant. Unoccupied I call it, for there was

[1] *prize money* Portion of the value of a enemy ship captured in war.

[2] *man-of-war* Warship.

[3] *sapphics or alcaics* Poetry in the verse form of the ancient Greek poets Sappho or Alcæus.

[4] *Shelley … old age* See Shelley's *Queen Mab* (Canto V).

no household or establishment in it; nor any furniture, indeed, except a table and a few chairs. But I found, on taking possession of my new quarters, that the house already contained one single inmate, a poor friendless child, apparently ten years old; but she seemed hunger-bitten, and sufferings of that sort often make children look older than they are. From this forlorn child I learned that she had slept and lived there alone for some time before I came; and great joy the poor creature expressed when she found that I was in future to be her companion through the hours of darkness. The house was large, and, from the want of furniture, the noise of the rats made a prodigious echoing on the spacious staircase and hall; and amidst the real fleshly ills of cold and, I fear, hunger, the forsaken child had found leisure to suffer still more (it appeared) from the self-created one of ghosts. I promised her protection against all ghosts whatsoever, but alas! I could offer her no other assistance. We lay upon the floor, with a bundle of cursed law papers for a pillow, but with no other covering than a sort of large horseman's cloak; afterwards, however, we discovered in a garret an old sofa cover, a small piece of rug, and some fragments of other articles, which added a little to our warmth. The poor child crept close to me for warmth, and for security against her ghostly enemies. When I was not more than usually ill I took her into my arms, so that in general she was tolerably warm, and often slept when I could not, for during the last two months of my sufferings I slept much in daytime, and was apt to fall into transient dozings at all hours. But my sleep distressed me more than my watching, for beside the tumultuousness of my dreams (which were only not so awful as those which I shall have to describe hereafter as produced by opium), my sleep was never more than what is called *dog-sleep*,[1] so that I could hear myself moaning, and was often, as it seemed to me, awakened suddenly by my own voice; and about this time a hideous sensation began to haunt me as soon as I fell into a slumber, which has since returned upon me at different periods of my life—viz., a sort of twitching (I know not where, but apparently about the region of the stomach) which compelled me violently to throw out my feet for the sake of relieving it. This sensation coming on as soon as I began to sleep, and the effort to relieve it constantly awaking me, at length I slept only from exhaustion; and from increasing weakness (as I said before) I was constantly falling asleep and constantly awaking. Meantime, the master of the house sometimes came in upon us suddenly, and very early, sometimes not till ten o'clock, sometimes not at all. He was in constant fear of bailiffs. Improving on the plan of Cromwell, every night he slept in a different quarter of London; and I observed that he never failed to examine through a private window the appearance of those who knocked at the door before he would allow it to be opened. He breakfasted alone; indeed, his tea equipage would hardly have admitted of his hazarding an invitation to a second person, any more than the quantity of esculent[2] *matériel*, which for the most part was little more than a roll or a few biscuits which he had bought on his road from the place where he had slept. Or, if he *had* asked a party—as I once learnedly and facetiously observed to him—the several members of it must have *stood* in the relation to each other (not *sat* in any relation whatever) of succession, as the metaphysicians have it, and not of a coexistence, in the relation of the parts of time, and not of the parts of space. During his breakfast I generally contrived a reason for lounging in, and, with an air of as much indifference as I could assume, took up such fragments as he had left; sometimes, indeed, there were none at all. In doing this I committed no robbery except upon the man himself, who was thus obliged (I believe) now and then to send out at noon for an extra biscuit; for as to the poor child, *she* was never admitted into his study (if I may give that name to his chief depository of parchments, law writings, &c.); that room was to her the Bluebeard room of the house, being regularly locked on his departure to dinner, about six o'clock, which usually was his final departure for the night. Whether this child were an illegitimate daughter of Mr. ——, or only a servant, I could not ascertain; she did not herself know; but certainly she was treated altogether as a menial servant. No sooner did Mr. —— make his appearance than she went below stairs, brushed his shoes, coat, &c.; and, except when she was summoned to run an errand, she never emerged from the dismal Tartarus[3] of the kitchen, &c., to the upper air until my welcome knock at night called up her little trembling footsteps to the front door. Of her life during the daytime, however, I knew little but what I gathered from her own account at

[1] *dog-sleep* Light sleep, frequently interrupted by periods of wakefulness.

[2] *esculent* Edible.

[3] *Tartarus* Hell.

night, for as soon as the hours of business commenced I saw that my absence would be acceptable, and in general, therefore, I went off and sat in the parks or elsewhere until nightfall.

But who and what, meantime, was the master of the house himself? Reader, he was one of those anomalous practitioners in lower departments of the law who— what shall I say?—who on prudential reasons, or from necessity, deny themselves all indulgence in the luxury of too delicate a conscience, (a periphrasis[1] which might be abridged considerably, but *that* I leave to the reader's taste); in many walks of life a conscience is a more expensive encumbrance than a wife or a carriage; and just as people talk of "laying down" their carriages, so I suppose my friend Mr. —— had "laid down" his conscience for a time, meaning, doubtless, to resume it as soon as he could afford it. The inner economy of such a man's daily life would present a most strange picture, if I could allow myself to amuse the reader at his expense. Even with my limited opportunities for observing what went on, I saw many scenes of London intrigues and complex chicanery, "cycle and epicycle, orb in orb,"[2] at which I sometimes smile to this day, and at which I smiled then, in spite of my misery. My situation, however, at that time gave me little experience in my own person of any qualities in Mr. ——'s character but such as did him honour; and of his whole strange composition I must forget everything but that towards me he was obliging, and to the extent of his power, generous.

That power was not, indeed, very extensive; however, in common with the rats, I sat rent free; and as Dr. Johnson has recorded that he never but once in his life had as much wall-fruit[3] as he could eat, so let me be grateful that on that single occasion I had as large a choice of apartments in a London mansion as I could possibly desire. Except the Bluebeard room, which the poor child believed to be haunted, all others, from the attics to the cellars, were at our service; "the world was all before us,"[4] and we pitched our tent for the night in any spot we chose. This house I have already described as a large one; it stands in a conspicuous situation and in a well-known part of London. Many of my readers will have passed it, I doubt not, within a few hours of reading this. For myself, I never fail to visit it when business draws me to London; about ten o'clock this very night, August 15, 1821—being my birthday—I turned aside from my evening walk down Oxford Street, purposely to take a glance at it; it is now occupied by a respectable family, and by the lights in the front drawing room I observed a domestic party assembled, perhaps at tea, and apparently cheerful and gay. Marvellous contrast, in my eyes, to the darkness, cold, silence, and desolation of that same house eighteen years ago, when its nightly occupants were one famishing scholar and a neglected child. Her, by the bye, in after-years I vainly endeavoured to trace. Apart from her situation, she was not what would be called an interesting child; she was neither pretty, nor quick in understanding, nor remarkably pleasing in manners. But, thank God! even in those years I needed not the embellishments of novel accessories to conciliate my affections; plain human nature, in its humblest and most homely apparel, was enough for me, and I loved the child because she was my partner in wretchedness. If she is now living she is probably a mother, with children of her own; but, as I have said, I could never trace her.

This I regret, but another person there was at that time whom I have since sought to trace with far deeper earnestness, and with far deeper sorrow at my failure. This person was a young woman, and one of that unhappy class who subsist upon the wages of prostitution. I feel no shame, nor have any reason to feel it, in avowing that I was then on familiar and friendly terms with many women in that unfortunate condition. The reader needs neither smile at this avowal nor frown; for, not to remind my classical readers of the old Latin proverb, "*Sine Cerere*," &c.,[5] it may well be supposed that in the existing state of my purse my connection with such women could not have been an impure one. But the truth is, that at no time of my life have I been a person to hold myself polluted by the touch or approach of any creature that wore a human shape; on the contrary, from my very earliest youth it has been my pride to converse familiarly,

[1] *periphrasis* Circumlocution; use of more words than required.

[2] *"cycle ... orb"* From Milton's *Paradise Lost* (8.84).

[3] *wall-fruit* Fruit that is espaliered, or grown against a wall; ergo, choice fruit.

[4] *the world was all before us* From Milton's *Paradise Lost* (12.646–67): "The world was all before them [Adam and Eve], where to choose / Their place of rest."

[5] *"Sine Cerere," &c.* Latin: "*Sine Cerere et Baccho friget Venus*": Without Ceres and Bacchus (food and wine), Venus (love) freezes.

more Socratio,[1] with all human beings, man, woman, and child, that chance might fling in my way, a practice which is friendly to the knowledge of human nature, to good feelings, and to that frankness of address which becomes a man who would be thought a philosopher. For a philosopher should not see with the eyes of the poor limitary creature calling himself a man of the world, and filled with narrow and self-regarding prejudices of birth and education, but should look upon himself as a catholic[2] creature, and as standing in equal relation to high and low, to educated and uneducated, to the guilty and the innocent. Being myself at that time of necessity a peripatetic, or a walker of the streets, I naturally fell in more frequently with those female peripatetics who are technically called streetwalkers. Many of these women had occasionally taken my part against watchmen who wished to drive me off the steps of houses where I was sitting. But one amongst them, the one on whose account I have at all introduced this subject—yet no! let me not class the, oh! noble-minded Ann—with that order of women. Let me find, if it be possible, some gentler name to designate the condition of her to whose bounty and compassion, ministering to my necessities when all the world had forsaken me, I owe it that I am at this time alive. For many weeks I had walked at nights with this poor friendless girl up and down Oxford Street, or had rested with her on steps and under the shelter of porticoes. She could not be so old as myself; she told me, indeed, that she had not completed her sixteenth year. By such questions as my interest about her prompted I had gradually drawn forth her simple history. Hers was a case of ordinary occurrence (as I have since had reason to think), and one in which, if London beneficence had better adapted its arrangements to meet it, the power of the law might oftener be interposed to protect and to avenge. But the stream of London charity flows in a channel which, though deep and mighty, is yet noiseless and underground, not obvious or readily accessible to poor houseless wanderers; and it cannot be denied that the outside air and framework of London society is harsh, cruel, and repulsive. In any case, however, I saw that part of her injuries might easily have been redressed, and I urged her often and earnestly to lay her complaint before a magistrate. Friendless as she was, I assured her that she would meet with immediate attention, and that English justice, which was no respecter of persons, would speedily and amply avenge her on the brutal ruffian who had plundered her little property. She promised me often that she would, but she delayed taking the steps I pointed out from time to time, for she was timid and dejected to a degree which showed how deeply sorrow had taken hold of her young heart; and perhaps she thought justly that the most upright judge and the most righteous tribunals could do nothing to repair her heaviest wrongs. Something, however, would perhaps have been done, for it had been settled between us at length, but unhappily on the very last time but one that I was ever to see her, that in a day or two we should go together before a magistrate, and that I should speak on her behalf. This little service it was destined, however, that I should never realize. Meantime, that which she rendered to me, and which was greater than I could ever have repaid her, was this: One night, when we were pacing slowly along Oxford Street, and after a day when I had felt more than usually ill and faint, I requested her to turn off with me into Soho Square. Thither we went, and we sat down on the steps of a house, which to this hour I never pass without a pang of grief and an inner act of homage to the spirit of that unhappy girl, in memory of the noble action which she there performed. Suddenly, as we sat, I grew much worse. I had been leaning my head against her bosom, and all at once I sank from her arms and fell backwards on the steps. From the sensations I then had, I felt an inner conviction of the liveliest kind, that without some powerful and reviving stimulus I should either have died on the spot, or should at least have sunk to a point of exhaustion from which all reascent under my friendless circumstances would soon have become hopeless. Then it was, at this crisis of my fate, that my poor orphan companion, who had herself met with little but injuries in this world, stretched out a saving hand to me. Uttering a cry of terror, but without a moment's delay, she ran off into Oxford Street, and in less time than could be imagined returned to me with a glass of port wine and spices, that acted upon my empty stomach, which at that time would have rejected all solid food, with an instantaneous power of restoration; and for this glass the generous girl without a murmur paid out of her humble purse at a time—be it remembered!—when she had scarcely wherewithal to purchase the bare neces-

[1] *more Socratio* In the Socratic way: through a dialogue, both listening and speaking.

[2] *catholic* Sharing sympathies with all people.

saries of life, and when she could have no reason to expect that I should ever be able to reimburse her.

Oh, youthful benefactress! how often in succeeding years, standing in solitary places, and thinking of thee with grief of heart and perfect love—how often have I wished that, as in ancient times, the curse of a father was believed to have a supernatural power, and to pursue its object with a fatal necessity of self-fulfilment; even so the benediction of a heart oppressed with gratitude might have a like prerogative, might have power given to it from above to chase, to haunt, to waylay,[1] to overtake, to pursue thee into the central darkness of a London brothel, or (if it were possible) into the darkness of the grave, there to awaken thee with an authentic message of peace and forgiveness, and of final reconciliation!

I do not often weep, for not only do my thoughts on subjects connected with the chief interests of man daily, nay hourly, descend a thousand fathoms "too deep for tears;"[2] not only does the sternness of my habits of thought present an antagonism to the feelings which prompt tears—wanting of necessity to those who, being protected usually by their levity from any tendency to meditative sorrow, would by that same levity be made incapable of resisting it on any casual access of such feelings; but also, I believe that all minds which have contemplated such objects as deeply as I have done, must, for their own protection from utter despondency, have early encouraged and cherished some tranquilizing belief as to the future balances and the hieroglyphic meanings of human sufferings. On these accounts I am cheerful to this hour, and, as I have said, I do not often weep. Yet some feelings, though not deeper or more passionate, are more tender than others; and often, when I walk at this time in Oxford Street by dreamy lamplight, and hear those airs played on a barrel organ which years ago solaced me and my dear companion (as I must always call her), I shed tears, and muse with myself at the mysterious dispensation which so suddenly and so critically separated us forever. How it happened the reader will understand from what remains of this introductory narration.

Soon after the period of the last incident I have recorded I met in Albemarle Street a gentleman of his late Majesty's[3] household. This gentleman had received hospitalities on different occasions from my family, and he challenged me upon the strength of my family likeness. I did not attempt any disguise; I answered his questions ingenuously, and, on his pledging his word of honour that he would not betray me to my guardians, I gave him an address to my friend the attorney. The next day I received from him a ten-pound banknote. The letter enclosing it was delivered with other letters of business to the attorney, but though his look and manner informed me that he suspected its contents, he gave it up to me honourably and without demur.

This present, from the particular service to which it was applied, leads me naturally to speak of the purpose which had allured me up to London, and which I had been (to use a forensic word) soliciting from the first day of my arrival in London to that of my final departure. In so mighty a world as London it will surprise my readers that I should not have found some means of starving off the last extremities, of penury; and it will strike them that two resources at least must have been open to me—viz., either to seek assistance from the friends of my family, or to turn my youthful talents and attainments into some channel of pecuniary emolument.[4] As to the first course, I may observe generally, that what I dreaded beyond all other evils was the chance of being reclaimed by my guardians; not doubting that whatever power the law gave them would have been enforced against me to the utmost—that is, to the extremity of forcibly restoring me to the school which I had quitted, a restoration which, as it would in my eyes have been a dishonour, even if submitted to voluntarily, could not fail, when extorted from me in contempt and defiance of my own wishes and efforts, to have been a humiliation worse to me than death, and which would indeed have terminated in death. I was therefore shy enough of applying for assistance even in those quarters where I was sure of receiving it, at the risk of furnishing my guardians with any clue of recovering me. But as to London in particular, though doubtless my father had in his lifetime had many friends there, yet (as ten years had passed since his death) I remembered few of them even by name; and never having seen London

[1] *to haunt, to waylay* Cf. Wordsworth's "She was a Phantom of Delight" (9–10): "A dancing shape, an image gay, / To haunt, to startle, and waylay."

[2] *"too deep for tears"* From Wordsworth's *Ode: Intimations of Immortality from Recollections of Early Childhood* (11.17): "Thoughts that do often lie too deep for tears."

[3] *his late Majesty* King George III (1738–1820).

[4] *pecuniary emolument* Financial reward.

before, except once for a few hours, I knew not the address of even those few. To this mode of gaining help, therefore, in part the difficulty, but much more the paramount fear which I have mentioned, habitually indisposed me. In regard to the other mode, I now feel half inclined to join my reader in wondering that I should have overlooked it. As a corrector of Greek proofs (if in no other way) I might doubtless have gained enough for my slender wants. Such an office as this I could have discharged with an exemplary and punctual accuracy that would soon have gained me the confidence of my employers. But it must not be forgotten that, even for such an office as this, it was necessary that I should first of all have an introduction to some respectable publisher, and this I had no means of obtaining. To say the truth, however, it had never once occurred to me to think of literary labours as a source of profit. No mode sufficiently speedy of obtaining money had ever occurred to me but that of borrowing it on the strength of my future claims and expectations. This mode I sought by every avenue to compass; and amongst other persons I applied to a Jew named D——.[1]

[1] [De Quincey's note] To this same Jew, by the way, some eighteen months afterwards, I applied again on the same business; and, dating at that time from a respectable college, I was fortunate enough to gain his serious attention to my proposals. My necessities had not arisen from any extravagance or youthful levities (these my habits and the nature of my pleasures raised me far above), but simply from the vindictive malice of my guardian, who, when he found himself no longer able to prevent me from going to the university, had, as a parting token of his good nature, refused to sign an order for granting me a shilling beyond the allowance made to me at school—viz., 100 pounds per annum. Upon this sum it was in my time barely possible to have lived in college, and not possible to a man who, though above the paltry affectation of ostentatious disregard for money, and without any expensive tastes, confided nevertheless rather too much in servants, and did not delight in the petty details of minute economy. I soon, therefore, became embarrassed, and at length, after a most voluminous negotiation with the Jew (some parts of which, if I had leisure to rehearse them, would greatly amuse my readers), I was put in possession of the sum I asked for, on the "regular" terms of paying the Jew seventeen and a half percent by way of annuity on all the money furnished; Israel, on his part, graciously resuming no more than about ninety guineas of the said money, on account of an attorney's bill (for what services, to whom rendered, and when, whether at the siege of Jerusalem, at the building of the second Temple, or on some earlier occasion, I have not yet been able to discover). How many perches [areas of land] this bill measured I really forget; but I still keep it in a cabinet of natural curiosities, and some time or other I believe I shall present it to the British Museum.

To this Jew, and to other advertizing moneylenders (some of whom were, I believe, also Jews),[2] I had introduced myself with an account of my expectations, which account, on examining my father's will at Doctors' Commons,[3] they had ascertained to be correct. The person there mentioned as the second son of —— was found to have all the claims (or more than all) that I had stated; but one question still remained, which the faces of the Jews pretty significantly suggested—was I that person? This doubt had never occurred to me as a possible one; I had rather feared, whenever my Jewish friends scrutinised me keenly, that I might be too well known to be that person, and that some scheme might be passing in their minds for entrapping me and selling me to my guardians. It was strange to me to find my own self materialiter considered (so I expressed it, for I doted on logical accuracy of distinctions), accused, or at least suspected, of counterfeiting my own self formaliter considered.[4] However, to satisfy their scruples, I took the only course in my power. Whilst I was in Wales I had received various letters from young friends; these I produced, for I carried them constantly in my pocket, being, indeed, by this time almost the only relics of my personal encumbrances (excepting the clothes I wore) which I had not in one way or other disposed of. Most of these letters were from the Earl of ——, who was at that time my chief (or rather only) confidential friend. These letters were dated from Eton. I had also some from the Marquis of ——, his father, who, though absorbed in agricultural pursuits, yet having been an Etonian himself, and as good a scholar as a nobleman needs to be, still retained an affection for classical studies and for youthful scholars. He had accordingly, from the time that I was fifteen, corresponded with me; sometimes upon the great improvements which he had made or was meditating in the counties of M——

[2] *Jews* The association of Jews with moneylending, and the prejudice against Jews on the basis of this association, had deep roots in Western culture by the time De Quincey was writing. Beginning in the Middle Ages, many professions had been closed off to Jews; one of the relatively few occupations left open to a Jewish person was that of moneylending, which Christian strictures against usury had made disreputable.

[3] *Doctors' Commons* Area of the civil courts in London, chiefly used for marriages, divorces, and the probating of wills.

[4] *materialiter considered ... formaliter considered* Scholastic terms suggesting the material and formal aspects of beings supposed to be real.

and Sl—— since I had been there, sometimes upon the merits of a Latin poet, and at other times suggesting subjects to me on which he wished me to write verses.

On reading the letters, one of my Jewish friends agreed to furnish me with two or three hundred pounds on my personal security, provided I could persuade the young Earl—who was, by the way, not older than myself—to guarantee the payment on our coming of age, the Jew's final object being, as I now suppose, not the trifling profit he could expect to make by me, but the prospect of establishing a connection with my noble friend, whose immense expectations were well known to him. In pursuance of this proposal on the part of the Jew, about eight or nine days after I had received the ten pounds, I prepared to go down to Eton. Nearly three pounds of the money I had given to my money-lending friend, on his alleging that the stamps must be bought, in order that the writings might be preparing whilst I was away from London. I thought in my heart that he was lying; but I did not wish to give him any excuse for charging his own delays upon me. A smaller sum I had given to my friend the attorney (who was connected with the moneylenders as their lawyer), to which, indeed, he was entitled for his unfurnished lodgings. About fifteen shillings I had employed in re-establishing (though in a very humble way) my dress. Of the remainder I gave one quarter to Ann, meaning on my return to have divided with her whatever might remain. These arrangements made, soon after six o'clock on a dark winter evening I set off, accompanied by Ann, towards Piccadilly; for it was my intention to go down as far as Salthill on the Bath or Bristol mail.[1] Our course lay through a part of the town which has now all disappeared, so that I can no longer retrace its ancient boundaries—Swallow Street, I think it was called. Having time enough before us, however, we bore away to the left until we came into Golden Square; there, near the corner of Sherrard Street, we sat down, not wishing to part in the tumult and blaze of Piccadilly. I had told her of my plans some time before, and I now assured her again that she should share in my good fortune, if I met with any, and that I would never forsake her as soon as I had power to protect her. This I fully intended, as much from inclination as from a sense of duty; for setting aside gratitude, which in any case must have made me her debtor for life, I loved her as affectionately as if she had been my sister; and at this moment with sevenfold tenderness, from pity at witnessing her extreme dejection. I had apparently most reason for dejection, because I was leaving the saviour of my life; yet I, considering the shock my health had received, was cheerful and full of hope. She, on the contrary, who was parting with one who had had little means of serving her, except by kindness and brotherly treatment, was overcome by sorrow, so that, when I kissed her at our final farewell, she put her arms about my neck and wept without speaking a word. I hoped to return in a week at farthest, and I agreed with her that on the fifth night from that, and every night afterwards, she would wait for me at six o'clock near the bottom of Great Titchfield Street, which had been our customary haven, as it were, of rendezvous, to prevent our missing each other in the great Mediterranean of Oxford Street. This and other measures of precaution I took; one only I forgot. She had either never told me, or (as a matter of no great interest) I had forgotten her surname. It is a general practice, indeed, with girls of humble rank in her unhappy condition, not (as novel-reading women of higher pretensions) to style themselves Miss Douglas, Miss Montague, &c., but simply by their Christian names—Mary, Jane, Frances, &c. Her surname, as the surest means of tracing her hereafter, I ought now to have inquired; but the truth is, having no reason to think that our meeting could, in consequence of a short interruption, be more difficult or uncertain than it had been for so many weeks, I had scarcely for a moment adverted to it as necessary, or placed it amongst my memoranda against this parting interview; and my final anxieties being spent in comforting her with hopes, and in pressing upon her the necessity of getting some medicines for a violent cough and hoarseness with which she was troubled, I wholly forgot it until it was too late to recall her.

It was past eight o'clock when I reached the Gloucester coffeehouse, and the Bristol mail being on the point of going off, I mounted on the outside. The fine fluent motion[2] of this mail soon laid me asleep; it is somewhat remarkable that the first easy or refreshing sleep which I had enjoyed for some months, was on the outside of a

[1] *mail* I.e., the mail coach.

[2] [De Quincey's note] The Bristol mail is the best appointed in the Kingdom, owing to the double advantages of an unusually good road and of an extra sum for the expenses subscribed by the Bristol merchants.

mail coach—a bed which at this day I find rather an uneasy one. Connected with this sleep was a little incident which served, as hundreds of others did at that time, to convince me how easily a man who has never been in any great distress may pass through life without knowing, in his own person at least, anything of the possible goodness of the human heart—or, as I must add with a sigh, of its possible vileness. So thick a curtain of *manners* is drawn over the features and expression of men's *natures*, that to the ordinary observer the two extremities, and the infinite field of varieties which lie between them, are all confounded; the vast and multitudinous compass of their several harmonies reduced to the meagre outline of differences expressed in the gamut or alphabet of elementary sounds. The case was this: for the first four or five miles from London I annoyed my fellow passenger on the roof by occasionally falling against him when the coach gave a lurch to his side; and indeed, if the road had been less smooth and level than it is, I should have fallen off from weakness. Of this annoyance he complained heavily, as perhaps, in the same circumstances, most people would; he expressed his complaint, however, more morosely than the occasion seemed to warrant, and if I had parted with him at that moment I should have thought of him (if I had considered it worthwhile to think of him at all) as a surly and almost brutal fellow. However, I was conscious that I had given him some cause for complaint, and therefore I apologized to him, and assured him I would do what I could to avoid falling asleep for the future; and at the same time, in as few words as possible, I explained to him that I was ill and in a weak state from long suffering, and that I could not afford at that time to take an inside place. This man's manner changed, upon hearing this explanation, in an instant; and when I next woke for a minute from the noise and lights of Hounslow (for in spite of my wishes and efforts I had fallen asleep again within two minutes from the time I had spoken to him) I found that he had put his arm round me to protect me from falling off, and for the rest of my journey he behaved to me with the gentleness of a woman, so that at length I almost lay in his arms; and this was the more kind, as he could not have known that I was not going the whole way to Bath or Bristol. Unfortunately, indeed, I *did* go rather farther than I intended, for so genial and so refreshing was my sleep, that the next time after leaving Hounslow that I fully awoke was upon the sudden pulling up of the mail (possibly at a post office), and on inquiry I found that we had reached Maidenhead—six or seven miles, I think, ahead of Salthill. Here I alighted, and for the half minute that the mail stopped I was entreated by my friendly companion (who, from the transient glimpse I had had of him in Piccadilly, seemed to me to be a gentleman's butler, or person of that rank) to go to bed without delay. This I promised, though with no intention of doing so; and in fact I immediately set forward, or rather backward, on foot. It must then have been nearly midnight, but so slowly did I creep along that I heard a clock in a cottage strike four before I turned down the lane from Slough to Eton. The air and the sleep had both refreshed me, but I was weary nevertheless. I remember a thought (obvious enough, and which has been prettily expressed by a Roman poet) which gave me some consolation at that moment under my poverty. There had been some time before a murder committed on or near Hounslow Heath. I think I cannot be mistaken when I say that the name of the murdered person was *Steele*,[1] and that he was the owner of a lavender plantation in that neighbourhood. Every step of my progress was bringing me nearer to the Heath, and it naturally occurred to me that I and the accused murderer, if he were that night abroad, might at every instant be unconsciously approaching each other through the darkness, in which case, said I—supposing I, instead of being (as indeed I am) little better than an outcast—

> Lord of my learning, and no land beside—[2]

were, like my friend Lord ——, heir by general repute to 70,000 pounds per annum, what a panic should I be under at this moment about my throat! Indeed, it was not likely that Lord ——should ever be in my situation. But nevertheless, the spirit of the remark remains true—that vast power and possessions make a man shamefully afraid of dying; and I am convinced that many of the most intrepid adventurers, who, by fortunately being poor, enjoy the full use of their natural courage, would, if at the very instant of going into action news were brought to them that they had unexpectedly succeeded to an estate in England of 50,000 pounds a year, feel their dislike to

[1] *Steele* John Cole Steele was robbed and murdered in 1802.

[2] *Lord ... beside* Adapted from Shakespeare's *The Life and Death of King John* 1.1.142: "Lord of thy presence and no land beside."

bullets considerably sharpened,[1] and their efforts at perfect equanimity and self-possession proportionably difficult. So true it is, in the language of a wise man whose own experience had made him acquainted with both fortunes, that riches are better fitted

> To slacken virtue, and abate her edge,
> Than tempt her to do ought may merit praise.
>
> *Paradise Regained*.[2]

I dally with my subject because, to myself, the remembrance of these times is profoundly interesting. But my reader shall not have any further cause to complain, for I now hasten to its close. In the road between Slough and Eton I fell asleep, and just as the morning began to dawn I was awakened by the voice of a man standing over me and surveying me. I know not what he was; he was an ill-looking fellow, but not therefore of necessity an ill-meaning fellow; or, if he were, I suppose he thought that no person sleeping out of doors in winter could be worth robbing. In which conclusion, however, as it regarded myself, I beg to assure him, if he should be among my readers, that he was mistaken. After a slight remark he passed on; and I was not sorry at his disturbance, as it enabled me to pass through Eton before people were generally up. The night had been heavy and lowering, but towards the morning it had changed to a slight frost, and the ground and the trees were now covered with rime. I slipped through Eton unobserved, washed myself, and as far as possible adjusted my dress at a little public-house in Windsor, and about eight o'clock went down towards Pote's.[3] On my road I met some junior boys, of whom I made inquiries. An Etonian is always a gentleman; and, in spite of my shabby habiliments, they answered me civilly. My friend Lord —— was gone to the University of ——. "*Ibi omnis effusus labor*!"[4] I had, however, other friends at Eton; but it is not to all that wear that name in prosperity that a man is willing to present himself in distress. On recollecting myself, however, I asked for the Earl of D——, to whom (though my acquaintance with him was not so intimate as with some others) I should not have shrunk from presenting myself under any circumstances. He was still at Eton, though I believe on the wing for Cambridge. I called, was received kindly, and asked to breakfast.

Here let me stop for a moment to check my reader from any erroneous conclusions. Because I have had occasion incidentally to speak of various patrician friends, it must not be supposed that I have myself any pretension to rank and high blood. I thank God that I have not. I am the son of a plain English merchant, esteemed during his life for his great integrity, and strongly attached to literary pursuits (indeed, he was himself, anonymously, an author). If he had lived it was expected that he would have been very rich; but dying prematurely, he left no more than about 30,000 pounds amongst seven different claimants. My mother I may mention with honor, as still more highly gifted, for though unpretending to the name and honors of a *literary* woman, I shall presume to call her (what many literary women are not) an *intellectual* woman; and I believe that if ever her letters should be collected and published, they would be thought generally to exhibit as much strong and masculine sense, delivered in as pure "mother English," racy and fresh with idiomatic graces, as any in our language—hardly excepting those of Lady M. W. Montague.[5] These are my honors of descent, I have no other; and I have thanked God sincerely that I have not, because, in my judgment, a station which raises a man too eminently above the level of his fellow creatures is not the most favorable to moral or to intellectual qualities.

Lord D—— placed before me a most magnificent breakfast. It was really so; but in my eyes it seemed trebly magnificent, from being the first regular meal, the first "good man's table," that I had sat down to for months. Strange to say, however, I could scarce eat anything. On the day when I first received my ten- pound banknote I had gone to a baker's shop and bought a couple of rolls; this very shop I had two months or six weeks before surveyed with an eagerness of desire which it was almost

[1] [De Quincey's note] It will be objected that many men, of the highest rank and wealth, have in our own day, as well as throughout our history, been amongst the foremost in courting danger in battle. True, but this is not the case supposed; long familiarity with power has to them deadened its effect and its attractions.

[2] *To slacken … Regained* From Milton's *Paradise Regained* (II.455–56): To slacken virtue and abate her edge / Than prompt her to do aught may merit praise."

[3] *Pote's* Bookstore owned by Joseph Pote.

[4] *Ibi omnis effusus labor!* Latin: from Virgil's *Georgics* 4; "Poured out was all his labor."

[5] *Lady M. W. Montague* I.e., Lady Mary Wortley Montagu (1689–1762), English author known primarily for her letters.

humiliating to me to recollect. I remembered the story about Otway,[1] and feared that there might be danger in eating too rapidly. But I had no need for alarm; my appetite was quite sunk, and I became sick before I had eaten half of what I had bought. This effect from eating what approached to a meal I continued to feel for weeks; or, when I did not experience any nausea, part of what I ate was rejected, sometimes with acidity, sometimes immediately and without any acidity. On the present occasion, at Lord D——'s table, I found myself not at all better than usual, and in the midst of luxuries I had no appetite. I had, however, unfortunately, at all times a craving for wine; I explained my situation, therefore, to Lord D——, and gave him a short account of my late sufferings, at which he expressed great compassion and called for wine. This gave me a momentary relief and pleasure; and on all occasions when I had an opportunity I never failed to drink wine, which I worshipped then as I have since worshipped opium. I am convinced, however, that this indulgence in wine contributed to strengthen my malady, for the tone of my stomach was apparently quite sunk, and by a better regimen it might sooner, and perhaps effectually, have been revived. I hope that it was not from this love of wine that I lingered in the neighbourhood of my Eton friends; I persuaded myself then that it was from reluctance to ask of Lord D——, on whom I was conscious I had not sufficient claims, the particular service in quest of which I had come down to Eton. I was, however, unwilling to lose my journey, and—I asked it. Lord D——, whose good nature was unbounded, and which, in regard to myself, had been measured rather by his compassion perhaps for my condition, and his knowledge of my intimacy with some of his relatives, than by an over-rigorous inquiry into the extent of my own direct claims, faltered, nevertheless, at this request. He acknowledged that he did not like to have any dealings with moneylenders, and feared lest such a transaction might come to the ears of his connections. Moreover, he doubted whether *his* signature, whose expectations were so much more bounded than those of ——, would avail with my unchristian friends. However, he did not wish, as it seemed, to mortify me by an absolute refusal; for after a little consideration he promised, under certain conditions which he pointed out, to give his security. Lord D—— was at this time not eighteen years of age; but I have often doubted, on recollecting since the good sense and prudence which on this occasion he mingled with so much urbanity of manner (an urbanity which in him wore the grace of youthful sincerity), whether any statesman—the oldest and the most accomplished in diplomacy—could have acquitted himself better under the same circumstances. Most people, indeed, cannot be addressed on such a business without surveying you with looks as austere and unpropitious as those of a Saracen's[2] head.

Recomforted by this promise, which was not quite equal to the best but far above the worst that I had pictured to myself as possible, I returned in a Windsor coach to London three days after I had quitted it. And now I come to the end of my story. The Jews did not approve of Lord D——'s terms; whether they would in the end have acceded to them, and were only seeking time for making due inquiries, I know not; but many delays were made, time passed on, the small fragment of my banknote had just melted away, and before any conclusion could have been put to the business I must have relapsed into my former state of wretchedness. Suddenly, however, at this crisis, an opening was made, almost by accident, for reconciliation with my friends; I quitted London in haste for a remote part of England; after some time I proceeded to the university, and it was not until many months had passed away that I had it in my power again to revisit the ground which had become so interesting to me, and to this day remains so, as the chief scene of my youthful sufferings.

Meantime, what had become of poor Ann? For her I have reserved my concluding words. According to our agreement, I sought her daily, and waited for her every night, so long as I stayed in London, at the corner of Titchfield Street. I inquired for her of everyone who was likely to know her, and during the last hours of my stay in London I put into activity every means of tracing her that my knowledge of London suggested and the limited extent of my power made possible. The street where she had lodged I knew, but not the house; and I remembered at last some account which she had given me of ill treat-

[1] *Otway* Thomas Otway (1652–85), English playwright, who died in poverty; one story holds that he choked upon eating a roll after having gone without food for a number of days.

[2] *Saracen* Originally, a member of a particular nomadic group of the Syrian desert, but by extension sometimes used to refer to any person of Arabic or Turkish descent.

ment from her landlord, which made it probable that she had quitted those lodgings before we parted. She had few acquaintances; most people, besides, thought that the earnestness of my inquiries arose from motives which moved their laughter or their slight regard; and others, thinking I was in chase of a girl who had robbed me of some trifles, were naturally and excusably indisposed to give me any clue to her, if indeed they had any to give. Finally as my despairing resource, on the day I left London I put into the hands of the only person who (I was sure) must know Ann by sight, from having been in company with us once or twice, an address to ——, in ——shire, at that time the residence of my family. But to this hour I have never heard a syllable about her. This, amongst such troubles as most men meet with in this life, has been my heaviest affliction. If she lived, doubtless we must have been some time in search of each other, at the very same moment, through the mighty labyrinths of London; perhaps even within a few feet of each other—a barrier no wider than a London street often amounting in the end to a separation for eternity! During some years I hoped that she *did* live; and I suppose that, in the literal and unrhetorical use of the word *myriad*, I may say that on my different visits to London I have looked into many, many myriads of female faces, in the hope of meeting her. I should know her again amongst a thousand, if I saw her for a moment, for though not handsome, she had a sweet expression of countenance and a peculiar and graceful carriage of the head. I sought her, I have said, in hope. So it was for years; but now I should fear to see her; and her cough, which grieved me when I parted with her, is now my consolation. I now wish to see her no longer, but think of her, more gladly, as one long since laid in the grave—in the grave, I would hope, of a Magdalen,[1] taken away, before injuries and cruelty had blotted out and transfigured her ingenuous nature, or the brutalities of ruffians had completed the ruin they had begun.

PART 2

So then, Oxford Street, stony-hearted stepmother! thou that listenest to the sighs of orphans and drinkest the tears of children, at length I was dismissed from thee; the time was come at last that I no more should pace in anguish thy never-ending terraces, no more should dream and wake in captivity to the pangs of hunger. Successors too many, to myself and Ann, have doubtless since then trodden in our footsteps, inheritors of our calamities; other orphans than Ann have sighed; tears have been shed by other children; and thou, Oxford Street, hast since doubtless echoed to the groans of innumerable hearts. For myself, however, the storm which I had outlived seemed to have been the pledge of a long fair weather—the premature sufferings which I had paid down to have been accepted as a ransom for many years to come, as a price of long immunity from sorrow; and if again I walked in London a solitary and contemplative man (as oftentimes I did), I walked for the most part in serenity and peace of mind. And although it is true that the calamities of my noviciate in London had struck root so deeply in my bodily constitution, that afterwards they shot up and flourished afresh, and grew into a noxious umbrage that has overshadowed and darkened my latter years, yet these second assaults of suffering were met with a fortitude more confirmed, with the resources of a maturer intellect, and with alleviations from sympathizing affection—how deep and tender!

Thus, however, with whatsoever alleviations, years that were far asunder were bound together by subtle links of suffering derived from a common root. And herein I notice an instance of the shortsightedness of human desires, that oftentimes on moonlight nights, during my first mournful abode in London, my consolation was (if such it could be thought) to gaze from Oxford Street up every avenue in succession which pierces through the heart of Marylebone to the fields and the woods; for *that*, said I, travelling with my eyes up the long vistas which lay part in light and part in shade, "*That* is the road to the North, and therefore to, and if I had the wings of a dove, *that* way I would fly for comfort." Thus I said, and thus I wished, in my blindness. Yet even in that very northern region it was, even in that very valley, nay, in that very house to which my erroneous wishes pointed, that this second birth of my sufferings began, and that they again threatened to besiege the citadel of life and hope. There it was that for years I was persecuted by visions as ugly, and as ghastly phantoms as ever haunted the couch of an

[1] *Magdalen* Common epithet for a prostitute who had repented, after Mary Magdalene.

Orestes;[1] and in this unhappier than he, that sleep, which comes to all as a respite and a restoration, and to him especially as a blessed balm for his wounded heart and his haunted brain, visited me as my bitterest scourge. Thus blind was I in my desires; yet if a veil interposes between the dim-sightedness of man and his future calamities, the same veil hides from him their alleviations, and a grief which had not been feared is met by consolations which had not been hoped. I therefore, who participated, as it were, in the troubles of Orestes (excepting only in his agitated conscience), participated no less in all his supports. My Eumenides, like his, were at my bed feet, and stared in upon me through the curtains; but watching by my pillow, or defrauding herself of sleep to bear me company through the heavy watches of the night, sat my Electra; for thou, beloved M., dear companion of my later years, thou wast my Electra! and neither in nobility of mind nor in long-suffering affection wouldst permit that a Grecian sister should excel an English wife. For thou thoughtest not much to stoop to humble offices of kindness and to servile ministrations of tenderest affection—to wipe away for years the unwholesome dews upon the forehead, or to refresh the lips when parched and baked with fever; nor even when thy own peaceful slumbers had by long sympathy become infected with the spectacle of my dread contest with phantoms and shadowy enemies that oftentimes bade me "sleep no more!"—not even then didst thou utter a complaint or any murmur, nor withdraw thy angelic smiles, nor shrink from thy service of love, more than Electra did of old. For she too, though she was a Grecian woman, and the daughter of the king[2] of men, yet wept sometimes, and hid her face[3] in her robe.

But these troubles are past; and thou wilt read records of a period so dolorous to us both as the legend of some hideous dream that can return no more. Meantime, I am again in London, and again I pace the terraces of Oxford Street by night; and oftentimes, when I am oppressed by anxieties that demand all my philosophy and the comfort of thy presence to support, and yet remember that I am separated from thee by three hundred miles and the length of three dreary months, I look up the streets that run northwards from Oxford Street, upon moonlight nights, and recollect my youthful ejaculation of anguish; and remembering that thou art sitting alone in that same valley, and mistress of that very house to which my heart turned in its blindness nineteen years ago, I think that, though blind indeed, and scattered to the winds of late, the promptings of my heart may yet have had reference to a remoter time, and may be justified if read in another meaning; and if I could allow myself to descend again to the impotent wishes of childhood, I should again say to myself, as I look to the North, "Oh, that I had the wings of a dove—"[4] and with how just a confidence in thy good and gracious nature might I add the other half of my early ejaculation—"And *that* way I would fly for comfort!"

The Pleasures of Opium

It is so long since I first took opium that if it had been a trifling incident in my life I might have forgotten its date; but cardinal events are not to be forgotten, and from circumstances connected with it I remember that it must be referred to the autumn of 1804. During that season I was in London, having come thither for the first time since my entrance at college. And my introduction to opium arose in the following way. From an early age I had been accustomed to wash my head in cold water at least once a day; being suddenly seized with toothache, I attributed it to some relaxation caused by an accidental intermission of that practice, jumped out of bed, plunged my head into a basin of cold water, and with hair thus wetted went to sleep. The next morning, as I need hardly say, I awoke with excruciating rheumatic pains of the head and face, from which I had hardly any respite for

[1] *Orestes* As told in Aeschylus's play *Eumenides*, (458 BCE), Orestes, with help from his sister, Electra, avenged the murder of his father, Agamemnon, by killing those responsible: his mother, Clytemnestra, and her lover, Aegisthus. This fracturing of family ties brought upon Orestes the wrath of the Eumenides (the Furies), who hounded him until he was eventually exonerated.

[2] [De Quincey's note] ἀναξ ἀνδρων Αγαμεμνων [Agamemnon].

[3] [De Quincey's note] ὀμμα θεισ᾽ ἐισω πεπλων. The scholar will know that throughout this passage I refer to the early scenes of the Orestes, one of the most beautiful exhibitions of the domestic affections which even the dramas of Euripides can furnish. To the English reader it may be necessary to say that the situation at the opening of the drama is that of a brother attended only by his sister during the demoniacal possession of a suffering conscience (or, in the mythology of the play, haunted by the Furies), and in circumstances of immediate danger from enemies, and of desertion or cold regard from nominal friends.

[4] *Oh … dove* From Psalm 55.6: "Oh that I had wings like a dove! for then would I fly away, and be at rest."

about twenty days. On the twenty-first day I think it was, and on a Sunday, that I went out into the streets, rather to run away, if possible, from my torments, than with any distinct purpose. By accident I met a college acquaintance, who recommended opium. Opium! dread agent of unimaginable pleasure and pain! I had heard of it as I had of manna or of ambrosia,[1] but no further. How unmeaning a sound was it at that time; what solemn chords does it now strike upon my heart! what heart-quaking vibrations of sad and happy remembrances! Reverting for a moment to these, I feel a mystic importance attached to the minutest circumstances connected with the place and the time and the man (if man he was) that first laid open to me the Paradise of Opium-eaters. It was a Sunday afternoon, wet and cheerless, and a duller spectacle this earth of ours has not to show than a rainy Sunday in London. My road homewards lay through Oxford Street; and near "the stately Pantheon"[2] (as Mr. Wordsworth has obligingly called it) I saw a druggist's shop. The druggist—unconscious minister of celestial pleasures!—as if in sympathy with the rainy Sunday, looked dull and stupid, just as any mortal druggist might be expected to look on a Sunday; and when I asked for the tincture of opium, he gave it to me as any other man might do, and furthermore, out of my shilling returned me what seemed to be real copper halfpence, taken out of a real wooden drawer. Nevertheless, in spite of such indications of humanity, he has ever since existed in my mind as the beatific vision of an immortal druggist, sent down to earth on a special mission to myself. And it confirms me in this way of considering him, that when I next came up to London I sought him near the stately Pantheon, and found him not; and thus to me, who knew not his name (if indeed he had one), he seemed rather to have vanished from Oxford Street than to have removed in any bodily fashion. The reader may choose to think of him as possibly no more than a sublunary[3] druggist; it may be so, but my faith is better—I believe him to have evanesced,[4] or evaporated. So unwillingly would I connect any mortal remembrances with that hour, and place, and creature, that first brought me acquainted with the celestial drug.

Arrived at my lodgings, it may be supposed that I lost not a moment in taking the quantity prescribed. I was necessarily ignorant of the whole art and mystery of opium-taking, and what I took I took under every disadvantage. But I took it—and in an hour—oh, heavens! what a revulsion! what an upheaving, from its lowest depths, of inner spirit! what an apocalypse of the world within me! That my pains had vanished was now a trifle in my eyes; this negative effect was swallowed up in the immensity of those positive effects which had opened before me—in the abyss of divine enjoyment thus suddenly revealed. Here was a panacea, a φαρμακον νήωενθες [5] for all human woes; here was the secret of happiness, about which philosophers had disputed for so many ages, at once discovered; happiness might now be bought for a penny, and carried in the waistcoat pocket; portable ecstacies might be had corked up in a pint bottle, and peace of mind could be sent down in gallons by the mail coach. But if I talk in this way the reader will think I am laughing, and I can assure him that nobody will laugh long who deals much with opium; its pleasures even are of a grave and solemn complexion, and in his happiest state the opium-eater cannot present himself in the character of L'Allegro; even then he speaks and thinks as becomes Il Penseroso.[6] Nevertheless, I have a very reprehensible way of jesting at times in the midst of my own misery; and unless when I am checked by some more powerful feelings, I am afraid I shall be guilty of this indecent practice even in these annals of suffering or enjoyment. The reader must allow a little to my infirm

[1] *manna* Biblical food that saved the Jews in their escape from Egypt; *ambrosia* Food of the Greek gods.

[2] *"the stately Pantheon"* From Wordsworth's "Power of Music" (3); London's Pantheon was then a concert hall.

[3] *sublunary* Earthly.

[4] [De Quincey's note] *Evanesced*: this way of going off the stage of life appears to have been well known in the 17th century, but at that time to have been considered a peculiar privilege of blood-royal, and by no means to be allowed to druggists. For about the year 1686 a poet of rather ominous name (and who, by-the-bye, did ample justice to his name), viz., Mr. *Flat-man*, in speaking of the death of Charles II expresses his surprise that any prince should commit so absurd an act as dying, because, says he, "Kings should disdain to die, and only *disappear*." They should *abscond*, that is, into the other world. [Cf. Thomas Flatman's *On the Death of our Late Sovereign Lord King Charles II of Blessed Memory: A Pindarique Ode* (1685): "*Princes* (like the wondrous *Enoch*) should be free / From death's unbounded tyranny, / And when their godlike race is run, / And nothing glorious left undone, / Never submit to fate, but only disappear."]

[5] φαρμακον νήωενθες Greek: soothing and healing drug.

[6] *L'Allegro … Il Penseroso* Poems by Milton (1645), whose titles mean "The Happy Man" and "The Brooding Man" respectively.

nature in this respect; and with a few indulgences of that sort I shall endeavour to be as grave, if not drowsy, as fits a theme like opium, so antimercurial as it really is, and so drowsy as it is falsely reputed.

And first, one word with respect to its bodily effects; for upon all that has been hitherto written on the subject of opium, whether by travellers in Turkey (who may plead their privilege of lying as an old immemorial right), or by professors of medicine, writing *ex cathedra*,[1] I have but one emphatic criticism to pronounce—Lies! lies! lies! I remember once, in passing a book stall, to have caught these words from a page of some satiric author: "By this time I became convinced that the London newspapers spoke truth at least twice a week, viz., on Tuesday and Saturday,[2] and might safely be depended upon for—the list of bankrupts." In like manner, I do by no means deny that some truths have been delivered to the world in regard to opium. Thus it has been repeatedly affirmed by the learned that opium is a dusky brown in colour; and this, take notice, I grant. Secondly, that it is rather dear, which also I grant, for in my time East Indian opium has been three guineas a pound, and Turkey eight. And thirdly, that if you eat a good deal of it, most probably you must do what is particularly disagreeable to any man of regular habits, viz., die.[3] These weighty propositions are, all and singular, true; I cannot gainsay them, and truth ever was, and will be, commendable. But in these three theorems I believe we have exhausted the stock of knowledge as yet accumulated by men on the subject of opium. And therefore, worthy doctors, as there seems to be room for further discoveries, stand aside, and allow me to come forward and lecture on this matter.

First, then, it is not so much affirmed as taken for granted, by all who ever mention opium, formally or incidentally, that it does or can produce intoxication. Now, reader, assure yourself, *meo perieulo*,[4] that no quantity of opium ever did or could intoxicate. As to the tincture of opium (commonly called laudanum) *that* might certainly intoxicate if a man could bear to take enough of it, but why? Because it contains so much proof spirit, and not because it contains so much opium. But crude opium, I affirm peremptorily, is incapable of producing any state of body at all resembling that which is produced by alcohol, and not in *degree* only incapable, but even in *kind*; it is not in the quantity of its effects merely, but in the quality, that it differs altogether. The pleasure given by wine is always mounting and tending to a crisis, after which it declines; that from opium, when once generated, is stationary for eight or ten hours: the first, to borrow a technical distinction from medicine, is a case of acute—the second, the chronic pleasure; the one is a flame, the other a steady and equable glow. But the main distinction lies in this, that whereas wine disorders the mental faculties, opium, on the contrary (if taken in a proper manner), introduces amongst them the most exquisite order, legislation, and harmony. Wine robs a man of his self-possession; opium greatly invigorates it. Wine unsettles and clouds the judgment, and gives a preternatural brightness and a vivid exaltation to the contempts and the admirations, the loves and the hatreds of the drinker; opium, on the contrary, communicates serenity and equipoise to all the faculties, active or passive, and with respect to the temper and moral feelings in general it gives simply that sort of vital warmth which is approved by the judgment, and which would probably always accompany a bodily constitution of primeval or antediluvian[5] health. Thus, for instance, opium, like wine, gives an expansion to the heart and the benevolent affections; but then, with this remarkable difference, that in the sudden development of kindheartedness which accompanies inebriation there is always more or less of a maudlin character, which exposes it to the contempt of the bystander. Men shake hands, swear eternal friendship, and shed tears, no mortal knows why; and the sensual creature is clearly uppermost. But the expansion of the benigner feelings incident to opium is no febrile access, but a healthy restoration to that state which the mind would naturally recover upon the removal of any deep-seated irritation of pain that had disturbed and quarrelled

[1] *ex cathedra* With authority (from the Latin, meaning, literally, "from the cathedral").

[2] *Tuesday and Saturday* Days on which the newspaper would publish a list of bankruptcies.

[3] [De Quincey's note] Of this, however, the learned appear latterly to have doubted; for in a pirated edition of Buchan's *Domestic Medicine*, which I once saw in the hands of a farmer's wife, who was studying it for the benefit of her health, the doctor was made to say—"Be particularly careful never to take above five-and-twenty *ounces* of laudanum [the liquid form of opium] at once;" the true reading being probably five-and-twenty *drops*, which are held equal to about one grain of crude opium.

[4] *meo perieulo* Latin: at my risk.

[5] *antediluvian* Before the Biblical flood, hence primitive.

with the impulses of a heart originally just and good. True it is that even wine, up to a certain point and with certain men, rather tends to exalt and to steady the intellect; I myself, who have never been a great wine drinker, used to find that half a dozen glasses of wine advantageously affected the faculties—brightened and intensified the consciousness, and gave to the mind a feeling of being "*ponderibus librata suis*;"[1] and certainly it is most absurdly said, in popular language, of any man that he is *disguised* in liquor; for, on the contrary, most men are disguised by sobriety, and it is when they are drinking (as some old gentleman says in Athenaeus), that men ἑαντούς ἐμφανίζουσιυ οἵτινες εἰσίν—display themselves in their true complexion of character, which surely is not disguising themselves. But still, wine constantly leads a man to the brink of absurdity and extravagance, and beyond a certain point it is sure to volatilize and to disperse the intellectual energies, whereas opium always seems to compose what had been agitated, and to concentrate what had been distracted. In short, to sum up all in one word, a man who is inebriated, or tending to inebriation, is, and feels that he is, in a condition which calls up into supremacy the merely human, too often the brutal part of his nature; but the opium-eater (I speak of him who is not suffering from any disease or other remote effects of opium) feels that the diviner part of his nature is paramount; that is, the moral affections are in a state of cloudless serenity, and overall is the great light of the majestic intellect.

This is the doctrine of the true church on the subject of opium, of which church I acknowledge myself to be the only member—the alpha and the omega;[2] but then it is to be recollected that I speak from the ground of a large and profound personal experience, whereas most of the unscientific[3] authors who have at all treated of opium, and even of those who have written expressly on the *materia medica*, make it evident, from the horror they express of it, that their experimental knowledge of its action is none at all. I will, however, candidly acknowledge that I have met with one person who bore evidence to its intoxicating power, such as staggered my own incredulity, for he was a surgeon, and had himself taken opium largely. I happened to say to him that his enemies (as I had heard) charged him with talking nonsense on politics, and that his friends apologized for him by suggesting that he was constantly in a state of intoxication from opium. Now the accusation, said I, is not *prima facie*[4] and of necessity an absurd one; but the defence *is*. To my surprise, however, he insisted that both his enemies and his friends were in the right. "I will maintain," said he, "that I *do* talk nonsense; and secondly, I will maintain that I do not talk nonsense upon principle, or with any view to profit, but solely and simply," said he, "solely and simply—solely and simply (repeating it three times over), because I am drunk with opium, and *that* daily." I replied that, as to the allegation of his enemies, as it seemed to be established upon such respectable testimony, seeing that the three parties concerned all agree in it, it did not become me to question it; but the defence set up I must demur to. He proceeded to discuss the matter, and to lay down his reasons; but it seemed to me so impolite to pursue an argument which must have presumed a man mistaken in a point belonging to his own profession, that I did not press him even when his course of argument seemed open to objection, not to mention that a man who talks nonsense, even though "with no view to profit," is not altogether the most agreeable partner in a dispute,

[1] "*ponderibus librata suis*" Latin: from Ovid's *Metamorphoses* (1.16): "[the earth, not] poised, did on its own foundations lie."

[2] *the alpha and the omega* The beginning and the end; from the first and last letters of the Greek alphabet.

[3] [De Quincey's note] Amongst the great herd of travellers, &c., who show sufficiently by their stupidity that they never held any intercourse with opium, I must caution my readers specially against the brilliant author [Thomas Hope] of *Anastasius* [(1819)]. This gentleman, whose wit would lead one to presume him an opium-eater, has made it impossible to consider him in that character, from the grievous misrepresentation which he gives of its effects at pp. 215–17 of vol. 1. Upon consideration it must appear such to the author himself, for, waiving the errors I have insisted on in the text, which (and others) are adopted in the fullest manner, he will himself admit that an old gentleman "with a snow-white beard," who eats "ample doses of opium," and is yet able to deliver what is meant and received as very weighty counsel on the bad effects of that practice, is but an indifferent evidence that opium either kills people prematurely or sends them into a madhouse. But for my part, I see into this old gentleman and his motives: the fact is, he was enamoured of "the little golden receptacle of the pernicious drug" which Anastasius carried about him; and no way of obtaining it so safe and so feasible occurred as that of frightening its owner out of his wits (which, by the bye, are none of the strongest). This commentary throws a new light upon the case, and greatly improves it as a story; for the old gentleman's speech, considered as a lecture on pharmacy, is highly absurd; but considered as a hoax on Anastasius, it reads excellently.

[4] *prima facie* Latin: on first impressions.

whether as opponent or respondent. I confess, however, that the authority of a surgeon, and one who was reputed a good one, may seem a weighty one to my prejudice; but still I must plead my experience, which was greater than his greatest by 7,000 drops a day; and though it was not possible to suppose a medical man unacquainted with the characteristic symptoms of vinous intoxication, it yet struck me that he might proceed on a logical error of using the word intoxication with too great latitude, and extending it generically to all modes of nervous excitement, instead of restricting it as the expression for a specific sort of excitement connected with certain diagnostics. Some people have maintained in my hearing that they had been drunk upon green tea; and a medical student in London, for whose knowledge in his profession I have reason to feel great respect, assured me the other day that a patient in recovering from an illness had got drunk on a beefsteak.

Having dwelt so much on this first and leading error in respect to opium, I shall notice very briefly a second and a third, which are, that the elevation of spirits produced by opium is necessarily followed by a proportionate depression, and that the natural and even immediate consequence of opium is torpor and stagnation, animal and mental. The first of these errors I shall content myself with simply denying, assuring my reader that for ten years, during which I took opium at intervals, the day succeeding to that on which I allowed myself this luxury was always a day of unusually good spirits.

With respect to the torpor supposed to follow, or rather (if we were to credit the numerous pictures of Turkish opium-eaters) to accompany the practice of opium-eating, I deny that also. Certainly opium is classed under the head of narcotics, and some such effect it may produce in the end; but the primary effects of opium are always, and in the highest degree, to excite and stimulate the system. This first stage of its action always lasted with me, during my noviciate, for upwards of eight hours, so that it must be the fault of the opium-eater himself if he does not so time his exhibition of the dose (to speak medically) as that the whole weight of its narcotic influence may descend upon his sleep. Turkish opium-eaters, it seems, are absurd enough to sit, like so many equestrian statues, on logs of wood as stupid as themselves. But that the reader may judge of the degree in which opium is likely to stupefy the faculties of an Englishman, I shall (by way of treating the question illustratively, rather than argumentatively) describe the way in which I myself often passed an opium evening in London during the period between 1804–1812. It will be seen that at least opium did not move me to seek solitude, and much less to seek inactivity, or the torpid state of self-involution ascribed to the Turks. I give this account at the risk of being pronounced a crazy enthusiast or visionary, but I regard *that* little. I must desire my reader to bear in mind that I was a hard student, and at severe studies for all the rest of my time; and certainly I had a right occasionally to relaxations as well as other people. These, however, I allowed myself but seldom.

The late Duke of —— used to say, "Next Friday, by the blessing of heaven, I purpose to be drunk"; and in like manner I used to fix beforehand how often within a given time, and when, I would commit a debauch of opium. This was seldom more than once in three weeks, for at that time I could not have ventured to call every day, as I did afterwards, for "*A glass of laudanum negus,*[1] *warm, and without sugar.*" No, as I have said, I seldom drank laudanum, at that time, more than once in three weeks. This was usually on a Tuesday or a Saturday night; my reason for which was this. In those days Grassini[2] sang at the opera, and her voice was delightful to me beyond all that I had ever heard. I know not what may be the state of the opera house now, having never been within its walls for seven or eight years, but at that time it was by much the most pleasant place of public resort in London for passing an evening. Five shillings admitted one to the gallery, which was subject to far less annoyance than the pit of the theatres; the orchestra was distinguished by its sweet and melodious grandeur from all English orchestras, the composition of which, I confess, is not acceptable to my ear, from the predominance of the clamorous instruments and the absolute tyranny of the violin. The choruses were divine to hear, and when Grassini appeared in some interlude, as she often did, and poured forth her passionate soul as Andromache at the tomb of Hector,[3] &c., I question whether any Turk, of all that ever entered the Paradise of Opium-eaters, can have had half the pleasure

[1] *negus* Mulled wine; a drink made with warm wine and spices.

[2] *Grassini* Giuseppina Grassini (1773–1850).

[3] *Andromache at the tomb of Hector* Andromache was the widow of Hector (son of the King of Troy), who was killed by Achilles during the Trojan War.

I had. But, indeed, I honour the barbarians too much by supposing them capable of any pleasures approaching to the intellectual ones of an Englishman. For music is an intellectual or a sensual pleasure according to the temperament of him who hears it. And, by the bye, with the exception of the fine extravaganza on that subject in *Twelfth Night*,[1] I do not recollect more than one thing said adequately on the subject of music in all literature; it is a passage in the *Religio Medici*[2] of Sir T. Brown, and though chiefly remarkable for its sublimity, has also a philosophic value, inasmuch as it points to the true theory of musical effects. The mistake of most people is to suppose that it is by the ear they communicate with music, and therefore that they are purely passive to its effects. But this is not so; it is by the reaction of the mind upon the notices of the ear (the *matter* coming by the senses, the *form* from the mind) that the pleasure is constructed, and therefore it is that people of equally good ear differ so much in this point from one another. Now, opium, by greatly increasing the activity of the mind, generally increases, of necessity, that particular mode of its activity by which we are able to construct out of the raw material of organic sound an elaborate intellectual pleasure. But, says a friend, a succession of musical sounds is to me like a collection of Arabic characters: I can attach no ideas to them. Ideas! my good sir? There is no occasion for them; all that class of ideas which can be available in such a case has a language of representative feelings. But this is a subject foreign to my present purposes; it is sufficient to say that a chorus, &c., of elaborate harmony displayed before me, as in a piece of arras[3] work, the whole of my past life—not as if recalled by an act of memory, but as if present and incarnated in the music; no longer painful to dwell upon; but the detail of its incidents removed or blended in some hazy abstraction, and its passions exalted, spiritualized, and sublimed. All this was to be had for five shillings. And over and above the music of the stage and the orchestra, I had all around me, in the intervals of the performance, the music of the Italian language talked by Italian women—for the gallery was usually crowded with Italians—and I listened with a pleasure such as that with which Weld the traveller lay and listened, in Canada,[4] to the sweet laughter of Indian women, for the less you understand of a language, the more sensible you are to the melody or harshness of its sounds. For such a purpose, therefore, it was an advantage to me that I was a poor Italian scholar, reading it but little, and not speaking it at all, nor understanding a tenth part of what I heard spoken.

These were my opera pleasures; but another pleasure I had which, as it could be had only on a Saturday night, occasionally struggled with my love of the opera, for at that time Tuesday and Saturday were the regular opera nights. On this subject I am afraid I shall be rather obscure, but I can assure the reader not at all more so than Marinus in his *Life of Proclus*,[5] or many other biographers and autobiographers of fair reputation. This pleasure, I have said, was to be had only on a Saturday night. What, then, was Saturday night to me more than any other night? I had no labours that I rested from, no wages to receive; what needed I to care for Saturday night, more than as it was a summons to hear Grassini? True, most logical reader; what you say is unanswerable. And yet so it was and is, that whereas different men throw their feelings into different channels, and most are apt to show their interest in the concerns of the poor chiefly by sympathy, expressed in some shape or other, with their distresses and sorrows, I at that time was disposed to express my interest by sympathizing with their pleasures. The pains of poverty I had lately seen too much of, more than I wished to remember; but the pleasures of the poor, their consolations of spirit, and their reposes from bodily toil, can never become oppressive to contemplate. Now Saturday night is the season for the chief, regular, and periodic return of rest of the poor; in this point the most hostile sects unite, and acknowledge a common link of brotherhood; almost all Christendom rests from its labours. It is

[1] *Twelfth Night* Duke Orsino's opening lines in the play by Shakespeare: "If music be the food of love, play on; / Give me excess of it, that, surfeiting, / The appetite may sicken, and so die."

[2] [De Quincey's note] I have not the book at this moment to consult, but I think the passage begins—"And even that tavern music, which makes one man merry, another mad, in me strikes a deep fit of devotion," &c. [From Thomas Browne's *Religio Medici* (1642).]

[3] *arras* Tapestry.

[4] *Weld ... Canada* Irishman Isaac Weld Jr., author of *Travels through the States of North America and the Provinces of Upper and Lower Canada during the Years 1795, 1796, and 1797* (1799).

[5] *Marinus ... Proclus* In the 5th century BCE, Marinus of Samaria wrote a biography of his teacher called *The Life of Proclus or Concerning Happiness; Being the Biographical Account of an Ancient Greek Philosopher Who Was Innately Loved by the Gods.*

a rest introductory to another rest, and divided by a whole day and two nights from the renewal of toil. On this account I feel always, on a Saturday night, as though I also were released from some yoke of labour, had some wages to receive, and some luxury of repose to enjoy. For the sake, therefore, of witnessing, upon as large a scale as possible, a spectacle with which my sympathy was so entire, I used often on Saturday nights, after I had taken opium, to wander forth, without much regarding the direction or the distance, to all the markets and other parts of London to which the poor resort of a Saturday night, for laying out their wages. Many a family party, consisting of a man, his wife, and sometimes one or two of his children, have I listened to, as they stood consulting on their ways and means, or the strength of their exchequer,[1] or the price of household articles. Gradually I became familiar with their wishes, their difficulties, and their opinions. Sometimes there might be heard murmurs of discontent, but far oftener expressions on the countenance, or uttered in words, of patience, hope, and tranquillity. And taken generally, I must say that, in this point at least, the poor are more philosophic than the rich—that they show a more ready and cheerful submission to what they consider as irremediable evils or irreparable losses. Whenever I saw occasion, or could do it without appearing to be intrusive, I joined their parties, and gave my opinion upon the matter in discussion, which, if not always judicious, was always received indulgently. If wages were a little higher or expected to be so, or the quartern-loaf[2] a little lower, or it was reported that onions and butter were expected to fall, I was glad; yet, if the contrary were true, I drew from opium some means of consoling myself. For opium (like the bee, that extracts its materials indiscriminately from roses and from the soot of chimneys) can overrule all feelings into compliance with the master key. Some of these rambles led me to great distances, for an opium-eater is too happy to observe the motion of time; and sometimes in my attempts to steer homewards, upon nautical principles, by fixing my eye on the polestar, and seeking ambitiously for a northwest passage, instead of circumnavigating all the capes and headlands I had doubled in my outward voyage, I came suddenly upon such knotty problems of alleys, such enigmatical entries, and such sphinx's riddles[3] of streets without thoroughfares, as must, I conceive, baffle the audacity of porters and confound the intellects of hackney coachmen. I could almost have believed at times that I must be the first discoverer of some of these *terrae incognitae*,[4] and doubted whether they had yet been laid down in the modern charts of London. For all this, however, I paid a heavy price in distant years, when the human face tyrannized over my dreams, and the perplexities of my steps in London came back and haunted my sleep, with the feeling of perplexities, moral and intellectual, that brought confusion to the reason, or anguish and remorse to the conscience.

Thus I have shown that opium does not of necessity produce inactivity or torpor, but that, on the contrary, it often led me into markets and theatres. Yet, in candour, I will admit that markets and theatres are not the appropriate haunts of the opium-eater when in the divinest state incident to his enjoyment. In that state, crowds become an oppression to him; music even, too sensual and gross. He naturally seeks solitude and silence, as indispensable conditions of those trances, or profoundest reveries, which are the crown and consummation of what opium can do for human nature. I, whose disease it was to meditate too much and to observe too little, and who upon my first entrance at college was nearly falling into a deep melancholy, from brooding too much on the sufferings which I had witnessed in London, was sufficiently aware of the tendencies of my own thoughts to do all I could to counteract them. I was, indeed, like a person who, according to the old legend, had entered the cave of Trophonius;[5] and the remedies I sought were to force myself into society, and to keep my understanding in continual activity upon matters of science. But for these remedies I should certainly have become hypochondriacally melancholy. In after years, however, when my cheerfulness was more fully re-established, I yielded to

[1] *exchequer* Here, private possessions; from Exchequer, royal or national Treasury of Great Britain.

[2] *quartern-loaf* Unit of measurement for the weight of bread: approximately four pounds.

[3] *sphinx's riddles* In Greek mythology, a creature with wings, the head of a woman, and body of a lion, who would pose riddles to passers-by and kill them when they were unable to solve the puzzles.

[4] *terrae incognitae* Latin: unknown lands.

[5] *cave of Trophonius* State of despair: in Greek mythology, Trophonius, who had killed his brother, was buried in a cave that became famous for its oracle that would overwhelm with melancholy all those who consulted it.

my natural inclination for a solitary life. And at that time I often fell into these reveries upon taking opium; and more than once it has happened to me, on a summer night, when I have been at an open window, in a room from which I could overlook the sea at a mile below me, and could command a view of the great town of L——, at about the same distance, that I have sat from sunset to sunrise, motionless, and without wishing to move.

I shall be charged with mysticism, Behmenism, quietism,[1] &c., but *that* shall not alarm me. Sir H. Vane, the younger,[2] was one of our wisest men; and let my reader see if he, in his philosophical works, be half as unmystical as I am. I say, then, that it has often struck me that the scene itself was somewhat typical of what took place in such a reverie. The town of L—— represented the earth, with its sorrows and its graves left behind, yet not out of sight, nor wholly forgotten. The ocean, in everlasting but gentle agitation, and brooded over by a dove-like calm, might not unfitly typify the mind and the mood which then swayed it. For it seemed to me as if then first I stood at a distance and aloof from the uproar of life, as if the tumult, the fever, and the strife were suspended; a respite granted from the secret burdens of the heart; a sabbath of repose; a resting from human labours. Here were the hopes which blossom in the paths of life reconciled with the peace which is in the grave; motions of the intellect as unwearied as the heavens, yet for all anxieties a halcyon calm; a tranquillity that seemed no product of inertia, but as if resulting from mighty and equal antagonisms; infinite activities, infinite repose.

Oh! just, subtle, and mighty opium![3] that to the hearts of poor and rich alike, for the wounds that will never heal, and for "the pangs that tempt the spirit to rebel,"[4] bringest an assuaging balm; eloquent opium! that with thy potent rhetoric stealest away the purposes of wrath; and to the guilty man for one night givest back the hopes of his youth, and hands washed pure from blood; and to the proud man a brief oblivion for

> Wrongs unredressed and insults unavenged;[5]

that summonest to the chancery[6] of dreams, for the triumphs of suffering innocence, false witnesses; and confoundest perjury, and dost reverse the sentences of unrighteous judges—thou buildest upon the bosom of darkness, out of the fantastic imagery of the brain, cities and temples beyond the art of Phidias and Praxiteles[7]—beyond the splendour of Babylon and Hekatómpylos,[8] and "from the anarchy of dreaming sleep"[9] callest into sunny light the faces of long-buried beauties and the blessed household countenances cleansed from the "dishonours of the grave."[10] Thou only givest these gifts to man; and thou hast the keys of Paradise, oh, just, subtle, and mighty opium!

Introduction to the Pains of Opium

Courteous, and, I hope, indulgent reader (for all *my* readers must be indulgent ones, or else I fear I shall shock them too much to count on their courtesy), having accompanied me thus far, now let me request you to move onwards for about eight years, that is to say, from 1804 (when I have said that my acquaintance with opium first began) to 1812. The years of academic life are now over and gone—almost forgotten; the student's cap no longer presses my temples; if my cap exist at all, it presses those of some youthful scholar, I trust, as happy as myself, and as passionate a lover of knowledge. My gown is by this time, I dare say, in the same condition with many thousand excellent books in the Bodleian,[11] viz., diligently

[1] *Behmenism* Following the mystical teachings of the German Lutheran philosopher Jakob Boehme (1575–1624); *quietism* State of tranquility, the mystical practice of the European Quietists of the seventeenth century.

[2] *Sir H. Vane, the younger* Statesman and Puritan leader Sir Henry Vane, author of *The Retired Man's Meditations* (1655).

[3] *Oh! ... opium!* Cf. Sir Walter Ralegh's *The History of the World* (10): "O eloquent, just and mighty death! Whom none could advise, thou hast persuaded! What none have dared, thou hast done!"

[4] *"the pangs ... rebel"* From Wordsworth's "The White Doe of Rylstone or, The Fate of the Nortons" (36).

[5] *Wrongs ... unavenged* From Wordsworth's "The Excursion" (3.374).

[6] *chancery* Court.

[7] *Phidias and Praxiteles* Ancient Greek sculptors.

[8] *Babylon and Hekatómpylos* Magnificent ancient cities of Mesopotamia and Persia (present-day Iran).

[9] *"from the anarchy of dreaming sleep"* From Wordsworth's "The Excursion" (27).

[10] *"dishonours of the grave"* From George Horne's *Commentary on the Psalms* (1776).

[11] *Bodleian* University of Oxford library.

perused by certain studious moths and worms, or departed, however (which is all that I know of his fate), to that great reservoir of *somewhere* to which all the teacups, tea caddies, teapots, tea kettles, &c., have departed (not to speak of still frailer vessels, such as glasses, decanters, bedmakers, &c.), which occasional resemblances in the present generation of teacups, &c., remind me of having once possessed, but of whose departure and final fate I, in common with most gownsmen of either university,[1] could give, I suspect, but an obscure and conjectural history. The persecutions of the chapel bell, sounding its unwelcome summons to six o'clock matins,[2] interrupts my slumbers no longer, the porter who rang it, upon whose beautiful nose (bronze, inlaid with copper) I wrote, in retaliation so many Greek epigrams whilst I was dressing, is dead, and has ceased to disturb anybody; and I, and many others who suffered much from his tintinnabulous[3] propensities, have now agreed to overlook his errors, and have forgiven him. Even with the bell I am now in charity; it rings, I suppose, as formerly, thrice a day, and cruelly annoys, I doubt not, many worthy gentlemen, and disturbs their peace of mind; but as to me, in this year 1812, I regard its treacherous voice no longer (treacherous I call it, for, by some refinement of malice, it spoke in as sweet and silvery tones as if it had been inviting one to a party); its tones have no longer, indeed, power to reach me, let the wind sit as favourable as the malice of the bell itself could wish, for I am 250 miles away from it, and buried in the depth of mountains. And what am I doing among the mountains? Taking opium. Yes, but what else? Why reader, in 1812, the year we are now arrived at, as well as for some years previous, I have been chiefly studying German metaphysics in the writings of Kant, Fichte, Schelling,[4] &c. And how and in what manner do I live?—in short, what class or description of men do I belong to? I am at this period—viz. in 1812—living in a cottage and with a single female servant (*honi soit qui mal y pense*[5]), who amongst my neighbours passes by the name of my "housekeeper." And as a scholar and a man of learned education, and in that sense a gentleman, I may presume to class myself as an unworthy member of that indefinite body called *gentlemen*. Partly on the ground I have assigned perhaps, partly because from my having no visible calling or business, it is rightly judged that I must be living on my private fortune, I am so classed by my neighbours; and by the courtesy of modern England I am usually addressed on letters, &c., "Esquire," though having, I fear, in the rigorous construction of heralds, but slender pretensions to that distinguished honour; yet in popular estimation I am X. Y. Z.,[6] Esquire, but not Justice of the Peace nor *Custos Rotulorum*.[7] Am I married? Not yet. And I still take opium? On Saturday nights. And perhaps have taken it unblushingly ever since "the rainy Sunday," and "the stately Pantheon," and "the beatific druggist" of 1804? Even so. And how do I find my health after all this opium-eating? In short, how do I do? Why, pretty well, I thank you, reader; in the phrase of ladies in the straw,[8] "as well as can be expected." In fact, if I dared to say the real and simple truth, though, to satisfy the theories of medical men, I *ought* to be ill, I never was better in my life than in the spring of 1812; and I hope sincerely that the quantity of claret, port, or "particular Madeira," which in all probability you, good reader, have taken, and design to take for every term of eight years during your natural life, may as little disorder your health as mine was disordered by the opium I had taken for eight years, between 1804 and 1812. Hence you may see again the danger of taking any medical advice from Anastasius; in divinity, for aught I know, or law, he may be a safe counsellor; but not in medicine. No; it is far better to consult Dr. Buchan, as I did; for I never forgot that worthy man's excellent suggestion, and I was "particularly careful not to take above five-and-twenty ounces of laudanum." To this moderation and temperate use of the article I may ascribe it, I suppose, that as yet, at least (i.e. in 1812), I am ignorant and unsuspicious of the avenging terrors which opium has in store for those who abuse its

[1] *gownsmen of either university* Members of Oxford or Cambridge.

[2] *matins* Morning church services.

[3] *tintinnabulous* Bell ringing.

[4] *Kant, Fichte, Schelling* German philosophers Immanuel Kant (1724–1804), Johann Gottlieb Fichte (1762–1814), and Friedrich Wilhelm Joseph von Schelling (1775–1854).

[5] *honi … pense* Old French: motto of the "Most Noble Order of the Garter," a British order of chivalry founded in the fourteenth century; translates to "Shame on him who thinks evil of it."

[6] *X. Y. Z.* De Quincey's pseudonym.

[7] *Custos Rotulorum* Latin: Keeper of the rolls, or court records.

[8] *"ladies in the straw"* Women in late pregnancy.

lenity.[1] At the same time, it must not be forgotten that hitherto I have been only a dilettante eater of opium; eight years' practice even, with a single precaution of allowing sufficient intervals between every indulgence, has not been sufficient to make opium necessary to me as an article of daily diet. But now comes a different era. Move on, if you please, reader, to 1813. In the summer of the year we have just quitted I have suffered much in bodily health from distress of mind connected with a very melancholy event.[2] This event being no ways related to the subject now before me, further than through the bodily illness which it produced, I need not more particularly notice. Whether this illness of 1812 had any share in that of 1813 I know not; but so it was, that in the latter year I was attacked by a most appalling irritation of the stomach, in all respects the same as that which had caused me so much suffering in youth, and accompanied by a revival of all the old dreams. This is the point of my narrative on which, as respects my own self-justification, the whole of what follows may be said to hinge. And here I find myself in a perplexing dilemma. Either, on the one hand, I must exhaust the reader's patience by such a detail of my malady, or of my struggles with it, as might suffice to establish the fact of my inability to wrestle any longer with irritation and constant suffering; or, on the other hand, by passing lightly over this critical part of my story, I must forego the benefit of a stronger impression left on the mind of the reader, and must lay myself open to the misconstruction of having slipped, by the easy and gradual steps of self-indulging persons, from the first to the final stage of opium-eating (a misconstruction to which there will be a lurking predisposition in most readers, from my previous acknowledgements). This is the dilemma, the first horn of which would be sufficient to toss and gore any column of patient readers, though drawn up sixteen deep and constantly relieved by fresh men; consequently that is not to be thought of. It remains, then, that I *postulate* so much as is necessary for my purpose. And let me take as full credit for what I postulate as if I had demonstrated it, good reader, at the expense of your patience and my own. Be not so ungenerous as to let me suffer in your good opinion through my own forbearance and regard for your comfort. No; believe all that I ask of you—viz., that I could resist no longer; believe it liberally and as an act of grace, or else in mere prudence; for if not, then in the next edition of my Opium Confessions, revised and enlarged, I will make you believe and tremble; and a *force d'ennuyer*,[3] by mere dint of pandiculation[4] I will terrify all readers of mine from ever again questioning any postulate that I shall think fit to make.

This, then, let me repeat, I postulate—that at the time I began to take opium daily I could not have done otherwise. Whether, indeed, afterwards I might not have succeeded in breaking off the habit, even when it seemed to me that all efforts would be unavailing, and whether many of the innumerable efforts which I did make might not have been carried much further, and my gradual reconquests of ground lost might not have been followed up much more energetically—these are questions which I must decline. Perhaps I might make out a case of palliation; but shall I speak ingenuously? I confess it, as a besetting infirmity of mine, that I am too much of an Eudaemonist;[5] I hanker too much after a state of happiness, both for myself and others; I cannot face misery, whether my own or not, with an eye of sufficient firmness, and am little capable of encountering present pain for the sake of any reversionary benefit.[6] On some other matters I can agree with the gentlemen in the cotton trade[7] at Manchester in affecting the Stoic philosophy,[8] but not in this. Here I take the liberty of an Eclectic philosopher, and I look out for some courteous and considerate sect that will condescend more to the infirm condition of an opium-eater; that are "sweet men," as Chaucer says, "to give absolution," and will show some conscience in the penances they inflict, and the efforts of abstinence they exact from poor sinners like myself. An inhuman moralist I can no more endure in my nervous

[1] *lenity* Soothing qualities.

[2] *very melancholy event* Death of the Wordsworths' daughter.

[3] *force d'ennuyer* French: power to bore.

[4] *pandiculation* Yawning.

[5] *Eudaemonist* Believer in the virtues of pleasure and happiness.

[6] *reversionary benefit* Later benefit.

[7] [De Quincey's note] A handsome newsroom, of which I was very politely made free in passing through Manchester by several gentlemen of that place, is called, I think, *The Porch*; whence I, who am a stranger in Manchester, inferred that the subscribers meant to profess themselves followers of Zeno [of Citium, ancient Greek Stoic philosopher]. But I have been since assured that this is a mistake.

[8] *Stoic philosophy* Ancient Greek and Roman philosophical movement, which held that people should lead peaceful, simple, and contented lives by practicing control, patience, and indifference to pain and pleasure.

state than opium that has not been boiled. At any rate, he who summons me to send out a large freight of self-denial and mortification upon any cruising voyage of moral improvement, must make it clear to my understanding that the concern is a hopeful one. At my time of life (six-and-thirty years of age) it cannot be supposed that I have much energy to spare; in fact, I find it all little enough for the intellectual labours I have on my hands, and therefore let no man expect to frighten me by a few hard words into embarking any part of it upon desperate adventures of morality.

Whether desperate or not, however, the issue of the struggle in 1813 was what I have mentioned, and from this date the reader is to consider me as a regular and confirmed opium-eater, of whom to ask whether on any particular day he had or had not taken opium, would be to ask whether his lungs had performed respiration, or the heart fulfilled its functions. You understand now, reader, what I am, and you are by this time aware that no old gentleman "with a snow-white beard" will have any chance of persuading me to surrender "the little golden receptacle of the pernicious drug."[1] No; I give notice to all, whether moralists or surgeons, that whatever be their pretensions and skill in their respective lines of practice, they must not hope for any countenance from me, if they think to begin by any savage proposition for a Lent or a Ramadan of abstinence from opium. This, then, being all fully understood between us, we shall in future sail before the wind. Now then, reader, from 1813, where all this time we have been sitting down and loitering, rise up, if you please, and walk forward about three years more. Now draw up the curtain, and you shall see me in a new character.

If any man, poor or rich, were to say that he would tell us what had been the happiest day in his life, and the why and the wherefore, I suppose that we should all cry out—Hear him! Hear him! As to the happiest *day*, that must be very difficult for any wise man to name, because any event that could occupy so distinguished a place in a man's retrospect of his life, or be entitled to have shed a special felicity on any one day, ought to be of such an enduring character as that (accidents apart) it should have continued to shed the same felicity, or one not distinguishably less, on many years together. To the happiest *lustrum*,[2] however, or even to the happiest *year*, it may be allowed to any man to point without discountenance from wisdom. This year, in my case, reader, was the one which we have now reached, though it stood, I confess, as a parenthesis between years of a gloomier character. It was a year of brilliant water (to speak after the manner of jewellers), set as it were, and insulated, in the gloom and cloudy melancholy of opium. Strange as it may sound, I had a little before this time descended suddenly, and without any considerable effort, from 320 grains of opium (i.e. eight[3] thousand drops of laudanum) per day, to forty grains, or one-eighth part. Instantaneously, and as if by magic, the cloud of profoundest melancholy which rested upon my brain, like some black vapours that I have seen roll away from the summits of mountains, drew off in one day (νυχθημερον[4]); passed off with its murky banners as simultaneously as a ship that has been stranded, and is floated off by a spring tide—

> That moveth altogether, if it move at all.[5]

Now, then, I was again happy; I now took only 1000 drops of laudanum per day; and what was that? A latter spring had come to close up the season of youth; my brain performed its functions as healthily as ever before; I read Kant again, and again I understood him, or fancied that I did. Again my feelings of pleasure expanded themselves to all around me; and if any man from Oxford or Cambridge, or from neither, had been announced to me in my unpretending cottage, I should have welcomed him with as sumptuous a reception as so poor a man could offer. Whatever else was wanting to a wise man's happiness, of laudanum I would have given him as much as he wished, and in a golden cup. And, by the way, now that I speak of

[1] *snow-white ... drug* From Thomas Hope's *Anastasius*.

[2] *lustrum* Five-year period.

[3] [De Quincey's note] I here reckon twenty-five drops of laudanum as equivalent to one grain of opium, which, I believe, is the common estimate. However, as both may be considered variable quantities (the crude opium varying much in strength, and the tincture still more), I suppose that no infinitesimal accuracy can be had in such a calculation. Teaspoons vary as much in size as opium in strength. Small ones hold about 100 drops, so that 8,000 drops are about eighty times a teaspoonful. The reader sees how much I kept within Dr. Buchan's indulgent allowance.

[4] νυχθημερον Greek: twenty-four hours.

[5] *That moveth ... at all* From Wordsworth's "Resolution and Independence" (11.7).

giving laudanum away, I remember about this time a little incident, which I mention because, trifling as it was, the reader will soon meet it again in my dreams, which it influenced more fearfully than could be imagined. One day a Malay[1] knocked at my door. What business a Malay could have to transact amongst English mountains I cannot conjecture, but possibly he was on his road to a seaport about forty miles distant.

The servant who opened the door to him was a young girl, born and bred amongst the mountains, who had never seen an Asiatic dress of any sort; his turban therefore confounded her not a little; and as it turned out that his attainments in English were exactly of the same extent as hers in the Malay, there seemed to be an impassable gulf fixed between all communication of ideas, if either party had happened to possess any. In this dilemma, the girl, recollecting the reputed learning of her master (and doubtless giving me credit for a knowledge of all the languages of the earth besides perhaps a few of the lunar ones), came and gave me to understand that there was a sort of demon below, whom she clearly imagined that my art could exorcise from the house. I did not immediately go down, but when I did, the group which presented itself, arranged as it was by accident, though not very elaborate, took hold of my fancy and my eye in a way that none of the statuesque attitudes exhibited in the ballets at the opera house, though so ostentatiously complex, had ever done. In a cottage kitchen, but panelled on the wall with dark wood that from age and rubbing resembled oak, and looking more like a rustic hall of entrance than a kitchen, stood the Malay—his turban and loose trousers of dingy white relieved upon the dark panelling. He had placed himself nearer to the girl than she seemed to relish, though her native spirit of mountain intrepidity contended with the feeling of simple awe which her countenance expressed as she gazed upon the tiger cat before her. And a more striking picture there could not be imagined than the beautiful English face of the girl, and its exquisite fairness, together with her erect and independent attitude, contrasted with the sallow and bilious skin of the Malay, enamelled or veneered with mahogany by marine air, his small, fierce, restless eyes, thin lips, slavish gestures and adorations. Half hidden by the ferocious-looking Malay was a little child from a neighbouring cottage who had crept in after him, and was now in the act of reverting its head and gazing upwards at the turban and the fiery eyes beneath it, whilst with one hand he caught at the dress of the young woman for protection. My knowledge of the Oriental tongues is not remarkably extensive, being indeed confined to two words—the Arabic word for barley and the Turkish for opium (*madjoon*), which I have learned from *Anastasius*; and as I had neither a Malay dictionary nor even Adelung's *Mithridates*,[2] which might have helped me to a few words, I addressed him in some lines from the *Iliad*, considering that, of such languages as I possessed, Greek, in point of longitude, came geographically nearest to an Oriental one. He worshipped me in a most devout manner, and replied in what I suppose was Malay. In this way I saved my reputation with my neighbours, for the Malay had no means of betraying the secret. He lay down upon the floor for about an hour and then pursued his journey. On his departure I presented him with a piece of opium. To him, as an Orientalist, I concluded that opium must be familiar, and the expression of his face convinced me that it was. Nevertheless, I was struck with some little consternation when I saw him suddenly raise his hand to his mouth, and, to use the schoolboy phrase, bolt the whole, divided into three pieces, at one mouthful. The quantity was enough to kill three dragoons[3] and their horses, and I felt some alarm for the poor creature, but what could be done? I had given him the opium in compassion for his solitary life, on recollecting that if he had travelled on foot from London it must be nearly three weeks since he could have exchanged a thought with any human being. I could not think of violating the laws of hospitality by having him seized and drenched with an emetic, and thus frightening him into a notion that we were going to sacrifice him to some English idol. No, there was clearly no help for it. He took his leave, and for some days I felt anxious, but as I never heard of any Malay being found dead, I became convinced that he was used to opium,[4] and that I must

[1] *Malay* Member of a people that inhabits Malaysia, Brunei, and parts of Indonesia.

[2] Adelung's *Mithridates* German linguistics and grammar scholar Johann Christoph Adelung (1732–1806), author of *Mithridate or the Universal Table of Languages, with the Lord's Prayer in 500 Dialects*, a four-volume book on Oriental languages.

[3] *dragoons* Mounted soldiers.

[4] [De Quincey's note] This, however, is not a necessary conclusion; the varieties of effect produced by opium on different constitutions are infinite. A London magistrate (Harriott's *Struggles through*

have done him the service I designed by giving him one night of respite from the pains of wandering.

This incident I have digressed to mention, because this Malay (partly from the picturesque exhibition he assisted to frame, partly from the anxiety I connected with his image for some days) fastened afterwards upon my dreams, and brought other Malays with him, worse than himself, that ran "a-muck"[1] at me, and led me into a world of troubles. But to quit this episode, and to return to my intercalary[2] year of happiness. I have said already, that on a subject so important to us all as happiness, we should listen with pleasure to any man's experience or experiments, even though he were but a ploughboy, who cannot be supposed to have ploughed very deep into such an intractable soil as that of human pains and pleasures, or to have conducted his researches upon any very enlightened principles. But I who have taken happiness both in a solid and liquid shape, both boiled and unboiled, both East India and Turkey—who have conducted my experiments upon this interesting subject with a sort of galvanic battery, and have, for the general benefit of the world, inoculated myself, as it were, with the poison of 8000 drops of laudanum per day (just for the same reason as a French surgeon inoculated himself lately with cancer, an English one twenty years ago with plague, and a third, I know not of what nation, with hydrophobia[3]), I (it will be admitted) must surely know what happiness is, if anybody does. And therefore I will here lay down an analysis of happiness; and as the most interesting mode of communicating it, I will give it, not didactically, but wrapped up and involved in a picture of one evening, as I spent every evening during the intercalary year when laudanum, though taken daily, was to me no more than the elixir of pleasure. This done, I shall quit the subject of happiness altogether, and pass to a very different one—*the pains of opium.*

Let there be a cottage standing in a valley, eighteen miles from any town—no spacious valley, but about two miles long by three-quarters of a mile in average width; the benefit of which provision is that all the family resident within its circuit will compose, as it were, one larger household, personally familiar to your eye, and more or less interesting to your affections. Let the mountains be real mountains, between 3,000 and 4,000 feet high, and the cottage a real cottage, not (as a witty author has it) "a cottage with a double coach-house;"[4] let it be, in fact (for I must abide by the actual scene), a white cottage, embowered with flowering shrubs, so chosen as to unfold a succession of flowers upon the walls and clustering round the windows through all the months of spring, summer, and autumn—beginning, in fact, with May roses, and ending with jasmine. Let it, however, *not* be spring, nor summer, nor autumn, but winter in his sternest shape. This is a most important point in the science of happiness. And I am surprised to see people overlook it, and think it matter of congratulation that winter is going, or, if coming, is not likely to be a severe one. On the contrary, I put up a petition annually for as much snow, hail, frost, or storm, of one kind or other, as the skies can possibly afford us. Surely everybody is aware of the divine pleasures which attend a winter fireside, candles at four o'clock, warm hearth rugs, tea, a fair tea maker, shutters closed, curtains flowing in ample draperies on the floor, whilst the wind and rain are raging audibly without,

> And at the doors and windows seem to call,
> As heav'n and earth they would together mell;
> Yet the least entrance find they none at all;
> Whence sweeter grows our rest secure in massy hall.
>
> *Castle of Indolence.*[5]

All these are items in the description of a winter

Life, vol. iii. p. 391, third edition) has recorded that, on the first occasion of his trying laudanum for the gout he took *forty* drops, the next night *sixty*, and on the fifth night *eighty*, without any effect whatever, and this at an advanced age. I have an anecdote from a country surgeon, however, which sinks Mr. Harriott's case into a trifle; and in my projected medical treatise on opium, which I will publish provided the College of Surgeons will pay me for enlightening their benighted understandings upon this subject, I will relate it; but it is far too good a story to be published gratis.

[1] [De Quincey's note] See the common accounts in any Eastern traveller or voyager of the frantic excesses committed by Malays who have taken opium, or are reduced to desperation by ill-luck at gambling. [The term "ran amuck" is based on the Malay word "amoq," meaning frenzied, so was originally used in English to refer to a "frenzied Malay."]

[2] *intercalary* Intervening; an intercalary year is one in which days have been added to synchronize with the solar year.

[3] *hydrophobia* Rabies.

[4] *"a cottage … house"* From "The Devil's Thoughts" (1799) by Robert Southey and Samuel Taylor Coleridge.

[5] *Castle of Indolence* By James Thomson (1748).

evening which must surely be familiar to everybody born in a high latitude. And it is evident that most of these delicacies, like ice-cream, require a very low temperature of the atmosphere to produce them; they are fruits which cannot be ripened without weather stormy or inclement in some way or other. I am not "*particular*," as people say, whether it be snow, or black frost, or wind so strong that (as Mr. —— says) "you may lean your back against it like a post." I can put up even with rain, provided it rains cats and dogs; but something of the sort I must have, and if I have it not, I think myself in a manner ill-used; for why am I called on to pay so heavily for winter, in coals and candles, and various privations that will occur even to gentlemen, if I am not to have the article good of its kind? No, a Canadian winter for my money, or a Russian one, where every man is but a co-proprietor with the north wind in the fee-simple[1] of his own ears. Indeed, so great an epicure am I in this matter that I cannot relish a winter night fully if it be much past St. Thomas's day,[2] and have degenerated into disgusting tendencies to vernal appearances. No, it must be divided by a thick wall of dark nights from all return of light and sunshine. From the latter weeks of October to Christmas Eve, therefore, is the period during which happiness is in season, which, in my judgment, enters the room with the tea tray; for tea, though ridiculed by those who are naturally of coarse nerves, or are become so from wine drinking, and are not susceptible of influence from so refined a stimulant, will always be the favourite beverage of the intellectual; and, for my part, I would have joined Dr. Johnson in a *bellum internecinum* against Jonas Hanway,[3] or any other impious person, who should presume to disparage it. But here, to save myself the trouble of too much verbal description, I will introduce a painter, and give him directions for the rest of the picture. Painters do not like white cottages, unless a good deal weather-stained, but as the reader now understands that it is a winter night, his services will not be required except for the inside of the house.

Paint me, then, a room seventeen feet by twelve, and not more than seven and a half feet high. This, reader, is somewhat ambitiously styled in my family the drawing room; but being contrived "a double debt to pay,"[4] it is also, and more justly, termed the library, for it happens that books are the only article of property in which I am richer than my neighbours. Of these I have about five thousand, collected gradually since my eighteenth year. Therefore, painter, put as many as you can into this room. Make it populous with books, and, furthermore, paint me a good fire, and furniture plain and modest, befitting the unpretending cottage of a scholar. And near the fire paint me a tea table, and (as it is clear that no creature can come to see one such a stormy night) place only two cups and saucers on the tea tray; and, if you know how to paint such a thing symbolically or otherwise, paint me an eternal teapot—eternal *a parte ante* and *a parte post*[5]—for I usually drink tea from eight o'clock at night to four o'clock in the morning. And as it is very unpleasant to make tea or to pour it out for oneself, paint me a lovely young woman sitting at the table. Paint her arms like Aurora's and her smiles like Hebe's.[6] But no, dear M., not even in jest let me insinuate that thy power to illuminate my cottage rests upon a tenure so perishable as mere personal beauty, or that the witchcraft of angelic smiles lies within the empire of any earthly pencil. Pass then, my good painter, to something more within its power; and the next article brought forward should naturally be myself—a picture of the opium-eater, with his "little golden receptacle of the pernicious drug" lying beside him on the table. As to the opium, I have no objection to see a picture of *that*, though I would rather see the original. You may paint it if you choose, but I apprise you that no "little" receptacle would, even in 1816, answer *my* purpose, who was at a distance from the "stately Pantheon," and all druggists (mortal or otherwise). No, you may as well paint the real receptacle, which was not of gold, but of glass, and as much like a wine decanter as possible. Into this you may put a quart of ruby-coloured laudanum;

[1] *fee-simple* Absolute ownership.

[2] *St. Thomas's day* December 21st, the shortest day of the year.

[3] *Dr. Johnson … Hanway* Jonas Hanway, known as the inventor of the umbrella, wrote "An Essay on Tea" (1756), in which he claimed that tea is bad for the health. Samuel Johnson, lexicographer, critic, and "a hardened and shameless tea-drinker," countered Hanway's argument in 1757; *bellum internecinum* War of extermination.

[4] *"a double debt to pay"* From Oliver Goldsmith's "The Deserted Village" (1770).

[5] *eternal … post* From John Wesley's 1776 Sermon 54, "On Eternity": "that eternity which is past, and that eternity which is to come."

[6] *Aurora* Roman goddess of the dawn; *Hebe* Greek goddess of youth.

that, and a book of German metaphysics placed by its side, will sufficiently attest my being in the neighbourhood. But as to myself—there I demur. I admit that, naturally, I ought to occupy the foreground of the picture; that being the hero of the piece, or (if you choose) the criminal at the bar, my body should be had into court. This seems reasonable; but why should I confess on this point to a painter? or why confess at all? If the public (into whose private ear I am confidentially whispering my confessions, and not into any painter's) should chance to have framed some agreeable picture for itself of the opium-eater's exterior, should have ascribed to him, romantically an elegant person or a handsome face, why should I barbarously tear from it so pleasing a delusion—pleasing both to the public and to me? No; paint me, if at all, according to your own fancy, and as a painter's fancy should teem with beautiful creations, I cannot fail in that way to be a gainer. And now, reader, we have run through all the ten categories of my condition as it stood about 1816–17, up to the middle of which latter year I judge myself to have been a happy man, and the elements of that happiness I have endeavoured to place before you in the above sketch of the interior of a scholar's library, in a cottage among the mountains, on a stormy winter evening.

But now, farewell—a long farewell—to happiness, winter or summer! Farewell to smiles and laughter! Farewell to peace of mind! Farewell to hope and to tranquil dreams, and to the blessed consolations of sleep. For more than three years and a half I am summoned away from these. I am now arrived at an Iliad of woes, for I have now to record—

THE PAINS OF OPIUM

—as when some great painter dips
His pencil in the gloom of earthquake and eclipse.
Shelley's *Revolt of Islam.*

Reader, who have thus far accompanied me, I must request your attention to a brief explanatory note on three points:

1. For several reasons I have not been able to compose the notes for this part of my narrative into any regular and connected shape. I give the notes disjointed as I find them, or have now drawn them up from memory. Some of them point to their own date, some I have dated, and some are undated. Whenever it could answer my purpose to transplant them from the natural or chronological order, I have not scrupled to do so. Sometimes I speak in the present, sometimes in the past tense. Few of the notes, perhaps, were written exactly at the period of time to which they relate; but this can little affect their accuracy, as the impressions were such that they can never fade from my mind. Much has been omitted. I could not, without effort, constrain myself to the task of either recalling, or constructing into a regular narrative, the whole burden of horrors which lies upon my brain. This feeling partly I plead in excuse, and partly that I am now in London, and am a helpless sort of person, who cannot even arrange his own papers without assistance; and I am separated from the hands which are wont to perform for me the offices of an amanuensis.[1]

2. You will think perhaps that I am too confidential and communicative of my own private history. It may be so. But my way of writing is rather to think aloud, and follow my own humors, than much to consider who is listening to me; and if I stop to consider what is proper to be said to this or that person, I shall soon come to doubt whether any part at all is proper. The fact is, I place myself at a distance of fifteen or twenty years ahead of this time, and suppose myself writing to those who will be interested about me hereafter; and wishing to have some record of time, the entire history of which no one can know but myself, I do it as fully as I am able with the efforts I am now capable of making, because I know not whether I can ever find time to do it again.

3. It will occur to you often to ask, why did I not release myself from the horrors of opium by leaving it off or diminishing it? To this I must answer briefly: it might be supposed that I yielded to the fascinations of opium too easily; it cannot be supposed that any man can be charmed by its terrors. The reader may be sure, therefore, that I made attempts innumerable to reduce the quantity. I add, that those who witnessed the agonies of those attempts, and not myself, were the first to beg me to desist. But could not have I reduced it a drop a day, or, by adding water, have bisected or trisected a drop? A thousand drops bisected would thus have taken nearly six years to reduce, and that way would certainly not have answered. But this is a common mistake of those who know

[1] *amanuensis* Latin: scribe or secretary.

nothing of opium experimentally; I appeal to those who do, whether it is not always found that down to a certain point it can be reduced with ease and even pleasure, but that after that point further reduction causes intense suffering. Yes, say many thoughtless persons, who know not what they are talking of, you will suffer a little low spirits and dejection for a few days. I answer, no; there is nothing like low spirits; on the contrary, the mere animal spirits are uncommonly raised; the pulse is improved; the health is better. It is not there that the suffering lies. It has no resemblance to the sufferings caused by renouncing wine. It is a state of unutterable irritation of stomach (which surely is not much like dejection), accompanied by intense perspirations, and feelings such as I shall not attempt to describe without more space at my command.

I shall now enter *in medias res*,[1] and shall anticipate, from a time when my opium pains might be said to be at their acme, an account of their palsying effects on the intellectual faculties.

* * *

My studies have now been long interrupted. I cannot read to myself with any pleasure, hardly with a moment's endurance. Yet I read aloud sometimes for the pleasure of others, because reading is an accomplishment of mine, and, in the slang use of the word "accomplishment" as a superficial and ornamental attainment, almost the only one I possess; and formerly, if I had any vanity at all connected with any endowment or attainment of mine, it was with this, for I had observed that no accomplishment was so rare. Players[2] are the worst readers of all: —— reads vilely; and Mrs. ——, who is so celebrated, can read nothing well but dramatic compositions, Milton she cannot read sufferably. People in general either read poetry without any passion at all, or else overstep the modesty of nature, and read not like scholars. Of late, if I have felt moved by anything it has been by the grand lamentations of *Samson Agonistes*, or the great harmonies of the Satanic speeches in *Paradise Regained*,[3] when read aloud by myself. A young lady sometimes comes and drinks tea with us; at her request and M.'s,[4] I now and then read W——'s poems to them. (W., by the bye, is the only poet I ever met who could read his own verses; often indeed he reads admirably.)

For nearly two years I believe that I read no book, but one; and I owe it to the author, in discharge of a great debt of gratitude, to mention what that was. The sublimer and more passionate poets I still read, as I have said, by snatches, and occasionally. But my proper vocation, as I well know, was the exercise of the analytic understanding. Now, for the most part analytic studies are continuous, and not to be pursued by fits and starts, or fragmentary efforts. Mathematics, for instance, intellectual philosophy, &c., were all become insupportable to me; I shrunk from them with a sense of powerless and infantine feebleness that gave me an anguish the greater from remembering the time when I grappled with them to my own hourly delight; and for this further reason, because I had devoted the labour of my whole life, and had dedicated my intellect, blossoms and fruits, to the slow and elaborate toil of constructing one single work, to which I had presumed to give the title of an unfinished work of Spinoza's—viz., *De Emendatione Humani Intellectus*.[5] This was now lying locked up, as by frost, like any Spanish bridge or aqueduct, begun upon too great a scale for the resources of the architect; and instead of reviving me as a monument of wishes at least, and aspirations, and a life of labour dedicated to the exaltation of human nature in that way in which God had best fitted me to promote so great an object, it was likely to stand a memorial to my children of hopes defeated, of baffled efforts, of materials uselessly accumulated, of foundations laid that were never to support a super-structure—of the grief and the ruin of the architect. In this state of imbecility I had, for amusement, turned my attention to political economy; my understanding, which formerly had been as active and restless as a hyena, could not, I suppose (so long as I lived at all) sink into utter lethargy; and political economy offers this advantage to a person in my state, that though it is eminently an organic science (no part, that is to say, but what acts on the whole as the whole again reacts on each part), yet the several parts may be detached and contemplated singly. Great as was the prostration of my powers at this time, yet I could not forget my knowledge; and my understanding had been for too many years intimate with severe thinkers, with logic, and the great

[1] *in medias res* Latin: in the midst of things.

[2] *Players* I.e., actors.

[3] *Samson Agonistes … Paradise Regained* Both by John Milton.

[4] *M.* Margaret, De Quincey's wife.

[5] *Spinoza's … Intellectus* Dutch philosopher Baruch Spinoza's *Treatise on the Improvement of the Understanding* (1677).

masters of knowledge, not to be aware of the utter feebleness of the main herd of modern economists. I had been led in 1811 to look into loads of books and pamphlets on many branches of economy; and, at my desire, M. sometimes read to me chapters from more recent works, or parts of parliamentary debates. I saw that these were generally the very dregs and rinsings of the human intellect, and that any man of sound head, and practised in wielding logic with a scholastic adroitness, might take up the whole academy of modern economists, and throttle them between heaven and earth with his finger and thumb, or bray their fungus heads[1] to powder with a lady's fan. At length, in 1819, a friend in Edinburgh sent me down Mr. Ricardo's book; and recurring to my own prophetic anticipation of the advent of some legislator for this science, I said, before I had finished the first chapter, "Thou art the man!" Wonder and curiosity were emotions that had long been dead in me. Yet I wondered once more: I wondered at myself that I could once again be stimulated to the effort of reading, and much more I wondered at the book. Had this profound work been really written in England during the nineteenth century? Was it possible? I supposed thinking[2] had been extinct in England. Could it be that an Englishman, and he not in academic bowers, but oppressed by mercantile and senatorial cares, had accomplished what all the universities of Europe and a century of thought had failed even to advance by one hair's breadth? All other writers had been crushed and overlaid by the enormous weight of facts and documents. Mr. Ricardo had deduced *a priori*[3] from the understanding itself laws which first gave a ray of light into the unwieldy chaos of materials, and had constructed what had been but a collection of tentative discussions into a science of regular proportions, now first standing on an eternal basis.

Thus did one single work of a profound understanding avail to give me a pleasure and an activity which I had not known for years. It roused me even to write, or at least to dictate what M. wrote for me. It seemed to me that some important truths had escaped even "the inevitable eye" of Mr. Ricardo; and as these were for the most part of such a nature that I could express or illustrate them more briefly and elegantly by algebraic symbols than in the usual clumsy and loitering diction of economists, the whole would not have filled a pocket-book; and being so brief, with M. for my amanuensis, even at this time, incapable as I was of all general exertion, I drew up my "Prolegomena[4] to all Future Systems of Political Economy." I hope it will not be found redolent of opium, though, indeed, to most people the subject is a sufficient opiate.

This exertion, however, was but a temporary flash, as the sequel showed, for I designed to publish my work. Arrangements were made at a provincial press, about eighteen miles distant, for printing it. An additional compositor was retained for some days on this account. The work was even twice advertised, and I was in a manner pledged to the fulfilment of my intention. But I had a preface to write, and a dedication, which I wished to make a splendid one, to Mr. Ricardo. I found myself quite unable to accomplish all this. The arrangements were countermanded, the compositor dismissed, and my "Prolegomena" rested peacefully by the side of its elder and more dignified brother.

I have thus described and illustrated my intellectual torpor in terms that apply more or less to every part of the four years during which I was under the Circean[5] spells of opium. But for misery and suffering, I might indeed be said to have existed in a dormant state. I seldom could prevail on myself to write a letter; an answer of a few words to any that I received was the utmost that I could accomplish, and often *that* not until the letter had lain weeks or even months on my writing table. Without the aid of M. all records of bills paid or *to be* paid must have perished, and my whole domestic economy, whatever became of Political Economy, must have gone into irretrievable confusion. I shall not afterwards allude to this part of the case. It is one, however, which the opium-eater will find, in the end, as oppressive and tormenting as any other, from the sense of incapacity and feebleness, from the direct embarrassments incident to the neglect or

[1] *bray their fungus heads* Beat their spongy heads.

[2] [De Quincey's note] The reader must remember what I here mean by *thinking*, because else this would be a very presumptuous expression. England, of late, has been rich to excess in fine thinkers, in the departments of creative and combining thought; but there is a sad dearth of masculine thinkers in any analytic path. A Scotchman of eminent name has lately told us that he is obliged to quit even mathematics for want of encouragement.

[3] *a priori* Latin: from first principles; without direct experience.

[4] *Prolegomena* Latin: introductory discussion.

[5] *Circean* Alluring, yet poisonous. In Homer's *Odyssey*, Circe was a mythological enchantress who turned Odysseus's sailors into swine.

procrastination of each day's appropriate duties, and from the remorse which must often exasperate the stings of these evils to a reflective and conscientious mind. The opium-eater loses none of his moral sensibilities or aspirations. He wishes and longs as earnestly as ever to realize what he believes possible, and feels to be exacted by duty, but his intellectual apprehension of what is possible infinitely outruns his power, not of execution only, but even of power to attempt. He lies under the weight of incubus[1] and nightmare; he lies in sight of all that he would fain perform, just as a man forcibly confined to his bed by the mortal languor of a relaxing disease, who is compelled to witness injury or outrage offered to some object of his tenderest love: he curses the spells which chain him down from motion; he would lay down his life if he might but get up and walk, but he is powerless as an infant and cannot even attempt to rise.

I now pass to what is the main subject of these latter confessions, to the history and journal of what took place in my dreams, for these were the immediate and proximate cause of my acutest suffering.

The first notice I had of any important change going on in this part of my physical economy was from the reawakening of a state of eye generally incident to childhood, or exalted states of irritability. I know not whether my reader is aware that many children, perhaps most, have a power of painting, as it were upon the darkness, all sorts of phantoms. In some that power is simply a mechanical affection of the eye; others have a voluntary or semi-voluntary power to dismiss or to summon them, or, as a child once said to me when I questioned him on this matter, "I can tell them to go, and they go; but sometimes they come when I don't tell them to come." Whereupon I told him that he had almost as unlimited a command over apparitions as a Roman centurion over his soldiers. In the middle of 1817, I think it was, that this faculty became positively distressing to me: at night, when I lay awake in bed, vast processions passed along in mournful pomp; friezes of never-ending stories, that to my feelings were as sad and solemn as if they were stories drawn from times before Oedipus or Priam, before Tyre, before Memphis.[2] And at the same time a corresponding change took place in my dreams; a theater seemed suddenly opened and lighted up within my brain, which presented nightly spectacles of more than earthly splendour. And the four following facts may be mentioned as noticeable at this time:

1. That as the creative state of the eye increased, a sympathy seemed to arise between the waking and the dreaming states of the brain in one point—that whatsoever I happened to call up and to trace by a voluntary act upon the darkness was very apt to transfer itself to my dreams, so that I feared to exercise this faculty, for, as Midas turned all things to gold that yet baffled his hopes and defrauded his human desires,[3] so whatsoever things capable of being visually represented I did but think of in the darkness, immediately shaped themselves into phantoms of the eye; and by a process apparently no less inevitable, when thus once traced in faint and visionary colours, like writings in sympathetic[4] ink, they were drawn out by the fierce chemistry of my dreams into insufferable splendour that fretted my heart.

2. For this and all other changes in my dreams were accompanied by deep-seated anxiety and gloomy melancholy, such as are wholly incommunicable by words. I seemed every night to descend, not metaphorically, but literally to descend, into chasms and sunless abysses, depths below depths, from which it seemed hopeless that I could ever re-ascend. Nor did I, by waking, feel that I *had* re-ascended. This I do not dwell upon because the state of gloom which attended these gorgeous spectacles, amounting at last to utter darkness, as of some suicidal despondency, cannot be approached by words.

3. The sense of space, and in the end the sense of time, were both powerfully affected. Buildings, landscapes, &c., were exhibited in proportions so vast as the bodily eye is not fitted to receive. Space swelled and was amplified to an extent of unutterable infinity. This, however, did not disturb me so much as the vast expan-

[1] *incubus* Burden or oppression; "incubi" were demons who tormented people in their sleep.

[2] *Oedipus* King of Thebes, a city in ancient Egypt; *Priam* King of Troy, a city in ancient Greece; *Tyre* Ancient city of Phoenicia, now Lebanon; *Memphis* Capital of ancient Egypt.

[3] *Midas … desires* The Greek god Dionysus granted King Midas his wish that everything he touched be turned to gold; the king was devastated when his food, wine, and eventually his daughter were all turned to gold.

[4] *sympathetic* Invisible.

sion of time; I sometimes seemed to have lived for 70 or 100 years in one night—nay, sometimes had feelings representative of a millennium passed in that time, or, however, of a duration far beyond the limits of any human experience.

4. The minutest incidents of childhood, or forgotten scenes of later years, were often revived; I could not be said to recollect them, for if I had been told of them when waking, I should not have been able to acknowledge them as parts of my past experience. But placed as they were before me, in dreams like intuitions, and clothed in all their evanescent circumstances and accompanying feelings, I *recognized* them instantaneously. I was once told by a near relative of mine, that having in her childhood fallen into a river, and being on the very verge of death but for the critical assistance which reached her, she saw in a moment her whole life, in its minutest incidents, arrayed before her simultaneously as in a mirror; and she had a faculty developed as suddenly for comprehending the whole and every part. This, from some opium experiences of mine, I can believe; I have indeed seen the same thing asserted twice in modern books, and accompanied by a remark which I am convinced is true, viz., that the dread book of account which the Scriptures speak of[1] is in fact the mind itself of each individual. Of this at least I feel assured, that there is no such thing as *forgetting* possible to the mind; a thousand accidents may and will interpose a veil between our present consciousness and the secret inscriptions on the mind; accidents of the same sort will also rend away this veil; but alike, whether veiled or unveiled, the inscription remains forever, just as the stars seem to withdraw before the common light of day, whereas in fact we all know that it is the light which is drawn over them as a veil, and that they are waiting to be revealed when the obscuring daylight shall have withdrawn.

Having noticed these four facts as memorably distinguishing my dreams from those of health, I shall now cite a case illustrative of the first fact, and shall then cite any others that I remember, either in their chronological order, or any other that may give them more effect as pictures to the reader.

I had been in youth, and even since, for occasional amusement, a great reader of Livy,[2] whom I confess that I prefer, both for style and matter, to any other of the Roman historians; and I had often felt as most solemn and appalling sounds, and most emphatically representative of the majesty of the Roman people, the two words so often occurring in Livy—Consul Romanus,[3] especially when the consul is introduced in his military character. I mean to say that the words king, sultan, regent, &c., or any other titles of those who embody in their own persons the collective majesty of a great people, had less power over my reverential feelings. I had also, though no great reader of history, made myself minutely and critically familiar with one period of English history, viz., the period of the Parliamentary War,[4] having been attracted by the moral grandeur of some who figured in that day, and by the many interesting memoirs which survive those unquiet times. Both these parts of my lighter reading, having furnished me often with matter of reflection, now furnished me with matter for my dreams. Often I used to see, after painting upon the blank darkness a sort of rehearsal whilst waking, a crowd of ladies, and perhaps a festival and dances. And I heard it said, or I said to myself, "These are English ladies from the unhappy times of Charles I. These are the wives and the daughters of those who met in peace, and sat at the same table, and were allied by marriage or by blood; and yet, after a certain day in August 1642, never smiled upon each other again, nor met but in the field of battle; and at Marston Moor, at Newbury, or at Naseby,[5] cut asunder all ties of love by the cruel sabre, and washed away in blood the memory of ancient friendship." The ladies danced, and looked as lovely as the court of George IV.[6] Yet I knew, even in my dream, that they had been in the grave for nearly two centuries. This pageant would suddenly dissolve; and at a clapping of hands would be heard the heart-quaking

[1] *dread … speak of* Cf. Revelation 20.12: "I saw the dead, small and great, stand before God; and the books were opened: and another book was opened, which is the book of life: and the dead were judged out of those things which were written in the books, according to their works."

[2] *Livy* Titus Livius (59 BCE–17 CE), author of *The History of Rome.*

[3] *Consul Romanus* I.e., Consul of Rome, who, with another consul, exercised supreme authority in the Roman Republic.

[4] *Parliamentary War* English Civil War, begun after King Charles I declared war on Parliament in 1642, and ending with his beheading in 1649.

[5] *Marston Moor, at Newbury, or at Naseby* Sites of civil war battles in which Royalist forces sustained heavy losses.

[6] *court of George IV* George IV ruled England from 1820 to 1830.

sound of *Consul Romanus*; and immediately came "sweeping by," in gorgeous paludaments, Paulus or Marius,[1] girt round by a company of centurions, with the crimson tunic[2] hoisted on a spear, and followed by the alalagmos[3] of the Roman legions.

Many years ago, when I was looking over Piranesi's *Antiquities of Rome*,[4] Mr. Coleridge, who was standing by, described to me a set of plates by that artist, called his *dreams*,[5] and which record the scenery of his own visions during the delirium of a fever. Some of them (I describe only from memory of Mr. Coleridge's account) represented vast Gothic halls, on the floor of which stood all sorts of engines and machinery, wheels, cables, pulleys, levers, catapults, &c. &c., expressive of enormous power put forth and resistance overcome. Creeping along the sides of the walls you perceived a staircase, and upon it, groping his way upwards, was Piranesi himself; follow the stairs a little further and you perceive it come to a sudden and abrupt termination without any balustrade, and allowing no step onwards to him who had reached the extremity except into the depths below. Whatever is to become of poor Piranesi, you suppose at least that his labours must in some way terminate here. But raise your eyes, and behold a second flight of stairs still higher, on which again Piranesi is perceived, but this time standing on the very brink of the abyss. Again elevate your eye, and a still more aerial flight of stairs is beheld, and again is poor Piranesi busy on his aspiring labours; and so on, until the unfinished stairs and Piranesi both are lost in the upper gloom of the hall. With the same power of endless growth and self-reproduction did my architecture proceed in dreams. In the early stage of my malady the splendours of my dreams were indeed chiefly architectural; and I beheld such pomp of cities and palaces as was never yet beheld by the waking eye unless in the clouds. From a great modern poet I cite part of a passage which describes, as an appearance actually beheld in the clouds, what in many of its circumstances I saw frequently in sleep:

The appearance, instantaneously disclosed,
Was of a mighty city—boldly say
A wilderness of building, sinking far
And self-withdrawn into a wondrous depth,
Far sinking into splendour—without end!
Fabric it seemed of diamond, and of gold,
With alabaster domes, and silver spires,
And blazing terrace upon terrace, high
Uplifted; here, serene pavilions bright
In avenues disposed; there towers begirt
With battlements that on their restless fronts
Bore stars—illumination of all gems!
By earthly nature had the effect been wrought
Upon the dark materials of the storm
Now pacified; on them, and on the coves,
And mountain steeps and summits, whereunto
The vapours had receded,—taking there
Their station under a cerulean sky.[6] &c. &c.

The sublime circumstance, "battlements that on their *restless* fronts bore stars," might have been copied from my architectural dreams, for it often occurred. We hear it reported of Dryden and of Fuseli,[7] in modern times, that they thought proper to eat raw meat for the sake of obtaining splendid dreams; how much better for such a purpose to have eaten opium, which yet I do not remember that any poet is recorded to have done, except the dramatist Shadwell;[8] and in ancient days Homer is I think rightly reputed to have known the virtues of opium.[9]

To my architecture succeeded dreams of lakes and silvery expanses of water; these haunted me so much that I feared (though possibly it will appear ludicrous to a medical man) that some dropsical state or tendency of the brain might thus be making itself (to use a metaphysical word) *objective*; and the sentient organ *project* itself as its own object. For two months I suffered greatly in my head,

[1] *paludaments* Military cloaks; *Paullus or Marius* Roman consuls.

[2] *crimson tunic* War signal.

[3] *alalagmos* War cries.

[4] *Piranesi's … Rome* Etchings by Italian architect and artist Giovanni Battista Piranesi (1720–78).

[5] plates … dreams From *Carceri* (1747–61), a series of etchings of "prisons of the imagination."

[6] *The appearance … sky* From Wordsworth's *The Excursion, Book Second*: "The Solitary" (834–51).

[7] *Dryden* English poet, playwright, and critic John Dryden (1631–1700); *Fuseli* Anglo-Swiss painter John Henry Fuseli (1741–1825).

[8] *Shadwell* English poet laureate and playwright Thomas Shadwell (c. 1642–92).

[9] *Homer … opium* Cf. Homer's *Odyssey* (trans. George Chapman) 4.293–97: "Helen now on new device did stand, / Infusing straight a medicine to their wine, / That, drowning cares and angers, did decline / All thought of ill. Who drunk her cup could shed / All that day not a tear."

a part of my bodily structure which had hitherto been so clear from all touch or taint of weakness (physically I mean) that I used to say of it, as the last Lord Orford[1] said of his stomach, that it seemed likely to survive the rest of my person. Till now I had never felt a headache even, or any the slightest pain, except rheumatic pains caused by my own folly. However, I got over this attack, though it must have been verging on something very dangerous.

The waters now changed their character—from translucent lakes shining like mirrors they now became seas and oceans. And now came a tremendous change, which, unfolding itself slowly like a scroll through many months, promised an abiding torment; and in fact it never left me until the winding up of my case. Hitherto the human face had mixed often in my dreams, but not despotically nor with any special power of tormenting. But now that which I have called the tyranny of the human face began to unfold itself. Perhaps some part of my London life might be answerable for this. Be that as it may, now it was that upon the rocking waters of the ocean the human face began to appear; the sea appeared paved with innumerable faces upturned to the heavens—faces imploring, wrathful, despairing, surged upwards by thousands, by myriads, by generations, by centuries; my agitation was infinite; my mind tossed and surged with the ocean.

* * *

May 1818

The Malay has been a fearful enemy for months. I have been every night, through his means, transported into Asiatic scenes. I know not whether others share in my feelings on this point, but I have often thought that if I were compelled to forego England and to live in China, and among Chinese manners and modes of life and scenery, I should go mad. The causes of my horror lie deep, and some of them must be common to others. Southern Asia in general is the seat of awful images and associations. As the cradle of the human race, it would alone have a dim and reverential feeling connected with it. But there are other reasons. No man can pretend that the wild, barbarous, and capricious superstitions of Africa, or of savage tribes elsewhere, affect him in the way that he is affected by the ancient, monumental, cruel, and elaborate religions of Indostan, &c. The mere antiquity of Asiatic things, of their institutions, histories, modes of faith, &c., is so impressive, that to me the vast age of the race and name overpowers the sense of youth in the individual. A young Chinese seems to me an antediluvian man renewed. Even Englishmen, though not bred in any knowledge of such institutions, cannot but shudder at the mystic sublimity of *castes* that have flowed apart, and refused to mix, through such immemorial tracts of time; nor can any man fail to be awed by the names of the Ganges or the Euphrates.[2] It contributes much to these feelings that southern Asia is, and has been for thousands of years, the part of the earth most swarming with human life, the great *officina gentium*.[3] Man is a weed in those regions. The vast empires also in which the enormous population of Asia has always been cast, give a further sublimity to the feelings associated with all Oriental names or images. In China, over and above what it has in common with the rest of southern Asia, I am terrified by the modes of life, by the manners, and the barrier of utter abhorrence and want of sympathy placed between us by feelings deeper than I can analyse. I could sooner live with lunatics or brute animals. All this, and much more than I can say or have time to say, the reader must enter into before he can comprehend the unimaginable horror which these dreams of Oriental imagery and mythological tortures impressed upon me. Under the connecting feeling of tropical heat and vertical sunlights I brought together all creatures, birds, beasts, reptiles, all trees and plants, usages and appearances, that are found in all tropical regions, and assembled them together in China or Indostan. From kindred feelings, I soon brought Egypt and all her gods under the same law. I was stared at, hooted at, grinned at, chattered at, by monkeys, by parroquets,[4] by cockatoos. I ran into pagodas, and was fixed for centuries at the summit or in secret rooms. I was the idol; I was the priest; I was worshipped; I was sacrificed. I fled from the wrath of Brama through all the forests of Asia; Vishnu hated me. Seeva[5] laid wait for me. I came suddenly upon Isis and Osiris. I had done a deed,

[1] *last Lord Orford* Author Horace Walpole (1717–97).

[2] *Ganges or the Euphrates* Major rivers of Asia.

[3] *officina gentium* Latin: factory of nations.

[4] *parroquets* I.e., parakeets.

[5] *Brama … Seeva* The Hindu triad: the gods Brahma, Vishnu, and Shiva.

they said, which the ibis and the crocodile[1] trembled at. I was buried for a thousand years in stone coffins, with mummies and sphinxes, in narrow chambers at the heart of eternal pyramids. I was kissed, with cancerous kisses, by crocodiles, and laid, confounded with all unutterable slimy things, amongst reeds and Nilotic mud.[2]

I thus give the reader some slight abstraction of my Oriental dreams, which always filled me with such amazement at the monstrous scenery that horror seemed absorbed for a while in sheer astonishment. Sooner or later came a reflux of feeling that swallowed up the astonishment, and left me not so much in terror as in hatred and abomination of what I saw. Over every form, and threat, and punishment, and dim sightless incarceration, brooded a sense of eternity and infinity that drove me into an oppression as of madness. Into these dreams only it was, with one or two slight exceptions, that any circumstances of physical horror entered. All before had been moral and spiritual terrors. But here the main agents were ugly birds, or snakes, or crocodiles, especially the last. The cursed crocodile became to me the object of more horror than almost all the rest. I was compelled to live with him, and (as was always the case almost in my dreams) for centuries. I escaped sometimes, and found myself in Chinese houses, with cane tables, &c. All the feet of the tables, sofas, &c., soon became instinct with life; the abominable head of the crocodile, and his leering eyes, looked out at me, multiplied into a thousand repetitions, and I stood loathing and fascinated. And so often did this hideous reptile haunt my dreams that many times the very same dream was broken up in the very same way: I heard gentle voices speaking to me (I hear everything when I am sleeping), and instantly I awoke. It was broad noon, and my children were standing, hand in hand, at my bedside—come to show me their coloured shoes, or new frocks, or to let me see them dressed for going out. I protest that so awful was the transition from the damned crocodile, and the other unutterable monsters and abortions of my dreams, to the sight of innocent *human* natures and of infancy, that in the mighty and sudden revulsion of mind I wept, and could not forbear it, as I kissed their faces.

[1] *Isis ... crocodile* Isis and Osiris were deities of ancient Egypt; Thoth, in the shape of an ibis, and Sobek, a crocodile, were also Egyptian gods.

[2] *Nilotic mud* I.e., mud of the river Nile.

June 1819

I have had occasion to remark, at various periods of my life, that the deaths of those whom we love, and indeed the contemplation of death generally, is (*caeteris paribus*[3]) more affecting in summer than in any other season of the year. And the reasons are these three, I think: first, that the visible heavens in summer appear far higher, more distant, and (if such a solecism may be excused) more infinite; the clouds, by which chiefly the eye expounds the distance of the blue pavilion stretched over our heads, are in summer more voluminous, massed and accumulated in far grander and more towering piles. Secondly, the light and the appearances of the declining and the setting sun are much more fitted to be types and characters of the Infinite. And thirdly (which is the main reason), the exuberant and riotous prodigality of life naturally forces the mind more powerfully upon the antagonist thought of death, and the wintry sterility of the grave. For it may be observed generally, that wherever two thoughts stand related to each other by a law of antagonism, and exist, as it were, by mutual repulsion, they are apt to suggest each other. On these accounts it is that I find it impossible to banish the thought of death when I am walking alone in the endless days of summer; and any particular death, if not more affecting, at least haunts my mind more obstinately and besiegingly in that season. Perhaps this cause, and a slight incident which I omit, might have been the immediate occasions of the following dream, to which, however, a predisposition must always have existed in my mind; but having been once roused it never left me, and split into a thousand fantastic varieties, which often suddenly reunited, and composed again the original dream.

I thought that it was a Sunday morning in May, that it was Easter Sunday, and as yet very early in the morning. I was standing, as it seemed to me, at the door of my own cottage. Right before me lay the very scene which could really be commanded from that situation, but exalted, as was usual, and solemnized by the power of dreams. There were the same mountains, and the same lovely valley at their feet; but the mountains were raised to more than Alpine height, and there was interspace far larger between them of meadows and forest lawns; the hedges were rich with white roses, and no living creature was to be seen, excepting that in the green churchyard there were cattle tranquilly reposing upon the verdant graves, and particu-

[3] *caeteris paribus* Latin: other things being equal.

larly round about the grave of a child whom I had tenderly loved, just as I had really beheld them, a little before sunrise in the same summer, when that child died. I gazed upon the well-known scene, and I said aloud (as I thought) to myself, "It yet wants much of sunrise, and it is Easter Sunday; and that is the day on which they celebrate the first fruits of resurrection. I will walk abroad; old griefs shall be forgotten today, for the air is cool and still, and the hills are high and stretch away to heaven; and the forest glades are as quiet as the churchyard, and with the dew I can wash the fever from my forehead, and then I shall be unhappy no longer." And I turned as if to open my garden gate, and immediately I saw upon the left a scene far different, but which yet the power of dreams had reconciled into harmony with the other. The scene was an Oriental one, and there also it was Easter Sunday, and very early in the morning. And at a vast distance were visible, as a stain upon the horizon, the domes and cupolas of a great city—an image or faint abstraction, caught perhaps in childhood from some picture of Jerusalem. And not a bowshot[1] from me, upon a stone and shaded by Judean palms, there sat a woman, and I looked, and it was—Ann! She fixed her eyes upon me earnestly, and I said to her at length: "So, then, I have found you at last." I waited, but she answered me not a word. Her face was the same as when I saw it last, and yet again how different! Seventeen years ago, when the lamplight fell upon her face, as for the last time I kissed her lips (lips, Ann, that to me were not polluted), her eyes were streaming with tears; the tears were now wiped away; she seemed more beautiful than she was at that time, but in all other points the same, and not older. Her looks were tranquil, but with unusual solemnity of expression, and I now gazed upon her with some awe; but suddenly her countenance grew dim, and turning to the mountains I perceived vapours rolling between us. In a moment all had vanished, thick darkness came on, and in the twinkling of an eye I was far away from mountains, and by lamplight in Oxford Street, walking again with Ann—just as we walked seventeen years before, when we were both children.

As a final specimen, I cite one of a different character, from 1820.

The dream commenced with a music which now I often heard in dreams—a music of preparation and of awakening suspense, a music like the opening of the Coronation Anthem, and which, like *that*, gave the feeling of a vast march, of infinite cavalcades filing off, and the tread of innumerable armies. The morning was come of a mighty day—a day of crisis and of final hope for human nature, then suffering some mysterious eclipse, and labouring in some dread extremity. Somewhere, I knew not where—somehow, I knew not how—by some beings, I knew not whom—a battle, a strife, an agony, was conducting, was evolving like a great drama or piece of music, with which my sympathy was the more insupportable from my confusion as to its place, its cause, its nature, and its possible issue. I, as is usual in dreams (where of necessity we make ourselves central to every movement), had the power, and yet had not the power, to decide it. I had the power, if I could raise myself to will it, and yet again had not the power, for the weight of twenty Atlantics was upon me, or the oppression of inexpiable guilt. "Deeper than ever plummet sounded,"[2] I lay inactive. Then like a chorus the passion deepened. Some greater interest was at stake, some mightier cause than ever yet the sword had pleaded, or trumpet had proclaimed. Then came sudden alarms, hurryings to and fro, trepidations of innumerable fugitives—I knew not whether from the good cause or the bad, darkness and lights, tempest and human faces, and at last, with the sense that all was lost, female forms, and the features that were worth all the world to me, and but a moment allowed—and clasped hands, and heartbreaking partings, and then—everlasting farewells! And with a sigh, such as the caves of Hell sighed when the incestuous mother uttered the abhorred name of death,[3] the sound was reverberated—everlasting farewells! And again and yet again reverberated—everlasting farewells!

And I awoke in struggles, and cried aloud—"I will sleep no more."[4]

[1] *bowshot* Measurement of distance: the span an arrow will fly from the bow.

[2] *"Deeper … sounded"* From Shakespeare's *The Tempest* 3.3.115.

[3] *incestuous … death* In Milton's *Paradise Lost* 2.787–89, Sin, the daughter of Satan, fled and: "cried out DEATH! / Hell trembled at the hideous name, and sighed / From all her caves, and back resounded, DEATH!"

[4] *"I will sleep no more."* From Shakespeare's *Macbeth* 2.2.46, in which the guilt-ridden Macbeth says: "Methought I heard a voice cry 'Sleep no more!'"

But I am now called upon to wind up a narrative which has already extended to an unreasonable length. Within more spacious limits the materials which I have used might have been better unfolded, and much which I have not used might have been added with effect. Perhaps, however, enough has been given. It now remains that I should say something of the way in which this conflict of horrors was finally brought to a crisis. The reader is already aware (from a passage near the beginning of the introduction to the first part) that the opium-eater has, in some way or other, "unwound almost to its final links the accursed chain which bound him." By what means? To have narrated this according to the original intention would have far exceeded the space which can now be allowed. It is fortunate, as such a cogent reason exists for abridging it, that I should, on a maturer view of the case, have been exceedingly unwilling to injure, by any such unaffecting details, the impression of the history itself, as an appeal to the prudence and the conscience of the yet unconfirmed opium-eater—or even (though a very inferior consideration) to injure its effect as a composition. The interest of the judicious reader will not attach itself chiefly to the subject of the fascinating spells, but to the fascinating power. Not the opium-eater, but the opium, is the true hero of the tale, and the legitimate centre on which the interest revolves. The object was to display the marvellous agency of opium, whether for pleasure or for pain; if that is done, the action of the piece has closed.

However, as some people, in spite of all laws to the contrary, will persist in asking what became of the opium-eater, and in what state he now is, I answer for him thus: The reader is aware that opium had long ceased to found its empire on spells of pleasure; it was solely by the tortures connected with the attempt to abjure it that it kept its hold. Yet, as other tortures, no less it may be thought, attended the non-abjuration of such a tyrant, a choice only of evils was left; and *that* might as well have been adopted which, however terrific in itself, held out a prospect of final restoration to happiness. This appears true, but good logic gave the author no strength to act upon it. However, a crisis arrived for the author's life, and a crisis for other objects still dearer to him—and which will always be far dearer to him than his life, even now that it is again a happy one. I saw that I must die if I continued the opium. I determined, therefore, if that should be required, to die in throwing it off. How much I was at that time taking I cannot say, for the opium which I used had been purchased for me by a friend, who afterwards refused to let me pay him, so that I could not ascertain even what quantity I had used within the year. I apprehend, however, that I took it very irregularly, and that I varied from about fifty or sixty grains to 150 a day. My first task was to reduce it to forty, to thirty, and as fast as I could to twelve grains.

I triumphed. But think not, reader, that therefore my sufferings were ended, nor think of me as of one sitting in a *dejected* state. Think of me as one, even when four months had passed, still agitated, writhing, throbbing, palpitating, shattered, and much perhaps in the situation of him who has been racked, as I collect the torments of that state from the affecting account of them left by a most innocent sufferer[1] of the times of James I. Meantime, I derived no benefit from any medicine, except one prescribed to me by an Edinburgh surgeon of great eminence, viz., ammoniated tincture of valerian. Medical account, therefore, of my emancipation I have not much to give, and even that little, as managed by a man so ignorant of medicine as myself, would probably tend only to mislead. At all events, it would be misplaced in this situation. The moral of the narrative is addressed to the opium-eater, and therefore of necessity limited in its application. If he is taught to fear and tremble, enough has been effected. But he may say that the issue of my case is at least a proof that opium, after a seventeen years' use and an eight years' abuse of its powers, may still be renounced, and that *he* may chance to bring to the task greater energy than I did, or that with a stronger constitution than mine he may obtain the same results with less. This may be true. I would not presume to measure the efforts of other men by my own. I heartily wish him more energy. I wish him the same success. Nevertheless, I had motives external to myself which he may unfortunately want, and these supplied me with conscientious supports which mere personal interests might fail to supply to a mind debilitated by opium.

[1] [De Quincey's note] William Lithgow. His book (*Travels*, &c.) is ill and pedantically written; but the account of his own sufferings on the rack at Malaga is overpoweringly affecting. [Lithgow was tortured in Malaga, Spain, after being accused of being a spy for King James I, who reigned from 1604–25.]

Jeremy Taylor[1] conjectures that it may be as painful to be born as to die. I think it probable; and during the whole period of diminishing the opium I had the torments of a man passing out of one mode of existence into another. The issue was not death, but a sort of physical regeneration; and I may add that ever since, at intervals, I have had a restoration of more than youthful spirits, though under the pressure of difficulties which in a less happy state of mind I should have called misfortunes.

One memorial of my former condition still remains—my dreams are not yet perfectly calm; the dread swell and agitation of the storm have not wholly subsided; the legions that encamped in them are drawing off, but not all departed; my sleep is still tumultuous, and, like the gates of Paradise to our first parents when looking back from afar, it is still (in the tremendous line of Milton)

> With dreadful faces thronged, and fiery arms.[2]

—1821

[1] *Jeremy Taylor* English bishop, theologian, and author (1613–67).

[2] *"With dreadful … thronged"* From Milton's *Paradise Lost* (12.644).

Mary Prince

1788 – 1833

Author of the earliest extant slave narrative by a woman, Mary Prince was born into bondage in the British colony of Bermuda, where for the first twelve years of her life she was spared the cruelty that dominated her adult years. Both her parents were also slaves, the property of Charles Myners. After Myners died, Mary and her mother were sold to a Captain Williams, whose daughter Betsey treated Mary as "her little nigger," yet with relative compassion. Williams sold Prince to another family to raise money for his marriage and in 1806 she was sent to work in the salt ponds of Turks Island: "This work was perfectly new to me. I was given a half barrel and shovel, and had to stand up to my knees in the water, from four o'clock in the morning till nine, when we were given some Indian corn boiled in water, which we were obliged to swallow as fast as we could for fear the rain should come on and melt the salt."

In 1818, Prince was sold for three hundred dollars to John Wood, a plantation owner in Antigua. On the plantation Prince contracted rheumatism and became essentially crippled, her legs covered with boils; these maladies stayed with her and eventually affected her eyesight. She was also beaten and sexually abused by her master. Prince began attending meetings held at the Moravian Church, where various women taught her to read: "After we had done spelling, we tried to read in the Bible. After reading was over, the missionary gave out a hymn for us to sing." Prince was married in this church to Daniel Jones, a former slave who had purchased his own freedom. Wood horsewhipped Prince when he discovered the marriage. In 1828 Wood took Prince to London as his servant. Abolitionist sympathizers helped her escape and she found employment as a domestic servant (slavery was illegal in England) of Thomas Pringle, a Methodist and secretary of the Anti-Slavery Society.

Pringle encouraged Prince to tell the story of her life and, in 1831, he arranged for the publication of her book, *The History of Mary Prince, a West-Indian Slave, Related by Herself.* In his "Preface" to the work, Pringle wrote: "The idea of writing Mary Prince's history was first suggested by herself. She wished it to be done, she said, that good people in England might hear from a slave what a slave had felt and suffered." Mary Prince told her story to Susanna Strickland (later Moodie), who recorded it in writing. It seems improbable that Strickland—who would later come to be regarded as one of Canada's most accomplished writers in the nineteenth century—would not at a minimum have edited the dictated narrative for grammar and syntax, and some have suggested that Pringle may have had some hand in shaping the manuscript so as to better serve abolitionist ends. (His insistence that the rhetorical flourish at the end of Prince's first paragraph is "given verbatim as uttered by Mary Prince" has struck more than one reader as rather forced.) But most scholars have stopped short of suggesting that material was fabricated by Pringle and Strickland, or that this is not in essence Prince's own narrative. Strickland herself attested that she had "been writing Mr. Pringle's black Mary's life from her own dictation and for her benefit adhering to her own simple story and language without deviating to the paths of flourish or romance."

The book was a great success, and gave rise to considerable controversy. *Blackwood's Magazine* and *The Glasgow Courier* claimed it was fraudulent and propagandistic. A number of libel suits resulted, with Wood suing Pringle and Pringle counter-suing. Wood claimed that the book had "endeavored to injure the character of my family by the most vile and infamous falsehoods." Wood lost the case and the libel scandal served only to make Prince's work more widely known. It reached a third edition in the same year it was published and it has since that time retained its place as one of the most moving, detailed, and comprehensive narratives of the life of a slave.

Slavery was abolished in all British colonies in 1833. Little is known of Prince's life after the publication of her *History*, and we do not know when, where, or how she died.

⌘⌘⌘

The History of Mary Prince
A West Indian Slave
Related by Herself

PREFACE [BY THOMAS PRINGLE]

The idea of writing Mary Prince's history was first suggested by herself. She wished it to be done, she said, that good people in England might hear from a slave what a slave had felt and suffered; and a letter of her late master's, which will be found in the Supplement, induced me to accede to her wish without farther delay. The more immediate object of the publication will afterwards appear.

The narrative was taken down from Mary's own lips by a lady who happened to be at the time residing in my family as a visitor. It was written out fully, with all the narrator's repetitions and prolixities,[1] and afterwards pruned into its present shape; retaining, as far as was practicable, Mary's exact expressions and peculiar phraseology. No fact of importance has been omitted, and not a single circumstance or sentiment has been added. It is essentially her own, without any material alteration farther than was requisite to exclude redundances and gross grammatical errors, so as to render it clearly intelligible.

After it had been thus written out, I went over the whole, carefully examining her on every fact and circumstance detailed; and in all that relates to her residence in Antigua I had the advantage of being assisted in this scrutiny by Mr. Joseph Phillips, who was a resident in that colony during the same period, and had known her there.

The names of all the persons mentioned by the narrator have been printed in full, except those of Capt. I—and his wife, and that of Mr. D—, to whom conduct of peculiar atrocity is ascribed. These three individuals are now gone to answer at a far more awful tribunal than that of public opinion, for the deeds of which their former bondwoman accuses them; and to hold them up more openly to human reprobation could no longer affect themselves, while it might deeply lacerate the feelings of their surviving and perhaps innocent relatives, without any commensurate public advantage.

Without detaining the reader with remarks on other points which will be adverted to more conveniently in the Supplement, I shall here merely notice farther, that the Anti-Slavery Society have no concern whatever with this publication, nor are they in any degree responsible for the statements it contains. I have published the tract, not as their Secretary, but in my private capacity; and any profits that may arise from the sale will be exclusively appropriated to the benefit of Mary Prince herself.

THOMAS PRINGLE[2]
7, Solly Terrace, Claremont Square,
January 25, 1831

P.S. Since writing the above, I have been furnished by my friend Mr. George Stephen, with the interesting narrative of Asa-Asa, a captured African, now under his protection; and have printed it as a suitable appendix to this little history.

T.P.

The History of Mary Prince

I was born at Brackish-Pond, in Bermuda, on a farm belonging to Mr. Charles Myners. My mother was a household slave; and my father, whose name was Prince, was a sawyer[3] belonging to Mr. Trimmingham, a shipbuilder at Crow-Lane. When I was an infant, old Mr. Myners died, and there was a division of the slaves and other property among the family. I was bought along with my mother by old Captain Darrel, and given to his

[1] *prolixities* Instances of wordiness.

[2] *Thomas Pringle* Also known as the "father of South African poetry," Pringle (1789–1834) was born in Scotland and lived in South Africa between 1820 and 1826, where he published a newspaper and a magazine. In 1826 he returned to England, where he devoted himself to the antislavery movement as secretary to the Society for the Abolition of Slavery.

[3] *sawyer* Worker whose job it is to saw timber.

grandchild, little Miss Betsey Williams. Captain Williams, Mr. Darrel's son-in-law, was master of a vessel which traded to several places in America and the West Indies, and he was seldom at home long together.

Mrs. Williams was a kind-hearted good woman, and she treated all her slaves well. She had only one daughter, Miss Betsey, for whom I was purchased, and who was about my own age. I was made quite a pet of by Miss Betsey, and loved her very much. She used to lead me about by the hand, and call me her little nigger. This was the happiest period of my life; for I was too young to understand rightly my condition as a slave, and too thoughtless and full of spirits to look forward to the days of toil and sorrow.

My mother was a household slave in the same family. I was under her own care, and my little brothers and sisters were my play-fellows and companions. My mother had us several fine children after she came to Mrs. Williams, three girls and two boys. The tasks given out to us children were light, and we used to play together with Miss Betsey, with as much freedom almost as if she had been our sister.

My master, however, was a very harsh, selfish man; and we always dreaded his return from sea. His wife was herself much afraid of him; and, during his stay at home, seldom dared to show her usual kindness to the slaves. He often left her, in the most distressed circumstances, to reside in other female society, at some place in the West Indies of which I have forgot the name. My poor mistress bore his ill-treatment with great patience, and all her slaves loved and pitied her. I was truly attached to her, and, next to my own mother, loved her better than any creature in the world. My obedience to her commands was cheerfully given: it sprung solely from the affection I felt for her, and not from fear of the power which the white people's law had given her over me.

I had scarcely reached my twelfth year when my mistress became too poor to keep so many of us at home; and she hired me out to Mrs. Pruden, a lady who lived about five miles off, in the adjoining parish, in a large house near the sea. I cried bitterly at parting with my dear mistress and Miss Betsey, and when I kissed my mother and brothers and sisters, I thought my young heart would break, it pained me so. But there was no help; I was forced to go. Good Mrs. Williams comforted me by saying that I should still be near the home I was about to quit, and might come over and see her and my kindred whenever I could obtain leave of absence from Mrs. Pruden. A few hours after this I was taken to a strange house, and found myself among strange people. This separation seemed a sore trial to me then; but oh! 'twas light, light to the trials I have since endured!—'twas nothing—nothing to be mentioned with them; but I was a child then, and it was according to my strength.

I knew that Mrs. Williams could no longer maintain me; that she was fain to part with me for my food and clothing; and I tried to submit myself to the change. My new mistress was a passionate woman; but yet she did not treat me very unkindly. I do not remember her striking me but once, and that was for going to see Mrs. Williams when I heard she was sick, and staying longer than she had given me leave to do. All my employment at this time was nursing a sweet baby, little Master Daniel; and I grew so fond of my nursling that it was my greatest delight to walk out with him by the sea-shore, accompanied by his brother and sister, Miss Fanny and Master James.—Dear Miss Fanny! She was a sweet, kind young lady, and so fond of me that she wished me to learn all that she knew herself; and her method of teaching me was as follows:—Directly she had said her lessons to her grandmamma, she used to come running to me, and make me repeat them one by one after her; and in a few months I was able not only to say my letters but to spell many small words. But this happy state was not to last long. Those days were too pleasant to last. My heart always softens when I think of them.

At this time Mrs. Williams died. I was told suddenly of her death, and my grief was so great that, forgetting I had the baby in my arms, I ran away directly to my poor mistress's house; but reached it only in time to see the corpse carried out. Oh, that was a day of sorrow—a heavy day! All the slaves cried. My mother cried and lamented her sore; and I (foolish creature!) vainly entreated them to bring my dear mistress back to life. I knew nothing rightly about death then, and it seemed a hard thing to bear. When I thought about my mistress I felt as if the world was all gone wrong; and for many days and weeks I could think of nothing else. I returned to Mrs. Pruden's; but my sorrow was too great to be comforted, for my own dear mistress was always in my mind. Whether in the house or abroad, my thoughts were always talking to me about her.

I stayed at Mrs. Pruden's about three months after this; I was then sent back to Mr. Williams to be sold. Oh, that was a sad sad time! I recollect the day well. Mrs. Pruden came to me and said, "Mary, you will have to go home directly; your master is going to be married, and he means to sell you and two of your sisters to raise money for the wedding." Hearing this I burst out a crying,—though I was then far from being sensible of the full weight of my misfortune, or of the misery that waited for me. Besides, I did not like to leave Mrs. Pruden, and the dear baby, who had grown very fond of me. For some time I could scarcely believe that Mrs. Pruden was in earnest, till I received orders for my immediate return.—Dear Miss Fanny! how she cried at parting with me, whilst I kissed and hugged the baby, thinking I should never see him again. I left Mrs. Pruden's, and walked home with a heart full of sorrow. The idea of being sold away from my mother and Miss Betsey was so frightful, that I dared not trust myself to think about it. We had been bought of Mrs. Myners, as I have mentioned, by Miss Betsey's grandfather, and given to her, so that we were by right *her* property, and I never thought we should be separated or sold away from her.

When I reached the house, I went in directly to Miss Betsey. I found her in great distress; and she cried out as soon as she saw me, "Oh, Mary! my father is going to sell you all to raise money to marry that wicked woman. You are *my* slaves, and he has no right to sell you; but it is all to please her." She then told me that my mother was living with her father's sister at a house close by, and I went there to see her. It was a sorrowful meeting; and we lamented with a great and sore crying our unfortunate situation. "Here comes one of my poor piccaninnies!"[1] she said, the moment I came in, "one of the poor slave-brood who are to be sold to-morrow."

Oh dear! I cannot bear to think of that day,— it is too much.—It recalls the great grief that filled my heart, and the woeful thoughts that passed to and fro through my mind, whilst listening to the pitiful words of my poor mother, weeping for the loss of her children. I wish I could find words to tell you all I then felt and suffered. The great God above alone knows the thoughts of the poor slave's heart, and the bitter pains which follow such separations as these. All that we love taken away from us—oh, it is sad, sad! and sore to be borne!—I got no sleep that night for thinking of the morrow; and dear Miss Betsey was scarcely less distressed. She could not bear to part with her old playmates and she cried sore and would not be pacified.

The black morning at length came; it came too soon for my poor mother and us. Whilst she was putting on us the new osnaburgs[2] in which we were to be sold, she said, in a sorrowful voice, (I shall never forget it!) "See, I am *shrouding* my poor children; what a task for a mother!"—She then called Miss Betsey to take leave of us. "I am going to carry my little chickens to market," (these were her very words) "take your last look of them; may be you will see them no more." "Oh, my poor slaves! my own slaves!" said dear Miss Betsey, "you belong to me; and it grieves my heart to part with you."—Miss Betsey kissed us all, and, when she left us, my mother called the rest of the slaves to bid us good bye. One of them, a woman named Moll, came with her infant in her arms. "Ay!" said my mother, seeing her turn away and look at her child with the tears in her eyes, "your turn will come next." The slaves could say nothing to comfort us; they could only weep and lament with us. When I left my dear little brothers and the house in which I had been brought up, I thought my heart would burst.

Our mother, weeping as she went, called me away with the children Hannah and Dinah, and we took the road that led to Hamble Town, which we reached about four o'clock in the afternoon. We followed my mother to the market-place, where she placed us in a row against a large house, with our backs to the wall and our arms folded across our breasts. I, as the eldest, stood first, Hannah next to me, then Dinah; and our mother stood beside, crying over us. My heart throbbed with grief and terror so violently, that I pressed my hands quite tightly across my breast, but I could not keep it still, and it continued to leap as though it would burst out of my body. But who cared for that? Did one of the many bystanders, who were looking at us so carelessly, think of the pain that wrung the hearts of the negro woman and her young ones? No, no! They were not all bad, I dare say, but slavery hardens white people's hearts towards the

[1] *piccaninnies* Children, usually applied derogatively to black children.

[2] *osnaburgs* Type of coarse linen used to make clothing.

blacks; and many of them were not slow to make their remarks upon us aloud, without regard to our grief—though their light words fell like cayenne on the fresh wounds of our hearts. Oh those white people have small hearts who can only feel for themselves.

At length the vendue[1] master, who was to offer us for sale like sheep or cattle, arrived, and asked my mother which was the eldest. She said nothing, but pointed to me. He took me by the hand, and led me out into the middle of the street, and, turning me slowly round, exposed me to the view of those who attended the vendue. I was soon surrounded by strange men, who examined and handled me in the same manner that a butcher would a calf or a lamb he was about to purchase, and who talked about my shape and size in like words—as if I could no more understand their meaning than the dumb beasts. I was then put up for sale. The bidding commenced at a few pounds, and gradually rose to fifty-seven, when I was knocked down to the highest bidder; and the people who stood by said that I had fetched a great sum for so young a slave.

I then saw my sisters led forth, and sold to different owners; so that we had not the sad satisfaction of being partners in bondage. When the sale was over, my mother hugged and kissed us, and mourned over us, begging of us to keep up a good heart, and do our duty to our new masters. It was a sad parting; one went one way, one another, and our poor mammy went home with nothing.

My new master was a Captain I—, who lived at Spanish Point. After parting with my mother and sisters, I followed him to his store, and he gave me into the charge of his son, a lad about my own age, Master Benjy, who took me to my new home. I did not know where I was going, or what my new master would do with me. My heart was quite broken with grief, and my thoughts went back continually to those from whom I had been so suddenly parted. "Oh, my mother! my mother!" I kept saying to myself, "Oh, my mammy and my sisters and my brothers, shall I never see you again!"

Oh, the trials! the trials! they make the salt water come into my eyes when I think of the days in which I was afflicted—the times that are gone; when I mourned and grieved with a young heart for those whom I loved.—It was night when I reached my new home. The house was large, and built at the bottom of a very high hill; but I could not see much of it that night. I saw too much of it afterwards. The stones and the timber were the best things in it; they were not so hard as the hearts of the owners.

Before I entered the house, two slave women, hired from another owner, who were at work in the yard, spoke to me, and asked who I belonged to? I replied, "I am come to live here." "Poor child, poor child!" they both said; "you must keep a good heart, if you are to live here."—When I went in, I stood up crying in a corner. Mrs. I— came and took off my hat, a little black silk hat Miss Pruden made for me, and said in a rough voice, "You are not come here to stand up in corners and cry, you are come here to work." She then put a child into my arms, and, tired as I was, I was forced instantly to take up my old occupation of a nurse.—I could not bear to look at my mistress, her countenance was so stern. She was a stout tall woman with a very dark complexion, and her brows were always drawn together into a frown. I thought of the words of the two slave women when I saw Mrs. I—, and heard the harsh sound of her voice.

The person I took the most notice of that night was a French Black called Hetty, whom my master took in privateering from another vessel, and made his slave. She was the most active woman I ever saw, and she was tasked to her utmost. A few minutes after my arrival she came in from milking the cows, and put the sweet-potatoes on for supper. She then fetched home the sheep, and penned them in the fold; drove home the cattle, and staked them about the pond side; fed and rubbed down my master's horse, and gave the hog and the fed cow their suppers; prepared the beds, and undressed the children, and laid them to sleep. I liked to look at her and watch all her doings, for her's was the only friendly face I had as yet seen, and I felt glad that she was there. She gave me my supper of potatoes and milk, and a blanket to sleep upon, which she spread for me in the passage before the door of Mrs. I—'s chamber.

I got a sad fright, that night. I was just going to sleep, when I heard a noise in my mistress's room; and she presently called out to inquire if some work was finished that she had ordered Hetty to do. "No, Ma'am, not yet," was Hetty's answer from below. On hearing this, my master started up from his bed, and just as he was, in his

[1] *vendue* Sale.

shirt, ran down stairs with a long cow-skin in his hand. I heard immediately after, the cracking of the thong, and the house rang to the shrieks of poor Hetty, who kept crying out, "Oh, Massa! Massa! me dead. Massa! have mercy upon me—don't kill me outright."—This was a sad beginning for me. I sat up upon my blanket, trembling with terror, like a frightened hound, and thinking that my turn would come next. At length the house became still, and I forgot for a little while all my sorrows by falling fast asleep.

The next morning my mistress set about instructing me in my tasks. She taught me to do all sorts of household work; to wash and bake, pick cotton and wool, and wash floors, and cook. And she taught me (how can I ever forget it!) more things than these; she caused me to know the exact difference between the smart of the rope, the cart-whip, and the cow-skin, when applied to my naked body by her own cruel hand. And there was scarcely any punishment more dreadful than the blows I received on my face and head from her hard heavy fist. She was a fearful woman, and a savage mistress to her slaves.

There were two little slave boys in the house, on whom she vented her bad temper in a special manner. One of these children was a mulatto, called Cyrus, who had been bought while an infant in his mother's arms; the other, Jack, was an African from the coast of Guinea, whom a sailor had given or sold to my master. Seldom a day passed without these boys receiving the most severe treatment, and often for no fault at all. Both my master and mistress seemed to think that they had a right to ill-use them at their pleasure; and very often accompanied their commands with blows, whether the children were behaving well or ill. I have seen their flesh ragged and raw with licks.—Lick—lick—they were never secure one moment from a blow, and their lives were passed in continual fear. My mistress was not contented with using the whip, but often pinched their cheeks and arms in the most cruel manner. My pity for these poor boys was soon transferred to myself; for I was licked, and flogged, and pinched by her pitiless fingers in the neck and arms, exactly as they were. To strip me naked—to hang me up by the wrists and lay my flesh open with the cow-skin, was an ordinary punishment for even a slight offence. My mistress often robbed me too of the hours that belong to sleep. She used to sit up very late, frequently even until morning; and I had then to stand at a bench and wash during the greater part of the night, or pick wool and cotton and often I have dropped down overcome by sleep and fatigue, till roused from a state of stupor by the whip, and forced to start up to my tasks.

Poor Hetty, my fellow slave, was very kind to me, and I used to call her my Aunt; but she led a most miserable life, and her death was hastened (at least the slaves all believed and said so,) by the dreadful chastisement she received from my master during her pregnancy. It happened as follows. One of the cows had dragged the rope away from the stake to which Hetty had fastened it, and got loose. My master flew into a terrible passion, and ordered the poor creature to be stripped quite naked, notwithstanding her pregnancy, and to be tied up to a tree in the yard. He then flogged her as hard as he could lick, both with the whip and cow-skin, till she was all over streaming with blood. He rested, and then beat her again and again. Her shrieks were terrible. The consequence was that poor Hetty was brought to bed before her time, and was delivered after severe labour of a dead child. She appeared to recover after her confinement, so far that she was repeatedly flogged by both master and mistress afterwards; but her former strength never returned to her. Ere long her body and limbs swelled to a great size; and she lay on a mat in the kitchen, till the water burst out of her body and she died. All the slaves said that death was a good thing for poor Hetty; but I cried very much for her death. The manner of it filled me with horror. I could not hear to think about it; yet it was always present to my mind for many a day.

After Hetty died all her labours fell upon me, in addition to my own. I had now to milk eleven cows every morning before sunrise, sitting among the damp weeds; to take care of the cattle as well as the children; and to do the work of the house. There was no end to my toils—no end to my blows. I lay down at night and rose up in the morning in fear and sorrow; and often wished that like poor Hetty I could escape from this cruel bondage and be at rest in the grave. But the hand of that God whom then I knew not, was stretched over me; and I was mercifully preserved for better things. It was then, however, my heavy lot to weep, weep, weep, and that for years; to pass from one misery to another, and from one cruel master to a worse. But I must go on with the thread of my story.

One day a heavy squall of wind and rain came on suddenly, and my mistress sent me round the corner of the house to empty a large earthen jar. The jar was already cracked with an old deep crack that divided it in the middle, and in turning it upside down to empty it, it parted in my hand. I could not help the accident, but I was dreadfully frightened, looking forward to a severe punishment. I ran crying to my mistress, "O mistress, the jar has come in two." "You have broken it, have you?" she replied; "come directly here to me." I came trembling: she stripped and flogged me long and severely with the cow-skin; as long as she had strength to use the lash, for she did not give over till she was quite tired.—When my master came home at night, she told him of my fault; and oh, frightful! how he fell a swearing. After abusing me with every ill name he could think of, (too, too bad to speak in England,) and giving me several heavy blows with his hand, he said, "I shall come home to-morrow morning at twelve, on purpose to give you a round hundred." He kept his word—Oh sad for me! I cannot easily forget it. He tied me up upon a ladder, and gave me a hundred lashes with his own hand, and master Benjy stood by to count them for him. When he had licked me for some time he sat down to take breath; then after resting, he beat me again and again, until he was quite wearied, and so hot (for the weather was very sultry), that he sank back in his chair, almost like to faint. While my mistress went to bring him drink, there was a dreadful earthquake. Part of the roof fell down, and every thing in the house went—clatter, clatter, clatter. Oh I thought the end of all things near at hand; and I was so sore with the flogging, that I scarcely cared whether I lived or died. The earth was groaning and shaking; every thing tumbling about; and my mistress and the slaves were shrieking and crying out, "The earthquake! the earthquake!" It was an awful day for us all.

During the confusion I crawled away on my hands and knees, and laid myself down under the steps of the piazza, in front of the house. I was in a dreadful state—my body all blood and bruises, and I could not help moaning piteously. The other slaves, when they saw me, shook their heads and said, "Poor child! poor child"—I lay there till the morning, careless of what might happen, for life was very weak in me, and I wished more than ever to die. But when we are very young, death always seems a great way off, and it would not come that night to me. The next morning I was forced by my master to rise and go about my usual work, though my body and limbs were so stiff and sore, that I could not move without the greatest pain.—Nevertheless, even after all this severe punishment, I never heard the last of that jar; my mistress was always throwing it in my face.

Some little time after this, one of the cows got loose from the stake, and eat one of the sweet-potato slips. I was milking when my master found it out. He came to me, and without any more ado, stooped down, and taking off his heavy boot, he struck me such a severe blow in the small of my back, that I shrieked with agony, and thought I was killed; and I feel a weakness in that part to this day. The cow was frightened by his violence, and kicked down the pail and spilt the milk all about. My master knew that this accident was his own fault, but he was so enraged that he seemed glad of an excuse to go on with his ill usage. I cannot remember how many licks he gave me then, but he beat me till I was unable to stand, and till he himself was weary.

After this I ran away and went to my mother, who was living with Mr. Richard Darrel. My poor mother was both grieved and glad to see me; grieved because I had been so ill used, and glad because she had not seen me for a long, long while. She dared not receive me into the house, but she hid me up in a hole in the rocks near, and brought me food at night, after every body was asleep. My father, who lived at Crow-Lane, over the salt-water channel, at last heard of my being hid up in the cavern, and he came and took me back to my master. Oh I was loath, loath to go back; but as there was no remedy, I was obliged to submit.

When we got home, my poor father said to Capt. I—, "Sir, I am sorry that my child should be forced to run away from her owner; but the treatment she has received is enough to break her heart. The sight of her wounds has nearly broke mine.—I entreat you, for the love of God, to forgive her for running away, and that you will be a kind master to her in future." Capt. I— said I was used as well as I deserved, and that I ought to be punished for running away. I then took courage and said that I could stand the floggings no longer; that I was weary of my life, and therefore I had run away to my mother; but mothers could only weep and mourn over their children, they could not save them from cruel masters—from the whip, the rope, and the cow-skin. He told me to hold my tongue and go about my work, or he would find a way to settle me. He did not, however, flog me that day.

For five years after this I remained in his house, and almost daily received the same harsh treatment. At length he put me on board a sloop,[1] and to my great joy sent me away to Turk's Island.[2] I was not permitted to see my mother or father, or poor sisters and brothers, to say good bye, though going away to a strange land, and might never see them again. Oh the Buckra[3] people who keep slaves think that black people are like cattle, without natural affection. But my heart tells me it is far otherwise.

We were nearly four weeks on the voyage, which was unusually long. Sometimes we had a light breeze, sometimes a great calm, and the ship made no way; so that our provisions and water ran very low, and we were put upon short allowance. I should almost have been starved had it not been for the kindness of a black man called Anthony, and his wife, who had brought their own victuals, and shared them with me.

When we went ashore at the Grand Quay, the captain sent me to the house of my new master, Mr. D—, to whom Captain I— had sold me. Grand Quay is a small town upon a sandbank; the houses low and built of wood. Such was my new master's. The first person I saw, on my arrival, was Mr. D—, a stout sulky looking man, who carried me through the hall to show me to his wife and children. Next day I was put up by the vendue master to know how much I was worth, and I was valued at one hundred pounds currency.

My new master was one of the owners or holders of the salt ponds, and he received a certain sum for every slave that worked upon his premises, whether they were young or old. This sum was allowed him out of the profits arising from the salt works. I was immediately sent to work in the salt water with the rest of the slaves. This work was perfectly new to me. I was given a half barrel and a shovel, and had to stand up to my knees in the water, from four o'clock in the morning till nine, when we were given some Indian corn boiled in water, which we were obliged to swallow as fast as we could for fear the rain should come on and melt the salt. We were then called again to our tasks, and worked through the heat of the day; the sun flaming upon our heads like fire, and raising salt blisters in those parts which were not completely covered. Our feet and legs, from standing in the salt water for so many hours, soon became full of dreadful boils, which eat down in some cases to the very bone, afflicting the sufferers with great torment. We came home at twelve; ate our corn soup, called *blawly,* as fast as we could, and went back to our employment till dark at night. We then shovelled up the salt in large heaps, and went down to the sea, where we washed the pickle from our limbs, and cleaned the barrows and shovels from the salt. When we returned to the house, our master gave us each our allowance of raw Indian corn, which we pounded in a mortar and boiled in water for our suppers. We slept in a long shed, divided into narrow slips, like the stalls used for cattle. Boards fixed upon stakes driven into the ground, without mat or covering, were our only beds. On Sundays, after we had washed the salt bags, and done other work required of us, we went into the bush and cut the long soft grass, of which we made trusses for our legs and feet to rest upon, for they were so full of the salt boils that we could get no rest lying upon the bare boards.

Though we worked from morning till night, there was no satisfying Mr. D—. I hoped, when I left Capt. I—, that I should have been better off, but I found it was but going from one butcher to another. There was this difference between them: my former master used to beat me while raging and foaming with passion; Mr. D— was usually quite calm. He would stand by and give orders for a slave to be cruelly whipped, and assist in the punishment, without moving a muscle of his face; walking about and taking snuff with the greatest composure. Nothing could touch his hard heart—neither sighs, nor tears, nor prayers, nor streaming blood; he was deaf to our cries, and careless of our sufferings.—Mr. D— has often stripped me naked, hung me up by the wrists, and beat me with the cow-skin, with his own hand, till my body was raw with gashes. Yet there was nothing very remarkable in this; for it might serve as a sample of the common usage of the slaves on that horrible island.

Owing to the boils in my feet, I was unable to wheel the barrow fast through the sand, which got into the sores,

[1] *sloop* Small ship.

[2] *Turk's Island* The southernmost and easternmost islands of the Bahamas.

[3] *Buckra* White.

and made me stumble at every step; and my master, having no pity for my sufferings from this cause, rendered them far more intolerable, by chastising me for not being able to move so fast as he wished me. Another of our employments was to row a little way off from the shore in a boat, and dive for large stones to build a wall round our master's house. This was very hard work; and the great waves breaking over us continually, made us often so giddy that we lost our footing, and were in danger of being drowned.

Ah, poor me!—my tasks were never ended. Sick or well, it was work—work—work!—After the diving season was over, we were sent to the South Creek, with large bills, to cut up mangoes to burn lime with. Whilst one party of slaves were thus employed, another were sent to the other side of the island to break up coral out of the sea.

When we were ill, let our complaint be what it might, the only medicine given to us was a great bowl of hot salt water, with salt mixed with it, which made us very sick. If we could not keep up with the rest of the gang of slaves, we were put in the stocks,[1] and severely flogged the next morning. Yet, not the less, our master expected, after we had thus been kept from our rest, and our limbs rendered stiff and sore with ill usage, that we should still go through the ordinary tasks of the day all the same.—Sometimes we had to work all night, measuring salt to load a vessel; or turning a machine to draw water out of the sea for the salt-making. Then we had no sleep—no rest—but were forced to work as fast as we could, and go on again all next day the same as usual. Work—work —work—Oh that Turk's Island was a horrible place! The people in England, I am sure, have never found out what is carried on there. Cruel, horrible place!

Mr. D— had a slave called old Daniel, whom he used to treat in the most cruel manner. Poor Daniel was lame in the hip, and could not keep up with the rest of the slaves; and our master would order him to be stripped and laid down on the ground, and have him beaten with a rod of rough briar till his skin was quite red and raw. He would then call for a bucket of salt, and fling upon the raw flesh till the man writhed on the ground like a worm, and screamed aloud with agony. This poor man's wounds were never healed, and I have often seen them full of maggots, which increased his torments to an intolerable degree. He was an object of pity and terror to the whole gang of slaves, and in his wretched case we saw, each of us, our own lot, if we should live to be as old.

Oh the horrors of slavery!—How the thought of it pains my heart! But the truth ought to be told of it; and what my eyes have seen I think it is my duty to relate; for few people in England know what slavery is. I have been a slave—I have felt what a slave feels, and I know what a slave knows; and I would have all the good people in England to know it too, that they may break our chains, and set us free.

Mr. D— had another slave called Ben. He being very hungry, stole a little rice one night after he came in from work, and cooked it for his supper. But his master soon discovered the theft; locked him up all night; and kept him without food till one o'clock the next day. He then hung Ben up by his hands, and beat him from time to time till the slaves came in at night. We found the poor creature hung up when we came home; with a pool of blood beneath him, and our master still licking him, but this was not the worst. My master's son was in the habit of stealing the rice and rum. Ben had seen him do this, and thought he might do the same, and when master found out that Ben had stolen the rice and swore to punish him, he tried to excuse himself by saying that Master Dickey did the same thing every night. The lad denied it to his father, and was so angry with Ben for informing against him, that out of revenge he ran and got a bayonet, and whilst the poor wretch was suspended by his hands and writhing under his wounds, he run it quite through his foot. I was not by when he did it, but I saw the wound when I came home, and heard Ben tell the manner in which it was done.

I must say something more about this cruel son of a cruel father.—He had no heart—no fear of God; he had been brought up by a bad father in a bad path, and he delighted to follow in the same steps. There was a little old woman among the slaves called Sarah, who was nearly past work; and, Master Dickey being the overseer of the slaves just then, this poor creature, who was subject to several bodily infirmities, and was not quite right in her head, did not wheel the barrow fast enough to please him. He threw her down on the ground, and after beating her severely, he took her up in his arms and flung her among

[1] *stocks* Device for confining the ankles and sometimes the wrists.

the prickly-pear[1] bushes, which are all covered over with sharp venomous prickles. By this her naked flesh was so grievously wounded, that her body swelled and festered all over, and she died in a few days after. In telling my own sorrows, I cannot pass by those of my fellow-slaves—for when I think of my own griefs, I remember theirs.

I think it was about ten years I had worked in the salt ponds at Turk's Island, when my master left off business, and retired to a house he had in Bermuda, leaving his son to succeed him in the island. He took me with him to wait upon his daughters; and I was joyful, for I was sick, sick of Turk's Island, and my heart yearned to see my native place again, my mother, and my kindred.

I had seen my poor mother during the time I was a slave in Turk's Island. One Sunday morning I was on the beach with some of the slaves, and we saw a sloop come in loaded with slaves to work in the salt water. We got a boat and went aboard. When I came upon the deck I asked the black people, "Is there any one here for me?" "Yes," they said, "your mother." I thought they said this in jest—I could scarcely believe them for joy; but when I saw my poor mammy my joy was turned to sorrow, for she had gone from her senses. "Mammy," I said, "is this you!" She did not know me. "Mammy," I said, "what's the matter?" She began to talk foolishly and said that she had been under the vessel's bottom. They had been overtaken by a violent storm at sea. My poor mother had never been on the sea before, and she was so ill, that she lost her senses, and it was long before she came quite to herself again. She had a sweet child with her—a little sister I had never seen, about four years of age, called Rebecca. I took her on shore with me, for I felt I should love her directly; and I kept her with me a week. Poor little thing! her's has been a sad life, and continues so to this day. My mother worked for some years on the island, but was taken back to Bermuda some time before my master carried me again thither.

After I left Turk's Island, I was told by some negroes that came over from it, that the poor slaves had built up a place with boughs and leaves, where they might meet for prayers, but the white people pulled it down twice, and would not allow them even a shed for prayers. A flood came down soon after and washed away many houses, filled the place with sand, and overflowed the ponds: and I do think that this was for their wickedness; for the Buckra men there were very wicked. I saw and heard much that was very very bad at that place.

I was several years the slave of Mr. D— after I returned to my native place. Here I worked in the grounds. My work was planting and hoeing sweet-potatoes, Indian corn, plaintains, bananas, cabbages, pumpkins, onions, &c. I did all the household work, and attended upon a horse and cow besides,—going also upon all errands. I had to curry the horse—to clean and feed him—and sometimes to ride him a little. I had more than enough to do—but still it was not so very bad as Turk's Island.

My old master often got drunk, and then he would get in a fury with his daughter, and beat her till she was not fit to be seen. I remember on one occasion, I had gone to fetch water, and when I was coming up the hill I heard a great screaming; I ran as fast as I could to the house, put down the water, and went into the chamber, where I found my master beating Miss D— dreadfully. I strove with all my strength to get her away from him; for she was all black and blue with bruises. He had beat her with his fist, and almost killed her. The people gave me credit for getting her away. He turned round and began to lick me. Then I said, "Sir, this is not Turk's Island." I can't repeat his answer, the words were too wicked—too bad to say. He wanted to treat me the same in Bermuda as he had done in Turk's Island.

He had an ugly fashion of stripping himself quite naked and ordering me then to wash him in a tub of water. This was worse to me than all the licks. Sometimes when he called me to wash him I would not come, my eyes were so full of shame. He would then come to beat me. One time I had plates and knives in my hand, and I dropped both plates and knives, and some of the plates were broken. He struck me so severely for this, that at last I defended myself, for I thought it was high time to do so. I then told him I would not live longer with him, for he was a very indecent man—very spiteful, and too indecent; with no shame for his servants, no shame for his own flesh. So I went away to a neighbouring house and sat down and cried till the next morning, when I went home again, not knowing what else to do.

After that I was hired to work at Cedar Hills, and every Saturday night I paid the money to my master. I

[1] *prickly-pear* Type of cactus.

had plenty of work to do there—plenty of washing; but yet I made myself pretty comfortable. I earned two dollars and a quarter a week, which is twenty pence a day.

During the time I worked there, I heard that Mr. John Wood was going to Antigua. I felt a great wish to go there, and I went to Mr. D—, and asked him to let me go in Mr. Wood's service. Mr. Wood did not then want to purchase me; it was my own fault that I came under him, I was so anxious to go. It was ordained to be, I suppose; God led me there. The truth is, I did not wish to be any longer the slave of my indecent master.

Mr. Wood took me with him to Antigua, to the town of St. John's, where he lived. This was about fifteen years ago. He did not then know whether I was to be sold; but Mrs. Wood found that I could work, and she wanted to buy me. Her husband then wrote to my master to inquire whether I was to be sold? Mr. D— wrote in reply, "that I should not be sold to any one that would treat me ill." It was strange he should say this, when he had treated me so ill himself. So I was purchased by Mr. Wood for 300 dollars (or £100 Bermuda currency).

My work there was to attend the chambers and nurse the child, and to go down to the pond and wash clothes. But I soon fell ill of the rheumatism, and grew so very lame that I was forced to walk with a stick. I got the Saint Anthony's fire,[1] also, in my left leg, and became quite a cripple. No one cared much to come near me, and I was ill a long long time; for several months I could not lift the limb. I had to lie in a little old out-house, that was swarming with bugs and other vermin, which tormented me greatly; but I had no other place to lie in. I got the rheumatism by catching cold at the pond side, from washing in the fresh water; in the salt water I never got cold. The person who lived in next yard, (a Mrs. Greene,) could not bear to hear my cries and groans. She was kind, and used to send an old slave woman to help me, who sometimes brought me a little soup. When the doctor found I was so ill, he said I must be put into a bath of hot water. The old slave got the bark of some bush that was good for pains, which she boiled in the hot water, and every night she came and put me into the bath, and did what she could for me; I don't know what I should have done, or what would have become of me, had it not been for her.—My mistress, it is true, did send me a little food; but no one from our family came near me but the cook, who used to shove my food in at the door, and say, "Molly, Molly, there's your dinner." My mistress did not care to take any trouble about me; and if the Lord had not put it into the hearts of the neighbours to be kind to me, I must, I really think, have lain and died.

It was a long time before I got well enough to work in the house. Mrs. Wood, in the meanwhile, hired a mulatto woman to nurse the child; but she was such a fine lady she wanted to be mistress over me. I thought it very hard for a coloured woman to have rule over me because I was a slave and she was free. Her name was Martha Wilcox; she was a saucy woman, very saucy; and she went and complained of me, without cause, to my mistress, and made her angry with me. Mrs. Wood told me that if I did not mind what I was about, she would get my master to strip me and give me fifty lashes: "You have been used to the whip," she said, "and you shall have it here." This was the first time she threatened to have me flogged; and she gave me the threatening so strong of what she would have done to me, that I thought I should have fallen down at her feet, I was so vexed and hurt by her words. The mulatto woman was rejoiced to have power to keep me down. She was constantly making mischief; there was no living for the slaves—no peace after she came.

I was also sent by Mrs. Wood to be put in the Cage one night, and was next morning flogged, by the magistrate's order, at her desire; and this all for a quarrel I had about a pig with another slave woman. I was flogged on my naked back on this occasion; although I was in no fault after all; for old Justice Dyett, when we came before him, said that I was in the right, and ordered the pig to be given to me. This was about two or three years after I came to Antigua.

When we moved from the middle of the town to the Point, I used to be in the house and do all the work and mind the children, though still very ill with the rheumatism. Every week I had to wash two large bundles of clothes, as much as a boy could help me to lift; but I could give no satisfaction. My mistress was always abusing and fretting after me. It is not possible to tell all her ill language.—One day she followed me foot after foot scolding and rating me. I bore in silence a great deal of ill words: at last my heart was quite full, and I told her that

[1] *Saint Anthony's fire* Erysipelas or ergotism, diseases that cause intense redness, swelling of the skin, and severe pain.

she ought not to use me so;—that when I was ill I might have lain and died for what she cared; and no one would then come near me to nurse me, because they were afraid of my mistress. This was a great affront. She called her husband and told him what I had said. He flew into a passion: but did not beat me then; he only abused and swore at me; and then gave me a note and bade me go and look for an owner. Not that he meant to sell me; but he did this to please his wife and to frighten me. I went to Adam White, a cooper,[1] a free black who had money, and asked him to buy me. He went directly to Mr. Wood, but was informed that I was not to be sold. The next day my master whipped me.

Another time (about five years ago) my mistress got vexed with me because I fell sick and I could not keep on with my work. She complained to her husband, and he sent me off again to look for an owner. I went to a Mr. Burchell, showed him the note, and asked him to buy me for my own benefit; for I had saved about 100 dollars, and hoped with a little help, to purchase my freedom. He accordingly went to my master: - "Mr. Wood," he said, "Molly has brought me a note that she wants an owner. If you intend to sell her, I may as well buy her as another." My master put him off and said that he did not mean to sell me. I was very sorry at this, for I had no comfort with Mrs. Wood, and I wished greatly to get my freedom.

The way in which I made my money was this.—When my master and mistress went from home, as they sometimes did, and left me to take care of the house and premises, I had a good deal of time to myself and made the most of it. I took in washing, and sold coffee and yams and other provisions to the captains of ships. I did not sit still idling during the absence of my owners; for I wanted, by all honest means, to earn money to buy my freedom. Sometimes I bought a hog cheap on board ship, and sold it for double the money on shore; and I also earned a good deal by selling coffee. By this means I by degrees acquired a little cash. A gentleman also lent me some to help to buy my freedom—but when I could not get free he got it back again. His name was Captain Abbot.

My master and mistress went on one occasion into the country, to Date Hill, for a change of air, and carried me with them to take charge of the children, and to do the work of the house. While I was in the country, I saw how the field negroes are worked in Antigua. They are worked very hard and fed but scantily. They are called out to work before daybreak, and come home after dark; and then each has to heave his bundle of grass for the cattle in the pen. Then, on Sunday morning, each slave has to go out and gather a large bundle of grass; and, when they bring it home, they have all to sit at the manager's door and wait till he comes out: often have they to wait there till past eleven o'clock without any breakfast. After that, those that have yams or potatoes, or fire-wood to sell, hasten to market to buy a dog's worth[2] of salt fish, or pork, which is a great treat for them. Some of them buy a little pickle out of the shad barrels, which they call sauce, to season their yams and Indian corn. It is very wrong, I know, to work on Sunday or go to market; but will not God call the Buckra men to answer for this on the great day of judgment—since they will give the slaves no other day?

While we were at Date Hill Christmas came; and the slave woman who had the care of the place (which then belonged to Mr. Roberts the marshal), asked me to go with her to her husband's house, to a Methodist meeting for prayer, at a plantation called Winthorps. I went; and they were the first prayers I ever understood. One woman prayed; and then they all sung a hymn; then there was another prayer and another hymn; and then they all spoke by turns of their own griefs as sinners. The husband of the woman I went with was a black driver. His name was Henry. He confessed that he had treated the slaves very cruelly; but said that he was compelled to obey the orders of his master. He prayed them all to forgive him, and he prayed that God would forgive him. He said it was a horrid thing for a ranger to have sometimes to beat his own wife or sister; but he must do so if ordered by his master.

I felt sorry for my sins also. I cried the whole night, but I was too much ashamed to speak. I prayed God to forgive me. This meeting had a great impression on my mind, and led my spirit to the Moravian church; so that when I got back to town, I went and prayed to have my name put down in the Missionaries' book; and I followed the church earnestly every opportunity. I did not then tell my mistress about it; for I knew that she would not give

[1] *cooper* Barrel-and tub-maker.

[2] *dog's worth* 72nd part of a dollar.

me leave to go. But I felt I *must* go. Whenever I carried the children their lunch at school, I ran round and went to hear the teachers.

The Moravian ladies (Mrs. Richter, Mrs. Olufsen, and Mrs. Sauter) taught me to read in the class; and I got on very fast. In this class there were all sorts of people, old and young, grey headed folks and children; but most of them were free people. After we had done spelling, we tried to read in the Bible. After the reading was over, the missionary gave out a hymn for us to sing. I dearly loved to go to the church, it was so solemn. I never knew rightly that I had much sin till I went there. When I found out that I was a great sinner, I was very sorely grieved, and very much frightened. I used to pray God to pardon my sins for Christ's sake, and forgive me for every thing I had done amiss; and when I went home to my work, I always thought about what I had heard from the missionaries, and wished to be good that I might go to heaven. After a while I was admitted a candidate for the holy Communion.—I had been baptized long before this, in August 1817, by the Rev. Mr. Curtin, of the English Church, after I had been taught to repeat the Creed and the Lord's Prayer. I wished at that time to attend a Sunday School taught by Mr. Curtin, but he would not receive me without a written note from my master, granting his permission. I did not ask my owner's permission, from the belief that it would be refused; so that I got no farther instruction at that time from the English Church.

Some time after I began to attend the Moravian Church, I met with Daniel James, afterwards my dear husband. He was a carpenter and cooper to his trade; an honest, hard-working, decent black man, and a widower. He had purchased his freedom of his mistress, old Mrs. Baker, with money he had earned whilst a slave. When he asked me to marry him, I took time to consider the matter over with myself, and would not say yes till he went to church with me and joined the Moravians. He was very industrious after he bought his freedom; and he had hired a comfortable house, and had convenient things about him. We were joined in marriage, about Christmas 1826, in the Moravian Chapel at Spring Gardens, by the Rev. Mr. Olufsen. We could not be married in the English Church. English marriage is not allowed to slaves; and no free man can marry a slave woman.

When Mr. Wood heard of my marriage, he flew into a great rage, and sent for Daniel, who was helping to build a house for his old mistress. Mr. Wood asked him who gave him a right to marry a slave of his? My husband said, "Sir, I am a free man, and thought I had a right to choose a wife; but if I had known Molly was not allowed to have a husband, I should not have asked her to marry me." Mrs. Wood was more vexed about my marriage than her husband. She could not forgive me for getting married, but stirred up Mr. Wood to flog me dreadfully with his horsewhip. I thought it very hard to be whipped at my time of life for getting a husband—I told her so. She said that she would not have nigger men about the yards and premises, or allow a nigger man's clothes to be washed in the same tub where hers were washed. She was fearful, I think, that I should lose her time, in order to wash and do things for my husband: but I had then no time to wash for myself; I was obliged to put out my own clothes, though I was always at the wash-tub.

I had not much happiness in my marriage, owing to my being a slave. It made my husband sad to see me so ill-treated. Mrs. Wood was always abusing me about him. She did not lick me herself, but she got her husband to do it for her, whilst she fretted the flesh off my bones. Yet for all this she would not sell me. She sold five slaves whilst I was with her; but though she was always finding fault with me, she would not part with me. However, Mr. Wood afterwards allowed Daniel to have a place to live in our yard, which we were very thankful for.

After this, I fell ill again with the rheumatism, and was sick a long time; but whether sick or well, I had my work to do. About this time I asked my master and mistress to let me buy my own freedom. With the help of Mr. Burchell, I could have found the means to pay Mr. Wood; for it was agreed that I should afterwards serve Mr. Burchell a while, for the cash he was to advance for me. I was earnest in the request to my owners; but their hearts were hard—too hard to consent. Mrs. Wood was very angry—she grew quite outrageous—she called me a black devil, and asked me who had put freedom into my head. "To be free is very sweet," I said: but she took good care to keep me a slave. I saw her change colour, and I left the room.

About this time my master and mistress were going to England to put their son in school, and bring their daughters home; and they took me with them to take care of the child. I was willing to come to England: I thought that by going there I should probably get cured of my rheumatism, and should return with my master and mistress, quite well, to my husband. My husband was willing for me to come away, for he had heard that my master would free me,—and I also hoped this might prove true; but it was all a false report.

The steward of the ship was very kind to me. He and my husband were in the same class in the Moravian Church. I was thankful that he was so friendly, for my mistress was not kind to me on the passage; and she told me, when she was angry, that she did not intend to treat me any better in England than in the West Indies—that I need not expect it. And she was as good as her word.

When we drew near to England, the rheumatism seized all my limbs worse than ever, and my body was dreadfully swelled. When we landed at the Tower, I showed my flesh to my mistress, but she took no great notice of it. We were obliged to stop at the tavern till my master got a house; and a day or two after, my mistress sent me down into the wash-house to learn to wash in the English way. In the West Indies we wash with cold water—in England with hot. I told my mistress I was afraid that putting my hands first into the hot water and then into the cold, would increase the pain in my limbs. The doctor had told my mistress long before I came from the West Indies, that I was a sickly body and the washing did not agree with me. But Mrs. Wood would not release me from the tub, so I was forced to do as I could. I grew worse, and could not stand to wash. I was then forced to sit down with the tub before me, and often through pain and weakness was reduced to kneel or to sit down on the floor, to finish my task. When I complained to my mistress of this, she only got into a passion as usual, and said washing in hot water could not hurt any one;—that I was lazy and insolent, and wanted to be free of my work; but that she would make me do it. I thought her very hard on me, and my heart rose up within me. However I kept still at that time, and went down again to wash the child's things; but the English washerwomen who were at work there, when they saw that I was so ill, had pity upon me and washed them for me.

After that, when we came up to live in Leigh Street, Mrs. Wood sorted out five bags of clothes which we had used at sea, and also such as had been worn since we came on shore, for me and the cook to wash. Elizabeth the cook told her, that she did not think that I was able to stand to the tub, and that she had better hire a woman. I also said myself, that I had come over to nurse the child, and that I was sorry I had come from Antigua, since mistress would work me so hard, without compassion for my rheumatism. Mr. and Mrs. Wood, when they heard this, rose up in a passion against me. They opened the door and bade me get out. But I was a stranger, and did not know one door in the street from another, and was unwilling to go away. They made a dreadful uproar, and from that day they constantly kept cursing and abusing me. I was obliged to wash, though I was very ill. Mrs. Wood, indeed once hired a washerwoman, but she was not well treated, and would come no more.

My master quarrelled with me another time, about one of our great washings, his wife having stirred him up to do so. He said he would compel me to do the whole of the washing given out to me, or if I again refused, he would take a short course with me: he would either send me down to the brig in the river, to carry me back to Antigua, or he would turn me at once out of doors, and let me provide for myself. I said I would willingly go back, if he would let me purchase my own freedom. But this enraged him more than all the rest: he cursed and swore at me dreadfully, and said he would never sell my freedom—if I wished to be free, I was free in England, and I might go and try what freedom would do for me, and be d—d. My heart was very sore with this treatment, but I had to go on. I continued to do my work, and did all I could to give satisfaction, but all would not do.

Shortly after, the cook left them, and then matters went on ten times worse. I always washed the child's clothes without being commanded to do it, and any thing else that was wanted in the family; though still I was very sick—very sick indeed. When the great washing came round, which was every two months, my mistress got together again a great many heavy things, such as bed-ticks, bed-coverlets, &c. for me to wash. I told her I was too ill to wash such heavy things that day. She said, she supposed I thought myself a free woman, but I was not; and if I did not do it directly I should be instantly turned out of doors. I stood a long time before I could answer, for I did not know well what to do. I knew that I was free in England, but I did not know where to go, or how to get my living; and therefore, I did not like to leave the house. But Mr. Wood said he would send for a constable to thrust me out; and at last I took courage and resolved that I would not be longer thus treated, but would go and trust to Providence. This was the fourth time they had threatened to turn me out, and, go where I might, I was determined now to take them at their word; though I thought it very hard, after I had lived with them for thirteen years, and worked for them like a horse, to be driven out in this way, like a beggar. My only fault was being sick, and therefore unable to please my mistress, who thought she never could get work enough out of her slaves; and I told them so: but they only abused me and drove me out. This took place from two to three months, I think, after we came to England.

When I came away, I went to the man (one Mash) who used to black the shoes of the family, and asked his wife to get somebody to go with me to Hatton Garden to the Moravian Missionaries: these were the only persons I knew in England. The woman sent a young girl with me to the mission house, and I saw there a gentleman called Mr. Moore. I told him my whole story, and how my owners had treated me, and asked him to take in my truck with what few clothes I had. The missionaries were very kind to me—they were sorry for my destitute situation, and gave me leave to bring my things to be placed under their care. They were very good people, and they told me to come to the church.

When I went back to Mr. Wood's to get my trunk, I saw a lady, Mrs. Pell, who was on a visit to my mistress. When Mr. and Mrs. Wood heard me come in, they set this lady to stop me, finding that they had gone too far with me. Mrs. Pell came out to me, and said, "Are you really going to leave, Molly? Don't leave, but come into the country with me." I believe she said this because she thought Mrs. Wood would easily get me back again. I replied to her, "Ma'am, this is the fourth time my master and mistress have driven me out, or threatened to drive me—and I will give them no more occasion to bid me go. I was not willing to leave them, for I am a stranger in this country, but now I must go—I can stay no longer to be used." Mrs. Pell then went up stairs to my mistress, and told that I would go, and that she could not stop me. Mrs. Wood was very much hurt and frightened when she found I was determined to go out that day. She said, "If she goes the people will rob her, and then turn her adrift." She did not say this to me, but she spoke it loud enough for me to hear; that it might induce me not to go, I suppose. Mr. Wood also asked me where I was going to. I told him where I had been, and that I should never have gone away had I not been driven out by my owners. He had given me a written paper some time before, which said that I had come with them to England by my own desire; and that was true. It said also that I left them of my own free will, because I was a free woman in England; and that I was idle and would not do my work— which was not true. I gave this paper afterwards to a gentleman who inquired into my case.

I went into the kitchen and got my clothes out. The nurse and the servant girl were there, and I said to the man who was going to take out my trunk, "Stop, before you take up this trunk, and hear what I have to say before these people. I am going out of this house, as I was ordered; but I have done no wrong at all to my owners, neither here nor in the West Indies. I always worked very hard to please them, both by night and day; but there was no giving satisfaction, for my mistress could never be satisfied with reasonable service. I told my mistress I was sick, and yet she has ordered me out of doors. This is the fourth time; and now I am going out."

And so I came out, and went and carried my trunk to the Moravians. I then returned back to Mash the shoeblack's house, and begged his wife to take me in. I had a little West Indian money in my trunk; and they got it changed for me. This helped to support me for a little while. The man's wife was very kind to me. I was very sick, and she boiled nourishing things up for me. She also sent for a doctor to see me, and sent me medicine, which did me good, though I was ill for a long time with the rheumatic pains. I lived a good many months with these poor people, and they nursed me, and did all that lay in their power to serve me. The man was well acquainted with my situation, as he used to go to and fro to Mr. Wood's house to clean shoes and knives; and he and his wife were sorry for me.

About this time, a woman of the name of Hill told me of the Anti-Slavery Society, and went with me to their office, to inquire if they could do any thing to get me my freedom, and send me back to the West Indies. The gentlemen of the Society took me to a lawyer, who examined very strictly into my case; but told me that the laws of England could do nothing to make me free in Antigua. However they did all they could for me: they gave me a little money from time to time to keep me from want; and some of them went to Mr. Wood to try to persuade him to let me return a free woman to my husband; but though they offered him, as I have heard, a large sum for my freedom, he was sulky and obstinate, and would not consent to let me go free.

This was the first winter I spent in England, and I suffered much from the severe cold, and from the rheumatic pains, which still at times torment me. However, Providence was very good to me, and I got many friends—especially some Quaker ladies, who hearing of my case, came and sought me out, and gave me good warm clothing and money. Thus I had great cause to bless God in my affliction.

When I got better I was anxious to get some work to do, as I was unwilling to eat the bread of idleness. Mrs. Mash, who was a laundress, recommended me to a lady for a charwoman. She paid me very handsomely for what work I did, and I divided the money with Mrs. Mash; for though very poor, they gave me food when my own money was done, and never suffered me to want.

In the spring, I got into service with a lady, who saw me at the house where I sometimes worked as a charwoman. This lady's name was Mrs. Forsyth. She had been in the West Indies, and was accustomed to Blacks, and liked them. I was with her six months, and went with her to Margate. She treated me well, and gave me a good character when she left London.

After Mrs. Forsyth went away, I was again out of place, and went to lodgings, for which I paid two shillings a week, and found coals and candle. After eleven weeks, the money I had saved in service was all gone, and I was forced to go back to the Anti-Slavery office to ask a supply, till I could get another situation. I did not like to go back—I did not like to be idle. I would rather work for my living than get it for nothing. They were very good to give me a supply, but I felt shame at being obliged to apply for relief whilst I had strength to work.

At last I went into the service of Mr. and Mrs. Pringle, where I have been ever since, and am as comfortable as I can be while separated from my dear husband, and away from my own country and all old friends and connections. My dear mistress teaches me daily to read the word of God, and takes great pains to make me understand it. I enjoy the great privilege of being enabled to attend church three times on the Sunday; and I have met with many kind friends since I have been here, both clergymen and others. The Rev. Mr. Young, who lives in the next house, has shown me much kindness, and taken much pains to instruct me, particularly while my master and mistress were absent in Scotland. Nor must I forget, among my friends, the Rev. Mr. Mortimer, the good clergyman of the parish, under whose ministry I have now sat for upwards of twelve months. I trust in God I have profited by what I have heard from him. He never keeps back the truth, and I think he has been the means of opening my eyes and ears much better to understand the word of God. Mr. Mortimer tells me that he cannot open the eyes of my heart, but that I must pray to God to change my heart, and make me to know the truth, and the truth will make me free.

I still live in the hope that God will find a way to give me my liberty, and give me back to my husband. I endeavour to keep down my fretting, and to leave all to Him, for he knows what is good for me better than I know myself. Yet, I must confess, I find it a hard and heavy task to do so.

I am often much vexed, and I feel great sorrow when I hear some people in this country say, that the slaves do not need better usage, and do not want to be free. They believe the foreign people, who deceive them, and say slaves are happy. I say, Not so. How can slaves be happy when they have the halter round their neck and the whip upon their back? and are disgraced and thought no more of than beasts?—and are separated from their mothers, and husbands, and children, and sisters, just as cattle are sold and separated? Is it happiness for a driver in the field to take down his wife or sister or child, and strip them, and whip them in such a disgraceful manner?—women that have had children exposed in the open field to shame! There is no modesty or decency shown by the owner to his slaves; men, women, and children are exposed alike. Since I have been here I have often wondered how English people can go out into the West Indies and act in such a beastly manner. But when they go to the West Indies, they forget God and all feeling of shame, I think, since they can see and do such things. They tie up slaves like hogs—moor them up like cattle, and they lick them, so as hogs, or cattle, or horses never were flogged;—and yet they come home and say, and make some good people believe, that slaves don't want to get out of slavery. But they put a cloak about the truth. It is not so. All slaves want to be free—to be free is very sweet. I will say the truth to English people who may read this history that my good friend, Miss S—, is now writing down for me. I have been a slave myself—I know what slaves feel—I can tell by myself what other slaves feel, and by what they have told me. The man that says slaves be quite happy in slavery—that they don't want to be free—that man is either ignorant or a lying person. I never heard a slave say so. I never heard a Buckra man say so, till I heard tell of it in England. Such people ought to be ashamed of themselves. They can't do without slaves they say. What's the reason they can't do without slaves as well as in England? No slaves here—no whips—no stocks—no punishment, except for wicked people. They hire servants in England; and if they don't like them, they send them away: they can't lick them. Let them work ever so hard in England, they are far better off than slaves. If they get a bad master, they give warning and go hire to another. They have their liberty. That's just what *we* want. We don't mind hard work, if we had proper treatment, and proper wages like English servants, and proper time given in the week to keep us from breaking the Sabbath. But they won't give it; they will have work—work—work, night and day, sick or well, till we are quite done up; and we must not speak up nor look amiss, however much we be abused. And then when we are quite done up, who cares for us, more than for a lame horse? This is slavery. I tell it to let English people know the truth; and I hope they will never leave off to pray God, and call loud to the great King of England, till all the poor blacks be given free, and slavery done up for evermore.

—1831

IN CONTEXT

Mary Prince and Slavery

Mary Prince's Petition Presented to Parliament on June 24, 1829

A Petition of Mary Prince or James, commonly called Molly Wood, was presented, and read; setting forth, That the Petitioner was born a Slave in the colony of Bermuda, and is now about forty years of age; That the Petitioner was sold some years go for the sum of 300 dollars to Mr. John Wood, by whom the Petitioner was carried to Antigua, where she has since, until lately resided as a domestic slave on his establishment; that in December 1826, the Petitioner who is connected with the Moravian Congregation, was married in a Moravian Chapel at Spring Gardens, in the parish of Saint John's, by the Moravian minister, Mr. Ellesen, to a free Black of the name of Daniel James, who is a carpenter at Saint John's, in Antigua, and also a member of the same congregation; that the Petitioner and the said Daniel James have lived together ever since as man and wife; that about ten months ago the Petitioner arrived in London, with her master and mistress, in the capacity of nurse to their child; that the Petitioner's master has offered to send her back in his brig to the West Indies , to work in the yard; that the Petitioner expressed her desire to return to the West Indies, but not as a slave, and has entreated her master to sell her, her freedom on account of her services as a nurse to his child, but he has refused, and still does refuse; further stating the particulars of her case; and praying the House to take the same into their consideration, and to grant such relief as to them may, under the circumstances, appear right. Ordered, That the said Petition do lie upon the Table.

from Thomas Pringle, Supplement to *The History of Mary Prince* (1831)

It was through the auspices of Thomas Pringle that Mary Prince's narrative came to be published, and that Prince found employment in London. Pringle contributed a substantial *Supplement* to the *History* when it was first published; excerpts are reproduced below.

By the Original Editor, Thomas Pringle

Leaving Mary's narrative, for the present, without comment to the reader's reflections, I proceed to state some circumstances connected with her case which have fallen more particularly under my own notice, and which I consider it incumbent now to lay fully before the public.

About the latter end of November, 1828, this poor woman found her way to the office of the Anti-Slavery Society in Aldermanbury, by the aid of a person who had become acquainted with her situation, and had advised her to apply there for advice and assistance. After some preliminary examination into the accuracy of the circumstances related by her, I went along with her to Mr. George Stephen, solicitor, and requested him to investigate and draw up a statement of her case, and have it submitted to counsel, in order to ascertain whether or not, under the circumstances, her freedom could be legally established on her return to Antigua. On this occasion, in Mr. Stephen's presence and mine, she expressed, in very strong terms, her anxiety to return thither if she could go as a free person, and, at the same time, her extreme apprehensions of the fate that would probably await her if she returned as a slave. Her words were, "I would rather go into my grave than go back a slave to Antigua, though I wish to go back to my husband very much—very much—very much! I am much afraid my owners would separate me from my husband, and use me very hard, or perhaps sell me for a field negro;—and slavery is too too bad. I would rather go into my grave!'

The paper which Mr. Wood had given her before she left his house, was placed by her in Mr. Stephen's hands. It was expressed in the following terms:—

"I have already told Molly, and now give it her in writing, in order that there may be no misunderstanding on her part, that as I brought her from Antigua at her own request and entreaty, and that she is consequently now free, she is of course at liberty to take her baggage and go where she pleases. And, in consequence of her late conduct, she must do one of two things—either quit the house, or return to Antigua by the earliest opportunity, as she does not evince a disposition to make herself useful. As she is a stranger in London, I do not wish to turn her out, or would do so, as two female servants are sufficient for my establishment. If after this she does remain, it will be only during her good behaviour; but on no consideration will I allow her wages or any other remuneration for her services.

"JOHN A. WOOD"

"London, August 18, 1828."

This paper, though not devoid of inconsistencies, which will be apparent to any attentive reader, is craftily expressed; and was well devised to serve the purpose which the writer had obviously in view, namely, to frustrate any appeal which the friendless black woman might make to the sympathy of strangers, and thus prevent her from obtaining an asylum, if she left his house, from any respectable family. As she had no one to refer to for a character in this country except himself, he doubtless calculated securely on her being speedily driven back, as soon as the slender fund she had in her possession was expended, to throw herself unconditionally upon his tender mercies; and his disappointment in this expectation appears to have exasperated his feelings of resentment towards the poor woman, to a degree which few persons alive to the claims of common justice, not to speak of Christianity or common humanity, could easily have anticipated. Such, at least, seems the only intelligible inference that can be drawn from his subsequent conduct.

The case having been submitted, by desire of the Anti-Slavery Committee, to the consideration of Dr. Lushington and Mr. Sergeant Stephen, it was found that there existed no legal means of compelling Mary's master to grant her manumission; and that if she returned to Antigua, she would inevitably fall again under his power, or that of his attorneys, as a slave. It was, however, resolved to try what could be effected for her by amicable negotiation; and with this view Mr. Ravenscroft, a solicitor, (Mr. Stephen's relative,) called upon Mr. Wood, in order to ascertain whether he would consent to Mary's manumission on any reasonable terms, and to refer, if required, the amount of compensation for her value to arbitration. Mr. Ravenscroft with some difficulty obtained one or two interviews, but found Mr. Wood so full of animosity against the woman, and so firmly bent against any arrangement having her freedom for its object, that the negotiation was soon broken off as hopeless. The angry slave-owner declared "that he would not move a finger about her in this country, or grant her manumission on any terms whatever; and that if she went back to the West Indies, she must take the consequences."

This unreasonable conduct of Mr. Wood, induced the Anti-Slavery Committee, after several other abortive attempts to effect a compromise, to think of bringing the case under the notice of Parliament. The heads of Mary's statement were accordingly engrossed in a Petition, which Dr. Lushington offered to present, and to give notice at the same time of his intention to bring in a Bill to provide for the entire emancipation of all slaves brought to England with the owner's consent. But before this step was taken, Dr. Lushington again had recourse to negotiation with the master; and, partly through the friendly intervention of Mr. Manning, partly by personal conference, used every persuasion in his power to induce Mr. Wood to relent and let the bondwoman go free. Seeing the matter thus seriously taken up, Mr. Wood became at length alarmed,—not relishing, it appears, the idea of having the case publicly discussed in the House of Commons; and to avert this result he submitted to temporize—assumed a demeanour of unwonted civility, and even hinted to Mr. Manning (as I was given to understand) that if he was not driven to utter hostility by the threatened exposure, he would probably meet our wishes "in his own time and way." Having gained time by these manoeuvres, he adroitly endeavoured to cool the ardour of Mary's new friends, in her cause, by representing her as an abandoned and worthless woman, ungrateful towards him, and undeserving of sympathy from others; allegations which he supported by the ready affirmation of some of his West India friends, and by one or two plausible letters procured from Antigua. By these and like artifices he appears completely to have imposed on Mr. Manning, the respectable West India merchant whom Dr. Lushington had asked to negotiate with him; and he prevailed so far as to induce Dr. Lushington himself (actuated by the benevolent view of thereby best serving Mary's cause), to abstain from any remarks upon his conduct when the petition was at last presented in Parliament. In this way he dextrously contrived to neutralize all our efforts, until the close of the Session of 1829; soon after which he embarked with his family for the West Indies.

Every exertion for Mary's relief having thus failed; and being fully convinced from a twelvemonth's observation of her conduct, that she was really a well-disposed and respectable woman; I engaged her, in December 1829, as a domestic servant in my own family. In this capacity she has remained ever since; and I am thus enabled to speak of her conduct and character with a degree of confidence I could not have otherwise done.…

I may here add a few words respecting the earlier portion of Mary Prince's narrative. The facts there stated must necessarily rest entirely,—since we have no collateral evidence,—upon their intrinsic claims to probability, and upon the reliance the reader may feel disposed, after perusing the foregoing pages, to place on her veracity. To my judgment, the internal evidence of the truth of her narrative appears remarkably strong. The circumstances are related in a tone of natural sincerity, and are accompanied in almost every case with characteristic and minute details, which must, I conceive, carry with them full conviction to every candid mind that this negro woman has actually seen, felt, and suffered all that she so impressively describes; and that the picture she has given of West Indian slavery is not less true than it is revolting.

But there may be some persons into whose hands this tract may fall, so imperfectly acquainted with the real character of Negro Slavery, as to be shocked into partial, if not absolute incredulity, by the acts of inhuman oppression and brutality related of Capt. I— and his wife, and of Mr. D—, the salt manufacturer of Turk's Island. Here, at least, such persons may be disposed to think, there surely must be *some* exaggeration; the facts are too shocking to be credible. The facts are indeed shocking, but unhappily not the less credible on that account. Slavery is a curse to the oppressor scarcely less than to the oppressed: its natural tendency is to brutalize both.

The Narrative of Ashton Warner

The History of Mary Prince was published in January of 1831. The following month Susanna Strickland recorded the narrative of the life of another slave, Ashton Warner, which was published March 1st. No doubt inevitably, there is some similarity in the descriptions of horrific abuse in the two narratives, but there is also a good deal to suggest that Strickland was not being disingenuous in her assertion that she was quite faithful in recording these narratives as they were related to her; certainly there are noticeable differences between the narrative style of Warner and that of Prince. (Strickland's note inviting readers to "see and converse with themselves" if they doubt that someone of Warner's background would be able to express himself so well is particularly interesting in this connection.)

Advertisement

In consequence of the unexpected decease of Ashton Warner, while this little volume was in the press, the profits that may arise from its sale will no longer be required, as was originally designed, for his personal benefit. But, in compliance with a wish expressed by the poor negro on his death-bed, it is now proposed to appropriate the proceeds to the benefit of his aged mother, and the enfranchisement (should the amount prove so considerable) of his enslaved wife and child. And I have the satisfaction of being authorized to add, for the information of benevolent individuals disposed to contribute liberally towards the objects now intimated—whether by the purchase of copies of this volume, or by pecuniary donations—that the little charitable fund thus contemplated, will be placed under the immediate management of George Stephen, Esq., Solicitor, 17, *King's Arms Yard, Coleman Street, and Thomas Pringle, Esq., Secretary of the Anti-Slavery Society,* 18, *Aldermanbury, who have kindly undertaken to superintend its proper application.*

S. STRICKLAND.

from Introduction

In writing Ashton's narrative, I have adhered strictly to the simple facts, adopting, wherever it could conveniently be done, his own language, which, for a person in his condition, is remarkably expressive and appropriate. Had I been inclined to give a recital of revolting cruelty, I should have chosen another case; and for such, unhappily, I had not far to seek. But those who wish to read such mournful narratives of human depravity will find enough for their information (far too many for the honour of human nature!) recorded in the publications of the Anti-Slavery Society.

The profits arising from the sale of this tract will be appropriated to the benefit of Ashton, who has been for the last three months in England, endeavouring to establish his claims to freedom; and who is at present suffering under severe illness, without any adequate means of subsistence.

With a view to render this Sketch of Colonial Slavery more complete, and to enable the reader to compare the details given by Ashton with those recorded by intelligent and conscientious eye-witnesses from England, I have subjoined, as an Appendix, the very important testimonies on this subject of three highly respectable clergymen of the established Church, and of an excellent Wesleyan Missionary—testimonies as yet but partially known to the public, and which comprise a mass of information equally recent and interesting.

Should this little tract assist, however feebly, in the diffusion of correct information in regard to the general condition and the feelings of the slaves, and thus tend to promote the great and good cause of justice and mercy, the writer's object will be fully accomplished. Like the widow's mite cast into the sacred treasury,[1] those who love the truth will not deem it unworthy because its value is but humble.

London, February 19, 1831.
S.S.

NEGRO SLAVERY
DESCRIBED
BY A NEGRO:
BEING
THE NARRATIVE OF ASHTON WARNER,
A NATIVE OF ST. VINCENT'S.
With an Appendix,
CONTAINING THE
TESTIMONY OF FOUR CHRISTIAN MINISTERS,
RECENTLY RETURNED FROM THE COLONIES,
ON THE SYSTEM OF SLAVERY AS IT NOW EXISTS.
BY
S. STRICKLAND.

"And tears and toil have been my lot
Since I the white man's thrall became;
And sorer griefs I wish forgot—
Harsh blows and burning shame!
Oh, Englishman! thou ne'er canst know
The injured bondman's bitter woe,
When round his heart, like scorpions, cling
Black thoughts that madden while they sting!"

LONDON:
SAMUEL MAUNDER, NEWGATE STREET.
1831.

from The Narrative of Ashton Warner (1831)

I was born in the Island of St. Vincent's, and baptized by the name of Ashton Warner, in the parish church, by the Rev. Mr. Gildon. My father and mother, at the time of my birth, were slaves on Cane Grove estate, in Bucumar Valley, then the property of Mr. Ottley. I was an infant at the breast when Mr. Ottley died; and shortly after the estate was put to sale, that the property might be divided among his family. Before Cane Grove was sold, my aunt, Daphne Crosbie, took the opportunity of buying my mother and me of Mr. Ottley's trustees. My aunt had been a slave, but a favoured one. She had money left her by a coloured gentleman of the name of Crosbie, with whom she lived, and whose name she took.

[1] *widow's ... treasury* See Luke 21.1–4.

After his death she went to reside at Kingston. Finding it a good thing to be free, aunt Daphne wished to make all her friends free also, particularly the slaves on the estate where she was born, and with whom she had shared, in her early days, all the sorrows of negro servitude. She had a large heart, and felt great kindness for her own people; but her means were not equal to her good wishes. She bought her old parents of Mr. Jackson, Mr. Ottley's executor; and, as it was her earnest desire to make us all happy, she would have bought my uncle John Baptiste (my mother's brother) too; but Mr. Wilson, the gentleman who purchased the estate, would not sell him, His reason for refusing my aunt never knew, for my uncle was an old man then, and nearly past work. Mr. Wilson sent him away to the Island of St. Lucia, and it was some years before aunt Daphne heard any tidings of him. At last some persons, coming from St. Lucia to St. Vincent's, told her that he lay very sick on Mr. Grant's estate. My aunt was glad to find that he was still living, and she went herself to make him free. She had never crossed the water, or been on the great sea, but she overcame her fears, and hired a small boat, and went directly to St. Lucia. She found my poor uncle in a very miserable state, and in this condition she bought him of his master, and brought him back to St. Vincent's. He was ill a long, long time; it was many long weary months before he could even take up a broom to sweep the house. He was very grateful to aunt Daphne for all that she had done for him; and so were we all. She was a very good, kind woman, and a Christian, though a black woman; and we (her relations) all loved her very, very much. We had no one else to love—she was all the world to us.

Whilst I lived with my aunt at Kingston I was very happy. I had no heavy tasks to do; and she was as careful over me as if she had been my own mother, and used to keep me with her in the house, that I might not be playing about in the streets with bad companions. My mother made sausages and *souse,*[1] and I used to help her to carry them to gentlemen's houses for sale. This was light labour to her, for she had been a field slave, kept at hard work, and driven to it by the whip. I am sure our best days were spent with my dear aunt; nor did she make us alone happy; all the money she could save went to purchase the freedom of slaves who had formerly been her companions in bondage at Cane Grove, or to make their condition better. There was not a person upon the island who did not speak well of Daphne Crosbie; black or white it was all the same. She bore a good character until the day she died.

I lived with my aunt till I was ten years old, when I was claimed as a slave belonging to the Cane Grove estate, by Mr. Wilson. This was a hard and unjust claim; but Mr. Wilson said, that though my mother was sold I was not—that the best slaves had been sold off the estate—that I was *his* property, and he would claim me wherever I was to be found. Now, he was wrong in all this, and I can prove to you, in two short minutes, that I did not belong to him. When my aunt manumitted my mother and me, Mr. Wilson had not-yet bought the estate; and in the Island of St. Vincent's it has always been a customary rule that the young child at the breast is sold as one with its mother, and does not become separate property till it is five or six years old; so that Mr. Wilson's claim was very unjust and oppressive.[2]

When my aunt found Mr. Wilson bent on taking me away by force, she went to Mr. Jackson, the gentleman from whom she had purchased my mother, and told him the state of the case, and he gave her a written paper to take to the Chief Justice of the island, to prove that I belonged to Daphne Crosbie, should Mr. Wilson continue to claim me. My aunt went to the Governor and showed him this paper, and also the manumission paper she had received from Mr. Jackson. The Governor, after looking at it, said that Mr. Wilson had no legal right to claim me upon the estate, and he promised my aunt that he would write to him to that effect. But we never knew whether he did or not, for we never got an answer from him. It is of no use trusting to what the white people in the West Indies say; they always forget their

---

[1] [Strickland's note] Slices of pig's head, salted and prepared in a particular manner, and sold in the markets by the slaves.

[2] [Strickland's note] This is poor Ashton's own statement. Whether the Colonial *Slave Law* will support his claim for freedom on this ground, is a question which remains to be determined.—S. S.

promises to slaves. Before this happened, my aunt had bound me apprentice to a cooper, to learn his trade. I was bound for seven years, and had signed the indenture myself, as a free black, by making a cross for my name.

My master's name was Pierre Wynn. He was a kind good master, and I never ceased to lament the cause which parted me from him. I had been with him between two and three months, and was busy one morning at work in the cooper's yard, helping the journeyman to truss a molasses-cask, when Mr. Wilson's manager, Mr. Donald, with two coloured men, and a white named Newman, came into the yard. This man, Newman, had informed Mr. Wilson where I was, and he sent his people to take me away by force. When the manager came into the yard, he said, "Which is Ashton?" I answered, quite innocently, not suspecting any mischief, "I am Ashton." Directly I said so the manager caught hold of me by the back of my neck. I did not know why he held me. I did not know what to think—I could not get my breath to speak—I was dreadfully frightened, and trembled all over. The other men got hold of me, and held me fast. They then led me away to Mr. Dalzell, Mr. Wilson's attorney, and shut me up in his office till Mr. Wilson came. Mr. Dalzell was afraid that I would try to make my escape, and to make sure of me one man kept watch at the window and another at the door. When Mr. Wilson came in he did not know me, and asked who I was. One of the men told him that I was Ashton. He said, "Very well; keep him here till I am ready to send him down to the estate." He then came up to the place where I was standing, and examined me from head to foot; then turned to Mr. Dalzell, and began talking to him about me. I was too young, and too much frightened at being stolen away, to remember much of their discourse; but I am very sure that I shall never forget that day.

Before Mr. Wilson left the office, my mother and Daphne Crosbie came to hear what was to be done with me, and why I had been taken away. But all they said was of no use; they could do no good where there was no justice to be had. Mr. Wilson insisted that I was a slave, and *his* slave, and he would have it so, in spite of my mother's tears and my aunt's entreaties. My poor mother was greatly distressed, and cried very bitterly. She entreated Mr. Wilson, if he thought he had a just claim for me, to put me in gaol till the question as to my freedom could be fairly settled; but he refused to do this, and when she continued her entreaties he grew angry, and ordered her not to stop in the yard, but to go away directly. And she and aunt Crosbie, on finding that nothing could be done for me there, were obliged to leave me in his hands.

The manager then put me into a boat, and took me down to the estate. It was rather late in the afternoon when we got there. I had nothing given me to do that day. It was Saturday, and I was not set to work till the Monday morning. I was very sad, and wished very much to run away. I could not bear the thought of being a slave, and I was very restless and unhappy.

On the Monday morning, John, the head cooper, took me down to the sugar works to help him; but I had no heart to work—I did nothing but think how I might run away. I was not knowing enough, however, to make my escape; and, after consulting with myself a long time, I found it would be the best plan to make myself as patient as I could. But still I was always thinking of my mother and aunt, and of Pierre Wynn, and the home I had been taken from. The estate of Cane Grove was in the middle of a deep valley, near the sea shore. Mr. Wilson's house stood upon the brow of the hill, and overlooked the whole sugar plantation. He had about three hundred slaves, and was considered one of the severest masters in the whole island.

As I have spoken of the condition of the field negroes as being so much worse than that of the mechanics among whom I was ranked on the estate, I shall here endeavour to describe the manner in which the field gang were worked on Cane Grove estate. They were obliged to be in the field before five o'clock in the morning; and, as the negro houses were at the distance of from three to four miles from the cane pieces, they were generally obliged to rise as early as four o'clock, to be at their work in time. The driver is first in the field, and calls the slaves together by cracking the whip or blowing the conch shell. Before five o'clock the overseer calls over the roll; and if any of the slaves are so unfortunate as to be too late, even by a few minutes, which, owing to the distance, is often the case, the driver flogs them as they come in, with the cart-whip, or with a scourge of tamarind rods. When flogged with the whip, they are stripped and held down upon the ground, and exposed in the most shameful manner.

In the cultivation of the canes the slaves work in a row. Each person has a hoe, and the women are expected to do as much as the men. This work is so hard that any slave, newly put to it, in the course of a month becomes so weak that often he is totally unfit for labour. If he falls back behind the rest, the driver keeps forcing him up with the whip.

They work from five o'clock to nine, when they are allowed to sit down for half an hour in the field, and take such food as they have been able to prepare over night. But many have no food ready, and so fast till mid-day.

They go to work again directly after half an hour's respite, and labour till twelve o'clock, when they leave off for dinner. They are allowed two hours of mid-day intermission, out of crop time, and an hour and a half in crop time.

During this interval every slave must pick a bundle of grass to bring home for the cattle at night. The grass grows in tufts, often scattered over a great space of ground, and, when the season is dry, it is very scarce and withered, so that the slaves collect it slowly and with difficulty, and are often employed most of the time allowed them for mid-day rest, in seeking for it. I have frequently known them occupied the whole two hours in collecting it.

They work again in gang from two till seven o'clock. It is then dark. When they return home the overseer calls over the roll, and demands of every man and woman their bundles of grass. He weighs with his hand each bundle as it is given in, and, if it be too light, the person who presents it is either instantly laid down and flogged severely with the cart-whip, or is put into the stocks for the whole night. If the slaves bring home no grass, they are not only put into the stocks all night, but are more severely flogged the next morning. This grass-picking is a very sore grievance to the field slaves.

When they are manuring the ground, the slaves are forced to carry the wet manure in open baskets upon their heads. This is most unpleasant as well as severe work. It is a usual occupation for wet weather, and the moisture from the manure drips constantly down upon the faces, and over the body and clothes of the slaves. They are forced to run with their loads as fast as they can; and, if they flag, the driver is instantly at their heels with the cart-whip.

The crop-time usually commences in January and lasts till June, and, if the season is wet, till July. During this season every slave must bring in a bundle of cane-tops for the cattle, instead of a bundle of grass. They then go immediately to the sugar works, where they have to take up the *mogass* which was spread out at nine o'clock in the morning to dry for fuel to boil the sugar. This mogass is the stalks of the cane after the juice has been squeezed out by the mill. The slaves are employed till ten at night in gathering in the mogass, that it may not be wetted with the dew and rendered unfit for immediate use. The overseer then calls over the roll, and issues orders for a certain spell of them to be up and at the works at one o'clock in the morning. After this the slaves have to prepare their suppers; for, if they have no very aged parents or friends belonging to them, they must do this themselves, which occupies them another hour. Every creature that is capable of work must take a part in the labours of the crop; and no person remains at home but those who are totally unfit for work. Slaves who are too old and weak to go to the field have to make up bundles of mogass, cut grass for the stock, &c.

During this season all the mechanics on the estate are employed to pot the sugar; carpenters, coopers, masons, and rum-distillers, even the pasture-boys who tend the cattle, are called in to assist. To the little people are given small tubs to carry the sugar into the curing house; and the grown-up slaves have shovels to fill the tubs for them. When employed in potting the sugar, we did not leave off to get our breakfast till ten or eleven o'clock, and I have known it mid-day before we have tasted food.

The whole gang of field slaves are divided into spells, and every man and woman able to work has not only to endure during crop-time the severe daily labour, but to work half the night also, or three whole nights in the week. The work is very severe, and great numbers of the slaves, during this period, sink under it, and become ill; but if they complain, their complaints are not readily believed, or are considered only a pretence to escape from labour. If they are so very ill that their inability to work can be no longer doubted, they are at length sent to the sick house.

The sick-house is just like a pen to keep pigs in; if you wish to keep yourself clean and decent, you cannot. It is one of the greatest punishments to the slaves to be sent there. When we were hard pressed, and had much sugar to pot, the manager would often send to the sick-house for the people who were sick, or lame with sores, to help us. If they refused to come, and said that they were unable to work, they were taken down and severely flogged, by the manager's order, with the cart-whip. There is nothing in slavery harder to bear than this. When you are ill and cannot work, your pains are made light of, and your complaints neither listened to, nor believed. I have seen people who were so sick that they could scarcely stand, dragged out of the sick-house, and tied up to a tree, and flogged in a shocking manner; then driven with the whip to the work. I have seen slaves in this state crawl away, and lie down among the wet trash to get a little ease, though they knew that it would most likely cause their death.

The quantity of food allowed the slaves is from two pounds and a half to three pounds of salt-fish per week, for each grown person. They could easily eat this in two days, but they must make it last till they receive a fresh allowance from the overseer. The rest of their food they raise upon their provision grounds. The owner gives to each slave from thirty to forty feet square of ground; not the best ground, but such as has been over-cropped, and is no longer productive for canes. This is taken from them the next year, when, by manuring and planting with yams and other things, it has been brought round, and recovered strength for the cultivation of sugar. The slaves are likewise permitted to cultivate waste pieces of ground, and the headlands of fields, that are unfit for planting. They work this ground every Sunday. It is generally given to them in March or April, and it is taken away in December or January. Besides the Sunday, they get part of twenty-six Saturdays, out of crop-time, to cultivate their grounds. What I mean by saying they get only *part* of these Saturdays is this—that they are employed in their master's work, such as carrying out trash, &c., from five to ten o'clock in the forenoon; and in the evening they must bring each his bundle of grass to deliver as usual at the calling of the lists; so that about seven hours, even of the day which is called their own, is occupied with their owner's work. They are obliged to work on these days at the provision grounds, if they wish ever so much for a holiday. If they are absent when the overseer inspects the grounds, they are flogged, or put in the stocks. The grounds produce plantains, yams, potatoes, pumpkins, calabashes, &c. On the Sunday, at every town, a market is held, in which the slaves are allowed to sell the produce of their grounds. Those that can save a little money, buy a pig and fatten it, that, in case of any death happening among their friends, they may sell the pig to provide a few necessaries for the funeral. They bury the dead during the night, being allowed no time during the day for their funerals.

In building their houses, they are allowed as much board as will form a window and a door. They go to the woods and cut wild canes, to form the walls and roof. The huts are thatched with cane-trash or tops.

For clothing, the owner gives to each slave in the year six yards of blue stuff, called bamboo, and six yards of brown. The young people and children are given a less allowance, in proportion to their size and age; the young children getting only a small stripe to tie round the waist. For bed-clothing, they give them only a blanket once in four or five years; and they are obliged to wear this till it falls in pieces. If the slaves require other clothes, they must buy them out of their own little savings. Many of the field negroes are very badly off for clothing. A good many are always to be seen with only a rag of cloth round their loins in all weathers.

People so hardly, so harshly, treated, and so destitute of every comfort, cannot be supposed to work with a willing mind. They have no home which they can well call their own. They are worked beyond their strength, and live in perpetual fear of the whip. They are insulted, tormented, and indecently exposed and degraded; yet English people wonder that they are not contented. Some have even said that they are happy! Let such people place themselves for a few minutes under the same yoke, and see if they could bear it. Such bondage is ruin both to the soul and body of the slave; and I hope every good Englishman will daily pray to God, that the yoke of slavery may soon be broken from off the necks of my unfortunate countrymen for ever.[1]

What made me feel more deeply for the sad condition of the field slaves was the circumstance of my having taken a wife from among them, after I had resided several years on Cane Grove estate. When I was about twenty-one years of age, finding my condition lonely, because I had no friends to manage for me, as the other slaves had, I wished to marry, and have a home of my own, and a kind partner to do for me. Among the field slaves there was a very respectable young woman, called Sally, for whom I had long felt a great deal of regard. At last I asked her to be my wife; and we stood up in her father's house, before her mother, and her uncle, and her sisters, and, holding each other by the hand, pledged our troth as husband and wife, and promised before God to be good and kind to each other, and to love and help each other, as long as we lived.

And so we married. And though it was not as white folks marry, before the parson, yet I considered her as much my wife, and I loved her as well, as though we had been married in the church; and she was as careful, and managed as well for me, as if she had been my mother. I could not bear to see her work in the field. It is, as I have already said, a very sad and hard condition of slavery; and the more my wife suffered, the more I wished to be free, and to make her so. When she was with child, she was flogged for not coming out early enough to work, and afterwards, when far advanced in pregnancy, she was put into the stocks by the manager, because she said she was unable to go to the field. My heart was almost broken to see her so treated, but I could do nothing to help her; and it would have made matters worse if I had attempted to speak up for her. She was twice punished in this cruel manner, though the overseer must have known that she was in no condition to work. After our child was born, she was again repeatedly flogged for not coming sooner to the field, though she had stopped merely to attend and suckle the baby. But they had no feeling for the mother or for her child, they cared only for the work. It is a dreadful thing to be a field negro; and it is scarcely less dreadful, if one's heart is not quite hardened, to have a wife, or a husband, or a child, in that condition. On this account I was often grieved that I had taken poor Sally to be my wife; for it caused her more suffering as a mother, while her cruel treatment wrung my heart, without my being able to move a finger, or utter a word, in her behalf.

[1] [Strickland's note] Such is the impressive language in which Ashton speaks of slavery. The above are his own expressions; for, though an uneducated, he is a very intelligent negro, and speaks remarkably good English. Any reader, who wishes it, may see and converse with himself, by making application through the publisher.—S.S.

The Abolition of Slavery

CONTEXTS

In the 1750s it was possible for John Newton, the author of the hymn "Amazing Grace," to write that neither he nor any of his friends had had any notion that "slavery could be considered unlawful and wrong." By 1807 the tide had turned sufficiently that the British Parliament (through the Slave Trade Act) prohibited British vessels from participating in the trading of humans. And in 1833 (through the Slavery Abolition Act) slavery in all British territory was ended.

What brought about such a vast change in such a relatively short time? In part the answer lies in the history of ideas; the Enlightenment gave birth to concepts of freedom and equality—of human rights which, as they were thought through, were widely recognized to apply to all humans, regardless of gender, regardless of race. But the abolition first of the slave trade and then of slavery itself was also the result of concerted political pressure. Some have identified the birth of the modern political movement and modern political lobbying in the campaign to abolish slavery. Certainly the Society for Effecting the Abolition of the Slave Trade, formed in 1787 and led by Thomas Clarkson and Granville Sharp, among others, played a hugely important role in acquiring and disseminating information as to the actual conditions endured by slaves, and in pressuring the government to take action. In Parliament, William Wilberforce became the *de facto* leader of the anti-slavery movement: Wilberforce, the author of *Practical Christianity*, was tireless in his efforts. The Society of Friends (also known as the Quakers) also played a leading role, both within the Society for Effecting the Abolition of the Slave Trade and independently, in shaping public opinion and pressing for change. And a number of authors—including William Wordsworth, Samuel Taylor Coleridge, Helen Maria Williams, Anna Letitia Barbauld, and Mary Robinson—lent their voices to the cause.

The legal system too played an important role in the process. In a landmark 1772 case the owner of one James Somerset lost his legal suit to regain ownership of Somerset, who had run away from servitude while in England. Lord Mansfield, the Lord Chief Justice ruled that, according to the established principles of English law, everyone in England was free. Proponents of slavery had suggested that villeinage, the state of servitude which had existed under feudalism and which had never been declared illegal, provided sufficient legal precedent. Mansfield decided, however, that no such justification could be deemed to exist under English Common Law. If Parliament wished to legalize slavery in England, that would require specific new legislation. Despite Mansfield's *caveat* against taking his ruling to apply to British possessions overseas, abolitionists had some reason to feel confident from that point on that the law would eventually support their arguments universally and unequivocally, in Britain's colonies as well as within Britain itself.

⌘⌘⌘

from John Newton, *A Slave Trader's Journal* (1751)

John Newton (1725–1807) first went to sea at the age of ten, sailing with his father, the captain of the vessel. By the age of twenty-eight he had wide experience both of the sea and of the slave trade, and was for the first time commanding a vessel himself. The *Duke of Argyll* left England for Bassa in West Africa (in what is now Guinea Bissau) in 1750, made the "middle passage" from Bassa to Antigua in the West Indies between 22 May and 2 July, and returned to Liverpool with a cargo of sugar, arriving in November. The following excerpts are from Newton's journal of that voyage. In later life, Newton came to regret deeply his life as a slave trader (which he had given up for health reasons in 1754). He became a Christian minister and wrote that he would have left the slave trade sooner "had I considered it as I now do to be unlawful and wrong. But I never had a scruple upon this head at the time; nor was such a thought ever suggested to me by any friend." In 1770 Newton wrote the famous hymn "Amazing Grace." He became a strong advocate for the abolition of the slave trade.

Thursday 16 May
… [A] long boat came on board from Grande Bassa. I sent Billinge [the second mate] chiefly to satisfy myself of the state and price of slaves. He says the glut we heard so much of is entirely over, the Brittannia and Ranger having met very few. About Settra Crue there is still plenty (upon the account of a war very probably begun with that view) but extravagantly dear … He brought me a sample of the prices in a woman slave he bought at Bassa, which upon costing up the goods I find cost 96 bars, and I ordered him to get one upon any terms for that reason. That I might not think he gave more than usual, he brought me a list of goods he saw Saunders pay for a man which amounts to 102 bars, and the farther to leeward the dearer still. I think I have sufficient reason not to go down, for setting aside the cost, the assortments in demand there would ruin me soon.

Tuesday 28 May
Secured the after bulkhead of the men's room, for they had started almost every stantient. Their plot was exceedingly well laid, and had they been let alone an hour longer, must have occasioned us a good deal of trouble and damage. I have reason to be thankful they did not make attempts upon the coast when we had often 7 or 8 of our best men out of the ship at a time and the rest busy. They still look very gloomy and sullen and have doubtless mischief in their heads if they could find every opportunity to vent it. But I hope (by the Divine Assistance) we are fully able to overawe them now. …

Wednesday 12 June
Got the slaves up this morn. Washed them all with fresh water. They complained so much that was obliged to let them go down again when the rooms were cleaned. Buryed a man slave (No. 84) of a flux, which he has been struggling with near 7 weeks. …

Saturday 22 June
Being pretty warm, got up the men and washed all the slaves with fresh water. I am much afraid of another ravage from the flux, for we have had 8 taken within these few days. Have seen 2 or 3 tropick birds and a few flying fish.

Monday 24 June
Buried a girl slave (No. 92). In the afternoon while we were off the deck, William Cooney seduced a woman slave down into the room and lay with her brutelike in view of the whole quarter deck, for which I put him in irons.[1] I hope this has been the first affair of the kind on board and I am determined to keep them quiet if possible. If anything happens to the woman I shall impute it to him, for she was big with child. Her number is 83. …

Friday 28 June
By the favour of Divine Providence made a timely discovery today that the slaves were forming a plot for an insurrection. Surprised 2 of them attempting to get off

[1] *for which … irons* In contrast to Newton, some captains actively encouraged their crew to rape the female slaves, since pregnant slaves could be sold at a higher price; mulatto children were especially highly valued as house servants.

their irons, and upon farther search in their rooms, upon the information of 3 of the boys, found some knives, stones, shot, etc., and a cold chissel. Upon enquiry there appeared 8 principally concerned to move in projecting the mischief and 4 boys in supplying them with the above instruments. Put the boys in irons and slightly in the thumbscrews to urge them to a full confession. We have already 36 men out of our small number....

Friday 5 July
... [I]n the morning Mr. Guichard went off with me to view the slaves. When came on shore again, after comparing orders and intelligence, he judged it best for the concern to sell here, if I approved it, without which, he was pleased to say, he would do nothing, tho my letters from the owners referred me wholly to his direction. It seems by all I can learn that this is likely to prove as good a market as any of the neighbouring islands; and as for Jamaica or America, I should be extremely loth to venture so far, for we have had the men slaves so long on board that their patience is just worn out, and I am certain they would drop fast had we another passage to make. Monday is appointed for the sale.

from Quobna Ottobah Cugoano, *Thoughts and Sentiments on the Evil and Wicked Traffic of the Slavery and Commerce of the Human Species* (1787)

Cugoano had been kidnapped in West Africa and sold into slavery in the West Indies. His owner travelled with him to England in 1772, and he declared himself a free man on English soil following the landmark Somerset case. His *Thoughts and Sentiments* is the first substantial anti-slavery work by a black writer.

But why should total abolition, and an universal emancipation of slaves, and the enfranchisement of all the Black People employed in the culture of the Colonies, taking place as it ought to do, and without any hesitation, or delay for a moment, even though it might have some seeming appearance of loss either to government or to individuals, be feared at all? Their labour, as freemen, would be as useful in the sugar colonies as any other class of men that could be found; and should it even take place in such a manner that some individuals, at first, would suffer loss as a just reward for their wickedness in slave-dealing, what is that to the happiness and good of doing justice to others; and, I must say, to the great danger, otherwise, that must eventually hang over the whole community? It is certain, that the produce of the labour of slaves, together with all the advantages of the West-India traffic, bring in an immense revenue to government; but let that amount be what it will, there might be as much or more expected from the labour of an equal increase of free people, and without the implication of any guilt attending it, and which, otherwise, must be a greater burden to bear, and more ruinous consequences to be feared from it, than if the whole national debt was to sink at once, and to rest upon the heads of all that might suffer by it. Whereas, if a generous encouragement were to be given to a free people, peaceable among themselves, intelligent and industrious, who by art and labour would improve the most barren situations, and make the most of that which is fruitful; the free and voluntary labour of many, would soon yield to any government, many greater advantages than any thing that slavery can produce. And this should be expected, wherever a Christian government is extended, and the true religion is embraced, that the blessings of liberty should be extended likewise, and that it should diffuse its influences first to fertilize the mind, and then the effects of its benignity would extend, and arise with exuberant blessings and advantages from all its operations. Was this to be the case, every thing would increase and prosper at home and abroad, and ten thousand times greater and greater advantages would arise to the state, and more permanent and solid benefit to individuals from the service of freemen, than ever they can reap, or in any possible way enjoy, by the labour of slaves....

from Alexander Falconbridge, *Account of the Slave Trade on the Coast of Africa* (1788)

Falconbridge sailed aboard slave trading vessels as a surgeon in the 1780s. The work from which the following excerpts are taken was given wide distribution by the Society for Effecting the Abolition of the Slave Trade. In 1789 Falconbridge also testified as to the horrors of the trade before the Parliamentary Committee investigating the issue.

The men negroes, on being brought aboard the ship, are immediately fastened together, two and two, by hand-cuffs on their wrists, and by irons rivetted on their legs. They are then sent down between the decks, and placed in an apartment partitioned off for that purpose. The women likewise are placed in a separate apartment between decks, but without being ironed. And an adjoining room, on the same deck, is besides appointed for the boys. Thus are they all placed in different apartments.

But at the same time, they are frequently stowed so close, as to admit of no other posture than lying on their sides. Neither will the height between decks, unless directly under the grating, permit them the indulgence of an erect posture; especially where there are platforms, which is generally the case. These platforms are a kind of shelf, about eight or nine feet in breadth, extending from the side of the ship towards the centre. They are placed nearly midway between the decks, at the distance of two or three feet from each deck. Upon these the negroes are stowed in the same manner as they are on the deck underneath.

In each of the apartments are placed three or four large buckets, of a conical form, being near two feet in diameter at the bottom, and only one foot at the top, and in depth about twenty-eight inches; to which, when necessary, the negroes have recourse. It often happens, that those who are placed at a distance from the buckets, in endeavouring to get to them, tumble over their companions, in consequence of their being shackled. These accidents, although unavoidable, are productive of continual quarrels, in which some of them are always bruised. In this distressed situation, unable to proceed, and prevented from getting to the tubs, they desist from the attempt; and, as the necessities of nature are not to be repelled, ease themselves as they lie. This becomes a fresh source of broils and disturbances, and tends to render the condition of the poor captive wretches still more uncomfortable. The nuisance arising from these circumstances, is not unfrequently increased by the tubs being much too small for the purpose intended, and their being usually emptied but once every day. The rule for doing this, however, varies in different ships, according to the attention paid to the health and convenience of the slaves by the captain ...

The diet of the negroes, while on board, consists chiefly of horse-beans, boiled to the consistence of a pulp; of boiled yams and rice, and sometimes of a small quantity of beef or pork. The latter are frequently taken from the provisions laid in for the sailors. They sometimes make use of a sauce, composed of palm-oil, mixed with flour, water, and pepper, which the sailors call *slabber-sauce.* Yams are the favourite food of the Eboe, or Bight negroes, and rice or corn, of those from the Gold and Windward Coasts; each preferring the produce of their native soil ...

They are commonly fed twice a day, about eight o'clock in the morning and four in the afternoon. In most ships they are only fed with their *own food* once a day. Their food is served up to them in tubs, about the size of a small water bucket. They are placed round these tubs in companies of ten to each tub, out of which they feed themselves with wooden spoons. These they soon lose, and when they are not allowed others, they feed themselves with their hands. In favourable weather they are fed upon deck, but in bad weather their food is given them below. Numberless quarrels take place among them during their meals; more especially when they are put upon short allowance ... Their allowance of water is about half a pint each at every meal. It is handed round in a bucket, and given to each negroe in a pannekin; a small utensil with a strait handle, somewhat similar to a sauce-boat....

Upon the negroes refusing to take sustenance, I have seen coals of fire, glowing hot, put on a shovel, and placed so near their lips, as to scorch and burn them. And this has been accompanied with threats, of forcing them to swallow the coals, if they any longer persisted in refusing to eat. These means have generally had the desired effect. I have also been credibly informed, that a certain captain in the slave trade, poured melted lead on such of the negroes as obstinately refused their food.

Exercise being deemed necessary for the preservation of their health, they are sometimes obliged to dance, when the weather will permit their coming on deck. If they go about it reluctantly, or do not move with agility, they are flogged; a person standing by them all the time with a cat-o'-nine-tails[1] in his hand for that purpose. Their musick, upon these occasions consists of a drum, sometimes with only one head; and when that is worn out, they do not scruple to make use of the bottom of one of the tubs before described. The poor wretches are frequently compelled to sing also; but when they do so, their songs are generally, as may naturally be expected, melancholy lamentations of their exile from their native country. …

On board some ships, the common sailors are allowed to have intercourse with such of the black women whose consent they can procure. And some of them have been known to take the inconstancy of their paramours so much to heart, as to leap overboard and drown themselves. The officers are permitted to indulge their passions among them at pleasure, and sometimes are guilty of such brutal excesses, as disgrace human nature.

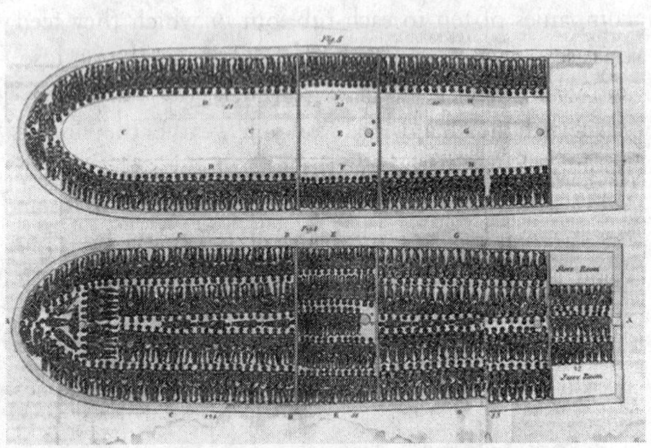

Diagram showing allotment of space for slaves on two decks of a late eighteenth-century sailing ship.

[1] *cat-o'-nine-tails* Switch with nine ropes attached, used as a beating implement.

William Cowper, Sweet Meat has Sour Sauce or, The Slave-Trader in the Dumps[2] (1788)

A trader I am to the African shore,
  But since that my trading is like to be o'er,
I'll sing you a song that you ne'er heard before,
  Which nobody can deny, deny,
  Which nobody can deny.

When I first heard the news it gave me a shock,
Much like what they call an electrical knock,
And now I am going to sell off my stock,
  Which nobody, &c.

'Tis a curious assortment of dainty regales,
To tickle the negroes with when the ship sails,
Fine chains for the neck, and a cat with nine tails,
  Which nobody, &c.

Here's supple-jack plenty, and store of rat-tan,[3]
That will wind itself round the sides of a man,
As close as a hoop round a bucket or can,
  Which nobody, &c.

Here's padlocks and bolts, and screws for the thumbs,
That squeeze them so lovingly till the blood comes,
They sweeten the temper like comfits or plums,[4]
  Which nobody, &c.

When a negro his head from his victuals withdraws,
And clenches his teeth and thrusts out his paws,
Here's a notable engine to open his jaws,
  Which nobody, &c.

Thus going to market, we kindly prepare
A pretty black cargo of African ware,

[2] *Sweet Meat … Dumps* The poem is one of several anti-slavery poems by Cowper. The Society for Effecting the Abolition of the Slave Trade distributed his ballad "The Negro's Complaint" widely; both that poem and this were set to music and sung as well as read.

[3] *supple-jack* Climbing vine; *rat-tan* Palm stem. Both supple-jack and rattan were used for switches or canes.

[4] *comfits or plums* Sweetmeats; sugarplums: fruits preserved with sugar.

For what they must meet with when they get there,
Which nobody, &c.

'Twould do your heart good to see 'em below
Lie flat on their backs all the way as we go,
Like sprats on a gridiron,[1] scores in a row,
Which nobody, &c.

But ah! if in vain I have studied an art
So gainful to me, all boasting apart,
I think it will break my compassionate heart,
Which nobody, &c.

For oh! how it enters my soul like an awl![2]
This pity, which some people self-pity call,
Is sure the most heart-piercing pity of all,
Which nobody, &c.

So this is my song, as I told you before;
Come buy off my stock, for I must no more
Carry Caesars and Pompeys[3] to Sugar-cane shore,
Which nobody can deny, deny,
Which nobody can deny.

from William Wilberforce, "Speech to the House of Commons," 13 May 1789

William Wilberforce began his long struggle to have the British Parliament abolish the slave trade with the speech excerpted below. In April of 1791, a bill put forward by Wilberforce was voted down by 163 votes to 88; not until 1807 were his efforts on this score successful. News of the passage of the Slavery Abolition Act reached Wilberforce on his deathbed in 1833.

A report has been made by his Majesty's Privy Council, which, I trust, every Gentleman has read, and which ascertains the Slave Trade to be just such in practice as we know, from theory, that it must be. What should we suppose must naturally be the consequence of our carrying on a Slave Trade with Africa? With a country, vast in its extent, not utterly barbarous, but civilized in a very small degree? Does any one suppose a Slave Trade would *help* their civilization? That Africa would *profit* by such an intercourse? Is it not plain, that she must *suffer* from it? That civilization must be checked; that her barbarous manners must be made more barbarous; and that the happiness of her millions of inhabitants must be prejudiced by her intercourse with Britain? Does not every one see, that a Slave Trade, carried on around her coasts, must carry violence and desolation to her very centre? That, in a Continent, just emerging from barbarism, if a Trade in Men is established—if her men are all converted into goods, and become commodities that can be bartered, it follows, they must be subject to ravage just as goods are; and this too, at a period of civilization, when there is no protecting Legislature to defend this their only sort of property, in the same manner as the rights of property are maintained by the legislature of every civilized country.

We see then, in the nature of things, how easily all the practices of Africa are to be accounted for. Her kings are never compelled to war, that we can hear of, by public principles,—by national glory—still less by the love of their people. In Europe it is the extension of commerce, the maintenance of national honor, or some great public object, that is ever the motive to war with every monarch; but, in Africa, it is the personal *avarice* and *sensuality* of their kings: these two vices of avarice and sensuality, (the most powerful and predominant in natures thus corrupt) we tempt, we stimulate in all these African Princes, and we depend upon these vices for the very maintenance of the Slave Trade....

Sir, the nature and all the circumstances of this trade are now laid open to us; we can no longer plead ignorance,—we cannot evade it,—it is now an object placed before us,—we cannot pass it; we may spurn it, we may kick it out of our way, but we cannot turn aside so as to avoid seeing it; for it is brought now so directly before our eyes, that this House must decide, and must justify to all the world, and to their own consciences, the rectitude of the grounds and principles of their decision.

A Society [the Society for Effecting the Abolition of the Slave Trade] has been established for the abolition of this trade, [in 1787] in which Dissenters, Quakers,

[1] *sprats on a gridiron* Small fish on a griddle or broiling-pan.

[2] *awl* Tool for piercing holes in leather.

[3] *Caesars and Pompeys* Names commonly given to African slaves.

Churchmen—in which the most conscientious of all persuasions have all united, and made a common cause in this great question. Let not Parliament be the only body that is insensible to the principles of national justice. Let us make reparation to Africa, so far as we can, by establishing a trade upon true commercial principles, and we shall soon find the rectitude of our conduct rewarded, by the benefits of a regular and a growing commerce.

Proponents of Slavery

It is often (and rightly) pointed out that appeals to Christian virtue were central to the abolitionist cause. As some of the following excerpts illustrate, appeals to Christian principles were also made on the other side of the argument—as were appeals of a variety of other sorts.

from Rev. Robert Boncher Nicholls, *Observations, Occasioned by the Attempts Made in England to Effect the Abolition of the Slave Trade* (1788)

[The author] thought it incumbent on him first to search the scriptures, to learn whether slavery was inconsistent with the revealed will of the Deity. The result of his enquiry was perfectly satisfactory to himself, and he thought it but right to point out some few of the many passages, to be found in the sacred volumes, which justify that commerce. Since the following observations went to the press the author has the great satisfaction to find, that he might have pursued his original plan without any injury to the cause he has endeavoured to support, as he has seen a pamphlet by the Rev. Mr. Harris, of Liverpool, who has so clearly proved, from the scriptures, that slavery is neither contrary to the law nor gospel, that it is scarcely possible for the most conscientious believer, who reads that tract, to doubt in future; whether the man servant or the maid servant is not as much a man's property as "*his ox or his ass, or any thing that is his.*" …

About the time of Lord Mansfield's determination in the case of Mr. Stuart's negro, [those in England who were attended by slaves] … had every right to suppose they were authorised, by the laws of Great Britain, as well as those of the colonies, to consider those people as their property; and that they had a right to their services in Europe, or to send, or accompany them back to the colonies, as they judged proper: They found themselves mistaken, and that it was permitted to debauch their slaves, to encourage or entice them to run away, with impunity. The ideas of liberty, the charms of novelty, and an ignorance of the country they had got to; where they found themselves upon a perfect equality, at least, with the inferior white people, could not fail of having pernicious effects upon their minds, and great numbers ran away from their masters. They in general plunged into vice and debauchery, and many of them, who were desirous of returning to their masters and mistresses, were refused to be received. The whole of those thus lost to their owners, and as to every useful purpose, to the community, cannot have been less in number than from 15,000 to 20,000.—As most of them were prime, young seasoned, or Creole slaves, the loss to their owners, the planters, have not been less than from 1,000,000 to 1,200,000 sterling. A large sum to be sacrificed, to the mere names of *liberty and humanity! What* has been the result of thus extending *the blessings of liberty* to so many *wretched slaves.* Let any body shew scarce a single instance of any one of these people being in so happy a situation as they were before. The greater part, it is known, died miserably, in a very short time. No parish was willing to receive them, so that the survivers, after begging about the streets of London, and suffering all those evils, and inconveniencies, consequent on idleness and poverty, famine, disease, and the inclemency of the weather; attracted the attention of the public, and government was prevailed upon to undertake the transportation of them to the country from whence they or their ancestors had been ravished *by the wicked traders* of London, Liverpool, and Bristol.

Equal unhappiness would be the lot of the slaves in the islands, if they were set free; what could they do to obtain a livelihood? To suppose they would hire themselves out to work, can only enter into the imagination of those who do not know the people, or the country: What has so lately passed in England is surely sufficient to shew that there can be no idea, they will, any of them, wish to return to their own country. Thousands of negroes have been made free by their masters in the colonies, and it may, with truth, be asserted, that, notwithstanding many of them were very capable of paying for a passage to any part of Africa they thought proper; scarce a single instance can be produced of any one of them desiring to return to the place of his nativity.

The present attempt to cram liberty down the throats of people who are incapable of digesting it, can with propriety, be resembled to nothing, so well as to the account of poor Gulliver, when he was carried out of his little cabinet to the top of the house, by the Brobdignag Monkey.

from Anonymous, *Thoughts on the Slavery of Negroes, as it Affects the British Colonies in the West Indies: Humbly Submitted to the Consideration of Both Houses of Parliament* (1788)

If I am able to shew that the blacks are really happy; that their condition (if the odious name of slave could be forgotten) is preferable to the lower orders of the people in Great Britain and Ireland; and that they enjoy the necessaries, and often the luxuries of life, I trust every honest man will feel a just indignation at any attempt to mislead his judgment, and to impose upon him an opinion of cruelty, which has no existence in any of the British West India islands. …

Let us take a view of the situation of the Africans, the nature of their country, their climate and government, and the genius and disposition of its inhabitants. The appearance of the slave-coast of Africa, when it was first visited by the Europeans, strongly marked the barbarous state of the people; a rude, inhospitable country, susceptible indeed of cultivation, but almost every way covered with thick, impenetrable forests. The wild luxuriance of nature was here portrayed in rich attire. The pruning hand of man was hardly seen. The peaceful labours of agriculture were little known.

It has been observed, that those countries most favoured by nature, often make the slowest progress to civilization; and that the people always groan under the weight of a cruel despotism. "This is an effect which springs from a natural cause. Great heat enervates the strength and courage of men, while in cold climates they have a certain vigour of body and mind, which renders them capable of long, painful, great, and intrepid actions. We ought not, then, to be astonished, that the effeminacy of the people in hot climates has almost always rendered them slaves; and that the bravery of those in colder regions has enabled them to maintain their liberties."

In those countries between the tropics, and especially under the equator, "the excess of heat renders men so slothful and dispirited, that nothing but the most pressing necessity can induce them to perform any laborious duty." An unconquerable indolence is universally felt and acknowledged. Sunk into the most deplorable degeneracy, they feel no incitements beyond the present moment. In vain may we represent to them the happiness of others. In vain may we attempt to rouse them to a sense of their own weakness. The soul, unwilling to enlarge itself, becomes the prey of every ignoble passion. Strangers to every virtuous and magnanimous sentiment, they are without fame—they are without glory.

The Africans have been always represented as a cruel and perfidious people, lazy, lascivious, faithless in their engagements, innate thieves, without morals, and without any just notion of any one religious duty. Their laws are founded on such principles as naturally flow from so impure a source. The government of the slave-coast of Africa is despotic. The will of the Prince must be obeyed. There is no appeal upon earth from his awful decree. The lives and fortunes of every one are absolutely at his disposal. These tyrants have thought fit to distinguish a number of crimes, but have taken no care to proportionate their degrees of punishment. Every offence is there punished with loss of life or liberty. Captives in war are deliberately murdered, or sold as slaves, as may most indulge the sanguinary caprice of the conqueror. Those convicted of adultery or theft, lose their liberty. He who is in debt, and unable to pay must either sell himself or his children to satisfy the creditor. It may be said, that the loss of life, or liberty, only commences with the injury done to society. I answer, "that in Africa, the civil liberty is already destroyed by the political slavery." A country like this, doomed to bear the weight of human misery, will always present a history of the most shocking cruelties, and of the severest slavery upon earth.

After viewing this melancholy picture, we ought not to be surprised at the extent of the present intercourse between the Africans and Europeans. For want of proper consideration, and from the influence of certain prejudices, the slave-trade has long been considered the scandal and reproach of every nation who have been anywise engaged in it, but without sufficient reason.

Men who enjoy the benefits of civilization, and who are protected in life, liberty, and property, by the wisdom of humane and equal laws, feel that spirit of liberty, and enthusiastic love of their country, which freedom only can inspire. Talk to them of banishment, and it is more terrible than death. Not so the poor African—he has few motives for wishing any longer to behold the distresses of his country; he is, alas! perhaps, the last witness of the sad misfortunes of his house— Already deprived of family, friends, and every other tender endearment, he has no relief but in banishment or death.

It is pleasant to mark the progress of the barbarian, from the moment he is put on shore in an English colony, to the time he becomes the master of a family, and acquires property of his own. He is first of all clothed (a thing unknown to him in his own country) and then instructed in the necessity of cleanliness. When carried to the plantation, he is shewn how to work in common with others. In a little time he chooses himself a wife, and has a house given to him, much better, allowing for the difference of climate, than what the peasants have in this country. When he is sufficiently instructed in the management of ground, a certain portion is allotted to the exclusive use of himself and family, which, with a moderate share of industry, is not only sufficient to supply every personal want, but leave a considerable part to be sent to market, to be sold, or exchanged for either necessaries or luxuries. The African now, finding himself a family man, and in possession of house and land, he begins to rear hogs, poultry, and other small stock, and either sells them to his master at a fair price, or carries them to market, for which one day in the week is allowed him. …

The African, no longer remembering a country to which he owes nothing but birth, becomes attached to the soil which is so propitious to his wants, and having few cares, and few desires, that are not completely satisfied, there is nothing so terrible to him as a change of situation. The master is the steward, the faithful guardian of all his wants and necessities. In sickness and in health—in youth and in old age, his assiduities are undiminished. The reader will anticipate the happiness of these people—and happy they must be, while their labours are directed by equity and humanity, and not by avarice.

God forbid that I should be an advocate for slavery, or servitude of any description, that can anywise limit the extent of human happiness: at the same time let me caution my countrymen against the weakness and folly of believing that happiness can only be sought in a constitution as free as their own. The history of all nations shew how extremely improper the laws of one country would be for those of another.

from Gordon Turnbull, *An Apology of Negro Slavery; or, the West India Planters Vindicated from the Charge of Inhumanity* (1786)

As a contrast to the horrid and fictitious picture, which has been drawn of the state of the negroes in the West-Indies, I shall here exhibit a true and more pleasing representation, taken from the life.

To begin then with the period of the Guinea negroe's arrival in one of the islands.—As soon as the ship that brings them is at anchor, the master or surgeon goes on shore to procure fresh provisions, fruit, and vegetables of all kinds, which are immediately sent on board for the slaves. Parties of them are sent on shore at different times, and conducted a little way into the country, where they frequently meet with many natives of their own country, who speak the same language, and sometimes with near and dear relations, who all appear very cheerful and happy. These agreeable and unexpected meetings are truly affecting, and excite the most tender and pleasing sensations in the breasts of the by-standers. It is not uncommon for these newly arrived guests, to mingle in the dance, or to join in the song, with their country people. If any of them appear dull or desponding, the old negroes endeavour to enliven them, by the most soothing and endearing expressions, telling them, in their own tongue, not to be afraid of the white men; that the white men are very good; that they will get plenty of *yam, yam,* (their general name for victuals) and that their work will be of the easiest kind. By these means, they are perfectly reconciled to the white men, and to a change of country, and of situation, which many of them declare, to be far superior to that which they had quitted. When the day of sale arrives, they not only meet the planter's looks, and answer his enquiries, by means of an interpreter, with great firmness, but they try, by offering their stout limbs to his inspection, jumping to shew their activity, and other allurements, to induce those, whose appearance pleases them, to buy them, and to engage, if possible, a preference in their favour …

As soon as the new negroes are brought home to the plantation, if a planter has purchased them they are properly clothed.—A sufficient quantity of wholesome food is prepared, and served to them three times a day. They are comfortably lodged in some room of the manager's own house, or in some other convenient place, where they can be immediately under his eye for a few days. During this time they are not put to any kind of labour whatever, but are regularly conducted to bathe in the river, or in the sea, if it is nigh, twice a day. In the evenings they sing and dance, after the manner of their own nation, together with the old negroes who happen to be from the same country, one or two of whom are commonly instrumental performers, in these very noisy, but very joyous assemblies. In a very short time, they are taken into the houses of the principal and best disposed negroes, who adopt one of two of these new subjects into each family, to assist them in all the little domestic offices of cookery, carrying water, wood, &c. This is almost the only work they are employed in for the first two or three months, at the expiration of which, they are put to the easiest kind of labour for some months more.…

from Mary Wollstonecraft, *A Vindication of the Rights of Men* (1790)

Wollstonecraft's more famous work, *A Vindication of the Rights of Woman*, was published two years after her much shorter work on the rights of men, which briefly discusses the issue of slavery.

Is it necessary to repeat, that there are rights which we received, at our birth, as men, when we were raised above the brute creation by the power of improving ourselves—and that we receive these not from our forefathers, but from God?

My father may dissipate his property, yet I have no right to complain;—but if he should attempt to sell me for a slave, or fetter me with laws contrary to reason; nature, in enabling me to discern good from evil, teaches me to break the ignoble chain.…

But on what principle Mr. Burke[1] could defend American independence, I cannot conceive; for the whole tenor of his … arguments settles slavery on an everlasting foundation. Allowing his servile reverence for antiquity, and prudent attention to self-interest, to have the force which he insists on, it ought never to be abolished; and, because our ignorant forefathers, not understanding the native dignity of man, sanctioned a traffic that outrages every suggestion of reason and religion, we are to submit to the inhuman custom, and term an atrocious insult to humanity the love of our country and a proper submission to those laws which secure our property.—Security of property! Behold, in a few words, the definition of English liberty. And to this selfish principle every nobler one is sacrificed.…

Anna Laetitia Barbauld, "Epistle to William Wilberforce, Esq. on the Rejection of the Bill for Abolishing the Slave Trade" (1791)[2]

Cease, Wilberforce, to urge thy generous aim!
Thy country knows the sin, and stands the shame!
The preacher, poet, senator in vain
Has rattled in her sight the Negro's chain;
With his deep groans assailed her startled ear,
And rent the veil that hid his constant tear;
Forced her averted eyes his stripes[3] to scan,
Beneath the bloody scourge laid bare the man,
Claimed Pity's tear, urged Conscience's strong control,
And flashed conviction on her shrinking soul.
The Muse too, soon awaked, with ready tongue

[1] *Mr. Burke* Edmund Burke (1729–97), Anglo-Irish statesman, author, and philosopher. Burke famously supported the right of the colonies to self-rule.

[2] *William Wilberforce … Slave Trade* This poem appeared shortly after the bill put forward by Wilberforce (and supported both by the Prime Minister, William Pitt, and the leader of the Opposition, Charles Fox), was defeated by a vote of 163 to 88.

[3] *stripes* Open wounds caused by the lash.

At Mercy's shrine applausive paeans rung;
And Freedom's eager sons, in vain foretold
A new Astraean[1] reign, an age of gold:
She knows and she persists—Still Afric bleeds,
Unchecked, the human traffic still proceeds;
She stamps her infamy to future time,
And on her hardened forehead seals the crime.
In vain, to thy white standard[2] gathering round,
Wit, Worth, and Parts° and Eloquence are found: *intelligence*
In vain, to push to birth thy great design,
Contending chiefs, and hostile virtues join;
All, from conflicting ranks, of power possest
To rouse, to melt, or to inform the breast.
Where seasoned tools of Avarice prevail,
A nation's eloquence, combined, must fail:
Each flimsy sophistry by turns they try;
The plausive° argument, the daring lie, *plausible*
The artful gloss,° that moral sense confounds, *explanation*
Th'acknowledged thirst of gain that honour wounds:
Bane of ingenuous minds, th'unfeeling sneer,
Which, sudden, turns to stone the falling tear:
They search assiduous, with inverted skill,
For forms of wrong, and precedents of ill;
With impious mockery wrest the sacred page,
And glean up crimes from each remoter age:
Wrung Nature's tortures, shuddering, while you tell,
From scoffing fiends bursts forth the laugh of hell;
In Britain's senate, Misery's pangs give birth
To jests unseemly, and to horrid mirth—[3]
Forbear!—thy virtues but provoke our doom,
And swell th'account of vengeance yet to come;
For, not unmarked in Heaven's impartial plan,
Shall man, proud worm, condemn his fellow man?
And injured Afric, by herself redrest,
Darts her own serpents at her tyrant's breast.
Each vice, to minds depraved by bondage known,
With sure contagion fastens on his own;
In sickly languors melts his nerveless frame,
And blows to rage impetuous Passion's flame:
Fermenting swift, the fiery venom gains
The milky innocence of infant veins;
There swells the stubborn will, damps learning's fire,
The whirlwind wakes of uncontrolled desire,
Sears the young heart to images of woe,
And blasts the buds of Virtue as they blow.
Lo! where reclined, pale Beauty courts the breeze,
Diffused on sofas of voluptuous ease;
With anxious awe, her menial train around,
Catch her faint whispers of half-uttered sound;
See her, in monstrous fellowship, unite
At once the Scythian, and the Sybarite;[4]
Blending repugnant vices, misallied,
Which frugal nature purposed to divide;
See her, with indolence to fierceness joined,
Of body delicate, infirm of mind,
With languid tones imperious mandates urge;
With arm recumbent wield the household scourge;
And with unruffled mien,° and placid sounds, *appearance*
Contriving torture, and inflicting wounds.
Nor, in their palmy walks and spicy groves,
The form benign of rural pleasure roves;
No milkmaid's song, or hum of village talk,
Soothes the lone poet in his evening walk:
No willing arm the flail unwearied plies,
Where the mixed sounds of cheerful labour rise;
No blooming maids, and frolic swains are seen
To pay gay homage to their harvest queen:
No heart-expanding scenes their eyes must prove
Of thriving industry, and faithful love:
But shrieks and yells disturb the balmy air,
Dumb sullen looks of woe announce despair,
And angry eyes through dusky features glare.
Far from the sounding lash the Muses fly,
And sensual riot drowns each finer joy.
Nor less from the gay East,° on essenced wings, *India*
Breathing unnamed perfumes, Contagion springs;
The soft luxurious plague alike pervades
The marble palaces, and rural shades;
Hence, thronged Augusta° builds her rosy bowers, *London*
And decks in summer wreaths her smoky towers;

[1] *Astraea* Greek goddess of justice.

[2] *standard* Flag.

[3] *To jests … mirth* Barbauld refers to some Members of Parliament who laughed in the House of Commons upon hearing of the suffering of slaves.

[4] *Scythian* Ancient nomadic Europeans: synonym for ferocity; *Sybarite* People from the ancient Greek city of Sybaris: synonym for pleasure-loving.

And hence, in summer bow'rs, Art's costly hand
Pours courtly splendours o'er the dazzled land:
The manners melt—One undistinguished blaze
O'erwhelms the sober pomp of elder days;
Corruption follows with gigantic stride,
And scarce vouchsafes his shameless front to hide:
The spreading leprosy taints ev'ry part,
Infects each limb, and sickens at the heart.
Simplicity! most dear of rural maids,
Weeping resigns her violated shades:
Stern Independence from his glebe° retires, *field*
And anxious Freedom eyes her drooping fires;
By foreign wealth are British morals changed,
And Afric's sons, and India's, smile avenged.
    For you, whose tempered ardour long has borne
Untired the labour, and unmoved the scorn;
In Virtue's fasti° be inscribed your fame, *calendar*
And uttered yours with Howard's[1] honoured name,
Friends of the friendless—Hail, ye generous band!
Whose efforts yet arrest Heav'n's lifted hand,
Around whose steady brows, in union bright,
The civic wreath, and Christian's palm unite:
Your merit stands, no greater and no less,
Without, or with the varnish of success;
But seek no more to break a nation's fall,
For ye have saved yourselves—and that is all.
Succeeding times your struggles, and their fate,
With mingled shame and triumph shall relate,
While faithful History, in her various page,
Marking the features of this motley age,
To shed a glory, and to fix a stain,
Tells how you strove, and that you strove in vain.

William Blake, Images of Slavery

The engravings reproduced below are among sixteen plates prepared by William Blake in 1792–93 as illustrations for John Stedman's *Narrative of Five Years' Expedition against the Revolted Negroes of Surinam* (1796).

[1] *Howard* John Howard (1726–90), prison reformer and philanthropist.

from Samuel Taylor Coleridge, *On the Slave Trade* (1796)

The article from which this excerpt is taken was delivered as a lecture in 1795, and published in Coleridge's magazine *The Watchman* the following year.

I have dwelt anxiously on this subject, with a particular view, to the slave-trade, which, I knew, has insinuated in the minds of many, uneasy doubts respecting the existence of a beneficent Deity. And indeed the evils arising from the formation of *imaginary* wants, have in no instance been so dreadfully exemplified, as in this inhuman traffic. We receive from the West-India Islands sugars, rum, cotton, logwood, cocoa, coffee, pimento, ginger, indigo, mahogany, and conserves. Not one of these articles are necessary; indeed with the exception of cotton and mahogany we cannot truly call them even useful: and not one of them is at present attainable by the poor and labouring part of Society. In return we export vast quantities of necessary tools, raiment, and defensive weapons, with great stores of provision. So that in this trade as in most others the poor are employed with unceasing toil first to raise, and then to send away the comforts, which they themselves absolutely want, in order to procure idle superfluities for their masters. If this trade had never existed, no one human being would have been less comfortably cloathed, housed, or nourished. Such is its value—they who would estimate the price which we pay for it, may consult the evidence delivered before the House of Commons.

from William Earle, *Obi; or, the History of Three-Fingered Jack* (1800)

Earle's novel is set against the background of a slave rebellion in Jamaica; it is based on the true story of Jack Mansong, an escaped slave who was said to have gained strength to lead the rebellion from the religion of "obeah," or "obi." The epistolary novel is for the most part made up of letters from one George Stanford, "a resident of Jamaica," to Charles, "his friend in England." The excerpt that appears here is from the letter with which the book opens.

Jack is a noble fellow, and in spite of every cruel hard-hearted planter, I shall repeat the same to the last hour of my life. "Jack is a Negro," say they. "Jack is a MAN," say I.

—"He is a slave."

—"MAN cannot be a slave to MAN."

—"He is my property."

—"How did you acquire that property?"

—"By paying for it."

—"Paying! Paying whom?"

—"Him who brought him from Africa."

—"How did he get possession of him?"

—"He caught him there."

—"Caught! what? Like a wild beast?"

—"No, but he contrived means to convey him into his ship?"

—"Contrived! Then he brought him without his consent?"

—"Very likely."

—"And what is become of that robber?"

—"Robber! He is a very respectable man, who has left off trade, has married the daughter of a rich planter, and now lives very comfortably, after the fatigues of an industrious life."

—"What! Do they hang a poor hard-labouring man, who, driven by despair at the sight of his numerous family ready to starve for want of a bit of bread, takes advantage of a dark night, goes on the highway and frightens the traveller out of a few pieces of gold; and shall a daring ruffian, who is openly guilty of a crime more heinous in its nature and baneful in its effects, get respected by every body and pass his days in the peaceable enjoyment of riches acquired by such infamous means?"

—"I don't understand you; I never heard that the traffic was infamous. Is it not authorised by all the nations of Europe, Asia and America? Have not regulations been made concerning it by all governments?"

—"Very true, but that does not make it more honorable."

Anti-slavery woodcut (c. 1790s).

Mary Robinson, Poems on Slavery (1798, 1800)

Robinson, one of the best-known writers of the age, published a substantial number of works devoted in whole or in part to anti-slavery themes, including "Captivity: A Poem" (1777), "The African" (1798), and "The Negro Girl" (1800). "The African" was published initially in the *Morning Post*, 2 August 1798 and later incorporated into the long poem *The Progress of Liberty*. "The Negro Girl" appeared in Robinson's collection of *Lyrical Tales*.

"The African" (1798)

Shall the poor AFRICAN, the passive Slave,
Born in the bland effulgence of broad day,
Cherish'd by torrid splendours, while around
The plains prolific teem with honey'd stores,
Sink prematurely to a grave obscure,
No tear to grace his ashes? Or suspire
To wear Submission's long and goading chain,
To drink the tear that down his swarthy cheek
Flows fast, to moisten his toil-fever'd lip
Parch'd by the noon-tide blaze? Shall HE endure
The frequent lash, the agonizing scourge,
The day of labour, and the night of pain;
Expose his naked limbs to burning gales;
Faint in the sun, and wither in the storm;
Traverse hot sands, imbibe the morbid breeze,
Wing'd with contagion; while his blister'd feet,
Scorch'd by the vertical and raging beam,
Pour the swift life-stream? Shall his frenzied eyes,
Oh! worst of mortal miseries! behold
The darling of his heart, his sable love,
Selected from the trembling timid throng,
By the wan TYRANT, whose licentious touch
Seals the dark fiat of the SLAVE's despair!

OH LIBERTY! From thee the suppliant claims
The meed of retribution! Thy pure flame
Would light the sense opaque, and warm the spring
Of boundless ecstacy: while Nature's laws,
So violated, plead immortal tongu'd,
For her dark-fated children! Lead them forth
From bondage infamous! Bid Reason own
The dignities of MAN, whate'er his clime,
Estate, or colour. And, O sacred TRUTH!
Tell the proud Lords of traffic, that the breast
Thrice ebon-tinted, owns a crimson tide
As pure,—as clear, as Europe's Sons can boast.

"The Negro Girl" (1800)

I

Dark was the dawn, and o'er the deep
The boist'rous whirlwinds blew;
The Sea-bird wheel'd its circling sweep,
And all was drear to view—
When on the beach that binds the western shore
The love-lorn ZELMA stood, list'ning the tempest's roar.

2

Her eager Eyes beheld the main,
While on her DRACO dear
She madly call'd, but call'd in vain,
No sound could DRACO hear,
Save the shrill yelling of the fateful blast,
While ev'ry Seaman's heart, quick shudder'd as it past.

3

White were the billows, wide display'd
The clouds were black and low;
The Bittern shriek'd, a gliding shade
Seem'd o'er the waves to go!
The livid flash illum'd the clam'rous main,
While ZELMA pour'd, unmark'd, her melancholy strain.

4

"Be still!" she cried, "loud tempest cease!
O! spare the gallant souls:
The thunder rolls—the winds increase—
The Sea, like mountains, rolls!
While, from the deck, the storm-worn victims leap,
And o'er their struggling limbs, the furious billows sweep.

5

"O! barb'rous Pow'r! relentless Fate!
Does Heav'n's high will decree
That some should sleep on beds of state,—
Some, in the roaring Sea?
Some, nurs'd in splendour, deal Oppression's blow,
While worth and DRACO pine—in Slavery and woe!

6

"Yon Vessel oft has plough'd the main
With human traffic fraught;
Its cargo,—our dark Sons of pain—
For worldly treasure bought!
What had they done?—O Nature tell me why—
Is taunting scorn the lot, of thy dark progeny?

7

"Thou gav'st, in thy caprice, the Soul
Peculiarly enshrin'd;
Nor from the ebon Casket stole
The Jewel of the mind!
Then wherefore let the suff'ring Negro's breast
Bow to his fellow, MAN, in brighter colours drest.

8

"Is it the dim and glossy hue
That marks him for despair?—
While men with blood their hands embrue,
And mock the wretch's pray'r?
Shall guiltless Slaves the Scourge of tyrants feel,
And, e'en before their GOD! unheard, unpitied kneel.

9

"Could the proud rulers of the land
Our Sable race behold;
Some bow'd by torture's Giant hand
And others, basely sold!
Then would they pity Slaves, and cry, with shame,
Whate'er their TINTS may be, their SOULS are still the same!

10

"Why seek to mock the Ethiop's face?
Why goad our hapless kind?
Can features alienate the race—
Is there no kindred mind?
Does not the cheek which vaunts the roseate hue
Oft blush for crimes, that Ethiops never knew?

11

"Behold! the angry waves conspire
To check the barb'rous toil!
While wounded Nature's vengeful ire—
Roars, round this trembling Isle!
And hark! her voice re-echoes in the wind—
Man was not form'd by Heav'n, to trample on his kind!

12

"Torn from my Mother's aching breast,
My Tyrant sought my love—
But, in the Grave shall ZELMA rest,
E'er she will faithless prove—
No DRACO!—Thy companion I will be
To that celestial realm, where Negroes shall be free!

13

"The Tyrant WHITE MAN taught my mind—
The letter'd page to trace;—
He taught me in the Soul to find
No tint, as in the face:
He bade my Reason, blossom like the tree—
But fond affection gave, the ripen'd fruits to thee.

14

"With jealous rage he mark'd my love;
He sent thee far away;—
And prison'd in the plantain grove—
Poor ZELMA pass'd the day—
But ere the moon rose high above the main,
ZELMA, and Love contriv'd, to break the Tyrant's chain.

15

"Swift, o'er the plain of burning Sand
My course I bent to thee;
And soon I reach'd the billowy strand
Which bounds the stormy Sea.—
DRACO! my Love! Oh yet, thy ZELMA's soul
Springs ardently to thee,—impatient of controul.

16

"Again the lightning flashes white—
The rattling cords among!
Now, by the transient vivid light,
I mark the frantic throng!
Now up the tatter'd shrouds my DRACO flies—
While o'er the plunging prow, the curling billows rise.

17

"The topmast falls—three shackled slaves—
Cling to the Vessel's side!
Now lost amid the madd'ning waves—
Now on the mast they ride—
See! on the forecastle my DRACO stands
And now he waves his chain, now clasps his bleeding hands.

18

"Why, cruel WHITE-MAN! when away
My sable Love was torn,
Why did you let poor ZELMA stay,
On Afric's sands to mourn?
No! ZELMA is not left, for she will prove
In the deep troubled main, her fond—her faithful LOVE."

19

The lab'ring Ship was now a wreck,
The Shrouds were flutt'ring wide!
The rudder gone, the lofty deck
Was rock'd from side to side—
Poor ZELMA's eyes now dropp'd their last big tear,
While, from her tawny cheek, the blood recoil'd with fear.

20

Now frantic, on the sands she roam'd,
Now shrieking stop'd to view
Where high the liquid mountains foam'd,
Around the exhausted crew—
'Till, from the deck, her DRACO's well known form
Sprung mid the yawning waves, and buffetted the Storm.

21

Long, on the swelling surge sustain'd
Brave DRACO sought the shore,
Watch'd the dark Maid, but ne'er complain'd,
Then sunk, to gaze no more!
Poor ZELMA saw him buried by the wave—
And, with her heart's true Love, plung'd in a wat'ry grave.

from Dorothy Wordsworth, *The Grasmere Journal*

As the following excerpt from Dorothy Wordsworth's journals indicates, brutality on slave ships could also be directed at members of the crew.

Monday Morning [March 15th] We sat reading the poems and I read a little German … During W's[1] absence a sailor who was travelling from Liverpool to Whitehaven called. He was faint and pale when he knocked at the door, a young man very well dressed. We sat by the kitchen fire talking with him for 2 hours—he told us most interesting stories of his life. His name was Isaac Chapel—he had been at sea since he was 15 years old. He was by trade a sail-maker. His last voyage was to the coast of Guinea. He had been on board a slave ship the captain's name Maxwell where one man had been killed a boy put to lodge with the pigs & was half eaten,

[1] *W's* William Wordsworth's.

one boy set to watch in the hot sun till he dropped down dead. He had been cast away in North America and had travelled 30 days among the Indians where he had been well treated. He had twice swum from a king's ship in the night & escaped, he said he would rather be in hell than be pressed.[1] He was now going to wait in England to appear against Captain Maxwell—"Oh he's a rascal, sir, he ought to be put in the papers!" The poor man had not been in bed since Friday night—he left Liverpool at 2 o'clock on Saturday morning. He had called at a farm house to beg victuals and had been refused. The woman said she would give him nothing—"Won't you? Then I can't help it." He was excessively like my brother John.

from Thomas Clarkson, *The History of the Rise, Progress and Accomplishment of the Abolition of the African Slave Trade* (1808)

In 1785, Clarkson (1760–1846) was the author of a prize-winning essay at Cambridge University on "slavery and commerce of the human species, particularly the African." Thereafter he devoted enormous energy to the abolitionist cause. He played a leading role in founding the Society for Effecting the Abolition of the Slave Trade in 1787, and in pressing for the abolition of slavery itself after the halting of the slave trade in 1807.

Let us examine the state of the unhappy Africans, reduced to slavery in this manner, while on board the vessels, which are to convey them across the ocean to other lands. And here I must observe at once, that, as far as this part of the evil is concerned, I am at a loss to describe it. Where shall I find words to express properly their sorrow, as arising from the reflection of being parted for ever from their friends, their relatives, and their country? Where shall I find language to paint in appropriate colours the horror of mind brought on by thoughts of their future unknown destination, of which they can augur nothing but misery from all that they have yet seen? How shall I make known their situation, while labouring under painful disease, or while struggling in the suffocating holds of their prisons, like animals inclosed in an exhausted receiver? How shall I describe their feelings as exposed to all the personal indignities, which lawless appetite or brutal passion may suggest? How shall I exhibit their sufferings as determining to refuse sustenance and die, or as resolving to break their chains, and, disdaining to live as slaves, to punish their oppressors? How shall I give an idea of their agony, when under various punishments and tortures for their reputed crimes? Indeed every part of this subject defies my powers, and I must therefore satisfy myself and the reader with a general representation, or in the words of a celebrated member of Parliament, that "Never was so much human suffering condensed in so small a space."

I now come to the evil, as it has been proved to arise in the third case; or to consider the situation of the unhappy victims of the trade, when their painful voyages are over, or after they have been landed upon their destined shores. And here we are to view them first under the degrading light of cattle. We are to see them examined, handled, selected, separated, and sold. Alas! relatives are separated from relatives, as if, like cattle, they had no rational intellect, no power of feeling the nearness of relationship, nor sense of the duties belonging to the ties of life! We are next to see them labouring, and this for the benefit of those, to whom they are under no obligation, by any law either natural or divine, to obey. We are to see them, if refusing the commands of their purchasers, however weary, or feeble, or indisposed, subject to corporal punishments, and, if forcibly resisting them, to death. We are to see them in a state of general degradation and misery. The knowledge, which their oppressors have of their own crime in having violated the rights of nature, and of the disposition of the injured to seek all opportunities of revenge, produces a fear, which dictates to them the necessity of a system of treatment by which they shall keep up a wide distinction between the two, and by which the noble feelings of the latter shall be kept down, and their spirits broken. We are to see them again subject to individual persecution, as anger, or malice, or any bad passion may suggest. Hence the whip—the chain—the iron-collar. Hence the various modes of private torture, of which so many accounts have been truly given. Nor can such horrible cruelties be discovered so as to be made punishable, while the testimony of any number of the

[1] *pressed* Forced into naval service. "Press gangs" were authorized to force men into the Navy at this period.

oppressed is invalid against the oppressors, however they may be offences against the laws. And, lastly, we are to see their innocent offspring, against whose person liberty the shadow of an argument cannot be advanced, inheriting all the miseries of their parents' lot.

from Matthew "Monk" Lewis, *Journal of A West India Proprietor* (1815–17)

Lewis, whose father was the absentee owner of sugar plantations in Jamaica and the Deputy Secretary of War, became well known with the publication of *The Monk*, a sensational Gothic novel written in a ten-week period when he was nineteen years old. Lewis inherited his father's property in 1812, and made two trips to Jamaica (in 1815–16 and 1817–18) with a view to ascertaining the condition of the plantations and ameliorating conditions for the slaves. His journals were first offered for publication in 1817, but did not appear in print until 1834, sixteen years after Lewis's death from yellow fever, during the return voyage after his second residence in Jamaica.

Though Lewis was clearly considerably more humane than most plantation owners, he opposed any move to abolish slavery, on the grounds that it was necessary to the plantation economy.

15 January 1815

The offspring of a white man and black woman is a *mulatto*; the mulatto and black produce a *sambo*; from the mulatto and white comes the *quadroon*; from the quadroon and white the *mustee*; the child of a mustee by a white man is called a *musteefino*; while the children of a musteefino are free by law, and rank as white persons to all intents and purposes. I think it is Long who asserts, that two mulattoes will never have children; but, as far as the most positive assurances can go, since my arrival in Jamaica, I have reason to believe the contrary, and that mulattoes breed together just as well as blacks and whites; but they are almost universally weak and effeminate persons, and thus their children are very difficult to rear. On a sugar estate one black is considered as more than equal to two mulattoes. Beautiful as are their forms in general, and easy and graceful as are their movements (which, indeed, appear to me so striking, that they cannot fail to excite the admiration of any one who has ever looked with delight on statues), still the women of colour are deficient in one of the most requisite points of female beauty. When Oromases[1] was employed in the formation of woman, and said,— "Let her enchanting bosom resemble the celestial spheres," he must certainly have suffered the negress to slip out of his mind. Young or old, I have not yet seen such a thing as a *bosom*.

16 January 1815

I never witnessed on the stage a scene so picturesque as a negro village. I walked through my own to-day, and visited the houses of the drivers, and other principal persons; and if I were to decide according to my own taste, I should infinitely have preferred their habitations to my own. Each house is surrounded by a separate garden, and the whole village is intersected by lanes, bordered with all kinds of sweet-smelling and flowering plants; but not such gardens as those belonging to our English cottages, where a few cabbages and carrots just peep up and grovel upon the earth between hedges, in square narrow beds, and where the tallest tree is a gooseberry bush: the vegetables of the negroes are all cultivated in their provision-grounds; these form their *kitchen*-gardens, and these are all for ornament or luxury, and are filled with a profusion of oranges, shaddocks, cocoa-nuts, and peppers of all descriptions: in particular I was shown the abba, or palm tree, resembling the cocoa-tree, but much more beautiful, as its leaves are larger and more numerous, and, feathering to the ground as they grow old, they form a kind of natural arbour. It bears a large fruit, or rather vegetable, towards the top of the tree, in shape like the cone of the pine, but formed of seeds, some scarlet and bright as coral, others of a brownish-red or purple. The abba requires a length of years to arrive at maturity: a very fine one, which was shown me this morning, was supposed to be upwards of an hundred years old; and one of a very moderate size had been planted at the least twenty years, and had only borne fruit once.

It appears to me a strong proof of the good treatment which the negroes on Cornwall have been accustomed to receive, that there are many very old people upon it; I saw to-day a woman near a hundred years of age; and I am

[1] *Oromases* The good principle, the god of light, in ancient Persian thought.

told that there are several of sixty, seventy, and eighty. I was glad, also, to find, that several negroes who have obtained their freedom, and possess little properties of their own in the mountains, and at Savannah la Mar, look upon my estate so little as the scene of their former sufferings while slaves, that they frequently come down to pass a few days in their ancient habitations with their former companions, by way of relaxation. One woman in particular expressed her hopes, that I should not be offended at her still coming to Cornwall now and then, although she belonged to it no longer; and begged me to give directions before my return to England, that her visits should not be hindered on the grounds of her having no business there.

My visit to Jamaica has at least produced one advantage to myself. Several runaways, who had disappeared for some time (some even for several months), have again made their appearance in the field, and I have desired that no questions should be asked. On the other hand, after enjoying herself during the Saturday and Sunday, which were allowed for holidays on my arrival, one of my ladies chose *to pull foot,* and did not return from her hiding-place in the mountains till this morning. Her name is Marcia; but so unlike is she to Addison's Marcia, that she is not only as black as Juba, (instead of being "fair, oh! how divinely fair!") but,—whereas Sempronius[1] complains, that "Marcia, the lovely Marcia, is left behind," the complaint against my heroine is, that "Marcia, the lovely Marcia" is always running away. In excuse for her disappearance she alleged, that so far was her husband from thinking that "she towered above her sex," that he had called her "a very bad woman," which had provoked her so much, that she could not bear to stay with him; and she assured me, that he was himself "a very bad man"; which, if true, was certainly enough to justify any lady, black or white, in making a little incognito excursion for a week or so; therefore, as it appeared to be nothing more than a conjugal quarrel, and as Marcia engaged never to run away any more (at the same time allowing that she had suffered her resentment to carry her too far, when it had carried her all the way to the mountains), I desired that an act of oblivion might be passed in favour of Cato's daughter, and away she went, quite happy, to pick hog's meat.

The negro houses are composed of wattles[2] on the outside, with rafters of sweet-wood, and are well plastered within and white-washed; they consist of two chambers, one for cooking and the other for sleeping, and are, in general, well furnished with chairs, tables, etc., and I saw none without a four-post bedstead and plenty of bed-clothes; for, in spite of the warmth of the climate, when the sun is not above the horizon the negro always feels very chilly. I am assured that many of my slaves are very rich (and their property is inviolable), and that they are never without salt provisions, porter, and even wine, to entertain their friends and their visitors from the bay or the mountains. As I passed through their grounds, many little requests were preferred to me: one wanted an additional supply of lime for the whitewashing his house; another was building a new house for a superannuated wife (for they have all so much decency as to call their sexual attachments by a conjugal name), and wanted a little assistance towards the finishing it; a third requested a new axe to work with; and several entreated me to negotiate the purchase of some relation or friend belonging to another estate, and with whom they were anxious to be reunited: but all their requests were for additional indulgences; not one complained of ill-treatment, hunger, or over-work.

Poor Nicholas gave me a fresh instance of his being one of those whom Fortune pitches upon to show her spite: he has had four children, none of whom are alive; and the eldest of them, a fine little girl of four years old, fell into the mill-stream, and was drowned before any one was aware of her danger. His wife told me that she had had fifteen children, had taken the utmost care of them, and yet had now but two alive: she said, indeed, fifteen at the first, but she afterwards corrected herself, and explained that she had had "twelve whole children and three half ones"; by which she meant miscarriages.

Besides the profits arising from their superabundance of provisions, which the better sort of negroes are enabled to sell regularly once a week at Savannah la Mar to a considerable amount, they keep a large stock of poultry, and pigs without number; which latter cost their owners

[1] *Addison's Marcia ... Sempronius* Marcia and Sempronius are characters in Joseph Addison's *Cato* (1713).

[2] *wattles* Woven branches.

but little, though they cost me a great deal; for they generally make their way into the cane-pieces, and sometimes eat me up an hogshead of sugar in the course of the morning: but the most expensive of the planter's enemies are the rats, whose numbers are incredible, and are so destructive that a reward is given for killing them. During the last six months my agent has paid for three thousand rats killed upon Cornwall. Nor is the sugar which they consume the worst damage which they commit; the worst mischief is, that if, through the carelessness of those whose business it is to supply the mill, one cane which has been gnawed by the rats is allowed admittance, that single damaged piece is sufficient to produce acidity enough to spoil the whole sugar.

24 February 1815

On the Sunday after my first arrival, the whole body of Eboe negroes came to me to complain of the attorney, and more particularly of one of the book-keepers. I listened to them, if not with unwearied patience, at least with unsubdued fortitude, for above an hour and a half; and finding some grounds for their complaint against the latter, in a few days I went down to their quarter of the village, told them that to please them I had discharged the book-keeper, named a day for examining their other grievances, and listened to them for an hour more. When the day of trial came, they sent me word that they were perfectly satisfied, and had no complaint to make. I was, therefore, much surprised to receive a visit from Edward, the Eboe, yesterday evening, who informed me, that during my absence his fellows had formed a plan of making a complaint *en masse* to a neighbouring magistrate; and that, not only against the attorney, but against myself "for not listening to them when they were injured"; and Edward claimed great merit with me for having prevented their taking this step, and convinced them, that while I was on the estate myself, there could be no occasion for applying to a third person. Now, having made me aware of my great obligations to him, here Edward meant the matter to rest; but being a good deal incensed at their ingratitude, I instantly sent for the Eboes, and enquired into the matter; when it appeared, that Edward (who is a clever fellow, and has great influence over the rest) had first goaded them into a resolution of complaining to a magistrate, had then stopped them from putting their plan into execution, and that the whole was a plot of Edward's, in order to make a merit with me for himself at the expense of his countrymen. However, as they confessed their having had the intention of applying to Mr. Hill as a magistrate, I insisted upon their executing their intention. I told them, that as Mr. Hill was the person whom they had selected for their protector, to Mr. Hill they should go; that they should either make their complaint to him against me, or confess that they had been telling lies, and had no complaint to make; and that, as the next day was to be a play-day given them by me, instead of passing it at home in singing and dancing, they should pass it at the Bay in stating their grievances.

This threw them into terrible confusion; they cried out that they wanted to make no complaint whatever, and that it was all Edward's fault, who had misled them. Three of them, one after the other, gave him the lie to his face; and each and all (Edward as well as the rest) declared that go to the Bay they absolutely would *not*. The next morning they were all at the door waiting for my coming out: they positively refused to go to Mr. Hill, and begged and prayed, and humbled themselves; now scraping and bowing to me, and then blackguarding Edward with all their might and main; and when I ordered the driver to take charge of them, and carry them to Mr. Hill, some of them fairly took to their heels, and ran away. However, the rest soon brought them back again, for they swore that if one went, all should go; and away they were marched, in a string of about twenty, with the driver at their head. When they got to the Bay, they told Mr. Hill that, as to their massa, they had no complaint to make against him, except that he had compelled them to make one; and what they said against the attorney was so trifling, that the magistrate bade the driver take them all back again. Upon which they slunk away to their houses, while the Creoles cried out "Shame! shame!" as they passed along.

Indeed, the Creoles could not have received a greater pleasure than the mortification of the Eboes; for the two bodies hate each other as cordially as the Guelphs and Ghibellines;[1] and after their departure for the Bay, I heard the head cook haranguing a large audience, and declaring it to be her fixed opinion, "that massa ought to sell all the Eboes, and buy Creoles instead." Probably, Mrs. Cook

[1] *Guelphs and Ghibellines* Opposing factions in political struggles between papal and imperial powers during the later Middle Ages.

was not the less loud in her exclamations against the ingratitude of the Eboes, from her own loyalty having lately been questioned. She had found fault one day in the hospital with some women who feigned sickness in order to remain idle. "You no work willing for massa," said Mrs. Cook, "and him so vex, him say him go to Kingston to-morrow, and him wish him neber come back again!"—"What!" cried Philippa, the mad woman, "you wish massa neber come back from Kingston?" So she gave Mrs. Cook a box on the ear with all her might; upon which Mrs. Cook snatched up a stick and broke the mad woman's pate with it. But though she could beat a hole in her head, she never could beat out of it her having said that she wished massa might never come back. And although Philippa has recovered her senses, in her belief of Mrs. Cook's disloyalty she continues firm; and they never meet without renewing the dispute.

To-day being a play-day, the gaiety of the negroes was promoted by a distribution of an additional quantity of salt-fish (which forms a most acceptable ingredient in their pepper-pots), and as much rum and sugar as they chose to drink. But there was also a dinner prepared at the house where the "white people" reside, expressly for none but the *piccaninny-mothers*; that is, for the women who had children living. I had taken care, when this play-day was announced by the head driver, to make him inform the negroes that they were indebted for it entirely to these mothers; and to show them the more respect, I went to them after dinner myself, and drank their healths. The most respectable blacks on the estate were also assembled in the room; and I then told them that clothes would wear out, and money would be spent, and that I wished to give them something more lasting than clothes or money. The law only allows them, as a matter of right, every alternate Saturday for themselves, and holidays for three days at Christmas, which, with all Sundays, forms their whole legal time of relaxation. I therefore granted them as a matter of right, and of which no person should deprive them on any account whatever, *every* Saturday to cultivate their grounds; and in addition to their holidays at Christmas, I gave them for play-days Good-Friday, the second Friday in October, and the second Friday in July. By which means, they will in future have the same number of holidays four times a year, which hitherto they have been allowed only once, *i.e.* at Christmas. The first is to be called "the royal play-day," in honour of that excellent Princess, the Duchess of York; and the negroes are directed to give three cheers upon the head driver's announcing "The health of our good lady, HRH the Duchess of York." And I told them, that before my leaving the island, I should hear them drink this health, and should not fail to let Her Royal Highness know, that the negroes of Cornwall drank her health every year. This evidently touched the right chord of their vanity, and they all bowed and courtesied down to the very ground, and said, that would do them much high honour. The ninth being my own birthday, the July play-day is to be called "the massa's"; and that in October is to be in honour of the piccaninny-mothers, from whom it is to take its name.

The poor creatures overflowed with gratitude; and the prospective indulgences which had just been announced, gave them such an increase of spirits, that on returning to my own residence, they fell to singing and dancing again with as much violence as if they had been a pack of French furies at the Opera. The favourite song of the light was, "Since massa come, we very well off"; which words they repeated in chorus, without intermission (dancing all the time), for hours together; till, at half-past three, neither my eyes nor my brain could endure it any longer, and I was obliged to send them word that I wanted to go to bed, and could not sleep till the noise should cease.

1 May 1815 (Friday)

This morning I signed the manumission of Nicholas Cameron, the best of my mulatto carpenters. He had been so often on the very point of getting his liberty, and still the cup was dashed from his lips, that I had promised to set him free, whenever he could procure an able negro as his substitute; although being a good workman, a single negro was by no means an adequate price in exchange. On my arrival this year I found that he had agreed to pay 150*l.* for a female negro, and the woman was approved of by my trustee. But on enquiry it appeared that she had a child, from which she was unwilling to separate, and that her owner refused to sell the child, except at a most unreasonable price. Here then was an insurmountable objection to my accepting her, and Nicholas was told to his great mortification, that he must look out for another substitute. The woman, on her part, was determined to belong to Cornwall estate and no other: so she told her owner, that if he attempted to sell her elsewhere she would make away with herself, and on his ordering her to prepare for a removal to a neighbouring proprietor's, she disappeared, and concealed herself so well, that for some time she was believed to have put her threats of suicide into execution. The idea of losing his 150*l.* frightened her master so completely, that he declared himself ready to let me have the child at a fair price, as well as the mother, if she ever should be found; and her friends having conveyed this assurance to her, she thought proper to emerge from her hiding-place, and the bargain was arranged finally. The titles, however, were not yet made out, and as the time of my departure for Hordley was arrived, these were ordered to be got ready against my return, when the negroes were to be delivered over to me, and Nicholas was to be set free. In the meanwhile, the child was sent by her mistress (a free mulatto) to hide some stolen ducks upon a distant property, and on her return blabbed out the errand: in consequence the mistress was committed to prison for theft; and no sooner was she released, than she revenged herself upon the poor girl by giving her thirty lashes with the cattle-whip, inflicted with all the severity of vindictive malice. This treatment of a child of such tender years reduced her to such a state, as made the magistrates think it right to send her for protection to the workhouse, until the conduct of the mistress should have been enquired into. In the meanwhile, as the result of the enquiry might be the setting the girl at liberty, the joint title for her and her mother could not be made out, and thus poor Nicholas's manumission was at a stand-still again. The magistrates at length decided, that although the chastisement had been severe, yet (according to the medical report) it was not such as to authorise the sending the mistress to be tried at the assizes. She was accordingly dismissed from farther investigation, and the girl was once more considered as belonging to me, as soon as the title could be made out. But the fatality which had so often prevented Nicholas from obtaining his freedom, was not weary yet. On the very morning, when he was to sign the title, a person whose signature was indispensable, was thrown out of his chaise, the wheel of which passed over his head, and he was rendered incapable of transacting business for several weeks. Yesterday, the titles were at length brought to me complete, and this morning put Nicholas in possession of the object, in the pursuit of which he has experienced such repeated disappointments. The conduct of the poor child's mulatto mistress in this case was most unpardonable, and is only one of numerous instances of a similar description, which have been mentioned to me. Indeed, I have every reason to believe, that nothing can be uniformly more wretched, than the life of the slaves of free people of colour in Jamaica; nor would any thing contribute more to the relief of the black population, than the prohibiting by law any mulatto to become the owner of a slave for the future. Why should not rich people of colour be served by poor people of colour, hiring them as domestics? It seldom happens that mulattoes are in possession of plantations; but when a white man dies, who happens to possess twenty negroes, he will divide them among his brown family, leaving (we may say) five to each of his four children. These are too few to be employed in plantation work; they are, therefore, ordered to maintain their owner by some means or other, and which means are frequently not the most honest, the most frequent being the travelling about as higglers, and exchanging the trumpery contents of their packs and boxes with plantation negroes for stolen rum and sugar. I confess I cannot see why, on such bequest being made, the law should not order the negroes to be sold, and the produce of the sale paid to the mulatto heirs, but absolutely prohibiting the mulattoes from becoming proprietors of the negroes themselves. Every man of humanity must wish that slavery, even in its best and most mitigated form, had never found a legal sanction, and must regret that its system is now so incorporated with the welfare of Great Britain as well as of Jamaica, as to make its extirpation an absolute impossibility, without the certainty of producing worse mischiefs than the one which we annihilate. But certainly there can be no sort of occasion for continuing in the colonies the existence of *domestic slavery,* which neither contributes to the security of the colonies themselves, nor to the opulence of the mother-country, the revenue of which derived from colonial duties would suffer no defalcation whatever, even if neither whites nor blacks in the West Indies were suffered to employ slaves, except in plantation labour.

George Gordon, Lord Byron

1788 – 1824

George Gordon, Lord Byron, was one of the most influential literary figures of the nineteenth century. His works—the long poems *Childe Harold's Pilgrimage* and *Don Juan* among them —were tremendous popular successes, and the Byronic Hero has become a cultural icon. Byron himself, handsome and charming, sexually unconventional, politically iconoclastic, has been alternately celebrated and reviled from his own time to the present.

Byron's beginnings were inauspicious. He was born in near-poverty on 22 January 1788, lame in one leg (probably the result of a form of cerebral palsy). His father, Captain John ("Mad Jack") Byron, a notorious spendthrift and rake, had married Byron's mother, the Scottish heiress Catherine Gordon, for her money. This he quickly squandered, afterward fleeing to France. Byron and his mother moved to Aberdeen. Here Byron lived out his first ten years, the object of his mother's capricious mixture of love and sudden overwhelming rages, deeply conscious of his lameness, and steeped in Calvinism. Here, too, at ten years old, he was regularly molested by his nursemaid.

In 1798 Byron's great-uncle, the fifth Lord Byron, died childless, and Byron inherited the title. He and his mother moved to the family's ancestral, debt-encumbered home, Newstead Abbey, in Nottinghamshire. Byron was sent to school, first to an academy in Dulwich, then to Harrow in 1801. Around 1801 he also met for the first time his half-sister Augusta, the product of an earlier marriage of his father's. In 1805 Byron entered Trinity College, Cambridge University, where he made the most lasting friendships of his life. He also contracted huge debts to which he would only add in the future.

Byron took a degree from Cambridge in 1807. In the same year, he published his first poetry collection, *Hours of Idleness*. The book was excoriated in the press as pretentious and derivative; Byron responded in 1809 with the verse satire *English Bards and Scotch Reviewers*, in which he attacked the most notable of his critics and many of the leading poets of the day. In that same year, Byron came of age and took possession of Newstead Abbey, where he held riotous parties; as a result of carousing and redecorating, his mountain of debt grew larger. In March he made his first appearance in the House of Lords, and in July, after having incurred more debt to finance himself, he set off on a trip through Europe and the Near East, areas largely closed to the English as a result of the Napoleonic Wars. This journey began an intense attachment to Greece that would color the rest of Byron's life and writing and allowed him to fulfill the homosexual desires that he had been unable to explore in England (where sodomy was a capital crime). During this time he also began *Childe Harold's Pilgrimage,* the work that would make him a celebrity.

Featuring a journey almost identical to that which Byron himself had just completed, undertaken by a mysteriously gloomy hero, *Childe Harold's Pilgrimage*, Cantos I&II, launched both the figure of the "Byronic Hero" and the association between that figure and Byron that the poet would alternately embrace and seek to evade for the remainder of his life. The poem cunningly managed to weave elements from familiar genres such as travel writing, gothic novels, and sentimental literature with experiments in mood and tone. It enthralled its readers. Byron wrote in Spenserian stanzas, but as the poem progressed he began to bend this stiff form so that it became his own. (Harold's discoveries and the narrator's own growing observational and meditative abilities find their mirror in the rhythms of the verse.) With its panoramic focus, high-flown tone, and alluringly aloof protagonist, *Childe Harold's Pilgrimage* marked an important moment in English and European literature.

Now a celebrity, Byron played that role with gusto. He became a darling of Whig society and indulged in a series of affairs, most scandalously with Lady Caroline Lamb. In addition, some time in 1813 Byron began a sexual relationship with his half-sister Augusta. This was to prove his undoing, but it was nonetheless the deepest and most lasting attachment of his life. He also continued writing, producing a collection of hugely popular works ranging from the short lyrics of *Hebrew Melodies* to the "Eastern Tales" produced in 1813 and 1814. In this series of long narrative poems, set in the Near East, he fleshed out the anti-heroic figure he had sketched in *Childe Harold's Pilgrimage*. The protagonists of the "Tales" stood aloof from those who surround them, tortured by a mysterious but deeply-felt guilt. Brave, glamorous, and in each case devoted utterly to one woman (who herself was an idealized romantic heroine), they were nonetheless fated to be outcasts. Described most fully in the first of the "Eastern Tales," "The Giaour," the hero reached his final refinement in the last, "Lara." The public embraced this figure, and a literary type entered into the canon with a vengeance: the writing of the next hundred years would be crowded with Byronic Heroes.

In January of 1815, Byron married Annabella Millbanke, a sheltered heiress. The marriage was based on a short courtship and false hopes, and the two participants were utterly unsuited. Byron was psychologically abusive to his wife, whose piety and conventionality were a constant irritant to him. At the end of 1815, a few weeks after the birth of their daughter, Ada Augusta, Annabella left him. A public scandal, aided by unauthorized publication of Byron's poems and his wife's revelations about his incest with Augusta Leigh, followed. Now a social outcast, Byron departed for Europe, never to return. He continued to communicate with his friends in England through a voluminous and revealingly frank series of letters that detailed his sexual adventures, his political and literary beliefs, and his continued involvement with affairs in England. Even if he had written no poetry, the letters would qualify Byron for a place as one of England's foremost authors: urbane, broad-ranging, dazzling, and hilarious, they make for riveting and delightful reading.

Landing in Belgium in April of 1816, Byron made his way through scenes—including a visit to Waterloo—which he would describe in the final two cantos of *Childe Harold*. At Geneva he met Mary and Percy Shelley. They had travelled to Switzerland accompanied by Mary's stepsister Claire Clairmont, who had had a brief sexual relationship with Byron in England. The two poets formed an intimate and intellectually rich friendship, and the four lived in close proximity during the summer. Byron resumed his involvement with Claire; she bore him a daughter, Allegra, in January of 1817.

When the Shelleys departed for England in August, Byron journeyed to Venice, where he lived for the next three years. Here he flung himself into a period of promiscuity (he estimated that he had sex with over two hundred women during this time), but continued to work as well, producing his verse drama *Manfred*, the fourth canto of *Childe Harold*, and the humorous *Beppo*, written in *ottava rima*. This colloquial Italian form was fiendishly ill-adapted to English, but Byron made it his own, also using it to produce his masterpiece, *Don Juan*, which he began in July of 1818.

Don Juan is the creation of an author who has found his *métier*. It is the longest satirical poem in English, a rollicking tale of a young hero who bears the same name as the seducer but resembles him in no other way. Juan, passive and sweet-natured, is seduced by women ranging from a family friend to Catherine the Great. His adventures take him on a journey from Spain to London by way of Greece and Russia. Byron was thus able to mock not only current social mores but also his own previous poems, Don Juan standing as a kind of anti-Byronic Hero. He took as his model for the poem a slight satire written in 1817 by John Hookham Frere in *ottava rima*, but *Don Juan* is also descended from Swift's *Gulliver's Travels*, and Sterne's *Tristram Shandy*. As with the latter, the focus of Byron's poem is not so much what is narrated as its narrator, a garrulous, easily distracted gentleman who at times bears a remarkable resemblance to the author. Byron's publisher, friends, and the critical establishment condemned *Don Juan* for its immorality, but he himself relished it, asserting that he had written it only "to giggle and make giggle"—a comment typically Byronic in its attempt to deny responsibility by invoking comedy. For all its author's disclaimers, *Don Juan* is no mere comic throwaway. It is a text of great cultural and political scope and a work of questing philosophy, arguably the best of its age.

In April of 1819 Byron met Countess Teresa Guiccioli, a young Italian woman married to a much older man. Almost immediately they began a socially-sanctioned affair that would last, with reasonable fidelity, until the end of Byron's life. Through her family, Byron was drawn into nationalist schemes to free Italy from the Austrians. When the family was exiled to Pisa in 1821 as a result of this plotting, Byron followed. The Shelleys were now based in Pisa, and Byron became one of their group. Soon, however, this "Pisan circle" fell apart, first because of Shelley's anger over Byron's callous treatment of Allegra (she had joined him in Venice in 1819, only for him first to neglect her and then send her to be brought up in a convent, where she died, unvisited by him, in 1822), then because of Byron's decision to follow the Gambas to Genoa, and finally because of Shelley's own death in July 1822.

Despite these upheavals, Byron wrote at a furious pace. Between 1819 and 1823 he produced numerous works, including a series of closet dramas (including *Sardanapalus*, *The Two Foscari*, and *Cain*), and his biting satire of England under George III, *The Vision of Judgment.* He also continued *Don Juan*, finishing sixteen cantos by the end of 1823.

In 1824 Byron organized an expedition to assist the Greeks in their fight for independence from the Turks. Settled in the marsh town of Missolonghi, he financed and trained soldiers. Exhausted and worn down, he contracted a fever and died on 19 April, aged thirty-six, his death hastened by copious bloodletting performed by his incompetent doctors.

⌘⌘⌘

Sun of the Sleepless

Sun of the sleepless! melancholy star!
Whose tearful beam glows tremulously far,
That show'st the darkness thou canst not dispel,
How like art thou to joy remembered well!
So gleams the past, the light of other days,
Which shines, but warms not with its powerless rays;
A night-beam Sorrow watcheth to behold,
Distinct, but distant—clear—but, oh how cold!
—1814

She walks in beauty

1

She walks in beauty, like the night
Of cloudless climes and starry skies;
And all that's best of dark and bright
Meet in her aspect and her eyes:
Thus mellow'd to that tender light
Which heaven to gaudy day denies.

2

One shade the more, one ray the less,
Had half impair'd the nameless grace
Which waves in every raven tress,
Or softly lightens o'er her face;

Where thoughts serenely sweet express
How pure, how dear their dwelling place.

3

And on that cheek, and o'er that brow,
So soft, so calm, yet eloquent,
The smiles that win, the tints that glow,
But tell of days in goodness spent,
A mind at peace with all below,
A heart whose love is innocent!

—1815 [WRITTEN 1814]

When we two parted [1]

1

When we two parted
In silence and tears,
Half broken-hearted
To sever for years,
Pale grew thy cheek and cold,
Colder thy kiss;
Truly that hour foretold
Sorrow to this.

2

The dew of the morning
Sunk chill on my brow—
It felt like the warning
Of what I feel now.
Thy vows are all broken,
And light is thy fame;
I hear thy name spoken,
And share in its shame.

3

They name thee before me,
A knell to mine ear;
A shudder comes o'er me—
Why wert thou so dear?
They know not I knew thee,
Who knew thee too well:—
Long, long shall I rue thee,
Too deeply to tell.

4

In secret we met—
In silence I grieve,
That thy heart could forget,
Thy spirit deceive.
If I should meet thee
After long years,
How should I greet thee!—
With silence and tears.

—1816

Stanzas for Music [2]

1

There's not a joy the world can give like that it takes away,
When the glow of early thought declines in feeling's dull decay;
'Tis not on youth's smooth cheek the blush alone, which fades so fast,
But the tender bloom of heart is gone, ere youth itself be past.

2

Then the few whose spirits float above the wreck of happiness,
Are driven o'er the shoals of guilt or ocean of excess:
The magnet of their course is gone, or only points in vain
The shore to which their shiver'd sail shall never stretch again.

[1] *When we two parted* This poem has a complex history, at least partially because Byron deliberately misdated the date of its composition as 1816, in order to hide its true subject. In fact, the lines were written in 1815, and their subject is Lady Frances Wedderburn Webster, the wife of a friend of Byron's; Byron had heard gossip about her affair with the Duke of Wellington. Byron himself had had a brief "platonic" affair with Lady Webster in 1813: a heated and exciting chase, kept secret from her husband and ending without consummation.

[2] *Stanzas for Music* Byron wrote this poem in 1815 to commemorate the death of one of the friends of his youth, the Duke of Dorset. He referred to it in an 1816 letter as "the truest, though the most melancholy, I ever wrote."

3

Then the mortal coldness of the soul like death
itself comes down;
It cannot feel for others' woes, it dare not dream
its own;
That heavy chill has frozen o'er the fountain of
our tears,
And tho' the eye may sparkle still, 'tis where the
ice appears.

4

Tho' wit may flash from fluent lips, and mirth
distract the breast,
Through midnight hours that yield no more their
former hope of rest;
'Tis but as ivy-leaves around the ruin'd turret wreath,
All green and wildly fresh without but worn and
grey beneath.

5

Oh could I feel as I have felt,—or be what I have been,
Or weep as I could once have wept, o'er many a
vanished scene:
As springs in deserts found seem sweet, all
brackish though they be,
So midst the wither'd waste of life, those tears
would flow to me.

—1816

Darkness[1]

I had a dream, which was not all a dream.
The bright sun was extinguish'd, and the stars
Did wander darkling in the eternal space,
Rayless, and pathless, and the icy earth
Swung blind and blackening in the moonless air;[2]
Morn came, and went—and came, and brought no day,
And men forgot their passions in the dread
Of this their desolation; and all hearts
Were chill'd into a selfish prayer for light:
And they did live by watchfires—and the thrones,
The palaces of crowned kings—the huts,
The habitations of all things which dwell,
Were burnt for beacons; cities were consumed,
And men were gathered round their blazing homes
To look once more into each other's face;
Happy were those who dwelt within the eye
Of the volcanos, and their mountain-torch:
A fearful hope was all the world contain'd;
Forests were set on fire—but hour by hour
They fell and faded—and the crackling trunks
Extinguish'd with a crash—and all was black.
The brows of men by the despairing light
Wore an unearthly aspect, as by fits
The flashes fell upon them; some lay down
And hid their eyes and wept; and some did rest
Their chins upon their clenched hands, and smiled;
And others hurried to and fro, and fed
Their funeral piles with fuel, and looked up
With mad disquietude on the dull sky,
The pall of a past world; and then again
With curses cast them down upon the dust,
And gnash'd their teeth and howl'd: the wild
birds shriek'd,
And, terrified, did flutter on the ground,
And flap their useless wings; the wildest brutes
Came tame and tremulous; and vipers crawl'd
And twined themselves among the multitude,
Hissing, but stingless—they were slain for food:
And War, which for a moment was no more,
Did glut himself again;—a meal was bought
With blood, and each sate sullenly apart
Gorging himself in gloom: no love was left;
All earth was but one thought—and that was death,
Immediate and inglorious; and the pang
Of famine fed upon all entrails—men
Died, and their bones were tombless as their flesh;
The meagre by the meagre were devoured,

[1] *Darkness* The dust thrown into the atmosphere in 1815 by Mount Tamboro, an Indonesian volcano, made the summer of 1816 the coldest and wettest on record. Influenced by the weather, and perhaps by recent warnings by an Italian astronomer that sunspots might lead to the extinction of the sun, Byron produced this prescient poem, which he labeled "a Fragment." The "last man" theme was a source of fascination for the Romantics, but Byron's poem is distinctive for its absence of a last man, its unrelentingly bleak vision, and its representation of a typically Byronic faithful dog.

[2] *icy earth ... moonless air* Cf. Ezekiel 32.7–8; Joel 2.31; Revelation 6.12.

Even dogs assail'd their masters, all save one,
And he was faithful to a corse,[1] and kept
The birds and beasts and famish'd men at bay,
Till hunger clung them, or the dropping dead
Lured their lank jaws; himself sought out no food,
But with a piteous and perpetual moan
And a quick desolate cry, licking the hand
Which answered not with a caress—he died.
The crowd was famish'd by degrees; but two
Of an enormous city did survive,
And they were enemies; they met beside
The dying embers of an altar-place
Where had been heap'd a mass of holy things
For an unholy usage; they raked up,
And shivering scraped with their cold skeleton hands
The feeble ashes, and their feeble breath
Blew for a little life, and made a flame
Which was a mockery; then they lifted up
Their eyes as it grew lighter, and beheld
Each other's aspects—saw, and shriek'd, and died—
Even of their mutual hideousness they died,
Unknowing who he was upon whose brow
Famine had written Fiend. The world was void,
The populous and the powerful was a lump,
Seasonless, herbless, treeless, manless, lifeless—
A lump of death—a chaos of hard clay.
The rivers, lakes, and ocean all stood still,
And nothing stirred within their silent depths;
Ships sailorless lay rotting on the sea,
And their masts fell down piecemeal; as they dropp'd
They slept on the abyss without a surge—
The waves were dead; the tides were in their grave,
The moon their mistress had expired before;
The winds were withered in the stagnant air,
And the clouds perish'd; Darkness had no need
Of aid from them—She was the universe.
—1816

[1] *corse* Corpse.

Prometheus[2]

1

Titan! to whose immortal eyes
The sufferings of mortality,
Seen in their sad reality,
Were not as things that gods despise;
What was thy pity's recompense?
A silent suffering, and intense;
The rock, the vulture, and the chain,
All that the proud can feel of pain,
The agony they do not show,
The suffocating sense of woe,
Which speaks but in its loneliness,
And then is jealous lest the sky
Should have a listener, nor will sigh
Until its voice is echoless.

2

Titan! to thee the strife was given
Between the suffering and the will,
Which torture where they cannot kill;
And the inexorable Heaven,
And the deaf tyranny of Fate,
The ruling principle of Hate,
Which for its pleasure doth create
The things it may annihilate,
Refused thee even the boon to die:
The wretched gift eternity
Was thine—and thou hast borne it well.
All that the Thunderer[3] wrung from thee
Was but the menace which flung back
On him the torments of thy rack;
The fate thou didst so well foresee
But would not to appease him tell;
And in thy Silence was his Sentence,
And in his Soul a vain repentance,
And evil dread so ill dissembled
That in his hand the lightnings trembled.

[2] *Prometheus* The Titan Prometheus stole fire from heaven and gave it to humanity. To punish him, Jupiter, King of the gods, had him chained to a rock in the Caucasus, where a vulture (in some versions, an eagle) tore at his liver. Each night Prometheus's liver grew afresh, to be torn out the next day.

[3] *Thunderer* Jupiter.

3

Thy Godlike crime was to be kind,
To render with thy precepts less
The sum of human wretchedness,
And strengthen Man with his own mind;
But baffled as thou wert from high,
Still in thy patient energy,
In the endurance, and repulse
Of thine impenetrable Spirit,
Which Earth and Heaven could not convulse,
A mighty lesson we inherit:
Thou art a symbol and a sign
To Mortals of their fate and force;
Like thee, Man is in part divine,
A troubled stream from a pure source;
And Man in portions can foresee
His own funereal destiny;
His wretchedness, and his resistance,
And his sad unallied existence:
To which his Spirit may oppose
Itself—an equal to all woes,
And a firm will, and a deep sense,
Which even in torture can descry
Its own concentered recompense,
Triumphant where it dares defy,
And making Death a Victory.
—1816

So, we'll go no more a roving[1]

1

So, we'll go no more a roving
So late into the night,
Though the heart be still as loving,
And the moon be still as bright.

2

For the sword outwears its sheath,
And the soul wears out the breast,
And the heart must pause to breathe,
And love itself have rest.

3

Though the night was made for loving,
And the day returns too soon,
Yet we'll go no more a roving
By the light of the moon.
—1817

When a man hath no freedom to fight for at home[2]

When a man hath no freedom to fight for at home,
Let him combat for that of his neighbors;
Let him think of the glories of Greece and of Rome,
And get knock'd on the head for his labours.

To do good to mankind is the chivalrous plan,
And is always as nobly requited;
Then battle for freedom wherever you can,
And, if not shot or hang'd, you'll get knighted.
—1820

[1] *When … home* Originally written as part of a letter from Byron to his friend Thomas Moore, 28 February 1817. Just before these lines Byron writes, "The Carnival … knocked me up a little. But it is over—and it is now Lent, with all its abstinence and sacred music. The mumming closed with a masked ball … and, though I did not dissipate much upon the whole, yet I find 'the sword wearing out the scabbard', though I have but just turned the corner of twenty-nine."

[2] *When a man … home* Byron first sent these lines in a letter to his friend Thomas Moore on 5 November 1820. They are based on Byron's activities with the Italian freedom-fighters, the Carbonari, and their abortive attempt to stage an uprising.

January 22nd 1842.
Missolonghi
On this day I complete my thirty sixth year[1]

I

'Tis time this heart should be unmoved
Since others it hath ceased to move,
Yet though I cannot be beloved
Still let me love.

2

My days are in the yellow leaf[2]
The flowers and fruits of love are gone—
The worm—the canker, and the grief
Are mine alone.

3

The fire that on my bosom preys
Is lone as some Volcanic Isle,
No torch is kindled at its blaze
A funeral pile!

4

The hope, the fear, the jealous care
The exalted portion of the pain
And power of Love I cannot share
But wear the chain.

5

But 'tis not *thus*—and 'tis not *here*
Such thoughts should shake my soul, nor *now*
Where Glory decks the hero's bier
Or binds his brow.

6

The Sword—the Banner—and the Field
Glory and Greece around us see!
The Spartan borne upon his shield[3]
Was not more free!

7

Awake! (not Greece—She *is* awake!)
Awake my spirit—think through *whom*
Thy life-blood tracks its parent lake
And then strike home!

8

Tread those reviving passions down
Unworthy Manhood;—unto thee
Indifferent should the smile or frown
Of Beauty be.

9

If thou regret'st thy youth, why *live?*
The land of honourable Death
Is here—up to the Field! and give
Away thy Breath.

10

Seek out—less often sought than found,
A Soldier's Grave—for thee the best,
Then look around and choose thy ground
And take thy Rest.

—1824

[1] *On this ... year* This poem was until recently most commonly known by its subtitle, but the date and place are the correct title. Byron wrote it on his 36th birthday, in Greece. A companion who was with him at the time says, "January 22.—Lord Byron came from his bedroom into the apartment ... where some friends were assembled, and said, with a smile, 'You were complaining, the other day, that I never write any poetry now:—this is my birthday, and I have just finished something which, I think, is better than what I usually write.'" The poem is informed by Byron's relationship with two people, his young Greek companion of the time, Loukas Chalandritsanos, and a Turkish girl, Hataje, whom he had taken into his care. Byron's feelings for Chalandritsanos are commonly understood to be the stronger influence of the two.

[2] *My days ... leaf* See *Macbeth* 5.3.21–22.

Epistle to Augusta[4]

I

My Sister—my sweet Sister—if a name
Dearer and purer were—it should be thine.
Mountains and seas divide us—but I claim

[3] [Byron's note] The slain were borne on their shields—witness the Spartan mother's speech to her son, delivered with his buckler—"Either *with* this or *on* this."

[4] *Augusta* Byron's sister, Augusta Leigh (1783–1857).

No tears, but tenderness to answer mine:
Go where I will, to me thou art the same—
A loved regret which I would not resign—
There yet are two things in my destiny
A world to roam through—and a home with thee.

2

The first were nothing—had I still the last
It were the haven of my happiness—
But other claims and other ties thou hast—
And mine is not the wish to make them less.
A strange doom is thy father's son's and past
Recalling—as it lies beyond redress—
Reversed for him our grandsire's fate of yore
He had no rest at sea—nor I on shore.[1]

3

If my inheritance of storms hath been
In other elements—and on the rocks
Of perils overlooked or unforeseen
I have sustained my share of worldly shocks
The fault was mine—nor do I seek to screen
My errors with defensive paradox—
I have been cunning in mine overthrow
The careful pilot of my proper woe.

4

Mine were my faults—and mine be their reward—
My whole life was a contest—since the day
That gave me being gave me that which marred
The gift—a fate, or will that walked astray—
And I at times have found the struggle hard
And thought of shaking off my bonds of clay—
But now I fain would for a time survive
If but to see what next can well arrive.

5

Kingdoms and empires in my little day
I have outlived, and yet I am not old—
And when I look on this, the petty spray
Of my own years of trouble, which have rolled
Like a wild bay of breakers, melts away:—
Something—I know not what—does still uphold
A spirit of slight patience;—not in vain,
Even for its own sake—do we purchase pain.

6

Perhaps—the workings of defiance stir
Within me, or perhaps a cold despair—
Brought on when ills habitually recur,—
Perhaps a kinder clime—or purer air—
For even to this may change of soul refer—
And with light armour we may learn to bear—
Have taught me a strange quiet which was not
The chief companion of a calmer lot.

7

I feel almost at times as I have felt
In happy childhood—trees, and flowers, and brooks
Which do remember me of where I dwelt
Ere my young mind was sacrificed to books—
Come as of yore upon me—and can melt
My heart with recognition of their looks—
And even at moments I could think I see
Some living thing to love—but none like thee.

8

Here are the Alpine landscapes—which create
A fund for contemplation;—to admire
Is a brief feeling of a trivial date—
But something worthier do such scenes inspire:
Here to be lonely is not desolate—
For much I view which I could most desire—
And, above all a Lake I can behold—
Lovelier—not dearer than our own of old.

9

Oh that thou wert but with me!—but I grow
The fool of my own wishes—and forget
The solitude which I have vaunted so
Has lost its praise in this but one regret—
There may be others which I less may show—
I am not of the plaintive mood—and yet
I feel an ebb in my philosophy
And the tide rising in my altered eye.

---

[1] *He had no ... on shore* Byron and Augusta's grandfather, Admiral John Byron, was renowned for never making a sea voyage without encountering a storm. He was known as "Foulweather Jack."

10

I did remind thee of our own dear lake
By the old Hall which may be mine no more—
Leman's is fair—but think not I forsake
The sweet remembrance of a dearer shore—
Sad havoc Time must with my memory make
Ere that or thou can fade these eyes before—
Though like all things which I have loved—they are
Resigned for ever—or divided far.

11

The world is all before me—I but ask
Of Nature that with which she will comply—
It is but in her Summer's sun to bask—
To mingle with the quiet of her sky—
To see her gentle face without a mask
And never gaze on it with apathy—
She was my early friend—and now shall be
My Sister—till I look again on thee.

12

I can reduce all feelings but this one,
And that I would not—for at length I see
Such scenes as those wherein my life begun
The earliest—were the only paths for me.
Had I but sooner learnt the crowd to shun
I had been better than I now can be
The passions which have torn me would have slept—
I had not suffered—and *thou* hadst not wept.

13

With false Ambition what had I to do?
Little with love, and least of all with fame!
And yet they came unsought and with me grew,
And made me all which they can make—a Name.
Yet this was not the end I did pursue—
Surely I once beheld a nobler aim.
But all is over—I am one the more
To baffled millions which have gone before.

14

And for the future—this world's future may
From me demand but little from my care;
I have outlived myself by many a day,
Having survived so many things that were—
My years have been no slumber—but the prey
Of ceaseless vigils;—for I had the share
Of life which might have filled a century
Before its fourth in time had passed me by.

15

And for the remnants which may be to come
I am content—and for the past I feel
Not thankless—for within the crowded sum
Of struggles—happiness at times would steal
And for the present—I would not benumb
My feelings farther—nor shall I conceal
That with all this I still can look around
And worship Nature with a thought profound.

16

For thee—my own sweet Sister—in thy heart
I know myself secure—as thou in mine
We were and are—I am—even as thou art—
Beings who ne'er each other can resign
It is the same together or apart
From Life's commencement to its slow decline—
We are entwined—let death come slow or fast
The tie which bound the first endures the last.

—1830

Don Juan

Byron worked on *Don Juan* from 1818 until his death, publishing it piecemeal from 1819 to 1824. His immediate poetic inspiration for his satirical reworking of the *Don Juan* legend was *The Monks and the Giants* (1817), by his friend John Hookham Frere. In this, he said, he discovered the power of the ottava rima rhyme scheme (abababcc) that drives his own poem. His models for *Don Juan*'s rambling episodic format were the serio-comic romances of the fifteenth- and sixteenth-century Italian writers Pulci, Ariosto, and Berni. Byron, however, did more with these influences than anyone could have hoped or dreamed. The flexible structure allowed him to range widely, moving with ease from high-flown philosophical reflections to the most trivial minutiae, and back again—sometimes within the same stanza. In the guise of a garrulous raconteur, Byron was able to comment seriously on English and European politics, the hypocrisy of sexual mores, the falseness of conventional morals, and the often painful complexities of human emotions. The philosophical aspects of *Don Juan* are only just beginning to be discussed, but they are an integral part of the poem.

At the same time, *Don Juan* remains a comic goldmine. All forms of wit—satire, wordplay, parody, just plain silliness—confront the reader, and no cultural shibboleth escapes Byron's mockery. For this reason, the poem was met with outrage and horror upon its publication. Indeed, Byron's own mistress, Teresa Guiccioli, found it immoral, but although he stopped writing it at her request in 1821, he resumed again in 1822. Friends and critics alike lamented what they saw as Byron's lack of tact, his lack of taste, and his lack of decency. He was attacked for making his personal life public (the portrait of Juan's mother, Donna Inez, in the first canto was agreed to be a satirical picture of Lady Byron), and for writing a poem "not ... didactic of any thing but mischief." Byron himself famously insisted that he had written the poem only "to giggle and make giggle," and continued writing.

Byron's protagonist is a many-layered creation. The story of the great seducer was first told by Tirso de Molina (Gabriel Téllez), *El Burlador de Sevilla y convidado di piedra* ("The Trickster of Seville and the Stone Guest," 1616?); it subsequently inspired such masterpieces as Molière's *Don Juan ou Le Festin de pierre* (1665), Thomas Shadwell's *The Libertine* (1676), and Mozart's *Don Giovanni* (1787). Apparently Byron first encountered the story in a pantomime (see Canto 1.7, below). But Byron's Don Juan (pronounced, in the English manner, Joo-an, with the stress on the first syllable), like his poem, is more than the sum of his sources. He is, first and foremost, a parody of the famous Don Juan, for he is a passive fellow, seduced and sweet-natured rather than seducing and ruthless. He is also a parodic version of the epic hero figure (including Byron's own most famous creation, Childe Harold), and by extension, of Byron himself; throughout the poem Byron uses Juan to play on the public notion of what it meant to be "Byron."

Don Juan incorporates three chronological levels: Byron wrote it from 1818-1824, using his memories of the England in which he moved from 1812–16, but Juan lives in the late eighteenth century. The narrative voice is carefully constructed; it evidently both is and is not meant to be Byron. This subversion of certainty pervades the poem at every level. Yet paradoxically, the effect it creates is often naturalistic. "Confess—you dog!" Byron wrote to his friend Douglas Kinnaird about the poem in 1819, "is it not life?—is it not the thing?"

Don Juan

"Difficile est proprie communia dicere." [1]

Horace, *Epistola ad Pisones*

Dedication[2]

1

Bob Southey! You're a poet—Poet Laureate,
And representative of all the race;
Although 'tis true that you turned out a Tory[3] at
Last—yours has lately been a common case:
And now, my epic renegade! what are ye at,
With all the Lakers[4] in and out of place?
A nest of tuneful persons, to my eye
Like "four and twenty Blackbirds in a pye;[5]

2

"Which pye being opened they began to sing"
(This old song and new simile holds good),
"A dainty dish to set before the King,"
Or Regent,[6] who admires such kind of food;
And Coleridge, too, has lately taken wing,
But like a hawk encumbered with his hood,
Explaining Metaphysics to the nation—
I wish he would explain his Explanation.[7]

3

You, Bob! are rather insolent, you know,
At being disappointed in your wish
To supersede all warblers here below,
And be the only Blackbird in the dish;
And then you overstrain yourself, or so,
And tumble downward like the flying fish
Gasping on deck, because you soar too high, Bob,
And fall, for lack of moisture quite a-dry, Bob![8]

4

And Wordsworth, in a rather long "Excursion"
(I think the quarto holds five hundred pages),[9]
Has given a sample from the vasty version
Of his new system to perplex the sages;
'Tis poetry—at least by his assertion,
And may appear so when the dog-star rages—[10]
And he who understands it would be able
To add a story to the Tower of Babel.

5

You—Gentlemen! by dint of long seclusion
From better company, have kept your own
At Keswick,[11] and, through still continued fusion
Of one another's minds, at last have grown
To deem as a most logical conclusion,

---

[1] *difficile ... dicere* Latin: "It is hard to treat in your own way what is common."

[2] *Dedicationi* This Dedication is an attack on Robert Southey (1774–1843), then England's Poet Laureate, although Byron also makes jokes at the expense of other poets (especially Coleridge and Wordsworth). Southey had spread the rumor that Byron and Shelley participated in a "league of incest" when they were living in Switzerland (Byron was at that time conducting an affair with Mary Shelley's stepsister, Clare Clairmont. Southey believed them to be half-sisters, and further believed that both had sex with both men). Less personally, Byron felt that Southey had played the part of a traitor when he abandoned his early republican ideals and became a wholehearted supporter of the increasingly conservative government. Nonetheless, when he decided to publish the first two cantos anonymously, Byron had the Dedication omitted; he felt it was cowardly to attack Southey anonymously. The stanzas were first published in 1833.

[3] *Tory* Supporter of the Conservative party in Parliament, here opposed to a more republican political stance, which Southey once assumed.

[4] *Lakers* The name applied by *The Edinburgh Review* to Coleridge, Southey, and Wordsworth, who all resided in the Lake District at one time or another.

[5] *pye* Byron here makes a pun on the familiar nursery rhyme. Henry James Pye (1745–1813) had been Poet Laureate before Southey.

[6] *Regent* The Prince of Wales (later George IV) was appointed Prince Regent in 1811, after his father, George III, had become permanently incapacitated for ruling.

[7] *I wish ... his Explanation* Coleridge's philosophical prose was notoriously vague and hard to follow.

[8] *dry-bob* Slang for sex without ejaculation.

[9] *Wordsworth ... pages* Byron here refers to Wordsworth's *The Excursion* (1814).

[10] *dog-star* Sirius, ascendant during the hottest days of the summer, was once believed to have a maddening influence.

[11] *Keswick* Of the Lake Poets only Southey lived at Keswick, in the Lake District; Coleridge had moved there with his family in 1800, but he was no longer living there in 1819. Wordsworth lived nearby, at Grasmere.

That Poesy has wreaths for you alone:
There is a narrowness in such a notion,
Which makes me wish you'd change your lakes
for Ocean.

6

I would not imitate the petty thought,
Nor coin my self-love to so base a vice,
For all the glory your conversion brought,
Since gold alone should not have been its price.
You have your salary; was't for that you wrought?
And Wordsworth has his place in the Excise.[1]
You're shabby fellows—true—but poets still,
And duly seated on the Immortal Hill.

7

Your bays may hide the baldness of your brows—[2]
Perhaps some virtuous blushes—let them go—
To you I envy neither fruit nor boughs—
And for the fame you would engross below,
The field is universal, and allows
Scope to all such as feel the inherent glow:
Scott, Rogers, Campbell, Moore and Crabbe,[3] will try
'Gainst you the question with posterity.

8

For me, who, wandering with pedestrian Muses,
Contend not with you on the winged steed,
I wish your fate may yield ye, when she chooses,
The fame you envy, and the skill you need;
And, recollect, a poet nothing loses
In giving to his brethren their full meed
Of merit, and complaint of present days
Is not the certain path to future praise.

9

He that reserves his laurels for posterity
(Who does not often claim the bright reversion)
Has generally no great crop to spare it, he
Being only injured by his own assertion;
And although here and there some glorious rarity
Arise like Titan[4] from the sea's immersion,
The major part of such appellants go
To—God knows where—for no one else can know.

10

If, fallen in evil days on evil tongues,
Milton appealed to the Avenger, Time,
If Time, the Avenger, execrates his wrongs,
And makes the word "Miltonic" mean "sublime,"
He deigned not to belie his soul in songs,
Nor turn his very talent to a crime;
He did not loathe the Sire to laud the Son,
But closed the tyrant-hater he begun.

11

Think'st thou, could he—the blind Old Man—arise
Like Samuel from the grave,[5] to freeze once more
The blood of monarchs with his prophecies
Or be alive again— again all hoar
With time and trials, and those helpless eyes,
And heartless daughters—worn—and pale—and
poor;[6]
Would *he* adore a sultan? *he* obey
The intellectual eunuch Castlereagh?[7]

[1] *Wordsworth … Excise* In 1813, Wordsworth had been appointed Distributor of Stamps for Westmoreland (a sinecure), through the influence of his patron Lord Lonsdale. In gratitude, he dedicated *The Excursion* to Lonsdale.

[2] *bay* Bay, or laurel, leaves were awarded both to military heroes and to poets (hence the term "poet laureate"). Julius Caesar was allegedly gratified with his because they hid the fact that he was bald. Southey was not bald, and this particular insult is striking, given that Byron himself had frequently commented on Southey's good looks.

[3] *Scott … Crabbe Scott* Sir Walter Scott, poet and novelist (1771–1832); *Rogers* Samuel Rogers, poet (1763–1855); *Campbell* Thomas Campbell, poet (1777–1844); *Moore* Thomas Moore, poet (1779–1852).

[4] *Titan* The Latin name for Helios, the Sun God.

[5] *Samuel from the grave* See 1 Samuel 28.13–14.

[6] [Byron's note] Pale, but not cadaverous:—Milton's two elder daughters are said to have robbed him of his books, besides cheating and plaguing him in the economy of his house, &c. His feelings on such an outrage, both as a parent and a scholar, must have been singularly painful. Hayley compares him to Lear. See part third, *Life of Milton*, by W. Hayley (or Hailey, as spelt in the edition before me).

[7] *Castlereagh* Conservative politician Robert Stewart, Lord Castlereagh (1769–1822).

12

Cold-blooded, smooth-faced, placid miscreant!
Dabbling its sleek young hands in Erin's gore,
And thus for wider carnage taught to pant,
Transferred to gorge upon a sister shore,
The vulgarest tool that Tyranny could want,
With just enough of talent, and no more,
To lengthen fetters by another fixed,
And offer poison long already mixed.

13

An orator of such set trash of phrase
Ineffably—legitimately vile,
That even its grossest flatterers dare not praise,
Nor foes—all nations—condescend to smile,
Not even a sprightly blunder's spark can blaze
From that Ixion grindstone's ceaseless toil,[1]
That turns and turns to give the world a notion
Of endless torments and perpetual motion.

14

A bungler even in its disgusting trade,
And botching, patching, leaving still behind
Something of which its masters are afraid,
States to be curbed, and thoughts to be confined,
Conspiracy or Congress to be made—
Cobbling at manacles for all mankind—
A tinkering slave-maker, who mends old chains,
With God and Man's abhorrence for its gains.

15

If we may judge of matter by the mind,
Emasculated to the marrow *It*
Hath but two objects, how to serve, and bind,
Deeming the chain it wears even men may fit,
Eutropius of its many masters,[2] blind
To worth as freedom, wisdom as to Wit,
Fearless—because *no* feeling dwells in ice,
Its very courage stagnates to a vice.

16

Where shall I turn me not to *view* its bonds,
For I will never *feel* them?—Italy!
Thy late reviving Roman soul desponds
Beneath the lie this State-thing breathed o'er thee—
Thy clanking chain, and Erin's yet green wounds,
Have voices—tongues to cry aloud for me.
Europe has slaves—allies—kings—armies still,
And Southey lives to sing them very ill.

17

Meantime—Sir Laureate—I proceed to dedicate,
In honest simple verse, this song to you,
And, if in flattering strains I do not predicate,
'Tis that I still retain my "buff and blue";[3]
My politics as yet are all to educate:
Apostasy's so fashionable, too,
To keep *one* creed's a task grown quite Herculean;
Is it not so, my Tory, ultra-Julian?[4]

Canto 1

1

I want a hero: an uncommon want,
When every year and month sends forth a new one,
Till, after cloying the gazettes with cant,
The age discovers he is not the true one;
Of such as these I should not care to vaunt,
I'll therefore take our ancient friend Don Juan—
We all have seen him in the pantomime,
Sent to the devil somewhat ere his time.

2

Vernon, the butcher Cumberland, Wolfe, Hawke,
Prince Ferdinand, Granby, Burgoyne, Keppel, Howe,
Evil and good, have had their tithe of talk,

[1] *Ixion ... toil* For attempting to rape Hera, Ixion was bound to a wheel that rolled forever through Hades.

[2] [Byron's note] For the character of Eutropius, the eunuch and minister at the court of Arcadius, see Gibbon. [See Edward Gibbon, *The Decline and Fall of the Roman Empire,* ch. 32.]

[3] *buff and blue* The colours of the Whig Club, and of the cover of the leading Whig periodical, the *Edinburgh Review*.

[4] [Byron's note] I allude not to our friend Landor's hero, the traitor Count Julian, but to Gibbon's hero, vulgarly yclept "The Apostate." [The Emperor Julian was raised as a Christian, but returned to the worship of the Roman gods before becoming emperor in 361.]

And filled their sign posts then, like Wellesley now;[1]
Each in their turn like Banquo's monarchs stalk,
Followers of fame, "nine farrow" of that sow:[2]
France, too, had Buonaparte and Dumourier[3]
Recorded in the Moniteur and Courier.

3

Barnave, Brissot, Condorcet, Mirabeau,
Petion, Clootz, Danton, Marat, La Fayette,[4]
Were French, and famous people, as we know:
And there were others, scarce forgotten yet,
Joubert, Hoche, Marceau, Lannes, Desaix, Moreau[5]
With many of the military set,
Exceedingly remarkable at times,
But not at all adapted to my rhymes.

4

Nelson was once Britannia's god of war,
And still should be so, but the tide is turned;
There's no more to be said of Trafalgar,
'T is with our hero quietly inurned;
Because the army's grown more popular,
At which the naval people are concerned;
Besides, the prince is all for the land-service,
Forgetting Duncan, Nelson, Howe, and Jervis.[6]

5

Brave men were living before Agamemnon[7]
And since, exceeding valorous and sage,
A good deal like him too, though quite the same none;
But then they shone not on the poet's page,
And so have been forgotten:—I condemn none,
But can't find any in the present age
Fit for my poem (that is, for my new one);
So, as I said, I'll take my friend Don Juan.

6

Most epic poets plunge "in medias res"[8]
(Horace makes this the heroic turnpike road),
And then your hero tells, whene'er you please,
What went before—by way of episode,
While seated after dinner at his ease,
Beside his mistress in some soft abode,
Palace, or garden, paradise, or cavern,
Which serves the happy couple for a tavern.

7

That is the usual method, but not mine—
My way is to begin with the beginning;
The regularity of my design
Forbids all wandering as the worst of sinning,
And therefore I shall open with a line
(Although it cost me half an hour in spinning)

[1] *Vernon* Admiral Edward Vernon (1684–1757); *Cumberland* William, Duke of Cumberland (1721–65), whose victory over the Young Pretender at Culloden (1746) was marred by ferocity, and whose nickname was "Billy the Butcher"; *Wolfe* General James Wolfe (1726–59); *Hawke* Edward, Lord Admiral Hawke (1715–81); *Ferdinand* Ferdinand, Duke of Brunswick (1721–92); *Granby* John Manners, Marquess of Granby (1721–90); *Burgoyne* General John Burgoyne (d. 1792); *Keppel* Augustus, Lord Admiral Keppel (1725–86); *Howe* Richard, Lord Admiral Howe (1725–99); *Wellington* Arthur Wellesley, Duke of Wellington. Wellington Street and Waterloo Bridge were both opened on the anniversary of Waterloo, in 1817.

[2] *Each in … sow* See Shakespeare, *Macbeth* 4.1.64–65, 112–24.

[3] *Dumourier* Charles-François Duperier Dumouriez (1739–1823), French general. The *Moniteur* and *Courier* were French newspapers.

[4] *Barnave* Antoine-Pierre-Joseph Barnave (1761–93; *Brissot* Jean-Pierre Brissot de Warville (1754–93); *Condorcet* Marie-Jean-Antoine, marquis de Condorcet (1743–94); *Mirabeau* Honoré-Gabriel Riquetti, comte de Mirabeau (1749–91); Petion Jérôme Petion de Villeneuve (1753–94); *Clootz* Jean-Baptiste, baron de Clootz (1755–94); *Danton* Georges-Jacques Danton (1759–94), Jean-Paul Marat (1744–93); *La Fayette* Marie-Jean-Paul, marquis de La Fayette (1757–1834), French Revolutionaries. Mirabeau died of natural causes, Marat was assassinated, and La Fayette was still alive; the rest all perished in the Terror that followed the French Revolution. Clootz, who changed his name to Anacharsis Clootz and nominated himself "l'orateur du genre humain," is a clue to Byron's plans for the conclusion of his unfinished epic: see his letter to John Murray on 16 February 1821, in this volume.

[5] *Joubert … Moreau* For Hoche and Marceau, see note to *Childe Harold's Pilgrimage* 3.541. Barthélemi-Catherine Joubert (1769–99), Jean Lannes, duc de Montebello (1769–1809), Louis-Charles-Antoine Desaix de Voygoux (1768–1800), Jean-Victor Moreau (1763–1813), French Revolutionary generals.

[6] *Duncan* Adam, Lord Admiral Duncan (1731–1804); *Nelson* Horatio, Lord Admiral Nelson (1758–1805), killed at Trafalgar (27); *Jervis* John, Lord Admiral Jervis (1735–1823); for Howe, see note to line 12.

[7] [Byron's note] "'Vixere fortes ante Agamemnona,' &c.—HORACE." [Agamemnon was the King of the Greeks and leader of the Greek expedition against Troy in Homer's *Iliad*.]

[8] *in medias res* Latin: in the middle of things.

Narrating somewhat of Don Juan's father,
And also of his mother, if you'd rather.

8

In Seville was he born, a pleasant city,
Famous for oranges and women—he
Who has not seen it will be much to pity,
So says the proverb—and I quite agree;
Of all the Spanish towns is none more pretty,
Cadiz[1] perhaps —but that you soon may see:
Don Juan's parents lived beside the river,
A noble stream, and called the Guadalquivir.

9

His father's name was Jóse[2]—*Don*,[3] of course,
A true Hidalgo,[4] free from every stain
Of Moor or Hebrew blood, he traced his source
Through the most Gothic gentlemen of Spain;
A better cavalier ne'er mounted horse,
Or, being mounted, e'er got down again,
Than Jóse, who begot our hero, who
Begot—but that's to come—Well, to renew:

10

His mother was a learned lady,[5] famed
For every branch of every science known—
In every Christian language ever named,
With virtues equalled by her wit alone,
She made the cleverest people quite ashamed,
And even the good with inward envy groan,
Finding themselves so very much exceeded
In their own way by all the things that she did.

11

Her memory was a mine: she knew by heart
All Calderon and greater part of Lopé,[6]
So that if any actor missed his part
She could have served him for the prompter's copy;
For her Feinagle's were an useless art,[7]
And he himself obliged to shut up shop—he
Could never make a memory so fine as
That which adorned the brain of Donna Inez.

12

Her favourite science was the mathematical,
Her noblest virtue was her magnanimity,
Her wit (she sometimes tried at wit) was Attic all,[8]
Her serious sayings darkened to sublimity;
In short, in all things she was fairly what I call
A prodigy—her morning dress was dimity,
Her evening silk, or, in the summer, muslin,
And other stuffs, with which I won't stay puzzling.

13

She knew the Latin—that is, "The Lord's Prayer,"
And Greek—the alphabet—I'm nearly sure;
She read some French romances here and there,
Although her mode of speaking was not pure;
For native Spanish she had no great care,
At least her conversation was obscure;
Her thoughts were theorems, her words a problem,
As if she deemed that mystery would ennoble 'em.

14

She liked the English and the Hebrew tongue,
And said there was analogy between 'em;
She proved it somehow out of sacred song,
But I must leave the proofs to those who've seen 'em,
But this I heard her say, and can't be wrong,
And all may think which way their judgments lean 'em,
"'Tis strange—the Hebrew noun which means 'I am,'
The English always used to govern d—n."[9]

[1] *Cadiz* Byron anglicizes the pronunciations of his Spanish words, so that Seville is pronounced "SEVil"; Cadiz to rhyme with "ladies."

[2] *Jóse* Byron changes the stress, so that José is pronounced in the English manner, with the emphasis on the first syllable.

[3] *Don* Spanish title, denoting high rank.

[4] *Hidalgo* Gentleman, by birth.

[5] *His mother … lady* Although Byron denied that the character of Donna Inez was a satiric portrait of his wife, a perceived resemblance to her was one of the chief complaints his friends made against these cantos.

[6] *Calderon … Lopé* Calderón de la Barca (1600–81) and Lopé de Vega (1562–1635), Spanish dramatists.

[7] *Feinagle's…art* Gregor von Feinagle (1765?–1819) invented a new method of memorization.

[8] *Her wit … Attic all* Attic, that is, Grecian, wit, refined and delicate.

[9] *d—n* Cf. Exodus 3.14. Byron is referring to "God damn."

15

Some women use their tongues—she *looked* a lecture,
    Each eye a sermon, and her brow a homily,
An all-in-all sufficient self-director,
    Like the lamented late Sir Samuel Romilly, [1]
The Law's expounder, and the State's corrector,
    Whose suicide was almost an anomaly—
One sad example more, that "All is vanity"
(The jury brought their verdict in "Insanity").

16

In short, she was a walking calculation,
    Miss Edgeworth's novels stepping from their covers,
Or Mrs. Trimmer's books on education,
    Or "Cœlebs' Wife" set out in quest of lovers,[2]
Morality's prim personification,
    In which not Envy's self a flaw discovers,
To others' share let "female errors fall,"
For she had not even one—the worst of all.

17

Oh! she was perfect past all parallel—
    Of any modern female saint's comparison;
So far above the cunning powers of hell,
    Her guardian angel had given up his garrison;
Even her minutest motions went as well
    As those of the best time-piece made by Harrison:[3]
In virtues nothing earthly could surpass her,
Save thine "incomparable oil," Macassar![4]

18

Perfect she was, but as perfection is
    Insipid in this naughty world of ours,
Where our first parents never learned to kiss
    Till they were exiled from their earlier bowers,
Where all was peace, and innocence, and bliss
    (I wonder how they got through the twelve hours)
Don Jóse, like a lineal son of Eve,
Went plucking various fruit without her leave.

19

He was a mortal of the careless kind,
    With no great love for learning, or the learned,
    Who chose to go where'er he had a mind,
And never dreamed his lady was concerned:
    The world, as usual, wickedly inclined
To see a kingdom or a house o'erturned,
Whispered he had a mistress, some said *two*,
But for domestic quarrels *one* will do.

20

Now Donna Inez had, with all her merit,
    A great opinion of her own good qualities;
Neglect, indeed, requires a saint to bear it,
    And such, indeed, she was in her moralities;
But then she had a devil of a spirit,
    And sometimes mixed up fancies with realities,
And let few opportunities escape
Of getting her liege lord into a scrape.

21

This was an easy matter with a man
    Oft in the wrong, and never on his guard;
And even the wisest, do the best they can,
    Have moments, hours, and days, so unprepared,
That you might "brain them with their lady's fan;"[5]
    And sometimes ladies hit exceeding hard,
And fans turn into falchions° in fair hands, *swords*
And why and wherefore no one understands.

22

'Tis pity learned virgins ever wed
    With persons of no sort of education,
Or gentlemen, who, though well-born and bred,

[1] *Romilly* Sir Samuel Romilly (1757–1818), lawyer and legal reformer, represented Lady Byron during the separation proceedings, despite having previously accepted a retainer from Byron. Byron never forgave him. Romilly's wife died in October 1818, and he committed suicide. This stanza was censored in the first edition.

[2] *Miss Edgeworth's … lovers* Byron here refers to three female writers famous for their didactic and moral works: Maria Edgeworth (1767–1849), author of *Moral Tales* (1801) and other fiction; Sarah Trimmer (1741–1810), author of books for children and publisher of *Guardian to Education* (1802–6), and Hannah More, to whose *Coelebs in Search of a Wife* (1809) he alludes.

[3] *Harrison* John Harrison (1693–1776) invented a chronometer so accurate that it could be used to calculate longitude.

[4] [Byron's note] 'description des *vertus incomparables* de l'Huile de Macassar.'—See the Advertisement. [Macassor oil, a dressing for the hair named after an Indonesian location said to be the source of its ingredients, was very popular through the nineteenth century.]

[5] *brain them … fan* Cf. Shakespeare, *1 Henry IV* 2.3.21.

Grow tired of scientific conversation:
I don't choose to say much upon this head,
I'm a plain man, and in a single station,
But—Oh! ye lords of ladies intellectual,
Inform us truly, have they not hen-pecked you all?

23

Don Jóse and his lady quarrelled—*why*,
Not any of the many could divine,
Though several thousand people chose to try,
'Twas surely no concern of theirs nor mine;
I loathe that low vice curiosity,
But if there's any thing in which I shine
'Tis in arranging all my friends' affairs,
Not having, of my own, domestic cares.

24

And so I interfered, and with the best
Intentions, but their treatment was not kind;
I think the foolish people were possessed,
For neither of them could I ever find,
Although their porter afterwards confessed—
But that's no matter, and the worst 's behind,
For little Juan o'er me threw, down stairs,
A pail of housemaid's water unawares.

25

A little curly-headed, good-for-nothing,
And mischief-making monkey from his birth;
His parents ne'er agreed except in doting
Upon the most unquiet imp on earth;
Instead of quarrelling, had they been but both in
Their senses, they'd have sent young master forth
To school, or had him soundly whipped at home,
To teach him manners for the time to come.

26

Don Jóse and the Donna Inez led
For some time an unhappy sort of life,
Wishing each other, not divorced, but dead;
They lived respectably as man and wife,
Their conduct was exceedingly well-bred,
And gave no outward signs of inward strife,
Until at length the smothered fire broke out,
And put the business past all kind of doubt.

27

For Inez called some druggists and physicians,
And tried to prove her loving lord was *mad*,
But as he had some lucid intermissions,
She next decided he was only *bad*;
Yet when they asked her for her depositions,
No sort of explanation could be had,
Save that her duty both to man and God
Required this conduct—which seemed very odd.

28

She kept a journal, where his faults were noted,
And opened certain trunks of books and letters,
All which might, if occasion served, be quoted;
And then she had all Seville for abettors,
Besides her good old grandmother (who doted);
The hearers of her case became repeaters,
Then advocates, inquisitors, and judges,
Some for amusement, others for old grudges. [1]

29

And then this best and meekest woman bore
With such serenity her husband's woes,
Just as the Spartan ladies did of yore,
Who saw their spouses killed, and nobly chose
Never to say a word about them more—
Calmly she heard each calumny that rose,
And saw *his* agonies with such sublimity,
That all the world exclaimed, "What magnanimity!"

30

No doubt, this patience, when the world is damning us,
Is philosophic in our former friends;
'Tis also pleasant to be deemed magnanimous,
The more so in obtaining our own ends;
And what the lawyers call a "*malus animus*"[2]
Conduct like this by no means comprehends:
Revenge in person's certainly no virtue,
But then 'tis not my fault, if *others* hurt you.

---

[1] *For Inez … grudges* During the months leading up to their separation, Lady Byron did, or was suspected by her husband of doing, all the things attributed to Donna Inez in these two stanzas.

[2] *malus animus* Latin: bad spirit.

31

And if our quarrels should rip up old stories,
And help them with a lie or two additional,
I'm not to blame, as you well know, no more is
Any one else—they were become traditional;
Besides, their resurrection aids our glories
By contrast, which is what we just were wishing all:
And science profits by this resurrection—
Dead scandals form good subjects for dissection.

32

Their friends had tried at reconciliation,
Then their relations, who made matters worse;
('Twere hard to tell upon a like occasion
To whom it may be best to have recourse—
I can't say much for friend or yet relation):
The lawyers did their utmost for divorce,
But scarce a fee was paid on either side
Before, unluckily, Don Jóse died.

33

He died: and most unluckily, because,
According to all hints I could collect
From counsel learned in those kinds of laws
(Although their talk's obscure and circumspect)
His death contrived to spoil a charming cause;
A thousand pities also with respect
To public feeling, which on this occasion
Was manifested in a great sensation.

34

But ah! he died; and buried with him lay
The public feeling and the lawyers' fees:
His house was sold, his servants sent away,
A Jew took one of his two mistresses,
A priest the other—at least so they say:
I asked the doctors after his disease,
He died of the slow fever called the tertian,
And left his widow to her own aversion.

35

Yet Jóse was an honourable man,
That I must say, who knew him very well;
Therefore his frailties I'll no further scan,
Indeed there were not many more to tell;
And if his passions now and then outran
Discretion, and were not so peaceable
As Numa's (who was also named Pompilius),[1]
He had been ill brought up, and was born bilious.

36

Whate'er might be his worthlessness or worth,
Poor fellow! he had many things to wound him,
Let's own, since it can do no good on earth;
It was a trying moment that which found him
Standing alone beside his desolate hearth,
Where all his household gods lay shivered round him;
No choice was left his feelings or his pride,
Save death or Doctors' Commons[2]—so he died.

37

Dying intestate, Juan was sole heir
To a chancery suit, and messuages, and lands,
Which, with a long minority and care,
Promised to turn out well in proper hands:
Inez became sole guardian, which was fair,
And answered but to nature's just demands;
An only son left with an only mother
Is brought up much more wisely than another.

38

Sagest of women, even of widows, she
Resolved that Juan should be quite a paragon,
And worthy of the noblest pedigree:
(His sire was of Castile, his dam from Aragon).
Then for accomplishments of chivalry,
In case our lord the king should go to war again,
He learned the arts of riding, fencing, gunnery,
And how to scale a fortress—or a nunnery.

39

But that which Donna Inez most desired,
And saw into herself each day before all
The learned tutors whom for him she hired,
Was, that his breeding should be strictly moral;
Much into all his studies she inquired,
And so they were submitted first to her, all,

[1] *Pompilius* The peaceable second king of Rome; see Plutarch, *Parallel Lives*.

[2] *Doctors' Commons* Divorce courts.

Arts, sciences, no branch was made a mystery
To Juan's eyes, excepting natural history.

40

The languages, especially the dead,
The sciences, and most of all the abstruse,
The arts, at least all such as could be said
To be the most remote from common use,
In all these he was much and deeply read;
But not a page of any thing that's loose,
Or hints continuation of the species,
Was ever suffered, lest he should grow vicious.

41

His classic studies made a little puzzle,
Because of filthy loves of gods and goddesses,
Who in the earlier ages raised a bustle,
But never put on pantaloons or boddices;
His reverend tutors had at times a tussle,
And for their Æneids, Iliads, and Odysseys,
Were forced to make an odd sort of apology,
For Donna Inez dreaded the mythology.

42

Ovid's a rake, as half his verses show him,
Anacreon's morals are a still worse sample,
Catullus scarcely has a decent poem,
I don't think Sappho's Ode a good example,
Although Longinus tells us there is no hymn
Where the sublime soars forth on wings more ample;[1]
But Virgil's songs are pure, except that horrid one
Beginning with "*Formosum Pastor Corydon.*"[2]

43

Lucretius' irreligion is too strong
For early stomachs, to prove wholesome food;
I can't help thinking Juvenal was wrong,
Although no doubt his real intent was good,
For speaking out so plainly in his song,
So much indeed as to be downright rude;
And then what proper person can be partial
To all those nauseous epigrams of Martial?[3]

44

Juan was taught from out the best edition,
Expurgated by learned men, who place,
Judiciously, from out the schoolboy's vision,
The grosser parts; but fearful to deface
Too much their modest bard by this omission,
And pitying sore his mutilated case,
They only add them all in an appendix,
Which saves, in fact, the trouble of an index.[4]

45

For there we have them all at one fell swoop,
Instead of being scattered through the pages;
They stand forth marshalled in a handsome troop,
To meet the ingenuous youth of future ages,
Till some less rigid editor shall stoop
To call them back into their separate cages,
Instead of standing staring altogether,
Like garden gods—and not so decent either.

46

The Missal too (it was the family Missal)
Was ornamented in a sort of way
Which ancient mass-books often are, and this all
Kinds of grotesques illumined; and how they,
Who saw those figures on the margin kiss all,
Could turn their optics to the text and pray
Is more than I know—but Don Juan's mother
Kept this herself, and gave her son another.

---

[1] [Byron's note] See Longinus, Section 10, "*hina me hen ti peri auten pathos phainetai, pathon de sunodos*]." [See Ovid's *Amores* and *Ars Amatoria*; the erotic lyrics then attributed to Anacreon; the erotic lyrics of Catullus; and the poem by Sappho beginning "To me he seems a peer of the gods," praised by Longinus in *On the Sublime* 10.]

[2] *Formosum ... Corydon* This is the first line of Virgil's second Eclogue, which may be translated, "The shepherd Corydon [burned for] fair [Alexis, his master's darling.]" The poem is about homosexual love.

[3] *Lucretius ... Martial* Byron here refers to three classical works which Inez certainly would have considered dangerous: Lucretius, *On the Nature of Things*, a philosophical poem; Juvenal, *Satires*, and Martial's epigrams, which are notoriously scurrilous and obscene.

[4] [Byron's note] Fact. There is, or was, such an edition, with all the obnoxious epigrams of Martial placed by themselves at the end. [The Delphin edition of Martial (Amsterdam, 1701) has an appendix entitled "Epigrammata Obscaena."]

47

Sermons he read, and lectures he endured,
And homilies, and lives of all the saints;
To Jerome and to Chrysostom[1] inured,
He did not take such studies for restraints;
But how faith is acquired, and then insured,
So well not one of the aforesaid paints
As Saint Augustine in his fine Confessions,
Which make the reader envy his transgressions.[2]

48

This, too, was a sealed book to little Juan—
I can't but say that his mamma was right,
If such an education was the true one.
She scarcely trusted him from out her sight;
Her maids were old, and if she took a new one
You might be sure she was a perfect fright,
She did this during even her husband's life—
I recommend as much to every wife.

49

Young Juan waxed in goodliness and grace;
At six a charming child, and at eleven
With all the promise of as fine a face
As e'er to man's maturer growth was given:
He studied steadily, and grew apace,
And seemed, at least, in the right road to heaven,
For half his days were passed at church, the other
Between his tutors, confessor, and mother.

50

At six, I said, he was a charming child,
At twelve he was a fine, but quiet boy;
Although in infancy a little wild,
They tamed him down amongst them; to destroy
His natural spirit not in vain they toiled,
At least it seemed so; and his mother's joy
Was to declare how sage, and still, and steady,
Her young philosopher was grown already.

51

I had my doubts, perhaps I have them still,
But what I say is neither here nor there:
I knew his father well, and have some skill
In character—but it would not be fair
From sire to son to augur good or ill:
He and his wife were an ill-sorted pair—
But scandal's my aversion—I protest
Against all evil speaking, even in jest.

52

For my part I say nothing—nothing—but
This I will say—my reasons are my own—
That if I had an only son to put
To school (as God be praised that I have none)
'Tis not with Donna Inez I would shut
Him up to learn his catechism alone,
No—no—I'd send him out betimes to college,
For there it was I picked up my own knowledge.

53

For there one learns—'tis not for me to boast,
Though I acquired—but I pass over *that*,
As well as all the Greek I since have lost:
I say that there's the place—but "*Verbum sat.*"[3]
I think, I picked up too, as well as most,
Knowledge of matters—but no matter *what*—
I never married—but, I think, I know
That sons should not be educated so.

54

Young Juan now was sixteen years of age,
Tall, handsome, slender, but well knit; he seemed
Active, though not so sprightly, as a page;
And every body but his mother deemed
Him almost man; but she flew in a rage,
And bit her lips (for else she might have screamed),
If any said so, for to be precocious
Was in her eyes a thing the most atrocious.

---

[1] *Jerome* St. Jerome (340?–420), translator of the Bible into Latin; *Chrysostom* St. John Chrysostom (347?–407); both were ascetics.

[2] [Byron's note] See his *Confessions*, lib. i. cap. ix. By the representation which Saint Augustine gives of himself in his youth, it is easy to see that he was what we should call a rake. He avoided the school as the plague; he loved nothing but gaming and public shows; he robbed his father of everything he could find; he invented a thousand lies to escape the rod, which they were obliged to make use of to punish his irregularities.

[3] *Verbum sat* Latin: a word [to the wise] is enough.

55

Amongst her numerous acquaintance, all
Selected for discretion and devotion,
There was the Donna Julia, whom to call
Pretty were but to give a feeble notion
Of many charms in her as natural
As sweetness to the flower, or salt to ocean,
Her zone to Venus, or his bow to Cupid,
(But this last simile is trite and stupid.)

56

The darkness of her oriental eye
Accorded with her Moorish origin;
(Her blood was not all Spanish, by the by;
In Spain, you know, this is a sort of sin.)
When proud Granada fell, and, forced to fly,
Boabdil wept,[1] of Donna Julia's kin
Some went to Africa, some staid in Spain,
Her great great grandmamma chose to remain.

57

She married (I forget the pedigree)
With an Hidalgo, who transmitted down
His blood less noble than such blood should be;
At such alliances his sires would frown,
In that point so precise in each degree
That they bred *in and in*, as might be shown,
Marrying their cousins—nay, their aunts and nieces,
Which always spoils the breed, if it increases.[2]

58

This heathenish cross restored the breed again,
Ruined its blood, but much improved its flesh;
For, from a root the ugliest in Old Spain
Sprung up a branch as beautiful as fresh;
The sons no more were short, the daughters plain:
But there's a rumour which I fain would hush,
'Tis said that Donna Julia's grandmamma
Produced her Don more heirs at love than law.

59

However this might be, the race went on
Improving still through every generation,
Until it centred in an only son,
Who left an only daughter; my narration
May have suggested that this single one
Could be but Julia (whom on this occasion
I shall have much to speak about), and she
Was married, charming, chaste, and twenty-three.

60

Her eye (I'm very fond of handsome eyes)
Was large and dark, suppressing half its fire
Until she spoke, then through its soft disguise
Flashed an expression more of pride than ire,
And love than either; and there would arise
A something in them which was not desire,
But would have been, perhaps, but for the soul
Which struggled through and chastened down the whole.

61

Her glossy hair was clustered o'er a brow
Bright with intelligence, and fair and smooth;
Her eyebrow's shape was like the aerial bow,
Her cheek all purple with the beam of youth,
Mounting, at times, to a transparent glow,
As if her veins ran lightning; she, in sooth,
Possessed an air and grace by no means common:
Her stature tall—I hate a dumpy woman.

62

Wedded she was some years, and to a man
Of fifty, and such husbands are in plenty;
And yet, I think, instead of such a ONE
'Twere better to have TWO of five-and-twenty,
Especially in countries near the sun:
And now I think on't, "mi vien in mente,"[3]
Ladies even of the most uneasy virtue
Prefer a spouse whose age is short of thirty.

63

'Tis a sad thing, I cannot choose but say,
And all the fault of that indecent sun,

[1] *Boabdil* Mohammed XI, the last Moorish king of Granada, defeated by the Spanish in 1492.

[2] *Marrying … increases* The Byron family frequently intermarried, cousins wedding cousins.

[3] *mi … mente* Italian: "It comes into my mind."

Who cannot leave alone our helpless clay,
    But will keep baking, broiling, burning on,
That howsoever people fast and pray
    The flesh is frail, and so the soul undone:
What men call gallantry, and gods adultery,
Is much more common where the climate's sultry.

64

Happy the nations of the moral north!
    Where all is virtue, and the winter season
Sends sin, without a rag on, shivering forth;
    ('Twas snow that brought St. Anthony to reason);[1]
Where juries cast up what a wife is worth
    By laying whate'er sum, in mulct, they please on
The lover, who must pay a handsome price,
Because it is a marketable vice.

65

Alfonso was the name of Julia's lord,
    A man well looking for his years, and who
Was neither much beloved, nor yet abhorred;
    They lived together as most people do,
Suffering each other's foibles by accord,
    And not exactly either *one* or *two*;
Yet he was jealous, though he did not show it,
For jealousy dislikes the world to know it.

66

Julia was—yet I never could see why—
    With Donna Inez quite a favourite friend;
Between their tastes there was small sympathy,
    For not a line had Julia ever penned:
Some people whisper (but, no doubt, they lie,
    For malice still imputes some private end)
That Inez had, ere Don Alfonso's marriage,
Forgot with him her very prudent carriage.

67

And that still keeping up the old connexion,
    Which time had lately rendered much more chaste,
She took his lady also in affection,
    And certainly this course was much the best:
She flattered Julia with her sage protection,
    And complimented Don Alfonso's taste;
And if she could not (who can?) silence scandal,
At least she left it a more slender handle.

68

I can't tell whether Julia saw the affair
    With other people's eyes, or if her own
Discoveries made, but none could be aware
    Of this, at least no symptom e'er was shown;
Perhaps she did not know, or did not care,
    Indifferent from the first, or callous grown:
I'm really puzzled what to think or say,
She kept her counsel in so close a way.

69

Juan she saw, and, as a pretty child,
    Caressed him often, such a thing might be
Quite innocently done, and harmless styled,
    When she had twenty years, and thirteen he;
But I am not so sure I should have smiled
    When he was sixteen, Julia twenty-three,
These few short years make wondrous alterations,
Particularly amongst sun-burnt nations.

70

Whate'er the cause might be, they had become
    Changed; for the dame grew distant, the youth shy,
Their looks cast down, their greetings almost dumb,
    And much embarrassment in either eye;
There surely will be little doubt with some
    That Donna Julia knew the reason why,
But as for Juan, he had no more notion
Than he who never saw the sea of ocean.

71

Yet Julia's very coldness still was kind,
    And tremulously gentle her small hand
Withdrew itself from his, but left behind
    A little pressure, thrilling, and so bland
And slight, so very slight, that to the mind
    'Twas but a doubt; but ne'er magician's wand

[1] [Byron's note] For the particulars of St. Anthony's recipe for hot blood in cold weather, see Mr. Alban Butler's Lives of the Saints. [It was actually St. Francis of Assisi who was reported to have thrown himself naked into the snow to counteract the temptations of the flesh.]

Wrought change with all Armida's fairy art[1]
Like what this light touch left on Juan's heart.

72

And if she met him, though she smiled no more,
  She looked a sadness sweeter than her smile,
As if her heart had deeper thoughts in store
  She must not own, but cherished more the while,
For that compression in its burning core;
  Even innocence itself has many a wile,
And will not dare to trust itself with truth,
And love is taught hypocrisy from youth.

73

But passion most dissembles yet betrays
  Even by its darkness; as the blackest sky
Foretells the heaviest tempest, it displays
  Its workings through the vainly guarded eye,
And in whatever aspect it arrays
  Itself, 'tis still the same hypocrisy;
Coldness or anger, even disdain or hate,
Are masks it often wears, and still too late.

74

Then there were sighs, the deeper for suppression,
  And stolen glances, sweeter for the theft,
And burning blushes, though for no transgression,
  Tremblings when met, and restlessness when left;
All these are little preludes to possession,
  Of which young Passion cannot be bereft,
And merely tend to show how greatly Love is
Embarrassed at first starting with a novice.

75

Poor Julia's heart was in an awkward state;
  She felt it going, and resolved to make
The noblest efforts for herself and mate,
  For honour's, pride's, religion's, virtue's sake;
Her resolutions were most truly great,
  And almost might have made a Tarquin quake;[2]
She prayed the Virgin Mary for her grace,
As being the best judge of a lady's case.

76

She vowed she never would see Juan more,
  And next day paid a visit to his mother,
And looked extremely at the opening door,
  Which, by the Virgin's grace, let in another;
Grateful she was, and yet a little sore—
  Again it opens, it can be no other,
'Tis surely Juan now—No! I'm afraid
That night the Virgin was no further prayed.

77

She now determined that a virtuous woman
  Should rather face and overcome temptation,
That flight was base and dastardly, and no man
  Should ever give her heart the least sensation;
That is to say, a thought beyond the common
  Preference, that we must feel upon occasion,
For people who are pleasanter than others,
But then they only seem so many brothers.

78

And even if by chance—and who can tell?
  The devil's so very sly—she should discover
That all within was not so very well,
  And, if still free, that such or such a lover
Might please perhaps, a virtuous wife can quell
  Such thoughts, and be the better when they're over;
And if the man should ask, 'tis but denial:
I recommend young ladies to make trial.

79

And then there are such things as love divine,
  Bright and immaculate, unmixed and pure,
Such as the angels think so very fine,
  And matrons, who would be no less secure,
Platonic, perfect, "just such love as mine:"
  Thus Julia said—and thought so, to be sure,
And so I'd have her think, were I the man
On whom her reveries celestial ran.

---

1 *Armida* The enchantress in Torquato Tasso's, *Jerusalem Delivered.*

2 *Tarquin* Sextus Tarquinius raped Lucretia, a Roman matron, who subsequently stabbed herself.

80

Such love is innocent, and may exist
Between young persons without any danger,
A hand may first, and then a lip be kist;
For my part, to such doings I'm a stranger,
But *hear* these freedoms form the utmost list
Of all o'er which such love may be a ranger:
If people go beyond, 'tis quite a crime,
But not my fault—I tell them all in time.

81

Love, then, but love within its proper limits,
Was Julia's innocent determination
In young Don Juan's favour, and to him its
Exertion might be useful on occasion;
And, lighted at too pure a shrine to dim its
Ethereal lustre, with what sweet persuasion
He might be taught, by love and her together—
I really don't know what, nor Julia either.

82

Fraught with this fine intention, and well fenced
In mail of proof—her purity of soul—
She, for the future of her strength convinced,
And that her honour was a rock, or mole,[1]
Exceeding sagely from that hour dispensed
With any kind of troublesome control;
But whether Julia to the task was equal
Is that which must be mentioned in the sequel.

83

Her plan she deemed both innocent and feasible,
And, surely, with a stripling of sixteen
Not scandal's fangs could fix on much that's seizable,
Or if they did so, satisfied to mean
Nothing but what was good, her breast was peaceable—
A quiet conscience makes one so serene!
Christians have burnt each other, quite persuaded
That all the Apostles would have done as they did.

84

And if in the mean time her husband died,
But heaven forbid that such a thought should cross
Her brain, though in a dream! (and then she sighed)
Never could she survive that common loss;
But just suppose that moment should betide,
I only say suppose it—*inter nos*.
(This should be *entre nous*,[2] for Julia thought
In French, but then the rhyme would go for nought.)

85

I only say suppose this supposition:
Juan being then grown up to man's estate
Would fully suit a widow of condition,
Even seven years hence it would not be too late;
And in the interim (to pursue this vision)
The mischief, after all, could not be great,
For he would learn the rudiments of love,
I mean the seraph way[3] of those above.

86

So much for Julia. Now we'll turn to Juan,
Poor little fellow! he had no idea
Of his own case, and never hit the true one;
In feelings quick as Ovid's Miss Medea,
He puzzled over what he found a new one,
But not as yet imagined it could be a
Thing quite in course, and not at all alarming,
Which, with a little patience, might grow charming.

87

Silent and pensive, idle, restless, slow,
His home deserted for the lonely wood,
Tormented with a wound he could not know,
His, like all deep grief, plunged in solitude:
I'm fond myself of solitude or so,
But then, I beg it may be understood,
By solitude I mean a sultan's, not
A hermit's, with a haram° for a grot. *harem*

88

"Oh Love! in such a wilderness as this,
Where transport and security entwine,
Here is the empire of thy perfect bliss,

[1] *mole* Massive structure, such as a pier or breakwater.

[2] *inter nos* Latin: between us; *entre nous* French: between us.

[3] *seraph way* I.e., angelic way.

And here thou art a god indeed divine."[1]
The bard I quote from does not sing amiss,
With the exception of the second line,
For that same twining "transport and security"
Are twisted to a phrase of some obscurity.

89

The poet meant, no doubt, and thus appeals
To the good sense and senses of mankind,
The very thing which every body feels,
As all have found on trial, or may find,
That no one likes to be disturbed at meals
Or love.—I won't say more about "entwined"
Or "transport," as we knew all that before,
But beg "Security" will bolt the door.

90

Young Juan wandered by the glassy brooks,
Thinking unutterable things; he threw
Himself at length within the leafy nooks
Where the wild branch of the cork forest grew;
There poets find materials for their books,
And every now and then we read them through,
So that their plan and prosody are eligible,
Unless, like Wordsworth, they prove unintelligible.

91

He, Juan (and not Wordsworth), so pursued
His self-communion with his own high soul,
Until his mighty heart,[2] in its great mood,
Had mitigated part, though not the whole
Of its disease; he did the best he could
With things not very subject to control,
And turned, without perceiving his condition,
Like Coleridge, into a metaphysician.[3]

92

He thought about himself, and the whole earth,
Of man the wonderful, and of the stars,
And how the deuce they ever could have birth;
And then he thought of earthquakes, and of wars,
How many miles the moon might have in girth,
Of air-balloons, and of the many bars
To perfect knowledge of the boundless skies;
And then he thought of Donna Julia's eyes.

93

In thoughts like these true wisdom may discern
Longings sublime, and aspirations high,
Which some are born with, but the most part learn
To plague themselves withal, they know not why:
'Twas strange that one so young should thus concern
His brain about the action of the sky;
If *you* think 'twas philosophy that this did,
I can't help thinking puberty assisted.

94

He pored upon the leaves, and on the flowers,
And heard a voice in all the winds; and then
He thought of wood nymphs and immortal bowers,
And how the goddesses came down to men:
He missed the pathway, he forgot the hours,
And when he looked upon his watch again,
He found how much old Time had been a winner—
He also found that he had lost his dinner.[4]

95

Sometimes he turned to gaze upon his book,
Boscan, or Garcilasso;[5]—by the wind
Even as the page is rustled while we look,
So by the poesy of his own mind
Over the mystic leaf his soul was shook,
As if 'twere one whereon magicians bind
Their spells, and give them to the passing gale,
According to some good old woman's tale.

96

Thus would he while his lonely hours away
Dissatisfied, nor knowing what he wanted;

[1] [Byron's note] Campbell's Gertrude of Wyoming, (I think) the opening of Canto II; but quote from memory. [Thomas Campbell, *Gertrude of Wyoming* 3.1.1–4.]

[2] *so pursued … heart* See Wordsworth, "Composed upon Westminster Bridge" (1802), 14.

[3] *turned … metaphysician* See Coleridge, "Dejection: an Ode," 87–93.

[4] *lost his dinner* I.e., was so late for dinner that he had missed it entirely.

[5] *Boscan* Spanish poet Juan Boscán (1500–44); *Garcilasso* Spanish poet Garcias Lasso or Garcilaso de la Vega (1503–36).

Nor glowing reverie, nor poet's lay,
    Could yield his spirit that for which it panted,
A bosom whereon he his head might lay,
    And hear the heart beat with the love it granted,
With—several other things, which I forget,
Or which, at least, I need not mention yet.

97

Those lonely walks, and lengthening reveries,
    Could not escape the gentle Julia's eyes;
She saw that Juan was not at his ease;
    But that which chiefly may, and must surprise,
Is, that the Donna Inez did not tease
    Her only son with question or surmise;
Whether it was she did not see, or would not,
Or, like all very clever people, could not.

98

This may seem strange, but yet 'tis very common;
    For instance—gentlemen, whose ladies take
Leave to o'erstep the written rights of woman,
    And break the—Which commandment is't they
        break?[1]
(I have forgot the number, and think no man
    Should rashly quote, for fear of a mistake.)
I say, when these same gentlemen are jealous,
They make some blunder, which their ladies tell us.

99

A real husband always is suspicious,
    But still no less suspects in the wrong place,
Jealous of some one who had no such wishes,
    Or pandering blindly to his own disgrace
By harbouring some dear friend extremely vicious;
    The last indeed's infallibly the case:
And when the spouse and friend are gone off wholly,
He wonders at their vice, and not his folly.

100

Thus parents also are at times short-sighted;
    Though watchful as the lynx, they ne'er discover,
The while the wicked world beholds delighted,
    Young Hopeful's mistress, or Miss Fanny's lover,
Till some confounded escapade has blighted
    The plan of twenty years, and all is over;
And then the mother cries, the father swears,
And wonders why the devil he got heirs.[2]

101

But Inez was so anxious, and so clear
    Of sight, that I must think, on this occasion,
She had some other motive much more near
    For leaving Juan to this new temptation;
But what that motive was, I shan't say here;
    Perhaps to finish Juan's education,
Perhaps to open Don Alfonso's eyes,
In case he thought his wife too great a prize.

102

It was upon a day, a summer's day;—
    Summer's indeed a very dangerous season,
And so is spring about the end of May;
    The sun, no doubt, is the prevailing reason;
But whatsoe'er the cause is, one may say,
    And stand convicted of more truth than treason,
That there are months which nature grows more
        merry in,
March has its hares, and May must have its heroine.

103

'Twas on a summer's day—the sixth of June:—
    I like to be particular in dates,
Not only of the age, and year, but moon;
    They are a sort of post-house, where the Fates
Change horses, making history change its tune,
    Then spur away o'er empires and o'er states,
Leaving at last not much besides chronology,
Excepting the post-obits[3] of theology.

104

'Twas on the sixth of June, about the hour
    Of half-past six—perhaps still nearer seven,
When Julia sat within as pretty a bower
    As e'er held houri in that heathenish heaven

[1] *Which commandment ... break?* They break the seventh commandment, "Thou shalt not commit adultery."

[2] *got heirs* I.e., begot children, heirs to his estate.

[3] *post-obits* Latin: after death; here, referring to a legacy, that which comes after a death.

Described by Mahomet, and Anacreon Moore,[1]
To whom the lyre and laurels have been given,
With all the trophies of triumphant song—
He won them well, and may he wear them long!

105

She sate, but not alone; I know not well
How this same interview had taken place,
And even if I knew, I should not tell—
People should hold their tongues in any case;
No matter how or why the thing befell,
But there were she and Juan, face to face—
When two such faces are so, 'twould be wise,
But very difficult, to shut their eyes.

106

How beautiful she looked! her conscious heart
Glowed in her cheek, and yet she felt no wrong.
Oh Love! how perfect is thy mystic art,
Strengthening the weak, and trampling on the strong,
How self-deceitful is the sagest part
Of mortals whom thy lure hath led along—
The precipice she stood on was immense,
So was her creed in her own innocence.

107

She thought of her own strength, and Juan's youth
And of the folly of all prudish fears,
Victorious virtue, and domestic truth,
And then of Don Alfonso's fifty years:
I wish these last had not occurred, in sooth,
Because that number rarely much endears,
And through all climes, the snowy and the sunny,
Sounds ill in love, whate'er it may in money.

108

When people say, "I've told you *fifty* times,"
They mean to scold, and very often do;
When poets say, "I've written *fifty* rhymes,"
They make you dread that they'll recite them too;
In gangs of *fifty*, thieves commit their crimes;
At *fifty* love for love is rare, 'tis true,
But then, no doubt, it equally as true is,
A good deal may be bought for fifty Louis.[2]

109

Julia had honour, virtue, truth, and love
For Don Alfonso; and she inly swore,
By all the vows below to powers above,
She never would disgrace the ring she wore,
Nor leave a wish which wisdom might reprove;
And while she pondered this, besides much more,
One hand on Juan's carelessly was thrown,
Quite by mistake—she thought it was her own;

110

Unconsciously she leaned upon the other,
Which played within the tangles of her hair;
And to contend with thoughts she could not smother,
She seemed by the distraction of her air.
'Twas surely very wrong in Juan's mother
To leave together this imprudent pair,
She who for many years had watched her son so—
I'm very certain *mine* would not have done so.

111

The hand which still held Juan's, by degrees
Gently, but palpably confirmed its grasp,
As if it said, "detain me, if you please;"
Yet there's no doubt she only meant to clasp
His fingers with a pure Platonic squeeze;
She would have shrunk as from a toad, or asp,
Had she imagined such a thing could rouse
A feeling dangerous to a prudent spouse.

112

I cannot know what Juan thought of this,
But what he did, is much what you would do;
His young lip thanked it with a grateful kiss,
And then, abashed at its own joy, withdrew
In deep despair, lest he had done amiss,
Love is so very timid when 'tis new:

[1] *Anacreon Moore* Byron's friend Thomas Moore was known as "Anacreon" Moore because he first became famous for translating the lyric poems then attributed to the Roman poet Anacreon. The reference is to "Paradise and the Peri," one of the tales in Moore's *Lalla Rookh* (1817).

[2] *Louis* French gold coin.

She blushed, and frowned not, but she strove to speak,
And held her tongue, her voice was grown so weak.

113

The sun set, and up rose the yellow moon:
The devil's in the moon for mischief; they
Who called her CHASTE, methinks, began too soon
Their nomenclature; there is not a day,
The longest, not the twenty-first of June,
Sees half the business in a wicked way
On which three single hours of moonshine smile—
And then she looks so modest all the while.

114

There is a dangerous silence in that hour,
A stillness, which leaves room for the full soul
To open all itself, without the power
Of calling wholly back its self-control;
The silver light which, hallowing tree and tower,
Sheds beauty and deep softness o'er the whole,
Breathes also to the heart, and o'er it throws
A loving languor, which is not repose.

115

And Julia sat with Juan, half embraced
And half retiring from the glowing arm,
Which trembled like the bosom where 'twas placed;
Yet still she must have thought there was no harm,
Or else 'twere easy to withdraw her waist;
But then the situation had its charm,
And then—God knows what next—I can't go on;
I'm almost sorry that I e'er begun.

116

Oh Plato! Plato! you have paved the way,
With your confounded fantasies, to more
Immoral conduct by the fancied sway
Your system feigns o'er the controlless core
Of human hearts, than all the long array
Of poets and romancers:—You're a bore,
A charlatan, a coxcomb—and have been,
At best, no better than a go-between.

117

And Julia's voice was lost, except in sighs,
Until too late for useful conversation;
The tears were gushing from her gentle eyes,
I wish, indeed, they had not had occasion,
But who, alas! can love, and then be wise?
Not that remorse did not oppose temptation,
A little still she strove, and much repented,
And whispering "I will ne'er consent"—consented.

118

'Tis said that Xerxes[1] offered a reward
To those who could invent him a new pleasure;
Methinks, the requisition's rather hard,
And must have cost His majesty a treasure:
For my part, I'm a moderate-minded bard,
Fond of a little love (which I call leisure);
I care not for new pleasures, as the old
Are quite enough for me, so they but hold.

119

Oh Pleasure! you're indeed a pleasant thing,
Although one must be damned for you, no doubt;
I make a resolution every spring
Of reformation, ere the year run out,
But, somehow, this my vestal vow takes wing,
Yet still, I trust, it may be kept throughout:
I'm very sorry, very much ashamed,
And mean, next winter, to be quite reclaimed.

120

Here my chaste Muse a liberty must take—
Start not! still chaster reader—she'll be nice
hence—
Forward, and there is no great cause to quake;
This liberty is a poetic licence,
Which some irregularity may make
In the design, and as I have a high sense
Of Aristotle and the Rules,[2] 'tis fit
To beg his pardon when I err a bit.

121

This licence is to hope the reader will
Suppose from June the sixth (the fatal day,

[1] *Xerxes* Xerxes was King of Persia from 486 to 465 BCE.

[2] *Rules* I.e., rules for literary composition set out in Aristotle's *Poetics*.

Without whose epoch my poetic skill
For want of facts would all be thrown away),
But keeping Julia and Don Juan still
In sight, that several months have passed; we'll say
'Twas in November, but I'm not so sure
About the day—the era's more obscure.

122

We'll talk of that anon.—'Tis sweet to hear
At midnight on the blue and moonlit deep
The song and oar of Adria's gondolier,
By distance mellowed, o'er the waters sweep;
'Tis sweet to see the evening star appear;
'Tis sweet to listen as the night-winds creep
From leaf to leaf; 'tis sweet to view on high
The rainbow, based on ocean, span the sky.

123

'Tis sweet to hear the watch-dog's honest bark
Bay deep-mouthed welcome as we draw near home;
'Tis sweet to know there is an eye will mark
Our coming, and look brighter when we come;
'Tis sweet to be awakened by the lark,
Or lulled by falling waters; sweet the hum
Of bees, the voice of girls, the song of birds,
The lisp of children, and their earliest words.

124

Sweet is the vintage, when the showering grapes
In Bacchanal profusion reel to earth
Purple and gushing: sweet are our escapes
From civic revelry to rural mirth;
Sweet to the miser are his glittering heaps,
Sweet to the father is his first-born's birth,
Sweet is revenge—especially to women,
Pillage to soldiers, prize-money to seamen.

125

Sweet is a legacy, and passing sweet
The unexpected death of some old lady
Or gentleman of seventy years complete,
Who've made "us youth" wait too—too long already
For an estate, or cash, or country-seat,
Still breaking, but with stamina so steady,
That all the Israelites are fit to mob its
Next owner for their double-damned post-obits.[1]

126

'Tis sweet to win, no matter how, one's laurels
By blood or ink; 'tis sweet to put an end
To strife; 'tis sometimes sweet to have our quarrels,
Particularly with a tiresome friend;
Sweet is old wine in bottles, ale in barrels;
Dear is the helpless creature we defend
Against the world; and dear the schoolboy spot
We ne'er forget, though there we are forgot.

127

But sweeter still than this, than these, than all,
Is first and passionate love—it stands alone,
Like Adam's recollection of his fall;
The tree of knowledge has been plucked—all's known—
And life yields nothing further to recall
Worthy of this ambrosial sin, so shown,
No doubt in fable, as the unforgiven
Fire which Prometheus filched for us from heaven.

128

Man's a strange animal, and makes strange use
Of his own nature, and the various arts,
And likes particularly to produce
Some new experiment to show his parts;
This is the age of oddities let loose,
Where different talents find their different marts;
You'd best begin with truth, and when you've lost your
Labour, there's a sure market for imposture.

129

What opposite discoveries we have seen!
(Signs of true genius, and of empty pockets.)
One makes new noses, one a guillotine,
One breaks your bones, one sets them in their sockets;
But vaccination certainly has been
A kind antithesis to Congreve's rockets,

[1] *post-obits* Here, loans repayable after a death; that is, when the borrower comes into an inheritance.

With which the Doctor paid off an old pox,
By borrowing a new one from an ox.[1]

130

Bread has been made (indifferent) from potatoes;
And galvanism has set some corpses grinning,
But has not answered like the apparatus
Of the Humane Society's beginning
By which men are unsuffocated gratis:
What wondrous new machines have late been spinning!
I said the small-pox has gone out of late;
Perhaps it may be followed by the great.

131

'Tis said the great came from America;
Perhaps it may set out on its return,—
The population there so spreads, they say
'Tis grown high time to thin it in its turn,
With war, or plague, or famine,[2] any way,
So that civilisation they may learn;
And which in ravage the more loathsome evil is—
Their real lues,° or our pseudo-syphilis? *syphilis*

132

This is the patent age of new inventions
For killing bodies, and for saving souls,[3]
All propagated with the best intentions;
Sir Humphry Davy's lantern, by which coals
Are safely mined for in the mode he mentions,[4]
Timbuctoo travels, voyages to the Poles,[5]
Are ways to benefit mankind, as true,
Perhaps, as shooting them at Waterloo.[6]

133

Man's a phenomenon, one knows not what,
And wonderful beyond all wondrous measure;
'Tis pity though, in this sublime world, that
Pleasure's a sin, and sometimes sin's a pleasure;
Few mortals know what end they would be at,
But whether glory, power, or love, or treasure,
The path is through perplexing ways, and when
The goal is gained, we die, you know—and then—

134

What then?—I do not know, no more do you—
And so good night.—Return we to our story:
'Twas in November, when fine days are few,
And the far mountains wax a little hoary,
And clap a white cape on their mantles blue;
And the sea dashes round the promontory,
And the loud breaker boils against the rock,
And sober suns must set at five o'clock.

135

'Twas, as the watchmen say, a cloudy night;
No moon, no stars, the wind was low or loud
By gusts, and many a sparkling hearth was bright
With the piled wood, round which the family crowd;
There's something cheerful in that sort of light,
Even as a summer sky's without a cloud:
I'm fond of fire, and crickets, and all that,
A lobster salad, and champagne, and chat.

136

'Twas midnight—Donna Julia was in bed,
Sleeping, most probably,—when at her door
Arose a clatter might awake the dead,
If they had never been awoke before,

---

[1] *new noses* Benjamin Charles Perkins, an American quack, alleged that his metallic "tractors" could cure toes afflicted with the gout, as well as broken legs, flatulence, and red noses; *Congreve's rocket* Sir William Congreve (1772–1828) invented the Congreve rocket, which terrified the French at the Battle of Leipzig (1813), although it did little actual harm; *old pox ... ox* Edward Jenner (1749–1823) first vaccinated against smallpox in 1796, using the related cow-pox virus as his inoculant.

[2] *war, or plague, or famine* Byron here refers to the theory propounded by Thomas Malthus in his *An Essay on the Principles of Population* (1798–1817).

[3] *killing bodies ... saving souls* The British and Foreign Bible Society was founded in 1804.

[4] *Sir Humphry ... mentions* Sir Humphrey Davy (1778–1829) invented the safety lantern in 1815.

[5] *Timbuctoo ... Poles* Byron here refers to voyages of exploration such as those recounted in James Grey Jackson, *An Account of the Empire of Marocco* (1809); and Sir John Ross (1777–1856), *A Voyage of Discovery ... for the Purpose of Exploring Baffin's Bay* (1819).

[6] *Waterloo* I.e., the Battle of Waterloo, 18 June 1815.

And that they have been so we all have read,
And are to be so, at the least, once more—
The door was fastened, but with voice and fist
First knocks were heard, then "Madam—Madam—
hist![1]

137

"For God's sake, Madam—Madam—here's my master,
With more than half the city at his back—
Was ever heard of such a curst disaster!
'Tis not my fault—I kept good watch—Alack!
Do, pray undo the bolt a little faster—
They're on the stair just now, and in a crack
Will all be here; perhaps he yet may fly—
Surely the window's not so *very* high!"

138

By this time Don Alfonso was arrived,
With torches, friends, and servants in great number;
The major part of them had long been wived,
And therefore paused not to disturb the slumber
Of any wicked woman, who contrived
By stealth her husband's temples to encumber:[2]
Examples of this kind are so contagious,
Were *one* not punished, *all* would be outrageous.

139

I can't tell how, or why, or what suspicion
Could enter into Don Alfonso's head;
But for a cavalier of his condition
It surely was exceedingly ill-bred,
Without a word of previous admonition,
To hold a levee[3] round his lady's bed,
And summon lackeys, armed with fire and sword,
To prove himself the thing he most abhorred.

140

Poor Donna Julia, starting as from sleep!
(Mind—that I do not say—she had not slept)
Began at once to scream, and yawn, and weep;
Her maid Antonia, who was an adept,[4]
Contrived to fling the bed-clothes in a heap,
As if she had just now from out them crept:
I can't tell why she should take all this trouble
To prove her mistress had been sleeping double.[5]

141

But Julia mistress, and Antonia maid,
Appeared like two poor harmless women, who
Of goblins, but still more of men afraid,
Had thought one man might be deterred by two,
And therefore side by side were gently laid,
Until the hours of absence should run through,
And truant husband should return, and say,
"My dear, I was the first who came away."

142

Now Julia found at length a voice, and cried,
"In heaven's name, Don Alfonso, what d'ye mean?
Has madness seized you? would that I had died
Ere such a monster's victim I had been!
What may this midnight violence betide,
A sudden fit of drunkenness or spleen?
Dare you suspect me, whom the thought would kill?
Search, then, the room!"—Alfonso said, "I will."

143

He searched, *they* searched, and rummaged every where,
Closet and clothes'-press, chest and window-seat,
And found much linen, lace, and several pair
Of stockings, slippers, brushes, combs, complete,
With other articles of ladies fair,
To keep them beautiful, or leave them neat:
Arras[6] they pricked and curtains with their swords,
And wounded several shutters, and some boards.

144

Under the bed they searched, and there they found—
No matter what—it was not that they sought;
They opened windows, gazing if the ground
Had signs or footmarks, but the earth said nought;
And then they stared each others' faces round:

[1] *hist!* I.e., listen!

[2] *temples to encumber* That is, to give him horns, the traditional symbol of a cuckold.

[3] *levee* Morning reception.

[4] *adept* Skilled person.

[5] *sleeping double* I.e., with Antonia.

[6] *Arras* Wall-hangings.

'Tis odd, not one of all these seekers thought,
And seems to me almost a sort of blunder,
Of looking *in* the bed as well as under.

145

During this inquisition, Julia's tongue
Was not asleep—"Yes, search and search," she cried,
"Insult on insult heap, and wrong on wrong!
It was for this that I became a bride!
For this in silence I have suffered long
A husband like Alfonso at my side;
But now I'll bear no more, nor here remain,
If there be law, or lawyers, in all Spain.

146

"Yes, Don Alfonso! husband now no more,
If ever you indeed deserved the name,
Is't worthy of your years?—you have threescore,
Fifty, or sixty—it is all the same—
Is't wise or fitting causeless to explore
For facts against a virtuous woman's fame?
Ungrateful, perjured, barbarous Don Alfonso,
How dare you think your lady would go on so?

147

"Is it for this I have disdained to hold
The common privileges of my sex?
That I have chosen a confessor so old
And deaf, that any other it would vex,
And never once he has had cause to scold,
But found my very innocence perplex
So much, he always doubted I was married—
How sorry you will be when I've miscarried!

148

"Was it for this that no Cortejo[1] ere
I yet have chosen from out the youth of Seville?
Is it for this I scarce went any where,
Except to bull-fights, mass, play, rout, and revel?
Is it for this, whate'er my suitors were,
I favoured none—nay, was almost uncivil?
Is it for this that General Count O'Reilly,
Who took Algiers, declares I used him vilely?[2]

149

"Did not the Italian Musico° Cazzani musician
Sing at my heart six months at least in vain?
Did not his countryman, Count Corniani,[3]
Call me the only virtuous wife in Spain?
Were there not also Russians, English, many?
The Count Strongstroganoff I put in pain,
And Lord Mount Coffeehouse, the Irish peer,
Who killed himself for love (with wine) last year.

150

"Have I not had two bishops at my feet?
The Duke of Ichar, and Don Fernan Nunez?
And is it thus a faithful wife you treat?
I wonder in what quarter now the moon is:
I praise your vast forbearance not to beat
Me also, since the time so opportune is—
Oh, valiant man! with sword drawn and cocked trigger,
Now, tell me, don't you cut a pretty figure?

151

"Was it for this you took your sudden journey,
Under pretence of business indispensible
With that sublime of rascals your attorney,
Whom I see standing there, and looking sensible
Of having played the fool? though both I spurn, he
Deserves the worst, his conduct's less defensible,
Because, no doubt, 'twas for his dirty fee,
And not from any love to you nor me.

152

"If he comes here to take a deposition,
By all means let the gentleman proceed;
You've made the apartment in a fit condition:—
There's pen and ink for you, sir, when you need—
Let every thing be noted with precision,

---

1 *Cortejo* The acknowledged lover of a married woman.

2 [Byron's note] Donna Julia here made a mistake. Count O'Reilly did not take Algiers—but Algiers very nearly took him: he and his army and fleet retreated with great loss, and not much credit, from before that city in the year 17[75]. [Alexander O'Reilly (1722–94), Irish-born Spanish general.]

3 *Cazzani … Corniani* "Cazzani" is from "cazzo" (penis); "Corniani," from "cornuto" (horned; i.e., cuckolded).

I would not you for nothing should be feed—
But, as my maid's undrest, pray turn your spies out."
"Oh!" sobbed Antonia, "I could tear their eyes out."

153

"There is the closet, there the toilet, there
The antechamber—search them under, over;
There is the sofa, there the great arm-chair,
The chimney—which would really hold a lover.
I wish to sleep, and beg you will take care
And make no further noise, till you discover
The secret cavern of this lurking treasure—
And when 'tis found, let me, too, have that pleasure.

154

"And now, Hidalgo! now that you have thrown
Doubt upon me, confusion over all,
Pray have the courtesy to make it known
Who is the man you search for? how d'ye call
Him? what's his lineage? let him but be shown—
I hope he's young and handsome—is he tall?
Tell me—and be assured, that since you stain
My honour thus, it shall not be in vain.

155

"At least, perhaps, he has not sixty years,
At that age he would be too old for slaughter,
Or for so young a husband's jealous fears—
(Antonia! let me have a glass of water.)
I am ashamed of having shed these tears,
They are unworthy of my father's daughter;
My mother dreamed not in my natal hour
That I should fall into a monster's power.

156

"Perhaps 'tis of Antonia you are jealous,
You saw that she was sleeping by my side
When you broke in upon us with your fellows:
Look where you please—we've nothing, sir, to hide;
Only another time, I trust, you'll tell us,
Or for the sake of decency abide
A moment at the door, that we may be
Drest to receive so much good company.

157

"And now, sir, I have done, and say no more;
The little I have said may serve to show
The guileless heart in silence may grieve o'er
The wrongs to whose exposure it is slow:—
I leave you to your conscience as before,
'Twill one day ask you *why* you used me so?
God grant you feel not then the bitterest grief!
Antonia! where's my pocket-handkerchief?"

158

She ceased, and turned upon her pillow; pale
She lay, her dark eyes flashing through their tears,
Like skies that rain and lighten; as a veil,
Waved and o'ershading her wan cheek, appears
Her streaming hair; the black curls strive, but fail,
To hide the glossy shoulder, which uprears
Its snow through all;—her soft lips lie apart,
And louder than her breathing beats her heart.

159

The Senhor Don Alfonso stood confused;
Antonia bustled round the ransacked room,
And, turning up her nose, with looks abused
Her master, and his myrmidons,[1] of whom
Not one, except the attorney, was amused;
He, like Achates,[2] faithful to the tomb,
So there were quarrels, cared not for the cause,
Knowing they must be settled by the laws.

160

With prying snub-nose, and small eyes, he stood,
Following Antonia's motions here and there,
With much suspicion in his attitude;
For reputations he had little care;
So that a suit or action were made good,
Small pity had he for the young and fair,
And ne'er believed in negatives, till these
Were proved by competent false witnesses.

[1] *myrmidons* Warriors led by Achilles to the siege of Troy.

[2] *Achates* Aeneas's companion in *The Aeneid*, famous for his faithfulness.

161

But Don Alfonso stood with downcast looks,
And, truth to say, he made a foolish figure;
When, after searching in five hundred nooks,
And treating a young wife with so much rigour,
He gained no point, except some self-rebukes,
Added to those his lady with such vigour
Had poured upon him for the last half-hour,
Quick, thick, and heavy—as a thunder-shower.

162

At first he tried to hammer an excuse,
To which the sole reply were tears and sobs,
And indications of hysterics, whose
Prologue is always certain throes, and throbs,
Gasps, and whatever else the owners choose:—
Alfonso saw his wife, and thought of Job's;[1]
He saw too, in perspective, her relations,
And then he tried to muster all his patience.

163

He stood in act to speak, or rather stammer,
But sage Antonia cut him short before
The anvil of his speech received the hammer,
With "Pray, sir, leave the room, and say no more,
Or madam dies."—Alfonso muttered, "D—n her,
But nothing else, the time of words was o'er;
He cast a rueful look or two, and did,
He knew not wherefore, that which he was bid.

164

With him retired his "*posse comitatus*,"[2]
The attorney last, who lingered near the door,
Reluctantly, still tarrying there as late as
Antonia let him—not a little sore
At this most strange and unexplained "*hiatus*"
In Don Alfonso's facts, which just now wore
An awkward look; as he revolved the case,
The door was fastened in his legal face.

165

No sooner was it bolted, than—Oh shame!
Oh sin! Oh sorrow! and Oh womankind!
How can you do such things and keep your fame,
Unless this world, and t'other too, be blind?
Nothing so dear as an unfilched good name!
But to proceed—for there is more behind:
With much heart-felt reluctance be it said,
Young Juan slipped, half-smothered, from the bed.

166

He had been hid—I don't pretend to say
How, nor can I indeed describe the where—
Young, slender, and packed easily, he lay,
No doubt, in little compass, round or square;
But pity him I neither must nor may
His suffocation by that pretty pair;
'Twere better, sure, to die so, than be shut
With maudlin Clarence in his Malmsey butt.[3]

167

And, secondly, I pity not, because
He had no business to commit a sin,
Forbid by heavenly, fined by human laws,
At least 'twas rather early to begin;
But at sixteen the conscience rarely gnaws
So much as when we call our old debts in
At sixty years, and draw the accompts of evil,
And find a deuced balance with the devil.

168

Of his position I can give no notion:
'Tis written in the Hebrew Chronicle,
How the physicians, leaving pill and potion,
Prescribed, by way of blister, a young belle,
When old King David's blood grew dull in motion,[4]
And that the medicine answered very well;
Perhaps 'twas in a different way applied,
For David lived, but Juan nearly died.

169

What's to be done? Alfonso will be back

[1] *Job's* See the Biblical book of Job.

[2] *posse comitatus* Latin: literally, "the power of the county," a group of deputies.

[3] *Clarence … butt* According to rumors that passed into legend, King Richard III of England, when Duke of Gloucester, arranged for his elder brother the Duke of Clarence to be drowned in a barrel of Malmsey wine, thus moving Richard closer to the throne.

[4] *When old … motion* See 1 Kings 1.1-4.

The moment he has sent his fools away.
Antonia's skill was put upon the rack,
But no device could be brought into play—
And how to parry the renewed attack?
Besides, it wanted but few hours of day:
Antonia puzzled; Julia did not speak,
But pressed her bloodless lip to Juan's cheek.

170

He turned his lip to hers, and with his hand
Called back the tangles of her wandering hair;
Even then their love they could not all command,
And half forgot their danger and despair:
Antonia's patience now was at a stand—
"Come, come, 'tis no time now for fooling there,"
She whispered, in great wrath—"I must deposit
This pretty gentleman within the closet.

171

"Pray, keep your nonsense for some luckier night—
Who can have put my master in this mood?
What will become on't—I'm in such a fright,
The devil's in the urchin, and no good—
Is this a time for giggling? this a plight?
Why, don't you know that it may end in blood?
You'll lose your life, and I shall lose my place,
My mistress all, for that half-girlish face.

172

"Had it but been for a stout cavalier
Of twenty-five or thirty—(Come, make haste)
But for a child, what piece of work is here!
I really, madam, wonder at your taste—
(Come, sir, get in)—my master must be near.
There, for the present, at the least he's fast,
And if we can but till the morning keep
Our counsel—(Juan, mind, you must not sleep.)"

173

Now, Don Alfonso entering, but alone,
Closed the oration of the trusty maid:
She loitered, and he told her to be gone,
An order somewhat sullenly obeyed;
However, present remedy was none,
And no great good seemed answered if she staid:
Regarding both with slow and sidelong view,
She snuffed the candle, curtsied, and withdrew.

174

Alfonso paused a minute—then begun
Some strange excuses for his late proceeding;
He would not justify what he had done,
To say the best, it was extreme ill-breeding;
But there were ample reasons for it, none
Of which he specified in this his pleading:
His speech was a fine sample, on the whole,
Of rhetoric, which the learned call "*rigmarole.*"

175

Julia said nought; though all the while there rose
A ready answer, which at once enables
A matron, who her husband's foible knows,
By a few timely words to turn the tables,
Which if it does not silence still must pose,
Even if it should comprise a pack of fables;
'Tis to retort with firmness, and when he
Suspects with *one*, do you reproach with *three.*

176

Julia, in fact, had tolerable grounds,
Alfonso's loves with Inez were well known;
But whether 'twas that one's own guilt confounds,
But that can't be, as has been often shown,
A lady with apologies abounds;
It might be that her silence sprang alone
From delicacy to Don Juan's ear,
To whom she knew his mother's fame was dear.

177

There might be one more motive, which makes two,
Alfonso ne'er to Juan had alluded,
Mentioned his jealousy, but never who
Had been the happy lover, he concluded,
Concealed amongst his premises; 'tis true,
His mind the more o'er this its mystery brooded;
To speak of Inez now were, one may say,
Like throwing Juan in Alfonso's way.

178

A hint, in tender cases, is enough;

Silence is best, besides there is a *tact*
(That modern phrase appears to me sad stuff,
But it will serve to keep my verse compact)
Which keeps, when pushed by questions rather rough,
A lady always distant from the fact—
The charming creatures lie with such a grace,
There's nothing so becoming to the face.

179

They blush, and we believe them; at least I
Have always done so; 'tis of no great use,
In any case, attempting a reply,
For then their eloquence grows quite profuse;
And when at length they're out of breath, they sigh,
And cast their languid eyes down, and let loose
A tear or two, and then we make it up;
And then—and then—and then—sit down and sup.

180

Alfonso closed his speech, and begged her pardon,
Which Julia half withheld, and then half granted,
And laid conditions, he thought, very hard on,
Denying several little things he wanted:
He stood like Adam lingering near his garden,
With useless penitence perplexed and haunted,
Beseeching she no further would refuse,
When, lo! he stumbled o'er a pair of shoes.

181

A pair of shoes!—what then? not much, if they
Are such as fit with lady's feet, but these
(No one can tell how much I grieve to say)
Were masculine; to see them, and to seize,
Was but a moment's act.—Ah! Well-a-day!
My teeth begin to chatter, my veins freeze—
Alfonso first examined well their fashion,
And then flew out into another passion.

182

He left the room for his relinquished sword,
And Julia instant to the closet flew.
"Fly, Juan, fly! for heaven's sake—not a word—
The door is open—you may yet slip through
The passage you so often have explored—
Here is the garden-key—Fly—fly—Adieu!
Haste—haste!—I hear Alfonso's hurrying feet—
Day has not broke—there's no one in the street."

183

None can say that this was not good advice,
The only mischief was, it came too late;
Of all experience 'tis the usual price,
A sort of income-tax laid on by fate:
Juan had reached the room-door in a trice,
And might have done so by the garden-gate,
But met Alfonso in his dressing-gown,
Who threatened death—so Juan knocked him down.

184

Dire was the scuffle, and out went the light,
Antonia cried out "Rape!" and Julia "Fire!"
But not a servant stirred to aid the fight.
Alfonso, pommelled to his heart's desire,
Swore lustily he'd be revenged this night;
And Juan, too, blasphemed an octave higher,
His blood was up; though young, he was a Tartar,
And not at all disposed to prove a martyr.

185

Alfonso's sword had dropped ere he could draw it,
And they continued battling hand to hand,
For Juan very luckily ne'er saw it;
His temper not being under great command,
If at that moment he had chanced to claw it,
Alfonso's days had not been in the land
Much longer.—Think of husbands', lovers' lives!
And how ye may be doubly widows—wives!

186

Alfonso grappled to detain the foe,
And Juan throttled him to get away,
And blood ('twas from the nose) began to flow;
At last, as they more faintly wrestling lay,
Juan contrived to give an awkward blow,
And then his only garment quite gave way;
He fled, like Joseph, leaving it; but there,
I doubt, all likeness ends between the pair.[1]

---

[1] *He fled ... the pair* See the story of Joseph and Potiphar's wife, Genesis 39.7–20.

187

Lights came at length, and men, and maids, who found
An awkward spectacle their eyes before;
Antonia in hysterics, Julia swooned,
Alfonso leaning, breathless, by the door;
Some half-torn drapery scattered on the ground,
Some blood, and several footsteps, but no more:
Juan the gate gained, turned the key about,
And liking not the inside, locked the out.

188

Here ends this canto.—Need I sing, or say,
How Juan, naked, favoured by the night,
Who favours what she should not, found his way,
And reached his home in an unseemly plight?
The pleasant scandal which arose next day,
The nine days' wonder which was brought to light,
And how Alfonso sued for a divorce,
Were in the English newspapers, of course.

189

If you would like to see the whole proceedings,
The depositions, and the cause at full,
The names of all the witnesses, the pleadings
Of counsel to nonsuit, or to annul,
There's more than one edition, and the readings
Are various, but they none of them are dull,
The best is that in short-hand ta'en by Gurney,[1]
Who to Madrid on purpose made a journey.

190

But Donna Inez, to divert the train
Of one of the most circulating scandals
That had for centuries been known in Spain,
At least since the retirement of the Vandals,
First vowed (and never had she vowed in vain)
To Virgin Mary several pounds of candles;
And then, by the advice of some old ladies,
She sent her son to be shipped off from Cadiz.

191

She had resolved that he should travel through
All European climes, by land or sea,
To mend his former morals, or get new,
Especially in France and Italy,
(At least this is the thing most people do.)
Julia was sent into a convent; she
Grieved, but, perhaps, her feelings may be better
Shown in the following copy of her letter:

192

"They tell me 'tis decided; you depart:
'Tis wise—'tis well, but not the less a pain;
I have no further claim on your young heart,
Mine is the victim, and would be again;
To love too much has been the only art
I used;—I write in haste, and if a stain
Be on this sheet, 'tis not what it appears,
My eyeballs burn and throb, but have no tears.

193

"I loved, I love you, for this love have lost
State, station, heaven, mankind's, my own esteem,
And yet can not regret what it hath cost,
So dear is still the memory of that dream;
Yet, if I name my guilt, 'tis not to boast,
None can deem harshlier of me than I deem:
I trace this scrawl because I cannot rest—
I've nothing to reproach, or to request.

194

"Man's love is of man's life a thing apart,
'Tis woman's whole existence; man may range
The court, camp, church, the vessel, and the mart;
Sword, gown, gain, glory, offer in exchange
Pride, fame, ambition, to fill up his heart,
And few there are whom these cannot estrange;
Men have all these resources, we but one,
To love again, and be again undone.

195

"You will proceed in pleasure, and in pride,
Beloved and loving many; all is o'er
For me on earth, except some years to hide
My shame and sorrow deep in my heart's core;
These I could bear, but cannot cast aside
The passion which still rages as before,

[1] *Gurney* William Brodie Gurney (1777–1855), official shorthand writer to the Houses of Parliament, also reported several notorious trials.

And so farewell—forgive me, love me—No,
That word is idle now—but let it go.

196

"My breast has been all weakness, is so yet;
But still I think I can collect my mind;
My blood still rushes where my spirit's set,
As roll the waves before the settled wind;
My heart is feminine, nor can forget—
To all, except one image, madly blind;
So shakes the needle, and so stands the pole,
As vibrates my fond heart to my fixed soul.

197

"I have no more to say, but linger still,
And dare not set my seal upon this sheet,
And yet I may as well the task fulfil,
My misery can scarce be more complete:
I had not lived till now, could sorrow kill;
Death shuns the wretch who fain the blow would meet,
And I must even survive this last adieu,
And bear with life, to love and pray for you!"

198

This note was written upon gilt-edged paper
With a neat little crow-quill, slight and new:
Her small white hand could hardly reach the taper,
It trembled as magnetic needles do,
And yet she did not let one tear escape her;
The seal a sun-flower; "*Elle vous suit partout*,"[1]
The motto, cut upon a white cornelian;
The wax was superfine, its hue vermilion.

199

This was Don Juan's earliest scrape; but whether
I shall proceed with his adventures is
Dependent on the public altogether;
We'll see, however, what they say to this,
Their favour in an author's cap's a feather,
And no great mischief's done by their caprice;
And if their approbation we experience,
Perhaps they'll have some more about a year hence.

200

My poem's epic, and is meant to be
Divided in twelve books; each book containing,
With love, and war, a heavy gale at sea,
A list of ships, and captains, and kings reigning,
New characters; the episodes are three:
A panorama view of hell's in training,
After the style of Virgil and of Homer,
So that my name of Epic's no misnomer.[2]

201

All these things will be specified in time,
With strict regard to Aristotle's rules,
The *Vade Mecum*[3] of the true sublime,
Which makes so many poets, and some fools;
Prose poets like blank-verse, I'm fond of rhyme,
Good workmen never quarrel with their tools;
I've got new mythological machinery,
And very handsome supernatural scenery.

202

There's only one slight difference between
Me and my epic brethren gone before,
And here the advantage is my own, I ween;
(Not that I have not several merits more,
But this will more peculiarly be seen)
They so embellish, that 'tis quite a bore
Their labyrinth of fables to thread through,
Whereas this story's actually true.

203

If any person doubt it, I appeal
To history, tradition, and to facts,
To newspapers, whose truth all know and feel,
To plays in five, and operas in three acts;
All these confirm my statement a good deal,
But that which more completely faith exacts
Is, that myself, and several now in Seville,
Saw Juan's last elopement with the devil.

[1] *Elle … partout* French: she follows you everywhere.

[2] *My poem's … no misnomer* Byron lists the traditional elements of an epic poem. See also the letter to John Murray, February 16, 1821, in this volume.

[3] *Vade mecum* Latin: literally, go with me; i.e., a guidebook.

204

If ever I should condescend to prose,
I'll write poetical commandments, which
Shall supersede beyond all doubt all those
That went before; in these I shall enrich
My text with many things that no one knows,
And carry precept to the highest pitch:
I'll call the work "Longinus o'er a Bottle,
Or, Every Poet his *own* Aristotle."[1]

205

Thou shalt believe in Milton, Dryden, Pope;
Thou shalt not set up Wordsworth, Coleridge,
Southey;
Because the first is crazed beyond all hope,
The second drunk, the third so quaint and mouthey:
With Crabbe it may be difficult to cope,
And Campbell's Hippocrene[2] is somewhat
drouthy:° *dry*
Thou shalt not steal from Samuel Rogers, nor
Commit—flirtation with the muse of Moore.

206

Thou shalt not covet Mr. Sotheby's Muse,[3]
His Pegasus, nor any thing that's his;
Thou shalt not bear false witness like "the Blues,"[4]
(There's *one*, at least, is very fond of this);
Thou shalt not write, in short, but what I choose:
This is true criticism, and you may kiss—
Exactly as you please, or not, the rod,
But if you don't, I'll lay it on, by G—d!

207

If any person should presume to assert
This story is not moral, first, I pray,
That they will not cry out before they're hurt,
Then that they'll read it o'er again, and say,
(But, doubtless, nobody will be so pert)
That this is not a moral tale, though gay;
Besides, in canto twelfth, I mean to show
The very place where wicked people go.

208

If, after all, there should be some so blind
To their own good this warning to despise,
Led by some tortuosity of mind,
Not to believe my verse and their own eyes,
And cry that they "the moral cannot find,"
I tell him, if a clergyman, he lies;
Should captains the remark or critics make,
They also lie too—under a mistake.

209

The public approbation I expect,
And beg they'll take my word about the moral,
Which I with their amusement will connect,
(So children cutting teeth receive a coral);[5]
Meantime, they'll doubtless please to recollect
My epical pretensions to the laurel:
For fear some prudish readers should grow skittish,
I've bribed my grandmother's review—the British.[6]

210

I sent it in a letter to the editor,
Who thanked me duly by return of post—
I'm for a handsome article his creditor;
Yet if my gentle Muse he please to roast,
And break a promise after having made it her,
Denying the receipt of what it cost,
And smear his page with gall instead of honey,
All I can say is—that he had the money.

211

I think that with this holy *new* alliance
I may ensure the public, and defy
All other magazines of art or science,
Daily, or monthly, or three monthly; I

[1] *Longinus … Aristotle* Longinus, *On the Sublime*, and Aristotle, *Poetics*: two renowned works of literary theory.

[2] *Hippocrene* A fountain sacred to the Muses, which started flowing when the winged horse Pegasus (see line 1642) struck the ground with his hoof.

[3] *Sotheby* William Sotheby (1757–1833), poet.

[4] *Blues* Group of intellectual women commonly called the "Bluestockings."

[5] *coral* Teething rings were commonly made of coral.

[6] *British* William Roberts, editor of the *British Review*, took this accusation seriously and contradicted it in his review of *Don Juan*, prompting Byron to write "Letter to the Editor of my Grandmother's Review" (1822).

Have not essayed to multiply their clients,
Because they tell me 'twere in vain to try,
And that the Edinburgh Review and Quarterly
Treat a dissenting author very martyrly.

212

"*Non ego hoc ferrem calida juventa*
Consule Planco," Horace said,[1] and so
Say I; by which quotation there is meant a
Hint that some six or seven good years ago
(Long ere I dreamt of dating from the Brenta)[2]
I was most ready to return a blow,
And would not brook at all this sort of thing
In my hot youth—when George the Third was King.

213

But now at thirty years my hair is gray—
(I wonder what it will be like at forty?
I thought of a peruke° the other day) *wig*
My heart is not much greener; and, in short, I
Have squandered my whole summer while 'twas May,
And feel no more the spirit to retort; I
Have spent my life, both interest and principal,
And deem not, what I deemed, my soul invincible.

214

No more—no more—Oh! never more on me
The freshness of the heart can fall like dew,
Which out of all the lovely things we see
Extracts emotions beautiful and new,
Hived in our bosoms like the bag o' the bee:
Think'st thou the honey with those objects grew?
Alas! 'twas not in them, but in thy power
To double even the sweetness of a flower.

215

No more—no more—Oh! never more, my heart,
Canst thou be my sole world, my universe!
Once all in all, but now a thing apart,
Thou canst not be my blessing or my curse:
The illusion's gone for ever, and thou art
Insensible, I trust, but none the worse,
And in thy stead I've got a deal of judgment,
Though heaven knows how it ever found a lodgement.

216

My days of love are over, me no more[3]
The charms of maid, wife, and still less of widow,
Can make the fool of which they made before,
In short, I must not lead the life I did do;
The credulous hope of mutual minds is o'er,
The copious use of claret is forbid too,
So for a good old-gentlemanly vice,
I think I must take up with avarice.

217

Ambition was my idol, which was broken
Before the shrines of Sorrow and of Pleasure;
And the two last have left me many a token
O'er which reflection may be made at leisure:
Now, like Friar Bacon's brazen head,[4] I've spoken,
"Time is, Time was, Time's past,"—a chymic° treasure *counterfeit gold*
Is glittering youth, which I have spent betimes—
My heart in passion, and my head on rhymes.

218

What is the end of Fame? 'tis but to fill
A certain portion of uncertain paper:
Some liken it to climbing up a hill,
Whose summit, like all hills, is lost in vapour;
For this men write, speak, preach, and heroes kill,
And bards burn what they call their "midnight taper,"
To have, when the original is dust,
A name, a wretched picture, and worse bust.[5]

---

[1] *Non…Planco* "I would not have borne with this in the heat of my youth, when Plancus was consul." Horace, *Odes* 3.14.27–28.

[2] *Brenta* River flowing into the Adriatic at Venice.

[3] [Byron's note] 'Me nec femina, nec puer
Jam, nec spes animi credula mutui,
Nec certare juvat mero;
Nec vincire novis tempora floribus.'
[Horace, *Odes* 4.1.30: "Now neither a woman nor a boy delights me, nor confident hope of love returned, nor drinking bouts, nor binding my temples with fresh flowers."]

[4] *Friar Bacon's brazen head* See Robert Greene's *Friar Bacon and Friar Bungay*.

[5] Byron sat for a number of busts and disliked all the results; he also found fault with most of his portraits.

219

What are the hopes of man? old Egypt's King
Cheops erected the first pyramid
And largest, thinking it was just the thing
To keep his memory whole, and mummy hid;
But somebody or other rummaging,
Burglariously broke his coffin's lid:
Let not a monument give you or me hopes,
Since not a pinch of dust remains of Cheops.

220

But I, being fond of true philosophy,
Say very often to myself, "Alas!
All things that have been born were born to die,
And flesh (which Death mows down to hay) is grass;[1]
You've passed your youth not so unpleasantly,
And if you had it o'er again—'twould pass—
So thank your stars that matters are no worse,
And read your Bible, sir, and mind your purse."

221

But for the present, gentle reader! and
Still gentler purchaser! the bard—that's I—
Must, with permission, shake you by the hand,
And so your humble servant, and good-bye!
We meet again, if we should understand
Each other; and if not, I shall not try
Your patience further than by this short sample—
'Twere well if others followed my example.

222

"Go, little book, from this my solitude!
I cast thee on the waters—go thy ways!
And if, as I believe, thy vein be good,
The world will find thee after many days."
When Southey's read, and Wordsworth, understood,
I can't help putting in my claim to praise—
The four first rhymes are Southey's every line:[2]
For God's sake, reader! take them not for mine.
—1819

[1] *flesh ... grass* See Isaiah 40.6.

[2] *Southey's every line* From Southey, *The Lay of the Laureate* (1816), "L'Envoy."

Canto 2

1

Oh ye! who teach the ingenuous youth of nations,
Holland, France, England, Germany, or Spain,
I pray ye flog them upon all occasions,
It mends their morals; never mind the pain:
The best of mothers and of educations
In Juan's case were but employed in vain,
Since in a way, that's rather of the oddest, he
Became divested of his native modesty.

2

Had he but been placed at a public school,
In the third form, or even in the fourth,
His daily task had kept his fancy cool,
At least, had he been nurtured in the north;
Spain may prove an exception to the rule,
But then exceptions always prove its worth—
A lad of sixteen causing a divorce
Puzzled his tutors very much, of course.

3

I can't say that it puzzles me at all,
If all things be considered: first, there was
His lady-mother, mathematical,
A—never mind; his tutor, an old ass;
A pretty woman—(that's quite natural,
Or else the thing had hardly come to pass);
A husband rather old, not much in unity
With his young wife—a time, and opportunity.

4

Well—well, the world must turn upon its axis,
And all mankind turn with it, heads or tails,
And live and die, make love and pay our taxes,
And as the veering wind shifts, shift our sails;
The king commands us, and the doctor quacks us,
The priest instructs, and so our life exhales,
A little breath, love, wine, ambition, fame,
Fighting, devotion, dust,—perhaps a name.

5

I said that Juan had been sent to Cadiz—
A pretty town, I recollect it well—

'Tis there the mart of the colonial trade is,
(Or was, before Peru learned to rebel)[1]
And such sweet girls—I mean, such graceful ladies,
Their very walk would make your bosom swell;
I can't describe it, though so much it strike,
Nor liken it—I never saw the like.

6

An Arab horse, a stately stag, a barb
New broke, a camelopard,° a gazelle, *giraffe*
No—none of these will do;—and then their garb!
Their veil and petticoat—Alas! to dwell
Upon such things would very near absorb
A canto—then their feet and ankles—well,
Thank Heaven I've got no metaphor quite ready,
(And so, my sober Muse—come, let's be steady—

7

Chaste Muse!—well, if you must, you must)—the veil
Thrown back a moment with the glancing hand,
While the o'erpowering eye, that turns you pale,
Flashes into the heart:—All sunny land
Of love! when I forget you, may I fail
To—say my prayers—but never was there planned
A dress through which the eyes give such a volley,
Excepting the Venetian Fazzioli.[2]

8

But to our tale: the Donna Inez sent
Her son to Cadiz only to embark;
To stay there had not answered her intent,
But why?—we leave the reader in the dark—
'Twas for a voyage the young man was meant,
As if a Spanish ship were Noah's ark,
To wean him from the wickedness of earth,
And send him like a dove of promise forth.

9

Don Juan bade his valet pack his things
According to direction, then received
A lecture and some money: for four springs
He was to travel; and though Inez grieved,
(As every kind of parting has its stings)
She hoped he would improve—perhaps believed:
A letter, too, she gave (he never read it)
Of good advice—and two or three of credit.[3]

10

In the mean time, to pass her hours away,
Brave Inez now set up a Sunday school
For naughty children, who would rather play
(Like truant rogues) the devil, or the fool;
Infants of three years old were taught that day,
Dunces were whipt, or set upon a stool:
The great success of Juan's education
Spurred her to teach another generation.

11

Juan embarked—the ship got under way,
The wind was fair, the water passing rough;
A devil of a sea rolls in that Bay,
As I, who've crossed it oft, know well enough;
And, standing upon deck, the dashing spray
Flies in one's face, and makes it weather-tough:
And there he stood to take, and take again,
His first—perhaps his last—farewell of Spain.

12

I can't but say it is an awkward sight
To see one's native land receding through
The growing waters; it unmans one quite,
Especially when life is rather new:
I recollect Great Britain's coast looks white,
But almost every other country's blue,
When gazing on them, mystified by distance,
We enter on our nautical existence.

13

So Juan stood, bewildered, on the deck:
The wind sung, cordage strained, and sailors swore,
And the ship creaked, the town became a speck,
From which away so fair and fast they bore.
The best of remedies is a beef-steak
Against sea-sickness; try it, sir, before

[1] *Peru learned to rebel* Peru rebelled against Spain in 1813, and would finally win its independence in 1824.

[2] [Byron's note] *Fazzioli*—literally, little handkerchiefs—the veils most availing of St. Mark.

[3] *letter … of credit* For presentation in order to procure funds.

You sneer, and I assure you this is true,
For I have found it answer—so may you.

14

Don Juan stood, and, gazing from the stern,
Beheld his native Spain receding far:
First partings form a lesson hard to learn,
Even nations feel this when they go to war;
There is a sort of unexpressed concern,
A kind of shock that sets one's heart ajar:
At leaving even the most unpleasant people
And places, one keeps looking at the steeple.

15

But Juan had got many things to leave,
His mother, and a mistress, and no wife,
So that he had much better cause to grieve
Than many persons more advanced in life;
And if we now and then a sigh must heave
At quitting even those we quit in strife,
No doubt we weep for those the heart endears—
That is, till deeper griefs congeal our tears.

16

So Juan wept, as wept the captive Jews
By Babel's waters, still remembering Sion:[1]
I'd weep, but mine is not a weeping Muse,
And such light griefs are not a thing to die on;
Young men should travel, if but to amuse
Themselves; and the next time their servants tie on
Behind their carriages their new portmanteau,
Perhaps it may be lined with this my canto.

17

And Juan wept, and much he sighed and thought,
While his salt tears dropped into the salt sea,
"Sweets to the sweet;" (I like so much to quote;
You must excuse this extract, 'tis where she,
The Queen of Denmark, for Ophelia brought
Flowers to the grave);[2] and, sobbing often, he
Reflected on his present situation,
And seriously resolved on reformation.

18

"Farewell, my Spain! a long farewell!" he cried,
"Perhaps I may revisit thee no more,
But die, as many an exiled heart hath died,
Of its own thirst to see again thy shore:
Farewell, where Guadalquivir's waters glide!
Farewell, my mother! and, since all is o'er,
Farewell, too, dearest Julia!"—(Here he drew
Her letter out again, and read it through.)

19

"And, oh! if e'er I should forget, I swear—
But that's impossible, and cannot be—
Sooner shall this blue ocean melt to air,
Sooner shall earth resolve itself to sea,
Than I resign thine image, Oh, my fair!
Or think of any thing excepting thee;
A mind diseased no remedy can physic—"
(Here the ship gave a lurch, and he grew sea-sick.)

20

"Sooner shall heaven kiss earth—(here he fell sicker)
Oh, Julia! what is every other woe?—
(For God's sake let me have a glass of liquor;—
Pedro, Battista, help me down below.)
Julia, my love!—(you rascal, Pedro, quicker)—
Oh Julia!—(this curst vessel pitches so)—
Beloved Julia, hear me still beseeching!"
(Here he grew inarticulate with retching.

21

He felt that chilling heaviness of heart,
Or rather stomach, which, alas! attends,
Beyond the best apothecary's art,
The loss of love, the treachery of friends,
Or death of those we dote on, when a part
Of us dies with them as each fond hope ends:
No doubt he would have been much more pathetic,
But the sea acted as a strong emetic.

22

Love's a capricious power; I've known it hold
Out through a fever caused by its own heat,
But be much puzzled by a cough and cold,
And find a quinsy very hard to treat;

[1] *Babel's waters ... Sion* See Psalm 137.1.

[2] *sweets to ... the grave* See Shakespeare's *Hamlet* 4.3.

Against all noble maladies he's bold,
    But vulgar illnesses don't like to meet,
Nor that a sneeze should interrupt his sigh,
Nor inflammations redden his blind eye.

23

But worst of all is nausea, or a pain
    About the lower region of the bowels;
Love, who heroically breathes a vein,
    Shrinks from the application of hot towels,
And purgatives are dangerous to his reign,
    Sea-sickness death: his love was perfect, how else
Could Juan's passion, while the billows roar,
Resist his stomach, ne'er at sea before?

24

The ship, called the most holy "Trinidada,"[1]
    Was steering duly for the port Leghorn;
For there the Spanish family Moncada
    Were settled long ere Juan's sire was born:
They were relations, and for them he had a
    Letter of introduction, which the morn
Of his departure had been sent him by
His Spanish friends for those in Italy.

25

His suite consisted of three servants and
    A tutor, the licentiate[2] Pedrillo,
Who several languages did understand,
    But now lay sick and speechless on his pillow,
And, rocking in his hammock, longed for land,
    His headache being increased by every billow;
And the waves oozing through the port-hole made
His berth a little damp, and him afraid.

26

'Twas not without some reason, for the wind
    Increased at night, until it blew a gale;
And though 'twas not much to a naval mind,
    Some landsmen would have looked a little pale,
For sailors are, in fact, a different kind:
    At sunset they began to take in sail,
For the sky showed it would come on to blow,
And carry away, perhaps, a mast or so.

27

At one o'clock the wind with sudden shift
    Threw the ship right into the trough of the sea,
Which struck her aft, and made an awkward rift,
    Started the stern-post, also shattered the
Whole of her stern-frame, and, ere she could lift
    Herself from out her present jeopardy,
The rudder tore away: 'twas time to sound
The pumps, and there were four feet water found.[3]

28

One gang of people instantly was put
    Upon the pumps, and the remainder set
To get up part of the cargo, and what not,
    But they could not come at the leak as yet;
At last they did get at it really, but
    Still their salvation was an even bet:
The water rushed through in a way quite puzzling,
While they thrust sheets, shirts, jackets, bales of muslin,

29

Into the opening; but all such ingredients
    Would have been vain, and they must have gone
        down,
Despite of all their efforts and expedients,
    But for the pumps: I'm glad to make them known
To all the brother tars[4] who may have need hence,
    For fifty tons of water were upthrown
By them per hour, and they had all been undone,
But for the maker, Mr. Mann, of London.

30

As day advanced the weather seemed to abate,
    And then the leak they reckoned to reduce,
And keep the ship afloat, though three feet yet
    Kept two hand and one chain-pump still in use.

[1] *Trinidada* Spanish: Trinity.

[2] *licenetiate* Graduate of a university.

[3] *At one o'clock … found* Byron was proud of the verisimilitude of his portrayal of a shipwreck, for which he drew many details from William Bligh, *A Narrative of the Mutiny of the Bounty* (1790), Sir John G. Dalyell, *Shipwrecks and Disasters at Sea* (1812), and Philip Aubin, *Remarkable Shipwrecks* (1813).

[4] *tars* Sailors.

The wind blew fresh again: as it grew late
A squall came on, and while some guns broke loose,
A gust—which all descriptive power transcends—
Laid with one blast the ship on her beam ends.

31

There she lay motionless, and seemed upset;
The water left the hold, and washed the decks,
And made a scene men do not soon forget;
For they remember battles, fires, and wrecks,
Or any other thing that brings regret,
Or breaks their hopes, or hearts, or heads, or necks:
Thus drownings are much talked of by the divers
And swimmers who may chance to be survivors.

32

Immediately the masts were cut away,
Both main and mizzen; first the mizzen went,
The main-mast followed: but the ship still lay
Like a mere log, and baffled our intent.
Foremast and bowsprit were cut down, and they
Eased her at last (although we never meant
To part with all till every hope was blighted),
And then with violence the old ship righted.

33

It may be easily supposed, while this
Was going on, some people were unquiet,
That passengers would find it much amiss
To lose their lives as well as spoil their diet;
That even the able seaman, deeming his
Days nearly o'er, might be disposed to riot,
As upon such occasions tars will ask
For grog, and sometimes drink rum from the cask.

34

There's nought, no doubt, so much the spirit calms
As rum and true religion; thus it was,
Some plundered, some drank spirits, some sung psalms,
The high wind made the treble, and as bass
The hoarse harsh waves kept time; fright cured the qualms
Of all the luckless landsmen's sea-sick maws:
Strange sounds of wailing, blasphemy, devotion,
Clamoured in chorus to the roaring ocean.

35

Perhaps more mischief had been done, but for
Our Juan, who, with sense beyond his years,
Got to the spirit-room, and stood before
It with a pair of pistols; and their fears,
As if Death were more dreadful by his door
Of fire than water, spite of oaths and tears,
Kept still aloof the crew, who, ere they sunk,
Thought it would be becoming to die drunk.

36

"Give us more grog," they cried, "for it will be
All one an hour hence." Juan answered, "No!
'Tis true that death awaits both you and me,
But let us die like men, not sink below
Like brutes;"—and thus his dangerous post kept he,
And none liked to anticipate the blow;
And even Pedrillo, his most reverend tutor,
Was for some rum a disappointed suitor.

37

The good old gentleman was quite aghast,
And made a loud and pious lamentation;
Repented all his sins, and made a last
Irrevocable vow of reformation;
Nothing should tempt him more (this peril past)
To quit his academic occupation,
In cloisters of the classic Salamanca,[1]
To follow Juan's wake, like Sancho Panca.[2]

38

But now there came a flash of hope once more;
Day broke, and the wind lulled: the masts were gone,
The leak increased; shoals round her, but no shore,
The vessel swam, yet still she held her own.
They tried the pumps again, and though before
Their desperate efforts seemed all useless grown,
A glimpse of sunshine set some hands to bale—
The stronger pumped, the weaker thrummed a sail.

39

Under the vessel's keel the sail was past,

[1] *Salamanca* Spanish university.

[2] *Sancho Panca* Don Quixote's page, in the novel by Miguel Cervantes (often spelled Sancho Panza).

And for the moment it had some effect;
But with a leak, and not a stick of mast,
Nor rag of canvas, what could they expect?
But still 'tis best to struggle to the last,
'Tis never too late to be wholly wrecked:
And though 'tis true that man can only die once,
'Tis not so pleasant in the Gulf of Lyons.

40

There winds and waves had hurled them, and from thence,
Without their will, they carried them away;
For they were forced with steering to dispense,
And never had as yet a quiet day
On which they might repose, or even commence
A jurymast or rudder, or could say
The ship would swim an hour, which, by good luck,
Still swam—though not exactly like a duck.

41

The wind, in fact, perhaps was rather less,
But the ship laboured so, they scarce could hope
To weather out much longer; the distress
Was also great with which they had to cope
For want of water, and their solid mess
Was scant enough: in vain the telescope
Was used—nor sail nor shore appeared in sight,
Nought but the heavy sea, and coming night.

42

Again the weather threatened,—again blew
A gale, and in the fore and after hold
Water appeared; yet, though the people knew
All this, the most were patient, and some bold,
Until the chains and leathers were worn through
Of all our pumps:—a wreck complete she rolled,
At mercy of the waves, whose mercies are
Like human beings during civil war.

43

Then came the carpenter, at last, with tears
In his rough eyes, and told the captain, he
Could do no more; he was a man in years,
And long had voyaged through many a stormy sea,
And if he wept at length, they were not fears
That made his eyelids as a woman's be,
But he, poor fellow, had a wife and children,
Two things for dying people quite bewildering.

44

The ship was evidently settling now
Fast by the head; and, all distinction gone,
Some went to prayers again, and made a vow
Of candles to their saints—but there were none
To pay them with; and some looked o'er the bow;
Some hoisted out the boats; and there was one
That begged Pedrillo for an absolution,
Who told him to be damned—in his confusion.

45

Some lashed them in their hammocks, some put on
Their best clothes, as if going to a fair;
Some cursed the day on which they saw the sun,
And gnashed their teeth, and, howling, tore their hair;
And others went on as they had begun,
Getting the boats out, being well aware
That a tight boat will live in a rough sea,
Unless with breakers close beneath her lee.

46

The worst of all was, that in their condition,
Having been several days in great distress,
'Twas difficult to get out such provision
As now might render their long suffering less:
Men, even when dying, dislike inanition;
Their stock was damaged by the weather's stress:
Two casks of biscuit, and a keg of butter,
Were all that could be thrown into the cutter.

47

But in the long-boat they contrived to stow
Some pounds of bread, though injured by the wet;
Water, a twenty-gallon cask or so;
Six flasks of wine; and they contrived to get
A portion of their beef up from below,
And with a piece of pork, moreover, met,
But scarce enough to serve them for a luncheon—
Then there was rum, eight gallons in a puncheon.

48

The other boats, the yawl and pinnace, had
Been stove in the beginning of the gale;
And the long-boat's condition was but bad,
As there were but two blankets for a sail,
And one oar for a mast, which a young lad
Threw in by good luck over the ship's rail;
And two boats could not hold, far less be stored,
To save one half the people then on board.

49

'Twas twilight, for the sunless day went down
Over the waste of waters; like a veil,
Which, if withdrawn, would but disclose the frown
Of one whose hate is masked but to assail,
Thus to their hopeless eyes the night was shown,
And grimly darkled o'er the faces pale,
And the dim desolate deep: twelve days had Fear
Been their familiar, and now Death was here.

50

Some trial had been making at a raft,
With little hope in such a rolling sea,
A sort of thing at which one would have laughed,
If any laughter at such times could be,
Unless with people who too much have quaffed,
And have a kind of wild and horrid glee,
Half epileptical and half hysterical:—
Their preservation would have been a miracle.

51

At half-past eight o'clock, booms, hencoops, spars,
And all things, for a chance, had been cast loose,
That still could keep afloat the struggling tars,
For yet they strove, although of no great use:
There was no light in heaven but a few stars,
The boats put off o'ercrowded with their crews;
She gave a heel, and then a lurch to port,
And, going down head foremost—sunk, in short.

52

Then rose from sea to sky the wild farewell,
Then shrieked the timid, and stood still the brave,
Then some leaped overboard with dreadful yell,
As eager to anticipate their grave;
And the sea yawned around her like a hell,
And down she sucked with her the whirling wave,
Like one who grapples with his enemy,
And strives to strangle him before he die.

53

And first one universal shriek there rushed,
Louder than the loud ocean, like a crash
Of echoing thunder; and then all was hushed,
Save the wild wind and the remorseless dash
Of billows; but at intervals there gushed,
Accompanied with a convulsive splash,
A solitary shriek, the bubbling cry
Of some strong swimmer in his agony.

54

The boats, as stated, had got off before,
And in them crowded several of the crew;
And yet their present hope was hardly more
Than what it had been, for so strong it blew
There was slight chance of reaching any shore;
And then they were too many, though so few—
Nine in the cutter, thirty in the boat,
Were counted in them when they got afloat.

55

All the rest perished; near two hundred souls
Had left their bodies; and what's worse, alas!
When over Catholics the ocean rolls,
They must wait several weeks before a Mass
Takes off one peck of purgatorial coals,
Because, till people know what's come to pass,
They won't lay out their money on the dead—
It costs three francs for every Mass that's said.

56

Juan got into the long-boat, and there
Contrived to help Pedrillo to a place;
It seemed as if they had exchanged their care,
For Juan wore the magisterial face
Which courage gives, while poor Pedrillo's pair
Of eyes were crying for their owner's case:

Battista, though, (a name called shortly Tita)[1]
Was lost by getting at some aqua-vita.° *spirits*

57

Pedro, his valet, too, he tried to save,
But the same cause, conducive to his loss,
Left him so drunk, he jumped into the wave
As o'er the cutter's edge he tried to cross,
And so he found a wine-and-watery grave;
They could not rescue him although so close,
Because the sea ran higher every minute,
And for the boat—the crew kept crowding in it.

58

A small old spaniel,—which had been Don Jóse's,
His father's, whom he loved, as ye may think,
For on such things the memory reposes
With tenderness, stood howling on the brink,
Knowing, (dogs have such intellectual noses!)
No doubt, the vessel was about to sink;
And Juan caught him up, and ere he stepped
Off, threw him in, then after him he leaped.

59

He also stuffed his money where he could
About his person, and Pedrillo's too,
Who let him do, in fact, whate'er he would,
Not knowing what himself to say, or do,
As every rising wave his dread renewed;
But Juan, trusting they might still get through,
And deeming there were remedies for any ill,
Thus re-embarked his tutor and his spaniel.

60

'Twas a rough night, and blew so stiffly yet,
That the sail was becalmed between the seas,
Though on the wave's high top too much to set,
They dared not take it in for all the breeze;
Each sea curled o'er the stern, and kept them wet,
And made them bale without a moment's ease,
So that themselves as well as hopes were damped,
And the poor little cutter quickly swamped.

61

Nine souls more went in her: the long-boat still
Kept above water, with an oar for mast,
Two blankets stitched together, answering ill
Instead of sail, were to the oar made fast:
Though every wave rolled menacing to fill,
And present peril all before surpassed,
They grieved for those who perished with the cutter,
And also for the biscuit casks and butter.

62

The sun rose red and fiery, a sure sign
Of the continuance of the gale: to run
Before the sea, until it should grow fine,
Was all that for the present could be done:
A few tea-spoonfuls of their rum and wine
Were served out to the people, who begun
To faint, and damaged bread wet through the bags,
And most of them had little clothes but rags.

63

They counted thirty, crowded in a space
Which left scarce room for motion or exertion;
They did their best to modify their case,
One half sat up, though numbed with the immersion,
While t'other half were laid down in their place,
At watch and watch; thus, shivering like the tertian
Ague° in its cold fit, they filled their boat, *flu*
With nothing but the sky for a great coat.

64

'Tis very certain the desire of life
Prolongs it; this is obvious to physicians,
When patients, neither plagued with friends nor wife,
Survive through very desperate conditions,
Because they still can hope, nor shines the knife
Nor shears of Atropos[2] before their visions:
Despair of all recovery spoils longevity,
And makes men's miseries of alarming brevity.

65

'Tis said that persons living on annuities
Are longer lived than others,—God knows why,

[1] *Tita* Byron's own servant Giovanni Battista Lusieri (1798–1874) was nicknamed "Tita."

[2] *Atropos* One of the three Fates: Clotho spun the thread of life, Lachesis measured it, and Atropos cut it off.

Unless to plague the grantors,—yet so true it is,
That some, I really think, *do* never die;
Of any creditors the worst a Jew it is,[1]
And *that's* their mode of furnishing supply:
In my young days they lent me cash that way,
Which I found very troublesome to pay.

66

'Tis thus with people in an open boat,
They live upon the love of life, and bear
More than can be believed, or even thought,
And stand like rocks the tempest's wear and tear;
And hardship still has been the sailor's lot,
Since Noah's ark went cruising here and there;
She had a curious crew as well as cargo,
Like the first old Greek privateer, the Argo.[2]

67

But man is a carnivorous production,
And must have meals, at least one meal a day;
He cannot live, like woodcocks, upon suction,[3]
But, like the shark and tiger, must have prey:
Although his anatomical construction
Bears vegetables, in a grumbling way,
Your labouring people think beyond all question,
Beef, veal, and mutton, better for digestion.

68

And thus it was with this our hapless crew;
For on the third day there came on a calm,
And though at first their strength it might renew,
And, lying on their weariness like balm,
Lulled them like turtles sleeping on the blue
Of ocean, when they woke they felt a qualm,
And fell all ravenously on their provision,
Instead of hoarding it with due precision.

69

The consequence was easily foreseen—
They ate up all they had, and drank their wine,
In spite of all remonstrances, and then
On what, in fact, next day were they to dine?
They hoped the wind would rise, these foolish men!
And carry them to shore; these hopes were fine,
But as they had but one oar, and that brittle,
It would have been more wise to save their victual.

70

The fourth day came, but not a breath of air,
And Ocean slumbered like an unweaned child:
The fifth day, and their boat lay floating there,
The sea and sky were blue, and clear, and mild—
With their one oar (I wish they had had a pair)
What could they do? and hunger's rage grew wild:
So Juan's spaniel, spite of his entreating,
Was killed, and portioned out for present eating.

71

On the sixth day they fed upon his hide,
And Juan, who had still refused, because
The creature was his father's dog that died,
Now feeling all the vulture in his jaws,
With some remorse received (though first denied)
As a great favour one of the fore-paws,
Which he divided with Pedrillo, who
Devoured it, longing for the other too.

72

The seventh day, and no wind—the burning sun
Blistered and scorched, and, stagnant on the sea,
They lay like carcasses; and hope was none,
Save in the breeze that came not; savagely
They glared upon each other—all was done,
Water, and wine, and food,—and you might see
The longings of the cannibal arise
(Although they spoke not) in their wolfish eyes.

---

[1] *Of any ... is* Since the middle ages European Christian society had condemned Jews for the practice of usury, or money-lending, which was in most European countries one of the few professions that Jews were allowed to follow. Discrimination against Jews was less severe in Britain than in many European jurisdictions, but, as Byron's casual slur here demonstrates, virulent anti-Semitism was common among the English as well. In his youth, Byron had borrowed from Jewish moneylenders; he did not pay these debts off for many years.

[2] *Argo* The ship in which Jason and the Argonauts sailed.

[3] *live ... upon suction* Woodcocks feed by probing the grass with their beaks.

73

At length one whispered his companion, who
 Whispered another, and thus it went round,
And then into a hoarser murmur grew,
 An ominous, and wild, and desperate sound,
And when his comrade's thought each sufferer knew,
 'Twas but his own, suppressed till now, he found:
And out they spoke of lots for flesh and blood,
And who should die to be his fellow's food.

74

But ere they came to this, they that day shared
 Some leathern caps, and what remained of shoes;
And then they looked around them, and despaired,
 And none to be the sacrifice would choose;
At length the lots were torn up, and prepared,
 But of materials that much shock the Muse—
Having no paper, for the want of better,
They took by force from Juan Julia's letter.

75

The lots were made, and marked, and mixed, and handed,
 In silent horror, and their distribution
Lulled even the savage hunger which demanded,
 Like the Promethean vulture,[1] this pollution;
None in particular had sought or planned it,
 'Twas nature gnawed them to this resolution,
By which none were permitted to be neuter—
And the lot fell on Juan's luckless tutor.

76

He but requested to be bled to death:
 The surgeon had his instruments, and bled
Pedrillo, and so gently ebbed his breath,
 You hardly could perceive when he was dead.
He died as born, a Catholic in faith,
 Like most in the belief in which they're bred,
And first a little crucifix he kissed,
And then held out his jugular and wrist.

77

The surgeon, as there was no other fee,
 Had his first choice of morsels for his pains;
But being thirstiest at the moment, he
 Preferred a draught from the fast-flowing veins:
Part was divided, part thrown in the sea,
 And such things as the entrails and the brains
Regaled two sharks, who followed o'er the billow—
The sailors ate the rest of poor Pedrillo.

78

The sailors ate him, all save three or four,
 Who were not quite so fond of animal food;
To these was added Juan, who, before
 Refusing his own spaniel, hardly could
Feel now his appetite increased much more;
 'Twas not to be expected that he should,
Even in extremity of their disaster,
Dine with them on his pastor and his master.

79

'Twas better that he did not; for, in fact,
 The consequence was awful in the extreme:
For they, who were most ravenous in the act,
 Went raging mad—Lord! how they did blaspheme!
And foam and roll, with strange convulsions racked,
 Drinking salt water like a mountain-stream,
Tearing, and grinning, howling, screeching, swearing,
And, with hyaena laughter, died despairing.[2]

80

Their numbers were much thinned by this infliction,
 And all the rest were thin enough, heaven knows;
And some of them had lost their recollection,
 Happier than they who still perceived their woes;
But others pondered on a new dissection,
 As if not warned sufficiently by those
Who had already perished, suffering madly,
For having used their appetites so sadly.

81

And next they thought upon the master's mate,
 As fattest; but he saved himself, because,

[1] *Promethean vulture* As a punishment for stealing fire from the gods, Prometheus was chained to a rock while a vulture pecked at his liver.

[2] *Went raging mad … despairing* It was believed that cannibalism produced madness.

Besides being much averse from such a fate,
There were some other reasons: the first was,
He had been rather indisposed of late;
And that which chiefly proved his saving clause,
Was a small present made to him at Cadiz,
By general subscription of the ladies.[1]

82

Of poor Pedrillo something still remained,
But was used sparingly,—some were afraid,
And others still their appetites constrained,
Or but at times a little supper made;
All except Juan, who throughout abstained,
Chewing a piece of bamboo, and some lead:
At length they caught two boobies, and a noddy,[2]
And then they left off eating the dead body.

83

And if Pedrillo's fate should shocking be,
Remember Ugolino condescends
To eat the head of his arch-enemy
The moment after he politely ends
His tale; if foes be food in hell, at sea
'Tis surely fair to dine upon our friends,
When shipwreck's short allowance grows too scanty,
Without being much more horrible than Dante.[3]

84

And the same night there fell a shower of rain,
For which their mouths gaped, like the cracks of earth
When dried to summer dust; till taught by pain,
Men really know not what good water's worth;
If you had been in Turkey or in Spain,
Or with a famished boat's-crew had your birth,
Or in the desert heard the camel's bell,
You'd wish yourself where Truth is—in a well.

85

It poured down torrents, but they were no richer
Until they found a ragged piece of sheet,
Which served them as a sort of spongy pitcher,
And when they deemed its moisture was complete,
They wrung it out, and though a thirsty ditcher
Might not have thought the scanty draught so sweet
As a full pot of porter, to their thinking
They ne'er till now had known the joys of drinking.

86

And their baked lips, with many a bloody crack,[4]
Sucked in the moisture, which like nectar streamed;
Their throats were ovens, their swol'n tongues were black,
As the rich man's in hell, who vainly screamed
To beg the beggar, who could not rain back
A drop of dew, when every drop had seemed
To taste of heaven—If this be true, indeed,
Some Christians have a comfortable creed.[5]

87

There were two fathers in this ghastly crew,
And with them their two sons, of whom the one
Was more robust and hardy to the view,
But he died early; and when he was gone,
His nearest messmate told his sire, who threw
One glance at him, and said, "Heaven's will be done!
I can do nothing," and he saw him thrown
Into the deep without a tear or groan.

88

The other father had a weaklier child,
Of a soft cheek and aspect delicate;
But the boy bore up long, and with a mild
And patient spirit held aloof his fate;
Little he said, and now and then he smiled,
As if to win a part from off the weight
He saw increasing on his father's heart,
With the deep deadly thought, that they must part.

89

And o'er him bent his sire, and never raised
His eyes from off his face, but wiped the foam
From his pale lips, and ever on him gazed,
And when the wished-for shower at length was come,

[1] *small present … ladies* I.e., venereal disease.

[2] *boobies … noddy* Birds.

[3] *Ugolino … Dante* See Dante's *Inferno*.

[4] *And … crack* Cf. Coleridge, *The Rime of the Ancient Mariner* 3.157.

[5] *As the rich man's … creed* See Luke 16.19–25.

And the boy's eyes, which the dull film half glazed,
Brightened, and for a moment seemed to roam,
He squeezed from out a rag some drops of rain
Into his dying child's mouth—but in vain.

90
The boy expired—the father held the clay,
And looked upon it long, and when at last
Death left no doubt, and the dead burthen lay
Stiff on his heart, and pulse and hope were past,
He watched it wistfully, until away
'Twas borne by the rude wave wherein 'twas cast;
Then he himself sunk down all dumb and shivering,
And gave no sign of life, save his limbs quivering.

91
Now overhead a rainbow, bursting through
The scattering clouds, shone, spanning the dark sea,
Resting its bright base on the quivering blue;
And all within its arch appeared to be
Clearer than that without, and its wide hue
Waxed broad and waving, like a banner free,
Then changed like to a bow that's bent, and then
Forsook the dim eyes of these shipwrecked men.

92
It changed, of course; a heavenly chameleon,
The airy child of vapour and the sun,
Brought forth in purple, cradled in vermilion,
Baptized in molten gold, and swathed in dun,
Glittering like crescents o'er a Turk's pavilion,
And blending every colour into one,
Just like a black eye in a recent scuffle,
(For sometimes we must box without the muffle.)

93
Our shipwrecked seamen thought it a good omen—
It is as well to think so, now and then;
'Twas an old custom of the Greek and Roman,
And may become of great advantage when
Folks are discouraged; and most surely no men
Had greater need to nerve themselves again
Than these, and so this rainbow looked like hope—
Quite a celestial kaleidoscope.[1]

94
About this time a beautiful white bird,
Webfooted, not unlike a dove in size
And plumage, (probably it might have erred
Upon its course) passed oft before their eyes,
And tried to perch, although it saw and heard
The men within the boat, and in this guise
It came and went, and fluttered round them till
Night fell:—this seemed a better omen still.

95
But in this case I also must remark,
'Twas well this bird of promise did not perch,
Because the tackle of our shattered bark
Was not so safe for roosting as a church;
And had it been the dove from Noah's ark,
Returning there from her successful search,
Which in their way that moment chanced to fall,
They would have eat[2] her, olive-branch and all.

96
With twilight it again came on to blow,
But not with violence; the stars shone out,
The boat made way; yet now they were so low,
They knew not where nor what they were about;
Some fancied they saw land, and some said "No!"
The frequent fog-banks gave them cause to doubt—
Some swore that they heard breakers, others guns,
And all mistook about the latter once.

97
As morning broke the light wind died away,
When he who had the watch sung out, and swore
If 'twas not land that rose with the suns ray,
He wished that land he never might see more;
And the rest rubbed their eyes, and saw a bay,

---

[1] *kaleidoscope* Sir David Brewster invented the kaleidoscope in 1817. Byron's lawyer, John Hanson, brought him one in November 1818.

[2] *eat* Pronounced "et," in England an acceptable past tense form of "eat."

Or thought they saw, and shaped their course for shore;
For shore it was, and gradually grew
Distinct, and high, and palpable to view.

98

And then of these some part burst into tears,
And others, looking with a stupid stare,
Could not yet separate their hopes from fears,
And seemed as if they had no further care;
While a few prayed—(the first time for some years)—
And at the bottom of the boat three were
Asleep; they shook them by the hand and head,
And tried to awaken them, but found them dead.

99

The day before, fast sleeping on the water,
They found a turtle of the hawk's-bill kind,
And by good fortune, gliding softly, caught her,
Which yielded a day's life, and to their mind
Proved even still a more nutritious matter,
Because it left encouragement behind:
They thought that in such perils, more than chance
Had sent them this for their deliverance.

100

The land appeared a high and rocky coast,
And higher grew the mountains as they drew,
Set by a current, toward it: they were lost
In various conjectures, for none knew
To what part of the earth they had been tost,
So changeable had been the winds that blew;
Some thought it was Mount Ætna, some the highlands
Of Candia,[1] Cyprus, Rhodes, or other islands.

101

Meantime the current, with a rising gale,
Still set them onwards to the welcome shore,
Like Charon's bark of spectres, dull and pale:[2]
Their living freight was now reduced to four,
And three dead, whom their strength could not avail
To heave into the deep with those before,
Though the two sharks still followed them, and dashed
The spray into their faces as they splashed.

102

Famine, despair, cold, thirst, and heat, had done
Their work on them by turns, and thinned them to
Such things a mother had not known her son
Amidst the skeletons of that gaunt crew;
By night chilled, by day scorched, thus one by one
They perished, until withered to these few,
But chiefly by a species of self-slaughter,
In washing down Pedrillo with salt water.

103

As they drew nigh the land, which now was seen
Unequal in its aspect here and there,
They felt the freshness of its growing green,
That waved in forest-tops, and smoothed the air,
And fell upon their glazed eyes like a screen
From glistening waves, and skies so hot and bare—
Lovely seemed any object that should sweep
Away the vast, salt, dread, eternal deep.

104

The shore looked wild, without a trace of man,
And girt by formidable waves; but they
Were mad for land, and thus their course they ran,
Though right ahead the roaring breakers lay:
A reef between them also now began
To show its boiling surf and bounding spray,
But finding no place for their landing better,
They ran the boat for shore,—and overset her.

105

But in his native stream, the Guadalquivir,
Juan to lave° his youthful limbs was wont; *wash*
And having learnt to swim in that sweet river,
Had often turned the art to some account:
A better swimmer you could scarce see ever,
He could, perhaps, have passed the Hellespont,
As once (a feat on which ourselves we prided)
Leander, Mr. Ekenhead, and I did.[3]

---

[1] *Candia* Crete.

[2] *Charon's bark … pale* Charon ferried the souls of the newly dead across the river Acheron in Hades.

[3] *Hellespont … did* In imitation of the classical hero Leander, who swam across the Hellespont to reach his lover, Byron swam the Hellespont on 3 May 1810, accompanied by Lieutenant Ekenhead

106

So here, though faint, emaciated, and stark,
He buoyed his boyish limbs, and strove to ply
With the quick wave, and gain, ere it was dark,
The beach which lay before him, high and dry:
The greatest danger here was from a shark,
That carried off his neighbour by the thigh;
As for the other two they could not swim,
So nobody arrived on shore but him.

107

Nor yet had he arrived but for the oar,
Which, providentially for him, was washed
Just as his feeble arms could strike no more,
And the hard wave o'erwhelmed him as 'twas dashed
Within his grasp; he clung to it, and sore
The waters beat while he thereto was lashed;
At last, with swimming, wading, scrambling, he
Rolled on the beach, half-senseless, from the sea.

108

There, breathless, with his digging nails he clung
Fast to the sand, lest the returning wave,
From whose reluctant roar his life he wrung,
Should suck him back to her insatiate grave:
And there he lay, full length, where he was flung,
Before the entrance of a cliff-worn cave,
With just enough of life to feel its pain,
And deem that it was saved, perhaps, in vain.

109

With slow and staggering effort he arose,
But sunk again upon his bleeding knee
And quivering hand; and then he looked for those
Who long had been his mates upon the sea,
But none of them appeared to share his woes,
Save one, a corpse from out the famished three,
Who died two days before, and now had found
An unknown barren beach for burial ground.

110

And as he gazed, his dizzy brain spun fast,
And down he sunk; and as he sunk, the sand
Swam round and round, and all his senses passed:
He fell upon his side, and his stretched hand
Drooped dripping on the oar, (their jury-mast)
And, like a withered lily, on the land
His slender frame and pallid aspect lay,
As fair a thing as e'er was formed of clay.

111

How long in his damp trance young Juan lay
He knew not, for the earth was gone for him,
And Time had nothing more of night nor day
For his congealing blood, and senses dim;
And how this heavy faintness passed away
He knew not, till each painful pulse and limb,
And tingling vein, seemed throbbing back to life,
For Death, though vanquished, still retired with strife.

112

His eyes he opened, shut, again unclosed,
For all was doubt and dizziness; methought
He still was in the boat, and had but dozed,
And felt again with his despair o'erwrought,
And wished it death in which he had reposed,
And then once more his feelings back were brought,
And slowly by his swimming eyes was seen
A lovely female face of seventeen.

113

'Twas bending close o'er his, and the small mouth
Seemed almost prying into his for breath;
And chafing him, the soft warm hand of youth
Recalled his answering spirits back from death;
And, bathing his chill temples, tried to soothe
Each pulse to animation, till beneath
Its gentle touch and trembling care, a sigh
To these kind efforts made a low reply.

114

Then was the cordial poured, and mantle flung
Around his scarce-clad limbs; and the fair arm
Raised higher the faint head which o'er it hung;
And her transparent cheek, all pure and warm,
Pillowed his death-like forehead; then she wrung
His dewy curls, long drenched by every storm;

of the Marines. See Byron's "Written after Swimming from Sestos to Abydos."

And watched with eagerness each throb that drew
A sigh from his heaved bosom—and hers, too.

115

And lifting him with care into the cave,
The gentle girl and her attendant,—one
Young, yet her elder, and of brow less grave,
And more robust of figure,—then begun
To kindle fire, and as the new flames gave
Light to the rocks that roofed them, which the sun
Had never seen, the maid, or whatsoe'er
She was, appeared distinct, and tall, and fair.

116

Her brow was overhung with coins of gold,
That sparkled o'er the auburn of her hair,
Her clustering hair, whose longer locks were rolled
In braids behind, and though her stature were
Even of the highest for a female mould,
They nearly reached her heel; and in her air
There was a something which bespoke command,
As one who was a lady in the land.

117

Her hair, I said, was auburn; but her eyes
Were black as death, their lashes the same hue,
Of downcast length, in whose silk shadow lies
Deepest attraction, for when to the view
Forth from its raven fringe the full glance flies,
Ne'er with such force the swiftest arrow flew;
'Tis as the snake late coiled, who pours his length,
And hurls at once his venom and his strength.

118

Her brow was white and low, her cheek's pure dye
Like twilight rosy still with the set sun;
Short upper lip—sweet lips! that make us sigh
Ever to have seen such; for she was one
Fit for the model of a statuary,
(A race of mere impostors, when all's done—
I've seen much finer women, ripe and real,
Than all the nonsense of their stone ideal.)

119

I'll tell you why I say so, for 'tis just
One should not rail without a decent cause:
There was an Irish lady,[1] to whose bust
I ne'er saw justice done, and yet she was
A frequent model; and if e'er she must
Yield to stern Time and Nature's wrinkling laws,
They will destroy a face which mortal thought
Ne'er compassed, nor less mortal chisel wrought.

120

And such was she, the lady of the cave:
Her dress was very different from the Spanish,
Simpler, and yet of colours not so grave;
For, as you know, the Spanish women banish
Bright hues when out of doors, and yet, while wave
Around them (what I hope will never vanish)
The basquiña[2] and the mantilla, they
Seem at the same time mystical and gay.

121

But with our damsel this was not the case:
Her dress was many-coloured, finely spun;
Her locks curled negligently round her face,
But through them gold and gems profusely shone;
Her girdle sparkled, and the richest lace
Flowed in her veil, and many a precious stone
Flashed on her little hand; but, what was shocking
Her small snow feet had slippers, but no stocking.

122

The other female's dress was not unlike,
But of inferior materials; she
Had not so many ornaments to strike,
Her hair had silver only, bound to be
Her dowry; and her veil, in form alike,
Was coarser; and her air, though firm, less free;
Her hair was thicker, but less long; her eyes
As black, but quicker, and of smaller size.

123

And these two tended him, and cheered him both
With food and raiment, and those soft attentions,
Which are (as I must own) of female growth,

---

1 *Irish lady* Perhaps a reference to Lady Adelaide Forbes (1798–1858), whom Byron compared to the Apollo Belvedere.

2 *basquiña* Beautiful outer petticoat.

And have ten thousand delicate inventions:
They made a most superior mess of broth,
A thing which poesy but seldom mentions,
But the best dish that e'er was cooked since Homer's
Achilles ordered dinner for new comers.[1]

124

I'll tell you who they were, this female pair,
Lest they should seem princesses in disguise;
Besides, I hate all mystery, and that air
Of clap-trap, which your recent poets prize;
And so, in short, the girls they really were
They shall appear before your curious eyes,
Mistress and maid; the first was only daughter
Of an old man, who lived upon the water.

125

A fisherman he had been in his youth,
And still a sort of fisherman was he;
But other speculations were, in sooth,
Added to his connexion with the sea,
Perhaps not so respectable, in truth:
A little smuggling, and some piracy,
Left him, at last, the sole of many masters
Of an ill-gotten million of piastres.[2]

126

A fisher, therefore, was he—though of men,
Like Peter the Apostle,[3]—and he fished
For wandering merchant-vessels, now and then,
And sometimes caught as many as he wished;
The cargoes he confiscated, and gain
He sought in the slave-market too, and dished
Full many a morsel for that Turkish trade,
By which, no doubt, a good deal may be made.

127

He was a Greek, and on his isle had built
(One of the wild and smaller Cyclades)
A very handsome house from out his guilt,
And there he lived exceedingly at ease;
Heaven knows what cash he got, or blood he spilt,
A sad old fellow was he, if you please;
But this I know, it was a spacious building,
Full of barbaric carving, paint, and gilding.

128

He had an only daughter, called Haidée,
The greatest heiress of the Eastern Isles;
Besides, so very beautiful was she,
Her dowry was as nothing to her smiles:
Still in her teens, and like a lovely tree
She grew to womanhood, and between whiles
Rejected several suitors, just to learn
How to accept a better in his turn.

129

And walking out upon the beach, below
The cliff, towards sunset, on that day she found,
Insensible,—not dead, but nearly so,—
Don Juan, almost famished, and half drowned;
But being naked, she was shocked, you know,
Yet deemed herself in common pity bound,
As far as in her lay, "to take him in,
A stranger" dying, with so white a skin.

130

But taking him into her father's house
Was not exactly the best way to save,
But like conveying to the cat the mouse,
Or people in a trance into their grave;
Because the good old man had so much "νοῦς,"[4]
Unlike the honest Arab thieves so brave,
He would have hospitably cured the stranger,
And sold him instantly when out of danger.

131

And therefore, with her maid, she thought it best
(A virgin always on her maid relies)
To place him in the cave for present rest:
And when, at last, he opened his black eyes,
Their charity increased about their guest;
And their compassion grew to such a size,
It opened half the turnpike-gates to heaven—
(St. Paul says, 'tis the toll which must be given).

---

[1] *since Homer's … comers* See Homer, *Iliad* 9.

[2] *piastres* Pieces of eight.

[3] *Like … Apostle* Cf. Matthew 4.18–19.

[4] νοῦς Intelligence, or, more cynically, cunning.

132

They made a fire, but such a fire as they
Upon the moment could contrive with such
Materials as were cast up round the bay,
Some broken planks, and oars, that to the touch
Were nearly tinder, since so long they lay
A mast was almost crumbled to a crutch;
But, by God's grace, here wrecks were in such plenty,
That there was fuel to have furnished twenty.

133

He had a bed of furs, and a pelisse,
For Haidée stripped her sables off to make
His couch; and, that he might be more at ease,
And warm, in case by chance he should awake,
They also gave a petticoat apiece,
She and her maid, and promised by day-break
To pay him a fresh visit, with a dish
For breakfast, of eggs, coffee, bread, and fish.

134

And thus they left him to his lone repose:
Juan slept like a top, or like the dead,
Who sleep at last, perhaps, (God only knows)
Just for the present; and in his lulled head
Not even a vision of his former woes
Throbbed in accursed dreams, which sometimes spread
Unwelcome visions of our former years,
Till the eye, cheated, opens thick with tears.

135

Young Juan slept all dreamless:—but the maid,
Who smoothed his pillow, as she left the den
Looked back upon him, and a moment staid,
And turned, believing that he called again.
He slumbered; yet she thought, at least she said,
(The heart will slip even as the tongue and pen)
He had pronounced her name—but she forgot
That at this moment Juan knew it not.

136

And pensive to her father's house she went,
Enjoining silence strict to Zoe, who
Better than her knew what, in fact, she meant,
She being wiser by a year or two:
A year or two's an age when rightly spent,
And Zoe spent hers, as most women do,
In gaining all that useful sort of knowledge
Which is acquired in Nature's good old college.

137

The morn broke, and found Juan slumbering still
Fast in his cave, and nothing clashed upon
His rest; the rushing of the neighbouring rill,
And the young beams of the excluded sun,
Troubled him not, and he might sleep his fill;
And need he had of slumber yet, for none
Had suffered more—his hardships were comparative
To those related in my grand-dad's Narrative.[1]

138

Not so Haidée: she sadly tossed and tumbled,
And started from her sleep, and, turning o'er,
Dreamed of a thousand wrecks, o'er which she stumbled,
And handsome corpses strewed upon the shore;
And woke her maid so early that she grumbled,
And called her father's old slaves up, who swore
In several oaths—Armenian, Turk, and Greek—
They knew not what to think of such a freak.

139

But up she got, and up she made them get,
With some pretence about the sun, that makes
Sweet skies just when he rises, or is set;
And 'tis, no doubt, a sight to see when breaks
Bright Phoebus,[2] while the mountains still are wet
With mist, and every bird with him awakes,
And night is flung off like a mourning suit
Worn for a husband, or some other brute.

140

I say, the sun is a most glorious sight,
I've seen him rise full oft, indeed of late
I have sat up on purpose all the night,

[1] *Narrative* Byron's grandfather, Admiral John Byron (1723–86), was famous for encountering a storm each time he sailed, and hence was nicknamed "Foulweather Jack." In 1768 he published *Narrative of Great Distresses on the Shores of Patagonia.*

[2] *Phoebus* Phoebus Apollo, god of the sun; i.e., the sun.

Which hastens, as physicians say, one's fate;
And so all ye, who would be in the right
In health and purse, begin your day to date
From day-break, and when coffined at fourscore,
Engrave upon the plate, you rose at four.

141

And Haidée met the morning face to face;
Her own was freshest, though a feverish flush
Had dyed it with the headlong blood, whose race
From heart to cheek is curbed into a blush,
Like to a torrent which a mountain's base,
That overpowers some Alpine river's rush,
Checks to a lake, whose waves in circles spread;
Or the Red Sea—but the sea is not red.

142

And down the cliff the island virgin came,
And near the cave her quick light footsteps drew,
While the sun smiled on her with his first flame,
And young Aurora[1] kissed her lips with dew,
Taking her for a sister; just the same
Mistake you would have made on seeing the two,
Although the mortal, quite as fresh and fair,
Had all the advantage, too, of not being air.

143

And when into the cavern Haidée stepped
All timidly, yet rapidly, she saw
That like an infant Juan sweetly slept;
And then she stopped, and stood as if in awe,
(For sleep is awful) and on tiptoe crept
And wrapt him closer, lest the air, too raw,
Should reach his blood, then o'er him still as death
Bent, with hushed lips, that drank his scarce-drawn breath.

144

And thus like to an angel o'er the dying
Who die in righteousness, she leaned; and there
All tranquilly the shipwrecked boy was lying,
As o'er him lay the calm and stirless air:
But Zoe the meantime some eggs was frying,
Since, after all, no doubt the youthful pair
Must breakfast, and betimes—lest they should ask it,
She drew out her provision from the basket.

145

She knew that the best feelings must have victual,
And that a shipwrecked youth would hungry be;
Besides, being less in love, she yawned a little,
And felt her veins chilled by the neighbouring sea;
And so, she cooked their breakfast to a tittle;
I can't say that she gave them any tea,
But there were eggs, fruit, coffee, bread, fish, honey,
With Scio wine,—and all for love, not money.

146

And Zoe, when the eggs were ready, and
The coffee made, would fain have wakened Juan;
But Haidée stopped her with her quick small hand,
And without word, a sign her finger drew on
Her lip, which Zoe needs must understand;
And, the first breakfast spoilt, prepared a new one
Because her mistress would not let her break
That sleep which seemed as it would ne'er awake.

147

For still he lay, and on his thin worn cheek
A purple hectic played like dying day
On the snow-tops of distant hills; the streak
Of sufferance yet upon his forehead lay,
Where the blue veins looked shadowy, shrunk, and weak;
And his black curls were dewy with the spray,
Which weighed upon them yet, all damp and salt,
Mixed with the stony vapours of the vault.

148

And she bent o'er him, and he lay beneath,
Hushed as the babe upon its mother's breast,
Drooped as the willow when no winds can breathe,
Lulled like the depth of ocean when at rest,
Fair as the crowning rose of the whole wreath,
Soft as the callow cygnet in its nest;
In short, he was a very pretty fellow,
Although his woes had turned him rather yellow.

[1] *Aurora* Goddess of the dawn.

149

He woke and gazed, and would have slept again,
    But the fair face which met his eyes forbade
Those eyes to close, though weariness and pain
    Had further sleep a further pleasure made;
For woman's face was never formed in vain
    For Juan, so that even when he prayed
He turned from grisly saints, and martyrs hairy,
To the sweet portraits of the Virgin Mary.

150

And thus upon his elbow he arose,
    And looked upon the lady, in whose cheek
The pale contended with the purple rose,
    As with an effort she began to speak;
Her eyes were eloquent, her words would pose,
    Although she told him, in good modern Greek,
With an Ionian accent, low and sweet,
That he was faint, and must not talk, but eat.

151

Now Juan could not understand a word,
    Being no Grecian; but he had an ear,
And her voice was the warble of a bird,
    So soft, so sweet, so delicately clear,
That finer, simpler music ne'er was heard;
    The sort of sound we echo with a tear,
Without knowing why—an overpowering tone,
Whence Melody descends as from a throne.

152

And Juan gazed as one who is awoke
    By a distant organ, doubting if he be
Not yet a dreamer, till the spell is broke
    By the watchman, or some such reality,
Or by one's early valet's cursed knock;
    At least it is a heavy sound to me,
Who like a morning slumber—for the night
Shows stars and women in a better light.

153

And Juan, too, was helped out from his dream,
    Or sleep, or whatso'er it was, by feeling
A most prodigious appetite: the steam
    Of Zoe's cookery no doubt was stealing
Upon his senses, and the kindling beam
    Of the new fire, which Zoe kept up, kneeling
To stir her viands, made him quite awake
And long for food, but chiefly a beef-steak.

154

But beef is rare within these oxless isles;
    Goat's flesh there is, no doubt, and kid, and mutton;
And, when a holiday upon them smiles,
    A joint upon their barbarous spits they put on:
But this occurs but seldom, between whiles,
    For some of these are rocks with scarce a hut on;
Others are fair and fertile, among which
This, though not large, was one of the most rich.

155

I say that beef is rare, and can't help thinking
    That the old fable of the Minotaur—
From which our modern morals, rightly shrinking,
    Condemn the royal lady's taste who wore
A cow's shape for a mask—was only (sinking
    The allegory) a mere type, no more,
That Pasiphae promoted breeding cattle,
To make the Cretans bloodier in battle.[1]

156

For we all know that English people are
    Fed upon beef—I won't say much of beer,
Because 'tis liquor only, and being far
    From this my subject, has no business here;
We know, too, they are very fond of war,
    A pleasure—like all pleasures—rather dear;
So were the Cretans—from which I infer
That beef and battles both were owing to her.

157

But to resume. The languid Juan raised
    His head upon his elbow, and he saw
A sight on which he had not lately gazed,
    As all his latter meals had been quite raw,

[1] *Minotaur ... battle* Pasiphaë, Queen of Crete, lusted after a bull sent by Poseidon. To fulfill her desires, she had herself enclosed in a hollow model of a cow to mate with the bull. She gave birth to the Minotaur, a creature with the body of a man and the head of a bull. Her husband Minos imprisoned the monster in a labyrinth built by Daedalus.

Three or four things, for which the Lord he praised,
And, feeling still the famished vulture gnaw,[1]
He fell upon whate'er was offered, like
A priest, a shark, an alderman, or pike.

158

He ate, and he was well supplied; and she,
Who watched him like a mother, would have fed
Him past all bounds, because she smiled to see
Such appetite in one she had deemed dead;
But Zoe, being older than Haidée,
Knew (by tradition, for she ne'er had read)
That famished people must be slowly nurst,
And fed by spoonfuls, else they always burst.

159

And so she took the liberty to state,
Rather by deeds than words, because the case
Was urgent, that the gentleman, whose fate
Had made her mistress quit her bed to trace
The sea-shore at this hour, must leave his plate,
Unless he wished to die upon the place—
She snatched it, and refused another morsel,
Saying, he had gorged enough to make a horse ill.

160

Next they—he being naked, save a tattered
Pair of scarce decent trousers—went to work,
And in the fire his recent rags they scatterd,
And dressed him, for the present, like a Turk,
Or Greek—that is, although it not much mattered,
Omitting turban, slippers, pistols, dirk,—
They furnished him, entire except some stitches,
With a clean shirt, and very spacious breeches.[2]

161

And then fair Haidée tried her tongue at speaking,
But not a word could Juan comprehend,
Although he listened so that the young Greek in
Her earnestness would ne'er have made an end;
And, as he interrupted not, went eking
Her speech out to her protegé and friend,
Till pausing at the last her breath to take,
She saw he did not understand Romaic.[3]

162

And then she had recourse to nods, and signs,
And smiles, and sparkles of the speaking eye,
And read (the only book she could) the lines
Of his fair face, and found, by sympathy,
The answer eloquent, where the soul shines
And darts in one quick glance a long reply;
And thus in every look she saw exprest
A world of words, and things at which she guessed.

163

And now, by dint of fingers and of eyes,
And words repeated after her, he took
A lesson in her tongue; but by surmise,
No doubt, less of her language than her look:
As he who studies fervently the skies
Turns oftener to the stars than to his book,
Thus Juan learned his alpha beta better
From Haidée's glance than any graven letter.

164

'Tis pleasing to be schooled in a strange tongue
By female lips and eyes—that is, I mean,
When both the teacher and the taught are young,
As was the case, at least, where I have been;
They smile so when one's right, and when one's wrong
They smile still more, and then there intervene
Pressure of hands, perhaps even a chaste kiss;—
I learned the little that I know by this:

165

That is, some words of Spanish, Turk, and Greek,
Italian not at all, having no teachers;
Much English I cannot pretend to speak,
Learning that language chiefly from its preachers,
Barrow, South, Tillotson, whom every week
I study, also Blair,[4] the highest reachers

[1] *feeling still ... gnaw* Jove sent an eagle to gnaw the vitals (guts) of Prometheus, chained to a mountainside.

[2] *breeches* Pronounced "britches."

[3] *Romaic* Modern Greek.

[4] *Barrow* Isaac Barrow (1630–77); *South* Robert South (1634–1716); *Tillotson* John Tillotson (1630–94); *Blair* Hugh Blair (1718–1800): British preachers.

Of eloquence in piety and prose—
I hate your poets, so read none of those.

166

As for the ladies, I have nought to say,
A wanderer from the British world of fashion,
Where I, like other "dogs, have had my day,"[1]
Like other men, too, may have had my passion—
But that, like other things, has passed away,
And all her fools whom I *could* lay the lash on,
Foes, friends, men, women, now are nought to me
But dreams of what has been, no more to be.

167

Return we to Don Juan. He begun
To hear new words, and to repeat them; but
Some feelings, universal as the sun,
Were such as could not in his breast be shut
More than within the bosom of a nun:
He was in love,—as you would be, no doubt,
With a young benefactress—so was she,
Just in the way we very often see.

168

And every day by day-break—rather early
For Juan, who was somewhat fond of rest—
She came into the cave, but it was merely
To see her bird reposing in his nest;
And she would softly stir his locks so curly,
Without disturbing her yet slumbering guest,
Breathing all gently o'er his cheek and mouth,
As o'er a bed of roses the sweet south.

169

And every morn his colour freshlier came,
And every day helped on his convalescence;
'Twas well, because health in the human frame
Is pleasant, besides being true love's essence,
For health and idleness to passion's flame
Are oil and gunpowder; and some good lessons
Are also learnt from Ceres and from Bacchus,
Without whom Venus will not long attack us.[2]

170

While Venus fills the heart (without heart really
Love, though good always, is not quite so good),
Ceres presents a plate of vermicelli,—
For love must be sustained like flesh and blood,—
While Bacchus pours out wine, or hands a jelly:
Eggs, oysters, too, are amatory food;
But who is their purveyor from above
Heaven knows,—it may be Neptune, Pan, or Jove.

171

When Juan woke he found some good things ready,
A bath, a breakfast, and the finest eyes
That ever made a youthful heart less steady,
Besides her maid's, as pretty for their size;
But I have spoken of all this already—
And repetition's tiresome and unwise,—
Well—Juan, after bathing in the sea,
Came always back to coffee and Haidée.

172

Both were so young, and one so innocent,
That bathing passed for nothing; Juan seemed
To her, as 'twere, the kind of being sent,
Of whom these two years she had nightly dreamed,
A something to be loved, a creature meant
To be her happiness, and whom she deemed
To render happy; all who joy would win
Must share it,—Happiness was born a twin.

173

It was such pleasure to behold him, such
Enlargement of existence to partake
Nature with him, to thrill beneath his touch,
To watch him slumbering, and to see him wake:
To live with him forever were too much;
But then the thought of parting made her quake:
He was her own, her ocean-treasure, cast
Like a rich wreck—her first love, and her last.

174

And thus a moon rolled on, and fair Haidée
Paid daily visits to her boy, and took
Such plentiful precautions, that still he
Remained unknown within his craggy nook;

[1] *dogs ... day* See Shakespeare, *Hamlet*, 5.1.279.

[2] *Ceres* Ceres, or Demeter, was the goddess of agriculture; *Bacchus* God of wine.

At last her father's prows put out to sea,
For certain merchantmen upon the look,
Not as of yore to carry off an Io,[1]
But three Ragusan vessels, bound for Scio.

175

Then came her freedom, for she had no mother,
So that, her father being at sea, she was
Free as a married woman, or such other
Female, as where she likes may freely pass,
Without even the incumbrance of a brother,
The freest she that ever gazed on glass:
I speak of Christian lands in this comparison,
Where wives, at least, are seldom kept in garrison.

176

Now she prolonged her visits and her talk
(For they must talk), and he had learnt to say
So much as to propose to take a walk,—
For little had he wandered since the day
On which, like a young flower snapped from the stalk,
Drooping and dewy on the beach he lay,—
And thus they walked out in the afternoon,
And saw the sun set opposite the moon.

177

It was a wild and breaker-beaten coast,
With cliffs above, and a broad sandy shore,
Guarded by shoals and rocks as by an host,
With here and there a creek, whose aspect wore
A better welcome to the tempest-tost;
And rarely ceased the haughty billow's roar,
Save on the dead long summer days, which make
The outstretched ocean glitter like a lake.

178

And the small ripple spilt upon the beach
Scarcely o'erpassed the cream of your champagne,
When o'er the brim the sparkling bumpers reach,
That spring-dew of the spirit! the heart's rain!
Few things surpass old wine; and they may preach
Who please,—the more because they preach in vain,—
Let us have wine and woman, mirth and laughter,
Sermons and soda-water the day after.

179

Man, being reasonable, must get drunk;
The best of life is but intoxication:
Glory, the grape, love, gold, in these are sunk
The hopes of all men, and of every nation;
Without their sap, how branchless were the trunk
Of life's strange tree, so fruitful on occasion:
But to return,—Get very drunk; and when
You wake with headache, you shall see what then.

180

Ring for your valet—bid him quickly bring
Some hock[2] and soda-water, then you'll know
A pleasure worthy Xerxes the great king;
For not the blest sherbet, sublimed with snow,
Nor the first sparkle of the desert-spring,
Nor Burgundy in all its sunset glow,
After long travel, ennui, love, or slaughter,
Vie with that draught of hock and soda-water.

181

The coast—I think it was the coast that I
Was just describing—Yes, it *was* the coast—
Lay at this period quiet as the sky,
The sands untumbled, the blue waves untost,
And all was stillness, save the sea-bird's cry,
And dolphin's leap, and little billow crost
By some low rock or shelve, that made it fret
Against the boundary it scarcely wet.

182

And forth they wandered, her sire being gone,
As I have said, upon an expedition;
And mother, brother, guardian, she had none,
Save Zoe, who, although with due precision
She waited on her lady with the sun,
Thought daily service was her only mission,
Bringing warm water, wreathing her long tresses,
And asking now and then for cast-off dresses.

[1] *Io* A nymph spirited away by Zeus.

[2] *hock* Wine from the area of Hochheim in Germany.

183

It was the cooling hour, just when the rounded
Red sun sinks down behind the azure hill,
Which then seems as if the whole earth it bounded,
Circling all nature, hushed, and dim, and still,
With the far mountain-crescent half surrounded
On one side, and the deep sea calm and chill
Upon the other, and the rosy sky,
With one star sparkling through it like an eye.

184

And thus they wandered forth, and hand in hand,[1]
Over the shining pebbles and the shells,
Glided along the smooth and hardened sand,
And in the worn and wild receptacles
Worked by the storms, yet worked as it were planned,
In hollow halls, with sparry roofs and cells,
They turned to rest; and, each clasped by an arm,
Yielded to the deep twilight's purple charm.

185

They looked up to the sky, whose floating glow
Spread like a rosy ocean, vast and bright;
They gazed upon the glittering sea below,
Whence the broad moon rose circling into sight;
They heard the wave's splash, and the wind so low,
And saw each other's dark eyes darting light
Into each other—and, beholding this,
Their lips drew near, and clung into a kiss;

186

A long, long kiss, a kiss of youth, and love,
And beauty, all concentrating like rays
Into one focus, kindled from above;
Such kisses as belong to early days,
Where heart, and soul, and sense, in concert move,
And the blood's lava, and the pulse a blaze,
Each kiss a heart-quake,—for a kiss's strength,
I think, it must be reckoned by its length.

187

By length I mean duration; theirs endured
Heaven knows how long—no doubt they never
reckoned;
And if they had, they could not have secured
The sum of their sensations to a second:
They had not spoken; but they felt allured,
As if their souls and lips each other beckoned,
Which, being joined, like swarming bees they clung—
Their hearts the flowers from whence the honey sprung.

188

They were alone, but not alone as they
Who shut in chambers think it loneliness;
The silent ocean, and the starlight bay,
The twilight glow, which momently grew less,
The voiceless sands, and dropping caves, that lay
Around them, made them to each other press,
As if there were no life beneath the sky
Save theirs, and that their life could never die.

189

They feared no eyes nor ears on that lone beach,
They felt no terrors from the night, they were
All in all to each other: though their speech
Was broken words, they *thought* a language there,—
And all the burning tongues the passions teach
Found in one sigh the best interpreter
Of nature's oracle—first love,—that all
Which Eve has left her daughters since her fall.

190

Haidée spoke not of scruples, asked no vows,
Nor offered any; she had never heard
Of plight and promises to be a spouse,
Or perils by a loving maid incurred;
She was all which pure ignorance allows,
And flew to her young mate like a young bird;
And, never having dreamt of falsehood, she
Had not one word to say of constancy.

191

She loved, and was beloved—she adored,
And she was worshipped; after nature's fashion,
Their intense souls, into each other poured,
If souls could die, had perished in that passion,—
But by degrees their senses were restored,
Again to be o'ercome, again to dash on;

[1] *They wandered … hand* Cf. Milton, *Paradise Lost* 12.645–49.

And, beating 'gainst *his* bosom, Haidée's heart
Felt as if never more to beat apart.

192

Alas! they were so young, so beautiful,
So lonely, loving, helpless, and the hour
Was that in which the heart is always full,
And, having o'er itself no further power,
Prompts deeds eternity can not annul,
But pays off moments in an endless shower
Of hell-fire—all prepared for people giving
Pleasure or pain to one another living.

193

Alas! for Juan and Haidée! they were
So loving and so lovely—till then never,
Excepting our first parents, such a pair
Had run the risk of being damn'd for ever;
And Haidée, being devout as well as fair,
Had, doubtless, heard about the Stygian river,[1]
And hell and purgatory—but forgot
Just in the very crisis she should not.

194

They look upon each other, and their eyes
Gleam in the moonlight; and her white arm clasps
Round Juan's head, and his around her lies
Half buried in the tresses which it grasps;
She sits upon his knee, and drinks his sighs,
He hers, until they end in broken gasps;
And thus they form a group that's quite antique,
Half naked, loving, natural, and Greek.

195

And when those deep and burning moments passed
And Juan sunk to sleep within her arms,
She slept not, but all tenderly, though fast,
Sustained his head upon her bosom's charms;
And now and then her eye to heaven is cast,
And then on the pale cheek her breast now warms,
Pillowed on her o'erflowing heart, which pants
With all it granted, and with all it grants.

196

An infant when it gazes on a light,
A child the moment when it drains the breast,
A devotee when soars the Host in sight,
An Arab with a stranger for a guest,
A sailor when the prize has struck in fight,
A miser filling his most hoarded chest,
Feel rapture; but not such true joy are reaping
As they who watch o'er what they love while sleeping.

197

For there it lies so tranquil, so beloved,
All that it hath of life with us is living;
So gentle, stirless, helpless, and unmoved,
And all unconscious of the joy 'tis giving;
All it hath felt, inflicted, passed, and proved,
Hushed into depths beyond the watcher's diving;
There lies the thing we love with all its errors
And all its charms, like death without its terrors.

198

The lady watched her lover—and that hour
Of Love's, and Night's, and Ocean's solitude,
O'erflowed her soul with their united power;
Amidst the barren sand and rocks so rude
She and her wave-worn love had made their bower,
Where nought upon their passion could intrude,
And all the stars that crowded the blue space
Saw nothing happier than her glowing face.

199

Alas! the love of women! it is known
To be a lovely and a fearful thing;
For all of theirs upon that die is thrown,
And if 'tis lost, life hath no more to bring
To them but mockeries of the past alone,
And their revenge is as the tiger's spring,
Deadly, and quick, and crushing; yet, as real
Torture is theirs, what they inflict they feel.

200

They are right; for man, to man so oft unjust,
Is always so to women; one sole bond
Awaits them, treachery is all their trust;
Taught to conceal, their bursting hearts despond

[1] *Stygian river* River Styx, in Hades.

Over their idol, till some wealthier lust
Buys them in marriage—and what rests beyond?
A thankless husband, next a faithless lover,
Then dressing, nursing, praying, and all's over.

201

Some take a lover, some take drams or prayers,
Some mind their household, others dissipation,
Some run away, and but exchange their cares,
Losing the advantage of a virtuous station;
Few changes e'er can better their affairs,
Theirs being an unnatural situation,
From the dull palace to the dirty hovel:
Some play the devil, and then write a novel.[1]

202

Haidée was Nature's bride, and knew not this;
Haidée was Passion's child, born where the sun
Showers triple light, and scorches even the kiss
Of his gazelle-eyed daughters; she was one
Made but to love, to feel that she was his
Who was her chosen: what was said or done
Elsewhere was nothing—She had nought to fear,
Hope, care, nor love beyond, her heart beat *here*.

203

And oh! that quickening of the heart, that beat!
How much it costs us! yet each rising throb
Is in its cause as its effect so sweet,
That Wisdom, ever on the watch to rob
Joy of its alchymy, and to repeat
Fine truths; even Conscience, too, has a tough job
To make us understand each good old maxim,
So good—I wonder Castlereagh don't tax 'em.

204

And now 't was done—on the lone shore were plighted
Their hearts; the stars, their nuptial torches, shed
Beauty upon the beautiful they lighted:
Ocean their witness, and the cave their bed,
By their own feelings hallowed and united,
Their priest was Solitude, and they were wed:
And they were happy, for to their young eyes
Each was an angel, and earth paradise.

205

Oh, Love! of whom great Caesar was the suitor,
Titus the master, Antony the slave,[2]
Horace, Catullus, scholars, Ovid tutor,[3]
Sappho the sage blue-stocking, in whose grave
All those may leap who rather would be neuter—[4]
(Leucadia's rock still overlooks the wave)
Oh, Love! thou art the very god of evil,
For, after all, we cannot call thee devil.

206

Thou mak'st the chaste connubial state precarious,
And jestest with the brows of mightiest men:
Caesar and Pompey, Mahomet, Belisarius[5]
Have much employed the muse of history's pen;
Their lives and fortunes were extremely various,
Such worthies Time will never see again;
Yet to these four in three things the same luck holds,
They all were heroes, conquerors, and cuckolds.

207

Thou mak'st philosophers; there's Epicurus
And Aristippus,[6] a material crew!
Who to immoral courses would allure us
By theories quite practicable too;
If only from the devil they would insure us,

[1] *write a novel* Byron's former lover, Lady Caroline Lamb, published *Glenarvon*, a roman-à-clef about their relationship, in 1816. Byron's comment on the book was, "I read 'Glenarvon,' too, by Caro. Lamb / *God damn*!"

[2] *great Caesar ... slave* Caesar and Antony were lovers of Cleopatra. Titus mastered his passion for Berenice, sending her away.

[3] *tutor* Because of his didactic poem, *Ars Amatoria* (*The Art of Love*).

[4] *Sappho ... neuter* An allusion to the legend of Sappho's suicide; *neuter* is a reference to her lesbianism.

[5] *Caesar ... Belisarius* Julius Caesar divorced his third wife, Pompeia, apparently for attempted adultery. Pompey divorced his third wife, Mucia, for committing adultery with Caesar. Mohammed's favourite wife, Ayesha, was suspected of impropriety, but he received a divine revelation of her purity. Antonina, the wife of Justinian's great general Belisarius, had several lovers before she married him.

[6] *Epicurus* (342–270 BCE) Greek philosopher; *Aristippus* (c. 370 BCE), pupil of Socrates. Byron thinks of them (unfairly in the case of Epicurus) as advocating the unrestrained pursuit of pleasure.

How pleasant were the maxim, (not quite new)
"Eat, drink, and love, what can the rest avail us?"
So said the royal sage Sardanapalus.[1]

208

But Juan! had he quite forgotten Julia?
And should he have forgotten her so soon?
I can't but say it seems to me most truly a
Perplexing question; but, no doubt, the moon
Does these things for us, and whenever newly a
Strong palpitation rises, 'tis her boon,
Else how the devil is it that fresh features
Have such a charm for us poor human creatures?

209

I hate inconstancy—I loathe, detest,
Abhor, condemn, abjure the mortal made
Of such quicksilver clay that in his breast
No permanent foundation can be laid;
Love, constant love, has been my constant guest,
And yet last night, being at a masquerade,
I saw the prettiest creature, fresh from Milan,
Which gave me some sensations like a villain.

210

But soon Philosophy came to my aid,
And whispered "think of every sacred tie!"
"I will, my dear Philosophy!" I said,
"But then her teeth, and then, Oh heaven! her eye!
I'll just inquire if she be wife or maid,
Or neither—out of curiosity."
"Stop!" cried Philosophy, with air so Grecian,
(Though she was masqued then as a fair Venetian.)

211

"Stop!" so I stopped.—But to return: that which
Men call inconstancy is nothing more
Than admiration due where nature's rich
Profusion with young beauty covers o'er
Some favoured object; and as in the niche
A lovely statue we almost adore,
This sort of adoration of the real
Is but a heightening of the "beau ideal."[2]

212

'Tis the perception of the beautiful,
A fine extension of the faculties,
Platonic, universal, wonderful,
Drawn from the stars, and filtered through the skies,
Without which life would be extremely dull;
In short, it is the use of our own eyes,
With one or two small senses added, just
To hint that flesh is formed of fiery dust.

213

Yet 'tis a painful feeling, and unwilling,
For surely if we always could perceive
In the same object graces quite as killing
As when she rose upon us like an Eve,
'Twould save us many a heartache, many a shilling,
(For we must get them any how, or grieve)
Whereas if one sole lady pleased for ever,
How pleasant for the heart, as well as liver!

214

The heart is like the sky, a part of heaven,
But changes night and day too, like the sky;
Now o'er it clouds and thunder must be driven,
And darkness and destruction as on high:
But when it hath been scorched, and pierced, and riven,
Its storms expire in water-drops; the eye
Pours forth at last the heart's-blood turned to tears,
Which make the English climate of our years.

215

The liver is the lazaret[3] of bile,
But very rarely executes its function,
For the first passion stays there such a while,
That all the rest creep in and form a junction,
Like knots of vipers on a dunghill's soil,
Rage, fear, hate, jealousy, revenge, compunction,
So that all mischiefs spring up from this entrail,
Like earthquakes from the hidden fire called "central."

[1] *Sardanapalus* A famously sybaritic Assyrian king. Byron wrote a tragedy about him in 1821.

[2] *beau ideal* French: ideal beauty.

[3] *lazaret* Hospital for those with infectious diseases, particularly leprosy.

216

In the mean time, without proceeding more
In this anatomy, I've finished now
Two hundred and odd stanzas as before,
That being about the number I'll allow
Each canto of the twelve, or twenty-four;
And, laying down my pen, I make my bow,
Leaving Don Juan and Haidée to plead
For them and theirs with all who deign to read.

from *Canto 3*

In this canto, Haidée takes Juan to the palace of her absent father, the fierce pirate Lambro (see Canto 1.174–75, above). He returns home to find them feasting, entertained by a bard. In the figure of the bard (who "lied with such a fervour of intention / There was no doubt he earned his laureate pension"), Byron again parodies Robert Southey, but he also mocks himself (see stanzas 84–85), and all poets. Byron's own fervent commitment to the cause of a free Greece finds expression in the poet's song.

1

Hail, Muse! *et cetera.*—We left Juan sleeping,
Pillowed upon a fair and happy breast,
And watched by eyes that never yet knew weeping,
And loved by a young heart, too deeply blest
To feel the poison through her spirit creeping,
Or know who rested there; a foe to rest,
Had soiled the current of her sinless years,
And turned her pure heart's purest blood to tears!

2

Oh, Love! what is it in this world of ours
Which makes it fatal to be loved? Ah why
With cypress[1] branches hast thou wreathed thy bowers,
And made thy best interpreter a sigh?
As those who dote on odours pluck the flowers,
And place them on their breast—but place to die—
Thus the frail beings we would fondly cherish
Are laid within our bosoms but to perish.

[1] *cypress* Tree traditionally symbolic of mourning.

3

In her first passion woman loves her lover,
In all the others all she loves is love,
Which grows a habit she can ne'er get over,
And fits her loosely—like an easy glove,
As you may find, whene'er you like to prove her:
One man alone at first her heart can move;
She then prefers him in the plural number,
Not finding that the additions much encumber.

4

I know not if the fault be men's or theirs;
But one thing's pretty sure; a woman planted—
(Unless at once she plunge for life in prayers)—
After a decent time must be gallanted;
Although, no doubt, her first of love affairs
Is that to which her heart is wholly granted;
Yet there are some, they say, who have had *none,*
But those who have ne'er end with only *one.*

5

Tis melancholy, and a fearful sign
Of human frailty, folly, also crime,
That love and marriage rarely can combine,
Although they both are born in the same clime;
Marriage from love, like vinegar from wine—
A sad, sour, sober beverage—by time
Is sharpened from its high celestial flavour
Down to a very homely household savour.

6

There's something of antipathy, as 'twere,
Between their present and their future state;
A kind of flattery that's hardly fair
Is used until the truth arrives too late—
Yet what can people do, except despair?
The same things change their names at such a rate;
For instance—passion in a lover's glorious,
But in a husband is pronounced uxorious.

7

Men grow ashamed of being so very fond;
They sometimes also get a little tired
(But that, of course, is rare), and then despond:
The same things cannot always be admired,

Yet 'tis "so nominated in the bond,"[1]
That both are tied till one shall have expired.
Sad thought! to lose the spouse that was adorning
Our days, and put one's servants into mourning.

8

There's doubtless something in domestic doings
Which forms, in fact, true love's antithesis;
Romances paint at full length people's wooings,
But only give a bust of marriages;[2]
For no one cares for matrimonial cooings,
There's nothing wrong in a connubial kiss:
Think you, if Laura had been Petrarch's wife,
He would have written sonnets all his life?[3]

9

All tragedies are finished by a death,
All comedies are ended by a marriage;
The future states of both are left to faith,
For authors fear description might disparage
The worlds to come of both, or fall beneath,
And then both worlds would punish their miscarriage;
So leaving each their priest and prayer-book ready,
They say no more of Death or of the Lady.[4]

...

70

Of all the dresses I select Haidée's:
She wore two jelicks[5]—one was of pale yellow;
Of azure, pink, and white was her chemise—
'Neath which her breast heaved like a little billow;
With buttons formed of pearls as large as peas,
All gold and crimson shone her jelick's fellow,
And the striped white gauze baracan[6] that bound her,
Like fleecy clouds about the moon, flowed round her.

71

One large gold bracelet clasped each lovely arm,
Lockless—so pliable from the pure gold
That the hand stretched and shut it without harm,
The limb which it adorned its only mould;
So beautiful—its very shape would charm,
And clinging as if loath to lose its hold,
The purest ore enclosed the whitest skin
That e'er by precious metal was held in.

72

Around, as princess of her father's land,
A like gold bar above her instep rolled
Announced her rank; twelve rings were on her hand;
Her hair was starred with gems; her veil's fine fold
Below her breast was fastened with a band
Of lavish pearls, whose worth could scarce be told;
Her orange silk full Turkish trousers furled
About the prettiest ankle in the world.

73

Her hair's long auburn waves down to her heel
Flowed like an Alpine torrent which the sun
Dyes with his morning light,—and would conceal
Her person if allowed at large to run,
And still they seem resentfully to feel
The silken fillet's° curb, and sought to shun *thin headband*
Their bonds whene'er some Zephyr[7] caught began
To offer his young pinion as her fan.

74

Round her she made an atmosphere of life,
The very air seemed lighter from her eyes,
They were so soft and beautiful, and rife
With all we can imagine of the skies,
And pure as Psyche ere she grew a wife—
Too pure even for the purest human ties;

---

[1] *Yet ... the bond* From Shakespeare's *The Merchant of Venice* 4.1.254. Byron here uses "bond" to mean "marriage bond."

[2] *Romances ... marriages* Romances detail all of courtship (as a full-length portrait does a person), but only mention marriage briefly (as a sculpted bust cuts off a person).

[3] *Think ... life* Petrarch (Francesco Petrarca, 1304–74), the Italian poet, fell passionately in love with a woman named Laura, who was already married. He wrote a series of sonnets in praise of her.

[4] *Death ... Lady* In the ballad *Death and the Lady*, Death demands the life of the Lady, despite her pleas. The ballad's conclusion asserts that the only hope for salvation is to have lived a moral life.

[5] *jelick* Bodice worn by Turkish women.

[6] *baracan* Byron means a veil of delicate material, but he uses the word incorrectly. The actual definition is a woolly garment.

[7] *Zephyr* Wind. Zephyrus was the Greek god of the west wind.

Her overpowering presence made you feel
It would not be idolatry to kneel.

75

Her eyelashes, though dark as night, were tinged
(It is the country's custom), but in vain;
For those large black eyes were so blackly fringed,
The glossy rebels mocked the jetty stain,
And in their native beauty stood avenged:
Her nails were touched with henna; but again
The power of art was turned to nothing, for
They could not look more rosy than before.

76

The henna should be deeply dyed to make
The skin relieved appear more fairly fair;
She had no need of this, day ne'er will break
On mountain tops more heavenly white than her:
The eye might doubt if it were well awake,
She was so like a vision; I might err,
But Shakespeare also says 'tis very silly
"To gild refined gold, or paint the lily."[1]

77

Juan had on a shawl of black and gold,
But a white baracan, and so transparent
The sparkling gems beneath you might behold,
Like small stars through the milky way apparent;
His turban, furled in many a graceful fold,
An emerald aigrette[2] with Haidée's hair in't
Surmounted, as its clasp, a glowing crescent,
Whose rays shone ever trembling, but incessant.

78

And now they were diverted by their suite,
Dwarfs, dancing girls, black eunuchs, and a poet,
Which made their new establishment complete;
The last was of great fame, and liked to show it:
His verses rarely wanted their due feet—
And for his theme—he seldom sung below it,
He being paid to satirise or flatter,
As the psalm says, "inditing a good matter."[3]

79

He praised the present, and abused the past,
Reversing the good custom of old days,
An Eastern Anti-Jacobin[4] at last
He turned, preferring pudding to *no* praise—
For some few years his lot had been o'ercast
By his seeming independent in his lays,
But now he sung the Sultan and the Pacha[5]
With truth like Southey, and with verse like Crashaw.[6]

80

He was a man who had seen many changes,
And always changed as true as any needle;[7]
His polar star being one which rather ranges,
And not the fixed—he knew the way to wheedle:
So vile he 'scaped the doom which oft avenges;
And being fluent (save indeed when feed ill),
He lied with such a fervour of intention—
There was no doubt he earned his laureate pension.

81

But he had genius,—when a turncoat has it,
The "Vates irritabilis"[8] takes care
That without notice few full moons shall pass it;
Even good men like to make the public stare:—
But to my subject—let me see—what was it?—
Oh!—the third canto—and the pretty pair—
Their loves, and feasts, and house, and dress, and mode
Of living in their insular abode.

---

[1] *To gild ... the lily* See Shakespeare's *King John* 4.2.11.

[2] *aigrette* Ornament worn on the head, consisting of gems clasping a spray of feathers. In this case, it seems, the piece incorporates some of Haidee's hair.

[3] *As the psalm ... matter* See Psalm 45.1.

[4] *Anti-Jacobin* The Anti-Jacobins fought against subversive thought brought into England after the French Revolution, urging the English to maintain conservative standards and institutions.

[5] *Pacha* In Turkey, a man of high rank or office. Usually spelt Pasha.

[6] *Crashaw* Richard Crashaw (1613–49), a poet then widely judged to have written verse of uneven quality.

[7] *needle* Compass needle.

[8] *Vates irritabilis* Latin: the irritability of men of genius.

82

Their poet, a sad trimmer, but no less
In company a very pleasant fellow,
Had been the favourite of full many a mess
Of men, and made them speeches when half mellow;
And though his meaning they could rarely guess,
Yet still they deigned to hiccup or to bellow
The glorious meed of popular applause,
Of which the first ne'er knows the second cause.

83

But now being lifted into high society,
And having picked up several odds and ends
Of free thoughts in his travels for variety,
He deemed, being in a lone isle, among friends,
That without any danger of a riot, he
Might for long lying make himself amends;
And singing as he sung in his warm youth,
Agree to a short armistice with truth.

84

He had travelled 'mongst the Arabs, Turks, and Franks,
And knew the self-loves of the different nations;
And having lived with people of all ranks,
Had something ready upon most occasions—
Which got him a few presents and some thanks.
He varied with some skill his adulations;
To "do at Rome as Romans do," a piece
Of conduct was which he observed in Greece.

85

Thus, usually, when he was asked to sing,
He gave the different nations something national;
'Twas all the same to him—"God save the King,"
Or "Ca ira,"[1] according to the fashion all:
His muse made increment of any thing,
From the high lyric down to the low rational:
If Pindar sang horse-races, what should hinder
Himself from being as pliable as Pindar?[2]

86

In France, for instance, he would write a chanson;[3]
In England a six canto quarto tale;
In Spain, heed make a ballad or romance on
The last war—much the same in Portugal;
In Germany, the Pegasus heed prance on
Would be old Goethe's—(see what says de Staël)[4]
In Italy heed ape the "Trecentisti";[5]
In Greece, heed sing some sort of hymn like this t'ye:

1

The isles of Greece, the isles of Greece!
Where burning Sappho loved and sung,
Where grew the arts of war and peace,—
Where Delos rose, and Phoebus sprung![6]
Eternal summer gilds them yet,
But all, except their sun, is set.

2

The Scian and the Teian muse,
The hero's harp, the lover's lute,[7]
Have found the fame your shores refuse;
Their place of birth alone is mute
To sounds which echo further west
Than your sires' "Islands of the Blest."

3

The mountains look on Marathon—
And Marathon looks on the sea;
And musing there an hour alone,
I dreamed that Greece might still be free;
For standing on the Persians' grave,[8]
I could not deem myself a slave.

[1] *Ça ira* French: "It will succeed," a song of the French Revolution.

[2] *Pindar … Pindar* The Greek poet Pindar (c.522–443 BC), was famous for his Odes. His first Olympian Ode celebrates the winner of a horse race.

[3] *chanson* French: "song," but here possibly a reference to the *chansons de geste*, poems in Old French detailing legends about historical figures.

[4] *see De Staël* In *De l'Allemagne* (1818), Madame de Staël (1766–1817) writes that Goethe "will be able to represent the whole of German literature."

[5] *Trecentisti* Italian poets of the fourteenth century.

[6] *Delos … sprung* Delos, the mythical birthplace of Phoebus Apollo, was called out of the ocean by Poseidon.

[7] *Scian … muse* Homer, primarily a poet of war and heroes, was born on Scio; Anacreon, famous for his poems of love, was born at Teos.

[8] *Persians' grave* The Greeks defeated the Persians at the Battle of Marathon in 490 BCE.

4

A king sat on the rocky brow
Which looks o'er sea-born Salamis;
And ships, by thousands, lay below,
And men in nations;—all were his!
He counted them at break of day—
And when the sun set where were they?[1]

5

And where are they? and where art thou,
My country? On thy voiceless shore
The heroic lay is tuneless now—
The heroic bosom beats no more!
And must thy lyre, so long divine,
Degenerate into hands like mine?

6

'Tis something, in the dearth of fame,
Though linked among a fettered race,
To feel at least a patriot's shame,
Even as I sing, suffuse my face;
For what is left the poet here?
For Greeks a blush—for Greece a tear.

7

Must we but weep o'er days more blest?
Must *we* but blush?—Our fathers bled.
Earth! render back from out thy breast
A remnant of our Spartan dead!
Of the three hundred grant but three,
To make a new Thermopylae![2]

8

What, silent still? and silent all?
Ah! no;—the voices of the dead
Sound like a distant torrent's fall,
And answer, "Let one living head,
But one arise,—we come, we come!"
'Tis but the living who are dumb.

9

In vain—in vain: strike other chords;
Fill high the cup with Samian wine![3]
Leave battles to the Turkish hordes,
And shed the blood of Scio's vine!
Hark! rising to the ignoble call—
How answers each bold Bacchanal!

10

You have the Pyrrhic dance as yet,
Where is the Pyrrhic phalanx[4] gone?
Of two such lessons, why forget
The nobler and the manlier one?
You have the letters Cadmus[5] gave—
Think ye he meant them for a slave?

11

Fill high the bowl with Samian wine!
We will not think of themes like these!
It made Anacreon's song divine:
He served—but served Polycrates—[6]
A tyrant; but our masters then
Were still, at least, our countrymen.

12

The tyrant of the Chersonese
Was freedom's best and bravest friend;
That tyrant was Miltiades![7]
Oh! that the present hour would lend
Another despot of the kind!
Such chains as his were sure to bind.

13

Fill high the bowl with Samian wine!
On Suli's rock, and Parga's shore,[8]
Exists the remnant of a line

---

[1] *A king ... they* At the Battle of Salamis in 480 BCE, the Persian king Xerxes watched from a promontory as the Greeks, although vastly outnumbered, defeated his men in a sea battle.

[2] *Spartan ... Thermopylae* In 480 BCE the Persians slaughtered 300 Spartans in the narrow pass of Thermopylae. The Spartan sacrifice, however, halted the Persian advance into Greece.

[3] *Samian wine* The Greek island of Samos was famous for its Muscat wine.

[4] *Pyrrhic dance* In the Pyrrhic dance, armed men perform quick acrobatic movements of attack and defense; *Pyrrhic phalanx* The Pyrrhic phalanx was a close massing of soldiers, a maneuver responsible for many Greek victories.

[5] *Cadmus* Phoenician prince who reputedly introduced the use of letters in Greece.

[6] *Polycrates* Greek tyrant and ruler of Samos, the island to which Anacreon fled after Teos was captured by Persians in 510 BCE.

[7] *tyrant ... Miltiades* In the fifth century BCE, Miltiades became the ruler of Chersonesus, now the peninsula of the Dardanelles.

[8] *Suli's rock ... Parga's shore* The Suliotes were a fierce Albanian tribe; Parga is a town on the Ionian coast.

Such as the Doric mothers bore;
And there, perhaps, some seed is sown,
The Heracleidan[1] blood might own.

14

Trust not for freedom to the Franks—[2]
They have a king who buys and sells:
In native swords, and native ranks,
The only hope of courage dwells;
But Turkish force, and Latin fraud,
Would break your shield, however broad.

15

Fill high the bowl with Samian wine!
Our virgins dance beneath the shade—
I see their glorious black eyes shine;
But gazing on each glowing maid,
My own the burning tear-drop laves,
To think such breasts must suckle slaves.

16

Place me on Sunium's[3] marbled steep,
Where nothing, save the waves and I,
May hear our mutual murmurs sweep;
There, swan-like, let me sing and die:
A land of slaves shall ne'er be mine—
Dash down yon cup of Samian wine!

87

Thus sung, or would, or could, or should have sung,
The modern Greek, in tolerable verse;
If not like Orpheus quite, when Greece was young,
Yet in these times he might have done much worse:
His strain displayed some feeling—right or wrong;
And feeling, in a poet, is the source
Of others' feeling; but they are such liars,
And take all colours—like the hands of dyers.

88

But words are things, and a small drop of ink,
Falling like dew, upon a thought, produces
That which makes thousands, perhaps millions, think;
'Tis strange, the shortest letter which man uses
Instead of speech, may form a lasting link
Of ages; to what straits old Time reduces
Frail man, when paper—even a rag like this,
Survives himself, his tomb, and all that's his.

—1821

from *Canto 7*

In Cantos 7 and 8 Byron describes the Siege of Ismail and Juan's participation in it. In December of 1790, Russian troops under the command of General Alexander Suvarov besieged and overpowered the Turkish fortress of Ismail in a quick, brutal attack. Byron's cantos vividly depict the action, confusion, brutality, and devastation of war.

78

—The work of glory still went on
In preparations for a cannonade
As terrible as that of Ilion,[4]
If Homer had found mortars ready made;
But now, instead of slaying Priam's son,[5]
We only can but talk of escalade,
Bombs, drums, guns, bastions, batteries, bayonets, bullets;
Hard words, which stick in the soft Muses' gullets.

79

Oh, thou eternal Homer! who couldst charm
All ears, though long; all ages, though so short,
By merely wielding with poetic arm
Arms to which men will never more resort,
Unless gunpowder should be found to harm
Much less than is the hope of every court,
Which now is leagued young Freedom to annoy;
But they will not find Liberty a Troy:—

80

Oh, thou eternal Homer! I have now
To paint a siege, wherein more men were slain,

[1] *Heracleidan blood* The Heracleidae, supposedly descendants of Hercules, conquered the Pelopennesus.

[2] *Franks* Western Europeans.

[3] *Sunium's* I.e., Cape Sounion's. Cape Sounion was the site of a temple of Poseidon.

[4] *Ilion* I.e., Troy.

[5] *Priam's son* I.e., Hector, Trojan hero and prince of Troy.

With deadlier engines and a speedier blow,
Than in thy Greek gazette of that campaign;
And yet, like all men else, I must allow,
To vie with thee would be about as vain
As for a brook to cope with ocean's flood;
But still we moderns equal you in blood;

81

If not in poetry, at least in fact;
And fact is truth, the grand desideratum![1]
Of which, howe'er the Muse describes each act,
There should be ne'ertheless a slight substratum.
But now the town is going to be attacked;
Great deeds are doing—how shall I relate 'em?
Souls of immortal generals! Phoebus watches
To colour up his rays from your despatches.
—1823

from *Canto 11*

In Canto 11 Juan, having passed through a Turkish harem, the Siege of Ismail (above), and the court of Catherine the Great, establishes himself in London among the upper classes. Byron uses this canto to describe Juan's experiences and, in the excerpt below, to muse on the changes that have occurred in his own life in the years since he left England.

55

In twice five years the "greatest living poet,"
Like to the champion in the fisty ring,[2]
Is called on to support his claim, or show it,
Although 'tis an imaginary thing.
Even I—albeit I'm sure I did not know it,
Nor sought of foolscap subjects to be king—
Was reckoned a considerable time,
The grand Napoleon of the realms of rhyme.[3]

[1] *desideratum* Latin: something desired or believed to be essential.

[2] *the fisty ring* The boxing ring. Byron was a keen amateur boxer.

[3] *Even I … rhyme* Byron frequently likens himself to Napoleon throughout his work. Here he makes ironic reference to both Napoleon's conspicuous success and his equally conspicuous fall.

56

But Juan was my Moscow,[4] and Faliero
My Leipsic,[5] and my Mount Saint Jean seems Cain:
"*La Belle Alliance*" of dunces down at zero,[6]
Now that the Lion's fall'n, may rise again:
But I will fall at least as fell my hero;
Nor reign at all, or as a *monarch* reign;
Or to some lonely isle of gaolers go,
With turncoat Southey for my turnkey Lowe.[7]

57

Sir Walter reigned before me; Moore and Campbell[8]
Before and after; but now grown more holy,
The Muses upon Sion's hill must ramble
With poets almost clergymen, or wholly;
And Pegasus hath a psalmodic amble
Beneath the very Reverend Rowley Powley,[9]
Who shoes the glorious animal with stilts,
A modern Ancient Pistol[10]—"by these hilts!"

58

Still he excels that artificial hard
Labourer in the same vineyard, though the vine
Yields him but vinegar for his reward,—
That neutralised dull Dorus of the Nine;
That swarthy Sporus, neither man nor bard;

[4] *Moscow* Napoleon attempted to conquer Russia by invading Moscow, but was defeated by the Russian winter.

[5] *Leipsic* The battle of Leipzig in October 1813 effectively broke the power of the French army. Byron draws a mocking parallel between this and his play *Marino Faliero*, which failed when it was performed against his wishes in 1821.

[6] *Cain … La Belle Alliance* Byron's *Cain* (1821), was condemned by critics for its blasphemy, and Byron likens it to Napoleon's defeat at Waterloo (crucial action occurred at Mont St. Jean). "La Belle Alliance" was the farmhouse in which the victors met after Waterloo; Byron is also punning on the alliance of England, Russia, Austria and Prussia, which combined to rout Napoleon.

[7] *Lowe* Sir Hudson Lowe, governor of St. Helena during Napoleon's exile.

[8] *Sir Walter … Campbell* Sir Walter Scott, Thomas Moore, and Thomas Campbell, contemporary poets.

[9] *Reverend Rowley Powley* The Rev. George Croly (1780–1860), a minor but prolific poet, fond of imitating Byron's work and known for his bombastic manner.

[10] *Pistol* In Shakespeare's *I Henry IV*, Pistol is a blustering friend of Falstaff.

That ox of verse, who *ploughs* for every line:—
Cambyses' roaring Romans beat at least
The howling Hebrews of Cybele's priest.—[1]

59

Then there's my gentle Euphues,[2] who, they say,
Sets up for being a sort of *moral me*;
He'll find it rather difficult some day
To turn out both, or either, it may be.
Some persons think that Coleridge hath the sway;
And Wordsworth has supporters, two or three;
And that deep-mouthed Boeotian "Savage Landor"[3]
Has taken for a swan rogue Southey's gander.

60

John Keats, who was killed off by one critique,
Just as he really promised something great,[4]
If not intelligible, without Greek
Contrived to talk about the gods of late,
Much as they might have been supposed to speak.[5]
Poor fellow! His was an untoward fate;
'T is strange the mind, that very fiery particle,
Should let itself be snuffed out by an article.

61

The list grows long of live and dead pretenders
To that which none will gain—or none will know
The conqueror at least; who, ere Time renders
His last award, will have the long grass grow
Above his burnt-out brain, and sapless cinders.
If I might augur, I should rate but low
Their chances; they're too numerous, like the thirty
Mock tyrants,[6] when Rome's annals waxed but dirty.

62

This is the literary *lower* empire,
Where the prætorian bands[7] take up the matter;—
A "dreadful trade," like his who "gathers samphire,"[8]
The insolent soldiery to soothe and flatter,
With the same feelings as you'd coax a vampire.
Now, were I once at home, and in good satire,
I'd try conclusions with those Janizaries,[9]
And show them *what* an intellectual war is.

63

I think I know a trick or two, would turn
Their flanks;—but it is hardly worth my while
With such small gear to give myself concern:
Indeed I've not the necessary bile;
My natural temper's really aught but stern,
And even my Muse's worst reproof's a smile;
And then she drops a brief and modern curtsy,
And glides away, assured she never hurts ye.

64

My Juan, whom I left in deadly peril
Amongst live poets and *blue* ladies, past
With some small profit through that field so sterile,
Being tired in time, and, neither least nor last,

[1] *Cybele's priest* Byron here attacks Henry Milman (1791–1868), author of *The Fall of Jerusalem*, and a reviewer whose criticism he resented. He offers him several different insults. *Dorus* was a eunuch in Terence's *Eunuchus*; effeminate *Sporus* was castrated, then married, by the emperor Nero; in the last two lines he suggests that the "howling Hebrews" of Milman's *Fall* are inferior even to the "roaring Romans" of George Croly. In the final line, he calls Milman "Cybele's priest," alluding to followers of the Asiatic goddess Cybele: these followers were often castrated.

[2] *gentle Euphues* Bryan Waller Proctor (1787–1874), whose poem *Diego de Montilla* was said to resemble *Don Juan*, but without the satire of social mores. Euphues, who gave his name to the "Euphuistic" style, is the hero of a prose romance by the Elizabethan writer John Lyly.

[3] *Savage Landor* Walter Savage Landor (1775–1864), a poet and friend of Robert Southey. He joined Southey in propagating rumors about Byron. *Boetian* The Athenians believed the Boetians to be stupid and boorish.

[4] *John Keats ... great* It was commonly believed that Keats's death was hastened by a savage attack by John Wilson Croker in the *Quarterly Review*, a popular journal. This notion came from Shelley (see *Adonais*).

[5] *Contrived to talk ... speak* Referring to Keats's *Hyperion*, which Byron admired.

[6] *thirty mock tyrants* The thirty pretenders to the throne of Rome during the third century.

[7] *praetorian bands* The Roman Emperor's guard, whose power was so strong during the Empire's decline that they had effective control over succession to the throne; in one case, they auctioned it off.

[8] *gathers samphire* Samphire is a European plant, used in cooking, that grows on rocks near the sea. In Shakespeare's *King Lear* 4.6.15–16, Edgar says that the man he pretends to see is engaged in a fearful trade because he must cling halfway down a cliff in order to gather samphire.

[9] *Janizaries* The sultan's guard.

Left it before he had been treated very ill;
And henceforth found himself more gaily classed
Amongst the higher spirits of the day,
The sun's true son, no vapour, but a ray.

65

His morns he passed in business—which, dissected,
Was like all business a laborious nothing
That leads to lassitude, the most infected
And Centaur Nessus garb[1] of mortal clothing,
And on our sofas makes us lie dejected,
And talk in tender horrors of our loathing
All kinds of toil, save for our country's good—
Which grows no better, though 't is time it should.

66

His afternoons he passed in visits, luncheons,
Lounging and boxing; and the twilight hour
In riding round those vegetable puncheons[2]
Called "Parks," where there is neither fruit nor flower
Enough to gratify a bee's slight munchings;
But after all it is the only "bower"
(In Moore's phrase), where the fashionable fair
Can form a slight acquaintance with fresh air.

67

Then dress, then dinner, then awakes the world!
Then glare the lamps, then whirl the wheels, then roar
Through street and square fast flashing chariots hurled
Like harnessed meteors; then along the floor
Chalk mimics painting;[3] then festoons are twirled;
Then roll the brazen thunders of the door,
Which opens to the thousand happy few
An earthly paradise of ormolu.[4]

68

There stands the noble hostess, nor shall sink
With the three-thousandth curtsy; there the waltz,
The only dance which teaches girls to think,
Makes one in love even with its very faults.
Saloon, room, hall, o'erflow beyond their brink,
And long the latest of arrivals halts,
'Midst royal dukes and dames condemned to climb,
And gain an inch of staircase at a time.

69

Thrice happy he who, after a survey
Of the good company, can win a corner,
A door that's *in* or boudoir *out* of the way,
Where he may fix himself like small "Jack Horner,"
And let the Babel round run as it may,
And look on as a mourner, or a scorner,
Or an approver, or a mere spectator,
Yawning a little as the night grows later.

70

But this won't do, save by and by; and he
Who, like Don Juan, takes an active share,
Must steer with care through all that glittering sea
Of gems and plumes and pearls and silks, to where
He deems it is his proper place to be;
Dissolving in the waltz to some soft air,
Or proudlier prancing with mercurial skill
Where Science marshals forth her own quadrille.

71

Or, if he dance not, but hath higher views
Upon an heiress or his neighbour's bride,
Let him take care that that which he pursues
Is not at once too palpably descried.
Full many an eager gentleman oft rues
His haste: impatience is a blundering guide,
Amongst a people famous for reflection,
Who like to play the fool with circumspection.

72

But, if you can contrive, get next at supper;
Or, if forestalled, get opposite and ogle:—
Oh, ye ambrosial moments! always upper
In mind, a sort of sentimental bogle,° *goblin*

[1] *Centaur Nessus garb* Hercules's wife gave him a garment dipped in the blood of the dying centaur Nessus, who told her it would win her back her husband's love. Instead, it caused Hercules unbearable pain.

[2] *puncheons* Large casks for liquids.

[3] *Chalk mimics painting* In ballrooms of the period, floors were decorated with elaborate chalk drawings.

[4] *ormolu* Gilded bronze decoration.

Which sits for ever upon memory's crupper,° *hindquarters*
The ghost of vanished pleasures once in vogue! Ill
Can tender souls relate the rise and fall
Of hopes and fears which shake a single ball.

73

But these precautionary hints can touch
Only the common run, who must pursue,
And watch, and ward; whose plans a word too much
Or little overturns; and not the few
Or many (for the number's sometimes such)
Whom a good mien, especially if new,
Or fame, or name, for wit, war, sense, or nonsense,
Permits whate'er they please, or *did* not long since.

74

Our hero, as a hero, young and handsome,
Noble, rich, celebrated, and a stranger,
Like other slaves of course must pay his ransom,
Before he can escape from so much danger
As will environ a conspicuous man. Some
Talk about poetry, and "rack and manger,"[1]
And ugliness, disease, as toil and trouble;—
I wish they knew the life of a young noble.

75

They are young, but know not youth—it is anticipated;
Handsome but wasted, rich without a sou;[2]
Their vigour in a thousand arms is dissipated;
Their cash comes *from*, their wealth goes *to* a Jew;
Both senates see their nightly votes participated
Between the tyrant's and the tribunes' crew;[3]
And having voted, dined, drunk, gamed, and whored,
The family vault receives another lord.

76

"Where is the world?" cries Young, at *eighty*[4]—"Where
The world in which a man was born?" Alas!
Where is the world of *eight* years past? '*T was there*—
I look for it—'t is gone, a globe of glass!
Cracked, shivered, vanished, scarcely gazed on, ere
A silent change dissolves the glittering mass.
Statesmen, chiefs, orators, queens, patriots, kings,
And dandies, all are gone on the wind's wings.

77

Where is Napoleon the Grand? God knows.
Where little Castlereagh?[5] The devil can tell:
Where Grattan, Curran, Sheridan,[6] all those
Who bound the bar or senate in their spell?
Where is the unhappy Queen, with all her woes?
And where the Daughter, whom the Isles loved well?[7]
Where are those martyred saints the Five per Cents?[8]
And where—oh, where the devil are the rents?

78

Where's Brummel? Dished. Where's Long Pole
Wellesley? Diddled.[9]
Where's Whitbread? Romilly?[10] Where's George the
Third?

---

[1] *rack and manger* Rack and ruin.

[2] *without a sou* Penniless.

[3] *Both … crew* The young noble does not express principles of his own, but simply votes the party line, a situation seen every night in both Houses of Parliament.

[4] *Where…eighty* Edward Young (1683–1765) was over eighty when he included this question in his poem, *Resignation*.

[5] *Castlereagh* Robert Stewart, Lord Castlereagh (1769–1822), Tory politician and Foreign Secretary during the Napoleonic Wars. Castlereagh committed suicide ("Where is little Castlereagh? The devil can tell").

[6] *Grattan* Henry Grattan (1746–1820), Whig statesman who supported Irish interests; *Curran* John Philpot Curran (1750–1814), who aided in the attempt to achieve Irish emancipation; *Sheridan* Richard Brinsley Sheridan (1751–1816), Whig M.P., playwright, and wit.

[7] *Queen* Caroline of Brunswick (1768–1821), whom George IV (1762–1830) married and then immediately repudiated, always treating with contempt. In 1820 he attempted to divorce her in a scandalous proceeding before the House of Lords; *the daughter* Princess Charlotte (1796–1817), daughter of George IV and Caroline and heir to the throne, was extremely popular. She died in childbirth in 1817.

[8] *Five per cents* Government bonds.

[9] *Brummel … Diddled* "Dished" and "diddled" both mean "ruined." George "Beau" Brummel (1788–1840), the famous dandy, was forced to flee to Calais in 1816 because of his enormous debts; William Pole Tylney Wellesley (1788–1857) was notorious for spending his money with abandon.

[10] *Whitbread* Samuel Whitbread (1758–1815), who supported Queen Caroline against the Prince Regent, committed suicide in 1815.

Where is his will? (That's not so soon unriddled.)[1]
And where is "Fum" the Fourth, our "royal bird?"[2]
Gone down, it seems, to Scotland to be fiddled
Unto by Sawney's[3] violin, we have heard:
"Caw° me, caw thee"—for six months hath been hatching   *scratch*
This scene of royal itch and loyal scratching.

79

Where is Lord This? And where my Lady That?
The Honourable Mistresses and Misses?
Some laid aside like an old Opera hat,
Married, unmarried, and remarried (this is
An evolution oft performed of late).
Where are the Dublin shouts—and London hisses?
Where are the Grenvilles? Turned as usual.[4] Where
My friends the Whigs? Exactly where they were.

80

Where are the Lady Carolines and Franceses?
Divorced or doing thereanent.[5] Ye annals
So brilliant, where the list of routs and dances is,—
Thou Morning Post, sole record of the panels
Broken in carriages, and all the phantasies
Of fashion,—say what streams now fill those channels?
Some die, some fly, some languish on the Continent,
Because the times have hardly left them *one* tenant.

81

Some who once set their caps[6] at cautious dukes,
Have taken up at length with younger brothers:
Some heiresses have bit at sharpers' hooks:[7]
Some maids have been made wives, some merely mothers;
Others have lost their fresh and fairy looks:
In short, the list of alterations bothers.
There's little strange in this, but something strange is
The unusual quickness of these common changes.

82

Talk not of seventy years as age; in seven
I have seen more changes, down from monarchs to
The humblest individual under heaven,
Than might suffice a moderate century through.
I knew that nought was lasting, but now even
Change grows too changeable, without being new:
Nought's permanent among the human race,
Except the Whigs *not* getting into place.

83

I have seen Napoleon, who seemed quite a Jupiter,
Shrink to a Saturn. I have seen a Duke
(No matter which) turn politician stupider,
If that can well be, than his wooden look.
But it is time that I should hoist my "blue Peter,"[8]
And sail for a new theme:—I have seen—and shook
To see it—the king hissed, and then caressed;
But don't pretend to settle which was best.

84

I have seen the Landholders without a rap—
I have seen Joanna Southcote[9]—I have seen—

[1] *Where … unriddled* King George III made two wills, one in 1770 and one in 1810. He left the later will unsigned. The earlier was thus official, although many of its provisions were outdated.

[2] *Fum … bird* George IV. The king's nickname was "Hum," while an apartment at the lavishly-decorated and ruinously expensive Brighton Pavilion contained an ornament called "Fum, the Chinese Bird of Royalty." Byron here alludes also to Moore's satire, *Fum and Hum, the Two Birds of Royalty* (1818).

[3] *Sawney's* Scotsman's. Sawney was a contemptuous term for a Scot.

[4] *Where are … usual* George Grenville (1712–70) first supported Pitt, then later broke with him; his son William Wyndam, Baron Grenville (1759–1834), was first a social reformer, then a repressive Tory.

[5] *doing thereanent* Doing something related to that. After her affair with Byron, Lady Caroline Lamb was for some years estranged from her husband; Lady Frances Wedderburn Webster (d. 1837), with whom Byron had once carried on a nearly-adulterous flirtation, left her husband in 1821; Byron helped to effect a reconciliation about the time that he wrote this canto.

[6] *set their caps* Set out to attract, with the sense of attracting into a marriage proposal.

[7] *bit at sharper's hooks* Been seduced into marriage by money-seeking rogues.

[8] *blue Peter* A blue flag with a white square in the center, raised as a sign of immediate sailing.

[9] *Southcote* Joanna Southcott (1750–1814), the founder of a fanatical sect, announced that she was about to give birth to the second messiah; in fact, she was suffering from dropsy and did not know it.

The House of Commons turned to a tax-trap[1]—
I have seen that sad affair of the late Queen—
I have seen crowns worn instead of a fool's cap—
I have seen a Congress doing all that's mean—
I have seen some nations like o'erloaded asses
Kick off their burthens, meaning the high classes.[2]

85

I have seen small poets, and great prosers, and
Interminable—*not eternal*—speakers—
I have seen the funds at war with house and land[3]—
I have seen the country gentlemen turn squeakers—
I have seen the people ridden o'er like sand
By slaves on horseback—I have seen malt liquors
Exchanged for "thin potations" by John Bull[4]—
I have seen John half detect himself a fool.—

86

But "*carpe diem*,"[5] Juan, "*carpe, carpe!*"
To-morrow sees another race as gay
And transient, and devoured by the same harpy.
"Life's a poor player,"—then "play out the play,
Ye villains!" above all keep a sharp eye
Much less on what you do than what you say:
Be hypocritical, be cautious, be
Not what you *seem*, but always what you *see*.

87

But how shall I relate in other cantos
Of what befell our hero in the land,
Which 't is the common cry and lie to vaunt as
A moral country? But I hold my hand—
For I disdain to write an Atalantis;[6]
But 't is as well at once to understand,
You are *not* a moral people, and you know it
Without the aid of too sincere a poet.

88

What Juan saw and underwent shall be
My topic, with of course the due restriction
Which is required by proper courtesy;
And recollect the work is only fiction,
And that I sing of neither mine nor me,
Though every scribe, in some slight turn of diction,
Will hint allusions never *meant*. Ne'er doubt
This—when I speak, I *don't hint*, but *speak out*.

89

Whether he married with the third or fourth
Offspring of some sage husband-hunting countess,
Or whether with some virgin of more worth
(I mean in Fortune's matrimonial bounties)
He took to regularly peopling Earth,
Of which your lawful awful wedlock fount is,—
Or whether he was taken in for damages,
For being too excursive in his homages,—

90

Is yet within the unread events of time.
Thus far, go forth, thou lay, which I will back
Against the same given quantity of rhyme,
For being as much the subject of attack
As ever yet was any work sublime,
By those who love to say that white is black.
So much the better!—I may stand alone,
But would not change my free thoughts for a throne.
—1823

[1] *tax trap* To pay for the Napoleonic Wars, Parliament levied extremely high taxes.

[2] *Congress* Probably the Congress of Vienna, which, after Napoleon's defeat, divided up Europe without regard for the wishes of the populace; *nations … classes* The recent revolts in Spain, Mexico, and South America.

[3] *funds at … land* The National Debt and the Sinking Fund, which unsuccessfully attempted to reduce it.

[4] *I have … horseback* Byron may be referring to scenes of political unrest he had witnessed in Italy or to the Peterloo Massacre in Manchester (1819), in which several peaceful protestors were murdered by the militia; *thin potations* Cf. Shakespeare, *2 Henry IV* 3.120–24. English brewers reduced the amount of malt they used in order to avoid the malt tax.

[5] *carpe diem* Latin: seize the day.

[6] *Atalantis* *The New Atalantis, or Memoirs and Manners of Several Persons of Quality* (1709) was an openly disrespectful book by Delarivier Manley (1663–1724).

In Context

Don Juan

"Remarks on *Don Juan*," from *Blackwood's Magazine*, August 1819

That Lord Byron has never written anything more decisively and triumphantly expressive of the greatness of his genius, will be allowed by all who have read this poem. That (laying all its manifold and grievous offences for a moment out of our view) it is by far the most admirable specimen of the mixture of ease, strength, gaiety, and seriousness extant in the whole body of English poetry, is a proposition to which, we are almost as well persuaded, very few of them will refuse their assent. With sorrow and humiliation do we speak it: the poet has devoted his powers to the worst of purposes and passions; and it increases his guilt and our sorrow, that he has devoted them entire. What the immediate effect of the poem may be on contemporary literature, we cannot pretend to guess—too happy could we hope that its lessons of boldness and vigour in language, and versification, and conception, might be attended to, as they deserve to be—without any stain being suffered to fall on the purity of those who minister to the general shape and culture of the public mind, from the mischievous insults against all good principle and all good feeling, which have been unworthily embodied in so many elements of fascination.

The moral strain of the whole poem is pitched in the lowest key, and if the genius of the author lifts him now and then out of his pollution, it seems as if he regretted the elevation, and made all haste to descend again. To particularize the offences committed in its pages would be worse than vain because the great genius of the man seems to have been throughout exerted to its utmost strength, in devising every possible method of pouring scorn upon every element of good or noble nature in the hearts of his readers. Love, honour, patriotism, religion, are mentioned only to be scoffed at and derided, as if their sole remaining resting-place were, or ought to be, in the bosoms of fools. It appears, in short, as if this miserable man, having exhausted every species of sensual gratification, having drained the cup of sin even to its bitterest dregs, were resolved to show us that he is no longer a human being, even in his frailties—but a cool unconcerned fiend, laughing with a detestable glee over the whole of the better and worse elements of which human life is composed; treating well nigh with equal derision the most pure of virtues, and the most odious of vices, dead alike to the beauty the one, and the deformity of the other; a mere heartless despiser of that frail but noble humanity, whose type was never exhibited in a shape of more deplorable degradation than in his own contemptuously distinct delineation of himself.

Selected Letters

Byron's letters are valuable literary artefacts in their own right. Only Keats rivalled him for breadth of subject matter and depth of thought in his personal correspondence, and even Keats could not match his dazzling wit. The letters are filled with gossip and scandal, with the most intimate details of Byron's life and those of his friends, all recounted with great shrewdness and relish. At the same time, however, Byron was not afraid to place his most intimate thoughts, and accounts of his greatest anguish, on paper for others to read. The letters record his minute observations on the foreign countries he passed through, his political beliefs, his growing involvement with revolutionary movements, his frank descriptions (and ratings of) his many sexual involvements, his sorrow and rage over the end of his marriage, his generosity and kindness toward both friends and strangers—all recounted with a dexterity of language that mirrors that of his poetical works.

from a letter To Francis Hodgson[1]

Newstead Abbey, September 13, 1811

My dear Hodgson

...I won't dispute with you on the arcana of your new calling; they are bagatelles,[2] like the King of Poland's rosary.[3] One remark and I have done: the basis of your religion is *injustice*; the *Son of God*, the *pure*, the *immaculate*, the *innocent*, is sacrificed for the *guilty*. This proves *His* heroism; but no more does away with *man's* guilt than a schoolboy's volunteering to be flogged for another would exculpate the dunce from negligence, or preserve him from the rod. You degrade the Creator, in the first place, by making him a begetter of children, and in the next you convert Him into a tyrant over an immaculate and injured being who is sent into existence to suffer death for the benefit of some millions of scoundrels, who, after all, seem as likely to be damned as ever. As to miracles, I agree with Hume, that it is more probable men should *lie* or be *deceived*, than that things out of the course of nature should so happen.[4] Mahomet wrought miracles; Brothers the prophet had *proselytes*; and so would Breslau the conjurer,[5] had he lived in the time of Tiberius.

Besides, I trust that God is not a *Jew*, but the God of all mankind; and, as you allow that a virtuous Gentile may be saved, you do away the necessity of being a Jew or a Christian.

I do not believe in any revealed religion, because no religion is revealed; and if it pleases the Church to damn me for not allowing a *nonentity*, I throw myself on the mercy of the "*Great First Cause, least understood,*"[6] who must do what is most proper, though I conceive He never made anything to be tortured in another life, whatever it may in this. I will neither read *pro* nor *con*. God would have made His will known without books, considering how very few could read them when Jesus of Nazareth lived, had it been His pleasure to ratify any peculiar mode of worship. As to your immortality, if people are to live, why die? And our carcasses, which are to rise again, are they worth raising? I hope, if mine is, that I shall have a better *pair of legs* than I have moved on these two-and-twenty years, or I shall be sadly behind in the squeeze into Paradise. Did you ever read "Malthus on Population?"[7] If he be right, war and pestilence are our best friends, to save us from being eaten alive, in

[1] *Hodgson* Francis Hodgson (1781–1832) was Provost of Eton College and one of Byron's closest friends.

[2] *bagatelles* Toys, trifles.

[3] *King of Poland's rosary* In 1683 the Muslims laid siege to Vienna. The city was saved by an army under the Polish King, John Sobieski, who was dedicated to the rosary. The King believed that the rosary, and this dedication, had been instrumental in his victory.

[4] *As to miracles ... happen* In his book, *An Enquiry Concerning Human Understanding* (1748), the Scottish philosopher David Hume (1711–76) argued that it was miraculous that so many believed in miracles.

[5] *Brothers* Richard Brothers (1757–1824) claimed that in 1795 he would be revealed as Prince of the Hebrews and ruler of the world; *Breslau the conjurer* Philip Breslaw was a German magician who performed in England in the 1760s. He wrote *Breslaw's Last Legacy; or, the Magical Companion* (1784).

[6] *Great First Cause ... understood* Cf. Alexander Pope, *The Universal Prayer*, st. 2.

[7] *Malthus on Population* Thomas Malthus (1766–1834) wrote in his *Essay on Population* (1798) that plague, famine, and war were necessary means of reducing the population. See also *Don Juan*, Canto 11.131.

this "best of all possible worlds."[1]

I will write, read, and think no more; indeed, I do not wish to shock your prejudices by saying all I do think. Let us make the most of life, and leave dreams to Emanuel Swedenborg. …[2]

Yours ever,

Byron

To Lady Byron

Byron's marriage was a disaster from the start, and his cruelty and bizarre behavior caused his wife to leave him after a year. He was at first devastated, then full of bitter rage. In the early weeks of their separation, he wrote her a number of letters expressing confusion at her, apologizing for his bad behavior, and pleading with her to return, or at least to meet with him. In the letter below he gives vent to both his sorrow and his rage.

February 8, 1816

All I can say seems useless—and all I could say might be no less unavailing—yet I still cling to the wreck of my hopes before they sink forever.——Were you then *never* happy with me? did you never at any times express yourself so? have no marks of affection—of the warmest & most reciprocal attachment passed between us? or did in fact hardly a day go down without some such on one side and generally on both?—do not mistake me—[two lines crossed out] I have not denied my state of mind, but you know it's causes. & were those deviations from calmness never followed by acknowledgment & repentance? was not the last which occurred more particularly so? & had I not—had we not—the days before & on the day when we parted—every reason to believe that we loved each other, that we were to meet again—were not your letters kind? had I not acknowledged to you all my faults and follies, & assured you that some had not & would not be repeated?—I do not require these questions to be answered to me, but to your own heart.——The day before I received your father's letter, I had fixed a day for rejoining you; if I did not write lately, Augusta did, and as you had been my proxy in correspondence with her—so did I imagine she might be the same for me to you. Upon your letter to me this day I surely may remark that it's expressions imply a treatment which I am incapable of inflicting, & you of imputing to me if aware of their latitude & the extent of the inferences to be drawn from them. This is not just——but I have no reproaches nor the wish to find cause for them. Will you see me?—when & where you please, in whose presence you please: the interview shall pledge you to nothing, & I will say & do nothing to agitate either; it is torture to correspond thus, & there are things to be settled & said which cannot be written. You say "it is my disposition to deem what I *have worthless*"—did I deem *you* so? did I ever express myself to you—or of you—to others? You are much changed within these twenty days or you would never have thus poisoned your own better feelings—and trampled on mine.

Ever yours most truly & affectionately

B

To Augusta Leigh

Byron's relationship with his half-sister was complex. He was closer to her than to any other woman in his life: she was for him the gentle mother he had never had, an ally against the world, a lover, and a reflection of himself. After they were separated by his departure from England in 1816, he used his letters to her to express his love. These letters are among his most tender writings.

Ouchy, September 17, 1816

My dearest Augusta,[3] I am thus far on my way to the Bernese Alps & the Grindewald[4] and the *Yungfrau*[5] (that is the "Wild woman" being interpreted, as it is so perverse a mountain that no other sex would suit it), which journey may occupy me eight days or so, and then it is my intention to return to Geneva, preparatory

[1] *best of all possible worlds* Cf. Voltaire, *Candide*, ch 30.

[2] *leave dreams … Swedenborg* The Swedish philosopher and theologian Emmanuel Swedenborg (1688–72) believed that he had received messages from God and Jesus Christ in a series of vivid waking dreams.

[3] *Augusta* Augusta Leigh, Byron's half-sister (1783–1851).

[4] *Grindewald* Town in Switzerland.

[5] *Yungfrau* I.e., Jungfrau, a mountain in the Alps.

to passing the Simplon.[1]

Continue to direct as usual to Geneva.[2] I have lately written to you several letters (3 or 4 by post and two by hand) and I have received all yours very safely. I rejoice to have heard that you are well. You have been in London too lately, & H[obhouse][3] tells me that at your levee he generally found Ld. F. Bentinck.[4] Pray why is that fool so often a visitor? is he in love with you? I have recently broken through my resolution of not speaking to you of Lady B[yron], but do not on that account name her to me. It is a relief, a partial relief to me to talk of her sometimes to you—but it would be none to hear of her. *Of* her you are to judge for yourself, but not altogether forget that she has destroyed your brother. Whatever my faults might or may have been—*She* was not the person marked out by providence to be their avenger. One day or another her conduct will recoil on her own head; *not* through *me*, for my feelings toward her are not those of Vengeance, but mark if she does not end miserably *tout ou tard*.[5] She may think, talk, or act as she will, and by any process of cold reasoning and jargon of "duty & acting for the best" &c., &c., impose upon her own feelings & those of others for a time—but woe unto her: the wretchedness she has brought upon the man to whom she has been everything evil will flow back into its fountain. I may thank the strength of my constitution that has enabled me to bear all this, but those who bear the longest and most do not suffer the least. I do not think a human being could endure more mental torture than that woman has directly & indirectly inflicted upon me within the present year.

She has (for a time at least) separated me from my child & from you but I turn from the subject for the present.

Tomorrow I repass Clarens & Vevey;[6] if in the new & more extended tour I am making, anything I think may please you occurs, I will detail it.

Scrope[7] has by this time arrived with my little presents for you and yours[8] & Ada. I still hope to be able to see you next Spring, perhaps you & one or two of the children could be spared some time next year for a little tour *here* or in France with me for a month or two. I think I could make it very pleasing to you, & it should be no expense to L[eigh][9] or to yourself. Pray think of this hint. You have no idea how very beautiful great part of this country is, and *women* and *children* traverse it with ease and expedition. I would return from any distance at any time to see you, an come to England for you; and when you consider the chances against our—but I won't relapse into the dismals and anticipate long absences—

The great obstacle would be that you are so admirably yoked, and necessary as a housekeeper, and a letter writer, & a place-hunter to that very helpless gentleman your Cousin,[10] that I suppose the usual self-love of an elderly person would interfere between you & any scheme of recreation or relaxation, for however short a period.

What a fool I was to marry, and *you* not very wise, my dear—we might have lived so single and so happy, as old maids and bachelors; I shall never find anyone like you—nor you (vain as it may seem) like me. We are just formed to pass our lives together, and therefore we—at least I—am by a crowd of circumstances removed from the only being who could ever have loved me, or whom I can unmixedly feel attached to.

Had you been a Nun and I a Monk, that we might have talked through a grate[11] instead of across the sea; no matter—my voice and my heart are

Ever thine,

B

[1] *Simplon* Simplon Pass, in the Alps.

[2] *Continue ... Geneva* I.e., continue to send your letters to Geneva.

[3] *Hobhouse* John Cam Hobhouse (1786–1869), Byron's best friend.

[4] *Ld. F. Bentinck* Lord Frederick Bentinck (1802–48), a friend of Augusta's husband.

[5] *tout ou tard* French: sooner or later.

[6] *Clarens and Vevey* Swiss towns.

[7] *Scrope* Scrope Berdmore Davies (1783–1852), a charming and feckless, but very loyal, friend of Byron's. His first name is pronounced "Scroop."

[8] *yours* Augusta's five children.

[9] *Leigh* Augusta's first cousin and husband, Colonel George Leigh.

[10] *that ... cousin* In 1807, Augusta married her first cousin Col. George Leigh (the Byrons frequently married their first cousins). Leigh's main activity was betting on horse-racing, and the marriage was not entirely happy.

[11] *grate* Cloistered monks and nuns spoke to visitors from behind a grate that separated the cloister from the rest of the world.

To Douglas Kinnaird[1]

Don Juan created a sensation among Byron's friends before it was published and among the public after it appeared in print. Byron, however, refused to yield either to the pleas to neutralize the poem by those who knew him, or to the horrified condemnations of the reviewers: he remained proud of it and convinced of its ultimate value. The two letters and review below give some sense of the public reaction to the poem, and of Byron's own thoughts about it.

Venice, October 26, 1818 [1819]

My dear Douglas, My late expenditure has arisen from living at a distance from Venice and being obliged to keep up two establishments, from frequent journeys, and buying some furniture and books as well as a horse or two, and not from any renewal of the EPICUREAN system as you suspect. I have been faithful to my honest liaison with Countess Guiccioli,[2] and I can assure you that *She* has never cost me directly or indirectly a sixpence—indeed the circumstances of herself and family render this no merit. I never offered her but one present, a broach of brilliants, and she sent it back to me with her *own hair* in it (I shall *not* say of *what part,* but *that* is an Italian custom)[3] and a note to say that she was not in the habit of receiving presents of that value, but hoped that I would not consider her sending it back as an affront, nor the value diminished by the enclosure. I have not had a whore this half-year, confining myself to the strictest adultery. Why should you prevent Hanson[4] from making a *peer* if he likes it—I think the "*Garretting*" would be far the best parliamentary privilege I know of. Damn your delicacy. It is a low commercial quality, and very unworthy a man who prefixes "honourable" to his nomenclature. If you say that I must sign the bonds, I suppose that I must, but it is very iniquitous to make me pay my debts—you have no idea of the pain it gives one. Pray do three things: get my property out of the *funds*; get Rochdale[5] sold; get me some information from Perry[6] about *South America*—and 4thly. ask Lady Noel[7] not to live so very long. As to Subscribing to Manchester, if I do that I will write a letter to Burdett[8] for publication to accompany the Subscription, which shall be more radical than anything yet rooted—but I feel lazy. I have thought of this for some time, but alas! the air of this cursed Italy enervates and disfranchises the thoughts of a man after nearly four years of respiration, to say nothing of emission. As to "Don Juan," confess, confess, you dog—and be candid—that it is the sublime of *that there* sort of writing. It may be bawdy, but is it not good English? it may be profligate, but is it not *life*, is it not *the thing*? Could any man have written it who has not lived in the world? and tooled in a post-chaise, in a hackney coach? in a Gondola? against a wall? in a court carriage? in a vis-a-vis?[9] on a table? and under it? I have written about a hundred stanzas of a third Canto, but it is damned modest—the outcry has frightened me. I had such projects for the Don, but the *Cant* is so much stronger than *Cunt* now a days, that the benefit of experience in a man who had well weighed the worth of both monosyllables must be lost to despairing posterity. After all what stuff this outcry is—Lalla Rookh and Little[10] are more dangerous than my burlesque poem can be. Moore has been here; we got tipsy together and were very amicable—he is gone on to Rome. I put my life (in M.S.) into his hands (*not* for publication); you or

---

[1] *Kinnaird* Douglas Kinnaird (1788–1830), Byron's friend and banker.

[2] *Countess Guiccioli* Teresa Gamba Ghiselli (1800–79) married Count Alessandro Guiccioli in 1818; in 1819, she and Byron began a love affair that lasted until his death.

[3] *own hair ... custom* There seems to have been something about Byron that inspired women to send him their pubic hair; Lady Caroline Lamb had done the same.

[4] *Hanson* John Hanson (d. 1841), Byron's lawyer.

[5] *Rochdale* One of Byron's estates. He had been trying to sell it since 1809.

[6] *Perry* James Perry (1756–1821), editor of the Whig *Morning Chronicle*. Byron expected him to have an interest in the South American independence movements in which he was contemplating taking part.

[7] *Lady Noel* Lady Judith Milbanke Noel (1751–1822), Byron's mother-in-law.

[8] *Burdett* Sir Francis Burdett (1770–1844), radical political leader.

[9] *vis-a-vis* French: face-to-face. Here, referring to a light carriage in which two persons sit face-to-face.

[10] *Lalla Rookh* (1817) and *Poems of the Late Thomas Little* (1801), poems by Thomas Moore.

any body else may see it at his return.[1] It only comes up to 1816. He is a noble fellow and looks quite fresh and poetical; nine years (the age of a poem's education) my Senior, he looks younger—this comes of marriage and being settled in the Country. I want to go to South America; I have written to Hobhouse all about it. I wrote to my wife three months ago under care to Murray[2]—has she got the letter, or is the letter got into Blackwood's magazine?[3] You ask after my Christmas pye; remit it any how—*Circulars* is the best. You are right about *income*; I must have it all—how the devil do I know that I may live a year or a month? I wish I knew that I might regulate my spending in more ways that one. As it is one always thinks that there is but a span. A man may as well break or be damned for a large sum as a small one; I should be loth to pay the devil or any other creditor more than sixpence in the pound.

P.S. I recollect nothing of "Davies's landlord," but what ever Davies *says* I will *swear* to, and *that's* more than *he* would. So pray pay—has he a landlady too? perhaps I may owe her something. With regard to the bonds I will sign them, but it goes against the grain. As to the rest, you *can't* err so long as you *don't* pay. Paying is executor's or executioner's work. You may write somewhat oftener. Mr. Galignani's messenger[4] gives the outline of your public affairs, but I see no results; you have no man yet (always excepting Burdett & you & H[obhouse] and the Gentlemanly leaven of your two-penny loaf of rebellion) don't forget however my charge of horse and commission for the Midland Counties and by the holies! You shall have your account in decimals. Love to Hobby[5]—but why leave the Whigs?

[1] *I put ... return* After his death, Byron's memoirs were burnt by his publisher, who had not read them, over the protests of Moore, who had.

[2] *Murray* John Murray II (1778–1843), Byron's publisher.

[3] *Blackwood's Edinburgh Magazine*, a Tory publication always critical of Byron, had just published a savage review of *Don Juan*. See the extract following *Don Juan*.

[4] *Galignani's Messenger* An English-language periodical published in Paris and available in Venice.

[5] *Hobby* I.e., John Cam Hobhouse.

from a letter To John Murray

Ravenna, February 16, 1821

Dear Moray[6]—In the month of March will arrive from Barcelona *Signor Curioni*[7] engaged for the Opera. He is an acquaintance of mine and a gentlemanly young man, high in his profession. I must request your personal kindness and patronage in his favour. Pray introduce him to such of the theatrical people, Editors of Papers, and others, as may be useful to him in his profession publicly and privately. He is accompanied by the Signora Arpalice Taruscelli,[8] a Venetian lady of great beauty and celebrity and a particular friend of mine; your natural gallantry will I am sure induce you to pay her proper attention. Tell Israeli that as he is fond of *literary* anecdotes she can tell him some of your acquaintance abroad.—I presume that he speaks Italian. Do not neglect this request, but do them and me a favour in their behalf. I shall write to some others to aid you in assisting them with your countenance.

I agree to your request of leaving in abeyance the terms for the three D.J.s till you can ascertain the effect of publication. If I refuse to alter, you have a claim to so much courtesy in return. I had let you off your proposal about the price of Cantos, last year (the 3d. & 4th. always to reckon as *one* only, which they originally were) and I do not call upon you to renew it. You have therefore no occasion to fight so shy of such subjects as I am not conscious of having given you occasion. The 5th. is so far from being the last of D.J. that it is hardly the beginning. I meant to take him the tour of Europe—with a proper mixture of siege, battle, and adventure—and to make him finish as *Anacharsis Cloots*[9] in the French revolution. To how many cantos this may extend I know not, nor whether (even if I live) I shall

[6] *Moray* Pun on Murray's name. A moray is a kind of eel.

[7] *Curioni* Alberico Curioni (1785–1875), an Italian tenor who sang in London from 1821 to 1832.

[8] *Arpalice Taruscelli* A woman with whom Byron had had a brief affair in Venice in 1818.

[9] *Anacharsis Cloots* Jean Baptiste Clootz (1755–94) was a Prussian baron who became involved in the French Revolution. He took the name "Anarcharsis" and described himself as "l'orateur de genre humaine" ("the orator of the human race"). He was executed by guillotine in 1794, during the reign of terror. See *Don Juan*, Canto 1.3, above.

complete it, but this was my notion. I meant to have made him a Cavalier Servente[1] in Italy and a cause for a divorce in England and a Sentimental "Werther-faced man"[2] in Germany, so as to show the different ridicules of the society in each of those countries, and to have displayed him gradually gaté and blasé as he grew older, as is natural. But I had not quite fixed whether to make him end in Hell, or in an unhappy marriage, not knowing which would be the severest. The Spanish tradition says hell, but it is probably only an Allegory of the other state. You are now in possession of my notions on the subject.

… How came George Bankes[3] to quote English Bards in the House of Commons? all the World keep flinging that poem in my face.—Belzoni[4] *is* a grand traveller and his English is very prettily broken.—As for News: the Barbarians[5] are marching on Naples, and if they lose a single battle, all Italy will be up. It will be like the Spanish war if they have any bottom.—"*Letters opened* !"[6] to be sure they are, and that's the reason why I always put in my opinion of the German Austrian Scoundrels; there is not an Italian who loathes them more than I do, and whatever I could do to scour Italy and the earth of their infamous oppression would be done "con amore."[7]

Yours ever & truly

BYRON

Recollect that the Hints[8] must be printed with the *Latin* otherwise there is no sense.

[1] *Cavaliere Servente* Official lover of a married woman. Byron was himself Teresa Guiccioli's cavaliere servente, and was often embarrassed by the servile nature of the position.

[2] *Werther-faced man* Byron here refers to the protagonist of Goethe's *The Sorrows of Young Werther* (1774), a depressive young man, but he borrows the phrase from Thomas Moore, who had first used it in his *Fudge Family in Paris* (1818).

[3] *George Bankes* George Bankes (1787–1856), an English Member of Parliament, quoted Byron's early satire, *English Bards and Scotch Reviewers,* in an address at the opening of Parliament in 1821.

[4] *Belzoni* Giovanni Battista Belzoni (1778–1823), an Italian explorer, insisted on writing his account of his travels in English, though he was far from a master of the language.

[5] *Barbarians* Germans.

[6] *Letters opened* Because Byron was connected with the Gamba family, known for its devotion to the Italian national cause, his mail might be secretly opened and read by the authorities.

[7] *con amorei* Italian: with love.

[8] *Hints* *Hints from Horace,* originally to be published in 1811, but superseded by the first two cantos of *Childe Harold's Pilgrimage.* Byron's interest in publishing it was revived in 1820, but lapsed. It was finally issued in 1831.

Percy Bysshe Shelley

1792 – 1822

Even more than Blake's, Percy Bysshe Shelley's progressive social and political ideas have been an inspiration to many readers, from nineteenth-century socialists like Marx and Engels to radical thinkers of the 1960s. Although he was born into wealth and privilege, Shelley opposed the powerful, from those who teased and harassed him in school at Eton to the Tory government and press whom he believed were responsible for the oppression of the working classes. He collaborated on *The Necessity of Atheism* (1811), a pamphlet destined to alienate not only his father, but also the bishops and authorities at Oxford, to whom Shelley sent the piece. Antagonistic to kings, priests, judges, the conservative press and aristocracy, he was called "Mad Shelley" at Oxford. He earned this sobriquet not only for his radicalism but also for his intense interest in science. These intellectual passions underwrite a body of remarkable visionary poetry characterized by an elegance and complexity that is at once very wonderful and very difficult.

Shelley was born in 1792 at Field Place in Sussex, the first of the six children of Elizabeth and Timothy Shelley, a Member of Parliament who became a baronet on the death of his father, Sir Bysshe Shelley. Percy grew up in the affluence befitting his role as heir to the estate and title of his father and grandfather. He spent his early years running free on the estate and entertaining his siblings, so he was unprepared for the rules of the boys' academy he attended, or the bullying he would suffer there. Shelley later attended Eton College, and there the teasing continued, further developing his allegiance to outcasts and the disenfranchised, and nurturing his rebellious spirit. He was still a student at Eton when he published *Zastrozzi* (1810), a Gothic romance novel. He continued to publish during his short stint at Oxford University, from which he and Thomas Jefferson Hogg, his friend and the co-author of *The Necessity of Atheism*, were expelled for writing the pamphlet.

In 1813 Shelley published his first important work: *Queen Mab*, a poetic dream-vision that vilified conventional morality and institutional religion in a utopian picture of humanity returned to a condition of innocence. Shelley's greatest utopian fantasy, *Prometheus Unbound* (1820), would essentially reprise the same picture, imagining a world grown young again as human beings learn to undo the curse of their acquired historical fears and hatreds and replace it with a program based on love, which he called "the great secret" of all morality.

Shelley's personal involvements with love, fueled by his ideals, were also fraught with that inherited curse. In 1811 Shelley married Harriet Westbrook, and the couple had a daughter born to them in 1813. But before long he would fall in love with another young woman, Mary Godwin, the daughter of the radical thinkers William Godwin and Mary Wollstonecraft.

In 1814 Shelley left Harriet and traveled to the continent with Mary and her half sister Clair Clairmont for a six-week tour. When they returned to England Shelley proposed that Harriet should live with Mary and himself as free lovers. When Harriet refused, Shelley, Mary, and Clair again traveled to Europe, where the three met Lord Byron in Switzerland in June. In the meantime, Harriet gave birth to Shelley's second child, a son, in late 1814, and at the end of 1816 she committed suicide. Mary and Percy were then married.

The summer of 1816 is one of the most famous in the history of English letters. Out of it came a series of stunning literary works: Mary's great novel *Frankenstein*; Byron's third canto of *Childe Harold* as well as various apocalyptic works, especially *Manfred*; and a series of key lyric poems by Shelley including "Mont Blanc" and the "Hymn to Intellectual Beauty." Later (1818) Shelley would write "Julian and Maddalo: A Conversation," a brilliant verse dialogue representing the conversations that he and Byron had been having since they met in 1816.

Upon this return to England from Switzerland, his life bristling with personal and political scandals, Shelley was denied custody of his two children from his first marriage. In 1818 the Shelleys moved to the Continent with their baby girl Clara in the hope of joining Byron in Italy and avoiding the judgment of English society. Unfortunately, Clara died in September, and William, born in 1816, died the following year. The only child to survive would be Percy Florence, born in 1819.

Shelley wrote his lyric masterpiece *Prometheus Unbound* that same year, to show how social life might and ought to be, and he wrote the political tragedy *The Cenci* (1819), to show the way it actually was. The distance between the two works is dialectical, as Shelley later attempted to explain in his important prose work, the *Defence of Poetry* (1821). During this prolific period Shelley also responded to the Peterloo Massacre—in which eleven workers were killed at what was meant to be a peaceful rally in Manchester—by writing "The Mask of Anarchy," "Song: To the Men of England," "A Philosophical View of Reform," and "Ode to the West Wind," a revolutionary lyric that recapitulates, in miniature, the argument and structure of *Prometheus Unbound*. Shelley hoped his verse would undermine the retrograde political institutions of his time and seed the future with a promise of rejuvenation. Enjoying scant fame or immediate influence, he nevertheless concluded his *Defence of Poetry* with the now-famous pronouncement that poets are "the unacknowledged legislators of the world."

In 1822 Shelley—who could not swim—went sailing on the Bay of Spezia in Italy with his friend Edward Williams. They were caught in a sudden squall and drowned. When Shelley's body washed up on the beach a few days later, a copy of Keats's poems was found in his pocket. A funeral pyre was hastily built and his corpse cremated—except for his heart, which was snatched from the pyre by his friend Edward Trelawney.

In a letter to some of his conservative English friends Byron famously declared: "You are all brutally mistaken about Shelley who was without exception—the *best* and least selfish man I ever knew." His ashes were placed near the recently buried Keats in the Protestant Cemetery in Rome. His inconsumable heart remained in Mary Shelley's possession, wrapped in the pages of *Adonais*, Shelley's elegy for Keats, until her death. It is buried with her in her tomb at St. Peter's Churchyard in Bournemouth.

⌘⌘⌘

To Wordsworth[1]

Poet of Nature, thou hast wept to know
That things depart which never may return:
Childhood and youth, friendship and love's first glow,
Have fled like sweet dreams, leaving thee to mourn.
These common woes I feel. One loss is mine
Which thou too feel'st, yet I alone deplore.
Thou wert as a lone star, whose light did shine
On some frail bark in winter's midnight roar:
Thou hast like to a rock-built refuge stood
Above the blind and battling multitude:
In honoured poverty thy voice did weave
Songs consecrate to truth and liberty—
Deserting these, thou leavest me to grieve,
Thus having been, that thou shouldst cease to be.
—1816

Alastor; or, The Spirit of Solitude

Preface

The poem entitled "Alastor" may be considered as allegorical of one of the most interesting situations of the human mind. It represents a youth of uncorrupted feelings and adventurous genius[2] led forth by an imagination inflamed and purified through familiarity with all that is excellent and majestic, to the contemplation of the universe. He drinks deep of the fountains of knowledge, and is still insatiate. The magnificence and beauty of the external world sinks profoundly into the frame of his conceptions, and affords to their modifications a variety not to be exhausted. So long as it is possible for his desires to point towards objects thus infinite and unmeasured, he is joyous, and tranquil, and self-possessed. But the period arrives when these objects cease to suffice. His mind is at length suddenly awakened and thirsts for intercourse with an intelligence similar to itself. He images to himself the Being whom he loves. Conversant with speculations of the sublimest and most perfect natures, the vision in which he embodies his own imaginations unites all of wonderful, or wise, or beautiful, which the poet, the philosopher, or the lover could depicture. The intellectual faculties, the imagination, the functions of sense, have their respective requisitions[3] on the sympathy of corresponding powers in other human beings. The Poet is represented as uniting these requisitions, and attaching them to a single image. He seeks in vain for a prototype of his conception. Blasted by his disappointment, he descends to an untimely grave.

The picture is not barren of instruction to actual men. The Poet's self-centred seclusion was avenged by the furies of an irresistible passion pursuing him to speedy ruin. But that Power which strikes the luminaries of the world with sudden darkness and extinction, by awakening them to too exquisite a perception of its influences, dooms to a slow and poisonous decay those meaner spirits that dare to abjure its dominion. Their destiny is more abject and inglorious as their delinquency is more contemptible and pernicious. They who, deluded by no generous error, instigated by no sacred thirst of doubtful knowledge, duped by no illustrious superstition, loving nothing on this earth, and cherishing no hopes beyond, yet keep aloof from sympathies with their kind, rejoicing neither in human joy nor mourning with human grief; these, and such as they, have their apportioned curse. They languish, because none feel with them their common nature. They are morally dead. They are neither friends, nor lovers, nor fathers, nor citizens of the world, nor benefactors of their country. Among those who attempt to exist without human sympathy, the pure and tender-hearted perish through the intensity and passion of their search after its communities, when the vacancy of their spirit suddenly makes itself felt. All else, selfish, blind, and torpid, are those unforeseeing multitudes who constitute, together with their own, the lasting misery and loneliness of the world. Those who love not their fellow-beings live unfruitful lives, and prepare for their old age a miserable grave.

"The good die first,
And those whose hearts are dry as summer dust,
Burn to the socket!"[4]

December 14, 1815

[1] *To Wordsworth* As a young man, Wordsworth identified himself as a political radical, but as his career progressed he gradually became more conservative. His 1814 poem *The Excursion* showed a marked change in his political and religious thinking, and was received with disappointment by many of his early admirers, such as Shelley.

[2] *youth of … genius* This protagonist is unnamed, although because of the poem's title he is often (incorrectly) assumed to be called Alastor. In his *Memoirs of Shelley*, Shelley's friend Thomas Love Peacock explains that Shelley was "at a loss for a title, and I proposed that which he adopted: Alastor, or the Spirit of Solitude. The Greek word *Alastor* is an evil genius."

[3] *requisitions* Claims.

[4] *The … socket* From Wordsworth's *Excursion*, 1.500–02.

Alastor; or, The Spirit of Solitude

Nondum amabam, et amare amabam, quaerebam quid amarem, amans amare.

—*Confess. St. August.*[1]

Earth, ocean, air, belovèd brotherhood!
If our great Mother[2] has imbued my soul
With aught of natural piety[3] to feel
Your love, and recompense the boon with mine;
If dewy morn, and odorous noon, and even,
With sunset and its gorgeous ministers,
And solemn midnight's tingling silentness;
If autumn's hollow sighs in the sere wood,
And winter robing with pure snow and crowns
Of starry ice the grey grass and bare boughs;
If spring's voluptuous pantings when she breathes
Her first sweet kisses, have been dear to me;
If no bright bird, insect, or gentle beast
I consciously have injured, but still loved
And cherished these my kindred; then forgive
This boast, belovèd brethren, and withdraw
No portion of your wonted favour now!

Mother of this unfathomable world!
Favour my solemn song, for I have loved
Thee ever, and thee only; I have watched
Thy shadow, and the darkness of thy steps,
And my heart ever gazes on the depth
Of thy deep mysteries. I have made my bed
In charnels[4] and on coffins, where black death *cemeteries*
Keeps record of the trophies won from thee,
Hoping to still these obstinate questionings[5]
Of thee and thine, by forcing some lone ghost,
Thy messenger, to render up the tale
Of what we are. In lone and silent hours,
When night makes a weird sound of its own stillness,
Like an inspired and desperate alchemist
Staking his very life on some dark hope,
Have I mixed awful talk and asking looks
With my most innocent love, until strange tears
Uniting with those breathless kisses, made
Such magic as compels the charmèd night
To render up thy charge: … and, though ne'er yet
Thou hast unveiled thy inmost sanctuary,
Enough from incommunicable dream,
And twilight phantasms, and deep noon-day thought,
Has shone within me, that serenely now
And moveless, as a long-forgotten lyre
Suspended in the solitary dome
Of some mysterious and deserted fane,° *temple*
I wait thy breath, Great Parent, that my strain
May modulate with murmurs of the air,
And motions of the forests and the sea,
And voice of living beings, and woven hymns
Of night and day, and the deep heart of man.

There was a Poet whose untimely tomb
No human hands with pious reverence reared,
But the charmed eddies of autumnal winds
Built o'er his mouldering bones a pyramid
Of mouldering leaves in the waste wilderness:
A lovely youth—no mourning maiden decked
With weeping flowers, or votive cypress wreath,[6]
The lone couch of his everlasting sleep:
Gentle, and brave, and generous—no lorn° bard *forlorn*
Breathed o'er his dark fate one melodious sigh:
He lived, he died, he sung, in solitude.
Strangers have wept to hear his passionate notes,
And virgins, as unknown he passed, have pined
And wasted for fond love of his wild eyes.
The fire of those soft orbs has ceased to burn,
And Silence, too enamoured of that voice,
Locks its mute music in her rugged cell.

[1] *Nondum … August* Latin: "I was not yet in love, and I loved to love, I sought what I might love, loving to love." From St. Augustine's *Confessions* 3.1, in which he describes his youthful desire for sexual love, rather than the spiritual love of God that he later found.

[2] *our great Mother* Cybele, goddess of the powers of nature and fertility.

[3] *natural piety* From Wordsworth's "My Heart Leaps Up," line 9.

[4] *charnels* Houses of death, mortuaries.

[5] *obstinate questionings* From Wordsworth's "Ode: Intimations of Immortality," lines 142–43: "Those obstinate questionings / Of sense and outward things."

[6] *cypress wreath* Worn to represent mourning.

By solemn vision, and bright silver dream,
His infancy was nurtured. Every sight
And sound from the vast earth and ambient air,
Sent to his heart its choicest impulses.
The fountains of divine philosophy
Fled not his thirsting lips, and all of great,
Or good, or lovely, which the sacred past
In truth or fable consecrates, he felt
And knew. When early youth had passed, he left
His cold fireside and alienated home
To seek strange truths in undiscovered lands.
Many a wide waste and tangled wilderness
Has lured his fearless steps; and he has bought
With his sweet voice and eyes, from savage men,
His rest and food. Nature's most secret steps
He like her shadow has pursued, where'er
The red volcano overcanopies
Its fields of snow and pinnacles of ice
With burning smoke, or where bitumen° lakes *pitch*
On black bare pointed islets ever beat
With sluggish surge, or where the secret caves
Rugged and dark, winding among the springs
Of fire and poison, inaccessible
To avarice or pride, their starry domes
Of diamond and of gold expand above
Numberless and immeasurable halls,
Frequent with crystal column, and clear shrines
Of pearl, and thrones radiant with chrysolite.[1]
Nor had that scene of ampler majesty
Than gems or gold, the varying roof of heaven
And the green earth lost in his heart its claims
To love and wonder; he would linger long
In lonesome vales, making the wild his home,
Until the doves and squirrels would partake
From his innocuous hand his bloodless food,
Lured by the gentle meaning of his looks,
And the wild antelope, that starts whene'er
The dry leaf rustles in the brake,° suspend *thicket*
Her timid steps to gaze upon a form
More graceful than her own.
His wandering step
Obedient to high thoughts, has visited
The awful ruins of the days of old:
Athens, and Tyre, and Balbec,[2] and the waste
Where stood Jerusalem,[3] the fallen towers
Of Babylon, the eternal pyramids,
Memphis and Thebes,[4] and whatsoe'er of strange
Sculptured on alabaster obelisk,
Or jasper tomb, or mutilated sphynx,
Dark Æthiopia in her desert hills
Conceals. Among the ruined temples there,
Stupendous columns, and wild images
Of more than man, where marble daemons[5] watch
The Zodiac's brazen mystery,[6] and dead men
Hang their mute thoughts on the mute walls around,
He lingered, poring on memorials
Of the world's youth, through the long burning day
Gazed on those speechless shapes, nor, when the moon
Filled the mysterious halls with floating shades
Suspended he that task, but ever gazed
And gazed, till meaning on his vacant mind
Flashed like strong inspiration, and he saw
The thrilling secrets of the birth of time.

Meanwhile an Arab maiden brought his food,
Her daily portion, from her father's tent,
And spread her matting for his couch, and stole
From duties and repose to tend his steps—
Enamoured, yet not daring for deep awe
To speak her love—and watched his nightly sleep,
Sleepless herself, to gaze upon his lips
Parted in slumber, whence the regular breath
Of innocent dreams arose: then, when red morn
Made paler the pale moon, to her cold home
Wildered,° and wan, and panting, she returned. *bewildered*

[1] *chrysolite* Green gemstone.

[2] *Tyre* Ancient capital of Phoenicia, located in present-day Lebanon, that was destroyed by Muslims in 1291; *Balbec* Ancient Phoenician city in eastern Lebanon that is known for its Roman ruins.

[3] *Jerusalem* Destroyed by Emperor Titus in 70 CE.

[4] *Memphis and Thebes* Ancient cities of lower and upper Egypt, respectively.

[5] *daemons* Supernatural beings, or minor deities, of Greek mythology.

[6] *Zodiac's brazen mystery* Representations of the Zodiac decorate the ceiling of the temple of Isis (goddess of fertility) at Denderah, in Egypt.

The Poet wandering on, through Arabie
And Persia, and the wild Carmanian waste,[1]
And o'er the aërial mountains which pour down
Indus and Oxus[2] from their icy caves,
In joy and exultation held his way;
Till in the vale of Cashmire, far within
Its loneliest dell, where odorous plants entwine
Beneath the hollow rocks a natural bower,
Beside a sparkling rivulet he stretched
His languid limbs. A vision on his sleep
There came, a dream of hopes that never yet
Had flushed his cheek. He dreamed a veilèd maid
Sate near him, talking in low solemn tones.
Her voice was like the voice of his own soul
Heard in the calm of thought; its music long,
Like woven sounds of streams and breezes, held
His inmost sense suspended in its web
Of many-coloured woof[3] and shifting hues.
Knowledge and truth and virtue were her theme,
And lofty hopes of divine liberty,
Thoughts the most dear to him, and poesy,
Herself a poet. Soon the solemn mood
Of her pure mind kindled through all her frame
A permeating fire: wild numbers[4] then
She raised, with voice stifled in tremulous sobs
Subdued by its own pathos: her fair hands
Were bare alone, sweeping from some strange harp
Strange symphony, and in their branching veins
The eloquent blood told an ineffable tale.
The beating of her heart was heard to fill
The pauses of her music, and her breath
Tumultuously accorded with those fits
Of intermitted song. Sudden she rose,
As if her heart impatiently endured
Its bursting burthen: at the sound he turned,
And saw by the warm light of their own life
Her glowing limbs beneath the sinuous veil
Of woven wind, her outspread arms now bare,
Her dark locks floating in the breath of night,
Her beamy bending eyes, her parted lips
Outstretched, and pale, and quivering eagerly.
His strong heart sunk and sickened with excess
Of love. He reared his shuddering limbs and quelled
His gasping breath, and spread his arms to meet
Her panting bosom … she drew back a while,
Then, yielding to the irresistible joy,
With frantic gesture and short breathless cry
Folded his frame in her dissolving arms.
Now blackness veiled his dizzy eyes, and night
Involved and swallowed up the vision; sleep,
Like a dark flood suspended in its course,
Rolled back its impulse on his vacant brain.

Roused by the shock he started from his trance—
The cold white light of morning, the blue moon
Low in the west, the clear and garish hills,
The distinct valley and the vacant woods,
Spread round him where he stood. Whither have fled
The hues of heaven that canopied his bower
Of yesternight? The sounds that soothed his sleep,
The mystery and the majesty of Earth,
The joy, the exultation? His wan eyes
Gaze on the empty scene as vacantly
As ocean's moon looks on the moon in heaven.
The spirit of sweet human love has sent
A vision to the sleep of him who spurned
Her choicest gifts. He eagerly pursues
Beyond the realms of dream that fleeting shade;
He overleaps the bounds. Alas! Alas!
Were limbs, and breath, and being intertwined
Thus treacherously? Lost, lost, for ever lost,
In the wide pathless desert of dim sleep,
That beautiful shape! Does the dark gate of death
Conduct to thy mysterious paradise,
O Sleep? Does the bright arch of rainbow clouds,
And pendent mountains seen in the calm lake,
Lead only to a black and watery depth,
While death's blue vault, with loathliest vapours hung,
Where every shade which the foul grave exhales
Hides its dead eye from the detested day,
Conducts, O Sleep, to thy delightful realms?
This doubt with sudden tide flowed on his heart,
The insatiate hope which it awakened, stung
His brain even like despair.

---

1 *Carmanian waste* Kerman Desert, in present-day Iran.

2 *Indus and Oxus* Rivers which flow from opposite sides of the Hindu Kush mountains in Asia.

3 *woof* Thread that crosses from side to side in a web of weaving.

4 *numbers* Verses, of song or poetry.

While daylight held
The sky, the Poet kept mute conference
With his still soul. At night the passion came,
Like the fierce fiend of a distempered dream,
And shook him from his rest, and led him forth
Into the darkness. As an eagle, grasped
In folds of the green serpent, feels her breast
Burn with the poison, and precipitates
Through night and day, tempest, and calm, and cloud,
Frantic with dizzying anguish, her blind flight
O'er the wide aëry° wilderness: thus driven *lofty*
By the bright shadow of that lovely dream,
Beneath the cold glare of the desolate night,
Through tangled swamps and deep precipitous dells,
Startling with careless step the moonlight snake,
He fled. Red morning dawned upon his flight,
Shedding the mockery of its vital hues
Upon his cheek of death. He wandered on
Till vast Aornos seen from Petra's steep[1]
Hung o'er the low horizon like a cloud;
Through Balk,[2] and where the desolated tombs
Of Parthian kings[3] scatter to every wind
Their wasting dust, wildly he wandered on,
Day after day a weary waste of hours,
Bearing within his life the brooding care
That ever fed on its decaying flame.
And now his limbs were lean; his scattered hair
Sered° by the autumn of strange suffering *made dry*
Sung dirges in the wind; his listless hand
Hung like dead bone within its withered skin;
Life, and the lustre that consumed it, shone
As in a furnace burning secretly
From his dark eyes alone. The cottagers,
Who ministered with human charity
His human wants, beheld with wondering awe
Their fleeting visitant. The mountaineer,
Encountering on some dizzy precipice
That spectral form, deemed that the Spirit of wind
With lightning eyes, and eager breath, and feet
Disturbing not the drifted snow, had paused
In its career: the infant would conceal
His troubled visage in his mother's robe
In terror at the glare of those wild eyes,
To remember their strange light in many a dream
Of after-times; but youthful maidens, taught
By nature, would interpret half the woe
That wasted him, would call him with false names
Brother, and friend, would press his pallid hand
At parting, and watch, dim through tears, the path
Of his departure from their father's door.

At length upon the lone Chorasmian shore[4]
He paused, a wide and melancholy waste
Of putrid marshes. A strong impulse urged
His steps to the sea-shore. A swan was there,
Beside a sluggish stream among the reeds.
It rose as he approached, and with strong wings
Scaling the upward sky, bent its bright course
High over the immeasurable main.
His eyes pursued its flight—"Thou hast a home,
Beautiful bird; thou voyagest to thine home,
Where thy sweet mate will twine her downy neck
With thine, and welcome thy return with eyes
Bright in the lustre of their own fond joy.
And what am I that I should linger here,
With voice far sweeter than thy dying notes,
Spirit more vast than thine, frame more attuned
To beauty, wasting these surpassing powers
In the deaf air, to the blind earth, and heaven
That echoes not my thoughts?" A gloomy smile
Of desperate hope wrinkled his quivering lips.
For sleep, he knew, kept most relentlessly
Its precious charge, and silent death exposed,
Faithless perhaps as sleep, a shadowy lure,
With doubtful smile mocking its own strange charms.

Startled by his own thoughts he looked around.
There was no fair fiend near him, not a sight
Or sound of awe but in his own deep mind.
A little shallop[5] floating near the shore
Caught the impatient wandering of his gaze.
It had been long abandoned, for its sides
Gaped wide with many a rift, and its frail joints
Swayed with the undulations of the tide.

---

[1] *Aornos* Mountain on the Indus; *Petra's steep* Probably the Rock of Soghdiana in Uzbekistan. ("Petra" is Latin for "rock.")

[2] *Balk* Balkh, in present-day Afghanistan.

[3] *Parthian kings* Rulers of northern Persia.

[4] *Chorasmian shore* Shore of the Caspian sea.

[5] *shallop* Small open boat or dinghy.

A restless impulse urged him to embark
And meet lone Death on the drear ocean's waste;
For well he knew that mighty Shadow loves
The slimy caverns of the populous deep.

The day was fair and sunny, sea and sky
Drank its inspiring radiance, and the wind
Swept strongly from the shore, blackening the waves.
Following his eager soul, the wanderer
Leaped in the boat, he spread his cloak aloft
On the bare mast, and took his lonely seat,
And felt the boat speed o'er the tranquil sea
Like a torn cloud before the hurricane.

As one that in a silver vision floats
Obedient to the sweep of odorous winds
Upon resplendent clouds, so rapidly
Along the dark and ruffled waters fled
The straining boat. A whirlwind swept it on,
With fierce gusts and precipitating force,
Through the white ridges of the chafèd sea.
The waves arose. Higher and higher still
Their fierce necks writhed beneath the tempest's scourge
Like serpents struggling in a vulture's grasp.
Calm and rejoicing in the fearful war
Of wave ruining on wave, and blast on blast
Descending, and black flood on whirlpool driven
With dark obliterating course, he sate:
As if their genii were the ministers
Appointed to conduct him to the light
Of those belovèd eyes, the Poet sate
Holding the steady helm. Evening came on,
The beams of sunset hung their rainbow hues
High 'mid the shifting domes of sheeted spray
That canopied his path o'er the waste deep;
Twilight, ascending slowly from the east,
Entwined in duskier wreaths her braided locks
O'er the fair front and radiant eyes of day;
Night followed, clad with stars. On every side
More horribly the multitudinous streams
Of ocean's mountainous waste to mutual war
Rushed in dark tumult thundering, as to mock
The calm and spangled sky. The little boat
Still fled before the storm; still fled, like foam
Down the steep cataract of a wintry river;
Now pausing on the edge of the riven wave;
Now leaving far behind the bursting mass
That fell, convulsing ocean: safely fled—
As if that frail and wasted human form
Had been an elemental god.

At midnight
The moon arose: and lo! the ethereal cliffs
Of Caucasus,[1] whose icy summits shone
Among the stars like sunlight, and around
Whose caverned base the whirlpools and the waves
Bursting and eddying irresistibly
Rage and resound for ever. Who shall save?
The boat fled on—the boiling torrent drove—
The crags closed round with black and jaggèd arms,
The shattered mountain overhung the sea,
And faster still, beyond all human speed,
Suspended on the sweep of the smooth wave,
The little boat was driven. A cavern there
Yawned, and amid its slant and winding depths
Ingulfed the rushing sea. The boat fled on
With unrelaxing speed. "Vision and Love!"
The Poet cried aloud, "I have beheld
The path of thy departure. Sleep and death
Shall not divide us long!"

The boat pursued
The windings of the cavern. Daylight shone
At length upon that gloomy river's flow;
Now, where the fiercest war among the waves
Is calm, on the unfathomable stream
The boat moved slowly. Where the mountain, riven,
Exposed those black depths to the azure sky,
Ere yet the flood's enormous volume fell
Even to the base of Caucasus, with sound
That shook the everlasting rocks, the mass
Filled with one whirlpool all that ample chasm;
Stair above stair the eddying waters rose,
Circling immeasurably fast, and laved° *bathed*
With alternating dash the gnarlèd roots
Of mighty trees, that stretched their giant arms
In darkness over it. I'the midst was left,
Reflecting, yet distorting every cloud,
A pool of treacherous and tremendous calm.

[1] *ethereal* Belonging to the upper air; *Caucasus* On the western shore of the Caspian sea, in present-day Georgia.

Seized by the sway of the ascending stream,
With dizzy swiftness, round, and round, and round,
Ridge after ridge the straining boat arose,
Till on the verge of the extremest curve,
Where, through an opening of the rocky bank,
The waters overflow, and a smooth spot
Of glassy quiet mid those battling tides
Is left, the boat paused shuddering. Shall it sink
Down the abyss? Shall the reverting stress
Of that resistless gulf embosom it?
Now shall it fall? A wandering stream of wind,
Breathed from the west, has caught the expanded sail,
And, lo! with gentle motion, between banks
Of mossy slope, and on a placid stream,
Beneath a woven grove it sails, and, hark!
The ghastly torrent mingles its far roar
With the breeze murmuring in the musical woods.
Where the embowering trees recede, and leave
A little space of green expanse, the cove
Is closed by meeting banks, whose yellow flowers
For ever gaze on their own drooping eyes,[1]
Reflected in the crystal calm. The wave
Of the boat's motion marred their pensive task,
Which nought but vagrant bird, or wanton wind,
Or falling spear-grass, or their own decay
Had e'er disturbed before. The Poet longed
To deck with their bright hues his withered hair,
But on his heart its solitude returned,
And he forbore. Not the strong impulse hid
In those flushed cheeks, bent eyes, and shadowy frame
Had yet performed its ministry: it hung
Upon his life, as lightning in a cloud
Gleams, hovering ere it vanish, ere the floods
Of night close over it.
                                        The noonday sun
Now shone upon the forest, one vast mass
Of mingling shade, whose brown° magnificence *dark*
A narrow vale embosoms. There, huge caves,
Scooped in the dark base of their aëry rocks
Mocking its moans, respond and roar for ever.
The meeting boughs and implicated° leaves *entwined*
Wove twilight o'er the Poet's path, as led
By love, or dream, or god, or mightier Death,
He sought in Nature's dearest haunt, some bank,
Her cradle, and his sepulchre. More dark
And dark the shades accumulate. The oak,
Expanding its immense and knotty arms,
Embraces the light beech. The pyramids
Of the tall cedar overarching, frame
Most solemn domes within, and far below,
Like clouds suspended in an emerald sky,
The ash and the acacia floating hang
Tremulous and pale. Like restless serpents, clothed
In rainbow and in fire, the parasites,
Starred with ten thousand blossoms, flow around
The grey trunks, and, as gamesome° infants' eyes, *playful*
With gentle meanings, and most innocent wiles,
Fold their beams round the hearts of those that love,
These twine their tendrils with the wedded boughs
Uniting their close union; the woven leaves
Make net-work of the dark blue light of day,
And the night's noontide clearness, mutable
As shapes in the weird clouds. Soft mossy lawns
Beneath these canopies extend their swells,
Fragrant with perfumed herbs, and eyed with blooms
Minute yet beautiful. One darkest glen
Sends from its woods of musk-rose, twined with jasmine,
A soul-dissolving odour, to invite
To some more lovely mystery. Through the dell,
Silence and Twilight here, twin-sisters, keep
Their noonday watch, and sail among the shades,
Like vaporous shapes half seen; beyond, a well,
Dark, gleaming, and of most translucent wave,
Images[2] all the woven boughs above,
And each depending leaf, and every speck
Of azure sky, darting between their chasms;
Nor aught else in the liquid mirror laves
Its portraiture, but some inconstant star
Between one foliaged lattice twinkling fair,
Or, painted bird, sleeping beneath the moon,
Or gorgeous insect floating motionless,
Unconscious of the day, ere yet his wings
Have spread their glories to the gaze of noon.

Hither the Poet came. His eyes beheld
Their own wan light through the reflected lines

[1] *yellow flowers* Narcissus flowers. According to Greek mythology, the handsome youth Narcissus fell in love with his own reflection in a pool of water and wasted away pining after his own image.

[2] *Images* Reflects; forms an image of.

Of his thin hair, distinct in the dark depth
Of that still fountain; as the human heart,
Gazing in dreams over the gloomy grave,
Sees its own treacherous likeness there. He heard
The motion of the leaves, the grass that sprung
Startled and glanced and trembled even to feel
An unaccustomed presence, and the sound
Of the sweet brook that from the secret springs
Of that dark fountain rose. A Spirit seemed
To stand beside him—clothed in no bright robes
Of shadowy silver or enshrining light.
Borrowed from aught the visible world affords
Of grace, or majesty, or mystery—
But, undulating woods, and silent well,
And leaping rivulet, and evening gloom
Now deepening the dark shades, for speech assuming,
Held commune with him, as if he and it
Were all that was,—only … when his regard
Was raised by intense pensiveness, … two eyes,
Two starry eyes, hung in the gloom of thought,
And seemed with their serene and azure smiles
To beckon him.

Obedient to the light
That shone within his soul, he went, pursuing
The windings of the dell. The rivulet
Wanton and wild through many a green ravine
Beneath the forest flowed. Sometimes it fell
Among the moss with hollow harmony
Dark and profound. Now on the polished stones
It danced; like childhood laughing as it went:
Then, through the plain in tranquil wanderings crept,
Reflecting every herb and drooping bud
That overhung its quietness. "O stream!
Whose source is inaccessibly profound,
Whither do thy mysterious waters tend?
Thou imagest my life. Thy darksome stillness,
Thy dazzling waves, thy loud and hollow gulfs,
Thy searchless° fountain,° and invisible course *undiscoverable / source*
Have each their type in me: and the wide sky,
And measureless ocean may declare as soon
What oozy cavern or what wandering cloud
Contains thy waters, as the universe
Tell where these living thoughts reside, when stretched
Upon thy flowers my bloodless limbs shall waste
I' the passing wind!"

Beside the grassy shore
Of the small stream he went; he did impress
On the green moss his tremulous step, that caught
Strong shuddering from his burning limbs. As one
Roused by some joyous madness from the couch
Of fever, he did move; yet, not like him,
Forgetful of the grave, where, when the flame
Of his frail exultation shall be spent,
He must descend. With rapid steps he went
Beneath the shade of trees, beside the flow
Of the wild babbling rivulet; and now
The forest's solemn canopies were changed
For the uniform and lightsome° evening sky. *luminous*
Grey rocks did peep from the spare moss, and stemmed
The struggling brook: tall spires of windlestrae[1]
Threw their thin shadows down the rugged slope,
And nought but gnarled roots[2] of ancient pines,
Branchless and blasted, clenched with grasping roots
The unwilling soil. A gradual change was here,
Yet ghastly. For, as fast years flow away,
The smooth brow gathers, and the hair grows thin
And white, and where irradiate° dewy eyes *illumined*
Had shone, gleam stony orbs: so from his steps
Bright flowers departed, and the beautiful shade
Of the green groves, with all their odorous winds
And musical motions. Calm, he still pursued
The stream, that with a larger volume now
Rolled through the labyrinthine dell; and there
Fretted a path through its descending curves
With its wintry speed. On every side now rose
Rocks, which, in unimaginable forms,
Lifted their black and barren pinnacles
In the light of evening, and, its precipice
Obscuring the ravine, disclosed above,
Mid toppling stones, black gulfs and yawning caves,
Whose windings gave ten thousand various tongues
To the loud stream. Lo! where the pass expands
Its stony jaws, the abrupt mountain breaks,
And seems, with its accumulated crags,

[1] *windlestrae* Windlestraw; withered grass stalks.

[2] *roots* Believed to be a misprint for "trunks" or "knots."

To overhang the world: for wide expand
Beneath the wan stars and descending moon
Islanded seas, blue mountains, mighty streams,
Dim tracts and vast, robed in the lustrous gloom
Of leaden-coloured even,° and fiery hills *evening*
Mingling their flames with twilight, on the verge
Of the remote horizon. The near scene,
In naked and severe simplicity,
Made contrast with the universe. A pine,
Rock-rooted, stretched athwart the vacancy
Its swinging boughs, to each inconstant blast
Yielding one only response, at each pause
In most familiar cadence, with the howl
The thunder and the hiss of homeless streams
Mingling its solemn song, whilst the broad river,
Foaming and hurrying o'er its rugged path,
Fell into that immeasurable void
Scattering its waters to the passing winds.

Yet the grey precipice and solemn pine
And torrent, were not all—one silent nook
Was there. Even on the edge of that vast mountain,
Upheld by knotty roots and fallen rocks,
It overlooked in its serenity
The dark earth, and the bending vault of stars.
It was a tranquil spot, that seemed to smile
Even in the lap of horror. Ivy clasped
The fissured stones with its entwining arms,
And did embower with leaves for ever green,
And berries dark, the smooth and even space
Of its inviolated floor, and here
The children of the autumnal whirlwind bore,
In wanton sport, those bright leaves, whose decay,
Red, yellow, or ethereally pale,
Rivals the pride of summer. 'Tis the haunt
Of every gentle wind, whose breath can teach
The wilds to love tranquillity. One step,
One human step alone, has ever broken
The stillness of its solitude; one voice
Alone inspired its echoes—even that voice
Which hither came, floating among the winds,
And led the loveliest among human forms
To make their wild haunts the depository
Of all the grace and beauty that endued[1]
Its motions, render up its majesty,
Scatter its music on the unfeeling storm,
And to the damp leaves and blue cavern mould,
Nurses of rainbow flowers and branching moss,
Commit the colours of that varying cheek,
That snowy breast, those dark and drooping eyes.

The dim and hornèd moon hung low, and poured
A sea of lustre on the horizon's verge
That overflowed its mountains. Yellow mist
Filled the unbounded atmosphere, and drank
Wan moonlight even to fulness: not a star
Shone, not a sound was heard; the very winds,
Danger's grim playmates, on that precipice
Slept, clasped in his embrace—O, storm of death!
Whose sightless speed divides this sullen night:
And thou, colossal Skeleton, that, still
Guiding its irresistible career
In thy devastating omnipotence,
Art king of this frail world, from the red field
Of slaughter, from the reeking hospital,
The patriot's sacred couch, the snowy bed
Of innocence, the scaffold and the throne,
A mighty voice invokes thee. Ruin calls
His brother Death. A rare and regal prey
He hath prepared, prowling around the world;
Glutted with which thou mayst repose, and men
Go to their graves like flowers or creeping worms,
Nor ever more offer at thy dark shrine
The unheeded tribute of a broken heart.

When on the threshold of the green recess
The wanderer's footsteps fell, he knew that death
Was on him. Yet a little, ere it fled,
Did he resign his high and holy soul
To images of the majestic past,
That paused within his passive being now,
Like winds that bear sweet music, when they breathe
Through some dim latticed chamber. He did place
His pale lean hand upon the rugged trunk
Of the old pine. Upon an ivied stone
Reclined his languid head, his limbs did rest,
Diffused and motionless, on the smooth brink
Of that obscurest chasm—and thus he lay,
Surrendering to their final impulses

[1] *endued* Were inherent in.

The hovering powers of life. Hope and despair,
The torturers, slept; no mortal pain or fear
Marred his repose, the influxes of sense,
And his own being unalloyed by pain,
Yet feebler and more feeble, calmly fed
The stream of thought, till he lay breathing there
At peace, and faintly smiling—his last sight
Was the great moon, which o'er the western line
Of the wide world her mighty horn suspended,
With whose dun° beams inwoven darkness seemed *dusky*
To mingle. Now upon the jaggèd hills
It rests, and still as the divided frame
Of the vast meteor[1] sunk, the Poet's blood,
That ever beat in mystic sympathy
With nature's ebb and flow, grew feebler still:
And when two lessening points[2] of light alone
Gleamed through the darkness, the alternate gasp
Of his faint respiration scarce did stir
The stagnate° night—till the minutest ray *stagnant*
Was quenched, the pulse yet lingered in his heart.
It paused—it fluttered. But when heaven remained
Utterly black, the murky shades involved
An image, silent, cold, and motionless,
As their own voiceless earth and vacant air.
Even as a vapour° fed with golden beams *cloud*
That ministered on sunlight, ere the west
Eclipses it, was now that wondrous frame—
No sense, no motion, no divinity—
A fragile lute, on whose harmonious strings
The breath of heaven did wander—a bright stream
Once fed with many-voicèd waves—a dream
Of youth, which night and time have quenched for ever,
Still, dark, and dry, and unremembered now.

O, for Medea's wondrous alchemy,[3]
Which wheresoe'er it fell made the earth gleam
With bright flowers, and the wintry boughs exhale
From vernal blooms fresh fragrance! O, that God,
Profuse of poisons, would concede the chalice
Which but one living man has drained, who now,
Vessel of deathless wrath, a slave that feels
No proud exemption in the blighting curse
He bears, over the world wanders for ever,
Lone as incarnate death![4] O, that the dream
Of dark magician in his visioned[5] cave,
Raking the cinders of a crucible
For life and power, even when his feeble hand
Shakes in its last decay, were the true law
Of this so lovely world! But thou art fled
Like some frail exhalation; which the dawn
Robes in its golden beams—ah! thou hast fled!
The brave, the gentle, and the beautiful,
The child of grace and genius. Heartless things
Are done and said i'the world, and many worms
And beasts and men live on, and mighty Earth
From sea and mountain, city and wilderness,
In vesper[6] low or joyous orison,° *prayer*
Lifts still its solemn voice—but thou art fled—
Thou canst no longer know or love the shapes
Of this phantasmal scene, who have to thee
Been purest ministers, who are, alas!
Now thou art not. Upon those pallid lips
So sweet even in their silence, on those eyes
That image sleep in death, upon that form
Yet safe from the worm's outrage, let no tear
Be shed—not even in thought. Nor, when those hues
Are gone, and those divinest lineaments,
Worn by the senseless° wind, shall live alone *unfeeling*
In the frail pauses of this simple strain,
Let not high verse, mourning the memory
Of that which is no more, or painting's woe
Or sculpture, speak in feeble imagery
Their own cold powers. Art and eloquence,
And all the shows o'the world are frail and vain

[1] *meteor* Formerly used to refer to any atmospheric phenomenon; here, the moon.

[2] *two lessening points* The horns, or curved points, of the crescent moon.

[3] *Medea's wondrous alchemy* According to Greek myth, the sorceress Medea brewed a magic potion to restore youth to the dying Aeson. In Ovid's version of the tale (*Metamorphosis* 7.275ff), some of the potion spills on the ground and has the effect described in the following lines.

[4] *one living … death* Reference to the legend of Ahasuerus, the Wandering Jew, who taunted Christ on the way to His crucifixion and as punishment was condemned to wander the earth until Christ's second coming.

[5] *visioned* I.e., in which he has visions.

[6] *vesper* Evening prayer.

To weep a loss that turns their lights to shade.
It is a woe too "deep for tears,"[1] when all
Is reft at once, when some surpassing Spirit,
Whose light adorned the world around it, leaves
Those who remain behind, not sobs or groans,
The passionate tumult of a clinging hope;
But pale despair and cold tranquillity,
Nature's vast frame, the web of human things,
Birth and the grave, that are not as they were.
—1816

Mutability

We are as clouds that veil the midnight moon;
How restlessly they speed, and gleam, and quiver,
Streaking the darkness radiantly! Yet soon
Night closes round, and they are lost for ever:

Or like forgotten lyres,[2] whose dissonant strings
Give various response to each varying blast,
To whose frail frame no second motion brings
One mood or modulation like the last.

We rest—A dream has power to poison sleep;
We rise—One wandering thought pollutes the day;
We feel, conceive or reason, laugh or weep;
Embrace fond woe, or cast our cares away:

It is the same! For, be it joy or sorrow,
The path of its departure still is free:
Man's yesterday may ne'er be like his morrow;
Nought may endure but Mutability.
—1816

Mont Blanc

Lines Written in the Vale of Chamouni[3]

1

The everlasting universe of things
Flows through the mind, and rolls its rapid waves,
Now dark—now glittering—now reflecting gloom—
Now lending splendour, where from secret springs
The source of human thought its tribute brings
Of waters—with a sound but half its own,
Such as a feeble brook will oft assume
In the wild woods, among the mountains lone,
Where waterfalls around it leap for ever,
Where woods and winds contend, and a vast river
Over its rocks ceaselessly bursts and raves.

2

Thus thou, Ravine of Arve—dark, deep Ravine—
Thou many-coloured, many-voicèd vale,
Over whose pines, and crags, and caverns sail
Fast cloud shadows and sunbeams: awful° scene, *awe-inspiring*
Where Power in likeness of the Arve comes down
From the ice gulfs that gird his secret throne,
Bursting through these dark mountains like the flame
Of lightning through the tempest—thou dost lie,
Thy giant brood of pines around thee clinging,
Children of elder time, in whose devotion
The chainless winds still come and ever came
To drink their odours, and their mighty swinging
To hear—an old and solemn harmony;
Thine earthly rainbows stretched across the sweep
Of the etherial waterfall, whose veil
Robes some unsculptured[4] image; the strange sleep
Which when the voices of the desert fail

[1] *deep for tears* From the last line of Wordsworth's "Ode: Intimations of Immortality": "Thoughts that do often lie too deep for tears."

[2] *lyres* Aeolian harps, stringed instruments that produce music when exposed to wind.

[3] *Mont Blanc … Chamouni* Mont Blanc, located near France's border with Italy, is the highest peak in the Alps. Shelley conceived the idea for the poem when standing on a bridge over the Arve River in the Valley of Chamonix in southeastern France. Of the poem, Shelley wrote, "It was composed under the immediate impression of the deep and powerful feelings excited by the objects which it attempts to describe; and, as an indisciplined overflowing of the soul, rests its claim to approbation on an attempt to imitate the untameable wildness and inaccessible solemnity from which those feelings sprang."

[4] *unsculptured* I.e., not shaped by humans.

Wraps all in its own deep eternity—
Thy caverns echoing to the Arve's commotion,
A loud, lone sound no other sound can tame;
Thou art pervaded with that ceaseless motion,
Thou art the path of that unresting sound—
Dizzy Ravine! and when I gaze on thee
I seem as in a trance sublime and strange
To muse on my own separate fantasy,
My own, my human mind, which passively
Now renders and receives fast influencings,
Holding an unremitting interchange
With the clear universe of things around;
One legion of wild thoughts, whose wandering wings
Now float above thy darkness, and now rest
Where that or thou art no unbidden guest,
In the still cave of the witch Poesy,
Seeking among the shadows that pass by,
Ghosts of all things that are, some shade of thee,
Some phantom, some faint image; till the breast
From which they fled recalls them, thou art there!

3

Some say that gleams of a remoter world
Visit the soul in sleep—that death is slumber,
And that its shapes the busy thoughts outnumber
Of those who wake and live. I look on high;
Has some unknown omnipotence unfurled
The veil of life and death? or do I lie
In dream, and does the mightier world of sleep
Spread far around and inaccessibly
Its circles? For the very spirit fails,
Driven like a homeless cloud from steep to steep
That vanishes among the viewless° gales! *invisible*
Far, far above, piercing the infinite sky,
Mont Blanc appears—still, snowy, and serene—
Its subject mountains their unearthly forms
Pile around it, ice and rock; broad vales between
Of frozen floods, unfathomable deeps,
Blue as the overhanging heaven, that spread
And wind among the accumulated steeps;
A desert peopled by the storms alone,
Save when the eagle brings some hunter's bone,
And the wolf tracks her there—how hideously
Its shapes are heaped around: rude, bare, and high,
Ghastly, and scarred, and riven. Is this the scene
Where the old Earthquake-daemon[1] taught her young
Ruin? Were these their toys? or did a sea
Of fire envelop once this silent snow?
None can reply—all seems eternal now.
The wilderness has a mysterious tongue
Which teaches awful doubt, or faith so mild,
So solemn, so serene, that man may be
But for such faith with nature reconciled;
Thou hast a voice, great Mountain, to repeal
Large codes of fraud and woe; not understood
By all, but which the wise, and great, and good
Interpret, or make felt, or deeply feel.

4

The fields, the lakes, the forests, and the streams,
Ocean, and all the living things that dwell
Within the daedal[2] earth; lightning, and rain,
Earthquake, and fiery flood, and hurricane,
The torpor of the year when feeble dreams
Visit the hidden buds, or dreamless sleep
Holds every future leaf and flower; the bound
With which from that detested trance they leap;
The works and ways of man, their death and birth,
And that of him and all that his may be;
All things that move and breathe with toil and sound
Are born and die; revolve, subside and swell.
Power dwells apart in its tranquillity
Remote, serene, and inaccessible:
And *this*, the naked countenance of earth,
On which I gaze, even these primeval mountains
Teach the adverting mind. The glaciers creep
Like snakes that watch their prey, from their far
fountains,
Slow rolling on; there, many a precipice,
Frost and the Sun in scorn of mortal power
Have piled: dome, pyramid, and pinnacle,
A city of death, distinct with many a tower
And wall impregnable of beaming ice.
Yet not a city, but a flood of ruin
Is there, that from the boundaries of the sky
Rolls its perpetual stream; vast pines are strewing

---

[1] *daemon* In Greek mythology, supernatural being or minor deity that controls some natural force.

[2] *daedal* Skillfully or intricately wrought. (From Daedalus of classical myth, who built the famous labyrinth in Crete.)

Its destined path, or in the mangled soil
Branchless and shattered stand; the rocks, drawn down
From yon remotest waste, have overthrown
The limits of the dead and living world,
Never to be reclaimed. The dwelling-place
Of insects, beasts, and birds, becomes its spoil;
Their food and their retreat for ever gone,
So much of life and joy is lost. The race
Of man flies far in dread; his work and dwelling
Vanish, like smoke before the tempest's stream,
And their place is not known. Below, vast caves
Shine in the rushing torrent's restless gleam,
Which from those secret chasms in tumult welling[1]
Meet in the vale, and one majestic River,
The breath and blood of distant lands, for ever
Rolls its loud waters to the ocean waves,
Breathes its swift vapours to the circling air.

5

Mont Blanc yet gleams on high—the power is there,
The still and solemn power of many sights
And many sounds, and much of life and death.
In the calm darkness of the moonless nights,
In the lone glare of day, the snows descend
Upon that Mountain; none beholds them there,
Nor when the flakes burn in the sinking sun,
Or the star-beams dart through them. Winds contend
Silently there, and heap the snow with breath
Rapid and strong, but silently! Its home
The voiceless lightning in these solitudes
Keeps innocently, and like vapour broods
Over the snow. The secret strength of things
Which governs thought, and to the infinite dome
Of heaven is as a law, inhabits thee!
And what were thou, and earth, and stars, and sea,
If to the human mind's imaginings
Silence and solitude were vacancy?
—1817

[1] *Which from … welling* Cf. Coleridge's *Kubla Khan*, lines 12–24.

Hymn to Intellectual Beauty[2]

I

The awful shadow of some unseen Power
Floats though unseen amongst us, visiting
This various world with as inconstant wing
As summer winds that creep from flower to flower.
Like moonbeams that behind some piny mountain shower,
It visits with inconstant glance
Each human heart and countenance;
Like hues and harmonies of evening,
Like clouds in starlight widely spread,
Like memory of music fled,
Like aught that for its grace may be
Dear, and yet dearer for its mystery.

2

Spirit of BEAUTY, that doth consecrate
With thine own hues all thou dost shine upon
Of human thought or form—where art thou gone?
Why dost thou pass away and leave our state,
This dim vast vale of tears, vacant and desolate?
Ask why the sunlight not forever
Weaves rainbows o'er yon mountain river,
Why aught should fail and fade that once is shown,
Why fear and dream and death and birth
Cast on the daylight of this earth
Such gloom—why man has such a scope
For love and hate, despondency and hope?

3

No voice from some sublimer world hath ever
To sage or poet these responses given—
Therefore the name of God, and ghosts, and Heaven,
Remain the records of their vain endeavour,
Frail spells—whose uttered charm might not avail to sever,
From all we hear and all we see,

[2] *Hymn … Beauty* Composed during the summer of 1816, the same summer in which Shelley wrote "Mont Blanc." The concept of "intellectual beauty" is Platonic in origin and was a popular one in contemporary writing. It denotes a beauty of the soul, or the mind and its inventions, that cannot be perceived by the senses and therefore must be grasped intuitively.

Doubt, chance, and mutability.
Thy light alone—like mist o'er mountains driven,
Or music by the night wind sent
Through strings of some still instrument,
Or moonlight on a midnight stream,
Gives grace and truth to life's unquiet dream.

4

Love, Hope, and Self-esteem, like clouds depart
And come, for some uncertain moments lent.
Man were° immortal, and omnipotent, *would be*
Didst thou,[1] unknown and awful as thou art,
Keep with thy glorious train firm state within his heart.
Thou messenger of sympathies
That wax and wane in lovers' eyes—
Thou—that to human thought art nourishment,
Like darkness to a dying flame!
Depart not as thy shadow came,
Depart not—lest the grave should be,
Like life and fear, a dark reality.

5

While yet a boy I sought for ghosts, and sped
Through many a listening chamber, cave and ruin,
And starlight wood, with fearful steps pursuing
Hopes of high talk with the departed dead.
I called on poisonous names with which our youth is fed,
I was not heard—I saw them not—
When musing deeply on the lot
Of life, at that sweet time when winds are wooing
All vital things that wake to bring
News of buds and blossoming—
Sudden, thy shadow fell on me;
I shrieked, and clasped my hands in ecstasy!

6

I vowed that I would dedicate my powers
To thee and thine—have I not kept the vow?
With beating heart and streaming eyes, even now
I call the phantoms of a thousand hours
Each from his voiceless grave: they have in visioned bowers
Of studious zeal or love's delight
Outwatched with me the envious night—

[1] *Didst thou* I.e., "if thou didst."

They know that never joy illumed my brow
Unlinked with hope that thou wouldst free
This world from its dark slavery,
That thou—O awful LOVELINESS,
Wouldst give whate'er these words cannot express.

7

The day becomes more solemn and serene
When noon is past—there is a harmony
In autumn, and a lustre in its sky,
Which through the summer is not heard or seen,
As if it could not be, as if it had not been!
Thus let thy power, which like the truth
Of nature on my passive youth
Descended, to my onward life supply
Its calm—to one who worships thee,
And every form containing thee,
Whom, SPIRIT fair, thy spells did bind
To fear° himself, and love all human kind. *revere*
—1817

Ozymandias[2]

I met a traveller from an antique land
Who said: Two vast and trunkless legs of stone
Stand in the desert … Near them, on the sand,
Half sunk, a shattered visage lies, whose frown,
And wrinkled lip, and sneer of cold command,
Tell that its sculptor well those passions read
Which yet survive, stamped on these lifeless things,
The hand that mocked them, and the heart that fed:
And on the pedestal these words appear:
"My name is Ozymandias, king of kings:
Look on my works, ye Mighty, and despair!"
Nothing beside remains. Round the decay
Of that colossal wreck, boundless and bare
The lone and level sands stretch far away.
—1818

[2] *Ozymandias* Greek name for King Ramses II of Egypt (1304–1237 BCE). First century BCE Greek historian Diodorus Siculus records the story of this monument (Ozymandias's tomb was in the shape of a male sphinx) and its inscription, which Diodorus says reads: "King of Kings am I, Ozymandias. If anyone would know how great I am and where I lie, let him surpass one of my exploits."

Ode to the West Wind[1]

1

O Wild West Wind, thou breath[2] of Autumn's being,
Thou, from whose unseen presence the leaves dead
Are driven, like ghosts from an enchanter fleeing,

Yellow, and black, and pale, and hectic° red, *feverish*
Pestilence-stricken multitudes: O thou,
Who chariotest to their dark wintry bed

The winged seeds, where they lie cold and low,
Each like a corpse within its grave, until
Thine azure sister of the Spring shall blow

Her clarion[3] o'er the dreaming earth, and fill
(Driving sweet buds like flocks to feed in air)
With living hues and odours plain and hill:

Wild Spirit, which art moving everywhere;
Destroyer and Preserver; hear, oh, hear!

2

Thou on whose stream, 'mid the steep sky's commotion,
Loose clouds like earth's decaying leaves are shed,
Shook from the tangled boughs of Heaven and Ocean,

Angels° of rain and lightning: there are spread *harbingers*
On the blue surface of thine aëry surge,
Like the bright hair uplifted from the head

Of some fierce Mænad,[4] even from the dim verge
Of the horizon to the zenith's height,
The locks of the approaching storm. Thou dirge

Of the dying year, to which this closing night
Will be the dome of a vast sepulchre,
Vaulted with all thy congregated might

Of vapours,° from whose solid atmosphere *clouds*
Black rain, and fire, and hail will burst: oh, hear!

3

Thou who didst waken from his summer dreams
The blue Mediterranean, where he lay,
Lulled by the coil of his chrystàlline streams,[5]

Beside a pumice isle in Baiae's bay,[6]
And saw in sleep old palaces and towers
Quivering within the wave's intenser day,

All overgrown with azure moss and flowers
So sweet, the sense faints picturing them! Thou
For whose path the Atlantic's level powers

Cleave themselves into chasms, while far below
The sea-blooms and the oozy woods which wear
The sapless foliage of the ocean, know

Thy voice, and suddenly grow gray with fear,
And tremble and despoil themselves:[7] oh, hear!

---

[1] [Shelley's note] This poem was conceived and chiefly written in a wood that skirts the Arno, near Florence, and on a day when that tempestuous wind, whose temperature is at once mild and animating, was collecting the vapours which pour down the autumnal rains. They began, as I foresaw, at sunset with a violent tempest of hail and rain, attended by that magnificent thunder and lightning peculiar to the Cispaline regions.

[2] *breath* The Latin word for wind, *spiritus,* also means "breath" and "soul," and is the root of the word "inspiration."

[3] *clarion* High-pitched trumpet.

[4] *Mænad* Female attendant of Bacchus, the Greek god of wine.

[5] *coil… streams* Currents of the Mediterranean, the color of which are often different from the surrounding water.

[6] *pumice* Porous stone made from cooled lava; *Baiae's Bay* Bay west of Naples that contains the ruins of several imperial villas.

[7] [Shelley's note] The phenomenon alluded to at the conclusion of the third stanza is well known to naturalists. The vegetation at the bottom of the sea, of rivers, and of lakes, sympathizes with that of the land in the change of seasons, and is consequently influenced by the winds which announce it.

4

If I were a dead leaf thou mightest bear;
If I were a swift cloud to fly with thee;
A wave to pant beneath thy power, and share

The impulse of thy strength, only less free
Than thou, O uncontrollable! If even
I were as in my boyhood, and could be

The comrade of thy wanderings over Heaven,
As then, when to outstrip thy skiey speed
Scarce seemed a vision; I would ne'er have striven

As thus with thee in prayer in my sore need.
Oh! lift me as a wave, a leaf, a cloud!
I fall upon the thorns of life! I bleed!

A heavy weight of hours has chained and bowed
One too like thee: tameless, and swift, and proud.

5

Make me thy lyre,[1] even as the forest is:
What if my leaves are falling like its own!
The tumult of thy mighty harmonies

Will take from both a deep, autumnal tone,
Sweet though in sadness. Be thou, Spirit fierce,
My spirit! Be thou me, impetuous one!

Drive my dead thoughts over the universe
Like withered leaves to quicken a new birth!
And, by the incantation of this verse,

Scatter, as from an unextinguished hearth
Ashes and sparks, my words among mankind!
Be through my lips to unawakened Earth

The trumpet of a prophecy! O, Wind,
If Winter comes, can Spring be far behind?
—1820

[1] *lyre* Aeolian harp, a stringed instrument that produces music when exposed to wind.

The Cloud

I bring fresh showers for the thirsting flowers,
From the seas and the streams;
I bear light shade for the leaves when laid
In their noonday dreams.
From my wings are shaken the dews that waken
The sweet buds every one,
When rocked to rest on their mother's breast,
As she dances about the sun.
I wield the flail of the lashing hail,
And whiten the green plains under,
And then again I dissolve it in rain,
And laugh as I pass in thunder.

I sift the snow on the mountains below,
And their great pines groan aghast;
And all the night 'tis my pillow white,
While I sleep in the arms of the blast,
Sublime on the towers of my skiey bowers,
Lightning my pilot sits;
In a cavern under is fettered the thunder,
It struggles and howls at fits;[2]
Over earth and ocean, with gentle motion,
This pilot is guiding me,
Lured by the love of the genii that move
In the depths of the purple sea;
Over the rills, and the crags, and the hills,
Over the lakes and the plains,
Wherever he dream, under mountain or stream,
The Spirit he loves remains;
And I all the while bask in Heaven's blue smile,
Whilst he is dissolving in rains.

The sanguine Sunrise, with his meteor eyes,
And his burning plumes outspread,
Leaps on the back of my sailing rack,[3]
When the morning star shines dead;
As on the jag of a mountain crag,
Which an earthquake rocks and swings,
An eagle alit one moment may sit
In the light of its golden wings.

[2] *at fits* Fitfully.

[3] *rack* Mass of clouds in the upper air.

And when Sunset may breathe, from the lit sea beneath,
Its ardours of rest and love,
And the crimson pall[1] of eve may fall
From the depth of Heaven above,
With wings folded I rest, on mine aëry nest,
As still as a brooding dove.

That orbèd maiden with white fire laden,
Whom mortals call the Moon,
Glides glimmering o'er my fleece-like floor,
By the midnight breezes strewn;
And wherever the beat of her unseen feet,
Which only the angels hear,
May have broken the woof° of my tent's thin roof, *weave*
The stars peep behind her and peer;
And I laugh to see them whirl and flee,
Like a swarm of golden bees,
When I widen the rent in my wind-built tent,
Till the calm rivers, lakes, and seas,
Like strips of the sky fallen through me on high,
Are each paved with the moon and these.

I bind the Sun's throne with a burning zone,° *belt*
And the Moon's with a girdle of pearl;
The volcanoes are dim, and the stars reel and swim,
When the whirlwinds my banner unfurl.
From cape to cape, with a bridge-like shape,
Over a torrent sea,
Sunbeam-proof, I hand like a roof—
The mountains its columns be.
The triumphal arch through which I march
With hurricane, fire, and snow,
When the Powers of the air are chained to my chair,
Is the million-coloured bow;
The sphere-fire[2] above its soft colours wove,
While the moist Earth was laughing below.

I am the daughter of Earth and Water,
And the nursing of the Sky;
I pass through the pores of the ocean and shores;
I change, but I cannot die.
For after the rain, when with never a stain
The pavilion of Heaven is bare,
And the winds and sunbeams with their convex gleams
Build up the blue dome of air,
I silently laugh at my own cenotaph,[3]
And out of the caverns of rain,
Like a child from the womb, like a ghost from the tomb,
I arise and unbuild it again.
—1820

To a Skylark[4]

Hail to thee, blithe Spirit!
Bird thou never wert,
That from Heaven, or near it,
Pourest thy full heart
In profuse strains of unpremeditated art.

Higher still and higher
From the earth thou springest
Like a cloud of fire;
The blue deep thou wingest,
And singing still dost soar, and soaring ever singest.

In the golden lightning
Of the sunken sun,
O'er which clouds are bright'ning,
Thou dost float and run;
Like an unbodied joy whose race is just begun.

The pale purple even
Melts around thy flight;
Like a star of Heaven,
In the broad daylight
Thou art unseen, but yet I hear thy shrill delight,

Keen as are the arrows
Of that silver sphere,[5]
Whose intense lamp narrows

[1] *pall* Rich cloth or canopy.

[2] *sphere-fire* I.e., sunlight.

[3] *cenotaph* Empty sepulcher; monument honoring a dead person whose body lies elsewhere.

[4] *Skylark* Small bird that sings only when in flight, and often flies so high that it cannot be easily seen.

[5] *silver sphere* I.e., the morning star.

In the white dawn clear
Until we hardly see—we feel that it is there.

All the earth and air
With thy voice is loud,
As, when night is bare,
From one lonely cloud
The moon rains out her beams, and Heaven is overflowed.

What thou art we know not;
What is most like thee?
From rainbow clouds there flow not
Drops so bright to see
As from thy presence showers a rain of melody.

Like a Poet hidden
In the light of thought,
Singing hymns unbidden,
Till the world is wrought
To sympathy with hopes and fears it heeded not:

Like a high-born maiden
In a palace-tower,
Soothing her love-laden
Soul in secret hour
With music sweet as love, which overflows her bower:

Like a glow-worm golden
In a dell of dew,
Scattering unbeholden
Its aëreal hue
Among the flowers and grass, which screen it from the view:

Like a rose embowered
In its own green leaves,
By warm winds deflowered,
Till the scent it gives
Makes faint with too much sweet these heavy-wingèd thieves:

Sound of vernal° showers *springtime*
On the twinkling grass,
Rain-awakened flowers,
All that ever was
Joyous, and clear, and fresh, thy music doth surpass:

Teach us, Sprite° or Bird, *fairy*
What sweet thoughts are thine:
I have never heard
Praise of love or wine
That panted forth a flood of rapture so divine.

Chorus Hymeneal,[1]
Or triumphal chaunt,° *chant*
Matched with thine would be all
But an empty vaunt,
A thing wherein we feel there is some hidden want.

What objects are the fountains
Of thy happy strain?
What fields, or waves, or mountains?
What shapes of sky or plain?
What love of thine own kind? what ignorance of pain?

With thy clear keen joyance
Languor cannot be:
Shadow of annoyance
Never came near thee:
Thou lovest—but ne'er knew love's sad satiety.

Waking or asleep,
Thou of death must deem
Things more true and deep
Than we mortals dream,
Or how could thy notes flow in such a crystal stream?

We look before and after,
And pine for what is not:
Our sincerest laughter
With some pain is fraught;
Our sweetest songs are those that tell of saddest thought.

Yet if we could scorn
Hate, and pride, and fear;
If we were things born
Not to shed a tear,
I know not how thy joy we ever should come near.

[1] *Hymeneal* Marital (Hymen is the Greek god of marriage).

Better than all measures
 Of delightful sound,
Better than all treasures
 That in books are found,
Thy skill to poet were, thou scorner of the ground!

Teach me half the gladness
 That thy brain must know,
Such harmonious madness
 From my lips would flow
The world should listen then—as I am listening now.
—1820

Adonais

In this pastoral elegy for fellow poet John Keats, Shelley calls the young poet Adonais after Adonis, the beautiful youth of classical myth who was loved by Venus and killed by a wild boar. In some versions of the story Venus asks Persephone, Queen of the underworld, to allow Adonis to return above ground for four months of every year, while in others she transforms his blood into the bright red anemone, enabling him to live on in this ever-blooming flower.

Shelley had known Keats only casually, through their mutual acquaintance Leigh Hunt, the editor of the radical *Examiner*, but he admired his poetry and agreed with many of his political views. Hearing of Keats's serious illness in 1820, Shelley had invited Keats to spend the winter with him in Pisa. Keats did journey to Italy, but died in Rome in February of 1812, before he could reach Pisa.

The beast whom Shelley blames for Keats's death is the anonymous critic who ridiculed Keats's *Endymion* in *The Quarterly Review* (April 1818); Shelley thus gave force to a sentimental myth that Keats's illness and death were brought on by demoralizing reviews, both in *The Quarterly Review* and *Blackwoods Magazine.* For many years after his death, it was commonly maintained that, as Byron said, Keats was "snuffed out by an article." Until the late 1840s, Keats was better known by *Adonais* and the legend of his death than by his own poetry.

Adonais
An Elegy on the Death of John Keats

Αστήρ πρὶν μέν ὲλαμπες ενι ζῶοισιν εῶος.
 Νυν δε θανῶν, λαμπεις ἕοπερος εν φθίμενοις. PLATO[1]

1

I weep for Adonais—he is dead!
 O, weep for Adonais! though our tears
Thaw not the frost which binds so dear a head!
And thou, sad Hour, selected from all years
To mourn our loss, rouse thy obscure compeers,
And teach them thine own sorrow, say: with me
Died Adonais; till the Future dares
Forget the Past, his fate and fame shall be
An echo and a light unto eternity!

2

Where wert thou mighty Mother, when he lay,
When thy Son lay, pierced by the shaft which flies
In darkness? Where was lorn° Urania[2] *forlorn*
When Adonais died? With veiled eyes,
'Mid listening Echoes, in her Paradise
She sate, while one, with soft enamoured breath,
Rekindled all the fading melodies,
With which, like flowers that mock the corse° *body*
 beneath,
He had adorned and hid the coming bulk of death.

3

O, weep for Adonais—he is dead!
Wake, melancholy Mother, wake and weep!
Yet wherefore? Quench within their burning bed
Thy fiery tears, and let thy loud heart keep
Like his, a mute and uncomplaining sleep;
For he is gone, where all things wise and fair

---

[1] Αστήρ ... *Plato* [Shelley's translation] Thou wert the morning star among the living, / Ere thy fair light had fled— / Now, having died, thou art as Hesperus, giving / New splendour to the dead. [Translation from the Greek of Plato's *Epigram on Aster*. The planet Venus appears in the sky as both the morning star, Vesper, and the evening star, Hesperus.]

[2] *Urania* Muse who is invoked near the beginning of Milton's *Paradise Lost.* Urania is also an epithet for the goddess Venus, who loved Adonis.

Descend—oh, dream not that the amorous Deep° *abyss*
Will yet restore him to the vital air;
Death feeds on his mute voice, and laughs at our
 despair.

4

Most musical of mourners, weep again!
Lament anew, Urania! He[1] died,
Who was the Sire of an immortal strain,
Blind, old, and lonely, when his country's pride,
The priest, the slave, and the liberticide,
Trampled and mocked with many a loathed rite
Of lust and blood; he went, unterrified,
Into the gulf of death; but his clear Sprite° *spirit*
Yet reigns o'er earth; the third among the sons of light.

5

Most musical of mourners, weep anew!
Not all to that bright station dared to climb;
And happier they their happiness who knew,
Whose tapers yet burn through that night of time
In which suns perished; others more sublime,
Struck by the envious wrath of man or God,
Have sunk, extinct in their refulgent° prime; *gleaming*
And some yet live, treading the thorny road,
Which leads, through toil and hate, to Fame's serene
 abode.

6

But now, thy youngest, dearest one, has perished,
The nursling of thy widowhood, who grew,
Like a pale flower by some sad maiden cherished,
And fed with true love tears, instead of dew;
Most musical of mourners, weep anew!
Thy extreme hope, the loveliest and the last,
The bloom, whose petals nipt before they blew,° *bloomed*
Died on the promise of the fruit, is waste;
The broken lily lies—the storm is overpast.

7

To that high Capital,[2] where kingly Death
Keeps his pale court in beauty and decay,
He came; and bought, with price of purest breath,
A grave among the eternal. Come away!
Haste, while the vault of blue Italian day
Is yet his fitting charnel°-roof! while still *mortuary*
He lies, as if in dewy sleep he lay;
Awake him not! surely he takes his fill
Of deep and liquid rest, forgetful of all ill.

8

He will awake no more, oh, never more!
Within the twilight chamber spreads apace,
The shadow of white Death, and at the door
Invisible Corruption waits to trace
His extreme way to her dim dwelling-place;
The eternal Hunger sits, but pity and awe
Soothe her pale rage, nor dares she to deface
So fair a prey, till darkness, and the law
Of mortal change, shall fill the grave which is her
 maw.° *stomach*

9

O, weep for Adonais! The quick° Dreams, *living*
The passion-wingèd Ministers of thought,
Who were his flocks, whom near the living streams
Of his young spirit he fed, and whom he taught
The love which was its music, wander not—
Wander no more, from kindling brain to brain,
But droop there, whence they sprung; and mourn their
 lot
Round the cold heart, where, after their sweet pain,
They ne'er will gather strength, or find a home again.

10

And one with trembling hands clasps his cold head,
And fans him with her moonlight wings, and cries,
"Our love, our hope, our sorrow, is not dead;
See, on the silken fringe of his faint eyes,
Like dew upon a sleeping flower, there lies
A tear some Dream has loosened from his brain."
Lost Angel of a ruined Paradise!

[1] *He* Poet John Milton (1608–74), who served in Cromwell's Parliamentary government and, as a result, was imprisoned when the monarchy was restored, although he was released quickly. At the end of this stanza, Shelley places Milton in a triumvirate with the earlier epic poets Homer and Dante ("the third among the sons of light").

[2] *high Capital* Rome, where Keats died.

She knew not 'twas her own; as with no stain
She faded, like a cloud which had outwept its rain.

11

One from a lucid° urn of starry dew *resplendent*
Washed his light limbs as if embalming them;
Another clipt her profuse locks, and threw
The wreath upon him, like an anadem,° *garland*
Which frozen tears instead of pearls begem;
Another in her wilful grief would break
Her bow and winged reeds,° as if to stem *arrows*
A greater loss with one which was more weak;
And dull the barbed fire against his frozen cheek.

12

Another Splendour on his mouth alit,
That mouth, whence it was wont to draw the breath
Which gave it strength to pierce the guarded wit,
And pass into the panting heart beneath
With lightning and with music: the damp death
Quenched its caress upon his icy lips;
And, as a dying meteor stains a wreath
Of moonlight vapour, which the cold night clips,° *clasps*
It flushed through his pale limbs, and passed to its
eclipse.

13

And others came ... Desires and Adorations,
Winged Persuasions and veiled Destinies,
Splendours, and Glooms, and glimmering Incarnations
Of hopes and fears, and twilight Phantasies;
And Sorrow, with her family of Sighs,
And Pleasure, blind with tears, led by the gleam
Of her own dying smile instead of eyes,
Came in slow pomp—the moving pomp might seem
Like pageantry of mist on an autumnal stream.

14

All he had loved, and moulded into thought,
From shape, and hue, and odour, and sweet sound,
Lamented Adonais. Morning sought
Her eastern watchtower, and her hair unbound,
Wet with the tears which should adorn the ground,
Dimmed the aerial eyes that kindle day;
Afar the melancholy thunder moaned,
Pale Ocean in unquiet slumber lay,
And the wild winds flew round, sobbing in their dismay.

15

Lost Echo sits amid the voiceless mountains,
And feeds her grief with his remembered lay,° *song*
And will no more reply to winds or fountains,
Or amorous birds perched on the young green spray,
Or herdsman's horn, or bell° at closing day; *church-bell*
Since she can mimic not his lips, more dear
Than those for whose disdain she pined away
Into a shadow of all sounds[1]—a drear
Murmur, between their songs, is all the woodmen hear.

16

Grief made the young Spring wild, and she threw down
Her kindling buds, as if she Autumn were,
Or they dead leaves; since her delight is flown
For whom should she have waked the sullen year?
To Phoebus was not Hyacinth so dear[2]
Nor to himself Narcissus, as to both
Thou Adonais: wan they stand and sere° *withered*
Amid the drooping comrades of their youth,
With dew all turned to tears; odour, to sighing ruth.° *pity*

17

Thy spirit's sister, the lorn nightingale
Mourns not her mate with such melodious pain;
Not so the eagle, who like thee could scale
Heaven, and could nourish in the sun's domain
Her mighty youth with morning,[3] doth complain,
Soaring and screaming round her empty nest,

---

[1] *those for ... sounds* Narcissus, whom the nymph Echo loved. Echo had been robbed of her voice by the goddess Hera, and could only repeat what others said. After falling in love with Narcissus, who rejected her in favor of his own reflection, she pined away until only her echoing voice remained.

[2] *To Phoebus ... dear* Phoebus Apollo, god of poetry and the sun, loved the beautiful youth Hyacinthus. When Hyacinthus was accidentally slain by a discus the god had thrown, Apollo caused the hyacinth flower to spring up from his spilt blood. It was said that Zephyrus (the west wind), a rejected suitor of Hyancinthus, blew the discus off course so that it would strike the youth. "Zephyr" was also the pen name of the reviewer of *Endymion*.

[3] *nourish ... morning* According to legend, the eagle could renew her youth by flying toward the sun until its heat burnt off her old plumage and cleared the film from her eyes.

As Albion[1] wails for thee: the curse of Cain[2]
Light on his head who pierced thy innocent breast,
And scared the angel soul that was its earthly guest!

18

Ah woe is me! Winter is come and gone,
But grief returns with the revolving year;
The airs and streams renew their joyous tone;
The ants, the bees, the swallows reappear;
Fresh leaves and flowers deck the dead Seasons' bier;
The amorous birds now pair in every brake,° *thicket*
And build their mossy homes in field and brere;° *briar*
And the green lizard, and the golden snake,
Like unimprisoned flames, out of their trance awake.

19

Through wood and stream and field and hill and Ocean
A quickening life from the Earth's heart has burst
As it has ever done, with change and motion,
From the great morning of the world when first
God dawned on Chaos; in its steam immersed
The lamps of Heaven flash with a softer light;
All baser things pant with life's sacred thirst;
Diffuse themselves; and spend in love's delight,
The beauty and the joy of their renewed might.

20

The leprous corpse touched by this spirit tender
Exhales itself in flowers of gentle breath;
Like incarnations of the stars, when splendour
Is changed to fragrance, they illumine death
And mock the merry worm that wakes beneath;
Nought we know, dies. Shall that alone which knows[3]
Be as a sword consumed before the sheath
By sightless[4] lightning?—th'intense atom glows
A moment, then is quenched in a most cold repose.

21

Alas! that all we loved of him should be,
But for our grief, as if it had not been,
And grief itself be mortal! Woe is me!
Whence are we, and why are we? of what scene
The actors or spectators? Great and mean
Meet massed in death, who lends what life must borrow.
As long as skies are blue, and fields are green,
Evening must usher night, night urge the morrow,
Month follow month with woe, and year wake year to
sorrow.

22

He will awake no more, oh, never more!
"Wake thou," cried Misery, "childless Mother, rise
Out of thy sleep, and slake,° in thy heart's core, *ease*
A wound more fierce than his with tears and sighs."
And all the Dreams that watched Urania's eyes,
And all the Echoes whom their sister's song
Had held in holy silence, cried: "Arise!"
Swift as a Thought by the snake Memory stung,
From her ambrosial[5] rest the fading Splendour sprung.

23

She rose like an autumnal Night, that springs
Out of the East, and follows wild and drear
The golden Day, which, on eternal wings,
Even as a ghost abandoning a bier,
Had left the Earth a corpse. Sorrow and fear
So struck, so roused, so rapt Urania;
So saddened round her like an atmosphere
Of stormy mist; so swept her on her way
Even to the mournful place where Adonais lay.

24

Out of her secret Paradise she sped,
Through camps and cities rough with stone, and steel,
And human hearts, which to her aery tread
Yielding not, wounded the invisible
Palms of her tender feet where'er they fell:
And barbed tongues, and thoughts more sharp than they
Rent the soft Form they never could repel,
Whose sacred blood, like the young tears of May,
Paved with eternal flowers that undeserving way.

---

[1] *Albion* England.

[2] *curse of Cain* For murdering his brother Abel, Cain was forced to wander the earth as a vagabond, unable to farm because no land would yield crops for him. See Genesis 4.

[3] *that alone which knows* I.e., the mind.

[4] *sightless* Invisible; blind.

[5] *ambrosial* Divine (ambrosia is the food of the gods); *the fading Splendour* Urania.

25

In the death chamber for a moment Death,
Shamed by the presence of that living Might,
Blushed to annihilation, and the breath
Revisited those lips, and life's pale light
Flashed through those limbs, so late her dear delight.
"Leave me not wild and drear and comfortless,
As silent lightning leaves the starless night!
Leave me not!" cried Urania: her distress
Roused Death: Death rose and smiled, and met her vain caress.

26

"Stay yet awhile! speak to me once again;
Kiss me, so long but as a kiss may live;
And in my heartless breast and burning brain
That word, that kiss shall all thoughts else survive,
With food of saddest memory kept alive,
Now thou art dead, as if it were a part
Of thee, my Adonais! I would give
All that I am to be as thou now art!
But I am chained to Time, and cannot thence depart!

27

"Oh gentle child, beautiful as thou wert,
Why didst thou leave the trodden paths of men
Too soon, and with weak hands though mighty heart
Dare° the unpastured dragon in his den? *challenge*
Defenceless as thou wert, oh where was then
Wisdom the mirrored shield,[1] or scorn the spear?
Or hadst thou waited the full cycle, when
Thy spirit should have filled its crescent sphere,
The monsters of life's waste had fled from thee like deer.

28

"The herded wolves, bold only to pursue;
The obscene ravens, clamorous o'er the dead;
The vultures to the conqueror's banner true
Who feed where Desolation first has fed,
And whose wings rain contagion—how they fled,
When like Apollo, from his golden bow,
The Pythian of the age[2] one arrow sped
And smiled! The spoilers tempt no second blow,
They fawn on the proud feet that spurn them as they go.

29

"The sun comes forth, and many reptiles spawn;
He sets, and each ephemeral insect then
Is gathered into death without a dawn,
And the immortal stars awake again;
So is it in the world of living men:
A godlike mind soars forth, in its delight
Making earth bare and veiling heaven, and when
It sinks, the swarms that dimmed or shared its light
Leave to its kindred lamps the spirit's awful° night." *awe-inspiring*

30

Thus ceased she: and the mountain shepherds came,
Their garlands sere, their magic mantles rent;
The Pilgrim of Eternity,[3] whose fame
Over his living head like Heaven is bent,
An early but enduring monument,
Came, veiling all the lightnings of his song
In sorrow; from her wilds Ierne° sent *Ireland*
The sweetest lyrist of her saddest wrong,
And love taught grief to fall like music from his tongue.[4]

31

Midst others of less note, came one frail Form,[5]
A phantom among men; companionless
As the last cloud of an expiring storm
Whose thunder is its knell;° he, as I guess, *funeral-bell*
Had gazed on Nature's naked loveliness,

---

[1] *mirrored shield* Because the stare of the Gorgon Medusa would turn men into stone, Perseus fought and defeated her by viewing her reflection in his shield.

[2] *Pythian of the age* Byron, who attacked the unfavorable reviewers of his *Hours of Idleness* in his satire *English Bards and Scotch Reviewers* (1809). The epithet "Pythian" was given to the god Apollo when he slew the dragon Python.

[3] *Pilgrim of Eternity* Byron.

[4] *The sweetest … tongue* Poet Thomas Moore (1779–1852), whose *Irish Melodies* deals with the oppression of his native Ireland by England.

[5] *one frail Form* Shelley.

Actæon-like,[1] and now he fled astray
With feeble steps o'er the world's wilderness,
And his own thoughts, along that rugged way,
Pursued, like raging hounds, their father and their prey.

32

A pardlike° Spirit beautiful and swift— *leopard-like*
A Love in desolation masked—a Power
Girt round with weakness; it can scarce uplift
The weight of the superincumbent hour;
It is a dying lamp, a falling shower,
A breaking billow—even whilst we speak
Is it not broken? On the withering flower
The killing sun smiles brightly: on a cheek
The life can burn in blood, even while the heart may break.

33

His head was bound with pansies overblown,
And faded violets, white, and pied, and blue;
And a light spear topped with a cypress cone,
Round whose rude shaft dark ivy tresses grew[2]
Yet dripping with the forest's noonday dew,
Vibrated, as the ever-beating heart
Shook the weak hand that grasped it; of that crew
He came the last, neglected and apart;
A herd-abandoned deer struck by the hunter's dart.

34

All stood aloof, and at his partial° moan *sympathetic*
Smiled through their tears; well knew that gentle band
Who in another's fate now wept his own;
As in the accents of an unknown land,
He sung new sorrow; sad Urania scanned
The Stranger's mien, and murmured: "who art thou?"
He answered not, but with a sudden hand
Made bare his branded and ensanguined° brow, *bloody*
Which was like Cain's or Christ's—Oh! that it should be so!

35

What softer voice is hushed over the dead?
Athwart what brow is that dark mantle thrown?
What form leans sadly o'er the white death-bed,
In mockery of monumental stone,
The heavy heart heaving without a moan?
If it be He, who, gentlest of the wise,
Taught, soothed, loved, honoured the departed one;[3]
Let me not vex, with inharmonious sighs
The silence of that heart's accepted sacrifice.

36

Our Adonais has drunk poison—oh!
What deaf and viperous murderer could crown
Life's early cup with such a draught of woe?
The nameless worm would now itself disown:
It felt, yet could escape the magic tone
Whose prelude held all envy, hate, and wrong,
But what was howling in one breast alone,
Silent with expectation of the song,
Whose master's hand is cold, whose silver lyre unstrung.[4]

37

Live thou, whose infamy is not thy fame!
Live! fear no heavier chastisement from me,
Thou noteless blot on a remembered name!
But be thyself, and know thyself to be!
And ever at thy season be thou free
To spill the venom when thy fangs o'er flow:
Remorse and Self-contempt shall cling to thee;
Hot Shame shall burn upon thy secret brow,
And like a beaten hound tremble thou shalt—as now.

38

Nor let us weep that our delight is fled
Far from these carrion kites[5] that scream below;
He wakes or sleeps with the enduring dead;
Thou canst not soar where he is sitting now.

---

[1] *Actæon-like* Actaeon was a hunter who accidentally came upon Diana, goddess of chastity, bathing naked. Angered, she turned him into a stag, and his own hounds chased him down and tore him apart.

[2] *pansies overblown* Pansies (a symbol of sorrow) past their bloom; *violets* Representing death; *light spear … tresses grew* Thyrsus, staff borne by Dionysus, the god of fertility, and his followers.

[3] *He who … one* Radical journalist Leigh Hunt, to whom Keats dedicated his first volume.

[4] *silver lyre unstrung* On Keats's tomb is engraved the image of a Greek lyre with half its strings broken. According to his friend Joseph Severn, this symbolizes "his classical genius cut off by death before its maturity."

[5] *kites* Falcon-like birds of prey.

Dust to the dust! but the pure spirit shall flow
Back to the burning fountain whence it came,
A portion of the Eternal, which must glow
Through time and change, unquenchably the same,
Whilst thy cold embers choke the sordid hearth of
shame.

39

Peace, peace! he is not dead, he doth not sleep—
He hath awakened from the dream of life—
'Tis we who lost in stormy visions keep
With phantoms an unprofitable strife,
And in mad trance, strike with our spirit's knife
Invulnerable nothings. *We* decay
Like corpses in a charnel; fear and grief
Convulse us and consume us day by day,
And cold hopes swarm like worms within our living
clay.

40

He has outsoared the shadow of our night;
Envy and calumny° and hate and pain, *slander*
And that unrest which men miscall delight,
Can touch him not and torture not again;
From the contagion of the world's slow stain
He is secure, and now can never mourn
A heart grown cold, a head grown grey in vain;
Nor, when the spirit's self has ceased to burn,
With sparkless ashes load an unlamented urn.

41

He lives, he wakes—'tis Death is dead, not he;
Mourn not for Adonais. Thou young Dawn
Turn all thy dew to splendour, for from thee
The spirit thou lamentest is not gone;
Ye caverns and ye forests, cease to moan!
Cease ye faint flowers and fountains, and thou Air
Which like a mourning veil thy scarf hadst thrown
O'er the abandoned Earth, now leave it bare
Even to the joyous stars which smile on its despair!

42

He is made one with Nature: there is heard
His voice in all her music, from the moan
Of thunder, to the song of night's sweet bird;[1]
He is a presence to be felt and known
In darkness and in light, from herb and stone,
Spreading itself where'er that Power may move
Which has withdrawn his being to its own;
Which wields the world with never wearied love,
Sustains it from beneath, and kindles it above.

43

He is a portion of the loveliness
Which once he made more lovely: he doth bear
His part, while the one Spirit's plastic° stress *formative*
Sweeps through the dull dense world, compelling there,
All new successions to the forms they wear;
Torturing th'unwilling dross° that checks *impure matter*
its flight
To its own likeness, as each mass may bear;
And bursting in its beauty and its might
From trees and beasts and men into the Heaven's light.

44

The splendours of the firmament of time
May be eclipsed, but are extinguished not;
Like stars to their appointed height they climb
And death is a low mist which cannot blot
The brightness it may veil. When lofty thought
Lifts a young heart above its mortal lair,
And love and life contend in it, for what
Shall be its earthly doom,° the dead live there *fate*
And move like winds of light on dark and stormy air.

45

The inheritors of unfulfilled renown
Rose from their thrones, built beyond mortal thought,
Far in the Unapparent. Chatterton[2]
Rose pale, his solemn agony had not
Yet faded from him; Sidney,[3] as he fought
And as he fell and as he lived and loved
Sublimely mild, a Spirit without spot,

---

[1] *night's sweet bird* I.e., the nightingale, in reference to Keats's "Ode to a Nightingale."

[2] *Chatterton* Poet Thomas Chatterton, who committed suicide in 1770 at the age of 17.

[3] *Sidney* Sir Philip Sidney (1554–86), who was killed in battle when he was 32.

Arose; and Lucan,[1] by his death approved:
Oblivion as they rose shrank like a thing reproved.

46

And many more, whose names on Earth are dark
But whose transmitted effluence cannot die
So long as fire outlives the parent spark,
Rose, robed in dazzling immortality.
"Thou art become as one of us," they cry,
"It was for thee yon kingless sphere has long
Swung blind in unascended majesty,
Silent alone amid an Heaven of song.
Assume thy winged throne, thou Vesper[2] of our
  throng!"

47

Who mourns for Adonais? Oh come forth
Fond° wretch! and know thyself and him aright. *foolish*
Clasp with thy panting soul the pendulous Earth;
As from a centre, dart thy spirit's light
Beyond all worlds, until its spacious might
Satiate the void circumference: then shrink
Even to a point within our day and night;
And keep thy heart light lest it make thee sink
When hope has kindled hope, and lured thee to the
  brink.

48

Or go to Rome, which is the sepulchre
O, not of him, but of our joy: 'tis nought
That ages, empires, and religions there
Lie buried in the ravage they have wrought;
For such as he can lend°—they borrow not *bestow*
Glory from those who made the world their prey;
And he is gathered to the kings of thought
Who waged contention with their time's decay,
And of the past are all that cannot pass away.

49

Go thou to Rome—at once the Paradise,
The grave, the city, and the wilderness;
And where its wrecks like shattered mountains rise,
And flowering weeds, and fragrant copses° dress *thickets*
The bones of Desolation's nakedness
Pass, till the Spirit of the spot shall lead
Thy footsteps to a slope of green access[3]
Where, like an infant's smile, over the dead,
A light of laughing flowers along the grass is spread.

50

And gray walls moulder round,[4] on which dull Time
Feeds, like slow fire upon a hoary° brand;[5] *white*
And one keen pyramid with wedge sublime,
Pavilioning the dust of him who planned
This refuge for his memory, doth stand
Like flame transformed to marble; and beneath,
A field is spread, on which a newer band
Have pitched in Heaven's smile their camp of death
Welcoming him we lose with scarce extinguished
  breath.

51

Here pause: these graves are all too young as yet
To have outgrown the sorrow which consigned
Its charge to each; and if the seal is set,
Here, on one fountain of a mourning mind,
Break it not thou! too surely shalt thou find
Thine own well full, if thou returnest home,
Of tears and gall. From the world's bitter wind
Seek shelter in the shadow of the tomb.
What Adonais is, why fear we to become?

52

The One remains, the many change and pass;
Heaven's light forever shines, Earth's shadows fly;
Life, like a dome of many-coloured glass,
Stains the white radiance of Eternity,
Until Death tramples it to fragments. Die,
If thou wouldst be with that which thou dost seek!

---

[1] *Lucan* First-century CE Roman poet Marcus Annaeus Lucan, who at the age of twenty-six killed himself to avoid being executed for conspiring against the tyrannical emperor Nero.

[2] *Vesper* The evening star.

[3] *slope of green access* The Protestant Cemetery in Rome, where Keats is buried. Shelley's son William, who died at age three, is also buried there.

[4] *gray … round* One of the boundaries of the cemetery incorporates the wall of ancient Rome, while another is formed by the pyramid-tomb of Roman tribune Caius Cestius.

[5] *brand* Burning log.

Follow where all is fled! Rome's azure sky,
Flowers, ruins, statues, music, words, are weak
The glory they transfuse with fitting truth to speak.

53

Why linger, why turn back, why shrink, my Heart?
Thy hopes are gone before: from all things here
They have departed; thou shouldst now depart!
A light is past from the revolving year,
And man, and woman; and what still is dear
Attracts to crush, repels to make thee wither.
The soft sky smiles—the low wind whispers near:
'Tis Adonais calls! Oh, hasten thither,
No more let Life divide what Death can join together.

54

That Light whose smile kindles the Universe,
That Beauty in which all things work and move,
That Benediction which the eclipsing Curse
Of birth can quench not, that sustaining Love
Which through the web of being blindly wove
By man and beast and earth and air and sea,
Burns bright or dim, as[1] each are mirrors of
The fire for which all thirst; now beams on me,
Consuming the last clouds of cold mortality.

55

The breath whose might I have invoked in song
Descends on me; my spirit's bark is driven,
Far from the shore, far from the trembling throng
Whose sails were never to the tempest given;
The massy earth and sphered skies are riven!
I am borne darkly, fearfully, afar;
Whilst burning through the inmost veil of Heaven,
The soul of Adonais, like a star,
Beacons from the abode where the Eternal are.
—1821

[1] *as* I.e., to the extent that.

from *Hellas*[2]

CHORUS[3]

Worlds on worlds are rolling ever
From creation to decay,
Like the bubbles on a river
Sparkling, bursting, borne away.
But they[4] are still immortal
Who, through birth's orient° portal *eastern*
And death's dark chasm hurrying to and fro,
Clothe their unceasing flight
In the brief dust and light
Gathered around their chariots as they go;
New shapes they still may weave,
New gods, new laws receive,
Bright or dim are they as the robes they last
On Death's bare ribs had cast.

A power from the unknown God,[5]

[2] *Hellas* Classical name for Greece. Shelley's inspiration for the poem was the 1821 Greek revolt (against the Turks), which began their eleven-year war for independence. He uses as a model fifth century BCE playwright Aeschylus's *Persians*, which details the Greek defeat of Xerxes and the invading Persians at Salamis in 480 BCE. In his preface to the play, Shelley explains that his interest in Greece results from his belief that the culture, religion, and laws of his society all have their roots in Greece (a belief, common at the time, often referred to now as "Romantic Hellenism"). He also declares his wholehearted support for the Greek cause in an age characterized by "war of the oppressed against the oppressors."

[3] *Chorus* Shelley's chorus is composed of Greek women in Constantinople, the city founded by Roman Emperor Constantine the Great but conquered by the Ottoman Empire in 1435.

[4] *they* "Living and thinking beings which inhabit the planets." In a note to *Hellas*, Shelley says that in this first stanza he contrasts the immortality of these beings with "the transience of the noblest manifestations of the external world." The following verses go on, he says, to "indicate a progressive state of more or less exalted existence, according to the degree of perfection which every distinct intelligence may have attained," and to "conjecture the condition of futurity towards which we are all impelled by an inextinguishable thirst for immortality."

[5] *unknown God* God is here "unknown" because this is before the coming of Christ. Shelley goes on to compare Christ to Prometheus, the classical god who stole fire from Mount Olympus (home of the gods) and gave it to humans. For this, Zeus, King of the gods, chained him to a rock and had an eagle eat out his liver, which grew

A Promethean conqueror, came;
Like a triumphal path he trod
The thorns of death and shame.
A mortal shape to him
Was like the vapour dim
Which the orient planet[1] animates with light;
Hell, Sin, and Slavery came,
Like bloodhounds mild and tame,
Nor preyed, until their Lord had taken flight;
The moon of Mahomet[2]
Arose, and it shall set:
While blazoned as on Heaven's immortal noon
The cross leads generations on.[3]

Swift as the radiant shapes of sleep
From one whose dreams are Paradise
Fly, when the fond° wretch° wakes to weep, *foolish / mortal*
And Day peers forth with her blank eyes;
So fleet, so faint, so fair,
The Powers of earth and air
Fled from the folding-star[4] of Bethlehem:
Apollo, Pan, and Love,
And even Olympian Jove[5]
Grew weak, for killing Truth had glared on them;
Our hills and seas and streams,
Dispeopled of their dreams,
Their waters turned to blood, their dew to tears.
Wailed for the golden years....

CHORUS[6]

The world's great age begins anew,
The golden years return,
The earth doth like a snake renew
Her winter weeds outworn:
Heaven smiles, and faiths and empires gleam,
Like wrecks of a dissolving dream.

A brighter Hellas rears its mountains
From waves serener far;
A new Peneus[7] rolls his fountains° *waters*
Against the morning star.
Where fairer Tempes bloom, there sleep
Young Cyclads[8] on a sunnier deep.

A loftier Argo[9] cleaves the main,° *sea*
Fraught with a later prize;
Another Orpheus[10] sings again,
And loves, and weeps, and dies.
A new Ulysses leaves once more
Calypso for his native shore.[11]

back daily only to be devoured again.

[1] *orient planet* Venus, which appears in the east as the morning star.

[2] *moon of Mahomet* Crescent moon, the emblem of Islam (which was founded by the prophet Mohammed in the sixth century CE).

[3] *While blazoned ... on* In 312 CE, Constantine is said to have beheld a flaming cross inscribed with the words "In this sign, thou shalt conquer." He converted to Christianity and won control of Rome.

[4] *folding-star* I.e., star that appears as shepherds are herding their sheep back to the pen (fold).

[5] *Apollo ... Jove* Greek and Roman gods.

[6] [From Shelley's note] The final chorus is indistinct and obscure, as the event of the living drama whose arrival it foretells. Prophesies of wars, and rumours of wars, etc., may safely be made by poet or prophet in any age, but to anticipate however darkly a period of regeneration and happiness is a more hazardous exercise of the faculty which bards possess or feign. [This chorus occurs after the Greek rebels have been defeated by the Turks.]

[7] *Peneus* River in Thessaly, also known as the Salambria, which flows from Mount Pindus (one of the homes of the Muses) through the Tempe Valley; also, god of that river.

[8] *Cyclads* Islands in the Aegean Sea off the southeast shore of Greece.

[9] *Argo* Ship of classical myth in which Jason sailed in search of the Golden Fleece.

[10] *Orpheus* Celebrated Thracian musician and poet of Greek mythology. When his beloved, Eurydice, was killed by a snake, he so charmed Hades with his lyre playing that Hades allowed him to lead Eurydice back with him, provided he not look at her on the journey from the underworld. When he could not resist making sure she was behind him, she was condemned to return to Hades forever. In his grief, Orpheus spent the rest of his life as a wandering recluse until the women of Thrace, enraged at his inattention, tore him to pieces.

[11] *A new ... shore* Ulysses (Odysseus) in Homer's *Odyssey* is shipwrecked on the nymph Calypso's island on his voyage home from the Trojan War. He spends seven years with her, entranced by her charms, until finally leaving to continue his voyage home.

Oh, write no more the tale of Troy,
If earth Death's scroll must be!
Nor mix with Laian rage the joy
Which dawns upon the free:
Although a subtler Sphinx renew
Riddles of death Thebes never knew.[1]

Another Athens shall arise,
And to remoter time
Bequeath, like sunset to the skies,
The splendour of its prime;
And leave, if nought so bright may live,
All earth can take or Heaven can give.

Saturn and Love their long repose
Shall burst, more bright and good
Than all who fell, than One who rose,
Than many unsubdued:[2]
Not gold, not blood, their altar dowers,° *dowries*
But votive tears and symbol flowers.

Oh, cease! must hate and death return?
Cease! must men kill and die?
Cease! drain not to its dregs the urn
Of bitter prophecy.
The world is weary of the past,
Oh, might it die or rest at last!
—1822

[1] *Nor mix … knew* Laius, King of Thebes, ordered the death of his son Oedipus after it was prophesied that the boy would later kill him. Oedipus was rescued and grew up in ignorance of his origin. As a grown man he became involved in a dispute with Laius, not knowing him to be his father, and killed him. He then married Laius's widow, similarly ignorant of her identity as his mother. When he discovered what he had done, he blinded himself, and his mother committed suicide. The Sphinx was a monster who challenged travelers on the road to Thebes with riddles. If they solved the riddle (as Oedipus did) they were allowed to pass. If they did not, they were slain.

[2] [From Shelley's note] Saturn and Love were among the deities of a real or imaginary state of innocence and happiness. *All* those *who fell,* or the Gods of Greece, Asia and Egypt; the *One who rose,* or Jesus Christ…; and *the many unsubdued,* or the monstrous objects of the idolatry of China, India, the Antarctic islands, and the native tribes of America.

Mutability

1

The flower that smiles to-day
To-morrow dies;
All that we wish to stay
Tempts and then flies.
What is this world's delight?
Lightning that mocks the night,
Brief even as bright.

2

Virtue, how frail it is!
Friendship how rare!
Love, how it sells poor bliss
For proud despair!
But we, though soon they fall,
Survive their joy, and all
Which ours we call.

3

Whilst skies are blue and bright,
Whilst flowers are gay,
Whilst eyes that change ere night
Make glad the day;
Whilst yet the calm hours creep,
Dream thou—and from thy sleep
Then wake to weep.
—1824

Stanzas

Written in Dejection – December 1818, near Naples

1

The sun is warm, the sky is clear,
The waves are dancing fast and bright,
Blue isles and snowy mountains wear
The purple noon's transparent might,
The breath of the moist earth is light,
Around its unexpanded buds;

Like many a voice of one delight,
The winds, the birds, the ocean floods,
The City's voice itself, is soft like Solitude's.

2

I see the Deep's untrampled floor
With green and purple seaweeds strown;
I see the waves upon the shore,
Like light dissolved in star-showers,[1] thrown:
I sit upon the sands alone—
The lightning of the noontide ocean
Is flashing round me, and a tone
Arises from its measured motion,
How sweet! did any heart now share in my emotion.

3

Alas! I have nor hope nor health,
Nor peace within nor calm around,
Nor that content surpassing wealth
The sage in meditation found,
And walked with inward glory crowned—
Nor fame, nor power, nor love, nor leisure.
Others I see whom these surround—
Smiling they live, and call life pleasure;—
To me that cup has been dealt in another measure.

4

Yet now despair itself is mild,
Even as the winds and waters are;
I could lie down like a tired child,
And weep away the life of care
Which I have borne and yet must bear,
Till death like sleep might steal on me,
And I might feel in the warm air
My cheek grow cold, and hear the sea
Breathe o'er my dying brain its last monotony.

5

Some might lament that I were cold.
As I, when this sweet day is gone,
Which my lost heart, too soon grown old,
Insults with this untimely moan;
They might lament—for I am one
Whom men love not—and yet regret,
Unlike this day, which, when the sun
Shall on its stainless glory set,
Will linger, though enjoyed, like joy in memory yet.
—1824

[1] *star-showers* Meteor showers.

Sonnet [Lift Not the Painted Veil]

Lift not the painted veil which those who live
Call Life: though unreal shapes be pictured there,
And it but mimic all we would believe
With colours idly spread—behind, lurk Fear
And Hope, twin Destinies; who ever weave
Their shadows, o'er the chasm, sightless and drear.
I knew one who had lifted it—he sought,
For his lost heart was tender, things to love,
But found them not, alas! nor was there aught
The world contains, the which he could approve.
Through the unheeding many he did move,
A splendour among shadows, a bright blot
Upon this gloomy scene, a Spirit that strove
For truth, and like the Preacher[2] found it not.
—1824

To Night

1

Swiftly walk o'er the western wave,
Spirit of Night!
Out of the misty eastern cave,
Where, all the long and lone daylight,
Thou wovest dreams of joy and fear,
Which make thee terrible and dear,
Swift be thy flight!

2

Wrap thy form in a mantle gray,
Star-inwrought!
Blind with thine hair the eyes of Day;
Kiss her until she be wearied out,

[2] *Preacher* Speaker of Ecclesiastes, who says, "I have seen all the works that are done under the sun; and, behold, all is vanity and vexation of spirit" (1.14).

Then wander o'er city, and sea, and land,
Touching all with thine opiate° wand— *sleep-inducing*
Come, long-sought!

3

When I arose and saw the dawn,
I sighed for thee;
When light rode high, and the dew was gone,
And noon lay heavy on flower and tree,
And the weary Day turned to his rest,
Lingering like an unloved guest,
I sighed for thee.

4

Thy brother Death came, and cried,
Wouldst thou me?
Thy sweet child Sleep, the filmy-eyed,
Murmured like a noontide bee,
Shall I nestle near thy side?
Wouldst thou me? And I replied,
No, not thee!

5

Death will come when thou art dead,
Soon, too soon—
Sleep will come when thou art fled;
Of neither would I ask the boon
I ask of thee, beloved Night—
Swift be thine approaching flight,
Come soon, soon!

—1824

To ——

Music, when soft voices die,
Vibrates in the memory—
Odours, when sweet violets sicken,
Live within the sense they quicken.° *vivify*

Rose leaves, when the rose is dead,
Are heaped for the beloved's bed;
And so thy thoughts, when thou art gone,
Love itself shall slumber on.

—1824

The Mask of Anarchy

On 16 August 1819, roughly 60,000 men, women, and children, led by radical orator Henry Hunt, peaceably gathered on St. Peter's Field in Manchester in support of Parliamentary reform and a repeal of the corn laws (restricting the import and export of grain). After ordering the meeting to disband, the magistrates sent out the militia to attack the crowd. Eleven people were killed and over four hundred injured. When the Home Office condoned this violent response, public outrage was widespread, and the radical journal *The Examiner* was filled with indignant reports on what became known as the "Peterloo Massacre," in mockery of the English victory in the Battle of Waterloo.

Though he was in Italy at the time, Shelley was inspired by the public outcry in *The Examiner* to write *The Mask of Anarchy*. He sent the poem to Leigh Hunt, editor of the journal, in September 1819, but Hunt thought its publication would be a risk to both Shelley's reputation and that of *The Examiner*. When Hunt did finally print the poem, in 1832, it was with the subtitle and the specific references to Jon Scott, Earl of Eldon and Lord Chancellor (who was responsible for depriving Shelley of access to his children with Harriet, his first wife) and Home Secretary Sidmouth removed. He gave the title as *The Masque of Anarchy*, which Shelley had called the poem in a letter to him, thus making explicit the reference to the literary genre of the masque, a courtly drama.

The Mask of Anarchy
Written on the Occasion of the Massacre at Manchester

1

As I lay asleep in Italy
There came a voice from over the Sea,
And with great power it forth led me
To walk in the visions of Poesy.

2

I met Murder on the way—
He had a mask like Castlereagh[1]—
Very smooth he looked, yet grim;
Seven bloodhounds[2] followed him:

3

All were fat; and well they might
Be in admirable plight,
For one by one, and two by two,
He tossed them human hearts to chew
Which from his wide cloak he drew.

4

Next came Fraud, and he had on,
Like Eldon, an ermined gown;[3]
His big tears, for he wept well,
Turned to mill-stones as they fell.[4]

5

And the little children, who
Round his feet played to and fro,
Thinking every tear a gem,
Had their brains knocked out by them.

6

Clothed with the Bible, as with light,
And the shadows of the night,
Like Sidmouth, next, Hypocrisy
On a crocodile rode by.[5]

7

And many more Destructions played
In this ghastly masquerade,
All disguised, even to the eyes,
Like Bishops, lawyers, peers, or spies.

8

Last came Anarchy: he rode
On a white horse, splashed with blood;
He was pale even to the lips,
Like Death in the Apocalypse.[6]

9

And he wore a kingly crown;
And in his grasp a sceptre shone;
On his brow this mark I saw—
"I AM GOD, AND KING, AND LAW!"

10

With a pace stately and fast,
Over English land he passed,
Trampling to a mire of blood
The adoring multitude.

11

And a mighty troop around,
With their trampling shook the ground,
Waving each a bloody sword,
For the service of their Lord.

12

And with glorious triumph, they
Rode through England proud and gay,
Drunk as with intoxication
Of the wine of desolation.

13

O'er fields and towns, from sea to sea,
Passed the Pageant swift and free,
Tearing up, and trampling down;
Till they came to London town.

[1] *Castlereagh* Robert Stuart Castlereagh, Foreign Secretary (1812–22), who was very unpopular with radicals such as Shelley. In 1815 he was responsible for Britain's joining with seven other European nations to postpone the final abolition of the slave trade.

[2] *bloodhounds* Faction of Parliament that supported war.

[3] *ermined gown* Traditional robe of office for the Lord Chancellor.

[4] *big tears ... fell* Lord Chancellor John Scott, Earl of Eldon (1751–1838), frequently shed tears during his public appearances.

[5] *Clothed with ... light* Home Secretary Henry Addington, 1st Viscount Sidmouth (1757–1844), invested in the construction of several churches for the poor, but did nothing to improve their living conditions; *crocodile* Animal often used to symbolize hypocrisy because it was fabled to shed tears as it devoured its victims.

[6] *he rode ... Apocalypse* See Revelation 6, in which John the Divine has a vision of the four horsemen of the Apocalypse. Of the fourth horse he says, "and behold a pale horse: and his name that sat on him was Death, and Hell followed him" (6.8).

14

And each dweller, panic-stricken,
Felt his heart with terror sicken
Hearing the tempestuous cry
Of the triumph of Anarchy.

15

For with pomp to meet him came,
Clothed in arms like blood and flame,
The hired murderers, who did sing
Thou art God, and Law, and King.

16

"We have waited, weak and lone
For thy coming, Mighty One!
Our purses are empty, our swords are cold,
Give us glory, and blood, and gold."

17

Lawyers and priests, a motley crowd,
To the earth their pale brows bowed;
Like a bad prayer not over loud,
Whispering—"Thou art Law and God."

18

Then all cried with one accord,
"Thou art King, and God, and Lord;
Anarchy, to thee we bow,
Be thy name made holy now!"

19

And Anarchy, the Skeleton,
Bowed and grinned to every one,
As well as if his education
Had cost ten millions to the nation.

20

For he knew the Palaces
Of our Kings were rightly his;
His the sceptre, crown, and globe,[1]
And the gold-inwoven robe.

21

So he sent his slaves before
To seize upon the Bank and Tower,[2]
And was proceeding with intent
To meet his pensioned Parliament

22

When one fled past, a maniac maid,
And her name was Hope, she said:
But she looked more like Despair,
And she cried out in the air:

23

"My father Time is weak and gray
With waiting for a better day;
See how idiot-like he stands,
Fumbling with his palsied hands!

24

"He has had child after child,
And the dust of death is piled
Over every one but me—
Misery, oh, Misery!"

25

Then she lay down in the street,
Right before the horses' feet,
Expecting, with a patient eye,
Murder, Fraud, and Anarchy.

26

When between her and her foes
A mist, a light, an image rose,
Small at first, and weak, and frail
Like the vapour of a vale:

27

Till as clouds grow on the blast,
Like tower-crowned giants striding fast,
And glare with lightnings as they fly
And speak in thunder to the sky,

[1] *globe* Golden ball that, like the scepter, is an emblem of sovereignty.

[2] *Bank* Bank of England, the national treasury; *Tower* Tower of London, where the crown jewels are kept.

28

It grew—a Shape arrayed in mail° *chain mail*
Brighter than the viper's scale,
And upborne on wings whose grain° *texture*
Was as the light of sunny rain.

29

On its helm, seen far away,
A planet, like the Morning's,[1] lay;
And those plumes its light rained through
Like a shower of crimson dew.

30

With step as soft as wind it passed
O'er the heads of men—so fast
That they knew the presence there
And looked—but all was empty air.

31

As flowers beneath May's footstep waken,
As stars from Night's loose hair are shaken,
As waves arise when loud winds call,
Thoughts sprung where'er that step did fall.

32

And the prostrate multitude
Looked—and ankle-deep in blood,
Hope, that maiden most serene,
Was walking with a quiet mien:° *countenance*

33

And Anarchy, the ghastly birth,
Lay dead earth upon the earth;
The Horse of Death tameless as wind
Fled, and with his hoofs did grind
To dust the murderers thronged behind.

34

A rushing light of clouds and splendour,
A sense awakening and yet tender
Was heard and felt—and at its close
These words of joy and fear arose

35

As if their own indignant Earth
Which gave the sons of England birth
Had felt their blood upon her brow,
And shuddering with a mother's throe

36

Had turnèd every drop of blood
By which her face had been bedewed
To an accent unwithstood—
As if her heart had cried aloud:

37

"Men of England, heirs of Glory,
Heroes of unwritten story,
Nurslings of one mighty Mother,
Hopes of her, and one another,

38

"Rise like Lions after slumber
In unvanquishable number,
Shake your chains to earth like dew
Which in sleep had fallen on you—
Ye are many, they are few.

39

"What is Freedom? Ye can tell
That which slavery is, too well—
For its very name has grown
To an echo of your own.

40

"'Tis to work and have such pay
As just keeps life from day to day
In your limbs, as in a cell
For the tyrants' use to dwell,

41

"So that ye for them are made
Loom, and plough, and sword, and spade,
With or without your own will bent
To their defence and nourishment.

---

[1] *Morning* Venus, as the morning star.

42

"'Tis to see your children weak
With their mothers pine° and peak,° *suffer / waste away*
When the winter winds are bleak—
They are dying whilst I speak.

43

"'Tis to hunger for such diet
As the rich man in his riot
Casts to the fat dogs that lie
Surfeiting beneath his eye;

44

"'Tis to let the Ghost of Gold[1]
Take from Toil a thousandfold
More than e'er its substance could
In the tyrannies of old.

45

"Paper coin—that forgery
Of the title-deeds, which ye
Hold to something of the worth
Of the inheritance of Earth.

46

"'Tis to be a slave in soul
And to hold no strong control
Over your own wills, but be
All that others make of ye.

47

"And at length when ye complain
With a murmur weak and vain
'Tis to see the Tyrant's crew
Ride over your wives and you—
Blood is on the grass like dew.

48

"Then it is to feel revenge
Fiercely thirsting to exchange
Blood for blood—and wrong for wrong—
Do not thus when ye are strong.

49

"Birds find rest, in narrow nest
When weary of their wingèd quest;
Beasts find fare, in woody lair
When storm and snow are in the air.

50

"Asses, swine, have litter spread
And with fitting food are fed;
All things have a home but one—
Thou, Oh, Englishman, hast none![2]

51

"This is Slavery—savage men,
Or wild beasts within a den,
Would endure not as ye do—
But such ills they never knew.

52

"What art thou Freedom? O! could slaves
Answer from their living graves
This demand—tyrants would flee
Like a dream's dim imagery:

53

"Thou art not, as impostors say,
A shadow soon to pass away,
A superstition, and a name
Echoing from the cave of Fame.° *rumor*

54

"For the labourer thou art bread,
And a comely table spread
From his daily labour come
In a neat and happy home.

55

"Thou art clothes, and fire, and food
For the trampled multitude—
No—in countries that are free
Such starvation cannot be
As in England now we see.

---

[1] *Ghost of Gold* Paper money. At the time paper money was regarded as unreliable currency, and was not backed by any gold reserves. Paper money was often used to pay laborers' wages.

[2] *Asses … none* See Matthew 8.20, in which Jesus says, "The foxes have holes, and the birds of the air have nests; but the Son of man hath not where to lay his head."

56

"To the rich thou art a check,
When his foot is on the neck
Of his victim, thou dost make
That he treads upon a snake.

57

"Thou art Justice—ne'er for gold
May thy righteous laws be sold
As laws are in England—thou
Shield'st alike the high and low.

58

"Thou art Wisdom—Freemen never
Dream that God will damn for ever
All who think those things untrue
Of which Priests make such ado.

59

"Thou art Peace—never by thee
Would blood and treasure wasted be
As tyrants wasted them, when all
Leagued to quench thy flame in Gaul.[1]

60

"What if English toil and blood
Was poured forth, even as a flood?
It availed, Oh, Liberty,
To dim, but not extinguish thee.

61

"Thou art Love—the rich have kissed
Thy feet, and like him following Christ,
Give their substance to the free
And through the rough world follow thee,[2]

62

"Or turn their wealth to arms, and make
War for thy belovèd sake
On wealth, and war, and fraud—whence they
Drew the power which is their prey.

63

"Science, Poetry, and Thought
Are thy lamps; they make the lot
Of the dwellers in a cot° *cottage*
So serene, they curse it not.

64

"Spirit, Patience, Gentleness,
All that can adorn and bless
Art thou—let deeds, not words, express
Thine exceeding loveliness.

65

"Let a great Assembly be
Of the fearless and the free
On some spot of English ground
Where the plains stretch wide around.

66

"Let the blue sky overhead,
The green earth on which ye tread,
All that must eternal be
Witness the solemnity.

67

"From the corners uttermost
Of the bounds of English coast;
From every hut, village, and town
Where those who live and suffer moan
For others' misery or their own,

68

"From the workhouse[3] and the prison
Where pale as corpses newly risen,
Women, children, young and old
Groan for pain, and weep for cold—

[1] *Gaul* France.

[2] *like him … thee* See Matthew 19.21, in which Jesus counsels a rich man to "go and sell that thou hast, and give to the poor, and thou shalt have treasure in heaven: and come and follow me."

[3] *workhouse* Institution established to provide work, shelter, and food for the parish poor; appalling conditions were the norm at most workhouses.

69

"From the haunts of daily life
Where is waged the daily strife
With common wants and common cares
Which sows the human heart with tares°— *weeds*

70

"Lastly from the palaces
Where the murmur of distress
Echoes, like the distant sound
Of a wind alive around

71

"Those prison halls of wealth and fashion,
Where some few feel such compassion
For those who groan, and toil, and wail
As must make their brethren pale—

72

"Ye who suffer woes untold,
Or° to feel, or to behold *either*
Your lost country bought and sold
With a price of blood and gold—

73

"Let a vast assembly be,
And with great solemnity
Declare with measured words that ye
Are, as God has made ye, free—

74

"Be your strong and simple words
Keen to wound as sharpened swords,
And wide as targes° let them be, *shields*
With their shade to cover ye.

75

"Let the tyrants pour around
With a quick and startling sound,
Like the loosening of a sea,
Troops of armed emblazonry.

76

"Let the charged artillery drive
Till the dead air seems alive
With the clash of clanging wheels,
And the tramp of horses' heels.

77

"Let the fixed bayonet
Gleam with sharp desire to wet
Its bright point in English blood
Looking keen as one for food.

78

"Let the horsemen's scimitars[1]
Wheel and flash, like sphereless stars
Thirsting to eclipse their burning
In a sea of death and mourning.

79

"Stand ye calm and resolute,
Like a forest close and mute,
With folded arms and looks which are
Weapons of unvanquished war,

80

"And let Panic, who outspeeds
The career of armèd steeds
Pass, a disregarded shade
Through your phalanx undismayed.

81

"Let the laws of your own land,
Good or ill, between ye stand
Hand to hand, and foot to foot,
Arbiters of the dispute,

82

"The old laws of England—they
Whose reverend heads with age are gray,
Children of a wiser day;
And whose solemn voice must be
Thine own echo—Liberty!

83

"On those who first should violate
Such sacred heralds in their state

[1] *scimitars* Short curved swords.

Rest the blood that must ensue,
And it will not rest on you.

84
"And if then the tyrants dare
Let them ride among you there,
Slash, and stab, and maim, and hew—
What they like, that let them do.

85
"With folded arms and steady eyes,
And little fear, and less surprise,
Look upon them as they slay
Till their rage has died away,

86
"Then they will return with shame
To the place from which they came,
And the blood thus shed will speak
In hot blushes on their cheek.

87
"Every woman in the land
Will point at them as they stand—
They will hardly dare to greet
Their acquaintance in the street.

88
"And the bold, true warriors
Who have hugged Danger in wars
Will turn to those who would be free,
Ashamed of such base company.

89
"And that slaughter to the Nation
Shall steam up like inspiration,
Eloquent, oracular;
A volcano heard afar.

90
"And these words shall then become
Like Oppression's thundered doom
Ringing through each heart and brain,
Heard again—again—again—

91
"Rise like Lions after slumber
In unvanquishable number—
Shake your chains to earth like dew
Which in sleep had fallen on you—
Ye are many, they are few."
—1832 (1819)

Song To The Men Of England[1]

1
Men of England, wherefore plough
For the lords who lay ye low?
Wherefore weave with toil and care
The rich robes your tyrants wear?

2
Wherefore feed, and clothe, and save,
From the cradle to the grave,
Those ungrateful drones who would
Drain your sweat—nay, drink your blood?

3
Wherefore, Bees of England, forge
Many a weapon, chain, and scourge,
That these stingless drones may spoil
The forced produce of your toil?

4
Have ye leisure, comfort, calm,
Shelter, food, love's gentle balm?
Or what is it ye buy so dear
With your pain and with your fear?

5
The seed ye sow, another reaps;
The wealth ye find, another keeps;
The robes ye weave, another wears;
The arms ye forge, another bears.

[1] *Song … England* Composed in 1819, during a time of economic depression and social turmoil following the end of the Napoleonic Wars. In this song, which became a hymn for the British labor movement, Shelley urges the proletariat to force change in the social and economic order.

6

Sow seed—but let no tyrant reap;
Find wealth—let no impostor heap;
Weave robes—let not the idle wear;
Forge arms—in your defence to bear.

7

Shrink to your cellars, holes, and cells;
In halls ye deck another dwells.
Why shake the chains ye wrought? Ye see
The steel ye tempered glance on[1] ye.

8

With plough and spade, and hoe and loom,
Trace your grave, and build your tomb,
And weave your winding-sheet, till fair
England be your sepulchre.
—1839 (1819)

England in 1819

An old, mad, blind, despised, and dying king,[2]
Princes, the dregs of their dull race, who flow
Through public scorn—mud from a muddy spring—
Rulers who neither see, nor feel, nor know,
But leech-like to their fainting country cling,
Till they drop, blind in blood, without a blow—
A people starved and stabbed in the untilled field[3]—
An army, which liberticide and prey
Makes as a two-edged sword to all who wield—
Golden and sanguine laws[4] which tempt and slay;
Religion Christless, Godless—a book sealed;
A Senate, Time's worst statute, unrepealed,[5]
Are graves, from which a glorious Phantom[6] may
Burst, to illumine our tempestuous day.
—1839

[1] *glance on* Strike obliquely.

[2] *old mad … king* George III, who was declared insane in 1811. His sons were known for their corruption and their licentious behavior.

[3] *A people … field* Reference to the massacre at St. Peter's Field on 16 August 1819 (the Peterloo Massacre), when the militia used undue force to disperse a crowd of men, women, and children who were peacefully demonstrating for political reform. Several people were killed and hundreds more injured (see "The Mask of Anarchy").

[4] *Gold … laws* I.e., laws, bought with gold, that lead to bloodshed.

[5] *Time's … unrepealed* Laws against Catholics and Dissenters.

A Defence of Poetry

This essay, begun in 1822 and never completed, was written in response to an 1820 essay by Shelley's friend Thomas Love Peacock called "The Four Ages of Poetry." In this partially-ironic essay, Peacock describes four cycles through which poetry passes: the first is an iron age of crude folk ballads, medieval romances, etc; the second, the gold age, contains the great epics of Homer, Dante, and Milton; the silver age contains the "derivative" poetry of the Augustan poets (who included John Dryden and Alexander Pope; and the fourth stage, the age of brass, is that of Peacock's contemporaries, whom he claimed were markedly inferior. Criticizing Romantic poets such as Byron, Coleridge, and Wordsworth, Peacock urged the men of his generation to apply themselves to new sciences, such as astronomy, economics, politics, mathematics, or chemistry, instead of poetry. Though Shelley recognized Peacock's satirical humor, he also acknowledged that Peacock had put his finger on a common bias of the time—both in the theories of Utilitarian philosophers and in general public opinion—in favor of economic growth and scientific progress over creativity and humanitarian concerns. It was this bias that he attempted to correct in his *Defence.*

from *A Defence of Poetry*, *or Remarks Suggested by an Essay Entitled "The Four Ages of Poetry"*

According to one mode of regarding those two classes of mental action which are called reason and imagination, the former may be considered as mind contemplating the relations borne by one thought to another, however produced; and the latter, as mind acting upon those thoughts so as to colour them with its own light, and composing from them, as from elements, other

[6] *a glorious Phantom* I.e., revolution.

thoughts, each containing within itself the principle of its own integrity. The one is the τὸ ποιειν,[1] or the principle of synthesis, and has for its objects those forms which are common to universal nature and existence itself; the other is the τὸ λογιζειν[2] or principle of analysis, and its action regards the relations of things, simply as relations; considering thoughts, not in their integral unity, but as the algebraical representations which conduct to certain general results. Reason is the enumeration of quantities already known; imagination is the perception of the value of those quantities, both separately and as a whole. Reason respects the differences, and imagination the similitudes of things. Reason is to Imagination as the instrument to the agent, as the body to the spirit, as the shadow to the substance.

Poetry, in a general sense, may be defined to be "the expression of the Imagination": and poetry is connate with the origin of man. Man is an instrument over which a series of external and internal impressions are driven, like the alternations of an ever-changing wind over an Æolian lyre,[3] which move it by their motion to ever-changing melody. But there is a principle within the human being, and perhaps within all sentient beings, which acts otherwise than in the lyre, and produces not melody alone, but harmony, by an internal adjustment of the sounds or motions thus excited to the impressions which excite them. It is as if the lyre could accommodate its chords to the motions of that which strikes them, in a determined proportion of sound; even as the musician can accommodate his voice to the sound of the lyre. A child at play by itself will express its delight by its voice and motions; and every inflexion of tone and every gesture will bear exact relation to a corresponding antitype in the pleasurable impressions which awakened it; it will be the reflected image of that impression; and as the lyre trembles and sounds after the wind has died away, so the child seeks, by prolonging in its voice and motions the duration of the effect, to prolong also a consciousness of the cause. In relation to the objects which delight a child, these expressions are what poetry is to higher objects. The savage (for the savage is to ages what the child is to years) expresses the emotions produced in him by surrounding objects in a similar manner; and language and gesture, together with plastic[4] or pictorial imitation, become the image of the combined effect of those objects, and of his apprehension of them. Man in society, with all his passions and his pleasures, next becomes the object of the passions and pleasures of man; an additional class of emotions produces an augmented treasure of expressions; and language, gesture, and the imitative arts become at once the representation and the medium, the pencil and the picture, the chisel and the statue, the chord and the harmony. The social sympathies, or those laws from which as from its elements society results, begin to develop themselves from the moment that two human beings coexist; the future is contained within the present as the plant within the seed; and equality, diversity, unity, contrast, mutual dependence, become the principles alone capable of affording the motives according to which the will of a social being is determined to action, inasmuch as he is social; and constitute pleasure in sensation, virtue in sentiment, beauty in art, truth in reasoning, and love in the intercourse of kind. Hence men, even in the infancy of society, observe a certain order in their words and actions, distinct from that of the objects and the impressions represented by them, all expression being subject to the laws of that from which it proceeds. But let us dismiss those more general considerations which might involve an enquiry into the principles of society itself, and restrict our view to the manner in which the imagination is expressed upon its forms.

In the youth of the world, men dance and sing and imitate natural objects, observing[5] in these actions, as in all others, a certain rhythm or order. And, although all men observe a similar, they observe not the same order, in the motions of the dance, in the melody of the song, in the combinations of language, in the series of their imitations of natural objects. For there is a certain order or rhythm belonging to each of these classes of mimetic representation, from which the hearer and the spectator

[1] τὸ ποιειν Greek: making.

[2] τὸ λογιζειν Greek: reasoning.

[3] *Æolian lyre* Stringed instrument that produces music when exposed to wind.

[4] *plastic* Formative.

[5] *observing* Following.

receive an intenser and purer pleasure than from any other: the sense of an approximation to this order has been called taste, by modern writers. Every man in the infancy of art observes an order which approximates more or less closely to that from which this highest delight results: but the diversity is not sufficiently marked, as that its gradations should be sensible, except in those instances where the predominance of this faculty of approximation to the beautiful (for so we may be permitted to name the relation between this highest pleasure and its cause) is very great. Those in whom it exists in excess are poets, in the most universal sense of the word; and the pleasure resulting from the manner in which they express the influence of society or nature upon their own minds, communicates itself to others, and gathers a sort of reduplication from that community. Their language is vitally metaphorical; that is, it marks the before unapprehended relations of things, and perpetuates their apprehension, until the words which represent them, become through time signs for portions or classes of thoughts instead of pictures of integral thoughts; and then if no new poets should arise to create afresh the associations which have been thus disorganized, language will be dead to all the nobler purposes of human intercourse. These similitudes or relations are finely said by Lord Bacon to be "the same footsteps of nature impressed upon the various subjects of the world"[1]—and he considers the faculty which perceives them as the storehouse of axioms common to all knowledge. In the infancy of society every author is necessarily a poet, because language itself is poetry; and to be a poet is to apprehend the true and the beautiful, in a word the good which exists in the relation, subsisting, first between existence and perception, and secondly between perception and expression. Every original language near to its source is in itself the chaos of a cyclic poem:[2] the copiousness of lexicography and the distinctions of grammar are the works of a later age, and are merely the catalogue and the form of the creations of Poetry.

But Poets, or those who imagine and express this indestructible order, are not only the authors of language and of music, of the dance and architecture and statuary and painting: they are the institutors of laws, and the founders of civil society and the inventors of the arts of life and the teachers, who draw into a certain propinquity with the beautiful and the true that partial apprehension of the agencies of the invisible world which is called religion. Hence all original religions are allegorical, or susceptible of allegory, and like Janus have a double face of false and true.[3] Poets, according to the circumstances of the age and nation in which they appeared, were called in the earlier epochs of the world legislators or prophets:[4] a poet essentially comprises and unites both these characters. For he not only beholds intensely the present as it is, and discovers those laws according to which present things ought to be ordered, but he beholds the future in the present, and his thoughts are the germs of the flower and the fruit of latest time. Not that I assert poets to be prophets in the gross sense of the word, or that they can foretell the form as surely as they foreknow the spirit of events: such is the pretence of superstition which would make poetry an attribute of prophecy, rather than prophecy an attribute of poetry. A Poet participates in the eternal, the infinite, and the one; as far as relates to his conceptions, time and place and number are not. The grammatical forms which express the moods of time, and the difference of persons and the distinction of place, are convertible with respect to the highest poetry without injuring it as poetry, and the choruses of Æschylus, and the book of Job, and Dante's Paradise[5] would afford, more than any other writings, examples of this fact, if the limits of this essay did not forbid citation. The creations of sculpture, painting, and music are illustra-

[1] *the same ... world* From Francis Bacon's *Of the Advancement of Learning* (1605) 3.1.

[2] *cyclic poem* Set of poems dealing with the same subject (though not always by the same author). The "Arthurian Cycle," a series of poems about the court of King Arthur, is one example of the genre.

[3] *like Janus ... true* Janus, the Roman god of war, of doorways, and of beginnings and endings (after whom the month of January is named) is generally depicted with two faces, one looking forward and one back.

[4] *were called ... prophets* Cf. Sir Philip Sidney's *Defence of Poesy* (1595), in which he points out that *vates*, the Latin word for poet, also means diviner or prophet.

[5] *Æschylus* Greek tragic dramatist (c. 525–456 BCE); *Dante's Paradise* Reference to Italian poet Dante Alighieri's fourteenth-century work, *The Divine Comedy*, which describes a journey from Hell, through Purgatory, to Paradise.

tions still more decisive.

Language, colour, form, and religious and civil habits of action are all the instruments and materials of poetry; they may be called poetry by that figure of speech which considers the effect as a synonym of the cause. But poetry in a more restricted sense expresses those arrangements of language, and especially metrical language, which are created by that imperial faculty whose throne is curtained within the invisible nature of man. And this springs from the nature itself of language, which is a more direct representation of the actions and passions of our internal being, and is susceptible of more various and delicate combinations, than colour, form, or motion, and is more plastic and obedient to the control of that faculty of which it is the creation. For language is arbitrarily produced by the Imagination and has relation to thoughts alone; but all other materials, instruments and conditions of art, have relations among each other, which limit and interpose between conception and expression. The former is as a mirror which reflects, the latter as a cloud which enfeebles, the light of which both are mediums of communication. Hence the fame of sculptors, painters and musicians, although the intrinsic powers of the great masters of these arts, may yield in no degree to that of those who have employed language as the hieroglyphic of their thoughts, has never equalled that of poets in the restricted sense of the term; as two performers of equal skill will produce unequal effects from a guitar and a harp. The fame of legislators and founders of religions, so long as their institutions last, alone seems to exceed that of poets in the restricted sense; but it can scarcely be a question whether, if we deduct the celebrity which their flattery of the gross opinions of the vulgar usually conciliates, together with that which belonged to them in their higher character of poets, any excess will remain.

We have thus circumscribed the meaning of the word Poetry within the limits of that art which is the most familiar and the most perfect expression of the faculty itself. It is necessary however to make the circle still narrower, and to determine the distinction between measured and unmeasured language; for the popular division into prose and verse is inadmissible in accurate philosophy. Sounds as well as thoughts have relation both between each other and towards that which they represent, and a perception of the order of those relations has always been found connected with a perception of the order of the relations of thoughts. Hence the language of poets has ever affected a certain uniform and harmonious recurrence of sound, without which it were not poetry, and which is scarcely less indispensable to the communication of its influence, than the words themselves, without reference to that peculiar order.…

A poem is the very image of life expressed in its eternal truth. There is this difference between a story and a poem, that a story is a catalogue of detached facts, which have no other bond of connection than time, place, circumstance, cause and effect; the other is the creation of actions according to the unchangeable forms of human nature, as existing in the mind of the creator, which is itself the image of all other minds. The one is partial, and applies only to a definite period of time, and a certain combination of events which can never again recur; the other is universal, and contains within itself the germ of a relation to whatever motives or actions have place in the possible varieties of human nature.…

Poetry is ever accompanied with pleasure: all spirits on which it falls open themselves to receive the wisdom which is mingled with its delight. In the infancy of the world, neither poets themselves nor their auditors are fully aware of the excellence of poetry: for it acts in a divine and unapprehended manner, beyond and above consciousness; and it is reserved for future generations to contemplate and measure the mighty cause and effect in all the strength and splendour of their union. Even in modern times, no living poet ever arrived at the fulness of his fame; the jury which sits in judgement upon a poet, belonging as he does to all time, must be composed of his peers: it must be impanelled by Time from the selectest of the wise of many generations. A Poet is a nightingale, who sits in darkness and sings to cheer its own solitude with sweet sounds; his auditors are as men entranced by the melody of an unseen musician, who feel that they are moved and softened, yet know not whence or why. The poems of Homer and his contemporaries were the delight of infant Greece; they were the elements of that social system which is the column upon which all succeeding civilization has reposed. Homer embodied the ideal perfection of his age in human character; nor can we doubt that those who read his verses were awakened to an ambition of becoming like to Achilles, Hector and Ulysses:[1] the truth and beauty of friendship, patriotism, and persevering devotion to an object were unveiled to the depths in these immortal creations: the sentiments of the auditors must have been refined and enlarged by a sympathy with such great and lovely impersonations, until from admiring they imitated, and from imitation they identified themselves with the objects of their admiration....

The whole objection, however, of the immorality of poetry[2] rests upon a misconception of the manner in which poetry acts to produce the moral improvement of man. Ethical science[3] arranges the elements which poetry has created, and propounds schemes and proposes examples of civil and domestic life: nor is it for want of admirable doctrines that men hate, and despise, and censure, and deceive, and subjugate one another. But Poetry acts in another and diviner manner. It awakens and enlarges the mind itself by rendering it the receptacle of a thousand unapprehended combinations of thought. Poetry lifts the veil from the hidden beauty of the world, and makes familiar objects be as if they were not familiar; it reproduces[4] all that it represents, and the impersonations clothed in its Elysian[5] light stand thenceforward in the minds of those who have once contemplated them, as memorials of that gentle and exalted content which extends itself over all thoughts and actions with which it coexists. The great secret of morals is Love; or a going out of our own nature, and an identification of ourselves with the beautiful which exists in thought, action, or person not our own. A man, to be greatly good, must imagine intensely and comprehensively; he must put himself in the place of another and of many others; the pains and pleasures of his species must become his own. The great instrument of moral good is the imagination; and poetry administers to the effect by acting upon the cause. Poetry enlarges the circumference of the imagination by replenishing it with thoughts of ever new delight, which have the power of attracting and assimilating to their own nature all other thoughts, and which form new intervals and interstices whose void for ever craves fresh food. Poetry strengthens that faculty which is the organ of the moral nature of man, in the same manner as exercise strengthens a limb. A Poet therefore would do ill to embody his own conceptions of right and wrong, which are usually those of his place and time, in his poetical creations, which participate in neither. By this assumption of the inferior office of interpreting the effect, in which perhaps after all he might acquit himself but imperfectly, he would resign the glory in a participation in the cause. There was little danger that Homer, or any of the eternal poets, should have so far misunderstood themselves as to have abdicated this throne of their widest dominion. Those in whom the poetical faculty, though great, is less intense, as Euripides, Lucan, Tasso, Spenser,[6] have frequently affected a moral aim, and the effect of their poetry is diminished in exact proportion to the degree in which they compel us to advert to this purpose....

The drama at Athens, or wheresoever else it may have approached to its perfection, coexisted with the moral and intellectual greatness of the age. The tragedies of the Athenian poets are as mirrors in which the spectator beholds himself, under a thin disguise of circumstance, stript of all but that ideal perfection and energy which every one feels to be the internal type of all that he loves, admires, and would become. The imagination is enlarged by a sympathy with pains and passions so mighty that they distend in their conception the capacity of that by which they are conceived; the good affections are strengthened by pity, indignation, terror and sorrow; and an exalted calm is prolonged from the satiety of this high exercise of them into the tumult of familiar life; even crime is disarmed of half its horror and all its contagion by being represented as the

[1] *Achilles, Hector and Ulysses* Trojan and Greek heroes in Homer's *Iliad* and *Odyssey*.

[2] *immorality of poetry* An objection voiced by Plato in his *Republic*, in which he says that poetry often depicts characters who are morally imperfect and whose actions do not provide suitable examples for readers.

[3] *Ethical science* Moral philosophy.

[4] *reproduces* I.e., produces or creates anew.

[5] *Elysian* I.e., paradisical. From Elysium, the paradise where the blessed reside after death, according to Greek myth.

[6] *Euripides* Greek tragedian of the fifth century BCE; *Lucan* Roman poet of the first century CE; *Tasso* Torquato Tasso, Italian epic poet of the sixteenth century; *Spenser* Edmund Spenser, sixteenth-century epic poet; author of *The Faerie Queene*.

fatal consequence of the unfathomable agencies of nature; error is thus divested of its wilfulness; men can no longer cherish it as the creation of their choice. In a drama of the highest order there is little food for censure or hatred; it teaches rather self-knowledge and self-respect. Neither the eye nor the mind can see itself, unless reflected upon that which it resembles. The drama, so long as it continues to express poetry, is as a prismatic and many-sided mirror, which collects the brightest rays of human nature and divides and reproduces them from the simplicity of these elementary forms, and touches them with majesty and beauty, and multiplies all that it reflects, and endows it with the power of propagating its like wherever it may fall.

But in periods of the decay of social life, the drama sympathizes with that decay. Tragedy becomes a cold imitation of the form of the great masterpieces of antiquity, divested of all harmonious accompaniment of the kindred arts; and often the very form misunderstood: or a weak attempt to teach certain doctrines, which the writer considers as moral truths; and which are usually no more than specious flatteries of some gross vice or weakness with which the author in common with his auditors are infected....

The drama being that form under which a greater number of modes of expression of poetry are susceptible of being combined than any other, the connection of poetry and social good is more observable in the drama than in whatever other form: and it is indisputable that the highest perfection of human society has ever corresponded with the highest dramatic excellence; and that the corruption or the extinction of the drama in a nation where it has once flourished, is a mark of a corruption of manners, and an extinction of the energies which sustain the soul of social life. But, as Machiavelli[1] says of political institutions, that life may be preserved and renewed, if men should arise capable of bringing back the drama to its principles. And this is true with respect to poetry in its most extended sense: all language, institution and form, require not only to be produced but to be sustained: the office and character of a poet participates in the divine nature as regards providence, no less than as regards creation.

... It is admitted that the exercise of the imagination is most delightful, but it is alleged that that of reason is more useful. Let us examine as the grounds of this distinction, what is here meant by Utility. Pleasure or good, in a general sense, is that which the consciousness of a sensitive and intelligent being seeks, and in which when found it acquiesces. There are two kinds of pleasure, one durable, universal, and permanent; the other transitory and particular. Utility may either express the means of producing the former or the latter. In the former sense, whatever strengthens and purifies the affections, enlarges the imagination, and adds spirit to sense, is useful. But the meaning in which the Author of the Four Ages of Poetry seems to have employed the word utility is the narrower one of banishing the importunity of the wants of our animal nature, the surrounding men with security of life, the dispersing the grosser delusions of superstition, and the conciliating such a degree of mutual forbearance among men as may consist with the motives of personal advantage.

Undoubtedly the promoters of utility in this limited sense have their appointed office in society. They follow the footsteps of poets, and copy the sketches of their creations into the book of common life. They make space, and give time. Their exertions are of the highest value so long as they confine their administration of the concerns of the inferior powers of our nature within the limits due to the superior ones. But whilst the sceptic destroys gross superstitions, let him spare to deface, as some of the French writers have defaced, the eternal truths charactered upon the imaginations of men. Whilst the mechanist abridges, and the political economist combines, labour, let them beware that their speculations, for want of correspondence with those first principles which belong to the imagination, do not tend, as they have in modern England, to exasperate at once the extremes of luxury and want. They have exemplified the saying, "To him that hath, more shall be given; and from him that hath not, the little that he hath shall be taken away."[2] The rich have become richer, and the poor have become poorer; and the vessel of the

[1] *Machiavelli* Niccolo Machiavelli (1469–1527), author of the political treatise *The Prince*.

[2] *To him ... away* Repeatedly said by Jesus (Matthew 25.29, Mark 4.25, Luke 8.18 and 19.26).

state is driven between the Scylla and Charybdis[1] of anarchy and despotism. Such are the effects which must ever flow from an unmitigated exercise of the calculating faculty.

It is difficult to define pleasure in its highest sense; the definition involving a number of apparent paradoxes. For, from an inexplicable defect of harmony in the constitution of human nature, the pain of the inferior is frequently connected with the pleasures of the superior portions of our being. Sorrow, terror, anguish, despair itself are often the chosen expressions of an approximation to the highest good. Our sympathy in tragic fiction depends on this principle; tragedy delights by affording a shadow of the pleasure which exists in pain. This is the source also of the melancholy which is inseparable from the sweetest melody. The pleasure that is in sorrow is sweeter than the pleasure of pleasure itself. And hence the saying, "It is better to go to the house of mourning, than to the house of mirth."[2] Not that this highest species of pleasure is necessarily linked with pain. The delight of love and friendship, the ecstasy of the admiration of nature, the joy of the perception and still more of the creation of poetry is often wholly unalloyed.

The production and assurance of pleasure in this highest sense is true utility. Those who produce and preserve this pleasure are Poets or poetical philosophers.

The exertions of Locke, Hume, Gibbon, Voltaire, Rousseau,[3] and their disciples, in favour of oppressed and deluded humanity, are entitled to the gratitude of mankind. Yet it is easy to calculate the degree of moral and intellectual improvement which the world would have exhibited, had they never lived. A little more nonsense would have been talked for a century or two; and perhaps a few more men, women, and children, burnt as heretics. We might not at this moment have been congratulating each other on the abolition of the Inquisition in Spain.[4] But it exceeds all imagination to conceive what would have been the moral condition of the world if neither Dante, Petrarch, Boccaccio, Chaucer, Shakespeare, Calderon,[5] Lord Bacon, nor Milton, had ever existed; if Raphael and Michael Angelo[6] had never been born; if the Hebrew poetry had never been translated; if a revival of the study of Greek literature had never taken place; if no monuments of ancient sculpture had been handed down to us; and if the poetry of the religion of the ancient world had been extinguished together with its belief. The human mind could never, except by the intervention of these excitements, have been awakened to the invention of the grosser sciences, and that application of analytical reasoning to the aberrations of society, which it is now attempted to exalt over the direct expression of the inventive and creative faculty itself.

... The cultivation of those sciences which have enlarged the limits of the empire of man over the external world, has, for want of the poetical faculty, proportionally circumscribed those of the internal world; and man, having enslaved the elements, remains himself a slave. To what but a cultivation of the mechanical arts in a degree disproportioned to the presence of the creative faculty, which is the basis of all knowledge, is to be attributed the abuse of all invention for abridging and combining labour, to the exasperation of the inequality of mankind? From what other cause has it arisen that the discoveries which should have lightened, have added a weight to the curse imposed on Adam? Poetry, and the principle of Self, of which money is the visible incarnation, are the God and the Mammon of the world.[7]

The functions of the poetical faculty are two-fold; by one it creates new materials of knowledge, and power

[1] *Scylla and Charybdis* A group of rocks and a whirlpool located at the Strait of Messina (between Sicily and mainland Italy).

[2] *It is ... mirth* From Ecclesiastes 7.2.

[3] *Locke ... Rousseau* John Locke, David Hume, Edward Gibbon, François-Marie Arouet Voltaire, and Jean-Jacques Rousseau, noted philosophers of the seventeenth and eighteenth centuries.

[4] *We might ... Spain* The Inquisition was suspended in 1820 (the year before Shelley wrote this essay) and abolished permanently in 1834.

[5] *Petrarch* Fourteenth-century Italian poet, famous for his love lyrics; *Boccaccio* Italian poet, author of the *Decameron* (1351–3); *Calderon* Seventeenth-century Spanish poet and dramatist.

[6] *Raphael and Michael Angelo* Italian Renaissance painters.

[7] *God and ... world* Cf. Matthew 6.24: "No man can serve two masters: for either he will hate the one, and love the other; or else he will hold to the one, and despise the other. Ye cannot serve God and Mammon," Mammon being the false idol of worldly possessions.

and pleasure; by the other it engenders in the mind a desire to reproduce and arrange them according to a certain rhythm and order which may be called the beautiful and the good. The cultivation of poetry is never more to be desired than at periods when, from an excess of the selfish and calculating principle, the accumulation of the materials of external life exceed the quantity of the power of assimilating them to the internal laws of human nature. The body has then become too unwieldy for that which animates it.

Poetry is indeed something divine. It is at once the centre and circumference of knowledge; it is that which comprehends all science, and that to which all science must be referred. It is at the same time the root and blossom of all other systems of thought: it is that from which all spring, and that which adorns all; and that which, if blighted, denies the fruit and the seed, and withholds from the barren world the nourishment and the succession of the scions[1] of the tree of life. It is the perfect and consummate surface and bloom of things; it is as the odour and the colour of the rose to the texture of the elements which compose it, as the form and the splendour of unfaded beauty to the secrets of anatomy and corruption. What were Virtue, Love, Patriotism, Friendship &c.—what were the scenery of this beautiful Universe which we inhabit—what were our consolations on this side of the grave—and what were our aspirations beyond it—if Poetry did not ascend to bring light and fire from those eternal regions where the owl-winged faculty of calculation dare not ever soar? Poetry is not like reasoning, a power to be exerted according to the determination of the will. A man cannot say, "I will compose poetry." The greatest poet even cannot say it: for the mind in creation is as a fading coal which some invisible influence, like an inconstant wind, awakens to transitory brightness: this power arises from within, like the colour of a flower which fades and changes as it is developed, and the conscious portions of our natures are unprophetic either of its approach or its departure. …

Poetry is the record of the best and happiest moments of the happiest and best minds. We are aware of evanescent visitations of thought and feeling sometimes associated with place or person, sometimes regarding our own mind alone, and always arising unforeseen and departing unbidden, but elevating and delightful beyond all expression: so that even in the desire and the regret they leave, there cannot but be pleasure, participating as it does in the nature of its object. It is as it were the interpenetration of a diviner nature through our own; but its footsteps are like those of a wind over a sea, which the coming calm erases, and whose traces remain only as on the wrinkled sand which paves it. These and corresponding conditions of being are experienced principally by those of the most delicate sensibility and the most enlarged imagination; and the state of mind produced by them is at war with every base desire. The enthusiasm of virtue, love, patriotism, and friendship is essentially linked with these emotions; and whilst they last, self appears as what it is, an atom to a Universe. Poets are not only subject to these experiences as spirits of the most refined organization, but they can colour all that they combine with the evanescent hues of this ethereal world; a word, a trait in the representation of a scene or a passion, will touch the enchanted chord, and reanimate, in those who have ever experienced these emotions, the sleeping, the cold, the buried image of the past. Poetry thus makes immortal all that is best and most beautiful in the world; it arrests the vanishing apparitions which haunt the interlunations[2] of life, and veiling them or in language or in form sends them forth among mankind, bearing sweet news of kindred joy to those with whom their sisters abide—abide, because there is no portal of expression from the caverns of the spirit which they inhabit into the universe of things. Poetry redeems from decay the visitations of the divinity in man.

Poetry turns all things to loveliness; it exalts the beauty of that which is most beautiful, and it adds beauty to that which is most deformed: it marries exultation and horror, grief and pleasure, eternity and change; it subdues to union under its light yoke all irreconcilable things. It transmutes all that it touches, and every form moving within the radiance of its presence is changed by wondrous sympathy to an incarnation of the spirit which it breathes; its secret

[1] *scions* Shoots.

[2] *interlunations* Period between an old and a new moon; period of darkness.

alchemy turns to potable[1] gold the poisonous waters which flow from death through life; it strips the veil of familiarity from the world, and lays bare the naked and sleeping beauty which is the spirit of its forms.

All things exist as they are perceived: at least in relation to the percipient. "The mind is its own place, and of itself can make a heaven of hell, a hell of heaven."[2] But poetry defeats the curse which binds us to be subjected to the accident of surrounding impressions. And whether it spreads its own figured curtain or withdraws life's dark veil from before the scene of things, it equally creates for us a being within our being. It makes us the inhabitants of a world to which the familiar world is a chaos. It reproduces the common universe of which we are portions and percipients, and it purges from our inward sight the film of familiarity which obscures from us the wonder of our being. It compels us to feel that which we perceive, and to imagine that which we know. It creates anew the universe after it has been annihilated in our minds by the recurrence of impressions blunted by reiteration....

The first part of these remarks has related to Poetry in its elements and principles; and it has been shown, as well as the narrow limits assigned them would permit, that what is called poetry, in a restricted sense, has a common source with all other forms of order and of beauty according to which the materials of human life are susceptible of being arranged, and which is poetry in an universal sense.

The second part[3] will have for its object an application of these principles to the present state of the cultivation of Poetry, and a defence of the attempt to idealize the modern forms of manners and opinion, and compel them into a subordination to the imaginative and creative faculty. For the literature of England, an energetic development of which has ever preceded or accompanied a great and free development of the national will, has arisen as it were from a new birth. In spite of the low-thoughted envy which would undervalue contemporary merit, our own will be a memorable age in intellectual achievements, and we live among such philosophers and poets as surpass beyond comparison any who have appeared since the last national struggle for civil and religious liberty.[4] The most unfailing herald, companion, and follower of the awakening of a great people to work a beneficial change in opinion or institution, is Poetry. At such periods there is an accumulation of the power of communicating and receiving intense and impassioned conceptions respecting man and nature. The persons in whom this power resides, may often, as far as regards many portions of their nature, have little apparent correspondence with that spirit of good of which they are the ministers. But even whilst they deny and abjure, they are yet compelled to serve the Power which is seated upon the throne of their own soul. It is impossible to read the compositions of the most celebrated writers of the present day without being startled with the electric life which burns within their words. They measure the circumference and sound the depths of human nature with a comprehensive and all-penetrating spirit, and they are themselves perhaps the most sincerely astonished at its manifestations, for it is less their spirit than the spirit of the age. Poets are the hierophants[5] of an unapprehended inspiration, the mirrors of the gigantic shadows which futurity casts upon the present, the words which express what they understand not; the trumpets which sing to battle, and feel not what they inspire: the influence which is moved not, but moves.[6] Poets are the unacknowledged legislators of the World.

—1820

[1] *potable* Drinkable. Alchemists sought a liquid form of gold that, when consumed, would be the elixir of life.

[2] *The mind ... heaven* From Satan's speech in Milton's *Paradise Lost* 1.254–55.

[3] *The second part* Shelley did not complete a second part.

[4] *the last ... liberty* I.e., the English Civil War of the 1640s.

[5] *hierophants* Interpreters of sacred mysteries.

[6] *is moved ... moves* Reference to Greek philosopher Aristotle's description of God as the "Unmoved Mover" of the universe.

IN CONTEXT

The Peterloo Massacre

Though Shelley's "The Mask of Anarchy" was not published until years after the Peterloo Massacre, many poems on the subject were published soon after the event—among them the four reprinted below. Robert Shorter's satire "The Bloody Fields of Peterloo! A New Song" appeared attributed to "R.S." in *The Theological and Political Comet*, which Shorter edited, as did the anonymous "A New Song," which in several respects takes an approach parallel to that of the "The Mask of Anarchy." "Stanzas Occasioned by the Manchester Massacre!" (the second stanza of which may be of particular interest in relation to Shelley's poem) and "The Peterloo Man" both appeared in *The Black Dwarf*, a radical weekly periodical, edited by Thomas Wooler, that was widely read among the laboring classes.

In stanza 87 of "The Mask of Anarchy" Shelley imagines that "Every woman in the land / Will point at" the tyrants in accusation. In fact, the role of women at St. Peter's Field and in the Radical Movement generally had already become substantial. In the first of the passages reprinted below from his biography, *Passages in the Life of a Radical*, Samuel Bamford (1788–1872), a prominent political radical, describes the part played by women in the Radical Movement at the time. Bamford led the Middleton contingent to St. Peter's Field the day of the Massacre, and was later charged with treason—though it was determined that his actions were peaceful and orderly, and he was only sentenced to a year in jail for inciting a riot. His account of the Massacre is also excerpted below, as is that of his wife, whose story he included in his biography.

Robert Shorter, The Bloody Field of Peterloo! A New Song (1819)

Heroes of Manchester, all hail!
    Your fame the astonished world shall know;
Th' immortalizing bard can't fail,
    To sing the *deeds* of Peterloo!

The Muse[1] shall soar on daring wing,
    And her ecstatic numbers flow;
But Pindar's[2] muse would fail to sing
    Your *glorious deeds* at Peterloo!

You all shall live in deathless fame,
    For chivalry you there did show;
Children shall lisp the Yeomen's name,
    As Heroes all of Peterloo!

[1] *Muse* In Greek mythology, one of nine daughters of Zeus and Mnemosyne, each of whom presided over and provided inspiration for an aspect of learning or the arts.

[2] *Pindar* Fifth-century BCE Greek poet celebrated for his odes.

How on that memorable day,
    Ye did with martial ardor glow;
And such heroic zeal display,
    All on the plains of Peterloo!

How swelled your breasts with rapture high,
    To meet the *well armed*, bannered foe;
What courage teemed in Yeoman's eye,
    When dashing on to Peterloo!

Methinks I see the mettled° steed, *spirited*
    Trampling the mangled corses° low, *corpses*
Whilst charging round, in furious speed,
    The *bloody field* of Peterloo!!

Methinks I hear the cries, the groans,
    (And view their fatal overthrow)
Heart-rending sighs, and piteous moans,
    Rise from the field of Peterloo!

Methinks I see the crimson flood,
    And mark the well aimed fatal blow,
The Yeoman's sabre died in blood,
    Reeking° on far famed Peterloo! *smeared*

Wives, mothers, children, on the plain,
    In one promiscuous heap, I view;
The husband, son, and father slain,
    Stretched on the field of Peterloo!

But Yeomen's hearts arc formed of steel,
    Ardent to fields of blood they go;
Their gallant souls disdain to feel,
    Whilst dealing death at Peterloo!

My muse the truth shall ne'er deny;
    The good, the wise, the just, we know,
Think you deserve promotion high,
    In *iron case* on Peterloo!!

Anonymous, A New Song (1819)

Rouse, rouse, loyal Britons, your fame to maintain
Nor tamely submit to wear Slavery's chain;
Like Britons stand firm in Humanity's cause,
Asserting with spirit your rights and your laws,

Chor. Thus united and free,
May we ever agree;
And man view each other
As friend and as brother;
And may Britons be happy, as happy can be!

By Justice supported, with rapturous eye,
See the banners of Liberty waving on high;
Her sons are all rallying round at her call,
Resolved by her standard to stand or to fall.

Chor. Thus united, &c.

To the traitors' perdition, whose merciless plan
Is, by Tyranny's force, to destroy Rights of Man,
Your freedom to shackle, your rights to invade,
And, by state-craft and trick, make religion a trade.

Chor. Thus united, &c.

Not long shall the demons o'er Britain have sway,
Not long on her vitals these vultures shall prey;[1]
United and firm all their efforts withstand,
And Oppression and Anarchy chase from our land.

Chor. Thus united, &c.

While Nature, in plenty, her riches doth pour,
And Providence kindly is blessing the store,
With the feelings of Britons, how shall we endure
To see Pride and Cruelty starving the poor?

Chor. Thus united, &c.

Old England, my country, may Heaven thee defend,
On each patriot heart all thy blessings descend;
Thy foes all confounded, thy triumphs secured,
That the sun of thy glory be never obscured!

Chor. Thus united, &c.

[1] *on her vitals … prey* Reference to the Greek myth of Prometheus, a Titan who stole fire from Olympus (the home of the gods) and gave it to humankind. As punishment Zeus chained him to a rock in Hades (the classical underworld), where a vulture fed on his liver, which grew back daily.

Hibernicus, Stanzas Occasioned by the Manchester Massacre! (21 August 1819)

Oh, weep not for those who are freed
From bondage so frightful as ours!
Let *tyranny* mourn for the deed,
And howl o'er the prey she devours!

The mask for a century worn,
Has fallen from her visage at last;
Of all its sham attributes shorn,
Her reign of delusion is past.

In native deformity now
Behold her, how shattered and weak!
With *murder* impressed on her brow,
And *cowardice* blanching her cheek.

With guilt's gloomy terrors bowed down,
She scowls on the smile of the slave!
She shrinks at the patriot's frown;
She *dies* in the grasp of the brave.

Then brief be our wail for the dead,
Whose blood has sealed tyranny's doom;
And the tears that affliction will shed,
Let vengeance, bright flashes illume.

And shame on the passionless thing
Whose soul can *now* slumber within him!
To slavery still let him cling,
For liberty scorns to win him.

Her manlier spirits arouse
At the summons so frightfully given!
And glory exults in their vows,
While virtue records them in Heaven.

Anonymous, The Peterloo Man (1819)

You have heard of the far-renowned Waterloo plains,
Where the sun, horror-struck at the slaughter, declined;
Where courage to frenzy abandoned the reins,
And liberty fell 'midst the tears of mankind.

But a scene still more dreadful remains to the story,
Where the blood of the helpless in wild torrents ran;

When women, and children, and grandsires hoary,° *grey-haired*
Fell beneath the fierce sword of the *Peterloo Man*!

How brave were the heroes, what muse can relate;
On the breast of its mother, he bade the babe bleed!
And the mother herself would in vain shun the fate,
That awaited her under the hoofs of his steed.

Stained deep with their gore, how he dashed along,
Of banditti° the first, since fell° murder began; *bandits / savage*
How tremble the feeble among the scared throng,
When they hear the fierce shout of the Peterloo Man!

What groups there assemble, what ferment prevails!
'Tis a nation in search of the savages base;
And justice demands, in her still even scales,
To balance the wretches who Britain disgrace.

Whether Yeomen, or Magistrates, forth be they brought,
Their deeds which a nation indignantly scan,
Well merit the doom to eternity fraught
With the vengeance of God on the Peterloo Man.

from Samuel Bamford, *Passages in the Life of a Radical* (1843)

CHAPTER 28

With the restoration of the Habeas Corpus Act, the agitation for reform was renewed.... Numerous meetings followed in various parts of the country; and Lancashire, and the Stockport borders of Cheshire, were not the last to be concerned in public demonstrations for reform. At one of these meetings, which took place at Lydgate, in Saddleworth, and at which Bagguley, Drummond, Fitton, Haigh, and others, were the principal speakers, I, in the course of an address, insisted on the right, and the propriety also, of females who were present at such assemblages voting, by show of hand, for or against the resolutions. This was a new idea; and the women, who attended numerously on that bleak ridge, were mightily pleased with it; and the men being nothing dissentient, when the resolution was put, the women held up their hands, amid much laughter; and ever from that time, females voted with the men at the radical meetings. I was not then aware that the new impulse thus given to political movement would in a short time be applied to charitable and religious purposes. But it was so; our females voted at every subsequent meetings; it became the practice—female political unions were formed, with their chair-women, committees, and other officials; and from us, the practice was soon borrowed, very judiciously no doubt, and applied in a greater or less degree to the promotion of religious and charitable institutions....

CHAPTER 35 [At the St. Peter's Field meeting, 16 August 1819]

In about half an hour after our arrival at the meeting, the sounds of music, and reiterated shouts, proclaimed the near approach of Mr. Hunt and his party; and in a minute or two they were seen coming from towards Deansgate, preceded by a band of music, and several flags.... Their approach was hailed by one universal shout from probably eighty thousand persons. They threaded their way slowly past us, and through the crowd, which Hunt eyed, I thought with almost as much of astonishment as satisfaction. This spectacle could not be otherwise in his view, than solemnly impressive. Such a mass of human beings he had never beheld till then.... Mr. Hunt, stepping towards the front of the stage, took off his white hat, and addressed the people.

Whilst he was doing so, I proposed to an acquaintance, that, as the speeches and resolutions were not likely to contain anything new to us, and as we could see them in the papers, we should retire awhile, and get some refreshment, of which I stood in much need, being in not very robust health. He assented, and we had got to nearly the outside of the crowd, when a noise and strange murmur arose towards the church. Some persons said it was the Blackburn people coming; and I stood on tip-toe, and looked in the direction whence the noise proceeded, and saw a party of cavalry in blue and white uniform, come trotting sword in hand, round the corner of a garden-wall, and to the front of a row of new houses, where they reined up in a line.

"The soldiers are here," I said, "we must go back and see what this means." "Oh," some one made reply, "they are only come to be ready if there should be any disturbance in the meeting." "Well, let us go back," I said, and we forced our way towards the colours.

On the cavalry drawing up they were received with a shout, of good will, as I understood it. They shouted again, waving their sabres over their heads; and then, slackening rein, and striking spur into their steeds, they dashed forward, and began cutting the people.

"Stand fast," I said, "they are riding upon us, stand fast." And there was a general cry in our quarter of "Stand fast." The cavalry were in confusion: they evidently could not, with all the weight of man and horse, penetrate that compact mass of human beings; and their sabres were plied to hew a way through naked held-up hands, and defenceless heads; and then chopped limbs, and wound-gaping skulls were seen; and groans and cries were mingled with the din of that horrid confusion. "Ah! ah!" "For shame! for shame!" was shouted. Then, "Break! break! they are killing them in front, and they cannot get away"; and there was a general cry of "Break! break." For a moment the crowd held back as in a pause; then was a rush, heavy and resistless as a headlong sea; and a sound like low thunder, with screams, prayers, and imprecations from the crowd-moiled[1] and sabre-doomed, who could not escape.

By this time Hunt and his companions had disappeared from the hustings,[2] and some of the yeomanry, perhaps less sanguinarily disposed than others, were busied in cutting down the flag-staves, and demolishing the flags at the hustings.

On the breaking of the crowd, the yeomanry wheeled; and dashing wherever there was an opening, they followed, pressing and wounding. Many females appeared as the crowd opened; and striplings or mere youths also were found. Their cries were piteous and heart-rending; and would, one might have supposed, have disarmed any human resentment: but here, their appeals were vain. Women, white-vested maids, and tender youths were indiscriminately sabred or trampled; and we have reason for believing that few were the instances in which that forbearance was vouchsafed which they so earnestly implored.

In ten minutes from the commencement of the havoc, the field was an open and almost deserted space. The sun looked down through a sultry and motionless air. The curtains and blinds of the windows within view were all closed. A gentleman or two might occasionally be seen looking out from one of the new houses before-mentioned, near the door of which, a group of persons, (special constables) were collected, and apparently in conversation; others were assisting the wounded, or

[1] *crowd-moiled* Harassed by, or worn out with toiling in, the crowd.

[2] *hustings* Platforms.

carrying off the dead. The hustings remained, with a few broken and hewed flag-staves erect, and a torn and gashed banner or two dropping; whilst over the whole field, were strewed caps, bonnets, hats, shawls, and shoes, and other parts of male and female dress; trampled, torn, and bloody....

from CHAPTER 36

... A number of our people were driven to some timber which lay at the foot of the wall of the Quakers' meeting house. Being pressed by the yeomanry, a number sprung over the balks and defended themselves with stones which they found there. It was not without difficulty, and after several were wounded, that they were driven out. A heroine, a young married woman of our party, with her face all bloody, her hair streaming about her, her bonnet hanging by the string, and her apron weighted with stones, kept her assailant at bay until she fell backwards and was near being taken; but she got away covered with severe bruises. It was near this place, and about this time, that one of the yeomanry was dangerously wounded, and unhorsed, by a blow from the fragment of a brick; and it was supposed to have been flung by this woman....

from CHAPTER 39 [The narrative of Bamford's wife, Jemima]

As a narrative collateral with these passages, the account given by my dear wife, of her attendance at the meeting on Saint Peter's Field, and of some incidents which befell her, may not be devoid of interest to the reader, and certainly will not be out of place, if introduced here. She says:

> I was determined to go to the meeting, and should have followed, even if my husband had refused his consent to my going with the procession. From what I, in common with others, had heard the week previous, "that if the country people went with their caps of liberty, and their banners, and music, the soldiers would be brought to them," I was uneasy, and felt persuaded, in my own mind, that something would be the matter, and I had best go with my husband, and be near him; and if I only saw him I should be more content than in staying at home. I accordingly, he having consented after much persuasion, gave my little girl something to please her, and, promising more on my return, I left her with a careful neighbour woman, and joined some other married females at the head of the procession.
>
> Every time I went aside to look at my husband, and that was often, an ominous impression smote my heart. He looked very serious, I thought, and I felt a foreboding of something evil to befall us that day.
>
> I was dressed plainly as a countrywoman, in my second best attire. My companions were also neatly dressed as the wives of working men; I had seen Mr. Hunt before that time; they had not, and some of them were quite eager to obtain good places, that they might see and hear one of whom so much had been reported.
>
> In going down Mosley Street, I lost sight of my husband. Mrs. Yates, who had hold of my arm, would keep hurrying forward to get a good place, and when the crowd opened for the Middleton procession, Mrs. Yates and myself, and some others of the women, went close to the hustings, quite glad that we had obtained such a situation for seeing and hearing all. My husband got on the stage, but when afterwards I saw him leap down, and lost sight of him, I began to be unhappy.
>
> The crowd seemed to have increased very much, for we became insufferably pressed. We were surrounded by men who were strangers; we were almost suffocated, and to me the heat was quite sickening; but Mrs. Yates, being taller than myself, supported it better.

I felt I could not bear this long, and I became alarmed. I reflected that if there was any more pressure I must faint, and then what would become of me? and I begged of the men to open a way and let me go out, but they would not move. Every moment I became worse, and I told some other men then, who stood in a row, that I was sick, and begged they would let me pass them, and they immediately made a way, and I went down a long passage betwixt two ranks of these men, many of them saying, "Make way, she's sick, she's sick, let her go out," and I passed quite out of the crowd, and, turning to my right, I got on some high ground, on which stood a row of houses—This was Windmill Street.

I thought if I could get to stand at the door of one of those houses, I should have a good view of the meeting, and should perhaps see my husband again; and I kept going further down the row, until I saw a door open, and I stepped within it, the people of the house making no objections.

By this time Mr. Hunt was on the hustings, addressing the people. In a minute or two some soldiers came riding up. The good folks of the house, and some who seemed to be visitors, said, "the soldiers were only come to keep order; they would not meddle with the people"; but I was alarmed. The people shouted, and then the soldiers shouted, waving their swords. Then they rode amongst the people, and there was a great outcry, and a moment after, a man passed without hat, and wiping the blood off his head with his hand, and it ran down his arm in a great stream.

The meeting was all in a tumult; there were dreadful cries; the soldiers kept riding amongst the people, and striking with their swords. I became faint, and turning from the door, I went unobserved down some steps into a cellared passage; and, hoping to escape from the horrid noise, and to be concealed, I crept into a vault, and sat down, faint and terrified, on some fire-wood.

The cries of the multitude outside still continued, and the people of the house, up stairs, kept bewailing most pitifully. They could see all the dreadful work through the window, and their exclamations were so distressing that I put my fingers in my ears to prevent my hearing more; and, on removing them, I understood that a young man had just been brought past, wounded. The front door of the passage before-mentioned soon after opened, and a number of men entered, carrying the body of a decent, middle-aged woman, who had been killed. I thought they were going to put her beside me, and was about to scream, but they took her forward, and deposited her in some premises at the back of the house.

I had sat in my hiding place some time, and the tumult seemed abated, when a young girl, one of the family, came into the vault, and suddenly crouching, she bumped against my knee, and starting up, and seeing another dead woman, as she probably thought, she ran up stairs quite terrified, and told her mother. The good woman, Mrs. Jones, came down with the girl and several others, and, having ascertained that I was living, but sadly distressed, she spoke very kindly, and assisted me to a chair in her front room....

from John Tyas, an account of the events leading up to the massacre, *The Times* 19 August 1819

A club of Female Reformers, amounting in numbers, according to our calculations, 150 came from Oldham; and another, not quite so numerous, from Royton. The first bore a white silk banner, by far the most elegant displayed during the day, inscribed "Major Cartwright's Bill, Annual Parliaments, Universal Suffrage, and Vote by Ballot." The females of Royton bore two red flags, the one inscribed "Let us die like men, and not sold like slaves"; the other "Annual Parliaments and Universal Suffrage."

A group of women of Manchester, attracted by the crowd, came to the corner of the street where we had taken our post. They viewed the Oldham Female Reformers for some time with a look in which compassion and disgust was equally blended, and at last burst out into an indignant exclamation—"Go home to your families, and leave sike-like as these to your husbands and sons, who better understand them." The women who addressed them were of the lower order of life.

Peterloo Massacre (detail), 1819, a print published by Richard Carlile (publisher of the radical newspaper *The Republican* and a speaker at the St. Peter's Field Meeting). The banners read (from left to right) "Manchester Female Reform [Group]," "Universal Suffrage," "Liberty or Death," and "Universal Civil and Religious Liberty." The woman in white on the stage is thought to be Mary Fildes, a leading campaigner for the expansion of the Manchester Female Reform Group. Fildes was slashed by a cavalryman and seriously wounded during the attack, but survived to become an active participant in the Chartist Movement, a working class movement for Parliamentary democracy.

In Context

Youth and Love

Thomas Jefferson Hogg was a close friend of Shelley (and later his biographer). The two were students together at Oxford at the time the following correspondence between the two occurred. Both were expelled from the university later that same year, after the publication of Shelley's *Necessity of Atheism*. Also included below is a long letter by Shelley to William Godwin. Profoundly influenced by Godwin's *Enquiry Concerning Political Justice* (1793), Shelley sought out a correspondence with the author, who would later become his father-in-law.

Letter to T.J. Hogg

Field Place, January 3, 1811

My Dear Friend,

Before we deny or believe the existence of anything, it is necessary that we should have a tolerably clear idea of what it is. The word "God," a vague word, has been, and will continue to be, the source of numberless errors, until it is erased from the nomenclature of philosophy. Does it not imply "the soul of the universe, the intelligent and *necessarily* beneficent, actuating principle"? This it is impossible not to believe in. I may not be able to adduce proofs; but I think that the leaf of a tree, the meanest insect on which we trample, are, in themselves, arguments more conclusive than any which can be advanced, that some vast intellect animates infinity. If we disbelieve *this,* the strongest argument in support of the existence of a future state instantly becomes annihilated. I confess that I think Pope's—

All are but parts of one stupendous whole,[1]

something more than poetry. It has ever been my favourite theory, for the immortal soul, "never to be able to die, never to escape from some shrine as chilling as the clay-formed dungeon which now it inhabits"; it is the future punishment which I can most easily believe in.

Love, love *infinite in extent,* eternal in duration, yet (allowing your theory in that point), perfectible, should be the reward; but can we suppose that this reward will arise, spontaneously, as a necessary appendage to our nature, or that our nature itself could be without cause—a first cause—a God? When do we see effects arise without causes? What causes are there without correspondent effects? Yet here, I swear—and as I break my oaths, may Infinity, Eternity blast me—here I swear that never will I forgive intolerance! It is the only point on which I allow myself to encourage revenge; every moment shall be devoted to my object, which I can spare; and let me hope that it will not be a blow which spends itself, and leaves the wretch at rest—but lasting, long revenge! I am convinced, too, that it is of great disservice to society—that it encourages prejudices, which strike at the root of the dearest, the tenderest of its ties. Oh! how I wish I were the avenger!—that it were mine to crush the demon; to hurl him to his native hell, never to rise again, and thus to establish for ever perfect and universal toleration. I expect to gratify some of this insatiable feeling in poetry. You shall see—you

[1] *All are … whole* Alexander Pope, *Essay on Man* 1.267.

shall hear—how it has injured me. She[1] is no longer mine! she abhors me as a sceptic, as what *she* was before! Oh, bigotry! When I pardon this last, this severest of thy persecutions, may Heaven (if there be wrath in Heaven) blast me! Has vengeance, in its armoury of wrath, a punishment more dreadful? Yet forgive me, I have done; and were it not for your great desire to know *why* I consider myself as the victim of severer anguish, I could not have entered into this brief recital.

I am afraid there is selfishness in the passion of love, for I cannot avoid feeling every instant as if my soul was bursting; but I *will* feel no more! It is selfish. I would feel for others, but for myself—oh! how much rather would I expire in the struggle! Yes, that were a relief! Is suicide wrong? I slept with a loaded pistol and some poison, last night, but did not die. I could not come on Monday, my sister would not part with me; but I must—I will see you soon. My sister is now comparatively happy; she has felt deeply for me. Had it not been for her—had it not been for a sense of what I owed to her, to *you*, I should have bidden you a final farewell some time ago. But can the dead feel; dawns any day-beam on the night of dissolution?

Adieu, my dear friend. Your sincere,

P.B.S.

Letter to T.J. Hogg, 1811

[Undated]

My Dear Friend—

You will perhaps see me before you can answer this; perhaps not; Heavens knows! I shall certainly come to York, but *Harriet Westbrook*[2] will decide whether now or in three weeks. Her father has persecuted her in a most horrible way, by endeavouring to compel her to go to school. She asked my advice: resistance was the answer, at the same time that I essayed to mollify Mr. W. in vain! And in consequence of my advice *she* has thrown herself upon *my* protection. I set off for London on Monday. How flattering a distinction!—I am thinking of ten million things at once.

What have I said? I declare, quite *ludicrous.* I advised her to resist. She wrote to say that resistance was useless, but that she would fly with me, and threw herself upon my protection. We shall have £200 a year: when we find it run short, we must live, I suppose, upon love! Gratitude and admiration all demand that I should love her *for ever.* We shall see you at York. I will hear your arguments for matrimonialism, by which I am now almost convinced. I can get lodgings at York, I suppose. Direct[3] to me at Graham's, 18 Sackville Street, Piccadilly.

Your inclosure of £10 has arrived; I am now indebted to you £30. In spite of philosophy, I am rather ashamed of this unceremonious exsiccation[4] of your financial river. But indeed, my dear friend, the gratitude which I owe you for your society and attachment ought so far to over-balance this consideration as to leave me nothing but that. I must, however, pay you when I can. I suspect that the *strain* is gone for ever. This letter will convince you that I am not under the influence of a *strain.* I am thinking at once of ten million things. I shall come to live near you, as Mr. Peyton.

Ever your most faithful friend,

P.B.S.

I shall be at 18 Sackville Street; at least direct there. Do not send more cash; I shall raise supplies in London.

---

1 *She* Shelley's cousin Harriet Grove, with whom he was briefly in love.

2 *Harriet Westbrook* With whom Shelley eloped on 28 August 1811.

3 *Direct* Send a message or letter.

4 *exsiccation* Complete drying out or absorption.

Joseph Severn, *Percy Bysshe Shelley* (detail), 1845.

Letter to William Godwin

Keswick, 10 January 1812

Sir—

It is not otherwise to be supposed than that I should appreciate your avocations far beyond the pleasure or benefit which can accrue to me from their sacrifice. The time, however, will be small which may be mis-spent in reading this letter; and much individual pleasure as an answer might give me, I have not the vanity to imagine that it will be greater than the happiness elsewhere diffused during the time which its creation will occupy.

You complain that the generalizing character of my letter renders it deficient in interest; that I am not an individual to you. Yet, intimate as I am with your character and your writings, intimacy with *yourself* must in some degree precede this exposure of my peculiarities. It is scarcely possible, however pure be the morality which he has endeavoured to diffuse, but that generalization must characterize the uninvited address of a stranger to a stranger.

I proceed to remedy the fault. I am the son of a man of fortune in Sussex. The habits of thinking of my father and myself never coincided. Passive obedience was inculcated and enforced in my childhood. I was required to love, because it was *my duty* to love: it is scarcely necessary to remark, that coercion obviated its own intention. I was haunted with a passion for the wildest and most extravagant romances. Ancient books of Chemistry and Magic were perused with an enthusiasm of wonder, almost amounting to belief. My sentiments were unrestrained by anything within me; external impediments were numerous and strongly applied; their effect was merely temporary. From a reader, I became a writer of romances; before the age of seventeen I had published two, *St. Irvyn* and *Zastrozzi*, each of which, though quite uncharacteristic of me as now I am, yet serves to mark the state of my mind at the period of their composition. I shall desire them to be sent to you: do not, however, consider this as any obligation to yourself to misapply your valuable time.

It is now a period of more than two years since first I saw your inestimable book of *Political Justice*; it opened to my mind fresh and more extensive views; it materially influenced my character, and I rose from its perusal a wiser and a better man. I was no longer the votary of romance; till then I had existed in an ideal world—now I found that in this universe of ours was enough to excite the interest of the heart, enough to employ the discussions of reason; I beheld, in short, that I had duties to perform. Conceive the effect which the *Political Justice* would have upon a mind before jealous of its independence, participating somewhat singularly in a peculiar susceptibility.

My age is now *nineteen*; at the period to which I allude I was at Eton. No sooner had I formed the principles which I now profess, than I was anxious to disseminate their benefits. This was done without the slightest caution. I was twice expelled,[1] but recalled by the interference of my father. I went to Oxford. Oxonian society was insipid to me, uncongenial with my habits of thinking. I could not descend to common life: the sublime interest of poetry, lofty and exalted achievements, the proselytism of the world, the equalization of its inhabitants, were to me the soul of my soul. You can probably form some idea of the contrast exhibited to my character by those with whom I was surrounded. Classical reading and poetical writing employed me during my residence at Oxford.

In the meantime I became, in the popular sense of the word, a sceptic. I printed a pamphlet, avowing my opinion, and its occasion. I distributed this anonymously to men of thought and

[1] *I was twice expelled* Shelley's friend Jefferson Hogg claimed that Shelley's letters "must be received with caution," not because he intended to deliberately tell falsehoods, but because "he was the creature, the unsuspecting and unresisting victim, of his irresistible imagination." According to Hogg, Shelley was never expelled from Eton, and he never published anything controversial there. He also states that the incident between Shelley and Mr. ——, described in the following paragraph, never occurred, and that Shelley's father never offered him a commission in the army.

learning, wishing that Reason should decide on the case at issue: it was never my intention to deny it. Mr.—, at Oxford, among others, had the pamphet; he showed it to the Master and the Fellows of University College, and *I* was sent for. I was informed, that in case I denied the publication, no more would be said. I refused, and was expelled.

It will be necessary, in order to elucidate this part of my history, to inform you that I am heir by entail to an estate of £6,000 per annum. My principles have induced me to regard the law of primogeniture as an evil of primary magnitude. My father's notions of family honour are incoincident with my knowledge of public good. I will never sacrifice the latter to any consideration. My father has ever regarded me as a blot, a defilement of his honour. He wished to induce me by poverty to accept of some commission in a distant regiment, and in the interim of my absence to prosecute the pamphlet, that a process of outlawry might make the estate, on his death, devolve to my younger brother. These are the leading points of the history of the man before you. Others exist, but I have thought proper to make some selection, not that it is my design to conceal or extenuate any part, but that I should by their enumeration quite outstep the bounds of modesty. Now, it is for you to judge whether, by permitting me to cultivate your friendship, you are exhibiting yourself more really useful than by the pursuance of those avocations, of which the time spent in allowing this cultivation would deprive you. I am now earnestly pursuing studious habits. I am writing "An inquiry into the causes of the failure of the French Revolution to benefit mankind." My plan is that of resolving to lose no opportunity to disseminate truth and happiness.

I am married to a woman whose views are similar to my own. To you, as the regulator and former of my mind, I must ever look with real respect and veneration.

Yours sincerely,

P.B. SHELLEY.

IN CONTEXT

Shelley and Keats

The unfinished letter excerpted below was written to the editor of the *Quarterly Review*, which had published unfavorable notices both of Shelley's own work and of that of Keats. It shows Shelley's conviction that Keats was of a fragile constitution, easily discouraged and demoralized by criticism—a conviction that, after Keats's death, spurred his composition of *Adonais*. Also excerpted below is the response of Leigh Hunt, editor of the radical journal *The Examiner*, to Shelley's *Adonais*.

from Letter to the Editor of the *Quarterly Review*, 1820

Sir,

Should you cast your eye on the signature of this letter before you read the contents, you might imagine that they related to a slanderous paper which appeared in your *Review* some time since. I never notice anonymous attacks....

The case is different with the unfortunate subject of this letter, the author of *Endymion*, to whose feelings and situations I entreat you to allow me to call your attention....

Poor Keats was thrown into a dreadful state of mind by this review, which, I am persuaded, was not written with any intention of producing the effect, to which it has, at least, greatly contributed, of embittering his existence, and inducing a disease, from which there are now but faint hopes of his recovery. The first effects are described to me to have resembled insanity, and it was by assiduous watching that he was restrained from effecting purposes of suicide. The agony of his sufferings at length produced the rupture of a blood vessel in the lungs, and the usual process of consumption[1] appears to have begun. He is coming to pay me a visit in Italy; but I fear that, unless his mind can be kept tranquil, little is to be hoped from the mere influence of climate.

But let me not extort anything from your pity. I have just seen a second volume,[2] published by him evidently in careless despair. I have desired my bookseller to send you a copy, and allow me to solicit your especial attention to the fragment of a poem entitled *Hyperion*, the composition of which was checked by the Review in question.[3] The great proportion of this piece is surely in the very highest style of poetry. I speak impartially, for the canons of taste to which Keats has conformed in his other compositions are the very reverse of my own. I leave you to judge for yourself; if would be an insult to you to suppose that, from motives however honourable, you would lend yourself to a deception of the public.

Leigh Hunt on "Mr. Shelley's New Poem Entitled *Adonais*" (1822)

Since I left London, Mr. Shelley's *Adonais, or Elegy on the Death of Mr. Keats*, has, I find, made its appearance. I have not seen the London edition; but I have an Italian one printed at Pisa, with which I must content myself at present. The other was to have had notes. It is not a poem calculated to be popular, any more than the *Prometheus Unbound*;[4] it is of too abstract and subtle a nature for that purpose; but it will delight the few, to whom Mr. Shelley is accustomed to address himself. Spenser would be pleased with it if he were living. A mere town reader and a Quarterly Reviewer will find it *caviare*.[5] *Adonais,* in short, is such an elegy as poet might be expected to write upon poet. The author has had before him his recollections of Lycidas, of Moschus and Bion, and of the doctrines of Plato; and in the stanza of the most poetical of poets, Spenser, has brought his own genius, in all its etherial beauty, to lead a pomp of Loves, Graces, and Intelligences, in honour of the departed.

Nor is the Elegy to be considered less sincere, because it is full of poetical abstractions. Dr. Johnson would have us believe, that *Lycidas*[6] is not "the effusion of real passion" "Passion," says he, in his usual conclusive tone (as if the force of critic could no further go) "plucks no berries from the myrtle and ivy; nor calls upon Arethuse and Mincius nor tells of rough Satyrs and Fauns with cloven heel. Where there is leisure for fiction, there is little grief."[7] This is on a more genteel commonplace, brought in to put down a vulgar one. Dr. Johnson, like most critics, had no imagination; and because he found nothing natural to his own impulses in the associations of poetry, and saw them so often

---

[1] *consumption* I.e., tuberculosis.

[2] *second volume* Keats's *Lamia and Other Poems* (1820).

[3] *the composition … question* This is not true. Keats had worked on *Hyperion* intermittently for several years and was having difficulty completing it. Shelley here great exaggerates the effects of the review on Keats, who did not attach much importance to the opinions of reviewers. He himself thought *Endymion* to be a mediocre and adolescent poetic attempt.

[4] *Prometheus Unbound* 1820 poem by Shelley.

[5] *caviare* Unpalatable. (Caviar is generally not appreciated by those who have not acquired a taste for it.)

[6] *Lycidas* Pastoral elegy by John Milton (1608–74).

[7] *Passion … little grief* From Samuel Johnson's "Life of Milton" (1779), in which he criticizes Milton's pastoral elegy *Lycidas* for a lack of passion and for "remote allusions and obscure opinions," such as those quoted here. (Myrtle and ivy are used to crown poets; Arethuse, a spring on Ortygia, and Mincius, a river of Mantua, symbolize Greek and Latin pastoral poetry.)

abused by the practice of versifiers inferior to himself, he was willing to conclude that on natural occasions they were always improper. But a poet's world is as real to him as the more palpable one to people in general. He spends his time in it as truly as Dr. Johnson did his in Fleet Street or at the club.[1] Milton felt that the happiest hours he had passed with his friend had been passed in the regions of poetry. He had been accustomed to be transported with him "beyond the visible diurnal sphere" of his fire-side and supper table, things which he could record nevertheless with a due relish. (See the *Epitaphium Damonis*.[2]) The next step was to fancy himself again among them, missing the dear companion of his walks; and then it is that the rivers murmur complainingly, and the flowers hang their heads—which to a truly poetical habit of mind, though to no other, they may literally be said to do, because such is the aspect which they present to an afflicted imagination. "I see nothing in the world but melancholy," is a common phrase with persons who are suffering under a great loss. With ordinary minds in this condition the phrase implies a vague feeling, but still an actual one. The poet, as in other instances, gives it a life and particularity. The practice has doubtless been abused; so much so, that even some imaginative minds may find it difficult at first to fall in with it, however beautifully managed. But the very abuse shows that it is founded in a principle in nature. And a great deal depends upon the character of the poet. What is mere frigidity and affectation in common magazine rhymers, or men of wit and fashion about town, becomes another thing in minds accustomed to live in the sphere I spoke of. It was as unreasonable in Dr. Johnson to sneer at Milton's grief in *Lycidas* as it was reasonable in him to laugh at Prior and Congreve for comparing Chloe to Venus and Diana, and pastoralizing about Queen Mary.[3] Neither the turn of their genius, nor their habits of life, included this sort of ground. We feel that Prior should have stuck to V tuckers and bodices, and Congreve appeared in his proper Court-mourning.

Milton perhaps overdid the matter a little when he personified the poetical enjoyments of his friend and himself under the character of actual shepherds. Mr. Shelley is the more natural in this respect, inasmuch as he is entirely abstract and imaginative, and recalls his lamented acquaintance to mind in no other shape than one strictly poetical. I say acquaintance, because such Mr. Keats was; and it happens, singularly enough, that the few hours which he and Mr. Shelley passed together were almost entirely of a poetical character. I recollect one evening in particular which they spent with the writer of these letters in composing verses on a given subject. But it is not as a mere acquaintance, however poetical, that Mr. Shelley records him. It is as the intimate acquaintance of all lovely and lofty thoughts, as the nursling of the Muse, the hope of her coming days, the creator of additional Beauties and Intelligences for the adornment and the inhabitation of the material world....

---

[1] *Fleet Street* Where Johnson lived; *the club* Johnson's famous Literary Club, which included prominent writers and thinkers such as Edmund Burke, Oliver Goldsmith, and Charles Burney.

[2] *Epitaphium Damonis* 1639 Latin poem by John Milton.

[3] *Prior* Poet Matthew Prior (1664–1721). The poem referred to is "To Chloe Jealous"; *Congreve* Poet and playwright William Congreve (1670–1729). The poem referred to is his "The Mourning Muse of Alexis," written upon the death of Queen Mary in 1694.

Felicia Hemans

1793 – 1835

Felicia Hemans was one of the first English poets to earn a living by writing. Her poetry was in many ways representative of the late Romantic and early Victorian eras, with an emphasis on religious, martial, and domestic themes, but several of her poems—perhaps most notably "Casabianca" and "The Homes of England"—remained enormously popular well into the twentieth century. Writing was in Hemans's day still widely considered incompatible with women's domestic bliss; some have argued that Hemans's own marriage failed because of her literary pursuits. It was certainly the case that, while her work was widely read and widely praised, it was also occasionally mocked, and that gender was at the root of much of the ridicule. (Byron, for example, parodied her as "Mrs. Hewoman.")

Hemans was born Felicia Browne, the fifth of seven children of a Liverpool wine merchant and his wife, the daughter of a foreign diplomat. The failure of her father's business in 1799 caused the family to move to Wales; Felicia adored the countryside and it became the inspiration for much of her poetry. She learned several languages and a great deal about music from her mother, and benefited from a well-stocked family library. She loved Shakespeare as a child and was said to have had an excellent memory for reciting verse. Her own first published volume appeared in 1808, when she was only 14. Although *Poems* received some negative reviews, it sold 1,000 copies and she was encouraged to continue writing. Two of her brothers were then engaged in the British war against Spain and many of the poems are patriotic depictions of Britain in battle. Her brothers passed the volume on to one of their colleagues, Captain Alfred Hemans; he later became her husband. Percy Bysshe Shelley also received her first volume and began a correspondence with the young poet.

Felicia Browne married in 1812, shortly after the publication of her third volume of poetry, *The Domestic Affections and Other Poems.* She and her husband initially lived in her mother's house in Wales, a situation that would eventually prove uncomfortable for Captain Hemans. While Hemans continued to publish and become more popular, Captain Hemans became disillusioned with Wales and moved to Italy in 1818 on grounds of "ill health," never to see his wife again. From this point onwards she supported herself solely by her writing.

Hemans was one of very few British poets to have been in the prime of their writing careers in the 1810s and 1820s. She occupies something of an uneasy position between the Romantics and the Victorians. That she lived into Victoria's era and that her poetry retained a high degree of popularity through the Victorian period may have encouraged modern critics to see Hemans in the light of the standards of a later period; in the past critics perceived her poetry as characterized by powerful rhythms and powerful passions (even by emotional "gush"). And certainly the strength of form and of feeling in poems of patriotic fervor such as "The Homes of England" and "Casabianca" (both of which were learnt by heart by English schoolchildren into the twentieth century) is unquestionable. Yet in her own day, seen against the backdrop of the extravagant passions of Byron and other poets associated with the Romantic Movement, her poetry was praised for its formal and emotional restraint.

Though Hemans's most famous poems are short, she was also successful with long narrative poems, most notably *The Siege of Valencia* (1823), which recounts the epic story of Elmira after her two sons are captured by a Moorish army. And she wrote innovative linked poems, such as those in *Records of Woman* (1828). Though she is often thought of as an important poet of domesticity, Hemans focused at least as much on women acting out their lives on a larger stage.

In 1821 Hemans was awarded the Royal Society of Literature's annual prize of £52.50 (a substantial amount at the time). She was then publishing regularly in British literary magazines, and from 1823, she was earning roughly £200 per year, enough to support herself and her five sons in some comfort. Her work was never out of print, and she was widely read in Britain and in America. The death of her mother in 1827 had a devastating effect on her, however, and from that point onwards she was plagued by poor health.

In her latter years, she rivaled Byron in popularity, and was highly sought after by budding poets and autograph-seekers. She found herself caught, however, between the success she needed to support herself and the masculine characteristics attributed to it, a theme she explores in "Women and Fame." In 1831 Hemans moved to Dublin to live with one of her brothers. She died there in 1835, of a weak heart and the effects of rheumatic fever.

⌘⌘⌘

The Homes of England

Where's the coward that would not dare
To fight for such a land? MARMION[1]

The stately Homes of England,
How beautiful they stand!
Amidst their tall ancestral trees,
O'er all the pleasant land.
The deer across their greensward° bound *turf*
Thro' shade and sunny gleam,
And the swan glides past them with the sound
Of some rejoicing stream.

The merry Homes of England!
Around their hearths by night,
What gladsome looks of household love
Meet, in the ruddy° light! *red-hued*
There woman's voice flows forth in song,
Or childhood's tale is told,
Or lips move tunefully along
Some glorious page of old.

The blessed Homes of England!
How softly on their bowers° *arbors*
Is laid the holy quietness
That breathes from Sabbath-hours!
Solemn, yet sweet, the church-bell's chime
Floats thro' their woods at morn;
All other sounds, in that still time,
Of breeze and leaf are born.

The Cottage Homes of England!
By thousands on her plains,
They are smiling o'er the silvery brooks,
And round the hamlet-fanes.[2]
Thro' glowing orchards forth they peep,
Each from its nook of leaves,
And fearless there the lowly sleep,
As the bird beneath their eaves.

---

[1] *Marmion* Walter Scott's *Marmion: A Tale of Flodden Field* (1808), 4.30. When first published in *Blackwood's Magazine*, the poem had instead the following epigraph from Joanna Baillie, *Ethwald: A Tragedy* (1802) 2.1.2.76–82:

A land of peace,
Where yellow fields unspoil'd, and pastures green,
Mottled with herds and flocks, who crop secure
Their native herbage, nor have ever known
A stranger's stall, smile gladly.
See through its tufted alleys to Heaven's roof
The curling smoke of quiet dwellings rise.

[2] *hamlet-fanes* Weather vanes of the village.

The free, fair Homes of England!
  Long, long, in hut and hall,
May hearts of native proof be rear'd
  To guard each hallow'd wall!
And green for ever be the groves,
  And bright the flowery sod,
Where first the child's glad spirit loves
Its country and its God![1]
—1812

The Land of Dreams

> And dreams, in their development, have breath,
> And tears and tortures, and the touch of joy;
> They leave a weight upon our waking thoughts,
> They make us what we were not—what they will,
> And shake us with the vision that's gone by. BYRON.[2]

Oh spirit land, thou land of dreams!
  A world thou art of mysterious gleams,
Of startling voices, and sounds at strife—
A world of the dead in the hues of life.

Like a wizard's magic-glass° thou art *mirror*
When the wavy shadows float by, and part—
Visions of aspects, now loved, now strange,
Glimmering and mingling in ceaseless change.

Thou art like a city of the past
With its gorgeous halls into fragments cast,
Amidst whose ruins there glide and play
Familiar forms of the world's today.

Thou art like the depths where the seas have birth,
Rich with the wealth that is lost from earth—
All the sere° flowers of our days gone by, *dry*
And the buried gems in thy bosom lie.

Yes, thou art like those dim sea-caves,
A realm of treasures, a realm of graves!
And the shapes through thy mysteries that come and go,
Are of beauty and terror, of power and woe.

But for me, oh thou picture-land of sleep,
Thou art all one world of affections deep—
And wrung from my heart is each flushing dye
That sweeps o'er thy chambers of imagery.

And thy bowers° are fair—even as Eden fair; *arbors*
All the beloved of my soul are there!
The forms my spirit most pines to see,
The eyes whose love hath been life to me:

They are there, and each blessed voice I hear,
Kindly, and joyous, and silvery clear;
But undertones are in each, that say,
"It is but a dream; it will melt away!"

I walk with sweet friends in the sunset's glow;
I listen to music of long ago;
But one thought, like an omen, breathes faint through
  the lay[3]—
"It is but a dream; it will melt away!"

I sit by the hearth of my early days;
All the home-faces are met by the blaze,
And the eyes of the mother shine soft, yet say,
"It is but a dream; it will melt away!"

And away, like a flower's passing breath, 'tis gone,
And I wake more sadly, more deeply lone—
Oh, a haunted heart is a weight to bear!
Bright faces, kind voices, where are ye, where?

Shadow not forth, oh thou land of dreams,
The past, as it fled by my own blue streams!
Make not my spirit within me burn
For the scenes and the hours that may ne'er return!

Call out from the future thy visions bright,
From the world o'er the grave, take thy solemn light,
And oh! with the loved, whom no more I see,
Show me my home as it yet may be!

[1] [Hemans's note] Originally published in *Blackwood's Magazine.* [1828.]

[2] *And dreams ... Byron* From "The Dream," by George Gordon, Lord Byron (1788–1824).

[3] *lay* Medieval narrative song or poem.

As it yet may be in some purer sphere,
No cloud, no parting, no sleepless fear;
So my soul may bear on through the long, long day,
Till I go where the beautiful melts not away!
—1821

Evening Prayer at a Girls' School

Now in thy youth, beseech of Him,
 Who giveth, upbraiding° not, *sharply scolding*
That his light in thy heart become not dim,
 And his love be unforgot;
And thy God, in the darkest of days, will be
Greenness, and beauty, and strength to thee.[1]
BERNARD BARTON.

Hush! 'tis a holy hour—the quiet room
 Seems like a temple, while yon soft lamp sheds
A faint and starry radiance, through the gloom
 And the sweet stillness, down on bright young heads,
With all their clust'ring locks, untouch'd by care,
And bow'd, as flowers are bow'd with night—in prayer.

Gaze on,—'tis lovely!—childhood's lip and cheek,
 Mantling[2] beneath its earnest brow of thought—
Gaze—yet what seest thou in those fair, and meek,
 And fragile things, as but for sunshine wrought?
—Thou seest what grief must nurture for the sky,
What death must fashion for eternity!

Oh! joyous creatures, that will sink to rest,
 Lightly, when those pure orisons° are done, *prayers*
As birds with slumber's honey-dew oppress'd,
 'Midst the dim folded leaves, at set of sun—
Lift up your hearts!—though yet no sorrow lies
Dark in the summer-heaven of those clear eyes;

Though fresh within your breasts th'untroubled springs
 Of hope make melody where'er ye tread;
And o'er your sleep bright shadows, from the wings
 Of spirits visiting but youth, be spread;
Yet in those flute-like voices, mingling low,
Is woman's tenderness—how soon her woe!° *sorrow*

Her lot° is on you—silent tears to weep, *fate*
 And patient smiles to wear through suffering's hour,
And sumless riches, from Affection's deep,
 To pour on broken reeds-a wasted shower!
And to make idols, and to find them clay,[3]
And to bewail that worship—therefore pray!

Her lot is on you—to be found untir'd,
 Watching the stars out by the bed of pain,
With a pale cheek, and yet a brow inspir'd,
 And a true heart of hope, though hope be vain.
Meekly to bear with wrong, to cheer decay,
And oh! to love through all things—therefore pray!

And take the thought of this calm vesper° *evening prayer*
 time,
 With its low murmuring sounds and silvery light,
Or through the dark days fading from their prime,
 As a sweet dew to keep your souls from blight.
Earth will forsake—oh! happy to have given
Th'unbroken heart's first fragrance unto Heaven!
–1825

Casabianca[4]

The boy stood on the burning deck,
 Whence all but him had fled;
The flame that lit the battle's wreck,
 Shone round him o'er the dead.

---

[1] *Now in ... strength to thee* "The Ivy, Addressed to a Young Friend" (1825), 43–48, by Bernard Barton (1784–1849).

[2] *Mantling* Blushing, coloring from emotion.

[3] *And to ... clay* See Daniel 2.31–45.

[4] [Hemans's note] Young Casabianca, a boy about thirteen years old, son to the admiral of the Orient, remained at his post (in the battle of the Nile), after the ship had taken fire, and all the guns had been abandoned; and perished in the explosion of the vessel, when the flames had reached the powder. [The British fleet, commanded by Horatio Nelson, defeated Napoleon's fleet, commanded by Louis de Casabianca, at the battle of the Nile on 1 August 1798. Among those killed when the French flagship, *L'Orient*, exploded were the Admiral and his son, Giacomo Jocante Casabianca (who in fact was only ten). Hemans's source is probably Southey, *Life of Horatio, Lord Nelson* (1813). The poem was first published in the *Monthly Magazine*.]

Yet beautiful and bright he stood,
As born to rule the storm;
A creature of heroic blood,
A proud, though child-like form.

The flames roll'd on—he would not go,
Without his father's word;
That father, faint in death below,
His voice no longer heard.

He call'd aloud—"Say, father, say
If yet my task is done?"
He knew not that the chieftain lay
Unconscious of his son.

"Speak, Father!" once again he cried,
"If I may yet be gone!"
—And but the booming shots replied,
And fast the flames roll'd on.

Upon his brow he felt their breath,
And in his waving hair;
And look'd from that lone post of death,
In still, yet brave despair.

And shouted but once more aloud,
"My father! must I stay?"
While o'er him fast, through sail and shroud,
The wreathing fires made way.

They wrapt the ship in splendor wild,
They caught the flag on high,
And stream'd above the gallant child,
Like banners in the sky.

There came a burst of thunder sound—
The boy—oh! where was he?
—Ask of the winds that far around
With fragments strew'd the sea!

With mast, and helm, and pennon[1] fair,
That well had borne their part—
But the noblest thing that perish'd there,
Was that young faithful heart.
—1826

[1] *pennon* Banner or flag.

Corinne at the Capitol[2]

Les femmes doivent penser qu'il est dans cette carrière bien peu de sort qui puissent valoir la plus obscure vie d'une femme aimée et d'une mère heureuse.—MADAME DE STAËL.[3]

Daughter of th'Italian heaven!
Thou, to whom its fires are given,
Joyously thy car° hath roll'd *chariot*
Where the conqueror's pass'd of old;
And the festal° sun that shone, *festive*
O'er three hundred triumphs gone,[4]
Makes thy day of glory bright,
With a shower of golden light.

Now thou tread'st th'ascending road,
Freedom's foot so proudly trode;[5]
While, from tombs of heroes borne,
From the dust of empire shorn,
Flowers upon thy graceful head,
Chaplets[6] of all hues, are shed,
In a soft and rosy rain,
Touch'd with many a gemlike stain.

Thou hast gain'd the summit now!
Music hails thee from below;
Music, whose rich notes might stir
Ashes of the sepulchre;° *tomb*
Shaking with victorious notes
All the bright air as it floats.

[2] *Corinne at the Capitol* Based on the novel *Corinne, ou l'Italie* (1807), by Germaine de Staël (1766–1817). Corinne is an Italian improvisatrice—a poet who improvises verses in public. The English Lord Nelvil first sees her when she is being honored at the Capitol, in Rome. They fall in love and he offers to marry her, but she declines, preferring her independence. When he marries her half-sister instead, she dies of a broken heart. The poem was first published in *The Literary Souvenir* for 1827 (1826) 189–91.

[3] *Les femmes … heureuse* French: "Women must reflect that there are in this career [of glory] very few destinies that can equal in worth the most obscure life of a beloved wife and happy mother." See Staël, *De l'Influence des passions sur le bonheur des individus et des nations* (1796) ch. 3.

[4] [Hemans's note] The trebly hundred triumphs.—Byron. [See "Childe Harold's Pilgrimage" 4.82 (1818)]; *triumph* Ancient Roman celebration of a military victory; there were a total of 320.

[5] *trode* Archaic past tense of "tread."

[6] *chaplets* Garlands of flowers worn on the head.

Well may woman's heart beat high
Unto that proud harmony!

Now afar it rolls—it dies—
And thy voice is heard to rise
With a low and lovely tone
In its thrilling power alone;
And thy lyre's deep silvery string,
Touch'd as by a breeze's wing,
Murmurs tremblingly at first,
Ere° the tide of rapture burst. *before*

All the spirit of thy sky
Now hath lit thy large dark eye,
And thy cheek a flush hath caught
From the joy of kindled thought;
And the burning words of song
From thy lip flow fast and strong,
With a rushing stream's delight
In the freedom of its might.

Radiant daughter of the sun!
Now thy living wreath is won.
Crown'd of Rome!—Oh! art thou not
Happy in that glorious lot?°— *fate*
Happier, happier far than thou,
With the laurel on thy brow,[1]
She that makes the humblest hearth
Lovely but to one on earth!
—1826

The Effigies[2]

Der rasche Kampf verewigt einen Mann:
Er falle gleich, so preiset ihn das Lied.
Allein die Thränen, die unendlichen
Der überbliebnen, der verlass'nen Frau,
Zählt keine Nachwelt. GOETHE[3]

Warrior! whose image on thy tomb,
With shield and crested head,
Sleeps proudly in the purple gloom
By the stain'd window shed;
The records of thy name and race
Have faded from the stone,
Yet, through a cloud of years, I trace
What thou hast been and done.

A banner, from its flashing spear,
Flung out o'er many a fight;
A war-cry ringing far and clear,
And strong to turn the flight;
An arm that bravely bore the lance
On for the holy shrine;
A haughty heart and a kingly glance—
Chief! were not these things thine?

A lofty place where leaders sate° *sat*
Around the council-board;° *table*
In festive halls a chair of state
When the blood-red wine was pour'd;
A name that drew a prouder tone
From herald, harp, and bard;° *court poet*
Surely these things were all thine own,—
So hadst thou thy reward.

Woman! whose sculptur'd form at rest
By the armed knight is laid,
With meek hands folded o'er a breast
In matron robes array'd;
What was thy tale?—Oh! gentle mate
Of him, the bold and free,
Bound unto his victorious fate,
What bard hath sung of *thee*?

He woo'd a bright and burning star—
Thine was the void, the gloom,
The straining eye that follow'd far
His fast-receding plume;
The heart-sick listening while his steed
Sent echoes on the breeze;
The pang—but when did *Fame* take heed
Of griefs obscure as these?

[1] *laurel on … brow* Poets were traditionally honored with crowns of laurel, which was sacred to Apollo.

[2] *Effigies* Sculptural representations of people, often upon their tombs.

[3] *Der rasche … Nachwelt* German: "Rash combat oft immortalizes man. / If he should fall, he is renowned in song; / But after ages reckon not the tears / Which ceaseless the forsaken woman sheds." (Goethe, *Iphigenie* 5.6. English translation by Anna Swanwick [1909-14].)

Thy silent and secluded hours
Thro' many a lonely day,
While bending o'er thy broider'd° flowers, *embroidered*
With spirit far away;
Thy weeping midnight prayers for him
Who fought on Syrian plains,
Thy watchings till the torch grew dim—
These fill no minstrel strains.

A still, sad life was thine!—long years
With tasks unguerdon'd° fraught, *unrewarded*
Deep, quiet love, submissive tears,
Vigils of anxious thought;
Prayer at the cross in fervour pour'd,
Alms[1] to the pilgrim given—
Oh! happy, happier than thy lord,
In that lone path to heaven!
—1826

The Image in Lava[2]

Thou thing of years departed!
What ages have gone by,
Since here the mournful seal was set
By love and agony!

Temple and tower have moulder'd,
Empires from earth have pass'd,—
And woman's heart hath left a trace
Those glories to outlast!

And childhood's fragile image
Thus fearfully enshrin'd,
Survives the proud memorials rear'd
By conquerors of mankind.

Babe! wert thou brightly slumbering
Upon thy mother's breast,
When suddenly the fiery tomb
Shut round each gentle guest?

A strange, dark fate o'ertook you,
Fair babe and loving heart!
One moment of a thousand pangs—
Yet better than to part!

Haply° of that fond bosom, *by chance*
On ashes here impress'd,
Thou wert the only treasure, child!
Whereon a hope might rest.

Perchance all vainly lavish'd,
Its other love had been,
And where it trusted, nought remain'd
But thorns on which to lean.

Far better then to perish,
Thy form within its clasp,
Than live and lose thee, precious one!
From that impassion'd grasp.

Oh! I could pass all relics
Left by the pomps of old,
To gaze on this rude° monument, *primitive*
Cast in affection's mould.

Love, human love! what art thou?
Thy print upon the dust
Outlives the cities of renown
Wherein the mighty trust!
Immortal, oh! immortal
Thou art, whose earthly glow
Hath given these ashes holiness—
It must, it must be so!
—1827

---

[1] *Alms* Money given in charity to the poor.

[2] [Hemans's note] The impression of a woman's form, with an infant clasped to the bosom, found at the uncovering of Herculaneum. [Herculaneum and Pompeii were destroyed by the eruption of Vesuvius in 79 BCE. The image is one of the casts made during the excavations (1763–1820) by pouring plaster into the holes left in the lava by the victims' bodies. The poem was first published in the *New Monthly Magazine* in 1827.]

Properzia Rossi

(Properzia Rossi,[1] a celebrated female sculptor of Bologna, possessed also of talents for poetry and music, died in consequence of an unrequited attachment.—A painting, by Ducis,[2] represents her showing her last work, a basso-relievo of Ariadne,[3] to a Roman knight, the object of her affection, who regards it with indifference.)

—Tell me no more, no more
Of my soul's lofty gifts! Are they not vain
To quench its haunting thirst for happiness?
Have I not lov'd, and striven, and fail'd to bind
One true heart unto me, whereon my own
Might find a resting-place, a home for all
Its burden of affections? I depart,
Unknown, tho' Fame goes with me; I must leave
The earth unknown. Yet it may be that death
Shall give my name a power to win such tears
As would have made life precious.[4]

I

One dream of passion and of beauty more!
And in its bright fulfilment let me pour
My soul away! Let earth retain a trace
Of that which lit my being, tho' its race
Might have been loftier far.—Yet one more dream!
From my deep spirit one victorious gleam
Ere I depart! For thee alone, for thee!
May this last work, this farewell triumph be,
Thou, loved so vainly! I would leave enshrined
Something immortal of my heart and mind,
That yet may speak to thee when I am gone,
Shaking thine inmost bosom with a tone
Of lost affection;—something that may prove
What she hath been, whose melancholy love
On thee was lavish'd; silent pang and tear,
And fervent song, that gush'd when none were near,
And dream by night, and weary thought by day,
Stealing the brightness from her life away,—
While thou—Awake! not yet within me die,
Under the burden and the agony
Of this vain tenderness,—my spirit, wake!
Ev'n for thy sorrowful affection's sake,
Live! in thy work breathe out!—that he may yet,
Feeling sad mastery there, perchance regret
Thine unrequited gift.

2

It comes,—the power
Within me born, flows back; my fruitless dower° *dowry*
That could not win me love. Yet once again
I greet it proudly, with its rushing train
Of glorious images:—they throng—they press—
A sudden joy lights up my loneliness,—
I shall not perish all![5]
The bright work grows
Beneath my hand, unfolding, as a rose,
Leaf after leaf, to beauty; line by line,
I fix my thought, heart, soul, to burn, to shine,
Thro' the pale marble's veins. It grows—and now
I give my own life's history to thy brow,
Forsaken Ariadne! thou shalt wear
My form, my lineaments;[6] but oh! more fair,
Touch'd into lovelier being by the glow
Which in me dwells, as by the summer-light
All things are glorified. From thee my woe
Shall yet look beautiful to meet his sight,
When I am pass'd away. Thou art the mould
Wherein I pour the fervent thoughts, th'untold,
The self-consuming! Speak to him of me,
Thou, the deserted by the lonely sea,
With the soft sadness of thine earnest eye,
Speak to him, lorn° one! deeply, mournfully, *forlorn*
Of all my love and grief! Oh! could I throw
Into thy frame a voice, a sweet, and low,
And thrilling voice of song! when he came nigh,
To send the passion of its melody
Thro' his pierced bosom—on its tones to bear
My life's deep feeling, as the southern air

[1] *Properzia Rossi* Properzia de'Rossi (c.1491–1530), Bolognese sculptor, painter, and poet.

[2] *Ducis* Louis Ducis (1775–1847), *Properzia de'Rossi and her Last Bas-relief.*

[3] *basso-relievo* Relief sculpture; *Ariadne* Cretan princess who helped Theseus find his way through the labyrinth and kill the Minotaur. They eloped, but he abandoned her on the island of Naxos. See Ovid (43–17 BCE), *Heroides* 10.

[4] *Tell me … precious* The epigraph is by Hemans herself.

[5] *I shall … all* Cf. Horace, *Odes* 3.30.6.

[6] *lineaments* Distinctive shapes.

Wafts the faint myrtle's[1] breath,—to rise, to swell,
To sink away in accents of farewell,
Winning but one, one gush of tears, whose flow
Surely my parted spirit yet might know,
If love be strong as death!

3

Now fair thou art,
Thou form, whose life is of my burning heart!
Yet all the vision that within me wrought,
I cannot make thee! Oh! I might have given
Birth to creations of far nobler thought,
I might have kindled, with the fire of heaven,
Things not of such as die! But I have been
Too much alone;[2] a heart whereon to lean,
With all these deep affections, that o'erflow
My aching soul, and find no shore below;
An eye to be my star, a voice to bring
Hope o'er my path, like sounds that breathe of spring,
These are denied me—dreamt of still in vain,—
Therefore my brief aspirings from the chain,
Are ever but as some wild fitful° song, *irregular*
Rising triumphantly, to die ere° long *before*
In dirge-like[3] echoes.

4

Yet the world will see
Little of this, my parting work, in thee,
Thou shalt have fame! Oh, mockery! give the reed
From storms a shelter,—give the drooping vine
Something round, which its tendrils may entwine,—
Give the parch'd flower a rain-drop, and the
meed° *reward*
Of love's kind words to woman! Worthless fame!
That in *his* bosom wins not for my name
Th'abiding place it ask'd! Yet how my heart,
In its own fairy world of song and art,
Once beat for praise!—Are those high longings o'er?
That which I have been can I be no more?—
Never, oh! never more; tho' still thy sky
Be blue as then, my glorious Italy!
And tho' the music, whose rich breathings fill
Thine air with soul, be wandering past me still,
And tho' the mantle° of thy sunlight streams, *cloak*
Unchang'd on forms, instinct with poet-dreams;
Never, oh! never more! Where'er I move,
The shadow of this broken-hearted love
Is on me and around! Too well *they* know,
Whose life is all within, too soon and well,
When there the blight hath settled;—but I go
Under the silent wings of peace to dwell;
From the slow wasting, from the lonely pain,
The inward burning of those words—"*in vain*,"
Sear'd on the heart—I go. 'Twill soon be past.
Sunshine, and song, and bright Italian heaven,
And thou, oh! thou, on whom my spirit cast
Unvalued wealth,—who know'st not what was given
In that devotedness,—the sad, and deep,
And unrepaid—farewell! If I could weep
Once, only once, belov'd one! on thy breast,
Pouring my heart forth ere I sink to rest!
But that were happiness, and unto me
Earth's gift is *fame*. Yet I was form'd to be
So richly blest! With thee to watch the sky,
Speaking not, feeling but that thou wert nigh;
With thee to listen, while the tones of song
Swept ev'n as part of our sweet air along,
To listen silently;—with thee to gaze
On forms, the deified of olden days,
This had been joy enough;—and hour by hour,
From its glad well-springs drinking life and power,
How had my spirit soar'd, and made its fame
A glory for thy brow!—Dreams, dreams!—the fire
Burns faint within me. Yet I leave my name—
As a deep thrill may linger on the lyre[4]
When its full chords are hush'd—awhile to live,
And one day haply in thy heart revive
Sad thoughts of me:—I leave it, with a sound,
A spell o'er memory, mournfully profound,
I leave it, on my country's air to dwell,—
Say proudly yet—"'Twas hers who lov'd me well!"
—1828

[1] *myrtle's* Belonging to the myrtle, a Mediterranean evergreen shrub bearing pink flowers and black berries.

[2] *Too ... alone* Cf. Byron, *Mazeppa* (1819), 839.

[3] *dirge-like* Like a funeral hymn, solemn and mournful.

[4] *lyre* Stringed instrument.

Woman and Fame

Happy—happier far than thou,
With the laurel on thy brow;[1]
She that makes the humblest hearth,
Lovely but to one on earth.[2]

Thou hast a charmed cup, O Fame!
A draught that mantles[3] high,
And seems to lift this earthly frame
Above mortality.
Away! to me—a woman—bring
Sweet waters from affection's spring.

Thou hast green laurel leaves, that twine
Into so proud a wreath;
For that resplendent gift of thine,
Heroes have smiled in death:
Give *me* from some kind hand a flower,
The record of one happy hour!

Thou hast a voice, whose thrilling tone
Can bid each life-pulse beat
As when a trumpet's note hath blown,
Calling the brave to meet:
But mine, let mine—a woman's breast,
By words of home-born love be bless'd.

A hollow sound is in thy song,
A mockery in thine eye,
To the sick heart that doth but long
For aid, for sympathy—
For kindly looks to cheer it on,
For tender accents that are gone.

Fame, Fame! thou canst not be the stay° *prop*
Unto the drooping reed,
The cool fresh fountain in the day
Of the soul's feverish need:
Where must the lone one turn or flee?—
Not unto thee—oh! not to thee!

—1829

[1] *laurel on … brow* Poets were traditionally honored with crowns of laurel, which was sacred to Apollo.

[2] *Happy—happier … earth* Paraphrased from Hemans's own "Corinne at the Capitol" (ll. 45–8).

[3] *mantles* Here, foams.

John Clare

1793 – 1864

Later in his life, farmer-poet John Clare recalled that, as a young aspiring poet, he had made a brief effort to master the rules of grammar; however, "finding a jumble of words classed together under this name, and that name and this such-a-figure of speech and that another-hard-worded figure, I turned from further notice of it in instant disgust." This decision to concentrate on the rhythms and sounds of his poetry (without concerning himself with grammatical correctness) and to steep his writings in the dialect and idiom of his home town while writing of his own rural experiences makes Clare unique.

Born in Northamptonshire, England in 1793, to Parker Clare (a poor thresher) and Ann Stimson (daughter of the town shepherd), John Clare grew up in a house where his love for reading and writing was an anomaly—though both his parents passed on to him numerous traditional hymns, ballads, and verses. While attempting to perfect the rhythms and meters of his first volume, *Poems Descriptive of Rural Life and Scenery* (1820), Clare would recite his poems to his parents for approval. When this volume was published, Clare was marketed as successor to Robert Burns as a poet shaped by the language and customs of rural life. The book enjoyed considerable success, and curious readers would often come to observe this "peasant poet" working in the fields.

With a keen eye for the natural world and its denizens, Clare wrote several poems celebrating the niches in which various animals flourish. If Clare is frequently regarded as a nature poet, it is largely because of his evocation of these habitats. As he saw many of these animals hunted, their habitats destroyed, and what he observed to be the delicate balance between humanity and nature threatened, the mood of Clare's nature poems became darker and the tone more indignant. Of particular concern to Clare was the increasing division of the commons—the closing off of public pathways, and the general enclosure of open land. Clare's home parish of Helpston was affected by the enclosures in 1809, and his protests against this can be seen in such poems as "Remembrances."

Building on the success of his debut, Clare brought out *The Village Minstrel* (1821), *The Shepherd's Calendar* (1827), and *The Rural Muse* (1835), but these works did not enjoy the popularity of Clare's first volume. The degree to which these successive disappointments, coupled with the pressures of providing for a steadily growing family, may have affected his mental health is unclear, but by 1830 Clare was unquestionably displaying symptoms of insanity. In that year, while watching a production of *The Merchant of Venice*, Clare became so incensed by the character Shylock demanding his pound of flesh that he began to upbraid the actor and had to be removed from the theater. Clare's form of mental illness would today probably be identified as bipolar affective disorder (manic depression). He often imagined himself to be Lord Byron (who may also have been manic-depressive) and in that connection wrote "Don Juan: A Poem," a continuation of Byron's unfinished *Don Juan*. Clare also insisted that he was possessed of (or by) two wives—one his actual wife, and the other his childhood sweetheart and muse, Mary Joyce (the subject of "To Mary").

Clare was placed in a private asylum in 1837 and later in the Northampton general lunatic asylum, where he continued to write poems. Having escaped from the first asylum in 1841, and walked eighty miles home, eating grass to survive, he was committed to a second institution, where he remained until his death some twenty-five years later.

Some of Clare's most interesting poems were written while he was institutionalized. In many of these later, "mad" lyrics, critics have found an inspired desolation and schizophrenic ingenuity; in others they have discerned interesting points of connection with his earlier work and with that of other poets. In "I Am," for example, Clare signals his increasing estrangement from the world; like some other Romantic poets, he sees in childhood an altogether different, and entirely blissful, form of asylum. Meanwhile, Clare's early "nesting" poems ("Mouse's Nest," for example) find analogues in later fantasies such as "Clock a Clay."

Clare died in May 1864 and was largely forgotten until the mid-twentieth century. Since that time, however, he has consistently been seen as one of the more important poetic voices of the first half of the nineteenth century. For many years his poems suffered at hands of editors who sought to standardize his spelling and punctuation and to remove his idiosyncratic use of dialect; recently, however, efforts been made to restore the poems, enabling readers to experience the poems as Clare intended.

⌘⌘⌘

Written In November

Autumn I love thy latter end to view
In cold novembers[1] day so bleak & bare
When like lifes dwindld thread worn nearly thro
Wi lingering pottering° pace & head bleachd bare *dawdling*
Thou like an old man bids the world adieu
I love thee well & often when a child
Have roamd the bare brown heath a flower to find
& in the moss clad vale & wood bank wild
Have cropt the little bell flowers paley blue
That trembling peept the sheltering bush behind
When winnowing north winds cold & blealy° blew *bleakly*
How have I joyd wi dithering° hands to find *shivering*
Each fading flower & still how sweet the blast
Woud bleak novembers hour Restore the joy thats past

—1821

Remembrances

Summer pleasures they are gone like to visions every one
& the cloudy days of autumn & of winter cometh on
I tried to call them back but unbidden they are gone
Far away from heart & eye & for ever far away
Dear heart & can it be that such raptures meet decay
I thought them all eternal when by Langley bush[2] I lay
I thought them joys eternal when I used to shout & play
On its bank at "clink & bandy" "chock" & "taw" & ducking stone[3]
Where silence sitteth now on the wild heath as her own
Like a ruin of the past all alone

When I used to lie & sing by old east wells boiling spring[4]
When I used to tie the willow boughs together for a "swing"
& fish with crooked pins & thread & never catch a thing
With heart just like a feather—now as heavy as a stone
When beneath old lea close oak I the bottom branches broke
To make our harvest cart like so many working folk
& then to cut a straw at the brook to have a soak
O I never dreamed of parting or that trouble had a sting

[1] *novembers* The usual practice of this anthology regarding modernization of spelling and punctuation has not been followed in the case of Clare; his idiosyncrasies have been retained.

[2] *Langley bush* An old whitethorn (a type of hawthorn with light-colored bark) tree that Clare claimed had stood for more than a century. It fell in 1823.

[3] *clink … stone* Three children's games played with marbles or stones.

[4] *old east … spring* Before the enclosures in Clare's home parish, Eastwell Spring was a popular place to meet on Sundays for sugar and water.

Or that pleasures like a flock of birds would ever take to wing
Leaving nothing but a little naked spring

When jumping time away on old cross berry way
& eating awes like sugar plumbs ere they had lost the may
& skipping like a leveret° before the peep of day *young hare*
On the rolly polly up & downs of pleasant swordy well[1]
When in round oaks narrow lane as the south got black again
We sought the hollow ash that was shelter from the rain
With our pockets full of peas we had stolen from the grain
How delicious was the dinner time on such a showry day
O words are poor receipts for what time hath stole away
The ancient pulpit trees & the play

When for school oer "little field" with its brook & wooden brig° *bridge*
Where I swaggered like a man though I was not half so big
While I held my little plough though twas but a willow twig
& drove my team along made of nothing but a name
"Gee hep" & "hoit" & "woi"—O I never call to mind
These pleasant names of places but I leave a sigh behind
While I see the little mouldywharps[2] hang sweeing° to the wind *swinging*
On the only aged willow that in all the field remains
& nature hides her face where theyre sweeing in their chains
& in a silent murmuring complains

Here was commons for their hills where they seek for freedom still
Though every commons gone & though traps are set to kill
The little homeless miners—O it turns my bosom chill
When I think of old "sneap green" puddocks° nook & hilly snow *buzzard's*
Where bramble bushes grew & the daisy gemmed° in dew *shone*
& the hills of silken grass like to cushions to the view
Where we threw the pissmire° crumbs when we'd nothing else to do *ants*
All leveled like a desert by the never weary plough
All vanished like the sun where that cloud is passing now
& settled here for ever on its brow

O I never thought that joys would run away from boys
Or that boys would change their minds & forsake such summer joys
But alack I never dreamed that the world had other toys
To petrify first feelings like the fable into stone
Till I found the pleasure past & a winter come at last
Then the fields were sudden bare & the sky got over cast
& boyhoods pleasing haunts like a blossom in the blast
Was shrivelled to a withered weed & trampled down & done
Till vanished was the morning spring & set that summer sun
& winter fought her battle strife & won

By Langley bush I roam but the bush hath left its hill
On cowper green I stray tis a desert strange & chill
& spreading lea close oak ere decay had penned its will
To the axe of the spoiler & self interest fell a prey
& cross berry way & old round oaks narrow lane
With its hollow trees like pulpits I shall never see again
Inclosure like a Buonaparte let not a thing remain
It levelled every bush & tree & levelled every hill
& hung the moles for traitors—though the brook is running still
It runs a naker° brook cold & chill[3] *more naked*

O had I known as then joy had left the paths of men
I had watched her night & day besure & never slept agen
& when she turned to [go] O I'd caught her mantle then
& wooed her like a lover by my lonely side to stay
Aye knelt & worshiped on as love in beautys bower
& clung upon her smiles as a bee upon a flower
& gave her heart my poesys all cropt in a sunny hour
As keepsakes & pledges all to never fade away
But love never heeded to treasure up the may
So it went the common road with decay

—1908 (WRITTEN C. 1832)

[1] *swordy well* An old stone quarry, also called Swaddy Well, where Clare used to watch butterflies and collect ferns.

[2] *mouldywharps* Moles. Mole-catchers would hang the dead moles they had caught from trees, to prove they had done their jobs.

[3] *though the … chill* Round Oak Waters, which flowed from Round Oak Spring, was surrounded by trees and meadows that were removed during enclosure.

from *The Flitting*

Ive left mine own old home of homes[1]
Green fields & every pleasant place
The summer like a stranger comes
I pause & hardly know her face
I miss the hazels happy green
The bluebells quiet hanging blooms
Where envys sneer was never seen
Where staring malice never comes

I miss the heath its yellow furze[2]
Molehills & rabbit tracts that lead
Through beesom ling[3] & teazle[4] burrs
That spread a wilderness indeed
The wood land oaks & all below
That their white powdered branches shield
The mossy paths—the very crow
Croaks music in my native field …

I dwell on trifles like a child
I feel as ill becomes a man
& still my thoughts like weedlings wild
Grow up to blossom where they can
They turn to places known so long
& feel that joy was dwelling there
So home fed pleasures fill the song
That has no present joys to heir° … *inherit*

Strange scenes mere shadows are to me
Vague unpersonifying things
I love with my old home to be
By quiet woods & gravel springs
Where little pebbles wear as smooth
As hermits beads° by gentle floods *rosary beads*
Whose noises doth my spirits sooth
& warms them into singing moods …

I love the verse that mild & bland
Breaths of green fields & open sky
I love the muse that in her hand
Bears wreaths of native poesy
Who walks nor skips the pasture brook
In scorn—but by the drinking horse
Leans oer its little brig° to look *bridge*
How far the sallows° lean across *willows*

& feels a rapture in her breast
Upon their root-fringed grains to mark
A hermit morehens° sedgy° nest *moorhen's / grassy*
Just like a naiads summer bark
She counts the eggs she cannot reach
Admires the spots & loves it well
& yearns so natures lessons teach
Amid such neighbourhoods to dwell

I love the muse who sits her down
Upon the molehills little lap
Who feels no fear to stain her gown
& pauses by the hedgrow[5] gap
Not with that affectation praise
Of song to sing & never see
A field flower grow in all her days
Or een° a forests aged tree *even*

Een here my simple feelings nurse
A love for every simple weed
& een this little "shepherds purse"[6]
Grieves me to cut it up—Indeed
I feel at times a love & joy
For every weed & every thing
A feeling kindred from a boy
A feeling brought with every spring

& why—this "shepherds purse" that grows
In this strange spot—In days gone bye
Grew in the little garden rows
Of my old home now left—And I
Feel what I never felt before
This weed an ancient neighbour here
& though I own the spot no more
Its every trifle makes it dear

---

[1] *Ive … homes* This was written after Clare had relocated from Helpston to Northborough.

[2] *furze* Type of flowering evergreen shrub found throughout Europe.

[3] *beesom ling* Besom-heather; heather used to make brooms ("besoms").

[4] *teazle* Type of plant with prickly leaves.

[5] *hedgrow* I.e., "hedgerow."

[6] *shepherds purse* A common type of weed.

The Ivy at the parlour end
The wood bine[1] at the garden gate
Are all & each affections friend
That rendered parting desolate
But times will change & friends must part
& nature still can make amends
Their memory lingers round the heart
Like life whose essence is its friends

Time looks on pomp with careless moods
Or killing apathys disdain
—So where old marble citys stood
Poor persecuted weeds remain
She feels a love for little things
That very few can feel beside
& still the grass eternal springs
Where castles stood & grandeur died
—1908 (WRITTEN 1832)

The Badger

The badger grunting on his woodland track
With shaggy hide & sharp nose scrowed° with black *marked*
Roots in the bushes & the woods & makes
A great hugh° burrow in the ferns & brakes *huge*
With nose on ground he runs a awkard pace
& anything will beat him in the race
The shepherds dog will run him to his den
Followed & hooted by the dogs & men
The wood man when the hunting comes about
Go round at night to stop the foxes out
& hurrying through the bushes ferns & brakes° *bracken*
Nor sees the many hol[e]s the badger makes
& often through the bushes to the chin
Breaks the old holes & tumbles headlong in

When midnight comes a host of dogs & men
Go out & track the badger to his den
& put a sack within the hole & lye
Till the old grunting badger passes bye
He comes & hears they let the strongest loose
The old fox hears the noise & drops the goose
The poacher shoots & hurrys from the cry
& the old hare half wounded buzzes bye
They get a forked stick to bear him down
& clapt the dogs & bore him to the town
& bait him all the day with many dogs
& laugh & shout & fright the scampering hogs
He runs along & bites at all he meets
They shout & hollo down the noisey streets

He turns about to face the loud uproar
& drives the rebels to their very doors
The frequent stone is hurled where ere they go
When badgers fight & every ones a foe
The dogs are clapt & urged to join the fray
The badger turns & drives them all away
Though scar[c]ely half as big dimute° & small *diminutive*
He fights with dogs for hours & beats them all
The heavy mastiff savage in the fray
Lies down & licks his feet & turns away
The bull dog knows his match & waxes cold
The badger grins & never leaves his hold
He drive[s] the crowd & follows at their heels
& bites them through the drunkard swears & reels

The frighted women takes the boys away
The blackguard[2] laughs & hurrys in the fray
He trys to reach the woods a awkard race
But sticks & cudgels quickly stop the chace
He turns agen & drives the noisey crowd
& beats the many dogs in noises loud
He drives away & beats them every one
& then they loose them all & set them on
He falls as dead & kicked by boys & men
Then starts & grins & drives the crowd agen
Till kicked & torn & beaten out he lies
& leaves his hold & cackles groans & dies
—1920 (WRITTEN C. 1835–7)

Written in a Thunder storm July 15th 1841[3]

The heavens are wrath—the thunders rattling peal
Rolls like a vast volcano in the sky

[1] *wood bine* Honeysuckle.

[2] *blackguard* Scoundrel; a worthless or vicious character.

[3] *July 15th 1841* Five days before Clare's escape from the asylum.

Yet nothing starts the apathy I feel
Nor chills with fear eternal destiny

My soul is apathy—a ruin vast
Time cannot clear the ruined mass away
My life is hell—the hopeless die is cast
& manhoods prime is premature decay

Roll on ye wrath of thunders—peal on peal
Till worlds are ruins & myself alone
Melt heart & soul cased in obdurate steel
Till I can feel that nature is my throne

I live in love sun of undying light
& fathom my own heart for ways of good
In its pure atmosphere day without night
Smiles on the plains the forest & the flood

Smile on ye elements of earth & sky
Or frown in thunders as ye frown on me
Bid earth & its delusions pass away
But leave the mind as its creator free

This twilight seems a veil of gause & mist
Trees seem dark hills between the earth & sky
Winds sob awake & then a gusty hist° *hissing*
Fanns through the wheat like serpents gliding bye
I love to stretch my length 'tween earth & sky
& see the inky foliage oer me wave
Though shades are still my prison where I lie
Long use grows nature which I easy brave
& think how sweet cares rest within the grave …
—1949 (WRITTEN 1841)

Don Juan A Poem[1]

"Poets are born"—& so are whores—the trade is
Grown universal—in these canting days
Women of fashion must of course be ladies
& whoreing is the business—that still pays
Playhouses Ball rooms—there the masquerade is
—To do what was of old—& now adays
Their maids—nay wives so innocent & blooming
Cuckold[2] their spouses to seem honest women

Milton sung Eden & the fall of man[3]
Not woman for the name implies a wh—e
& they would make a ruin of his plan
Falling so often they can fall no lower
Tell me a worse delusion if you can
For innocence—& I will sing no more
Wherever mischief is tis womans brewing
Created from manself—to be mans ruin

The flower in bud hides from the fading sun
& keeps the hue of beauty on its cheek
But when full blown they into riot run
The hue turns pale & lost each ruddy streak
So 't'is with woman who pretends to shun
Immodest actions which they inly seek
Night hides the wh—e—cupboards tart & pasty
Flora was p-x-d—& womans quite as nasty

Marriage is nothing but a driveling hoax
To please old codgers when they're turned of forty
I wed & left my wife like other folks
But not untill I found her false & faulty
O woman fair—the man must pay thy jokes
Such makes a husband very often naughty
Who falls in love will seek his own undoing
The road to marriage is—"the road to ruin"

Love worse then debt or drink or any fate
It is the damnest smart of matrimony
A hell incarnate is a woman-mate
The knot is tied—& then we loose the honey
A wife is just the protetype to hate
Commons for stock° & warrens for the coney° *cattle / rabbit*
Are not more tresspassed over in rights plan
Then this incumberance on the rights of man

There's much said about love & more of women
I wish they were as modest as they seem
Some borrow husbands till their cheeks are blooming
Not like the red rose blush—but yellow cream

[1] *Don Juan a Poem* After Byron's death in 1824, many poets experimented with writing continuations of his "Don Juan." Parts of this poem demonstrate Clare's belief that he and Byron were one and the same person.

[2] *Cuckold* Commit adultery.

[3] *Milton … man* In *Paradise Lost.*

Lord what a while those good days are in coming—
Routs[1] Masques & Balls—I wish they were a dream
—I wish for poor men luck—an honest praxis
Cheap food & cloathing—no corn laws[2] or taxes

I wish—but there is little got bye wishing
I wish that bread & great coats ne'er had risen
I wish that there was some such word as "pishun"
For ryhme sake for my verses must be dizen° *adorned*
With dresses fine—as hooks with baits for fishing
I wish all honest men were out of prison
I wish M.P's. would spin less yarn—nor doubt
But burn false bills & cross bad taxes out

I wish young married dames were not so frisky
Nor hide the ring to make believe they're single
I wish small beer[3] was half as good as whiskey
& married dames with buggers would not mingle
There's some too cunning far & some too frisky
& here I want a ryhme—so write down "jingle"
& there's such putting in—in whores crim con[4]
Some mouths would eat forever & eat on

Childern are fond of sucking sugar candy
& maids of sausages—larger the better
Shopmen are fond of good sigars & brandy
& I of blunt°—& if you change the letter *money*
To C or K it would be quite as handy
& throw the next away—but I'm your debtor
For modesty—yet wishing nought between us
I'd hawl close to a she as vulcan did to venus[5]

I really cant tell what this poem will be
About—nor yet what trade I am to follow
I thought to buy old wigs[6]—but that will kill me
With cold starvation—as they're beaten hollow[7]
Long speeches in a famine will not fill me
& madhouse traps° still take me by the collar *warders*
So old wig bargains now must be forgotten
The oil that dressed them[8] fine has made them rotten

I wish old wigs were done with ere they're mouldy
I wish—but heres the papers large & lusty
With speeches that full fifty times they've told ye
—Noble Lord John to sweet Miss Fanny Fusty
Is wed[9]—a lie good reader I ne'er sold ye
—Prince Albert[10] goes to Germany & must he
Leave the queens snuff box where all fools are strumming
From addled eggs no chickens can be coming

Whigs strum state fiddle strings untill they snap
With cuckoo cuckold cuckoo year by year
The razor plays it on the barbers strap
—The sissars° grinder thinks it rather quere *scissors*
That labour wont afford him "one wee drap"
Of ale or gin or half & half[11] or beer
—I wish prince Albert & the noble dastards° *despicable cowards*
Who wed the wives—would get the noble bastards

I wish prince Albert on his german journey
I wish the Whigs were out of office &
Pickled in law books of some good atorney
For ways & speeches few can understand
They'll bless ye when in power—in prison scorn ye
& make a man rent his own house & land—
I wish prince Alberts queen was undefiled
—& every man could get his *wife* with child

I wish the devil luck with all my heart
As I would any other honest body
His bad name passes bye me like a f—t

---

[1] *Routs* Fashionable gatherings or evening parties, very popular in the late eighteenth and early nineteenth centuries.

[2] *corn laws* Series of British laws, repealed in 1846, regulating the trade of grain and restricting its import. One of the effects of these laws was to keep the price of bread very high.

[3] *small beer* Weak beer.

[4] *crim con* Criminal conversation (a legal term for adultery).

[5] *hawl close to* I.e., sleep with ("hawl" meaning "haul"); *as vulcan … venus* Vulcan, the Roman god of fire, was married to Venus, the goddess of love.

[6] *wigs* Slang for "heads"; also a pun on "Whigs."

[7] *beaten hollow* The Whigs were defeated in the election of July 1841.

[8] *oil … them* Reference to the expression "to oil someone's wig," meaning to make them drunk.

[9] *Noble … wed* The marriage of Lord John Russell to Lady Fanny Elliott, daughter of the Earl of Minto, was announced in the papers in July 1841.

[10] *Prince Albert* Consort of Queen Victoria (1819–61).

[11] *half & half* Mixture of ale and porter, or any other two malt liquors.

Stinking of brimstone—then like whisky toddy[1]
We swallow sin which seems to warm the heart
—There's no imputing any sin to God—he
Fills hell with work—& is'n't it a hard case
To leave old whigs & give to hell the carcass

Me-b—ne may throw his wig to little Vicky[2]
& so resign his humbug & his power
& she with the young princess mount the dickey[3]
On ass milk diet[4] for her german tour
Asses like ministers are rather tricky
I & the country proves it every hour
W-ll—gt-n[5] & M-lb—n in their station
Coblers to queens—are phisic to the nation

These batch of toadstools on this rotten tree
Shall be the cabinet of any queen
Though not such coblers as her servants be
They're of Gods making—that is plainly seen
Nor red nor green nor orange—they are free
To thrive & flourish as the Whigs have been
But come tomorrow—like the Whigs forgotten
You'll find them withered stinking dead and rotten

Death is an awfull thing it is by God
I've said so often & I think so now
Tis rather droll to see an old wig nod
Then doze & die the devil don't know how
Odd things are wearisome & this is odd—
Tis better work then kicking up a row
I'm weary of old Whigs & old whigs heirs
& long been sick of teazing God with prayers

I've never seen the cow turn to a bull
I've never seen the horse become an ass
I've never seen an old brawn[6] cloathed in whool—
But I have seen full many a bonny lass
& wish I had one now beneath the cool
Of these high elms—Muse tell me where I was
O—talk of turning I've seen Whig & Tory
Turn imps of hell—& all for Englands glory

I love good fellowship & wit & punning
I love "true love" & God my taste defend
I hate most damnably all sorts of cunning—
I love the Moor & Marsh & Ponders end[7]—
I do not like the song of "cease your funning"[8]
I love a modest wife & trusty friend
—Bricklayers want lime as I want ryhme for fillups
—So here's a health to sweet Eliza Phillips[9]

Song

Eliza now the summer tells
Of spots where love & beauty dwells
Come & spend a day with me
Underneath the forest tree
Where the restless water flushes
Over mosses mounds & rushes
& where love & freedom dwells
With orchis° flowers & fox glove bells *orchid*
Come dear Eliza set me free
& oer the forest roam with me

Here I see the morning sun
Among the beachtree's shadows run
That into gold the short sward° turns *turf, grass*
Where each bright yellow blossom burns
With hues that would his beams out shine
Yet nought can match those smiles of thine
I try to find them all the day
But none are nigh when thou'rt away
Though flowers bloom now on every hill
Eliza is the fairest still

[1] *whisky toddy* Whiskey mixed with warm water and sugar.

[2] *Me-b—ne* Lord Melbourne, who resigned as Prime Minister in August 1841; *little Vicky* Queen Victoria.

[3] *young princess* Victoria Adelaide, the Queen's first-born daughter; *dickey* back seat of a carriage.

[4] *ass milk diet* Common diet for babies, asses' milk being the closest of all mammals' milk to that of humans.

[5] *W-ll-gt-n* Arthur Wellesley, Duke of Wellington, a former prime minister who became a cabinet minister in 1841 under Peel, and then Commander-in-Chief of the army.

[6] *brawn* Boar (also a male prostitute).

[7] *Ponders end* Ponders End is located three miles west of High Beach.

[8] *cease … funning* From John Gay's *Beggar's Opera* (1728), Air 19, 2.13.

[9] *Eliza Phillips* In a letter written after this poem, Clare dedicates "Don Juan" to Eliza, who has not been identified.

The sun wakes up the pleasant morn
& finds me lonely & forlorn
Then wears away to sunny noon
The flowers in bloom the birds in tune
While dull & dowie° all the year *dreary*
No smiles to see no voice to hear
I in this forest prison lie
With none to heed my silent sigh
& underneath this beachen tree
With none to sigh for Love but thee

Now this new poem is entirely new
As wedding gowns or money from the mint
For all I know it is entirely true
For I would scorn to put a lie in print
—I scorn to lie for princes—so would you
& ere I shoot I try my pistol flint
—The cattle salesman—knows the way in trying
& feels his bullocks ere he thinks of buying

Lord bless me now the day is in the gloaming
& every evil thought is out of sight
How I should like to purchase some sweet woman
Or else creep in with my two wives[1] to night —
Surely that wedding day is on the comeing
Abscence like phisic poisons all delight —
Mary & Martha both an evil omen
Though both my own—they still belong to no man

But to our text again—& pray where is it
Begin as parsons do at the beginning
Take the first line friend & you cannot miss it
"Poets are born" & so are whores for sinning
—Here's the court circular—o Lord is this it
Court cards like lists of—not the naked meaning
Here's Albert going to germany they tell us
& the young queen down in the dumps & jealous

Now have you seen a tramper° on race courses *vagrant*
Seeking an honest penny as his trade is
Crying a list of all the running horses
& showing handbills of the sporting ladies
—In bills of fare you'll find a many courses
Yet all are innocent as any maid is
Put these two dishes into one & dress it
& if there is a meaning—you may guess it

Don Juan was Ambassador from russia
But had no hand in any sort of tax
His orders hung like blossoms of the fushia
& made the ladies hearts to melt like wax
He knew Napoleon & the king of prusia
& blowed a cloud oer spirits wine or max° *gin*
But all his profits turned out losses rather
To save one orphan which he forced to father

Theres Docter Bottle imp who deals in urine
A keeper of state prisons for the queen
As great a man as is the Doge° of Turin *Chief Magistrate*
& save in London is but seldom seen
Yclep'd° old A-ll-n[2]—mad brained ladies curing *called*
Some p-x-d like Flora & but seldom clean
The new road oer the forest is the right one
To see red hell & further on the white one[3]

Earth hells or b-gg-r sh-ps or what you please
Where men close prisoners are & women ravished
I've often seen such dirty sights as these
I've often seen good money spent & lavished
To keep bad houses up for docters fees
& I have known a b-gg-rs tally travers'd[4]
Till all his good intents began to falter
—When death brought in his bill & left the halter° *noose*

O glorious constitution what a picking
Ye've had from your tax harvest & your tythe[5]
Old hens which cluck about that fair young chicken
— Cocks without spurs[6] that yet can crow so blythe° *cheerfully*

---

[1] *my two wives* Reference to Clare's delusional belief that he possessed two wives—one being Martha ("Peggy"), his real wife, and the other being Mary, his dead childhood sweetheart.

[2] *A-ll-n* Dr. Matthew Allen, superintendent of the asylum. He would collect urine samples from patients, which were often used to diagnose venereal diseases.

[3] *To see … one* Reference to the two other houses of High Beach, the first for female patients and the second for male, which Clare could see from his residence.

[4] *tally travers'd* I.e., examined his list of wrong-doings or backslidings.

[5] *tythe* Tithe, tax amounting to one tenth of one's income.

[6] *spurs* Back claws.

Truth is shut up in prison while ye're licking
The gold from off the gingerbread—be lythe
In winding that patched broken old state clock up
Playhouses open—but mad houses lock up

Give toil more pay where rank starvation lurches
& pay your debts & put your books to rights
Leave whores & playhouses & fill your churches
Old clovenfoot your dirty victory fights
Like theft he still on natures manor poaches
& holds his feasting on anothers rights
To show plain truth you act in bawdy farces
Men show their tools—& maids expose their arses

Now this day is the eleventh of July
& being sunday I will seek no flaw
In man or woman—but prepare to die
In two days more I may that ticket draw
& so may thousands more as well as I
To day is here—the next who ever saw
& In a madhouse I can find no mirth pay
—Next tuesday used to be Lord Byrons birthday[1]

Lord Byron poh—the man wot rites the werses
& is just what he is & nothing more
Who with his pen lies like the mist disperses
& makes all nothing as it was before
Who wed two wives[2] & oft the truth rehearses
& might have had some twenty thousand more
Who has been dead so fools their lies are giving
& still in Allens madhouse caged & living

If I do wickedness to day being sunday
Can I by hearing prayers or singing psalms
Clear off all debts twixt god & man on monday
& lie like an old hull that dotage calms
& is there such a word as Abergundy
I've read that poem called the "Isle of Palms"[3]
—But singing sense pray tell me if I can
Live an old rogue & die an honest man

I wish I had a quire of foolscap paper
Hot pressed[4]—& crowpens°—how I could endite *quill pens*
A silver candlestick & green wax taper
Lord bless me what fine poems I would write
The very tailors they would read & caper
& mantua[5] makers would be all delight
Though laurel wreaths[6] my brows did ne'er environ
I think myself as great a bard as Byron

I have two wives & I should like to see them
Both by my side before another hour
If both are honest I should like to be them
For both are fair & bonny as a flower
& one o Lord—now do bring in the tea mem° *ma'am*
Were bards pens steamers[7] each of ten horse power
I could not bring her beautys fair to weather
So I've towed both in harbour blest together

Now i'n't this canto worth a single pound
From anybodys pocket who will buy
As thieves are worth a halter I'll be bound
Now honest reader take the book & try
& if as I have said it is not found
I'll write a better canto bye & bye
So reader now the money till unlock it
& buy the book & help to fill my pocket
—1949 (WRITTEN 1841)

Sonnet
[I am]

I feel I am;—I only know I am,
And plod upon the earth, as dull and void:
Earth's prison chilled my body with its dram[8]
Of dullness, and my soaring thoughts destroyed,
I fled to solitudes from passions dream,
But strife persued—I only know, I am,

---

[1] *Next ... birthday* 13 July was Clare's birthday, but Lord Byron was born on 22 January.

[2] *Who ... wives* Byron only married only once, though he was known for his sexual adventures.

[3] *Isle of Palms* Poem by John Wilson (published under the pseudonym "Christopher North").

[4] *Hot pressed* Made smooth and shiny by being pressed between two hot plates.

[5] *mantua* Type of fashionable, loose-fitting gown.

[6] *laurel wreaths* Bestowed as a mark of honor upon poets, heroes, and victorious athletes in ancient Greece.

[7] *steamers* Steam boats.

[8] *dram* Measurement of weight.

I was a being created in the race
Of men disdaining bounds of place and time:—
A spirit that could travel o'er the space
Of earth and heaven,—like a thought sublime,
Tracing creation, like my maker, free,—
A soul unshackled—like eternity,
Spurning earth's vain and soul debasing thrall
But now I only know I am,—that's all.
—1932 (WRITTEN C. 1842–46)

"I Am"

I am—yet what I am, none cares or knows;
My friends forsake me like a memory lost:—
I am the self-consumer of my woes;—
They rise and vanish in oblivion's host,
Like shadows in love's frenzied stifled throes:—
And yet I am, and live—like vapours tost

Into the nothingness of scorn and noise,—
Into the living sea of waking dreams,
Where there is neither sense of life or joys,
But the vast shipwreck of my lifes esteems;
Even the dearest, that I love the best
Are strange—nay, rather stranger than the rest.[1]

I long for scenes, where man hath never trod
A place where woman never smiled or wept
There to abide with my Creator, God;
And sleep as I in childhood, sweetly slept,
Untroubling, and untroubled where I lie,
The grass below—above the vaulted sky.
—1848

[1] *Even the ... rest* Apparently Clare's family never came to visit him in the Northampton asylum.

Clock A Clay[2]

In the cowslips peeps I lye[3]
Hidden from the buzzing fly
While green grass beneath me lies
Pearled wi' dew like fishes eyes
Here I lye a Clock a clay
Waiting for the time o' day[4]

While grassy forests quake surprise
And the wild wind sobs and sighs
My gold home rocks as like to fall
On its pillars green and tall
When the pattering rain drives bye
Clock a Clay keeps warm and dry

Day by day and night by night
All the week I hide from sight
In the cowslips peeps I lye
In rain and dew still warm and dry
Day and night and night and day
Red black spotted clock a clay

My home it shakes in wind and showers
Pale green pillar top't wi' flowers
Bending at the wild winds breath
Till I touch the grass beneath
Here still I live lone clock a clay
Watching for the time of day
—1873 (WRITTEN C. 1848)

[2] *Clock A Clay* Ladybug.

[3] *In ... lye* Cf. the spirit Ariel's song in Shakespeare, *The Tempest*, 5.1.88–9: "Where the bee sucks, there suck I: / In the cowslip's bell I lie" ; *cowslip* Yellow primrose; *peeps* Pips; blossoms.

[4] *Waiting ... day* In a popular game, children would tell the time by counting the number of taps necessary to make the ladybug fly home.

To Mary[1]

I sleep with thee, and wake with thee,
And yet thou art not there:—
I fill my arms, with thoughts of thee,
And press the common air.—
Thy eyes are gazing upon mine,
When thou art out of sight;
My lips are always touching thine,
At morning, noon, and night.

I think, and speak of other things,
To keep my mind at rest:
But still to thee, my memory clings,
Like love in womans breast;—
I hide it from the worlds-wide eye;
And think, and speak contrary;
But soft, the wind comes from the sky,
And wispers tales of Mary.—

The night wind wispers in my ear,
The moon shines in my face;
A burden still of chilling fear,
I find in every place.—
The breeze is wispering in the bush;
And the dew-fall from the tree,
All; sighing on, and will not hush,
Some pleasant tales of thee.—
—1984 (WRITTEN C. 1844)

[1] *Mary* Clare's childhood sweetheart, who had died years earlier. Clare often believed that she was still alive and that he had married her.

An Invite to Eternity

Wilt thou go with me sweet maid
Say maiden wilt thou go with me
Through the valley depths of shade
Of night and dark obscurity
Where the path hath lost its way
Where the sun forgets the day
Where there's nor life nor light to see
Sweet maiden wilt thou go with me

Where stones will turn to flooding streams
Where plains will rise like ocean waves
Where life will fade like visioned dreams
And mountains darken into caves
Say maiden wilt thou go with me
Through this sad non-identity
Where parents live and are forgot
And sisters live and know us not

Say maiden wilt thou go with me
In this strange death of life to be
To live in death and be the same
Without this life, or home, or name
At once to be, & not to be
That was, and is not—yet to see
Things pass like shadows—and the sky
Above, below, around us lie

The land of shadows wilt thou trace
And look—nor know each others face
The present mixed with reasons gone
And past, and present all as one
Say maiden can thy life be led
To join the living with the dead
Then trace thy footsteps on with me
We're wed to one eternity
—1984 (WRITTEN 1848)

John Keats

1795 – 1821

John Keats has come to epitomize the popular conception of the Romantic poet as a passionate dreamer whose intense, sensuous poetry celebrates the world of the imagination over that of everyday life. Keats published only 54 poems in his short lifetime, but his work ranges across a number of poetic genres, including sonnets, odes, romances, and epics. In each of these genres his poetry seeks beauty and truth that will transcend the world of suffering, always questioning its own process of interpretation.

The eldest of four children, John Keats was born in London on 31 October 1795. He lost both his parents by the time he was fourteen—his father in a riding accident and his mother of tuberculosis (then commonly known as consumption). After his mother's death, Keats came under the care of two guardians. He continued to attend Enfield School, a liberal institution where he first became acquainted with Leigh Hunt's radical paper *The Examiner*, and where his interest in poetry grew, particularly after reading the poetry of Edmund Spenser. Keats's friend Charles Brown said it was *The Faerie Queene* that awakened Keats's talent for expressing the "acute sense of beauty" he possessed.

After a promising but incomplete schooling, Keats apprenticed himself in 1815 to a surgeon at Guy's Hospital in London. (He remained licensed as an apothecary until 1817.) Having befriended some of the most prolific artists and critics of his day, among them radical publisher Leigh Hunt, essayist Charles Lamb, painter Benjamin Haydon, and poets John Hamilton Reynolds and Percy Shelley (later to eulogize Keats in *Adonais*), Keats was spurred to further develop his own creative abilities. In 1816, after spending a night reading a translation of Homer with his school friend Cowden Clarke, Keats wrote "On First Looking Into Chapman's Homer" (1816), a sonnet that presents a poet reflecting on poetic tradition and discovering his talent, as an explorer surveys "with a wild surmise" another ocean of possibility.

Shortly thereafter, Keats composed "Sleep and Poetry" (1817), a poetic manifesto of sorts in which he proclaims his devotion to a new type of poetry, one in the style of Wordsworth, devoted to nature and the human heart. By aligning himself with Wordsworth's naturalism, Keats ensured the condemnation of critics; nevertheless, that same year he chose to give up surgery and devote himself entirely to poetry. This decision was most likely sealed by Leigh Hunt's first "Young Poets" article (*Examiner*, December 1816), in which he identified Keats, Shelley, and Reynolds as the leaders of a new generation of poets.

Keats's first volume, *Poems* (1817), received little critical attention. The following year he published the long and ambitious romance *Endymion* (1818), about a shepherd-prince who pursues his elusive feminine ideal. The book was sharply criticized in a famous review published in the *Quarterly Review*, where Keats and his friend Hunt were ridiculed as representing "the Cockney school of poetry." Keats endured further criticism when he read "Hymn to Pan" from *Endymion* to the contemporary poet he most admired, Wordsworth; the elder poet ungenerously dismissed it as "a very pretty piece of paganism."

His hopes undimmed, Keats continued to pursue his poetic ideals. In a series of now-famous letters to Benjamin Bailey, he explored his aesthetic ideas and sought to define the purpose of literature for modern life. Keats's letters to his friends and family are justly acclaimed for their intuitions about life, suffering, and poetry. To Keats we owe the concepts of "negative capability," the "chameleon poet," and "the vale of Soul-making." He particularly admired what he saw as Shakespeare's chameleon-like ability to escape from his personality and enter fully into the being of his characters.

During this time, Keats fell in love with the lively and flirtatious Fanny Brawne, who became a kind of muse. Though they became engaged, Keats wanted to gain financial security before marrying. He had begun as well to be haunted by fears of his own early death. (Throat ulcers that had appeared during a walking tour in poor weather the previous summer had become chronic.) It was in this set of tumultuous emotional circumstances that Keats began one of the most extraordinary periods of creativity in the history of English literature. Between January and September of 1819 he composed all seven of his "great Odes"—"Ode to Psyche," "Ode to a Nightingale," "Ode on a Grecian Urn," "Ode on Indolence," "Ode on Melancholy," and "To Autumn"—as well as "The Eve of St. Agnes," "La Belle Dame sans Merci," "Lamia," and a number of sonnets. "The Eve of St. Agnes" remains Keats's best-known narrative poem. Suffused with amorous feeling and lush imagery, "The Eve of St. Agnes" recounts a romantic story with affinities to the story of Romeo and Juliet. Generations of readers have been seduced by the sensuous immediacy of this poetry.

Keats's largest poetic project was *Hyperion*, a blank-verse epic on Jupiter's dethroning of Saturn and Apollo's overthrow of Hyperion. An intense study of cultural loss, the poem is a self-consciously Miltonic exercise that Keats kept returning to but never completed. He began the poem in the autumn of 1818, but put the manuscript aside in April of the following year. (This first fragmentary version of the poem was published as "Hyperion: A Fragment" in the 1820 volume of his verse.)

In the summer he resumed work on the project, this time casting the story within the frame of a poet's dream vision, but he stopped for a second time in September. (This second version, also fragmentary, was finally published in 1856 as "The Fall of Hyperion.")

As Keats's extraordinary poetic outpouring of 1819 was coming to a close, he began to suspect himself inadequate to the task of undertaking a Miltonic epic. As he wrote to a friend John Reynolds on 21 September 1819:

> I have given up Hyperion ... Miltonic verse cannot be written but in an artful or rather artist's humour. I wish to give myself up to other sensations. English ought to be kept up.

Keats wrote little after September of 1819, but he published his third volume of poetry, *Lamia, Isabella, The Eve of St. Agnes, and Other Poems*, in 1820—defiantly advertising himself on the cover as "the author of *Endymion*." Critics were gradually acquiring a taste for Keats's work, but by this time Keats was very ill, having contracted tuberculosis. His lungs weakened and his throat still ulcerating, Keats in August of 1820 declined an invitation to join Shelley and his circle in Pisa, and instead went to Rome, where he died in the house at the base of the Spanish Steps that is now the Keats-Shelley Memorial House. Keats was buried in the Protestant Cemetery in Rome.

In the generations since his death many have wondered what Keats would have accomplished had he lived. Such thoughts, however, focus on the tragedy of the poet's death, rather than on the sustained richness of his achievement. Before his death, Keats asked that his epitaph be "Here lies one whose name was writ in water." (Though his friends complied, they added above, "This Grave contains all that was Mortal of a YOUNG ENGLISH POET, Who on his Death Bed in the Bitterness of his Heart at the Malicious Power of his Enemies, Desired these Words to be incised on his Tomb Stone.") On visiting his gravesite in 1877, Oscar Wilde supplied another epitaph: "A Priest of Beauty slain before his time." But the last sentences of Keats's last letter to Charles Brown are perhaps more evocative: "I can scarcely bid you good bye even in a letter. I always made an awkward bow."

⌘⌘⌘

On First Looking into Chapman's Homer[1]

Much have I travell'd in the realms of gold,
And many goodly states and kingdoms seen;
Round many western islands have I been
Which bards in fealty to Apollo[2] hold.
Oft of one wide expanse had I been told
That deep-brow'd Homer ruled as his demesne;
Yet never did I breathe its pure serene,
Till I heard Chapman speak out loud and bold:
Then felt I like some watcher of the skies
When a new planet swims into his ken;[3]
Or like stout Cortez[4] when with eagle eyes
He star'd at the Pacific—and all his men
Look'd at each other with a wild surmise—
Silent, upon a peak in Darien.
—1816

On the Grasshopper and Cricket

The poetry of earth is never dead:
When all the birds are faint with the hot sun,
And hide in cooling trees, a voice will run
From hedge to hedge about the new-mown mead;
That is the Grasshopper's—he takes the lead
In summer luxury—he has never done
With his delights; for when tired out with fun
He rests at ease beneath some pleasant weed.
The poetry of earth is ceasing never:
On a lone winter evening, when the frost
Has wrought a silence, from the stove there shrills
The Cricket's song, in warmth increasing ever,
And seems to one in drowsiness half lost,
The Grasshopper's among some grassy hills.
—1817

[1] *On ... Homer* Written in October 1816, on the morning after Keats and his friend and mentor Charles Cowden Clarke had stayed up all night reading the 1614 translation of Homer by George Chapman (1559–1634).

[2] *Apollo* Greek god of poetry.

[3] *a new ... ken* William Herschel had discovered Uranus in 1781.

[4] *Cortez* The first European to see the Pacific (from the Isthmus of Darien in Panama) was not actually Hernán Cortez (1485–1547), the conqueror of Mexico, but Vasco Nuñez de Balboa in 1513 (1475–1519).

Sleep And Poetry

As I lay in my bed slepe full unmete° *unallotted*
Was unto me, but why that I ne might
Rest I ne wist,° for there n'as° erthly *knew / was no*
wight° *creature*
[As I suppose] had more of hertis ese° *heart's ease*
Than I, for I n'ad° sicknesse nor disese.[5] *had not*
CHAUCER

What is more gentle than a wind in summer?
What is more soothing than the pretty hummer
That stays one moment in an open flower,
And buzzes cheerily from bower to bower?
What is more tranquil than a musk-rose
blowing° *blossoming*
In a green island, far from all men's knowing?
More healthful than the leafiness of dales?
More secret than a nest of nightingales?
More serene than Cordelia's[6] countenance?
More full of visions than a high romance?
What, but thee Sleep? Soft closer of our eyes!
Low murmurer of tender lullabies!
Light hoverer around our happy pillows!
Wreather of poppy buds, and weeping willows!

[5] *As ... disese* From *The Floure and the Leafe* 17–21, which was then thought to have been written by Chaucer.

[6] *Cordelia* Daughter of King Lear in Shakespeare's *King Lear*.

Silent entangler of a beauty's tresses!
Most happy listener! when the morning blesses
Thee for enlivening all the cheerful eyes
That glance so brightly at the new sun-rise.

But what is higher beyond thought than thee?
Fresher than berries of a mountain tree?
More strange, more beautiful, more smooth, more
regal,
Than wings of swans, than doves, than dim-seen eagle?
What is it? And to what shall I compare it?
It has a glory, and naught else can share it:
The thought thereof is awful, sweet, and holy,
Chasing away all worldliness and folly;
Coming sometimes like fearful claps of thunder,
Or the low rumblings earth's regions under;
And sometimes like a gentle whispering
Of all the secrets of some wond'rous thing
That breathes about us in the vacant air;
So that we look around with prying stare,
Perhaps to see shapes of light, aërial limning,[1]
And catch soft floatings from a faint-heard hymning;
To see the laurel wreath,[2] on high suspended,
That is to crown our name when life is ended.
Sometimes it gives a glory to the voice,
And from the heart up-springs, "Rejoice! rejoice!"
Sounds which will reach the Framer of all things,
And die away in ardent mutterings.

No one who once the glorious sun has seen,
And all the clouds, and felt his bosom clean
For his great Maker's presence, but must know
What 'tis I mean, and feel his being glow:
Therefore no insult will I give his spirit,
By telling what he sees from native merit.

O Poesy! For thee I hold my pen
That am not yet a glorious denizen
Of thy wide heaven—Should I rather kneel
Upon some mountain-top until I feel
A glowing splendour round about me hung,
And echo back the voice of thine own tongue?
O Poesy! For thee I grasp my pen
That am not yet a glorious denizen
Of thy wide heaven; yet, to my ardent prayer,
Yield from thy sanctuary some clear air,
Smoothed for intoxication by the breath
Of flowering bays, that I may die a death
Of luxury, and my young spirit follow
The morning sun-beams to the great Apollo[3]
Like a fresh sacrifice; or, if I can bear
The o'erwhelming sweets, 'twill bring to me the fair
Visions of all places: a bowery nook
Will be elysium[4]—an eternal book
Whence I may copy many a lovely saying
About the leaves, and flowers—about the playing
Of nymphs in woods, and fountains; and the shade
Keeping a silence round a sleeping maid;
And many a verse from so strange influence
That we must ever wonder how, and whence
It came. Also imaginings will hover
Round my fire-side, and haply there discover
Vistas of solemn beauty, where I'd wander
In happy silence, like the clear Meander[5]
Through its lone vales; and where I found a spot
Of awfuller shade, or an enchanted grot,° *grotto*
Or a green hill o'erspread with chequered dress
Of flowers, and fearful from its loveliness,
Write on my tablets all that was permitted,
All that was for our human senses fitted.
Then the events of this wide world I'd seize
Like a strong giant, and my spirit tease
Till at its shoulders it should proudly see
Wings to find out an immortality.

Stop and consider! Life is but a day;
A fragile dew-drop on its perilous way
From a tree's summit; a poor Indian's sleep
While his boat hastens to the monstrous steep

[1] *limning* Painting.

[2] *laurel wreath* Wreaths made of leaves of the bay laurel were traditionally bestowed upon those who distinguished themselves in poetry.

[3] *Apollo* Greek god of poetry.

[4] *elysium* State of perfect happiness. From the Elysium of Greek mythology, the place where the blessed reside after death.

[5] *Meander* Winding river in Asia Minor.

Of Montmorenci.[1] Why so sad a moan?
Life is the rose's hope while yet unblown;
The reading of an ever-changing tale;
The light uplifting of a maiden's veil;
A pigeon tumbling in clear summer air;
A laughing school-boy, without grief or care,
Riding the springy branches of an elm.

O for ten years, that I may overwhelm
Myself in poesy; so I may do the deed
That my own soul has to itself decreed.
Then will I pass the countries that I see
In long perspective, and continually
Taste their pure fountains. First the realm I'll pass
Of Flora, and old Pan:[2] sleep in the grass,
Feed upon apples red, and strawberries,
And choose each pleasure that my fancy sees;
Catch the white-handed nymphs in shady places,
To woo sweet kisses from averted faces,
Play with their fingers, touch their shoulders white
Into a pretty shrinking with a bite
As hard as lips can make it: till agreed,
A lovely tale of human life we'll read
And one will teach a tame dove how it best
May fan the cool air gently o'er my rest;
Another, bending o'er her nimble tread,
Will set a green robe floating round her head,
And still will dance with ever varied ease,
Smiling upon the flowers and the trees:
Another will entice me on, and on
Through almond blossoms and rich cinnamon;
Till in the bosom of a leafy world
We rest in silence, like two gems upcurl'd
In the recesses of a pearly shell.

And can I ever bid these joys farewell?
Yes, I must pass them for a nobler life,
Where I may find the agonies, the strife
Of human hearts: for lo! I see afar,
O'er sailing the blue cragginess, a car° *chariot*
And steeds with streamy manes—the charioteer
Looks out upon the winds with glorious fear:
And now the numerous tramplings quiver lightly
Along a huge cloud's ridge; and now with sprightly
Wheel downward come they into fresher skies,
Tipt round with silver from the sun's bright eyes.
Still downward with capacious whirl they glide,
And now I see them on the green-hill's side
In breezy rest among the nodding stalks.
The charioteer with wond'rous gesture talks
To the trees and mountains; and there soon appear
Shapes of delight, of mystery, and fear,
Passing along before a dusky space
Made by some mighty oaks: as they would chase
Some ever-fleeting music on they sweep.
Lo! how they murmur, laugh, and smile, and weep:
Some with upholden hand and mouth severe;
Some with their faces muffled to the ear
Between their arms; some, clear in youthful bloom,
Go glad and smilingly athwart the gloom;
Some looking back, and some with upward gaze;
Yes, thousands in a thousand different ways
Flit onward—now a lovely wreath of girls
Dancing their sleek hair into tangled curls;
And now broad wings. Most awfully intent
The driver of those steeds is forward bent,
And seems to listen: O that I might know
All that he writes with such a hurrying glow.

The visions all are fled—the car is fled
Into the light of heaven, and in their stead
A sense of real things comes doubly strong,
And, like a muddy stream, would bear along
My soul to nothingness: but I will strive
Against all doubtings, and will keep alive
The thought of that same chariot, and the strange
Journey it went.

Is there so small a range
In the present strength of manhood, that the high
Imagination cannot freely fly
As she was wont of old? prepare her steeds,
Paw up against the light, and do strange deeds
Upon the clouds? Has she not shown us all?

[1] *Montmorenci* Montmorency Falls near Québec City, Canada.

[2] *Flora ... Pan* In Greek mythology, the goddess of flowers and the shepherd god of nature, respectively. The realm of Flora and Pan is that of pastoral poesy, which, according to Virgil, should be the genre with which the aspiring poet begins, eventually working his way up to the epic.

From the clear space of ether, to the small
Breath of new buds unfolding? From the meaning
Of Jove's[1] large eyebrow, to the tender greening
Of April meadows? Here her altar shone,
E'en in this isle; and who could paragon
The fervid choir that lifted up a noise
Of harmony, to where it aye will poise
Its mighty self of convoluting sound,
Huge as a planet, and like that roll round,
Eternally around a dizzy void?
Ay, in those days the Muses[2] were nigh cloy'd
With honours; nor had any other care
Than to sing out and sooth their wavy hair.

Could all this be forgotten? Yes, a schism
Nurtured by foppery and barbarism,
Made great Apollo blush for this his land.
Men were thought wise who could not understand
His glories: with a puling infant's force
They sway'd about upon a rocking horse,
And thought it Pegasus.[3] Ah dismal soul'd!
The winds of heaven blew, the ocean roll'd
Its gathering waves—ye felt it not. The blue
Bared its eternal bosom, and the dew
Of summer nights collected still to make
The morning precious: beauty was awake!
Why were ye not awake? But ye were dead
To things ye knew not of—were closely wed
To musty laws lined out with wretched rule
And compass vile: so that ye taught a school
Of dolts to smooth, inlay, and clip, and fit,
Till, like the certain wands of Jacob's wit,[4]
Their verses tallied. Easy was the task:
A thousand handicraftsmen wore the mask
Of Poesy. Ill-fated, impious race!
That blasphemed the bright Lyrist[5] to his face,
And did not know it—no, they went about,
Holding a poor, decrepit standard out
Mark'd with most flimsy mottos, and in large
The name of one Boileau![6]

O ye whose charge
It is to hover round our pleasant hills!
Whose congregated majesty so fills
My boundly[7] reverence, that I cannot trace
Your hallowed names, in this unholy place,
So near those common folk; did not their shames
Affright you? Did our old lamenting Thames° *river*
Delight you? Did ye never cluster round
Delicious Avon,° with a mournful sound, *river*
And weep? Or did ye wholly bid adieu
To regions where no more the laurel grew?
Or did ye stay to give a welcoming
To some lone spirits[8] who could proudly sing
Their youth away, and die? 'Twas even so:
But let me think away those times of woe:
Now 'tis a fairer season; ye have breathed
Rich benedictions o'er us; ye have wreathed
Fresh garlands: for sweet music has been heard
In many places—some has been upstirr'd
From out its crystal dwelling in a lake,
By a swan's ebon bill;[9] from a thick brake,° *thicket*
Nested and quiet in a valley mild,
Bubbles a pipe;[10] fine sounds are floating wild
About the earth: happy are ye and glad.

---

[1] *Jove* Roman king of the gods.

[2] *Muses* In Greek mythology, nine daughters of Zeus and Mnemosyne, each of whom presided over and provided inspiration for an aspect of learning or the arts.

[3] *Pegasus* Great winged horse of Greek mythology. This line is a reference to William Hazlitt's essay "On Milton's Versification" (1815), in which he says, on the use of the heroic couplet by eighteenth-century poets, "Dr. Johnson and Pope would have turned [Milton's] vaulting Pegasus into a rocking-horse."

[4] *Jacob's wit* See Genesis 30.27–43, in which Jacob increases his wealth at the expense of Laban.

[5] *the bright Lyrist* I.e., Apollo.

[6] *Boileau* French literary critic Nicolas Boileau Despréaux (1636–1711), whose *L'Art Poétique* (1674), a verse treatise on literary aesthetics, was extremely influential among English poets.

[7] *boundly* Term coined by Keats, meaning either "boundless" or "bounden."

[8] *some lone spirits* Reference to poets Thomas Chatterton (1752–70), Henry White (1785–1806), and others, who died young, without receiving the critical attention their work deserved.

[9] *swan's ebon bill* Reference to William Wordsworth (1770–1850), who, along with Coleridge and Southey, was known as a "Lake Poet."

[10] *from a … pipe* Reference to poet Leigh Hunt (1784–1859).

These things are doubtless: yet in truth we've had
Strange thunders from the potency of song;
Mingled indeed with what is sweet and strong,
From majesty: but in clear truth the themes
Are ugly clubs, the poets Polyphemes[1]
Disturbing the grand sea. A drainless shower
Of light is poesy; 'tis the supreme of power;
'Tis might half slumb'ring on its own right arm.
The very archings of her eye-lids charm
A thousand willing agents to obey,
And still she governs with the mildest sway:
But strength alone though of the Muses born
Is like a fallen angel: trees uptorn,
Darkness, and worms, and shrouds, and sepulchres
Delight it; for it feeds upon the burrs,
And thorns of life; forgetting the great end
Of poesy, that it should be a friend
To sooth the cares, and lift the thoughts of man.

Yet I rejoice: a myrtle fairer than
E'er grew in Paphos,[2] from the bitter weeds
Lifts its sweet head into the air, and feeds
A silent space with ever sprouting green.
All tenderest birds there find a pleasant screen,
Creep through the shade with jaunty fluttering,
Nibble the little cupped flowers and sing.
Then let us clear away the choking thorns
From round its gentle stem; let the young fawns,
Yeaned° in after times, when we are flown, *brought forth*
Find a fresh sward° beneath it, overgrown *turf*
With simple flowers: let there nothing be
More boisterous than a lover's bended knee;
Nought more ungentle than the placid look
Of one who leans upon a closed book;
Nought more untranquil than the grassy slopes
Between two hills. All hail delightful hopes!
As she was wont, th'imagination
Into most lovely labyrinths will be gone,
And they shall be accounted poet kings
Who simply tell the most heart-easing things.
O may these joys be ripe before I die.
Will not some say that I presumptuously
Have spoken? that from hastening disgrace
'Twere better far to hide my foolish face?
That whining boyhood should with reverence bow
Ere the dread thunderbolt could reach? How!
If I do hide myself, it sure shall be
In the very fane, the light of Poesy:
If I do fall, at least I will be laid
Beneath the silence of a poplar shade;
And over me the grass shall be smooth shaven;
And there shall be a kind memorial graven.
But off Despondence! miserable bane!
They should not know thee, who athirst to gain
A noble end, are thirsty every hour.
What though I am not wealthy in the dower
Of spanning wisdom; though I do not know
The shiftings of the mighty winds that blow
Hither and thither all the changing thoughts
Of man: though no great minist'ring reason sorts
Out the dark mysteries of human souls
To clear conceiving: yet there ever rolls
A vast idea before me, and I glean
Therefrom my liberty; thence too I've seen
The end and aim of Poesy. 'Tis clear
As any thing most true; as that the year
Is made of the four seasons—manifest
As a large cross, some old cathedral's crest,
Lifted to the white clouds. Therefore should I
Be but the essence of deformity,
A coward, did my very eyelids wink
At speaking out what I have dared to think.
Ah! rather let me like a madman run
Over some precipice; let the hot sun
Melt my Dedalian wings,[3] and drive me down
Convuls'd and headlong! Stay! an inward frown
Of conscience bids me be more calm awhile.
An ocean dim, sprinkled with many an isle,
Spreads awfully before me. How much toil!
How many days! what desperate turmoil!
Ere I can have explored its widenesses.

[1] *Polyphemes* One-eyed, club-wielding giant in Homer's *Odyssey*.

[2] *Paphos* City in Cyprus that is the site of a famous temple to Venus, goddess of love and beauty. Myrtle (line 248) is also associated with Venus.

[3] *Dedalian wings* According to Greek mythology, the sculptor Daedalus built wings of wax and feathers so that he and his son Icarus could escape from the island of Crete, where they were imprisoned. Icarus flew too close to the sun, and his wings melted, causing him to fall into the sea.

Ah, what a task! upon my bended knees,
I could unsay those—no, impossible!
Impossible!
For sweet relief I'll dwell
On humbler thoughts, and let this strange assay
Begun in gentleness die so away.
E'en now all tumult from my bosom fades:
I turn full hearted to the friendly aids
That smooth the path of honour; brotherhood,
And friendliness the nurse of mutual good.
The hearty grasp that sends a pleasant sonnet
Into the brain ere one can think upon it;
The silence when some rhymes are coming out;
And when they're come, the very pleasant rout:
The message certain to be done to-morrow.
'Tis perhaps as well that it should be to borrow
Some precious book from out its snug retreat,
To cluster round it when we next shall meet.
Scarce can I scribble on; for lovely airs
Are fluttering round the room like doves in pairs;
Many delights of that glad day recalling,
When first my senses caught their tender falling.
And with these airs come forms of elegance
Stooping their shoulders o'er a horse's prance,
Careless, and grand—fingers soft and round
Parting luxuriant curls—and the swift bound
Of Bacchus from his chariot, when his eye
Made Ariadne's cheek look blushingly.[1]
Thus I remember all the pleasant flow
Of words at opening a portfolio.

Things such as these are ever harbingers
To trains of peaceful images: the stirs
Of a swan's neck unseen among the rushes:
A linnet starting all about the bushes:
A butterfly, with golden wings broad parted,
Nestling a rose, convuls'd as though it smarted
With over pleasure—many, many more,
Might I indulge at large in all my store
Of luxuries: yet I must not forget
Sleep, quiet with his poppy coronet:[2]
For what there may be worthy in these rhymes
I partly owe to him: and thus, the chimes
Of friendly voices had just given place
To as sweet a silence, when I 'gan retrace
The pleasant day, upon a couch at ease.
It was a poet's house who keeps the keys
Of pleasure's temple.[3] Round about were hung
The glorious features of the bards who sung
In other ages—cold and sacred busts
Smiled at each other. Happy he who trusts
To clear Futurity his darling fame!
Then there were fauns and satyrs taking aim
At swelling apples with a frisky leap
And reaching fingers, 'mid a luscious heap
Of vine leaves. Then there rose to view a fane° *temple*
Of liny° marble, and thereto a train *veined*
Of nymphs approaching fairly o'er the sward:
One, loveliest, holding her white hand toward
The dazzling sun-rise: two sisters sweet
Bending their graceful figures till they meet
Over the trippings of a little child:
And some are hearing, eagerly, the wild
Thrilling liquidity of dewy piping.
See, in another picture, nymphs are wiping
Cherishingly Diana's[4] timorous limbs;
A fold of lawny mantle dabbling swims
At the bath's edge, and keeps a gentle motion
With the subsiding crystal: as when ocean
Heaves calmly its broad swelling smoothness o'er
Its rocky marge, and balances once more
The patient weeds; that now unshent° *unharmed*
by foam
Feel all about their undulating home.

Sappho's[5] meek head was there half smiling down
At nothing; just as though the earnest frown

[1] *Of Bacchus … blushingly* Adriane, daughter of King Minos of Crete, was abandoned by her lover, Theseus, on the island of Naxos. Bacchus, god of wine, found her there, consoled her, and married her (Ovid, *Metamorphses* 8.172–82). Keats would also have been familiar with the painting *Bacchus and Ariadne* (1523) by Venetian painter Titian (1490–1576).

[2] *poppy coronet* The seed capsules of some species of poppy contain opium, and therefore were associated with sleep.

[3] *It was … temple* Poet Leigh Hunt kept a bed for Keats in his study. Hunt's cottage was filled with busts and pictures, on which the following descriptions are probably based.

[4] *Diana* Roman goddess of chastity, childbirth, and the hunt.

[5] *Sappho* Greek lyric poet of the sixth century BCE.

Of over thinking had that moment gone
From off her brow, and left her all alone.

Great Alfred's[1] too, with anxious, pitying eyes,
As if he always listened to the sighs
Of the goaded world; and Kosciusko's[2] worn
By horrid suffrance—mightily forlorn.

Petrarch, outstepping from the shady green,
Starts at the sight of Laura;[3] nor can wean
His eyes from her sweet face. Most happy they!
For over them was seen a free display
Of out-spread wings, and from between them shone
The face of Poesy: from off her throne
She overlook'd things that I scarce could tell.
The very sense of where I was might well
Keep Sleep aloof: but more than that there came
Thought after thought to nourish up the flame
Within my breast; so that the morning light
Surprised me even from a sleepless night;
And up I rose refresh'd, and glad, and gay,
Resolving to begin that very day
These lines; and howsoever they be done,
I leave them as a father does his son.
—1817

On Seeing the Elgin Marbles[4]

My spirit is too weak; mortality
Weighs heavily on me like unwilling sleep,
And each imagined pinnacle and steep
Of godlike hardship, tells me I must die
Like a sick Eagle looking at the sky.
Yet 'tis a gentle luxury to weep,
That I have not the cloudy winds to keep
Fresh for the opening of the morning's eye.
Such dim-conceived glories of the brain
Bring round the heart an indescribable feud;
So do these wonders a most dizzy pain,
That mingles Grecian grandeur with the rude
Wasting of old Time—with a billowy main,° *sea*
A sun, a shadow of a magnitude.
—1817

On Sitting Down to Read King Lear Once Again

O golden tongued Romance, with serene lute!
Fair plumed Syren![5] Queen of far-away!
Leave melodizing on this wintry day,
Shut up thine olden pages, and be mute:
Adieu! for once again the fierce dispute
Betwixt damnation and impassion'd clay
Must I burn through; once more humbly assay
The bitter-sweet of this Shakespearian fruit.
Chief Poet! and ye clouds of Albion,[6]
Begetters of our deep eternal theme,
When through the old oak forest I am gone,
Let me not wander in a barren dream,
But when I am consumed in the fire,
Give me new Phœnix[7] wings to fly at my desire.
—1838

When I Have Fears That I May Cease To Be

When I have fears that I may cease to be
Before my pen has glean'd my teeming brain,
Before high piled books, in charact'ry,[8]
Hold like rich garners the full-ripen'd grain;

[1] *Great Alfred* Alfred the Great, King of Wessex from 871 to 899.

[2] *Kosciusko* Polish patriot Tadeusz Kosciusko (1746–1817), who led his countrymen in an uprising against Russia, and also fought for the United States Army in the American struggle for independence.

[3] *Petrarch … Laura* Italian poet Petrarch (1304–74) wrote odes and sonnets in celebration of his beloved, Laura.

[4] *Elgin Marbles* In 1806 Lord Elgin brought friezes and other sculptures that had decorated the exterior of the Parthenon, in Athens, to England. In 1816 the government purchased them for display in the British Museum, where they remain today. See the "In Context" section on this topic.

[5] *Syren* Monster of classical mythology who is half woman, half serpent, and whose enchanted singing lures sailors to their deaths.

[6] *Albion* England.

[7] *Phoenix* Mythical Egyptian bird that is consumed by fire, and then reborn, once every 500 years.

[8] *charact'ry* Symbols or characters.

When I behold, upon the night's starr'd face,
Huge cloudy symbols of a high romance,
And think that I may never live to trace
Their shadows, with the magic hand of chance;
And when I feel, fair creature of an hour!
That I shall never look upon thee more,
Never have relish in the fairy power
Of unreflecting love—then on the shore
Of the wide world I stand alone, and think
Till love and fame to nothingness do sink.
—1848 (WRITTEN 1818)

Epistle to John Hamilton Reynolds[1]

Dear Reynolds! as last night I lay in bed,
There came before my eyes that wonted thread
Of shapes, and shadows, and remembrances,
That every other minute vex and please:
Things all disjointed come from north and south—
Two witch's eyes above a cherub's mouth,
Voltaire with casque and shield and habergeon,[2]
And Alexander[3] with his night-cap on;
Old Socrates[4] a-tying his cravat,
And Hazlitt playing with Miss Edgeworth's cat;[5]
And Junius Brutus, pretty well so so,[6]
Making the best of's way towards Soho.[7]

Few are there who escape these visitings—
Perhaps one or two whose lives have patent wings,
And through whose curtains peeps no hellish nose,
No wild-boar tushes,° and no mermaid's toes; *tusks*
But flowers bursting out with lusty pride,
And young Æolian harps[8] personified;
Some, Titian[9] colours touch'd into real life—
The sacrifice goes on; the pontiff knife
Gleams in the sun, the milk-white heifer lows,
The pipes go shrilly, the libation flows:
A white sail shows above the green-head cliff,
Moves round the point, and throws her anchor stiff;
The mariners join hymn with those on land.

You know the Enchanted Castle[10]—it doth stand
Upon a rock, on the border of a lake,
Nested in trees, which all do seem to shake
From some old magic like Urganda's sword.[11]
O Phoebus![12] that I had thy sacred word
To show this Castle, in fair dreaming wise,
Unto my friend, while sick and ill he lies!

You know it well enough, where it doth seem
A mossy place, a Merlin's Hall,[13] a dream;
You know the clear lake, and the little isles,
The mountains blue, and cold near neighbour rills,
All which elsewhere are but half animate;
There do they look alive to love and hate,
To smiles and frowns; they seem a lifted mound
Above some giant, pulsing underground.

Part of the building was a chosen see,° *dwelling-place*
Built by a banish'd Santon° of Chaldee; *holy man*
The other part, two thousand years from him,
Was built by Cuthbert de Saint Aldebrim;[14]
Then there's a little wing, far from the sun,

[1] *John Hamilton Reynolds* Poet and lawyer (1794–1852) who was a close friend of Keats. Reynolds was ill at the time, and Keats sent him this verse letter to cheer him.

[2] *Voltaire* French philosopher François-Marie Arouet de Voltaire (1694–1778); *casque* Helmet; *habergeon* Sleeveless jacket of chain mail.

[3] *Alexander* Poet Alexander Pope (1688–1744).

[4] *Socrates* Greek philosopher of the fifth century BCE.

[5] *Hazlitt* Painter and writer William Hazlitt (1778–1830); *Miss Edgeworth* Novelist Maria Edgeworth (1767–1849).

[6] *Junius Brutus* Actor Junius Brutus Booth (1796–1852); *so so* Tipsy.

[7] *Soho* Area in London, then rather disreputable.

[8] *Æolian harps* Harps that produce sound when exposed to the wind or open air. From Æolus, the Greek god of the winds.

[9] *Titian* I.e, rich; in the style of Titian, a Venetian Renaissance painter whose work was characterized by bold colors. The following lines most likely describe *Sacrifice to Apollo*, by French painter Claude Lorraine (1600–82).

[10] *the Enchanted Castle* Painting by Claude Lorraine.

[11] *Urganda's sword* Enchantress figure in *Amadis of Gaul*, a fifteenth-century romance.

[12] *Phoebus* Apollo, Greek god of poetry and of the sun.

[13] *Merlin's Hall* I.e., a hall built by magicians such as the sorcerer Merlin, from Arthurian legend.

[14] *Cuthbert … Aldebrim* Character invented by Keats.

Built by a Lapland witch[1] turn'd maudlin nun;
And many other juts of aged stone
Founded with many a mason-devil's groan.

The doors all look as if they oped themselves,
The windows as if latched by fays° and elves, *fairies*
And from them comes a silver flash of light,
As from the westward of a summer's night;
Or like a beauteous woman's large blue eyes
Gone mad through olden songs and poesies.

See! what is coming from the distance dim!
A golden galley all in silken trim!
Three rows of oars are lightening, moment whiles,
Into the verd'rous bosoms of those isles;
Towards the shade, under the Castle wall,
It comes in silence—now 'tis hidden all.
The clarion sounds, and from a postern-gate
An echo of sweet music doth create
A fear in the poor herdsman, who doth bring
His beasts to trouble the enchanted spring—
He tells of the sweet music, and the spot,
To all his friends, and they believe him not.

O that our dreamings all, of sleep or wake,
Would all their colours from the sunset take:
From something of material sublime,
Rather than shadow our own soul's daytime
In the dark void of night. For in the world
We jostle—but my flag is not unfurl'd
On the admiral-staff—and to philosophise
I dare not yet! Oh, never will the prize,
High reason, and the lore of good and ill,
Be my award! Things cannot to the will
Be settled, but they tease us out of thought;
Or is it that imagination brought
Beyond its proper bound, yet still confin'd,
Lost in a sort of Purgatory blind,
Cannot refer to any standard law
Of either earth or heaven? It is a flaw
In happiness, to see beyond our bourn—
It forces us in summer skies to mourn,
It spoils the singing of the nightingale.

[1] *Lapland witch* Lapland was supposed to be the dwelling-place of witches.

Dear Reynolds! I have a mysterious tale,
And cannot speak it: the first page I read
Upon a lampit° rock of green sea-weed *limpet*
Among the breakers; 'twas a quiet eve,
The rocks were silent, the wide sea did weave
An untumultuous fringe of silver foam
Along the flat brown sand; I was at home
And should have been most happy—but I saw
Too far into the sea, where every maw° *throat, gullet*
The greater on the less feeds evermore.
But I saw too distinct into the core
Of an eternal fierce destruction,
And so from happiness I far was gone.
Still am I sick of it, and tho', to-day,
I've gather'd young spring-leaves, and flowers gay
Of periwinkle and wild strawberry,
Still do I that most fierce destruction see—
The shark at savage prey, the hawk at pounce,
The gentle robin, like a pard° or ounce,° *leopard / lynx*
Ravening a worm—Away, ye horrid moods!
Moods of one's mind! You know I hate them well.
You know I'd sooner be a clapping bell
To some Kamschatkan[2] missionary church,
Than with these horrid moods be left i'the lurch.
Do you get health—and Tom the same—I'll dance,
And from detested moods in new romance[3]
Take refuge—Of bad lines a centaine[4] dose
Is sure enough—and so "here follows prose."[5]
—1848

To Homer[6]

Standing aloof in giant ignorance,
Of thee I hear and of the Cyclades,[7]
As one who sits ashore and longs perchance

[2] *Kamschatkan* From the Kamchatka Peninsula in Siberia.

[3] *new romance* Probably Keats's *Isabella* (1820), a romance based on a tale from Italian poet Giovanni Boccaccio's *Decameron* (written 1348–53).

[4] *centaine* Company of one hundred.

[5] *here follows prose* See Shakespeare's *Twelfth Night* 2.5.154.

[6] *Homer* Early Greek poet, believed to be the author of *The Iliad* and *Odyssey*.

[7] *Cyclades* Group of islands in the Aegean Sea, off the southeast coast of Greece.

To visit dolphin-coral in deep seas.
So thou wast blind![1]—but then the veil was rent;
For Jove[2] uncurtain'd Heaven to let thee live,
And Neptune[3] made for thee a spumy[4] tent,
And Pan[5] made sing for thee his forest-hive;
Aye, on the shores of darkness there is light,
And precipices show untrodden green;
There is a budding morrow in midnight;
There is a triple sight in blindness keen;
Such seeing hast thou, as it once befell
To Dian, Queen of Earth, and Heaven, and Hell.[6]
—1848 (WRITTEN C.1818)

The Eve of St. Agnes[7]

1

St. Agnes' Eve—Ah, bitter chill it was!
The owl, for all his feathers, was a-cold;
The hare limp'd trembling through the frozen grass,
And silent was the flock in woolly fold:
Numb were the Beadsman's[8] fingers, while he told
His rosary, and while his frosted breath,
Like pious incense from a censer[9] old,
Seem'd taking flight for heaven, without a death,
Past the sweet Virgin's[10] picture, while his prayer he saith.

2

His prayer he saith, this patient, holy man;
Then takes his lamp, and riseth from his knees,
And back returneth, meagre, barefoot, wan,
Along the chapel aisle by slow degrees:
The sculptur'd dead, on each side, seem to freeze,
Emprison'd in black, purgatorial rails:
Knights, ladies, praying in dumb orat'ries,° *chapels*
He passeth by; and his weak spirit fails
To think how they may ache in icy hoods and mails.

3

Northward he turneth through a little door,
And scarce three steps, ere Music's golden tongue
Flatter'd to tears this aged man and poor;
But no—already had his deathbell rung:
The joys of all his life were said and sung:
His was harsh penance on St. Agnes' Eve:
Another way he went, and soon among
Rough ashes sat he for his soul's reprieve,
And all night kept awake, for sinners' sake to grieve.

4

That ancient Beadsman heard the prelude soft;
And so it chanc'd, for many a door was wide,
From hurry to and fro. Soon, up aloft,
The silver, snarling trumpets 'gan to chide:
The level chambers, ready with their pride,
Were glowing to receive a thousand guests:
The carved angels, ever eager-eyed,
Star'd, where upon their heads the cornice rests,
With hair blown back, and wings put cross-wise on their breasts.

5

At length burst in the argent[11] revelry,
With plume, tiara, and all rich array,
Numerous as shadows haunting fairily
The brain, new stuff'd, in youth, with triumphs gay
Of old romance. These let us wish away,

---

1 *thou wast blind* Homer was said to have been blind.

2 *Jove* Roman King of the gods.

3 *Neptune* Roman god of the sea.

4 *spumy* Covered in sea foam.

5 *Pan* Greek shepherd god of nature who was half goat and half man. After the nymph Syrinx turned herself into a bed of reeds in order to escape him, Pan created an instrument (the panpipe) out of the reeds.

6 *To Dian ... Hell* Diana was sometimes envisioned as a three-figured goddess, presiding over the moon, childbirth, and the hunt, and hell.

7 *St. Agnes* Fourth-century Christian martyr, executed at the age of thirteen, who is the patron saint of virgins. It was tradition that young women could obtain a vision of their future husbands if they performed the proper rituals on 20 January, the night before St. Agnes's Feast Day.

8 *Beadsman* Pensioner paid to say prayers for the souls of his benefactors. He "tells," or counts, the beads of his rosary, saying a prayer at each bead.

9 *censer* Incense burner.

10 *Virgin* I.e., Mary, virgin mother of Christ.

11 *argent* Adorned with silver.

And turn, sole-thoughted, to one Lady there,
Whose heart had brooded, all that wintry day,
On love, and wing'd St. Agnes' saintly care,
As she had heard old dames full many times declare.

6

They told her how, upon St. Agnes' Eve,
Young virgins might have visions of delight,
And soft adorings from their loves receive
Upon the honey'd middle of the night,
If ceremonies due they did aright;° *arranged properly*
As, supperless to bed they must retire,
And couch supine their beauties, lily white;
Nor look behind, nor sideways, but require
Of Heaven with upward eyes for all that they desire.

7

Full of this whim was thoughtful Madeline:
The music, yearning like a God in pain,
She scarcely heard: her maiden eyes divine,
Fix'd on the floor, saw many a sweeping train
Pass by—she heeded not at all: in vain
Came many a tiptoe, amorous cavalier,
And back retir'd; not cool'd by high disdain,
But she saw not: her heart was otherwhere:
She sigh'd for Agnes' dreams, the sweetest of the year.

8

She danc'd along with vague, regardless eyes,
Anxious her lips, her breathing quick and short:
The hallow'd hour was near at hand: she sighs
Amid the timbrels,° and the throng'd resort *tambourines*
Of whisperers in anger, or in sport;
'Mid looks of love, defiance, hate, and scorn,
Hoodwink'd° with faery fancy; all *blindfolded*
amort,° *dead*
Save to St. Agnes and her lambs unshorn,[1]
And all the bliss to be before to-morrow morn.

9

So, purposing each moment to retire,
She linger'd still. Meantime, across the moors,
Had come young Porphyro, with heart on fire
For Madeline. Beside the portal doors,
Buttress'd from moonlight, stands he, and implores
All saints to give him sight of Madeline,
But for one moment in the tedious hours,
That he might gaze and worship all unseen;
Perchance speak, kneel, touch, kiss—in sooth such things have been.

10

He ventures in: let no buzz'd whisper tell:
All eyes be muffled, or a hundred swords
Will storm his heart, Love's fev'rous citadel:
For him, those chambers held barbarian hordes,
Hyena foemen, and hot-blooded lords,
Whose very dogs would execrations howl
Against his lineage: not one breast affords
Him any mercy, in that mansion foul,
Save one old beldame,[2] weak in body and in soul.

11

Ah, happy chance! the aged creature came,
Shuffling along with ivory-headed wand,° *staff*
To where he stood, hid from the torch's flame,
Behind a broad hall-pillar, far beyond
The sound of merriment and chorus bland:° *soft*
He startled her; but soon she knew his face,
And grasp'd his fingers in her palsied hand,
Saying, "Mercy, Porphyro! hie thee from this place;
They are all here to-night, the whole blood-thirsty race!"

12

"Get hence! get hence! there's dwarfish Hildebrand;
He had a fever late, and in the fit
He cursed thee and thine, both house and land:
Then there's that old Lord Maurice, not a whit
More tame for his gray hairs—Alas me! flit!
Flit like a ghost away."—"Ah, Gossip[3] dear,
We're safe enough; here in this arm-chair sit,
And tell me how"—"Good Saints! not here, not here;
Follow me, child, or else these stones will be thy bier."

13

He follow'd through a lowly arched way,
Brushing the cobwebs with his lofty plume,

[1] *St. Agnes … unshorn* The Latin for lamb is *agnus*; thus the traditional association of St. Agnes with lambs, which also carry connotations of whiteness and purity.

[2] *beldame* Grandmother, old woman, or elderly nurse.

[3] *Gossip* Good friend; godmother.

And as she mutter'd "Well-a—well-a-day!"
He found him in a little moonlight room,
Pale, lattic'd, chill, and silent as a tomb.
"Now tell me where is Madeline," said he,
"O tell me, Angela, by the holy loom
Which none but secret sisterhood may see,
When they St. Agnes' wool are weaving piously."

14

"St. Agnes! Ah! it is St. Agnes' Eve—
Yet men will murder upon holy days:
Thou must hold water in a witch's sieve,
And be liege-lord of all the Elves and Fays,° *fairies*
To venture so: it fills me with amaze
To see thee, Porphyro!—St. Agnes' Eve!
God's help! my lady fair the conjuror plays
This very night: good angels her deceive!
But let me laugh awhile, I've mickle° time to grieve. *much*

15

Feebly she laugheth in the languid moon,
While Porphyro upon her face doth look,
Like puzzled urchin on an aged crone
Who keepeth clos'd a wond'rous riddle-book,
As spectacled she sits in chimney nook.
But soon his eyes grew brilliant, when she told
His lady's purpose; and he scarce could brook° *prevent*
Tears, at the thought of those enchantments cold
And Madeline asleep in lap of legends old.

16

Sudden a thought came like a full-blown rose,
Flushing his brow, and in his pained heart
Made purple riot: then doth he propose
A stratagem, that makes the beldame start:
"A cruel man and impious thou art:
Sweet lady, let her pray, and sleep, and dream
Alone with her good angels, far apart
From wicked men like thee. Go, go!—I deem
Thou canst not surely be the same that thou didst seem."

17

"I will not harm her, by all saints I swear,"
Quoth Porphyro: "O may I ne'er find grace
When my weak voice shall whisper its last prayer,
If one of her soft ringlets I displace,
Or look with ruffian passion in her face:
Good Angela, believe me by these tears;
Or I will, even in a moment's space,
Awake, with horrid shout, my foemen's ears,
And beard° them, though they be more fang'd than wolves and bears." *oppose*

18

"Ah! why wilt thou affright a feeble soul?
A poor, weak, palsy-stricken, churchyard thing,
Whose passing-bell may ere the midnight toll;
Whose prayers for thee, each morn and evening,
Were never miss'd."—Thus plaining,° doth she bring *complaining*
A gentler speech from burning Porphyro;
So woeful, and of such deep sorrowing,
That Angela gives promise she will do
Whatever he shall wish, betide her weal or woe.

19

Which was, to lead him, in close secrecy,
Even to Madeline's chamber, and there hide
Him in a closet, of such privacy
That he might see her beauty unespied,
And win perhaps that night a peerless bride,
While legion'd fairies pac'd the coverlet,
And pale enchantment held her sleepy-eyed.
Never on such a night have lovers met,
Since Merlin paid his Demon all the monstrous debt.[1]

20

"It shall be as thou wishest," said the Dame:
"All cates° and dainties shall be stored there *delicacies*
Quickly on this feast-night: by the tambour frame[2]
Her own lute thou wilt see: no time to spare,
For I am slow and feeble, and scarce dare
On such a catering trust my dizzy head.
Wait here, my child, with patience; kneel in prayer
The while: Ah! thou must needs the lady wed,
Or may I never leave my grave among the dead."

---

[1] *Since … debt* Probably a reference to the episode in Arthurian legend in which the enchanter Merlin falls in love with the enchantress Vivien, or Nimue, who turns one of his spells against him and imprisons him in a cave.

[2] *tambour frame* Circular frame for embroidery.

21

So saying, she hobbled off with busy fear.
The lover's endless minutes slowly pass'd:
The dame return'd, and whisper'd in his ear
To follow her; with aged eyes aghast
From fright of dim espial. Safe at last,
Through many a dusky gallery, they gain
The maiden's chamber, silken, hush'd, and chaste;
Where Porphyro took covert, pleas'd amain.° *completely*
His poor guide hurried back with agues° *fever*
in her brain.

22

Her falt'ring hand upon the balustrade,
Old Angela was feeling for the stair,
When Madeline, St. Agnes' charmed maid,
Rose, like a mission'd spirit, unaware:
With silver taper's light, and pious care,
She turn'd, and down the aged gossip led
To a safe level matting. Now prepare,
Young Porphyro, for gazing on that bed;
She comes, she comes again, like ring-dove
fray'd° and fled. *frightened*

23

Out went the taper° as she hurried in; *candle*
Its little smoke, in pallid moonshine, died:
She clos'd the door, she panted, all akin
To spirits of the air, and visions wide:
No uttered syllable, or, woe betide!
But to her heart, her heart was voluble,
Paining with eloquence her balmy side;
As though a tongueless nightingale should swell
Her throat in vain, and die, heart-stifled, in her dell.

24

A casement high and triple-arch'd there was,
All garlanded with carven imag'ries
Of fruits, and flowers, and bunches of knot-grass,
And diamonded with panes of quaint device,
Innumerable of stains and splendid dyes,
As are the tiger-moth's deep-damask'd wings;
And in the midst, 'mong thousand heraldries,[1]
And twilight saints, and dim emblazonings,
A shielded scutcheon blush'd with blood of queens
and kings.[2]

25

Full on this casement shone the wintry moon,
And threw warm gules[3] on Madeline's fair breast,
As down she knelt for heaven's grace and boon;° *blessing*
Rose-bloom fell on her hands, together prest,
And on her silver cross soft amethyst,
And on her hair a glory, like a saint:
She seem'd a splendid angel, newly drest,
Save wings, for heaven—Porphyro grew faint:
She knelt, so pure a thing, so free from mortal taint.

26

Anon his heart revives: her vespers° done, *evening prayers*
Of all its wreathed pearls her hair she frees;
Unclasps her warmed jewels one by one;
Loosens her fragrant boddice; by degrees
Her rich attire creeps rustling to her knees:
Half-hidden, like a mermaid in sea-weed,
Pensive awhile she dreams awake, and sees,
In fancy, fair St. Agnes in her bed,
But dares not look behind, or all the charm is fled.

27

Soon, trembling in her soft and chilly nest,
In sort of wakeful swoon, perplex'd[4] she lay,
Until the poppied° warmth of sleep oppress'd *narcotic*
Her soothed limbs, and soul fatigued away;
Flown, like a thought, until the morrow-day;
Blissfully haven'd both from joy and pain;
Clasp'd like a missal[5] where swart Paynims[6] pray;
Blinded alike from sunshine and from rain,
As though a rose should shut, and be a bud again.

28

Stol'n to this paradise, and so entranced,
Porphyro gazed upon her empty dress,
And listen'd to her breathing, if it chanced

---

[1] *heraldries* Emblems of rank and genealogy.

[2] *scutcheon* I.e., escutcheon: shield; *blushed ... kings* I.e., indicates she is of royal blood.

[3] *gules* Red bars (a heraldic device).

[4] *perplexed* I.e., between sleep and waking.

[5] *missal* Christian mass- or prayer-book.

[6] *swart Paynims* Dark-skinned pagans.

To wake into a slumberous tenderness;
Which when he heard, that minute did he bless,
And breath'd himself: then from the closet crept,
Noiseless as fear in a wide wilderness,
And over the hush'd carpet, silent, stept,
And 'tween the curtains peep'd, where, lo!—how fast she slept.

29

Then by the bed-side, where the faded moon
Made a dim, silver twilight, soft he set
A table, and, half anguish'd, threw thereon
A cloth of woven crimson, gold, and jet—
O for some drowsy Morphean amulet![1]
The boisterous, midnight, festive clarion,° *trumpet*
The kettle-drum, and far-heard clarinet,
Affray his ears, though but in dying tone—
The hall door shuts again, and all the noise is gone.

30

And still she slept an azure-lidded sleep,
In blanched linen, smooth, and lavender'd,
While he from forth the closet brought a heap
Of candied apple, quince, and plum, and gourd;° *melon*
With jellies soother[2] than the creamy curd,
And lucent° syrops, tinct° with cinnamon; *clear / imbued*
Manna[3] and dates, in argosy[4] transferr'd
From Fez;[5] and spiced dainties, every one,
From silken Samarkand[6] to cedar'd Lebanon.

31

These delicates he heap'd with glowing hand
On golden dishes and in baskets bright
Of wreathed silver: sumptuous they stand
In the retired quiet of the night,
Filling the chilly room with perfume light.
"And now, my love, my seraph° fair, awake! *angel*
Thou art my heaven, and I thine eremite:° *hermit*
Open thine eyes, for meek St. Agnes' sake,
Or I shall drowse beside thee, so my soul doth ache."

32

Thus whispering, his warm, unnerved arm
Sank in her pillow. Shaded was her dream
By the dusk curtains—'twas a midnight charm
Impossible to melt as iced stream:
The lustrous salvers° in the moonlight gleam; *trays*
Broad golden fringe upon the carpet lies:
It seem'd he never, never could redeem
From such a stedfast spell his lady's eyes;
So mus'd awhile, entoil'd in woofed° phantasies. *woven*

33

Awakening up, he took her hollow lute—
Tumultuous—and, in chords that tenderest be,
He play'd an ancient ditty, long since mute,
In Provence call'd, "La belle dame sans mercy":[7]
Close to her ear touching the melody—
Wherewith disturb'd, she utter'd a soft moan:
He ceased—she panted quick—and suddenly
Her blue affrayed eyes wide open shone:
Upon his knees he sank, pale as smooth-sculptured stone.

34

Her eyes were open, but she still beheld,
Now wide awake, the vision of her sleep:
There was a painful change, that nigh expell'd
The blisses of her dream so pure and deep,
At which fair Madeline began to weep,
And moan forth witless words with many a sigh;
While still her gaze on Porphyro would keep;
Who knelt, with joined hands and piteous eye,
Fearing to move or speak, she look'd so dreamingly.

35

"Ah, Porphyro!" said she, "but even now
Thy voice was at sweet tremble in mine ear,
Made tuneable with every sweetest vow;
And those sad eyes were spiritual and clear:

[1] *Morphean amulet* Sleep-inducing medicine or charm. (Morpheus is the god of dreams.)

[2] *soother* A word of Keats's own invention, meaning more soothing, softer.

[3] *Manna* Dried, sweet gum taken from various plants.

[4] *argosy* Merchant vessels.

[5] *Fez* City in Morocco.

[6] *Samarkand* City in Uzbekistan.

[7] *La belle … mercy* French: "The beautiful woman without pity." Title of a long poem by medieval poet Alain Chartier (c. 1385–1433); Keats had not yet written his own poem with this title.

How chang'd thou art! how pallid, chill, and drear!
Give me that voice again, my Porphyro,
Those looks immortal, those complainings° *lamentings*
dear!
Oh leave me not in this eternal woe,
For if thou diest, my Love, I know not where to go."

36

Beyond a mortal man impassion'd far
At these voluptuous accents, he arose,
Ethereal, flush'd, and like a throbbing star
Seen mid the sapphire heaven's deep repose;
Into her dream he melted, as the rose
Blendeth its odour with the violet—
Solution sweet: meantime the frost-wind blows
Like Love's alarum° pattering the sharp sleet *warning bell*
Against the window-panes; St. Agnes' moon hath set.

37

'Tis dark: quick pattereth the flaw-blown° sleet: *gust-driven*
"This is no dream, my bride, my Madeline!"
'Tis dark: the iced gusts still rave and beat:
"No dream, alas! alas! and woe is mine!
Porphyro will leave me here to fade and pine.
Cruel! what traitor could thee hither bring?
I curse not, for my heart is lost in thine,
Though thou forsakest a deceived thing—
A dove forlorn and lost with sick unpruned wing."

38

"My Madeline! sweet dreamer! lovely bride!
Say, may I be for aye° thy vassal blest? *ever*
Thy beauty's shield, heart-shap'd and
vermeil° dyed? *vermilion (red)*
Ah, silver shrine, here will I take my rest
After so many hours of toil and quest,
A famish'd pilgrim, saved by miracle.
Though I have found, I will not rob thy nest
Saving of thy sweet self; if thou think'st well
To trust, fair Madeline, to no rude infidel.

39

"Hark! 'tis an elfin-storm from faery land,
Of haggard° seeming, but a boon indeed: *wild*
Arise—arise! the morning is at hand;
The bloated wassaillers° will never heed— *drinkers*
Let us away, my love, with happy speed;
There are no ears to hear, or eyes to see—
Drown'd all in Rhenish and the sleepy mead:[1]
Awake! arise! my love, and fearless be,
For o'er the southern moors I have a home for thee."

40

She hurried at his words, beset with fears,
For there were sleeping dragons all around,
At glaring watch, perhaps, with ready spears—
Down the wide stairs a darkling[2] way they found.
In all the house was heard no human sound.
A chain-droop'd lamp was flickering by each door;
The arras,° rich with horseman, hawk, and *tapestries*
hound,
Flutter'd in the besieging wind's uproar;
And the long carpets rose along the gusty floor.

41

They glide, like phantoms, into the wide hall;
Like phantoms, to the iron porch, they glide;
Where lay the Porter, in uneasy sprawl,
With a huge empty flaggon by his side:
The wakeful bloodhound rose, and shook his hide,
But his sagacious eye an inmate owns:
By one, and one, the bolts full easy slide—
The chains lie silent on the footworn stones—
The key turns, and the door upon its hinges groans.

42

And they are gone: ay, ages long ago
These lovers fled away into the storm.
That night the Baron dreamt of many a woe,
And all his warrior-guests, with shade and form
Of witch, and demon, and large coffin-worm,
Were long be-nightmar'd. Angela the old
Died palsy-twitch'd, with meagre face deform;
The Beadsman, after thousand aves[3] told,
For aye unsought for slept among his ashes cold.
—1820

[1] *Rhenish* Wine from the Rhine region; *mead* Alcoholic beverage made from fermented honey and water.

[2] *darkling* Obscure, gloomy.

[3] *aves* Latin: abbreviation for *Ave Marias*, or Hail Marys, prayers to the Virgin Mary.

Bright Star

Bright star, would I were steadfast as thou art—
Not in lone splendour hung aloft the night
And watching, with eternal lids apart,
Like nature's patient, sleepless Eremite,° *hermit*
The moving waters at their priestlike task
Of pure ablution[1] round earth's human shores,
Or gazing on the new soft fallen mask
Of snow upon the mountains and the moors—
No—yet still steadfast, still unchangeable,
Pillow'd upon my fair love's ripening breast,
To feel for ever its soft fall and swell,
Awake for ever in a sweet unrest,
Still, still to hear her tender-taken breath,
And so live ever—or else swoon to death.
—1838 (WRITTEN 1819)

La Belle Dame Sans Merci[2]

O what can ail thee, knight-at-arms,
Alone and palely loitering?
The sedge[3] has wither'd from the lake,
And no birds sing.

O what can ail thee, knight-at-arms,
So haggard, and so woe-begone?
The squirrel's granary is full,
And the harvest's done.

I see a lily[4] on thy brow,
With anguish moist and fever dew
And on thy cheeks a fading rose
Fast withereth too.

I met a lady in the meads,° *meadows*
Full beautiful—a faery's child,
Her hair was long, her foot was light,
And her eyes were wild.

I made a garland for her head,
And bracelets too, and fragrant zone;° *belt*
She look'd at me as she did love,
And made sweet moan.

I set her on my pacing steed,
And nothing else saw all day long,
For sidelong would she bend and sing
A faery's song.

She found me roots of relish sweet,
And honey wild, and manna dew,[5]
And sure in language strange she said
"I love thee true."

She took me to her elfin grot,° *grotto*
And there she wept and sigh'd full sore,
And there I shut her wild wild eyes
With kisses four.

And there she lulled me asleep,
And there I dream'd—Ah! woe betide!
The latest° dream I ever dream'd *last*
On the cold hill side.

I saw pale kings and princes too,
Pale warriors, death-pale were they all;
They cried, "La belle dame sans merci
Hath thee in thrall!"° *captivity*

I saw their starved lips in the gloam,° *twilight*
With horrid warning gaped wide,
And I awoke, and found me here,
On the cold hill's side.

And this is why I sojourn here,
Alone and palely loitering,
Though the sedge is wither'd from the lake,
And no birds sing.
—1848 (WRITTEN 1819)

---

[1] *ablution* Religious ritual washing of the body.

[2] *La Belle Dame Sans Merci* French: the beautiful lady without pity. This original version of the poem, found in a journal letter to George and Georgiana Keats, was first published in 1848. Keats's revised version was published in 1820.

[3] *sedge* Rush-like grass.

[4] *lily* Flower traditionally symbolic of death.

[5] *manna dew* See Exodus 16, in which God provides the Israelites with a food that falls from heaven, called manna.

La Belle Dame Sans Mercy[1]

Ah, what can ail thee, wretched wight,° *being*
Alone and palely loitering;
The sedge[2] is wither'd from the lake,
And no birds sing.

Ah, what can ail thee, wretched wight,
So haggard and so woe-begone?
The squirrel's granary is full,
And the harvest's done.

I see a lily[3] on thy brow,
With anguish moist and fever dew;
And on thy cheek a fading rose
Fast withereth too.

I met a lady in the meads° *meadows*
Full beautiful, a fairy's child;
Her hair was long, her foot was light,
And her eyes were wild.

I set her on my pacing steed,
And nothing else saw all day long;
For sideways would she lean, and sing
A fairy's song.

I made a garland for her head,
And bracelets too, and fragrant zone:° *belt*
She look'd at me as she did love,
And made sweet moan.

She found me roots of relish sweet,
And honey wild, and manna[4] dew;
And sure in language strange she said,
"I love thee true."

She took me to her elfin grot,° *grotto*
And there she gaz'd and sighed deep.
And there I shut her wild sad eyes—
So kiss'd to sleep.

And there we slumber'd on the moss,
And there I dream'd, ah woe betide,
The latest dream I ever dream'd
On the cold hill side.

I saw pale kings, and princes too,
Pale warriors, death-pale were they all;
Who cry'd—"La belle dame sans mercy
Hath thee in thrall!"° *captivity*

I saw their starv'd lips in the gloom
With horrid warning gaped wide,
And I awoke, and found me here
On the cold hill side.

And this is why I sojourn here
Alone and palely loitering,
Though the sedge is wither'd from the lake,
And no birds sing.

—1820 (WRITTEN 1819)

Incipit Altera Sonneta[5]

I have been endeavouring to discover a better sonnet stanza than we have. The legitimate[6] does not suit the language over-well from the pouncing rhymes—the other kind appears too elegaiac—and the couplet at the end of it has seldom a pleasing effect—I do not pretend to have succeeded—it will explain itself—

If by dull rhymes our English must be chain'd
And, like Andromeda,[7] the Sonnet sweet
Fetter'd in spite of pained loveliness;
Let us find out, if we must be constrain'd
Sandals more interwoven & complete

---

[1] *La Belle ... Mercy* French: the beautiful lady without pity. Keats's revised version was published in 1820.

[2] *sedge* Rush-like grass.

[3] *lily* Flower traditionally symbolic of death.

[4] *manna* See Exodus 16, in which God provides the Israelites with a food that falls from heaven, called manna.

[5] *Incipit Altera Sonneta* Latin: another sonnet begins.

[6] *The legitimate* I.e., the Petrarchan sonnet. The "other kind" to which Keats refers is the Shakespearean sonnet.

[7] *Andromeda* In Greek myth, Andromeda is tied to a rock to be devoured by a sea serpent after her mother boasts that she is more beautiful than the sea nymphs. Perseus, on his winged horse Pegasus (a symbol of poetic inspiration), rescues her.

To fit the naked foot of Poesy;
Let us inspect the Lyre,[1] & weigh the stress
Of every chord & see what may be gain'd
By ear industrious & attention meet;° *fitting*
Misers of sound & syllable, no less
Than Midas of his coinage,[2] let us be
Jealous of dead leaves in the bay wreath Crown;[3]
So if we may not let the Muse[4] be free,
She will be bound with Garlands of her own.
—1836 (WRITTEN 1819)

Ode To Psyche [5]

O Goddess! hear these tuneless numbers, wrung
By sweet enforcement and remembrance dear,
And pardon that thy secrets should be sung
Even into thine own soft-conched[6] ear:
Surely I dreamt to-day, or did I see
The winged Psyche with awaken'd eyes?
I wander'd in a forest thoughtlessly,
And, on the sudden, fainting with surprise,
Saw two fair creatures, couched side by side
In deepest grass, beneath the whisp'ring roof
Of leaves and trembled blossoms, where there ran
A brooklet, scarce espied:

'Mid hush'd, cool-rooted flowers, fragrant-eyed,
Blue, silver-white, and budded Tyrian,[7]
They lay calm-breathing on the bedded grass;
Their arms embraced, and their pinions° too; *wings*
Their lips touch'd not, but had not bade adieu,
As if disjoined by soft-handed slumber,
And ready still past kisses to outnumber
At tender eye-dawn of aurorean[8] love:
The winged boy° I knew; *Cupid*
But who wast thou, O happy, happy dove?
His Psyche true!

O latest born and liveliest vision far
Of all Olympus'[9] faded hierarchy!
Fairer than Phœbe's[10] sapphire-region'd star,
Or Vesper,[11] amorous glow-worm of the sky;
Fairer than these, though temple thou hast none,
Nor altar heap'd with flowers;
Nor virgin-choir to make delicious moan
Upon the midnight hours;
No voice, no lute, no pipe, no incense sweet
From chain-swung censer° teeming; *incense burner*
No shrine, no grove, no oracle, no heat
Of pale-mouth'd prophet dreaming.

O brightest! Though too late for antique vows,
Too, too late for the fond believing
lyre,° *stringed instrument*
When holy were the haunted forest boughs,
Holy the air, the water, and the fire;
Yet even in these days so far retir'd
From happy pieties, thy lucent fans,° *wings*
Fluttering among the faint Olympians,
I see, and sing, by my own eyes inspired.
So let me be thy choir, and make a moan
Upon the midnight hours;
Thy voice, thy lute, thy pipe, thy incense sweet
From swinged censer teeming;
Thy shrine, thy grove, thy oracle, thy heat
Of pale-mouth'd prophet dreaming.

Yes, I will be thy priest, and build a fane° *temple*
In some untrodden region of my mind,

[1] *Lyre* Stringed instrument.

[2] *Midas … coinage* In Ovid's *Metamorphoses*, King Midas of Phrygia gets his wish that everything he touches will turn to gold.

[3] *bay wreath Crown* Wreaths made of leaves of the bay laurel were traditionally bestowed upon those who distinguished themselves in poetry.

[4] *Muse* One of nine daughters of Zeus and Mnemosyne, each of whom presided over and provided inspiration for an aspect of learning or the arts.

[5] *Psyche* In classical mythology, a young woman who was beloved by Cupid, winged god of love and son of Venus. After winning over Venus, who was jealous of Psyche's beauty, Psyche was granted immortality by Jupiter. In Greek myth she is often a personification of the soul: her name in Greek means soul or mind as well as butterfly.

[6] *soft-conched* Shaped like a conch shell, but soft.

[7] *Tyrian* Purple. From the Phoenician city of Tyre, where purple or crimson dyes were made in ancient times.

[8] *aurorean* I.e., dawning. Aurora was the goddess of the dawn.

[9] *Olympus* Mount Olympus, home of the gods.

[10] *Phoebe* Diana, goddess of the moon.

[11] *Vesper* Venus, the evening star.

Where branched thoughts, new grown with pleasant pain,
Instead of pines shall murmur in the wind:
Far, far around shall those dark-cluster'd trees
Fledge the wild-ridged mountains steep by steep;
And there by zephyrs,° streams, and birds, and bees, *breezes*
The moss-lain Dryads° shall be lull'd to sleep; *wood nymphs*
And in the midst of quietness
A rosy sanctuary will I dress
With the wreath'd trellis of a working brain,
With buds, and bells, and stars without a name,
With all the gardener Fancy e'er could feign,
Who breeding flowers, will never breed the same:
And there shall be for thee all soft delight
That shadowy thought can win,
A bright torch, and a casement ope° at night, *window opened*
To let the warm Love in!
—1820

Ode To A Nightingale [1]

1

My heart aches, and a drowsy numbness pains
My sense, as though of hemlock° I had drunk, *poison*
Or emptied some dull opiate to the drains
One minute past, and Lethe-wards[2] had sunk:
'Tis not through envy of thy happy lot,
But being too happy in thine happiness—
That thou, light-winged Dryad° of the trees, *wood-nymph*
In some melodious plot
Of beechen green, and shadows numberless,
Singest of summer in full-throated ease.

2

O, for a draught of vintage! that hath been
Cool'd a long age in the deep-delved earth,
Tasting of Flora[3] and the country green,
Dance, and Provençal song,[4] and sunburnt mirth!
O for a beaker full of the warm South,
Full of the true, the blushful Hippocrene,[5]
With beaded bubbles winking at the brim,
And purple-stained mouth;
That I might drink, and leave the world unseen,
And with thee fade away into the forest dim:

3

Fade far away, dissolve, and quite forget
What thou among the leaves hast never known,
The weariness, the fever, and the fret
Here, where men sit and hear each other groan;
Where palsy shakes a few, sad, last gray hairs,
Where youth grows pale, and spectre-thin, and dies;
Where but to think is to be full of sorrow
And leaden-eyed despairs,
Where Beauty cannot keep her lustrous eyes,
Or new Love pine at them beyond to-morrow.

4

Away! away! for I will fly to thee,
Not charioted by Bacchus and his pards,[6]
But on the viewless wings of Poesy,
Though the dull brain perplexes and retards:
Already with thee! tender is the night,
And haply° the Queen-Moon is on her throne, *maybe*
Cluster'd around by all her starry Fays;° *fairies*

[1] *Ode to a Nightingale* Written about 1 May 1819. Twenty years later, Keats's friend and housemate Charles Armitage Brown remembered the composition of the poem: "In the spring of 1819 a nightingale had built her nest near my house. Keats felt a tranquil and continual joy in her song; and one morning he took his chair from the breakfast-table to the grass-plot under a plum-tree, where he sat for two or three hours. When he came into the house, I perceived he had some scraps of paper in his hand, and these he was quietly thrusting behind the books. On enquiry, I found those scraps, four or five in number, contained his poetic feeling on the song of our nightingale."

[2] *Lethe-wards* Towards Lethe, the river of forgetfulness which, in classical mythology, the dead must cross to reach Hades, the underworld.

[3] *Flora* Roman goddess of flowers.

[4] *Provençal song* The region of Provençe, in southern France, was known in the Middle Ages for its poet-singers, or troubadours.

[5] *Hippocrene* Fountain of the Muses (nine sister goddesses who presided over aspects of learning and the arts) located on the sacred Mount Helicon. Its waters were said to provide poetic inspiration.

[6] *Bacchus … pards* Bacchus, the god of wine, rides a chariot drawn by pards, or leopards.

But here there is no light,
Save what from heaven is with the breezes blown
Through verdurous glooms and winding mossy ways.

5

I cannot see what flowers are at my feet,
Nor what soft incense hangs upon the boughs,
But, in embalmed° darkness, guess each sweet *fragrant*
Wherewith the seasonable month endows
The grass, the thicket, and the fruit-tree wild;
White hawthorn, and the pastoral eglantine;
Fast fading violets cover'd up in leaves;
And mid-May's eldest child,
The coming musk-rose, full of dewy wine,
The murmurous haunt of flies on summer eves.

6

Darkling[1] I listen; and, for many a time
I have been half in love with easeful Death,
Call'd him soft names in many a mused rhyme,
To take into the air my quiet breath;
Now more than ever seems it rich to die,
To cease upon the midnight with no pain,
While thou art pouring forth thy soul abroad
In such an ecstasy!
Still wouldst thou sing, and I have ears in vain—
To thy high requiem[2] become a sod.

7

Thou wast not born for death, immortal Bird!
No hungry generations tread thee down;
The voice I hear this passing night was heard
In ancient days by emperor and clown:° *rustic*
Perhaps the self-same song that found a path
Through the sad heart of Ruth, when, sick for home,
She stood in tears amid the alien corn;[3]
The same that oft-times hath
Charm'd magic casements, opening on the foam
Of perilous seas, in faery lands forlorn.

8

Forlorn! the very word is like a bell
To toll me back from thee to my sole self!
Adieu! the fancy cannot cheat so well
As she is fam'd to do, deceiving elf.
Adieu! adieu! thy plaintive anthem fades
Past the near meadows, over the still stream,
Up the hill-side; and now 'tis buried deep
In the next valley-glades:
Was it a vision, or a waking dream?
Fled is that music—Do I wake or sleep?

—1819

Ode On A Grecian Urn

1

Thou still unravish'd bride of quietness,
Thou foster-child of silence and slow time,
Sylvan° historian, who canst thus express *woodland*
A flowery tale more sweetly than our rhyme:
What leaf-fring'd legend haunts about thy shape
Of deities or mortals, or of both,
In Tempe or the dales of Arcady?[4]
What men or gods are these? What maidens loth?
What mad pursuit? What struggle to escape?
What pipes and timbrels?° What *tambourines*
wild ecstasy?

2

Heard melodies are sweet, but those unheard
Are sweeter; therefore, ye soft pipes, play on;
Not to the sensual° ear, but, more endear'd, *physical*
Pipe to the spirit ditties of no tone:
Fair youth, beneath the trees, thou canst not leave
Thy song, nor ever can those trees be bare;
Bold Lover, never, never canst thou kiss,
Though winning near the goal—yet, do not grieve;
She cannot fade, though thou hast not thy bliss,
For ever wilt thou love, and she be fair!

---

[1] *Darkling* In the dark.

[2] *requiem* Mass sung for the dead.

[3] *Ruth ... corn* Widow in the Book of Ruth (1-4) who leaves Moab for Judah with her mother-in-law Naomi because of famine.

[4] *Tempe* Valley in ancient Greece renowned for its beauty; *Arcady* Ideal region of rural life, named for a mountainous district in Greece.

3

Ah, happy, happy boughs! that cannot shed
 Your leaves, nor ever bid the Spring adieu;
And, happy melodist, unwearied,
 For ever piping songs for ever new;
More happy love! more happy, happy love!
 For ever warm and still to be enjoy'd,
  For ever panting, and for ever young;
All breathing human passion far above,
 That leaves a heart high-sorrowful and cloy'd,
  A burning forehead, and a parching tongue.

4

Who are these coming to the sacrifice?
 To what green altar, O mysterious priest,
Lead'st thou that heifer lowing at the skies,
 And all her silken flanks with garlands drest?
What little town by river or sea shore,
 Or mountain-built with peaceful citadel,
  Is emptied of this folk, this pious morn?
And, little town, thy streets for evermore
 Will silent be; and not a soul to tell
  Why thou art desolate, can e'er return.

5

O Attic[1] shape! Fair attitude! with brede° *interwoven design*
 Of marble men and maidens overwrought,° *overlaid*
With forest branches and the trodden weed;
 Thou, silent form, dost tease us out of thought
As doth eternity: Cold Pastoral!
 When old age shall this generation waste,
  Thou shalt remain, in midst of other woe
Than ours, a friend to man, to whom thou say'st,
 "Beauty is truth, truth beauty,"—that is all
  Ye know on earth, and all ye need to know.[2]

—1820

[1] *Attic* I.e., Greek. Attica was an ancient region of Greece that had Athens as its capital.

[2] *Beauty is … know* The quotation marks in line 49 are present in Keats's 1820 volume of poems, but are absent in transcripts of the poem made by Keats's friends and in the version of the poem published in *Annals of the Fine Arts* in 1820. As a result, their presence has engendered much critical debate. It is unclear whether Keats meant the last line and a half to be spoken by the poet, or whether the entire final two lines are the imagined declaration of the urn.

Ode On Melancholy[3]

I

No, No, go not to Lethe,[4] neither twist
 Wolf's-bane,[5] tight-rooted, for its poisonous wine;
Nor suffer thy pale forehead to be kiss'd
By nightshade, ruby grape of Proserpine;[6]
Make not your rosary of yew-berries,[7]
 Nor let the beetle, nor the death-moth[8] be
  Your mournful Psyche,[9] nor the downy owl
A partner in your sorrow's mysteries;[10]

[3] *Ode on Melancholy* In the original manuscript version, the poem opened with the following stanza:

Though you should build a bark of dead men's bones,
 And rear a phantom gibbet for a mast,
Stitch creeds together for a sail, with groans
 To fill it out, bloodstained and aghast;
Although your rudder be a Dragon's tail,
 Long sever'd, yet still hard with agony,
Your cordage large uprootings from the skull
Of bald Medusa; certes you would fail
 To find Melancholy, whether she
  Dreameth in any isle of Lethe dull.

(Medusa was one of the Gorgons, three monstrous, winged sisters who had snakes for hair.)

[4] *Lethe* River in Hades, the classical underworld, whose waters produce forgetfulness.

[5] *Wolf's-bane* Poisonous plant native to Europe.

[6] *nightshade* Plants with poisonous berries; *Proserpine* Daughter of Demeter who was abducted by Pluto, god of the underworld, and made queen of Hades. Her mother, goddess of the harvest, mourned for her daughter and so caused an eternal winter until Pluto was prevailed upon to allow Proserpine to return to her mother six months of every year.

[7] *yew-berries* Poisonous berries of the yew tree, which is commonly planted in graveyards and is therefore often regarded as symbolic of death or sadness.

[8] *beetle* The scarab, a large black beetle that Egyptians placed in their tombs as a symbol of resurrection; *death-moth* Death's-head moth, whose wings carry a mark resembling a human skull.

[9] *Psyche* In classical mythology, a young woman who was beloved by Cupid, winged god of love and son of Venus. After winning over Venus, who was jealous of Psyche's beauty, Psyche was granted immortality by Jupiter. In Greek myth she is often a personification of the soul. Her name in Greek means butterfly as well as soul. Psyche was often represented as a butterfly flying out of a dying person's mouth.

[10] *mysteries* I.e., secret rites or ceremonies.

For shade to shade will come too drowsily,
And drown the wakeful anguish of the soul.

2

But when the melancholy fit shall fall
Sudden from heaven like a weeping cloud,
That fosters the droop-headed flowers all,
And hides the green hill in an April shroud;
Then glut thy sorrow on a morning rose,
Or on the rainbow of the salt sand-wave,
Or on the wealth of globed peonies;
Or if thy mistress some rich anger shows,
Emprison her soft hand, and let her rave,
And feed deep, deep upon her peerless eyes.

3

She dwells with Beauty—Beauty that must die;
And Joy, whose hand is ever at his lips
Bidding adieu; and aching Pleasure nigh,
Turning to poison while the bee-mouth sips:
Ay, in the very temple of Delight
Veil'd Melancholy has her sovran° shrine, *sovereign*
Though seen of none save him whose strenuous tongue
Can burst Joy's grape against his palate fine;° *refined*
His soul shall taste the sadness of her might,
And be among her cloudy trophies hung.

—1820

Ode On Indolence[1]

"They toil not, neither do they spin."[2]

I

One morn before me were three figures seen,
With bowed necks, and joined hands, side-faced;
And one behind the other stepp'd serene,
In placid sandals, and in white robes graced;
They pass'd, like figures on a marble urn,
When shifted round to see the other side;
They came again; as when the urn once more
Is shifted round, the first seen shades return;
And they were strange to me, as may betide
With vases, to one deep in Phidian lore.[3]

2

How is it, shadows, that I knew ye not?
How came ye muffled in so hush a masque?° *play*
Was it a silent deep-disguised plot
To steal away, and leave without a task
My idle days? Ripe was the drowsy hour;
The blissful cloud of summer-indolence
Benumb'd my eyes; my pulse grew less and less;
Pain had no sting, and pleasure's wreath no flower:
O, why did ye not melt, and leave my sense
Unhaunted quite of all but—nothingness?

3

A third time pass'd they by, and, passing, turn'd
Each one the face a moment whiles to me;
Then faded, and to follow them I burn'd
And ached for wings because I knew the three;
The first was a fair Maid, and Love her name;
The second was Ambition, pale of cheek,
And ever watchful with fatigued eye;
The last, whom I love more, the more of blame
Is heap'd upon her, maiden most unmeek,
I knew to be my demon Poesy.

4

They faded, and, forsooth! I wanted wings:
O folly! What is Love! and where is it?
And for that poor Ambition! It springs
From a man's little heart's short fever-fit;
For Poesy! No—she has not a joy—
At least for me—so sweet as drowsy noons,
And evenings steep'd in honeyed indolence;
O, for an age so shelter'd from annoy,° *harm*
That I may never know how change the moons,
Or hear the voice of busy common sense!

[1] *Ode on Indolence* See the 1919 letter to George and Georgiana Keats, reprinted below, in which Keats describes the bout of indolence that is thought to have inspired this poem.

[2] *They toil… spin* From Matthew 6.28–89: "Consider the lilies of the field, how they grow; they toil not, neither do they spin: And yet I say unto you, That even Solomon in all his glory was not arrayed like one of these."

[3] *Phidian lore* Lore concerning Phidias, the fifth-century Athenian sculptor of what were later named the Elgin Marbles, the marble sculptures that decorated the outside of the Parthenon and were brought to England by Lord Elgin.

5

A third time came they by—alas! wherefore?
  My sleep had been embroider'd with dim dreams;
My soul had been a lawn besprinkled o'er
  With flowers, and stirring shades, and baffled beams:
The morn was clouded, but no shower fell,
  Tho' in her lids hung the sweet tears of May;
    The open casement press'd a new-leav'd vine,
Let in the budding warmth and
    throstle's° lay; *thrush's / song*
  O shadows! 'twas a time to bid farewell!
  Upon your skirts had fallen no tears of mine.

6

So, ye three ghosts, adieu! Ye cannot raise
  My head cool-bedded in the flowery grass;
For I would not be dieted with praise,
  A pet-lamb in a sentimental farce!
Fade softly from my eyes, and be once more
  In masque-like figures on the dreamy urn;
    Farewell! I yet have visions for the night,
And for the day faint visions there is store;
  Vanish, ye phantoms! from my idle spright,° *spirit*
    Into the clouds, and never more return!
—1848 (WRITTEN 1819)

To Autumn

1

Season of mists and mellow fruitfulness,
  Close bosom-friend of the maturing sun;
Conspiring with him how to load and bless
  With fruit the vines that round the thatch-eves run;
To bend with apples the moss'd cottage-trees,
  And fill all fruit with ripeness to the core;
    To swell the gourd, and plump the hazel shells
With a sweet kernel; to set budding more,
  And still more, later flowers for the bees,
  Until they think warm days will never cease,
    For Summer has o'er-brimm'd their clammy cells.

2

Who hath not seen thee oft amid thy store?
  Sometimes whoever seeks abroad may find
Thee sitting careless on a granary floor,
  Thy hair soft-lifted by the winnowing wind;
Or on a half-reap'd furrow sound asleep,
  Drows'd with the fume of poppies, while thy hook[1]
  Spares the next swath and all its twined flowers:
And sometimes like a gleaner[2] thou dost keep
  Steady thy laden head across a brook;
  Or by a cider-press, with patient look,
    Thou watchest the last oozings hours by hours.

3

Where are the songs of Spring? Ay, where are they?
  Think not of them, thou hast thy music too—
While barred clouds bloom the soft-dying day,
  And touch the stubble-plains with rosy hue;
Then in a wailful choir the small gnats mourn
  Among the river sallows,° borne aloft *willows*
    Or sinking as the light wind lives or dies;
And full-grown lambs loud bleat from hilly bourn;° *realm*
  Hedge-crickets sing; and now with treble soft
  The red-breast whistles from a
      garden-croft;° *enclosed garden*
    And gathering swallows twitter in the skies.
—1820

Lamia

Philostratus, in his fourth book *de Vita Apollonii*, hath a memorable instance in this kind, which I may not omit, of one Menippus Lycius, a young man of twenty-five years of age, that going betwixt Cenchreas and Corinth, met such a phantasm in the habit of a fair gentlewoman, which taking him by the hand, carried him home to her house, in the suburbs of Corinth, and told him she was a Phoenician by birth, and if he would tarry with her, he should hear her sing and play, and drink such wine as never any drank, and no man should molest him; but she, being fair and lovely, would live and die with him, that was fair and lovely to behold. The young man, a philosopher, otherwise staid and discreet, able to moderate his passions, though not this of love, tarried with her a while to his great content, and at last married her, to whose wedding, among other guests, came Apollonius; who, by some probable conjectures, found her out to be a serpent, a lamia; and that all her furniture was, like Tantalus' gold, described by Homer, no substance but

[1] *hook* I.e., a reaping-hook or scythe.

[2] *gleaner* One who gathers the grain left by the reaper.

mere illusions. When she saw herself descried, she wept, and desired Apollonius to be silent, but he would not be moved, and thereupon she, plate, house, and all that was in it, vanished in an instant: many thousand took notice of this fact, for it was done in the midst of Greece.[1]

Part I

Upon a time, before the faery broods
Drove Nymph and Satyr from the prosperous woods,
Before King Oberon's bright diadem,° *crown*
Sceptre, and mantle, clasp'd with dewy gem,
Frighted away the Dryads and the Fauns
From rushes green, and brakes,° and cowslip'd lawns,[2] *ferns*
The ever-smitten Hermes[3] empty left
His golden throne, bent warm on amorous theft:
From high Olympus had he stolen light,
On this side of Jove's clouds,[4] to escape the sight
Of his great summoner, and made retreat
Into a forest on the shores of Crete.[5]
For somewhere in that sacred island dwelt
A nymph, to whom all hoofed Satyrs knelt;
At whose white feet the languid Tritons[6] poured
Pearls, while on land they wither'd and adored.
Fast by the springs where she to bathe was wont,
And in those meads° where sometime she might haunt, *meadows*
Were strewn rich gifts, unknown to any Muse,[7]
Though Fancy's casket were unlock'd to choose.
Ah, what a world of love was at her feet!
So Hermes thought, and a celestial heat
Burnt from his winged heels to either ear,
That from a whiteness, as the lily clear,
Blush'd into roses 'mid his golden hair,
Fallen in jealous curls about his shoulders bare.
From vale to vale, from wood to wood, he flew,
Breathing upon the flowers his passion new,
And wound with many a river to its head,
To find where this sweet nymph prepar'd her secret bed:
In vain; the sweet nymph might nowhere be found,
And so he rested, on the lonely ground,
Pensive, and full of painful jealousies
Of the Wood-Gods, and even the very trees.
There as he stood, he heard a mournful voice,
Such as once heard, in gentle heart, destroys
All pain but pity: thus the lone voice spake:
"When from this wreathed tomb shall I awake!
When move in a sweet body fit for life,
And love, and pleasure, and the ruddy strife
Of hearts and lips! Ah, miserable me!"
The God, dove-footed, glided silently
Round bush and tree, soft-brushing, in his speed,
The taller grasses and full-flowering weed,
Until he found a palpitating snake,
Bright, and cirque-couchant[8] in a dusky brake.

She was a gordian[9] shape of dazzling hue,
Vermilion°-spotted, golden, green, and blue; *scarlet*
Striped like a zebra, freckled like a pard,° *leopard*
Eyed like a peacock, and all crimson barr'd;
And full of silver moons, that, as she breathed,
Dissolv'd, or brighter shone, or interwreathed
Their lustres with the gloomier tapestries—
So rainbow-sided, touch'd with miseries,
She seem'd, at once, some penanced lady elf,
Some demon's mistress, or the demon's self.

[1] In a footnote originally placed at the end of *Lamia*, Keats provides the above quote from Robert Burton's *Anatomy of Melancholy* 3.2.1.1. (1621), his source for this narrative poem about a young man who falls in love with a lamia, a monster in the body of a woman.

[2] *before the ... lawns* In classical mythology, nymphs, dryads (wood nymphs), and satyrs and fauns (half-men, half-goats) were all minor deities. Oberon, in Shakespeare's *A Midsummer Night's Dream*, is king of the fairies, who were immortal beings of a later period.

[3] *Hermes* Wing-footed messenger of the gods (called Mercury in Roman mythology).

[4] *From high ... clouds* Jove is the King of the Roman gods, all of whom reside on Mt. Olympus.

[5] *Crete* Island in the Aegean Sea.

[6] *Tritons* Sea-gods, usually half-men and half-fish.

[7] *Muse* One of nine daughters of Zeus and Mnemosyne, each of whom presided over and provided inspiration for an aspect of learning or the arts.

[8] *cirque-couchant* French: lying in coils.

[9] *gordian* I.e., like the Gordian knot, tied by King Gordius of Phrygia and said to be impossible to untie. Alexander the Great eventually severed it with his sword.

Upon her crest she wore a wannish fire
Sprinkled with stars, like Ariadne's tiar:[1]
Her head was serpent, but ah, bitter-sweet!
She had a woman's mouth with all its pearls[2] complete:
And for her eyes: what could such eyes do there
But weep, and weep, that they were born so fair?
As Proserpine still weeps for her Sicilian air.[3]
Her throat was serpent, but the words she spake
Came, as through bubbling honey, for Love's sake,
And thus; while Hermes on his pinions° lay, *wings*
Like a stoop'd[4] falcon ere he takes his prey.

"Fair Hermes, crown'd with feathers, fluttering light,
I had a splendid dream of thee last night:
I saw thee sitting, on a throne of gold,
Among the Gods, upon Olympus old,
The only sad one; for thou didst not hear
The soft, lute-finger'd Muses chaunting clear,
Nor even Apollo when he sang alone,
Deaf to his throbbing throat's long, long melodious moan.
I dreamt I saw thee, robed in purple flakes,
Break amorous through the clouds, as morning breaks,
And, swiftly as a bright Phoebean dart,[5]
Strike for the Cretan isle; and here thou art!
Too gentle Hermes, hast thou found the maid?"
Whereat the star of Lethe[6] not delay'd
His rosy eloquence, and thus inquired:
"Thou smooth-lipp'd serpent, surely high inspired!
Thou beauteous wreath, with melancholy eyes,
Possess whatever bliss thou canst devise,
Telling me only where my nymph is fled—
Where she doth breathe!" "Bright planet, thou hast said,"
Return'd the snake, "but seal with oaths, fair God!"
"I swear," said Hermes, "by my serpent rod,[7]
And by thine eyes, and by thy starry crown!"
Light flew his earnest words, among the blossoms blown.
Then thus again the brilliance feminine:
"Too frail of heart! for this lost nymph of thine,
Free as the air, invisibly, she strays
About these thornless wilds; her pleasant days
She tastes unseen; unseen her nimble feet
Leave traces in the grass and flowers sweet;
From weary tendrils, and bow'd branches green,
She plucks the fruit unseen, she bathes unseen:
And by my power is her beauty veil'd
To keep it unaffronted, unassail'd
By the love-glances of unlovely eyes,
Of Satyrs, Fauns, and blear'd Silenus'[8] sighs.
Pale grew her immortality, for woe
Of all these lovers, and she grieved so
I took compassion on her, bade her steep
Her hair in weïrd° syrops, that would keep *magical*
Her loveliness invisible, yet free
To wander as she loves, in liberty.
Thou shalt behold her, Hermes, thou alone,
If thou wilt, as thou swearest, grant my boon!"
Then, once again, the charmed God began
An oath, and through the serpent's ears it ran
Warm, tremulous, devout, psalterian.[9]
Ravish'd, she lifted her Circean head,[10]
Blush'd a live damask,[11] and swift-lisping said,
"I was a woman, let me have once more
A woman's shape, and charming as before.
I love a youth of Corinth—O the bliss!
Give me my woman's form, and place me where he is.
Stoop, Hermes, let me breathe upon thy brow,
And thou shalt see thy sweet nymph even now."
The God on half-shut feathers sank serene,
She breath'd upon his eyes, and swift was seen

[1] *Ariadne's tiar* According to myth, after Ariadne married the god Bacchus she was converted into a constellation. In his painting of her, Italian painter Titian (c. 1488–1576) shows Ariadne wearing a crown of seven stars.

[2] *pearls* I.e., teeth.

[3] *As Proserpine … air* Hades, god of the underworld, abducted Proserpine from her home in Sicily to be his queen.

[4] *stoop'd* Swooping.

[5] *Phoeban dart* Sunbeam, after Phoebus Apollo, god of the sun.

[6] *star of Lethe* Hermes, who, like a star, guided the souls of the dead to the dark underworld (in which Lethe is a river).

[7] *my serpent rod* On Hermes's wand, or a caduceus, two serpents were entwined.

[8] *Silenus* Foster-father of Bacchus, god of wine, who is typically portrayed drunk.

[9] *psalterian* Like the sound of a psaltery (a stringed instrument); or, possibly, like a psalm, which were printed in psalters.

[10] *Circean head* Like that of Circe, the enchantress who turns men into beasts in Homer's *Odyssey*, Book 10.

[11] *damask* Pink, like the color of a damask rose.

Of both the guarded nymph near-smiling on the green.
It was no dream; or say a dream it was,
Real are the dreams of Gods, and smoothly pass
Their pleasures in a long immortal dream.
One warm, flush'd moment, hovering, it might seem
Dash'd by the wood-nymph's beauty, so he burn'd;
Then, lighting on the printless verdure, turn'd
To the swoon'd serpent, and with languid arm,
Delicate, put to proof the lithe Caducean charm.
So done, upon the nymph his eyes he bent
Full of adoring tears and blandishment,
And towards her stept: she, like a moon in wane,
Faded before him, cower'd, nor could restrain
Her fearful sobs, self-folding like a flower
That faints into itself at evening hour:
But the God fostering her chilled hand,
She felt the warmth, her eyelids open'd bland,° *soft*
And, like new flowers at morning song of bees,
Bloom'd, and gave up her honey to the lees.° *dregs*
Into the green-recessed woods they flew;
Nor grew they pale, as mortal lovers do.

Left to herself, the serpent now began
To change; her elfin blood in madness ran,
Her mouth foam'd, and the grass, therewith
besprent,° *besprinkled*
Wither'd at dew so sweet and virulent;
Her eyes in torture fix'd, and anguish drear,
Hot, glaz'd, and wide, with lid-lashes all sear,° *withered*
Flash'd phosphor and sharp sparks, without one
cooling tear.
The colours all inflam'd throughout her train,° *tail*
She writh'd about, convuls'd with scarlet pain:
A deep volcanian yellow took the place
Of all her milder-mooned[1] body's grace;
And, as the lava ravishes the mead,
Spoilt all her silver mail, and golden
brede;° *interwoven pattern*
Made gloom of all her frecklings, streaks and bars,
Eclips'd her crescents, and lick'd up her stars:
So that, in moments few, she was undrest
Of all her sapphires, greens, and amethyst,
And rubious-argent:° of all these bereft, *reddish-silver*
Nothing but pain and ugliness were left.
Still shone her crown; that vanish'd, also she
Melted and disappear'd as suddenly;
And in the air, her new voice luting soft,
Cried, "Lycius! gentle Lycius!" Borne aloft
With the bright mists about the mountains hoar° *ancient*
These words dissolv'd: Crete's forests heard no more.

Whither fled Lamia, now a lady bright,
A full-born beauty new and exquisite?
She fled into that valley they pass o'er
Who go to Corinth from Cenchreas' shore;[2]
And rested at the foot of those wild hills,
The rugged founts of the Peraean rills,
And of that other ridge whose barren back
Stretches, with all its mist and cloudy rack,
South-westward to Cleone.[3] There she stood
About a young bird's flutter from a wood,
Fair, on a sloping green of mossy tread,
By a clear pool, wherein she passioned[4]
To see herself escap'd from so sore ills,
While her robes flaunted with the daffodils.

Ah, happy Lycius!—for she was a maid
More beautiful than ever twisted braid,
Or sigh'd, or blush'd, or on spring-flowered lea° *pasture*
Spread a green kirtle° to the minstrelsy: *gown*
A virgin purest lipp'd, yet in the lore
Of love deep learned to the red heart's core:
Not one hour old, yet of sciential° brain *knowledgeable*
To unperplex° bliss from its neighbour pain; *extricate*
Define their pettish° limits, and estrange *uncertain*
Their points of contact, and swift counterchange;
Intrigue with the specious° chaos, and dispart° *seeming/cleave*
Its most ambiguous atoms with sure art;
As though in Cupid's[5] college she had spent
Sweet days a lovely graduate, still unshent,° *unspoiled*
And kept his rosy terms in idle languishment.

Why this fair creature chose so fairily
By the wayside to linger, we shall see;
But first 'tis fit to tell how she could muse
And dream, when in the serpent prison-house,

[1] *milder-mooned* I.e., of a milder, silver-moon color.

[2] *Cenchreas' shore* Shore of Cenchrea, the eastern harbor of Corinth, in southern Greece.

[3] *Cleone* Village between Corinth and Argos.

[4] *passioned* Was moved by intense passion.

[5] *Cupid* God of love.

Of all she list,° strange or magnificent: *desired*
How, ever, where she will'd, her spirit went;
Whether to faint Elysium,[1] or where
Down through tress-lifting waves the Nereids fair
Wind into Thetis' bower[2] by many a pearly stair;
Or where God Bacchus drains his cups divine,
Stretch'd out, at ease, beneath a glutinous pine;
Or where in Pluto's[3] gardens palatine° *palatial*
Mulciber's columns gleam in far piazzian line.[4]
And sometimes into cities she would send
Her dream, with feast and rioting to blend;
And once, while among mortals dreaming thus,
She saw the young Corinthian Lycius
Charioting foremost in the envious race,
Like a young Jove with calm uneager face,
And fell into a swooning love of him.
Now on the moth-time of that evening dim
He would return that way, as well she knew,
To Corinth from the shore; for freshly blew
The eastern soft wind, and his galley now
Grated the quaystones with her brazen prow
In port Cenchreas, from Egina isle
Fresh anchor'd; whither he had been awhile
To sacrifice to Jove, whose temple there
Waits with high marble doors for blood and incense
    rare.
Jove heard his vows, and better'd his desire;
For by some freakful chance he made retire
From his companions, and set forth to walk,
Perhaps grown wearied of their Corinth talk:
Over the solitary hills he fared,
Thoughtless at first, but ere eve's star appeared
His phantasy was lost, where reason fades,
In the calm'd twilight of Platonic shades.° *ghosts*
Lamia beheld him coming, near, more near—
Close to her passing, in indifference drear,
His silent sandals swept the mossy green;
So neighbour'd to him, and yet so unseen
She stood: he pass'd, shut up in mysteries,
His mind wrapp'd like his mantle, while her eyes
Follow'd his steps, and her neck regal white
Turn'd—syllabling thus, "Ah, Lycius bright,
And will you leave me on the hills alone?
Lycius, look back! and be some pity shown."
He did; not with cold wonder fearingly,
But Orpheus-like at an Eurydice;[5]
For so delicious were the words she sung,
It seem'd he had lov'd them a whole summer long:
And soon his eyes had drunk her beauty up,
Leaving no drop in the bewildering cup,
And still the cup was full—while he, afraid
Lest she should vanish ere his lip had paid
Due adoration, thus began to adore;
Her soft look growing coy, she saw his chain so sure:
"Leave thee alone! Look back! Ah, Goddess, see
Whether my eyes can ever turn from thee!
For pity do not this sad heart belie°— *deceive*
Even as thou vanishest so I shall die.
Stay! though a Naiad° of the rivers, stay! *water nymph*
To thy far wishes will thy streams obey:
Stay! though the greenest woods be thy domain,
Alone they can drink up the morning rain:
Though a descended Pleiad,[6] will not one
Of thine harmonious sisters keep in tune
Thy spheres, and as thy silver proxy shine?
So sweetly to these ravish'd ears of mine
Came thy sweet greeting, that if thou shouldst fade
Thy memory will waste me to a shade—
For pity do not melt!" "If I should stay,"
Said Lamia, "here, upon this floor of clay,
And pain my steps upon these flowers too rough,
What canst thou say or do of charm enough
To dull the nice remembrance of my home?
Thou canst not ask me with thee here to roam
Over these hills and vales, where no joy is—
Empty of immortality and bliss!
Thou art a scholar, Lycius, and must know
That finer spirits cannot breathe below
In human climes, and live: Alas! poor youth,
What taste of purer air hast thou to soothe

[1] *Elysium* Paradise of the classical underworld.

[2] *Nereids … bower* Thetis, the mother of Achilles, is a sea-nymph, or Nereid.

[3] *Pluto* Another name for Hades, god of the underworld.

[4] *Mulciber* Also called Vulcan, god of fire and metalworking; *piazzan line* Line of columns surrounding piazzas.

[5] *But … Eurydice* The poet Orpheus won the right to lead his wife, Eurydice, back from the underworld on the condition that he not turn around to look at her on the journey back. When he could not resist doing so, she was forced to return to the underworld forever.

[6] *Pleiad* One of the seven stars, daughters of the Titan Atlas, that comprise the constellation Pleiades.

My essence? What serener palaces,
Where I may all my many senses please,
And by mysterious sleights a hundred thirsts appease?
It cannot be—Adieu!" So said, she rose
Tiptoe with white arms spread. He, sick to lose
The amorous promise of her lone complain,° *complaint*
Swoon'd, murmuring of love, and pale with pain.
The cruel lady, without any show
Of sorrow for her tender favourite's woe,
But rather, if her eyes could brighter be,
With brighter eyes and slow amenity,
Put her new lips to his, and gave afresh
The life she had so tangled in her mesh:
And as he from one trance was wakening
Into another, she began to sing,
Happy in beauty, life, and love, and every thing,
A song of love, too sweet for earthly lyres,
While, like held breath, the stars drew in their panting fires.
And then she whisper'd in such trembling tone,
As those who, safe together met alone
For the first time through many anguish'd days,
Use other speech than looks; bidding him raise
His drooping head, and clear his soul of doubt,
For that she was a woman, and without
Any more subtle fluid in her veins
Than throbbing blood, and that the self-same pains
Inhabited her frail-strung heart as his.
And next she wonder'd how his eyes could miss
Her face so long in Corinth, where, she said,
She dwelt but half retir'd, and there had led
Days happy as the gold coin could invent
Without the aid of love; yet in content
Till she saw him, as once she pass'd him by,
Where 'gainst a column he leant thoughtfully
At Venus'[1] temple porch, 'mid baskets heap'd
Of amorous herbs and flowers, newly reap'd
Late on that eve, as 'twas the night before
The Adonian feast;[2] whereof she saw no more,
But wept alone those days, for why should she adore?
Lycius from death awoke into amaze,
To see her still, and singing so sweet lays;
Then from amaze into delight he fell
To hear her whisper woman's lore so well;
And every word she spake entic'd him on
To unperplex'd° delight and pleasure known. *certain*
Let the mad poets say whate'er they please
Of the sweets of Fairies, Peris,[3] Goddesses,
There is not such a treat among them all,
Haunters of cavern, lake, and waterfall,
As a real woman, lineal indeed
From Pyrrha's pebbles[4] or old Adam's seed.
Thus gentle Lamia judg'd, and judg'd aright,
That Lycius could not love in half a fright,
So threw the goddess off, and won his heart
More pleasantly by playing woman's part,
With no more awe than what her beauty gave,
That, while it smote, still guaranteed to save.
Lycius to all made eloquent reply,
Marrying to every word a twinborn sigh;
And last, pointing to Corinth, ask'd her sweet,
If 'twas too far that night for her soft feet.
The way was short, for Lamia's eagerness
Made, by a spell, the triple league decrease
To a few paces; not at all surmised
By blinded Lycius, so in her comprized.° *absorbed*
They pass'd the city gates, he knew not how,
So noiseless, and he never thought to know.

As men talk in a dream, so Corinth all,
Throughout her palaces imperial,
And all her populous streets and temples lewd,[5]
Mutter'd, like tempest in the distance brew'd,
To the wide-spreaded night above her towers.
Men, women, rich and poor, in the cool hours,
Shuffled their sandals o'er the pavement white,
Companion'd or alone; while many a light
Flared, here and there, from wealthy festivals,
And threw their moving shadows on the walls,
Or found them cluster'd in the corniced shade
Of some arch'd temple door, or dusky colonnade.

[1] *Venus* Goddess of love.

[2] *Adonian feast* Festival in honor of Adonis, a beautiful young man who was loved by Venus and was killed when hunting a boar.

[3] *Peris* Beautiful women inhabiting the world of the Persian afterlife.

[4] *Pyrrha's pebbles* In classical myth, Jupiter exterminated humanity in a flood. Deucalion and his wife Pyrrha, the only two survivors, repopulated the earth by throwing pebbles, which turned into people.

[5] *temples lewd* Temples of Venus, goddess of love.

Muffling his face, of greeting friends in fear,
Her fingers he press'd hard, as one came near
With curl'd gray beard, sharp eyes, and smooth bald
crown,
Slow-stepp'd, and robed in philosophic gown:
Lycius shrank closer, as they met and past,
Into his mantle, adding wings to haste,
While hurried Lamia trembled: "Ah," said he,
"Why do you shudder, love, so ruefully?
Why does your tender palm dissolve in dew?"
"I'm wearied," said fair Lamia: "tell me who
Is that old man? I cannot bring to mind
His features—Lycius! wherefore did you blind
Yourself from his quick eyes?" Lycius replied,
"'Tis Apollonius sage, my trusty guide
And good instructor; but to-night he seems
The ghost of folly haunting my sweet dreams."

While yet he spake they had arrived before
A pillar'd porch, with lofty portal door,
Where hung a silver lamp, whose phosphor glow
Reflected in the slabbed steps below,
Mild as a star in water; for so new,
And so unsullied was the marble hue,
So through the crystal polish, liquid fine,
Ran the dark veins, that none but feet divine
Could e'er have touch'd there. Sounds Æolian[1]
Breath'd from the hinges, as the ample span
Of the wide doors disclos'd a place unknown
Some time to any, but those two alone,
And a few Persian mutes, who that same year
Were seen about the markets: none knew where
They could inhabit; the most curious
Were foil'd, who watch'd to trace them to their house:
And but the flitter-winged verse must tell,
For truth's sake, what woe afterwards befell,
'Twould humour many a heart to leave them thus,
Shut from the busy world of more incredulous.

Part 2

Love in a hut, with water and a crust,
Is—Love, forgive us!—cinders, ashes, dust;
Love in a palace is perhaps at last
More grievous torment than a hermit's fast—
That is a doubtful tale from faery land,
Hard for the non-elect to understand.
Had Lycius liv'd to hand his story down,
He might have given the moral a fresh frown,
Or clench'd it quite: but too short was their bliss
To breed distrust and hate, that make the soft voice hiss.
Besides, there, nightly, with terrific glare,
Love, jealous grown of so complete a pair,
Hover'd and buzz'd his wings, with fearful roar,
Above the lintel[2] of their chamber door,
And down the passage cast a glow upon the floor.

For all this came a ruin: side by side
They were enthroned, in the even tide,
Upon a couch, near to a curtaining
Whose airy texture, from a golden string,
Floated into the room, and let appear
Unveil'd the summer heaven, blue and clear,
Betwixt two marble shafts—there they reposed,
Where use had made it sweet, with eyelids closed,
Saving a tithe[3] which love still open kept,
That they might see each other while they almost slept;
When from the slope side of a suburb hill,
Deafening the swallow's twitter, came a thrill
Of trumpets—Lycius started—the sounds fled,
But left a thought, a buzzing in his head.
For the first time, since first he harbour'd in
That purple-lined palace of sweet sin,
His spirit pass'd beyond its golden bourn° *realm*
Into the noisy world almost forsworn.
The lady, ever watchful, penetrant,
Saw this with pain, so arguing a want
Of something more, more than her empery° *empire*
Of joys; and she began to moan and sigh
Because he mused beyond her, knowing well
That but a moment's thought is passion's passing bell.[4]
"Why do you sigh, fair creature?" whisper'd he:
"Why do you think?" return'd she tenderly:
"You have deserted me;—where am I now?
Not in your heart while care weighs on your brow:
No, no, you have dismiss'd me; and I go

[1] *Sounds Aeolian* Sounds resembling those of an Aeolian harp, which produces music when exposed to currents of air. Aeolus was god of the winds.

[2] *lintel* Horizontal support beam.

[3] *tithe* I.e., a tenth, or very small part.

[4] *passing bell* Bell tolled following a death.

From your breast houseless: ay, it must be so."
He answer'd, bending to her open eyes,
Where he was mirror'd small in paradise,
"My silver planet, both of eve and morn![1]
Why will you plead yourself so sad forlorn,
While I am striving how to fill my heart
With deeper crimson, and a double smart?
How to entangle, trammel up and snare
Your soul in mine, and labyrinth you there
Like the hid scent in an unbudded rose?
Ay, a sweet kiss—you see your mighty woes.
My thoughts! shall I unveil them? Listen then!
What mortal hath a prize, that other men
May be confounded and abash'd withal,
But lets it sometimes pace abroad majestical,
And triumph, as in thee I should rejoice
Amid the hoarse alarm of Corinth's voice.
Let my foes choke, and my friends shout afar,
While through the thronged streets your bridal car
Wheels round its dazzling spokes." The lady's cheek
Trembled; she nothing said, but, pale and meek,
Arose and knelt before him, wept a rain
Of sorrows at his words; at last with pain
Beseeching him, the while his hand she wrung,
To change his purpose. He thereat was stung,
Perverse, with stronger fancy to reclaim
Her wild and timid nature to his aim:
Besides, for all his love, in self despite,
Against his better self, he took delight
Luxurious in her sorrows, soft and new.
His passion, cruel grown, took on a hue
Fierce and sanguineous as 'twas possible
In one whose brow had no dark veins to swell.
Fine was the mitigated fury, like
Apollo's presence when in act to strike
The serpent[2]—Ha, the serpent! certes,° she *certainly*
Was none. She burnt, she lov'd the tyranny,
And, all subdued, consented to the hour
When to the bridal he should lead his paramour.
Whispering in midnight silence, said the youth,
"Sure some sweet name thou hast, though, by my truth,
I have not ask'd it, ever thinking thee
Not mortal, but of heavenly progeny,
As still I do. Hast any mortal name,
Fit appellation for this dazzling frame?
Or friends or kinsfolk on the citied earth,
To share our marriage feast and nuptial mirth?"
"I have no friends," said Lamia, "no, not one;
My presence in wide Corinth hardly known:
My parents' bones are in their dusty urns
Sepulchred, where no kindled incense burns,
Seeing all their luckless race are dead, save me,
And I neglect the holy rite for thee.
Even as you list° invite your many guests; *desire to*
But if, as now it seems, your vision rests
With any pleasure on me, do not bid
Old Apollonius—from him keep me hid."
Lycius, perplex'd at words so blind and blank,
Made close inquiry; from whose touch she shrank,
Feigning a sleep; and he to the dull shade
Of deep sleep in a moment was betray'd.

It was the custom then to bring away
The bride from home at blushing shut of day,
Veiled, in a chariot, heralded along
By strewn flowers, torches, and a marriage song,
With other pageants: but this fair unknown
Had not a friend. So being left alone
(Lycius was gone to summon all his kin),
And knowing surely she could never win
His foolish heart from its mad pompousness,
She set herself, high-thoughted, how to dress
The misery in fit magnificence.
She did so, but 'tis doubtful how and whence
Came, and who were her subtle servitors.
About the halls, and to and from the doors,
There was a noise of wings, till in short space
The glowing banquet-room shone with wide-arched grace.
A haunting music, sole perhaps and lone
Supportress of the faery-roof, made moan
Throughout, as fearful the whole charm might fade.
Fresh carved cedar, mimicking a glade
Of palm and plantain, met from either side,
High in the midst, in honour of the bride:
Two palms and then two plantains, and so on,
From either side their stems branch'd one to one

[1] *My silver ... morn* I.e., my Venus (the planet that appears as both the morning and the evening star).

[2] *Apollo's ... serpent* Apollo killed a serpent, named Python, at Delphi; when his oracle was established there, the priestess was known as the Pythian.

All down the aisled place; and beneath all
There ran a stream of lamps straight on from wall to
 wall.
So canopied, lay an untasted feast
Teeming with odours. Lamia, regal drest,
Silently paced about, and as she went,
In pale contented sort of discontent,
Mission'd her viewless servants to enrich
The fretted[1] splendour of each nook and niche.
Between the tree-stems, marbled plain at first,
Came jasper panels; then, anon, there burst
Forth creeping imagery of slighter trees,
And with the larger wove in small intricacies.
Approving all, she faded at self-will,
And shut the chamber up, close, hush'd and still,
Complete and ready for the revels rude,
When dreadful guests would come to spoil her solitude.

The day appear'd, and all the gossip rout.
O senseless Lycius! Madman! wherefore flout
The silent-blessing fate, warm cloister'd hours,
And show to common eyes these secret bowers?
The herd approach'd; each guest, with busy brain,
Arriving at the portal, gaz'd amain,° *intently*
And enter'd marveling: for they knew the sheet,
Remember'd it from childhood all complete
Without a gap, yet ne'er before had seen
That royal porch, that high-built fair demesne;° *estate*
So in they hurried all, maz'd,° curious and keen: *bewildered*
Save one, who look'd thereon with eye severe,
And with calm-planted steps walk'd in austere;
'Twas Apollonius: something too he laugh'd,
As though some knotty problem, that had daft° *confounded*
His patient thought, had now begun to thaw,
And solve and melt—'twas just as he foresaw.

He met within the murmurous vestibule
His young disciple. "'Tis no common rule,
Lycius," said he, "for uninvited guest
To force himself upon you, and infest
With an unbidden presence the bright throng
Of younger friends; yet must I do this wrong,
And you forgive me." Lycius blush'd, and led
The old man through the inner doors broad-spread;
With reconciling words and courteous mien° *manner*
Turning into sweet milk the sophist's° *philosopher's*
 spleen.° *ill-humor*

Of wealthy lustre was the banquet-room,
Fill'd with pervading brilliance and perfume:
Before each lucid panel fuming stood
A censer[2] fed with myrrh and spiced wood,
Each by a sacred tripod held aloft,
Whose slender feet wide-swerv'd upon the soft
Wool-woofed° carpets: fifty wreaths of smoke *woven*
From fifty censers their light voyage took
To the high roof, still mimick'd as they rose
Along the mirror'd walls by twin-clouds odorous.
Twelve sphered tables, by silk seats ensphered,° *encircled*
High as the level of a man's breast rear'd
On libbard's° paws, upheld the heavy gold *leopard's*
Of cups and goblets, and the store thrice told
Of Ceres' horn,[3] and, in huge vessels, wine
Come from the gloomy° tun° with merry *dark / cask*
 shine.
Thus loaded with a feast the tables stood,
Each shrining in the midst the image of a God.

When in an antechamber every guest
Had felt the cold full sponge to pleasure press'd,
By minist'ring slaves, upon his hands and feet,
And fragrant oils with ceremony meet
Pour'd on his hair, they all mov'd to the feast
In white robes, and themselves in order placed
Around the silken couches, wondering
Whence all this mighty cost and blaze of wealth could
 spring.

Soft went the music the soft air along,
While fluent Greek a vowel'd undersong
Kept up among the guests, discoursing low
At first, for scarcely was the wine at flow;
But when the happy vintage touchd' their brains,
Louder they talk, and louder come the strains
Of powerful instruments—the gorgeous dyes,
The space, the splendour of the draperies,
The roof of awful richness, nectarous cheer,
Beautiful slaves, and Lamia's self, appear,

---

[1] *fretted* Adorned with elaborate carved patterns.

[2] *censer* Vessel for burning incense.

[3] *Ceres' horn* Ceres, goddess of grain and agriculture, is sometimes depicted with a horn of plenty, overflowing with produce.

Now, when the wine has done its rosy deed,
And every soul from human trammels freed,
No more so strange; for merry wine, sweet wine,
Will make Elysian shades not too fair, too divine.
Soon was God Bacchus at meridian height;
Flush'd were their cheeks, and bright eyes double bright:
Garlands of every green, and every scent
From vales deflower'd, or forest-trees branch-rent,
In baskets of bright osier'd° gold were brought *woven*
High as the handles heap'd, to suit the thought
Of every guest; that each, as he did please,
Might fancy-fit his brows, silk-pillow'd at his ease.

What wreath for Lamia? What for Lycius?
What for the sage, old Apollonius?
Upon her aching forehead be there hung
The leaves of willow and of adder's tongue;[1]
And for the youth, quick, let us strip for him
The thyrsus,[2] that his watching eyes may swim
Into forgetfulness; and, for the sage,
Let spear-grass and the spiteful thistle wage
War on his temples. Do not all charms fly
At the mere touch of cold philosophy?[3]
There was an awful° rainbow once in heaven: *awe-inspiring*
We know her woof, her texture; she is given
In the dull catalogue of common things.
Philosophy will clip an angel's wings,
Conquer all mysteries by rule and line,
Empty the haunted air, and gnomed[4] mine—
Unweave a rainbow, as it erewhile made
The tender-person'd Lamia melt into a shade.

By her glad Lycius sitting, in chief place,
Scarce saw in all the room another face,
Till, checking his love trance, a cup he took
Full brimm'd, and opposite sent forth a look
'Cross the broad table, to beseech a glance
From his old teacher's wrinkled countenance,
And pledge him. The bald-head philosopher
Had fix'd his eye, without a twinkle or stir
Full on the alarmed beauty of the bride,
Brow-beating her fair form, and troubling her sweet
 pride.
Lycius then press'd her hand, with devout touch,
As pale it lay upon the rosy couch:
'Twas icy, and the cold ran through his veins;
Then sudden it grew hot, and all the pains
Of an unnatural heat shot to his heart.
"Lamia, what means this? Wherefore dost thou start?
Know'st thou that man?" Poor Lamia answer'd not.
He gaz'd into her eyes, and not a jot
Own'd they the lovelorn piteous appeal:
More, more he gaz'd: his human senses reel:
Some hungry spell that loveliness absorbs;
There was no recognition in those orbs.
"Lamia!" he cried—and no soft-toned reply.
The many heard, and the loud revelry
Grew hush; the stately music no more breathes;
The myrtle sicken'd in a thousand wreaths.
By faint degrees, voice, lute, and pleasure ceased;
A deadly silence step by step increased,
Until it seem'd a horrid presence there,
And not a man but felt the terror in his hair.
"Lamia!" he shriek'd; and nothing but the shriek
With its sad echo did the silence break.
"Begone, foul dream!" he cried, gazing again
In the bride's face, where now no azure vein
Wander'd on fair-spaced temples; no soft bloom
Misted the cheek; no passion to illume
The deep-recessed vision—all was blight;
Lamia, no longer fair, there sat a deadly white.
"Shut, shut those juggling° eyes, thou *beguiling*
 ruthless man!
Turn them aside, wretch! or the righteous ban
Of all the Gods, whose dreadful images
Here represent their shadowy presences,
May pierce them on the sudden with the thorn
Of painful blindness; leaving thee forlorn,
In trembling dotage to the feeblest fright
Of conscience, for their long offended might,
For all thine impious proud-heart sophistries,
Unlawful magic, and enticing lies.
Corinthians! look upon that gray-beard wretch!
Mark how, possess'd, his lashless eyelids stretch
Around his demon eyes! Corinthians, see!
My sweet bride withers at their potency."
"Fool!" said the sophist, in an undertone

[1] *adder's tongue* Fern that bears spikes resembling a snake's tongue.

[2] *thyrsus* Staff tipped with a pine cone and wreathed with vine leaves; carried by the followers of Bacchus.

[3] *philosophy* I.e., science.

[4] *gnomed* I.e., inhabited by gnomes.

Gruff with contempt; which a death-nighing moan
From Lycius answer'd, as heart-struck and lost,
He sank supine beside the aching ghost.
"Fool! Fool!" repeated he, while his eyes still
Relented not, nor mov'd; "from every ill
Of life have I preserv'd thee to this day,
And shall I see thee made a serpent's prey?"
Then Lamia breath'd death breath; the sophist's eye,
Like a sharp spear, went through her utterly,
Keen, cruel, perceant,° stinging: she, as well *piercing*
As her weak hand could any meaning tell,
Motion'd him to be silent; vainly so,
He look'd and look'd again a level—No!
"A serpent!" echoed he; no sooner said,
Than with a frightful scream she vanished:
And Lycius' arms were empty of delight,
As were his limbs of life, from that same night.
On the high couch he lay! His friends came round—
Supported him—no pulse, or breath they found,
And, in its marriage robe, the heavy body wound.
—1820

The Fall Of Hyperion
A Dream

CANTO I

Fanatics have their dreams, wherewith they weave
A paradise for a sect; the savage, too,
From forth the loftiest fashion of his sleep
Guesses at Heaven; pity these have not
Trac'd upon vellum° or wild Indian leaf *parchment*
The shadows of melodious utterance.
But bare of laurel[1] they live, dream, and die;
For Poesy alone can tell her dreams—
With the fine spell of words alone can save
Imagination from the sable chain
And dumb enchantment. Who alive can say,
"Thou art no poet—may'st not tell thy dreams"?
Since every man whose soul is not a clod
Hath visions, and would speak, if he had lov'd
And been well nurtured in his mother tongue.
Whether the dream now purpos'd to rehearse
Be poet's or fanatic's will be known
When this warm scribe, my hand, is in the grave.

Methought I stood where trees of every clime,
Palm, myrtle, oak, and sycamore, and beech,
With plantane, and spice-blossoms, made a screen;
In neighbourhood of fountains, by the noise
Soft-showering in mine ears, and, by the touch
Of scent, not far from roses. Turning round,
I saw an arbour with a drooping roof
Of trellis vines, and bells, and larger blooms,
Like floral censers,[2] swinging light in air;
Before its wreathed doorway, on a mound
Of moss, was spread a feast of summer fruits,
Which, nearer seen, seemed refuse of a meal
By angel tasted or our Mother Eve;[3]
For empty shells were scatter'd on the grass,
And grape-stalks but half bare, and remnants more,
Sweet-smelling, whose pure kinds I could not know.
Still was more plenty than the fabled horn[4]
Thrice emptied could pour forth, at banqueting
For Proserpine[5] return'd to her own fields,
Where the white heifers low. And appetite,
More yearning than on earth I ever felt,
Growing within, I ate deliciously;
And, after not long, thirsted; for thereby
Stood a cool vessel of transparent juice,
Sipp'd by the wander'd bee, the which I took,
And, pledging all the mortals of the world,
And all the dead whose names are in our lips,
Drank. That full draught is parent of my theme.
No Asian poppy[6] nor elixir fine° *subtle*
Of the soon-fading, jealous Caliphat,[7]
No poison gender'd in close monkish cell,

---

[1] *laurel* Wreaths made of leaves of the bay laurel were traditionally bestowed upon those who distinguished themselves in poetry.

[2] *censers* Vessels in which incense is burnt.

[3] *By angel … Eve* See Milton, *Paradise Lost* 5.3, in which Eve serves a meal to Adam and the angel Raphael.

[4] *fabled horn* I.e., cornucopia, or horn of plenty, the symbol of Ceres, goddess of the harvest.

[5] *Proserpine* Daughter of Ceres who was kidnapped by Pluto, god of the underworld, and forced to become his queen. As a concession to Ceres, Pluto allows Proserpine to return to earth for half of every year. In the fall and winter, when Proserpine is in the underworld, the grief-stricken Ceres prevents crops from growing.

[6] *Asian poppy* I.e., opium poppy.

[7] *Caliphat* Council of Caliphs, or Muslim rulers.

To thin the scarlet conclave[1] of old men,
Could so have rapt unwilling life away.
Among the fragrant husks and berries crush'd
Upon the grass, I struggled hard against
The domineering potion, but in vain.
The cloudy swoon came on, and down I sunk,
Like a Silenus[2] on an antique vase.
How long I slumber'd 'tis a chance to guess.
When sense of life return'd, I started up
As if with wings, but the fair trees were gone,
The mossy mound and arbour were no more:
I look'd around upon the carved sides
Of an old sanctuary with roof august,
Builded so high, it seem'd that filmed clouds
Might spread beneath, as o'er the stars of heaven.
So old the place was, I remember'd none
The like upon the earth: what I had seen
Of gray cathedrals, buttress'd walls, rent towers,
The superannuations of sunk realms,
Or Nature's rocks toil'd hard in waves and winds,
Seem'd but the faulture° of decrepit things *failing*
To that eternal domed monument.
Upon the marble at my feet there lay
Store of strange vessels, and large draperies,
Which needs had been of dyed asbestos[3] wove,
Or in that place the moth could not corrupt,[4]
So white the linen, so, in some, distinct
Ran imageries from a sombre loom.
All in a mingled heap confus'd there lay
Robes, golden tongs, censer and chafing-dish,
Girdles, and chains, and holy jewelries.

Turning from these with awe, once more I rais'd
My eyes to fathom the space every way;
The embossed roof, the silent massy range
Of columns north and south, ending in mist
Of nothing; then to eastward, where black gates
Were shut against the sunrise evermore.
Then to the west I look'd, and saw far off
An image, huge of feature as a cloud,
At level of whose feet an altar slept,
To be approach'd on either side by steps
And marble balustrade, and patient travail
To count with toil the innumerable degrees.
Towards the altar sober-pac'd I went,
Repressing haste, as too unholy there;
And, coming nearer, saw beside the shrine
One minist'ring; and there arose a flame.
When in mid-May the sickening east wind
Shifts sudden to the south, the small warm rain
Melts out the frozen incense from all flowers,
And fills the air with so much pleasant health
That even the dying man forgets his shroud;
Even so that lofty sacrificial fire,
Sending forth Maian[5] incense, spread around
Forgetfulness of everything but bliss,
And clouded all the altar with soft smoke;
From whose white fragrant curtains thus I heard
Language pronounc'd: "If thou canst not ascend
These steps,[6] die on that marble where thou art.
Thy flesh, near cousin to the common dust,
Will parch for lack of nutriment—thy bones
Will wither in few years, and vanish so
That not the quickest eye could find a grain
Of what thou now art on that pavement cold.
The sands of thy short life are spent this hour,
And no hand in the universe can turn
Thy hourglass, if these gummed° leaves be burnt *aromatic*
Ere thou canst mount up these immortal steps."
I heard, I look'd: two senses both at once,
So fine, so subtle, felt the tyranny
Of that fierce threat and the hard task proposed.
Prodigious seem'd the toil; the leaves were yet
Burning, when suddenly a palsied chill
Struck from the paved level up my limbs,
And was ascending quick to put cold grasp
Upon those streams that pulse beside the throat!
I shriek'd, and the sharp anguish of my shriek
Stung my own ears—I strove hard to escape
The numbness, strove to gain the lowest step.

[1] *scarlet conclave* College of Cardinals, which elects the Pope.

[2] *Silenus* Satyr (half-man, half-goat), a drunken companion of Bacchus, the wine god.

[3] *asbestos* Fibrous mineral able to be woven into incombustible fabric.

[4] *Which needs … corrupt* See Matthew 6.20, in which Jesus instructs, "Lay up for yourselves treasures in heaven, where neither moth nor rust doth corrupt."

[5] *Maian incense* Incense burnt for Maia, Greek goddess of spring.

[6] *These steps* Cf. Dante's *Purgatory*, in which the poet must ascend to the seven terraces of the Mount of Purgatory, purging a deadly sin on each terrace.

Slow, heavy, deadly was my pace: the cold
Grew stifling, suffocating, at the heart;
And when I clasp'd my hands I felt them not.
One minute before death, my iced foot touch'd
The lowest stair; and, as it touch'd, life seem'd
To pour in at the toes: I mounted up,
As once fair angels on a ladder flew
From the green turf to heaven.[1] "Holy Power,"
Cried I, approaching near the horned shrine,[2]
"What am I that should so be saved from death?
What am I that another death come not
To choke my utterance, sacrilegious here?"
Then said the veiled shadow: "Thou hast felt
What 'tis to die and live again before
Thy fated hour; that thou hadst power to do so
Is thy own safety; thou hast dated on[3]
Thy doom." "High Prophetess," said I, "purge off,
Benign, if so it please thee, my mind's film."
"None can usurp this height," returned that shade,
"But those to whom the miseries of the world
Are misery, and will not let them rest.
All else who find a haven in the world,
Where they may thoughtless sleep away their days,
If by a chance into this fane° they come, *temple*
Rot on the pavement where thou rotted'st half."
"Are there not thousands in the world," said I,
Encourag'd by the sooth° voice of the shade, *truthful*
"Who love their fellows even to the death,
Who feel the giant agony of the world,
And more, like slaves to poor humanity,
Labour for mortal good? I sure should see
Other men here, but I am here alone."
"Those whom thou spak'st of are no visionaries,"
Rejoin'd that voice, "they are no dreamers weak;
They seek no wonder but the human face,
No music but a happy-noted voice—
They come not here, they have no thought to come—
And thou art here, for thou art less than they.
What benefit canst thou do, or all thy tribe,
To the great world? Thou art a dreaming thing,
A fever of thyself—think of the earth;
What bliss, even in hope, is there for thee?
What haven? Every creature hath its home;
Every sole man hath days of joy and pain,
Whether his labours be sublime or low—
The pain alone, the joy alone, distinct:
Only the dreamer venoms all his days,
Bearing more woe than all his sins deserve.
Therefore, that happiness be somewhat shar'd,
Such things as thou art are admitted oft
Into like gardens thou didst pass erewhile,
And suffer'd° in these temples: for that cause *allowed*
Thou standest safe beneath this statue's knees."
"That I am favour'd for unworthiness,
By such propitious parley medicin'd
In sickness not ignoble, I rejoice,
Aye, and could weep for love of such award."
So answered I, continuing, "If it please,
Majestic shadow, tell me: sure not all
Those melodies sung into the world's ear
Are useless: sure a poet is a sage;
A humanist, physician to all men.
That I am none I feel, as vultures feel
They are no birds when eagles are abroad.
What am I then: thou spakest of my tribe:
What tribe?" The tall shade veil'd in drooping white
Then spake, so much more earnest, that the breath
Moved the thin linen folds that drooping hung
About a golden censer from the hand
Pendent—"Art thou not of the dreamer tribe?
The poet and the dreamer are distinct,
Diverse, sheer opposite, antipodes.
The one pours out a balm upon the world,
The other vexes it." Then shouted I
Spite of myself, and with a Pythia's spleen,[4]
"Apollo! faded! O far-flown Apollo!
Where is thy misty pestilence[5] to creep
Into the dwellings, through the door crannies
Of all mock lyrists, large self-worshippers,
And careless hectorers[6] in proud bad verse?
Though I breathe death with them it will be life

[1] *As once … heaven* See Genesis 28.12, in which Jacob dreams of a ladder from earth to heaven, with angels ascending and descending on it. Milton also alludes to this ladder in *Paradise Lost* 3.510–11.

[2] *horned shrine* Horns were often placed on ancient thrones. See Exodus 27.2.

[3] *dated on* Postponed.

[4] *Pythia's spleen* The anger of a Pythia, the priestess and oracle of Apollo, god of poetry and the sun, at Delphi.

[5] *thy misty pestilence* In Homer's *Iliad*, Apollo is also the sender of plagues.

[6] *hectorers* Bullies; blusterers.

To see them sprawl before me into graves.[1]
Majestic shadow, tell me where I am,
Whose altar this, for whom this incense curls;
What image this whose face I cannot see
For the broad marble knees; and who thou art,
Of accent feminine so courteous?"

Then the tall shade, in drooping linens veil'd,
Spake out, so much more earnest, that her breath
Stirr'd the thin folds of gauze that drooping hung
About a golden censer, from her hand
Pendent; and by her voice I knew she shed
Long-treasured tears. "This temple, sad and lone,
Is all spar'd from the thunder of a war
Foughten long since by giant hierarchy
Against rebellion: this old image here,
Whose carved features wrinkled as he fell,
Is Saturn's; I, Moneta,[2] left supreme,
Sole priestess of his desolation."
I had no words to answer, for my tongue,
Useless, could find about its roofed home
No syllable of a fit majesty
To make rejoinder to Moneta's mourn:
There was a silence, while the altar's blaze
Was fainting for sweet food. I look'd thereon,
And on the paved floor, where nigh were piled
Faggots of cinnamon, and many heaps
Of other crisped spicewood: then again
I look'd upon the altar, and its horns
Whiten'd with ashes, and its lang'rous flame,
And then upon the offerings again;
And so by turns—till sad Moneta cried:
"The sacrifice is done, but not the less
Will I be kind to thee for thy good will.
My power, which to me is still a curse,
Shall be to thee a wonder; for the scenes
Still swooning vivid through my globed brain,
With an electral changing misery,
Thou shalt with these dull mortal eyes behold
Free from all pain, if wonder pain thee not."
As near as an immortal's sphered words
Could to a mother's soften, were these last:
And yet I had a terror of her robes,
And chiefly of the veils, that from her brow
Hung pale, and curtain'd her in mysteries,
That made my heart too small to hold its blood.
This saw that Goddess, and with sacred hand
Parted the veils. Then saw I a wan face,
Not pined by human sorrows, but bright-blanch'd
By an immortal sickness which kills not;
It works a constant change, which happy death
Can put no end to; deathwards progressing
To no death was that visage; it had pass'd
The lily and the snow; and beyond these
I must not think now, though I saw that face.
But for her eyes I should have fled away.
They held me back with a benignant light,
Soft mitigated by divinest lids
Half closed, and visionless entire they seem'd
Of all external things—they saw me not,
But, in blank splendour, beam'd like the mild moon,
Who comforts those she sees not, who knows not
What eyes are upward cast. As I had found
A grain of gold upon a mountain's side,
And, twing'd with avarice, strain'd out my eyes
To search its sullen entrails rich with ore,
So, at the view of sad Moneta's brow,
I ached to see what things the hollow brain
Behind enwombed: what high tragedy
In the dark secret chambers of her skull
Was acting, that could give so dread a stress
To her cold lips, and fill with such a light
Her planetary eyes, and touch her voice
With such a sorrow. "Shade of Memory!"
Cried I, with act adorant at her feet,
"By all the gloom hung round thy fallen house,
By this last temple, by the golden age,
By great Apollo, thy dear foster-child,
And by thyself, forlorn divinity,
The pale Omega[3] of a wither'd race,
Let me behold, according as thou saidst,
What in thy brain so ferments to and fro."
No sooner had this conjuration pass'd
My devout lips, than side by side we stood

[1] *Majestic shadow … graves* Lines 187–210 were crossed out by Keats's friend Richard Woodhouse, who believed Keats intended to delete them. Some of the content of these lines is repeated in lines 211 and 216–20.

[2] *Saturn* King of the Titans who was overthrown by his son Jupiter; *Moneta* Mnemosyne (Greek: memory), mother of the nine Muses, patrons of learning and the arts.

[3] *Omega* The last letter of the Greek alphabet.

(Like a stunt bramble by a solemn pine)
Deep in the shady sadness of a vale[1]
Far sunken from the healthy breath of morn,
Far from the fiery noon and eve's one star.
Onward I look'd beneath the gloomy boughs,
And saw what first I thought an image huge,
Like to the image pedestall'd so high
In Saturn's temple; then Moneta's voice
Came brief upon mine ear, "So Saturn sat
When he had lost his realms—" whereon there grew
A power within me of enormous ken,° *range*
To see as a god sees, and take the depth
Of things as nimbly as the outward eye
Can size and shape pervade. The lofty theme
Of those few words hung vast before my mind
With half-unravell'd web. I sat myself
Upon an eagle's watch, that I might see,
And seeing ne'er forget. No stir of life
Was in this shrouded vale, not so much air
As in the zoning° of a summer's day *course*
Robs not one light seed from the feather'd grass;
But where the dead leaf fell, there did it rest:
A stream went voiceless by, still deaden'd more
By reason of the fallen Divinity
Spreading more shade; the Naiad° 'mid *water nymph*
her reeds
Press'd her cold finger closer to her lips.

Along the margin sand large footmarks went
No farther than to where old Saturn's feet
Had rested, and there slept, how long a sleep!
Degraded, cold, upon the sodden ground
His old right hand lay nerveless, listless, dead,
Unsceptred, and his realmless eyes were clos'd;
While his bow'd head seem'd listening to the Earth,
His antient mother,[2] for some comfort yet.

It seem'd no force could wake him from his place;
But there came one who, with a kindred hand,
Touch'd his wide shoulders, after bending low
With reverence, though to one who knew it not.
Then came the griev'd voice of Mnemosyne,
And griev'd I hearken'd. "That divinity
Whom thou saw'st step from yon forlornest wood,
And with slow pace approach our fallen king,
Is Thea,[3] softest-natur'd of our brood."
I mark'd the Goddess, in fair statuary° *stature*
Surpassing wan Moneta by the head,
And in her sorrow nearer woman's tears.
There was a list'ning fear in her regard,
As if calamity had but begun;
As if the vanward clouds[4] of evil days
Had spent their malice, and the sullen rear
Was with its stored thunder labouring up.
One hand she press'd upon that aching spot
Where beats the human heart; as if just there,
Though an immortal, she felt cruel pain;
The other upon Saturn's bended neck
She laid, and to the level of his ear
Leaning with parted lips, some words she spoke
In solemn tenour and deep organ-tone;
Some mourning words, which in our feeble tongue
Would come in this like accenting; how frail
To that large utterance of the early Gods!

"Saturn, look up! and for what, poor lost king?
I have no comfort for thee; no—not one;
I cannot cry, *Wherefore thus sleepest thou?*
For Heaven is parted from thee, and the Earth
Knows thee not, so afflicted, for a God.
The Ocean, too, with all its solemn noise,
Has from thy sceptre pass'd; and all the air
Is emptied of thine hoary majesty.
Thy thunder, captious° at the new command, *objecting*
Rumbles reluctant o'er our fallen house;
And thy sharp lightning in unpractised hands
Scorches and burns our once serene domain.
With such remorseless speed still come new woes,
That unbelief has not a space to breathe.
Saturn! sleep on—Me thoughtless,[5] why should I
Thus violate thy slumbrous solitude?
Why should I ope thy melancholy eyes?
Saturn! sleep on, while at thy feet I weep."

As when upon a tranced summer night
Forests, branch-charmed by the earnest stars,

[1] *Deep in … vale* The opening line of the original *Hyperion*, of which the rest of the poem is a revision.

[2] *Earth … mother* The Titans were the offspring of Heaven and Earth.

[3] *Thea* Hyperion's wife and sister.

[4] *vanward clouds* I.e., the front line of clouds.

[5] *Me thoughtless* I.e., thoughtless me.

Dream, and so dream all night, without a noise,
Save from one gradual solitary gust
Swelling upon the silence; dying off;
As if the ebbing air had but one wave;
So came those words and went; the while in tears
She press'd her fair large forehead to the earth,
Just where her fallen hair might spread in curls,
A soft and silken mat for Saturn's feet.
Long, long these two were postured motionless,
Like sculpture builded up upon the grave
Of their own power. A long awful time
I look'd upon them: still they were the same;
The frozen God still bending to the earth,
And the sad Goddess weeping at his feet,
Moneta silent. Without stay or prop,
But my own weak mortality, I bore
The load of this eternal quietude,
The unchanging gloom and the three fixed shapes
Ponderous upon my senses, a whole moon;
For by my burning brain I measured sure
Her silver seasons shedded on the night,
And every day by day methought I grew
More gaunt and ghostly. Oftentimes I pray'd
Intense, that death would take me from the vale
And all its burthens—Gasping with despair
Of change, hour after hour I curs'd myself;
Until old Saturn rais'd his faded eyes,
And look'd around, and saw his kingdom gone,
And all the gloom and sorrow of the place,
And that fair kneeling Goddess at his feet.
As the moist scent of flowers, and grass, and leaves
Fills forest-dells with a pervading air,
Known to the woodland nostril, so the words
Of Saturn fill'd the mossy glooms around,
Even to the hollows of time-eaten oaks,
And to the windings in the foxes' holes,
With sad, low tones, while thus he spake, and sent
Strange musings to the solitary Pan.[1]
"Moan, brethren, moan; for we are swallow'd up
And buried from all godlike exercise
Of influence benign on planets pale,
And peaceful sway above man's harvesting,
And all those acts which Deity supreme
Doth ease its heart of love in. Moan and wail,
Moan, brethren, moan; for lo! the rebel spheres
Spin round, the stars their antient courses keep,
Clouds still with shadowy moisture haunt the earth,
Still suck their fill of light from sun and moon,
Still buds the tree, and still the sea-shores murmur.
There is no death in all the universe,
No smell of death—there shall be death—moan, moan;
Moan, Cybele,[2] moan, for thy pernicious babes
Have changed a god into a shaking palsy.
Moan, brethren, moan, for I have no strength left;
Weak as the reed—weak—feeble as my voice—
O, O, the pain, the pain of feebleness.
Moan, moan, for still I thaw—or give me help:
Throw down those imps, and give me victory.
Let me hear other groans; and trumpets blown
Of triumph calm, and hymns of festival,
From the gold peaks of heaven's high piled clouds;
Voices of soft proclaim, and silver stir
Of strings in hollow shells; and let there be
Beautiful things made new, for the surprise
Of the sky-children—"So he feebly ceas'd,
With such a poor and sickly-sounding pause,
Methought I heard some old man of the earth
Bewailing earthly loss; nor could my eyes
And ears act with that pleasant unison of sense
Which marries sweet sound with the grace of form,
And dolorous accent from a tragic harp
With large-limb'd visions. More I scrutinized.
Still fix'd he sat beneath the sable trees,
Whose arms spread straggling in wild serpent forms,
With leaves all hush'd; his awful presence there
(Now all was silent) gave a deadly lie
To what I erewhile heard: only his lips
Trembled amid the white curls of his beard.
They told the truth, though, round, the snowy locks
Hung nobly, as upon the face of heaven
A mid-day fleece of clouds. Thea arose,
And stretch'd her white arm through the hollow dark,
Pointing some whither: whereat he too rose
Like a vast giant seen by men at sea
To grow° pale from the waves at dull midnight. *arise*
They melted from my sight into the woods:
Ere I could turn, Moneta cried, "These twain° *two*

[1] *Pan* Greek shepherd god of nature who was half goat and half man. After the nymph Syrinx turned herself into a bed of reeds in order to escape him, Pan created an instrument (the panpipe) out of the reeds.

[2] *Cybele* Consort of Saturn and mother of the Olympian gods.

Are speeding to the families of grief,
Where, roof'd in by black rocks, they waste in pain
And darkness for no hope." And she spake on,
As ye may read who can unwearied pass
Onward from the antechamber of this dream,
Where even at the open doors awhile
I must delay, and glean my memory
Of her high phrase—perhaps no further dare.

CANTO 2

"Mortal, that thou mayst understand aright,
I humanize my sayings to thine ear,
Making comparisons of earthly things;[1]
Or thou might'st better listen to the wind,
Whose language is to thee a barren noise,
Though it blows legend-laden through the trees—
In melancholy realms big tears are shed,
More sorrow like to this, and such like woe,
Too huge for mortal tongue, or pen of scribe.
The Titans fierce, self-hid or prison-bound,
Groan for the old allegiance once more,
Listening in their doom for Saturn's voice.
But one of the whole eagle-brood still keeps
His sov'reignty, and rule, and majesty;
Blazing Hyperion on his orbed fire
Still sits, still snuffs the incense teeming up
From man to the Sun's God—yet unsecure,
For as upon the earth dire prodigies[2]
Fright and perplex, so also shudders he;
Nor at dog's howl, or gloom-bird's even screech,
Or the familiar visitings of one
Upon the first toll of his passing bell:[3]
But horrors, portion'd° to a giant nerve, *proportioned*
Make great Hyperion ache. His palace bright,
Bastion'd with pyramids of glowing gold,
And touched with shade of bronzed obelisks,
Glares a blood-red through all the thousand courts,
Arches, and domes, and fiery galleries;
And all its curtains of Aurorian clouds[4]
Flush angerly; when he would taste the wreaths
Of incense breath'd aloft from sacred hills,
Instead of sweets, his ample palate takes
Savour of poisonous brass and metals sick.
Wherefore when harbour'd in the sleepy west,
After the full completion of fair day,
For rest divine upon exalted couch
And slumber in the arms of melody,
He paces through the pleasant hours of ease,
With strides colossal, on from hall to hall,
While, far within each aisle and deep recess,
His winged minions in close clusters stand
Amaz'd, and full of fear; like anxious men,
Who on a wide plain gather in sad troops,
When earthquakes jar their battlements and towers.
Even now while Saturn, roused from icy trance,
Goes, step for step, with Thea from yon woods,
Hyperion, leaving twilight in the rear,
Is sloping to the threshold of the west.
Thither we tend." Now in clear light I stood,
Relieved from the dusk vale. Mnemosyne
Was sitting on a square-edg'd polish'd stone,
That in its lucid depth reflected pure
Her priestess-garments. My quick eyes ran on
From stately nave[5] to nave, from vault to vault,
Through bowers of fragrant and enwreathed light,
And diamond-paved lustrous long arcades.
Anon rush'd by the bright Hyperion;
His flaming robes stream'd out beyond his heels,
And gave a roar, as if of earthly fire,
That scared away the meek ethereal hours,
And made their dove-wings tremble. On he flared.[6]
—1856 (WRITTEN 1819)

This Living Hand[7]

This living hand, now warm and capable
Of earnest grasping, would, if it were cold

[1] *Mortal that ... things* Cf. Milton, *Paradise Lost* 5.571–76, in which Raphael likens "spiritual to corporeal forms" to explain the war in Heaven to Adam.

[2] *dire prodigies* Ominous omens.

[3] *passing bell* Bell rung to announce a death.

[4] *Aurorian clouds* Clouds of the dawn (Aurora is goddess of the dawn).

[5] *nave* Main body of a church.

[6] *On he flared* Keats's manuscript breaks off here.

[7] *This Living Hand* A fragment whose context is unknown.

And in the icy silence of the tomb,
So haunt thy days and chill thy dreaming nights
That thou would wish thine own heart dry of blood
So in my veins red life might stream again,
and thou be conscience-calme'd—see here it is—
I hold it towards you—
—1898 (WRITTEN C. 1819)

Selected Letters

TO BENJAMIN BAILEY[1]

22 November 1817

My Dear Bailey,

... O I wish I was as certain of the end of all your troubles as that of your momentary start about the authenticity of the Imagination. I am certain of nothing but of the holiness of the Heart's affections and the truth of imagination—What the imagination seizes as Beauty must be truth—whether it existed before or not—for I have the same Idea of all our Passions as of Love they are all in their sublime, creative of essential Beauty—In a Word, you may know my favourite Speculation by my first Book and the little song I sent in my last[2]—which is a representation from the fancy of the probable mode of operating in these Matters—The Imagination may be compared to Adam's dream[3]—he awoke and found it truth. I am the more zealous in this affair, because I have never yet been able to perceive how any thing can be known for truth by consequitive[4] reasoning—and yet it must be—Can it be that even the greatest Philosopher ever arrived at his goal without putting aside numerous objections—However it may be, O for a Life of Sensations rather than of Thoughts! It is "a Vision in the form of Youth" a Shadow of reality to come—and this consideration has further convinced me for it has come as auxiliary to another favourite Speculation of mine, that we shall enjoy ourselves here after by having what we called happiness on Earth repeated in a finer tone and so repeated—And yet such a fate can only befall those who delight in sensation rather than hunger as you do after Truth—Adam's dream will do here and seems to be a conviction that Imagination and its empyreal[5] reflection is the same as human Life and its spiritual repetition. But as I was saying—the simple imaginative Mind may have its rewards in the repetition of its own silent Working coming continually on the spirit with a fine suddenness—to compare great things with small—have you never by being surprised with an old Melody—in a delicious place—by a delicious voice, felt over again your very speculations and surmises at the time it first operated on your soul—do you not remember forming to yourself the singer's face more beautiful [than] it was possible and yet with the elevation of the Moment you did not think so—even then you were mounted on the Wings of Imagination so high—that the Prototype must be here after—that delicious face you will see—What a time! I am continually running away from the subject—sure this cannot be exactly the case with a complex Mind—one that is imaginative and at the same time careful of its fruits—who would exist partly on sensation partly on thought—to whom it is necessary that years should bring the philosophic Mind[6]—such an one I consider yours and therefore it is necessary to your eternal Happiness that you not only have drink this old Wine of Heaven which I shall call the redigestion of our most ethereal Musings on Earth; but also increase in knowledge and know all things. I am glad to hear you are in a fair Way for Easter—you will soon get through your unpleasant reading and then!—but the world is full of troubles and I have not much reason to think myself pestered with many—I think Jane or Marianne has a better opinion of me than I deserve—for really and truly I do not think my Brother's illness connected with

[1] *Benjamin Bailey* Undergraduate student in Divinity at Oxford University. Keats had stayed with him in September while he was working on *Endymion*.

[2] *my first book* I.e., the first book of *Endymion*; *little song ... last* The first five stanzas of "Ode to Sorrow," from Book 4 of *Endymion*, which Keats had enclosed with his previous letter.

[3] *Adam's dream* See Milton, *Paradise Lost* 78.460–90, in which Adam dreams about Eve and wakes to find she has been created.

[4] *consequitive* Consecutive and consequent: a word of Keats's invention.

[5] *empyreal* Celestial; pertaining to the highest heavens.

[6] *philosophic Mind* Cf. Wordsworth, *Ode: Intimations of Immortality*, line 186.

mine[1]—you know more of the real Cause than they do—nor have I any chance of being rack'd as you have been[2]—you perhaps at one time thought there was such a thing as Worldly Happiness to be arrived at, at certain periods of time marked out—you have of necessity from your disposition been thus led away—I scarcely remember counting upon any Happiness—I look not for it if it be not in the present hour—nothing startles me beyond the Moment. The setting sun will always set me to rights—or if a Sparrow come before my Window I take part in its existence and pick about the Gravel. The first thing that strikes me on hearing a Misfortune having befalled another is this. Well it cannot be helped.—he will have the pleasure of trying the resources of his spirit, and I beg now my dear Bailey that hereafter should you observe any thing cold in me not to [put] it to the account of heartlessness but abstraction—for I assure you I sometimes feel not the influence of a Passion or Affection during a whole week—and so long this sometimes continues I begin to suspect myself and the genuineness of my feelings at other times—thinking them a few barren Tragedy-tears—My Brother Tom is much improved—he is going to Devonshire—whither I shall follow him—at present I am just arrived at Dorking to change the Scene—change the Air and give me a spur to wind up my Poem, of which there are wanting 500 Lines. [...]

Your affectionate friend
John Keats—

I want to say much more to you—a few hints will set me going
Direct Burford Bridge near dorking

To George and Thomas Keats
21, 27 (?) December 1817
Hampstead Sunday

My Dear Brothers,

... I spent Friday evening with Wells[3] & went the next morning to see *Death on the Pale horse*. It is a wonderful picture, when West's[4] age is considered; But there is nothing to be intense upon; no women one feels mad to kiss; no face swelling into reality. the excellence of every Art is its intensity, capable of making all disagreeables evaporate, from their being in close relationship with Beauty & Truth—Examine *King Lear*[5] & you will find this exemplified throughout; but in this picture we have unpleasantness without any momentous depth of speculation excited, in which to bury its repulsiveness—The picture is larger than *Christ rejected*—I dined with Haydon[6] the sunday after you left, & had a very pleasant day, I dined too (for I have been out too much lately) with Horace Smith[7] & met his two Brothers with Hill & Kingston & one Du Bois, they only served to convince me, how superior humour is to wit in respect to enjoyment—These men say things which make one start, without making one feel, they are all alike; their manners are alike; they all know fashionables; they have a mannerism in their very eating & drinking, in their mere handling a Decanter—They talked of Kean[8] & his low company—Would I were with that company instead of yours said I to myself! I know such like acquaintance will never do for me & yet I am going to Reynolds,[9] on Wednesday—Brown & Dilke[10] walked with me & back from the Christmas pantomime. I had not a dispute but a disquisition[11] with Dilke, on various subjects; several things dovetailed in my mind, & at once it struck me, what quality went to form a Man of Achievement especially in Literature & which Shake-

[1] *Jane or ... mine* Jane and Marianne Reynolds, two friends of Keats, were afraid that his illness was a sign of tuberculosis, from which Keats's youngest brother, Tom, was suffering.

[2] *rack'd ... been* Bailey was upset over a love affair that had recently ended.

[3] *Wells* Charles Wells, a school friend of Tom Keats.

[4] *West* American painter Benjamin West (1738–1820), who moved to England and became President of the Royal Academy. The painting *Christ Rejected*, mentioned later in this letter, is West's.

[5] *King Lear* Painting by West that depicts the storm scene in Shakespeare's play.

[6] *Haydon* Painter Benjamin Haydon (1786–1846).

[7] *Horace Smith* Famous literary wit (1779–1849). The other men mentioned are all minor writers or literary critics.

[8] *Kean* Shakespearean actor Edmund Kean (1787–1833).

[9] *Reynolds* Lawyer and poet John Hamilton Reynolds (1796–1852).

[10] *Brown and Dilke* Writers Charles Wentworth Dilke (1789–1864) and Charles Armitage Brown (1786–1842), a close friend and housemate of Keats who cared for him after he first became ill and who later wrote his biography.

[11] *disquisition* Systematic investigation.

Benjamin West, *King Lear* (1788).

speare possessed so enormously—I mean *Negative Capability*, that is when man is capable of being in uncertainties, Mysteries, doubts, without any irritable reaching after fact & reason—Coleridge, for instance, would let go by a fine isolated verisimilitude caught from the Penetralium[1] of mystery, from being incapable of remaining content with half knowledge. This pursued through Volumes would perhaps take us no further than this, that with a great poet the sense of Beauty overcomes every other consideration, or rather obliterates all consideration.

Shelley's poem[2] is out, & there are words about its being objected too, as much as Queen Mab was. Poor Shelley I think he has his Quota of good qualities, in sooth la!![3] Write soon to your most sincere friend & affectionate Brother.

John

[1] *Penetralium* I.e., the innermost part. From the Latin *penetralia,* the innermost parts of a temple.

[2] *Shelley's poem* Shelley's *Laon and Cythna* (*The Revolt of Islam*), which he was forced to withdraw because readers objected to the poem's description of incestuous love between its hero and heroine.

[3] *in sooth la* In truth.

TO JOHN HAMILTON REYNOLDS
3 February 1818
Hampstead

My Dear Reynolds,

I thank you for your dish of Filberts[1]—Would I could get a basket of them by way of dessert every day for the sum of two pence—Would we were a sort of ethereal Pigs, & turn'd loose to feed upon spiritual Mast[2] & Acorns—which would be merely being a squirrel & feeding upon filberts. for what is a squirrel but an airy pig, or a filbert but a sort of archangelical acorn. About the nuts being worth cracking, all I can say is that where there are a throng of delightful Images ready drawn simplicity is the only thing. the first is the best on account of the first line, and the "arrow—foil'd of its antler'd food"[3]—and moreover (and this is the only word or two I find fault with, the more because I have had so much reason to shun it as a quicksand) the last has "tender and true"—We must cut this, and not be rattle-snaked into any more of the like—It may be said that we ought to read our Contemporaries. that Wordsworth &c should have their due from us. but for the sake of a few fine imaginative or domestic passages, are we to be bullied into a certain Philosophy engendered in the whims of an Egotist—Every man has his speculations, but every man does not brood and peacock over them till he makes a false coinage and deceives himself—Many a man can travel to the very bourne[4] of Heaven, and yet want confidence to put down his halfseeing. Sancho[5] will invent a Journey heavenward as well as any body. We hate poetry that has a palpable design upon us—and if we do not agree, seems to put its hand in its breeches pocket.[6] Poetry should be great & unobtrusive, a thing which enters into one's soul, and does not startle it or amaze it with itself but with its subject.—How beautiful are the retired flowers! how would they lose their beauty were they to throng into the highway crying out, "admire me I am a violet! dote upon me I am a primrose!" Modern poets differ from the Elizabethans in this. Each of the moderns like an Elector of Hanover governs his petty state, & knows how many straws are swept daily from the Causeways in all his dominions & has a continual itching that all the Housewives should have their coppers well scoured: the antients were Emperors of vast Provinces, they had only heard of the remote ones and scarcely cared to visit them.—I will cut all this—I will have no more of Wordsworth or Hunt in particular—Why should we be of the tribe of Manasseh, when we can wander with Esau?[7] why should we kick against the Pricks, when we can walk on Roses? Why should we be owls, when we can be Eagles? Why be teased with "nice Eyed wagtails," when we have in sight "the Cherub Contemplation"?[8]—Why with Wordsworths "Matthew with a bough of wilding in his hand" when we can have Jacques "under an oak &c"?[9]—The secret of the Bough of Wilding will run through your head faster than I can write it —Old Matthew spoke to him some years ago on some nothing, & because he happens in an Evening Walk to imagine the figure of the old man—he must stamp it down in black & white, and it is henceforth sacred—I don't mean to deny Wordsworth's grandeur & Hunt's merit, but I mean to say we need not be teazed with grandeur & merit—when we can have them uncontaminated & unobtrusive. Let us have the old Poets, & robin Hood Your letter and its sonnets gave me more pleasure than will the 4th Book of Childe Harold[10] & the whole of any body's life & opinions. In return for your dish of filberts, I have gathered a few

[1] *Filberts* Hazelnuts.

[2] *Mast* Fruit of certain woodland trees, such as beech, oak, and chestnut.

[3] *arrow ... food* Keats is commenting on Reynolds's "Sonnet on Robin Hood 1," which Reynolds had sent to Keats.

[4] *bourne* Realm.

[5] *Sancho* Sancho Panza, squire of the naive and idealistic Don Quixote in Miguel de Cervantes's *Don Quixote*.

[6] *put its ... pocket* I.e., refuse to fight (by putting one's fists away).

[7] *Why should ... Esau* In the Old Testament, the tribe of Manasseh lived according to the old way of life, while in Genesis 25 Esau sold his birthright and became an outlaw.

[8] *nice Eyed wagtails* From Leigh Hunt's *The Nymphs* 2.170; *the Cherub Contemplation* From Milton's *Il Penseroso* 54.

[9] *Matthew ... hand* From Wordsworth's *The Two April Mornings* 57–60; *under ... etc* From Shakespeare's *As You Like It* 2.1.31.

[10] *4th ... Harold* Canto 4 of Byron's *Childe Harold's Pilgrimage*, whose publication was eagerly anticipated at the time.

Catkins, I hope they'll look pretty.[1]

Y[r] sincere friend and Coscribbler
John Keats

TO JOHN TAYLOR[2]
27 February 1818
Hampstead

My Dear Taylor,

Your alteration strikes me as being a great improvement —the page looks much better. And now I will attend to the Punctuations you speak of—the comma should be at *soberly*, and in the other passage the comma should follow *quiet*.[3] I am extremely indebted to you for this attention and also for your after admonitions—It is a sorry thing for me that any one should have to overcome Prejudices in reading my Verses—that affects me more than any hyper-criticism on any particular Passage. In *Endymion* I have most likely but moved into the Gocart from the leading strings. In Poetry I have a few Axioms, and you will see how far I am from their Centre. 1st I think Poetry should surprise by a fine excess and not by Singularity—it should strike the Reader as a wording of his own highest thoughts, and appear almost a Remembrance—2nd Its touches of Beauty should never be half way thereby making the reader breathless instead of content: the rise, the progress, the setting of imagery should like the Sun come natural natural too him—shine over him and set soberly although in magnificence leaving him in the Luxury of twilight—but it is easier to think what Poetry should be than to write it—and this leads me on to another axiom. That if Poetry comes not as naturally as the Leaves to a tree it had better not come at all. However it may be with me I cannot help looking into new countries with "O for a Muse of fire to ascend!"[4]— If *Endymion* serves me as a Pioneer perhaps I ought to be content. I have great reason to be content, for thank God I can read and perhaps understand Shakespeare to his depths, and I have I am sure many friends, who, if I fail, will attribute any change in my Life and Temper to Humbleness rather than to Pride—to a cowering under the Wings of great Poets rather than to a Bitterness that I am not appreciated. I am anxious to get *Endymion* printed that I may forget it and proceed. I have copied the 3rd Book and have begun the 4th. On running my Eye over the Proofs—I saw one Mistake I will notice it presently and also any others if there be any—There should be no comma in "the raft branch down sweeping from a tall Ash top"[5]—I have besides made one or two alterations and also altered the 13 Line Page 32 to make sense of it as you will see. I will take care the Printer shall not trip up my Heels—There should be no dash after Dryope in this Line "Dryope's lone lulling of her Child."[6] Remember me to Percy Street.

Your sincere and oblig[d] friend
John Keats—

P. S. You shall have a short *Preface* in good time—

TO BENJAMIN BAILEY
13 March 1818
Teignmouth

My dear Bailey,

... I have never had your Sermon[7] from Wordsworth but Mrs. Dilke lent it me—You know my ideas about Religion—I do not think myself more in the right than other people and that nothing in this world is proveable. I wish I could enter into all your feelings on the subject merely for one short 10 Minutes and give you a Page or two to your liking. I am sometimes so very sceptical as to think Poetry itself a mere Jack a lantern to amuse whoever may chance to be struck with its brilliance—As Tradesmen say every thing is worth what it will fetch, so probably every mental pursuit takes its reality and worth

[1] *In return ... pretty* In return for the sonnets on Robin Hood that Reynolds had sent, Keats enclosed two poems of his own, *Robin Hood* and *Lines on the Mermaid Tavern.*

[2] *John Taylor* Partner in the publishing firm of Taylor and Hessey, who were publishing Keats's poem *Endymion* at this time.

[3] *soberly ... quiet* References to *Endymion* 1.149 and 1.247.

[4] *O for ... ascend* Cf. Shakespeare, *Henry V* Prologue 1: "O for a Muse of fire, that would ascend / The brightest heaven of invention."

[5] *the raft ... top* From *Endymion* 1.334–5.

[6] *Dryope's ... Child* From *Endymion* lines 334–5.

[7] *your Sermon* Bailey, like many clergymen at the time, had written a memorial sermon for Princess Charlotte, who died in childbirth in 1817.

from the ardour of the pursuer—being in itself a nothing—Ethereal things may at least be thus real, divided under three heads—Things real—things semireal—and no things—Things real—such as existences of Sun Moon & Stars and passages of Shakespeare—Things semireal such as Love, the Clouds &c which require a greeting of the Spirit to make them wholly exist—and Nothings which are made Great and dignified by an ardent pursuit—Which by the by stamps the burgundy mark on the bottles of our Minds, insomuch as they are able to "*consecrate whate'er they look upon*"[1] I have written a Sonnet here of a somewhat collateral nature—so don't imagine it an a propos des bottes.[2]

[*The Human Seasons* is included here.]

Aye this may be carried—but what am I talking of—it is an old maxim of mine and of course must be well known that every point of thought is the centre of an intellectual world—the two uppermost thoughts in a Man's mind are the two poles of his World he revolves on them and every thing is southward or northward to him through their means—We take but three steps from feathers to iron. Now my dear fellow I must once for all tell you I have not one Idea of the truth of any of my speculations—I shall never be a Reasoner because I care not to be in the right, when retired from bickering and in a proper philosophical temper [...] My Brother Tom desires to be remember'd to you—he has just this moment had a spitting of blood poor fellow —Remember me to [Gleig] and Whitehead—

Your affectionate friend
John Keats—

TO BENJAMIN BAILEY

18 July 1818

My dear Bailey,

... I am certain I have not a right feeling towards Women—at this moment I am striving to be just to them but I cannot—Is it because they fall so far beneath my Boyish imagination? When I was a Schoolboy I thought a fair Woman a pure Goddess, my mind was a soft nest in which some one of them slept though she knew it not—I have no right to expect more than their reality. I thought them ethereal above Men—I find them perhaps equal.... I do not like to think insults in a Lady's Company—I commit a Crime with her which absence would have not known—is it not extraordinary? When among Men I have no evil thoughts, no malice, no spleen[3]—I feel free to speak or to be silent—I can listen and from every one I can learn—my hands are in my pockets I am free from all suspicion and comfortable. When I am among Women I have evil thoughts, malice spleen—I cannot speak or be silent—I am full of Suspicions and therefore listen to no thing—I am in a hurry to be gone—You must be charitable and put all this perversity to my being disappointed since Boyhood—Yet with such feelings I am happier alone among Crowds of men, by myself or with a friend or two—With all this trust me Bailey I have not the least idea that Men of different feelings and inclinations are more short sighted than myself—I never rejoiced more than at my Brother's Marriage[4] and shall do so at that of any of my friends—. I must absolutely get over this—but how? The only way is to find the root of evil, and so cure it "with backward mutters of dissevering Power."[5] That is a difficult thing; for an obstinate Prejudice can seldom be produced but from a gordian complication[6] of feelings, which must take time to unravell and care to keep unravelled—I could say a good deal about this but I will leave it in hopes of better and more worthy dispositions—and also content that I am wronging no one, for after all I do think better of Womankind than to suppose they care whether Mister John Keats five feet high likes them or not....

Your affectionate friend
John Keats—

[1] *consecrate ... upon* From Percy Shelley's *Hymn to Intellectual Beauty* 13–14.

[2] *a propos des bottes* French: on the subject of boots.

[3] *spleen* Irritability; ill-humor; melancholy.

[4] *my Brother's Marriage* Keats's brother George had recently married, as had Bailey.

[5] *with ... Power* From Milton's *Comus* 816–17, in which the author describes the spells that will release a lady from the enchantment of Comus.

[6] *gordian complication* I.e., as difficult to undo as the intricate knot tied by King Gordias.

To Richard Woodhouse[1]

27 October 1818

My Dear Woodhouse,

Your Letter gave me a great satisfaction; more on account of its friendliness, than any relish of that matter in it which is accounted so acceptable in the "genus irritabile."[2] The best answer I can give you is in a clerklike manner to make some observations on two principle points, which seem to point like indices into the midst of the whole pro and con, about genius, and views and achievements and ambition and coetera.[3] 1st As to the poetical Character itself, (I mean that sort of which, if I am any thing, I am a Member; that sort distinguished from the wordsworthian or egotistical sublime; which is a thing per se and stands alone) it is not itself—it has no self—it is every thing and nothing—It has no character—it enjoys light and shade; it lives in gusto, be it foul or fair, high or low, rich or poor, mean or elevated—It has as much delight in conceiving an Iago as an Imogen.[4] What shocks the virtuous philosopher delights the chameleon Poet. It does no harm from its relish of the dark side of things any more than from its taste for the bright one; because they both end in speculation. A Poet is the most unpoetical of any thing in existence; because he has no Identity—he is continually in for—and filling some other Body—The Sun, the Moon, the Sea and Men and Women who are creatures of impulse are poetical and have about them an unchangeable attribute—the poet has none; no identity—he is certainly the most unpoetical of all God's Creatures. If then he has no self, and if I am a Poet, where is the Wonder that I should say I would write no more? Might I not at that very instant [have] been cogitating on the Characters of saturn and Ops?[5] It is a. wretched thing to confess; but is a very fact that not one word I ever utter can be taken for granted as an opinion growing out of my identical nature—how can it, when I have no nature? When I am in a room with People if I ever am free from speculating on creations of my own brain, then not myself goes home to myself: but the identity of every one in the room begins [so] to press upon me that, I am in a very little time annihilated—not only among Men; it would be the same in a Nursery of children: I know not whether I make myself wholly understood: I hope enough so to let you see that no dependence is to be placed on what I said that day.[6]

In the second place I will speak of my views, and of the life I purpose to myself—I am ambitious of doing the world some good: if I should be spared that may be the work of maturer years—in the interval I will assay to reach to as high a summit in Poetry as the nerve bestowed upon me will suffer. The faint conceptions I have of Poems to come brings the blood frequently into my forehead—All I hope is that I may not lose all interest in human affairs—that the solitary indifference I feel for applause even from the finest Spirits, will not blunt any acuteness of vision I may have. I do not think it will—I feel assured I should write from the mere yearning and fondness I have for the Beautiful even if my night's labours should be burnt every morning and no eye ever shine upon them. But even now I am perhaps not speaking from myself; but from some character in whose soul I now live. I am sure however that this next sentence is from myself. I feel your anxiety, good opinion and friendliness in the highest degree, and am

Yours most sincerely
John Keats

---

[1] *Richard Woodhouse* Young lawyer who worked with Keats's publishers. Woodhouse was struck by Keats's talent and preserved manuscript copies of many of his poems and letters.

[2] *genus irritabile* Latin: irritable tribe. The phrase, in reference to poets, was coined by the Roman poet Horace in his *Epistles* 2.2.102.

[3] *coetera* Latin: the following; the next.

[4] *Iago* Villain of Shakespeare's *Othello*; *Imogen* Heroine of Shakespeare's *Cymbeline*.

[5] *saturn* In Greek mythology, king of the Titan gods, who were overthrown by their children, the Olympians. The Titans figure prominently in Keats's *Hyperion*; *Ops* Titan goddess of the harvest.

[6] *what I … day* Keats had told Woodhouse that he felt preempted by great poets of the past.

To GEORGE AND GEORGIANA KEATS[1]
14 February – 3 May 1819

My dear Brother & Sister—

… [19 March] Yesterday I got a black eye—the first time I took a Cricket bat—Brown who is always one's friend in a disaster applied a leech to the eyelid, and there is no inflammation this morning though the ball hit me directly on the sight—'t was a white ball—I am glad it was not a clout—This is the second black eye I have had since leaving school—during all my school days I never had one at all—we must eat a peck before we die[2]—This morning I am in a sort of temper indolent and supremely careless: I long after a stanza or two of Thomson's *Castle of indolence*[3]—My passions are all asleep from my having slumbered till nearly eleven and weakened the animal fibre all over me to a delightful sensation about three degrees on this side of faintness—if I had teeth of pearl and the breath of lilies I should call it langour—but as I am[4] I must call it Laziness—In this state of effeminacy the fibres of the brain are relaxed in common with the rest of the body, and to such a happy degree that pleasure has no show of enticement and pain no unbearable frown. Neither Poetry, nor Ambition, nor Love have any alertness of countenance as they pass by me: they seem rather like three figures on a greek vase—a Man and two women—whom no one but myself could distinguish in their disguisement. This is the only happiness; and is a rare instance of advantage in the body overpowering the Mind. I have this moment received a note from Haslam[5] in which he expects the death of his Father who has been for some time in a state of insensibility—his mother bears up he says very well—I shall go to [town] tomorrow to see him. This is the world—thus we cannot expect to give way many hours to pleasure—Circumstances are like Clouds continually gathering and bursting—While we are laughing the seed of some trouble is put into the wide arable land of events—while we are laughing it sprouts [it] grows and suddenly bears a poison fruit which we must pluck—Even so we have leisure to reason on the misfortunes of our friends; our own touch us too nearly for words. Very few men have ever arrived at a complete disinterestedness[6] of Mind: very few have been influenced by a pure desire of the benefit of others—in the greater part of the Benefactors of & to Humanity some meretricious motive has sullied their greatness—some melodramatic scenery has fascinated them—From the manner in which I feel Haslam's misfortune I perceive how far I am from any humble standard of disinterestedness—Yet this feeling ought to be carried to its highest pitch, as there is no fear of its ever injuring society—which it would do I fear pushed to an extremity—For in wild nature the Hawk would loose his Breakfast of Robins and the Robin his of Worms The Lion must starve as well as the swallow—The greater part of Men make their way with the same instinctiveness, the same unwandering eye from their purposes, the same animal eagerness as the Hawk—The Hawk wants a Mate, so does the Man—look at them both they set about it and procure one in the same manner—They want both a nest and they both set about one in the same manner—they get their food in the same manner—The noble animal Man for his amusement smokes his pipe—the Hawk balances about the Clouds—that is the only difference of their leisures. This it is that makes the Amusement of Life—to a speculative Mind. I go among the Fields and catch a glimpse of a stoat[7] or a fieldmouse peeping out of the withered grass—the creature hath a purpose and its eyes are bright with it—I go amongst the buildings of a city and I see a Man hurrying along—to what? The Creature has a purpose and his eyes are bright with it. But then as Wordsworth says, "we have all one human heart"[8]— there is an electric fire in human nature tending to purify—so that among these human creatures there is continually some birth of new heroism—The pity is that we must wonder at it: as

[1] *George and Georgiana Keats* Keats's brother and sister-in-law, who had emigrated to America. Keats would compose long letters to them, each of which spanned several months, and in which he would include transcriptions of his poems.

[2] *eat a peck … die* Proverbial: everyone must eat a peck of dirt before he or she dies.

[3] *Thomson … indolence* James Thomson's *The Castle of Indolence*, in which a wizard named Indolence puts a spell of indolence on tired travelers who are lured into his castle.

[4] [Keats's note] Especially as I have a black eye.

[5] *Haslam* Keats's friend William Haslam, a businessman.

[6] *disinterestedness* State unmotivated by self-interest.

[7] *stoat* Weasel-like creature.

[8] *we have … heart* From *The Old Cumberland Beggar* 152–53.

we should at finding a pearl in rubbish—I have no doubt that thousands of people never heard of have had hearts completely disinterested: I can remember but two—Socrates and Jesus—their Histories evince it—What I heard a little time ago, Taylor observe with respect to Socrates, may be said of Jesus—That he was so great as man that though he transmitted no writing of his own to posterity, we have his Mind and his sayings and his greatness handed to us by others. It is to be lamented that the history of the latter was written and revised by Men interested in the pious frauds of Religion. Yet through all this I see his splendour. Even here though I myself am pursuing the same instinctive course as the veriest human animal you can think of—I am however young writing at random—straining at particles of light in the midst of a great darkness—without knowing the bearing of any one assertion of any one opinion. Yet may I not in this be free from sin? May there not be superior beings amused with any graceful, though instinctive attitude my mind my fall into, as I am entertained with the alertness of a Stoat or the anxiety of a Deer? Though a quarrel in the streets is a thing to be hated, the energies displayed in it are fine; the commonest Man shows a grace in his quarrel—By a superior being our reasoning may take the same tone—though erroneous they may be fine—This is the very thing in which consists poetry; and if so it is not so fine a thing as philosophy—For the same reason that an eagle is not so fine a thing as a truth—Give me this credit—Do you not think I strive—to know myself? Give me this credit— and you will not think that on my own account I repeat Milton's lines

> How charming is divine Philosophy
> Not harsh and crabbed as dull fools suppose
> But musical as is Apollo's lute—[1]

No—no for myself—feeling grateful as I do to have got into a state of mind to relish them properly—Nothing ever becomes real till it is experienced—Even a Proverb is no proverb to you till your Life has illustrated it— …

[21 April] I have been reading lately two very different books Robertson's *America* and Voltaire's *Siecle De Louis xiv* It is like walking arm and arm between Pizzarro and the great-little Monarch.[2] In How lamentable a case do we see the great body of the people in both instances: in the first, where Men might seem to inherit quiet of Mind from unsophisticated sense; from uncontamination of civilisation; and especially from their being as it were estranged from the mutual helps of Society and its mutual injuries—and thereby more immediately under the Protection of Providence—even there they had mortal pains to bear as bad; or even worse than Baliffs, Debts and Poverties of civilised Life—The whole appears to resolve into this—that Man is originally "a poor forked creature"[3] subject to the same mischances as the beasts of the forest, destined to hardships and disquietude of some kind or other. If he improves by degrees his bodily accommodations and comforts—at each stage, at each accent there are waiting for him a fresh set of annoyances—he is mortal and there is still a heaven with its Stars above his head. The most interesting question that can come before us is, How far by the persevering endeavours of a seldom appearing Socrates Mankind may be made happy—I can imagine such happiness carried to an extreme—but what must it end in?—Death—and who could in such a case bear with death—the whole troubles of life which are now frittered away in a series of years, would then be accumulated for the last days of a being who instead of hailing its approach, would leave this world as Eve left Paradise—But in truth I do not at all believe in this sort of perfectibility—the nature of the world will not admit of it—the inhabitants of the world will correspond to itself—Let the fish philosophise the ice away from the Rivers in winter time and they shall be at continual play in the tepid delight of summer. Look at the Poles and at the sands of Africa, Whirlpools and volcanoes—Let men exterminate them and I will say that they may arrive at earthly Happiness—The point at which Man may arrive is as far as the parallel state in inanimate nature and no further—For instance suppose a rose to have sensation,

[1] *How charming … lute* Milton's *Comus* 475–77.

[2] *Robertson's … Monarch* William Robertson's *History of the Discovery and Settlement of America* (1777) describes the Spanish conquistadors, including Francisco Pizarro, who conquered the Incas in the sixteenth century. French philosopher Voltaire's *Le Siècle de Louis XIV* (1751) describes the rule of Louis XIV, who was often called "The Great Monarch."

[3] *a poor forked creature* From *King Lear* 3.4.112–13, in which Lear looks at "Poor Tom" and says "Unaccommodated man is no more but such a poor, bare, forked animal as though art."

it blooms on a beautiful morning it enjoys itself—but there comes a cold wind, a hot sun—it can not escape it, it cannot destroy its annoyances—they are as native to the world as itself: no more can man be happy in spite, the worldly elements will prey upon his nature—The common cognomen of this world among the misguided and superstitious is "a vale of tears" from which we are to be redeemed by a certain arbitrary interposition of God and taken to Heaven—What a little circumscribed straightened notion! Call the world if you Please "The vale of Soul-making" Then you will find out the use of the world (I am speaking now in the highest terms for human nature admitting it to be immortal which I will here take for granted for the purpose of showing a thought which has struck me concerning it) I say "*Soul making*" Soul as distinguished from an Intelligence—There may be intelligences or sparks of the divinity in millions—but they are not Souls till they acquire identities, till each one is personally itself. Intelligences are atoms of perception—they know and they see and they are pure, in short they are God—how then are Souls to be made? How then are these sparks which are God to have identity given them—so as ever to possess a bliss peculiar to each ones individual existence? How, but by the medium of a world like this? This point I sincerely wish to consider because I think it a grander system of salvation than the christian religion—or rather it is a system of Spirit-creation—This is effected by three grand materials acting the one upon the other for a series of years—These three Materials are the *Intelligence*—the *human heart* (as distinguished from intelligence or Mind) and the *World* or *Elemental space* suited for the proper action of *Mind and Heart* on each other for the purpose of forming the *Soul or Intelligence destined to possess the sense of Identity*. I can scarcely express what I but dimly perceive—and yet I think I perceive it—that you may judge the more clearly I will put it in the most homely form possible—I will call the world a School instituted for the purpose of teaching little children to read—I will call the *human heart* the *horn Book*[1] used in that School—and I will call the *Child able to read, the Soul* made from that *school* and its *hornbook*. Do you not see how necessary a World of Pains and troubles is to school an Intelligence and make it a soul? A Place where the heart must feel and suffer in a thousand diverse ways! Not merely is the Heart a Hornbook, It is the Minds Bible, it is the Minds experience, it is the teat from which the Mind or intelligence sucks its identity—As various as the Lives of Men are—so various become their souls, and thus does God make individual beings, Souls, Identical Souls of the sparks of his own essence—This appears to me a faint sketch of a system of Salvation which does not affront our reason and humanity—I am convinced that many difficulties which christians labour under would vanish before it—there is one which even now Strikes me—the Salvation of Children—In them the Spark or intelligence returns to God without any identity—it having had no time to learn of, and be altered by, the heart—or seat of the human Passions—It is pretty generally suspected that the christian scheme has been copied from the ancient persian and greek Philosophers. Why may they not have made this simple thing even more simple for common apprehension by introducing Mediators and Personages in the same manner as in the heathen mythology abstractions are personified—Seriously I think it probable that this System of Soul-making—may have been the Parent of all the more palpable and personal Schemes of Redemption, among the Zoroastrians the Christians and the Hindus. For as one part of the human species must have their carved Jupiter; so another part must have the palpable and named Mediatior and saviour, their Christ their Oromanes and their Vishnu[2]—If what I have said should not be plain enough, as I fear it may not be, I will but [put] you in the place where I began in this series of thoughts—I mean, I began by seeing how man was formed by circumstances—and what are circumstances?—but touchstones of his heart?—and what are touchstones?—but provings of his heart? and what are provings of his heart but fortifiers or alterers of his nature? and what is his altered nature but his soul?—and what was his soul before it came into the world and had These provings and alterations and perfectionings?—An intelligence—without Identity—and how is this Identity to be made? Through the medium of the Heart? And how is the heart to become this Medium but in a

[1] *horn Book* Child's primer, originally made of a sheet of paper mounted on wood and protected by a thin sheet of transparent horn.

[2] *Oromanes* Ahriman, the chief evil spirit in Zoroastrianism, who is locked in perpetual struggle with Ahura Mazda; *Vishnu* Hindu deity who protects and preserves the world.

world of Circumstances?—There now I think what with Poetry and Theology you may thank your Stars that my pen is not very long winded— …

… this is the 3^d of May & every thing is in delightful forwardness; the violets are not withered, before the peeping of the first rose; You must let me know every thing, how parcels go &. come, what papers you have, &. what Newspapers you want, & other things—God bless you my dear Brother & Sister

Your ever Affectionate Brother
John Keats—

To Fanny Brawne[1]

25 July 1819
Sunday Night
Isle of Wight

My Sweet Girl,

I hope you did not blame me much for not obeying your request of a Letter on Saturday: we have had four in our small room playing at cards night and morning leaving me no undisturb'd opportunity to write. Now Rice and Martin are gone I am at liberty. Brown to my sorrow confirms the account you give of your ill health. You cannot conceive how I ache to be with you: how I would die for one hour—for what is in the world? I say you cannot conceive; it is impossible you should look with such eyes upon me as I have upon you: it cannot be. Forgive me if I wander a little this evening, for I have been all day employ'd in a very abstract Poem[2] and I am in deep love with you—two things which must excuse me. I have, believe me, not been an age in letting you take possession of me; the very first week I knew you I wrote myself your vassal; but burnt the Letter as the very next time I saw you I thought you manifested some dislike to me. If you should ever feel for Man at the first sight what I did for you, I am lost. Yet I should not quarrel with you, but hate myself if such a thing were to happen—only I should burst if the thing were not as fine as a Man as you are as a Woman. Perhaps I am too vehement, then fancy me on my knees, especially when I mention a part of your Letter which hurt me; you say speaking of Mr. Severn[3] "but you must be satisfied in knowing that I admired you much more than your friend." My dear love, I cannot believe there ever was or ever could be any thing to admire in me especially as far as sight goes—I cannot be admired, I am not a thing to be admired. You are, I love you; all I can bring you is a swooning admiration of your Beauty. I hold that place among Men which snubnos'd brunettes with meeting eyebrows do among women—they are trash to me—unless I should find one among them with a fire in her heart like the one that burns in mine. You absorb me in spite of myself—you alone: for I look not forward with any pleasure to what is call'd being settled in the world; I tremble at domestic cares—yet for you I would meet them, though if it would leave you the happier I would rather die than do so. I have two luxuries to brood over in my walks, your Loveliness and the hour of my death. O that I could have possession of them both in the same minute. I hate the world: it batters too much the wings of my self-will, and would I could take a sweet poison from your lips to send me out of it. From no others would I take it. I am indeed astonish'd to find myself so careless of all charms but yours—remembering as I do the time when even a bit of ribband was a matter of interest with me. What softer words can I find for you after this—what it is I will not read. Nor will I say more here, but in a Postscript answer any thing else you may have mentioned in your Letter in so many words—for I am distracted with a thousand thoughts. I will imagine you Venus tonight and pray, pray, pray to your star like a Heathen.

Yours ever, fair Star,
John Keats

[1] *Fanny Brawne* Young woman whom Keats met in the summer of 1818, and to whom he was engaged by the end of the year (though the couple was waiting to marry until Keats felt he was financially secure). From October to May 1819 Keats stayed in his friend Charles Brown's apartment in Hampstead, which was next door to the Brawnes, who took care of him throughout the summer.

[2] *very abstract Poem* Most likely *The Fall of Hyperion.*

[3] *Mr. Severn* Joseph Severn, an artist and a friend of Keats. He cared for Keats during his final illness in Rome and was present when he died.

To Percy Bysshe Shelley[1]

16 August 1820

Hampstead

My Dear Shelley,

I am very much gratified that you, in a foreign country, and with a mind almost over occupied, should write to me in the strain of the Letter beside me. If I do not take advantage of your invitation it will be prevented by a circumstance I have very much at heart to prophesy—There is no doubt that an english winter would put an end to me, and do so in a lingering hateful manner, therefore I must either voyage or journey to Italy as a soldier marches up to a battery. My nerves at present are the worst part of me, yet they feel soothed when I think that come what extreme may, I shall not be destined to remain in one spot long enough to take a hatred of any four particular bedposts. I am glad you take any pleasure in my poor Poem;[2]—which I would willingly take the trouble to unwrite, if possible, did I care so much as I have done about Reputation. I received a copy of the Cenci,[3] as from yourself from Hunt. There is only one part of it I am judge of; the Poetry, and dramatic effect, which by many spirits now a days is considered the mammon.[4] A modern work it is said must have a purpose, which may be the God—*an artist* must serve Mammon—he must have "self concentration" selfishness perhaps. You I am sure will forgive me for sincerely remarking that you might curb your magnanimity and be more of an artist, and "load every rift" of your subject with ore.[5] The thought of such discipline must fall like cold chains upon you, who perhaps never sat with your wings furl'd for six Months together. And is not this extraordinary talk for the writer of *Endymion*? whose mind was like a pack of scattered cards—I am pick'd up and sorted to a pip.[6] My Imagination is a Monastry and I am its Monk—you must explain my [metaphysics] to yourself. I am in expectation of *Prometheus*[7] every day. Could I have my own wish for its interest effected you would have it still in manuscript—or be but now putting an end to the second act. I remember you advising me not to publish my first-blights, on Hampstead heath—I am returning advice upon your hands. Most of the Poems in the volume I send you[8] have been written above two years, and would never have been publish'd but from a hope of gain; so you see I am inclined enough to take your advice now. I must express once more my deep sense of your kindness, adding my sincere thanks and respects for Mrs. Shelley. In the hope of soon seeing you I remain

most sincerely yours,

John Keats—

To Charles Brown

30 November 1820

Rome

My Dear Brown,

'Tis the most difficult thing in the world to me to write a letter. My stomach continues so bad, that I feel it worse on opening any book,—yet I am much better than I was in Quarantine.[9] Then I am afraid to encounter the proing and conning of any thing interesting to me in England. I have an habitual feeling of my real life having past, and that I am leading a posthumous existence. God knows how it would have been—but it appears to me—however, I will not speak of that subject. I must have been at Bedhampton nearly at the time you were writing to me from Chichester—how unfortunate—and to pass on the river too! There was

[1] *To … Shelley* This letter is written in response to one from Shelley, in which he, having learned of Keats's serious illness, invites Keats to stay with him in Pisa for the winter.

[2] *my poor Poem* Keats's *Endymion*, which had received several negative reviews but which Shelley had praised in his letter.

[3] *Cenci* Shelley's blank-verse tragedy (1820).

[4] *mammon* Wealth and profit, regarded as a false god. Cf. Matthew 6.24, in which Jesus says, "Ye cannot serve God and Mammon."

[5] *load … ore* Reference to Spenser's *Faerie Queene* 2.7.28, in which he describes the Palace of Mammon: "Embost with massy gold of glorious gift, / And with rich metal loaded every rift."

[6] *sorted to a pip* Put in order. Pips are the markings on playing cards.

[7] *Prometheus* Shelley's *Prometheus Unbound* (1820), a copy of which he had promised to send to Keats.

[8] *the volume … you* Keats's 1820 volume, which Shelley had in his pocket when he drowned.

[9] *in Quarantine* Keats's ship was quarantined for ten days outside Naples, in extremely hot weather. Keats was writing this letter from Rome, where he was being cared for by Joseph Severn.

my star predominant! I cannot answer any thing in your letter, which followed me from Naples to Rome, because I am afraid to look it over again. I am so weak (in mind) that I cannot bear the sight of any hand writing of a friend I love so much as I do you. Yet I ride the little horse,[1]—and, at my worst, even in Quarantine, summoned up more puns, in a sort of desperation, in one week than in any year of my life. There is one thought enough to kill me—I have been well, healthy, alert &c, walking with her[2]—and now—the knowledge of contrast, feeling for light and shade, all that information (primitive sense) necessary for a poem are great enemies to the recovery of the stomach. There, you rogue, I put you to the torture,—but you must bring your philosophy to bear—as I do mine, really—or how should I be able to live? Dr Clarke is very attentive to me; he says, there is very little the matter with my lungs, but my stomach, he says, is very bad. I am well disappointed in hearing good news from George,—for it runs in my head we shall all die young. I have not written to * * * *[3] yet, which he must think very neglectful; being anxious to send him a good account of my health, I have delayed it from week to week. If I recover, I will do all in my power to correct the mistakes made during sickness; and if I should not, all my faults will be forgiven. I shall write to * * * * tomorrow, or next day. I will write to * * * * in the middle of next week. Severn is very well, though he leads so dull a life with me. Remember me to all friends, and tell * * * * I should not have left London without taking leave of him, but from being so low in body and mind. Write to George as soon as you receive this, and tell him how I am, as far as you can guess; and also a note to my sister—who walks about my imagination like a ghost—she is so like Tom.[4] I can scarcely bid you good bye even in a letter. I always made an awkward bow.

God bless you!

John Keats.

In Context

Politics, Poetry, and the "Cockney School Debate"

As literary journals and magazines of the time demonstrate, in the nineteenth century politics and literary theory were often inextricably intertwined. At the time, only a small minority of adult males had been granted the vote, and the political system was widely perceived to be corrupt. Leigh Hunt, John Keats, William Hazlitt, and Percy Bysshe Shelley were among those who pressed strongly for political reform. Leigh Hunt, with his brothers John and Robert, edited the *Examiner*, a liberal weekly journal that frequently riled the government. After offending the Prince of Wales, Leigh and John spent two years in prison (1813–15) for libel.

In August 1817 the *Edinburgh Review* began to refer to Wordsworth, Coleridge, and Robert Southey as "The Lake School"—all three had lived in and been inspired by England's Lake District. Those poets and some others—Lord Byron in particular—had been identified the previous year by Leigh Hunt as representative of a school of poets "who go directly to Nature for inspiration." Hunt had written his article "Young Poets" to bring to the attention of the public "three young writers [Shelley, Keats, and John Hamilton Reynolds] who appear to us to promise a considerable addition of strength to the new school." Hunt had not named

[1] *Yet … horse* Recommended by Keats's doctor for exercise.

[2] *her* Fanny Brawne.

[3] * * * * Brown, whose transcription of this letter is the only surviving copy, deleted the names of Keats's friends in order to conceal their identities.

[4] *my sister … Tom* Keats's sister Fanny closely resembled his youngest brother Tom, who had died of tuberculosis in December 1818.

himself as a member of this new group, but it was on him that John Gibson Lockhart focused in launching an attack on the group that was as much political as literary. Lockhart's series of articles on "The Cockney School of Poetry" appeared in *Blackwood's Edinburgh Magazine*, a conservative journal founded in response to the *Edinburgh Review*.

from Leigh Hunt, "Young Poets" (*Examiner*, 1 December 1816)

In sitting down to this subject, we happen to be restricted by time to a much shorter notice than we could wish: but we mean to take it up again shortly. Many of our readers however have perhaps observed for themselves, that there has been a new school of poetry rising of late, which promises to extinguish the French one that has prevailed among us since the time of Charles the 2d. It began with something excessive, like most revolutions, but this gradually wore away; and an evident aspiration after real nature and original fancy remained, which called to mind the finer times of the English Muse. In fact it is wrong to call it a new school, and still more so to represent it as one of innovation, its only object being to restore the same love of Nature, and of *thinking* instead of mere *talking*, which formerly rendered us real poets, and not merely versifying wits, and bead-rollers of couplets.

We were delighted to see the departure of the old school acknowledged in the number of the *Edinburgh Review* just published—a candour the more generous and spirited, inasmuch as that work has hitherto been the greatest surviving ornament of the same school in prose and criticism, as it is now destined, we trust, to be still the leader in the new.

We also felt the same delight at the third canto of Lord Byron's *Childe Harold*, in which, to our conceptions at least, he has fairly renounced a certain leaven of the French style, and taken his place where we always said he would be found—among the poets who have a real feeling for numbers,[1] and who go directly to Nature for inspiration. But more of this poem in our next.

The object of the present article is merely to notice three young writers, who appear to us to promise a considerable addition of strength to the new school. Of the first who came before us, we have, it is true, yet seen only one or two specimens, and these were no sooner sent us than we unfortunately mislaid them; but we shall procure what he has published, and if the rest answer to what we have seen, we shall have no hesitation in announcing him for a very striking and original thinker. His name is Percy Bysshe Shelley, and he is the author of a poetical work entitled *Alastor, or the Spirit of Solitude*.

The next with whose name we became acquainted was John Henry Reynolds, author of a tale called *Safie*, written, we believe, in imitation of Lord Byron, and more lately of a small set of poems published by Taylor and Hessey, the principal of which is called the *Naiad*. It opens thus:

The gold sun went into the west,
And soft airs sang him to his rest;
And yellow leaves all loose and dry,
Play'd on the branches listlessly:
The sky wax'd palely blue, and high
A cloud seem'd touch'd upon the sky—
A spot of cloud—blue, thin, and still,
And silence bask'd on vale and hill. …

We shall give another extract or two in a future number. The author's style is too artificial, though he is evidently an admirer of Mr. Wordsworth. Like all young poets too, properly so called, his love

---

[1] *numbers* I.e., metrical harmony, rhythm.

of detail is too overwrought and indiscriminate; but still he is a young poet, and only wants a still closer attention to things as opposed to the seduction of words, to realize all that he promises. His nature seems very true and amiable.

The last of these young aspirants who we have met with, and who promise to help the new school to revive Nature and

> "To put a spirit of youth in every thing,"

is, we believe, the youngest of them all, and just of age. His name is John Keats. He has not yet published anything except in a newspaper; but a set of his manuscripts was handed us the other day, and fairly surprised us with the truth of their ambition, and ardent grappling with Nature. In the following sonnet there is one incorrect rhyme, which might be easily altered, but which shall serve in the mean time as a peace-offering to the rhyming critics. The rest of the composition, with the exception of a little vagueness in calling the regions of poetry "the realms of gold," we do not hesitate to pronounce excellent, especially the last six lines. The word *swims* is complete; and the whole conclusion is equally powerful and quiet

[Quotes "On First Looking Into Chapman's Homer"]

We have spoken with the less scruple of these poetical promises, because we really are not in the habit of lavishing praises and announcements, and because we have no fear of any pettier vanity on the part of young men who promise to understand human nature so well.

from John Gibson Lockhart ("Z."),"On the Cockney School of Poetry, No. 1" (*Blackwood's Edinburgh Magazine*, October 1817)

> Our talk shall be (a theme we never tire on)
> Of Chaucer, Spenser, Shakespeare, Milton, Byron,
> (Our England's Dante)—Wordsworth—Hunt, and Keats,
> The Muses' son of promise; and of what feats
> He yet may do.
>
> —CORNELIUS WEBB

While the whole critical world is occupied with balancing the merits, whether in theory or in execution, of what is commonly called The Lake School, it is strange that no one seems to think it at all necessary to say a single word about another new school of poetry which has of late sprung up amongst us. This school has not, I believe, as yet received any name; but if I may be permitted to have the honour of christening it, it may henceforth be referred to by the designation of The Cockney School. Its chief Doctor and Professor is Mr. Leigh Hunt, a man certainly of some talents, of extravagant pretensions both in wit, poetry, and politics, and withal of exquisitely bad taste, and extremely vulgar modes of thinking and manners in all respects. He is a man of little education. He knows absolutely nothing of Greek, almost nothing of Latin, and his knowledge of Italian literature is confined to a few of the most popular of Petrarch's sonnets, and an imperfect acquaintance with Ariosto, through the medium of Mr. Hoole. As to the French poets, he dismisses them in the mass as a set of prim, precise, unnatural pretenders. The truth is, he is in a state of happy ignorance about them and all that they have done. …

With this stock of knowledge, Mr. Hunt presumes to become the founder of a new school of poetry, and throws away entirely the chance he might have had of gaining some true poetic fame, had he been less lofty in his pretensions.…

All the great poets of our country have been men of some rank in society, and there is no vulgarity in any of their writings; but Mr. Hunt cannot utter a dedication, or even a note, without betraying the *Shibboleth*[1] of low birth and low habits. He is the ideal of a Cockney Poet. He raves perpetually about "green fields," "jaunty streams," and "o'er-arching leafiness," exactly as a Cheapside shop-keeper does about the beauties of his box[2] on the Camberwell road. Mr. Hunt is altogether unacquainted with the face of nature in her magnificent scenes; he has never seen any mountain higher than Highgate-hill,[3] nor reclined by any stream more pastoral than the Serpentine River.[4] But he is determined to be a poet eminently rural, and he rings the changes—till one is sick of him, on the beauties of the different "high views" which he has taken of God and nature, in the course of some Sunday dinner parties, at which he has assisted in the neighbourhood of London. His books are indeed not known in the country; his fame as a poet (and I might almost say, as a politician too) is entirely confined to the young attorneys and embryo-barristers about town. In the opinion of these competent judges, London is the world—and Hunt is a Homer.

Mr. Hunt is not disqualified by his ignorance and vulgarity alone, for being the founder of a respectable sect in poetry. He labours under the burden of a sin more deadly than either of these. The two great elements of all dignified poetry, religious feeling and patriotic feeling, have no place in his writings. His religion is a poor tame dilution of the blasphemies of the *Encyclopaedie*[5]—his patriotism a crude, vague, ineffectual, and sour Jacobinism.[6] His works exhibit no reverence either for God or man; neither altar nor throne have any dignity in his eyes. He speaks well of nobody but two or three great dead poets, and in so speaking of them he does well; but alas! Mr. Hunt is no conjurer τεχνη ὃ λανθανει.[7] He pretends, indeed, to be an admirer of Spenser and Chaucer, but what he praises in them is never what is most deserving of praise—it is only that which he humbly conceives bears some resemblance to the more perfect productions of Mr. Leigh Hunt; and we can always discover in the midst of his most violent ravings about the Court of Elizabeth, and the days of Sir Philip Sidney, and the Fairy Queen, that the real objects of his admiration are the Coterie of Hampstead and the Editor of the Examiner. When he talks about chivalry and King Arthur, he is always thinking of himself, and "*a small party of friends, who meet once a week at a Round Table, to discuss the merits of a leg of mutton, and of the subjects upon which we are to write.*"[8]—Mr. Leigh Hunt's ideas concerning the sublime, and concerning his own powers, bear a considerable resemblance to those of his friend Bottom, the weaver, on the same subjects; "I will roar, that it shall do any man's heart good to hear me."—"I will roar you an 'twere any nightingale."[9]

The poetry of Mr. Hunt is such as might be expected from the personal character and habits of its author. As a vulgar man is perpetually labouring to be genteel—in like manner, the poetry of this

[1] *Shibboleth* Word distinguishing a certain class or party.

[2] *box* Boxwood.

[3] *Highgate-hill* Hill (and district) in the north of London.

[4] *Serpentine River* Lake in Hyde Park, in the center of London.

[5] *Encylopaedie* Great manifesto of the French *philosophes*, prepared by Denis Diderot and Jean le Rond d'Alembert (1751).

[6] *Jacobinism* Extreme democratic principles; belief in complete equality (after the practice of the French political sect the Jacobins).

[7] τεχνη ὃ λανθανει Greek: his technique does not escape notice.

[8] *a small … write* From a feature in the *Examiner*, initiated by Leigh Hunt, called "The Round Table."

[9] *I will … nightingale* From Shakespeare's *A Midsummer Night's Dream* 1.2, in which Bottom the weaver (who is later transformed into an ass) desires to play the lion's part in a play.

man is always on the stretch to be grand. He has been allowed to look for a moment from the antechamber into the salon, and mistaken the waving of feathers and the painted floor for the *sine qua non*'s[1] of elegant society. He would fain be always tripping and waltzing, and is sorry that he cannot be allowed to walk about in the morning with yellow breeches and flesh-coloured silk-stockings. He sticks an artificial rosebud into his button hole in the midst of winter. …

How such an indelicate writer as Mr. Hunt can pretend to be an admirer of Mr. Wordsworth, is to us a thing altogether inexplicable. One great charm of Wordsworth's noble compositions consists in the dignified purity of thought, and the patriarchal simplicity of feeling, with which they are throughout penetrated and imbued. We can conceive a vicious[2] man admiring with distant awe the spectacle of virtue and purity; but if he does so sincerely, he must also do so with the profoundest feeling of the error of his own ways, and the resolution to amend them. His admiration must be humble and silent, not pert and loquacious. Mr. Hunt praises the purity of Wordsworth as if he himself were pure, his dignity as if he also were dignified. …

The founder of the Cockney School would fain claim poetical kindred with Lord Byron and Thomas Moore.[3] Such a connection would be as unsuitable for them as for William Wordsworth. The days of Mr. Moore's follies are long since over; and, as he is a thorough gentleman, he must necessarily entertain the greatest contempt for such an under-bred person as Mr. Leigh Hunt. But Lord Byron! … We dare say Mr. Hunt has some fine dreams about the true nobility being the nobility of talent, and flatters himself, that with those who acknowledge only that sort of rank, he himself passes for being the *peer* of Byron. He is sadly mistaken. He is as completely a Plebeian[4] in his mind as he is in his rank and station in society. To that highest and unalienable nobility which the great Roman satirist styles "*sola atque unica*,"[5] we fear his pretensions would be equally unavailing.

The shallow and impotent pretensions, tenets, and attempts of this man—and the success with which his influence seems to be extending itself among a pretty numerous, though certainly a very paltry and pitiful, set of readers—have for the last two or three years been considered by us with the most sickening aversion. The very culpable manner in which his chief poem was reviewed in the *Edinburgh Review* (we believe it is no secret, at his own impatient and feverish request, by his partner in the Round Table[6]), was matter of concern to more readers than ourselves. The masterly pen which inflicted such signal chastisement on the early licentiousness of Moore, should not have been idle on that occasion. Mr. Jeffrey[7] does ill, when he delegates his important functions into such hands as those of Mr. Hazlitt. It was chiefly in consequence of that gentleman's allowing Leigh Hunt to pass unpunished through the scene of slaughter, which his execution might so highly have graced, that we came to the resolution of laying before our readers a series of essays on *the Cockney School*—of which here terminates the first.

---

[1] *sine qua non* Latin: without which, not.

[2] *vicious* Immoral.

[3] *Thomas Moore* Irish poet (1779–1852).

[4] *Plebian* In ancient Rome, a commoner, a person of low birth or rank.

[5] *sola atque unique* Latin: alone and only. See Juvenal's *Satire* 8: "Virtue alone is the only true nobility."

[6] *partner … Table* William Hazlitt, who contributed to both the *Examiner* and the *Edinburgh Review*. Hazlitt frequently wrote for the *Examiner* feature "The Round Table," and his first book-length collection of essays appeared in 1817 under that title.

[7] *Mr. Jeffrey* Francis Jeffrey (1773–1850), founder and editor of the *Edinburgh Review*.

from John Lockhart ("Z."), "On the Cockney School of Poetry, No. 4." (*Blackwood's Edinburgh Magazine*, August 1818)

——————— Of Keats,
The Muses' son of promise, and what feats
He yet may do, &c.
—CORNELIUS WEBB

Of all the manias of this mad age, the most incurable, as well as the most common, seems to be no other than the *Metromanie*.[1] The just celebrity of Robert Burns and Miss Baillie[2] has had the melancholy effect of turning the heads of we know not how many farm-servants and unmarried ladies; our very footmen compose tragedies, and there is scarcely a superannuated governess in the island that does not leave a roll of lyrics behind her in her band-box. To witness the disease of any human understanding, however feeble, is distressing; but the spectacle of an able mind reduced to a state of insanity is of course ten times more afflicting. It is with such sorrow as this that we have contemplated the case of Mr. John Keats. This young man appears to have received from nature talents of an excellent, perhaps even of a superior order—talents which, devoted to the purpose of any useful profession, must have rendered him a respectable, if not an eminent citizen. His friends, we understand, destined him to the career of medicine, and he was bound apprentice some years ago to a worthy apothecary in town. But all has been undone by a sudden attack of the malady to which we have alluded. Whether Mr. John had been sent home with a diuretic or composing draught to some patient far gone in the poetical mania, we have not heard. This much is certain, that he has caught the infection, and that thoroughly. For some time we were in hopes that he might get off with a violent fit or two; but of late the symptoms are terrible. The frenzy of the "Poems"[3] was bad enough in its way; but it did not alarm us half so seriously as the calm, settled, imperturbable drivelling idiocy of "Endymion." We hope, however, that in so young a person, and with a constitution originally so good, even now the disease is not utterly incurable. Time, firm treatment, and rational restraint, do much for many apparently hopeless invalids; and if Mr. Keats should happen, at some interval of reason, to cast his eye upon our pages, he may perhaps be convinced of the existence of his malady, which in such cases is often all that is necessary to put the patient in a fair way of being cured. …

[Keats's] Endymion is not a Greek shepherd, loved by a Grecian goddess;[4] he is merely a young Cockney rhymester, dreaming a fantastic dream at the full of the moon. Costume, were it worth while to notice such a trifle, is violated in every page of this goodly octavo. From his prototype Hunt, Keats has acquired a sort of vague idea that the Greeks were a most tasteful people, and that no mythology can be so finely adapted for the purposes of poetry as theirs. It is amusing to see what a hand the two Cockneys make of this mythology; the one confesses that he never read the Greek Tragedians, and the other knows Homer only from Chapman;[5] and both of them write about Apollo, Pan, Nymphs, Muses, and Mysteries, as might be expected from persons of their education. We shall not, however, enlarge at present upon this subject, as we mean to dedicate an entire paper to the classical attainments and attempts of the Cockney poets. As for Mr. Keats' "Endymion," it has just as much

[1] *Metromanie* Mania for writing poetry.

[2] *Miss Baillie* Scottish poet and playwright Joanna Baillie (1762–1851).

[3] *Poems* Keats's first volume of poetry, which was published in March 1817.

[4] *Endymion … goddess* "Endymion" retells the story of the goddess of the moon falling in love with a shepherd, as told by the Roman poet Ovid.

[5] *Homer … Chapman* Keats knew very little Greek, and read it only in translation. George Chapman's edition of Homer's *Iliad* appeared in 1612, and his edition of the *Odyssey* in 1616.

to do with Greece as it has with "old Tartary the fierce;" no man whose mind has ever been imbued with the smallest knowledge or feeling of classical poetry or classical history could have stooped to profane and vulgarise every association in the manner which has been adopted by this "son of promise." Before giving any extracts, we must inform our readers that this romance is meant to be written in English heroic rhyme. To those who have read any of Hunt's poems, this hint might indeed be needless. Mr. Keats has adopted the loose, nerveless versification and Cockney rhymes of the poet of *Rimini*;[1] but, in fairness to that gentleman, we must add that the defects of the system are tenfold more conspicuous in his disciple's work than in his own. Mr. Hunt is a small poet, but he is a clever man. Mr. Keats is a still smaller poet, and he is only a boy of pretty abilities, which he has done every thing in his power to spoil.

IN CONTEXT

The Death of Keats

Keats's friend Joseph Severn had accompanied him to Italy in September of 1820, and was with him when he died of tuberculosis on 23 February 1821.

Joseph Severn to Charles Brown

Rome
27 February 1821

My Dear Brown,

He is gone—he died with the most perfect ease—he seemed to go to sleep. On the 23rd, about 4, the approaches of death came on. "Severn—I—lift me up—I am dying—I shall die easy—don't be frightened—be firm, and thank God it has come!" I lifted him up in my arms. The phlegm seemed boiling in his throat, and increased until 11, when he gradually sunk into death—so quiet—that I still thought he slept. I cannot say now—I am broken down from four nights' watching, and no sleep since, and my poor Keats gone. Three days since, the body was opened; the lungs were completely gone. The Doctors could not conceive by what means he had lived these two months. I followed his poor body to the grave on Monday, with many English. They take such care of me here—that I must, else, have gone into a fever. I am better now—but still quite disabled.

The police have been. The furniture, the walls, the floor, everything must be destroyed by order of the law. But this is well looked to by Dr. C.

The letters I put into the coffin with my own hand.

I must leave off.

[1] *Rimini* Hunt's long poem *The Story of Rimini* (1816).

Mary Shelley

1797 – 1851

As Mary Wollstonecraft Shelley wrote in her introduction to the second edition of *Frankenstein*, readers constantly asked her "How I, then a young girl, came to think of, and to dilate upon, so hideous an idea." At the age of nineteen, Shelley created one of the most extraordinary and powerful horror stories in Western literature, one that continues to pervade our popular culture.

Frankenstein continues to overshadow all her other work, but Shelley has also come to be recognized as having produced a large body of fiction of vivid imaginative power that grapples in penetrating fashion with the political and social concerns of her day.

If Shelley's writing is extraordinary, nor is there anything of the ordinary in her famous parentage or her tumultuous life. She was born Mary Wollstonecraft Godwin in August of 1797. The only child of radical feminist Mary Wollstonecraft and the philosopher, author, and political journalist William Godwin, Shelley felt the weight of her parents' controversial reputations throughout her life. Her mother died just after giving birth, and Shelley came to know her only through her works—in particular the *Vindication of the Rights of Woman* (1792). Godwin, for whom Shelley later said she bore an "excess of attachment," raised Mary and her half-sister Fanny, educating them with the help of several friends and regular visitors—a group of supremely qualified teachers that included poet Samuel Taylor Coleridge, painter Thomas Lawrence, novelist Maria Edgeworth, and scientist Humphrey Davy.

After Godwin married Mary Jane Clairmont in 1801, Mary, who did not get along with her stepmother, spent extended periods of time with family friends in Scotland. On a visit home in 1814, she became acquainted with Percy Bysshe Shelley, a radical poet and admirer of Godwin's principles, who had become a regular visitor to the Godwin home. Although Percy was married at the time, within months the two declared their love for each other and eloped to France, taking Mary's stepsister Claire Clairmont with them. Godwin disowned his daughter upon her elopement and was only slightly mollified when the two married in 1816, following the suicide of Percy's first wife, Harriet.

The couple toured France, Switzerland, and Germany (a trip described in Shelley's first publication, *History of a Six Weeks' Tour*) before eventually settling in Italy near Lord Byron, with whom Claire was having an affair. The subsequent years in Italy were turbulent ones. Two of Shelley's children died in infancy, her three-year-old son William died in 1819, and Claire's daughter by Byron died in a convent in 1822. A life-threatening miscarriage that same year plunged Shelley into severe depression, and she and her husband became increasingly distant. When Percy drowned with his friend Edward Williams in July of 1822, her sorrow at his death was further augmented by her guilt at their estrangement.

Although she wrote some poetry and verse dramas, Shelley's only publication during these years was *Frankenstein, or The Modern Prometheus,* first published in 1818 and revised for a new edition in 1831. This novel about a motherless creature rejected by its father, cast out by society, and parented largely by books has clear points of connection with Shelley's own unusual upbringing and her anxiety concerning familial relationships, origins, and parental responsibility. But the enduring appeal of the novel lies in its narrative power and its ability to stimulate ideas in rich profusion. With its themes of repression and doubling it can be read as a psychodrama, and its unspoken preoccupation with incest allies it with other Gothic thrillers. As a reworking of both Milton's story of the fall of man in *Paradise Lost* and the Greek myth of Prometheus (who stole fire from the gods and gave it to humans, saving them from servility), Shelley's novel shows the consequences of using one's power over others without acknowledging the attendant responsibilities. *Frankenstein* can also be read as a moral tale, advising us to treat others in the way we would like to be treated; if we assume those who are unfamiliar or different are evil, we may ourselves create evil where none existed before. The novel also calls into question the Enlightenment celebration of scientific advancement and articulates a deep-seated fear of the consequences of interfering with the natural order.

As a result of the scandalous events in her past, the radicalism of her parents, and the unsavory reputation of her husband, Shelley felt exiled from society. After the death of Byron in 1824 she found herself without friendship or support. She had a small allowance from her father-in-law, Sir Timothy Shelley, but it was hardly enough to support her, and had been given on the stipulation that she not bring her husband's name before the public. Consequently, although Shelley was eager to see her husband's talent appreciated, his *Posthumous Poems* (1824) had to be withdrawn from circulation only a few months after its release.

Shelley had always felt that "as the daughter of two persons of distinguished literary celebrity" she should be a writer, so she turned to writing for income. She returned to London and began producing book reviews, essays, and short biographies while continuing to write novels. *The Last Man* (1826) presents a view of humanity in which a plague destroys the earth, leaving only one man, Lionel Verney. Shelley's novels *Valperga* (1823) and *The Fortunes of Perkin Warbeck: A Romance* (1830) experiment with the genre of historical fiction—a mode that had recently been made popular by Walter Scott—combining romance and fiction with historical and political analysis. In these novels, as well as in *The Last Man*, critics found evidence of the "unsavory politics" they expected from one of the Godwin circle. Critics and readers alike preferred Shelley's more traditional domestic fictions, such as *Lodore* (1835) and *Falkner* (1837).

In 1844 the concerns that had plagued Shelley since the death of her husband were relieved by the death of his father. Her son, Percy Florence, inherited Sir Thomas's title and estate, and Shelley was free to produce biographical work on her husband. In his final years Sir Thomas had allowed her to publish editions of Percy Shelley's work, and in 1839 she had released his four-volume *Poetical Works*, as well as his *Essays and Letters from Abroad, Translations and Fragments*. In writing about her husband, Shelley endeavored to rationalize his radical attitudes and behavior—particularly his atheism and sedition—in order to mediate his poetry for his audience and redeem his public image. Although she has been accused of altering his manuscripts and misrepresenting his politics, she succeeded in her goal of bringing his work to public notice.

Shelley spent her final years traveling with her son and helping him manage his estate. In 1848 he married Jane St. John, a widow and friend of Shelley. Jane nursed Shelley in the months before her death of a brain tumor in 1851.

⌘⌘⌘

The Last Man

Other than *Frankenstein*, Mary Shelley's 1824 novel *The Last Man* is the work that has excited the greatest critical interest and enjoyed the most attention from her readership over the past generation. In part this may relate to increased interest in apocalyptic visions around the turn of the millennium; it may also speak to humanity's perpetual fascination with the idea of its own extinction. Additional interest may stem from the parallels between the lives of Shelley and her companions and those of the characters in the novel—the circumstances of Percy Shelley's death are strikingly similar to those surrounding the drowning of Lionel Verney's companions. While Shelley's novel can be seen as a depiction of her own grief on a universal scale, her wistful look back at an idealized, but ultimately untenable, past may also be read as a political critique, and a disillusioned examination of Romanticism.

Shelley's protagonist, Lionel Verney, is the last man in the world, looking back on human history from 2100. During the final years of the twenty-first century the world has been devastated by plague. In its wake, humans have descended into brutality: American survivors have attacked Ireland; the Irish have invaded England; and, finally, small bands of English survivors have been wandering the now-ruined continent of Europe. Lionel Verney and his party suspect themselves to be the last of these groups of survivors. As the final two chapters open, Verney has two remaining companions, Adrian and Clara, the latter distraught after the death of her child. The party has been staying in an abandoned villa at Lake Como in the Alps.

---

from *The Last Man*

CHAPTER 29

Now—soft awhile—have I arrived so near the end? Yes! it is all over now—a step or two over those new-made graves, and the wearisome way is done. Can I accomplish my task? Can I streak my paper with words capacious of the grand conclusion? Arise, black Melancholy! quit thy Cimmerian solitude![1] Bring with thee murky fogs from hell, which may drink up the day; bring blight and pestiferous exhalations, which, entering the hollow caverns and breathing places of earth, may fill her stony veins with corruption, so that not only herbage may no longer flourish, the trees may rot, and the rivers run with gall—but the everlasting mountains be decomposed, and the mighty deep putrify, and the genial atmosphere which clips the globe, lose all powers of generation and sustenance. Do this, sad visaged power, while I write, while eyes read these pages.

And who will read them? Beware, tender offspring of the re-born world—beware, fair being, with human heart, yet untamed by care, and human brow, yet unploughed by time—beware, lest the cheerful current of thy blood be checked, thy golden locks turn grey, thy sweet dimpling smiles be changed to fixed, harsh wrinkles! Let not day look on these lines, lest garish day waste, turn pale, and die. Seek a cypress grove, whose moaning boughs will be harmony befitting; seek some cave, deep embowered in earth's dark entrails, where no light will penetrate, save that which struggles, red and flickering, through a single fissure, staining thy page with grimmest livery of death.

There is a painful confusion in my brain, which refuses to delineate distinctly succeeding events. Sometimes the irradiation of my friend's gentle smile comes before me; and methinks its light spans and fills eternity—then, again, I feel the gasping throes—

We quitted Como, and in compliance with Adrian's earnest desire, we took Venice in our way to Rome. There was something to the English peculiarly attractive in the idea of this wave-encircled, island-enthroned city.

[1] *Cimmerian solitude* Referring to the Cimmerians, mythical people of Homer's *Odyssey* who inhabit the dark, misty fringes of the world.

Adrian had never seen it. We went down the Po and the Brenta[1] in a boat; and, the days proving intolerably hot, we rested in the bordering palaces during the day, travelling through the night, when darkness made the bordering banks indistinct, and our solitude less remarkable; when the wandering moon lit the waves that divided before our prow, and the night-wind filled our sails, and the murmuring stream, waving trees, and swelling canvass, accorded in harmonious strain. Clara, long overcome by excessive grief, had to a great degree cast aside her timid, cold reserve, and received our attentions with grateful tenderness. While Adrian with poetic fervour discoursed of the glorious nations of the dead, of the beauteous earth and the fate of man, she crept near him, drinking in his speech with silent pleasure. We banished from our talk, and as much as possible from our thoughts, the knowledge of our desolation. And it would be incredible to an inhabitant of cities, to one among a busy throng to what extent we succeeded. It was as a man confined in a dungeon, whose small and grated rift at first renders the doubtful light more sensibly obscure, till, the visual orb having drunk in the beam, and adapted itself to its scantiness, he finds that clear noon inhabits his cell. So we, a simple triad on empty earth, were multiplied to each other, till we became all in all. We stood like trees, whose roots are loosened by the wind, which support one another, leaning and clinging with increased fervour while the wintry storms howl.

Thus we floated down the widening stream of the Po, sleeping when the cicale[2] sang, awake with the stars. We entered the narrower banks of the Brenta, and arrived at the shore of the Laguna[3] at sunrise on the sixth of September. The bright orb slowly rose from behind its cupolas and towers, and shed its penetrating light upon the glassy waters. Wrecks of gondolas, and some few uninjured ones, were strewed on the beach at Fusina.[4] We embarked in one of these for the widowed daughter of ocean,[5] who, abandoned and fallen, sat forlorn on her propping isles, looking towards the far mountains of Greece. We rowed lightly over the Laguna, and entered Canale Grande.[6] The tide ebbed sullenly from out the broken portals and violated halls of Venice: sea weed and sea monsters were left on the blackened marble, while the salt ooze defaced the matchless works of art that adorned their walls, and the sea gull flew out from the shattered window. In the midst of this appalling ruin of the monuments of man's power, nature asserted her ascendancy, and shone more beauteous from the contrast. The radiant waters hardly trembled, while the rippling waves made many sided mirrors to the sun; the blue immensity, seen beyond Lido,[7] stretched far, unspecked by boat, so tranquil, so lovely, that it seemed to invite us to quit the land strewn with ruins, and to seek refuge from sorrow and fear on its placid extent.

We saw the ruins of this hapless city from the height of the tower of San Marco, immediately under us, and turned with sickening hearts to the sea, which, though it be a grave, rears no monument, discloses no ruin. Evening had come apace. The sun set in calm majesty behind the misty summits of the Apennines, and its golden and roseate hues painted the mountains of the opposite shore. "That land," said Adrian, "tinged with the last glories of the day, is Greece." Greece! The sound had a responsive chord in the bosom of Clara. She vehemently reminded us that we had promised to take her once again to Greece, to the tomb of her parents. Why go to Rome? what should we do at Rome? We might take one of the many vessels to be found here, embark in it, and steer right for Albania.

I objected the dangers of ocean, and the distance of the mountains we saw, from Athens; a distance which, from the savage uncultivation of the country, was almost impassable. Adrian, who was delighted with Clara's proposal, obviated these objections. The season was favourable; the north-west that blew would take us transversely across the gulph; and then we might find, in

[1] *the Po and the Brenta* Both rivers flow from the Alps down into the Venetian plain.

[2] *cicale* Cicada.

[3] *the Laguna* The Laguna Veneta, which surrounds Venice.

[4] *Fusina* Located on the coast of the mainland, south of Venice.

[5] *widowed daughter of ocean* I.e., Venice. In an ancient ceremony, the ruler of Venice threw a ring into the sea each Ascension Day to symbolize the marriage of Venice and the ocean.

[6] *Canale Grande* Canal that runs through Venice.

[7] *Lido* Island that forms a breakwater between the sea and the Laguna Veneta.

some abandoned port, a light Greek caique,[1] adapted for such navigation, and run down the coast of the Morea, and, passing over the Isthmus of Corinth, without much land-travelling or fatigue, find ourselves at Athens. This appeared to me wild talk; but the sea, glowing with a thousand purple hues, looked so brilliant and safe; my beloved companions were so earnest, so determined, that, when Adrian said, "Well, though it is not exactly what you wish, yet consent, to please me"—I could no longer refuse. That evening we selected a vessel, whose size just seemed fitted for our enterprize; we bent the sails and put the rigging in order, and, reposing that night in one of the city's thousand palaces, agreed to embark at sunrise the following morning.

When winds that move not its calm surface, sweep
The azure sea, I love the land no more;
The smiles of the serene and tranquil deep
Tempt my unquiet mind—

Thus said Adrian, quoting a translation of Moschus's poem, as, in the clear morning light, we rowed over the Laguna, past Lido, into the open sea—I would have added in continuation,

But, when the roar
Of ocean's gray abyss resounds, and foam
Gathers upon the sea, and vast waves burst—[2]

But my friends declared that such verses were evil augury; so in cheerful mood we left the shallow waters, and, when out at sea, unfurled our sails to catch the favourable breeze. The laughing morning air filled them while sun-light bathed earth, sky and ocean—the placid waves divided to receive our keel, and playfully kissed the dark sides of our little skiff, murmuring a welcome; as land receded, still the blue expanse, most waveless, twin sister to the azure empyrean, afforded smooth conduct to our bark.[3] As the air and waters were tranquil and balmy, so were our minds steeped in quiet. In comparison with the unstained deep, funereal earth appeared a grave, its high rocks and stately mountains were but monuments, its trees the plumes of a hearse, the brooks and rivers brackish with tears for departed man. Farewell to desolate towns—to fields with their savage intermixture of corn and weeds—to ever multiplying relics of our lost species. Ocean, we commit ourselves to thee—even as the patriarch of old[4] floated above the drowned world, let us be saved, as thus we betake ourselves to thy perennial flood.

Adrian sat at the helm; I attended to the rigging, the breeze right aft filled our swelling canvas, and we ran before it over the untroubled deep. The wind died away at noon; its idle breath just permitted us to hold our course. As lazy, fair-weather sailors, careless of the coming hour, we talked gaily of our coasting voyage, of our arrival at Athens. We would make our home of one of the Cyclades,[5] and there in myrtle-groves, amidst perpetual spring, fanned by the wholesome sea-breezes — we would live long years in beatific union—Was there such a thing as death in the world?—

The sun passed its zenith and lingered down the stainless floor of heaven. Lying in the boat, my face turned up to the sky, I thought I saw on its blue white, marbled streaks, so slight, so immaterial, that now I said—"They are there"—and now, "It is a mere imagination." A sudden fear stung me while I gazed; and, starting up, and running to the prow—as I stood, my hair was gently lifted on my brow—a dark line of ripples appeared to the east, gaining rapidly on us—my breathless remark to Adrian was followed by the flapping of the canvas, as the adverse wind struck it, and our boat lurched—swift as speech, the web of the storm thickened overhead, the sun went down red, the dark sea was strewed with foam, and our skiff rose and fell in its increasing furrows.

Behold us now in our frail tenement, hemmed in by hungry, roaring waves, buffeted by winds. In the inky east two vast clouds, sailing contrary ways, met; the lightning leapt forth, and the hoarse thunder muttered. Again in the south, the clouds replied, and the forked stream of fire, running along the black sky, showed us the appalling piles of clouds, now met and obliterated by the heaving waves. Great God! And we alone—we three—alone—alone—sole dwellers on the sea and on the earth, we three must perish! The vast universe, its

[1] *caique* Small row-boat or sail-boat.

[2] *When winds … burst* From Percy Shelley's sonnet "Translated from the Greek of Moschus" (1816), 2.1–6.

[3] *bark* Boat.

[4] *the patriarch of old* I.e., Noah.

[5] *Cyclades* Group of islands in the Aegean Sea.

myriad worlds, and the plains of boundless earth which we had left—the extent of shoreless sea around—contracted to my view—they and all that they contained, shrunk up to one point, even to our tossing bark, freighted with glorious humanity.

A convulsion of despair crossed the love-beaming face of Adrian, while with set teeth he murmured, "Yet they shall be saved!" Clara, visited by a human pang, pale and trembling, crept near him—he looked on her with an encouraging smile—"Do you fear, sweet girl? O, do not fear, we shall soon be on shore!"

The darkness prevented me from seeing the changes of her countenance; but her voice was clear and sweet, as she replied, "Why should I fear? Neither sea nor storm can harm us, if mighty destiny or the ruler of destiny does not permit. And then the stinging fear of surviving either of you is not here—one death will clasp us undivided."

Meanwhile we took in all our sails, save a jib;[1] and, as soon as we might without danger, changed our course, running with the wind for the Italian shore. Dark night mixed everything; we hardly discerned the white crests of the murderous surges, except when lightning made brief noon, and drank the darkness, showing us our danger, and restoring us to double night. We were all silent, except when Adrian, as steersman, made an encouraging observation. Our little shell obeyed the rudder miraculously well, and ran along on the top of the waves as if she had been an offspring of the sea, and the angry mother sheltered her endangered child.

I sat at the prow, watching our course; when suddenly I heard the waters break with redoubled fury. We were certainly near the shore—at the same time I cried, "About there!" and a broad lightning, filling the concave, showed us for one moment the level beach ahead, disclosing even the sands, and stunted, ooze-sprinkled beds of reeds, that grew at high water mark. Again it was dark, and we drew in our breath with such content as one may, who, while fragments of volcano-hurled rock darken the air, sees a vast mass plowing the ground immediately at his feet. What to do we knew not—the breakers here, there, everywhere, encompassed us—they roared, and dashed, and flung their hated spray in our faces. With considerable difficulty and danger we succeeded at length in altering our course, and stretched out from shore. I urged my companions to prepare for the wreck of our little skiff, and to bind themselves to some oar or spar which might suffice to float them. I was myself an excellent swimmer—the very sight of the sea was wont to raise in me such sensations as a huntsman experiences when he hears a pack of hounds in full cry; I loved to feel the waves wrap me and strive to overpower me; while I, lord of myself, moved this way or that, in spite of their angry bufferings. Adrian also could swim—but the weakness of his frame prevented him from feeling pleasure in the exercise, or acquiring any great expertness.

But what power could the strongest swimmer oppose to the overpowering violence of ocean in its fury? My efforts to prepare my companions were rendered nearly futile—for the roaring breakers prevented our hearing one another speak, and the waves that broke continually over our boat obliged me to exert all my strength in lading the water out, as fast as it came in. The while darkness, palpable and rayless, hemmed us round, dissipated only by the lightning; sometimes we beheld thunderbolts, fiery red, fall into the sea, and at intervals vast spouts stooped from the clouds, churning the wild ocean, which rose to meet them; while the fierce gale bore the rack[2] onwards, and they were lost in the chaotic mingling of sky and sea. Our gunwales had been torn away, our single sail had been rent to ribbands[3] and borne down the stream of the wind. We had cut away our mast, and lightened the boat of all she contained—Clara attempted to assist me in heaving the water from the hold, and, as she turned her eyes to look on the lightning, I could discern by that momentary gleam that resignation had conquered every fear. We have a power given us in any worst extremity, which props the else feeble mind of man, and enables us to endure the most savage tortures with a stillness of soul which in hours of happiness we could not have imagined. A calm, more dreadful in truth than the tempest, allayed the wild beatings of my heart—a calm like that of the gamester, the suicide, and the murderer, when the last die is on the point of being cast—while the poisoned cup is at the lips, as the death-blow is about to be given.

Hours passed thus—hours which might write old

[1] *jib* Triangular sail to the fore of a ship.

[2] *rack* Mass of clouds.

[3] *ribbands* I.e., ribbons.

age on the face of beardless youth, and grizzle the silky hair of infancy—hours, while the chaotic uproar continued, while each dread gust transcended in fury the one before, and our skiff hung on the breaking wave, and then rushed into the valley below, and trembled and spun between the watery precipices that seemed most to meet above her. For a moment the gale paused, and ocean sank to comparative silence—it was a breathless interval; the wind which, as a practised leaper, had gathered itself up before it sprung, now with terrific roar rushed over the sea, and the waves struck our stern. Adrian exclaimed that the rudder was gone—"We are lost," cried Clara, "Save yourselves—O save yourselves!" The lightning showed me the poor girl half buried in the water at the bottom of the boat; as she was sinking in it Adrian caught her up, and sustained her in his arms. We were without a rudder—we rushed prow foremost into the vast billows piled up ahead—they broke over and filled the tiny skiff; one scream I heard—one cry that we were gone, I uttered; I found myself in the waters; darkness was around. When the light of the tempest flashed, I saw the keel of our upset boat close to me—I clung to this, grasping it with clenched hand and nails, while I endeavoured during each flash to discover any appearance of my companions. I thought I saw Adrian at no great distance from me, clinging to an oar; I sprung from my hold, and with energy beyond my human strength, I dashed aside the waters as I strove to lay hold of him. As that hope failed, instinctive love of life animated me, and feelings of contention, as if a hostile will combated with mine. I breasted the surges, and flung them from me as I would the opposing front and sharpened claws of a lion about to enfang my bosom. When I had been beaten down by one wave, I rose on another, while I felt bitter pride curl my lip.

Ever since the storm had carried us near the shore, we had never attained any great distance from it. With every flash I saw the bordering coast; yet the progress I made was small, while each wave, as it receded, carried me back into ocean's far abysses. At one moment I felt my foot touch the sand, and then again I was in deep water; my arms began to lose their power of motion; my breath failed me under the influence of the strangling waters—a thousand wild and delirious thoughts crossed me: as well as I can now recall them, my chief feeling was, how sweet it would be to lay my head on the quiet earth, where the surges would no longer strike my weakened frame, nor the sound of waters ring in my ears—to attain this repose, not to save my life, I made a last effort—the shelving shore suddenly presented a footing for me. I rose, and was again thrown down by the breakers—a point of rock, to which I was enabled to cling, gave me a moment's respite; and then, taking advantage of the ebbing of the waves, I ran forwards—gained the dry sands, and fell senseless on the oozy reeds that sprinkled them.

I must have lain long deprived of life; for when first, with a sickening feeling, I unclosed my eyes, the light of morning met them. Great change had taken place meanwhile: grey dawn dappled the flying clouds, which sped onwards, leaving visible at intervals vast lakes of pure ether. A fountain of light arose in an increasing stream from the east, behind the waves of the Adriatic, changing the grey to a roseate hue, and then flooding sky and sea with aerial gold.

A kind of stupor followed my fainting; my senses were alive, but memory was extinct. The blessed respite was short—a snake lurked near me to sting me into life. On the first retrospective emotion I would have started up, but my limbs refused to obey me; my knees trembled, the muscles had lost all power. I still believed that I might find one of my beloved companions cast like me, half alive, on the beach; and I strove in every way to restore my frame to the use of its animal functions. I wrung the brine from my hair; and the rays of the risen sun soon visited me with genial warmth. With the restoration of my bodily powers, my mind became in some degree aware of the universe of misery, henceforth to be its dwelling. I ran to the water's edge, calling on the beloved names. Ocean drank in and absorbed my feeble voice, replying with pitiless roar. I climbed a near tree: the level sands bounded by a pine forest, and the sea clipped round by the horizon, was all that I could discern. In vain I extended my researches along the beach; the mast we had thrown overboard, with tangled cordage, and remnants of a sail, was the sole relic land received of our wreck. Sometimes I stood still, and wrung my hands. I accused earth and sky—the universal machine and the Almighty power that misdirected it. Again I threw myself on the sands, and then the sighing wind, mimicking a human cry, roused me to bitter, fallacious hope. Assuredly if any little bark or smallest canoe had been near, I should have sought the savage plains of ocean, found the dear remains of my lost ones, and, clinging round them, have shared their grave.

The day passed thus; each moment contained eternity; although when hour after hour had gone by, I wondered at the quick flight of time. Yet even now I had not drunk the bitter potion to the dregs; I was not yet persuaded of my loss; I did not yet feel in every pulsation, in every nerve, in every thought, that I remained alone of my race—that I was the LAST MAN.

The day had clouded over, and a drizzling rain set in at sunset. Even the eternal skies weep, I thought; is there any shame then, that mortal man should spend himself in tears? I remembered the ancient fables, in which human beings are described as dissolving away through weeping into ever-gushing fountains. Ah! that so it were; and then my destiny would be in some sort akin to the watery death of Adrian and Clara. Oh! grief is fantastic; it weaves a web on which to trace the history of its woe from every form and change around; it incorporates itself with all living nature; it finds sustenance in every object; as light, it fills all things, and, like light, it gives its own colours to all.

I had wandered in my search to some distance from the spot on which I had been cast, and came to one of those watch-towers, which at stated distances line the Italian shore. I was glad of shelter, glad to find a work of human hands, after I had gazed so long on nature's drear barrenness; so I entered, and ascended the rough winding staircase into the guard-room. So far was fate kind, that no harrowing vestige remained of its former inhabitants; a few planks laid across two iron tressels, and strewed with the dried leaves of Indian corn, was the bed presented to me; and an open chest, containing some half mouldered biscuit, awakened an appetite, which perhaps existed before, but of which, until now, I was not aware. Thirst also, violent and parching, the result of the sea-water I had drank, and of the exhaustion of my frame, tormented me. Kind nature had gifted the supply of these wants with pleasurable sensations, so that I—even I!—was refreshed and calmed as I ate of this sorry fare, and drank a little of the sour wine which half filled a flask left in this abandoned dwelling. Then I stretched myself on the bed, not to be disdained by the victim of shipwreck. The earthy smell of the dried leaves was balm to my sense after the hateful odour of sea-weed. I forgot my state of loneliness. I neither looked backward nor forward; my senses were hushed to repose; I fell asleep and dreamed of all dear inland scenes, of hay-makers, of the shepherd's whistle to his dog when he demanded his help to drive the flock to fold; of sights and sounds peculiar to my boyhood's mountain life, which I had long forgotten.

I awoke in a painful agony—for I fancied that ocean, breaking its bounds, carried away the fixed continent and deep rooted mountains, together with the streams I loved, the woods, and the flocks—it raged around, with that continued and dreadful roar which had accompanied the last wreck of surviving humanity. As my waking sense returned, the bare walls of the guard room closed round me, and the rain pattered against the single window. How dreadful it is to emerge from the oblivion of slumber and to receive as a good morrow the mute wailing of one's own hapless heart—to return from the land of deceptive dreams to the heavy knowledge of unchanged disaster!—Thus was it with me, now, and for ever! The sting of other griefs might be blunted by time; and even mine yielded sometimes during the day, to the pleasure inspired by the imagination or the senses; but I never look first upon the morning-light but with my fingers pressed tight on my bursting heart, and my soul deluged with the interminable flood of hopeless misery. Now I awoke for the first time in the dead world—I awoke alone—and the dull dirge of the sea, heard even amidst the rain, recalled me to the reflection of the wretch I had become. The sound came like a reproach, a scoff—like the sting of remorse in the soul—I gasped—the veins and muscles of my throat swelled, suffocating me. I put my fingers to my ears, I buried my head in the leaves of my couch, I would have dived to the centre to lose hearing of that hideous moan.

But another task must be mine—again I visited the detested beach, again I vainly looked far and wide, again I raised my unanswered cry, lifting up the only voice that could ever again force the mute air to syllable the human thought.

What a pitiable, forlorn, disconsolate being I was! My very aspect and garb told the tale of my despair. My hair was matted and wild, my limbs soiled with salt ooze; while at sea, I had thrown off those of my garments that encumbered me, and the rain drenched the thin summer-clothing I had retained—my feet were bare, and the stunted reeds and broken shells made them bleed—the while, I hurried to and fro, now looking earnestly on some distant rock which, islanded in the sands, bore for a moment a deceptive appearance—now with flashing eyes reproaching the murderous ocean for its unutterable cruelty.

For a moment I compared myself to that monarch of the waste—Robinson Crusoe.[1] We had been both thrown companionless—he on the shore of a desolate island: I on that of a desolate world. I was rich in the so-called goods of life. If I turned my steps from the near barren scene, and entered any of the earth's million cities, I should find their wealth stored up for my accommodation—clothes, food, books, and a choice of dwelling beyond the command of the princes of former times. Every climate was subject to my selection, while he was obliged to toil in the acquirement of every necessary, and was the inhabitant of a tropical island, against whose heats and storms he could obtain small shelter. Viewing the question thus, who would not have preferred the Sybarite[2] enjoyments I could command, the philosophic leisure, and ample intellectual resources, to his life of labour and peril? Yet he was far happier than I: for he could hope, nor hope in vain—the destined vessel at last arrived to bear him to countrymen and kindred, where the events of his solitude became a fire-side tale. To none could I ever relate the story of my adversity; no hope had I. He knew that, beyond the ocean which begirt his lonely island, thousands lived whom the sun enlightened when it shone also on him: beneath the meridian sun and visiting moon, I alone bore human features; I alone could give articulation to thought; and, when I slept, both day and night were unbeheld of any. He had fled from his fellows, and was transported with terror at the print of a human foot. I would have knelt down and worshipped the same. The wild and cruel Caribbee, the merciless Cannibal[3]—or worse than these, the uncouth, brute, and remorseless veteran in the vices of civilization, would have been to me a beloved companion, a treasure dearly prized. His nature would be kin to mine; his form cast in the same mould; human blood would flow in his veins; a human sympathy must link us for ever. It cannot be that I shall never behold a fellow being more!—never!—never!—not in the course of years!—Shall I wake, and speak to none, pass the interminable hours, my soul, islanded in the world, a solitary point, surrounded by vacuum? Will day follow day endlessly thus? No! no! a God rules the world—providence has not exchanged its golden sceptre for an aspic's[4] sting. Away! let me fly from the ocean-grave, let me depart from this barren nook, paled in,[5] as it is, from access by its own desolateness; let me tread once again the paved towns; step over the threshold of man's dwellings, and most certainly I shall find this thought a horrible vision—a maddening, but evanescent, dream.

I entered Ravenna[6] (the town nearest to the spot whereon I had been cast) before the second sun had set on the empty world; I saw many living creatures: oxen, and horses, and dogs, but there was no man among them. I entered a cottage, it was vacant; I ascended the marble stairs of a palace, the bats and the owls were nestled in the tapestry; I stepped softly, not to awaken the sleeping town. I rebuked a dog, that by yelping disturbed the sacred stillness; I would not believe that all was as it seemed—The world was not dead, but I was mad; I was deprived of sight, hearing, and sense of touch; I was labouring under the force of a spell, which permitted me to behold all sights of earth, except its human inhabitants; they were pursuing their ordinary labours. Every house had its inmate; but I could not perceive them. If I could have deluded myself into a belief of this kind, I should have been far more satisfied. But my brain, tenacious of its reason, refused to lend itself to such imaginations—and though I endeavoured to play the antic to myself, I knew that I, the offspring of man, during long years one among many—now remained sole survivor of my species.

The sun sank behind the western hills; I had fasted

[1] *Robinson Crusoe* Shipwrecked protagonist of Daniel Defoe's *The Life and Adventures of Robinson Crusoe* (1719).

[2] *Sybarite* Luxurious; from the Greek city of Sybaris, noted for its luxury.

[3] *Caribbee* Caribs, inhabitants of the southern West Indies; *Cannibal* Originally also a form of the word "Carib." The fierce inhabitants of this region were rumored to eat human flesh; thus the evolution of the word "cannibal" to its present meaning.

[4] *aspic* Asp, a poisonous snake.

[5] *paled in* Fenced in.

[6] *Ravenna* Town on the Adriatic Sea, approximately 80 miles south of Venice.

since the preceding evening, but, though faint and weary, I loathed food, nor ceased, while yet a ray of light remained, to pace the lonely streets. Night came on, and sent every living creature but me to the bosom of its mate. It was my solace to blunt my mental agony by personal hardship—of the thousand beds around, I would not seek the luxury of one; I lay down on the pavement—a cold marble step served me for a pillow—midnight came; and then, though not before, did my wearied lids shut out the sight of the twinkling stars, and their reflex on the pavement near. Thus I passed the second night of my desolation.

CHAPTER 30

I awoke in the morning, just as the higher windows of the lofty houses received the first beams of the rising sun. The birds were chirping, perched on the window sills and deserted thresholds of the doors. I awoke, and my first thought was, Adrian and Clara are dead. I no longer shall be hailed by their good-morrow, or pass the long day in their society. I shall never see them more. The ocean has robbed me of them—stolen their hearts of love from their breasts, and given over to corruption what was dearer to me than light, or life, or hope.

I was an untaught shepherd-boy when Adrian deigned to confer on me his friendship. The best years of my life had been passed with him. All I had possessed of this world's goods, of happiness, knowledge, or virtue, I owed to him. He had, in his person, his intellect, and rare qualities, given a glory to my life, which without him it had never known. Beyond all other beings he had taught me that goodness, pure and single, can be an attribute of man. It was a sight for angels to congregate to behold, to view him lead, govern, and solace the last days of the human race.

My lovely Clara also was lost to me—she who, last of the daughters of man, exhibited all those feminine and maiden virtues which poets, painters, and sculptors have in their various languages strove to express. Yet, as far as she was concerned, could I lament that she was removed in early youth from the certain advent of misery? Pure she was of soul, and all her intents were holy. But her heart was the throne of love, and the sensibility her lovely countenance expressed was the prophet of many woes, not the less deep and drear because she would have for ever concealed them.

These two wondrously endowed beings had been spared from the universal wreck to be my companions during the last year of solitude. I had felt, while they were with me, all their worth. I was conscious that every other sentiment, regret, or passion had by degrees merged into a yearning, clinging affection for them. I had not forgotten the sweet partner of my youth, mother of my children, my adored Idris; but I saw at least a part of her spirit alive again in her brother;[1] and after, that by Evelyn's[2] death I had lost what most dearly recalled her to me; I enshrined her memory in Adrian's form, and endeavoured to confound the two dear ideas. I sound the depths of my heart, and try in vain to draw thence the expressions that can typify my love for these remnants of my race. If regret and sorrow came athwart me, as well it might in our solitary and uncertain state, the clear tones of Adrian's voice, and his fervent look, dissipated the gloom; or I was cheered unaware by the mild content and sweet resignation Clara's cloudless brow and deep blue eyes expressed. They were all to me—the suns of my benighted soul, repose in my weariness, slumber in my sleepless woe. Ill, most ill, with disjointed words, bare and weak, have I expressed the feeling with which I clung to them. I would have wound myself like ivy inextricably round them, so that the same blow might destroy us. I would have entered and been a part of them—so that

> If the dull substance of my flesh were thought,[3]

even now I had accompanied them to their new and incommunicable abode.

Never shall I see them more. I am bereft of their dear converse—bereft of sight of them. I am a tree rent by lightning; never will the bark close over the bared fibres—never will their quivering life, torn by the winds, receive the opiate of a moment's balm. I am alone in the world—but that expression as yet was less pregnant with misery than that Adrian and Clara are dead.

The tide of thought and feeling rolls on for ever the same, though the banks and shapes around, which

---

1 *her brother* I.e., Adrian.

2 *Evelyn* Lionel and Idris's youngest son.

3 *If … thought* From Shakespeare's Sonnet 44, line 1.

govern its course, and the reflection in the wave, vary. Thus the sentiment of immediate loss in some sort decayed, while that of utter, irremediable loneliness grew on me with time. Three days I wandered through Ravenna—now thinking only of the beloved beings who slept in the oozy caves of ocean, now looking forward on the dread blank before me; shuddering to make an onward step, writhing at each change that marked the progress of the hours.

For three days I wandered to and fro in this melancholy town. I passed whole hours in going from house to house, listening whether I could detect some lurking sign of human existence. Sometimes I rang at a bell; it tinkled through the vaulted rooms, and silence succeeded to the sound. I called myself hopeless, yet still I hoped; and still disappointment ushered in the hours, intruding the cold, sharp steel, which first pierced me, into the aching festering wound. I fed like a wild beast, which seizes its food only when stung by intolerable hunger. I did not change my garb, or seek the shelter of a roof, during all those days. Burning heats, nervous irritation, a ceaseless but confused flow of thought, sleepless nights, and days instinct with a frenzy of agitation, possessed me during that time.

As the fever of my blood increased, a desire of wandering came upon me. I remember that the sun had set on the fifth day after my wreck when, without purpose or aim, I quitted the town of Ravenna. I must have been very ill. Had I been possessed by more or less of delirium, that night had surely been my last; for, as I continued to walk on the banks of the Mantone,[1] whose upward course I followed, I looked wistfully on the stream, acknowledging to myself that its pellucid waves could medicine my woes for ever, and was unable to account to myself for my tardiness in seeking their shelter from the poisoned arrows of thought that were piercing me through and through. I walked a considerable part of the night, and excessive weariness at length conquered my repugnance to the availing myself of the deserted habitations of my species. The waning moon, which had just risen, showed me a cottage, whose neat entrance and trim garden reminded me of my own England. I lifted up the latch of the door and entered. A kitchen first presented itself, where, guided by the moon beams, I found materials for striking a light. Within this was a bed room; the couch was furnished with sheets of snowy whiteness; the wood piled on the hearth, and an array as for a meal might almost have deceived me into the dear belief that I had here found what I had so long sought—one survivor, a companion for my loneliness, a solace to my despair. I steeled myself against the delusion; the room itself was vacant: it was only prudent, I repeated to myself, to examine the rest of the house. I fancied that I was proof against the expectation; yet my heart beat audibly as I laid my hand on the lock of each door, and it sunk again, when I perceived in each the same vacancy. Dark and silent they were as vaults; so I returned to the first chamber, wondering what sightless host had spread the materials for my repast, and my repose. I drew a chair to the table and examined what the viands were of which I was to partake. In truth it was a death feast! The bread was blue and mouldy; the cheese lay a heap of dust. I did not dare examine the other dishes; a troop of ants passed in a double line across the table cloth; every utensil was covered with dust, with cobwebs, and myriads of dead flies. These were object each and all betokening the fallaciousness of my expectations. Tears rushed into my eyes; surely this was a wanton display of the power of the destroyer. What had I done, that each sensitive nerve was thus to be anatomized? Yet why complain more now than ever? This vacant cottage revealed no new sorrow—the world was empty; mankind was dead—I knew it well—why quarrel therefore with an acknowledged and stale truth? Yet, as I said, I had hoped in the very heart of despair, so that every new impression of the hard-cut reality on my soul brought with it a fresh pang, telling me the yet unstudied lesson, that neither change of place nor time could bring alleviation to my misery, but that, as I now was, I must continue, day after day, month after month, year after year, while I lived. I hardly dared conjecture what space of time that expression implied. It is true, I was no longer in the first blush of manhood; neither had I declined far in the vale of years—men have accounted mine the prime of life: I had just entered my thirty-seventh year; every limb was as well knit, every articulation as true, as when I had acted the shepherd on the hills of Cumberland; and with these advantages I was to commence the train of solitary life. Such were the reflections that ushered in my slumber on that night.

[1] *Mantone* River that flows through Ravenna and into the Adriatic.

The shelter, however, and less disturbed repose which I enjoyed, restored me the following morning to a greater portion of health and strength than I had experienced since my fatal shipwreck. Among the stores I had discovered on searching the cottage the preceding night, was a quantity of dried grapes; these refreshed me in the morning as I left my lodging and proceeded towards a town which I discerned at no great distance. As far as I could divine, it must have been Forli. I entered with pleasure its wide and grassy streets. All, it is true, pictured the excess of desolation; yet I loved to find myself in those spots which had been the abode of my fellow creatures. I delighted to traverse street after street, to look up at the tall houses, and repeat to myself, once they contained beings similar to myself—I was not always the wretch I am now. The wide square of Forli, the arcade around it, its light and pleasant aspect, cheered me. I was pleased with the idea, that, if the earth should be again peopled, we, the lost race, would, in the relics left behind, present no contemptible exhibition of our powers to the newcomers.

I entered one of the palaces and opened the door of a magnificent saloon. I started—I looked again with renewed wonder. What wild-looking, unkempt, half-naked savage was that before me? The surprise was momentary.

I perceived that it was I myself whom I beheld in a large mirror at the end of the hall. No wonder that the lover of the princely Idris should fail to recognize himself in the miserable object there portrayed. My tattered dress was that in which I had crawled half alive from the tempestuous sea. My long and tangled hair hung in elf locks on my brow; my dark eyes, now hollow and wild, gleamed from under them; my cheeks were discoloured by the jaundice, which (the effect of misery and neglect) suffused my skin, and were half hid by a beard of many days' growth.

Yet why should I not remain thus, I thought; the world is dead, and this squalid attire is a fitter mourning garb than the foppery of a black suit. And thus, methinks, I should have remained, had not hope, without which I do not believe man could exist, whispered to me that in such a plight I should be an object of fear and aversion to the being, preserved I knew not where, but, I fondly trusted, at length to be found by me. Will my readers scorn the vanity that made me attire myself with some care, for the sake of this visionary being? Or will they forgive the freaks of a half crazed imagination? I can easily forgive myself—for hope, however vague, was so dear to me, and a sentiment of pleasure of so rare occurrence, that I yielded readily to any idea that cherished the one, or promised any recurrence of the former to my sorrowing heart.

After such occupation, I visited every street, alley, and nook of Forli. These Italian towns presented an appearance of still greater desolation than those of England or France. Plague had appeared here earlier—it had finished its course and achieved its work much sooner than with us. Probably the last summer had found no human being alive in all the track included between the shores of Calabria and the northern Alps. My search was utterly vain, yet I did not despond. Reason methought was on my side; and the chances were by no means contemptible that there should exist in some part of Italy a survivor like myself—of a wasted, depopulate land. As therefore I rambled through the empty town, I formed my plan for future operations. I would continue to journey on towards Rome. After I should have satisfied myself, by a narrow search, that I left behind no human being in the towns through which I passed, I would write up in a conspicuous part of each, with white paint, in three languages, that "Verney, the last of the race of Englishmen, had taken up his abode in Rome."

In pursuance of this scheme, I entered a painter's shop and procured myself the paint. It is strange that so trivial an occupation should have consoled and even enlivened me. But grief renders one childish, despair fantastic. To this simple inscription, I merely added the adjuration, "Friend, come! I wait for thee!—*Deh, vieni! ti aspetto!*"

On the following morning, with something like hope for my companion, I quitted Forli on my way to Rome. Until now, agonizing retrospect and dreary prospects for the future had stung me when awake, and cradled me to my repose. Many times I had delivered myself up to the tyranny of anguish—many times I resolved a speedy end to my woes; and death by my own hands was a remedy whose practicability was even cheering to me. What could I fear in the other world? If there were a hell, and I were doomed to it, I should come an adept to the sufferance of its tortures—the act were easy, the speedy and certain end of my deplorable tragedy. But now these thoughts faded before the new-born expectation. I went on my way, not as before, feeling each hour, each minute, to be an age instinct with incalculable pain.

As I wandered along the plain, at the foot of the Appennines—through their valleys, and over their bleak summits—my path led me through a country which had been trodden by heroes, visited and admired by thousands. They had, as a tide, receded, leaving me blank and bare in the midst. But why complain? Did I not hope?—so I schooled myself, even after the enlivening spirit had really deserted me, and thus I was obliged to call up all the fortitude I could command, and that was not much, to prevent a recurrence of that chaotic and intolerable despair that had succeeded to the miserable shipwreck, that had consummated every fear, and dashed to annihilation every joy.

I rose each day with the morning sun, and left my desolate inn. As my feet strayed through the unpeopled country, my thoughts rambled through the universe, and I was least miserable when I could, absorbed in reverie, forget the passage of the hours. Each evening, in spite of weariness, I detested to enter any dwelling, there to take up my nightly abode—I have sat, hour after hour, at the door of the cottage I had selected, unable to lift the latch and meet face to face blank desertion within. Many nights, though autumnal mists were spread around, I passed under an ilex[1]—many times I have supped on arbutus berries and chestnuts, making a fire, gypsy-like, on the ground—because wild natural scenery reminded me less acutely of my hopeless state of loneliness. I counted the days, and bore with me a peeled willow-wand, on which, as well as I could remember, I had notched the days that had elapsed since my wreck, and each night I added another unit to the melancholy sum.

I had toiled up a hill which led to Spoleto. Around was spread a plain, encircled by the chestnut-covered Apennines. A dark ravine was on one side, spanned by an aqueduct, whose tall arches were rooted in the dell below and attested that man had once deigned to bestow labour and thought here, to adorn and civilize nature. Savage, ungrateful nature, which in wild sport defaced his remains, protruding her easily renewed and fragile growth of wild flowers and parasite plants around his eternal edifices. I sat on a fragment of rock and looked round. The sun had bathed in gold the western atmosphere, and in the east the clouds caught the radiance, and budded into transient loveliness. It set on a world that contained me alone for its inhabitant. I took out my wand—I counted the marks. Twenty-five were already traced—twenty-five days had already elapsed since human voice had gladdened my ears or human countenance met my gaze. Twenty-five long, weary days, succeeded by dark and lonesome nights, had mingled with foregone years and had become a part of the past—the never to be recalled—a real, undeniable portion of my life—twenty-five long, long days.

Why this was not a month!—Why talk of days—or weeks—or months—I must grasp years in my imagination, if I would truly picture the future to myself—three, five, ten, twenty, fifty anniversaries of that fatal epoch might elapse—every year containing twelve months, each of more numerous calculation in a diary, than the twenty-five days gone by—Can it be? Will it be?—We had been used to look forward to death tremulously—wherefore, but because its place was obscure? But more terrible, and far more obscure, was the unveiled course of my lone futurity. I broke my wand; I threw it from me. I needed no recorder of the inch and barley-corn growth of my life, while my unquiet thoughts created other divisions than those ruled over by the planets—and, in looking back on the age that had elapsed since I had been alone, I disdained to give the name of days and hours to the throes of agony which had in truth portioned it out.

I hid my face in my hands. The twitter of the young birds going to rest, and their rustling among the trees, disturbed the still evening-air—the crickets chirped, the aziolo cooed at intervals. My thoughts had been of death—these sounds spoke to me of life. I lifted up my eyes—a bat wheeled round—the sun had sunk behind the jagged line of mountains, and the paly[2] crescent moon was visible, silver white amidst the orange sunset, and accompanied by one bright star, prolonged thus the twilight. A herd of cattle passed along in the dell below, untended, towards their watering place—the grass was rustled by a gentle breeze, and the olive-woods, mellowed into soft masses by the moonlight, contrasted

[1] *ilex* Evergreen oak.

[2] *paly* Pale.

their sea-green with the dark chestnut foliage. Yes, this is the earth; there is no change, no ruin, no rent made in her verdurous expanse; she continues to wheel round and round, with alternate night and day, through the sky, though man is not her adorner or inhabitant. Why could I not forget myself like one of those animals, and no longer suffer the wild tumult of misery that I endure? Yet, ah! what a deadly breach yawns between their state and mine! Have not they companions? Have not they each their mate—their cherished young, their home, which, though unexpressed to us, is, I doubt not, endeared and enriched, even in their eyes, by the society which kind nature has created for them? It is I only that am alone—I, on this little hilltop, gazing on plain and mountain recess; on sky, and its starry population, listening to every sound of earth, and air, and murmuring wave—I only cannot express to any companion my many thoughts, nor lay my throbbing head on any loved bosom, nor drink from meeting eyes an intoxicating dew that transcends the fabulous nectar of the gods. Shall I not then complain? Shall I not curse the murderous engine which has mowed down the children of men, my brethren? Shall I not bestow a malediction on every other of nature's offspring, which dares live and enjoy, while I live and suffer?

Ah, no! I will discipline my sorrowing heart to sympathy in your joys; I will be happy, because ye are so. Live on, ye innocents, nature's selected darlings; I am not much unlike to you. Nerves, pulse, brain, joint, and flesh, of such am I composed, and ye are organized by the same laws. I have something beyond this, but I will call it a defect, not an endowment, if it leads me to misery, while ye are happy. Just then, there emerged from a near copse two goats and a little kid, by the mother's side; they began to browze[1] the herbage of the hill. I approached near to them without their perceiving me; I gathered a handful of fresh grass and held it out; the little one nestled close to its mother, while she timidly withdrew. The male stepped forward, fixing his eyes on me: I drew near, still holding out my lure, while he, depressing his head, rushed at me with his horns. I was a very fool; I knew it, yet I yielded to my rage. I snatched up a huge fragment of rock; it would have crushed my rash foe. I poised it—aimed it—then my heart failed me. I hurled it wide of the mark; it rolled clattering among the bushes into dell. My little visitants, all aghast, galloped back into the covert of the wood; while I, my very heart bleeding and torn, rushed down the hill, and by the violence of bodily exertion sought to escape from my miserable self.

No, no, I will not live among the wild scenes of nature, the enemy of all that lives. I will seek the towns—Rome, the capital of the world, the crown of man's achievements. Among its storied streets, hallowed ruins, and stupendous remains of human exertion, I shall not, as here, find every thing forgetful of man; trampling on his memory, defacing his works, proclaiming from hill to hill, and vale to vale—by the torrents freed from the boundaries which he imposed, by the vegetation liberated from the laws which he enforced, by his habitation abandoned to mildew and weeds—that his power is lost, his race annihilated for ever.

I hailed the Tiber, for that was, as it were, an unalienable possession of humanity. I hailed the wild Campagna,[2] for every rood[3] had been trod by man; and its savage uncultivation, of no recent date, only proclaimed more distinctly his power, since he had given an honourable name and sacred title to what else would have been a worthless, barren track. I entered Eternal Rome by the Porta del Popolo,[4] and saluted with awe its time-honoured space. The wide square, the churches near, the long extent of the Corso, the near eminence of Trinita de' Monti[5] appeared like fairy work, they were so silent, so peaceful, and so very fair. It was evening, and the population of animals which still existed in this mighty city had gone to rest; there was no sound, save the murmur of its many fountains, whose soft monotony was harmony to my soul. The knowledge that I was in Rome soothed me; that wondrous city, hardly more illustrious for its heroes and sages than for the power it exercised over the imaginations of men. I went to rest that night; the eternal burning of my heart quenched, my senses tranquil.

The next morning I eagerly began my rambles in

[1] *browze* Feed on.

[2] *Campagna* Plain to the north of Rome through which the Tiber River flows before entering the city.

[3] *rood* Measure of land, varying from six to eight yards.

[4] *Porta del Popolo* Italian: "Gate of the People."

[5] *Corso* Via del Corso, main street of central Rome; a fashionable promenade in Shelley's time; *Trinita de' Monti* Church located at the top of the Spanish Steps.

search of oblivion. I ascended the many terraces of the garden of the Colonna Palace,[1] under whose roof I had been sleeping; and, passing out from it at its summit, I found myself on Monte Cavallo. The fountain sparkled in the sun; the obelisk above pierced the clear dark-blue air. The statues on each side, the works, as they are inscribed, of Phidias and Praxiteles, stood in undiminished grandeur, representing Castor and Pollux,[2] who with majestic power tamed the rearing animal at their side. If those illustrious artists had in truth chiselled these forms, how many passing generations had their giant proportions outlived! and now they were viewed by the last of the species they were sculptured to represent and deify. I had shrunk into insignificance in my own eyes, as I considered the multitudinous beings these stone demigods had outlived, but this after-thought restored me to dignity in my own conception. The sight of the poetry eternized in these statues, took the sting from the thought, arraying it only in poetic ideality.

I repeated to myself—I am in Rome! I behold, and, as it were, familiarly converse with the wonder of the world, sovereign mistress of the imagination, majestic and eternal survivor of millions of generations of extinct men. I endeavoured to quiet the sorrows of my aching heart by even now taking an interest in what in my youth I had ardently longed to see. Every part of Rome is replete with relics of ancient times. The meanest streets are strewed with truncated columns, broken capitals—Corinthian and Ionic—and sparkling fragments of granite or porphyry. The walls of the most penurious dwellings enclose a fluted pillar or ponderous stone, which once made part of the palace of the Caesars; and the voice of dead time, in still vibrations, is breathed from these dumb things, animated and glorified as they were by man.

I embraced the vast columns of the temple of Jupiter Stator,[3] which survives in the open space that was the Forum, and leaning my burning cheek against its cold durability, I tried to lose the sense of present misery and present desertion by recalling to the haunted cell of my brain vivid memories of times gone by. I rejoiced at my success, as I figured Camillus, the Gracchi, Cato, and last the heroes of Tacitus,[4] which shine meteors of surpassing brightness during the murky night of the empire; as the verses of Horace and Virgil, or the glowing periods of Cicero,[5] thronged into the opened gates of my mind, I felt myself exalted by long forgotten enthusiasm. I was delighted to know that I beheld the scene which they beheld—the scene which their wives and mothers, and crowds of the unnamed, witnessed, while at the same time they honoured applauded, or wept for these matchless specimens of humanity. At length, then, I had found a consolation. I had not vainly sought the storied precincts of Rome—I had discovered a medicine for my many and vital wounds.

I sat at the foot of these vast columns. The Coliseum,[6] whose naked ruin is robed by nature in a verdurous and glowing veil, lay in the sunlight on my right. Not far off, to the left, was the Tower of the Capitol.[7] Triumphal arches, the falling walls of many temples, strewed the ground at my feet. I strove, I resolved, to force myself to see the Plebeian multitude and lofty Patrician forms congregated around; and, as the diorama of ages passed across my subdued fancy, they were replaced by the modern Roman: the Pope, in his white stole, distributing benedictions to the kneeling worshippers; the friar in his cowl; the dark-eyed girl, veiled by

[1] *Colonna Palace* Located on Monte Cavallo (also called Quirinal Hill), it contains an art gallery of sixteenth- and seventeeth- century paintings.

[2] *The statues … Pollux* The statues of Castor and Pollux, the twin sons of Zeus and Leda, were then commonly (but incorrectly) ascribed to the fifth- and sixth-century BCE Greek sculptors Phidias and Praxiteles.

[3] *Jupiter Stator* Three large Corinthian columns remain of this temple, which is now thought to belong to Castor, rather than to Jupiter Stator (Jupiter the Stayer, or the Steadfast). The Forum, in which these columns stand, was the location of the marketplace and the center for political, economic, and religious activities.

[4] *Camillus* Roman statesman and general of the fourth century BCE; *the Gracci* Brothers Tiberius and Caius Gracchus, second-century BCE supporters of the plebian cause; *Cato* Either Cato the Elder (234–149 BCE), a famous politician and orator, or Cato the Younger (95–46 BCE), a Roman statesman who committed suicide rather than submit to the tyranny of Octavius Caesar; *Tacitus* Roman historian (c. 55–115 CE) whose heroes include Alexander, Julius Caesar, Mithridates, and Seneca.

[5] *Horace … Cicero* Horace and Virgil were two famous Roman poets of the first century BCE, famous for, respectively, *Odes* and *The Aeneid.* Cicero was a great orator, statesman, and prose writer who was assassinated by Caesar in 43 BCE.

[6] *Coliseum* Great amphitheater completed in 80 CE and used for gladiatorial combat.

[7] *Tower of the Capitol* Citadel located on Mons Capitolinus, one of the seven hills of Rome.

her mezzera;[1] the noisy, sun-burnt rustic, leading his herd of buffaloes and oxen to the Campo Vaccino.[2] The romance with which, dipping our pencils in the rainbow hues of sky and transcendent nature, we to a degree gratuitously endow the Italians, replaced the solemn grandeur of antiquity. I remembered the dark monk, and floating figures of "The Italian," and how my boyish blood had thrilled at the description.[3] I called to mind Corinna ascending the Capitol to be crowned,[4] and, passing from the heroine to the author, reflected how the Enchantress Spirit of Rome held sovereign sway over the minds of the imaginative, until it rested on me—sole remaining spectator of its wonders.

I was long wrapt by such ideas; but the soul wearies of a pauseless flight; and, stooping from its wheeling circuits round and round this spot, suddenly it fell ten thousand fathom deep, into the abyss of the present—into self-knowledge—into tenfold sadness. I roused myself—I cast off my waking dreams; and I, who just now could almost hear the shouts of the Roman throng, and was hustled by countless multitudes, now beheld the desert ruins of Rome sleeping under its own blue sky. The shadows lay tranquilly on the ground; sheep were grazing untended on the Palatine, and a buffalo stalked down the Sacred Way that led to the Capitol.[5] I was alone in the Forum; alone in Rome; alone in the world. Would not one living man—one companion in my weary solitude, be worth all the glory and remembered power of this time-honoured city? Double sorrow—sadness, bred in Cimmerian caves, robed my soul in a mourning garb. The generations I had conjured up to my fancy contrasted more strongly with the end of all—the single point in which, as a pyramid, the mighty fabric of society had ended, while I, on the giddy height, saw vacant space around me.

From such vague laments I turned to the contemplation of the minutiae of my situation. So far, I had not succeeded in the sole object of my desires, the finding a companion for my desolation. Yet I did not despair. It is true that my inscriptions were set up, for the most part, in insignificant towns and villages; yet, even without these memorials, it was possible that the person who, like me, should find himself alone in a depopulate land, should, like me, come to Rome. The more slender my expectation was, the more I chose to build on it, and to accommodate my actions to this vague possibility.

It became necessary, therefore, that for a time I should domesticate myself at Rome. It became necessary that I should look my disaster in the face—not playing the school-boy's part of obedience without submission; enduring life, and yet rebelling against the laws by which I lived.

Yet how could I resign myself? Without love, without sympathy, without communion with any, how could I meet the morning sun, and with it trace its oft repeated journey to the evening shades? Why did I continue to live—why not throw off the weary weight of time, and with my own hand let out the fluttering prisoner from my agonized breast? It was not cowardice that withheld me; for the true fortitude was to endure, and death had a soothing sound accompanying it that would easily entice me to enter its demesne. But this I would not do. I had, from the moment I had reasoned on the subject, instituted myself the subject to fate, and the servant of necessity, the visible laws of the invisible God—I believed that my obedience was the result of sound reasoning, pure feeling, and an exalted sense of the true excellence and nobility of my nature. Could I have seen in this empty earth, in the seasons and their change, the hand of a blind power only, most willingly would I have placed my head on the sod and closed my eyes on its loveliness for ever. But fate had administered life to me when the plague had already seized on its prey—she had dragged me by the hair from out the strangling waves. By such miracles she had bought me for her own; I admitted her authority, and bowed to her decrees. If, after mature consideration, such was my resolve, it was doubly necessary that I should not lose the end of life, the improvement of my faculties, and poison its flow by repinings without end. Yet how cease to repine, since there was no hand near to extract the

---

[1] *mezzera* Mesèro (Italian), a shawl worn by women over the head and shoulders.

[2] *Campo Vaccino* Italian: "Cattle Pasture," the original function of the Roman Forum.

[3] *I remember … description* References to the novel *The Italian* (1797), by Ann Radcliffe.

[4] *Corinna … crowned* Reference to the heroine of Anne-Louise-Germaine de Staël's novel *Corinne, ou l'Italie* (1807).

[5] *Palatine* Most important of the seven hills of Rome, it was the location of the earliest Roman settlement; *Sacred Way* Sacra Via (Latin), the oldest street in Rome.

barbed spear that had entered my heart of hearts? I stretched out my hand, and it touched none whose sensations were responsive to mine. I was girded, walled in, vaulted over, by seven-fold barriers of loneliness. Occupation alone, if I could deliver myself up to it, would be capable of affording an opiate to my sleepless sense of woe. Having determined to make Rome my abode, at least for some months, I made arrangements for my accommodation—I selected my home. The Colonna Palace was well adapted for my purpose. Its grandeur—its treasure of paintings, its magnificent halls were objects soothing and even exhilarating.

I found the granaries of Rome well stored with grain, and particularly with Indian corn; this product, requiring less art in its preparation for food, I selected as my principal support. I now found the hardships and lawlessness of my youth turn to account. A man cannot throw off the habits of sixteen years. Since that age, it is true, I had lived luxuriously, or at least surrounded by all the conveniences civilization afforded. But before that time, I had been "as uncouth a savage as the wolf-bred founder of old Rome"[1]—and now, in Rome itself, robber and shepherd propensities, similar to those of its founder, were of advantage to its sole inhabitant. I spent the morning riding and shooting in the Campagna; I passed long hours in the various galleries; I gazed at each statue, and lost myself in a reverie before many a fair Madonna or beauteous nymph. I haunted the Vatican, and stood surrounded by marble forms of divine beauty. Each stone deity was possessed by sacred gladness and the eternal fruition of love. They looked on me with unsympathizing complacency, and often in wild accents I reproached them for their supreme indifference—for they were human shapes, the human form divine was manifest in each fairest limb and lineament. The perfect moulding brought with it the idea of colour and motion; often, half in bitter mockery, half in self-delusion, I clasped their icy proportions, and, coming between Cupid and his Psyche's lips,[2] pressed the unconceiving marble.

I endeavoured to read. I visited the libraries of Rome. I selected a volume, and, choosing some sequestered, shady nook on the banks of the Tiber, or opposite the fair temple in the Borghese Gardens, or under the old pyramid of Cestius,[3] I endeavoured to conceal me from myself, and immerse myself in the subject traced on the pages before me. As if in the same soil you plant nightshade and a myrtle tree, they will each appropriate the mould, moisture, and air administered, for the fostering their several properties—so did my grief find sustenance, and power of existence, and growth, in what else had been divine manna, to feed radiant meditation. Ah! while I streak this paper with the tale of what my so-named occupations were—while I shape the skeleton of my days—my hand trembles, my heart pants, and my brain refuses to lend expression, or phrase, or idea, by which to image forth the veil of unutterable woe that clothed these bare realities. O worn and beating heart, may I dissect thy fibres, and tell how in each unmitigable misery, sadness dire, repinings, and despair, existed? May I record my many ravings—the wild curses I hurled at torturing nature, and how I have passed days shut out from light and food, from all except the burning hell alive in my own bosom?

I was presented, meantime, with one other occupation, the one best fitted to discipline my melancholy thoughts, which strayed backwards, over many a ruin, and through many a flowery glade, even to the mountain recess from which in early youth I had first emerged.

During one of my rambles through the habitations of Rome, I found writing materials on a table in an author's study. Parts of a manuscript lay scattered about. It contained a learned disquisition on the Italian language; one page an unfinished dedication to posterity, for whose profit the writer had sifted and selected the niceties of this harmonious language—to whose everlasting benefit he bequeathed his labours.

I also will write a book, I cried—for whom to read?—to whom dedicated? And then with silly flourish (what so capricious and childish as despair?) I wrote,

DEDICATION

TO THE ILLUSTRIOUS DEAD.

SHADOWS, ARISE, AND READ YOUR FALL!

[1] *as … Rome* Romulus, the founder of Rome, and his brother Remus were said to have been reared by a she-wolf. Lionel quotes a statement made earlier by himself, in Chapter 1.

[2] *Cupid … lips* Cupid, god of love, and his mortal lover, Psyche.

[3] *old … Cestius* Tomb of Praetor Gaius Cestius Epulo (d. 12 BCE), next to which is the Protestant cemetery in which Percy Shelley was buried.

BEHOLD THE HISTORY OF THE LAST MAN.

Yet, will not this world be re-peopled, and the children of a saved pair of lovers, in some to me unknown and unattainable seclusion, wandering to these prodigious relics of the ante-pestilential race, seek to learn how beings so wondrous in their achievements, with imaginations infinite, and powers godlike, had departed from their home to an unknown country?

I will write and leave in this most ancient city, this "world's sole monument,"[1] a record of these things. I will leave a monument of the existence of Verney, the Last Man. At first I thought only to speak of plague, of death, and last, of desertion; but I lingered fondly on my early years, and recorded with sacred zeal the virtues of my companions. They have been with me during the fulfilment of my task. I have brought it to an end—I lift my eyes from my paper—again they are lost to me. Again I feel that I am alone.

A year has passed since I have been thus occupied. The seasons have made their wonted round, and decked this eternal city in a changeful robe of surpassing beauty. A year has passed; and I no longer *guess* at my state or my prospects—loneliness is my familiar, sorrow my inseparable companion. I have endeavoured to brave the storm—I have endeavoured to school myself to fortitude—I have sought to imbue myself with the lessons of wisdom. It will not do. My hair has become nearly grey—my voice, unused now to utter sound, comes strangely on my ears. My person, with its human powers and features, seem to me a monstrous excrescence of nature. How express in human language a woe human being until this hour never knew! How give intelligible expression to a pang none but I could ever understand!—No one has entered Rome. None will ever come. I smile bitterly at the delusion I have so long nourished, and still more when I reflect that I have exchanged it for another as delusive, as false, but to which I now cling with the same fond trust.

Winter has come again; and the gardens of Rome have lost their leaves—the sharp air comes over the Campagna, and has driven its brute inhabitants to take up their abode in the many dwellings of the deserted city. Frost has suspended the gushing fountains, and Trevi[2] has stilled her eternal music. I had made a rough calculation, aided by the stars, by which I endeavoured to ascertain the first day of the new year. In the old outworn age, the Sovereign Pontiff[3] was used to go in solemn pomp, and mark the renewal of the year by driving a nail in the gate of the temple of Janus.[4] On that day I ascended St. Peter's, and carved on its topmost stone the aera 2100, last year of the world!

My only companion was a dog, a shaggy fellow, half water- and half shepherd's-dog, whom I found tending sheep in the Campagna. His master was dead, but nevertheless he continued fulfilling his duties in expectation of his return. If a sheep strayed from the rest, he forced it to return to the flock, and sedulously kept off every intruder. Riding in the Campagna I had come upon his sheep-walk, and for some time observed his repetition of lessons learned from man, now useless, though unforgotten. His delight was excessive when he saw me. He sprung up to my knees; he capered round and round, wagging his tail, with the short, quick bark of pleasure: he left his fold to follow me, and from that day has never neglected to watch by and attend on me, showing boisterous gratitude whenever I caressed or talked to him. His pattering steps and mine alone were heard when we entered the magnificent extent of nave and aisle of St. Peter's.[5] We ascended the myriad steps together when on the summit I achieved my design, and in rough figures noted the date of the last year. I then turned to gaze on the country, and to take leave of Rome. I had long determined to quit it, and I now formed the plan I would adopt for my future career, after I had left this magnificent abode.

A solitary being is by instinct a wanderer, and that I would become. A hope of amelioration always attends on change of place, which would even lighten the burden of my life. I had been a fool to remain in Rome all this time: Rome noted for malaria, the famous caterer for death. But it was still possible, that, could I visit the

[1] *world's sole monument* From Edmund Spenser's *Ruins of Rome* (1591): "Rome living, was the world's sole ornament, / And dead, is now the world's sole monument" (lines 405-6).

[2] *Trevi* Fountain on the Quirinal Hill, built in 1762 by Nicola Salvi.

[3] *Sovereign Pontiff* I.e., the Pontifex Maximus, the Roman High Priest, a title later given to the pope.

[4] *Janus* Roman god of gates, of doorways, and of the new year.

[5] *nave* Main body of a church; *St Peter's* Basilica of the Vatican.

whole extent of earth, I should find in some part of the wide extent a survivor. Methought the sea-side was the most probable retreat to be chosen by such a one. If left alone in an inland district, still they could not continue in the spot where their last hopes had been extinguished; they would journey on, like me, in search of a partner for their solitude, till the watery barrier stopped their further progress.

To that water—cause of my woes—perhaps now to be their cure I would betake myself. Farewell, Italy!—farewell, thou ornament of the world, matchless Rome, the retreat of the solitary one during long months!—to civilized life—to the settled home and succession of monotonous days, farewell! Peril will now be mine; and I hail her as a friend—death will perpetually cross my path, and I will meet him as a benefactor; hardship, inclement weather, and dangerous tempests will be my sworn mates. Ye spirits of storm, receive me! ye powers of destruction, open wide your arms, and clasp me for ever! if a kinder power have not decreed another end, so that after long endurance I may reap my reward, and again feel my heart beat near the heart of another like to me.

Tiber, the road which is spread by nature's own hand, threading her continent, was at my feet, and many a boat was tethered to the banks. I would with a few books, provisions, and my dog, embark in one of these and float down the current of the stream into the sea; and then, keeping near land, I would coast the beauteous shores and sunny promontories of the blue Mediterranean, pass Naples, along Calabria,[1] and would dare the twin perils of Scylla and Charybdis;[2] then with fearless aim, (for what had I to lose?) skim ocean's surface towards Malta and the further Cyclades. I would avoid Constantinople, the sight of whose well-known towers and inlets belonged to another state of existence from my present one; I would coast Asia Minor, and Syria, and, passing the seven-mouthed Nile, steer northward again, till, losing sight of forgotten Carthage and deserted Lybia, I should reach the pillars of Hercules.[3] And then, no matter where—the oozy caves and soundless depths of ocean may be my dwelling before I accomplish this long-drawn voyage, or the arrow of disease find my heart as I float singly on the weltering Mediterranean; or, in some place I touch at, I may find what I seek—a companion; or, if this may not be, to endless time, decrepit and grey headed— youth already in the grave with those I love—the lone wanderer will still unfurl his sail, and clasp the tiller, and, still obeying the breezes of heaven, for ever round another and another promontory, anchoring in another and another bay, still ploughing seedless ocean, leaving behind the verdant land of native Europe, adown the tawny shore of Africa, having weathered the fierce seas of the Cape,[4] I may moor my worn skiff in a creek, shaded by spicy groves of the odorous islands of the far Indian ocean.

These are wild dreams. Yet since, now a week ago, they came on me, as I stood on the height of St. Peter's, they have ruled my imagination. I have chosen my boat, and laid in my scant stores. I have selected a few books; the principal are Homer and Shakespeare—but the libraries of the world are thrown open to me, and in any port I can renew my stock. I form no expectation of alteration for the better; but the monotonous present is intolerable to me. Neither hope nor joy are my pilots—restless despair and fierce desire of change lead me on. I long to grapple with danger, to be excited by fear, to have some task, however slight or voluntary, for each day's fulfilment. I shall witness all the variety of appearance that the elements can assume—I shall read fair augury in the rainbow, menace in the cloud, some lesson or record dear to my heart in everything. Thus around the shores of deserted earth, while the sun is high, and the moon waxes or wanes, angels, the spirits of the dead, and the ever-open eye of the Supreme, will behold the tiny bark, freighted with Verney—the LAST MAN.

THE END

—1826

[1] *Calabria* Region of southern Italy.

[2] *Scylla and Charybdis* From Greek mythology, a sea monster, later turned into rock cliffs, and a whirlpool, located in the Straits of Messina.

[3] *the pillars of Hercules* The Rock of Gibraltar and the Hill of Ceuta, two promontories flanking the eastern end to the Strait of Gibraltar, which were considered in ancient times to mark the ends of the earth.

[4] *Cape* Cape of Good Hope.

In Context

The "Last Man" Theme in the Nineteenth Century

The theme of "the last man" was one that captured a great many imaginations in the 1820s and 1830s. Shelley's 1826 novel followed on the heels of Thomas Campbell's 1823 poem of the same name (to which, according to Campbell, Byron's poem "Darkness" owes its inspiration). Also in 1826 a number of magazine pieces were published on the same theme, including "The Last Man" (*Blackwoods*) and "The Death of the World" (*European Magazine*). That same year the painter John Martin, whose work often focused on apocalyptic visions, painted an initial study (now lost) of "The Last Man," a watercolor of which he completed in 1832, and an oil painting in 1849. The Campbell poem and the Martin painting are reproduced below; both envisage the end of the world occurring as a result of the sun's light being extinguished, rather than as a result of plague or other natural disaster.

Thomas Campbell, "The Last Man," *New Monthly Magazine* 8 (1823)

All worldly shapes shall melt in gloom,
The Sun himself must die,
Before this mortal shall assume
Its Immortality!
I saw a vision in my sleep,
That gave my spirit strength to sweep
Adown the gulf of Time!
I saw the last of human mould,
That shall Creation's death behold,
As Adam saw her prime!

The Sun's eye had a sickly glare,
The Earth with age was wan,
The skeletons of nations were
Around that lonely man!
Some had expir'd in fight—the brands
Still rusted in their bony hands;
In plague and famine some!
Earth's cities had no sound nor tread;
And ships were drifting with the dead
To shores where all was dumb!

Yet, prophet like, that lone one stood,
With dauntless words and high,
That shook the sere° leaves from the wood *withered*
As if a storm pass'd by,
Saying, we are twins in death, proud Sun,
Thy face is cold, thy race is run,
'Tis Mercy bids thee go.
For thou ten thousand thousand years
Hast seen the tide of human tears,
That shall no longer flow.

What though beneath thee man put forth
His pomp, his pride, his skill;
And arts that made fire, flood, and earth,
The vassals of his will—
Yet mourn I not thy parted sway,
Thou dim discrownèd king of day:
For all those trophied arts
And triumphs that beneath thee sprang,
Heal'd not a passion or a pang
Entail'd on human hearts.

Go, let oblivion's curtain fall
Upon the stage of men,
Nor with thy rising beams recall
Life's tragedy again.
Its piteous pageants bring not back,
Nor waken flesh, upon the rack
Of pain anew to writhe;
Stretch'd in disease's shapes abhorr'd,
Or mown in battle by the sword,
Like grass beneath the scythe.

Ev'n I am weary in yon skies
To watch thy fading fire;
Test of all sumless agonies,
Behold not me expire.
My lips that speak thy dirge of death—
Their rounded gasp and gurgling breath
To see thou shalt not boast.
The eclipse of Nature spreads my pall—
The majesty of Darkness shall
Receive my parting ghost!

This spirit shall return to Him
That gave its heavenly spark;
Yet think not, Sun, it shall be dim
When thou thyself art dark!
No! it shall live again, and shine
In bliss unknown to beams of thine,
By Him recall'd to breath,
Who captive led captivity,
Who robb'd the grave of Victory—
And took the sting from Death!

Go, Sun, while Mercy holds me up
On Nature's awful waste
To drink this last and bitter cup
Of grief that man shall taste—
Go, tell the night that hides thy face,
Thou saw'st the last of Adam's race,
On Earth's sepulchral clod,
The dark'ning universe defy
To quench his Immortality,
Or shake his trust in God!

from Thomas Campbell's letter to the editor of the *Edinburgh Review*, 28 February 1825

… You say that my poem, "The Last Man," seems to have been suggested by Lord Byron's poem "Darkness." Now the truth is, that fifteen, or it may be more, years ago, I called on Lord Byron, who at that time had lodgings near St. James's Street; and we had a long, and to me a very memorable, conversation, from which I have not a doubt that his Lordship imbibed those few ideas in the poem "Darkness" which have any resemblance to mine in "The Last Man." I remember my saying to him that I thought the idea of a being witnessing the extinction of his species and of the Creation, and of his looking, under the fading eye of nature, at desolate cities, ships floating at sea with the dead, would make a striking subject for a poem. I met those very ideas, many years afterwards, when I read Lord Byron's poem "Darkness."

John Martin, *The Last Man* (1849).

In Context

Shelley's Life and *The Last Man*

Many critical discussions of *The Last Man* touch on the connections between its images of waste and desolation and the extraordinary series of losses that Shelley herself suffered—including the deaths of three of her children, a life-threatening miscarriage, and the drowning of her husband in Italy in 1822. The selections from her letters reprinted below convey Shelley's impressions of Italy as well as of these tragic events, and highlight some of the connections between her own life and the plot of *The Last Man* (which Shelley began soon after returning to England in 1823). In her diary entry for 14 May 1824, she makes the connection between her own situation and that portrayed in the novel explicit: "The last man! Yes, I may well describe that solitary being's feelings, feeling myself as the last relic of a beloved race, my companions extinct before me."

Selected Letters

To Thomas Jefferson Hogg[1]
13 Arabella Road, Pimlico
6 March 1815

My dearest Hogg my baby is dead[2]—will you come to me as soon as you can—I wish to see you—It was perfectly well when I went to bed—I awoke in the night to give it suck it appeared to be sleeping so quietly that I would not awake it—it was dead then but we did not find that out till morning—from its appearance it evidently died of convulsions—

Will you come—you are so calm a creature & Shelley is afraid of a fever from the milk—for I am no longer a mother now.

Mary

To Thomas Jefferson Hogg
Windmill Inn, Salt Hill
25 April 1815

My Dear Jefferson

... Do you mean to come down to us—I suppose not, Prince Prudent; well, as you please, but remember I should be *very* happy to see you. If you had not been a lawyer you might have come with us.[3]

Rain has come after a mild beautiful day but Shelley & I are going to walk as it is only showery.

How delightful it is to read poetry among green shades. "Tintern Abbey"[4] thrilled me with delight—

But Shelley calls me to come for
The sun it is set
And night is coming

I will write perhaps by a night coach or at least early tomorrow—

I shall return soon & remain till then an affectionate but

Runaway Dormouse

To Maria Gisborne[5]
Este
2 Nov. 1818

My Dear Mrs. Gisborne

I have not heard from you since we parted—but I hope that nothing has occasioned this, except your dislike of letter writing—Several events have occurred to us since then, and the principal one, the death of my little Clara—I wrote to tell you of her illness, and the dreadful state of weakness that succeeded to it—In this state she began to cut all her teeth at once—pined a few weeks, and died.

Soon after this, William[6] grew rather ill, and as we were now soon frightened, and there is no good doctor at Este, Shelley and I took him to Venice, where we stayed about a fortnight. It is a pleasant town to visit—its appearance is so new and strange—but the want of walks and variety must render it disagreeable for a continuous residence. The Hoppners find it so—they have lived between four and five years here, and are heartily sick of it. We liked almost everything—however I must here except three things, as the disagreements of the city—1st its inhabitants, 2nd its streets to walk in, 3rd its canals at low water. These are tolerable deductions, and yet there is enough to like without liking these. The inhabitants I dislike, because they are some of the worst specimens of Italians, and to you, who have lived so long in the country, and know their characteristics, this is saying everything. The streets I dislike because they are narrow and dirty, and above all because they carry

[1] *Thomas Jefferson Hogg* Hogg (1792–1862) was a close friend of both Mary and Percy Shelley. He attended Oxford with Percy, and was introduced to Mary after the two had eloped.

[2] *my baby is dead* The name of this child, who was a few weeks old, and the cause of her death are unknown. Percy Shelley had recorded in his journal, however, that she was not expected to live.

[3] *If you ... us* Percy Shelley's grandfather had recently died, leaving his estate to his son and grandson, and Shelley was in the midst of negotiating an agreement with his father, in which he would sell his part of the estate in exchange for an annual income.

[4] *Tintern Abbey* 1798 poem by William Wordsworth entitled "Lines Composed a Few Miles Above Tintern Abbey, On Revisiting the Banks of the Wye During a Tour. July 13, 1978."

[5] *Maria Gisborne* Friend of Mary Shelley's who had been visiting her at Bagni to Lucca and who had accompanied Shelley as far as Lucca when Shelley set out to join her sister, Claire Clairmont, and Percy at Este.

[6] *William* The Shelleys' son, who was two at the time.

zucche[1] about to sell, the sight of which always makes me sick, and I dislike the canals at low water, because they are never cleaned, and the horrid smell makes my head ache, and so now, I daresay, you will think me reasonable enough in all my dislikes—

Well; tomorrow, God permitting, we set out for Naples—but having been forced to delay our journey so long, we must give up the hope of seeing you until next June, when we think of coming north again.…

Yours affectionately and
Sincerely,
M.W.S.

TO MARIA GISBORNE

Naples
c. 3 Dec. 1818

My Dear Mrs. Gisborne

I hasten to answer your kind letter as soon as we are a little recovered from the fatigue of our long journey, although I still feel wearied and overcome by it—so you must expect a very stupid letter. We set out from Este the day after I wrote to you—we remained one day at Ferrara & two at Bologna looking at the memorials preserved of Tasso and Ariosto[2] in the former town and at the most exquisite pictures in the latter. Afterwards we proceeded along the Coast Road by Rimini, Fano, Fossombrone, &c—We saw the divine (aqueduct) waterfall of Terni[3]—And arrived safely at Rome. We performed this journey with our own horses, with Paolo[4] to drive us, which we found a very economical & a very disagreeable way so we shall not attempt it again—To you who have seen Rome I need not say how enchanted we were with the first view of Rome and its antiquities—one drawback they have at present, which I hope will be fully compensated for in the future—The ruins are filled with galley slaves at work—They are propping the Coliseum & making very deep excavations in the Forum.[5] We remained a week at Rome and our fears for the journey to Naples were entirely removed; they said there that there had not been a robbery on the road for 8 months—This we found afterwards to be an exaggeration, but it tranquillized us so much that Shelley went on first to secure us lodgings and we followed a day or two after—We found the road guarded, and the only part of the road where there was any talk of fear was between Terracina and Fondi, where it was not thought advisable that we should set out from the former place before daylight—Shelley travelled with a Lombard merchant & a Neapolitan priest—he remained only two nights on the road—and he went veterino,[6] so you may guess he had to travel early & late—The priest, a great strong muscular fellow, was almost in convulsions with fear to travel before daylight along the Pomptine Marshes—There was talk of two bishops murdered & that touched him nearly—The robbers spare foreigners but never Neapolitan men if they are young & strong, so he was the worst off of the party—the merchant did not feel very comfortable & they were both surprised at Shelley's quietness—That quiet was disturbed however between Capua & Naples by an assassination committed in broad daylight before their eyes—a young man ran out of a shop on the road followed by a woman armed with a great stick & a man with a great knife—the man overtook him & stabbed him in the nape of the neck so that he fell down instantly stone dead—The fearful priest laughed heartily at Shelley's horror on the occasion— …

Use our little purse in paying for our letters & parcels—William is very well—S. & Claire send their kindest remembrances—Excuse this stupid scrawl.

Ever yours affectionately,
Mary W. Shelley

[1] *zucche* Gourds.

[2] *Tasso* Italian poet Torquato Tasso (1544–95); *Ariosto* Ludovico Ariosto, poet; author of *Orlando Furioso* (1474–1533).

[3] *aqueduct … Terni* The Marmore Falls, located approximately four miles outside of Terni, is an artificial waterfall, constructed in 290 BCE by the Romans, who dug a canal from the stagnant Velino River to the Marmore cliff. From the cliff the water falls 540 feet into the bed of the river Nera.

[4] *Paolo* Paolo Foggi, the Shelleys' Italian servant.

[5] *Coliseum* Great amphitheater completed in 80 CE and used for gladiatorial combat; *Forum* Public square and marketplace of ancient Rome.

[6] *veterino* Owner of a coach who could be contracted to drive passengers a certain distance and also to provide food and accommodation.

To Maria Gisborne

Rome

9 April 1819

My Dear Mrs. Gisborne,

You will have received Shelley's letter inviting you to Naples—but you will not come—I wish you would; but how many things do I wish as uselessly as I do this. We shall stay all the summer and perhaps the autumn somewhere on the shores of the bay—I am with child—and an eminent English surgeon will be there—that is one reason for going, for we have no faith in the Italians.

We are delighted with Rome, and nothing but the malaria would drive us from it for many months—It is very busy now with the funzioni[1] of the holy week, and the arrival of the Emperor of Austria,[2] who goes about to see these things preceded by an officer, who rudely pushes the people back with a drawn sword, a curious thing that a fellow, whose power only subsists through the supposed conveniences of the state of the complaisance of his subjects, should be thus insolent—Of course, we keep out of his track; for our English blood, would, I am afraid, boil over at such insolence.

The place is full of English, rich, noble—important and foolish. I am sick of it—I am sick of seeing the world in dumb show, and but that I am in Rome, in the city where stocks and stones defeat a million of times over my father's quoted maxim, "that a man is better than a stock or a stone,"[3] who could see the Apollo, and a dandy spying at it, and not be of my opinion—Our little Will is delighted with the goats and the horses and the men rotti, and the ladies' white marble feet.

We saw the illuminated cross in St Peter's last night, which is very beautiful; but how much more beautiful is the Pantheon by moonlight![4] As superior, in my opinion, as is the ancient temple to the modern church! I don't think much of S. Peter's after all—I cannot—it is so cut up—it is large—and not simple....

Affectionately yours,

MWS

[1] *funzioni* Italian: functions.

[2] *Emperor of Austria* Francis I, Emperor of Austria from 1804 to 1835, and Holy Roman Emperor (as Francis II) from 1792 to 1806.

[3] *a stock or a stone* Here, sacred images, such as statues of gods (like the Apollo).

[4] *St. Peter's* St. Peter's Basilica, in the Vatican; *Pantheon* Circular temple in Rome, constructed in 27 BCE in dedication to all the gods.

To Marianne Hunt[5]

Leghorn

29 June 1819

My dear Marianne

Although we have not heard from you or of you for some time I hope you are going on well—that you enjoy [y]our health and see your children lively about you—

You see by our hap[6] how blind we mortals are when we go seeking after what we think our good—We came to Italy thinking to do Shelley's health good—but the climate is not any means warm enough to be of benefit to him & yet it is that that has destroyed my two children[7]—We went from England comparatively prosperous & happy—I should return broken hearted & miserable—I never know one moment's ease from the wretchedness & despair that possesses me—May you my dear Marianne never know what it is to lose two only & lovely children in one year—to watch their dying moments—& then at last to be left childless & for ever miserable.

It is useless complaining & I shall therefore only write a short letter, for as all my thoughts are nothing but misery it is not kind to transmit them to you—Since Shelley wrote to Hunt we have taken a house in the neighbourhood of Leghorn; be so kind as to inform Peacock[8] of this—and that he must direct to us Ferma in Posta, Livorno, & to let us know whether he has sent any letter to Florence—I am very anxious to know whether or not I am to receive the clothes[9] I wrote to you about—for if we do not I must provide others and

[5] *Marianne Hunt* Wife of Leigh Hunt, poet, essayist, and co-owner of the weekly newspaper the *Examiner*. He had been a close friend of Percy Shelley for several years.

[6] *hap* Luck; chance.

[7] *my two children* Clara Everina Shelley, born in September 1817, died in Venice in September 1818. William Shelley, born in January 1816, died in Rome on 7 June 1819.

[8] *Peacock* Percy Shelley's friend Thomas Love Peacock.

[9] *clothes* For the baby Mary Shelley was expecting in November.

although that will be a great expense & trouble yet it would be better for me to know as soon as possible if anyone can or will send them— …

I am sorry to write to you all about these petty affairs, yet if I would write anything else about myself it would be a list of hours spent in tears and grief—Hunt used to call me serious what would he say to me now?—I feel that I am not fit for anything & therefore not fit to live, but how must that heart be moulded which would not be broken by what I have suffered—William was so good so beautiful so entirely attached to me—To the last moment almost he was in such abounding health & spirits—and his malady appeared of so slight a nature—and as arising simply from worms inspired no fear of danger that the blow was as sudden as it was terrible—Did you ever know a child with a fine colour—wonderful spirits—breeding worms (and those of the most innocent kind) that would kill him in a fortnight—we had a most excellent English surgeon to attend him and he allowed that these were the fruits of this hateful Italy—

But all this is all nothing to anyone but myself & I wish that I were incapable of feeling that or any other sorrow—Give my love to Hunt keep yourselves well and happy.

Yours—MW Shelley

To Maria Gisborne

Casa Magni, presso a Lerici

2 June 1822

My Dear Mrs. Gisborne

We received a letter from Mr. G.[1] the other day, which promised one from you—It is not yet come, and although I think that you are two or three in my debt, yet I am good enough to write to you again, and thus to increase your debit—nor will I allow you, with one letter, to take advantage of the Insolvent act,[2] and thus to free yourself from all claims at once. …

About a month ago Claire came to visit us at Pisa, and went, with the Williamses,[3] to find a house in the Gulf of Spezia; when, during her absence, the disastrous news came of the death of Allegra[4]—She died of a typhus fever, which had been raging in the Romagna;[5] but no one wrote to say it was there—she had no friends, except the nuns of the convent, who were kind to her, I believe, but you know Italians—If half of the convent had died of the plague, they would never have written to have had her removed, and so the poor child fell a sacrifice. Lord B—felt the loss, at first, bitterly—he also felt remorse, for he felt that he had acted against everybody's councils and wishes, and death had stamped with truth the many and often urged prophecies of Claire, that the air of the Romagna, joined to the ignorance of the Italians, would prove fatal to her. Shelley wished to conceal the fatal news from her, as long as possible, so when she returned from Spezia, he resolved to remove thither without delay—with so little delay, that he packed me off with Claire and Percy the very next day. She wished to return to Florence, but he persuaded her to accompany me—The next day, he packed up all our goods and chattels (for a furnished house was not to be found in this part of the world), and like a torrent, hurrying everything in it's course, he persuaded the W's to do the same. They came here—but one house was to be found for us all—It is beautifully situated on the seashore, under a woody hill. But such a place as this is! The poverty of the people is beyond anything—Yet, they do not appear unhappy, but go on in dirty content, or contented dirt, while we find it hard work to purvey, miles around for a few eatables—We were in wretched discomfort at first, but now we are in a kind of disorderly order, living from day to day as we can—After the first day or two, Claire insisted on returning to Florence—so S. was obliged to disclose the truth—You may judge of what was her first burst of grief, and despair—however she reconciled herself to her fate, sooner than we expected; and although, of course, until she forms new ties, she will always grieve, yet she is now tranquil—more tranquil than, when prophesying her disaster, she was forever forming plans for getting her child from a place she judged, but too truly, would be fatal to her. She has now

[1] *Mr. G.* I.e., Mr. Gisborne.

[2] *Insolvent act* I.e., for bankrupts.

[3] *the Williamses* Edward and Jane Williams, both of whom had been close friends of the Shelleys for many years.

[4] *Allegra* Daughter of Claire and Lord Byron, born in January 1817.

[5] *the Romagna* Region in north-central Italy.

returned to Florence, and I do not know whether she will join us again....

I have not even heard of the arrival of my novel;[1] but I suppose, for his own sake, Papa will dispose of it to the best advantage—If you see it advertised, pray tell me—also its publisher, &c &c. We have heard from Hunt the day he was to sail, and anxiously and daily now await his arrival—S—will go over to Leghorn to him, and I also, if I can so manage it—We shall be at Pisa next winter, I believe—fate so decrees—Of course you have heard that the lawsuit went against my father. This was the summit and crown of our spring misfortunes—but he writes in so few words, and in such a manner, that any information that I could get, through anyone, would be a great benefit to me.

Adieu—Pray write now, and at length—remember both S. and I to Hogg—Did you get *Matilda*[2] from Papa?

Yours ever,

Mary W. Shelley

To Maria Gisborne

Pisa
15 August 1822

I said in a letter to Peacock, my dear Mrs. Gisborne, that I would send you some account of the last miserable months of my disastrous life. From day to day I have put this off, but I will now endeavour to fulfill my design. The scene of my existence is closed, & though there be no pleasure in retracing the scenes that have preceded the event which has crushed my hopes, yet there seems to be a necessity in doing so, and I obey the impulse that urges me. I wrote to you either at the end of May or the beginning of June. I described to you the place we were living in—Our desolate house, the beauty yet strangeness of the scenery and the delight Shelley took in all this—he never was in better health or spirits than during this time. I was not well in body or mind. My nerves were wound up to the utmost irritation, and the sense of misfortune hung over my spirits. No words can tell you how I hated our house & the country about it. Shelley reproached me for this—his health was good & the place was quite after his own heart—What could I answer—that the people were wild & hateful, that though the country was beautiful yet I liked a more countrified place, that there was great difficulty in living—that all our Tuscans would leave us, & that the very jargon of these Genovese was disgusting—This was all I had to say but no words could describe my feelings—the beauty of the woods made me weep & shudder—so vehement was my feeling of dislike that I used to rejoice when the winds & waves permitted me to go out in the boat so that I was not obliged to take my usual walk among tree shaded paths, alleys of vine festooned trees—all that before I doted on—& that now weighed on me. My only moments of peace were on board that unhappy boat, when lying down with my head on his knee I shut my eyes & felt the wind & our swift motion alone. My ill health might account for much of this—bathing in the sea somewhat relieved me—but on the 8th of June (I think it was) I was threatened with a miscarriage, & after a week of great ill health on Sunday the 16th this took place at eight in the morning. I was so ill that for seven hours I lay nearly lifeless—kept from fainting by brandy, vinegar, eau de cologne, &c—at length ice was brought to our solitude—it came before the doctor so Claire & Jane[3] were afraid of using it but Shelley overruled them & by an unsparing application of it I was restored. They all thought & so did I at one time that I was about to die—I hardly wish that I had, my own Shelley could never have lived without me, the sense of eternal misfortune would have pressed to heavily upon him, & what would have become of my poor babe? My convalescence was slow and during it a strange occurence happened to retard it.... As I said Shelley was at first in perfect health, but having over-fatigued himself one day, & then the fright my illness gave him caused a return of nervous sensations & visions as bad as in his worst times. I think it was the Saturday after my illness, while yet unable to walk I was confined to my bed—in the middle of the night I was awoke by hearing him scream & come rushing into my room; I was sure that he was

[1] *my novel* Shelley's novel *Valperga*, which William Godwin was publishing for his daughter. He withheld the book from publishers until February 1823, fearing that news of his financial problems (the result of a legal decision against him) would cause booksellers to offer less than its real value.

[2] *Matilda* I.e., *Mathilda*, novella by Shelley.

[3] *Jane* Jane Williams.

asleep & tried to waken him by calling on him, but he continued to scream which inspired me with such a panic that I jumped out of bed & ran across the hall to Mrs. W.'s room, where I fell through weakness, though I was so frightened that I got up again immediately—she let me in & Williams went to S. who had been wakened by my getting out of bed—he said that he had not been asleep & that it was a vision that he saw that had frightened him—But as he declared that he had not screamed it was certainly a dream & no waking vision—What had frightened him was this—He dreamt that lying as he did in bed Edward & Jane came into him, they were in the most horrible condition, their bodies lacerated—their bones starting through their skin, the faces pale yet stained with blood, they could hardly walk, but Edward was the weakest & Jane was supporting him—Edward said—"Get up, Shelley, the sea is flooding the house & it is all coming down." S. got up, he thought, & went to his window that looked on the terrace & the sea & thought he saw the sea rushing in. Suddenly his vision changed & he saw the figure of himself strangling me, that had made him rush into my room, yet fearful of frightening me he dared not approach the bed, when my jumping out awoke him, or as he phrased it, caused his vision to vanish....

Well, we thought no more of these things & I slowly got better. Having heard from Hunt that he had sailed from Genoa, on Monday July 1st, S., Edward, & Captain Roberts (the gent. who built our boat) departed in our boat for Leghorn to receive him—I was then just better, had begun to crawl from my bedroom to the terrace; but bad spirits succeeded to ill health, and this departure of Shelley's seemed to add insufferably to my misery. I could not endure that he should go—I called him back two or three times, & told him that if I did not see him soon I would go to Pisa with the child—I cried bitterly when he went away. They went, & Jane, Claire, & I remained alone with the children—I could not walk out, & though I gradually gathered strength it was slowly & my ill spirits increased; in my letters to him I entreated him to return—"the feeling that some misfortune would happen," I said, "haunted me": I feared for the child, for the idea of danger connected with him never struck me—When Jane & Claire took their evening walk I used to patrol the terrace, oppressed with wretchedness, yet gazing on the most beautiful scene in the world. This Gulf of Spezia is subdivided into many small bays of which ours was far the most beautiful—the two horns of the bay (so to express myself) were wood-covered promontories crowned with castles—at the foot of these on the furthest was Lerici, on the nearest San Arenzo—Lerici being above a mile by land from us & San Arenzo about a hundred or two yards—trees covered the hills that enclosed this bay, & then beautiful groups were picturesquely contrasted with the rocks, the castle, and the town—the sea lay far extended in front while to the west we saw the promontory & islands which formed one of the extreme boundaries of the gulf—to see the sun set upon this scene, the stars shine & the moon rise was a sight of wondrous beauty, but to me it added only to my wretchedness—I repeated to myself all that another would have said to console me, & told myself the tale of love peace & competence which I enjoyed—but I answered myself by tears—did not my William die? & did I hold my Percy by a firmer tenure?—Yet I thought when he, when my Shelley returns I shall be happy—he will comfort me, if my boy be ill he will restore him & encourage me. I had a letter or two from Shelley mentioning the difficulties he had in establishing the Hunts, & that he was unable to fix the time of his return. Thus a week past. On Monday 8th Jane had a letter from Edward, dated Saturday; he said that he waited at Leghorn for S. who was at Pisa. That S.'s return was certain, "but" he continued, "if he should not come by Monday I will come in a felucca,[1] & you may expect me Tuesday evening at furthest." This was Monday, the fatal Monday, but with us it was stormy all day, & we did not at all suppose that they could put to sea. At twelve at night we had a thunderstorm; Tuesday it rained all day & was calm—the sky wept on their graves—on Wednesday the wind was fair from Leghorn & in the evening several feluccas arrived thence—one brought word that they had sailed Monday, but we did not believe them—Thursday was another day of fair wind & when twelve at night came & we did not see the tall sails of the little boat double the promontory before us we began to fear not the truth, but some illness—some disagreeable news for their detention. Jane got so uneasy that she determined to proceed the next day to Leghorn in a boat to see what was the matter—Friday came &

[1] *felucca* Small Mediterranean vessel propelled by oars or sails.

with it a heavy sea & bad wind—Jane however resolved to be rowed to Leghorn (since no boat could sail) and busied herself in preparations—I wished her to wait for letters, since Friday was letter day—she would not—but the sea detained her, the swell rose so that no boat would venture out—At 12 at noon our letters came—there was one from Hunt to Shelley, it said—"pray write to tell us how you got home, for they say that you had bad weather after you sailed Monday & we are anxious"—the paper fell from me—I trembled all over—Jane read it—"Then it is all over!" she said. "No, my dear Jane," I cried, "it is not all over, but this suspense is dreadful—come with me, we will go to Leghorn, we will post to be swift & learn our fate." We crossed to Lerici, despair in our hearts; they raised our spirits there by telling us that no accident had been heard of & that it must have been known &c—but still our fear was great—& without resting we posted to Pisa. It must have been fearful to see us—two poor, wild, aghast creatures—driving (like Matilda[1]) towards the sea to learn if we were to be for ever doomed to misery. I knew that Hunt was at Pisa at Lord Byron's house but I thought that L.B. was at Leghorn.... L.B. was in Pisa—Hunt was in bed, so I was to see L.B. instead of him—This was a great relief to me; I staggered upstairs—the Guiccioli[2] came to meet me smiling while I could hardly say—"Where is he—Sapete alcuna cosa di Shelley?"—They knew nothing—he had left Pisa on Sunday—on Monday he had sailed—there had been bad weather Monday afternoon—more they knew not. Both L.B. & the lady have told me since—that on that terrific evening I looked more like a ghost than a woman—light seemed to emanate from my features, my face was very white. I looked like marble—Alas. I had risen almost from a bed of sickness for this journey—I had travelled all day—it was now 12 at night—& we, refusing to rest, proceeded to Leghorn—not in despair—no, for then we must have died; but with sufficient hope to keep up the agitation of the spirits which was all my life. It was past two in the morning when we arrived—They took us to the wrong inn—neither Trelawny[3] or Capn. Roberts were there nor did we exactly know where they were so we were obliged to wait until daylight. We threw ourselves dressed on our beds & slept a little but at 6 o'clock we went to one or two inns to ask for one or the other of these gentlemen. We found Roberts at the Globe. He came down to us with a face which seemed to tell us that the worst was true, and here we learned all that had occurred during the week they had been absent from us, & under what circumstances they had departed on their return—Shelley had passed most of the time at Pisa—arranging the affairs of the Hunts—& screwing L.B.'s mind to the sticking place about the journal.[4] He had found this a difficult task at first but at length he had succeeded to his heart's content with both points. Mrs. Mason said that she saw him in better health and spirits than she had ever known him, when he took leave of her Sunday July 7th. His face burnt by the sun, & his heart light that he had succeeded in rendering the Hunts tolerably comfortable. Edward had remained at Leghorn. On Monday July 8th during the morning they were employed in buying many things—eatables &c for our solitude. There had been a thunderstorm early but about noon the weather was fine & the wind right fair for Lerici—They were impatient to be gone. Roberts said, "Stay until tomorrow to see if the weather is settled; & S. might have stayed but Edward was in so great an anxiety to reach home—saying they would get there in seven hours with that wind—that they sailed! S. being in one of those extravagant fits of good spirits in which you have sometimes seen him. Roberts went out to the end of the mole[5] & watched them out of sight—they sailed at one & went off at the rate of about 7 knots—About three—Roberts, who was still on the mole—saw wind coming from the gulf—or rather what the Italians call a temporale—anxious to know how the boat would weather the storm, he got leave to go up the tower & with the glass discovered them about ten miles out at sea, off Via Reggio, they were taking in their topsails—"The haze of the storm," he said, "hid them

[1] *Matilda* I.e., Mathilda, the protagonist of Mary Shelley's novella of that name; in an attempt to prevent her father's suicide, she follows his rush "towards the sea."

[2] *the Guiccioli* Count Alessandro Guiccioli and Countess Teresa Guiccioli, who was Byron's lover.

[3] *Trelawny* Edward Trelawny, friend of the Shelleys and a former navy midshipman who lived in Pisa.

[4] *the journal* Percy Shelley and Byron had agreed to start a liberal periodical, which would be owned by Shelley and Hunt, and to which Byron, Hunt, and Shelley would contribute.

[5] *mole* Pier.

from me & I saw them no more—when the storm cleared I looked again fancying that I should see them on their return to us—but there was no boat on the sea."—This then was all we knew, yet we did not despair—they might have been driven over to Corsica & not knowing the coast & gone god knows where. Reports favoured this belief—it was even said that they had been seen in the gulf—We resolved to return with all possible speed—We sent a courier to go from tower to tower along the coast to know if anything had been seen or found, & at 9 a.m. we quitted Leghorn—stopped but one moment at Pisa & proceeded towards Lerici. When at 2 miles from Via Reggio we rode down to that town to know if they knew anything—here our calamity first began to break on us—a little boat[1] & a water cask had been found five miles off— … We journeyed on and reached the Magra about ½ past ten p.m. I cannot describe to you what I felt in the first moment when, fording this river, I felt the water splash about our wheels—I was suffocated—I gasped for breath—I thought I should have gone into convulsions, & I struggled violently that Jane might not perceive it—looking down the river I saw two great lights burning at the *foce*—A voice from within me seemed to cry aloud that is his grace. After passing the river I gradually recovered. Arriving at Lerici we were obligated to cross our little bay in a boat—… we landed; nothing had been heard of them. This was Saturday July 13. & thus we waited until Thursday July 25th thrown about by hope & fear. We sent messengers along the coast towards Genoa & to Via Reggio— nothing had been found more than the *lancetta*; reports were brought us—we hoped—& yet to tell you all the agony we endured during those 12 days would be to make you conceive a universe of pain—each moment intolerable & giving place to one still worse.… On Thursday 25th Trelawny left us to go to Leghorn to see what was doing or what could be done. On Friday I was very ill but as evening came on I said to Jane—"If anything had been found on the coast Trelawny would have returned to let us know. He has not returned so I hope." About 7 o'clock p.m. he did return—all was over—all was quiet now, they had been found washed on shore—Well all this was to be endured.

Well what more have I to say? The next day we returned to Pisa. And here we are still—days pass away—one after another—& we live thus. We are all together—we shall quit Italy together. Jane must proceed to London—if letters do not alter my views I shall remain in Paris. Thus we live—Seeing the Hunts now & then. Poor Hunt has suffered terribly as you may guess. Lord Byron is very kind to me & comes with the Guiccioli to see me often.

Today—this day—the sun shining in the sky—they are gone to the desolate sea coast to perform the last offices to their earthly remains. Hunt, L.B. & Trelawny. The quarantine laws would not permit us to remove them sooner—& now only on condition that we burn them to ashes. That I do not dislike—His rest shall be at Rome beside my child—where one day I also shall join them—"Adonais"[2] is not Keats's, it is his own elegy—he bids you there go to Rome. I have seen the spot where he now lies—the sticks that mark the spot where the sands cover him—he shall not be there it is too near Via Reggio—They are now about this fearful office—& I live! …

Well here is my story—the last story I shall have to tell—all that might have been bright in my life is now despoiled—I shall live to improve myself, to take care of my child, & render myself worthy to join him. Soon my weary pilgrimage will begin—I rest now—but soon I must leave Italy—& then—there is an end of all despair. Adieu I hope you are well & happy. I have an idea that while he was at Pisa that he received a letter from you that I have never seen—so not knowing where to direct I shall send this letter to Peacock—I shall send it open—he may be glad to read it—

Yours ever truly, Mary WS.—Pisa

I shall probably write to you soon again.

I have left out a material circumstance—A fishing boat saw them go down—It was about 4 in the afternoon—they saw the boy at mast head, when baffling winds struck the sails, they had looked away a moment & looking again the boat was gone—This is their story but there is little doubt that these men might have saved them, at least Edward who could swim. They

[1] *a little boat* The small vessel (the "lancetta") of thin planks which had been constructed to allow the Shelleys to get from their boat (which drew four feet of water) to shore.

[2] *Adonais* Percy Shelley's "Adonais: An Elegy on the Death of John Keats" (1821).

could not they said get near her—but 3 quarters of an hour after passed over the spot where they had seen her—they protested no wreck of her was visible, but Roberts going on board their boat found several spars belonging to her—perhaps they let them perish to obtain these. Trelawny thinks he can get her up, since another fisherman thinks that he has found the spot where she lies, having drifted near shore. T. does this to know perhaps the cause of her wreck—but I care little about it.

Letitia Elizabeth Landon

1802–1838

When Letitia Elizabeth Landon began publishing poetry she did so under her initials, L.E.L., and these "three magic letters" (as one admirer referred to them) soon attracted a reputation and a following all their own. Her melancholy verses described dark and passionate young heroines, usually forsaken by the ones they loved, and earned L.E.L. the epithet "the Byron of our poetesses"; like Byron she chose love and sorrow as her topics, and intimately detailed her characters' emotions. But the passivity and the distinctively feminine insights of her heroines as they observe the society around them—"cold spectators of a cold spectacle repeatedly masked in the warm colors of dissimulating love" (as Jerome McGann has memorably put it), sets Landon's work apart from that of Byron or of any other poet of the time.

Readers constructed a romantic image of L.E.L. as a delicate, love-sick woman, but behind this highly idealized conception was an intelligent literary mind and a hard-working woman who knew how to please her audience. Landon was a great success as a professional writer; her work supported her family and enabled her brother to attend Oxford.

Letitia Elizabeth Landon was the daughter of John Landon and Catherine Bishop. Landon had little formal schooling, but her education was closely supervised by her older cousin, Elizabeth Landon. From an early age she began composing stories and verses that were highly influenced by the popular work of Sir Walter Scott. When the Landons moved from East Barnet to Old Brompton in 1815, one of their new neighbors was William Jerdan, editor of the new weekly journal *The Literary Gazette*. Jerdan, impressed with Landon's poetry, provided her with helpful advice and criticism and eventually published her poem "Rome" in the March 1818 issue of his journal. In the following months Landon (then only 18) published increasing amounts of verse in the *Gazette*, and in 1821 she released her first volume of poetry, *The Fate of Adelaide: A Swiss Tale of Romance*.

Amidst a favorable critical reception and increasing public attention, Landon followed her first verse collection with five others—*The Improvisatrice* (1824), *The Troubadour* (1825), *The Golden Violet* (1827), *The Venetian Bracelet* (1828), and *The Vow of the Peacock* (1835)—in each case signing herself L.E.L. Soon the editors of nearly every gift book and annual anthology (two increasingly popular literary forms) sought L.E.L. as a regular contributor. Landon produced an almost unprecedented amount of poetry during these years. She was able to compose her poems quickly and she rarely revised or edited; her writing, as a result, has a distinctive style in which punctuation and grammar vary widely, and verses often ramble without extensive narrative structure through moods and moments of passion. But her eloquent plainness of diction and lyrical intensity convey a sense of emotions pouring unbidden and unobstructed onto the page, and this unique style was soon the height of fashion.

In addition to the poetry of L.E.L., Landon published under her own name a children's book called *Traits and Trials of Early Life* (1836) and three novels, *Romance and Reality* (1831), *Francesca Carrara* (1834), and *Ethel Churchill* (1837); the latter in particular established her as a gifted writer of romantic fiction. Writing anonymously, Landon also tackled other literary genres, including essays on the history of poetry and critical reviews. In fact, from the age of twenty Landon had been the primary reviewer for *The Literary Gazette*, thus wielding an enormous amount of influence.

Landon was skilled at adapting her style to suit the demands of these various forms, but the place of a female writer in nineteenth-century London society was a precarious one, and much of the appeal of L.E.L.'s verses lay in the perceived authenticity of the dark and passionate emotions they expressed. As Landon became known, her gaiety and wit shocked and disillusioned former admirers of L.E.L. Public opinion gradually turned against Landon, and her detailed poetic examinations of female passion came to be seen as more indecorous than romantic. The literary community was further disconcerted when Landon was discovered to be Jerdan's reviewer; several male authors whose work she had criticized were particularly outraged.

Malicious gossip began to circulate concerning the nature of Landon's association with Jerdan and with several other young men, and her engagement to John Forster, editor of the *Daily News* and future biographer of Dickens, was broken off as a result. Though Landon had unconventional habits that fueled the gossip—including calling male friends by their first names and receiving them alone in private—she maintained, as she wrote to a friend, that the root of these allegations was "envy, malice, and all uncharitableness—these are the fruits of a successful literary career for a woman." No doubt there was some envy and uncharitableness—but recent scholarship has also established that there was some truth to the rumors. Landon, it turns out, had three illegitimate children by William Jerdan.

Landon was eventually married in 1838 to George Maclean, governor of the British settlement at Cape Coast Castle, West Africa. She sailed to Africa with him that July, planning to continue her writing career away from the merciless public scrutiny she had been subject to. Landon arrived in Africa in August and died in October of an overdose of prussic acid. Such a sudden death, strange in any circumstances, was doubly mysterious when coupled with the already sensational rumors surrounding Landon's life. Suicide and murder have both been suggested, but the truth has never been uncovered. The coroner's report stated the cause of death as accidental overdose.

⌘⌘⌘

Lines Written Under a Picture of a Girl Burning a Love Letter

The lines were filled with many a tender thing,
All the impassioned heart's fond communing.

I took the scroll: I could not brook
An eye to gaze on it, save mine;
I could not bear another's look
Should dwell upon one thought of thine.
My lamp was burning by my side,
I held thy letter to the flame,
I marked the blaze swift o'er it glide,
It did not even spare thy name.
Soon the light from the embers past,
I felt so sad to see it die,
So bright at first, so dark at last,
I feared it was love's history.

—1824

A Child Screening a Dove From a Hawk

By Stewardson[1]

Ay, screen thy favourite dove, fair child,
Ay, screen it if you may,—
Yet I misdoubt° thy trembling hand *doubt*
Will scare the hawk away.

That dove will die, that child will weep—
Is this their destiny?

[1] *By Stewardson* This poem was written in response to a painting by British artist Thomas Stewardson (1781–1859).

Ever amid the sweets of life
Some evil thing must be.

Ay, moralize—is it not thus
We've mourned our hope and love?
Alas! there's tears for every eye,
A hawk for every dove!
—1825

Love's Last Lesson

"Teach it me, if you can,—forgetfulness![1]
I surely shall forget, if you can bid me;
I who have worshipped thee, my god on earth,
I who have bowed me at thy lightest word.
Your last command, 'Forget me,' will it not
Sink deeply down within my inmost soul?
Forget thee!—ay, forgetfulness will be
A mercy to me. By the many nights
When I have wept for that I dared not sleep,
A dream had made me live my woes again,
Acting my wretchedness, without the hope
My foolish heart still clings to, though that hope
Is like the opiate which may lull a while,
Then wake to double torture; by the days
Passed in lone watching and in anxious fears,
When a breath sent the crimson to my cheek,
Like the red gushing of a sudden wound;
By all the careless looks and careless words
Which have to me been like the scorpion's stinging;
By happiness blighted, and by thee, forever;
By thy eternal work of wretchedness;
By all my withered feelings, ruined health,
Crushed hopes, and rifled heart, I will forget thee!
Alas! my words are vanity. Forget thee!
Thy work of wasting is too surely done.
The April shower may pass and be forgotten,
The rose fall and one fresh spring in its place,
And thus it may be with light summer love.
It was not thus with mine: it did not spring,
Like the bright colour on an evening cloud,
Into a moment's life, brief, beautiful;
Not amid lighted halls, when flatteries
Steal on the ear like dew upon the rose,
As soft, as soon dispersed, as quickly passed;
But you first called my woman's feelings forth,
And taught me love ere I had dreamed love's name.
I loved unconsciously; your name was all
That seemed in language, and to me the world
Was only made for you; in solitude,
When passions hold their interchange together,
Your image was the shadow of my thought;
Never did slave, before his Eastern lord,
Tremble as I did when I met your eye,
And yet each look was counted as a prize;
I laid your words up in my heart like pearls
Hid in the ocean's treasure-cave. At last
I learned my heart's deep secret: for I hoped,
I dreamed you loved me; wonder, fear, delight
Swept my heart like a storm; my soul, my life,
Seemed all too little for your happiness;
Had I been mistress of the starry worlds
That light the midnight, they had all been yours,
And I had deemed such boon but poverty.
As it was, I gave all I could—my love,
My deep, my true, my fervent, faithful love;
And now you bid me learn forgetfulness:
It is a lesson that I soon shall learn.
There is a home of quiet for the wretched,
A somewhat dark, and cold, and silent rest,
But still it is rest, for it is the grave."

She flung aside the scroll, as it had part
In her great misery. Why should she write?
What could she write? Her woman's pride forbade
To let him look upon her heart and see
It was an utter ruin; and cold words,
And scorn and slight, that may repay his own,
Were as a foreign language, to whose sound
She might not frame her utterance. Down she bent
Her head upon an arm so white that tears
Seemed but the natural melting of its snow,
Touched by the flushed cheek's crimson; yet life-blood
Less wrings in shedding than such tears as those.

And this then is love's ending! It is like
The history of some fair southern clime.

[1] *Teach … forgetfulness* One of the many echoes in this poem of Byron's *Manfred*. Cf. 1.1.135–36, in which Manfred is asked, "What wouldst thou with us, son of mortals, say?" to which he replies, "Forgetfulness."

Hot fires are in the bosom of the earth,
And the warmed soil puts forth its thousand flowers,
Its fruits of gold, summer's regality,
And sleep and odours float upon the air.
At length the subterranean element
Breaks from its secret dwelling-place, and lays
All waste before it; the red lava stream
Sweeps like the pestilence, and that which was
A garden in its colours and its breath,
Fit for the princess of a fairy tale,
Is as a desert in whose burning sands,
And ashy waters, who is there can trace
A sign, a memory of its former beauty?
It is thus with the heart; love lights it up
With hopes like young companions, and with joys
Dreaming deliciously of their sweet selves.

This is at first, but what is the result?
Hopes that lie mute in their own sullenness,
For they have quarrelled even with themselves;
And joys indeed like birds of Paradise:[1]
And in their stead despair coils scorpion-like,
Stinging itself; and the heart, burnt and crushed
With passion's earthquake, scorched and withered up,
Lies in its desolation,—this is love.

What is the tale that I would tell? Not one
Of strange adventure, but a common tale
Of woman's wretchedness; one to be read
Daily in many a young and blighted heart.
The lady whom I spake of rose again
From the red fever's couch, to careless eyes
Perchance the same as she had ever been.
But oh, how altered to herself! She felt
That bird-like pining for some gentle home
To which affection might attach itself,
That weariness which hath but outward part
In what the world calls pleasure, and that chill
Which makes life taste the bitterness of death.

And he she loved so well,—what opiate
Lulled consciousness into its selfish sleep?—
He said he loved her not; that never vow
Or passionate pleading won her soul for him;
And that he guessed not her deep tenderness.

Are words, then, only false? are there no looks,
Mute but most eloquent; no gentle cares
That win so much upon the fair weak things
They seem to guard? And had he not long read
Her heart's hushed secret in the soft dark eye
Lighted at his approach, and on the cheek
Colouring all crimson at his lightest look?
This is the truth; his spirit wholly turned
To stern ambition's dream, to that fierce strife
Which leads to life's high places, and reck'd not
What lovely flowers might perish in his path.

And here at length is somewhat of revenge:
For man's most golden dreams of pride and power
Are vain as any woman-dreams of love;
Both end in weary brow and withered heart,
And the grave closes over those whose hopes
Have lain there long before.
—1827

Lines of Life

Orphan in my first years, I early learnt
To make my heart suffice itself, and seek
Support and sympathy in its own depths.

Well read my cheek and watch my eye—
Too strictly schooled are they
One secret of my soul to show,
One hidden thought betray.

I never knew the time my heart
Looked freely from my brow;
It once was checked by timidness,
'Tis taught by caution now.

I live among the cold, the false,
And I must seem like them;
And such I am, for I am false
As those I most condemn.

[1] [Landon's note] In Eastern tales, the bird of Paradise never rests on the earth.

I teach my lip its sweetest smile,
My tongue its softest tone;
I borrow others' likeness, till
Almost I lose my own.

I pass through flattery's gilded sieve,
Whatever I would say;
In social life, all, like the blind,
Must learn to feel their way.

I check my thoughts like curbed steeds
That struggle with the rein;
I bid my feelings sleep, like wrecks
In the unfathomed main.

I hear them speak of love, the deep,
The true, and mock the name;
Mock at all high and early truth,
And I too do the same.

I hear them tell some touching tale,
I swallow down the tear;
I hear them name some generous deed,
And I have learnt to sneer.

I hear the spiritual, the kind,
The pure, but named in mirth;
Till all of good, ay, even hope,
Seems exiled from our earth.

And one fear, withering ridicule,
Is all that I can dread;
A sword hung by a single hair
Forever o'er the head.

We bow to a most servile faith
In a most servile fear,
While none among us dares to say
What none will choose to hear.

And if we dream of loftier thoughts,
In weakness they are gone;
And indolence and vanity
Rivet our fetters on.

Surely I was not born for this!
I feel a loftier mood
Of generous impulse, high resolve,
Steal o'er my solitude!

I gaze upon the thousand stars
That fill the midnight sky;
And wish, so passionately wish,
A light like theirs on high.

I have such eagerness of hope
To benefit my kind,
And feel as if immortal power
Were given to my mind.

I think on that eternal fame,
The sun of earthly gloom,
Which makes the gloriousness of death,
The future of the tomb—

That earthly future, the faint sign
Of a more heavenly one;
A step, a word, a voice, a look—
Alas! my dream is done.

And earth, and earth's debasing stain,
Again is on my soul;
And I am but a nameless part
Of a most worthless whole.

Why write I this? Because my heart
Towards the future springs,
That future where it loves to soar
On more than eagle wings.

The present, it is but a speck
In that eternal time,
In which my lost hopes find a home,
My spirit knows its clime.

Oh! not myself, for what am I?
The worthless and the weak,
Whose every thought of self should raise
A blush to burn my cheek.

But song has touched my lips with fire,
And made my heart a shrine;
For what, although alloyed,[1] debased
Is in itself divine.

I am myself but a vile link
Amid life's weary chain;
And I have spoken hallowed words,
O do not say in vain!

My first, my last, my only wish—
Say, will my charmed chords
Wake to the morning light of fame,
And breathe again my words?

Will the young maiden, when her tears
Alone in moonlight shine
(Tears for the absent and the loved),
Murmur some song of mine?

Will the pale youth by his dim lamp,
Himself a dying flame,
From many an antique scroll beside,
Choose that which bears my name?

Let music make less terrible
The silence of the dead;
I care not, so my spirit last
Long after life has fled.
—1828

Revenge

Ay, gaze upon her rose-wreathed hair,
And gaze upon her smile;
Seem as you drank the very air
Her breath perfumed the while;

And wake for her the gifted line,
That wild and witching lay,
And swear your heart is as a shrine,
That only holds her sway.

'Tis well: I am revenged at last,
Mark you that scornful cheek—
The eye averted as you passed
Spoke more than words could speak.

Ay, now by all the bitter tears
That I have shed for thee,
The racking doubts, the burning fears,
Avenged they well may be—

By the nights passed in sleepless care,
The days of endless woe;
All that you taught my heart to bear,
All that yourself will know.

I would not wish to see you laid
Within an early tomb;
I should forget how you betrayed,
And only weep your doom:

But this is fitting punishment,
To live and love in vain—
O my wrung heart, be thou content,
And feed upon his pain.

Go thou and watch her lightest sigh,
Thine own it will not be;
And bask beneath her sunny eye,
It will not turn on thee.

'Tis well: the rack, the chain, the wheel,
Far better had'st thou proved;
Even I could almost pity feel,
For thou art not beloved.
—1828

The Little Shroud

She put him on a snow-white shroud,
A chaplet° on his head; *garland*
And gathered early primroses
To scatter o'er the dead.

She laid him in his little grave—
'Twas hard to lay him there,

[1] *alloyed* Mixed with a baser metal.

When spring was putting forth its flowers,
And every thing was fair.

She had lost many children—now
The last of them was gone;
And day and night she sat and wept
Beside the funeral stone.

One midnight, while her constant tears
Were falling with the dew,
She heard a voice, and lo! her child
Stood by her, weeping too!

His shroud was damp, his face was white;
He said, "I cannot sleep,
Your tears have made my shroud so wet;
Oh, mother, do not weep!"

Oh, love is strong! the mother's heart
Was filled with tender fears;
Oh, love is strong! and for her child
Her grief restrained its tears.

One eve a light shone round her bed,
And there she saw him stand—
Her infant, in his little shroud,
A taper° in his hand. *candle*

"Lo! mother, see my shroud is dry,
And I can sleep once more!"
And beautiful the parting smile
The little infant wore.

And down within the silent grave
He laid his weary head;
And soon the early violets
Grew o'er his grassy bed.

—1832

Reading Poetry

WHAT IS A POEM?

Most of us know what a poem is when we see one. Still, even poets find it difficult to define a poem, or poetry. In a lecture on "The Name and Nature of Poetry" (1933), the English poet A.E. Housman stated that he could "no more define poetry than a terrier can define a rat"; however, he added, "we both recognize the object by the symptoms which it provokes in us." Housman knew he was in the presence of poetry if he experienced a shiver down the spine, or "a constriction of the throat and a precipitation of water to the eyes." Implicit in Housman's response is a recognition that we have to go beyond mere formal characteristics—stanzas, rhymes, rhythms—if we want to know what poetry is, or why it differs from prose. Poetry both represents and *creates* emotions in a highly condensed way. Therefore, any definition of the genre needs to consider, as much as possible, the impact of poetry on us as readers or listeners.

Worth consideration too is the role of the listener or reader not only as passive recipient of a poem, but also as an active participant in its performance. Poetry is among other things the locus for a communicative exchange. A section below deals with the sub-genre of performance poetry, but in a very real sense all poetry is subject to performance. Poems are to be read aloud as well as on the page, and both in sensing meaning and in expressing sound the reader plays a vital role in bringing a poem to life, no matter how long dead its author may be; as W.H. Auden wrote memorably of his fellow poet W.B. Yeats, "the words of a dead man / Are modified in the guts of the living."

For some readers, poetry is, in William Wordsworth's phrase, "the breath and finer spirit of all knowledge" ("Preface" to the *Lyrical Ballads*). They look to poetry for insights into the nature of human experience, and expect elevated thought in carefully-wrought language. In contrast, other readers distrust poetry that seems moralistic or didactic. "We hate poetry that has a palpable design upon us," wrote John Keats to his friend J.H. Reynolds; rather, poetry should be "great & unobtrusive, a thing which enters into one's soul, and does not startle it or amaze it with itself but with its subject." The American poet Archibald MacLeish took Keats's idea a step further: in his poem "Ars Poetica" he suggested that "A poem should not mean / But be." MacLeish was not suggesting that a poem should lack meaning, but rather that meaning should inhere in the poem's expressive and sensuous qualities, not in some explicit statement or versified idea.

Whatever we look for in a poem, the infinitude of forms, styles, and subjects that make up the body of literature we call "poetry" is, in the end, impossible to capture in a definition that would satisfy all readers. All we can do, perhaps, is to agree that a poem is a discourse that is characterized by a heightened attention to language, form, and rhythm, by an expressiveness that works through figurative rather than literal modes, and by a capacity to stimulate our imagination and arouse our feelings.

THE LANGUAGE OF POETRY

To speak of "the language of poetry" implies that poets make use of a vocabulary that is somehow different from the language of everyday life. In fact, all language has the capacity to be "poetic," if by poetry we understand a use of language to which some special importance is attached. The ritualistic utterances of religious ceremonies sometimes have this force; so do the skipping rhymes of children in the schoolyard. We can distinguish such uses of language from the kind of writing we find in, say, a computer user's manual: the author of the manual can describe a given function in a variety of ways, whereas the magic of the skipping rhyme can be invoked only by getting the right words in the right order. So with the poet: he or she chooses particular words in a particular order; the *way* the poet speaks is as important to our understanding as what is said. This doesn't mean that an instruction manual couldn't have poetic qualities—indeed, modern poets have created "found" poems from even less likely materials—but it does mean that in poetry there is an intimate relation amongst language, form, and meaning, and that the writer deliberately structures and manipulates language to achieve very particular ends.

THE BEST WORDS IN THE BEST ORDER

Wordsworth provides us with a useful example of the way that poetry can invest quite ordinary words with a high emotional charge:

> No motion has she now, no force,
> She neither hears nor sees;
> Rolled round in earth's diurnal course
> With rocks, and stones, and trees.

To paraphrase the content of this stanza from "A Slumber Did My Spirit Seal," "she" is dead and buried. But the language and structures used here give this prosaic idea great impact. For example, the regular iambic meter of the two last lines conveys something of the inexorable motion of the earth and of Lucy embedded in it; the monosyllabic last line is a grim reminder of her oneness with objects in nature; the repeated negatives in the first two lines drive home the irreparable destructiveness of death; the alliteration in the third and fourth lines gives a tangible suggestion of roundness, circularity, repetition in terms of the earth's shape and motion, suggesting a cycle in which death is perhaps followed by renewal. Even the unusual word "diurnal" (which would not have seemed so unusual to Wordsworth's readers) seems "right" in this context; it lends more weight to the notion of the earth's perpetual movement than its mundane synonym "daily" (which, besides, would not scan here). It is difficult to imagine a change of any kind to these lines; they exemplify another attempted definition of poetry, this time by Wordsworth's friend Samuel Taylor Coleridge: "the best words in the best order" (*Table Talk*, 1827).

POETIC DICTION AND THE ELEVATED STYLE

Wordsworth's diction in the "Lucy" poem cited above is a model of clarity; he has chosen language that, in its simplicity and bluntness, conveys the strength of the speaker's feelings far more strongly than an elaborate description of grief in more conventionally "poetic" language might have done. Wordsworth, disturbed by what he felt was a deadness and artificiality in the poetry of his day, sought to "choose incidents and situations from common life" and to describe them in "a selection of language really used by men" ("Preface" to *Lyrical Ballads*). His plan might seem an implicit reproach of the "raised" style, the elevated diction of epic poetry we associate with John Milton's *Paradise Lost*:

> Anon out of the earth a fabric huge
> Rose like an exhalation, with the sound
> Of dulcet symphonies and voices sweet,

Built like a temple, where pilasters round
Were set, and Doric pillars overlaid
With golden architrave; nor did there want
Cornice or frieze, with bossy sculptures graven;
The roof was fretted gold.

(*Paradise Lost* I.710–17)

At first glance this passage, with its Latinate vocabulary and convoluted syntax, might seem guilty of inflated language and pretentiousness. However, Milton's description of the devils' palace in Hell deliberately seeks to distance us from its subject in order to emphasize the scale and sublimity of the spectacle, far removed from ordinary human experience. In other words, language and style in *Paradise Lost* are well adapted to suit a particular purpose, just as they are in "A Slumber Did My Spirit Seal," though on a wholly different scale. Wordsworth criticized the poetry of his day, not because of its elevation, but because the raised style was too often out of touch with its subject; in his view, the words did not bear any significant relation to the "truths" they were attempting to depict.

"PLAIN" LANGUAGE IN POETRY

Since Wordsworth's time, writers have been conscious of a need to narrow the apparent gap between "poetic" language and the language of everyday life. In much of the poetry of the past century, especially free verse, we can observe a growing approximation to speech—even to conversation—in the diction and rhythms of poetry. This may have something to do with the changed role of the poet, who today has discarded the mantle of teacher or prophet that was assumed by poets of earlier times, and who is ready to admit all fields of experience and endeavor as appropriate for poetry. The modern poet looks squarely at life, and can often find a provoking beauty in even the meanest of objects.

We should not assume, however, that a greater concern with the "ordinary," with simplicity, naturalness, and clarity, means a reduction in complexity or suggestiveness. A piece such as Stevie Smith's "Mother, Among the Dustbins," for all the casual and playful domesticity of some of its lines, skilfully evokes a range of emotions and sense impressions defying simple paraphrase.

IMAGERY, SYMBOLISM, AND FIGURES OF SPEECH

The language of poetry is grounded in the objects and phenomena that create sensory impressions. Sometimes the poet renders these impressions quite literally, in a series of *images* that seek to recreate a scene in the reader's mind:

Only a man harrowing clods
In a slow silent walk
With an old horse that stumbles and nods
Half asleep as they stalk.

Only thin smoke without flame
From the heaps of couch-grass;
Yet this will go onward the same
Though Dynasties pass.

Yonder a maid and her wight
Come whispering by:
War's annals will cloud into night
Ere their story die.

(Thomas Hardy, "In Time of 'The Breaking of Nations'")

Here, the objects of everyday life are re-created with sensory details designed to evoke in us the sensations or responses felt by the speaker viewing the scene. At the same time, the writer invests the objects with such significance that the poem's meaning extends beyond the literal to the symbolic: that is, the images come to stand for something much larger than the objects they represent. Hardy's poem moves from the presentation of stark images of rural life to a sense of their timelessness. By the last stanza we see the ploughman, the burning grass, and the maid and her companion as symbols of recurring human actions and motives that defy the struggles and conflicts of history.

IMAGISM

The juxtaposition of clear, forceful images is associated particularly with the Imagist movement that flourished at the beginning of the twentieth century. Its chief representatives (in their early work) were the American poets H.D. and Ezra Pound, who defined an image as "that which represents an intellectual and emotional complex in an instant of time." Pound's two-line poem "In a Station of the Metro" provides a good example of the Imagists' goal of representing emotions or impressions through the use of concentrated images:

The apparition of these faces in the crowd,
Petals on a wet, black bough.

As in a Japanese *haiku,* a form that strongly influenced the Imagists, the poem uses sharp, clear, concrete details to evoke both a sensory impression and the emotion or the atmosphere of the scene. Though the Imagist movement itself lasted only a short time (from about 1912 to 1917), it had a far-reaching influence on modern poets such as T. S. Eliot, and William Carlos Williams.

FIGURES OF SPEECH

Imagery often works together with figurative expression to extend and deepen the meaning or impact of a poem. "Figurative" language means language that is metaphorical, not literal or referential. Through "figures of speech" such as metaphor and simile, metonymy, synecdoche, and personification, the writer may alter the ordinary, denotative meanings of words in order to convey greater force and vividness to ideas or impressions, often by showing likenesses between unlike things.

With *simile*, the poet makes an explicit comparison between the subject (called the *tenor*) and another object or idea (known as the *vehicle*), using "as" or "like":

It is a beauteous evening, calm and free,
The holy time is quiet as a Nun
Breathless with adoration. …

In this opening to a sonnet, Wordsworth uses a visual image of a nun in devout prayer to convey in concrete terms the less tangible idea of evening as a "holy time." The comparison also introduces an emotional dimension, conveying something of the feeling that the scene induces in the poet. The simile can thus illuminate and expand meaning in a compact way. The poet may also extend the simile to elaborate at length on any points of likeness.

In *metaphor*, the comparison between tenor and vehicle is implied: connectives such as "like" are omitted, and a kind of identity is created between the subject and the term with which it is being compared. Thus in John Donne's "The Good-Morrow," a lover asserts the endless joy that he and his beloved find in each other:

My face in thine eye, thine in mine appears,
And true plain hearts do in the faces rest;
Where can we find two better hemispheres,
Without sharp north, without declining west?

Here the lovers are transformed into "hemispheres," each of them a half of the world not subject to the usual natural phenomena of wintry cold ("sharp north") or the coming of night ("declining west"). Thus, they form a perfect world in balance, in which the normal processes of decay or decline have been arrested. Donne renders the abstract idea of a love that defies change in pictorial and physical terms, making it more real and accessible to us. The images here are all the more arresting for the degree of concentration involved; it is not merely the absence of "like" or "as" that gives the metaphor such direct power, but the fusion of distinct images and emotions into a new idea.

Personification is the figure of speech in which the writer endows abstract ideas, inanimate objects, or animals with human characteristics. In other words, it is a type of implied metaphorical comparison in which aspects of a non-human subject are compared to the feelings, appearance, or actions of a human being. In the second stanza of his ode "To Autumn," Keats personifies the concept of autumnal harvesting in the form of a woman, "sitting careless on a granary floor, / Thy hair soft-lifted by the winnowing wind." Personification may also help to create a mood, as when Thomas Gray attributes human feelings to a hooting owl in "Elegy Written in a Country Church-Yard"; using such words as "moping" and "complain," Gray invests the bird's cries with the quality of human melancholy:

... from yonder ivy-mantled tow'r
The moping owl does to the moon complain
Of such, as wand'ring near her secret bow'r,
Molest her ancient solitary reign.

In his book *Modern Painters* (1856), the English critic John Ruskin criticized such attribution of human feelings to objects in nature. Calling this device the "pathetic fallacy," he objected to what he saw as an irrational distortion of reality, producing "a falseness in all our impressions of external things." Modern criticism, with a distrust of any notions of an objective "reality," tends to use Ruskin's term as a neutral label simply to describe instances of extended personification of natural objects.

Apostrophe, which is closely related to personification, has the speaker directly addressing a non-human object or idea as if it were a sentient human listener. Blake's "The Sick Rose," Shelley's "Ode to the West Wind" and his ode "To a Sky-Lark" all employ apostrophe, personifying the object addressed. Keats's "Ode on a Grecian Urn" begins by apostrophizing the urn ("Thou still unravish'd bride of quietness"), then addresses it in a series of questions and reflections through which the speaker attempts to unravel the urn's mysteries.

Apostrophe also appeals to or addresses a person who is absent or dead. W. H. Auden's lament "In Memory of W. B. Yeats" apostrophizes both the earth in which Yeats is to be buried ("Earth, receive an honoured guest") and the dead poet himself ("Follow, poet, follow right / To the bottom of the night ..."). Religious prayers offer an illustration of the usefulness of apostrophe, since they are direct appeals from an earth-bound supplicant to an invisible god. The suggestion of strong emotion associated with such appeals is a common feature of apostrophe in poetry also, especially poetry with a religious theme, like Donne's "Holy Sonnets" (e.g., "Batter My Heart, Three-Personed God").

Metonymy and *synecdoche* are two closely related figures of speech that further illustrate the power of metaphorical language to convey meaning more intensely and vividly than is possible with prosaic statement. *Metonymy* (from the Greek, meaning "change of name") involves referring to an object or concept by substituting the name of another object or concept with which it is usually associated: for example, we might speak of "the Crown" when we mean the monarch, or describe the U.S. executive branch as "the White House." When the writer uses only part of something to signify the whole, or an individual to represent a class, we have an instance of *synecdoche*: T. S. Eliot provides an example in "The Love Song of J. Alfred Prufrock" when a crab is described as "a pair of ragged claws." Similarly, synecdoche is present in Milton's contemptous term "blind mouths" to describe the "corrupted clergy" he attacks in "Lycidas."

Dylan Thomas employs both metonymy and synecdoche in his poem "The Hand That Signed the Paper":

> The hand that signed the paper felled a city;
> Five sovereign fingers taxed the breath,
> Doubled the globe of dead and halved a country;
> These five kings did a king to death.
>
> The mighty hand leads to a sloping shoulder,
> The finger joints are cramped with chalk;
> A goose's quill has put an end to murder
> That put an end to talk.
>
> The hand that signed the treaty bred a fever,
> And famine grew, and locusts came;
> Great is the hand that holds dominion over
> Man by a scribbled name.
>
> The five kings count the dead but do not soften
> The crusted wound nor stroke the brow;
> A hand rules pity as a hand rules heaven;
> Hands have no tears to flow.

The "hand" of the poem is evidently a synecdoche for a great king who enters into treaties with friends and foes to wage wars, conquer kingdoms, and extend his personal power—all at the expense of his suffering subjects. The "goose quill" of the second stanza is a metonymy, standing for the pen used to sign the treaty or the death warrant that brings the war to an end.

Thomas's poem is an excellent example of the power of figurative language, which, by its vividness and concentrated force, can add layers of meaning to a poem, make abstract ideas concrete, and intensify the poem's emotional impact.

THE POEM AS PERFORMANCE: WRITER AND PERSON

Poetry is always dramatic. Sometimes the drama is explicit, as in Robert Browning's monologues, in which we hear the voice of a participant in a dialogue; in "My Last Duchess" we are present as the Duke reflects on the portrait of his late wife for the benefit of a visitor who has come to negotiate on behalf of the woman who is to become the Duke's next wife. Or we listen with amusement and pity as the dying Bishop addresses his venal and unsympathetic sons and tries to bargain with them for a fine burial ("The Bishop Orders His Tomb at St. Praxed's"). In such poems, the notion of a speaking voice is paramount: the speaker is a personage in a play, and the poem a means of conveying plot and character.

Sometimes the drama is less apparent, and takes the form of a plea, or a compliment, or an argument addressed to a silent listener. In Donne's "The Flea" we can infer from the poem the situation that has called it forth: a lover's advances are being rejected by his beloved, and his poem is an argument intended to overcome her reluctance by means of wit and logic. We can see a similar example in Marvell's "To His Coy Mistress": here the very shape of the poem, its three-paragraph structure, corresponds to the stages of the speaker's argument as he presents an apparently irrefutable line of reasoning. Much love poetry has this kind of background as its inspiration; the yearnings or lamentations of the lover are part of an imagined scene, not merely versified reflections about an abstraction called "love."

Meditative or reflective poetry can be dramatic too. Donne's "Holy Sonnets" are pleas from a tormented soul struggling to find its god; Tennyson's "In Memoriam" follows the agonized workings of a mind tracing a path from grief and anger to acceptance and renewed hope.

We should never assume that the speaker, the "I" of the poem, is simply a voice for the writer's own views. The speaker in W. H. Auden's "To an Unknown Citizen," presenting a summary of the dead citizen's life, appears to be an official spokesperson for the society which the citizen served ("Our report on his union"; "Our researchers ..." etc.). The speaker's words are laudatory, yet we perceive immediately that Auden's own views of this society are anything but approving. The speaker seems satisfied with the highly regimented nature of his society, one in which every aspect of the individual's life is under scrutiny and subject to correction. The only things necessary to the happiness of the "Modern Man," it seems, are "A phonograph, a radio, a car, and a frigidaire." The tone here is subtly ironic, an irony created by the gap between the imagined speaker's perception and the real feelings of the writer.

PERFORMANCE POETRY

Poetry began as an oral art, passed on in the form of chants, myths, ballads, and legends recited to an audience of listeners rather than readers. Even today, the dramatic qualities of a poem may extend beyond written text. "Performance poets" combine poetry and stagecraft in presenting their work to live audiences. Dramatic uses of voice, rhythm, body movement, music, and sometimes other visual effects make the "text" of the poem multi-dimensional. For example, Edith Sitwell's poem-sequence *Façade* (1922) was originally set to music: Sitwell read from behind a screen, while a live orchestra played. This performance was designed to enhance the verbal and rhythmic qualities of her poetry:

Beneath the flat and paper sky
The sun, a demon's eye
Glowed through the air, that mask of glass;
All wand'ring sounds that pass

Seemed out of tune, as if the light
Were fiddle-strings pulled tight.
The market-square with spire and bell
Clanged out the hour in Hell.
(from *Façade*)

By performing their poetry, writers can also convey cultural values and traditions. The cultural aspect of performance is central to Black poetry, which originates in a highly oral tradition of folklore and storytelling. From its roots in Africa, this oral tradition has been manifested in the songs and stories of slaves, in spirituals, in the jazz rhythms of the Twenties and the Thirties and in the rebelliousness of reggae and of rap. Even when it remains "on the page," much Black poetry written in the oral tradition has a compelling rhythmic quality. The lines below from Linton Kwesi Johnson's "Mi Revalueshanary Fren," for example, blur the line between spoken poetry and song. Johnson often performs his "dub poetry" against reggae or hip-hop musical backings.

yes, people powa jus a showa evry howa
an evrybady claim dem democratic
but some a wolf an some a sheep
an dat is problematic

The chorus of Johnson's poems, with its constant repetitions, digs deeply into the roots of African song and chant. Its performance qualities become clearer when the poem is read aloud:

Husak
e ad to go
Honnicka
e ad to go
Chowcheskhu
e ad to go
Just like apartied
will av to go

To perform a poem is one way to see and hear poetry as multi-dimensional, cultural, historical, and often also political. Performance is also another way to discover how poetic "meaning" can be constructed in the dynamic relation between speaker and listener.

TONE: THE SPEAKER'S ATTITUDE

In understanding poetry, it is helpful to imagine a poem as having a "voice." The voice may be close to the poet's own, or that of an imagined character, a *persona* adopted by the poet. The tone of the voice will reveal the speaker's attitude to the subject, thus helping to shape our understanding and response. In speech we can indicate our feelings by raising or lowering our voices, and we can accompany words with physical actions. In writing, we must try to convey the tonal inflections of the speaking voice through devices of language and rhythm, through imagery and figures of speech, and through allusions and contrasts.

THE IRONIC TONE

Housman's poem "Terence, This Is Stupid Stuff" offers a useful example of ways in which manipulating tone can reinforce meaning. When Housman, presenting himself in the poem as "Terence," imagines himself to be criticized for writing gloomy poems, his response to his critics takes the form of an ironic alternative: perhaps they should stick to drinking ale:

> Oh, many a peer of England brews
> Livelier liquor than the Muse,
> And malt does more than Milton can
> To justify God's ways to man.

The tone here is one of heavy scorn. The speaker is impatient with those who refuse to look at the realities of life and death, and who prefer to take refuge in simple-minded pleasure. The ludicrous comparisons, first between the brewers who have been made peers of England and the classical Muse of poetry, then between malt and Milton, create a sense of disproportion and ironic tension; the explicit allusion to *Paradise Lost* ("To justify God's ways to man") helps to drive home the poet's bitter recognition that his auditors are part of that fallen world depicted by Milton, yet unable or unwilling to acknowledge their harsh condition. The three couplets that follow offer a series of contrasts: in each case, the first line sets up a pleasant expectation and the second dashes it with a blunt reminder of reality:

> Ale, man, ale's the stuff to drink
> For fellows whom it hurts to think:
> Look into the pewter pot
> To see the world as the world's not.
> And faith, 'tis pleasant till 'tis past:
> The mischief is that 'twill not last.

These are all jabs at the "sterling lads" who would prefer to lie in "lovely muck" and not think about the way the world is. Housman's sardonic advice is all the more pointed for its sharp and ironic tone.

POETIC FORMS

In poetry, language is intimately related to form, which is the structuring of words within identifiable patterns. In prose we speak of phrases, sentences, and paragraphs; in poetry, we identify structures by lines, stanzas, or complete forms such as the sonnet or the ode (though poetry in complete or blank verse has paragraphs of variable length, not formal stanzas: see below).

Rightly handled, the form enhances expression and meaning, just as a frame can define and enhance a painting or photograph. Unlike the photo frame, however, form in poetry is an integral part of the whole work. At one end of the scale, the term "form" may describe the *epic*, the lengthy narrative governed by such conventions as division into books, a lofty style, and the interplay between human and supernatural characters. At the other end lies the *epigram*, a witty and pointed saying whose distinguishing characteristic is its brevity, as in Alexander Pope's famous couplet,

I am his Highness' dog at Kew;
Pray tell me sir, whose dog are you?

Between the epic and the epigram lie many other poetic forms, such as the sonnet, the ballad, or the ode. "Form" may also describe stanzaic patterns like *couplets* and *quatrains.*

"FIXED FORM" POEMS

The best-known poetic form is probably the sonnet, the fourteen-line poem inherited from Italy (the word itself is from the Italian *sonetto*, little song or sound). Within those fourteen lines, whether the poet chooses the "Petrarchan" rhyme scheme or the "English" form (see below in the section on "Rhyme"), the challenge is to develop an idea or situation that must find its statement and its resolution within the strict confines of the sonnet frame. Typically, there is an initial idea, description, or statement of feeling, followed by a "turn" in the thought that takes the reader by surprise, or that casts the situation in an unexpected light. Thus in Sonnet 130, "My Mistress' Eyes Are Nothing Like the Sun," William Shakespeare spends the first three quatrains apparently disparaging his lover in a series of unfavorable comparisons—"If snow be white, why then her breasts are dun"—but in the closing couplet his point becomes clear:

And yet, by heaven, I think my love as rare
As any she belied with false compare.

In other words, the speaker's disparaging comparisons have really been parodies of sentimental clichés which falsify reality; his mistress has no need of the exaggerations or distortions of conventional love poetry.

Other foreign forms borrowed and adapted by English-language poets include the *ghazal* and the *pantoum*. The *ghazal*, strongly associated with classical Urdu literature, originated in Persia and Arabia and was brought to the Indian subcontinent in the twelfth century. It consists of a series of couplets held together by a refrain, a simple rhyme scheme (a/a, b/a, c/a, d/a…), and a common rhythm, but only loosely related in theme or subject. Some English-language practitioners of the form have captured the epigrammatic quality of the ghazal, but most do not adhere to the strict pattern of the classical form.

The *pantoum*, based on a Malaysian form, was imported into English poetry via the work of nineteenth-century French poets. Typically it presents a series of quatrains rhyming *abab*, linked by a pattern of repetition in which the second and fourth lines of a quatrain become the first and third lines of the stanza that follows. In the poem's final stanza, the pattern is reversed: the second line repeats the third line of the first stanza, and the last line repeats the poem's opening line, thus creating the effect of a loop.

Similar to the pantoum in the circularity of its structure is the *villanelle,* originally a French form, with five *tercets* and a concluding *quatrain* held together by only two rhymes (aba, aba, aba, aba, aba, abaa) and by a refrain that repeats the first line at lines 6, 12, and 18, while the third line of the first tercet reappears as lines 9, 15, and 19. With its interlocking rhymes and elaborate repetitions, the villanelle can create a variety of tonal effects, ranging from lighthearted parody to the sonorous and earnest exhortation of Dylan Thomas's "Do Not Go Gentle Into That Good Night."

STANZAIC FORMS

Recurring formal groupings of lines within a poem are usually described as "stanzas." Both the recurring and the formal aspects of stanzaic forms are important; it is a common misconception to think that any group of lines in a poem, if it is set off by line spaces, constitutes a stanza. If such a group of lines is not patterned as one of a recurring group sharing similar formal characteristics, however, then it may be more appropriate to refer to such irregular groupings in the way we do for prose—as paragraphs. A ballad is typically divided into stanzas; a prose poem or a poem written in free verse, on the other hand, will rarely be divided into stanzas.

A stanza may be identified by the number of lines and the patterns of rhyme repeated in each grouping. One of the simpler traditional forms is the *ballad stanza*, with its alternating four and three-foot lines and its *abcb* rhyme scheme. Drawing on this form's association with medieval ballads and legends, Keats produces the eerie mystery of "La Belle Dame Sans Merci":

> I saw pale kings and princes too,
> Pale warriors, death-pale were they all;
> They cried—"La Belle Dame sans Merci
> Hath thee in thrall!"

Such imitations are a form of literary allusion; Keats uses a traditional stanza form to remind us of poems like "Sir Patrick Spens" or "Barbara Allen" to dramatize the painful thralldom of love by placing it within a well-known tradition of ballad narratives with similar forms and themes.

The four-line stanza, or *quatrain*, may be used for a variety of effects: from the elegiac solemnity of Gray's "Elegy Written in a Country Churchyard" to the apparent lightness and simplicity of some of Emily Dickinson's poems. Tennyson used a rhyming quatrain to such good effect in *In Memoriam* that the form he employed (four lines of iambic tetrameter rhyming *abba*) is known as the "In Memoriam stanza."

Other commonly used forms of stanza include the *rhyming couplet*, *terza rima*, *ottava rima*, *rhyme royal*, and the *Spenserian stanza*. Each of these is a rhetorical unit within a longer whole, rather like a paragraph within an essay. The poet's choice among such forms is dictated, at least in part, by the effects that each may produce. Thus the *rhyming couplet* often expresses a complete statement within two lines, creating a sense of density of thought, of coherence and closure; it is particularly effective where the writer wishes to set up contrasts, or to achieve the witty compactness of epigram:

> Of all mad creatures, if the learn'd are right,
> It is the slaver kills, and not the bite.
> A fool quite angry is quite innocent:
> Alas! 'tis ten times worse when they repent.
>
> (from Pope, "Epistle to Dr. Arbuthnot")

Ottava rima, as its Italian name implies, is an eight-line stanza, with the rhyme scheme *abababcc*. Like the sonnet, it is long enough to allow the development of a single thought in some detail and complexity, with a concluding couplet that may extend the central idea or cast it in a wholly unexpected light. W.B. Yeats uses this stanza form in "Sailing to Byzantium" and "Among Schoolchildren." Though much used by Renaissance poets, it is particularly associated with George Gordon, Lord Byron's *Don Juan*, in which the poet exploits to the full its potential for devastating irony and bathos. It is long enough to allow the development of a single thought in some detail and complexity; the concluding couplet can then, sonnet-like, turn that thought upon its head, or cast it in a wholly unexpected light:

Sagest of women, even of widows, she
    Resolved that Juan should be quite a paragon,
And worthy of the noblest pedigree
    (His sire was of Castile, his dam from Aragon).
Then for accomplishments of chivalry,
    In case our lord the king should go to war again,
He learned the arts of riding, fencing, gunnery,
And how to scale a fortress—or a nunnery.

(*Don Juan* I.38)

FREE VERSE

Not all writers want the order and symmetry—some might say the restraints and limitations—of traditional forms, and many have turned to *free verse* as a means of liberating their thoughts and feelings. Deriving its name from the French "vers libre" made popular by the French Symbolistes at the end of the nineteenth century, free verse is characterized by irregularity of metre, line length, and rhyme. This does not mean that it is without pattern; rather, it tends to follow more closely than other forms the unforced rhythms and accents of natural speech, making calculated use of spacing, line breaks, and "cadences," the rhythmic units that govern phrasing in speech.

Free verse is not a modern invention. Milton was an early practitioner, as was Blake; however, it was the great modern writers of free verse—first Walt Whitman, then Pound, Eliot, and William Carlos Williams (interestingly, all Americans, at least originally)—who gave this form a fluidity and flexibility that could free the imagination to deal with any kind of feeling or experience. Perhaps because it depends so much more than traditional forms upon the individual intuitions of the poet, it is the form of poetic structure most commonly found today. The best practitioners recognize that free verse, like any other kind of poetry, demands clarity, precision, and a close connection between technique and meaning.

PROSE POETRY

At the furthest extreme from traditional forms lies poetry written in prose. Contradictory as this label may seem, the two have much in common. Prose has at its disposal all the figurative devices available to poetry, such as metaphor, personification, or apostrophe; it may use structuring devices such as verbal repetition or parallel syntactical structures; it can draw on the same tonal range, from pathos to irony. The difference is that prose poetry accomplishes its ends in sentences and paragraphs, rather than lines or stanzas. First given prominence by the French poet Charles Baudelaire (*Petits Poèmes en prose*, 1862), the form is much used to present fragments of heightened sensation, conveyed through vivid or impressionistic description. It draws upon such prosaic forms as journal entries, lists, even footnotes. Prose poetry should be distinguished from "poetic prose," which may be found in a variety of settings (from the King James Bible to the fiction of Jeanette Winterson); the distinction—which not all critics would accept—appears to lie in the writer's intention.

Christan Bok's *Eunoia* is an interesting example of the ways in which a writer of prose poetry may try to balance the demands of each medium. *Eunoia* is an avowedly experimental work in which each chapter is restricted to the use of a single vowel. The text is governed by a series of rules described by the author in an afterword; they include a requirement that all chapters "must allude to the art of writing. All sentences must accent internal rhyme through the use of syntactical parallelism. The text must exhaust the lexicon for each vowel, citing at least 98% of the available repertoire...." Having imposed such constraints upon the language and form of the work, Bok then sets himself the task of showing that "even under such improbable conditions of duress, language can still express an uncanny, if not sublime, thought." The result is a surrealistic narrative that blends poetic and linguistic devices to almost hypnotic effect.

THE POEM AS A MATERIAL OBJECT

Both free verse and prose poetry pay attention in different ways to the poem as a living thing on the printed page. But the way in which poetry is presented in material form is an important part of the existence of almost any form of poetry. In the six volumes of this anthology the material form of the poem is highlighted by the inclusion of a number of facsimile reproductions of poems of other eras in their earliest extant material form.

RHYTHM AND SCANSION

When we read poetry, we often become aware of a pattern of rhythm within a line or set of lines. The formal analysis of that rhythmic pattern, or "metre," is called *scansion.* The verb "to scan" may carry different meanings, depending upon the context: if the *critic* "scans" a line, he or she is attempting to determine the metrical pattern in which it is cast; if the *line* "scans," we are making the observation that the line conforms to particular metrical rules. Whatever the context, the process of scansion is based on the premise that a line of verse is built on a pattern of stresses, a recurring set of more or less regular beats established by the alternation of light and heavy accents in syllables and words. The rhythmic pattern so distinguished in a given poem is said to be the "metre" of that poem. If we find it impossible to identify any specific metrical pattern, the poem is probably an example of free verse.

QUANTITATIVE, SYLLABIC, AND ACCENTUAL-SYLLABIC VERSE

Although we owe much of our terminology for analyzing or describing poetry to the Greeks and Romans, the foundation of our metrical system is quite different from theirs. They measured a line of verse by the duration of sound ("quantity") in each syllable, and by the combination of short and long syllables. Such poetry is known as *quantitative* verse.

Unlike Greek or Latin, English is a heavily accented language. Thus poetry of the Anglo-Saxon period, such as *Beowulf,* was *accentual:* that is, the lines were based on a fixed number of accents, or stresses, regardless of the number of syllables in the line:

Oft Scyld Scefing   sceapena þreatum
monegum maegþum   meodosetla ofteah.

Few modern poets have written in the accentual tradition. A notable exception was Gerard Manley Hopkins, who based his line on a pattern of strong stresses that he called "sprung rhythm." Hopkins experimented with rhythms and stresses that approximate the accentual quality of natural speech; the result is a line that is emphatic, abrupt, even harsh in its forcefulness:

I caught this morning morning's minion, kingdom of daylight's dauphin, dapple-dawn-drawn
Falcon, in his riding

Of the rolling level underneath him steady air ....
(from "The Windhover")

Under the influence of French poetry, following the Norman invasion of the eleventh century, English writers were introduced to *syllabic* prosody: that is, poetry in which the number of syllables is the determining factor in the length of any line, regardless of the number of stresses or their placement. A few modern writers have successfully produced syllabic poetry.

However, the accentual patterns of English, in speech as well as in poetry, were too strongly ingrained to disappear. Instead, the native accentual practice combined with the imported syllabic conventions to produce the *accentual-syllabic* line, in which the writer works with combinations of stressed and unstressed syllables in lines of equal syllabic length. Geoffrey Chaucer was the first great writer to employ the accentual-syllabic line in English poetry:

Ther was also a Nonne, a Prioresse,
That of hir smiling was ful simple and coy.
Hir gretteste ooth was but by sainté Loy,
And she was clepéd Madame Eglantine.
(from *The Canterbury Tales*)

The fundamental pattern here is the ten-syllable line (although the convention of sounding the final "e" at the end of a line in Middle English verse sometimes produces eleven syllables). Each line contains five stressed syllables, each of which alternates with one or two unstressed syllables. This was to become the predominant metre of poetry in English until the general adoption of free verse in the twentieth century.

IDENTIFYING POETIC METER

Conventionally, meter is established by dividing a line into roughly equal parts, based on the rise and fall of the rhythmic beats. Each of these divisions, conventionally marked by a bar, is known as a "foot," and within the foot there will be a combination of stressed and unstressed syllables, indicated by the prosodic symbols / (stressed) and x (unstressed).

I know | that I | shall meet | my fate
Somewhere | among | the clouds | above ...
(from *Yeats*, "An Irish Airman Foresees His Death")

To describe the meter used in a poem, we must first determine what kind of foot predominates, and then count the number of feet in each line. To describe the resultant meter we use terminology borrowed from classical prosody. In identifying the meter of English verse we commonly apply the following labels:

iambic (x /): a foot with one weak stress followed by one strong stress

("Look home | ward, Ang | el, now, | and melt | with ruth")

trochaic (/ x): strong followed by weak

("Ty | ger! Ty | ger! bur | ning bright")

anapaestic (x x /): two weak stresses, followed by a strong

("I have passed | with a nod | of the head")

dactylic (/ x x): strong stress followed by two weak

("Hickory | dickory | dock")

spondaic (/ /): two strong stresses

("If hate | killed men,| Brother | Lawrence,
God's blood,| would not | mine kill | you?")

We also use classical terms to describe the number of feet in a line. Thus, a line with one foot is *monometer*; with two feet, *dimeter*; three feet, *trimeter*; four feet, *tetrameter*; five feet, *pentameter*; and six feet, *hexameter*.

Scansion of the two lines from Yeats's "Irish Airman" quoted above shows that the predominant foot is iambic (x /), that there are four feet to each line, and that the poem is therefore written in *iambic tetrameters*. The first foot of the second line, however, may be read as a trochee ("Somewhere"); the variation upon the iambic norm here is an example of *substitution*, a means whereby the writer may avoid the monotony that would result from adhering too closely to a set rhythm. We very quickly build up an expectation about the dominant meter of a poem; the poet will sometimes disturb that expectation by changing the beat, and so through substitution create a pleasurable tension in our awareness.

The prevailing meter in English poetry is iambic, since the natural rhythm of spoken English is predominantly iambic. Nonetheless, poets may employ other rhythms where it suits their purpose. Thus W.H. Auden can create a solemn tone by the use of a trochaic meter(/ x):

Earth, receive an honoured guest;
William Yeats is laid to rest:
Let the Irish vessel lie
Emptied of its poetry.

The same meter may be much less funereal, as in Ben Jonson's song "*To Celia*":

Come, my Celia, let us prove,
While we may, the sports of love.
Time will not be ours forever;
He, at length, our good will sever.

The sense of greater pace in this last example derives in part from the more staccato phrasing, and also from the greater use of monosyllabic words. A more obviously lilting, dancing effect is obtained from anapaestic rhythm (x x /):

I sprang to the stirrup, and Joris, and he;
I galloped, Dirck galloped, we galloped all three.
"Good speed!" cried the watch, as the gatebolts undrew;
"Speed!" echoed the wall to us galloping through.
(from *Browning*, "How They Brought the Good News from Ghent to Aix")

Coleridge wittily captured the varying effects of different meters in "Metrical Feet: Lesson for a Boy," which the poet wrote for his sons, and in which he marked the stresses himself:

Trochee trips from long to short;
From long to long in solemn sort
Slow Spondee stalks; strong foot! yet ill able
Ever to come up with Dactyl trisyllable.
Iambics march from short to long:—
With a leap and a bound the swift Anapaests throng....

A meter which often deals with serious themes is unrhymed iambic pentameter, also known as *blank verse*. This is the meter of Shakespeare's plays, notably his great tragedies; it is the meter, too, of Milton's *Paradise Lost*, to which it lends a desired sonority and magnificence; and of Wordsworth's "Lines Composed a Few Miles above Tintern Abbey," where the flexibility of the meter allows the writer to move by turns from description, to narration, to philosophical reflection.

RHYME, CONSONANCE, ASSONANCE, AND ALLITERATION

Perhaps the most obvious sign of poetic form is rhyme: that is, the repetition of syllables with the same or similar sounds. If the rhyme words are placed at the end of the line, they are known as *end-rhymes*. The opening stanza of Housman's "To an Athlete Dying Young" has two pairs of end-rhymes:

The time you won your town the *race*
We chaired you through the market-*place*;
Man and boy stood cheering *by*,
And home we brought you shoulder-*high*.

Words rhyming within a line are *internal rhymes*, as in the first and third lines of this stanza from Coleridge's "The Rime of the Ancient Mariner":

The fair breeze *blew*, the white foam *flew*
The furrow followed free;
We were the *first* that ever *burst*
Into that silent sea.

When, as is usually the case, the rhyme occurs in a stressed syllable, it is known as a *masculine rhyme*; if the rhyming word ends in an unstressed syllable, it is referred to as *feminine*. The difference is apparent in the opening stanzas of Alfred Tennyson's poem "The Lady of Shalott," where the first stanza establishes the basic iambic meter with strong stresses on the rhyming words:

On either side the river *lie*
Long fields of barley and of *rye*,
That clothe the wold and meet the *sky*;
And through the field the road runs *by*
To many-towered Camelot ...

In the second stanza Tennyson changes to trochaic lines, ending in unstressed syllables and feminine rhymes:

> Willows whiten, aspens *quiver*,
> Little breezes dusk and *shiver*
> Through the wave that runs *forever*
> By the island in the *river*
> Flowing down to Camelot.

Not only does Tennyson avoid monotony here by his shift to feminine rhymes, he also darkens the mood by using words that imply a contrast with the bright warmth of day—"quiver," "dusk," "shiver"—in preparation for the introduction of the "silent isle" that embowers the Lady.

NEAR RHYMES

Most of the rhymes in "The Lady of Shalott" are exact, or "*perfect*" rhymes. However, in the second of the stanzas just quoted, it is evident that "forever" at the end of the third line is not a "perfect" rhyme; rather, it is an instance of "*near*" or "*slant*" rhyme. Such "*imperfect*" rhymes are quite deliberate; indeed, two stanzas later we find the rhyming sequence "early," "barley," "cheerly," and "clearly," followed by the rhymes "weary," "airy," and "fairy." As with the introduction of feminine rhymes, such divergences from one dominant pattern prevent monotony and avoid a too-mechanical sing-song effect.

More importantly, near-rhymes have an oddly unsettling effect, perhaps because they both raise and frustrate our expectation of a perfect rhyme. Their use certainly gives added emphasis to the words at the end of these chilling lines from Wilfred Owen's "*Strange Meeting*":

> For by my glee might many men have laughed,
> And of my weeping something had been left,
> Which must die now. I mean the truth untold,
> The pity of war, the pity war distilled.
> Now men will go content with what we spoiled,
> Or, discontent, boil bloody, and be spilled.

CONSONANCE AND ASSONANCE

In Owen's poem, the near-rhymes "laughed / left" and "spoiled / spilled" are good examples of *consonance*, which pairs words with similar consonants but different intervening vowels. Other examples from Owen's poem include "groined / groaned," "hall / Hell," "years / yours," and "mystery / mastery."

Related to consonance as a linking device is *assonance*, the echoing of similar vowel sounds in the stressed syllables of words with differing consonants (lane/hail, penitent/reticence). A device favored particularly by descriptive poets, it appears often in the work of the English Romantics, especially Shelley and Keats, and their great Victorian successor Tennyson, all of whom had a good ear for the musical quality of language. In the following passage, Tennyson makes effective use of repeated "o" and "ow" sounds to suggest the soft moaning of the wind as it spreads the seed of the lotos plant:

> The Lotos blooms below the barren peak,
> The Lotos blows by every winding creek;

All day the wind breathes low with mellower tone;
Through every hollow cave and alley lone
Round and round the spicy downs the yellow Lotos dust is blown.
(from "The Lotos-Eaters")

ALLITERATION

Alliteration connects words which have the same initial consonant. Like consonance and rhyme, alliteration adds emphasis, throwing individual words into strong relief, and lending force to rhythm. This is especially evident in the work of Gerard Manley Hopkins, where alliteration works in conjunction with the heavy stresses of *sprung rhythm*:

Brute beauty and valour and act, oh, air, pride, plume, here
Buckle! AND the fire that breaks from thee then, a billion
Times told lovelier, more dangerous, O my chevalier!
(from "The Windhover")

Like assonance, alliteration is useful in descriptive poetry, reinforcing an impression or mood through repeated sounds:

Thou on whose stream, 'mid the steep sky's commotion,
Loose clouds like Earth's decaying leaves are shed,
Shook from the tangled boughs of Heaven and Ocean ....
(from Percy Shelley, "Ode to the West Wind")

The repetition of "s" and "sh" sounds conveys the rushing sound of a wind that drives everything before it. This effect is also an example of *onomatopoeia*, a figure of speech in which the sound of the words seems to echo the sense.

RHYME AND POETIC STRUCTURE

Rhyme may play a central role in the structure of a poem. This is particularly apparent in the *sonnet* form, where the expression of the thought is heavily influenced by the poet's choice of rhyme-scheme. The "English" or "Shakespearean" sonnet has three quatrains rhyming *abab*, *cdcd*, *efef*, and concludes with a rhyming couplet, *gg*. This pattern lends itself well to the statement and restatement of an idea, as we find, for example, in Shakespeare's sonnet "That time of year thou mayst in me behold." Each of the quatrains presents an image of decline or decay—a tree in winter, the coming of night, a dying fire; the closing couplet then relates these images to the thought of an impending separation and attendant feelings of loss.

The organization of the "Italian" or "Petrarchan" sonnet, by contrast, hinges on a rhyme scheme that creates two parts, an eight-line section (the *octave*) typically rhyming *abbaabba*, and a concluding six-line section (the *sestet*) rhyming *cdecde* or some other variation. In the octave, the writer describes a thought or feeling; in the sestet, the writer may elaborate upon that thought, or may introduce a sudden "turn" or change of direction. A good example of the Italian form is Donne's "Batter My Heart, Three-Personed God."

The rhyming pattern established at the beginning of a poem is usually followed throughout; thus the opening sets up an expectation in the reader, which the poet may sometimes play on by means of an unexpected or surprising rhyme. This is especially evident in comic verse, where peculiar or unexpected rhymes can contribute a great deal to the comic effect:

> I shoot the Hippopotamus
> with bullets made of platinum,
> Because if I use leaden ones
> his hide is sure to flatten 'em.
>
> (*Hilaire Belloc,* "The Hippopotamus")

Finally, one of the most obvious yet important aspects of rhyme is its sound. It acts as a kind of musical punctuation, lending verse an added resonance and beauty. And as anyone who has ever had to learn poetry by heart will testify, the sound of rhyme is a powerful aid to memorization and recall, from helping a child to learn numbers—

> One, two,
> Buckle my shoe,
> Three, four,
> Knock at the door—

—to selling toothpaste through an advertising jingle in which the use of rhyme drives home the identity of a product:

> You'll wonder where the yellow went,
> When you brush your teeth with Pepsodent.

OTHER FORMS WITH INTERLOCKING RHYMES

Other forms besides the sonnet depend upon rhyme for their structural integrity. These include the *rondeau*, a poem of thirteen lines in three stanzas, with two half lines acting as a refrain, and having only two rhymes. The linking effect of rhyme is also essential to the three-line stanza called *terza rima*, the form chosen by Shelley for his "Ode to the West Wind," where the rhyme scheme (*aba, bcb, cdc* etc.) gives a strong sense of forward movement. But a poet need not be limited to particular forms to use interlocking rhyme schemes.

THE POET'S TASK

The poet's task, in Sir Philip Sidney's view, is to move us to virtue and well-doing by coming to us with

> words set in delightful proportion, either accompanied with, or prepared for, the well-enchanting skill of music; and with a tale forsooth he cometh unto you, with a tale which holdeth children from play, and old men from the chimney corner; and pretending no more,

> doth intend the winning of the mind from wickedness to virtue: even as the child is often brought to take most wholesome things by hiding them in such other as have a pleasant taste.
>
> (*The Defence of Poesy,* 1593)

Modern poets have been less preoccupied with the didactic or moral force of poetry, its capacity to win the mind to virtue; nonetheless, like their Renaissance counterparts, they view poetry as a means to understanding, a point of light in an otherwise dark universe. To Robert Frost, a poem "begins in delight and ends in wisdom":

> It begins in delight, it inclines to the impulse, it assumes direction with the first line laid down, it runs a course of lucky events, and ends in a clarification of life—not necessarily a great clarification, such as sects and cults are founded on, but in a momentary stay against confusion.
>
> ("The Figure a Poem Makes," *Collected Poems,* 1939)

Rhyme and metre are important tools at the poet's disposal, and can be valuable aids in developing thought as well as in creating rhythmic or musical effects. However, the technical skills needed to turn a good line or create metrical complexities should not be confused with the ability to write good poetry. Sidney wryly observes in his *Defence of Poesy* that "there have been many excellent poets that never versified, and now swarm many versifiers that need never answer to the name of poets.…it is not rhyming and versing that maketh a poet, no more than a long gown maketh an advocate." Technical virtuosity may arouse our admiration, but something else is needed to bring that "constriction of the throat and … precipitation of water to the eyes" that A.E. Housman speaks about. What that "something" is will always elude definition, and is perhaps best left for readers and listeners to determine for themselves through their own encounters with poetry.

Maps

N
S
E
W
ORKNEY
ORKNEY ISLANDS
HEBRIDES
ISLE OF SKYE
WESTERN ISLES
HIGHLAND
GRAMPIAN
SCOTLAND
North Sea
Atlantic Ocean
TAYSIDE
FIFE
Firth of Forth
CENTRAL
LOTHIAN
Clyde
STRATHCLYDE
BORDERS
Tweed
ARRAN ISLAND
North Channel
NORTH-UMBERLAND
DUMFRIES AND GALLOWAY
Tyne
DERRY (LONDONDERRY)
ANTRIM
DONEGAL
NORTHERN IRELAND (ULSTER)
TYRONE
Donegal Bay
FERMANAGH
ARMAGH
DOWN
SLIGO
MONAGHAN
LEITRIM
CAVAN
MAYO
ROSCOMMON
LONGFORD
LOUTH
MEATH
WESTMEATH
DUBLIN
GALWAY
OFFALY
KILDARE
IRELAND
LAOIGHIS
WICKLOW
CLARE
TIPPERARY
CARLOW
LIMERICK
KILKENNY
WEXFORD
KERRY
CORK
WATERFORD
St. George's Channel
Irish Sea
ISLE OF MAN
DURHAM
CUMBRIA
CLEVELAND
NORTH YORKSHIRE
Ouse
Aire
HUMBERSIDE
WEST YORKSHIRE
LANCASHIRE
SOUTH YORKSHIRE
CHESHIRE
DERBYSHIRE
LINCOLNSHIRE
The Wash
CLWYD
NOTTING-HAMSHIRE
GWYNEDD
Trent
ENGLAND
SHROPSHIRE
LEICESTER-SHIRE
Great Ouse
NORFOLK
POWYS
Severn
STAFFORD-SHIRE
NORTH-AMPTON-SHIRE
CAMBRIDGE-SHIRE
SUFFOLK
WORCESTER
WARWICK SHIRE
WALES
HEREFORD
BEDFORD-SHIRE
Wye
DYFED
BUCKING-HAMSHIRE
HERTFORD-SHIRE
ESSEX
GLOUCESTER-SHIRE
GWENT
OXFORD-SHIRE
Thames
London
WEST GLAMORGAN
SOUTH GLAMORGAN
AVON
WILTSHIRE
BERKSHIRE
SURREY
KENT
SOMERSET
HAMPSHIRE
WEST SUSSEX
EAST SUSSEX
Strait of Dover
DEVON
DORSET
CORNWALL
ISLE OF WIGHT
English Channel
ISLES OF SCILLY
CHANNEL ISLANDS
FRANCE
COUNTIES OF BRITAIN AND IRELAND

THE BRITISH ISLES
ORKNEY ISLANDS
HEBRIDES
ISLE OF SKYE
Elgin
Inverness
HIGHLANDS
Aberdeen
North Sea
SCOTLAND
Dunkeld
Dundee
Perth
St. Andrews
Stirling
Loch Lomond
Dunfermline
Firth of Forth
Glasgow
Edinburgh
Clyde R.
Ayr
Urr
Londonderry
Donegal
ULSTER
Donegal Bay
BEN BULBEN
Sligo
Armagh
Belfast
Dundalk
Croagh Patrick
CONNAUGHT
Kells
Tara
IRELAND
Dublin
ARAN ISLANDS
Kilkenny
Glendalough
LEINSTER
Limerick
Monaincha
Tipperary
Waterford
Wexford
MUNSTER
Cork
Dungarvan
Irish Sea
ISLE OF MAN
Tyne R.
Newcastle upon Tyne
THE LAKE DISTRICT
Grasmere
Durham
PENNINES
Leeds
York
Hull
Wakefield
Humber
Liverpool
Mersey R.
Manchester
THE PEAKS
Sheffield
Trent R.
Lincoln
Holyhead
Bangor
Chester
ENGLAND
Wrexham
Dee R.
Harlech
Derby
Nottingham
The Wash
NORFOLK BROADS
Lynn
Norwich
Stoke-on-Trent
Leicester
WALES
Birmingham
Severn R.
Coventry
Rugby
Warwick
Avon R.
Stratford-upon-Avon
Ely
Cambridge
Aberystwyth
Cardigan
Ipswich
Tintern Abbey
Gloucester
Oxford
St. Albans
Pembroke
Swansea
Thames R.
Reading
Eton
London
Greenwich
Milford Haven
Cardiff
Bristol
SALISBURY PLAIN
Windsor
Richmond
Canterbury
Bath
Royal Tunbridge Wells
Rochester
Dover
Salisbury
Ouse
Strait of Dover
Southampton
Winchester
THE WEALD
Winchelsea
Bournemouth
SOUTH DOWNS
Hastings
Exeter
DORSET DOWNS
Chichester
Lewes
Lyme Regis
Portsmouth
Brighton
DARTMOOR
ISLE OF WIGHT
Plymouth
St. Ives
LAND'S END
Penzance
English Channel
Amsterdam
The Hague
Oostende
Bruges
Antwerp
FLANDERS
Calais
Ghent
Cherbourg
GUERNSEY
Le Havre
Rouen
CHANNEL ISLANDS
JERSEY
Caen
NORMANDY
Paris
Brest
BRITTANY
Orléans
Nantes
N
W
E
S

GREATER LONDON
Finchley
Tottenham
Harrow
EPPING FOREST
Hampstead Heath
Wembley
Islington
Twyford Abbey
West Ham
London
Tower
Millenium Dome
Westminster
Fulham
Chelsea
Woolwich
Greenwich
Heathrow Airport
Richmond
Battersea
Deptford
Twickenham
Wandsworth
Dartford
Crystal Palace
Sydenham
Kingston
Wimbledon
Hampton Court
Merton
Bromley
Croydon

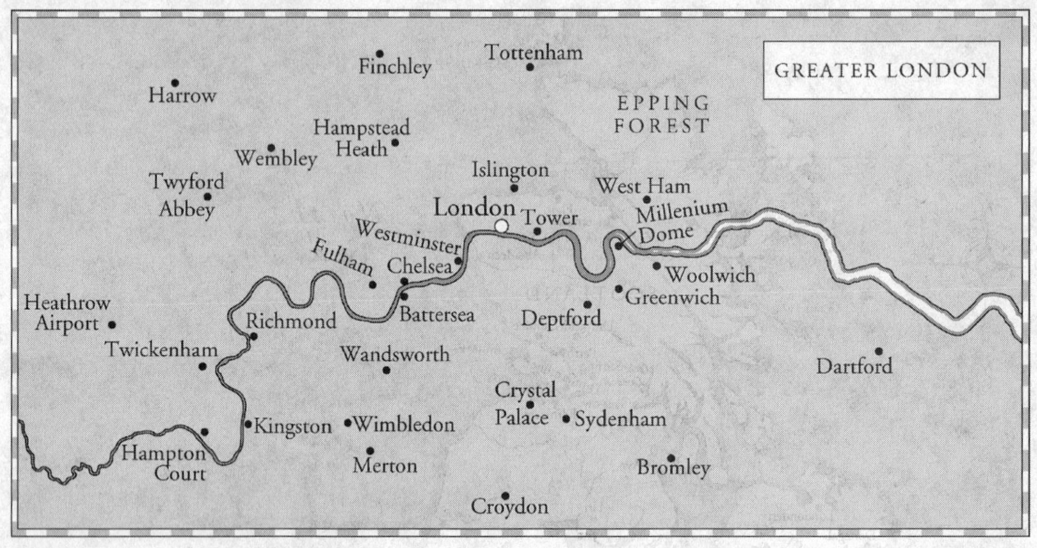

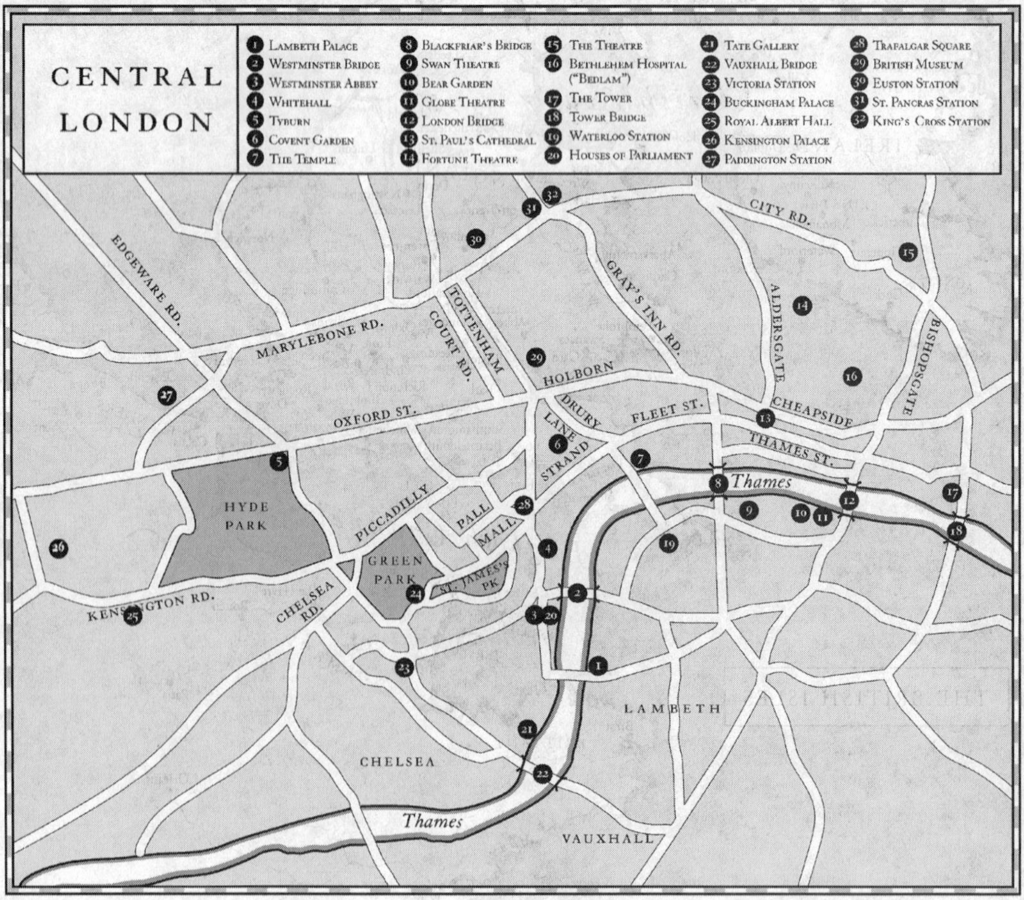

CENTRAL LONDON
1 Lambeth Palace
2 Westminster Bridge
3 Westminster Abbey
4 Whitehall
5 Tyburn
6 Covent Garden
7 The Temple
8 Blackfriar's Bridge
9 Swan Theatre
10 Bear Garden
11 Globe Theatre
12 London Bridge
13 St. Paul's Cathedral
14 Fortune Theatre
15 The Theatre
16 Bethlehem Hospital ("Bedlam")
17 The Tower
18 Tower Bridge
19 Waterloo Station
20 Houses of Parliament
21 Tate Gallery
22 Vauxhall Bridge
23 Victoria Station
24 Buckingham Palace
25 Royal Albert Hall
26 Kensington Palace
27 Paddington Station
28 Trafalgar Square
29 British Museum
30 Euston Station
31 St. Pancras Station
32 King's Cross Station
City Rd.
Edgeware Rd.
Gray's Inn Rd.
Aldersgate
Bishopsgate
Tottenham Court Rd.
Marylebone Rd.
Holborn
Drury Lane
Fleet St.
Cheapside
Oxford St.
Thames St.
Strand
Thames
Hyde Park
Piccadilly
Pall Mall
Green Park
St. James's Pk
Kensington Rd.
Chelsea Rd.
Lambeth
Chelsea
Thames
Vauxhall

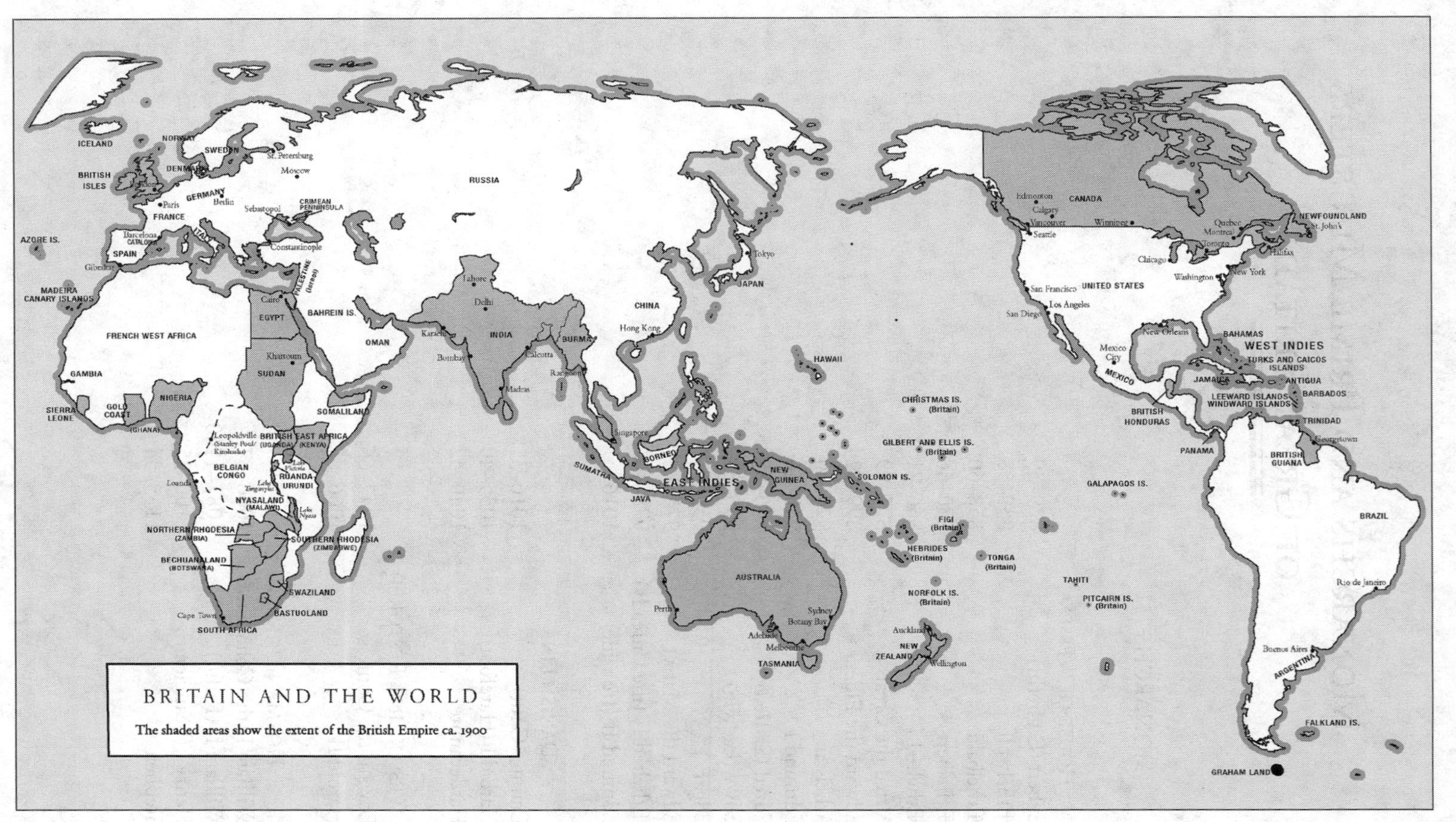

BRITAIN AND THE WORLD

The shaded areas show the extent of the British Empire ca. 1900

Monarchs and Prime Ministers of Great Britain

MONARCHS

House of Wessex

Egbert (Ecgberht)	829–39
Æthelwulf	839–58
Æthelbald	858–60
Æthelbert	860–66
Æthelred I	866–71
Alfred the Great	871–99
Edward the Elder	899–924
Athelstan	924–40
Edmund I	940–46
Edred (Eadred)	946–55
Edwy (Eadwig)	955–59
Edgar	959–75
Edward the Martyr	975–78
Æthelred II (the Unready)	978–1016
Edmund II (Ironside)	1016

Danish Line

Canute (Cnut)	1016–35
Harold I (Harefoot)	1035–40
Hardecanute	1040–42

Wessex Line, Restored

Edward the Confessor	1042–66
Harold II	1066

Norman Line

William I (the Conqueror)	1066–87
William II (Rufus)	1087–1100
Henry I (Beauclerc)	1100–35
Stephen	1135–54

MONARCHS

PLANTAGENET, ANGEVIN LINE	
Henry II	1154–89
Richard I (Coeur de Lion)	1189–99
John (Lackland)	1199–1216
Henry III	1216–72
Edward I (Longshanks)	1272–1307
Edward II	1307–27
Edward III	1327–77
Richard II	1377–99
PLANTAGENET, LANCASTRIAN LINE	
Henry IV	1399–1413
Henry V	1413–22
Henry VI	1422–61
PLANTAGENET, YORKIST LINE	
Edward IV	1461–83
Edward V	1483
Richard III	1483–85
HOUSE OF TUDOR	
Henry VII	1485–1509
Henry VIII	1509–47
Edward VI	1547–53
Mary I	1553–58
Elizabeth I	1558–1603
HOUSE OF STUART	
James I	1603–25
Charles I	1625–49
(The Commonwealth)	1649–60
Oliver Cromwell	1649–58
Richard Cromwell	1658–59

Henry VIII

Mary I

MONARCHS		PRIME MINISTERS	
HOUSE OF STUART, RESTORED			
Charles II	1660–85		
James II	1685–88		
HOUSE OF ORANGE AND STUART			
William III and Mary II	1689–94		
William III	1694–1702		
HOUSE OF STUART			
Anne	1702–14		
HOUSE OF BRUNSWICK, HANOVER LINE			
George I	1714–27	Sir Robert Walpole (Whig)	1721–42
George II	1727–60	Earl of Wilmington (Whig)	1742–43
		Henry Pelham (Whig)	1743–54
		Duke of Newcastle (Whig)	1754–56
		Duke of Devonshire (Whig)	1756–57
George III	1760–1820	Duke of Newcastle (Whig)	1757–62
		Earl of Bute (Tory)	1762–63
		George Grenville (Whig)	1763–65
		Marquess of Rockingham (Whig)	1765–66
		William Pitt the Elder (Earl of Chatham) (Whig)	1766–68
		Duke of Grafton (Whig)	1768–70
		Frederick North (Lord North) (Tory)	1770–82
		Marquess of Rockingham (Whig)	1782
		Earl of Shelburne (Whig)	1782–83
		Duke of Portland	1783
		William Pitt the Younger (Tory)	1783–1801
		Henry Addington (Tory)	1801–04
		William Pitt the Younger (Tory)	1804–06
		William Wyndham Grenville (Baron Grenville) (Whig)	1806–07

George III

George, Prince of Wales, Prince Regent

MONARCHS	
George, Prince of Wales, Prince Regent	1811–20
George IV	1820–30
William IV	1830–37
Victoria	1837–1901
HOUSE OF SAXE-COBURG-GOTHA	
Edward VII	1901–10
HOUSE OF WINDSOR	
George V	1910–36

Victoria

PRIME MINISTERS	
Duke of Portland (Whig)	1807–09
Spencer Perceval (Tory)	1809–12
Earl of Liverpool (Tory)	1812–27
George Canning (Tory)	1827
Viscount Goderich (Tory)	1827–28
Duke of Wellington (Tory)	1828–30
Earl Grey (Whig)	1830–34
Viscount Melbourne (Whig)	1834
Sir Robert Peel (Tory)	1834–35
Viscount Melbourne (Whig)	1835–41
Sir Robert Peel (Tory)	1841–46
Lord John Russell (later Earl) (Liberal)	1846–52
Earl of Derby (Con.)	1852
Earl of Aberdeen (Tory)	1852–55
Viscount Palmerston (Lib.)	1855–58
Earl of Derby (Con.)	1858–59
Viscount Palmerston (Lib.)	1859–65
Earl Russell (Liberal)	1865–66
Earl of Derby (Con.)	1866–68
Benjamin Disraeli (Con.)	1868
William Gladstone (Lib.)	1868–74
Benjamin Disraeli (Con.)	1874–80
William Gladstone (Lib.)	1880–85
Marquess of Salisbury (Con.)	1885–86
William Gladstone (Lib.)	1886
Marquess of Salisbury (Con.)	1886–92
William Gladstone (Lib.)	1892–94
Earl of Rosebery (Lib.)	1894–95
Marquess of Salisbury (Con.)	1895–1902
Arthur Balfour (Con.)	1902–05
Sir Henry Campbell-Bannerman (Lib.)	1905–08
Herbert Asquith (Lib.)	1908–15
Herbert Asquith (Lib.)	1915–16

MONARCHS		PRIME MINISTERS	
		Andrew Bonar Law (Con.)	1922–23
		Stanley Baldwin (Con.)	1923–24
		James Ramsay MacDonald (Labour)	1924
		Stanley Baldwin (Con.)	1924–29
		James Ramsay MacDonald (Labour)	1929–31
		James Ramsay MacDonald (Labour)	1931–35
		Stanley Baldwin (Con.)	1935–37
Edward VIII	1936	Neville Chamberlain (Con.)	1937–40
George VI	1936–52	Winston Churchill (Con.)	1940–45
		Winston Churchill (Con.)	1945
		Clement Attlee (Labour)	1945–51
		Sir Winston Churchill (Con.)	1951–55
Elizabeth II	1952–	Sir Anthony Eden (Con.)	1955–57
		Harold Macmillan (Con.)	1957–63
		Sir Alex Douglas-Home (Con.)	1963–64
		Harold Wilson (Labour)	1964–70
		Edward Heath (Con.)	1970–74
		Harold Wilson (Labour)	1974–76
		James Callaghan (Labour)	1976–79
		Margaret Thatcher (Con.)	1979–90
		John Major (Con.)	1990–97
		Tony Blair (Labour)	1997–

Glossary of Terms

Accent: the natural emphasis (stress) speakers place on a syllable.

Accentual Verse: poetry in which a line is measured only by the number of accents or stresses, not by the number of syllables.

Accentual-Syllabic Verse: the most common metrical system in traditional English verse, in which a line is measured by the number of syllables and by the pattern of accented (stressed) and unaccented (unstressed) syllables.

Aesthetes: members of a late nineteenth-century movement that valued "art for art's sake"—for its purely aesthetic qualities, as opposed to valuing art for the moral content it may convey, for the intellectual stimulation it may provide, or for a range of other qualities.

Alexandrine: a line of verse that is 12 syllables long. In English verse, the alexandrine is always an iambic hexameter: that is, it has six iambic feet. The most-often quoted example is the second line in a couplet from Alexander Pope's "Essay on Criticism" (1711): "A needless Alexandrine ends the song / That, like a wounded snake, drags its slow length along." See also *Spenserian stanza.*

Allegory: a narrative with both a literal meaning and secondary, often symbolic meaning or meanings. Allegory frequently employs personification to give concrete embodiment to abstract concepts or entities, such as feelings or personal qualities. It may also present one set of characters or events in the guise of another, using implied parallels for the purposes of satire or political comment, as in John Dryden's poem "Absalom and Achitophel."

Alliteration: the grouping of words with the same initial consonant (e.g., "break, blow, burn, and make me new"). The repetition of sound acts as a connector. See also *assonance* and *consonance.*

Alliterative Verse: poetry that employs alliteration of stressed syllables in each line as its chief structural principle.

Allusion: a reference, often indirect or unidentified, to a person, thing, or event. A reference in one literary work to another literary work, whether to its content or its form, also constitutes an allusion.

Ambiguity: an "opening" of language created by the writer to allow for multiple meanings or differing interpretations. In literature, ambiguity may be deliberately employed by the writer to enrich meaning; this differs from any unintentional, unwanted, ambiguity in non-literary prose.

Amphibrach: a metrical foot with three syllables, the second of which is stressed: x / x (e.g., sensation).

Analogy: a broad term that refers to our processes of noting similarities among things or events. Specific forms of analogy in poetry include *simile* and *metaphor* (see below).

Anapaest: a metrical foot containing two unstressed syllables followed by one stressed syllable: xx / (e.g., underneath, intervene).

Anglican Church / Church of England: formed after Henry VIII's break with Rome in the 1530s, the Church of England had acquired a permanently Protestant cast by the 1570s. There has remained considerable variation within the Church, however, with distinctions often drawn among High Church, Broad Church, and Latitudinarian. At one extreme High Church Anglicans (some of whom prefer to be known as "Anglo-Catholics") prefer relatively elaborate church rituals not dissimilar in form to those of the Roman Catholic Church and place considerable emphasis on church hierarchy, while in the other direction Latitudinarians prefer relatively informal religious services and tend far more towards egalitarianism.

Antistrophe: from Greek drama, the chorus's countermovement or reply to an initial movement (strophe). See *ode* below.

Apostrophe: a figure of speech (a trope; see figures of speech below) in which a writer directly addresses an object—or a dead or absent person—as if the imagined audience were actually listening.

Archetype: in literature and mythology, a recurring idea, symbol, motif, character, or place. To some scholars and psychologists, an archetype represents universal human thought-patterns or experiences.

Assonance: the repetition of identical or similar vowel sounds in stressed syllables in which the surrounding consonants are different: for example, "shame" and "fate"; "gale" and "cage"; or the long "i" sounds in "Beside the pumice isle..."

Aubade: a lyric poem that greets or laments the arrival of dawn.

Ballad: a folk song, or a poem originally recited to an audience, which tells a dramatic story based on legend or history.

Ballad Stanza: a quatrain with alternating four-stress and three-stress lines, rhyming *abcb*. A variant is "common measure," in which the alternating lines are strictly iambic, and rhyme *abab*.

Ballade: a fixed form most commonly characterized by only three rhymes, with an 8-line stanza rhyming *ababbcbc* and an envoy rhyming *bcbc*. Both Chaucer and Dante Gabriel Rossetti ("Ballad of the Dead Ladies") adopted this form.

Baroque: powerful and heavily ornamented in style. "Baroque" is a term from the history of visual art and of music that is sometimes also used to describe certain literary styles, such as that of Richard Crashaw.

Bathos: an anticlimactic effect brought about by a writer's descent from an elevated subject or tone to the ordinary or trivial.

Benedictine Rule: set of instructions for monastic communities, composed by Saint Benedict of Nursia (died c. 457).

Blank Verse: unrhymed lines written in iambic pentameter, a form introduced to English verse by Henry Howard, Earl of Surrey, in his translation of parts of Virgil's *Aeneid* in 1547.

Bombast: inappropriately inflated or grandiose language.

Broadside: individual sheet of paper printed on only one side. From the sixteenth through to the eighteenth centuries broadsides of a variety of different sorts (e.g., ballads, political tracts, short satires) were sold on the streets.

Broken Rhyme: in which a multi-syllable word is split at the end of a line and continued onto the next, to allow an end-rhyme with the split syllable.

Burlesque: satire of a particularly exaggerated sort, particularly that which ridicules its subject by emphasising its vulgar or ridiculous aspects.

Caesura: a pause or break in a line of verse occurring where a phrase, clause, or sentence ends, and indicated in scansion by the mark II. If it occurs in the middle of the line, it is known as a "medial" caesura.

Canon: in literature, those works that are commonly accepted as possessing authority or importance. In practice, "canonical" texts or authors are those that are discussed most frequently by scholars and taught most frequently in university courses.

Canto: a sub-section of a long (usually epic) poem.

Canzone: a short song or poem, with stanzas of equal length and an envoy.

Carpe Diem: Latin (from Horace) meaning "seize the day." The idea of enjoying the moment is a common one in Renaissance love poetry. See, for example, Marvell's "To His Coy Mistress."

Catalexis: the omission of unstressed syllables from a line of verse (such a line is referred to as "catalectic"). In iambic verse it is usually the first syllable of the line that is omitted; in trochaic, the last. For example, in the first stanza of Housman's "To an Athlete Dying Young" the third line is catalectic: i.e., it has dropped the first, unstressed syllable called for by the poem's iambic tetrameter form: "The time you won your town the race / We chaired you through the market-place; / Man and boy stood cheering by, / And home we brought you shoulder-high."

Catharsis: the arousal through the performance of a dramatic tragedy of "emotions of pity and fear" to a point where "purgation" or "purification" occurs and the feelings are released or transformed. The concept was developed by Aristotle in his *Poetics* from an ancient Greek medical concept, and adapted by him into an aesthetic principle.

Chiasmus: a figure of speech (a scheme) that reverses word order in successive parallel clauses. If the word order is A-B-C in the first clause, it becomes C-B-A in the second: for example, Donne's line "She is all states, and all princes, I" ("The Sun Rising") incorporates this reversal (though with an ellipsis).

Classical: originating in or relating to ancient Greek or Roman culture. As commonly conceived, *classical* implies a strong sense of formal order. The term *neoclassical* is often used with reference to literature of the Restoration and eighteenth century that was strongly influenced by ancient Greek and Roman models.

Closet Drama: a play (typically in verse) written for private performance. The term came into use in the first half of the nineteenth century.

Colored Narrative: alternative term for *free indirect discourse.*

Comedy: as a literary term, used originally to denote that class of ancient Greek drama in which the action ends happily. More broadly the term has been used to describe a wide variety of literary forms of a more or less light-hearted character.

***Commedia dell'arte*:** largely improvised comic performances conducted by masked performers and involving considerable physical activity. The genre of *commedia dell'arte* originated in Italy in the sixteenth century; it was influential throughout Europe for more than two centuries thereafter.

Commonwealth: from the fifteenth century, a term roughly equivalent to the modern "state," but tending to emphasize the commonality of interests among all citizens. In the seventeenth century Britain was named a commonwealth under Oliver Cromwell. In the twentieth century, the term came to be applied to associations of many nations; the British Commonwealth became the successor to the British Empire.

Conceit: an unusually elaborate metaphor or simile that extends beyond its original tenor and vehicle, sometimes becoming a "master" analogy for the entire poem (see, for example, Donne's "The Flea," and Robert Frost's sonnet "She is as in a field a silken tent"). Ingenious or fanciful images and comparisons were especially popular with the metaphysical poets of the seventeenth century, giving rise to the term "metaphysical conceit."

Concrete Poetry: an experimental form, most popular during the 1950s and 60s, in which the printed type itself forms a visual image of the poem's key words or ideas. See also *pattern poetry, assonance.*

Connotation: the implied, often unspoken meaning(s) of a given word, as distinct from its denotation, or literal meaning. Connotations may have highly emotional undertones and are usually culturally specific.

Conservative Party: See *Political Parties.*

Consonance: the pairing of words with similar initial and ending consonants, but with different vowel sounds (live/love, wander/wonder). See also *alliteration.*

Convention: aesthetic approach, technique, or practice accepted as characteristic and appropriate for a particular form. It is a convention of certain sorts of plays, for example, that the characters speak in blank verse, of other sorts of plays that characters speak in rhymed couplets, and of still other sorts of dramatic performances that characters frequently break into song to express their feelings.

Couplet: a pair of rhyming lines, usually in the same meter. If they form a complete unit of thought and are grammatically complete, the lines are known as a closed couplet. See also *heroic couplet* below.

Dactyl: a metrical foot containing one strong stress followed by two weak stresses: / xx (e.g., muttering, helplessly). A minor form known as "double dactyls" makes use of this meter for humorous purposes, e.g., "Jiggery pokery" or "Higgledy Piggledy."

Denotation: See *connotation* above.

Devolution: process through which a degree of political power was transferred in the late twentieth and early twenty-first centuries from the British government to assemblies in Scotland and in Wales.

Dialogue: words spoken by characters to one another. (When a character is addressing him or her self or the audience directly, the words spoken are referred to as a *monologue*.)

Diction: word choice. Whether the diction of a literary work (or of a literary character) is colloquial, conversational, formal, or of some other type contributes significantly to the tone of the text as well as to characterization.

Didacticism: aesthetic approach emphasizing moral instruction.

Dimeter: a poetic line containing two metrical feet.

Dirge: a song or poem that mourns someone's death. See also *elegy* and *lament* below.

Disestablishmentarianism: movement opposing an official state-supported religion, in particular the Church of England in that role.

Dissonance: harsh, unmusical sounds or rhythms which poets may use deliberately to achieve certain effects.

Dramatic Irony: this form of irony occurs when the audience's reception of a speech by a character on the stage is affected by the possession by the audience of information not available to the character.

Dramatic Monologue: a lyric poem that takes the form of an utterance by a single person addressing a silent listener. The speaker may be an historical personage (as in some of Robert Browning's dramatic monologues), a figure drawn from myth or legend (as in some of Tennyson's), or an entirely imagined figure, as in Webster's "A Castaway."

Dub Poetry: a form of protest poetry originating in Jamaica, with its roots in dance rhythms, especially reggae, and often accompanied in performance by drums and music. See also *rap* and *hip-hop*.

Duple Foot: A duple foot of poetry has two syllables. The possible duple forms are iamb (in which the stress is on the second of the two syllables), trochee (in which the stress is on the first of the two syllables), spondee (in which both are stressed equally), and pyrrhic (in which both syllables are unstressed).

Eclogue: now generally used simply as an alternative name for a pastoral poem. In classical times and in the early modern period, however, an *eclogue* (or *idyll*) was a specific type of pastoral poem—a dialogue or dramatic monologue involving rustic characters. (The other main sub-genre of the pastoral was the *georgic*.)

Elegiac Stanza: a quatrain of iambic pentameters rhyming *abab*, often used in poems meditating on death or sorrow. The best-known example is Thomas Gray's "Elegy Written in a Country Churchyard."

Elegy: a poem which formally mourns the death of a particular person (e.g., Tennyson's "In Memoriam") or in which the poet meditates on other serious subjects (e.g., Gray's "Elegy"). See also *dirge*.

Elision: omitting or suppressing a letter or an unstressed syllable at the beginning or end of a word, so that a line of verse may conform to a given metrical scheme. For example, the three syllables at the beginning of Shakespeare's sonnet 129 are reduced to two by the omission of the first vowel: "Th' expense of spirit in a waste of shame." See also *syncope*.

Ellipsis: the omission of a word or words necessary for the complete grammatical construction of a sentence, but not necessary for our understanding of the sentence.

End-Rhyme: See *rhyme*.

End-stopped: a line of poetry is said to be end-stopped when the end of the line coincides with a natural pause in the syntax, such as the conclusion of a sentence; e.g., in this couplet from Pope's "Essay on Criticism," both lines are end-stopped: "A little learning is a dangerous thing; / Drink deep, or taste not the Pierian spring." Compare this with *enjambement*.

Enjambement: the "running-on" of the sense from one line of poetry to the next, with no pause created by punctuation or syntax. (The more commonly found alternative is referred to as an *end-stopped line*.)

Envoy (Envoi): a stanza or half-stanza that forms the conclusion of certain French poetic forms, such as the *sestina* or the *ballade*. It often sums up or comments upon what has gone before.

Epic: a lengthy narrative poem, often divided into books and sub-divided into cantos. It generally celebrates heroic deeds or events, and the style tends to be lofty and grand. Examples in English include Spenser's *The Faerie Queene* and Milton's *Paradise Lost*.

Epic Simile: an elaborate simile, developed at such length that the vehicle of the comparison momentarily displaces the primary subject with which it is being compared.

Epigram: a very short poem, sometimes in closed couplet form, characterized by pointed wit.

Epigraph: a quotation placed at the beginning of a discourse to indicate or foreshadow the theme.

Epiphany: a moment at which matters of significance are suddenly illuminated for a literary character (or for the reader), typically triggered by something small and seemingly of little import. The term first came into wide currency in connection with the fiction of James Joyce.

Episodic Plot: plot comprising a variety of episodes that are only loosely connected by threads of story material (as opposed to plots that present one or more continually unfolding narratives where successive episodes build one on another).

Epithalamion: a poem celebrating a wedding. The best-known example in English is probably Edmund Spenser's "Epithalamion" (1595).

Eulogy: text expressing praise, especially for a distinguished person recently deceased.

Euphemism: mode of expression through which aspects of reality considered to be vulgar, crudely physical, or unpleasant are referred to indirectly rather than named explicitly. A variety of euphemisms exist for the processes of urination and defecation; *passed away* is often used as a euphemism for *died.* (The word *euphemism* has the same root as *Euphuism* (see below), but has taken on a different meaning.)

Euphony: pleasant, musical sounds or rhythms—the opposite of dissonance.

Euphuism: In the late sixteenth century John Lyly published a prose romance, *Euphues*, which employed a style that featured long sentences filled with balanced phrases and clauses, many of them adding little to the content. This highly mannered style was popular in the court of Elizabeth I for a few years following the publication of Lyly's famous work, and the style became known as *Euphuism*.

European Union: (EU) Group of nations formed in 1993 as the successor to the European Economic Community (Common Market). Britain first applied for membership in the latter in 1961; at first its efforts to join were blocked by the French government, but in 1973 Prime Minister Edward Heath successfully negotiated Britain's entry into the group. Britain has resisted some moves towards full integration with the European community, in particular retaining its own currency when other European nations adopted the Euro on 1 January 2002.

Exchequer: In earlier eras, the central royal financial office, responsible for receiving and keeping track of crown revenues. In later eras, part of the bureaucracy equivalent to the Ministry of Finance in Canada or the Treasury in the United States (the modern post of Chancellor of the Exchequer is equivalent to the American post of Secretary of the Treasury, the Canadian post of Minister of Finance or the Australian post of Treasurer).

Exposition: the setting out of material in an ordered form, either in speech or in writing. In a play those parts of the action that do not occur on stage but are rather recounted by the characters are frequently described as being presented in exposition. Similarly, when the background narrative is filled in near the beginning of a novel, such material is often described as having been presented in exposition. Somewhat confusingly, however, the term "expository prose" is usually used with reference not to fiction but to the setting forth of arguments or descriptions in the context of essays or other works of prose non-fiction.

Eye-Rhyme: See *rhyme* below.

Feminine Ending: the ending of a line of poetry on an "extra," and, especially, on an unstressed syllable. See, for example, the first line of Keat's "Ode on a Grecian Urn": "A thing of beauty is a joy forever," a line of iambic pentameter in which the final foot is an amphibrach rather than an iamb.

Feminine Rhyme: See *rhyme* below.

Figures of Speech: deliberate, highly concentrated uses of language to achieve particular purposes or effects on an audience. There are two kinds of figures: schemes and tropes. Schemes involve changes in word-sound and word-order, such as *alliteration* and *chiasmus*. Tropes play on our understandings of words to extend, alter, or transform meaning, as in *metaphor* and *personification*.

First-Person Narrative: narrative recounted using *I* and *me*. See also *narrative perspective*.

Fixed Forms: the term applied to a number of poetic forms and stanzaic patterns, many derived from French models, such as *ballade, rondeau, sestina, triolet,* and *villanelle*. Other "fixed forms" include the *sonnet, rhyme royal, haiku,* and *ottava rima*.

Folio: largest of several sizes of book page commonly used in the first few centuries after the introduction of the printing press. A folio size results from sheets of paper of at least 14 inches by 20 inches being folded in half (a folio page size will thus be at least 7 inches by 10 inches). When the same sheet is folded twice a quarto is produced, and when it is folded 3 times an octavo.

Foot: a unit of a line of verse which contains a particular combination of stressed and unstressed syllables. Dividing a line into metrical feet (*iambs, trochees,* etc.), then counting the number of feet per line, is part of *scansion*. See also *meter*.

Franklin: in the late medieval period, a landholder of free status, but ranking below the gentry.

Free Indirect Discourse: in prose fiction, commentary in which a seemingly objective and omniscient narrative voice assumes the point of view of one or more characters. When we hear through the third person narrative voice of Jane Austen's *Pride and Prejudice*, for example, that Mr. Darcy "was the proudest, most disagreeable man in the world, and every body hoped that he would never come there again," the narrative voice has assumed the point of view of "every body" in the community; we as readers are not meant to take it that Mr. Darcy is indeed the most disagreeable man in the world. Similarly, in the following passage from the same novel, we are likely to take it to read it as being the view of the character Charlotte that marriage is "the only honourable provision for well-educated young women of small fortune," not to take it to be an objective statement of perceived truth on the part of the novel's third person narrative voice:

> [Charlotte's] reflections were in general satisfactory. Mr. Collins to be sure was neither sensible nor agreeable; his society was irksome, and his attachment to her must be imaginary. But still he would be her husband. Without thinking highly either of men or of matrimony, marriage had always been her object; it was the only honourable provision for well-educated young women of small fortune, and however uncertain of giving happiness, must be their pleasantest preservative from want.

The term free indirect discourse may also be applied to situations in which it may not be entirely clear if the thoughts expressed emanate from the character, the narrator, or some combination of the two. (In the above-quoted passage expressing Charlotte's thoughts, indeed, some might argue that the statement concerning marriage should be taken as the expression of a belief that the narrative voice shares, at least in part.)

Free Verse: poetry that does not follow any regular meter, line length, or rhyming scheme. In many respects, though, free verse follows the complex natural "rules" and rhythmic patterns (or cadences) of speech.

Gaelic: Celtic language, variants of which are spoken in Ireland and Scotland.

Genre: a particular literary form. The concept of genre may be used with different levels of generality. At the most general, poetry, drama, and prose fiction are distinguished as separate genres. At a lower level of generality various sub-genres are frequently distinguished, such as (within drama) comedy and tragedy, or, at a still lower level of generality, Elizabethan domestic tragedy, Edwardian drawing-room comedy, and so on.

Georgic: (from Virgil's *Georgics*) a poem that celebrates the natural wealth of the countryside and advises how to cultivate and live in harmony with it. Pope's *Windsor Forest* and James Thomson's *Seasons* are classed as georgics. They were often said to make up, with eclogues, the two alliterative forms of pastoral poetry.

Ghazal: derived from Persian and Indian precedents, the ghazal presents a series of thoughts in closed couplets joined by a simple rhyme-scheme: *ab bb cb eb fb*, etc.

Gothic: in architecture and the visual arts, a term used to describe styles prevalent from the twelfth to the fourteenth centuries, but in literature a term used to describe work with a sinister or grotesque tone that seeks to evoke a sense of terror on the part of the reader or audience. Gothic literature originated as a genre in the eighteenth century with works such as Horace Walpole's *The Castle of Otranto*. To some extent the notion of the medieval itself then carried with it associations of the dark and the grotesque, but from the beginning an element of intentional exaggeration (sometimes verging on self-parody) attached itself to the genre. The Gothic trend of youth culture that began in the late twentieth century is less clearly associated with the medieval, but shares with the various varieties of Gothic literature (from Walpole in the eighteenth century, to Bram Stoker in the early twentieth, to Stephen King and Anne Rice in the late twentieth) a fondness for the sensational and the grotesque, as well as a propensity to self-parody.

Guilds: non-clerical associations that arose in the late Anglo-Saxon period, devoted both to social purposes (such as the organization of feasts for the members) and to piety. In the later medieval period guilds developed strong associations with particular occupations.

Haiku: a Japanese form, using three unrhymed lines of five, seven, and five syllables. Conventionally, it uses precise, concentrated images to suggest states of feeling.

Heptameter: a line containing seven metrical feet.

Heroic Couplet: a pair of rhymed iambic pentameters, so called because the form was much used in seventeenth and eighteenth-century poems and plays on heroic subjects.

Hexameter: a line containing six metrical feet.

Home Rule: movement dedicated to making Ireland politically independent from Britain.

Horatian Ode: inspired by the work of the Roman poet Horace, an ode that is usually calm and meditative in tone, and homostrophic (i.e., having regular stanzas) in form. Keats's odes are English examples.

House of Commons: elected legislative body, in Britain currently consisting of six hundred and fifty-nine members of Parliament. See also *Parliament*.

House of Lords: the "Upper House" of the British Houses of Parliament. Since the nineteenth century the House of Lords has been far less powerful than the elected House of Commons. The House of Lords is currently made up of both hereditary peers (Lords whose title is passed on from generation to generation) and life peers. As a result of legislation enacted by the Labour government of Tony Blair, the role of hereditary peers in Parliament is being phased out.

Humors: The four humors were believed in until the sixteenth and seventeenth centuries to be elements in the makeup of all humans; a person's temperament was thought to be determined by the way in which the humors were combined. When the *choleric* humor was dominant, the person would tend towards anger; when the *sanguine* humor was dominant, towards pleasant affability; when the *phlegmatic* humor was dominant, towards a cool and calm attitude and/or a lack of feeling or enthusiasm; and when the *melancholic* humor was dominant, towards withdrawal and melancholy.

Hymn: a song whose theme is usually religious, in praise of divinity. Literary hymns may praise more secular subjects.

Hyperbole: a *figure of speech* (a trope) that deliberately exaggerates or inflates meaning to achieve particular effects, such as the irony in A.E. Housman's claim (from "Terence, this is stupid stuff") that "malt does more than Milton can / To justify God's ways to man."

Iamb: the most common metrical foot in English verse, containing one unstressed syllable followed by a stressed syllable: x / (e.g., between, achieve).

Idyll: traditionally, a short pastoral poem that idealizes country life, conveying impressions of innocence and happiness.

Image: the recreation in words of objects perceived by the senses, sometimes thought of as "pictures," although other senses besides sight are involved. Besides this literal application, the term also refers more generally to the descriptive effects of figurative language, especially in *metaphor* and *simile*.

Imagism: a poetic movement that was popular mainly in the second decade of the twentieth century. The goal of Imagist poets (such as H.D. and Ezra Pound in their early work) was to represent emotions or impressions through highly concentrated imagery.

In Memoriam Stanza: a four-line stanza in iambic tetrameter, rhyming *abba*: the type of stanza used by Tennyson in *In Memoriam*.

Incantation: a chant or recitation of words that are believed to have magical power. A poem can achieve an "incantatory" effect through a compelling rhyme scheme and other repetitive patterns.

Interlocking Rhyme: See *rhyme*.

Internal Rhyme: See *rhyme*.

Irony: a subtle form of humor in which a statement is understood to convey a quite different (and often entirely opposite) meaning. A writer achieves this by carefully making sure that the statement occurs in a context which undermines or twists the statement's "literal" meaning. *Hyperbole* and *litotes* are often used for ironic effect. *Sarcasm* is a particularly strong or crude form of irony (usually spoken), in which the meaning is conveyed largely by the tone of voice adopted; something said sarcastically is meant clearly to imply its opposite.

Labour Party: See *Political Parties*.

Lament: a poem which expresses profound regret or grief either because of a death, or because of the loss of a former, happier state.

Language Poetry: a movement that defies the usual lyric and narrative conventions of poetry, and that challenges the structures and codes of everyday language. Often seen as both politically and aesthetically subversive, its roots lie in the works of modernist writers like Ezra Pound and Gertrude Stein.

Liberal Party: See *Political Parties*.

Litotes: a *figure of speech* (a trope) in which a writer deliberately uses understatement to highlight the importance of an argument, or to convey an ironic attitude.

Liturgical Drama: drama based on and/or incorporating text from the liturgy—the text recited during religious services.

Lollard: member of the group of radical Christians that took its inspiration from the ideas of John Wyclif (c. 1330–84). The Lollards, in many ways precursors of the Protestant Reformation, advocated making the Bible available to all, and dedication to the principles of evangelical poverty in imitation of Christ.

Luddites: protestors against the mechanization of industry on the grounds that it was leading to the loss of employment and to an increase in poverty. In the years 1811 to 1816 there were several Luddite protests in which machines were destroyed.

Lyric: a poem, usually short, expressing an individual speaker's feelings or private thoughts. Originally a song performed with accompaniment on a lyre, the lyric poem is often noted for musicality of rhyme and rhythm. The lyric genre includes a variety of forms, including the *sonnet*, the *ode*, the *elegy*, the *madrigal*, the *aubade*, the *dramatic monologue*, and the *hymn*.

Madrigal: a lyric poem, usually short and focusing on pastoral or romantic themes. A madrigal is often set to music.

Masculine Ending: a metrical line ending on a stressed syllable. *Masculine Rhyme*: see *rhyme*.

Masque: an entertainment typically combining music and dance, with a limited script, extravagant costumes and sets, and often incorporating spectacular special effects. Masques, which were performed before court audiences in the early seventeenth century, often focused on royal themes and frequently drew on classical mythology.

Mass: Within Christianity, a church service that includes the sacrament of the Eucharist (Holy Communion), in which bread and wine are consumed which are believed by those of many Christian denominations to have been transubstantiated into the body and blood of Christ. Anglicans (Episcopalians) are more likely to believe the bread and wine merely symbolizes the body and blood.

Melodrama: originally a term used to describe nineteenth-century-plays featuring sensational story lines and a crude separation of characters into moral categories, with the pure and virtuous pitted against evil villains. Early melodramas employed background music throughout the action of the play as a means of heightening the emotional response of the audience. By extension, certain sorts of prose fictions or poems are often described as having melodramatic elements.

Metaphor: a *figure of speech* (in this case, a trope) in which a comparison is made or identity is asserted between two unrelated things or actions without the use of "like" or "as." The primary subject is known as the *tenor*; to illuminate its nature, the writer links it to wholly different images, ideas, or actions referred to as the *vehicle*. Unlike a *simile*, which is a direct comparison of two things, a metaphor "fuses" the separate qualities of two things, creating a new idea. For example, Shakespeare's "Let slip the dogs of war" is a metaphorical statement. The tenor, or primary subject, is "war"; the vehicle of the metaphor is the image of hunting dogs released from their leash. The line fuses the idea of war with the qualities of ravening bloodlust associated with hunting dogs.

Metaphysical Poets: a group of seventeenth-century English poets, notably Donne, Cowley, Marvell, and Herbert, who employed unusual difficult imagery and *conceits* (see above) in order to develop intellectual and religious themes. The term was first applied to these writers to mark as far-fetched their use of philosophical and scientific ideas in a poetic context.

Meter: the pattern of stresses, syllables, and pauses that constitutes the regular rhythm of a line of verse. The meter of a poem written in the English accentual-syllabic tradition is determined by identifying the stressed and unstressed syllables in a line of verse, and grouping them into recurring units known as feet. See *accent*, *accentual-syllabic*, *caesura*, *elision*, and *scansion*. For some of the better known meters, see *iamb*, *trochee*, *dactyl*, *anapaest*, and *spondee*. See also *monometer*, *dimeter*, *trimeter*, *tetrameter*, *pentameter*, and *hexameter*.

Methodist: Protestant denomination formed in the eighteenth century as part of the religious movement led by John and Charles Wesley. Originally a movement within the Church of England, Methodism entailed enthusiastic evangelism, a strong emphasis on free will, and a strict regimen of Christian living.

Metonymy: a *figure of speech* (a trope), meaning "change of name," in which a writer refers to an object or idea by substituting the name of another object or idea closely associated with it: for example, the substitution of "crown" for monarchy, "the press" for journalism, or "the pen" for writing. *Synecdoche* (see below) is a kind of metonymy.

Mock-heroic: a style applying the elevated diction and vocabulary of epic poetry to low or ridiculous subjects. An example is Alexander Pope's "The Rape of the Lock."

Monologue: words spoken by a character to him or herself or to an audience directly.

Monometer: a line containing one metrical foot.

Mood: This can describe the writer's attitude, implied or expressed, towards the subject (see *tone* below); or it may refer to the atmosphere that a writer creates in a passage of description or narration.

Motif: an idea, image, action, or plot element that recurs throughout a literary work, creating new levels of meaning and strengthening structural coherence. The term is taken from music, where it describes recurring melodies or themes. See also *theme*.

Narrative Perspective: in fiction, the point of view from which the story is narrated. A first-person narrative is recounted using *I* and *me*, whereas a third person narrative is recounted using *he, she, they*, and so on. When a narrative is written in the third person and the narrative voice evidently "knows" all that is being done and thought, the story is typically described as being recounted by an "omniscient narrator."

Neoclassical: adapted from or substantially influenced by the cultures of ancient Greece and Rome. The term *neoclassical* is often used to describe the ideals of Restoration and eighteenth-century writers and artists who looked to ancient Greek and Roman civilization for models.

Nobility: privileged class, the members of which are distinguished by the holding of titles. Dukes, Marquesses, Earls, Viscounts, and Barons (in that order of precedence) are all holders of hereditary titles—that is to say, in the British patrilineal tradition, titles passed on from generation to generation to the eldest son. The title of Baronet, also hereditary, was added to this list by James I. Holders of non-hereditary titles include Knights and Dames.

Nonconformist: general term used to describe one who does subscribe to the Church of England.

Nonsense Verse: light, humorous poetry which contradicts logic, plays with the absurd, and invents words for amusing effects. Lewis Carroll is one of the best-known practitioners of nonsense verse.

Octave: also known as "octet," the first eight lines in an Italian/Petrarchan sonnet, rhyming *abbaabba*. See also *sestet* and *sonnet*.

Octosyllabic: a line of poetry with eight syllables, as in iambic tetrameter.

Ode: originally a classical poetic form, used by the Greeks and Romans to convey serious themes. English poetry has evolved three main forms of ode: the Pindaric (imitative of the odes of the Greek poet Pindar); the Horatian (modeled on the work of the Roman writer Horace); and the irregular ode.

The Pindaric ode was an irregular stanza in English, has a tripartite structure of "strophe," "anti-strophe," and "epode" (meaning turn, counterturn, and stand), modeled on the songs and movements of the Chorus in Greek drama. The Horatian ode is more personal, reflective, and literary, and employs a pattern of repeated stanzas. The irregular ode, as its name implies, avoids a recurrent stanza pattern, and is sometimes irregular in line length also (see, for example, Wordsworth's "Ode: Intimations of Immortality").

Onomatopoeia: a *figure of speech* (a scheme) in which a word "imitates" a sound, or in which the sound of a word seems to reflect its meaning.

Ottava Rima: an 8-line stanza, usually in iambic pentameter, with the rhyme scheme *abababcc*. For an example, see Byron's *Don Juan*, or Yeats's "Sailing to Byzantium."

Oxymoron: a *figure of speech* (a trope) in which two words whose meanings seem contradictory are placed together, a paradox: for example, the phrase "darkness visible," from Milton's *Paradise Lost*.

Paean: a triumphant, celebratory song, often associated with a military victory.

Pale: in the medieval period, term for a protective zone around a fortress. As of the year 1500 three of these had been set up to guard frontiers of territory controlled by England—surrounding Calais in France, Berwick-upon-Tweed on the Scottish frontier, and Dublin in Ireland. The Dublin Pale was the largest of the three, and the term remained in use for a longer period there.

Pantoum: a poem in linked quatrains that rhyme *abab*. The second and fourth lines of one stanza are repeated as the first and third lines of the stanza that follows. In the final stanza the pattern is reversed: the second line repeats the third line of the first stanza, the fourth and final line repeats the first line of the first stanza.

Parliament: in Britain, the legislative body, comprising both the House of Commons and the House of Lords. Since the eighteenth century, the most powerful figure in the British government has been the Prime Minister rather than the monarch, the House of Commons has been the dominant body in Parliament, and members of the House of Commons have been organized in political parties. Since the mid-nineteenth century the effective executive in the British Parliamentary system has been the Cabinet, each member of which is typically in charge of a department of government. Unlike the American system, the British Parliamentary system (sometimes called the "Westminster system," after the location of the Houses of Parliament) brings together the executive and legislative functions of government, with the Prime Minister leading the government party in the House of Commons as well as directing the cabinet. By convention it is understood that the House of Lords will not contravene the wishes of the House of Commons in any fundamental way, though the "Upper House," as it is often referred to, may sometimes modify or reject legislation.

Parody: a close, usually mocking imitation of a particular literary work, or of the well-known style of a particular author, in order to expose or magnify weaknesses. Parody is a form of satire—that is, humor that may ridicule and scorn its object.

Pastiche: a discourse which borrows or imitates other writers' characters, forms, style, or ideas. Unlike a parody, a pastiche is usually intended as a compliment to the original writer.

Pastoral: in general, pertaining to country life; in prose, drama, and poetry, a stylized type of writing that idealizes the lives and innocence of country people, particularly shepherds and shepherdesses. Also see *eclogue, georgic, idyll*, above.

Pastoral Elegy: a poem in which the poet uses the pastoral style to lament the death of a friend, usually represented as a shepherd. Milton's "Lycidas" provides a good example of the form, including its use of such conventions as an invocation of the muse and a procession of mourners.

Pathetic Fallacy: a form of personification in which inanimate objects are given human emotions: for example, rain clouds "weeping." The word "fallacy" in this connection is intended to suggest the distortion of reality or the false emotion that may result from an exaggerated use of personification.

Pathos: the emotional quality of a discourse; or the ability of a discourse to appeal to our emotions. It is usually applied to the mood conveyed by images of pain, suffering, or loss that arouse feelings of pity or sorrow in the reader.

Pattern Poetry: a predecessor of modern concrete poetry, in which the shape of the poem on the page is intended to suggest or imitate an aspect of the poem's subject. George Herbert's "Easter Wings" is an example of pattern poetry.

Penny Dreadful: Victorian term for a cheap and poorly produced work of short fiction, usually of a sensational nature.

Pentameter: a line of verse containing five metrical feet.

Performance Poetry: poetry composed primarily for oral performance, often very theatrical in nature. See also *dub poetry* and *rap*.

Persona: the assumed identity or "speaking voice" that a writer projects in a discourse. The term "persona" literally means "mask." Even when a writer speaks in the first person, we should be aware that the attitudes or opinions we hear may not necessarily be those of the writer in real life.

Personification: a *figure of speech* (a trope), also known as "prosopopoeia," in which a writer refers to inanimate objects, ideas, or animals as if they were human, or creates a human figure to represent an abstract entity such as Philosophy or Peace.

Petrarchan Sonnet: the earliest form of the sonnet, also known as the Italian sonnet, with an 8-line octave and a 6-line sestet. The Petrarchan sonnet traditionally focuses on love and descriptions of physical beauty.

Phoneme: a linguistic term denoting the smallest unit of sound that it is possible to distinguish. The words *fun* and *phone* each have three phonemes, though one has three letters and one has five. (Each makes up a single syllable.)

Pindaric: See *ode*.

Plot: the organization of story materials within a literary work. The order in which story material is presented (especially causes and consequences); the inclusion of elements that allow or encourage the reader or audience to form expectations as to what is likely to happen; the decision to present some story material through exposition rather than in more extended form as part of the main action of the narrative—all these are matters of plotting.

Political Parties: The party names "Whig" and "Tory" began to be used in the late seventeenth century; before that time members of the House of Commons acted individually or through shifting and very informal factions. At first the Whigs and Tories had little formal organization either, but by the mid-eighteenth century parties had acknowledged leaders, and the leader of the party with the largest number of members in the House of Commons had begun to be recognized as the Prime Minister. The Tories evolved into the modern Conservative Party, and the Whigs into the Liberal Party. In the late nineteenth century the Labour Party was formed in an effort to provide better representation in Parliament for the working class, and since the 1920s Labour and the Conservatives have alternated as the party of government, with the Liberals reduced to third-party status. (Since 1988, when the Liberals merged with a breakaway faction from Labour known as the Social Democrats, this third party has been named the Liberal Democrats.)

Pre-Raphaelites: originally a group of Victorian artists and writers, formed in 1848. Their goal was to revive what they considered the simpler, fresher, more natural art that existed before Raphael (1483-1520). The poet Dante Gabriel Rossetti was one of the founders of the group.

Presbyterian: term applied to a group of Protestants (primarily English and Scottish) who advocated replacing the traditional hierarchical church in which bishops and archbishops governed lower level members of the clergy with a system in which all presbyters (or ministers) would be equal. The Presbyterians, originally led by John Knox, were strongly influenced by the ideas of John Calvin.

Prose Poem: a poetic discourse that uses prose formats (e.g., it may use margins and paragraphs rather than line breaks or stanzas) yet is written with the kind of attention to language, rhythm and cadence that characterizes verse.

Prosody: the study and analysis of meter, rhythm, rhyme, stanzaic pattern, and other devices of versification.

Protagonist: the central character in a literary work.

Prothalamion: a wedding song; a term coined by the poet Edmund Spenser, adapted from "epithalamion" (see above).

Public School: See *schools* below.

Pun: a play on words, in which a word with two or more distinct meanings, or two words with similar sounds, may create humorous ambiguities. Also known as *paranomasia*.

Puritan: term, originally applied only in a derogatory fashion but later widely accepted as descriptive, referring to those in England who favored religious reforms that went beyond those instituted as part of the Protestant Reformation, or, more generally, who were more forceful and uncompromising in pressing for religious purity both within the Church and in society as a whole.

Pyrrhic: a metrical foot containing two weak stresses: xx.

Quadrivium: group of four academic subjects (arithmetic, astronomy, geometry, and music) that made up part of the university coursework in the Middle Ages. There were studied after the more basic subjects of the *Trivium*.

Quantitative Meter: a metrical system used by Greek and Roman poets, in which a line of verse was measured by the "quantity," or length of sound of each syllable. A foot was measured in terms of syllables classed as long or short.

Quantity: duration of syllables in poetry. The line "There is a Garden in her face" (the first line from the poem of the same name by Thomas Campion) is characterized by the short quantities of the syllables. The last line of Thomas Hardy's "During Wind and Rain" has the same number of syllables as the line by Campion, but the quantities of the syllables are much longer—in other words, the line take much longer to say: "Down their carved names the rain drop ploughs."

Quatrain: a four-line stanza, usually rhymed.

Quintet: a five-line stanza. Sometimes given as *quintain*.

Rap: originally coined to describe informal conversation, "rap" now usually describes a style of performance poetry in which a poet will chant rhymed verse, sometimes improvised and usually with musical accompaniment that has a heavy beat.

Realism: as a literary term, the presentation through literature of material closely resembling real life. As notions both of what constitutes "real life" and of how it may be most faithfully represented in literature have varied widely, "realism" has taken a variety of meanings. The term *naturalistic* has sometimes been used a synonym for *realistic*; *naturalism* originated in the nineteenth century as a term denoting a form of realism focusing in particular on grim, unpleasant, or ugly aspects of the real.

Refrain: one or more words or lines repeated at regular points throughout a poem, often at the end of each stanza or group of stanzas. Sometimes a whole stanza may be repeated to create a refrain, like the chorus in a song.

Reggae: a style of heavily-rhythmic music from the West Indies with lyrics that are colloquial in language and often anti-establishment in content and flavor. First popularized in the 1960s and 1970s, reggae has had a lasting influence on performance poetry, rap, and dub.

Rhetoric: in classical Greece and Rome, the art of persuasion and public speaking. From the Middle Ages onwards, the study of rhetoric gave greater attention to style, particularly figures of speech. Today in poetics, the term rhetoric may encompass not only figures of speech, but also the persuasive effects of forms, sounds and word choices.

Rhyme: the repetition of identical or similar sounds, usually in pairs and generally at the ends of metrical lines.

End-rhyme: a rhyming word or syllable at the end of a line.

Eye Rhyme: rhyming that pairs words whose spellings are alike but whose pronunciations are different: for example, though/slough.

Feminine Rhyme: a two-syllable (also known as "double") rhyme. The first syllable is stressed and the second unstressed: for example, hasty/tasty. See also *triple rhyme* below.

Interlocking Rhyme: the repetition of rhymes from one stanza to the next, creating links that add to the poem's continuity and coherence. Examples may be found in Shelley's use of *terza rima* in "Ode to the West Wind" and in Dylan Thomas's villanelle "Do Not Go Gentle Into That Good Night."

Internal Rhyme: the placement of rhyming words within lines so that at least two words in a line rhyme with each other.

Masculine Rhyme: a correspondence of sound between the final stressed syllables at the end of two or more lines, as in grieve/leave, arr-ive/sur-vive.

Slant Rhyme: an imperfect or partial rhyme (also known as "near" or "half" rhyme) in which the final consonants of stressed syllables match but the vowel sounds do not. E.g., spoiled / spilled, taint / stint.

Triple Rhyme: a three-syllable rhyme in which the first syllable of each rhyme-word is stressed and the other two unstressed (e.g., lottery / coterie).

True Rhyme: a rhyme in which everything but the initial consonant matches perfectly in sound and spelling.

Rhyme Royal: a stanza of seven iambic pentameters, with a rhyme-scheme of *ababbcc*. This is also known as the Chaucerian stanza, as Chaucer was the first English poet to use this form. See also *septet*.

Rhythm: in speech, the arrangement of stressed and unstressed syllables creates units of sound. In song or verse, these units usually form a regular rhythmic pattern, a kind of beat, described in prosody as *meter*.

Romanticism: a major social and cultural movement, originating in Europe, that shaped much of Western artistic thought in the late eighteenth and nineteenth centuries. Opposing the ideal of controlled, rational order of the Enlightenment, Romanticism emphasizes the importance of spontaneous self-expression, emotion, and personal experience in producing art. In Romanticism, the "natural" is privileged over the conventional or the artificial.

Rondeau: a fifteen-line poem, generally octosyllabic, with only two rhymes throughout its three stanzas, and an unrhymed refrain at the end of the ninth and fifteenth lines, repeating part of the opening line.

Sarcasm: See *irony*.

Satire: literary work designed to make fun of or seriously criticize its subject. According to many literary theories of the Renaissance and neoclassical periods, the ridicule through satire of a certain sort of behavior may function for the reader or audience as a corrective of such behavior.

Scansion: the formal analysis of patterns of rhythm and rhyme in poetry. Each line of verse will have a certain number of fairly regular "beats" consisting of alternating stressed and unstressed syllables. To "scan" a poem is to count the beats in each line, to mark stressed and unstressed syllables and indicate their combination into "feet," to note pauses, and to identify rhyme schemes with letters of the alphabet.

Scheme: See *figures of speech*.

Schools: In the sixteenth and seventeenth centuries the different forms of school in England included Cathedral schools (often founded with a view to the education of members of the choir); grammar schools (often founded by towns or by guilds, and teaching a much broader curriculum than the modern sense of "grammar" might suggest, private schools, operated by private individuals out of private residences; and public schools, which (like the private schools and the grammar schools) operated independent of any church authority, but unlike the grammar schools and private schools were organized as independent charities, and often offered free education. Over the centuries certain of these public schools, while remaining not-for-profit institutions, began to accept fee-paying students and to adopt standards that made them more and more exclusive. In the eighteenth and nineteenth century attendance at such prestigious public boarding schools as Eton, Westminster, and Winchester had become almost exclusively the preserve of the upper classes; by the nineteenth century such "public" schools were the equivalent of private schools in North America. Though a few girls attended some early grammar schools, the greater part of this educational system was for boys only. Though a number of individuals of earlier periods were concerned to increase the number of private schools for girls, the movement to create a parallel girls' system of public schools and grammar schools dates from the later nineteenth century.

Septet: a stanza containing seven lines.

Serf: in the medieval period, a person of unfree status, typically engaged in working the land.

Sestet: a six-line stanza that forms the second grouping of lines in an Italian / Petrarchan sonnet, following the octave. See *sonnet* and *sestina*.

Sestina: an elaborate unrhymed poem with six 6-line stanzas and a 3-line envoy.

Shire: originally a multiple estate; since the late medieval period a larger territory forming an administrative unit—also referred to as a county.

Simile: a *figure of speech* (a trope) which makes an explicit comparison between a particular object and another object or idea that is similar in some (often unexpected) way. A simile always uses "like" or "as" to signal the connection. Compare with *metaphor* above.

Sonnet: a highly structured lyric poem, which normally has fourteen lines of iambic pentameter. We can distinguish four major variations of the sonnet.

Italian/Petrarchan: named for the 14th-century Italian poet Petrarch, has an octave rhyming *abbaabba*, and a sestet rhyming *cdecde*, or *cdcdcd* (other arrangements are possible here). Usually, a turn in argument takes place between octave and sestet.

Miltonic: developed by Milton and similar to the Petrarchan in rhyme scheme, but eliminating the turn after the octave, thus giving greater unity to the poem's structure of thought.

Shakespearean: often called the English sonnet, this form has three quatrains and a couplet. The quatrains rhyme internally but do not interlock: *abab cdcd efef gg*. The turn may occur after the second quatrain, but is usually revealed in the final couplet. Shakespeare's sonnets are the best-known examples of this form.

Spenserian: after Edmund Spenser, who developed the form in his sonnet cycle *Amoretti*. This sonnet form has three quatrains linked through interlocking rhyme, and a separately rhyming couplet: *abab bcbc cdcd ee*.

Speaker: in the late medieval period, a member of the Commons in Parliament who spoke on behalf of that entire group. (The Commons first elected a Speaker in 1376.) In later eras the role of Speaker became one of chairing debates in the House of Commons and arbitrating disputes over matters of procedure.

Spenserian Stanza: a nine-line stanza, with eight iambic pentameters and a concluding alexandrine, rhyming *ababbcbcc*.

Spondee: a metrical foot containing two strong stressed syllables: // (e.g., blind mouths).

Sprung Rhythm: a modern variation of accentual verse, created by the English poet Gerard Manley Hopkins, in which rhythms are determined largely by the number of strong stresses in a line, without regard to the number of unstressed syllables. Hopkins felt that sprung rhythm more closely approximated the natural rhythms of speech than did conventional poetry.

Stanza: any lines of verse that are grouped together in a poem and separated from other similarly-structured groups by a space. In metrical poetry, stanzas share metrical and rhyming patterns; however, stanzas may also be formed on the basis of thought, as in irregular odes. Conventional stanza forms include the *tercet*, the *quatrain*, *rhyme royal*, the *Spenserian stanza*, the *ballad stanza*, and *ottava rima*.

Stream of Consciousness: narrative technique that attempts to convey in prose fiction a sense of the progression of the full range of thoughts and sensations occurring within a character's mind. Twentieth-century pioneers in the use of the stream of consciousness technique include Dorothy Richardson, Virginia Woolf, and James Joyce.

Stress: See *accent*.

Strophe: the first stanza in a Pindaric ode. This is followed by an *antistrophe* (see above), which presents the same metrical pattern and rhyme scheme, and finally by an *epode*, differing in meter from the preceding stanzas. Upon completion of this "triad," the entire sequence can recur. *Strophe* may also describe a stanza or other subdivision in other kinds of poem.

Sublime: a concept, most popular in eighteenth-century England, of the qualities of grandeur, power, and awe that may be inherent in or produced by undomesticated nature or great art. The sublime was thought of as higher and loftier than something that is merely beautiful.

Subplot: a line of story that is subordinate to the main storyline of a narrative. (Note that properly speaking a subplot is a category of story material, not of plot.)

Substitution: a deliberate change from the dominant pattern of stresses in a line of verse to create emphasis or variation. Thus the first line of Shakespeare's sonnet "'Shall I compare thee to a summer's day?' is decidedly iambic in meter (x / x / x / x / x /), whereas the second line substitutes a trochee (/ x) in the opening foot: "Thou art more lovely and more temperate."

Subtext: implied or suggested meaning of a passage of text, or of an entire work.

Syllabic Verse: poetry in which the length of a line is measured solely by the number of syllables, regardless of accents or patterns of stress.

Syllable: vocal sound or group of sounds forming a unit of speech; a syllable may be formed with a single effort of articulation. Some syllables consist of a single phoneme (e.g., the word *I*, or the first syllable in the word *u*-ni-ty) but others may be made up of several phonemes (as with one-syllable words such as *lengths*, *splurged*, and *through*). By contrast, the much shorter words *ago*, *any*, and *open* each have two syllables.

Symbol: a word, image, or idea that represents something more, or other, than for what it at first appears to stand. Like metaphor, the symbol extends meaning; but while the tenor and vehicle of metaphor are bound in a specific relationship, a symbol may have a range of connotations. For example, the image of a rose may call forth associations of love, passion, transience, fragility, youth and beauty, among others. Depending upon the context, such an image could be interpreted in a variety of ways, as in Blake's lyric, "The Sick Rose." Though this power of symbolic representation characterizes all language, poetry most particularly endows the concrete imagery evoked through language with a larger meaning. Such meaning is implied rather than explicitly stated; indeed, much of the power of symbolic language lies in the reader's ability to make meaningful sense of it.

Syncope: in poetry, the dropping of a letter or syllable from the middle of a word, as in "trav'ler." Such a contraction allows a line to stay within a metrical scheme. See also *catalexis* and *elision*.

Synecdoche: a kind of *metonymy* in which a writer substitutes the name of a part of something to signify the whole: for example, "sail" for ship or "hand" for a member of the ship's crew.

Tercet: a group, or stanza, of three lines, often linked by an interlocking rhyme scheme as in *terza rima*. See also *triplet.*

Terza Rima: an arrangement of tercets interlocked by a rhyme scheme of *aba bcb cdc ded*, etc., and ending with a couplet that rhymes with the second-last line of the final tercet (for example, *efe*, *ff*). See, for example, Percy Shelley's "Ode to the West Wind."

Tetrameter: a line of poetry containing four metrical feet.

Theme: the governing idea of a discourse, conveyed through the development of the subject, and through the recurrence of certain words, sounds, or metrical patterns. See also *motif.*

Third-Person Narrative: See *narrative perspective.*

Tone: the writer's attitude toward a given subject or audience, as expressed though an authorial persona or "voice." Tone can be projected through particular choices of wording, imagery, figures of speech, and rhythmic devices. Compare *mood.*

Tories: See *Political Parties.*

Tragedy: in the traditional definition originating in discussions of ancient Greek drama, a serious narrative recounting the downfall of the protagonist. More loosely, the term has been applied to a wide variety of literary forms in which the tone is predominantly a dark one and the narrative does not end happily.

Transcendentalism: a philosophical movement that influenced such Victorian writers as Thomas Carlyle and Robert Browning. Also a mode of Romantic thought, Transcendentalism places the supernatural and the natural within one great Unity and believes that each individual person embodies aspects of the divine.

Trimeter: a line of poetry containing three metrical feet.

Triolet: a French form in which the first line appears three times in a poem of only eight lines. The first line is repeated at lines 4 and 7; the second line is repeated in line 8. The triolet has only two rhymes: *abaaabab.*

Triple Foot: poetic foot of three syllables. The possible varieties of triple foot are the anapest (in which two unstressed syllables are followed by a stressed syllable), the dactyl (in which a stressed syllable is followed by two unstressed lines), and the mollossus (in which all three syllables are stressed equally). English poetry tends to use duple rhythms far more frequently than triple rhythms.

Triplet: a group of three lines with the same end-rhyme, much used by eighteenth-century poets to vary or punctuate the flow of couplets. See also *tercet.*

Trivium: group of three academic subjects (dialectic, grammar, and rhetoric) that were part of the university curriculum in the Middle Ages. Their study precedes that of the more advanced subjects of the *quadrivium.*

Trochee: a metrical foot containing one strong stress followed by one weak stress: / x (heaven, lover).

Trope: any figure of speech that plays on our understandings of words to extend, alter, or transform "literal" meaning. Common tropes include *metaphor*, *simile*, *personification*, *hyperbole*, *metonymy*, *oxymoron*, *synecdoche*, and *irony*. See also *figures of speech*, above.

Turn (Italian "volta"): the point in a *sonnet* where the mood or argument changes. The turn may occur between the octave and sestet, i.e., after the eighth line, or in the final couplet, depending on the kind of sonnet.

Unities: Many literary theorists of the late sixteenth through late eighteenth centuries held that a play should ideally be presented as representing a single place, and confining the action to a single day and a single dominant event. They disapproved of plots involving gaps or long periods of time, shifts in place, or subplots. These concepts, which came to be referred to as the unities of space, time, and action, were based on a misreading of classical authorities (principally of Aristotle).

Vers de societé: French: literally, "verse about society." The term originated with poetry written by aristocrats and upper-middle-class poets that specifically disavows the ambition of creating "high art" while treating the concerns of their own group in verse forms that demonstrate a high degree of formal control (e.g., artful rhymes, surprising turns of diction).

Vers libre (French): See *free verse* above.

Verse: a general term for works of poetry, usually referring to poems that incorporate some kind of metrical structure. The term may also describe a line of poetry, though more frequently it is applied to a stanza.

Villanelle: a poem usually consisting of 19 lines, with five 3-line stanzas (tercets) rhyming *aba*, and a concluding quatrain rhyming *abaa*. The first and third lines of the first tercet are repeated at fixed intervals throughout the rest of the poem. See, for example, Dylan Thomas's "Do Not Go Gentle Into That Good Night."

Whigs: See *Political Parties.*

Workhouse: public institution in which the poor were provided with a minimal level of sustenance and with lodging in exchange for work performed. Early workhouses were typically administered by individual parishes. In 1834 a unified system covering all of England and Wales was put into effect.

Zeugma: a *figure of speech* (trope) in which one word links or "yokes" two others in the same sentence, often to comic or ironic effect. For example, a verb may govern two objects, as in Pope's line "Or stain her honour, or her new brocade."

Permissions Acknowledgments

Illustration Credits

Page 1: Reproduced by permission of the National Portrait Gallery, London. Page 11: Reproduced by permission of the National Portrait Gallery, London. Page 59: Reproduced by permission of the National Portrait Gallery, London. Page 365: Reproduced by permission of the National Portrait Gallery, London. Page 418: Reproduced by permission of the National Portrait Gallery, London. Page 433: Reproduced by permission of the National Portrait Gallery, London. Page 526: Reproduced by permission of the National Portrait Gallery, London. Page 791: Reproduced by permission of the National Portrait Gallery, London.

Information on all translations used is provided in footnotes at the beginning of selections. Copyright permission to reproduce material translated or edited for this anthology and material reproduced or adapted here that originally appeared in other books published by Broadview Press may be sought from Broadview.

The publisher has endeavored to contact rights holders of all copyright material and would appreciate receiving any information as to errors or omissions.

Index of First Lines

Index of Authors and Titles